1950

Theaters
of
History

McGraw-Hill Series in Political Science

JOSEPH P. HARRIS, *Consulting Editor*

INTERNATIONAL RELATIONS

In the Age of the Conflict between
Democracy and Dictatorship

McGraw-Hill Series in Political Science

JOSEPH P. HARRIS, *Consulting Editor*

INTERNATIONAL RELATIONS

In the Age of the Conflict between Democracy and Dictatorship

ROBERT STRAUSZ-HUPÉ

University of Pennsylvania

STEFAN T. POSSONY

Georgetown University

ORIGINAL DRAWINGS BY LESLIE ROSENZWEIG

SECOND EDITION

McGRAW-HILL BOOK COMPANY, INC.

NEW YORK   TORONTO   LONDON

1954

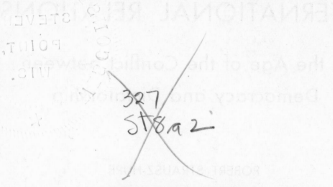

327
St8a2

INTERNATIONAL RELATIONS

To the Memory of

JAMES FORRESTAL

STATESMAN OF HEROIC MOLD

One must will the
consequences of what
one wants.
Jacques Bainville

The true character of
liberty is independence,
maintained by force.
Voltaire

PREFACE

This book is an introduction to the theory and practice of international relations. Like all texts, it is incomplete and cannot take the place of the live teacher, who will make use of it in accordance with his own sense of fitness. It is the authors' hope that the arrangement of the materials assembled in this book is elastic enough to leave teacher and student sufficient scope to exercise discretion as well as imagination.

Since international relations are human relations and, therefore, enmeshed in an infinite variety of social activities, their essence is change. Again and again, the best-laid plans and the most carefully formulated and reasonable policies are foiled by the unexpected and the absurd. In view of the volatile properties of the subject matter, the authors do not pretend to know which are the "lasting" documents of international affairs. The only documents reproduced in this volume, unabridged or in part, are those which bear upon the topical discussion. The Covenant of the League of Nations, the Charter of the United Nations, the North Atlantic Pact, and lesser compacts presumed to be of contemporary significance are easily accessible in numerous places. The tide in international affairs these documents recorded, the order they sanctioned, and the hopes they kindled or disappointed are the very stuff of which international politics are made. But in order to get at the substance, it is hardly necessary to learn "documents" paragraph by paragraph, article by article, just as it is unnecessary to memorize municipal ordinances in order to understand the problems of a city government.

The planning of this text—a thoroughly recast and rewritten edition of the book published in 1950—against the limitations of space and the ravages of time posed various problems of scholarly apparatus. In the making of the bibliographies the authors stuck to the sources which fed the individual chapters. They are aware of the gaps which open on every page of this book. These can be filled only by impressment of auxiliaries such as globes, maps, atlases, current publications, and "fugitive materials." Since international relations are still confined to this earth, their study presupposes at least an elementary knowledge of geographical relationships. Hence the importance of globes and maps. Since international relations are never made but always in the making, their study presupposes familiarity with current issues. Hence the importance of periodicals, pamphlets, and reports by competent newspapermen and commentators. They may be consulted profitably wherever this text appears to require expansion, emphasis—and the intervention of that "opinion to the contrary" which lends zest to all discussion.

International relations are intensely controversial. The authors hope that they have resisted the temptation of ducking behind that "impartiality" which goes by the name of scholarly objectivity. It is preposterous nonsense to assert that the writer on international politics can ply his trade without taking sides. If he does he will merely compound the confusion of the public with his own. The authors of this book have sought to formulate their conclusions by scientific methods. Once they arrived at their conclusions they saw no reason for softening them by weasel words. The chips fell where they fell. The authors' estimates may be proved wrong, but that, too, should prove instructive to the student. Estimates of the future are to the foreign-policy maker what the forecast of the weather is to the pilot.

The authors do not profess that they stand aside in scholarly detachment where the issue between freedom and tyranny is concerned. That issue is still a battle to be won. So far, the side of freedom has not scored decisively. To the contrary, for more than thirty years the initiative in world affairs has not been in the hands of free, representative, and progressive governments. Nor have the free peoples aroused themselves to the creative effort of adjusting the worn machinery of democracy to the exacting conditions of the air and atomic age. The progress of dictatorship does not prove the excellence of the principles of tyrannical government, for the advance of dictatorship was due to the default of democracy. The democratic nations, with surprising indifference to their own survival, condoned—indeed, sometimes abetted— the spreading of dictatorial government. In the rare cases when they opposed the danger, they indulged in those untimely half measures of which the present generation of democratic statesmen has the unique secret.

The authors thought it necessary, therefore, to subject the foreign policies of the democracies to a searching and explicit critique, no less searching and explicit than the critique, contained in this volume, of the foreign policies of the dictatorships. The authors are fully aware that they will thus give offense to the preconceptions of at least a few among their readers. But the great issues of international politics are far too important and too pressing to be handled with noncommittal delicacy. There are indeed alternatives, but there is also the ineluctable necessity of choosing between them.

The authors are confident that they have not succumbed to the greatest temptation to which the writer on world affairs is exposed: to write in an oracular or in an illusionist vein. Evidently, this or that policy can lead to defeat or victory; to cultural annihilation or progress; to *Weltuntergang* or eternal peace. Statements of this kind are fetching, but they do not help in making up one's mind as to which practical policy should be chosen. It is easy to blueprint policies which would lead to the enrichment of all mankind and insure universal peace, were we able to afford the costs and were not other peoples emphatically unenthusiastic about our conception of universal bliss. It is more difficult to remain pragmatical. Policies must aim to advance the cause of freedom. But such policies also must satisfy the criteria of practicality—economic and human cost, timeliness, and acceptability. Policies must be shaped so as to fit the intense desires, the urgent problems, and the scarce resources of concrete societies. They cannot be composed like a painting, a poem—or a book on political science. The authors tried their best to steer clear of irrational and emotional involvements with exclusive and final "solutions" of the world's problems. Instead they attempted to fashion a textbook which is what textbooks are supposed to be, namely, *expository*.

The science of international relations is in its infancy. Most of its findings are in the nature of first approximations: Some of the simplest, albeit most pressing, problems still remain unsolved. In no other field of human knowledge is the challenge fraught with vaster and more critical implications. No other field calls more urgently for sober, almost clinical objectivity and broad knowledge. And were we to advance along the path of science far beyond the present and wretched state of universal ignorance, we would still fail to reach the goal. Faith, courage, and forbearance must arm the knowledge that guides us to the summit of our task: a world order under peace and freedom.

ROBERT STRAUSZ-HUPÉ
STEFAN T. POSSONY

ACKNOWLEDGMENTS

Our thanks go to Vally Possony, without whose scholarly competence and unstinting devotion to an exacting task this book could not have been written; to Franz G. Lassner who supplied the authors with numerous documents here published for the first time; to Paul W. Blackstock for his assistance in helping us locate long-forgotten books; to Elaine Day who read and prepared the manuscript and whose cogent and vigorous criticism left its mark on several chapters; to Mary Francis Harvey who furnished a valuable political analysis of foreign trade problems; to Professor Joseph P. Harris who is the cause of many and considerable improvements, precisely because his view did not always agree with that set forth in these pages; to Monica Stevens and Joan H. Wise for their thoughtful editing of the manuscript; and with particular gratitude to Les Rosenzweig who in a most unusual combination unites creative artistic skill with profound scientific insight.

Alvin J. Cottrell not only contributed valuable insights in Soviet foreign policy but also undertook, while the authors were absent on foreign travel, the delicate and difficult task of reviewing the manuscript in order to bring it within the limits set by the publisher. The authors gratefully acknowledge his skillful and judicious intervention which speeded the publication of the book and suggested many improvements in this text.

We acknowledge Harold Faye's contribution of the four maps which were prepared for the first edition.

We are indebted to the following publishers and editors: G. P. Putnam's Sons, who gave permission to quote from Robert Strausz-Hupé, *The Balance of Tomorrow* (New York, 1945); William L. Neumann, editor of *American Perspective;* the Editors of the *Department of State Bulletin;* the Infantry Journal Press (Combat Forces Press) which gave permission to quote from Stefan T. Possony, *Strategic Air Power* (Washington, D.C., 1949); and to William Hodge & Co., Ltd., of London, who gave permission to reproduce Professor Eucken's table on page 31.

R. S.-H.
S. T. P.

CONTENTS

PART ONE

THEORY OF INTERNATIONAL RELATIONS

PART TWO

THE ELEMENTS OF POWER

PART THREE

THE ART OF THE POSSIBLE

PART FOUR

TECHNIQUES OF FOREIGN POLICY

Part Five

TECHNIQUES OF REVOLUTION AND THE COLD WAR

Part Six

INTERNATIONAL ECONOMICS

Part Seven

THE AGE OF CONFLICT

Part Eight

THE QUEST FOR PEACE

Part Nine

THE GOOD SOCIETY IN THE MAKING

Part One

THEORY OF INTERNATIONAL RELATIONS

Chapter 1

THE MOTIVATIONS OF CONTEMPORARY FOREIGN POLITICS: A STUDY IN VICIOUS CIRCLES

The science of international politics studies the mutual relationships between states. It also studies the actions by members of one society which are related to, or directed against, one or more foreign societies, either in part or as a whole. The underlying assumptions are, first, that these relationships and actions can be studied in a scientific manner and, secondly, that it is possible to describe, classify, analyze, and determine the interconnectibility [1] between those relationships and actions. Furthermore, it is assumed that many of the relationships between states and their interconnections show patterns of regularity and that these patterns may serve as bases of cautious and tentative forecasts. There are, however, numerous interstate relationships and actions which are unique and nonrecurrent and must be described as individual phenomena. As a study of nonrepetitive events, international politics becomes a historical science. As a study of human action, it is part of the sciences of psychology and praxiology.

The study of the international behavior of states is a relatively new science. Is this science necessary? Nations, states, and governments exist, and since they do exist, they also have interrelationships. Everything that exists and every relationship between existing things is a proper subject of scientific inquiry. The science of international politics does not require more justification than the science of botany or meteorology.

Sciences do not arise by accident. Meteorology is the result of mankind's need to know the future weather; it made real progress only when, in the air age, this need became a matter of life and death. The utility of a science

[1] Richard von Mises, *Positivism, A Study in Human Understanding,* Cambridge, Mass., Harvard University Press, 1951, p. 73.

often acts as a brake on scientific progress: the need to forecast tomorrow's weather imposed on the meteorologist the compulsion to make predictions *before* he had a thorough command of his weather data. Similarly, the science of international politics owes its emergence to the deplorable state of the "international situation." It is supported and studied because we hope to find solutions to our international problems. Unfortunately, before proper solutions can be worked out, we must first collect and analyze scientific data. At present, the science of international politics cannot do more than gather the knowledge which at some future date could serve as the basis for the improvement of the world.

The modern practitioners of foreign policy have little to go on but traditions and rules of thumb which, they hope, summarize the lessons of experience. They must act like primitive man, who organized his economic life by trial and error. These methods offered a certain limited control over events, but what a difference there is between a coppersmith of 2500 B.C. and a modern nuclear engineer! The progress from the former to the latter can be achieved only by observing facts, practicing the scientific method, and pushing aside the hopes, confusions, unprovable concepts, and downright deceptions which obstruct the application of science. This word of caution applies not only to those who cannot see the need for change and improvement and who want to go back to situations of which they possess illusional but not realistic images. It applies with equal force to those who advocate change without realizing the implications of their proposals, particularly those who think that *everything* must be changed and that *everything* can be improved. Changes, no doubt, are necessary. But what changes? What do they cost? And what will be their over-all result? Slogans, however attractive, do not provide the answers.

The first question to which we must address ourselves is, who is it that has the relationships which are pertinent to our science? We stated our intent to study the interrelationships and interactions between states. But it is necessary to explain the meaning of the term "state" in greater detail. A state is the political organization which a social group—in many cases a nation—establishes in order to manage its public life and safeguard the over-all interests of the group. The state functions through the government. In addition, it comprises the complex apparatus necessary for the management of public affairs, including executive administration per se, the legislatures, the political parties, the political opposition, special-interest groups, the armed forces, and the legal, moral, and intellectual conventions supplying the framework within which the government exercises its authority and the nongovernmental groups wield their influence. The state also comprises the degree of support which the rulers find among the ruled.

Thus, while the science of international politics studies the relationships between governments, a dynamic analysis must take into account that governments change, that they do not always possess the monopoly of authority but must share their decision-making powers with other groups, that decisions of a government may not reflect the consent of the entire social group, the "nation," or conversely, may be forced upon it by public pressure. The question, "Who stands in political relations with whom?" can be answered only as a first approximation by saying that the interrelationships between governments are the proper object of the science of international politics. In many instances, political groups of *any* kind—parties, religious organizations, business firms, trade unions, military officers, and revolutionary conspirators —may enter into relations with foreign governments or political groups, including groups of their own kind (*e.g.,* organized religious groups with foreign religious groups) and thus influence the happenings on the international scene.

It would be a grave mistake to talk about "governments" or "groups" as though they were anything but first-order abstractions. *"Governments" or "groups" consist of individuals;* they exist but conditionally, if they exist at all, outside of these individuals. There always may be a "government"; the mere existence of a continuing organization imposes certain behavior patterns on its discontinuous, changing membership. Just the same, decisions are made and executed by individuals, who alone are concrete [2] and who are subject not only to organizational or framework pressures but also to the much more direct and powerful pressures of their own bodies, thoughts, and emotions. Thus, while we must concentrate on relationships between "governments," the science of international politics also must study the relationships between individuals, above all between politically influential individuals and, to a certain extent, also the attenuated, fleeting, and indirect relationships between the average citizens of the different nations. What the prime ministers of two states think about each other may determine the course of many events; but the attitude of an industrial worker in one nation vis-à-vis the peasant in another state may also become a significant factor.

What do we mean when we talk about relations among nations? We mean, first, that actions undertaken by any of the citizens of one nation in one way or another, directly or indirectly, may affect the citizens of other nations. We mean, secondly, that many decisions made by a government or by other significant political groups deal with, or have a direct or indirect bearing on, the decisions and the lives of foreign governments and political groups. Decisions of this type may be made intentionally or unintentionally. Thirdly, we mean that there is pressure exerted on governments and other political groups, compelling them to make decisions relating to foreign states. These decisions spring from a desire to secure advantages for one's own group or to prevent foreign groups from accomplishing their intentions at the

[2] "A social collective has no existence and reality outside of the individual members' actions. The life of a collective is lived in the actions of the individuals constituting its body. . . . Thus the way to cognition of collective wholes is through analysis of the individuals' actions." Ludwig von Mises, *Human Action: A Treatise on Economics,* New Haven, Yale University Press, 1949, p. 42.

expense of one's own nation. People who are joined together in a state have many interests in common. Above all, they do not want their society to be exploited for the benefit of foreigners, to be put under foreign rule, or to be broken up. There are exceptions to this rule, as for example, when the meaning of the word "foreign" becomes blurred or when the loyalty to an existing society has been weakened critically. But in general, the members of any society want to maintain their social structure as a going and growing concern. *Foreign policy is that part of a government's activity which keeps the state—and, in a wider sense, the society—a going and growing concern as against the desires, interests, and activities of other states and societies.* At any given time, a government must put more emphasis on keeping its society a going rather than a growing concern. But occasionally the desire to grow predominates. Very rarely, a government will be motivated by conscious or subconscious self-destructive tendencies, in which case we are confronted by "treachery" or "social decomposition." Whenever considerations of "growth" or "destruction" outweigh the interest in the "going concern," a severe crisis must ensue.

At any time and place, foreign policy must deal with *economics* and *power*. These are the two main areas of decision in the field of foreign policy. Legal, cultural, and personal international relations are subsidiary in nature. There are other topics on the agenda of the makers of foreign policy, but these two are all-inclusive.

Each nation must trade with other nations. Otherwise it could not exist with any degree of comfort, and often it could not survive at all.[3] Each nation must sell commodities which foreigners cannot produce themselves, or cannot produce as cheaply. Each nation must buy goods which it cannot procure within its own territory. These goods may be foodstuffs, minerals, vegetable raw materials, transport, trade services, money, labor, patent rights, technical know-how, etc. The exchange may be on a small or a large scale. Foreign trade may account for a low or high percentage of the national income. It may embrace necessaries or luxuries. It may take place in a friendly fashion or as the result of a hostile tug of war. It may assume the form of barter or monetary settlement. But it always goes on, and it always is of key importance, however small the volume of trade may be. Even in time of war, when the exigencies of conflict make it advisable to deprive the opponent of vital commodities, these same exigencies may require that indirect trading *in certain commodities* be continued between the warring camps.

The need to trade is reflected throughout the entire economy. To be a successful trader, a nation must produce high-quality goods cheaply and in adequate quantities. It must possess transportation and distribution facilities, be able to extend credit, own banking and clearing facilities, and display

[3] Some understanding of the importance of trade even among illiterate or "primitive" societies may be gained from Melville J. Herskovits, *Economic Anthropology: A Study in Comparative Economics,* New York, Knopf, 1952, Part III.

social and political stability. A productive and well-run economy is a condition of extensive trade, and the power of a state, in its material aspects, is dependent on economic productivity, including trade. Economic productivity presupposes cooperation within the nation, which, in turn, it stimulates. Hence, many of the decisions concerning economic life at home bear significantly upon the international position of a state. There is a chain linking cooperation through productivity and trade to power; the position of each of these links may change, but all of these factors are interdependent.

If market economies trade with each other, the governments must make only a few decisions. They need only define the legal framework within which business is done. If trading takes place between centrally administered or state-directed economies,[4] the governments must make most of the economic decisions themselves. In both cases, the governments must protect the economic security of the nation and regulate trade in such a fashion that, in case of emergency, the nation will not be deprived suddenly of necessary materials and services, or will not support unwittingly the aggressive design of a prospective opponent. It is debatable whether governments *should* protect the economic interests of individual producers at home and regulate trade to exclude foreign competitors, but it is a fact that they *do* so very frequently and thereby engender, in practically each case, important repercussions in foreign countries.

POWER

While a government's routine decisions in the foreign field deal with economics and other international *relations,* the key decisions deal with international *politics* in the proper sense, *i.e.,* with power politics. No decisions can be of higher importance than the resolution to enter into, or abrogate, alliances and federations; to engage in international conflict; to go to war; and to offer or to sue for peace. Decisions of this type always are made to avoid a real or imaginary threat to national security and, in the case of dynamic or aggressive states, to exploit a unique opportunity. Such crucial decisions are motivated by the desire to increase power or to prevent power increases on the part of competing nations. They are tied together with innumerable preceding, simultaneous, and successive acts, all aiming at the accumulation and preservation of power. While the remote and immediate causes of war are most varied, the basic cause of each war—and major international crisis—always must be sought in the power domain. No modern nation has ever gone to war unless its power interests were at stake. It is these acts and decisions in the power domain which decide the fate of nations and which determine what is known as the "world situation."

International politics is dominated by the quest for power and, therefore, in its essential aspects, is tantamount to conflict. This statement does not

4 On this typology of economics, see Walter Eucken, *The Foundations of Economics, History and Theory in the Analysis of Economic Reality,* London, Hodge, 1950, Part III.

imply approval of such a state of affairs, any more than the doctor's diagnosis means approval of the disease. It is a simple protocol sentence, describing the fact that, at any given period of known history, there were several states locked in deadly conflict, all desiring the augmentation or preservation of their power. Some periods of history were characterized by the appearance of "natural aggressors," [5] states or rulers whose acts were motivated almost exclusively by the urge to increase power and establish power monopolies in large geographic regions and, in some cases, over the entire globe. This tendency always has been resisted by nations whom the power monopolist threatened to victimize, not only by counteraction against the existing natural aggressor, but also by preventive action aiming at keeping the strength of each nation within limits, regardless of currently prevailing aggressive or peaceful intentions; this type of preventive action is known as the *balance of power policy*. It is also a restatement of the fact that throughout known history key states spent almost half of their time in military conflict,[6] while in the other half of the time the struggle was continued by nonviolent techniques. If we define international peace as the absence of organized violence, the periods of peace were very rare indeed.

This domination of international politics by power conflict has two important consequences. First, since struggle is the law of international society, the survival of each state must depend on adequacy of power. Hence the most basic decisions of each state must aim at reaching the optimum power level. An optimum power level is reached when defensive requirements can be satisfied without detracting significantly from offensive strength. A nation which tries to maximize its power usually overcommits itself; it must allocate most of its strength to defensive purposes. Hence it reduces or loses its freedom of offensive action and becomes highly vulnerable. Optimum power is thus maximum offensive power projected against a minimum of hostile threat.

Occasionally, rational policy requires a contraction of power, as happened in the splitting of the Roman Empire or the transformation of the British Empire into the Commonwealth. Most states, however, operate from a power level which is too low to guarantee their security. Finding themselves directly or indirectly engaged in incessant struggle, they must aim at increasing the level of their power through expansion or alliance, or at eliminating themselves from the conflict through neutralization. We are confronted by a vicious circle: the compulsive desire to accumulate more power leads to an ever greater concentration on power politics. Attempts to break the circle

---

[5] The phenomenon of the "natural aggressor" was pointed out first by Admiral Raoul Castex in his *Théories stratégiques*, 5 vols., Paris, Societé d'Éditions Géographiques, Maritimes et Coloniales, 1927–1935.

[6] See Pitirim A. Sorokin, *Social and Cultural Dynamics*, 4 vols., New York, American Book, 1937–1941, especially Vol. III, Chaps. 9–11; and Quincy Wright, *A Study of War*, Chicago, University of Chicago Press, 1942, Vol. I, pp. *232ff.;* Tables 31–46, pp. 641–652.

entail the danger of strengthening the most power-hungry competitor and pose the risk of self-destruction.

Secondly, within an international conflict society, each member is forced to divide all the other members into three major groups: actual or potential friends, actual or potential enemies, and neutrals.[7] Politics between states are determined basically by the friend-enemy-and-neutral constellation, regardless of whether this is detrimental to social, economic, and cultural relations and even to the common interests of all peoples.

It is clear then, that foreign policy is dominated by two contradictory requirements. The need for economic and cultural relations can be satisfied only through cooperation among nations. Paradoxically, it is this cooperation which produces the necessary surplus energy and wealth which allows nations to engage in power conflict. The recognition of the fact that it is power that prompts the crucial decisions of history should not blind us to the other equally important fact that conflicts must be temporarily smothered into compromise if nations are to survive. The decision to arm, mobilize, and fight must be preceded and accompanied by cultivation, production, and trade. Conflict never can supersede any of these cooperative economic activities, although it restricts them in scope and success and may be fought for the purpose of economic gain. Power may be the law of states and the mode of life in the international society, but cooperation is the substance of power and the condition of physical survival. The fundamental rule is, therefore, that the makers of foreign policy neither can with impunity concentrate on cooperation and neglect power competition, nor without inviting disaster aim at accumulating power and neglect cooperation.

HISTORY OF POWER

In discussing the two key factors, power and cooperation, we must recognize that we are dealing with historical phenomena. The meaning and role of these factors have been changing with time and society. Both have shown the tendency to become more important and pervasive as mankind moved from less to more complex civilizations. In "primitive" societies, characterized by a mere subsistence economy, trade is a means of exchanging limited surpluses and of acquiring a few commodities in which there is a stringent shortage. Market economies are based on the division of labor, and hence on an ever-growing specialization of individual producers and producing groups. Trade becomes the *sine qua non* of economic existence. Without exchange, there would be no division of labor, and without division of labor, man would sink back to the level of the primitive food gatherer or herder. Society could not revert to those levels without the annihilation of perhaps more than nine-tenths of mankind. By the same token, as population in-

---

[7] For the concept of friend-foe relationship see Carl Schmitt, *Der Begriff des Politischen,* Hamburg, Hanseatische Verlagsanstalt, 1933, p. 9 and *passim.*

creases and specialization advances, economic cooperation becomes ever more essential.

The history of power is, first of all, the history of the physical instruments of power. In ancient civilization, an individual ruler or a government possessed but rudimentary implements of strength. His military forces were small and, more often than not, had to be disbanded during the winter. Weapons had a range of a few yards and negligible lethal effect. The government apparatus was small, inefficient, and incapable of bending the population as a whole to its will. Orders could be transmitted and carried out but slowly, and the execution of complex programs was nearly impossible.

Throughout the centuries, the implements of power developed from the club, the spear, and the bow and arrow to the airplane, the guided missile, the submarine, and the nuclear explosive. The government apparatus not only has grown in relative strength but has acquired knowledge and efficiency far superior to that possessed by single individuals or groups. Orders can be transmitted with the speed of light and executed with the speed of sound. The contacts between rulers and ruled have been moved from the oak tree and the forum to the newspaper, radio, and television set. Today, entire countries and continents are within the range of one man's voice. A modern government can execute complex programs and, if it so chooses, exercise control for long periods over most of the happenings within its borders. The power wielded by an ancient tyrant was almost entirely arbitrary but very limited in reach. The power wielded by a modern government need not be arbitrary and may be excessively legalistic—the ability to exercise power arbitrarily distinguishes a modern dictatorship from a democracy—but it is of almost limitless dimensions.[8]

This development of the instruments of power has had far-reaching sociological consequences. In former times, no ruling class was capable of extending its physical control over truly large territories. The Greek and Italian city-states illustrate this point, as does the proverbial impotence of medieval kings and emperors. Exceptions to this rule were either short-lived, like Alexander's empire, or due to exceptional circumstances. Rome retained its empire for several centuries because it possessed *one* vital power instrument which its competitors failed to develop: organization. This science— or art—of organization enabled the Romans to develop the legion, and with it to defeat all comers; it enabled them to govern efficiently and justly, and thus to consolidate their conquests. Even so, Rome did not expand beyond the confines of the Mediterranean. Sallies into other areas were short-lived. At the maximum point of its expansion this so-called "world empire" was inhabited by less people than are living today in France and Spain.

In the modern age, limitations on physical power have been receding at a rapid pace. It is feasible today to rule over entire continents; it may become

[8] The progressive increase of power is traced by Bertrand de Jouvenel in *Du Pouvoir, histoire naturelle de sa croissance*, Geneva, Éditions du Cheval Ailé, 1947.

possible to establish effective control over the entire globe. This is the fundamental reason why modern power conflicts have a far more inexorable and
relentless character than the struggles of yore. The expedients to which
vanquished groups could resort in former times in order to stage a comeback
no longer may be applicable. Today, success or failure is fraught with considerable finality. The price which must be paid for the struggle by both
victor and vanquished no longer is partial destruction; it may be obliteration
of entire countries and the reduction of mankind to universal bondage. The
stakes of modern conflict are, truly, the highest in history.

There also is a new development in the psychosociological motivation of
power. There probably never was a society without power stratification,
without individuals who gave the orders and others who obeyed. But in its
early form power was more in the nature of authority, a voluntary subordi-
nation to those who had performed outstanding service and who were able
to offer disinterested, wise counsel. The ruler was a *primus inter pares,* a
patriarch. His authority was modeled after that of a father in a large family.
There is no evidence to suggest that, in its youth, mankind walked with
oppression as its inseparable companion. Oppressive power is a social technique which could be applied only after mankind had "matured" to the point
that one individual was able to produce more than he needed for his bare
subsistence. This technique is designed to appropriate the fruit of somebody else's labor and to profit from the service of other persons. The oppressive ruler is divided by social status and legal privilege from the ruled.
The situation is that of the master and the servant, the commander and the
soldier, the exploiter and the exploited, and, in extreme cases, the deified,
exalted lord and the fettered slave. Throughout history as we know it from
written documents and artifacts, power moved between these two poles:
freely accepted, benign exercise of authority by a respected patriarch or by a
group of freely chosen trustees; and unlimited dominion over rightless,
powerless, and hapless serfs.

According to recent historical investigations, it seems as though oppressive power was invented by the nomadic peoples which at the end of the
glacial period surged forth from Central Asia, where for about 20,000 to
25,000 years they had been locked in by glaciers, snow-capped mountains,
and unconquerable arctic rivers and seas. These nomadic tribes, probably the
ancestors of the white "race," were formidable warriors. In order to survive
in their forbidding surroundings, they developed exceptional skills of orientation and mobility. To a greater extent than their contemporaries living in
moderate climates, they dominated nature. They tamed huge animals like the
bovines, the onager, and the equines which they used for transportation and
fighting. Their discipline and mobility were unmatched, as was their desire
to lead a more pleasant life.

As the glaciers were receding, the erstwhile prairies in North Africa and
the Middle East dried out and gradually became deserts. Hunting was no

longer possible. The inhabitants of the desiccated areas had to turn to agriculture. In many cases they moved away, taking the invention of seed culture to other peoples. The peasant entered the history of the race.[9]

When the nomadic peoples sallied forth from Central Asia, through many
thousands of years in wave after wave, they met, defeated, and subjugated
sedentary peasants. They superimposed their rule over the infrastructure of
producers who were of a different race and culture. For a while these two
groups lived together in separation, speaking different languages, abiding by
different customs and never mixing socially, let alone maritally. The conqueror constituted himself as the master, proclaimed that he belonged to a
superior "pure race," and exercised his rule, often through middlemen, from
unapproachable strong points and castles. The subjugated group was held in
bondage and compelled to toil for the benefit of the masters. The Norman
invasion of the British Isles (1066) furnishes a vivid and instructive
though belated illustration of this process.[10]

Gradually, however, this unnatural state of affairs ended. The cultures of
the peasant and the nomad, the economies of the plant grower and the
hunter, and the societies of the herder and warrior merged. The "races"
mixed, usually through the "middle group." The "lower" and most numerous
group, the sedentary peasant, swallowed up the erstwhile conqueror. The
rulers' castles became market places which grew into cities. Urbanization
began and opened the road for the great civilizations of mankind.

As the rule of race over race tended to disappear in the cauldron of sexual
and social intercourse, "racially" homogeneous peoples were split into social
"classes," the upper class inheriting some of the status and much of the
behavior pattern of the erstwhile foreign conqueror. The rule was of the rich
over the poor, the privileged over the nonprivileged, the learned over the
ignorant, and the armed over the disarmed. New invasions took place and
new conquerors subjugated sedentary peoples which, however, no longer
were socially unified but had become stratified. In many cases, the old
ruling classes were divested of their privileges and joined the ranks of the
nonprivileged, harboring their rancors and sowing the seeds of class warfare.
In other cases, the old ruling classes were pushed down only one notch and
became a solidly entrenched "middle class." Each foreign conquest tended to
accentuate stratification and cleavage—naturally enough, for conquest was
designed to appropriate wealth and to transfer property, services, and titles
from the vanquished to the new master.

[9] For the detailed historical reconstruction of these momentous events, see Alexander
Rüstow, *Ortsbestimmung der Gegenwart, eine universalgeschichtliche Kulturkritik,* Vol. I,
"Ursprung der Herrschaft," Zurich, Rentsch, 1950, Part I; also Shepard B. Clough, *The
Rise and Fall of Civilization: An Inquiry into the Relationship between Economic Devel-
opment and Civilization,* New York, McGraw-Hill, 1951, p. 23.

[10] For a comparatively recent example and for the better understanding of the
workings of such a society, see Gilberto Freyre, *The Masters and the Slaves: A Study on
the Development of Brazilian Civilization,* New York, Knopf, 1946.

FREEDOM AND POWER

Just as racial stratification within one territory proved to be an unworkable system, so the undivided possession of power privilege and economic command, and the unrestricted domination of a ruling class, proved to be impractical; the master needed the cooperation of the servants. Nor were the serving classes, and especially the *déclassés* among them, satisfied with their inferior status. Since they were unable to use force in order to escape their ignominious lot, they employed ideas to limit and circumscribe the exercise of power. The world religions emerged, with their emphasis on the metaphysical equality of all men. Ultimately the idea of freedom was born. The idea of freedom does not contradict the idea of power. In fact, a man is free only if he possesses the power to make his own decisions. Freedom acknowledges the necessity of political rule. But it seeks to define the conditions in which power can be exercised without being oppressive or exploitative and in which all members of society can work together in common effort without destroying the privacy or the independence of the individual. The idea of freedom sets limits to the arbitrariness of power and defines the scope of the individual's power. It denies the right of any person or group to wield power for personal or group benefit, or to wield it in an unorganized, undeterminable fashion, or to wield more of it than necessary for the common purpose. In short, it defines power as a social function and seeks a compromise between the exigencies of authority and the inalienable rights of the individual.

This battle between freedom and power is not predominantly a conflict of ideas—if only because power is not a tenable argument. It is, to a large measure, a social conflict in which the ability to convince is less important than the power to oppress or defeat oppression. The oppressor usually denies being an oppressor, but he enjoys his ability to oppress and command. There is an innate urge for power in many individuals, the much-debated *Wille zur Macht,* an urge which is derived from the more basic urge at self-aggrandizement or self-assertion. It may take the form of personal ambition, a quest for prestige and gratification, or simply a desire to profit from other people's work. If authority and power are indispensable functions of society, the *Wille zur Macht* is equally indispensable, since without it no one would exercise these functions, no one would aim at making the exercise of power a successful undertaking, and no one would strive to depose, and take the place of, the bad ruler. There never lived an effective statesman, strategist, economic or even cultural producer who did not obey a highly developed power urge. Indeed, the will to freedom is nourished by the power urges of the disenfranchised. Social progress would end if personal ambition and power urges were to disappear. But in extreme forms, the power urge becomes a psychological aberration or obsession.

The rationalism of the 18th century and the "progressive" convictions of the 19th century led to an interpretation of politics in which the power urge found scant acknowledgment. If its existence was recognized at all, power was decried as a corrupting force, a hindrance to good government, and the bane of peaceful international relations. In that epoch, most men of good will and not a few students of the social sciences thought that power was a psychological residual from the past which had to be discarded together with totem poles, mail coaches, and alchemy. They failed to understand that government *is* power: power to make and execute decisions, to punish the evildoer, and to restrain the power-hungry.

The act of creating a government consists in the transfer of power from a large group—for example, a nation—to a small number of men who presumably can act more wisely, quickly, and effectively than the large group. It is a recognition of the fact that large numbers of people are incapable of action unless directed. There is no "administration," or representation, or law without power.

"Rationalism" and "progressism" also overlooked the fact that people do enjoy and seek power—and this regardless of the criticism by reformers—and that only the power-hungry choose politics as their career. Politics without power is as unthinkable as astronomy without gravitation, physics without energy,[11] and biology without procreation. It remains true, however, and bears repetition, that power is *not* the only factor explaining politics, that the term has many meanings, that there are several distinct types of power, and that power is subject to historical change.

As a reaction to the theories extolling human reason, there emerged, between 1880 and 1920, a contradictory doctrine associated especially with the names of Friedrich Nietzsche and Vilfredo Pareto. According to this theory, power and the power instinct, not reason, are the prime movers of political behavior. In its popularized and simplified version, this theory proclaimed that politics is nothing but power competition, a game in which the players should not observe any limiting rules lest they be destroyed. Arguments, appeals to reason, and political programs are mere ideological devices; they serve to screen the brutal power instincts, or to make the exercise of power acceptable to the ruled, or to provide the masters with a good conscience. The sheep must be ruled by the wolves, and the wolfish rulers cannot behave but as beasts of prey. The purpose of politics was seen to be the satisfaction of the power instinct. International politics, a part of general politics, presumably must obey the same laws; it is an incessant struggle for survival. "Homo homini lupus, ergo societas societati hostis." This theory, though sound in part, is rendered implausible by gross exaggeration; power is a privilege which, at least in the long run, is granted for performance. Regardless of how power-hungry an individual or group may be, it will hold its

---

[11] Bertrand Russell, *Power: A New Social Analysis,* New York, Norton, 1938, p. 2.

power position only as long as it administers society effectively. Food must be grown and distributed, industry must be managed, law must be applied, and the large mass of people must be allowed minimum satisfaction of its spiritual and material needs and aspirations. There may not be an electoral or public-opinion poll, yet the ruler is dependent on the confidence of the ruled—to a large extent, on their willing cooperation. The most ruthless rulers are aware of this fatal limitation on their power. While mismanagement never leads to dissatisfaction immediately, while dissatisfaction never results forthwith in a change of government or ruling class, and while, lastly, it is possible for a time to dress up a poor administration as good government, misrule leads inexorably to loss of power: the holder of power must pay a price for its possession. Needless to add, many attempt to get by with paying the least price.

Yet it would be a mistake to explain the impact of Pareto's theory on contemporary politics merely as a negation of unrealistic rationalism. The distasteful fact is that power has assumed a more central importance than it seems to have ever had in the past. This is due to the increased physical force of power and, above all, to the circumstance that many of the limitations which in former times have contained the power instinct have fallen or have been pushed back. The power urge has become unbridled and licentious. Ancient and medieval society consisted of small numbers of people. More often than not there was a direct relationship between the rulers and the ruled, a personal and even intimate type of contact—illustrated, for example, in the stories of Harun al-Rashid—which tempered the acts of government by fatherly care and natural humanism. The smallness of society then made it unnecessary to maintain intermediate layers of power which execute decisions and control the populace. Nowadays, the emergence of a ruling middle class has offered to *more* people the possibility of striving for the satisfaction of the power urge than could formerly engage in that pursuit.

The German *Unteroffizier* and the Russian *chinovnik* have made a large and dismal contribution to the growth of rigidly stratified, power-mad societies. In the old lands of democracy, too, the proliferation of vast bureaucracies—wielding their power behind the shield of anonymity and often arbitrarily—has increased the weight of authority and has made the quest for power a popularly meaningful pursuit.

THE GROWTH OF THE POWER URGE

It would be rash to assert categorically that the hunger for power has become more voracious than it was in the past. But there is some evidence which makes such an assertion seem plausible. In earlier society, power was institutionalized as a profession; only the original or coopted members of the aristocracy were admitted to the levers of command. This meant that, by and large, people making the important political decisions did not suffer from the psychosis of the parvenu, the snob, or the frustrated job hunter, but had accustomed themselves, at least to a point, to take power in their stride. To them, power was a matter of routine—rarely a psychological climax. It also meant that, having fallen from political power, they still enjoyed a large measure of privilege as members of a ruling aristocracy. Therefore, the involvement of their private with their public life was less than that of today's statesman. By contrast, the modern politician often reaches the levers of command without ever having tasted the joys of power before. His private life merges with his public life, and upon fall from power he has little more than the status of an "ex," perhaps losing his wealth, connections, and conscience in the process.

In previous centuries, the circle of people from whom rulers could be chosen was limited by extreme inequality in knowledge and know-how. The ruler had to be an educated man or a soldier of high accomplishment. Gradually these types have been disappearing from the political scene. People who in previous times never could have thought of climbing up the political ladder have taken over the political profession, less perhaps in the cabinets than in the legislatures and administrations. The run-of-the-mill individual today receives enough schooling so that his power instincts are stimulated. He is provided with a minimum ability to fulfill the duties of a public position. In a modern society the relative and absolute number of persons who are eligible to satisfy their personal ambitions through a public career has increased considerably. This free-for-all competition has accentuated the significance of power.

The religious or metaphysical limitations on the power instinct have been broken down. The ruler of former times either was deeply religious himself and tried to comply with religious virtues, among which humility, but not ambition, is one; [12] or, if he was a skeptic, he had to pay his respects to the power of religious organization and to the religious convictions of his subjects. In any event, the ancient ruler was sufficiently superstitious to believe in *hubris*. In general, therefore, there was a tendency to tame the power instinct and to live up to the tenets of the faith. With the gradual weakening of religious faith, the decline of the material power of the church, and the indifference of modern nations to ethics, there was no longer a damper on power ambitions. If anything, the newly emerging doctrine of the *raison d'état*, the deification of the state, Paretian sociology, and the various forms of political Darwinism proclaiming the survival of the fittest strengthened the power urge as against all other interests and considerations. Humility and moderation ceased being virtues and became manifestations of weakness.

Internationally, the same trends promote an even more intense power struggle. The power tensions within each individual society react on its for-

[12] Romano Guardini, *Die Macht, Versuch einer Wegweisung*, Würzburg, Werkbund, 1951, pp. 37 *ff.*

eign policy. The quest for power and the struggles among and between the elites make the entire society more aggressive. The policy makers no longer belong to the one and only international elite. They no longer share certain minimum beliefs and standards. The domestic power struggle leads often, because of intolerable pressures or ultimate stalemates in internal politics, to a projection of domestic issues onto the international scene. The participants in the international struggle take advantage of domestic rivalries, and the ever tighter meshing of international conflict with civil and class warfare has brought to mankind unity of a kind, the unity of a panconflict world.

THE WEAKNESS OF THE FREEDOM URGE

We are thus confronted by the possibility that the relentless struggle may become ever more fierce, ever more limitless, and ever more senseless. To be sure, we are dealing with historical phenomena—the eagerness to fight may weaken again. But who can predict when the trend will change? Who can predict whether a turn toward peace will follow only upon the destruction of our resources because incessant struggle will have become too much of a luxury? Who can tell when the power urges will be brought again under control by a new ethical orientation and a return to the virtue of moderation? Modern psychology tells us that overemphasis on the power urge reflects personal immaturity and, not infrequently, insanity. Modern man is racked by neuroses, obsessions, compulsions, sado-masochistic and suicidal tendencies.[13] But this insight does not give us the complete diagnosis of our modern predicament. It simply elaborates on the psychological manifestations of a crisis which permeates the entire social fabric.

Theoretically, the power urge of the few could be restrained by the freedom urge of the many. After all, the basic objection against policy motivated by power considerations is not that such a policy is contrary to the nature of man but that it aims at satisfying the desires of small numbers of men to the detriment of the interests of the majority, i.e., that it benefits the few and does not serve the many. But it is futile to castigate the acts of the power-hungry when the evil is also caused, and perhaps to a greater measure, by the inactivity of the "herd." The overbearing impositions of the masters are a derivative of the submissiveness of the subjugated [14] in defending their own freedom.

That there is a basic freedom urge or instinct seems probable from Pavlov's celebrated experiments.[15] This urge manifests itself in strong tendencies to overcome obstacles, the refusal to adjust easily to a given milieu, the wish to remodel surroundings, and the desire to remain largely inde-

[13] See H. A. Overstreet, *The Mature Mind,* New York, Norton, 1949; Karen Horney, *The Neurotic Personality of Our Time,* New York, Norton, 1937.

[14] Rüstow, *op. cit.,* p. 116.

[15] W. Dabrovitch, *Fragilité de la liberté et séduction des dictateurs,* Paris, Mercure de France, 1934, pp. 56ff.

pendent from outside compulsion. Only a minority of Pavlov's dogs was possessed of this urge, which could be destroyed permanently by pain, frustration, and hunger. We do not know yet how widely distributed this urge is among the subspecies of *Homo sapiens,* but probably it exists only in relatively few individuals. Quite often, it merges with the power urge—only the powerful are free—and frequently it is rendered impotent by the contradictory urge to seek protection and shed responsibility. The satisfaction of the freedom urge requires high-tension work. But under many circumstances human beings are quite unable to produce the energy needed to operate within a psychological field of high tension. Persons under psychological pressure or suffering from traumas do not seek freedom and independence, *i.e.,* responsibility and the faculty to make their own decisions, but are waiting for orders. Their aim is adjustment and compliance, not initiative and leadership.

Throughout centuries the vast majority of mankind has been conditioned to carry out orders without questioning. Even in the United States, slavery was abolished less than ninety years ago. The inclination to obey still shapes conduct in most countries for most of the people. Where it no longer is the response to legal compulsion, there it is enforced by economic pressure. Where it no longer is the result of economic pressure, there it remains as a social habit. Compliance is demanded by most child-rearing and educational systems. It has become a psychological trait which is perpetuated by cultural and social structures.

Even in a democracy where there is great latitude of action, adjustment is an easier mode of life than any activity aiming at curbing the power instincts of the mighty. Anxiety and insecurity are the soil on which the power-hungry thrive. The frightened and the insecure allow the strong free rein not only because they do not dare oppose the strong but, more important, because they are seeking compensation in the protection which only the strong can give them. They are the more ready to forgo their own desires for self-assertion the greater their fear and the less trained their minds to accept or reject a proposition on the basis of its logical or factual validity alone.

Fear breeds suggestibility. Suggestion was defined by William McDougall as the "communication of any proposition from one person (or persons) to another in such a way as to secure its acceptance with conviction, in the absence of adequate logical ground for its acceptance." [16] Since in modern society the number of politically relevant people has grown, both in absolute and relative numbers, and since the faculty of logical discrimination is still restricted to a very small circle of people, it is obvious that suggestions presently wield a significant influence on events. Propaganda has become a vital tool of the power-elite. It preserves their security, secures compliance

[16] "Suggestion," *Encyclopaedia Britannica,* edition of 1944, Vol. 21, p. 531.

with their orders, enlists support for their actions—and stimulates, in feedback fashion, their own power urges.

ALIENATION

As man progressed from a relatively static to a highly dynamic society, he was deprived of patterns of regularity and social stability that he knew and was able to use for his own purposes. His life might have been short and dreary, but it was calculable, predictable, and relatively unexciting. Modern social developments have swept away most of the subordinate collectivities, so that man now has to move in the unfamiliar and almost abstract framework of a depersonalized state. The tempo of his life has increased. He is offered the choice between conflicting creeds and ideologies, is compelled every day to make decisions vitally affecting his own life, and finds himself confronted with rapidly changing situations. Worst of all, he moves from one soul-stirring excitement to the other. His inability to plan his life, to foresee his "station" in society and to operate under conditions of "normalcy," and not primarily his economic fears, make him psychologically insecure, isolated, and overstimulated. The implausibility of the old thought patterns deprives him of his intellectual crutches and throws him back on his own mental resources. All this cannot fail to produce states of anxiety. He becomes a stranger in his own society and in the world of his own thoughts and emotions; and this precisely is the phenomenon of alienation.

ANOMY

The political organization and procedures of modern states are inadequate for the accomplishment of the governmental function. This is partly the result of the rapid social change but partly a manifestation of poorly developed social inventiveness. The public discussion about suitable forms of political organization still is couched in terms dating from the 18th century —terms which, more often than not, have become simple clichés. The inertia of the existing structure resists modification and reform other than aggrandizement and enlargement. The government machinery is being improved by trial-and-error methods. Where a problem cannot be solved, the bureaucratic apparatus simply becomes bigger. The political "philosophers" of the 18th century recognized the needs of the age and proposed workable solutions. Their latter-day heirs cannot boast that they are coming to grips with the problems of political organization.

The organization of the state itself is highly deficient; a modern legislature, for example, is physically incapable of transacting the total volume of its business with the thoroughness and competence required. Laws limp behind developments. In some countries the books are being filled with contradictory laws, and everywhere laws are left unrepealed although they are no longer applicable. The political ideas on which most people, including government officials and Cabinet ministers, are acting are partially or totally false, often superficial, and always far short of the best available knowledge. At best, they reflect concepts which were valid one or two generations ago. The economic system, too, has changed its form since the beginning of the Industrial Revolution, progressing in some areas and regressing in others. There does not exist now anywhere an economic system which satisfies remotely scientific standards.

The inability to manage public life properly has been, and still is, creating untold psychological frustrations. Anomy—organizational ineffectiveness or breakdown—increases mental alienation and deprives the individual of the sense of belonging, cohesion, and common purpose. The social mind and the social structure are transforming themselves into mental orphanages. We know from Durkheim's studies [17] that anomy stimulates the suicidal tendencies of individuals. Is it too farfetched to assume that suicidal tendencies push nations toward war or allow the natural aggressors to satisfy their instincts in destructive ventures? The urge to self-destruction, to the "liquidation" of "classes," to genocide, to the annihilation of order, and to the elimination of property and the wish to create a social *tabula rasa* and to remake the world in fire and blood manifest insanity. The increase in the incidence of war and aggressiveness is paced by a significant growth of suicidal mania.

At the present time social change occurs in all corners of the globe. So do anomy and social disorganization. In the Western countries this change has been going on, at gradually increasing speed, since the Industrial and French Revolutions, that is, for 200-odd years. The Western nations have acquired some experience in developing adjustable institutions and an open society attuned to a continually expanding technology. Yet even the best-organized Western nations have failed to accommodate their societies to the rapid acceleration of change. The other nations and peoples who for centuries have been living in closed societies and caste systems, and whose cultures were not oriented toward the mastery of nature through technology but rather toward the mastery of hunger through asceticism and abnegation, suddenly find themselves confronted with what can be described only as a sociological holocaust. Beliefs, totems, taboos, habits, social relationships—all have been breaking up with incredible rapidity. Value systems are collapsing. Little is left but fear, insecurity, and helplessness.

The Western world has been adjusting itself mentally to the pace of modern technology and the discipline of scientific inquiry. Slow step by slow step, attitudes are being adopted which are compatible with, and ultimately may lead to, a rational organization of society. Other peoples are compelled to jump over several generations of human development. The advance from Lord Rutherford's Cavendish Laboratory to the isotope-separation plants

---

[17] Emile Durkheim, *Suicide: A Study in Sociology,* Glencoe, Ill., Free Press, first published 1897, Book 2, Chap. 5.

at Oak Ridge, Tennessee, is an exceptional but still a plausible performance. The transformation of a Russian muzhik into an operator of electronic computers, or of an illiterate Chinese coolie into an aircraft mechanic, or an animistic African native into a radio listener and supplier of a market economy, is a terrifying psychological catastrophe. Small wonder that the upheaval of culture and society transforms itself into aggressiveness! Contacts and conflicts with alien civilizations, which broke down the traditional structures, were the immediate cause of social change. Social and cultural disintegration now triggers international conflict.

THE STAGE OF HUMAN HISTORY

Human society is presently undergoing perhaps the greatest transformation of history. Any study of international politics must begin with the recognition that we live in a crisis of unparalleled dimensions. This crisis manifests itself in the impact of uncurbed power urges upon contemporary societies and in the impotence of the individual and the small group.

Furthermore, the modern crisis manifests itself in the fields of technology. Industrialization and electrification now reach into even the most backward areas; modern agricultural methods destroy the oldest traditions of work; motor transport, especially air transport, multiplies the contacts among people and makes entire societies mobile; electronics, especially radio and television, make most members of society participants in political and cultural life; and modern weapons of mass destruction pose a universal threat of annihilation.

Connected with these technological changes, there is an ever greater insistence on material well-being, while spiritual and aesthetic values are being lightly and indolently cast aside. There is the inadequacy (or at least instability) of economic and political organizations. There is the dynamics of the international "order," characterized by the disappearance of the balance of power among half a dozen great nations, the emergence of political oligopoly in the form of two "superpowers," the eclipse of small nations, and the stirring of the colored world. And there is the gradual merging of numerous, previously distinct, societies. Mankind reels under the impact of competitive and aggressive mass movements agitated by perniciously simplified and false ideas.[18]

This situation is being exploited to the hilt by international communism, itself a product and symptom of social disintegration. Communism proposes to intensify the crisis and to lead mankind by violent revolution and liquidation of the cultural and political elites to a new life. In fighting communism as a "solution" which would permanently install oppressive and violent power as the supreme arbiter of human affairs, the Western world must accelerate the decomposition of the existing order. It has failed so far to

[18] Hendrik de Man, *Vermassung und Kulturzerfall, eine Diagnose unserer Zeit,* Bern, Francke, 1951, Chap. 6.

TABLE 1. FACTORS CHARACTERIZING MODERN CRISIS *

Technology: Nuclear explosives
                Weapons with global range } High-offensive striking power
                Weapons with high speed
                Air transportation
                Radio and television
                Emerging nuclear technology (electric power)

Economic: Rapid industrialization
                Irrational organization of economic life
                Inadequate production } In backward areas
                Poor distribution systems
                Fluctuating role of ownership

Sociological: Breakdown of traditional societies
                Ideological, race, and class cleavages
                Mass movements
                Disappearing differences between city and country
                Merging of disparate societies
                Rapid population increases
                Mobility versus immobility

Psychological: Alienation
                Sado-masochism, compulsions, and other neurotic disturbances
                Cynical attitudes to value systems
                Deep anxieties

Political: Structural anomy
                Lack of organizational creativeness
                Change of international power balance

Threats: Communism and Soviet military and conspiratorial aggressiveness
                Disintegration of existing civilizations
                Revolt of backward and colored areas

Remedies: Scientific method
                Military power
                Constitutional government
                Organizational reform
                Stimulation of freedom desire

* This list is not complete. As the crisis develops, some of these factors may lose their importance. New factors, some of them now entirely unknown, will emerge.

bring about a definite reversal of the trend toward catastrophe; it has not yet overcome its own anomy.

This is the grim diagnosis of our times. Is the outlook hopeless? We are dealing with historical phenomena. Our present crisis had a beginning; hence it will have an end. The causes which presently are intensifying the power urge may change. If so, the infatuation with power may yield to cool detachment, and indeed the character of power may change too. Great changes are impending in the field of technology, especially in that of the civilian uses of nuclear energy, which herald an age of economic plenty. Yet the political and economic consequences of technological change depend in a large measure on mental attitudes. The Industrial Revolution of the 18th century did not suggest—as a self-explanation, so to speak—a new doctrine of economic management,[19] but followed upon, and was made possible by, the formulation of that doctrine. Similarly, the present crisis must be solved in the mind if we do not want to fight it out on the battlefields. History is not predetermined. Alienation, once properly diagnosed, can be cured. The mind of modern man is capable of submitting itself to the discipline of scientific inquiry. He can resolve to abide by the requirements of the scientific method, even in politics. In fact, the modern mind is quite incapable of attaching itself permanently to anything *but* the scientific ideal. Fundamentally, our political crisis signifies a break with political metaphysics and pseudomysticism. It is a mobilization of all the forces of all the societies.

It is not proposed here to design outlines for the future [20] except to repeat that there is only *one* way by which the spell of disaster can be broken and the great human potentialities of modern civilization be realized: the application of the scientific method to the problems of our time. We have no other choice but to identify and analyze the various factors which together create our difficulties. A clear understanding of these problems often will suggest, as a matter of course, practical methods of solution. In some cases, unfortunately, solutions may not be available; then, and only then, must we fall back on force and power to defend the values and institutions which we cherish—possibly for irrational reasons. This approach may not satisfy the crusader. Probably it will satisfy no one. But the insistence that infantile paralysis is a scourge does not by itself produce a cure. Slow, imperfect, and psychologically unrewarding, the scientific method is nevertheless the one and only instrument with which we can master our task. Slogans, blueprints, schemes, and exhortations concerning the improvement of mankind [21] do not advance but retard the solution of the international problem. The scientific method has as much appeal as the surgeon's knife or the mathematician's formulas. Yet, like Ulysses, the political scientist must tie himself to the mast in order not to succumb to the wiles of the sirens of emotion.

The ultimate objective of human society has been known at least since the Sermon on the Mount. It does not require restatement, although it may need elaboration. What it does require is the recognition and understanding of the facts. And no single fact is clearer than that, at present, the behavior of nations toward each other is motivated by the desire to dominate or by the fear of being dominated.

---

[19] Ludwig von Mises, *op. cit.*, p. 8.

[20] A serious discussion of historical alternatives may be found in Karl Jaspers, *Vom Ursprung und Ziel der Geschichte,* Munich, Piper, 1949.

[21] The origins of political verbalism are discussed by Carl Schmitt, in his *Romantisme politique,* Paris, Valois, 1928.

BIBLIOGRAPHY

Adler, Mortimer J.: *How to Think about War and Peace,* New York, Simon and Schuster, 1944.

Becker, Carl: *How New Will the Better World Be?* New York, Knopf, 1944.

Burckhardt, Jakob: *Grösse, Glück und Unglück in der Weltgeschichte,* Leipzig, Insel Verlag, 1932.

————: *Weltgeschichtliche Betrachtungen,* 2d ed., Berlin, Speman, 1910.

Burke, Edmund: *Reflections on the French Revolution* (various editions).

Burnham, James: *The Struggle for the World,* New York, John Day, 1947.

Croce, Benedetto: *Politics and Morals,* New York, Philosophical Library, 1945.

Ferrero, Guglielmo: *The Principles of Power: The Great Political Crises of History,* New York, Putnam, 1942.

Hamilton, Alexander, John Jay, and James Madison: *The Federalist* (Max Beloff, ed.), New York, Macmillan, 1948.

Hitler, Adolf: *Mein Kampf,* Munich, Eher Verlag, 1925.

Kirk, Russell: *The Conservative Mind from Burke to Santayana,* Chicago, Regnery, 1953.

Lasswell, H. D.: *Power and Personality,* New York, Norton, 1948.

Lea, Homer: *The Day of the Saxon,* New York, Harper, 1942.

Lenin, V. I.: *"Left-wing" Communism, an Infantile Disorder: An Experimental Popular Talk on Marxian Strategy and Tactics,* Moscow, Cooperative Publishing Society, 1935.

Machiavelli, Niccoló: *The Prince and the Discourses,* New York, Modern Lib., 1940.

Maistre, Joseph de: *Les soirées de Saint Petersbourg,* Paris, Renaissance du Livre, no date.

Muller, H. J.: *The Uses of the Past,* New York, Oxford, 1952.

Politis, Nicolas: *La Morale internationale,* New York, Brentano, 1944.

Reich, Emil: *Success among Nations,* New York, Harper, 1904.

Russell, Bertrand: *Power: A New Social Analysis,* New York, Norton, 1938.

Ryan, John K.: *Modern War and Basic Ethics,* Milwaukee, Bruce Pub., 1940.

Schmitt, Carl: *Der Begriff des Politischen,* Hamburg, Hanseatische Verlagsanstalt, 1933.

Schwarzschild, Leopold: *Primer of the Coming World,* New York, Knopf, 1944.

Shridharani, Krishnalal: *War without Violence,* New York, Duell, Sloan & Pearce, 1939.

Sorel, Georges: *Reflexions on Violence,* New York, Richard R. Smith, 1941.

Sorokin, Pitirim A.: *Man and Society in Calamity,* New York, Harper, 1942.

Stanton, A. H., and S. E. Perry: *Personality and Political Crisis,* Glencoe, Ill., Free Press, 1951.

Treitschke, Heinrich von: *Selections from Treitschke's Lectures on Politics,* Philadelphia, Stokes, 1914.

Walsh, Edmund A., S.J.: *Total Power,* New York, Doubleday, 1948.

Wright, Quincy: *A Study of War,* 2 vols., Chicago, University of Chicago Press, 1942.

Chapter 2

A GENERAL THEORY OF FOREIGN POLICY: ONE-STATE PERSPECTIVE POLICY MAKING

Foreign policy can be divided into the two broad categories of decision and execution. Government A may make the decision to increase the duty on a commodity imported from B. Once the decision has been made, the execution will consist in levying the newly imposed duty. Let us turn, first, to the decision-making process.

DECISION

Schematically, the government is apprised of a problem relating to foreign relations. A decision is made by the head of the state or the Cabinet, and the foreign minister communicates it to the affected foreign government through "diplomatic channels." An even simpler case is a decision of relatively minor importance which is made in the foreign ministry itself without prior discussion in the Cabinet. Rarely nowadays are decisions made by diplomats—"plenipotentiaries"—on foreign missions. In the past, diplomats were frequently allowed wide discretion in making decisions on the spot without consultation with the home office.

Matters seldom develop so simply. How is a problem put on the agenda of the Cabinet? The diplomatic representative abroad may inform the ministry of an occurrence requiring new decisions. The foreign minister may then transmit this message to the Prime Minister (or, in the United States, to the President) and a proposed solution may be submitted to the entire Cabinet. The question may be brought up by the military establishment or by any other of the governmental departments, every single one of which may be involved in foreign relations. In carrying out a previously adopted program, the government may, in the course of its deliberations and analyses, discover that a certain action in the field of foreign policy is required. Action may thus be initiated by the Cabinet without impulsion from abroad.

In many cases, there will be need for approval from the legislature and for the authorization of funds. The government may ask the legislature to support a decision, or the legislature may initiate action itself and tell the government what to do. Occasionally, the courts also get into the act.

However, we are still dealing with relatively simple cases. Suppose that there is a difference of opinion within the Cabinet, or between the Cabinet

and the legislature. It may then be necessary to amend the decision or tie it
to other decisions in order to compromise with the opposition. A disputed
decision may be subdivided into several smaller decisions, each of which
appears to involve a commitment less final or less costly than would the
single "package." Such a controversial measure can thus be presented to
public and parliament in seemingly innocuous instalments and pushed
through the legislative machinery without precipitating a major crisis. In
the case of cleavages between the government and the legislature, the government may try to put pressure on some of the legislators in order to obtain
a favorable vote. Or the government may carry out the legislature's decision
in a perfunctory and ineffectual manner.

In making foreign-policy decisions, the government, as well as the legislature, must protect its rear in the domestic field. Unpopular decisions may
endanger the tenure of the government, while popular decisions may endanger the security of the state. Public opinion, especially the press, exercises
considerable influence. Quite often, journalists identify problems which must
be acted upon, much earlier than does the government. They also propose,
criticize, praise, and advertise solutions. The same is true of businessmen,
industrialists and financiers, regional interests, religious organizations, and
other groups which frequently constitute themselves as pressure groups fighting for their vested interest or their ideas. Nationals residing abroad, such as
missionaries, writers, and traders, and mere tourists, often influence policy.

A state's foreign-policy decision always aims at another state. Accordingly,
it is preceded, regardless of whether the decision has a friendly or hostile
intent, by discussions between the two governments. Nearly always a decision is designed to obtain a follow-up decision on the part of the *other* government. The discussions between the two states may take place among
diplomats, foreign ministers, Cabinet members, nondiplomatic government
officials, or, more informally, between prominent private persons, private
emissaries, unofficial agents, and trusted individuals who have an entree to
important foreign groups. The immediate reactions and anticipated attitudes of the foreign government react on the precise nature of the decision.

It is possible that a decision will be supported by most of the domestic
groups interested in that particular phase of foreign policy. It is possible, too,
that this decision will be acceptable to the foreign government. But frequently the decision runs into opposition at home and proves unacceptable
to the foreign government. In this case the government may attempt to
shelve the original decision or to delay its execution. The foreign government may resort to countermeasures. It may, for example, exert pressure
in the economic field, or launch a propaganda campaign, or stimulate opposition in the press and among political parties. Further complications will
arise if there are, in any of the two states, conspiratorial and revolutionary
groups hoping to derive advantages from a blunder or an international crisis.

For that matter, even a "loyal opposition" is not always beyond pushing the government into an erroneous decision. Persons interested in such a turn of events may operate from any vantage point in the government, the legislature, or the public.[1]

EXECUTION

In the field of execution, there arises first the technical difficulty that the decision may not be understood properly by the numerous persons intrusted with executing its various parts. No decision can ever be applied forthwith; the execution must be carried out against time. This means that changes in the situation may negate the original intent of the decision and that, as other decisions are being made, the original decision, its intent, or its intended methods of execution may become inapplicable. For that matter, the wisdom of a decision can be tested only in application. Unforeseen difficulties and obstacles may arise requiring modifications, amendments, and supplementary decisions.

The effective implementation of a decision requires the wholehearted cooperation of the bureaucracy. Such cooperation does not always exist, especially if there are conflicting responsibilities (*Kompetenzstreit*) or if several government agencies and private institutions must participate in the act. A decision can be sabotaged or negated, executed too late or only partially. By the same token, the "administrator" can transform a barren decision, or a decision poorly and illogically phrased in its written form, into effective political action. Many programs can be carried out in the absence of a formal decision, or the decision may be applied to the letter but be negated through the absence of moderation and common sense. Then again, the program may be executed as planned but the intent not be realized because another program is pursued simultaneously. Complications of this type arise, for example, if politicians make decisions requiring military actions or if soldiers make decisions requiring political support, or if both make decisions requiring the cooperation of industrial management. Many types of technicians, including budget administrators, scientists, and police officials, possess a *de facto* power to make or break political programs.

Foreign-policy decisions always aim at foreign *targets*. The government does not necessarily project its act against the other government. It may deal with, or aim at, the foreign army or a political party. Military men of one country may contact their colleagues in the other. Important transactions resulting in modifications of foreign policy may take place between businessmen. There is an infinite variety of possibilities in all fields of economic, social, and cultural life, *e.g.*, banking, labor organizations, religion, science,

---

[1] On the concept of policy sabotage, see Stefan T. Possony, *A Century of Conflict, Communist Techniques of World Revolution*, Chicago, Regnery, 1953, pp. 404*f*.

and agriculture, and in all ranges of political power, *e.g.*, ex-ministers, cabinet-members-designate, and nationals of third countries acting as intermediaries.

The methods by which the message articulating the decision can be transmitted are most variable. The most conventional methods are the various types of diplomatic notes and communications as well as of diplomatic conferences, culminating in agreements and treaties. But there are communiqués, speeches, timed publication of documents and books, enactments of laws, propaganda campaigns, informal meetings, the application of pressure, performance of symbolic acts, secret communications of information, conspiracy, terror, rupture or intensification of diplomatic and economic relations, conclusion of military alliances with third parties, and finally military actions. There also is the dismissal or appointment of specifically oriented personalities to key positions, including changes of government and parliamentary groupings. A revolution often redefines a country's foreign policy and therefore is, in its results, a foreign political act. By its mere existence, a government represents a specific foreign policy.

THE BASIC RELATIONSHIPS BETWEEN SOCIETIES

Let us take the simple case of two states whose social organization is more or less identical. Their inhabitants have roughly the same income per head of population and enjoy similar educational standards. Their types of government are closely related, and their over-all security interests are parallel. The two states are contiguous to each other. In such a case, conflicts may emerge from competitive territorial claims, inexact delineation of rights, diverging economic interests, domestic struggles which are projected abroad, and animosity between ruling groups. This list is by no means complete, but it illustrates the point that conflict between more or less "identical" states rarely becomes too serious. The quasi identity of two societies, however, need not last. As each state leads a separate life, each one develops its own traditions, practices, and prejudices. All that needs to happen is a fundamental change in the political system of one of the neighbors or, for example, the coming to power of an aggressive party, and a major crisis is in the making.

Let us take a similar case and stipulate that the two neighbors belong to different religions and that the population of one of the states is increasing rapidly! After a while the surplus population may migrate into the "empty" neighboring country and settle close to the frontier. Let us assume that a generation passes and the host state takes discriminatory action against the newly established religious minority, or that the country of origin claims special rights for its citizens living beyond the frontier. Again a crisis is developing. We may take any two states and introduce additional variables; complications would arise in a similar manner.

However, in actual life, states which are in mutual contact usually represent two different types of society. It happens that one state may break apart and its successor states develop from similarity to ever greater diversification. In the primitive world, the alien was an enemy whose visit usually signified plunder or invasion. In modern times, the foreigner speaks with a different tongue, and his mind operates somewhat differently from the home-grown variety: he is not trustworthy because he differs from the national norm. Not that all mankind does not possess the same logic and, to a degree, the same mind! But the mind is not always used in the same fashion. There are more or less highly developed minds. There are areas of knowledge and experience, and areas of ignorance and traditions. There are differences in value systems, desires, ambitions, codes of behavior, procedures, business methods. As it is perfectly obvious to the member of one nation that he ought to take off his shoes upon entering a private home, so, too, it may be no less obvious to him that to purify one's drinking water is to offend one's most sacred tradition. One nation may be interested in the improvement of economic well-being, another may worry about the salvation of the soul. One nation may consider all people as equal human beings, another may restrict the rights of "low" castes and women. Even allies fighting on the same side against the same enemy have different ideas as to how they should proceed and about the limits of ruthlessness to which they should go. Differences in social organization, religious beliefs, and avowed or unavowed national objectives cause distrust and often hatred. And while in more than one respect we are discussing, objectively, petty matters, these differences in mentality [2] and outlook not only keep nations apart but also provoke active conflict.

AREAS OF CONFLICT

There are ten major areas of conflict between states. States may quarrel on account of differences in their *mental* outlook, especially if one of the two tries to impose upon the other its ideas—political ideologies—as the dominant ones. *Psychological* differences, especially fear, hatred, arrogance, or divergent manners and customs, may produce misunderstandings which can degenerate into conflict. Differences in the *social* structure evoke opposition as a result of the apprehension on the part of one state about the security of its own social organization. For example, a caste state may fear that the ascendancy of an egalitarian state may put an end to social stratification and caste privilege. *Cultural* differences arise when one culture—the sway of a language, a literature, and a national "style"—is more dynamic than the other and when there are cultural minorities in either one of the states. *Population* pressures and freedom of, or barriers to, migration easily lead to disputes. Conflicts over *economic* issues occur in many types: com-

[2] Gaston Bouthol, *Traité de sociologie,* 2d ed., Paris, Payot, 1949, Part II, Chaps. 3 and 4.

petition for markets and supplies; disputes over trade terms and conditions of payment; quarrels over joint property rights; and controversies over such highly technical matters as, for example, restrictions on exchange, transit rights, and reinvestment of earned surpluses. Economic disputes between industrial states usually center upon trade restrictions, monopoly exploitation, and currency regulations, while disputes between an economically advanced and a backward country may concern mining concessions, trade monopolies, defaulting on loans, reinvestment of locally earned profits, native comanagement rights, and expropriation of foreign property. Historically, conflict about *territorial claims* has been perhaps the single most potent cause of enmity between states. Territory may be disputed on historic, economic, demographic, ethnic, military, and numerous other grounds. Strictly *political* disputes arise if the objectives of two states are not compatible (the maintenance of the *status quo* versus the change of the *status quo*) or if their political systems (dictatorship versus democracy) differ and one deems itself threatened, potentially or actually, by the other. The *security interests* of states may lead into conflict by many routes: armaments may call for counterarmaments; troop movements for counter troop movements; and the conclusion of foreign alliances for counteralliances. All kinds of actions may be answered by a new spiral of actions and counteractions. Lastly, a state may harbor *aggressive designs* against another state and thus produce a conflict which is more comprehensive than all the other types of conflict. The naked power struggle tends to embrace all other disputes and litigations. It is undertaken for its own sake, *l'art pour l'art* in politics, the conflict *an sich*.

On the basis of these different types of conflict, the ultimate objectives of political action can be simplified as follows: A state may aim at:

1. The rectification of its borders by redrawing them at a different geographic location or by changing the regime in the disputed area.

2. The modification of another state's economic system and the expansion of its own in order to strengthen its supply base, broaden its markets, increase its profits, and provide outlets for its population.

3. The modification of another state's political, social, and cultural system and the expansion of its own system with the purpose of changing the other state's basic policy, government, political institutions, or, ultimately, its social structure.

4. Increasing its security by defeating or diverting possible threats, or by establishing its own decisive power superiority.

As a variant of the last objective, the aggressor state may aim at establishing regional or global power monopoly. It is characteristic of all major conflicts that the four different objectives are usually pursued simultaneously.

Theoretically, cooperation could obtain in the same areas in which we find conflict-*minus*-aggression. In reality, however, cooperation usually is restricted to economics and to security matters. There was hardly ever, and there is not now, any large-scale attempt to cooperate in the amelioration of boundaries, in the exploitation and development of territories, or in the equitable distribution of population. Cooperation in the intellectual, psychological, and cultural fields is restricted to a few haphazard contacts. In the field of political structures, systems, and techniques cooperation is very rare; each state, quite uncritically, presupposes that its system is perfect and that other systems are inapplicable. It is a triumph of rationality when two states with different systems agree to cooperate at all.

To understand the difficulty of international cooperation, we must look at the differences of state structures. We can distinguish six broad categories: political structure, economic structure, social structure, national composition, degree of uniformity, and cultural status.

1. *Political structure.* There is the broad distinction between authoritarian and free governments. There are furthermore regimes which fit neither description. Some of these represent surviving historical forms of government such as feudalism, tribalism, and theocracy. There is a great diversity of colonial and nonsovereign structures.

2. *Economic structure.* The historic distinction between industrial and agricultural societies gradually ceases to be meaningful; mechanization is transforming agriculture into an industry. Yet productionwise the distinction still holds. There are, of course, differences in the degree of industrialization and agricultural techniques. Industrial development in Asia differs from European patterns which, in turn, deviate from the United States model.

3. *Social structure.* The basic difference is between changing, advancing, and egalitarian societies, on one hand, and static, stagnant, and stratified societies, on the other hand, or, to use different labels, between positive or metaphysical, open or closed, experimental or traditional societies.

4. *National composition.* The principal distinction is between nation-states and multination-states. Nations may be domiciled in clearly defined territories or be dispersed in several territories. The rule of the multination-state may be exercised by one dominant nation or may be organized along various lines of federal government.

5. *Degree of uniformity.* A nation may be religiously, ideologically, culturally uniform or multiform. For example, it may profess several religions but one and the same political ideology, or it may be riven by ideological conflict that does not preclude unanimity in religious and cultural matters.

6. *Cultural status.* A nation may have high or low literacy standards—literacy defined in its broadest meaning. It may or may not be using modern techniques and procedures in its everyday life. It may plan or program its life or live by improvisation. It may be guided, in varying degrees, by tradition or by the scientific method.

Each state is unique as it possesses some of these elements and lacks others. Cooperation or conflict, therefore, does not take place between abstract states. In practice we are confronted, for example, by not a few situations involving relationships between an agricultural, authoritarian, static, multinational, religiously homogeneous, and culturally primitive state, on one hand, and an industrial, republican, dynamic, single-national, ideologically split, and highly literate state, on the other hand. Even between similar types of states, there are noteworthy differences: one free government may have a majority-republican system with fixed government tenure; another a proportional-representation, parliamentary system with frequent government changes. These various sociopolitical systems are not attuned to each other and are, in many respects, quite incompatible. This is the fundamental reason why international cooperation is haphazard, restricted, and unstable. We have "one world" only in an astronomical sense.

In this divided world of states, economic cooperation must take place between different types of markets and economic systems. Disregarding the differences in monetary systems, a competitive, free-enterprise national economy, for example, may transact business with a monopolistic or oligopolistic supplier, or two monopolies may trade with each other. The possible combinations have been worked out by Walter Eucken.[3]

On the basis of these different types of cooperation between discrete structures, the objectives of cooperative political action can be simplified as follows:

1. Integration of elements of strength in order to enhance mutual security and reduce defense costs.

2. Stimulation of trade in commodities in order to improve living standards and enhance other economic advantages.

3. Stimulation of exchange of techniques and cultural goods in order to improve cultural and intellectual standards.

4. Slow, adaptive transformation of society in order to eliminate preventively causes of conflict.

5. Transaction of all types of business to the mutual benefit of the several states.

TYPES OF POLITICAL ACTION

A situation is given which causes the government uneasiness; or the government's actions are motivated by an image of a more satisfactory state.[4] The uneasiness leads to remedial, the image to creative, action. Both uneasiness and image are connected with any, several, or all of the conflict or cooperation situations and the conflict or cooperation objectives. The task now is to decide upon the *means* by which these *ends* are to be reached.

Usually, there are alternate means. The choice of the means depends on five considerations.

1. *Motivation of the policy.* How important is it to reach the desired end? Is there a strong desire within the state or a strong compulsion from the out-

[3] Walter Eucken, *The Foundations of Economics, History and Theory in the Analysis of Economic Reality,* London, Hodge, 1950, p. 158.

[4] Ludwig von Mises, *Human Action: A Treatise on Economics,* New Haven, Yale University Press, 1949, p. 14.

TABLE 2. FORMS OF MARKET*

Form of demand	Form of supply				
	Competition	Partial oligopoly	Oligopoly	Partial monopoly	Monopoly, individual or collective
Competition	Perfect (complete) competition	Partial oligopoly of supply	Supply oligopoly	Partial monopoly of supply	Supply monopoly
Partial oligopoly (oligopoly)	Partial oligopoly of demand	Bilateral partial oligopoly	Supply oligopoly limited by partial oligopoly of demand	Partial monopoly of supply limited by partial oligopoly of demand	Supply monopoly limited by partial oligopoly of demand
Oligopoly (oligopsony)	Demand oligopoly	Demand oligopoly limited by partial oligopoly of supply	Bilateral oligopoly	Partial monopoly of supply limited by oligopoly of demand	Supply monopoly limited by oligopoly of demand
Partial monopoly (monopsony)	Partial monopoly of demand	Partial monopoly of demand limited by partial oligopoly of supply	Partial monopoly of demand limited by oligopoly of supply	Bilateral partial monopoly	Supply monopoly limited by partial monopoly of demand
Monopoly (monopsony), individual or collective	Demand monopoly	Demand monopoly limited by partial oligopoly of supply	Demand monopoly limited by oligopoly of supply	Demand monopoly limited by partial monopoly of supply	Bilateral monopoly

* Copyright 1951 by the University of Chicago.

side? Is the policy designed to widen the spheres of cooperation or to enhance power? Suppose improved cooperation is the goal. In this case radical means of conflict should be ruled out and an earnest attempt be made to proceed, for example, through diplomatic or economic arrangements. Occasionally, propaganda and political warfare could be employed. But open violence should be shunned. Suppose, however, that the attainment of more power is a stringent requirement of security. Then only employment of radical means may bring the desired objective within reach. In general, the more imperative is the objective and the greater the latent or actual hostility between the states, the more ruthless are the methods.

2. *Timing*. The achievement of an objective may be imperative, yet it may not matter if the goal be reached within ten or twenty years. In such a case, gradual and moderate means will be preferred. By the same token, the faster an objective must be attained, the more radical and violent must be the means.

3. *Cost*. Means selected under the two previous headings must be within the financial, industrial, social, political, and military capability of a nation. A technique may be feasible economically, but the political or social structure could not bear the cost. A politically sensible procedure may be economically quite impractical. Cost considerations may force a scaling down of the objective and may require a "stretch-out" of the program. Conversely, they may compel the adoption of techniques which may be expected to be effective rapidly and which may require a costly, albeit brief, effort. Indirect costs also must be considered, such as those incurred when a particular course of action affects adversely relations with third states.

4. *Risk*. Each course of action entails risks. It may be risky to let the situation continue without applying remedies; it may be equally risky to apply these remedies. In general, a state will choose those methods which entail minimum risks, but this does not mean that it will therefore select the least violent techniques. The greatest violence coupled with utmost rapidity often presents the minimum of risk. It may happen that the least violence coupled with the slowest speed spells complete ruin. While radical methods will be fraught with immediate risk, they also increase the chance of success; evolutionary methods may postpone the risk but may cause a greater and more permanent hazard in the future. In some cases, however, slow evolutionary methods may entail the least risk and yield the surest result.

5. *Conflicting policies*. There may be contradictory motivations and conflicting time, cost, and risk estimates. The execution of one policy may interfere with the execution of another equally important policy. The selection of one course of action may—through the necessities of industrial "lead times," for example—preclude a change to another course, although the alternate action may prove more desirable. Most important is the consideration that upon completion of the adopted action, a second and third series of actions must follow. Specifically, peaceful cooperation may be succeeded by

military conflict which in turn may lead to another round of cooperation. Political affairs are so much in flux that overcommitment to one policy or course of action may be as dangerous as frequent changes of policy.

The balancing of these criteria is a most delicate art. It is complicated by the fact that all choices must be based on anticipation of future events, which means that each choice involves forecasting. It is quite possible to make forecasts about phenomena which occur with statistical or cyclical regularity or which develop according to trend curves. Within general orders of magnitude, the growth of industrial output can be predicted within *one* known technological period, though basic changes in technology must invalidate forecasts. Prediction is an uncertain business. In most cases forecasts prove too low or too high, too early or too late. In the really relevant areas of political action, they are quite useless—and yet, paradoxically, the maker of foreign policy must constantly seek to plan against the unknown future.

The choice from among alternate means is a "rational" undertaking. Means are selected nearly always after *some* rational consideration. Governments which are run in an orderly manner will always employ means selected on the basis of elaborate staff work. This does not mean, of course, that reason is always most lucidly employed, that it is used in its full range, and that it is applied at the exclusion of other human factors and frailties. The question now is as to method.

Let us assume that, objectively, there are available ten different methods by which the desired end can be achieved. Let us assume also that, of these ten methods, seven had heretofore never been employed by a particular government, and let us assume furthermore that, in its current deliberations, this government now focuses its attention only on those three methods which it has employed in the past. In this case, the government would comply with custom and habit and apply a traditional mode of action. Such traditionalism also may affect the choice of ends. For example, the government never has given thought to overthrowing a hostile government but has always been obsessed by the idea of so rectifying its boundaries that it will hold a decisive strategic advantage in relation to the strategic geography of that potential opponent. Or a government persists in an attitude toward another state which corresponds to issues and necessities which were alive in previous periods. Thus, it may regard the other state as an hereditary enemy or as an eternally faithful ally. If a statesman defines ends on the basis of such dated assumptions, he is acting by the force of habit but is not proceeding rationally; *i.e.*, he does not use the full range of his reasoning powers but allows his mind to be blocked by "fixations."

Suppose a government is highly emotional about the decision it has to make. It hates or fears the other state, or wishfully closes its eyes to danger, or believes strongly that history is predetermined either in its own or in its opponent's favor. Suppose, too, that such a government has a preconceived notion or an "unconscious" urge for a particular type of action and that therefore it marshals its evidence merely in order to arrive at the preconceived decision. In this case it is acting with a minimum of reason—logic is being used mechanically and functionally but not substantially—and its decisions conform to preexisting attitudes rather than to realities. It happens frequently that the key decision makers are headstrong and stubborn individuals who do not consider the facts or fail to discriminate between primary and secondary factors. In such cases, too, action will not be rational in the proper sense of the term.

Not a few rulers are themselves ruled by ideals, values, moral precepts, and world conceptions and images to which they wish to conform in their acts. A statesman who cherishes peace will eschew military techniques. An ethically oriented government may spurn devious procedures in diplomacy and propaganda. A statesman trying to accomplish an utopian design may be willing to act on the doctrine that the end justifies the means, although in so doing he may defeat the basic purpose of the entire operation. On the other hand, being conscious of his goal, he may employ only those means which are compatible with the objective and which nevertheless are sufficient to accomplish the purpose. In this case, we have what Max Weber called *wertrationales Handeln,*[5] or value-oriented rational action. This can be defined as the choice of means compatible with one's ethical norms, yet adequate for the realization of the goal.

Lastly, we have rational action in the proper sense of the term. The objective is chosen on the basis of a thorough appraisal of alternate objectives, and it is selected in conformity with the purpose of the going or the growing concern. It is clearly spelled out whether the purpose is to enhance cooperation, to prevent conflict, or to win a conflict. Consideration is given to the interrelationships between cooperation and conflict. Can improved cooperation prevent the conflict, smother it, or enhance the chances of winning it? Is success in conflict an objective in itself, or is it a step on the road to ultimate cooperation?

On the basis of these determinations, all the available means are examined with a clear awareness of mental "soft spots" which may result from preexisting attitudes, emotions, or traditions. Methods are selected which will be sufficient for the purpose, both in scope and in time, as distinguished from a semirational action which, for example, would choose the right methods as to type but apply them in the manner of "too little and too late." Cost and risk factors will be given due consideration, with a clear realization that under certain circumstances both have only relative value: overemphasis on cost may increase the risk, while overemphasis on risk may either increase the cost or lead to inaction and thus augment the risk.

Under certain conditions, a rational course of action cannot be charted at all. A situation may be so fluid that ends cannot be fixed or the task of attain-

[5] Max Weber, *The Theory of Social and Economic Organization,* New York, Oxford, 1947, p. 115.

ing determined objectives may be so difficult that it is beyond immediate capability. In such a case the characteristic British doctrine of "wait and see"—the pragmatic method—offers the only practical solution, *provided* the proper precautions are taken and a rational policy formulated as soon as it is feasible.

A proper understanding of one's own objective is a necessary step in the elaboration of rational action. The rejection or acceptance of an objective may not be due to fully rational analysis and, in fact, usually hinges on the decision maker's value system and metaphysical convictions. But in making the choice according to his metaphysics, he should perceive his alternatives and the implications of his selection.

In a formal sense the ultimate alternative is between the *going* and the *growing* concern. But it does not follow that choosing the growing concern as the objective of foreign policy requires the waging of conflict, or that preoccupation with the going concern excludes the possibility of struggle. If cooperation and conflict are the two alternate modes of "coexistence," cooperation may be chosen as the means to achieve a growing concern, but conflict may be the sole means to defend the *status quo*. There is no sense in pairing conflict and growing concern, or cooperation and going concern. Furthermore, the operational modes are interrelated: cooperation may be a method aiming at avoiding conflict or, conversely, a method of preparing for conflict. By the same token, conflict may be resorted to in order to open the way for more intimate cooperation.

In opting for a cooperative effort, a decision must be made concerning the *purpose* of cooperation. Cooperation may be undertaken for the enhancement of mutual security or for economic benefit, or for both. Cooperation for security demands cooperation between governments as to the identification of the danger and the selection of the methods to avert or reduce it. It requires cooperation in the military field and in many cases must take the form of a written or formal alliance.

Of the many considerations which go into the forging of an effective alliance, let us consider briefly the geographic factor.

Assume that states A, B, C, D are situated along one geographical axis and that A is contiguous to B, B to C, C to D, and that there is major conflict, or actual war, between A and B. The following possibilities arise: A and B fight, and C and D remain neutral; A and C are allied against B, and D remains neutral; A, C, D are allied against B; C and B are allied against A, and D remains neutral; A and C are allied against B and D; A and D are allied against B and C; and B, C, and D are allied against A.

The policy of A will be aimed at alliances with C and possibly D, or at their neutrality. The policy of B will be directed at alliances with D to neutralize C, or with C to neutralize a hostile D, or at alliances with both C and D, or at their neutrality.

If the major conflict shifts from A:B to B:C or C:D, these relationships will be rearranged accordingly.

Under certain conditions, noncontiguous alliances will be replaced by contiguous alliances, and the set of four states may split up into two hostile "blocs," A,B versus C,D. These spatial and geographic arrangements must be taken into account in determining the policies of nations whose intentions are fixed; often rational choices will arise from geography (see page 37).

Under modern technical conditions, military alliances restricted to cooperation between armed forces of different composition and organization and to delivery of equipment and logistic support may not prove a practical device wherewith to meet military aggression. Such loose arrangements may have to be replaced by close integration among military establishments (*e.g.*, adoption of similar organizational patterns and identical equipment), or by "military federation," or by outright merger which in due time could lead to political federation. Cooperation for conflict extends, of course, to nonmilitary fields, especially to economics, where it requires the pooling of resources and joint planning for production and distribution.

Cooperation for mutual economic benefit proceeds primarily through the stimulation of exchange. It can take numerous forms, such as trade agreements, loans, exchange of patents, technical aid, and lifting of trade and currency restrictions. Cooperation will be the more successful the more fully the interest of each partner is being satisfied, an axiom which often argues against abstract and generalized solutions (*e.g.*, free trade any time, anywhere) and may require intermediate and compromise solutions which are applicable only to one case and only to a limited period. Rational action requires that the problem which cooperation is to solve should be analyzed properly and that solutions be worked out which do not conform to theoretical concepts alone. Solutions must prove to be politically acceptable. They must constitute steps forward on the road to the ultimate, the "ideal" solution. Statesmanship cannot operate by rote; its practice calls for creative thinking.

Conflict management requires action in many fields, and it is unnecessary to enumerate the entire gamut of actions designed to overcome an opponent. Conflict action can be violent or nonviolent in nature. It can be directed against hostile organizations, groups, and personalities, or it can be designed to reduce the opponent's human and material sources of power. It aims at frustrating the accomplishment of the opponent's purpose and at facilitating the attainment of one's own objective. These ends are reached by changing the opponent's motivation, the programs of hostile ruling groups and decision makers, or, to put it differently, by influencing and changing the opponent's mind or government; or by crippling the opponent's capabilities.

There are *four* basic techniques which may be employed to accomplish these conflict objectives:

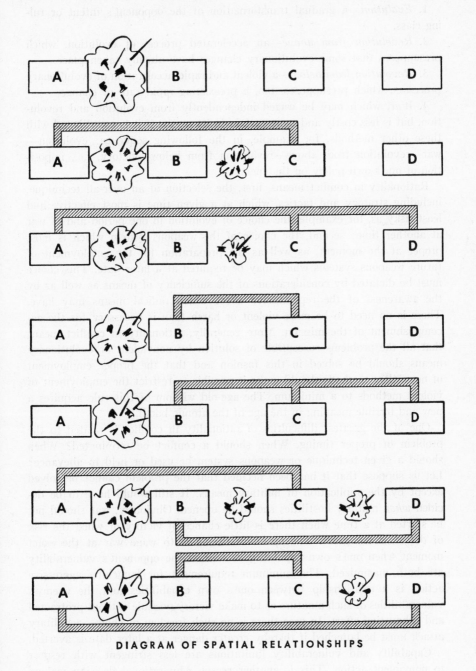

DIAGRAM OF SPATIAL RELATIONSHIPS

1. *Evolution*—a gradual transformation of the opponent's intent or ruling class.

2. *Revolution from above*—an accelerated process of evolution, which presupposes that some evolutionary changes have already taken place.

3. *Revolution from below*—a violent and rapid acceleration of evolutionary processes, which presupposes, too, a preexisting rapid rate of change.

4. *War,* which may be waged independently from evolution and revolution, but is less costly and more certain in its results if it is coordinated with these other methods, for example, in the following sequence: evolution—war—revolution from above—revolution from below—victory, *i.e.,* imposition of one's own policy on the enemy.

Rationality in conflict means, first, the selection of an over-all technique, including strategy and tactics, which at a given time is most effective and least risky as, for example, the choice of evolution in one period and of war at another time; second, the choice of the weapons system which is most proper at the moment, as well as the preparation for the employment of future weapons systems which may be required at a later date. This choice must be dictated by considerations of the sufficiency of means as well as by the awareness of the repercussive effect which radical means may have. There is no need to be more violent or harsh than is necessary for the accomplishment of the mission. More generally, rationality in conflict means that all the problems susceptible of solution by nonviolent or evolutionary means should be solved in this fashion and that the proper employment of nonviolent methods should make it possible to restrict the employment of violent methods to a minimum. The age-old wisdom of this rule acquires a new and terrible meaning in the age of the atomic bomb.

One of the greatest difficulties of rationality in conflict is related to the problem of proper timing. When should a conflict be terminated? When should a given technique or weapons system be used or held in abeyance? Let us suppose that it has been decided that the problem cannot be solved except by the application of military means. It still would have to be decided *when* military hostilities should be opened. Obviously, war should not be started at a time when there is little chance of victory or when the risk of defeat is too great. The optimum timing is to wage war at the exact moment when one's own capability as well as the opponent's vulnerability are both maximized. The minimum requirement for launching aggressive action is a relationship between one's own capabilities and the enemy's vulnerabilities of such a nature as to make victory possible without protracted and exhausting effort. In case there is no such freedom of choice, a military attack must be launched if thereby *greater* danger at a later date is averted.

Capability and vulnerability limitations are less stringent with respect to nonviolent action. This is another reason why rational decision makers should exploit nonviolent techniques to the fullest. Moreover, the outcome of a violent action can never be estimated accurately. Hence, control over violent operations is much more difficult to maintain than control over non-violent types of action.

Conflict actions, as they are projected abroad, require concurrent actions at home. These actions should be designed to enhance one's own capabilities, reduce vulnerabilities, avoid giving the opponent openings, and prepare opportunities for one's own initiatives. Only a strong society can engage successfully in the deadly serious conflicts of modern power politics.

BIBLIOGRAPHY

Hayek, F. A.: *The Counter-revolution of Science,* Glencoe, Ill., Free Press, 1952.

Klingberg, Frank L.: "Studies in Measurement of the Relations among Sovereign States," *Psychometrika,* Vol. 6, No. 6, 1941.

Lerner, Daniel, and Harold D. Lasswell (eds.): *The Policy Sciences,* Stanford, Calif., Stanford University Press, 1951.

Madariaga, Salvador de: *Theory and Practice in International Relations,* Philadelphia, University of Pennsylvania Press, 1937.

Morgenthau, Hans J.: *Scientific Man vs. Power,* Chicago, University of Chicago Press, 1946.

————, and Kenneth W. Thompson: *Principles and Problems of I..ternational Politics,* New York, Knopf, 1952.

Richardson, Lewis F.: "Generalized Foreign Politics," *British Journal of Psychology,* Monograph Supplement, Vol. 23, 1939.

Russell, Frank M.: *Theories of International Relations,* New York, Appleton-Century, 1936.

Schwarzenberger, Georg: *Power Politics: A Study of International Society,* New York, Praeger, 1951.

United Nations Educational, Scientific, and Cultural Organization, Massimo Salvadori (ed.): *Contemporary Political Science: A Survey of Methods, Research and Teaching,* Paris, 1950.

Wiese, Leopold von: *Systematic Sociology: or the Basis of the Bezichungslehre und Gebildelehre,* amplified by Howard Becker, New York, Wiley, 1932.

Chapter 3

A GENERAL THEORY OF FOREIGN POLICY: A SITUATIONAL PERSPECTIVE

Economic actions of individuals, producers, traders, government "planners," and consumers are at the basis of the formation of prices. Similarly, the actions of individual governments or internationally significant groups produce what, for the want of a better term, could be called the general or world situation. As economic man must orient his action toward prevailing or expected prices, so the maker of foreign policy must take into account all the relationships of his own state and most of the relationships among the other states and cannot confine his attention to the single relationship between two or three nations. If he fails to do so, his actions easily may come to grief and he may overlook opportunities for effective action.

There are at present in existence about 100 legally independent states and about two dozen semi-independent or quasi-sovereign units. Restricting ourselves to the 100-odd states and assuming that at any given moment there is only one relationship between two governments, the "world situation" could be described as the sum of 9,900 individual bilateral relations. We must assume that in each state there is an opposition to the government; it is conceivable that this opposition maintains relations with all the foreign nations. Assuming only one opposition per state, and assuming that the opposition groups maintain relations among each other, the theoretical number of relationships would rise to 39,800.

Actually, the real number would be much lower: there will be only limited or occasional contacts between opposition groups and foreign governments as well as among opposition groups. Applying common sense to these figures we can say that many sovereign nations do not maintain more than fictitious contacts with the majority of other governments. For example, the relations between Paraguay and Trucial Oman are quite irrelevant. Nevertheless, 50 states, in rough estimate, are really important. Hence 2,450 primary intergovernmental relationships must be considered, to which sum several hundred interrelationships between governments and opposition groups must be added. If the interrelationships between trade unions, business firms, religious groups, etc., are taken into consideration, as they must be, the world situation at any given moment would have to be described by 5,000 to 10,000 internationally relevant interconnections.

The analysis can be simplified through the identification of the *dominant issue* or a limited number of crucial issues. It is a historical fact that, with the exception of genuine periods of peace, one issue usually has primed all others in importance. For example, in the 1930's, the dominant issue was the aggressiveness of National Socialist Germany. The aggressiveness of Japan, while the main issue in Asia, was, globally speaking, derivative. In the late forties, Soviet aggressiveness had become the dominant issue. Subsidiary issues, such as the Franco-Italian dispute about Tunis or the nationalization of the tin mines in Bolivia, should not be overlooked, but they derived their international, as distinguished from their bilateral, significance from their "tie-in" into the global problem.

Whether or not isolated issues can be settled "on their own merits" depends on the scope and intensity of the dominant issue. But world events cannot be understood without reference to the primary issues, and the handling of subsidiary problems must depend on their interrelationship with the most relevant conflict. There is no dominant issue which does not affect, to a greater or lesser degree, the great powers, which number between three and nine, depending on the criteria of measurement. Since the cleavages between these powers usually bear on their relations with other nations, *the analysis of the relationships between ten to twenty nations is the absolute minimum for the adequate description of the international situation.* This "simple" case still requires the analysis of several hundred internationally significant interrelationships.

International relations are in constant flux. From one moment to the other, cooperation may supersede conflict and conflict cooperation. Within the one or other broad category, there are many gradations and policies continuously moving along the scale between one absolute state (perfect cooperation) and the other (all-out conflict). The analysis of this constant flux is necessary for the orientation of the policy makers. How can this analysis be performed?

Let us take the simplest case, two states A and B, and assume again that they have the choice between two fundamental attitudes, cooperation and conflict. We can then construct a scale to indicate the intensity of these attitudes. Descending downward from the cooperation maximum, we find that A and B can have the following friendly relations:

A:B Friendly Attitude Implementations

Union	Cultural and social merger
	Political
Federation	Political
	Military
	Economic
Confederation	
Alliance	Formal
	Informal
Long-term exchange agreements	
Coordinated policy	
Frequent cooperation	
Intermittent cooperation	
No contacts	

The precise quality of these attitudes will be more clearly defined if neither A nor B maintains significant contacts with third powers; that is, if A and B coordinate their policy only among themselves and do not coordinate it with $C, D. . . .$

Turning to the second basic attitude, conflict, we find the following scale:

A:B Inimical Attitude Implementations

Military aggression	Unlimited
	Limited
Counteroffensive, including preventive war	
Intervention by offensive means	
Defensive	Active resistance to aggression
	Defensive resistance
	Passive defensive
Defense by nonviolent techniques and preparedness	
Power competition	
Intermittent nonviolent opposition	
Appeasement	
(Occupation)	
(Surrender)	
(Annexation)	
(Extinction)	

It is clear that the four relations listed in parentheses can occur only after conflict already has led to victory through aggression; they would then move to the top of the list. All these attitudes are changeable in time, with the exception of extinction, which is irreversible.

The relationship between A and B can be called the primary power relationship. But there are third states which maintain vis-à-vis A and B a derivative relationship that may be called a third-power relationship. We shall illustrate this relationship by introducing state C.[1]

---

[1] Leopold von Wiese points out the social importance of the "pair," of which the husband-wife, parent-child, superior-subordinate, teacher-pupil types are most illustra-

It is apparent that *C*'s relations with *A* and *B* are dependent on whether *C* is a strong state, and whether the attitudes of *A* and *B* toward each other are friendly or hostile. Let us list first a weak *C*'s possible policies in case of *A* : *B* hostility:

WEAK C (A:B HOSTILE)

Alliance to help victory of *A* (or *B*)
Nonbelligerency to help victory of *A* (or *B*)
Full support to *A* (or *B*)
Limited support to *A* (or *B*)
Limited support to both *A* and *B*
Neutrality

    Armed—application of nonviolent techniques
    Unarmed—no application of nonviolent techniques

Economic, cultural, psychological neutrality
No connection

The time element is of great importance, since *C* may, whenever it is deemed advisable, switch from the support of *A* to the support of *B*. Also, *C*'s policies may move up and down the scale, depending on the success of *A* (or *B*).

A strong *C* will, according to his friendly or hostile attitudes, have different relations with *A* and *B*.

STRONG C WITH HOSTILE ATTITUDES (A:B HOSTILE)

Balance of power to prevent full victory of *A* (or *B*)
Military intervention if required
Temporary alliance with *A* (or *B*) and reversal of alliances
Temporary full nonmilitary support
Temporary limited support
Action to prolong conflict between *A* and *B*
Active nonmilitary or nonviolent measures to reap fruits from *A* : *B* conflict
Economically profitable neutrality
Insulation

A strong *C* may have friendly intentions with respect to the conflict between *A* and *B*. In such a case *C* may resort to the following types of action:

---

tive; if the pair has a mutually hostile attitude but cannot be dissolved (unhappy marriage), Wiese calls it the "antipair." Of great importance is the behavior of the pair toward third persons: there is a change in the pair pattern, almost without exception, when a third person comes into close relation with the pair, no matter whether the pair relation is permanent or transitory (see his *Systematic Sociology: or the Basis of the Beziehungslehre und Gebildelehre,* amplified by Howard Becker, New York, Wiley, 1932, p. 521). There is no "pair" pattern in international relations, except occasionally, and then it is rarely of a "closed" characteristic. "Friendship" or cooperation is always of an "open" type. As in human relations, the appearance of the "third" modifies the original relationship.

STRONG C WITH FRIENDLY ATTITUDES (A:B HOSTILE)

Balance of power to prevent war or make peace
Temporary alliances to prevent war or make peace
Friendly help to both belligerents (type: Red Cross)
Mediation, arbitration, and other good services
Strict neutrality, even at cost to self, especially in the economic sphere
No contacts

If C is an exceptionally strong nation, it can impose its will on the belligerents without resorting to balance of power policies.

If the attitudes between A and B are friendly, C may have hostile or friendly intentions. In the case of hostile intentions, C will try to embroil A and B with each other; or slowly undermine their friendship; or act in such a way that the power relationships between A and B will change, with incipient enmity resulting.

In the case of friendly intentions, C will be a true neutral and attempt to promote friendship between A and B, obtain maximum advantage for himself, and contribute to all-around cooperation; C also may remain in isolation. A weak and friendly C can act similarly in the case of friendship between A and B. But a hostile C, even if he is weaker than A or B, can embroil them under certain conditions. In most cases of weakness, C will pursue a policy of trade and friendly services.

The relations which C maintains with A and B are of an asymmetric nature, that is, C's actions are *reactions* to the attitudes between A and B. This usually happens when C is weaker than A or B. Yet if C possesses parity of strength with A or B, it may happen that C becomes a member of the primary power relationship and that either A or B reverts to the role of the "third power." A or B, or both at the same time, may be seeking an alliance with C, who will be inclined to side with the highest bidder. Often relations are complicated by the fact that one state may be a "third party" in one constellation, but a primary power element in another constellation. Every state has several frontiers and may have to pursue different policies in each direction, not to mention its relations with more distant states.

In any event, the relationships which states maintain with one another do not come about by magic but are the result, or rather the manifestation, of one of the various basic types of social action (discussed in the preceding chapter).

We now have the elements which would enable us to describe the world situation graphically. The purpose of such a graphic description is to be able to grasp the world situation with one look—Napoleon's celebrated *coup d'oeil*—and to check whether or not all the relevant relationships are being considered. Let us select those states and oppositional groups which are affected by the dominant issues either directly or indirectly and neglect those others which, on the basis of our judgment, have no present significance. Let us take, second, four types of social action and call them w, x, y, z; w standing for routine, x for emotional, y for value-determined, and z for rational action. Three types of attitudes—cooperation, indifference, and conflict—can be arranged as numerical coefficients ranging from $+10$ to -10, whereby the attitudes of indifference would be defined by the coefficients ranging from, say, $+2$ to -2. We also want to indicate whether between two powers there is a primary or a third-power relationship or neutrality. We arrange these as the main factors, giving them the notation Q, R, and S, respectively. Thus, a state may engage in a rational action z, waging unlimited military aggression, denoted by -10, against an enemy with whom it has a primary power relationship Q; the entire notation would then be written $-10Q_z$. Another state may engage in routine action w, carrying out mediation $+3$, in a neutrality power relationship S; the entire notation would then be written $+3S_w$.

The selected states and opposition groups could be listed in an array having the form of a matrix, and the following entries may be made:

	A	B	C	D	E	F
A		$-10Q_z$	$-5R_z$	$+2S_w$	$+3S_y$	$-6R_x$
B	$-6Q_x$		$+3S_w$	$+2S_w$	$+2S_y$	$+5R_z$
C	$-8R_z$	$+5Q_z$		$+2S_w$	$-1S_y$	$+2S_w$
D	$+3S_x$	$+3S_x$	$+2S_w$		$-2S_y$	$+2S_w$
E	$+2S_w$	$+4S_z$	$+1S_w$	$+1S_w$		$+2S_w$
F	$+2R_w$	$+4S_z$	$-1S_w$	$+1S_w$	$+4S_y$	

Notations

States and Groups: $A, B, C, D. \ldots$
Social action:
  Routine: w
  Emotional: x
  Value-determined: y
  Rational: z
Power relationship:
  Primary: Q
  Third-power: R
  Neutral: S
Coefficients for Q relationships (examples):
  Union: $+10$
  Alliances: $+5$
  Intermittent cooperation: $+2$
  Competition in power orbits: -3
  Counteroffensive: -7
  Limited Aggression: -9
  Extinction: -10
Similarly for R and S relationships.

The matrix is read vertically for the policy *initiated* by the state listed at the top. The matrix is read horizontally for the policies *directed* by the various states *against* the state listed at the left.

With the notations as defined, such an array can list 240 *types* of international relationships. In our example, it shows that B is waging by rational action an unlimited military aggression against A and that A and B have a primary power relationship. A answers this aggression by emotional defense. C is rationally hostile to A, that is, it supports, in a third-power relation, B short of military aggression. F gives B even greater support, also in a third-power relation, but is prompted by emotional action. A counters C by offensive intervention through rational action and tries, by routine action, to maintain neutrality against F. E is a neutral and is prompted in its actions by ethical or other valuations. Both A and B maintain partly routine, partly emotional, and partly rational neutrality vis-à-vis D, E, and F. The other entries show largely indifference in the form of limited and moderately friendly routine relations.

The numerical notations, if added, would give an *index* of the effectiveness of a state's foreign policy. Since the vertical lines indicate the foreign policy initiated by the state itself, and the horizontal lines the policies initiated by the other states against it, we can see that the success of A's foreign policy is indexed by -7, while the combined success of B, C, D, E, and F's policies against the same state puts A in a -16 position. By contrast, the two values for B are both $+6$. This indicates that B has gained a position of superiority against A and is pressing its advantage.

To indicate the "temperature" of the international situation as a whole, it is permissible to neglect the neutral states; hence we disregard the S factors. We get then, as sums both of the vertical and horizontal Q and R, a coefficient of -23, indicating, of course, a most adverse international situation. The notations could be refined by vectors indicating rising or falling trends.

The true significance of the international situation would become clearer if strength and weakness factors were listed in a similar fashion on separate arrays. It should be possible (though difficult) to construct a scale for both *relative* strength and weakness, and to enter it in the matrix in such a manner that the *relative* power position between two states would become clear. For example, the matrix could show that D is twice as strong as E but only half as strong as C, and that it is highly vulnerable to attack by B but not vulnerable to attack by A.

It is very important to understand that this array is a *tool* that can be applied for many different problems. Here, we proposed to use the matrix to indicate attitude relations among six groups. Yet by a suitable change in the notations, the matrix could be used to show, for example, comparative armaments, types and extent of mutual interventions and propagandas, exchanges of raw materials, foreign trade, exchange of technical information, population movements, and many other things.

Just to indicate how this can be done, let us assume that we analyze propaganda. We could use a minus notation for hostile propaganda, a plus notation for friendly propaganda (for example, of the "cultural" type), and zero for the complete absence of propaganda effort. It would then appear, let us say, that E undertakes a -5 propaganda effort against D, which counters by a $+2$ effort, meaning that E is fairly aggressive and that D makes a lame counterpropaganda appealing to E's "higher" motives.

International relations can be analyzed in this manner by several dozen of arrays. The sum total of the significant matrices would provide a *simultaneous* picture that may be comprehended *visually*. It must be underscored that this graphic analysis is simply a shorthand notation. It should prove useful for comprehensive surveys and especially for an analysis of current international changes.

It must be supplemented, however, by an analysis of the geographic factors and statistical as well as qualitative treatment of the respective capabilities and vulnerabilities in time (velocity, acceleration, and direction). Furthermore, there is required an analysis of immediate intentions and basic motivations as well as of the nuances within the broad types of political action and interrelationships. Last but not least, the policies between states cannot be understood without taking into account the *historical* development which led to the situation described in the array. In other words, *each* block in the matrix must be taken out and analyzed by *all* the tools of *all* the pertinent sciences.

Graphic description cannot and should not replace analysis by the *discursive* method, using a maximum of information rather than a minimum of schematized data.

Graphic representation merely should *supplement* the discursive method, refine it, and compensate for its main shortcoming, the quasi impossibility of perceiving a multitude of simultaneous events. It is a tool which is not always applicable but which, whenever applicable, can be used to great advantage. No more is claimed for it here than its usefulness and handiness for describing the "world situation," a term which heretofore had no concrete meaning.

The analysis of one given interstate relationship remains incomplete unless this *one* relationship is connected with the *whole, i.e.,* the product or integral of all relationships. It can, therefore, be argued that the term "world situation"—if described and defined as a composite of phenomena—must assume the same importance which the *Ganzheit* or *Gestalt* concepts have in biology and psychology. Elusive concepts of this type are most difficult to manage. The graphic method here proposed is a beginning. Its very imperfections illustrate the immaturity of our science.[2]

[2] The reader familiar with the history of science will recall that progress in biology, *i.e.,* the working out of biological theories leading to successful experimentation, was

The practicality of analyzing the world situation may be doubted by those who think that political science is essentially a matter of literary writing and a projection forward of the historical method of understanding. So it is—in part. The point is that the traditional methodology of the political sciences is limited in its effectiveness and erects obstacles to the full understanding of the over-all sociopsychopolitical processes which the statesman is supposed to influence. Economics, for example, was forced to develop beyond the literary method and, precisely in order to understand the economy as a *whole,* resorted to graphic descriptions and equilibrium analyses. It takes a while to work out such methods. Since they were successful in economics, there is no reason to assume that they would not be useful in the political sciences.[3]

Let us assume that it may be possible to describe the world situation with scientific accuracy. The difficulty would arise that the data will be reliable for *past* events but fragmentary and often inaccurate with respect to *current* events. We may *know* yesterday's situation; we may *estimate* and *infer* today's events. Yet in order to make rational policy, we can but *anticipate* the situation of the future. We should be able to visualize changes in the intentions of various groups, in the dominant issues, in the alignments of coalitions, and in the relative strengths and weaknesses of all groups, including our own. It is not quite enough to anticipate the nature of these changes; it is also necessary to make correct estimates concerning the *timing* of these events. On the basis of such anticipations, one's own intentions may be modified and the timing for the implementation of new plans and programs be determined. To complicate matters further, there is the "feed-back" problem: as soon as decisions have been made by one group, the entire situation changes, for other groups modify their decisions and timetables, and a new adaptation on the part of the first group has become necessary. It is an infinite, never-ending process.

For these very basic reasons no foreign policy can be fully rational. From time to time, it is possible to act with a measure of rationality. The simpler a situation, the greater is our ability to act in accordance with reason. It is frequently possible to indicate that a political action is not rational. Yet, by and large, we have neither the knowledge nor the method to understand the ultimate significance of current social and political events, to forecast future

---

preceded by Linnaeus's classifications of plants. The political sciences are in dire need of similar classification work as a condition of true progress. The array is a tool to break the "whole" of the world situation into its component parts—to classify and arrange the data.

[3] An excellent discussion of such a method may be found in Wassily W. Leontief, "Input-Output Economics," *Scientific American,* Vol. 185, No. 4, October, 1951, pp. 15–21. Concerning the practicality of this analytical tool, see the same author's *The Structure of the American Economy 1919–1939: An Empirical Application of Equilibrium Analysis,* 2d ed., New York, Oxford, 1951.

trends, let alone to *control* sociopolitical change.[4] This limitation of our reason and the incompleteness of our control are the most fundamental, and perhaps the eternal, causes subjecting social and international reform schemes to so high a probability of failure. The maker of foreign policy, who is the guardian over war, peace, and progress, must act, in his most significant decisions, by *intuition*. The art of predicting change should be his foremost skill—so long as science deserts him in the hour of need. This forced reliance on the "inner light" is the statesman's danger as well as his opportunity. The fate of the world is not as yet placed in the hands of scientific man. Success is dependent on insight, skill, perseverance, courage, and faith. *Non eritis sicut dii.*

See Bibliography at end of Chapter 2.

[4] Lately there has been some progress in the direction of the elaboration of more adequate theoretical tools. Von Neumann and Morgenstern's *Theory of Games and Economic Behavior* (Princeton, N.J., Princeton University Press, 1947), and Norbert Wiener's *Cybernetics: Or Control and Communication in the Animal and Machine* (New York, Wiley, 1948) point toward new and promising possibilities. However, these tools have not yet been perfected and cannot, without a great deal of additional research, be applied to the political sciences. A creative synthesis of the prediction problem may be found in Edward R. Dewey and Edwin F. Dakin, *Cycles: The Science of Prediction* (New York, Holt, 1947). In addition to a fascinating analysis of tides and growth curves, the authors found four major rhythms in the American economy: a 54-year, an $18\frac{1}{3}$-year, a 9-year, and a 41-month rhythm (p. 188 and *passim*). The 54-year rhythm is the Kondratieff cycle to which Joseph Schumpeter assigned such great importance in his *Business Cycles* (New York, McGraw-Hill, 1939). Every "Kondratieff" was characterized by an important innovation: the first known cycle was that of the Industrial Revolution of the 18th century; the second, that of steam and steel; the third, that of chemistry, electricity, and combustion engines. A new Kondratieff cycle started around 1952; is it hazardous to predict that it will be the Kondratieff of nucleonics? In any event, before the theory of combined rhythms can be used for practical foreign policy, it will be necessary to discover a few dozen pertinent cyclical movements in the political field. At present no such movements are known, and it is open to doubt that there are periodicities in the field of international politics proper, as contrasted, perhaps, to economics. In this connection attention may be drawn to the techniques of operational research that proved so successful during the war. See, for example, Lincoln R. Thiesmeyer and John E. Burchard, *Combat Scientists,* Boston, Little, Brown, 1947; and J. G. Crowther and R. Whiddington, *Science at War,* New York, Philosophical Library, 1948, Chap. 2. Since foreign policy consists of "operations" and is dependent on the effectiveness of its "operations" to an even higher degree than on the appropriateness of its "principles," operational analysis not only would give good results if applied to diplomacy, but sooner or later must become one of its most important tools.

Part Two

THE ELEMENTS OF POWER

Chapter 4

GEOGRAPHY AND THE FOREIGN POLICY OF NATIONS

Political society is earth-bound and time-bound. It embraces all human beings who live within given boundaries at a particular time. The citizen has no choice, except by emigration—which today is made difficult nearly everywhere by stringent state-imposed restrictions. The state, *i.e.,* national political society, as well as its subsidiary components, is peculiarly geographic in character. On a map, the geographical otherness of states lends itself to simple differentiations, and thus to interpretation of relationships according to size and location of states and of how these relationships can be changed by changing the boundaries of the multicolored areas on the map. Though the lessons of geography are not as simple as the best maps suggest and the interpretation of maps involves considerable technical and philosophical difficulties, the study of international politics is wedded to the study of political geography. History is inseparable from its geographic setting. The scene and prize of international politics is the earth.[1]

Napoleon's epigram, "The foreign policy of a country is determined by its geography," has been paraphrased by innumerable statesmen, diplomats, and soldiers. The concreteness of the geographical environment intrudes in any discussion on foreign policy, however abstract. Sir Austen Chamberlain wrote: ". . . Geographical facts have been decisive for the course of British history and explain, just as they dictate, the main principles of British policy and the preoccupations of British statesmen."[2]

[1] An original and profound discussion of the area limitations of political society and a bold outline of geographical techniques of analysis applied to modern world problems are contained in S. Whittemore Boggs's "Geographic and Other Scientific Techniques for Political Science," *American Political Science Review* (Vol. 47, No. 2, pp. 223–238).

[2] "First, Great Britain is an island, but, secondly, this island is separated only by a narrow streak of water from the Continent of Europe. Thirdly, this island has become

Specific dangers which threaten a country materialize through geography; effective countermeasures must be selected in accord with geographic configuration. To be more specific, in the geography of every country can be found adverse features, avenues of invasion through which it may be attacked. Foreign policy should be aimed at closing these avenues. Of course, in the air age the open sky is the avenue of approach. And in any period of revolutionary upheaval, the approach is not of a geographical but of a sociological or psychological nature—through the revolutionaries.

Geographic determination appears in historic form; alliances and enmities may develop independently from ideological and political affinities or dissimilarities. No effective policy of security can rely exclusively on political factors while neglecting geography. For example, alliances between conservative and revolutionary countries are fraught with logical and ethical contradictions, yet history shows that such alliances proved effective when they were in harmony with geographical facts. In such cases, geography primed ideology. Alliances concluded on the basis of ideological or racial affinity alone nearly always foundered on the rock of geographical realities.

It is tempting to fashion from the case histories of political geography a theory of geographical determinism. German *Geopolitik* surrendered only too willingly to the temptation. It is not necessary here to refute the fallacies of historical determinism, be they woven from the web of an economic, geographic, or any other theory. The axiom of geographic determination of foreign policy does not have as clear a meaning as a simple cause-effect relationship must contain by definition. Very often the axiom does not apply. Geographical facts are persistent but not immutable. Moreover, some geographical peculiarities are losing their importance in modern times. What constitutes a pertinent geographical fact, and what does not, is a matter of interpretation. It is in itself an ideological question whether geography, economics, political ideology, or military strategy should guide foreign policy. All that can be said is that under any conceivable circumstances geographical conditions must be taken into account, because no foreign policy, of whatever kind, can be effective, if, and when, it is carried out in disregard of geography. Even here, however, complications arise because "geography" may point in several directions: the geography of peace is often "determined" by the fact that distant countries may be economically interdependent, while the geography of war is "determined" by the fact that in the past the neighbor was the most frequent and the most likely enemy.

---

the center of a wide-flung empire whose arterial roads are on the oceans and through the narrow seas" (*The Permanent Bases of British Foreign Policy,* reprinted in *Foundations of National Power,* edited by Harold and Margaret Sprout, Princeton, N.J., Princeton University Press, 1945, p. 197). It should be readily apparent that the third fact cited by Sir Austen is by no means of a "geographical" character: the establishment of an empire by the British is only in part due to geographical circumstances.

APPROACHES

It is a historical fact that a country which has to surmount considerable geographical obstacles in order to attack its neighbor very rarely chooses aggression as a means for settling issues in dispute, while a country which can reach its neighbor without great difficulties attacks often, other things being equal.[3] For example, the configuration of Alpine valleys makes it almost impossible to attack France from Italy. It is therefore not surprising that aggressive wars were almost never launched against France from Italian bases. France was successfully invaded from the south in antiquity, when she was not yet organized politically and when Rome, being immensely stronger, also controlled the most practical avenue of approach—the sea leading to the Rhône Valley. A similar condition obtained when in 1944 the Allies invaded southern France. Yet these were the exceptions that prove the rule.

The configuration of the valleys did not, however, preclude invasions of Italy from southern France. On the contrary, it favored them, for the trans-Alpine valleys fan out toward the Lombard Plain. Many such invasions took place—those of the Cimbri and Teutons, Hannibal, Charles VIII, François I, Napoleon I, and Napoleon III, to mention only a few. French relations with Italy were no better than French relations with Germany, yet the number of French-Italian wars has been small. Conversely, Germany has easy approaches to France via the Low Countries and Alsace.

The existence of an avenue of approach is a neutral fact; whether or not accessibility constitutes a danger is dependent on political factors. For example, up to the middle of the 17th century, France fought many wars against Spain, then an aggressive power. After the Battle of Rocroi (1643), Spain ceased to be "dynamic," and friendly relations were gradually established; in many wars of the 18th century the two powers fought as allies. The only major Franco-Spanish conflicts to arise since then were due to Napoleon's aggressiveness (1808) and to peace enforcement carried out on behalf of the European powers (1822). For all practical purposes, the Spanish border became for both countries a safe frontier, although it offers good avenues of approach (as those for Wellington's march from Spain into France in 1814).

The Low Countries are another case in point. As long as the Low Countries were under the control of Spain and Austria, both of whom were hostile to France, wars swept incessantly across the hapless area. The reconciliation of France and Austria in the 18th century afforded the peoples of that region a long respite from war.

[3] Derwent Whittlesey, *The Earth and the State: A Study of Political Geography,* New York, Holt, 1939, pp. 1–22. See also Jacques Ancel, *Manuel géographique de politique européenne,* 2 vols. published, Paris, Delagrave, 1936–1940; also Ellsworth Huntington, *Mainsprings of Civilization,* New York, Wiley, 1945, Part III.

European Approaches

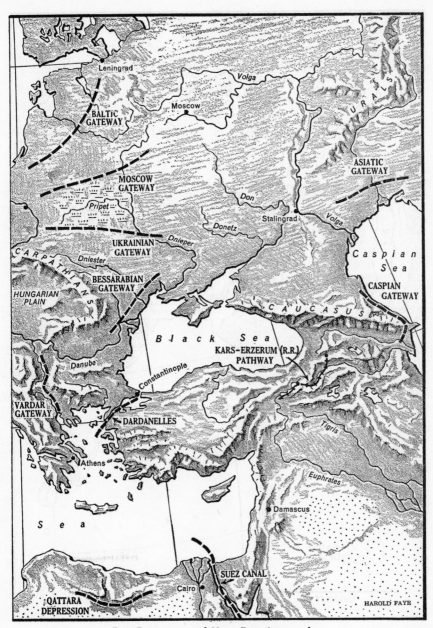

East European and Near East Approaches

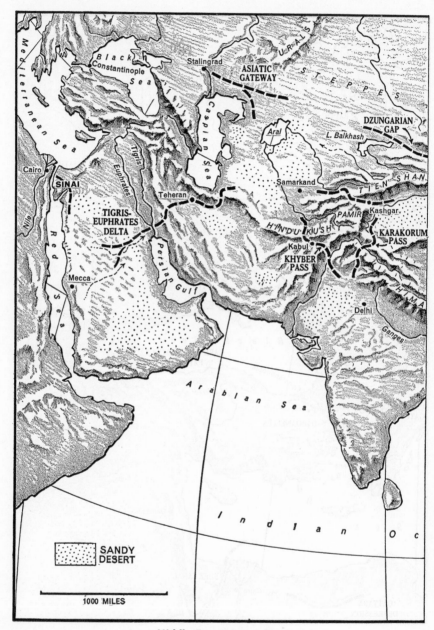

Middle East Approaches

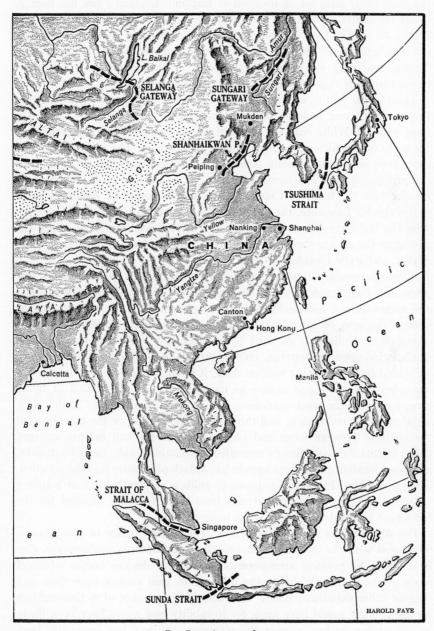

Far East Approaches

HAROLD FAYE

With the exception of the French Channel ports, the Low Countries are the most likely base for an invasion of England. England's aim has been to insure the neutrality of these countries or their control by a remote or peaceful nation. As soon as they fall into the hands of a dynamic power, Britain must act. The integrity of the Low Countries is of common concern to Britain and France, and they are immediately drawn together if an aggressive third power threatens this approach to Paris and London.

The Danish Straits with the Baltic; the West Russian rivers with Lakes Peipus, Ilmen, and Ladoga; the Dardanelles with the Black Sea; the North Cape with the White Sea; the Strait of Tsushima; and the Dzungarian gap are some of the historic avenues leading into Russia. The pass of Shanhai-kuan gave access to invaders from the Mongolian and Manchurian plains to the Peiping area and North China. A river, the Yangtze, can carry an invader into the heart of China, just as in the period of shallow-draught navies the St. Lawrence, the Hudson, Chesapeake Bay, and the Mississippi were the highways of invasion to the North American continent. Since the advent of the air age the roads into North America lead through Greenland, Alaska, and arctic Canada.

Although terrain no longer is all-important, there still remain considerable problems of approach even in the air age. The shortest line between base and target is not necessarily the best approach. The *location* of base is selected because of aircraft ranges and transportation facilities. But the *approach* route itself is dictated by meteorology, especially by prevailing winds, wind-pressure patterns, temperatures, the height of the tropopause, fog, cloud cover, and other weather data; it is furthermore defined by the distance between bases and targets as modified, for the calculation of flying time, by prevailing wind conditions, and by aircraft ranges as modified by aerial refueling techniques; and third, by the suitability or the actual use of the territory between bases and targets for warning and defense systems. Other factors such as magnetic anomalies, navigational aids, radar landmarks, and exact location and feature knowledge, or lack of it, enter into the selection. The geographical knowledge required to guide a modern bomber or a guided missile to its target is quite different from the knowledge required for the movement of cavalry units; it is far more exacting.

The Approaches and Their Politics. The foreign policy of most powers must deal with the problem of approach. Two concerns predominate. One is to block by political arrangements or military devices hostile advances along strategic thoroughfares; the other is to gain control over them and exclude other countries. Where the exclusive possession of a thoroughfare by one country would have made for instability and would have been likely to unite other nations against the possessor, recourse has frequently been made to the expedient of "neutralization." Switzerland is an illustration. It not only protects the most important passes through the Alps, and the only practical ones for large-scale military traffic, but also controls the communi-

Geography of the Air

Long Range Air Travel

5th Leg

The
CYCLO-GENETIC
ZONE

4th Leg

POLAR
CONTINENTAL
ZONE

3rd Leg

NORTHERN
CONTINENTAL
ZONE

2nd Leg

HURRICANE
ZONE

1st Leg

TROPICAL
DOLDRUM
ZONE

Route: 1. Tropical doldrum zone—predominantly still air with frequent upward movements of heated air. 2. Hurricane zone—during fall, hurricanes over Atlantic; typhoons over Pacific, also the zone of monsoons and trade winds. 3. Northern continental zone—magnetic anomalies, strong irregular winds and jet streams (narrow streams of fast, high-altitude winds) largely in a N.W.–S.E. direction; frequent radio interference; heavy cloud cover and turbulence. 4. Polar continental zone—same conditions as in 3rd leg, but intensified; in addition, severe icing and navigational difficulties. 5. The cyclo-genetic zone—the world's weather corner; zone of violent weather disturbances of all kinds. As a rule, there is a weather change between the 4th and 5th legs. The entire route is subject to patterned seasonal fluctuations and air-mass movements. Every route has a particular "geography." Routes crossing high mountains are subject to strong up and down drafts. Routes crossing Central Asia run into seasonal alternating air currents, largely in a S.E.–N.W. direction. However, jet aircraft (which fly above 35,000 feet) are, by and large, beyond the "weather" zone.

cations between Austria and France, France and Italy, Germany and Italy, and, to some extent, Austria and Italy. Switzerland was neutralized in 1474 by treaty with Austria and in 1516 by treaty with France; in 1648, upon formal severance from the Empire, it was recognized by the powers as a neutral and independent state.

In 1831, when a revolution had torn Belgium from Holland, Belgium was declared a neutral country on the assumption that the security of both Britain and France (who enforced the decision by their arms) would be best served by that settlement. The arrangement was reinforced by the accession to the throne of a minor German dynasty that could be counted upon not to favor any side. It should be noted, however, that this settlement was workable only if and when the Belgians were willing to play the role assigned to them.

In 1867, Luxembourg was neutralized when, after the dissolution of the German Confederacy, Prussian garrison troops were not withdrawn while France by political maneuvers sought to incorporate the country. These neutral countries, Belgium and Luxembourg (as well as Switzerland), theoretically separated France from Prussia (or Germany). In 1870, the German armies, advancing through Alsace, respected their neutrality, but in 1914 and 1940 violated it for reasons of "military necessity." On the other hand, both in 1914 and 1940, the neutrality of Switzerland remained inviolate, largely because violation would have brought little advantage to Germany. Again, it is worth noting that the situation would probably have developed differently if, for example, the German-Swiss population had assumed pro-German attitudes—which only indicates that geographical position alone is not decisive.

Till the end of the Second World War, the arctic served as a barrier of neutrality between the United States and Russia. This region is ceasing to be a zone of effective separation. Both competitors have been establishing air routes, sea routes, military bases, and trade settlements in the erstwhile wastelands; both sides attempt to put the northern wealth to work. The Russians even claim rights of possession over the frozen Arctic Ocean and its "ice islands" and, by a somewhat casuistic interpretation of international law, consider the area from their shores to the North Pole as their own. It is highly probable that the Arctic Ocean will become as much an apple of discord as was the Mediterranean throughout history. Incidentally, we seem to live in a climatic cycle during which the arctic is warming up.

In a future air war, neutrality may become quite meaningless. The belligerent air fleets can with impunity overfly most countries, or by-pass them, as may be more convenient. Modern aircraft ranges give a wide latitude of choice. Small neutral states have neither the technological means nor the distribution of air bases in depth required to defend themselves in the upper atmosphere; nor do they necessarily have to fight, since their geographic position rarely would be of real importance to the belligerents. Air war—like naval war—

Equiareal
Air Boundary

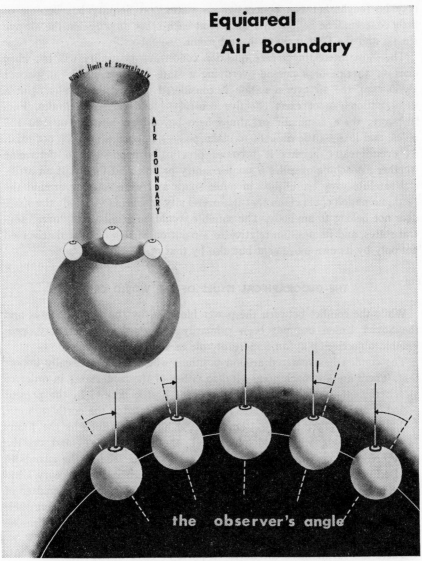

upper limit of sovereignty

AIR BOUNDARY

the observer's angle

The area which a nation "owns" in the air is stipulated to be of identical size as the nation's territory on the ground. Moreover, it is stipulated that the air space of each individual nation should not overlay that of another nation. This condition is fulfilled if a cylinder is projected skyward along an axis erected perpendicularly to the tangent touching the center of the country. Hence the air over each observation point which is "owned" by the nation cannot be determined by glancing upward at a 90° angle, but the angle of observation must change with the observer's position. In the center of the country this angle is 90°, but as the observer moves away from the center, the angle decreases. At the border of a country with a diameter of 1,000 miles it is 84°.

61

may be fought between noncontiguous states; propinquity has become of little concern. The belligerents can get at each other *directly*—in the air age Russia and the United States have become "neighbors."

The most interesting *future* question concerning neutrality will be, when does an aircraft or a missile overflying a state violate neutral "airspace"? By custom, the air over a nation is considered to be its possession. But a small nation cannot exert effective control beyond certain altitudes. Furthermore, there is no air or atmosphere beyond an altitude of 100–125 miles, and it is a little difficult to claim possession over what does not exist. At even greater heights it becomes practically impossible to determine whether a machine overflies a small country or not. And finally, if an artificial satellite were established in outer space and were rotating around the earth, no nation could claim that its sovereignty was being violated; the space does not belong to anybody. The satellite would be at all times "over" several states, and its position relative to a point on earth would be determined not only by its own movement but also by that of the earth.

THE GEOGRAPHICAL ISSUES OF THE WORLD CRISIS

While the conflict between the power blocs led by the United States and the Soviet Union has not been primarily concerned with territory, geographic objectives play an important role as intermediate goals.

The conflict has centered around positions which are strategically important. There are approach areas vital to either of the contestants in order to attack the other or, defensively, to prevent hostile access. In the present period of aerial war many of these positions are located in the northern arctic and subarctic. There are the islands of the high north such as the Franz Josef archipelago, with Rudolph Island, the northernmost land on the globe; Novaya Zemlya; Severnaya Zemlya; Wrangel Island; the islands in the Bering Sea; Svalbard; the northern parts of Greenland, with Peary Land and Thule; and the north Canadian islands. It is not so much a matter of taking political possession of these locations—all these territories have their rightful owners—but of developing some of them as forward air bases, rescue and electronic stations, and weather posts.

There are furthermore the northern parts of terra firma, such as Alaska north of Brooks range, the Canadian territories south of Victoria, Baffin and Ellesmere Islands, and, on the Russian side, the long coast line which connects Petsamo with Anadyr. Farther to the south, in the relatively sheltered arctic and subarctic regions, there are the somewhat more hospitable areas on which hinges the logistic support of the forward bases: Alaska south of Brooks range, middle and southern Canada, northern Maine, Iceland, the White Sea and the southern Kola peninsula areas, Yakutsk, the Magadan region, and Kamchatka. These areas in turn are backed up by the main centers of power in the United States and Russia respectively.

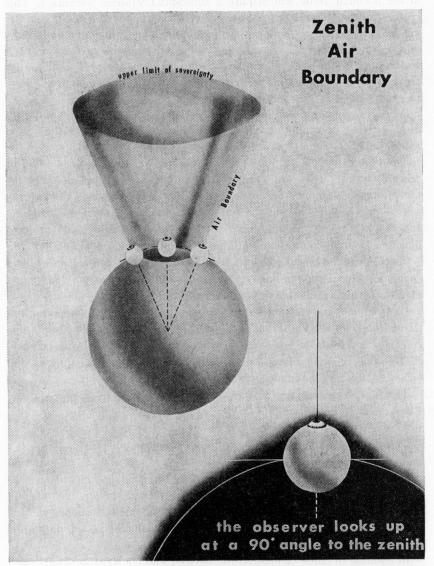

Zenith Air Boundary

upper limit of sovereignty

Air Boundary

the observer looks up at a 90° angle to the zenith

The air vertically over each point of the territory belongs to the nation on the ground. Hence, as we go up, the area increases. For example, a nation with a ground surface of 785,400 square miles (1,000 miles diameter), would "own" 2,010,624 square miles at 250 miles altitude.

The side which will achieve a stronger offensive and defensive posture in the northern arctic will acquire a substantial strategic advantage. This posture will be defined (1) by the number and location of bases in the north; (2) by the size and accessibility of these bases; (3) by the number of days during which these bases can be operated throughout the year and in each season; (4) by the scope of operations these bases can support; and (5) by the military equipment, including aircraft, to be used on and from these bases.

A second group of positions can be described as the *places d'armes*—bases of operations—of further expansion. Sakhalin and Korea are positions from which Japan can be menaced, while Tibet, Nepal, and Afghanistan threaten India. The creation of an autonomous Thai area in China's Yünnan, and of other Thai states in Tonkin, Laos, and the Burmese Shan states would be the prelude to the disintegration of the various states in Southeast Asia and the seizure of Thailand, paving the way for an advance through Malaya into Indonesia (whence a similar campaign could be undertaken in a northward direction by means of national disintegration and reintegration).

Third, there are places which, if they were to fall into Soviet hands under communist control, would create a dispersal of Western strength. Such areas are located in Central America, Africa, and the Philippines.

Lenin argued and the communists believe that, ultimately, manpower will prove to be the decisive factor in the struggle for the world. At present, the communists already control three of the most populous areas in the world—Russia itself, Eastern Europe, and China. India would be their greatest and Indonesia their second greatest prize in the "manpower resource areas."

The Mohammedan peoples, not counting Mohammedans in Russia and China, number between 275 and 300 million, living in north, northern central, and eastern Africa, throughout the Middle East including Pakistan, in Indonesia, and as a large minority in India. There is no islamitic "bloc," any more than there is a Christian "bloc." But these countries have, to a certain extent, a similarity in attitude. Cooperating with or against one major contestant, or remaining neutral, they are a considerable factor, not only on account of their numbers, but above all because of their location and their resources. The strategic function which the arctic fulfills in the north, the islamitic belt is fulfilling in the south.

In addition to crude manpower, the Soviets, who are short in skilled manpower and technicians, seek to absorb groups possessing a high productive proficiency. The biggest prize in this respect would be Western Germany, Belgium, Holland, France, and northern Italy—assuming that both the United States and Britain as well as the British Dominions would remain beyond the reach of Soviet conquest capabilities. Though Japanese crude and skilled manpower is a tempting objective, the conquest of Japan is fraught with considerable difficulties.

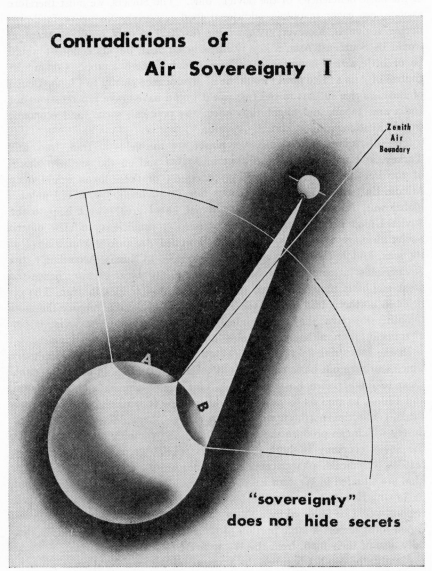

Contradictions of Air Sovereignty I

Zenith
Air
Boundary

"sovereignty"
does not hide secrets

If the air is divided by zenith boundaries, an observer from country A 2,875 miles up in the air can control visually a neighboring country B of 785,400 square miles in its entirety. A is still within his "airtory," but B cannot hide his secrets.

In so far as raw materials are concerned, food must be considered as one of the basic deficiencies of the Soviet "bloc." The Soviets, we must therefore assume, are eager to obtain additional food resources. No major food-producing region is, however, within their reach. The only possible exception would be Southeast Asia, a key rice-producing area, but its conquest would be of little *direct* importance to Russia and Eastern Europe. Communist control of Asia's "rice bowl" would be of significance chiefly to China. Denial of Burma's rice surplus to the free world would have grave repercussions for India and Japan, and might thus affect the political, social, and economic world situation.

The oil regions closest to Soviet power are the fields in Iran, Iraq, and Turkey, and somewhat more distant in Arabia and on the southern shores of the Persian Gulf. Soviet military conquest of these areas would deny Middle Eastern oil to the free nations but, in all likelihood, would unleash global war. In war, these areas would not be of great direct help to the Soviet Union because, under present transport conditions, in view of the Soviet shortage of tankers, and given continued Anglo-American control of the seas, Middle Eastern oil could not be shipped to Russia. Accordingly, the Soviets must attempt to obtain this oil by means *short of war;* hence the great emphasis they have been placing on their activities in Iran. The oil fields in northern Iran, *i.e.*, in the Persian parts of Azerbaijan, are the most tempting objective: they can be integrated most easily into the Soviet system of transportation, although the fields in that area still need development.

In the industrial field, the Soviets' two basic needs are (1) an industry which can turn out basic capital goods in large quantities in order to enable them to industrialize Eastern Siberia, Sinkiang, Mongolia and Manchuria, and China, as well as to establish firm transportation links, including railroads, connecting northern with eastern and southern Asia; and (2) an industry which can produce the multitudinous and complex products of which the Soviet economy is short, *e.g.*, electric appliances, automobiles, plastics, textiles, chemicals, pharmaceuticals, leather wares, etc. Industries of this kind are situated in Western Europe and Scandinavia and, to a lesser extent, in Japan. However, it must be borne in mind that the conquest of these regions would be followed by a sharp decline in output. Western Europe and Japan must import a large portion of their basic raw materials, and incidentally also of their food, from the Western Hemisphere and Africa.

Finally, the conflict between the Soviets and the free world centers around key transportation bottlenecks. The most important of these are the Dardanelles and the Suez Canal. The Dardanelles have been one of the oldest Russian territorial objectives, although at times Turkish control of the straits was to Russia's military advantage. Under modern conditions, and assuming that the Soviets cannot build up their own oil industry to the levels necessary and therefore in case of protracted war would have to rely on imports of Middle Eastern oil, possession of the straits alone would not help

Contradictions of Air Sovereignty II

Equiareal
Air Boundary

Zenith
Air
Boundary

no man's
air space

A

B

m

If the air is divided by equiareal boundaries, no man's air spaces will come into existence. Legally, these no man's air spaces would be in the same position as the high seas; i.e., they would be open to travel without restrictions on movement. Accordingly, an observer at *m* can overlook the entire territory of B without violating B's "airtory."

them as long as the Suez Canal remained under free-world control. By contrast, a Soviet strategy of denial could severely hamper Western traffic through the straits of Gibraltar, the Panama Canal, and the Malacca straits.

The territorial objectives of world communism can be summarized as follows: the build-up of the northern arctic as a base structure for aerial warfare; acquisition of additional sources of oil in the Middle East; control of the eastern Mediterranean, including the Suez Canal; acquisition of additional industrial resources; the establishment of control over large manpower reserves; the seizure of any areas anywhere as flanking positions. Ultimately, their objective would be continental Western Europe, Britain, and the United States.

The Soviets are a long way from their goal. Since the decisive factor would be Russian capability to knock out the United States in direct air warfare and to prevent an American knockout blow at Soviet Russia, the effective domination and utilization of the northern arctic is by far the most important of the intermediate objectives. Depending on the expansion of their native oil industry, the oil fields of Azerbaijan probably rank second in importance.

BUFFER STATES

Buffer states are a time-honored device to keep two potential enemies apart by appointing a third party as occupant of a contested thoroughfare. In the ideal case, this guardian remains independent of both contestants and may pursue an active policy of alliances with third countries. An early example of a historically important buffer state was the "Middle Kingdom," later called Lotharingia, established by the treaty of Verdun (843), which separated Germany from France. From the territory of this state were carved the states of Burgundy, Switzerland, Flanders, Lorraine, Belgium, Holland, and Luxembourg—the buffer states of western Europe.[4]

A series of buffer states came into existence when the Turkish Empire was pushed back from the Danube plains. Serbia, Rumania, Bulgaria, and Greece served to keep Austria, Russia, and Turkey apart, although in truth the quarrels between these minor states and the intrigues between the major powers led frequently to hostilities and major wars.

The southern approaches to the United States are "protected" by a string of buffer states or dependencies, serving in fact as a strategic zone. The liberation of Cuba actually transformed the base most suited for naval invasion of the United States into a buffer state no longer available for an attack by European powers.

[4] See Johan Huizinga, *Die Mittlerstellung der Niederlande zwischen West- und Mitteleuropa*, Leipzig, B. G. Teubner, 1933. For a general history and a description of the commercial advantages inherent in such a "Mittlerstellung," see Henri Pirenne, *Les Anciennes démocraties des Pays-Bas*, Paris, Flammarion, 1910. On the much-neglected history of Burgundy, see Henri Pirenne, *Histoire de l'Europe des invasions au XVIe siècle*, 3d ed., Paris, Alcan, 1936, pp. 338ff.

The Franco-German
Air Boundary
(the equiareal concept)

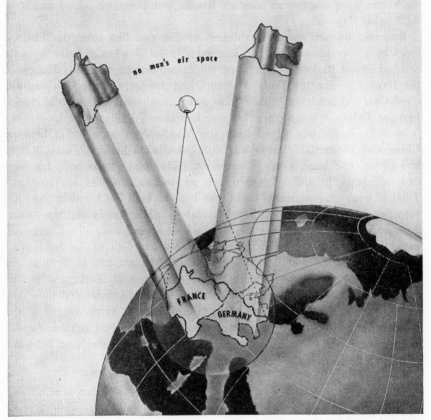

no man's air space

FRANCE

GERMANY

With an angle of observation of 30°, an observer at an altitude of 2,125 miles can overlook both France and Germany without violating their respective equiareal air boundaries.

Prussia, Austria, and Russia were in the 18th century separated by Poland, once a great power but by then weakened by internal dissension. Fearing that they might be drawn into internal Polish quarrels and spurred by territorial ambitions, they divided Poland step by step. The disappearance of the buffer state did not improve appreciably their mutual relations.[5]

After 1918 when the Bolsheviks established their rule over Russia, a string of buffer states, the so-called *cordon sanitaire,* was established by the Western powers for three reasons: to prevent the Bolshevization of Germany; to divest Russia of control over non-Russian nations; and to gain allies in eastern Europe, who were to be employed according to need, either against Germany or against Russia. These states were politically and militarily weak and were overrun as soon as Russia and Germany joined hands in liquidating them.

Rumania originally was established as the guardian over the Danube estuary, a function which it no longer could fulfill when Russia, in 1940, reached one of its long-coveted geographical objectives, the Kilia branch of the Danube mouth.[6] Similarly, Denmark and Sweden, in the 19th century, owed their independence to their joint guardianship of the Balts, the entries into the Baltic—a compromise keeping Russia and England apart.

In Asia, Korea has served since the Middle Ages as a buffer between China and Japan; Manchuria was established as a buffer between Russia and China, and later, Japan. Communist China and Russia have not seen fit to eliminate the buffers between their territories: Mongolia, Sinkiang, and Tibet. Afghanistan separates India and Russia; Iran lies between the Caspian Sea and the Persian Gulf and insulates Asiatic Russia and the Anglo-American sphere of interest in the Middle East against each other; Siam was maintained by France and Britain partly as a guardian of the Isthmus of Kra and partly as a buffer between the colonial empires of France and Britain in Southeast Asia; while the independence of Turkey, after the decline and dissolution of the Ottoman Empire, was safeguarded paradoxically by the conflicting interests of Britain and Russia in the Straits of the Dardanelles and by the largely fortuitous circumstance that neither of these great powers was either strong enough or determined enough to fight the other to a finish over the issue of sole control.

FRONTIERS

Another means of closing the avenues of approach is the "military border," an artificially created or maintained belt of wasteland. The potential aggres-

[5] In his memoirs, Frederick II comments on the partition of Poland as follows: "It is the first example which history furnishes of a partition, regulated and terminated peaceably between three Powers" (quoted by R. B. Mowat in *A History of European Diplomacy, 1451–1789,* New York, Longmans, 1928, p. 273). See also, Albert Sorel, *L'Europe et la Revolution Française,* Paris, Plon, 1927, Vol. 1, p. 545 and *passim.*

[6] See Grégoire Gafenco, *Préliminaires de la guerre à l'est,* Paris, Egloff, 1944, p. 94.

The Air over the Open Seas belongs
to no one

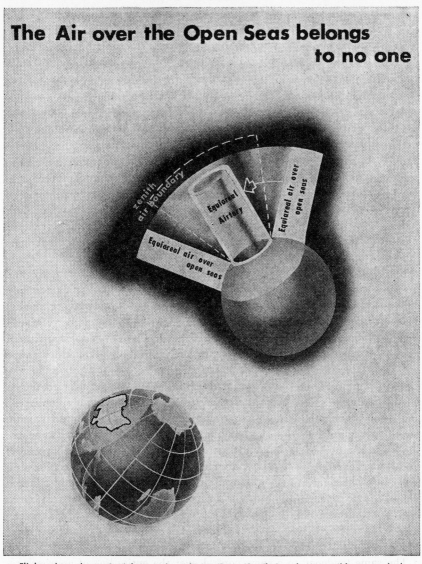

Flights along the territorial water boundaries (3 to 40 miles) make it possible to overlook vast territories. Assuming adoption of equiareal air boundaries by international convention, flights at 4,250 miles altitude (with a 30° angle of observation) along the water boundaries of Australia would allow a complete aerial check of all activities on that continent. If the zenith air boundary were adopted, flights at altitudes of 3,200 miles would allow the same amount of observation, although at a more distorted angle. The zenith and equiareal boundaries each offer distinct advantages of observation depending on the size of the territory, angle of observation, and altitude of observation point. If it is desired to achieve complete observation of a given territory, with a minimum of distortion, the observation point at the equiareal boundary will be situated at a lower altitude than the observation point at the zenith boundary.

sor is supposed to be stopped or slowed down by impassable terrain. Afghanistan is partly a military or waste frontier, partly a buffer state. Austria-Hungary maintained, until World War I, its borders in the Balkans, especially Bosnia-Herzegovina, roadless for the same reasons. Rumania kept her roads intentionally in poor shape and held the number of bridges over her eastern rivers at a minimum, while Russia left her western border regions undeveloped, especially the region of the Pripet marshes and, like Spain, built non-standard-gauge railways to impede the progress of hostile armies.

The diplomatic wranglings over the Berlin-Baghdad railway at the beginning of the 20th century can be traced to Germany's intention to establish a strategic link with the Persian Gulf, and to British desire to prevent this, since it would have brought the threat of German land power within dangerous proximity of the Middle Eastern focal points of the Empire.[7] Similarly, the British acted to prevent the Chinese from building a railroad connecting southern China with Burma; and for the same reason, there is no railroad connection between India and Burma.

Fortresses are built chiefly to block the main approaches. France and Belgium time and again attempted at great expense to make their territory impregnable by this means, sometimes with success, more often without a commensurate gain in security. Nowadays, a hostile air force can be "blocked" only by *impenetrable* air defense, which as yet has never been devised; or it must be stopped on the ground either through "preventive" offensive action or through the threat of overwhelming retaliation.

Another objective of "approach policy" is to gain control over the entire line of approach. Rome controlled the southern shores of the Mediterranean and thence dominated that entire sea. Medieval England for centuries maintained bridgeheads in France. The United States systematically eliminated the French and Spanish footholds in North America. France has tried frequently to maintain bridgeheads across the Rhine. In 1871 Bismarck drew a frontier which facilitated a German advance into Lorraine. Italy annexed Zara in 1919 (as a bridgehead into Yugoslavia) and Albania in 1939 (as a back door into the Balkan Peninsula).

In 1939–1940 Russia took Hangö in Finland and Riga in Latvia, a move which combined the offensive and defensive aspects of the "approach policy."

The same tendency to assume control over the entire line of approach reappeared in the foreign policy of major powers after the end of the Second World War as, for example, Russia's activities in the Middle East and its annexation of Königsberg (Kaliningrad) and the Kuril Islands, as well as the establishment of American bases in Greenland, Okinawa, Western Europe, and the Mediterranean.

[7] Edward Meade Earle, *Turkey, the Great Powers and the Baghdad Railway: A Study in Imperialism,* New York, Macmillan, 1935, pp. 196–199.

SIZE

Problems of frontier making and approach control—the topography of international relations—are the ever-recurring topics of the foreign policies of all states. It is, however, size, the expanse of the physical area which constitutes the sovereign realm of a state, and location, the location of a state on the globe and in relation to other states, which determine the questions, *who* makes history, and *where* is history made?

Size is a relative value, and the large states of ancient times appear small today. Yet the ancient empires were each in turn the largest states within the known world of antiquity. The power of small states, like Venice and the Netherlands, rested largely if not exclusively on the strength of their fleets and their trade advantages. Their rule was relatively short-lived as the life cycles of great empires go, and they succumbed to powers of larger territorial size. Yet mere size is not power. The strong states of history were those which had been built around a nuclear core—as, for example, France around the Île de France, England around the valley of the Thames, and Prussia around the Mark of Brandenburg. The potential strength of size was made effective by centralized control exerted from the kernel area. Mere possession of underdeveloped territory adds only *potentially* to power. If the territory exceeds a nation's capability of development, size becomes a factor of weakness, as demonstrated by centuries of Chinese history.

The establishment and maintenance of centralized control over wide space depends on an effective system of communications. Among the ancient empires, Rome and Persia spanned large and difficult mountainous areas by a system of military roads. Egypt and Babylonia were lowland empires controlled through excellent inland waterways. The technical means which made faster and more secure communications possible exerted a profound influence on "geography." They made space shrink. It is in this respect that the effective size of states and the geopolitical structure of a given age must be measured against the prevailing state of technology.

The great empire builders built roads and canals. The Roman roads, long after the decline of Roman power, weathered centuries of neglect. So well laid were the routes of the courier service of King Cyrus that the tracks of the Baghdad railway today faithfully follow the road along which the King's messengers rode.

The Roman road has left its impress on the political physiognomy of Europe. Hundreds of towns arose on the sites of the Roman camps. The average day's march of the Roman legion was 20 or 25 miles, depending on the nature of the terrain. Thus, the towns which succeeded the camp sites marked the roads at intervals of 20 to 25 miles—a fact that has determined the pattern of European civilization up to our time.

Hand in hand with the construction of roads went the organization of mail and transport services. So great was the speed with which the great Asiatic rulers spanned tremendous distances that, in many instances, only the airplane has been able to beat the records established many centuries ago. When Marco Polo returned from China, his story of how the great Mongol Khan controlled the vast reaches of Asia met with mocking disbelief. Yet it was true that the couriers of the Khan carried messages over thousands of miles at a pace exceeding 30 miles an hour.

Marco Polo's medieval Europe had lost the art of building good roads. It was largely a Europe of small states, a Europe patched together from the debris of the Roman Empire. The decay of that empire had coincided with the deterioration of the system of Roman roads as well as with the decline of the skills and techniques which had gone into its construction, and the successors of Charlemagne, floundering along muddy cart tracks across their sprawling realm, were emperors in name only.

Later the same difficulty in overcoming great distances contributed considerably toward the success of the American Revolution. It proved to be beyond the strength of Britain to maintain effective communications with so distant and so vast a continent as North America.

It was the railroad that made possible effective integration over wider land areas. Before the development of the railroad, few continental states were able to maintain control over territories lying more than 300 miles by land from the seat of the central government. Hence, the large states immediately availed themselves of the new instrument and built railway lines for political and strategic reasons long before the economic significance of the outlying areas warranted their construction.

The large continental powers, in fact, consolidated their unity by the development of their railroad systems. Transcontinental lines were flung across the United States, Canada, and Australia, and the Trans-Siberian and the Turksib lines brought Asiatic Russia within the reach of the central Russian government. It was no accident that Siberia, where climate adds its decentralizing influence to that of topography (most rivers flow to the Arctic Ocean and Lake Aral, which are closed to navigation), did not become an integrated part of the Russian Empire until the development of these railroads.[8]

At the present time, technological progress in railroad, steamship, and airplane development has made it possible to overcome topographical barriers which in the past had proved formidable obstacles to expansion and integration. A global net of almost a hundred air lines, regular and daily flights across the oceans and between continents, as well as the range and speed capabilities of modern air-borne forces testify to that proficiency in "bridging space" which the geopolitikers extol as the glory of Western civili-

[8] Nicholas J. Spykman, "Geography and Foreign Policy," *American Political Science Review,* Vol. 32, Nos. 1 and 2, February and April, 1938.

The Shrinking World

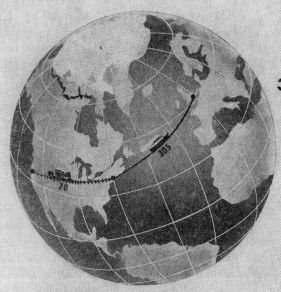

375 hours

25 hours

zation. The political implications of this transport revolution—its bearing on such questions as frontiers, national sovereignty, customs barriers—have as yet been apprehended only dimly.

In certain parts of the globe, particularly in the tropics and in the arctic, the change from ancient to modern means of transportation skipped the phases which characterize the development of Western civilization. It has been suggested that modern civilization has experienced three technological phases, those of eotechnics, paleotechnics, and neotechnics. According to Eugene Staley: [9]

Eotechnics, or the dawn age of modern technics, stretched roughly from the year 1000 to the latter part of the 18th century, and in some respects into the mid-19th century. It was a water-wind-and-wood complex. The express mail coach on land and the perfected sailing vessel on the sea were its highest achievements in the field of travel and transport. Paleotechnics dominated the 19th and early 20th centuries. It was a coal-and-iron complex, and produced the steam railway and the steamship. Neotechnics, of which we have been experiencing the beginnings since the late 19th century, is an electricity-and-alloy complex. It has produced radio communication, the modern automobile, the Diesel-electric stream-lined train, and the airplane.

It is a foregone conclusion that neotechnics will be followed by nucleo-technics.

So well has air communication served certain regions in Latin America, Asia, Africa, and in the arctic that their geopolitical characteristics are now being determined by the exigencies of neotechnics without ever having been affected by those of paleotechnics. It is probable that the Cape-to-Cairo Railroad, the dream of Cecil Rhodes and the issue behind so much of Britain's policy in Africa, never will be built. The airplane has replaced it for fast passenger and mail service and is now replacing it for freight. If in due time nuclear electric power reduces the need for coal—many African areas can obtain power from their hydrological resources—the last argument for railroad construction across Africa or South America will lose its plausibility.

The strategy of air communications—hardly less than that of rail communications—places a high premium on control of the territory between the taking-off place and the landing ground. Control of the African interior remains as desirable for Britain's trans-African air communications as it would have been for the protection of the projected Cape-to-Cairo Railroad. But the topographical requirements of ports on the sky route are different from those of railroad yards, and climatic conditions pose, for the plotting of a practicable air route, problems different from those to be considered in laying out a rail line. What might have become an important strategic locality

[9] Eugene Staley, *World Economy in Transition,* New York, Council on Foreign Relations, 1939, p. 4. The classification was suggested by Professor Patrick Geddes and enlarged upon by Lewis Mumford in *Technics and Civilization* (New York, Harcourt, Brace, 1934).

in innermost Africa, had the Cape-to-Cairo Railroad been built, will now remain a nameless point on the map; conversely, nameless sites in the heart of the African continent are, because of their suitability as airports, in the process of becoming strategic traffic centers.

The geopolitical changes produced by the fast development of modern technology are still in the making and as yet are only vaguely understood. There is the new phenomenon of the relativity of space with its incalculable strategic, political, and economic implications. An airplane, flying from Cairo to Capetown, may be scheduled to land at one of the relay ports within twenty minutes; its passengers may be looking for their hats and pleasurably anticipating a stroll on the grass; if, however, their plane is forced at this moment to make an emergency landing, it may take them days to reach a place from which they can continue their journey—if they ever reach such a place at all.

Whereas the railroad pushed through territory step by step and imparted the benefits of improved communications to the contiguous areas, the development of air routes does not necessarily benefit the area between airports. That area is "bridged"; it need not be "opened." The railroad developments in the West of the United States, and in some parts of Siberia, were accompanied by the development of roads which linked the hinterland with rail points. By contrast, transcontinental airlines across certain parts of South America and Africa have thus far effected little change as regards local transportation facilities. For the practical purposes of the resident populations the airlines might not exist. In other areas, local airlines have intensified contacts between formerly isolated settlements. In countries like Haiti the airplane rapidly is becoming a glorified version of an overland bus. Regional separation is being broken down, and civilization is being carried forward into areas heretofore inaccessible. The Amazon Basin and the Andes highlands are good examples. But local traffic in the proper sense still depends—as it does, for example, in equatorial Africa—on roads, which even in areas "opened up" by the plane may not exist. In the age of neotechnics a nearer place may be "farther" away than a farther place.

While modern technology is rapidly revising the value of strategic locations—including the value of maritime straits or narrows—it places an increasingly higher value on mere spaciousness. In this era of wars of matériel, when productive capacity overshadows most other considerations, big states have infinitely more chances for survival than small ones. Even a great productive capacity and ample natural resources do not alone suffice to achieve victory unless complemented by space in depth. Countries controlling comparatively small space but great productive capacity—e.g., Holland and Belgium—were crushed by fast and efficient war machines because they could not organize that defense in depth without which there seems to be no defense against modern attack.

The invisible ally of the German war machine in its European campaigns from 1939 to the spring of 1941 was the contradiction between Europe's political development and the development of modern technology. The frontiers of the states of Europe, Russia excepted, had been generally fixed in the communication era of stagecoach and canals. Their size did not correspond to the modern forms of communications, either in peace or in war. The United States and Russia, believed by most people a hundred years ago to be too vast for effective control, have proved to be the right size for modern states.

Productive capacity, self-sufficiency in raw materials, and defense in depth thus do not only call for large size but lure the large states on to further expansion at the expense of the small nations. The history of our times appears to reflect, with malignant fatality, the trend toward empires and superstates predicted by the Ratzels, Spenglers, and Mackinders. Whether the era of nucleotechnics will reverse this trend remains to be seen. But it is conceivable that the nuclear weapon may equalize nations just as the six-shooter equalized men, and that nuclear electric power may go a long way toward equalizing the conditions for industrial development. For the time being, however, the trend to big states continues strong, and it imposes on small nations the inevitable requirement to seek safety in alliances, blocs, or federations.

LOCATION

History has been made between the latitudes of twenty degrees and sixty degrees north. It has been made in the north latitudes simply because the greater proportion of the land is in the Northern Hemisphere. Most of the communities that have mattered in history have been situated in an almost continuous belt encircling the globe between these two latitudes. Exceptions occurred in favorable locations in the tropics, such as highlands and islands in the Trades, or in the temperate zones of the Southern Hemisphere. Granted these exceptions, there is no doubt that the relevant cultural, economic, political, and military history was made in the northern temperate zones. The historical centers of gravity have moved from south to north but largely within the latitudes of the moderate zone. The river states of Mesopotamia and Egypt were succeeded by the city-states of Greece. Greece yielded its hegemony of the ancient world to Rome, which extended its power beyond the Alps, conquered Gaul, invaded the Germanies, and established its northernmost frontier across the north of England. The history of the Occident, during the last four centuries, has recorded the gradual passing of world political initiative from the capitals of the Mediterranean states to Paris, London, Stockholm, St. Petersburg, and Berlin. This migration of the historical fulcrum has not occurred in straight progression, but its south-north passage is nevertheless clearly marked.

All of the civilization of antiquity was bounded between twenty and forty-five degrees north latitude. The Chinese civilization of the valley of the

Yangtze Kiang, the empire of Asoka on the banks of the Ganges River, the Kingdoms of Mesopotamia and Egypt flourished in subtropical latitudes. The later civilization of China on the banks of the Hwang Ho, of Rome and Greece on the shores of the Mediterranean, developed between thirty-five degrees and forty-five degrees latitude north. The great capitals of northwestern and north central Europe, of Russia, and of Japan are situated between forty-five degrees and sixty degrees latitude, *i.e.*, in the cool temperate zone.

This displacement from south to north of the historical centers of gravity has shaped the destiny of individual countries and of whole world regions. The countries of the Levant once lay at the center of world civilization and were the strategic passage lands between the great empires of Egypt, Assyria, and Persia. The cartographers of medieval Europe still centered their maps on Jerusalem; but in the 19th century Jerusalem lay on the periphery of the power area centered upon northwestern Europe. During the Middle Ages, long after the empire of the Romans had fallen, the rising states to the north still sought to obtain the sanction of Rome for their power. A few centuries later the capitals of northwestern Europe had assumed world leadership. For with the circumnavigation of Africa and the discovery of the Americas, the center of political power had moved northwestward. From the beginning of the 16th century to the beginning of the 20th century the world's political and cultural center lay in Europe. From that center the great west-east and east-west advances of European power around the entire globe had been set in motion.

British supremacy, gained by sea power based on the British Isles, marked the zenith of Europe's universal rule. With the rise of the United States to the position of a great power after the Spanish-American War, a new condition appeared. For the United States lay outside the European system which heretofore had alone mattered in world history. After the defeat of Russia in 1905, Japan too took her place as a great non-European power in the western Pacific.

With the emergence of these non-European powers the historic center of gravity shifted from northwestern Europe, or rather, there were several such centers where for four centuries there had been only one. The unitary rule of Europe gave way to world regions each centered upon a different core of power.

It is an axiom of the geopolitical theories formulated by certain scholars that a young, vital people controlling a strategic locality is in line for the career of empire. The peoples of the older empires are forced to step down from their place of world political preeminence because their "historical energies" are consumed.

It is difficult to reconcile this theory with the changes in the power position of, for instance, the Netherlands, Venice, and, in ancient times, Palestine and Syria. History plus geography, and clearly not national virtue and vitality alone, had been responsible for these power-position changes. No perceptible traits of biological or moral excellence on the part of the Netherlanders could have brought their land in the time of Caesar to the rank of a great power. They did attain this rank when the center of world political gravity had shifted to northwestern Europe for a complex of reasons entirely outside of their control: the decline of Rome, the discovery of America, the technical improvements of navigation, and their possession of the mouth of the Rhine.[10]

This same northward movement of the center of world political gravity away from the Mediterranean demoted the Republic of Venice when it was actually at the height of its vitality to the rank of a third-rate power. In the 18th century, Venice, which had exerted naval and commercial predominance in the Mediterranean and had been by the standards of the 15th century a great power, was still an important port on the Adriatic, but only a hollow shell of former might. For the Mediterranean epoch had come to an end, and the sun stood high over the distant shores of the Atlantic where first Portugal and Spain, then Holland, France, and England occupied the sunny side of the high road of national opportunities. The political thinking of the times was slow to adjust itself to the changes wrought by the opening of the transoceanic routes. Up to the beginning of the 18th century Venice remained an important factor in the calculations of the chancelleries of Europe, and in the rooted conceptions of many generations Venice retained her international "value"—prestige—long after she had lost her geopolitical position.

Similarly, the decline of Spain was hidden for almost two centuries even to the shrewdest practitioners of power politics. The impotence of Spain throughout the 19th century consistently surprised her opponents no less than her allies, awed by the grandeur of her past might. Viewed from the easy chair of the historian, the weakness of Spain's geopolitical structure was plainly perceptible long before that structure crashed. The resources of the motherland had become grotesquely inadequate for the maintenance of Spain's global interests. Yet the immense prestige of the Spanish kingdom screened its actual enfeeblement from friend and foe alike. The Spanish Empire was impressive even as a ruin, and for generations international opinion accorded Madrid the respect due to a great power. For history is not only a function of natural conditions but also of man's beliefs, traditions, and morals.

In the light of history, strategic location, even if it is at the disposal of an energetic people, is not an automatic guarantee of imperial greatness. When the canals of Suez and Panama had been completed, the great land masses of the world experienced a considerable geopolitical displacement. There were now five continental islands where before there had been only three. Of these five, Africa, South America, and Australia were for the pur-

[10] See Spykman, *op. cit.*

pose of common navigation true islands. The icecap of the polar sea barred the circumnavigation of Eurasia and North America, which hence functioned as true peninsulas. The strategic locations of states were profoundly affected by this man-made regrouping of the land masses, as can be easily seen from its effects on South Africa and Japan. It is not difficult to imagine how much more favorable Japan's strategic position would have been had the two canals never been built. Yet neither of the two canals was planned with any strategic considerations vis-à-vis Japan; for when the Suez Canal was completed and the construction of the Panama Canal was begun, Japan was not yet thought of as a great power. Nonetheless, the construction of the Panama Canal—for Japan a geopolitical accident—proved to be a most fateful event in Japanese history.

As for the future, it is unlikely that the northward passage of empire will continue. The arctic, to be sure, will be opened up, but it hardly will become an independent center of power, at least not so long as it is as sparsely inhabited as it is now. Conversely, as modern technology copes successfully with the debilitating and disease-producing conditions of the tropics, the chances are that more and more "history" will be made in the tropical zones where there are to be found the richest economic prizes of the future. Whether tropical countries will become true world powers remains to be seen, but Brazil and India (which are not entirely tropical) certainly possess some of the most important elements of power.

It is thus indisputable that "climate" exerts a great deal of influence on "history," but this influence is variable and not constant. It is a function of human technology. Man had to stay in warm zones so long as he could not protect himself against cold. Later he was able to move to healthier and more invigorating regions, the moderate zones. Today he is acquiring almost complete freedom of choice: even the hottest and dampest climate can be made bearable through air conditioning (electric power) and fast transportation to the healthier uplands. Man changes "climate" through the drying of swamps, the clearing of woods, the extermination of insects, and the control of endemic disease. Less than 200 years ago, many parts of Europe and America were malaria-infested. In the short run, man may have to submit to geography; in the long run, he creates many so-called geographic conditions to his liking. Geography determines where history is made. Yet man increasingly, throughout his history, has modified his environment and made geography to suit his history.

From early times political theorists and propagandists have tried to show that the political aspirations of certain nations were consonant with or contradictory to the larger tendencies of history. These larger tendencies indeed reflect the powerful influence of geography. History began where it did because of geographic conditions. But all throughout history these geographical conditions can be shown to have been susceptible, in varying degrees, to the modifying influence of man. Geographic conditions determine largely *where* history is made, but *it is always man who makes it.*

The empire of Alexander the Great crumbled when he died because it had been built without regard for the geographical cohesion of its component parts and for the demographic strength of the Macedonian people. The dream of Asiatic empire which haunted Alexander was his alone and not that of his Macedonian warriors. As he penetrated into Asia, the point of gravity of his empire shifted away from its sources of strength. Alexander's great empire did not survive its creator. Nothing remained of it but the tale of a king and the idea of empire.

Julius Caesar, by contrast, was keenly aware of the limitations which geography imposed upon his conquests. These limits he never overstepped. Alexander halted at the gates of India, Napoleon at Moscow, because they had to. Caesar, by his own will, retreated from the Thames and right bank of the Rhine. His were not limitless dreams of world conquest. He sought to gain for Rome's empire strong frontiers and a compact area. The empire he built endured for centuries; its Latin basis of speech and civilization endures to this day. For Caesar had made of geography, the enemy which had destroyed the empire of Alexander, an ally of Roman power.

BIBLIOGRAPHY

Bowman, Isaiah: *The New World: Problems in Political Geography,* 4th ed., Yonkers, N.Y., World, 1928.
Colby, C. C. (ed.): *Geography and the Foreign Policy of Nations: Geographic Aspects of International Relations,* Chicago, University of Chicago Press, 1938.
Fairgrieve, James: *Geography and World Power,* 8th ed., Bickley, Kent, England, University of London Press, Ltd., 1941.
Fitzgerald, Walter: *The New Europe,* New York, Harper, 1946.
György, Andrew: *Geopolitics,* Berkeley, University of California Press, 1944.
Hartshorne, Richard: *The Nature of Geography,* Ann Arbor, Mich., Edwards Bros., Inc., 1946.
Hassinger, H.: *Geographische Grundlagen der Geschichte,* Freiburg, Herder, 1953.
Mackinder, Sir Halford J.: *Democratic Ideals and Reality* (introduction by Edward Meade Earle), New York, Holt, 1942.
———: "The Geographical Pivot of History," *Geographical Journal,* Vol. 23, 1904.
Pearcy, G. Etzel, and Russell H. Fifield: *Political Geography,* New York, Crowell, 1948.
Sprout, Harold, and Margaret Sprout (eds.): *Foundations of National Power,* 2d ed., New York, Van Nostrand, 1951.
Spykman, Nicholas John (Helen R. Nicholl, ed.): *The Geography of the Peace,* New York, Harcourt, Brace, 1944.
———: *America's Strategy in World Politics,* New York, Harcourt, Brace, 1940.
———: "Geography and Foreign Policy," *American Political Science Review,* Vol. 22, Nos. 1 and 2, February and April, 1938.
——— and Abbie R. Rollins: "Geographic Objectives and Foreign Policy," *American Political Science Review,* Vol. 33, No. 3, June, 1939.
Strausz-Hupé, Robert: *Geopolitics: The Struggle for Space and Power,* New York, Putnam, 1942.
Weigert, Hans W.: *Generals and Geographers,* New York, Oxford, 1942.
———, R. E. Harrison, and Vilhjalmur Steffansson (eds.): *New Compass of the World,* New York, Macmillan, 1949.
Whittlesey, Derwent: *The Earth and the States,* New York, Holt, 1939.

Chapter 5

POPULATION AND POWER

Size and structure of population are datum points from which the modern state must reckon its power-political position. History is replete with illustrations of nations with enormous manpower which were outpaced in economic and cultural development and defeated in war by far smaller nations. But if we let the factor of manpower vary while we hold all other factors constant, then the relative size of populations and, perhaps more important still, the dynamics of population growth furnish valuable insights into the current and prospective power relationships of nations. Evidently, mere size of population is not a valid index of state power. *However, among states fairly evenly matched in the possession of technical skills, superiority in manpower spells military, hence political, preponderance.*

Sheer numbers of men have counted heavily in the struggles for power. Rome drew upon a large reservoir of manpower, recruited large armies, and manned large navies. The effectives of the Roman legion (4,000 men) were approximately those of the modern infantry regiment. Several Roman armies, roughly the size of a modern army corps, frequently kept the field at the same time. Large armories at home and at outlying bases, and permanent shipyards and storage facilities, serviced the forces operating in Europe, Africa, and Asia. Rome thus marshaled an integrated, well-trained force larger than that of any other power of the ancient world. Conversely, the decrease of Rome's population and subsequent reliance upon foreign mercenaries weakened the fiber of Roman power, and the fall of the empire coincided with a period of protracted population crisis. Was it cause? Was it effect? No one knows the answers.

Throughout history, decline in population has entailed decline in national power. A sudden preoccupation with population questions on the part of statesmen, scholars, and publicists generally signals crisis. Overpopulation is an economic problem; Malthus was not a demographer but an economist.

In antiquity, once the disastrous consequences of population decline had become apparent, the problem caused grave concern. Aristotle observed that "Sparta perished because of a lack of people." Polybius held that depopulation of the countryside and emptying of cities were the fundamental causes of the decline of Greece. Celibacy and debt, the two great scourges of the ancient world, which always suffered from want of capital and from diminished population in the most prosperous epochs, had brought desolation to the countryside. Large estates worked by slaves replaced prosperous communities of sturdy farmers. "In the towns art languished and morals deteriorated," and birth control and contraceptive practices were rapidly thinning the ranks of urban populations. On the road to slow extinction, Rome was only a lap behind her victim, Greece. As early as the year 37 B.C., Marcus Terentius Varro, senator and landholder, deplored the flight from the land and the shortage of agricultural labor, which he considered to be the general causes of Rome's decay.

Population decline resembles the slow process of subterranean erosion. The damage is done long before the surface begins to crack. Two generations after Augustus, the decline of Roman manpower had assumed alarming proportions. Imperial policy was henceforth haunted by the specter of an enfeebled race and dwindling legions. Trajan wished to force every Roman to marry. A hundred years later, Caracalla deemed it necessary to grant citizenship to all the freeborn within the empire. In the middle of the 4th century the population of Rome and her Italian dependencies had fallen below 5 million, a drop of approximately one-quarter from Augustus's Golden Age, and a large part of that population consisted of unassimilated immigrants from across the Alps. The "desolation of the countryside" had by then become the stock lament of Roman writers. The barbarians did not overrun the empire; they were sucked into a vacuum.

A similar catastrophe overtook Europe in the Thirty Years' War. Its brunt was borne by Germany. Epidemics and famine took a toll of about two-fifths of Germany's total rural population. In Pomerania, Thuringia, Hesse, Pfalz, and Württemburg about two-thirds of the inhabitants perished, and in Brandenburg, Saxony, Alsace, Bavaria, and Franconia about one-half. The campaigns having been fought mostly on German soil, other European nations were less afflicted. Yet France, the Netherlands, and Scandinavia also lost heavily. Montesquieu meditated 100 years later upon the significant analogies of European and Roman history, and declared population decline to be the most deadly disease of nations. Indeed, some of the deep scars of that disease, inflicted 300 years ago, still disfigure the countenance of Germany.

DEMOGRAPHIC DYNAMICS AND POWER POLITICAL CHANGE

The historic struggles for supremacy were waged by populous states, and victory seems to have favored rising populations.

The struggle for power in 15th- and 16th-century Italy was mainly waged between the most populous states such as Florence, Venice, Milan, the Papal states, and Naples. The Italian principalities and city republics fell prey in turn to the emergent nation states, Spain and France, whose military and economic might sprang from their more numerous, better integrated peoples.

The supremacy of the Austro-Spanish Empire throughout the 16th century was based on a population larger than that of any rival European state.

When France, under the rule of the Bourbon kings, became Europe's most populous country, she also attained military dominance of Europe. The peak of French manpower in relation to the rest of Europe lies somewhere between the conquests of Louis XIV and those of Napoleon. This also was France's bountiful century of great men. In 1800 the population of France was 27 million; every seventh European—Russians included—was a Frenchman.[1] It was Russia, with more than 40 million inhabitants in 1812, which vanquished Napoleon's *Grande Armée* of close to 500,000, the largest force Europe had ever seen marching under a single commander.

The rise of Britain and Germany during the 19th century can be traced along the steep curve of increasing populations. When, in 1870, Germany defeated Napoleon III, her population had already overtaken that of France. Henceforth French public opinion was never to shake off a profound concern over the nation's waning strength in numbers with respect to the resurrected *Reich*. The alliance with Russia concluded in 1892 and ratified in 1894 joined 38 million Frenchmen and 92 million Russians in military coalition. This step was not altogether pleasing to Frenchmen sensitive to the crudities of Tsarist autocracy, but it gratified the French general staff.

In the last decade of the 19th century the population of the United Kingdom crossed the 40-million mark, advancing slightly over that of France. The British Isles and the Dominions together accounted for approximately 56 million people, and the empire, including all of Britain's possessions and dependencies, for more than 400 million. The geographical distribution exposed the empire even then to strains which, as in the Boer War, severely taxed not only British economic but also manpower resources. However, Britain's might was boosted out of proportion to that of other states by the fact that it was based on sea power. Naval supremacy underwrote British wealth, secured Britain's unique bargaining position, and was the prerequisite for the successful application of the policy of the balance of power. Naval predominance invested Britain with greater military power than corresponded to her effective strength in men. It is a fact, however, that the crisis of Fashoda in 1898, which brought the long chapter of Anglo-French imperialist rivalries to a close with Britain's bloodless but decisive victory, followed hard upon the heels of Britain's victory in the contest of the cradles. In that contest, France now held fifth place in Europe. Even after the destruction of the Austro-Hungarian monarchy, France stood fifth, facing in growing Italy a new and impetuous rival.

There is no need to labor the plus and minus signs of Europe's numerical relationships; France's European hegemony after World War I, or what

[1] See Joseph J. Spengler, *France Faces Depopulation,* Durham, N.C., Duke University Press, 1938, pp. 19–21.

passed for it in the chancelleries of Europe, stemmed from the brief unanimity of the victorious Allies and the preconceptions of the past. France purported to do what the history of power and populations showed could not be done for any length of time. While in 1800 one Frenchman had faced six Europeans, in 1930 he faced twelve.

Germany's first bid for world power in 1914 was backed by the combined forces of the *Reich,* Austria-Hungary, Bulgaria, and Turkey. This coalition, at the height of its fortunes, controlled between 150 and 160 million people. And it took superiority in numbers, ultimately attained by the end of World War I, to enable the Allies and associated powers to defeat the Central Powers. German defeat, then, as exactly twenty-seven years later, was heralded by manpower shortages and impressment of children, women, the cripples, foreigners, the aged, and prisoners of war to free men for war duty. Military selection boards called to arms the middle-aged and did not cavil at pronouncing fit for battle men afflicted with disease. By contrast, the Allies in 1918, despite Russia's collapse and 2 million Anglo-French casualties, had at their disposal reserves not yet fully mobilized equaling 200 divisions. The manpower of the United States, only part of which had as yet been committed to European battlefields, tipped the scales. True, large contingents of American troops had not yet seen battle. Nonetheless, the German general staff saw the inevitable, and the worn-out German units were demoralized by the knowledge that fresh troops, eager to fight, were entering the lines of battle. Manpower-in-being, to borrow a term from naval strategy, thus helped to crush the enemy's will to resist.

MANPOWER DIFFERENTIALS AND WORLD WAR II

The history of World War II appears to confirm the saying attributed to Voltaire: "God is always on the side of the biggest battalions." Only against peoples inferior in manpower, such as Poland, Denmark, Norway, Belgium, France, Holland, Yugoslavia, and Greece, could the *Wehrmacht* achieve its spectacular successes, while it was unable to defeat any country equal or superior in numbers. Germany defeated her opponents singly or in batches.

Whatever the shortcomings of the Red Army in June, 1941, they were compensated for by the quantitative inferiority of the *Wehrmacht.* It was vast military manpower which enabled the Soviet high command to maintain strong strategic reserves and repeatedly throw fresh troops into the battle. In 1941, 80 million Germans, including Austrians and Sudetenlanders, faced 196 million Russians, including Latvians, Letts, Lithuanians, Poles, Ukrainians, Rumanians, and Asiatics.[2] However, the ratio of military man-

---

[2] These figures are based on the estimated populations of Germany and the U.S.S.R. for 1940, to which the estimated populations of territories annexed by Germany (1938–1940) and the U.S.S.R. (1939–1940) have been added. See Frank Notestein, *The Future Population of Europe and the Soviet Union,* Geneva, League of Nations, 1944, tables,

power did not correspond to these figures. Differences in age structure—larger proportions of younger age groups and a smaller ratio of the aged to the total population—accounted for a decisive Russian superiority in military as well as productive manpower. While Germany could muster 13.9 million males between twenty and forty-five years of age, Russia could draw upon 34.4 million—without counting her newly acquired territories in the Baltic and in southeastern Europe.

No one knew better than the Germans themselves how greatly Russian human reserves exceeded their own. German demographers had compiled detailed studies of Russia's changing population. Their findings were well known to, and impressed, the leaders of Nazi Germany. Why, then, did Germany attack Russia against such heavy numerical odds? Disregarding Hitler's intuitive whimseys, the strategical advantage hoped for from surprise attack, and Germany's trust in tactical mobility and technological superiority, the answer is simple: for Germany, the manpower ratio could only turn from bad to worse. In spite of frantic efforts toward stimulating the birth rate, no German expert seriously expected that the population of the *Reich* would grow substantially in the future. Even at the height of Hitler's drive for babies—which was, indeed, attended by a measure of success—the population of the *Reich* failed to reproduce itself.

A net reproduction rate shows the net increase or decrease of a population within one generation. It was clear when Hitler came into power that, were the German rate maintained at the 1933 level throughout one generation, Germany's population would decline by more than one-quarter. By 1939, improved economic conditions and the Nazi government's natality policies had raised it to 0.98, or 2 per cent less than the rate required for maintaining the population at a stationary level. Russia's net rate of reproduction stood then at approximately 1.70. Both rates served to forecast roughly the future population status of both nations: had the German general staff chosen to postpone war until 1950, 82 million Germans would have stood against 203 million Russians. The slight increase in the German population would be due to the survival of the older age groups, a carry-over from the higher fertility of preceding generations. By 1970 the surplus of the past would have been consumed, and absolute decline would have set in; 79 million Germans would be facing 250 million Russians.

These figures, like all projections of future population growth, are based on a number of assumptions, chief among them being that the rate of change remains constant and that political frontiers remain unaltered. Migration, wars, social and economic changes, and a host of other variables modify projected lines of growth.[3]

---

pp. 304–319; and Dudley Kirk, *Europe's Population in the Inter-war Years*, Geneva, League of Nations, 1946, p. 27.

[3] The fallibility of population forecasting was revealed by observed population trends in France during World War II. See J. Bourgeois-Pichat, "La Situation démographique

Hitler hoped to safeguard Germany's future by waging a demographic "preventive war." Not only did he lose, but he also erred by ascribing to demographic trend curves more finality than they possess. His error was abetted by the scientists, who were only too eager to advertise the efficacy of newly forged sociological and statistical methods. Of course, the statisticians should have emphasized that trends not only change but frequently are reversed, but apparently they preferred to pose as prophets. They should have been more careful in making sweeping deductions from only *one* set of curves—reliable population statistics are not quite 100 years old. What was considered normal, namely, a regularly and gradually declining birth rate, may turn out to be the exception, while oscillations of the birth rate may be the normal thing. The demographers should have foreseen that birth-rate curves must reach a minimum somewhere, but they managed to convey the impression that nations with declining birth rates would, sooner or later, usually sooner, disappear altogether. At the same time, certain population experts sounded fearsome warnings concerning "overpopulation" and the "rising tide of color" swamping mankind, although the birth rates of the colored peoples, too, must be expected to decline. In many cases, indeed, they *have* begun to decline.

In any case, events did not conform to the forecasts. The birth rate of Italy, previously a fast-growing country, fell below the birth rate of France, previously a declining nation. The resilience of the American birth rate and the increase of the United States' population by nearly 15 per cent between 1940 and 1950 [4] came as a complete surprise to the demographers. More significant perhaps than statistics is the fact that the *attitude* of the American people changed; where there had been before World War II some reluctance to bring up large families, postwar America appears to proceed on the cheerful assumption that "babies are fun." A similar change in attitude occurred in France.

The upshot is that while previously demographic events, and partially birth rates, were considered to be independent variables, it appears now that birth rates are partly dependent upon other factors, especially economic situations and mental attitudes. Fertility, which influences birth rates, seems to be connected with diet.[5] Sociologically, it is still true that the country produces relatively more children than the city, but modern man is becoming a suburbanite; his return to the suburbanized land may be accompanied by a return to the family.

All of which means that curves presenting population trends are *no forecasts*. The growth or decline of population can be predicted as little

---

de la Grande Bretagne: comparaison avec celle de la France," *Population,* Vol. 3, No. 4, October–December, 1948, pp. 672–673; also Alfred Sauvy, *Richesse et population,* Paris, Payot, 1944, pp. 279–281.

[4] The Bureau of the Census gives the following figures: 131,788,275 for 1940, and 151,132,361 for 1950, an increase of 14.68%.

[5] Josué de Castro, *The Geography of Hunger,* Boston, Little, Brown, 1952, pp. 67–72.

as anything else. There is some probability that events will conform to the predicted trend. In the absence of modifying factors, actual events and predicted trends may indeed coincide, but modifying factors are nearly always at work. What is perhaps most significant from the political point of view is this: the population decline of the Western nations is no more a foregone conclusion than the continued growth of the Slavs or the Asiatics. Even if it were, assuming the absence of modifying factors, there are many things which could be done to *stimulate* Western population growth.

QUANTITY AND QUALITY

Crude manpower is of little military significance. No matter how large their populations, backward countries do not make power-political history but must suffer it. Without natural resources, without developed industries, and without the requisite industrial skills and scientific knowledge, a large population weighs down the national economy; in war, it is a source of military weakness.

Malthus held that man's sex passion and material needs were in everlasting conflict, and that there would always be more people born than could be provided for. Population is necessarily limited by the means of subsistence. The last hundred years' boom in pessimistic social philosophies favored the wide dissemination of Malthus's doctrines.[6] Malthusianism permeates modern thinking on all kinds of economic, political, and military problems. It is generally expressed in terms of "too many people" or "too many goods" or "too few jobs." "Mature economy," "oversaving," and "underinvestment" are essentially Malthusian concepts in modern economics. Similarly, "too many soldiers" and *"l'armée de métier"* are Malthusian adaptations to military policy. The restrictive practices of organized labor, discrimination against aliens and racial groups, and bars to immigration are examples of modern Malthusianism in action. This "sophisticated" Malthusianism is not based on a correct understanding of the dynamics of modern industrial society. In its original and simpler form the theory of Malthus applies only to a primitive agricultural economy, but even there its significance should not be overrated. While, for example, the standard of living in India and China is deplorably low, it is nevertheless far higher than it was fifty or one hundred years ago—and that despite very substantial increases in population.

In China, crop failures and a poor system of distribution have resulted frequently, even in peacetime, in famines affecting millions. Approximately 80 per cent of China's 350 to 450 million inhabitants are engaged directly in agriculture. Yet China has imported food for a number of years. While

---

[6] See Thomas Robert Malthus, *An Essay on the Principle of Population as It Affects the Future Improvement of Society, with Remarks on the Speculations of Mr. Goodwin, M. Condorcet, and other Writers,* first published in 1798, reprinted by the Royal Economic Society, London, 1926.

these imports were small compared to total consumption, they were increasing in the 1920's and 1930's. And even if one concedes that the Chinese standard of living "for fully 90 per cent of the population is sub-human as compared only to the standard of an English unemployed worker on relief (in 1937)," [7] a situation of this type can be understood only if it is seen as a dynamic development rather than viewed as a static position. By 1940, the manpower potential of China could be utilized for guerrilla war, airfield building, and "coolie logistics." There were some moderately well-trained divisions—equipped largely with Western munitions—but their combat effectiveness was kept down by illiteracy, by poor administrative procedures, and in general by the backward conditions of the country as a whole. By 1950, the Korean War revealed a militarily stronger China. To the extent that China will be industrialized and modern techniques be introduced—a development which will occur *regardless* of China's political orientation—the country's huge manpower will provide it with considerable military strength. The chances are that China will become one of the truly powerful nations.

India, next to China, is the most populous country of the globe. The Indian census of 1941 reports a population of 389 million and a ten-year increase of more than 50 million, *i.e.*, a number larger than the total population of the United Kingdom. The Indian population, unlike the Chinese, has been growing rapidly. It has doubled within less than a hundred years and has increased from 300 million in 1921 to nearly 400 million in 1945. In length of mileage, India's railways stand first in Asia. India possesses a nucleus of heavy industry and large proven deposits of strategic raw materials. Yet the military strength of India, in terms of fighters as well as producers, stands in no relationship to her huge reservoir of manpower.

While during World War II the output of the Indian agricultural worker was substantially higher than that of the Chinese,[8] India nevertheless imported large quantities of foodstuffs, particularly rice from Burma, for consumption in the densely populated Bengal province. When, in 1942, Japanese occupation of Burma coincided with crop failure in the Ganges Valley, catastrophe overtook millions of Indians. India's growing population had turned into a liability; the Malthusian "limit of subsistence" effectively limited India's military power. The Indian government is well aware of this most pressing problem. Various plans are under way to increase agricultural production by land reclamation, improved farming methods, rural electrification, the development of a fertilizer industry, and the decrease in the number of useless cattle—the millions of "holy" cows which the Hindus refuse to eat but which devour a great portion of India's agricultural products. Only the future can tell the success of these measures. But it would be a grave mis-

[7] W. Burton, "Natural Resources of the Far East: A Qualitative Summary," *Asiatic Review,* Vol. 33, October, 1937, p. 791.

[8] Colin Clark, *The Economics of 1960,* London, 1943, p. 36. See also Professor Rao's figures for Indian food production and consumption in *Sankhya,* Vol. 4, Part 2.

take to disregard the fact that India—which, incidentally, is still a member of the British Commonwealth and participates in the latter's highly developed economic organization—gradually is acquiring significant military strength.

SOVIET MANPOWER STRATEGY

At the core of Soviet economic and strategic policies is a revolutionary redistribution of manpower. In 1913, 85 per cent of the Russian population lived in villages and only 15 per cent in towns. Twice as many people were employed in village handicraft industries as in factories. In 1939, urban population amounted to 33 per cent of the whole. Between 1913 and 1939, the Russian people increased from 130 million to 170 million, despite World War I losses in lives and territory.[9] By 1950, the Russian population, despite new war losses, was estimated at 200 million, with perhaps 40 per cent or 80-odd million people living in cities and hence an urban population four and one-half times larger than in 1913.

Increase went hand in hand with qualitative change. Expanding industry recruited labor from the ranks of the peasantry and the female population of the towns. During the first Five-Year Plan, industrial labor increased by 12.5 million, of whom 4 million came from the cities and 8.5 million from the villages. Soviet economic development depends upon the annual addition of 1–2 million industrial workers to the labor force. More critical than the problem of drafting illiterate peasants and housewives into factory work was that of turning them into skilled workers. Soviet leadership established hundreds of trade schools which were to train workers in six-month to two-year courses, and decreed that trainees were to be drafted not only from towns but also from the collective farms. By and large, the system of turning backward muzhiks into industrial laborers worked. The quality of the workers measured in output per head is still low compared with Western standards, and the training system, though exacting and cruel, hardly was efficient, but enough was accomplished to release latent potentialities—a large reservoir of manpower and plentiful raw materials—of industrial growth.

From 1926 to 1939, more than 3 million people moved from the densely populated districts of European Russia to the Urals, Siberia, and the Soviet Far East. During and after World War II this population movement was continued. In the process of "planning" the new Soviet order of national minorities, millions of Balts, Poles, and Ukrainians were forced to become Siberian "colonizers." The predominantly industrial character of this migration is borne out by the growth of cities in Siberia and the Far East.

Regarded from the long-range point of view, Soviet policy on the indus-

---

[9] Russia lost, as a result of World War I, territories containing approximately 30 million inhabitants. The population of Russia was estimated at 160 million in 1910. It had increased threefold in the last hundred years of Tsarist rule. Manpower estimated at several millions was also lost as a result of the civil war and the collectivization of agriculture.

trial and agricultural fronts stacks up to a gigantic struggle for a mobile reserve and manpower. The goal of Soviet agricultural policy was the freeing of men for factory work and the army; that of Soviet migration policy, the filling up of the eastern and northern areas, and of distant borderlands.

Strategically, these vastly conceived policies were put to the test in the war against Germany. Russia was able to draw upon unused reserves long after Germany had reached the peak of her manpower utilization.[10] It was Russia's eastern reserves which pressed upon the Germans when victory over Russian armies in the field seemed to have put final victory within their grasp. Paradoxically, the very incompleteness of Russia's early mobilization of manpower may have been one reason why Russia was able to sustain terrible defeats and to fall with new vigor upon the enemy.

Because she succumbed to the same power that Russia vanquished, the case of France invites comparison. It appears from the Red Army's disasters in 1941 in Western Russia and the Ukraine that Russia, notwithstanding the lessons of the Finnish War and the warning example of Allied defeats in the West, was no better prepared for war than France. Yet Russia could retrieve herself, even after she had made the very military mistakes which had sealed the fate of France. From that fate Russia was saved by space and population. Russia lost entire armies; she set up new ones. Russia lost her best agricultural districts; she created new ones in the East. The frequently low quality of Russian weapons was partly compensated for by their quantity, because Russia was able to maintain heavy production. The Russians, unlike France, could accept heavy losses yet afford to repair their mistakes.

As regards men fit for military service, the German-French manpower ratio was 3 to 1 in 1940; to wit, approximately 15 million against 5 million. Germany in the twenty to thirty age class, which is most fit in the active prosecution of war, could muster almost as many soldiers as France in all age classes from twenty to fifty combined. French war plans provided for the mobilization of at least 5 million men, or the withdrawal of approximately 40 per cent of all the employed male population from its previous occupation. It is estimated that Germany, before the war, employed in armament industries 3.5 times as many workers as France; the mobilization of 5 million men in each country is calculated to have increased that ratio to 5 to 1 in Germany's favor.[11] In short, France went to war close to the limit of her capacity, while Germany possessed a comfortable margin. Significantly, the man-power relationship of Germany to France is approximately the same as that of Russia to Germany, namely, 3 to 1, and the ultimate realities of the two military

[10] Surprisingly enough, Germany did not mobilize fully in 1941 and reached the maximum point of manpower efficiency only in 1944. The Germans' high command counted initially on a short and relatively easy war (see *U.S. Strategic Bombing Survey*, Government Printing Office, 1946).

[11] A. Reithinger, *Why France Lost the War*, New York, Veritas Press, 1941, p. 23.

situations did not lie far apart. Germany was able to conquer France; she was unable to defeat Russia.

MANPOWER AND THE DIFFERENTIATION OF SKILLS

Large forces can be raised only from large populations, and a large force was, and perhaps still is, one of the main conditions of victory. The larger the population, the greater the quantity and variety of weapons it can produce. Strenuous effort and higher quality weigh heavily against mere numerical superiority. Yet as the spread of technological proficiency rapidly turns quantity into quality, larger numbers are transformed into greater military power. The more populous a country is, the larger the industrial plant it can man. If it is geared to mass production, the old and rigid difference between skilled and unskilled labor all but vanishes. The problem of marshaling the labor force is transferred to the level of job planning and occupational schooling. The training of the fighting man, who, also, is made increasingly to handle precision tools, resembles closely the "processing" of skilled workers. Just as war and farming in the advanced countries have become mechanized, so the technician-soldier is replacing the peasant-horseman-soldier who, for centuries, was the backbone of military power.

As the production engineer succeeded in breaking down manufacturing processes into a great number of single operations, it became possible to convert, in a comparatively short period of time, a nation's potential of manpower into an effective force of "skilled" workers. However, the bulk of these recruits to skilled labor are skilled in single operations only. It is this distribution of the productive process over a great many single operations which enables industry to integrate the potential of crude manpower rapidly and smoothly. There is no "average" man or woman who cannot be trained to one or another of these thousands of single operations. The monopoly of crafts and the bottlenecks of skills are made to yield to a multiplicity of separate functions performed by different workers, *i.e.*, to numbers.

Dilution of jobs that formerly were the domain of craftsmen risen from long and exacting apprenticeships enables such industries as shipbuilding, aircraft production, and manufacture of electronic devices to employ as many housewives, waitresses, salesmen, lawyers, and cosmeticians as cared to take the proffered jobs. No less important was the shortening of the training period required for learning the simpler kinds of multiple operations. More workers could be trained without increasing the number of instructors, and the "unskilled" adult's aversion to lengthy schooling could thus be overcome. By these and similar methods a phenomenal mobility of manpower has been accomplished; virtually the entire able-bodied population not already engaged in war industries now forms a mobile labor reserve, available for productive use upon short notice. The bars to full utilization are socioeconomic, not technological, problems.

In peacetime, industries are rarely operated at capacity. Each modern war creates its own new devices, requiring unforeseen changes in established industries and the development of new ones. Manpower, too, is never put to maximum productive use in peacetime. The smooth meshing of surplus manpower and machine power in rapid response to the exigencies of war is a basic condition of military power.

The United States military establishment in 1945, with approximately 12 million men, was the largest on earth next to Russia, and probably equal to the combined effectives of Germany and Japan.

The line of demarcation separating, in various countries, military from civilian manpower is not clearly drawn. Not only do large numbers of civilians man the merchant marine, but many are also directly employed as maintenance and logistics workers by the armed forces. Domestic transportation, shipping, and the garrisoning of bases and outposts absorb large portions of military effectives. So do air and antisabotage defenses. And the manpower requirements of the basic industries, including food production, must be met adequately in order to satisfy the needs of the civilian and military population.

In the United States, approximately 200,000 persons—among them some of the country's most brilliant scientists and most highly skilled technicians —were employed in a gigantic experiment in applied physics, the making of an atomic bomb. Only a country able to draw on vast reserves of skilled manpower could divert at the height of a global war so large a contingent for so long a time to so uncertain an enterprise. The most advanced technology places a premium on vast and skilled manpower reserves even greater than that put on the national labor force by the mass production of "conventional" weapons.

Numerical strength acquires strategic value only with reference to the military situation; the requirements of sea, land, triphibian, and atomic warfare are not the same, as regards either quantity or quality of effectives. Nevertheless, these special cases are far from supporting the case for military Malthusianism, *i.e.*, a small, highly trained army of professionals.[12]

Long training periods are inadequate substitutes for a broad range of selection. A populous country can afford to select only those best fit for military service and may shorten training periods, as only the best human material need be taken. Three times within seventy years France tried unsuccessfully to overcome the handicap of numerical inferiority by extending the period of military service and creating elite formations of highly trained professionals.

Historically, the idea of the "small but highly trained and exceptionally mobile professional force," *l'armée de métier,* took root in those countries where either political conditions or lack of manpower, or both, stood in the

---

[12] The concept of military Malthusianism was fully elaborated by the French military theorist Ardant du Picq (see Stefan T. Possony and Étienne Mantoux: "Du Picq and Foch: The French School," in *Makers of Modern Strategy: Military Thought from Machiavelli to Hitler,* edited by Edward M. Earle, Princeton, N.J., Princeton University Press, 1943, pp. 206–216.

way of the mobilization of a large national army. After World War I, Germany was not permitted to have a large standing army; the British public thought it did not need one; and France feared that she would soon lack the recruits to keep up a strong one. The theories of Generals von Seeckt, Fuller, and de Gaulle, each a proponent of a small hard-hitting force of professionals, proposed to solve the insoluble problem: how to be strong without being strong in numbers.

But the Second World War showed that, while only a small band of men did the actual fighting,[13] large numbers were needed for support, logistics, and production. The problem was *not* to restore mobility in war by creating small elite armies; for all belligerents, the problem was to make *huge masses mobile*. Only the "elite" fought—though this "elite" consisted of millions of fighters. But it was supported by twice as many men in uniform. And the uniformed masses were supported by five to six times as many men in overalls.

MANPOWER AND TECHNOLOGICAL CHANGE

The appearance of nuclear weapons has given rise to the question of whether technological progress has invalidated the axiom of the superiority of numbers. It is demonstrably true that in an atomic war far fewer bombs need be delivered on enemy targets than in a war of conventional explosives. It does not necessarily follow that fewer aircraft, ships, guns, etc., may be required, for it may be far more difficult to break through to the target. There is no doubt that huge masses of manpower will be required to shift from the offensive to the defensive. Precisely because the new weapons are so powerful, it is of the utmost importance to ward off the attacker. Since hits cannot be avoided even with the best defensive system, and since the destruction resulting from only a few hits would be enormous, large numbers of people are required for repair, industrial recuperation, and aid to the civilian population. The biggest job would be to keep the country a going concern *after* atomic attack.

Naturally, it would be folly to assume that a future war will be fought exclusively by aerial and atomic means. There is still the naval threat, especially the submarine, and the threat of ground battle aiming at occupation. Victory in the air—as even the earliest prophet of air power, the Italian General Giulio Douhet, understood clearly—presupposes that the ground be held and that, at a minimum, the attacker on the ground be prevented from gaining a blitz victory. Loss of territory equals defeat. Territory must be defended—not all of it, but its vital parts. While formerly wars started at the national frontier, the potentialities of airborne operations pose an immediate threat to many sensitive points inland. Hence in addition to the

---

[13] Only 3 to 4 million of the total in American uniform were trained as fighters in the proper sense and only a fraction of these trained fighting men actually fought (see S. L. A. Marshall, *Men against Fire,* Washington, D.C., Infantry Journal, 1947, p. 56 and *passim*).

defense of the border, there exists in modern war a need for the ground defense of the entire territory. The effectiveness with which these various jobs will be accomplished will depend on the quantity and quality of manpower. There is no prospect whatever that future wars can be fought—and won—with small professional armies. A future war will be a contest between *entire societies.*

In summary, there is no way of dodging the weight of numbers either on the battlefield or on the home front. Ever since the United States entered world politics as a great power, *i.e.,* since the Spanish-American War in 1898, it has ranked as the most populous among Western nations. Even before World War I, it numbered more inhabitants than Great Britain and France combined, then the strongest powers in Europe. In 1944, the United States Army Air Force was numerically larger than the German army which in 1939 was launched against Poland. The American Navy exceeded in 1944 the combatant strength of the French army of 1940. The ground forces were larger than the combined German *Wehrmacht*—army, navy, and *Luftwaffe.* The War and Navy departments were staffed, in Washington alone, by more officers and men than served in the army of the Austrian Republic. These are crude figures of manpower relationships. Power contests are a crude business in which accounts are settled in numbers of men regardless of the weapons used. The hopes that Western Europe can become strong again by relying on small but well-equipped forces will prove to be illusions of decadence.

BIBLIOGRAPHY

Beloch, Julius: *Die Bevölkerung der Griechich-Römischen Welt,* Leipzig, 1886.

Davis, Shelby Cullom: *The French War Machine,* London, G. Allen, 1937.

Dietz, Walter: "Training within Industry," *Factory Management,* Washington, 1943.

Dodd, Alvin E., and James O. Rice: *How to Train Workers for War Industries,* New York, Harper, 1942.

Fedotoff-White, D.: *The Growth of the Red Army,* Princeton, N.J., Princeton University Press, 1944.

Gaulle, Charles de: *L'Armée de métier,* Paris, Payot, 1936.

Gibbon, Edward: *The Decline and Fall of the Roman Empire,* edited by Bury, London, 1900–1903, Vol. I.

Haufe, H.: *Die Bevölkerung Europas,* Berlin, 1936.

Lorimer, Frank: *The Population of the Soviet Union: History and Prospects,* Geneva and Princeton, N.J., League of Nations, 1946.

Notestein, Frank H., and Others: *The Future Population of Europe and the Soviet Union,* Geneva, League of Nations, 1944.

———: "Population and Power in Postwar Europe," *Foreign Affairs,* Vol. 22, No. 3, April, 1944.

Possony, Stefan T.: *Strategic Air Power,* Washington, D.C., Armed Forces Journal Press, 1949.

Prokopovicz, S. N.: "Changes in the Location of Population and Industry in the U.S.S.R.," *Quarterly Bulletin of Soviet Russian Economics,* No. 4, April, 1940.

———: "Results of the Census of 1939," *Quarterly Bulletin of Soviet Russian Economics,* No. 5, 1940.

Sorokin, Pitirim A.: *Social and Cultural Dynamics,* Cincinnati, 1936, Vol. III.

Strausz-Hupé, Robert: *The Balance of Tomorrow,* New York, Putnam, 1945.

Thompson, Warren S.: *Population Problems,* 4th ed., New York, McGraw-Hill, 1953.

Chapter 6

INTERNATIONAL POLITICS AND TOMORROW'S POPULATION: CALCULUS OF PROBABILITY

Four centuries ago, world population was little more than half a billion. It has grown at an increasing rate since the Industrial Revolution, and by 1950 it came close to 2.5 billion. The mid-century annual rate of 0.85 per cent for world growth compares with a corresponding rate of 0.29 per cent for the century ending in 1750. At the rate of growth prevailing from 1900 to 1950, world population would total within 300 years over 20 billion. Naturally, this is just a calculation and not a forecast. Yet world population is growing rapidly, and there is, at present, no convincing evidence showing that this growth has been slowing significantly. The growth rate may oscillate widely, and in some places growth may come to a stop. For the time being, the continuing increase of the world population is one of the secular phenomena of our time. Population increase will force drastic revisions in our political, social, and economic techniques.

The present distribution of population among the various continents and skin colors will not persist. The zenith of growth may have been passed by several white nations. Even if the earth's white population were to maintain or even somewhat better its present rate of growth, some of the most important colored peoples are growing at a far more rapid pace. Hence the white population will not be able to preserve its present relative position. The major areas of future population growth are in Asia, Africa, and South America, especially in the tropical parts.[1] In addition to an advance of the colored peoples, it is quite probable that we shall witness an advance of the "mixed races." The "racial" shape of things to come is hardly presaged by the fanciful image of the "pure" nordic—long-headed and blonde—or the "pure" Mongolian or Negro, but rather by the complicated reality of "melting pots" as they now exist in areas like Hawaii, Trinidad, Brazil, and Malaya. Since mankind has a single origin, the process of its separation into "races" is a historical phenomenon. As mentioned before, the white "race" owes its existence to the "challenge" of the glacial periods. Being a historical phenomenon, it will have an end as it had a beginning. It is likely

---

[1] It may be noted that the population growth in the cold climates also has been considerable: Alaska, 5.61 per cent yearly (1939–1950) ; Greenland, 1.56 per cent (1930–1945) ; and Svalbard, 6.74 per cent (1930–1946). Since these populations are small, the figures are not very significant.

that the present distribution of skin pigmentation will leave its traces for ever, but it is also likely that the areas inhabited by "pure races" will become more and more isolated islands in an ocean of new types of humanity. This process can be reversed only through forced depopulation and through the extermination of competing "races" by one victorious "race," a remote possibility even granting the hypothetical consequences of massive extermination and atomic sterilization.

PROJECTION OF POPULATION GROWTH

What will be the situation a quarter of a century hence? No one can hope to predict accurately the growth of population.

The United States and the United Kingdom together would account for about a twelfth of world population growth in the next two decades. The net growth of population in Asia and in the U.S.S.R. of about 200 million in this period is equivalent to only slightly less than the present population of the United States, the United Kingdom, Canada, Australia, New Zealand, and South Africa.[2]

However, it is possible, given the current trends of birth and death rates, to estimate future population within a margin of error not exceeding, on the basis of the most divergent estimates, 12 per cent over the next twenty-five years. From these estimates of growth it is possible to deduce, within a similar range of probability, the place the United States will hold by, let us say, 1970, in the international line-up of manpower.

The United States. With the dissolution of the European system, the United States was confronted with a fundamental change in the realities underlying its foreign policy. United States security depends no longer upon the width of oceans or upon traditional alignments, but upon American strength and therefore upon manpower.

Assuming a continuation of the population increase between 1945 and 1953 (when the 160 million mark was passed), the population of the United States could rise to 180 million by about 1960.[3] Before the end of the century,

[2] See *America's Resources for World Leadership,* New York, National Industrial Conference Board, Inc., 1948, p. 6.

[3] The Bureau of the Census forecast a population of 144.7 by 1950, when the U.S. population actually reached 151.1, an error of no less than 50 per cent (see J. Frederic Dewhurst and Associates, *America's Needs and Resources,* New York, Twentieth Century Fund, 1947, p. 35). Yet it does not follow that forecasts can now be based on the trend of the forties more confidently than on the trend of the thirties. Somewhat chastened by its experience, the Bureau of the Census has adopted the method of making short-term forecasts and basing them on three sets of conditions. Thus it is projected that by 1960 the United States would have a population of 161, 169, or 180 million, depending on whether the "low," "medium," or "high" assumptions prove correct (see *Statistical Abstract of the United States 1952,* p. 22). Obviously, demographers have gone out of the forecasting business. It appears that, contrary to Malthusian expectations, a highly urbanized population like that of the United States can be so influenced as to increase natality substantially.

the American population easily could rise to as high as 250 million or more, unless there is again a reversal of this trend. The American birth rate rose from 16.7 in 1936 (per 1,000) to 25.7 in 1947 and 23.4 in 1950. However, fertility and birth rates may decline again and fall back to the level of the thirties. Death rates may rise as the biological limits of longevity are reached by medical and dietary science; the U.S. death rate of 9.6 (1950) may be compared with the death rate of Israel (6.5 in 1950), the lowest on record. Regardless of the actual figures—which, incidentally, are conjectural—the trend indicates a continuous population growth in the United States. Significantly, the reversal of the birth rate in the United States coincided with a similar reversal in fourteen European countries.

Great Britain. Compared with other Western nations, the United States holds a privileged position. Forecasts for Great Britain envisage an outright decline before 1970; Britain's population may decline from 47 million to between 42 and 38 million. Natural increase declined steadily in England from 405,000 a year in 1900 to 120,000 a year in 1935, although the total population increased by one-fifth. This increase tended to disappear in the postwar world. The age composition favorable to births, unfavorable to deaths, was passing, and at the same time the population was failing to avail itself of the favorable age composition to replenish its lower age groups. The general shape of the future structure is therefore clear. During the present generation the largest part of the population will move into the upper age groups, and deaths will increase; the heavily populated younger middle-aged groups will pass into the upper middle-aged ranks, but because of the fall of the birth rate in the past generation, their places cannot be filled, since too few children have been born. The younger middle-aged groups will be numerically weaker than their predecessors. Thus the production of a future population of the present size would demand a very considerable rise in the birth rate. It is doubtful whether this can be achieved soon enough to counterbalance the increase of deaths which must take place in the immediate future. Therefore the population of England is entering a period in which age composition will be unfavorable to births, favorable to deaths, and possibly be marked by a *natural decrease* instead of continued growth. Actually, Britain's demographic situation—a birth rate of 16.1 in 1950—is one of the most alarming in the world.[4] Immigration could change this situation, and Britain has indeed permitted immigrants to settle in the country. At the same time, many Britishers leave the United Kingdom and settle overseas.

The population of Canada, South Africa, Australia, and New Zealand is still increasing and may keep, during the next generation, the white popu-

[4] Many statistical data in this chapter are based on *United Nations Demographic Yearbook 1951,* Statistical Office of the United Nations, Department of Economic Affairs, New York, 1951.

lation of the British Empire as a whole at about the present level, *i.e.,* 75–80 million.

The Latin Bloc. It is not impossible that the decline of French manpower has been halted. The French population, 42 million in 1938, fell to about 40 million in 1945—war losses were estimated to be 820,000 [5]—but by 1951 had risen again to 42.4 million, an astonishing rate of growth of 1 per cent per annum. Fertility and birth rates improved considerably. In 1950, the birth rate stood at 20.5, as compared to an average rate of 15 for the period 1933–1941; the death rate has been brought down from 15.8 (1938) to 12.2 (1952). However, it is impossible at the time of this writing to state whether this demographic recovery is going to be permanent, or to assess the inroads on French population growth made by war, enemy occupation, malnutrition, dearth of medical supplies, forced migration of French workers to Germany, and the consequences of a long period of postwar political and economic instability, including colonial conflict. With each man killed in battle, two births are lost. [6]

Some experts hold that France faces drastic depopulation and that by 1970 her people will have shrunk to 30–35 million. This view may prove too gloomy. The postwar resiliency of a people which many experts had condemned to slow extinction is all the more remarkable for the conditions wherein it has taken place. Whether this phenomenon of demographic recuperation is the result of improved economic conditions or a transformation of the social and psychological climate wrought by deeper-lying causes is largely a matter of speculation. However, the development confounds over-pessimistic prognostications. [7] Long-range trends indicate that French manpower *may* decline; they do not point to a catastrophic diminishment within the life span of the next generation.

Up to World War I, Italy lagged behind the average increase of European population. Only after 1918 did the Italian population increase more quickly than that of other European countries (with the exception of the Slavic group). It was a high death rate which weighed heavily against the comparatively large number of births. The slowing up of population increase in other European countries, more than any factor inherent in these countries or in Italian population growth itself, enabled Italy to overtake France and close in on the United Kingdom. World War II and the postwar crisis pressed heavily against the Italian birth rate, which fell from 26.7 in 1930

---

[5] See Committee for the Study of European Questions, *The Results of the War of 1939–1945 as Regards the Population of Germany and of the Allied Countries of Europe* (1946), as quoted by Dudley Kirk in *Europe's Population in the Interwar Years,* Geneva, League of Nations, 1946, p. 69.

[6] L. Hirsch, "Demographic Effects of Modern Warfare," *What Would Be the Character of a New War,* New York, 1933. See also Horst Mendershausen's discussion of the "Hollow Age Classes" in *Economics of War,* New York, Prentice-Hall, 1943, pp. 321–323.

[7] See J. Bourgeois-Pichat, "La Situation demographique de la Grande Bretagne: comparaison avec celle de France," *Population,* Vol. 3, No. 4, October–December, 1948, pp. 672–673.

to 19.6 in 1950—below the French level. The Italian death rate stands at the United States level. Between 1936 and 1951, Italy, with a total population of 47 million, grew on the average of 0.73 per cent yearly, which is less than the world's rate of growth. Italian statistical data thus do not indicate a vitality more exuberant than that of other European peoples, as has been so frequently and boisterously alleged by Fascist propaganda. Although Italian urban populations have low birth rates, the high fertility of the peasants in southern Italy, Sicily, and Sardinia appears to justify expectation of a net gain. By 1970 the Italian people may have grown to 50 or 53 million. This forecast does not take emigration into account, although this factor has played a considerable role in Italian population movements.

Italy's demographic future is uncertain, because the country's capacities for industrialization are in doubt. Agriculturally, the country is overpopulated, especially if the high percentage of nonarable land is given its due weight. But industrialization is hampered by lack of capital, raw-material deposits, and especially energy resources. Whether or not this crucial limitation can be overcome will depend, to a certain extent, on the degree to which Italy can benefit from the development of nuclear energy, a development over which the Italians have little control. Nor does Italy control the immigration policies of France, Great Britain, the United States, and Latin America, which will decide to what extent Italians will be able to escape from their economic strait jacket. No estimate of Italy's future manpower can hope to gauge accurately the effects of these most problematic and unstable factors.

Spain's population, like that of Italy, is growing and is slated to increase from 29 million in 1951 to 33 million in 1970. Spain, too, has been a country of emigration; in 1930, 2.5 million Spaniards, or 10 per cent of the homeland's population, lived outside the country while maintaining Spanish citizenship. Gradually Spanish relations with some of the Latin-American countries have become more intimate and may result in accelerated emigration, although Spain's birth rate, oscillating around 20, does not make for serious demographic pressure. However, Spain is far richer in industrial raw materials and is only half as densely settled in relation to arable soil as Italy. Thus, industrialization and land reclamation could absorb population increase more readily in Spain than in Italy.

Portugal, the second Iberian power, has a rapidly increasing population. The yearly growth rate is about 1 per cent and the birth rate 24–25. Portugal's "absorption potential" is only moderate.

By 1970 the combined population of the "Latin bloc"—France, Italy, Portugal, and Spain—may have increased from less than 120 million in 1940 to about 140 million. This small growth—which, be it repeated, is quite problematical—signifies a relative decline of the Latin bloc and indicates a waning influence of its member nations. The fact is of importance not only because the Latin powers hold vast "dependent" territories, peopled by a fair number of white "Latin" settlers, but also because their cultural influence in Latin America and in many other countries heretofore was decisive. Moreover, the Latin countries are Catholic and traditionally played a leading role in the Catholic world. The supranational ideas of Latinity and Catholicism will continue to evoke in many minds—in spite of, or perhaps because of, the many divisions of the Latin world—visions of a political community of interests. While most of the thinking done on that topic has so far been confined to intellectual, and mainly conservative, circles in Europe as well as in Latin America, its influence may prove a far from negligible factor in world politics.

Germany. Available estimates of Germany's future population disagree widely. Experts disagree as to which period is the one most representative of Germany's recent fertility trends. There is the question, too, of the delineation of German territory. For example, should we assume that the parts which Poland has occupied since 1945 will become Slavicized? Will Königsberg remain Russian? Territorial change was accompanied by large-scale, two-way migrations and appears to have affected the vital trends of the *Altreich, i.e.,* Germany within her 1936 boundaries.

During the war, German population rose, largely because of "immigration" of slave labor and displaced persons, and not because of a high birth rate. The *Bundesrepublik*'s population continued to increase, but this growth was due to influx of *Volksdeutsche* from the Baltic and Balkan countries and Czechoslovakia, and of refugees from East Germany and the Eastern Zone of Berlin, as well as Russian "nonreturners." There is a considerable surplus of women. The areas with the highest birth rates fell into Soviet hands. But it is conceivable that the refugees who escaped to Western Germany might cling to their cultural patterns and that their rate of growth might, at least for some time to come, remain on the Rhine what it had been on the Oder. In 1949, the West German birth rate stood at 17. It fell during the next year to 16.2; however, the death rate of about 13 was surprisingly low. The highly unsettled political conditions, housing shortages, and the presence of large numbers of foreign troops, as well as Soviet policies in Eastern Germany, threw the demographic picture into complete confusion.

Up to 1910 Germany's birth rate was still the highest in northwestern and central Europe. In 1933, it was one of the lowest in Europe and fell short, by one-quarter, of the rate required for keeping the population stationary. If an estimate of German population in 1970 were to be based on the low fertility levels of 1925–1933, it would hardly exceed 60 million. Before the war and during the early war years, subsidies and honors to large families, stringent laws against abortion, and official benevolence toward procreation out of wedlock met with some success. But in 1943 the birth rate, which according to Nazi statistics had stood at 20.3 in 1939, had fallen to 14 per 1,000 inhabitants, lower even than the French of the same year.

In France and Britain, population increase has been declining for several generations, but has declined more slowly as birth rates became smaller. By contrast, German population change has been more abrupt—a consequence of abrupt social and economic changes. Are the years 1925–1933, a phase of postwar reconstruction and economic and social crisis, or the years 1933–1939, a phase of reemployment through militarization, the most suitable base period for projecting future German growth?

In 1936, Germany was not an overpopulated country, and the German population, far from growing as lustily as Nazi propaganda fancied, showed signs of impending decline—as did, incidentally, every predominantly urban-industrial nation of Europe. In 1947, the German national standard of living, measured by the 1,500 calories per mouth provided by official ration, sank to the level of Asia, and there was, for the first time in German history, a real, not a propaganda-manufactured, doubt as to the ability of German economy to feed, clothe, and shelter an overcrowded population.

By 1945 Germany had received 7.5 million immigrants, *i.e.*, *Volksdeutsche* and "displaced persons." In the postwar period this influx remained heavy, adding a total of about 3.7 million, if the number of D.P.'s who left the country is taken into account. Hence the German population (all parts) rose from 60.8 million in 1945 to 67.7 million in 1947. Yet in 1950, when the census in Western Germany showed a population of 47.6 million, the number was half a million *below* the official estimate based on ration cards.[8]

After the German economic reforms of 1948 and the resumption of normal economic production, the standard of living rose sharply—and the ghost of overpopulation receded. Germany had resumed her place as one of the wealthiest and most productive countries of the world. Population density had risen from 372 per square mile in 1939 to about 500 per square mile of the *Bundesrepublik*, and yet, to confound the Malthusians, economic catastrophe was averted. This was the result not of a miracle but of sound economics.[9]

The principal effects of the war as regards the composition of the German population were (1) the precipitous decrease of the proportion of adult males in relation to the total population; (2) the massive increase of the female over the male component; and (3) the rise of the proportion of aged people in relation to the total population, the result mainly of the "disappearance" of a large contingent of young males.

The census of 1946 revealed a 5:6 ratio of male and female population. In 1950, this ratio, in the *Bundesrepublik* alone, still was 9:10. Yet these figures do not convey the far more significant distribution of the sexes in the

[8] Gregory Frumkin, *Population Changes in Europe since 1939*, London, G. Allen, 1951, p. 81.

[9] It is true that Germany was helped by the United States. Yet this help was balanced in large part by the direct and indirect costs of the occupation and the various economic restrictions, especially limitations on output and foreign trade, and by "dismantling" of machinery.

reproductive age groups. Between the ages of twenty and forty that ratio is probably 2:3. Every third woman of childbearing age hence would be, by the ruling preconceptions of a monogamous civilization, relegated to spinsterhood.

The abrupt and massive diminution of the young and productive male age groups resulted in an increased average age of the German population; the average German is older than he was in 1936, and there is a correspondingly larger quota of nonproducers in relation to producers. It is these circumstances and the fact that the German population at the height of Hitler's drive for babies failed by about one-tenth to reproduce itself which tend to slate Germany for a real decrease in population.

While it is probably safe to assume that the German population will not show any pronounced increase—unless there is continuous large-scale immigration from Soviet lands—it is by no means a foregone conclusion that there will be a real or significant population decline.

But it has become somewhat meaningless to talk of "Germany" when, in fact, there are two Germanies and two countries with divergent developments. For all practical purposes, Eastern Germany has become a Soviet province. Western Germany is a country which, manpowerwise, is approximately of the same size as Britain, Italy, and France. The influx of Slavic and Eastern elements, the predominance of Catholicism, the destruction of German cities, and the Soviet threat have changed the cultural and political aspirations of the German people. To a point, a *new* nation has emerged.

During a brief historical period, shorter than Western man's expectancy of life, the military effectives of Germany held the balance of power upon the European continent. It was that concentration of human force which pressed upon the rest of Europe, worked the expanding German plant, and energized the latent strategic possibilities of a central geographic position. For a recrudescence of that power, international trends would have to run backward, like a film being run off the wrong way around. These trends point, for the middle and long run, to new centers of population growth and political power.

The Soviet Union. The last reliable population figure for the U.S.S.R. was that of the census of January 17, 1939, which showed a population of 170,500,000. Since that date there have been incorporated into the Soviet Union, both before and after the war, territories with a population of about 24 million. The population of the enlarged territory was estimated at 201 million in 1950. It was estimated that the population of the U.S.S.R. and the Soviet-annexed territories would have risen to about 215 million, had prewar trends continued. Hence the figure of 193 million—the official Soviet estimate of population in 1946—shows a loss of 22 million. According to Eugen Kulischer, the excess mortality during the war years was 14 million, distributed between military and civilian deaths, and the deficit of births was approxi-

TABLE 3. EUROPEAN POPULATION CHANGES, 1937–1950 *

European Population Losses, 1939–1945
(In millions)

```
Territories ceded to Soviet Union (minus repatriates).... −17.9
Excess of births over deaths........................... +12.0
War losses (military and civilian).................... −15.1
Prisoners in captivity................................ − 5.0
Other population shifts (net)......................... + 0.3
                                                       ────────
                                                        −25.7
```

Changes in Density of Population, 1938–1947
(Within constant borders)

Nation	Per cent	Nation	Per cent
Finland	+19	Austria	+5
Germany	+15	U.K.	+4
Denmark	+12	Belgium	+1
Netherlands	+11	France	0
Switzerland	+10	Hungary	0
Portugal	+9	Rumania	0
Sweden	+8	Yugoslavia	−3
Bulgaria	+8	Czechoslovakia	−16
Norway	+8	Poland	−27
Italy	+7		

Excess of Births over Deaths
(In thousands)

Nation	1937–1938	1946–1947	1948–1949	1950
France	−47	622	655	327
Italy	796	956	946	442
U.K.	302	786	627	225
Belgium	41	75	79	36
Netherlands	199	394	331	154
Finland	54	122	122	56
Totals	1,345	2,955	2,760	1,240

Population Changes, 1938–1947
(In thousands)

Nations	1938	1947
Belgium, Luxembourg, France, Netherlands, U.K., Malta, Italy, Trieste	150.959	155.832
Austria, Germany	75.153	75.572
Poland, Czechoslovakia, Hungary, Rumania, Bulgaria...	74.550	68.001
Yugoslavia, Greece	22.785	23.192
Denmark, Norway, Finland, Sweden	16.729	18.405
Ireland, Portugal, Spain, Switzerland	40.232	42.853
Totals	380.406	383.915

* Based on Gregory Frumkin, *Populati* ɹ *Changes in Europe since 1939*, London, G. Allen, 1951.

mately 10 million.[10] Though these calculations appear not only to indicate terrible real population losses but also suggest a radical revision of earlier estimates of *future* growth, it is a fact that population gains by annexation have largely compensated the Soviet Union for population losses in war. Hence an earlier estimate, based on prewar trends, may still serve, in the absence of reliable Soviet statistics, as a first approximation of the future growth of the Soviet population.[11] According to this estimate the population of the Soviet Union within its 1939 borders will have increased from 174 million in 1940 to 251 million in 1970.[12]

This estimate is based on the following conditions: Though in Russia the average size of the family is declining and direct war losses (casualties) total at least 10 and perhaps 14 million, there are still so many families that the number of births will remain high. Moreover the number of children and young people now living will, for another generation at least, form a solid base for growth. Thus the age composition is favorable to births, and as the old-age group is relatively small, deaths will be proportionately few. It is precisely this condition which obtained in Western Europe up to thirty years ago, *i.e.,* during the period of large natural increase. However, many factors may cause this estimate to be invalidated. Unlike the United States, the Soviet Union is limping *behind* demographic forecasts. This probably is the result of the communist policies of purges, class liquidations, massive slave labor, famine, and war. If these policies continue, Russian population growth will be delayed; if they do not, a change of regime would have to be assumed with a resultant modification of demographic trends. Second, forced and rapid industrialization, coupled with extremely poor housing conditions, may advance the date of the decline. Third, Russian food production will have difficulty keeping pace with population increases; food shortages may well act as brakes. If the demographic situation of Russia really were favorable, the Soviets would not keep their census data secret.

It is important to remember that the population of Russia does not only comprise Russians. Depending on differing data and assumptions, the Great Russians may account for only 50 or, as a maximum, for 58 per cent of the Soviet population. At least one-fifth consists of non-Russian Slavs, particularly

[10] Eugen M. Kulischer, "The Russian Population Enigma," *Foreign Affairs,* Vol. 27, No. 23, April, 1949, p. 500. "Estimates concerning population in the Soviet Union of 1945/46 vary between 180 and 194 million. By 1950 the population of the Soviet Union—including the 23-odd million annexed since 1939—is estimated at 200–210 million. However, due to the probable gaps in the 1926 census—the first taken by the Soviets—prewar figures may have exaggerated Russia's rate of growth." Frumkin, *op. cit.,* p. 160.

[11] Assuming Russian war losses to have been 20 million, and gains by annexation to have canceled out war losses, Frank Lorimer arrives at an estimated population for 1970 of 251.4 million (see Frank Lorimer, "Population Prospects of the Soviet Union," *New Compass of the World,* New York, Macmillan, 1949, p. 167).

[12] See Frank Notestein, *The Future Population of Europe and the Soviet Union,* Geneva, League of Nations, 1944, p. 312.

Ukrainians; and the rest comprises various Turki, Caucasian, and Mongolian peoples (who probably have the highest birth rates in the Soviet Union). Hence, it is likely that, by 1970, the Russians themselves will not have grown much beyond the 120 million mark. This vitally important fact should be kept in mind when estimates of future Soviet cultural and political, economic and social developments are made.

Furthermore, Russia controls the Slavic states of Eastern Europe which may increase, *if* we accept prewar demographic estimates at face value, from 65 million in 1940 to 85 million in 1970 (including Yugoslavia). The fact, however, is that the growth rate of these nations has declined considerably. Czechoslovakia suffered a loss of population, although her birth rate (22 in 1949) has improved from prewar times. But this Slavic bloc is riven by non-Slavic nationalities: Rumanians, Hungarians (both declining nations), Germans, Finns, Balts. Moreover, since these Slavs are in opposition against each other (and also among themselves), we may find in 1970 that within the area currently known as the Soviet orbit, 120 million Russians will be outnumbered by non-Russian Slavs and by non-Slavs in a relation of 1:2.8.

Against this prospect it must be borne in mind that Soviet nationality policy aims at mixing and breaking up potentially hostile nationalities, apparently in the hope that ultimately many of them will become Russians through cultural and political assimilation—unless it be in the hope that they may be creating a new "communist" or "Soviet" nationality. The success of such a policy is quite problematical. But in the meantime, it is a serious mistake to talk about a "Slavic bloc" as though it represented a definite political reality rather than communist domination or a statistical classification.

In 1939, 38 million Soviet citizens lived in Asia. Recent estimates put this figure at 62 million in 1950, or about one-third of the total Soviet population. This increase by 63 per cent in eleven years may or may not have occurred in fact, but the development of industries in the shelter of the Urals, beyond the reach of hostile European powers, and the strengthening of the Asiatic border regions most certainly have dominated the strategic thinking of the Soviet regime since its earliest days. Industrialization and mechanization of agriculture in Russian Asia set in motion mass migration not only from the land to the towns but also from densely settled rural regions of Russian Europe. When the Red Army fell back before the German invader, it shielded the withdrawal of many war-important industries. Whole plants, together with their skilled personnel, were moved to Asia. In addition, millions of people uprooted by the war, villagers with their livestock, skilled workers, peasants and slave laborers streamed eastward. After the war Poles, Balts, Ruthenians, Ukrainians, Caucasians, and even Germans and Japanese were moved into Siberia. Soviet economic planners put new factories and cities "beyond the Urals." New deposits of raw materials were opened up in the arctic and subarctic wastes. While many legends have been spun around these developments, and while "dispersal" of this kind makes much less sense in the air age than in the age of the ground invader, a powerful historic trend has been accelerated: the "Asiatification" of Russia.

Already under the Tsars there was a distinct Siberian nation in the making, "Russian in the core, but modified also by the influx of foreign blood." [13] The opening of the Russian East, unlike the American West, with which it is so often and loosely compared, extended Russian domination not only to sparsely settled regions but also over a large part of central Asia inhabited by Turco-Islamic peoples. In the Far East, the settlers from the West meet with Mongolian peoples and even, it seems, with relatively large numbers of Asiatic immigrants into the Soviet Union. If and when Chinese labor were to be used in Siberia, the importance of the Mongolian element would increase. In the Far North, too, there is intermingling with increasing numbers of aboriginal inhabitants.

The "frontier" to the east will, for decades to come, mitigate whatever Malthusian tendencies may assert themselves in the social pattern of the Soviet Union, but it will not fail to modify the "racial" composition as well as the geographic structure of that country, or, rather, agglomeration of countries. Age structure and "frontier" appear to favor a rapid growth of the Soviet population. The climate of oppression, the mechanics of slave labor, and the practices of genocide or "class" liquidations militate against the demographic vitality of the peoples living in the Soviet orbit. Nevertheless, there seems to be little doubt that the population of Russia will continue to grow. For the time being we must base our thinking on the hypothesis that by 1970 the Soviet Union will have a population of 250 million and, within its orbit (except China, East Germany, and Albania), about 320 million.

Asia. Japan borrowed the mechanics of Western progress, not its inwardness. She began to acquire the former when the West forced her gates in the 1850's, and to transform, with the Meiji restoration in 1868, a feudal agrarian regime into an industrial state. Changes in population growth and structure followed the general lines of the Western pattern. Japan's population increased from 27 million in 1852 to 73 million in 1940. By 1950, Japan's population stood at 83 million (borders of 1945); this increase included, however, all the people repatriated from Japan's former possessions.

About half of the population lives in towns, one-eighth in the five great cities of Tokyo, Osaka, Yokohama, Nagoya, and Kobe. While the Japanese population continues to increase, the rate of growth has been declining gradually. The birth rate went down from 32.4 in 1930 to 28.4 in 1950 (although it stood again at 34.3 in 1947). For the period of 1945–1951 it stood at 0.82 per cent of the "replacement rate," as compared with 1.4 per cent for the

[13] Eric Fischer, *The Passing of the European Age,* Cambridge, Mass., Harvard University Press, 1943, p. 129.

period 1940–1945. At the same time the death rate declined from 18.2 (1930) to 11.0 (1950). In the big cities the birth rates have declined most rapidly. Were rural fertility to decline at the same rate as urban (for which assumption, thus far, conclusive evidence is lacking), Japan's population in 1970 would be 90–95 million, which estimate, like each foregoing one, projects past trends into the future and does not pretend to foretell what the future will be.

The transformation of Japan was wrought by the impact of Western civilization; Japan, however, has not absorbed all of it. Population increase is slackening, but the Western cliché will not fit Japanese conditions so long as habits of life and thought formed in the age of Japan's secluded feudalism retain their hold on the masses. The fertility of the industrial areas *has* been declining, chiefly, some experts believe, because of the increasing age of marriage, which in turn is due to young women's employment as factory labor and the long periods of military service for men.[14] But in Japan, factories and cities, patriarchal family and medieval village exist side by side. The state stimulated and directed the development of industry; it also guarded the traditional structure of a feudal-military society. Neither is wholly assimilated to the other. Hence the contradictions of modern Japan; hence, also, the doubtful value of analogies derived from the experience of Western peoples.

Many Japanese and Western students have argued that population pressure generated the expansionist tendencies that turned Japan to foreign conquest. It is quite true that Japan cannot feed her population and that, while food production has increased, population has grown even faster. Japanese agriculture still can be improved, but again the increase of population will tend to perpetuate the food deficit. The answer would be reduction of the Japanese population through emigration—peaceful emigration or military conquest—or expanding markets for trade. The demolition of the Japanese Empire, in and of itself, need not affect the situation, for only a fraction of the population increase has been diverted into the conquered territories, or for that matter to any other areas overseas. In 1938, only 1.5 million Japanese resided in Japan's overseas possessions, and of these a goodly number were officials. Barriers to Oriental immigration, before World War II, had closed Australia, North America, and many Latin-American states, except Brazil and Peru, to Japanese would-be settlers. But it is by no means clear that they would have settled abroad as readily as Japanese propagandists claimed they would have, had Western countries relaxed their discriminatory policies. Still, emigration may be an expedient. Of great concern for the future is the fact that much of the Asiatic mainland, chiefly China and Manchuria, may remain closed to large-scale Japanese trade. Japan must find—or be given—markets in South-

---

14 In 1935, the rate of net reproduction was for towns what it had been in 1920, namely, 1.2; for rural Japan it had risen from 1.8 to 1.9. (Irene B. Taeuber and Edwin G. Beal, "The Dynamics of Population in Japan," *Milbank Memorial Fund Quarterly*, Vol. 22, No. 3, July, 1944.)

east Asia, Africa, and other tropical areas; else its stability would be threatened. Otherwise, prospects of future Japanese population growth are determined by the economic future of the Japanese homeland with its askew Oriental-Western, agrarian-urban, medieval-industrial countenance. It is safe to say that this population will continue to increase; and also, given the topography of the land, that Japan's population growth will cause considerable social and international difficulties.

Forecasts of China's population are entirely impossible. For one thing, no one knows the present population of China. The current estimate is 475 million; probably, this number may be much smaller. Whether China's population will or will not increase will depend partly on the communist regime's policy (it has been said that the Chinese communists favor depopulation), on its economic success, on its tenure, and, in case of a political change, on the nature and extent of the crisis accompanying the change. It seems as though China has had for a long time an only slowly growing population; this growth may increase gradually.

By contrast, the populations of Pakistan and India have been increasing at the annual rate of 0.75 per cent and 1.3 per cent respectively between 1941 and 1951. The Indian subcontinent has a population of about 425 million (1951) and by 1970 undoubtedly will exceed 500 million. The death rates, too, have been declining relatively fast from 24.8 (1930) to 16 (1949) in India and 12.3 (1948) in Pakistan. The conventional picture of the excessively high birth and death rates no longer corresponds to reality. In so far as the future is concerned, much will depend on political circumstances, on economics, and, particularly, on the solution of the pressing food problem. Similar remarks apply to Indonesia, while, by and large, other Asiatic countries seem to have a much slower rate of growth than is commonly supposed. Israel, with a growth rate over 8 per cent (birth rate 30–33 and death rate 6–7 during 1945–1950), is an exception which is due predominantly to immigration.

There can be no doubt about the fact that the population of Asia is increasing; the current rate of growth for Asia (excluding the U.S.S.R.) is about 1.5 per cent per year. The growth, however, may follow possibly the pattern of Japan, which could serve Asia as an object lesson in Westernization. This can be said confidently: Japanese history does not warrant the belief that increase of the Asian peoples will halt in the near future or that all such increase must necessarily remain fallow industrially and militarily.

If this reading of the manpower realities of Asia is correct, there are being added to the two major centers of growing populations possessed of advanced technological skills—Russia in Asia and Japan, each slated to exceed in numbers the largest European nation—two new cores of skilled manpower, India and China. Their populations are slated for substantial increases.

From the first Tokugawa census count in 1721 to the last in 1850 the Japanese population remained stationary, fluctuating between 27 and 30 million.[15] This stability was not due to human foresight and birth control but to the action of famines and diseases, *i.e.*, the regulating factors of orthodox Malthusian theory. This situation is precisely that in which large parts of Asia still find themselves today. Yet the Japanese people so perilously close to the subsistence level were transformed within less than one generation into the industrial and military manpower which defeated first China, then the Russian Empire, and dared the mighty United States.

Africa. For the African continent as a whole, statistics are quite incomplete, but a gradual, albeit slow, population increase is observable. It can be estimated, on the base of the best data, at 1.5 per cent per year. By 1970, Africa should be approaching the 250-million mark. It should be noted, however, that the African population is not one entity but consists of many different races and cultures.

Latin America. The most rapid increase takes place in Latin America, which in 1951 reached a population of 160 million. The rate of growth is greater than 2.5 per cent per year, with some countries reaching considerably higher rates (*i.e.*, Mexico, 2.9; Argentina, 3.2 per cent). Accordingly, Latin America should have considerably more than 250 million inhabitants by 1970. It should be added that, throughout Latin America, the conditions of growth are perhaps more favorable than in any other continent, especially from the economic point of view. Honduras, for example, shows a record growth rate of 5 per cent (1945–1950). Birth rates have been rising rapidly in British Guiana, Argentina, Colombia, Peru, and Nicaragua. Venezuela's birth rate rose from 29.7 in 1930 to 43.1 in 1950, while its death rate declined from 17 (1930) to 11 (1950). It is highly probable that the Latin-American growth rate will be accelerated through immigration. On the other hand, some of the non-self-governing areas have shown declines, *e.g.*, Guadeloupe and French Guiana (a loss rate of 0.86 from 1936 to 1946).

Summary. By 1970, the global population may reach 3 billion people, of which 54 per cent will live in Asia, 15 per cent in the Americas, 12 per cent in Europe, 10 per cent in the Soviet orbit (minus China), 8 per cent in Africa, and the rest in Australia. Applying this hypothetical distribution to the political alignment of 1953—strictly an intellectual exercise—we would see that the Western world, *i.e.*, the Americas, Western Europe, Australia, and parts of Africa, account for 30 per cent of the world population; Russia with its European satellites, for 10 per cent; Russia together with China, for 28 per cent; and the "noncommitted" areas of Asia and Africa, for 42 per cent. This means that the balance of the world may be moving into the hands of the

[15] *Ibid.*

colored nations—other things being equal. Needless to repeat that the meaning of these figures might be different if there were major shifts in the Western or Soviet orbits, or if the colored nations were unable to make their influence felt. The forces set free by the demographical revolution which began 150 years ago in Western Europe and now encompass the whole globe are far from spent. The United States and Western Europe are faced by growing population pressure upon the landlocked areas of Eurasia as well as the Asiatic rimlands framed by the Indian and Pacific Oceans, and upon the Americas south of the Rio Grande. Is not this shift of highs and lows bound to make the weather of international politics?

POPULATION PRESSURES

Malthusian concepts have left their imprints on many minds. Hence numerous people shudder at the thought that population will continue to increase. Regardless of these fears, however, there seems to be very little that can be done about it. If population growth were to be slowed up at all, it would be to the detriment of the most civilized nations in Western Europe and perhaps of the United States. Such a deceleration of growth would lead to a deterioration of the power position of the Occident, to the extinction, in due course, of Western civilization, and certainly to the catastrophic reduction of the economic stature of the presently leading industrial nations. It is fortunate for the Western world that the population decline which loomed so ominously in the statistics of the 1930's seems to have been delayed. Depending on the success of the policy aiming at the cultural and economic restoration of Western Europe, this decline may be averted altogether, but, on the other hand, a relatively minor crisis may push the white nations again onto the downward slope.

There is no question that population increases pose very considerable economic problems. Resources must be opened up, production must be augmented, and food output must be raised. However, if the economic problem of increasing population is couched in the term of the concept of optimum population, very erroneous conclusions will be reached.

This conception can be briefly expressed as follows: at any given time the population which can exist on a given extent of land, consistently with the attainment of the maximum return of industry possible at the time, is finite. In other words, for any given area of land under any given set of circumstances there is an optimum population. If population is at an optimum number, the greatest return per head possible under the circumstances will be attained. Since the equilibrium of population and productive resources, implied by the notion "optimum," depends on the behavior of numerous variables such as technological change, foreign trade, and social development, the conception of optimum population is not particularly helpful beyond formulating a truism, namely, overpopulation and underpopulation alike imply a smaller income per head than could be attained by smaller and larger numbers respectively. Unfortunately attempts to determine whether underpopulation or overpopulation exist never yet have met with success. Moreover, the "optimum" for peace may not be the "optimum" for war; in fact, nobody has ever calculated an "optimum." Evidently, a country's optimum population under conditions prevailing in, let us say, 1955 is not the same as that in 1935 or 1895. These different "optimums" were determined as much by the intervention of political and military factors as by economic and technological circumstances. Although it was suggested by certain economists, as, for example, Alvin Hansen, that a population smaller than that now living in the United States constitutes an "optimum," neither wartime experiences nor the national income formation of the postwar years confirmed their contention.[16] And who can state categorically what is the "optimum" of the United States at any given time in relation to the political and economic commitments of the United States abroad, in relation to the requirements of national defense, and in relation to a host of contingencies with which the position of world leadership is fraught? An optimum population must be static if it is to be statistically measurable at all; if it is conceived of as dynamic, then the concept is not of very much practical use since the workings of innumerable variable factors preclude accurate measurement. The United States is one of the most sparsely populated countries in the world. It has the population density of underdeveloped areas, such as Afghanistan, Yemen, Iraq, and Estonia. Among the industrialized countries, it is the most sparsely populated one, excepting the Soviet Union, most of whose territory is useless. If the United States had the population density of Belgium, one of Europe's most prosperous countries, it would carry a population of two and one-half billion people. If the United States had the population density of the State of New York, which perhaps may be a more relevant example, its population would exceed 900 million. In summary, the notion of optimum population belongs to neo-Malthusian speculation. It fails not only to account for population change as a result of change in techniques of production but also to supply a formula for adjusting the populations of several countries to each other, *i.e.*, to a common optimum. A. M. Carr-Saunders commented on the "optimum" conception—which incidentally he held to be a valuable one—as follows: "It is not possible to say whether or not England and the United States are over- or underpopulated. It is, however, generally held that parts of India and China are overpopulated. It is, in other words, probably true that the inhabitants of these countries would be better off if the population was less dense." There is little in this definition which will aid in understanding why Japan, for example, managed to break the vicious circle of Malthusian reasoning.[17]

[16] Alvin H. Hansen, "Progress and Declining Population," *American Economic Review,* Vol. 29, No. 1, pp. 1–15.

[17] For a vigorous critique of the conception of optimum population, see Alfred Sauvy, *Richesse et population,* Paris, Payot, 1944, pp. 15–38.

It can be argued that whatever gains are being scored by backward peoples through better sanitation, transportation, and administration are quickly absorbed by additional growth, and that hence the population problems of colonial and semicolonial Asia have been created by the very improvements bestowed upon them by the West. Yet Japan waxed strong in the face of the very Malthusian controls, famine and disease, which curbed the growth of its population and now still curb the preindustrial societies of China and India.

The main tool of the Malthusian demographer is the concept of population density. High densities are considered a major threat to social and economic stability. They are deemed particularly burdensome for the tropical countries which, according to the legend, are already vastly overpopulated. A closer look at the figures, however, shows that the theoreticians have failed to analyze their facts properly. It appears that high population densities occur in the countries of Western Europe, which are among the most prosperous in the world. In the Orient, high concentrations of population occur in the valleys of the Nile and the Yangtze, and in the deltas of the rivers of tropical Asia. Yet strangely enough, these delta populations are much more prosperous than the less densely settled people who live some distance away from the rivers. There are, indeed, individual cases of plausible correlation between economic distress and high population densities, such as Java and Barbados. Yet the over-all density of Indonesia is 15 per cent of that of Java; while the "surplus" population of Barbados (which does suffer from food shortages) could be resettled easily in scores of underpopulated Caribbean islands or in British Guiana. The majority of the Indo-Chinese population is concentrated along the coast, but 85 per cent of the country has a population density of 18 inhabitants per square mile. Even India, which allegedly is overpopulated, has a lesser density than Italy or Belgium. While undoubtedly there are heavy population pressures, about one-third of the arable soil of India is not yet under cultivation.

It is quite erroneous to single out population density as the main factor of analysis. In the temperate zones, industrial and trading areas carry a far higher density of population than agricultural countries, and yet they enjoy a far higher standard of living. Comparisons between densities in temperate and in tropical climates are meaningless: the tropical farmer brings in more harvests than his colleague in the colder climate. He needs less clothing, building materials, or fuel. He probably needs less calories. He is less dependent on agricultural exchange, since it is easy for him to produce, on one lot, a well-rounded staple diet. Needless to say, other factors, such as quality of the soil, water supply, agricultural techniques, capital resources, availability of fertilizer, productivity of fisheries, etc., also must be taken into consideration. There does not exist a correlation between population density and unemployment, certainly not in industrialized countries. Even in tropical agricultural areas, density and unemployment are by no means clearly linked in a cause-effect relationship. For example, Jamaica has a far higher unemployment rate than Barbados, yet it is much less densely populated.

To determine how many people can be "carried" on a given territory, it would be necessary to analyze the relationships among arable land, technology, financial strength, markets, production and trade policies, invisible imports and exports, possibilities of industrialization, consumption patterns, labor skills, administrative maturity, etc., and to compare these factors with various levels of population. No investigation of this type ever has been made, and probably none ever will be made. Hence, the terms overpopulation or underpopulation and the significance ascribed to population density are meaningless as theoretical tools. They are as metaphysical as the angels on the point of a needle. However, it is possible to determine that, within a *given* framework of conditions, there are "chronic" food deficits or a surplus of population which cannot be gainfully employed. By the same token, there are areas which cannot be developed by the limited populations which now occupy them. Their improvement depends on the influx of additional people.

THE DILEMMA OF ASIA

From a humanitarian point of view, gradual and uniform growth is far more desirable than sweeping change. Yet it is in the latter form that progress has come to Asia.

The population dynamics of Asia confront the Western powers with a serious problem. Can the industrial development of these Asiatic regions proceed rapidly enough to provide a living for increased populations? Will not accelerated industrial development in turn improve living standards, hence reduce mortality, and thus annul whatever temporary relief it affords from population pressure? Granted even that industrialization will reform the social milieu and that Indian and Chinese peasants, who have newly become wage earners, will adjust with docility and speed their habits of procreation to an urban-industrial environment, fertility will not be reduced in advance of mortality.

The Malthusian concept of "too many people" has found its way into the vocabulary of the average man of the West. Because it has been for a long time part and parcel of his mental baggage, it determines his behavior—a behavior which is far from simple or natural. There is as yet no counterpart in the East for this set pattern which rules Western man. It cannot be reproduced in any and all climates by packaging industrialization—particularly when superimposed on ancient civilization—in educational programs. Perhaps Western technology will produce the identical effects wherever it spreads, independent of the indigenous culture. The Japanese experiment is far from furnishing a clear answer. For that matter, even under the apparent uniformity of the European pattern, puzzling contradictions are hidden. In the Caribbean area, on the other hand, experience seems to indicate that as living standards rise, literacy is becoming more widespread, organization is improving, and diets are becoming more diversified, fertility and birth rates begin to decline.[18] Greater participation in cultural life also has its effect. As marriages tend progressively to be contracted later in life, demographic pressures are being eased.

Nevertheless, it is doubtful that the demographical impact of industrialization can be cushioned by planning or persuasion, especially when foreigners do the planning and persuading. The consequences of industrialization in the East will, beyond the shadow of a doubt, be cataclysmic. The current growth precludes all gradualness of transition; prevailing political and social tensions are making certain that the transition will be convulsive. If solicitous aids, advisory and financial, extended by foreigners to an industrializing Asiatic country are guarantees of its peaceable evolution, then Japan should have been the most peaceful country in Asia.

Amid a host of imponderables, only one near certainty emerges. It has the concreteness, at least, of a sound military estimate. The introduction of Western techniques will, within two or three decades, make Asiatic manpower effective; to be sure, not in every country and not all of it in any country. But a fraction, only, of so large a mass will weigh heavily in the scales of world power.

THE LIMITATIONS OF POPULATION POLICIES

Population policies aim at controlling the rate of growth of a nation. Nazi Germany and Fascist Italy undertook measures to stimulate the birth rates; so did France and, to a limited degree, Great Britain. These measures consist, by and large, in giving economic advantages to big families and in propagandizing the idea of parenthood. There may be tax exemptions for each additional child as there are in most countries, including the United States; and there may be higher salaries, educational facilities, allocation of living quarters, and public honors for large families. The facts show that Mussolini's policy was quite unsuccessful. In the case of Nazi Germany and France, these policies were followed by an increase in the birth rates, but it is difficult to say whether this change was due to these demographic policies or to other factors, such as, in the case of Germany, confidence in victory. Considering, however, that a rather startling increase of the French birth rate occurred within a highly unsettled epoch and amidst the strains of war and enemy occupation, it seems permissible to assume that such demographic policies *can* be successful. In the United States, the upward change of the birth rate occurred without benefit of a population policy and was appar-

---

[18] For details see "Appendix on Demography," *Caribbean Statistical Digest,* Branch of the Central Secretariat, Caribbean Commission, first issue, Port of Spain, Trinidad, September, 1951.

ently motivated by a change in attitudes toward family life.[19] Even in Sweden, for generations the country most addicted to Malthusianism, the birth rate turned upward. The results of the demographic policies of the Soviet Union are uncertain, since the effect of strict laws against abortion and aid for large families are partly offset by the shifting around of people, inadequate housing, and slave-labor practices. So far as it is known, the satellite areas in Eastern Europe are at present—in addition to some isolated colonial regions—the only ones which show a loss of population.

In Asia, Japan has encouraged the use of contraceptive practices. The Indian government has made similar, though more timid, efforts at influencing the birth rates, which indeed have been declining slowly. The relatively slow growth of China's population appears to be due, in part, to habits of procreation and not solely to high death rates.

The possible gains from population policies should not be underrated. The conduct of people *can* be influenced through persuasion and economic rewards. A great deal will depend on the energy with which these policies are being pursued. As more is being learned about the motivations which lead people in the various areas to accept or reject large families, the effectiveness of appeals for larger or smaller families may be heightened. On the other hand, restrictive population policies run counter to religious convictions and cultural traditions, while policies aiming at the increase of numbers are not necessarily compatible with the mores of liberal-individualist societies. In any event, the secular trends of demographic events probably are related to the basic factors which make societies dynamic or static. Hence under the best conceivable circumstances, there will be limits to the effectiveness of population policies. While it may be possible to speed up population growth in one area and slow it down in another—which would be a remarkable achievement—the over-all situation hardly will change, except as its *basic* factors are altered. From this point of view the demographic upsurge in Western Europe and in the Americas certainly deserves the closest attention. Is it indicative of a more dynamic attitude and of moral and cultural rejuvenation? Within the next two generations, however, the *over-all* situation probably will continue to be characterized by the increasing pressure of the Asiatic and colored nations.

MIGRATIONS

There is one *other* method to prevent major population crises: migrations. Throughout history, population pressure has led to emigration and lack of population to immigration. Throughout history, too, barriers have

[19] Some of the basic modifications which occur in the American way of life are discussed by Frederick Lewis Allen in his *The Big Change: America Transforms Itself 1900–1950*, New York, Harper, 1952.

been raised against population movements. Since we are dealing again with *secular* events, these restrictions have proved none too successful.

If the problem is to increase the population of the Western nations substantially, or at least of some Western nations, and, at the same time, to reduce the population pressure of a country like Italy, migration would be the least expensive method and yield the quickest result. Although migration has taken place on a massive scale throughout the Western world during the last hundred years, it has not been viewed by receiving countries as an unmixed blessing. The objections which are being most frequently opposed to its manifest advantages are twofold: it destroys the cultural and political homogeneity of the receiving country; it sharpens the competition for jobs and adds needlessly to the social charges of the community.

It is not proposed here to review the pros and cons of this hotly debated issue. The broader question of whether immigration enhances or diminishes the military strength of the receiving country can be examined on the basis of abundant historical evidence at hand.

Athens and Rome admitted large numbers of foreigners to citizenship. The emperors of Rome accorded citizens' rights first to the inhabitants of Gaul, then to ever larger contingents of foreigners. For centuries these "barbarians," Romans by assimilation, defended the empire against the onslaughts of the barbarians from outside.

The princes of the Middle Ages called foreigners to provinces depopulated by plague or famine, employed foreign warriors in their military establishments, and invited foreigners to settle in backward regions and mount the defense of remote borders. The rulers of northern Europe welcomed Flemish weavers and Dutch shipwrights to their lands. The Huguenots, driven from France by religious discrimination culminating in the revocation of the Edict of Nantes, brought their skills to Prussia, an inestimable contribution to the power of that barren, predominantly Slavic principality. German gold- and silversmiths, glass blowers, and ironmongers plied their trades in England and Russia. From among the *émigrés* from revolutionary France, not all of whom were nobles, the receiving countries drew some of their most celebrated public servants, scholars, and soldiers. After Catherine the Great took the Crimea, the expansion of Russia's population was speeded by wholesale assimilation of alien populations. From the amalgamation of diverse European elements arose the largest nation of European stock, the United States. Yet modern migration is not exclusively bound up with the filling up of vast, thinly settled regions overseas, nor is the melting pot a specifically American institution.

The United States is the most powerful nation of European stock; it is a congeries of all the races of Europe. Their innate characteristics as well as those developed in the process of adjustment to the new environment have gone into the new solution, the American character. One catalyst was language—which caused Bismarck to observe that the most important fact in modern world politics was that Americans spoke English. No less important was a broad tolerance of, and capacity for, absorbing an unlimited number of races, religions, and folkways. So trite is this statement that it should not require emphasis beyond the primer stage. Yet it contains a fundamental truth, no less fundamental because it is obvious. To dismiss it as a mere historical incident is to miss the essence of American power, past, present, and future. Had immigration ceased after the Civil War, the population of the United States would hardly now exceed that of the larger European states and would probably have fallen behind that of Germany.

Regardless of what yardsticks are being applied and regardless of how optimistic we may be concerning the population growth of the United States, the fact remains that the demographic component is the *weakest* link in the American structure of power. The United States possesses all the elements needed to secure for it an unassailable position—all, that is, *except* manpower. It is true that we can anticipate dissensions within the Soviet orbit; the ultimate political alignment of China is uncertain. It is also true that the United States in alliance with a growing Latin America, with Western Europe, and with some of the Asiatic countries would be in a position of overwhelming power. Yet we cannot discount the possibility of a consolidation and even of expansion of the Soviet bloc. Some of the strong Asiatic countries may become hostile to the United States. European nations may waver in their loyalty to the idea of a West United. Opposition may emerge in Latin America. Decline may, after all, overtake Western Europe. If such dangers should materialize, the manpower weakness of the United States, even if it were to include Canada, would prove a serious handicap.

Foreign Migration Policies. The decreasing rate of immigration to the United States since 1924 is not due to the goal's having become less attractive. It is due to a political decision which reduced immigration from southern and eastern Europe to one-fifth of that from northern and western Europe, whereas still in 1914 the former had been six times as large as the latter. American immigration policy favors those nations whose population growth is declining and restricts immigration from those nations which are experiencing an accelerated rate of growth.

Emergency measures in favor of displaced persons and refugees from Central Europe and Russia have somewhat blunted the edge of the contradiction inherent in American immigration policy. So have laws facilitating the entrance of war brides and their relatives. Hence immigration has continued to be a factor which undoubtedly contributed its share to the recovery of the American rate of growth. Yet these timid policies are inadequate to balance the population growth of countries which are, or may become in the future, competitors of the United States. In the postwar period, countries like Canada and Australia opened their doors to a substantial number of European immigrants. But they stand ever ready, at the slightest sign of unemployment, to close their doors again. France admitted some immigration and in this fashion reduced its war losses. There is little doubt that France would be a nation with far greater vitality and higher military security if she were to adopt a policy similar to the one which the United States practiced before the First World War. France easily could resume her place as a great power if she were to raise her population to 50–60 million. Large-scale immigration would lead to an expanding and dynamic economy, breaking the grip of lethargy, if not senility, upon the country, and restore to productivity the large fertile areas now lying fallow in metropolitan France and in the French overseas possessions. The population problem of Italy still is unsolved, though it could be solved to the mutual advantage of Italy and the traditional immigration countries and their colonies. Apparently, in international politics it is quite impossible to put two and two together.

The drying up of world trade in the desert of protectionism parallels closely the stagnation of international migration induced by legislation. Yet the migratory urges of Europe had not subsided; they had shifted. "It is an apparent coincidence," W. D. Forsyth writes, "that the overseas countries should have lost their capacity to absorb vast masses of immigrants in the very generation in which European population growth had declined. Some underlying unity may still be traced between these two phenomena." [20] The coincidence is indeed only apparent.

The overseas countries have not lost their capacity to absorb large numbers of people. For example, the Caribbean islands are often described as "overpopulated." However, if all of them had the population density of Puerto Rico—and every single one of them has an almost identical natural endowment—these islands could support 60 million people instead of the 16 million now constituting their total population. If the Guianas and British Honduras, which both possess considerable natural resources, had the density of Trinidad, they could support 56 million people rather than 1.3 million. French Guiana has about the same conditions as British Guiana; yet it has only one-seventh of the density of the latter. More incomprehensible still, throughout these areas there are islands with *declining* population.

Of Costa Rica's exceptionally good volcanic soil, only 10 per cent is being cultivated; there is room for an estimated minimum of 2 million immigrants. Very favorable conditions exist in the eastern Andes, in the African highlands, and even in parts of Asia. That the British dominions, particularly Australia and South Africa,[21] could support millions of additional peo-

---

[20] W. D. Forsyth, *The Myth of Open Spaces,* Melbourne University Press, 1942, p. 167.

[21] The South African whites view with alarm the restiveness of the colored races and their demographic advances; yet they make no effort to increase the number of whites rapidly and substantially. The annual immigration rate oscillates around 1 per cent of the white population, or less than 0.2 per cent of the over-all population. The birth rate of the whites stands at over 25, but the birth rate of the colored in South Africa is unknown. The white rate of increase is consistently (though not dramatically) below the colored rate of growth. The *apartheid* (segregation) policy has been driving the half-caste population (more than 50 per cent of the whites) into a political alliance with the

ple has been disputed on spurious Malthusian grounds. By similar reasoning, it might have been argued, in 1776, that the United States could never support more than 20 to 30 million inhabitants. Are there indeed valid reasons why Africa could not support a density similar to that of the Soviet Union, or South America not one similar to the world average, or Oceania not one approaching the density of Africa (see Table 4)?

TABLE 4. POPULATION DENSITIES

Area	Density per square mile
World	45
Europe	200
Tropical Asia	175
Asia (except U.S.S.R.)	117
U.S.S.R.	23
North America	23
Africa	18
South America	15
Oceana	5

The point is that the population pressures—those which do exist and those which most certainly will emerge in the future—can be alleviated. There is enough room in Indonesia to solve Java's population problem. There is enough room in Africa to take a considerable load from the shoulders of India. There is ample space in Latin America for Japanese settlers. Given proper irrigation methods and installation of electric power, there is enough space in the Middle East to relieve the population pressure in the Nile Valley. In so far as the surplus population of Italy, the Slavic countries, and possibly Germany is concerned, there is ample space in the United States, France, and the British Dominions and in the British, Belgian, and French colonies. If we remember that, for example, in Indo-China there is only one doctor for 49,000 people (as compared to one doctor for 1,300 people in France), we see that there is still considerable *Lebensraum* even for members of the liberal professions.

A redistribution of population not only would help to reduce population pressures, but also would supply the manpower for the necessary development of presently unexploited resources. The industrial economy of the United States and Western Europe has been relying, to an ever-increasing degree, on minerals which are procured from underdeveloped areas, such as the Belgian Congo. As the hunger for minerals will not be quenched in the foreseeable future, new deposits must be opened up. Hence new lands must be settled. Moreover, as the world population increases, food requirements

---

natives (largely Bantus) and the Asiatics. Can there be any doubt as to the outcome of this "Alice in Wonderland" race struggle? See Jan H. Hofmeyr, *South Africa,* 2d ed., rev. by J. P. Cope, New York, McGraw-Hill, 1953, p. 216.

will soar. While they may be satisfied in part by more intensive agriculture, there is little doubt that new areas must be taken under cultivation.

This is not to belittle the enormous difficulties which militate against the solution of the demographic problem through migration. Yet these difficulties are neither geographic nor economic in nature. *They arise from cultural taboos and racial idiosyncrasies.* Whether or not it will be possible to reduce or overcome these idiosyncrasies remains to be seen. The resettlement of huge numbers of people requires very considerable financial investments and large organizations. Even if successful, its completion will take a long time, not to mention the fact that the resettlement process will spark many crises and political conflicts. It is merely suggested here that, through proper identification of the true problem, many steps be taken *gradually*. It is a primary interest of the United States to restore the circulatory system of Europe's population and to assist in composing the demographic crisis of Western Europe in order to check an all too rapid demographic shift in favor of nations profoundly different culturally. It is also in the interest of the United States to strengthen the population of the British Dominions and to forestall a population crisis in Germany. The need for the United States to help Japan solve its demographic problem is highlighted by the sole alternative: Japan's drift, as a mere appendage, into the orbit of Soviet Russia and Red China. The same argument applies, though perhaps with less force, to India, where a great deal can be done through internal colonization. Migration thus becomes a crucially important field of American foreign policy, both as regards the United States' own domestic strength and as regards the threats which may be developing from overseas. In the United States, the importance of this problem has never yet received its due recognition.

Several agencies of the United Nations are concerned with international demographical and migration problems. Although their activities are largely confined to the gathering and dissemination of information, highly pertinent recommendations and resolutions, which have issued from the Economic and Social Council, reflect awareness of the ramifications and the urgency of population problems. Thus, for example, the Advisory Committee on Planning and Co-ordination of the Social Commission, which met from March 8 to March 18, 1948, "considered migration as one of seven major fields of activity which it considered as requiring priority of consideration by the Secretariat."

The preceding chapters attempted to survey the broad trends which are reshaping the population distribution of the globe. Manpower, we observed, is but one among the many factors of power. It is the one which supplies the animate force transforming all the elements of power into political realities. Contemporary power relationships, unlike the stabler, more predictable conditions a hundred years ago, cannot be frozen, because manpower relationships will not stay put. Strength in numbers becomes, by virtue of modern production and training methods, increasingly synonymous with economic and military power. Malthusian ideas—a "stable" population, a "stable" economy—beget, inexorably, static foreign and military policies. Yet strategic bases, weapons-in-being, stockpiles of raw materials, and the world's most colossal wealth in inanimate assets cannot assure the future power of the United States. The security of the United States rests upon the growth, creativeness, and stamina of its people, not upon Maginot Lines, be they fashioned of concrete and steel or the figments of the Malthusian mind.

The populous nations of Eurasia will sooner or later, as a result of industrialization and urbanization, pass the maximum point of their demographical development. The United States must seek to maintain its relative position until the rate of increase of the other powers, too, diminishes. If this delaying action is successful, the equilibrium has been maintained.

In the past, attempts to influence population trends by government policies were mostly unsuccessful, although a good case may be made for the view that intervention was either too late, as in ancient Rome, or too timid and inept, as more recently in European countries. By contrast, there is the tremendous improvement effected within the last 100 years in mortality rates and expectancy of life, which obviously has been influenced by political decisions, *i.e.*, by sanitary and educational measures of all kinds. Recent experience in population policy has shown that limited successes can be achieved. If financial assistance to large families and generous maternity benefits are enacted into law, and if provisions similar to those proposed for Britain by Sir William Beveridge should be adopted by the United States, the population trend may be altered substantially. It has been said that babies cannot be bought. This is true in a sense. Pronatalist policies will fail if they rely on purely materialistic incentives. A population policy must operate in several sectors at once. Ideologies, habits, and customs are not fixed for all eternity and are subject to human control.

The United States has no population policy worthy of the name. On the contrary, the policy of the United States, as made into law, *aims* at restricting population growth. Throughout history, population growth has followed increase of wealth and productivity, partly because more children could be reared, partly because it stimulated immigration. The United States still exerts a powerful pull on surplus populations and uprooted peoples. A huge capital of manpower, brains, and skills is America's for the asking. An intelligent policy of *laissez passer* is today as much in the true interest of the United States as it ever was in its history.

BIBLIOGRAPHY

Carr-Saunders, A. M.: *World Population: Past Growth and Present Trends,* New York, Oxford, 1936.
Clark, Colin: *The Economics of 1960,* London, Macmillan & Co., Ltd., 1943.
Davis, J.: *The Population Upsurge in the United States,* Food Research Institute, Stamford University, December, 1949.

Food and Agricultural Organization, United Nations: *Second World Food Survey,* New York, Columbia University Press, 1952.

Forsyth, W. D.: *The Myth of Open Spaces,* Melbourne, Melbourne University Press, 1942.

International Labor Office, "Post-war Manpower Problems in Europe," *International Labor Review,* Vol. 55, June, 1947.

Isaacs, Julius: *Economics of Migration,* New York, Oxford, 1947.

Kirk, Dudley: *Europe's Population in the Interwar Years,* Geneva and Princeton, N.J., League of Nations, 1946.

Kulischer, Eugen M.: *Europe on the Move,* New York, Columbia University Press, 1948.

Ledermann, Sully: "La Population allemande," *Population,* Vol. 2, No. 1, 1947.

Lorimer, Frank: *The Population of the Soviet Union: History and Prospects,* Geneva, League of Nations, 1946.

———, E. E. B. Winston, and L. K. Kiser: *Foundations of American Population Policy,* New York, Harper, 1940.

Notestein, Frank W., and Others: *The Future Population of Europe and the Soviet Union,* Geneva and Princeton, N.J., League of Nations, 1944.

Peters, Clarence A. (ed.): *The Immigration Problem,* The Reference Shelf, Vol. 19, No. 17, New York, H. W. Wilson, 1948.

Sauvy, Alfred: *Richesse et population,* Paris, Payot, 1944.

———: *Théorie générale de la population,* Vol. 1, Paris, Presses Universitaires, 1952.

Schechtman, Joseph B.: *Population Transfers in Asia,* London, Halesby, 1949.

Spengler, J. J.: *France Faces Depopulation,* Durham, N.C., Duke University Press, 1938.

Thompson, Warren S.: *Population Problems,* 4th ed., New York, McGraw-Hill, 1953.

———: *Population and Peace in the Pacific,* Chicago, Chicago University Press, 1946.

United Nations, Economic and Social Council, *Report of the Secretary General on the Allocation of Functions among the Various Organs Concerned in the Field of Migration,* May 28, 1948.

Wilcox, W. F. (ed.): *International Migrations,* 2 vols., New York, National Bureau of Economic Research, Inc., 1929, 1931.

Chapter 7

RAW MATERIALS IN INTERNATIONAL POLITICS

THE IMPORTANCE OF RAW MATERIALS

Industrial capacity is determined in part by the available raw materials which a nation can maintain at its disposal. Thus state power, based as it is on industrial power, is a function not only of size and skill of population and geographical conditions, but also of access to or control of basic raw materials. These raw materials are unequally distributed upon the earth's surface and among nations. This condition—or rather geologic accident—may determine with considerable finality the importance of a nation's role in international politics.

Raw materials may be utilized for different objectives. A nation may attempt to utilize its supplies in the development of economic strength dedicated to providing a higher standard of living for its people, or these same raw materials may be employed as an instrument of political and military power; then the purpose of the economy is to make the nation as strong as conditions may permit in order to prepare for war. The first objective can be reached most effectively by stimulating trade—the free movement of goods and people—and production for the purpose of individual consumption, largely through competition and systematic elimination of restrictions on markets and initiative. The attainment of the second objective requires controls on trade and financial transactions, including foreign investments, as well as the channeling of production into capital equipment and military end products. It also may require a policy of stockpiling raw materials which must be imported from abroad or a policy of stimulating marginal raw-materials production at home although, in a purely civilian economy, it would be cheaper to procure these materials from abroad. Under modern conditions where war is an ever-present threat, policy must be designed to meet *both* purposes: it must provide for the security of the nation and at the same time, as far as practical, enhance the standards of living and the property resources (*i.e.*, the economic security) of the individual.

RAW MATERIAL PROBLEMS AND POLICIES IN THE INTERWAR PERIOD

Following both world wars the nations of the world faced the tremendous problems involved in restoring the international flow of raw materials. These problems were twofold. The first was essentially of a transitory nature; raw materials were needed for immediate use in economic rehabilitation and reconstruction of war-torn economies. It involved the movement of large quantities of foodstuffs for human consumption as well as the distribution of primary industrial products in order to generate the national and international economic machinery of the world. These were considered as normal economic conditions following termination of a widespread war. The other problem was of a long-range nature, concerned with the development of national economies. The problems in this category involved capital investments both at home and abroad, essential to the acquisition of needed supplies, and the creation of sufficiently large export markets in which to dispose of finished goods.

Accompanying these two conditions was the belief that one of the economic origins of both wars was the inability of some nations to obtain equal access to raw materials in all areas. This belief was expressed in the third of the Fourteen Points which in 1918 were laid down by the President of the United States: "The removal, so far as possible, of all economic barriers and the establishment of an equality of trade among all the nations consenting to the peace and associating themselves for its maintenance."

The history of the international raw-material problem consists, in the main, of constantly reiterated charges by the "have-not" nations that they were being discriminated against by the "haves" and were being refused access to needed industrial raw materials, and by assertions in rebuttal of the "haves" that legitimate demands could be satisfied in free markets. For example, the Provisional Economic and Financial Committee of the League of Nations concluded in September, 1921, that no country which needed raw materials urgently should suffer shortages because of discrimination. It pointed out that the difficulties involved stemmed from the credit and exchange problems arising out of the international trade rather than from political discriminations. However, ever since 1918, raw-material control schemes have been flourishing. They developed into two principal types: those schemes organized and operated by private enterprise in cartel form, and those set up, supervised, or operated by governments themselves. Very often the line between these two types of control schemes became blurred, since governments, by subsidy or tacit approval, sponsored the actions of private organizations.

Cartels had existed before World War I; however, the 1920's saw a multiplication of such instruments of raw-material control. The manufacture of war implements had caused a rapid increase in the volume of demand for primary products which resulted in the expansion of production facilities, and, in turn, the expansion of the power of the existing cartel organizations. This chain of events was reflected in the rise of such control schemes as the Bandung Tin Mining Pool, Stephenson Rubber Plan, United States Copper Exporters Association, Chadbourne Sugar Agreement, Coffee Cartel, New Zealand Kauri Gum Control Act of 1925, Chilean Nitrate Producers' Association, Argentina-Paraguay Quebracho Restriction Agreement of 1916, Reorganized European

Steel Cartel of 1926, the Yucatan Export and Production Agreements, and the European Zinc Cartel of 1928. The restrictions imposed by such agreements were strenuously opposed by consuming countries.

The economic slump in late 1929 hit countries dependent upon the export of raw materials very heavily. In the depression period from 1929 to 1935, the leading industrial countries resorted to protective legislation, which sought to insulate the remaining markets of domestic producers from intrusion by foreign-made goods, quota systems, and, finally, the reorganization of raw-material control schemes. Such control schemes now appeared in new forms for such commodities as: aluminum, potash, petroleum, jute, pineapple, zinc, tin, platinum, lumber, silver, cotton, rubber, cinchona bark, and coke. Simultaneously new raw-material control schemes were added to the existing ones, namely, for the regulation of trade in copper (1935), lead (1935–1938), coffee (1936), sugar (1937), and wheat (1938).

These events were accompanied by increasing demands by certain nations for territories as the sole equitable means of satisfying alleged raw-material needs. The Italian government, preparing to attack Ethiopia in 1935, used the argument that the pressure of her population on existing raw-material resources forced her to territorial expansion. The Japanese government supported its expansionist claims by pointing to the alarming increase in the rate of population bearing heavily upon domestic resources. Germany demanded the return of its former colonies because of an expanding birth rate, and reinforced its demands by racialistic, pan-German propaganda. These nations argued that the living standards of their populations were being depressed through the restrictive actions of control schemes.

The importance of these arguments was reflected in the thorough investigation of raw-material problems by the League of Nations.[1] The report of this investigation concluded that the difficulty involved stemmed not from the inability to obtain equal access to raw materials, but rather from the foreign-exchange situation. It is interesting to note that the countries which had most vociferously objected to the findings of the report were the first ones which resorted to some of the most flagrant restrictions through the use of controlled currency schemes, exchange restrictions, and quota and allotment schemes.

The investigation of the League of Nations was the last attempt to find a rational and peaceful solution for the raw-material problems before the outbreak of World War II. The importance of providing equal access to raw materials for all nations was acknowledged by the Prime Minister of Great Britain and the President of the United States on August 14, 1941, in the wording of the Atlantic Charter, Article 4: ". . . they [the United States and Great Britain] will endeavor, with due respect for existing obligations, to further the enjoyment by all the States, great or small, victor or vanquished, of

[1] "Report of the League of Nations Committee for the Study of the Raw Material Problems," *League of Nations Official Journal,* December, 1937.

access, on equal terms, to the trade and to the raw materials of the world which are needed for their economic prosperity."

The Charter of the United Nations Organization gives no direct guarantee of equality of access to raw materials, though a vaguely phrased provision may be construed to cover this principle. According to Chapter I, Purpose and Principles, Article 1 (2), the purposes of the United Nations are: "To develop friendly relations among nations based on respect for the principle of equal rights and self-determination of peoples, and to take other appropriate measures to strengthen universal peace."

However, the countries of the world remained unwilling, and in many cases unable, to surrender control-of-raw-material policies and practices to an international agency. This fact is reflected by the failure of the International Trade Organization to alter materially the existing pattern of trade restrictions and raw-material control schemes. The program for European economic recovery outlined by the European Recovery Act of 1948 was developed *within* the framework of existing control schemes.

There occurred, however, after 1945 the following changes: (1) countries closely associated with the United States claimed that they could not purchase raw materials because of real or fancied "dollar shortages" and were helped financially by the United States; (2) raw-materials demands increased everywhere, with the result that, in contrast to the depression years, there were shortages rather than surpluses and, consequently, higher prices of raw materials; (3) new types of raw materials, especially minerals, have become highly important; (4) raw-materials production was expanded everywhere. Hence, while monopolistic practices continue to flourish in the raw-materials field, the clamor for "easy access" to the materials themselves was superseded by agitation for cheap prices and long-term credits.

"SUBSTITUTES"

"Substitutes" are an integral part of a country's raw-material supply. This fact has given rise to a somewhat stultifying discussion, a "conservative" faction rejecting *ersatz* in any form, and an "alchemist" faction taking the diametrically opposite point of view. One side maintains that substitutes (1) are too expensive, (2) are of inferior quality, and (3) do not offer a solution of the raw-material problem when really serious shortages occur. The other side advocates a general use of substitutes and insists that military and economic security may not be assured unless the country has completely freed itself from the bondage of foreign trade.

The history of technical progress may be conceived of as a procession of substitutes. The gasoline motor is a substitute for the steam engine, which in turn was a substitute for the mail coach; fuel oil is a substitute for coal, which in turn replaced wood burning. An analogous process has transformed military technology; the tank, for instance, may be considered as a substitute for heavy cavalry. In a general sense, the economy of substitutes with its concomitant diffusion of technological skills turned inventive genius toward new ways and techniques. In a more narrow sense, substitution often eased the requirements of armament production and sometimes eliminated raw-material shortages altogether. Without Haber's invention for producing nitrogen from air, the British naval blockade and the subsequent loss of access to Chile's saltpeter would have forced Germany out of the First World War within six months. Without synthetic gasoline production, Germany could not have started the Second World War. Without synthetic rubber industrial plants at home, the loss of Malaya would have been an almost fatal blow to American war economy. Some countries, especially the United States, Great Britain, and Germany, successfully replaced scarce minerals with plastics.

There were other, less successful, attempts at replacing important but scarce materials by more abundant ones. Germany, for example, attempted to produce clothing and food, notably sugar, out of wood—with which, incidentally, she was not overabundantly supplied. Despite this feat of alchemy, the German people appear to have favored wool and beet sugar over wood fiber in any guise.

Perhaps the greatest promise of "substitution" lies in the field of nutrition. A good case can be made for the contention that food is what a good deal of international politics is about. Were it possible to duplicate the process of photosynthesis and thus to produce by "artificial" photosynthesis carbohydrates, sugars, and proteins, "food factories" could be set up, turning out food in whatever quantities were desired. Their products might not for a long time rival the nutritive and culinary properties of creamery butter and steaks, but they should alleviate the emergency food problems posed by population growth. The production of synthetic vitamins permits a nation to improve the nutritive value of the food it possesses. A better exploitation of the food contained in the sea, adoption of tank-farming techniques, and even the replacement of animal through vegetable food (or vice versa) are examples of substitution.

Substitution may be complete or partial. For example, Russia, which is short in some alloys, relies on "natural alloys," i.e., highly complex iron compounds found in the ores. The Soviet Union also may be short in high-grade bauxite and hence may try to place greater reliance on magnesium as a second light metal in addition to aluminum. The substitution of peat or lignite for coal is quite commonplace, although it is paid for by a loss in B.t.u.'s. By contrast, a substitution of bagasse (sugar-cane residuals) for wood as raw material for cellulose and paper may constitute technological progress—and transform the economies of many tropical countries.

A number of inflexible rules govern the workings of any substitute economy. In the early phase of the substitution process, when the technology of the new product is less satisfactory than that of the old, the substitute is more expensive and more difficult to produce. This was the case of Buna rubber. Although the price may decline and become competitive with the original or "natural" product, the technology of both products may tend to merge, with the products becoming complementary. This happened with natural and synthetic rubber. In other cases, the original product may be pushed into the background; nylon must win out over natural silk if for no other reason than that silk cannot be produced in large enough quantities. Many substitutes are inferior and more costly products, and will remain so forever. For example, beet sugar is far more costly than cane sugar; rye and corn are less nutritive than wheat; wood is a poor substitute for coal, which in turn is a poor substitute for oil.

Secondly, substitutes do not necessarily improve the over-all raw-material supply. Let us suppose that, to meet heavy demands for electric wiring, methods have been developed for replacing copper by aluminum; this would be a great advantage if copper were scarce but aluminum abundant. Yet the substitution creates a heavy demand for aluminum, and to satisfy it, aluminum production may have to be doubled or tripled. Hence a shortage in aluminum might occur, and transportation equipment and electric power, the most expensive "raw materials" in aluminum manufacture,[2] would have to be diverted from other, no less vital, economic tasks; or electric power production would have to be increased, exactly as it happened during the early years of the Korean War in the United States.

Thirdly, there are materials for which no substitutes can be found and which, on the contrary, are themselves the foundation of substitute economy. The most important of these materials have been, till now, coal and iron. Oil, too, is not as easily replaced as the "alchemists" may wish. For one thing, coal, lignite, shale, or other suitable materials must be available in adequate quantities; for another, there must be an abundant supply of vegetable matter to replace oil fuel by alcohol. Third, oil is not used as fuel only, but is also, in its various forms and with its thirty-odd derivatives, essential to the chemical industry. There are many minor minerals which cannot be dispensed with; prominent among these are manganese and, to a lesser extent, nickel and tin. More important still, there must be an ample supply of a variety— be it *any* variety—of these "minor" metals.

Fourthly, countries in need of substitutes are usually not rich enough to afford vast investments in huge industries which cannot produce cheaply enough to compete in peacetime with the natural product, and which thus must be kept idle on government subsidy until an emergency arrives.

One alternative to substitutions proposed by certain military and economic experts is stockpiling.[3]

[2] Robert Mosse, "Aluminum—A World Industry," *World Economics*, Vol. 2, Nos. 5–6.
[3] See p. 154.

COAL AND IRON IN WORLD POLITICS

Coal and iron are the fundamental minerals of every civilian and military activity today. These raw materials are needed in ever-increasing quantities in the manufacture of producers' goods, construction and industrial equipment, and consumers' goods. Their importance has continued to increase in modern warfare and civilian industry. While world coal production has approached a comparatively stable upper limit and during the 1940's reached an output of 1.5 to 2.0 billion short tons, iron and steel production has increased by leaps and bounds since the termination of World War II: pig-iron production nearly doubled within six years, while steel production increased by two-thirds. Within seventy-five-odd years world steel production soared from practically nothing to over 200 million tons by 1950; and the demand for steel and iron continues high.

Since coal and iron are unequally distributed over the surface of the earth, all nations, except a favored few, are forced to obtain supplies of one or both of these minerals from areas outside their borders. However, the mere presence of these raw materials within the territorial confines of a nation has not been sufficient in the past for the development of heavy industry, the basis of state power. It was the juxtaposition of these raw materials, their availability in relation to each other and to existing concentrations of labor and to markets, which determined their effective use in the development of heavy industry. Only a few nations on the earth possessed this fortuitous combination of quantitative and location factors. Hence only a few nations possessed real industrial power. The emergence of nuclear power as a source of energy is bound to change this traditional pattern profoundly.

Coal. While great strides have been made in replacing coal by petroleum, by hydroelectric power, and, more recently, by atomic energy, coal still remains, for the time being, the most important source of energy.

The preeminence of coal as a major energizer in the past 200 years has been due to a variety of circumstances. The most important impetus given to the utilization of coal was the destruction of the European forests and the discovery of a cheap "substitute" in the form of coal. In addition, with the invention of the Watt steam engine in 1769, coal became, in the form of steam power, the chief source of energy for industrial use. Further technological improvements in the iron and steel-making industry as a result of the Bessemer and the Siemens-Martin electric-furnace processes, and the widespread use of automatic or semiautomatic machinery demanding great amounts of dependable energy, raised the world demand for coal until annual consumption exceeded in bulk that for any other commodity.

The United States holds a favorable position regarding its coal resources at the present time. United States coal supplies include a superior grade of bituminous (soft) coal with adequate stocks of anthracite (hard) deposited in the eastern and northeastern sections of the United States. These superior grade reserves are backed by very large quantities of low-grade bituminous, subbituminous, and lignite coal deposits distributed among several states. The tremendous demand for high-grade, low-volatile coal during World Wars I and II has created, however, a sufficient scarcity in coking coals as to require supplementing high-grade coking coals with inferior grades. Some of the best seams of coal already have been depleted or shortly will become so.

Great quantities of coal are found in Nova Scotia. These coal reserves are of high-grade quality and may be used for coking in industry. The Canadian supplies include low-grade coals found in central and western Canada.

Nature has been exceedingly niggardly in supplying the southern half of the Western Hemisphere with coal. Some coal deposits exist in the northeastern coastal section of Mexico in the Sabina field. Small quantities of coal are also found throughout the countries of South America, chiefly of inferior grade.

Canada and the United States account for about 40 per cent of the world's coke and 30 per cent of the world's coal production. The other coal-production leaders are to be found in Europe and Asia. Germany, Russia, the United Kingdom, and Poland account for almost one-half of total world production today.

Formerly the second largest coal producer in the world, the United Kingdom has moved to the fourth place. British coal mines are located chiefly in the Lowlands of Scotland, northeastern England near the rivers Tees and Tyne, the eastern Midlands, the Birmingham-Coventry areas, and southern Wales. All of them have been worked extensively since the Industrial Revolution. The present reserves are to be found in thin seams, badly tilted, which makes for difficulty in recovering coal from these deposits cheaply. The high cost of production and the prevalence of obsolete mining equipment as well as nationalization have resulted in the economic decay of the British coal industry.

On the Continent, the heartland of industrial activity in Western Europe lies in the Ruhr Valley. The West German fields with their thick, easily workable coal seams provide great amounts of excellent coking and steaming coal. This is also true to a lesser extent of the Saar fields. After the United States, Germany has the second largest coal output in the world.

The German leadership in coal production may well be contrasted with the extremely weak position of France. French supplies of coal are in the northern areas adjoining Belgium in the Sambre-Meuse area. These coal supplies are of medium quality. They are insufficient to sustain the needs of the French iron and steel industry. The result has been French reliance on British and German coal. This dependence on outside coal supplies limited the expansion of the steel industry and resulted in the constant shipment of French iron ores from the Lorraine district to the coal deposits of the Ruhr Valley in Germany. The effect has been the development of an international complex of raw-material exchanges and processing which is centered upon the coal mines and steel mills of the Ruhr. The international organization developed under the Schuman Plan, the Coal and Steel Community (CSC), created in 1952, is designed to bring about a politicoeconomic integration of these industries.

Russian coal and coke production still lags behind that of the United States and Germany. It has overtaken, however, the output of the United Kingdom. The principal coal areas of Russia are the Donets Basin, the Kuznetsk region, the Moscow-Tula area, and Kazakhstan. The goal of the postwar Five-Year Plan (1946–1951) was to achieve a production volume in 1950 of 250 million tons of coal. According to Soviet claims, this goal was exceeded and the mines destroyed during the war were rehabilitated. Some time between 1951 and 1953 production apparently exceeded 300 million tons, to which must be added about 150 million tons from Poland, including former German Silesia, and Czechoslovakia. The Soviet bloc thus reached about three-quarters of the North American coal output.

Data on the coal supplies in the Asiatic continent are scant and notorious for their unreliability. Workable coal deposits in China are found in Manchuria, Hunan, Szechwan, Shensi, Yünnan, Kweichow, North China, and southwestern China. Chinese coal is generally of poor coking quality. In addition, China is faced with the problem of transporting large amounts of coal supplies over railroad systems that may remain for a long time inadequate to meet the increased volume of freight traffic, though the Chinese communists appear to have launched an ambitious program of railroad construction. In 1953, they claimed to have increased freight capacity by 50 per cent over 1951.

Japanese coal deposits have in the past been insufficient to meet the needs of the Japanese iron and steel industries. Deposits in the northwest part of Kyushu and Hokkaido occur in coal beds which are thin in seam and dipped at a considerable angle. Japan has become dependent on imports of high-grade coking coal. Indian coal is somewhat better qualitatively, but reserves are small. Nevertheless, coal production still can be expanded considerably.

Australian coal deposits are mainly of a bituminous and lignite quality. Production, though insignificant as compared with that of the major world producers, is sufficient to meet Australian home requirements. South Africa has been expanding its coal production gradually, and East Africa has appeared on the scene as the producer of a significant quantity of low-grade coal.

An economy based on coal would not permit areas like South America or Africa to achieve a strong industrial position; the exhaustion of coal fields in England and France may force these nations into a highly unpleasant "readjustment," i.e., into economic regression.

Fortunately, it no longer is necessary to stay within the strait jacket of coal technology: nuclear power shows the way out. *The total energy available in recoverable uranium is about 23 times larger than the energy stored in coal.*[4]

Nuclear power must be expected to be introduced gradually; it will not replace coal but *supplement* it, especially in areas which have no coal resources or in industries which are huge power consumers. Wherever coal is expensive, there will be a strong incentive to convert rapidly to nuclear power. For example, in 1951, the cost of power in Alaska was 6–7 cents per kilowatthour, as compared to an average of 1 cent in the United States.

The full international implications of such a development cannot be assessed beforehand. But mobile energy destroys the basis of the conventional theory of location: henceforth energy can be obtained at *any* place selected, and in any quantity desired, at competitive prices. The industrial predominance of the coal nations will lose one of its most important pillars. It also means that the economic future of the world looks much brighter than heretofore and that areas as yet unavailable to large-scale development (including areas requiring huge irrigation projects) can be put to productive uses.

Iron. The United States, the world's largest iron-ore producer, draws upon deposits located in the Great Lakes region, Alabama, the Pennsylvania–New York–New Jersey region, and in the Western states including Wyoming, Utah, California, Colorado, South Dakota, and Washington. Vast quantities of high-grade ores mined at low cost have been shipped from the Mesabi Range, Minnesota, by barge through the Great Lakes for refining in the Pennsylvania-Ohio-Illinois area. Because of civilian demands for steel, which have increased tenfold over the past seventy years, and the tremendous requirements of two world wars, the limits of the reserves in the Mesabi Range have come within sight. Their exhaustion will mean reliance upon inferior-grade ores near the Mesabi Range, or in the southeastern United States.

An estimated 5 billion tons of usable low-grade ore—taconite—are available at the upper end of the Great Lakes. But until recently there was no practical method of freeing the iron imbedded in the extremely hard taconite. The high-grade iron ore which has been the mainstay of steel's raw material runs about 50 per cent pure iron. It can be used in the iron-making blast furnaces just as it comes from the ground. Taconite, however, is about 25 per cent iron. It requires considerable processing before it can be used.

The importation of superior-grade ores from Labrador was scheduled to begin during 1954. Large-scale imports from Venezuela and Chile began in 1951. By 1953 foreign imports accounted for about one-tenth of the domestic

[4] John W. Landis, "Nuclear Energy as a Source of Power," *Atomic Power and Private Enterprise,* Joint Committee on Atomic Energy, 82d Cong., 2d Sess., December, 1952, pp. 381*f.* If true breeding becomes possible, the nuclear-energy reserve would be even greater; this also would be the case and production costs would decrease if the technology of mining low-grade uranium were to be improved or if uranium-bearing oil shales were to be processed for oil. "Recoverable" means in this context "recoverable at the price of $100 per pound of uranium metal."

Energy Resources of the World

23 units

1 unit

Coal
Oil
Natural Gas

6 Trillion Tons

Uranium

25 Million Tons

iron-ore production. Appreciable quantities of iron ore have been located in the Alaskan Territory.

Canada's ore reserves are available to the United States economy. In addition to Venezuela's large reserves—substantially a postwar discovery —there are major iron-ore deposits in Cuba and Brazil as well as smaller ones in Mexico and Chile. Even assuming a rapid industrialization of Latin America, a large portion of these reserves may be counted on by the United States in its future economic development.

The older of the Russian ore centers lie in the Urals and in the Donets Basin. Great quantities of iron ores are worked close to coal deposits. Large iron and steel industries were developed in the Magnitogorsk and Kuznetsk regions. Russian objectives are to increase production by developing new mines and by improving the transportation system linking coal and iron-ore deposits. In 1945, the U.S.S.R. produced 11 million tons of pig iron, which by 1950 had risen to 19.4 million tons (figures on ore production are unavailable), about one-third of U.S. output. The Russian increase of 75 per cent within five years certainly was remarkable; but the American increase during the same time was 45 per cent—starting from a far higher level. For that matter the world increase during the period was 70 per cent, indicating that indeed a revolution in production is taking place.

With the exception of the United States and possibly the Soviet Union, France is the greatest iron-ore producer. French production exceeds the output of all other European nations by a broad margin. The Lorraine ore deposits are connected with the deposits in Luxembourg, which in turn are not too distant from the German deposits. The output of this Western European iron base in 1950, shown in Table 5, was about 46 per cent of the American

TABLE 5. OUTPUT OF IRON ORE, RHINE-LORRAINE BASINS, 1950

Area	Millions of short tons
France	33.3
Germany	12.3
Luxembourg	4.2
Total	49.8

output. For pig iron, the production, shown in Table 6, was 45 per cent of the American or 123 per cent of the Soviet-Polish-Czech output.

A third major source of iron ore in Western Europe is found in the United Kingdom. Iron-ore deposits are located in the eastern, south-central, and northwest sections of England, and around Glasgow, Scotland. The British ores are produced from mines which have been worked extensively for about two centuries. Domestic low-grade ores are mixed with higher-grade imports from Sweden, Spain, and Africa.

TABLE 6. OUTPUT OF PIG IRON, RHINE-LORRAINE BASINS, 1950

Area	Millions of short tons
France	8.6
Saar	1.8
Germany	10.7
Luxembourg	2.7
Belgium	4.1
Total	27.9

Large deposits—high-grade magnetite and hematitic ore—lie in the northern and central parts of Sweden. Production conditions resemble those of the Mesabi Range, and the ore may be shipped at relatively low cost to Atlantic ports or to harbors in the Gulf of Bothnia for transshipment to continental Europe.

The Spanish position in the European market resembles that of Sweden. Spanish ore, which is of superior metallic content and contains few impurities, is mined in northern Spain in the Bay of Biscay area. Because of low shipment costs and control by foreign capital, the bulk of Spanish ore was formerly exported to other European countries, especially the United Kingdom and Germany, and now mostly to the United Kingdom.[5]

Taking the Western European iron industry as a whole and paying attention to its chief sources of supply, the picture in Table 7 emerges. Western

TABLE 7. PRODUCTION OF IRON, WESTERN EUROPE

Area	Millions of short tons of iron ore
Rhine-Lorraine basins	49.8
Great Britain	14.5
Spain	2.3
Sweden	15.3
Algeria	2.8
French and Spanish Morocco	1.3
Sierra Leone (half of production)	0.6
Total	86.6

Europe's metropolitan and overseas controlled output is 80 per cent of the United States output; pig-iron production accounts for about 57 per cent, and steel production (including the Italian output) for 56 per cent, of the American production. North America and Western Europe produce four times more steel than the Soviet Union and its European satellites.

[5] U.S. Department of the Interior, Bureau of Mines, "The Iron and Steel Industries of Europe," *Economic Paper* 19, 1939, pp. 72–73.

In Asia extensive iron deposits are located in India's northeastern provinces of Bihar and Orissa. The development of Indian heavy industry is favored by an ideal combination of rich ore deposits in close vicinity of good coal deposits, cheap labor, and potential markets, joined by Asia's most highly developed railroad system.[6] China is far less fortunate than India. Much of her iron ore is produced in the northern provinces within the Great Wall and in Manchuria. These mines, except those of Manchuria, are comparatively remote from available coal supplies. Their exploitation is hampered by unsatisfactory transportation conditions. However, the deposits near Hankow are considered among the best in the world. The ores in Shansi are located near large anthracite deposits. Shansi has the world's oldest iron industry and may emerge in the future as a major industrial complex.

Japanese iron-ore deposits are limited and are not of superior quality. The ores are essentially low-grade magnetite and must be sintered and concentrated before they become usable for processing into steel. Japanese steel industry placed great reliance on the development of the iron-ore deposits of Manchuria, and the expansionist policy of Japan on the Asiatic mainland aimed first and foremost at securing the mineral wealth of Manchuria. The future development of the Japanese iron and steel industry depends on the political future of the Far East and more particularly on Japan's ability to secure sources of supply.

In Australia large deposits of high-grade ores are located outside of Sydney. These ores are considered adequate for the satisfaction of Australia's own peacetime needs.

The estimates in Table 8 require some modification, taking into account the iron content of the areas. For example, Sweden, India, and Canada, and possibly China, rank probably higher than these figures indicate. Moreover, reliable estimates about many important producers, such as Luxembourg, Venezuela, Chile, Sierra Leone, and Liberia, are not available.

The figures show a very significant change from earlier times: the erstwhile major producers of iron ore have lost much of their standing, while new areas, particularly Africa and Latin America, begin to loom large. Given the anticipated reduced significance of coal, *the location of iron ore may very well determine the location of heavy industry, and hence the location of military power.*

If so, the Soviet Union and the United States (together with Canada and Cuba) certainly possess the wherewithal of military and economic strength. Western Europe, while still favored by the present locational requirement of contiguous coal and iron deposits, would have difficulty holding its own unless it continues to control Africa; British possession of Rhodesia should prove to be a significant factor. Within Europe, Germany's position—speaking strictly in terms of iron—should continue to decline, while France, if she

[6] See C. H. Behre, "The Iron Deposits of Bihar and Orissa," *Foreign Affairs,* Vol. 22, No. 1, pp. 78–93.

TABLE 8. IRON ORE ESTIMATES

Area	Billions of metric tons
Soviet Union	70.0
Southern Rhodesia	52.0
United States	25.0
Brazil	12.0
India	11.0
Canada	9.0
Cuba	6.0
France	3.0
French West Africa	2.5
United Kingdom	2.0
China	1.5
Sweden	1.2
South Africa	1.2
Germany	1.0
Turkey	0.8
Australia	0.6
Spain	0.5

manages to develop her potential, should gain. Turkey might improve her situation. India, it appears, has a far better chance to equip herself with heavy industry than China, though the unreliability of Chinese figures should be taken into account before placing China second to India. Finally, Brazil (and Venezuela), South Africa, Australia, Spain, and Sweden should be able to develop significant local heavy industries. Much will depend on developments in Africa which, in terms of iron alone, may indeed become crucial. The future of Japan within an iron-steel technology seems far from bright. Needless to say the ultimate distribution of industry does not depend exclusively on the location of deposits. The emergence of nuclear power is bound to change transport economics and thus, among other factors, will influence the choice of industrial location. One thing is certain: *new* industrial centers are arising.

THE INTERNATIONAL POLITICS OF OIL

Petroleum ranks third in importance to coal and iron as regards the operation of modern industrial economy as well as the successful prosecution of war, be it fought on land, at sea, or in the air. Modern farming and home living no less than water, highway, and railroad transportation and the chemical industry depend on the continued flow of petroleum. Nuclear propulsion will modify this picture. There is little doubt that sooner or later it will become all important in naval ships and in the merchant marine, reducing the need for oil and the cost of transportation. It may become significant for large airplanes and perhaps locomotives. But whatever inroads nuclear propulsion may make, there is no doubt whatsoever that petroleum consumption will continue to increase very rapidly. In 1910, United States crude petroleum production stood at 210 million (42 gallon) barrels. Early in 1951, it passed the 2-billion-barrel mark, a ten-fold increase within forty years. (The American oil industry invested 19 billion dollars between 1945 and 1952.)[7] At the same time, world oil-refining capacity almost reached 600 million tons, with about half of it located in North America. It is believed that the American oil production will be doubled between 1950 and 1975, and because of the time lag in motorization, oil consumption in the rest of the world may increase even faster. In any event, world production rose from 330 million barrels in 1910 to 3.8 billion in 1950, an 11.5-fold increase within forty years.

World petroleum supplies are located in relatively few areas. There are two major oil areas in the world. The first extends from North to South America, including the Caribbean and the Gulf of Mexico. This region includes the deposits of the United States, Canada, Mexico, Colombia, and Venezuela. The second and larger area comprises the Near and Middle East, *i.e.*, the region bounded by the Caspian Sea, the Black Sea, the Red Sea, and the Persian Gulf. Included in this area are the vast deposits of Kuwait, Iran, Iraq, Arabia, Qatar, Egypt, Turkey, Rumania, and Russia. This area possesses 49 per cent of the world's reserves, while the American zone possesses about 45 per cent; however, estimates of Middle Eastern oil constantly have been corrected upward. In addition there are two minor producing areas. The first includes the shallow depression lying between Asia and Australia including the deposits of Sumatra, Borneo, New Guinea, and Java; the second, the northern arctic, is still undeveloped but believed to contain large petroleum deposits, especially in Alaska and in the Yenisei and Lena Basins of Siberia.

It is not essential for military purposes that nations have large quantities of oil deposits within their territorial confines. Of greater importance is *assured access to supplies*. The German experience of 1933–1945 would point to the possibility of storing adequate supplies of imported petroleum, of creating additional petroleum reserves from coal and imported oil residuals, and of conquest (Rumania). Japan, desperately short of domestic reserves, seized upon large petroleum areas by conquest (Indonesia). The military victory of the United Nations in World War II was undoubtedly based, in part, upon the fact that they controlled, despite losses of refineries, deposits, and tankers, an overwhelming quantity of petroleum.

Throughout history, the United States has dominated the world's petroleum production. With about 30 per cent of the world reserves, it has been producing more than half, and occasionally two-thirds, of the world's crude oil and about two-thirds of the refined products (not to mention three-quarters of the natural gas output). In addition, American interests control 75 per

[7] This figure was supplied by T. S. Petersen, President of Standard Oil of California, in a speech at the annual meeting of the American Petroleum Institute, 1952.

cent of proved South American reserves, 40 per cent of the Middle East proved reserves, and 30 per cent of the proved reserves of the Far East. Generally speaking, aggregate American petroleum deposits are of all-purpose variety, usable for many industrial purposes. The outstanding significance of American petroleum production is the rapid rate of consumption, which has somewhat exceeded the rate of increase of domestic output. The net result has been the change in the character of international trade of petroleum. Since the end of World War II the United States has become a net importer of petroleum. This trend has been accompanied by the rise in productivity of the Caribbean and the Middle East.

The United States now draws increasingly upon the petroleum resources of Latin America. The greatest petroleum reserves in South America are located in Venezuela in the Lake Maracaibo, Apure, and Orinoco Basins. The Venezuelan fields supplied the critical margin of U.S. and British requirements in excess of U.S. production in World War II. Their output may be counted upon by the United States in future emergencies, provided production and lines of transportation can be guarded against hostile interference.

In Europe, the industrial nations such as the United Kingdom, France, Germany, Belgium, Holland, and the Scandinavian countries produce domestically but a fraction of the oil they consume. The most important European producers are Rumania, Austria, Hungary, Poland, and the U.S.S.R. German and Austrian drives for increased production have not been unsuccessful: both countries went beyond the 1-million-ton-per-year mark by 1950. Italian and French hopes for oil always have proved disappointing.

Rumania's wells have been worked extensively for long periods. Reorganization of the industry and application of modern techniques (e.g., repressurization) have not been without success. The Rumanian fields now produce about as much as their pre-1939 output, and production is increasing again. Furthermore, it is believed that Austrian oil production has reached, or is about to reach, the 3-million-ton mark. Oil production in Hungary in 1953 was about 850,000 tons, while Polish oil production hovers around 200,000 to 250,000 tons. All of which means that the Eastern European satellites by the end of 1953 had a total petroleum output of 13 million tons or roughly 98 million barrels.

For many years the most important oil-producing areas of the Soviet Union were the Baku, Grozny, and Maikop regions. Since the early thirties a second Baku has been developed in the Kirov-Molotov-Kuibyshev and Chkalov-Saratov areas. A third important area is being worked in Turkmenistan. Oil is also produced on Sakhalin, in the northern Urals, at Ferghana, and at Krasnovodsk and Emba on the Caspian Sea. Geological investigation points to petroleum deposits along the arctic coast, Lena River, Tolba River, and Sea of Okhotsk (Kamchatka) and in Bashkiria. The Russian objective under the fourth Five-Year Plan was to produce a total of 35,400,000 tons of petroleum *annually* by 1950. Allegedly an output of 37.8 million tons was reached, which during 1951 was upped to 42.3 million tons.[8] The United States *monthly* average for 1951 was 25 million tons. While the petroleum production of the U.S.S.R. lags behind that of the United States, it must be kept in mind that the Russian petroleum resources have not been as fully explored and as effectively exploited as those of the United States. Moreover, the Soviet Union produces annually only about 500,000 trucks, busses, and motor cars and 600,000-odd tractors and other agricultural vehicles, as compared to about 6.8 million cars, trucks, and busses in the United States. Russia's commercial air traffic is smaller; she operates fewer Diesel locomotives. Few Russian homes are heated with oil. While the Soviet oil production does not permit the improvement, through motorization, of living standards, it seems to be quite ample for military purposes. In any event, Russia's situation as regards oil is far superior to that of the Axis powers during World War II. Russia is definitely a major oil power, and her rate of growth seems to be considerable.

The newest addition to the group of large oil-producing regions is the area of the Middle East. It requires little imagination to perceive the leverage Middle Eastern oil must give to the powers who control it. The convergence of power interests in this area is as old as recorded history; modern techniques of transportation and the incidence of oil have added a new chapter to that history, without, however, breaking its continuity.

The area between Egypt and Afghanistan, including Iran, Iraq, Syria, Saudi Arabia, Kuwait, Sarawak, Bahrein, Qatar, and Trucial Oman, appears to be fated to play the role of the world's largest oil-producing region. In 1938 this region produced approximately 5 per cent of the world's total petroleum supplies. By 1950, production expanded to about one-fifth of the world's total, a production larger than that of South America. Operations are carried out principally under joint Anglo-American private corporate control, with the most modern techniques known in petroleum engineering. Transportation is accomplished by a huge system of pipe lines and seagoing tankers, most of which are directly or indirectly under Anglo-American control. The area possesses close to 10 per cent of the world's refining capacity.

In 1951, the development of the area was interrupted when the Iranian government decreed the nationalization of the mining and refining properties of the Anglo-Iranian Company. Iran temporarily dropped out as a producer of oil; its place was taken, largely through increased output, by Saudi Arabia and Venezuela. Lack of political stability in the area militates strongly against a really satisfactory growth of the Middle Eastern oil industry, although despite these handicaps, progress has been rapid, especially in the Arabic countries.

The Middle East has been the object of Russian attempts at political and economic penetration. It is difficult to say whether Soviet intervention in northern Iran in 1945–1946 was prompted by strategic consideration or by

[8] United Nations, *Economic Survey of Europe in 1951*, Geneva, 1952, p. 127.

desire to exploit the oil resources of that area. Shortly after V-E Day the Soviet Union, the United States, and Great Britain were requested by the Iranian government to withdraw their troops in accordance with the three-power pledge contained in the Teheran declaration of 1943. The Soviet Union agreed to the withdrawal of its troops under the terms of the treaty, *i.e.,* by March 2, 1946. Shortly thereafter a revolt broke out in the Azerbaijan province, and a United States proposal that the troops of the occupying powers be withdrawn by January 1, 1946, was rejected by the Soviet Union. Underlying these moves was the failure of a Soviet mission to Teheran in 1944 to secure an oil concession in northern Iran. Iran took the controversy before the United Nations Security Council.

In the diplomatic negotiations between the first meeting of the United Nations Security Council in January, 1946, and the evacuation of Soviet troops from Iran, May 23, 1946, petroleum seems to have been—next to the territorial integrity of Iran—the most important issue. During this period it was disclosed that the Russian government had made a counterproposal for the immediate removal of Soviet troops from Iran by demanding, first, that Iran recognize the internal autonomy of the province of Azerbaijan; secondly, that a joint Iranian-Russian oil company be established and that Russian troops be stationed for unspecified periods in certain areas of Iran. It also came to light that the U.S.S.R. had attempted to coerce the Premier of Iran into dropping the Iranian complaint before the United Nations. The United States and the United Kingdom managed, by considerable pressure on the Security Council and the Iranians, to keep the Soviet-Iranian controversy on the United Nations agenda for an indefinite period. The Soviet-sponsored government of Iranian Azerbaijan collapsed, and the Soviet Union at long last withdrew its forces from Iran. During the nationalization crisis of 1951 and 1952, the Soviets stayed in the background, although Soviet intervention, it has been asserted, would have been a distinct possibility had Britain asserted her rights by force. The increased reliance on Middle Eastern oil of the United States and Great Britain tends to involve both powers ever more deeply in the affairs of that region.

Although the United States and Britain have gained and, thus far, have managed to retain, by a complicated web of diplomatic, political, financial, and strategic arrangements, control over the oil-producing areas of the Middle East, their position is neither a comfortable one politically nor, as regards likely military contingencies, a reassuring one. It is far from certain that the Middle East could be held in the face of a Soviet thrust launched from the shores of the Caspian or that refining facilities could be successfully guarded against air attack and sabotage.

It is these circumstances which counsel caution as regards the *strategic* potentialities of Middle Eastern oil. They suggest that the United States can, as a last resort, place reliance safely only upon resources at home, in northern Canada, possibly in Alaska, and in Latin America and upon the increased production of fuel from sources other than crude petroleum, *e.g.*, coal or oil shales, with which the United States is richly endowed.[9] If only because of transportation costs and military safety, the Latin-American oil fields are of greater significance to the security of the United States than the Middle East which, however, is crucial for Europe and Asia.

In Asia proper there is little hope for the development of extensive additional reserves of petroleum. China, except for the shale deposits of Manchuria and possibly deposits in Sinkiang, Shensi, and the upper Yangtze region, has no large sources of supply, nor is Japan's domestic production even remotely sufficient to meet her domestic needs. The oil fields of northeastern India supply at present part of India's needs, but their output is inadequate for satisfying the requirements of projected industrialization. This is also true of Pakistan.

The world's oil reserves are currently estimated at about 12 billion tons.[10] Though current estimates on oil reserves are not always reliable nations must develop their policies in accordance with these known orders of magnitude, incomplete though they may be.

Table 9 reveals the dominant position of the Western Hemisphere, the relative long-range oil weakness of the Soviet Union, and the key significance of the Persian Gulf area which possesses greater reserves than the United States and which, therefore, must constitute the most significant expansionist goal of the Soviet Union. The table also shows that Europe, wide parts of Asia and Africa, and parts of South America will be greatly handicapped both industrially and militarily unless they can continue trading with the owners of oil, improve oil technology,[11] or produce fuel synthetically. On the other hand, the dominant position of the United States and Britain (and to a lesser extent France and Holland) is dependent on satisfactory political and economic relations with independent countries in Latin America and Asia, or on the employment of force. This situation is far from being satisfactory as regards the present world balance of power and forebodes conflict.

[9] Increasing attention has been given to the development of the synthetic-liquid-fuels program by the U.S. Congress, which has encouraged a program of investigating the convertibility of low-grade bituminous coal, lignite, and shale into petroleum. See Public Law 443, 80th Cong., 2d Sess., Mar. 15, 1948.

[10] T. S. Petersen, a leading expert, pointed out that "oil may be found anywhere within an estimated 2,400,000 square miles of sedimentary formation. Yet all of our present reserve is scattered over just one per cent of that tremendous expanse."

[11] According to T. S. Petersen "Technology and scientific research in the manufacturing end of our industry will remain tremendously important factors for the future. There was a day when only 10 to 20 per cent of each barrel of crude oil could be converted to gasoline; today we turn almost half of every barrel to gasoline, and even that figure can be increased if the need arises."

TABLE 9. OIL RESERVES

Area	Billions of metric tons	Per cent of world total
United States.....	3.7	31.0
Kuwait..........	1.7	14.0
Venezuela.........	1.6	13.0
Saudi Arabia......	1.5	12.0
Iran.............	1.1	9.0
Iraq.............	0.8	6.6
U.S.S.R..........	0.7	5.7
Indonesia........	0.16	1.3
Mexico..........	0.14	1.2
Turkey..........	0.09	0.8
Canada..........	0.08	0.6
Qatar...........	0.08	0.6
Total..........	11.65	95.8

RAW MATERIALS AND ATOMIC ENERGY

The significance of atomic energy within the international power struggle no longer is doubted by anyone. A great nation involved in a major war cannot hope to survive unless it possesses atomic weapons. It is not certain that atomic bombs ever will be used again. The fear of retaliation is, however, the strongest argument against trigger-happiness. A ruthless aggressor would not hesitate to employ these weapons against a nation which cannot retaliate in kind. Accordingly, survival in the modern age is dependent on the possession of atomic weapons.

In addition to the production of electric power, nuclear energy may become important for ship propulsion; ships driven by nuclear reactors can carry considerably more freight and possess a greater flexibility of movement. Whether nuclear reactors will be used in vehicles of land transportation, such as locomotives, or in aircraft, is not yet absolutely certain. Nuclear reactors will become important as sources of industrial heat. Isotopes (identical chemical elements differing in atomic weight like U^{233}, U^{235}, U^{238} and U^{239}), which are by-products of fissile materials output, are being employed on an ever larger scale in industry and agriculture, as research aids, as measuring and control devices, and in medicine. It is a fact that the nuclear industry is already the largest among all industries in the United States.

A reliable assessment of the raw-material needs of the nuclear industry is impossible at this time. It is known that early estimates concerning the scarcity of natural uranium have proved false and that, globally speaking, there should be enough uranium for any desired expansion of the nuclear industry, especially if breeding techniques (which use the rare isotope U^{235} to transform the common U^{238} into fissile matter) were employed.[12] In addition to large deposits of high-grade uranium, there are very large occurrences of low-grade uranium in oil shales and in the ocean. Thorium, too, is available in substantial quantities.

An assessment of the nuclear raw-material situation is furthermore made difficult because the quantitative needs of the atomic industry have not been revealed. Nor has it as yet been stated with certainty which minerals or other types of raw materials will remain, or will become, necessary for nuclear production. It is not only a question of the fissile materials themselves but of the chemicals needed for processing and of the metals needed in the reactors, heat exchangers, shields, etc. Metals with anticorrosive and heat-resisting characteristics have become increasingly important for the nuclear (and for the jet aircraft) industry.

According to the few statistics which have been published, the Belgian Congo must be considered as the main supplier of high-grade uranium. It is followed by Canada, Czechoslovakia, and the United States.[13] Despite sporadically published figures, the actual output is not known—if only because the uranium content of the ores has been kept secret. The following additional nations are supposed to have substantial uranium deposits: South Africa, Australia, Soviet Union, Portugal, France, Argentina, Mozambique, Spain, Madagascar, Germany, United Kingdom, Bulgaria, New Zealand, and possibly Israel and China. It is believed that, by and large, the African deposits under Belgian and British control are the most important, although little is known about the Soviet Union. Sensational claims were made by many nations, including Australia, South Africa, and Canada, but whatever the truth, there seems to be a more than ample supply of uranium.

In so far as thorium is concerned, the main deposits are located in Brazil, India, the United States, Ceylon, Indonesia, Soviet Union, Korea, Portugal, Australia, and New Zealand.[14] It may be assumed that nations like Brazil and India which apparently do not possess uranium will be inclined to use thorium as the base material for their future nuclear industry.

It has been determined that uranium often appears in oil shales and phosphate rocks. The following countries possess considerable deposits: United States, Great Britain, Soviet Union (including Estonia), Sweden, France, Spain, Italy, Australia, Southern Manchuria, and China (Shensi). The United States has initiated the full industrial utilization of uranium-bearing phosphate rocks, of which there are large deposits in Florida. Huge quantities of phos-

[12] Joint Committee on Atomic Energy, *Atomic Power and Private Enterprise,* pp. 227, 381.

[13] *Atlas International Larousse, Politique et Economique,* Paris, Larousse, 1950, statistical tables, p. 16.

[14] *Ibid.*

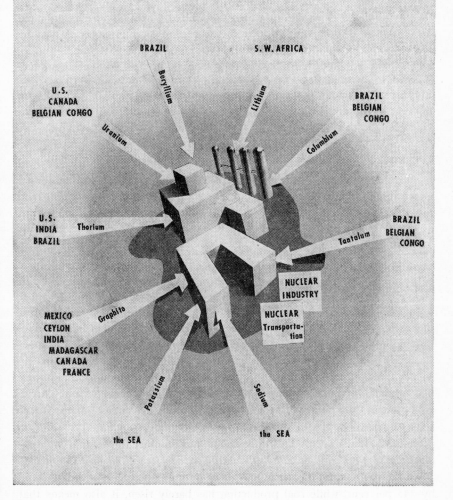

Trade Structure of Nucleonics

phate rock are found in French North Africa, Soviet Union, Egypt, French Oceania, Japan, Nauru Island, and numerous other places.

It has been reported that graphite is indispensable in some segments of the atomic industry. The United States is a heavy importer of this material. Main suppliers are Mexico, Ceylon, Madagascar, Canada, India, and France. Zirconium, a radiation- and corrosion-resisting material, has been imported from Australia and Brazil—but there are large deposits in Ceylon, India, and the Soviet Union. This ore, of which the United States obtains its principal domestic supply from sands dug from the beaches of Florida, is deemed by scientists to be second only to uranium as a key atomic material.

It should be noted that many of the materials needed for nuclear production seem to be found in Africa (notably in the Belgian Congo and the South African Union), in Brazil, and in India. While these nations can do little with their own materials so long as the atomic industries are located in the United States, the Soviet Union, and Great Britain only, these fortuitous deposits certainly enhance their international position.[15]

The main points to retain from this discussion are that (1) nucleonics will require many materials which in the past had only marginal use and were mined in only relatively small quantities; (2) the nuclear industry will tend to reduce further the capacity of any nation to become self-sufficient except as it may reduce dependence on coal.

NONFERROUS MINERALS

The hunger of world industry for minerals and metals is now more rapacious than it ever has been. As the world is being industrialized, the need for metals increases very rapidly. Between 1929 and 1951 the industrial production index of the world rose by 108 per cent. However, the production of practically all metals rose at a far faster rate, coal and lead, which increased by 31 per cent and 26 per cent respectively, being the only notable exceptions. The production of iron ore rose by 360 per cent, while manganese and bauxite rose each by 900 per cent. Molybdenum, showing the largest increase, rose by 1,350 per cent. The average for the metals and other materials listed in Table 10 is 420 per cent. This table shows, among other things, that *industrialization means increased emphasis on high-grade steels and on light metals.* Since the production of electric energy rose by 275 per cent, and that of oil by 245 per cent, while coal production has barely risen, it also means that the energy production has shifted away from coal. In other words, the world is being electrified and motorized.[16]

[15] For these and preceding data on minerals, see *Harwell, the British Atomic Energy Establishment, 1946 to 1951,* London, H.M. Stationery Office, 1952; p. 40.

[16] These figures are based on *United Nations Statistical Yearbook, 1952,* New York, 1952; the *United Nations Statistical Yearbook, 1949–1950,* New York, 1950; and *Minerals' Yearbook 1949,* Government Printing Office, 1950.

TABLE 10. PRODUCTION INCREASES, 1929–1951

Material	Per cent
Molybdenum	1,350
Manganese	900
Bauxite	900
Chromium	800
Asbestos	650
Tin	560
Nickel	500
Tungsten	430
Iron ore	360
Vanadium	280
Potash	250
Oil	245
Titanium (10 years)	200
Phosphate	215
Copper	190
Antimony	180
Zinc	164
Sulphur	125
Coal	31
Lead	26

What this signifies in terms of production and trade patterns may be illustrated by the example of manganese. Manganese is an essential ingredient of steel and has become, with an output increase of 900 per cent, one of the most important minerals. Disregarding the production of Russia, about which little is known except that the Soviet Union is perhaps the world's foremost producer, it appears that in 1929 about 90 per cent of the world's manganese was produced by seven nations: India, the Gold Coast, Brazil, South Africa, the United States, Egypt, and Morocco.[17] There were furthermore a number of small European producers working on marginal deposits. By 1951, the bulk of the manganese was coming from thirteen states (again disregarding the Soviet Union): India, the Gold Coast, South Africa, Morocco, Brazil, Cuba, Japan, the United States, Egypt, Portuguese India, the Belgian Congo, Turkey, and Angola. The marginal European producers, Italy, Rumania, Spain, Sweden, and Britain, practically have dropped out of the picture, while Mexico, Chile, China, Indonesia, the Philippines, and Yugoslavia are coming to the fore as significant producers. India and Brazil, formerly the most important producers, have lost ground, while the Gold Coast remains the second important producer. Africa's share was boosted from 35 to 52 per cent in world production; producers in South America and Asia are gaining at a fast rate.

The meaning of these statistics seems to be clear:

[17] *Statistisches Jahrbuch für das Deutsche Reich, 1935,* Berlin, 1935, p. 57 of International Survey.

1. As the requirements for minerals are growing and the deposits within the industrialized countries are nearing depletion and prove unable to satisfy the increasing demand, the underdeveloped countries become the world's major suppliers of important minerals. Specifically, it is noticeable that tropical countries, in Africa, South America, and some parts of Asia, are developing mining industries of truly global importance.

In any scheme for the expansion of the raw-material resources, upon which the very existence of Western industrial society depends, Africa must be given the highest priority. The Belgian Congo, to cite but one example illustrative of the potentials of the vast continent, supplies more than half of the uranium needs of the United States, 75 per cent of the free world's cobalt, 70 per cent of the industrial diamonds, 9 per cent of the tin, 7 per cent of the copper, and 30 per cent of the palm oil used not only for margarine but increasingly for industrial, especially metallurgical, purposes. This wealth—750 million dollars a year—is only the beginning, for there is a far greater wealth as yet unexplored or undeveloped.

The mineral deposits of Africa not only are huge, they are also accessible to the West strategically and economically. The West still dominates Africa militarily and politically; American and European capital still controls the bulk of African wealth. The military, political, and economic system of controls rests, however, upon shaky foundations. Nationalist ferment in North Africa and the disintegration of tribal society to the south of the Sahara, the increasing tensions between the races and the antagonisms and rivalries of Western interests and national groups—all these disintegrationist forces threaten to engulf the "tragic continent" in a crisis which could doom the hopes of the West and gravely impair Western strategic defenses as well as bring terrible suffering to the native peoples. There is virtually universal agreement that such a crisis is in the making and that the position of the white race—which accounts for only one-fiftieth of Africa's total population of 250 million—has become precarious. There is, however, no agreement as to how these dangers are to be met.

In Nigeria and the Gold Coast, Britain has answered the African question forthrightly by the grant of local autonomy; in the Congo, Belgium has answered it by a paternalism which, by colonial standards, is lavish in its ministrations to the natives' needs; in South Africa, the Afrikander government has answered it by denying that it exists and riding roughshod over those—blacks, whites, Hindus, and mixed—who persist in asking it. In British Central Africa, composed of the mineral-rich Rhodesias and Nyasaland, the idea has been gaining ground that the solution to the problem of racial relationships and the development of the area's wealth which waits upon the increase of foreign investment, Western settlers, and willing native labor, must be sought on the road to federation and Dominion status.

In sum, the problem of satisfying the boundless appetite of Western industry for raw materials, especially minerals, is, in Africa and to some extent

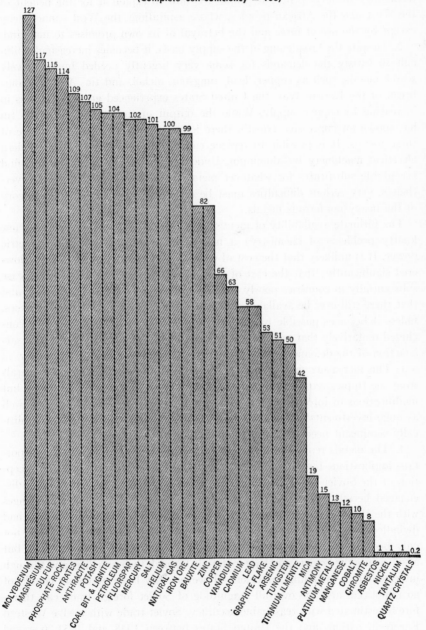

U.S. SELF SUFFICIENCY IN MINERALS, 1945
(Figures in per cent)
(Complete self-sufficiency = 100)

MOLYBDENUM	127
MAGNESIUM	117
SULFUR	115
PHOSPHATE ROCK	114
NITRATES	109
ANTHRACITE	107
POTASH	105
PETROLEUM	104
COAL, BIT. & LIGNITE	102
FLUORSPAR	101
MERCURY	100
SALT	99
HELIUM	82
NATURAL GAS	66
IRON ORE	63
BAUXITE	58
ZINC	53
COPPER	51
VANADIUM	50
CADMIUM	42
LEAD	19
GRAPHITE FLAKE	15
ARSENIC	13
TUNGSTEN	12
TITANIUM ILMENITE	10
MICA	8
ANTIMONY	1
PLATINUM METALS	1
MANGANESE	1
COBALT	0.2
CHROMITE	
ASBESTOS	
NICKEL	
TANTALUM	
QUARTZ CRYSTALS	

151

in the Middle East, not a technical or military one, but rather one of a political, social, and ethical nature. The wealth is there. The West has the technology to develop it. The problem is how to exploit it for the benefit of the West *and* the African peoples, whose aspirations the West cannot deny except by the use of force and the betrayal of its own promises to mankind.

2. Despite the broadening of the supply basis, it becomes increasingly difficult to satisfy the demands for some very urgently needed but relatively scarce metals, such as copper, lead, tungsten, nickel, and tin. After the outbreak of the Korean War, the United States experienced great difficulties in increasing its copper supply. While the output of tungsten, nickel, and tin has shown an impressive growth, there is some question as to the future of these metals. It is possible to replace copper wires in much of the modern electrical machinery by aluminum. Undoubtedly, it will be feasible to find acceptable substitutes for whatever metals may be in short supply. Nevertheless, very serious difficulties must be expected, especially in the category of the heavy nonferrous metals.

The ultimate availability of metals for all countries is (disregarding a few knotty problems of chemistry) a matter of availability of cheap electric power. It is unlikely that the cost of coal- or oil-generated power can be lowered significantly; that the cost of coal- or oil-generated power will decrease substantially in countries poorly supplied with either of these materials; and that there will ever be available sufficient dependable hydroelectric resources, unless it becomes possible to harness the ocean tides. It may hence be concluded tentatively that nuclear power alone holds the key to the ultimate satisfaction of the demand for many minerals which are now in short supply.

3. The increasing dependence of the industrialized countries on minerals from the tropics requires not only an enlargement of international trade but modifications of international trade patterns, including tariff policies, as well as huge investments in the supplier countries. That these changes are politically significant need not be labored.

4. The metals requirements of modern technology are fraught with important implications for the position of the Soviet Union. Ever since the inception of the Soviet regime and disregarding a few exceptions, Russia has disengaged herself tradewise from the outside world. By 1952, her exchanges with the Western industrialized nations and their allies and dependencies had dwindled to the vanishing point. Exact import figures are not obtainable, not only because the Soviet Union does not publish foreign-trade statistics but also because the Soviets purchase materials through their satellites and through intermediaries, including smugglers. However, very large purchases could not go unnoticed, and the over-all magnitude of Soviet foreign trade can therefore be estimated with reasonable accuracy. Soviet trade with twelve Western European nations and the United States between 1948 and 1951 averaged about 300 million dollars (imports plus exports). It was estimated to have been, in 1950, about 900 million dollars, *i.e.,* less than the foreign trade of

New Zealand. Hence the per capita rate would be about $4.30 of foreign trade per inhabitant of Russia. (Australia has a rate of about $375, the United Kingdom of $310, and the United States of $178 per inhabitant, with the world's per capita rate standing at about $64 in 1950.) Russia's share in world trade is only 0.65 per cent. The share of the Soviet bloc, excluding China, is about 5 billion dollars, or about 3.2 per cent as against a population amounting to 12 per cent of the world's total.

The Soviet Union controls a very considerable area and is theoretically less dependent than other nations on foreign suppliers. It is possible, though not probable, that the Soviets are finding all the metals needed for their industrial expansion within their territory. The Soviets have been suffering from a "chronic shortage of minerals." In 1944, lend-lease provided one-fourth of Russia's visible minerals supplies.[18]

The country has not been geologically explored in full; hence the Soviets may possess greater riches than they can be credited with in 1953. But even if every metal were found in the Soviet Union, it is likely that many deposits will be located in practically inaccessible areas and, therefore, could be worked only if transportation facilities had been established. If the Soviets persist in their drive for self-sufficiency they will, at a minimum, incur the penalty of greater production costs.

It is believed that the Soviet Union has some definite shortages. The country has become increasingly a minerals-importing country; the shortages in petroleum products, sulphur minerals, and nonferrous metals are especially pronounced. Some of these deficiencies could be alleviated by imports from satellites.[19] The satellites also suffer from deficits which would have to be covered by the Soviet Union. If anything, the enlargement of the Soviet orbit to Eastern Europe made the dependence on outside supplies worse, especially if industrialization is to be pushed.

There is no need to speculate about the precise nature and the extent of these shortages. The point is that, as Russian industrialization progresses, dependence on foreign minerals probably will increase. This has happened in all other countries, and the Soviet orbit hardly will prove to be an exception. If the Soviet rulers do not enlarge their foreign trade, they will be compelled to slow down industrialization or channel it into technologically less satisfactory fields. If, however, they seek to broaden their foreign trade, they will have to modify not only some of their economic procedures but also some of their political practices. *They could afford maximum isolation only during the first phase of their industrialization.* Economically at least, the future of the "iron curtain" does not look very promising.[20]

[18] Demitri B. Shimkin, *Minerals: A Key to Soviet Power,* Cambridge, Mass., Harvard University Press, 1953, pp. 302, 314.

[19] *Ibid.,* pp. 341f.

[20] Adolf Weber, *Marktwirtschaft und Sowjetwirtschaft, Ein Vergleich neuzeitlicher Wirtschaftordnungen,* 2d ed., Munich, Pflaum, 1951, pp. 391f. Weber called attention to the fact that Soviet production of manganese declined before World War II, although

STOCKPILING

One of the essential conditions of national security is the availability of raw-material stocks sufficient to develop long-range civilian and military programs. The United States has been a late-comer in the field of methodical stockpiling and conservation. The first modern stockpiling legislation was passed under the shadow of the disaster at Pearl Harbor. This program set up agencies to stockpile strategic and critical materials for national defense. At the outset, small purchases of tin, ferromanganese, tungsten ore, chromite, optical glass, and manila fiber were made.

Under the terms of the National Security Act of 1947 the government was given the duty of developing policies for the establishment of reserves of *strategic* and *critical* raw materials and for the relocation of vital industries for emergency periods.[21]

Stockpiling programs, to be both practical and effective, must consider the length of time in which the supply of the needed materials will not be forthcoming. Estimates of needed materials based on a calculated emergency period would be a most precarious venture in prediction, since no one knows how long a future emergency will last. A program for the development of natural resources within the territorial confines of neighboring countries (in the case of the United States, especially Canada and the Caribbean states) may provide more effectively for those unpredictable contingencies which a stockpiling program cannot cover.

Stockpiling programs were stepped up greatly during the Korean War. Whether all the needs were forecast correctly and whether the stockpiles were of an adequate size only the future can tell. While the program costs several billions of dollars and requires continued expenditures for storage, stockpiling is one of the answers to prolonged intercontinental war. The Soviet Union is known to invest heavily in stockpiles, not only of raw materials but also of finished products. Other nations have made little if any efforts in this field.

---

the deposits may well be the largest in the world. The neglect of sound methods of mining and the infatuation with speed-up systems to the detriment of adequate maintenance led to output declines.

[21] The classification "strategic raw materials" is applied to those materials which are essential to the national defense of the United States, the supply of which, in war, is obtained in whole or in substantial part from sources outside the continental limits of the United States. The term "critical raw materials" is applied to those materials still important to national defense but involving procurement problems which in times of emergency would be less difficult than those of strategic materials, either because they may be obtained from domestic supplies in greater quantities or because they are not so essential to national defense as are the strategic materials. See U.S. Military Academy, Department of Economics, Government, and History, *Strategic and Critical Raw Materials,* West Point, N.Y., 1942, pp. 10–11.

BIBLIOGRAPHY

American Institute of Mining and Metallurgical Engineers: *Seventy-five Years of Progress in the Mineral Industry, 1871–1946,* New York, 1947.

Armstrong, Willis C.: *The International Minerals Conference,* Government Printing Office, 1951.

Balzak, S. S., V. F. Vasyutin, and Ya. G. Feigin, *Economic Geography of the U.S.S.R.,* New York, Macmillan, 1949.

Cressey, George B.: *The Basis of Soviet Strength,* New York, Whittlesey, 1945.

De Mille, John B.: *Strategic Minerals,* New York, McGraw-Hill, 1947.

Emeny, Brooks: *The Strategy of Raw Materials,* New York, Macmillan, 1938.

Feis, Herbert: *Petroleum and American Foreign Policy,* Food Research Institute, Stanford University, 1944.

Fourth World Power Conference: *Transactions,* London, 1950.

Friedensburg, Ferdinand: *Die Mineralischen Bodenschätze als Weltpolitische und Militärische Machtfaktoren,* Stuttgart, Enke, 1936.

———: *Kohle und Eisen im Weltkrieg und in den Friedenschlüssen,* Berlin, 1934.

Gerschenkron, Alexander: "Russia's Trade in the Postwar Years," *The Annals,* May, 1949, pp. 85–100.

Great Britain, Board of Trade: *Raw Materials Guide, Jan., 1948,* London, H.M. Stationery Office, 1948.

Hanson, Earl Parker: *New Worlds Emerging,* New York, Duell, Sloan & Pearce, 1949.

Hoselitz, B. F. (ed.): *Progress of Underdeveloped Areas,* Chicago, University of Chicago Press, 1953.

Isard, Walter, and Vincent Whitney: *Atomic Power, An Economic and Social Analysis,* New York, Blakiston, 1952.

League of Nations: *Raw Materials Problems and Policies,* Geneva, 1946.

Lovering, T. S.: *Minerals in World Affairs,* New York, Prentice-Hall, 1943.

Mather, K. F.: *Enough and to Spare,* New York, Harper, 1944.

Osborn, F.: *Our Plundered Planet,* Boston, Little, Brown, 1948.

Pratt, Wallace E., and Dorothy Good: *World Geography of Petroleum,* Princeton, N.J., Princeton University Press, 1950.

Putnam, Palmer C.: *Energy in the Future,* New York, Van Nostrand, 1953.

Rostow, E. V.: *A National Policy for the Oil Industry,* New Haven, Yale University Press, 1948.

Schwartz, Harry: *Russia's Soviet Economy,* New York, Prentice-Hall, 1950.

Sharp, Walter R.: *International Technical Assistance: Programs and Organization,* Public Administration Clearing House, 1952.

Shimkin, Demitri B.: *Minerals: A Key to Soviet Power,* Cambridge, Mass., Harvard University Press, 1953.

Sovani, N. V.: *The International Position of India's Raw Materials,* New Delhi, Indian Council of World Affairs, 1948.

Staley, Eugene: *Raw Materials in Peace and War,* New York, Council on Foreign Relations, 1937.

U.S. Department of Interior, Bureau of Mines: *Minerals Yearbook, 1953,* Government Printing Office, 1953.

———: "The Iron and Steel Industries of Europe," *Economic Paper* 19, Government Printing Office, 1939.

U.S. Federal Trade Commission: *Foreign Ownership in the Petroleum Industry,* Government Printing Office, 1923.

U.S. International Development Advisory Board: *Partners in Progress; A Report to the President,* Government Printing Office, 1951.

U.S. Military Academy, Department of Social Sciences: *Raw Materials in War and Peace,* West Point, 1947.

Van Royen, William, and others: *The Mineral Resources of the World,* New York, Prentice-Hall, 1952.

Vogt, W.: *Road to Survival,* New York, Sloane, 1948.

Welsh, Anne (ed.): *Africa South of the Sahara: An Assessment of Human and Material Resources,* Capetown, Oxford University Press, 1951.
World Production of Raw Materials, New York, Royal Institute of International Affairs, 1953.
Zimmerman, Erich W.: *World Resources and Industries; A Functional Appraisal of the Availability of Agricultural and Industrial Materials,* rev. ed., New York, Harper, 1951.
————: *World Resources and Industries,* New York, Harper, 1933.
Zischka, Anton: *Länder der Zukunft; eine weltweite Analyse der Aussichtsreichsten,* Graz, L. Stocker, 1950.

Chapter 8

THE INDUSTRIAL AND TECHNOLOGICAL STRENGTH
OF NATIONS

PROBLEMS OF MEASUREMENT

Prior to the Industrial Revolution the military worth of a state was measured by the size of its standing army and, more crudely, by the size of its population. The First World War proved that the over-all productivity of a nation, including its ability, for the duration of hostilities, to produce weapons and procure supplies from abroad, was a factor to be considered in addition to military strength-in-being. If a war was not decided speedily with the forces and equipment available at the beginning of the conflict, the outcome would be dependent on the strength which a nation could mobilize in the course of hostilities. A greater mobilization potential ultimately meant more troops and munitions on the battlefield and promised victory in the last, the decisive, battle of the war. The resources of the Western world and Russia, far superior to the resources which Germany and her allies could muster in both world wars, determined the outcome of both struggles, although Germany's greater strength-*in-being* enabled her to win initial victories.

Ever since the First World War attempts were made to calculate the size of industrial war potentials and to measure the "rank" of nations. Early estimates were based on comparisons between coal, oil, and steel outputs, the assumption being that these three materials were the sinews of war. This type of calculation undervalued the importance of manpower. Moreover, there are many other materials which may be of crucial importance—especially if they are in short supply. To calculate war potentials accurately, it would be necessary to find common denominators for different materials. Since one cannot add apples and oranges, this is impossible. Moreover, it would be necessary to express qualitative elements, such as organizational efficiency, rapidity of decision, compliance with orders, workers' morale, etc., in quantitative terms. This is not feasible. Nevertheless, attempts to appraise the material strength of nations are not futile: they have about the same value as, for example, the classification of prize fighters under the categories of heavyweight, middleweight, and lightweight. The over-all productivity of a nation is undoubtedly an important factor, both in war and peace, and comparisons are highly useful, provided they are used with care: calculations may show that nation A has a productivity potential three times greater than nation B, but it would not necessarily follow that A can defeat B. Overreliance on *potential* strength is an easy method of losing in warfare as well as in peacetime competition.

ENERGY INDEX

It is total *energy production and consumption,* rather than coal and oil, which qualify as indices of economic and, therefore, of military strength. The statistics of the various forms in which energy is produced and consumed are available, and fortunately it is possible to calculate energy consumption on the basis of one common denominator as, for example, coal. Tables 11 and 12 present the energy production of the leading nations. It must be kept in mind that these tables do not show the energies stored up in fissile materials. On the other hand, they indicate the energy *produced* in a given country. Since many countries import fuels from abroad, the energy consumed (Table 13) is higher than the energy produced.

TABLE 11. TOTAL ENERGY PRODUCTION, 1948 *

(Coal, wood, oil, natural gas, and electricity in terms of coal equivalents)

Area	Millions of tons of coal equivalents	Index
United States.................	1,306	65
U.S.S.R......................	397	22
Germany (pre-1938 borders)......	248	12.5
United Kingdom................	214	11
France.......................	92	4.5
Poland.......................	80	4
Canada.......................	75	4
Japan........................	71	3.5
India........................	42	2
China........................	31	1.5
Italy........................	20	1

* *Atlas International Larousse,* statistical section, Table 96.

Since 1946 [1] the relative position of the various nations scarcely has changed, except that both the United States and Russia probably improved their relative status. The military worth of the Western nations, especially the United States and Canada, may have been exaggerated in these tables because some energy is used for luxuries such as driving cars for pleasure;

[1] Data based on U.S. Department of State, *Energy Resources of the World,* Government Printing Office, 1949, p. 27.

TABLE 12. TOTAL ENERGY PRODUCTION PER CAPITA, 1948

(Coal, wood, oil, natural gas, and electricity in terms of coal equivalents)

Area	Tons of coal equivalents per capita	Index per capita
United States..................	8.8	150
Canada.........................	5.5	92
United Kingdom................	4.3	72
Germany (pre-1938 borders)......	3.7	62
Poland.........................	3.4	57
France.........................	2.2	37
U.S.S.R........................	2	33
Japan..........................	0.9	15
Italy...........................	0.4	7
India *.........................	0.1	1.5
China..........................	0.06	1

* Countries with warm climates need less fuel for home heating.

TABLE 13. ENERGY CONSUMPTION, 1946

(All types of animate and inanimate energy in electric equivalents, assuming uniform 20 per cent efficiency)

	Billion kilowatt-hours		Kilowatt-hours per capita, in thousands
United States.............	1,843	United States........	13
Soviet Union..............	470	Canada..............	12.2
United Kingdom *.........	368	United Kingdom *....	7.6
Germany..................	363	Germany *...........	5.5
France *..................	162	France *.............	3.8
China and Manchuria *....	149	Soviet Union.........	2.6
Canada...................	140	Poland..............	2.4
Japan *...................	137	Japan *..............	1.7
India....................	131	Italy *..............	1.1
Poland...................	66	China *..............	0.3
Italy *...................	52	India................	0.3

* 1937 figures, to eliminate distortions due to war conditions.

in the Soviet Union practically all the energy consumed serves "utilitarian" purposes. Table 14 demonstrates, however, that this assumption may be less

TABLE 14. APPARENT USES OF ENERGY IN 1937 *

(In percentage)

Area	Military,† local and overseas bunkers	Railroads	Auto-motive vehicles	Domestic commercial public and agricultural uses	Industry	Lost and stored
World............	4	11	6	36	41	2
United States ‡.....	3	12	11 §	29	41	4
U.S.S.R...........	3	19	2	34	41	1

* Based on U.S. Department of State, *Energy Resources of the World*, pp. 86f., 1949.
† The share of the military has increased in the United States and in the Soviet Union; it is more questionable whether it has gone up in the rest of the world.
‡ Total American energy consumption was about four times greater than that of Russia.
§ Based on about 25 million private automobiles which by 1950 had risen to 40 million.

pertinent than would be expected; the United States allocated 23 per cent of its energy to transportation, while Russia allocated 21 per cent. The high American figures for losses probably indicate more honest bookkeeping, while the high Russian investment of energy in domestic, commercial, and agricultural uses partly reflects the colder Russian climate.

Perhaps it may not be unimportant to look briefly at the geographic location of progress in energetics as shown in Table 15. The rapid rise of

TABLE 15. INCREASE OF ENERGY PRODUCTION PER CAPITA, 1937–1951 *

Area	Per cent
South America................	64
Africa......................	47
Australia and Oceania.........	42
Europe.....................	35
North America and Mexico.....	24
Asia.......................	0

* Excluding U.S.S.R., China, and Korea.

South America is as astounding as the stagnation of Asia. The growing importance of Africa again is emphasized, as are the difficulties of Europe and the "maturity" of North America. The table suggests considerable future shifts in world power.

Man and Horse Power Census*

(In index numbers based on 1948–1950 figures)

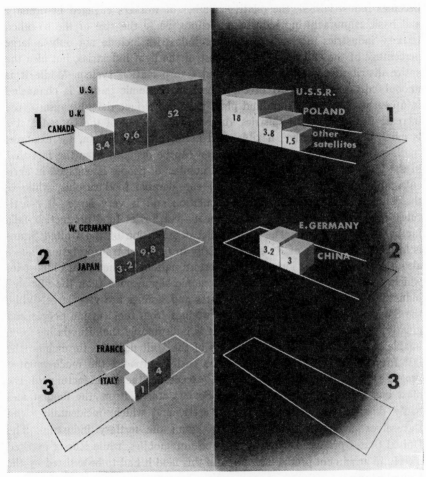

According to this calculation, the United States, Canada, and the United Kingdom possess 16.4 billion hypothetical inhabitants; Russia, Poland, China, and East Germany 7.4; and Western Germany, France, and Italy 3.5; i.e., the Western group, in terms of man and horse power, is 2.3 times stronger than the Soviet bloc.

* Population plus produced energy (1 ton of coal equivalent to 11 men/year
1 working man equivalent to 150 kwh/year).

ECONOMIC PROGRESS AND NATIONAL POWER

In evaluating the economic strength of nations, it would be an error to consider the basic products of energy and steel exclusively. As a nation becomes industrialized, the relative number of workers engaged in primary and basic manufacturing industries declines, while the size of the so-called tertiary industries increases. The latter industries include not only a large percentage of the end products and most of the light industries, but also the entire distribution, communication, and transportation system. While it is undoubtedly true that part of the American economic output is channeled into consumption for leisure and play, it is also a fact that, because of the increase in the tertiary industries, the economic system of the United States is much more productive, flexible, and better organized than, for example, that of the Soviet Union. This conclusion can be deduced from the fact that in the United States only a very small number of people is engaged in agricultural pursuits and produces a very considerable food surplus, while in the Soviet Union the agricultural population still is very large—it constitutes, in fact, camouflaged unemployment—yet Soviet food production falls far below requirements. The distribution organization of the United States is far superior to that of Russia, especially in terms of transportation. There also is a clear-cut superiority of the Western nations in the "light" industries which are not of lesser military or economic significance than the "heavy" industries. United States investment rates and savings are very large. While the Soviet government extracted large savings from the Russian people and greatly increased capital investments, it is indisputable that Russia has been unable to match the economic progress of the United States throughout the last fifty years. The United States has easily outpaced the much-vaunted progress under socialist management, except in the manufacture of the most basic commodities in which the Soviets started from the modest and badly damaged bequest of Tsarist Russia, and which, incidentally, lend themselves much better to "planning" than the tertiary industries. The United States produced guns, butter, and automobiles, while Russia excelled merely in armament production. Even in this field it had to be assisted by the United States.

It is possible to define economic progress in quantitative terms; first, the productivity per average man-hour can be calculated, and second, the growth of productivity can be determined. It appears from Table 16 that productivity per man-hour in the Soviet Union, taking into consideration all factors, has barely grown at all, while productivity in the United States, Britain, and Germany has been rising rapidly. Russian productivity may have been growing faster after the Second World War, but so has the productivity in the United States, which through this entire period was able to accentuate its lead at an ever-increasing rate.

TABLE 16. PRODUCTIVITY

Real Product per Man-hour in Colin Clark's International Units *

Area	1940	1913	Increase, per cent
U.S...........	.997	.506	50
U.K...........	.570	.365	59
Germany......	.470	.319	48
U.S.S.R.......	.178	.166	5

Productivity Indices

Area	1940	1913
U.S...........	5.6	3
U.K...........	3.3	2.2
Germany......	2.7	1.9
U.S.S.R.......	1	1

* Colin Clark, *The Conditions of Economic Progress*, 2d ed., London, Macmillan & Co., Ltd., 1951, pp. 47, 63, 101, 191.

TECHNOLOGY

To remain for a long period militarily and economically strong, a nation must possess an effective technology. Many people believe that in the modern industrialized world, technology per se is the key to power. Hence they assume that heavy investment in scientific research rather than in immediate preparedness provides the best long-range security. This, however, is an oversimplification; one can fight only with available weapons, not with blueprints. Research provides security only if and when its results are incorporated in actual weapons which must be produced in sufficient quantity and with which troops must be equipped in time sufficient to permit training and deployment.

By technology is meant, first and foremost, the variety, quality, longevity, and usefulness of industrial end products; secondly, the ability to produce commodities which perform a service heretofore never performed; and, thirdly, the ability to produce goods which serve a conventional purpose but do so in a manner superior to the goods previously in use. Modern means of transport, from the bicycle to the jet airliner, constitute a great variety of dependable and useful end products. The airplane and the submarine perform functions which were not performed before our time. The famous French 75-millimeter field gun performed the same function as its counterpart, the German 77-millimeter gun, but in a far superior manner.

Economic progress as well as military striking power is dependent on a continuous flow of "new" and "better" commodities. The broad field of electronics (radio, radar, television), nucleonics, and guided missiles are new developments which gave to the first users a great and immediate military advantage. The British pioneering development of radar saved the United Kingdom in 1940. The German advance in guided missiles almost saved Hitler from final destruction. The development of the atomic bomb hastened the defeat of Japan and, in the immediate postwar period, held in check Soviet expansionist desires. Ever since the invention of the club and the bow and arrow, and the training of the horse, technological surprise and superiority have contributed decisively to victory. Many of the great captains of history were predominantly men with technological vision, inventors and protagonists of new weapons.

As to the simply "better" commodities, we merely need think about German and British small cars, German chemical and pharmaceutical products, German photographic and optical equipment, Swiss watches, French perfumes, British textiles, Swedish ball bearings, American machine tools, Russian tanks, British commercial jet aircraft and merchant ships, and Dutch radio equipment to obtain a good notion of the economic advantages of technology.

Technology is not merely a matter of quality and unprecedented service. It is also one of the main conditions of increasing quantitative output. For example, James Watt's first steam engine required 4 tons of coal in order to produce 1,000 kilowatthours of energy; 150 years later, the same amount of energy could be produced by a high-pressure turbine from about 400 kilograms of coal. Technological progress meant in this case that the energy value of one coal unit had increased tenfold.

Technological performance contributes in other ways to high output. Without constantly improved technology, minerals could not be mined in adequate quantities. It has become very difficult to discover mineral deposits through conventional geological exploration. To identify deposits deep underground, complicated tools are necessary, including aircraft, high-performance photography, and even nuclear devices. The mineral wealth of a country, while in part the result of geographic accident, is also a function of the technology employed to determine it.

The technology of production control, distribution, and storage as well as scientific management (pioneered by Frederick W. Taylor), training of the labor force and building the morale of the worker influence directly the output performance of an industry. It is not only the basic inventions which count; production techniques, reliability of the product, and a whole range of laborsaving and control devices are necessary for large-scale production.

The enormous American output is due to rationalization and mechanization of practically all productive and distributive processes. No doubt, besides manpower, technology *is* the greatest resource.

Hence the question arises: who owns this resource or who possesses superiority in the technological field? It should be possible to measure technological performance in terms of a nation's employment of various techniques and in terms of usefulness, performance, durability, and diversity of end products. No figures are known beyond very rough quantitative statistics. Statements that the United States produces many more types of goods and qualitatively far superior commodities than the Soviet Union are probably true but cannot be buttressed by reliable figures. However, there is little doubt that the Western industrialized nations hold a considerable lead over the Soviet Union, especially in terms of "diversity." To a large extent, the Soviets achieve their output levels by a rigorous standardization of commodities and by a minimum of effort in the field of highly priced, high-precision, and specialized goods. This is just another reason why comparisons between the outputs of basic raw materials can lead to very erroneous conclusions. The quantity of coal mined is less significant than the value of the end products fabricated by a nation, but unfortunately reliable figures are lacking.

MEASUREMENTS OF TECHNOLOGICAL PROGRESS

National income figures (Table 17) should give some clue to the technological performance of a nation. The technological status of nations can be determined somewhat more accurately by considering the strength of the industrial labor force or, rather, the nonagricultural labor force, and establishing its relative position within the total population (Table 18). The size of the labor force also may serve as an indicator of a country's military potential.

Table 20 reveals Britain as the most industrialized country in the world, closely followed by the United States. Surprisingly, France is more industrialized than Germany, though the respective figures reflect oversized government employment in France and postwar chaos in Germany. The Soviet Union shows up as the least industrialized great power.

One of the most consequential industrial innovations of the last fifteen years is the introduction and spread of the continuous strip mill for making flat steel products. American companies pushed this great invention and, in the words of a present study, used its lower costs "as a lever to raise production, consumption and thus the standard of living to new levels." [2] Europe has now eleven of these huge and complicated installations in various stages of completion. Seven of them are now in production. In the United States 65 per cent of all flat products—24 million tons out of a total of 37 million—

[2] United Nations, Industry Division, Economic Commission for Europe, *The European Steel Industry and the Wide-strip Mill: A Study of Production and Consumption Trends in Flat Products*, Geneva, 1953, p. 8.

TABLE 17. NATIONAL INCOMES IN CURRENT DOLLARS *

Nation	Billions of dollars	Index
United States (1948).......	$223.5	248
Soviet Union (1948— hypothetical estimate) †..	60.0	66
United Kingdom (1947)....	35.2	39
France (1946).............	21.2	24
West Germany (1948–1949).	19.2	21
Japan (1944)..............	18.1	20
India (1942)..............	10.3	11
Canada (1946)............	9.5	10
China (1936)..............	8	9
Italy (1936)..............	6.2	7
Poland (1946).............	0.9	1

* Figures are based on United Nations Secretariat Statistical Office, *National Income Statistics of Various Countries, 1938–1947*, Lake Success, 1948, pp. 123–129. The reader is warned against using these figures as anything more than approximations to global orders of magnitude. Statistical methods in the various countries are different; hence results are not strictly comparable. Calculating foreign currencies in dollars is open to many objections, including the fact that exchange rates are variable and that comparisons between different types of economic systems and price formations may be relatively meaningless. Estimates from pre–World War II years in the above table have not been adjusted because they give a more reliable picture of China's and Italy's productivity than postwar figures. On the other hand, the figure for India may understate that country's postwar strength. The German figure definitely understates the productivity of that country, which at that time had not yet recovered from war, production ceilings, dismantling, occupation, and partition.

† The accurate determination of the Russian national income is impossible. Since for this discussion rough figures are sufficient, there is no point in writing a dissertation on the errors of available estimates. The figure given here is based on (1) Jasny's 1948 estimate of Russian agricultural, industrial, and construction output; (2) Jasny's estimate of transportation, trade, and "other" activities; (3) Wyler's dollar estimate of 1940 adjusted to 1948 according to the Russian index; (4) adjustment of Wyler's figure to allow for repaired war damage. The figure given here is the mean of the two estimates. See Naum Jasny, *The Soviet Economy during the Plan Era*, Stanford, Calif., Stanford University Press, 1951, pp. 7, 17, 36.

were produced, in 1952, in wide-strip mills. In Russia, only three strip mills with a capacity of 3–4 million tons are reported to have been completed, the Novomoskvosk Steel Works and the Zaparozhstal Works in the Dnieper Basin and the Kuibyshev Metallurgical Works.[3] Just what the continuous strip mill —one particular technological improvement in one industry—means to a nation's economy is shown by Table 19.

The teamwork of scientists and engineers and the courage and ingenuity of entrepreneurs stand for much in this particular achievement of America's per-

[3] *Izvestia*, Jan. 23, 1953.

TABLE 18. NONAGRICULTURAL LABOR FORCE

Country	Millions	Per cent of total population
United States (1948)........	51.4	35
Soviet Union (1948).........	36.0 *	19
India (1947)...............	30.0 *	7
United Kingdom (1948).....	19.0	38
Japan (1947)...............	16.0	20
West Germany (1946).......	13.6	28
France (1946)..............	13.0	32
Italy (1936)................	9.9	22
Canada (1946).............	3.5	27
Poland (1947).............	3.0	12
China....................	Unknown	Unknown

* Approximate.

TABLE 19. WAGE SCALES PER MAN-HOUR AND PRICES OF STEEL SHEETS

(In U.S. dollars)

Nation	Wage scale per man-hour (1951)*	Price of sheets per ton (July, 1952)
United States.......	$2.20	$117
Belgium............	0.65	143
France.............	0.63	136
West Germany......	0.62	142
United Kingdom †...	0.59	110

* Economic Commission for Europe, *Economic Survey of Europe since the War*, Geneva, 1953, Table 79, p. 228.

† British sheet prices were under United States levels with $110 a ton. But in contrast to the American workingman's $2.20 wage package the British mill hand got only 59 cents.

manent technological revolution. The story of the continuous strip mill illustrates to what extent the United States has overtaken, in the race of productivity and rising standards of living, the older industrial nations and has maintained its technological lead over the Soviet Union.

Comparing national incomes with nonagricultural labor forces, we obtain the indicators of productivity shown in Table 20. Not surprisingly, these fig-

TABLE 20. NATIONAL INCOME: NONAGRICULTURAL LABOR FORCE

(Hypothetical productivity of operatives and white-collar workers)

Nation	Per capita annual income	Index
United States (1948)	$4,350	14.5
Canada (1948)	2,700	9.0
United Kingdom (1948)	1,860	6.2
Soviet Union (1948)	1,665	5.5
France (1946)	1,630	5.4
West Germany (1946)	1,410	4.7
Japan (1947)	1,130	3.8
Italy (1936)	630	2.1
India (1947)	343	1.1
Poland (1947)	300	1.0

ures show a few anomalies. French productivity probably was high on account of American help, while the German figure was low because of production and trade ceilings. The relatively high Russian figure might be explained by a probable exaggeration of the Russian national income. The relatively low British figure may reflect the obsolescence of the British industrial plant. Japan's high performance reflects, at least in part, the undetermined contributions of Manchuria. But otherwise these figures are in accord with the prima-facie impression derived from the analysis of the technological performance of the various countries. It appears that, while the Soviet Union still is far behind North American technology, it has reached, or is about to reach, the level of the highest Continental technological performance—though Germany again may be pulling ahead.

Another way to measure "technology" would be to count the patents which are granted by the various nations. Unfortunately patent laws and procedures differ so widely that no common standard can be applied. Moreover, available data are, to say the least, fragmentary.

Modern industry is based on about 400 fundamental inventions. According to the compilation of the *World Almanac* (1953), a compilation which goes back to the times of Kepler and Galileo, inventiveness was distributed as shown in Table 21. According to this table, Italy ranks high on the list, because it is the cradle of modern science. Czechoslovakia now enters the ranks as an Eastern European nation not previously listed; Brazil now joins the non-European countries. But Russia's contribution still remains negligible. Four nations—the United States, the United Kingdom, Germany, and France—account for 90 per cent of all basic inventions. The list is marred by inaccuracies, inasmuch as some of the American inventors are of German and—

TABLE 21. MOST IMPORTANT SCIENTIFIC DISCOVERIES AND INVENTIONS, 1593 TO 1952

United States	205	Russia	2
United Kingdom	73	Spain	1
Germany	47	Brazil	1
France	33	Switzerland	1
Italy	15	Canada	1
Austria	7	Poland	1
Sweden	4	Denmark	1
Belgium	3	Czechoslovakia	1
Holland	3		

in one or two cases—of Russian origin. It also must be borne in mind that the most important inventions on which civilization is based, such as the fire, the wheel, writing, and mathematics, were made by peoples long since buried by the sands of time, peoples who for the most part lived throughout the Middle East.

It matters little whether Russia is given, on the basis of the tenuous arguments of her propagandists, a far higher credit for technological performance— or whether even a few of the fantastic Russian claims to "firsts" are accepted as having some basis of fact; up to now the Western nations have enjoyed almost a complete monopoly in scientific discovery and technological inventiveness.

We now may attempt to summarize our findings. Taking the nonagricultural population as the base of our calculations and weighing it, on the one hand, on the basis of its average food intake, total steel production, and the kilowatt hour energy production per worker, and, on the other, on the basis of the dollar value of its output, the material and technological strengths of the great powers can be described by the index numbers in Table 22.

Naturally, these figures cannot be read to mean that, for example, the United States is 47 times stronger than Poland. These indices describe merely orders of magnitude; if another statistical method had been chosen, the numbers might have come out somewhat differently. They describe only the potential power available to these nations within their own territory, but not the strength which they can bring to bear on distant battlefields. The figures do suggest, however, that even without allowing for atomic factors, there was, in the post World War II period, only *one superpower,* the United States. Russia and Britain were great powers; West Germany, France, Japan, China, Canada, and India were medium powers; Belgium, Italy, and Poland were the largest of the small nations.[4]

[4] The figures for Poland reflect some of the material strength which was formerly Germany's. Poland's geographic location deprives that country of much of its genuine potentialities. If it were located in the Balkans or in Scandinavia, its true power would be more impressive. Despite their relatively small total manpower, Canada and Belgium show up as extraordinarily strong.

TABLE 22. MATERIAL AND TECHNOLOGICAL STRENGTH INDEX OF GREAT POWERS

(Approximately 1948)

United States	47
U.S.S.R.*	14
United Kingdom	10.6
Western Germany *	6.2
France	5.2
Japan	3.8
China	2.6
Canada	2.4
India	2.3
Belgium	2.2
Italy	1.9
Poland	1

* At the present time, the strength of these countries probably is significantly greater.

CONDITIONS OF TECHNOLOGICAL PROGRESS

Technology does not depend exclusively on intellectual ingenuity and on the ability to discover new scientific concepts. These intellectual propensities are not necessarily, and certainly not exclusively, the result of specific biological or even cultural heredity. They are to a large extent functions of social conditions, among which education plays a primary role. Without going into elaborate statistics, it can be said that the educational standards as well as the numbers of academic degrees have been increasing in the United States, both absolutely and relatively, while in Europe they have been more or less stationary. Educational standards improved in some of the Latin American and Asiatic countries. In Eastern Europe, the educated classes have suffered terrible losses, and large numbers of the educated have migrated to the West. Statistically, educational standards in the Soviet Union have been ameliorated; the numbers of academic institutions and students have increased greatly. On the other hand, there is reason to question the qualitative standards of Soviet education and, in particular, the efficacy of an educational process geared to nonscientific basic assumptions. Nevertheless, the drawing of a larger segment of the population into academic pursuits is bound to increase scientific performance of a nation.

The growth of education everywhere tends to accelerate technological progress. It is bound to benefit those countries most where there is already a basis of literacy but where education was heretofore restricted to a few privileged groups. Large-scale migrations of the educated classes tend, however, to "export" educational assets to other areas. Since approximately 1933 the "brain reserve" of continental Europe has been depleted to the advantage of the United States and other non-European countries, although this stock may be replenished in time. (During the First World War there was a considerable and permanent depletion due to war losses, especially in France.) The Soviet

Union profited from a small and partly compulsory immigration of German, Czech, Hungarian, and Polish scientists, particularly after 1945, but has been losing a large portion of its educated classes since 1917. Hence the enlargement of educational facilities in the Soviet Union is not a net gain. It is partly a compensation for a huge deficit. Moreover, the gain may not be so great as Soviet propaganda claims.[5]

Under the impact of modern industry, the role of the individual inventor has declined in favor of the research group and the laboratory. For example, in 1948, the du Pont Corporation employed, at a cost of 35 million dollars, 2,000 scientists in its laboratories. In the same year, du Pont paid out 15 million dollars for the purchase of patents. Developments such as guided missiles or atomic weapons are the result of collective research, although one should guard against underrating the continued function of the "one-man team" or the scientific genius; atomic energy would not have been developed but for the highly individualistic efforts of about a dozen scientists working independently in different countries.

Collective research and large laboratories are indispensable in order to make possible the transformation of a theoretical concept into its practical application. This means that relatively large numbers of highly qualified personnel, huge sums of capital, and fair quantities of materials, including costly and rare ones, must be withdrawn from current production. After an invention has been made, costly development work must be undertaken to prepare it for industrial production. It is true that the research investment in the atomic bomb which ran into several hundred million dollars (the total investment for the first atomic bomb was about 2 billion dollars) may be considered as particularly high, and that the vast initial outlay might not have been made had it not been called for by an overriding military necessity. However, important new inventions have always required bold investments. The basic investment, in 1780, for Watt's steam engine was about 40,000 pounds, which, in terms of purchasing power and available capital resources, is not far below the staggering costs of developing the revolutionary devices of modern technology.

A great deal of research and development is required in correlated fields; in order to be usable, end products should not exceed a certain size and should be cheap. Materials must be used which are obtainable easily. Protection against early wear and frequent breakdowns must be given. Safety in the

---

[5] Jasny, *op. cit.*, pp. 80*ff.* The funds spent by the Soviet Union on "education" probably include vast outlays for political propaganda. In 1948, the outlay for education *and* health was 75 billion rubles. Allocating half of this sum for health and allowing 20 per cent of the rest for propaganda, the educational expenditure may be estimated at 30 billion rubles, or 6–10 billion dollars. The United States was then spending about 6.2 billion dollars on education (elementary and higher, not counting industrial research) which, corrected to the Russian population figure, would be the equivalent of 8.2 billion dollars. To this must be added, in the United States, an expenditure of about 6 billion dollars for printing and publishing, an item probably included in the Soviet educational budget.

manufacturing processes and in the employment of the end product must be provided. The by-products which accrue in fabrication should be exploitable commercially. More often than not, the emergence of new commodities requires reorganization in the field of industrial management. There may arise needs for labor-training programs, improvement of working conditions, measures for coping with "technological" unemployment, rearrangement of production lines, and development of new distribution methods.

Thus it appears that technological progress in itself is a commodity, an end product, of large industries. Only a strong nation endowed with large industries can set aside the manpower, raw materials, capital, and organization which modern research and development require. The basic invention still may be made on a university campus or by a scientific hermit, but it will not be useful unless large resources are brought to bear. Nowadays, scientific research and its practical application are themselves Big Business.

There are exceptions from the rule, for the human mind remains the greatest single technological resource. A small nation may specialize in one particular line of technology and may succeed in almost monopolizing progress in the field of its specialization. Yet the over-all rule still stands: the large industrial nations are placed most favorably for accomplishing technological advances. This means that, despite a historically poor showing, Russia must be given credit for a large technological capability. It also means that non-European nations will become technologically significant if and when their industry has grown to maturity. By the same token, Western European countries whose industries now stagnate will experience difficulties in maintaining their technological status despite their superior historical accomplishments.[6]

On the other side of the ledger, it must be remembered that technological achievement does not remain a national possession, let alone a national

---

[6] That mere bigness of industry does not by itself provide technological superiority may be seen from this consideration: while mass production allows a sizable drop in production costs, relatively cheap output can be achieved with small series. Based on various commodities, the following magnitudes of cost reduction may be considered as typical:

COST REDUCTIONS IN MASS FABRICATIONS, PER CENT

Nonrepetitive single manufacture	100
Repetitive single manufacture	55
Serial production in threes	39
Serial production in tens	30
Serial production in fifteens	28
Serial production in thirties	27
Serial production in sixties	26
Continuous serial production with modifications	23
Continuous serial production	21

It appears therefore that the bigness of the American market is not a sufficient explanation of the technological performance of the American industry as compared with Continental industries. More than anything else, it is the result of technological planning on a broad front, including production and distribution management. See Walter G. Waffenschmidt, *Technik und Wirtschaft der Gegenwart*, Berlin, Springer, 1952, p. 157.

monopoly. A country may pioneer in technological improvements and for a while gain economic and military advantages. It may try, through secrecy and other means, to lengthen this period of technological predominance. Yet sooner or later, through trade, war, or espionage, the new commodity will become known to the competitor. The latter will then be in a position to build a replica which may neither be an exact copy nor achieve the performance of the original, but which will render approximately the same services and which, for that matter, may be a *superior* product.

Superiority in technology does not by itself give the United States a safe margin of security. Historically, the Soviet Union, a technological parasite, has sponged on the inventiveness of other nations and has developed great skills in adapting foreign inventions to its own uses. For example, its World War II tanks were combinations of German, French, British, and American tank designs and proved superior to the tanks of any of these nations. Parasitic technology is an effective way to economize resources and yet to achieve high military capabilities. This method merely requires that the technological parasite be able to afford the time lag between the making of inventions in foreign countries and the redesigning and production of the replica. If war occurs before the start of a *new* technological cycle, the technological inventor may be armed with superior weapons but the weapons of the technological parasite still would be in the same performance class. If, however, war occurs at a time when the technological inventor has entered into a new technological phase, while the parasite still remains within the preceding cycle, the latter would have to fight at a disadvantage.

All in all, while the technological superiority of the United States and its allies is the pillar of their strength, the technological capability of the Soviet Union must be assessed as fairly high. At the same time, some weaknesses in the American technological performance should not be overlooked, including the inadequacy of cooperation with European scientists and inventors. In so far as the rest of the world is concerned, it is still critically dependent on Western technology. However, this should not blind us to the fact that, nowadays, most nations—except the most primitive—can build automobiles, guns, and even airplanes. The Chinese and Indo-Chinese guerrillas contrived to fashion by hand, in the jungle and in rock caves, effective weapons, employing primitive tools and captured parts.

What then, in summary, is the power significance of industrial and technological potentials?

It is one thing to evaluate the economic strength of a nation in relation to its peacetime pursuits. It is another to equate economic strength with warmaking ability. The warmaking capacity of a nation does not depend uniquely on manpower and on economic and technological output factors, but in part on geographic position, including forward bases, administrative efficiency, military organization and strength-in-being, alliances, strategy and tactics, and weapons systems. It would be a grave mistake to seek to evaluate the military strength of nations on the basis of peacetime statistics alone. It is less important to know what is the output of a nation on D Day *minus* 2 months than what it will be on D Day *plus* 3 months. By means of atomic warfare, the attacker may secure such a considerable initial advantage and reduce his opponent's economic production so effectively that the war potential of the latter never will come into play. If so, military forces-*in-being* become the decisive factor. If both sides reduce or destroy each other's economic capability without being able to end the struggle, the significant question would be, which nation possesses a greater *ability to recuperate,* economically, militarily, and morally, from atomic destruction? War potentials in the conventional sense were of extreme importance in conflicts in which the *last* battle was decisive. In an atomic war the *first* battle may decide the outcome of the struggle. Under modern conditions, therefore, a nation truly "possesses" its own war potential only if it is able to protect it against devastating atomic blows. A nation without adequate forces-in-being holds a war potential only in theory. In practice, it is powerless.

BIBLIOGRAPHY

Baker, John R.: *Science and the Planned State,* New York, Macmillan, 1945.

Bush, Vannevar: *Modern Arms and Free Men,* New York, Simon and Schuster, 1949.

Christman, Ruth C. (ed.): *Soviet Science, A Symposium,* Washington, American Association for the Advancement of Science, 1952.

Conference on Industrial Research: *Proceedings,* Vol. 1, 1950, King's Crown Press, Columbia University, 1951.

Edwards, Ronald S.: *Cooperative Industrial Research: A Study of the Economic Aspects of the Research Associations, Grant-aided by the Department of Scientific and Industrial Research,* London, Pitman, 1950.

Great Britain, Department of Scientific and Industrial Research: *Report for the Year 1950–1951,* London, H.M. Stationery Office, 1952.

Hamilton, R. T., and R. Strausz-Hupé: "International Technological Progress," *American Journal of Economics and Sociology,* Vol. 11, No. 2.

Hertz, David B.: *The Theory and Practice of Industrial Research,* New York, McGraw-Hill, 1950.

Hill, Douglas: *Cooperative Research in Industry,* London, Hutchinson, 1947.

Industrial Research, London, Todd Pub. Co., Ltd., annual.

Little, Arthur D., Inc.: *Management of Industrial Research: A Selected and Annotated Bibliography,* Cambridge, Mass., 1950.

Manchester Joint Research Council: *Operational Research, Its Application to Peace-time Industry,* Manchester, England, 1950.

Mees, Charles E. K., and John A. Leermakers: *The Organization of Industrial Scientific Research,* 2d ed., New York, McGraw-Hill, 1950.

"Thought Control in the Soviet Union," Part I, "The Educational System," Part II, "Science and Scholarship," *U.S. Department of State Bulletin,* Nov. 5 and 26, 1951.

United Nations Educational, Scientific and Cultural Organization: *The Field Scientific Liaison Work of Unesco* (UNESCO publication 361), Paris, no date.

Part Three

THE ART OF THE POSSIBLE

Chapter 9

THE GREAT ISSUES OF FOREIGN POLICY

In addition to regular duties and routine responsibilities, the makers of foreign policy are confronted by crucial, ever-recurring issues. These issues transcend in scope most technical questions and strategic decisions. Attitudes to these issues are basic determinants of over-all policy. All statesmen must take a stand on tradition, compromise, war, law, and ethics.

TRADITIONS OF FOREIGN POLICY

How constant is the foreign policy of nations? The notion sometimes is put forth that foreign policy follows a straight unwavering course. In many cases this is indeed true. The Monroe Doctrine, for example, has been a constant factor in American foreign policy since 1823. For centuries, French foreign policy was shaped by the overriding concern with the defense of the northeastern and eastern borders of France against Germany and the conclusion of countervailing alliances with nations in eastern, southeastern, and northern Europe. Italian foreign policy is less easily defined in geographic terms, but in general the Italians attempted to remain aloof from European conflicts in their initial stages and then side with the winner. Imperial Germany's foreign policy for a long time was characterized by close cooperation with Austria, the other major Germanic power, and with Russia, the other major autocratic power. Britain's outstandingly successful foreign policy was based on four propositions: (1) that no major power should be allowed to control the Channel ports and the Netherlands; (2) that there should be a balance of power in Europe, that hence no one Continental power should be allowed to become predominant, and that, if one nation grew too strong, Britain should intervene against it on the side of the weaker powers; (3) that Britain should expand her trade, establish possessions in underdeveloped areas, guard the "lifelines" joining motherland and possessions, and, hence, be the predominant seapower of the world; and (4) that British policies should be in accord with the aspirations of mankind and not oppose the basic political trends of the times.

These traditions often go beyond specific techniques such as countervailing alliances and become identified with specific objectives. During the first half of the 19th century the United States strove for a geographic objective assigned to it by "manifest destiny," the establishment of one dominion from the Atlantic to the Pacific. "Manifest destiny," if interpreted in an uncompromising spirit, could have meant the establishment of one single power in North America, i.e., the absorption of Canada into the United States, but this was not within the tradition. Throughout centuries the policy of Russia was motivated by the idea that Constantinople should be secured for Slavdom and Greek Orthodox Christianity. The quest for access to the sea and to warmwater ports has been a significant element in the political tradition of such countries as Russia, Poland, Bulgaria, Bolivia, and Abyssinia. Similarly many countries are concerned about vital communication routes such as the Straits of Gibraltar, the Dardanelles, the Alpine passes, key river crossings, and, in modern times, oil concessions.

A closer look shows, however, that these traditions are far less firmly grounded than people are prone to believe. The French tradition of countervailing alliances with eastern European nations made sense only if France was threatened by Germany. If the threat came from Britain, as it did during the Middle Ages, or from Spain, as it did in the 16th and 17th centuries, the protection of the eastern frontiers and an alliance with a nation situated to the east of Germany were of little use. Even if Germany was a competitor, countervailing alliances did not necessarily offer France the best protection. Napoleon I, following the medieval tradition of interposing a "Middle Empire"—a 19th-century version of Burgundy—between the French and German domain, created the *Rheinbund*, a confederation of small west German states. Napoleon III sought the friendship of Prussia and helped to forge German unity. When he came into conflict with Prussia Napoleon III tried, unsuccessfully, for an alliance with Italy and Austria. During the Hitler era some French politicians attempted to appease Germany, in the hope that the Nazis might turn against the East rather than the West.

Germany's traditional policy of keeping on good terms with Russia was broken in both world wars, with sorry results. It is true that Germany was caught in the pincers of France's countervailing alliances, but the more fundamental reason was that the "tradition" of Russo-German friendship lasted only as long as the domestic policies of both countries were alike. When in 1912 the Social Democrats became the strongest party in Germany, a continuing friendship with autocratic Russia had become impossible. After 1918, some of the ruling parties of the democratic Weimar Republic opposed cooperation with Bolshevik Russia though the latter, a defeated "have-not" and "outcast" nation, was Germany's willing would-be partner.

Britain's traditional policy of denying the control of the Channel ports to any major Continental power certainly was reduced to inconsequential folklore by the simple fact that France has been in possession of most of these ports for more than 400 years. The balance of power policy occasionally was applied in such a way that Britain helped the stronger rather than the weaker power. While Britain kept her policy attuned to the demands of the liberal conscience, she did not hesitate to oppose the French Revolution, to back— at least temporarily—all kinds of antiliberal regimes, and to drag her feet with respect to a European federation.

In so far as Russia's traditional quest for Constantinople is concerned, it is surely remarkable that this goal has remained unattained for more than 600 years.

The Monroe Doctrine, hallowed tradition of United States foreign policy, has remained in force, but its meaning has been changed. It was enunciated as the defensive policy of a small nation whose very existence was an anathema to the great autocratic powers of the Old World. But what is its meaning in a period when no European or Asiatic nation has the power to establish itself in the Western Hemisphere and when the United States, now the leading conservative power, maintains more than one-half of its air and naval bases in overseas territories?

The tradition of foreign policy usually is a product of geographic and political conditions. As long as these conditions do not change, tradition retains its hold on the minds of statesmen and peoples. In the pre-air age, island powers, like Britain, the United States, and Japan, could be threatened only from the sea; hence naval power was necessarily their first-line defense. Similarly, Russia could be threatened most effectively by amphibious attack, hence she was always determined to deny the Dardanelles as well as the Baltic and White Sea approaches to hostile powers.

Yet geography and politics do change. Whenever they do, tradition must yield to the logic of fact. Air power has superseded naval power. For the French, the source of aggression, a political factor, has moved from London to Madrid, from Madrid to Vienna and Berlin, and then from Central Europe to Moscow. The geography of alliances had to be adapted to this migration of the political threat. The geographic traditions of a foreign policy may increasingly be at odds with political and social traditions. Thus, geography may demand the conclusion of a countervailing alliance with a nation different in social and political outlook. Often, geography wins out. French history supplies numerous examples of the mighty pull exerted by strategic geography against ideological affinity: the alliances of Francis I with the Turkish Sultan; the alliance of Cardinal Richelieu with Sweden, then the chief Protestant power; and the alliance of republican France with autocratic Russia. Such alliances have proved useful; they tend to be short-lived. Often politics primes geography, as shown by the failure of the Franco-Russian alliance of 1935 and by the German-Italian alliance, disastrous for both partners, during World War II. Geography may yield to ideology, as shown by the vagaries of 19th-century British-Turkish relations, Franco-Italian relations before 1940, and the attitude of the United States in both world wars. If the United States had joined Germany, the two nations could have divided the world between them. Had American foreign policy been purely geography-oriented *and* could the United States have turned itself into an autocratic state, then a German alliance would indeed have been the most logical policy. This "logical" policy would have destroyed American democracy and thus the basis of American power. The traditional cooperation between Britain and the United States, which is based almost exclusively on political, social, and cultural traditions and hardly on any geographic "necessity," has proved highly beneficial to both partners.

Countries cherish and perpetuate traditions in the field of foreign-policy techniques. Throughout centuries, France, homeland of Cartesian thought, has shown herself eager to conclude *formal* military alliances. The British have shown marked preference for freedom of action, although in some cases, such as the Anglo-Japanese alliance of 1902, they did not hesitate to undertake firm commitments. The United States has shied away from military alliances and considered itself even during the First World War to be only an "associated" rather than an "allied" power of the Triple Entente. Generations of American statesmen placed their hopes mainly on the efficacy of trade agreements and moral suasion and eschewed the example of other nations who inclined traditionally to seek solutions "by the sword."

These traditional differences extend into the sphere of colonial relations. The English-speaking peoples abhor uniform patterns and incline to cultural and racial segregation. Among the Latin powers, there is a tendency to impose relatively uniform patterns of colonial rule, but at the same time to allow full cultural assimilation and racial as well as social intermingling.

Finally, there are the traditional differentiations between predominantly friendly and predominantly hostile powers. There are "hereditary enemies" and perennial friends, nations who can be trusted and nations whose actions are always suspect, as well as nations with whom one must trade, regardless of political sympathies, and others with whom one must not trade because they are apt to take unfair advantage or, simply, will not pay their bills. Quite often these economic "traditions" are based on fancy rather than fact. For example, Germany looked to Eastern Europe as the "natural market" for her trade, when actually most of Germany's trade was done with Western Europe and the Americas. The United States often exaggerated the importance of China as against Europe, and, after 1945, favored Europe at the expense of Latin America.

The roots of foreign-policy traditions are deep. In the first place, there is generally a good reason why a certain attitude or act—a response to a specific situation—is being endowed by successive generations with the authority of a tradition. A foreign-policy tradition was rarely, if ever, the result of an intellectual exercise in political ideas, but almost always was forced upon its heirs by circumstances. France did not hit on the device of countervailing alliances by rigorous argument such as the inferences which led Pascal to discover his philosophical insights. Time and again, France, when she was threatened from beyond the Rhine, was able to find support in Eastern Europe. If a situation tends to repeat itself, and if, moreover, departures from an established tradition frequently lead to disaster (such as France suffered each time she failed to conclude countervailing alliances), it is not too farfetched to deduce that such traditions correspond to a country's fundamental interests.

Secondly, once the tradition has become accepted, a great deal of national life is oriented to support it. Once tradition hallows friendship with another nation, statesmen and their propagandists will seek to reinforce political and military attraction by strengthening economic and cultural ties. Political, trade, and cultural associations, chambers of commerce, literary clubs, tourist agencies, and exchange professors will do their best to extol and cement that particular friendship. If, on the other hand, hostility toward another nation becomes the accepted norm, a comparable effort goes into alerting one's own country against this danger and persuading one's countrymen that they should avoid those economic and cultural contacts which, in case of conflict, might prove harmful.

Thirdly, as time goes on, the thought pattern of policy makers, political theorists, and the man in the street increasingly conforms to the given tradition. Anyone criticizing it risks himself severe criticism, and indeed those who have made light of it often can be shown to have been in the service of a hostile power or to have pursued objectives incompatible with the national interest.

Despite the imposing strength of political traditions, however, there usually comes the time when policies must be reviewed and modified. Circumstances which brought the tradition to life no longer exist; hence the tradition has become an obstacle to effective foreign policy. For example, toward the end of the 19th century, one French political faction advocated an aggressive colonial policy. France had secured Indo-China and large parts of Africa. The colonial enthusiasts wanted to prevent Britain from joining her possessions in North and South Africa and constructing a railroad which would have linked Capetown with Cairo. They dreamed of creating for France a contiguous empire reaching from the western to the eastern coasts of Africa. They proposed to cut straight across Britain's line of colonial expansion. Their policy was virulently anti-British and drew its domestic support from the secular anti-British tradition of French foreign policy. The so-called Fashoda incident (1898) brought Britain and France face to face on the upper reaches of the Nile and to the verge of armed conflict. When the British threatened war, the French gave in. The traditional anti-British policy, then represented by Gabriel Hanotaux, foreign minister and well-known historian, was abandoned and replaced by a policy designed to win British friendship. The new policy was masterminded by Théophile Delcassé who, incidentally, was subjected to vicious personal attacks for his presumed lack of respect toward a venerable tradition. The old thought pattern, however, remained imbedded in the minds of many Frenchmen. Resentment toward Britain has kept on rankling among Frenchmen ever since. Occasionally, as, for example, in 1940 and 1941, old grudges burst forth in open and violent reactions.

France did manage to shake off the grip of an outworn tradition, especially when confronted by issues which mattered vitally. The Germans were not so sensible. Weimar Germany (1918–1933) was unable to break with the traditional pro-Russian orientation which, given Germany's need for reconciling the West, was most injudicious, and could therefore not reestablish intimate and friendly relations with the Western countries. At the same time, Germany's democratic government could not go through with plans for close cooperation with Russia. Thus the Weimar Republic, led by vacillating though well-intentioned men, embarked upon that ambiguous diplomacy which neither gained the respect of the Western democracies nor forged a firm alliance with the Soviet Union. Incidentally, it was this diplomatic schizophrenia which contributed, at least in part, to the fall of German democracy and the rise of Hitler.

One becomes as much attached to one's old enemies as to one's old friends. The removal of a familiar threat may demoralize a nation even more effectively than the rise of a new one. More important still, a traditional foe supplies a nation with emotional outlets into which domestic frustrations can be channeled, and, in certain cases, with a welcome diversion from such tedious economic problems as, for example, how to balance the budget. This peculiar dilemma is illustrated aptly by the behavior of France after World War II. It is as if not a few French politicians felt a sense of bereavement at losing Germany as a traditional foe and of irritation at winning her as an ally. After 1945, France was confronted with the need of scrapping the bitterest of her old enmities, namely, that against Germany. The process proved difficult. The French collective mind seemed incapable of realizing that the threat to French security was coming from Russia, while Germany was rallying, *de facto,* to the defense of the West and thus by geographic necessity, though not by inclination, to the defense of France. Yet in times past the French were quite capable of reacting smartly to a shift in the locus of aggression. When in the 18th century Austria ceased to be a threat to French security while Prussia emerged as a dangerous aggressor, France dismantled her old diplomatic system designed to keep Austria in check, and substituted for it an alliance with Austria, the erstwhile hereditary enemy. Yet popular resentment about this *renversement des alliances* was so strong that it was a contributory factor to the outbreak of the French Revolution.

In the case of Britain, the circumstances favoring the traditional balance of power policy gave way, after World War II, to a situation wherein it was to Britain's interest to strengthen the powers of Western Europe collectively, not only as a substitute for the time-honored British policy of neutralizing the Channel ports, but also as a defense against possible threats from the Eurasian heartland. In the United States, the conditions which, up to the close of the 19th century, had made a policy of isolation practical and advisable, changed so much that, in the 20th century, a diametrically opposite policy was inaugurated. The policy of isolation had been adopted by the end of the 18th century. How could this policy remain applicable at a time when this country had become both an Atlantic and a Pacific power, had emerged as the most populous Western nation, possessed the strongest industrial structure in the world, enjoyed the highest standard of living, and could be threatened effectively by devastating, long-range weapons? Still, the tradition lives on in American psychological reactions.

Abandonment of traditional policies may be required by technological and military changes, as well as by changes in political and social structures. For example, Russia was unable to embark on a dynamic policy in Asia before she extended her railroad communications into Siberia. Conversely, an island empire, like the British or Japanese, could be established and held only in a period when sea communications were the superior form of transport. As to social and political changes, suffice it to recall that the transformation of the multinational Ottoman Empire into nationalist Turkey required a complete revamping of Turkish policies, including the transfer of the capital from Constantinople to Ankara.

The termination of traditional policy is one of the most difficult operations of statesmanship. A new policy cannot be launched except for compelling reasons. But if these reasons exist, tradition must be set aside lest national security be jeopardized critically. In autocratic regimes, change in policy requires simply an act by the Cabinet, followed by indoctrination of the public and sometimes by changes in personnel. Often these changes are made initially through secret treaties in order not to hurt the susceptibilities of the population too brutally; but, ultimately, the truth must out. In democratically governed nations changes of foreign-policy traditions are much more difficult to carry through. Usually they require a considerable time and a gradual adjustment of the popular mind. A democracy may find it as impossible to proceed without secret understandings and tactics of camouflage as does an autocracy: there is a time lag before public opinion in a democratic country adjusts itself to new conditions. Moreover, changes of traditional policy are tied to domestic struggles inasmuch as both the traditional and new policies enjoy strong partisan support. In order to change policy, a democracy usually must change its government.

Changes in traditional policy may be against the best interests of the nation. In a series of *coups d'état* through assassination, Japan changed its traditional pro-British policy into an alliance with Germany; the experiment hardly can be considered to have been a success. Similarly, the change of traditional Russian foreign policy from one of increasing regional power in northern Asia and, perhaps, in the Balkans, and maintaining close friendship with major Western nations, into a policy aiming at world domination certainly contradicts Russian national interests. Paradoxically, the willful change of traditional policy which often is carried out in an atmosphere of enthusiasm and national exuberance [1] may be accomplished more easily than a logical—and perhaps painful—change necessitated by a new set of circumstances.

Policies supported by traditions and reason are firm, while policies shaped by tradition at the neglect of reason tend to be weak, at least initially. Nontraditional, irrational policies often are successful for short periods. Most fortunate are those countries which are wedded to the tradition of rational analysis of the national interest. This is another way of saying that statesmanship should prevent any tradition, however justified it may be at certain times and under certain circumstances, from becoming ossified, and that, while it should shun erratic and frequent change, it must persevere in a broad policy which allows ample room for modification and flexible adjustment.

COMPROMISE

Compromise is an essential ingredient of politics.[2] It is perhaps no exaggeration to say that it is the political method par excellence. Yet little thinking is done about the matter. It is not generally recognized that the art of making compromises, or lack of skill in this art, can have very far-reaching consequences. Both uncompromising zeal and supine readiness to enter into compromises can jeopardize the security of the state. The former may lead into unnecessary conflicts; the latter, to the loss of vital positions.

The importance of political compromise derives from the very nature of politics. In the first place, not all issues to be solved by political means admit of clear-cut scientific solutions. In biology, the alternative is either a boy or a girl, but political questions rarely display this disarming simplicity. Let us suppose that a frontier incident is to be settled, that it has been established that the soldiers of state A fired first at the soldiers of state B, and that therefore state A is the guilty party. If, however, the soldiers of state B engaged in provocative demonstrations, the affair no longer is quite so simple. Not all issues need to be so complicated as the Danish question of which Bismarck allegedly said that only three men understood it: one who

[1] Jacob Burckhardt, in his *Weltgeschichtliche Betrachtungen, 1868–1871*, rev. ed., Stuttgart, Kroener, 1949, p. 172, decries *"das brilliante Narrenspiel der Hoffnung."*

[2] John Viscount Morley, *On Compromise*, 1921, rev. ed., London, Watts, 1946.

was dead, another who had forgotten all about it, and he—Bismarck—himself.

Secondly, prejudices, opinions, and beliefs tend to confuse political issues. However convinced one side may be of its rights, it hardly will succeed in convincing the other side. Most militant religions call for the forceful conversion or the extermination of the infidels, and many totalitarian countries accept the statements of their masters as the last word. Democratic peoples lean toward self-righteousness about the purity of their intentions. Yet in practice, lest conflict become interminable, radical positions—or as the French call them, *parti pris*—must be compromised and the other side must be granted concessions which are incompatible with one's own original position.

An uncompromising, radical attitude can be sustained only if there is strong support from the population. Such support may be forthcoming in a serious crisis. But history teaches that it usually occurs in the form of a reaction to unsuccessful, albeit vigorous, efforts to compromise the conflict beforehand, while refusal to compromise at all may be rewarded by lack of popular support. In the Munich crisis (1938), for example, Hitler felt that his rigid attitude deprived him of a great deal of German mass support. He recaptured this support by agreeing to what he could describe as a reasonable compromise. Similarly, the British supported their government unequivocally when in 1939 it declared war on Nazi Germany, but they hardly would have approved a preventive attack in 1933 or 1934; the failure of a long-standing policy of compromise convinced them that war was unavoidable. Such an attitude may not be reasonable or rational, but it is a fact of life with which most policy makers have to reckon. Occasionally, public restraint upon a government is beneficial. A ruling class which may be convinced of the validity of its ideology, and may be willing to go to any length to impose the blessings of its system on the rest of the world, may be held back by a populace which does not share this belief. Such an attitude has characterized the relationship between the Soviet government and the Russian people since 1917.

Thirdly, all interests of one and the same state are never compatible with each other. Two states may be united in the desire to settle one specific issue, but the advantage of one party may mean the detriment of the other. Suppose the title to a territorial possession is in doubt and the drawing of a new frontier is being negotiated. If the entire territory falls to state A, B would not feel interested in the arrangement, though its interest in avoiding conflict is as genuine as is that of A. If B is forced to accept the arrangement, it might become resentful, with the result that sooner or later the question will be reopened. In such a situation it is more advantageous to devise a settlement by which key interests of both sides are satisfied partially: each gives and loses a little.

Fourthly, complete subjugation of the other party is the implied consequence of a policy of noncompromise; if one's conditions are not acceptable and settlement cannot be postponed, these conditions must be imposed—if need be, by force, and force is usually needed. Furthermore, the other side must be prevented from sabotaging the settlement. But to do so is impossible except through an Assyrian or Morgenthau-ian settlement of ruination—which in an age of interdependence is not a sensible solution. This is why peace treaties which give the victor less than he would desire, and the vanquished more than he could expect, display a far more permanent character than radical, absolute solutions. Thus, compromise is the prerequisite of the durability of political arrangements.

Resistance against compromise usually is stubborn, especially in modern times, when broad segments of the population have become politically conscious. Modern nations are influenced by abstract ideas and, especially in times of acute conflict, fall easy prey to simplified notions which always foreshadow radical solutions. Once a struggle has been joined, the nation is unanimously agreed that it must defeat the enemy. Uncritically, it assumes that the other nation is *nothing* but an enemy, always has been bent on mischief, and always will be a deadly foe. Accordingly, the opponent must be destroyed. Victory must be final and complete. By contrast, partial victory does not seem worth the effort; concessions to the opponent smack of treason.

Outside of violent conflict, difficulties and discomforts usually are explained by one or two simple causes which are singled out as the primary sources of all evil. The unsophisticated mind concludes that these causes must be eliminated fast and radically. For instance, the management of the system of international payments is fraught with difficulties. The solution obviously must be to abolish it and to establish a system of national self-sufficiency. Many troubles are caused by governments acting with or against other governments; hence if "sovereignty" were abolished, international society would enjoy eternal peace.

The idea of gradual change or evolution is alien to this type of thinking. To make things worse, it is considered necessary that nations commit themselves to positive programs of action in which they must believe firmly. Nations tend to be adamant about such "programs," especially when they are more amply endowed with enthusiasm than with experience. The thought that gradualness and deliberate compromise may lead to the goal faster and more securely is repulsive to impatient thought cluttered with either-or concepts. In order to improve the moral stamina of a nation, governments often are forced, or believe themselves to be forced, to propagandize simple, deceptively simple, ideas. The pathos of a "holy mission," a national or revolutionary duty, an obligation to "*la terre et les morts*," keeping faith with past sacrifices and solemn promises make compromise all but impossible.[3] Rarely is an effort made to keep the political thinking of a nation on the straight and narrow path of reality and practicality, and to make it clear—if

---

[3] The Peloponnesian War which destroyed Greece resulted from inability to compromise (see Burckhardt, *op. cit.*, p. 177).

need be, *ad nauseam*—that politics cannot be practiced effectively except as the art of the possible. Under these circumstances, it is most difficult for a statesman to negotiate compromises. All too frequently, peoples accept compromises only after lengthy and exhausting struggles. They are the fruit of fatigue rather than reason.

We may have, therefore, a situation where, on the one hand, a government tries to compromise a conflict but is unable to do so because of political and public pressure. Classic cases are attempts to forestall a futile war or to terminate a war, more or less futile, before the opponent's "unconditional surrender." On the other hand, the population may not at all be interested in doing and dying for a certain policy, while the government may insist on a radical solution and play all kinds of tricks to enlist public support for its rigid attitude. The converse of this situation exists when the nation, or an influential political party, wants to effect a compromise which would be harmful to the national interest, while the government is resisting attempts to force its hand and to make ruinous concessions. Examples are the attitude of the German populace in 1918 which wanted to end the war immediately, although further resistance still was possible and probably would have led to far more favorable peace terms, and the apathy of the French masses in 1939 who really did not understand the Nazi threat and therefore saw no reason to "die for Danzig." Finally, we have the case of a government which is ready to make too many compromises, including harmful ones, while the political parties and the public are kept uninformed, do not understand the issue, or remain inert for other reasons. The example in point is the policy of the American government culminating in the agreements at Yalta and Potsdam.

Overeagerness to compromise may result from considerations of domestic politics (impending elections), underrating of one's own relative strength, a conscious policy of appeasement, lack of political purpose, demagogy, and, occasionally, even sympathy with the opponent's cause. Depending on the situation, there must be limits on a government's willingness to compromise. These limits may be territorial, economic, military, social, cultural, or ethical in character. While a government may go out of its way to prevent a struggle through compromise, it cannot always and under all circumstances shirk the struggle unless the preservation of peace at any price, even at the price of subjugation, is considered the highest value. The danger of ill-considered compromise is that important power positions are traded away without a proper *quid pro quo* and that humoring the opponent makes him ever more demanding. The danger for a nation of such a policy is that the conflict which it sought to avoid becomes inevitable and will be fought with diminished moral and material strength. The effectiveness of compromise depends, to a large degree, on cultural, political, and social structures. There must be a predisposition to compromise, or else compromise must fail. Compromises between nations whose word can be relied upon, and who are showing in their transactions a high degree of moderation, usually will redound to the benefit of all. Compromises with a radical government, strongly influenced by an aggressive ideology and unaccustomed in its domestic dealings to techniques of live-and-let-live and toleration, usually are doomed to failure. Such governments are prone to misunderstand a compromise as a partial defeat or a surrender and as a way station along the road to further concessions. They often misinterpret compromise as a sign of weakness and thus as an opportunity for aggression. Such compromises usually must be paid for heavily. It is one of the tragedies of the world that the Anglo-Saxon nations have been willing to compromise far too often on too many important points and that their motivations were misunderstood. By contrast, ideologically oriented nations, especially those of Central and Eastern Europe and Asia, have not learned the art of compromise and are as yet incapable of accepting a situation in which their demands are not fulfilled in their entirety. They tend to confuse willingness to compromise with lack of character and rigidity of attitude with heroism. Nor are they as yet able to understand that reluctance to stand fully on one's rights does not necessarily denote stupidity, weakness, or lack of resolve. To find the *juste-milieu* between too much and too little compromising is a matter of tact and political intuition.

WAR

War is the alternative to compromise. If an urgent problem cannot be settled or, if left unsolved, cannot be lived with honorably, safely, and sanely, nations have recourse to the verdict of arms.[4] The military victor imposes his solution. This solution is rarely "absolute" and undiluted by compromise, but the concessions made by the victor are far smaller than those the defeated could have obtained had he elected to negotiate rather than fight. On the other hand, the victor must pay a high price for his success, and, initially, has had to take the risk of costly failure.

War is not an act of God nor is it a "natural catastrophe." It results from a conscious decision taken by a government. Heretofore, there always were governments who acknowledged no scruples about the employment of military means. Having formulated an objective and having obtained no satisfaction from other governments, they stood forever ready to let the arms decide. It is perhaps exaggerated to say that war always has been a *routine*

---

[4] Conceivably, Britain and France could have kept on living indefinitely with the problem posed by the unscrupulous tactics and pathological and provocative rantings of Hitler. For Britain and France, some sort of uneasy truce—a lengthy Cold War—might, in the end, have proved less costly than World War II. The British and French peoples, however, were unwilling to stand (or incapable of standing) the strains imposed upon them by Nazi blackmail and terror strategy. They went to war not so much for safety and honor as for sanity. In 1939, the French took to arms with the cry *"Il faut en finir."* D. W. Brogan, *France under the Republic: The Development of Modern France 1870–1939*, New York, Harper, no date, p. 729.

technique of foreign policy. Certainly, it was a measure which governments employed frequently and which they never ceased to consider as an entirely legitimate and often unavoidable technique of international politics. Since in the 20th century there has been more fighting than in any other period of history, it must be assumed that this attitude still prevails—despite interminable protestations of pacific intentions, especially on the part of the aggressive governments. However, the advent of nuclear weapons has changed the character of war fundamentally. This change must affect the standing of war as a political technique. Wars may still occur, but it will be quite impossible to consider atomic conflict as a "routine measure."

It is true that, throughout the ages, governments of civilized nations never *admitted* that they employed war—often quite frivolously—as a routine measure. It always was *claimed* that war is the ultima ratio of politics, to be employed only where vital interests are at stake and when no other solutions prove practical. These apologetics of war were largely a verbal tribute to the idealistic and humanistic motivations of mankind and were necessitated partly by the need to placate the instinct of self-preservation of those who must do the fighting, suffering, and dying. Yet such an attitude also occasionally accorded with practical, earthy considerations. War is a doubtful business; no one can guarantee victory, and no one can foretell the cost and duration of the conflict. Even if a victory is won, war may transform the society as a whole. The changes resulting from the conflict may be so far-reaching that the government which started the war may not be in a position to end it.

Accordingly, if war entails serious social consequences—though this need *not* be true in all times or places—it should be resorted to only if there is a direct or indirect threat to the highest values of a society: national and cultural independence, the integrity of the political system, the economic safety of the society, the freedom of the individual, and the inviolability of man's natural rights. The more devastating war becomes, the more imperative is the requirement to fight *only* for the preservation of these supreme values. Minor territorial or economic disputes which in former times might have been settled by military conflict, no longer are acceptable as sufficient causes of large-scale war. Governments hardly will display the recklessness of waging atomic war unless the fundamental tenets of civilization and personal freedom (as distinguished from serfdom) will be in jeopardy. The issue clearly must be of a nature that it is preferable to die rather than to give in and "live."

If an aggressor government were acting logically, it would ask itself whether its objectives are worth a military conflict, whether these objectives are at all attainable through military means, and whether these goals cannot be reached by less sanguinary methods. The fact is that most revolutionary objectives, such as the remaking of society, cannot be attained through violent techniques, and these utopian aims definitely include the dream of limitless power. War can be a rewarding method only if it is waged for limited objectives. Modern war tends to transcend all limits. War no longer is a dependably effective method; desire and attainment tend to contradict one another.

Unfortunately, modern aggressor governments do not necessarily act rationally but are influenced by the emotional power urges of a small elite. Acceptance of the elite's program—boundless as are its ambitions—cannot be obtained by persuasion but only by force. The structure of a power-oriented political system may drive it into military conflict regardless of other considerations. *Hence war remains an ever-present danger even in the atomic age.*

This situation imposes on fundamentally peaceful governments the exacting burden of a policy designed to discourage the bellicose ambitions of would-be aggressors. Unhappily, democratic governments, or, simply, governments which do not themselves harbor projects of conquest, usually ignore the military problem and fail, except in times of acute crisis, to pay serious heed to their military security. In fact, the more they worry about economic security the less they are inclined to protect the economic and social systems as a whole. This paradoxical attitude is as much to blame for the brutality of history and the frailty of freedom as are the dreams of glory of the conquerors and aggressors.

Democratic countries indulge in the nonrational habit of gainsaying the fact that war may be the *only* solution of a given problem; of proclaiming objectives which cannot be reached except by war while assuming that the price—always an exorbitant one—of living up to one's own convictions need not be paid; and of believing that war—which is a technique of statecraft— is not compatible with the democratic code. Yet democracies go to war as often as autocracies and, occasionally, even oftener. Once involved in war, democrats feel cheated and betrayed—it should not have happened to them! Hence the erstwhile pacifists transform themselves into rabid (and pathetic) militarists fighting without restraint for an absolute victory and an atrociously harsh peace. In short, democrats have a bad conscience about war; this is why modern wars are so particularly bloody and costly—and frequent.

Both democracies and autocracies tend to mistake the basic nature of war. They are inclined to feel that war is, or should be, a *constructive* activity, the creator of a "better" world. War is supposed to eliminate oppression, help the downtrodden, establish justice, make the world "safe" for democracy (or any other system), and produce a "better peace"—ideas of the kind which the ancient Romans politely described as *flatus vocis*. In fact, war is as constructive (or destructive) as surgery. It is designed to remove a *specific* dangerous condition. The operation is as unpleasant as it is necessary. Once it is all over, the patient, provided he lives, will be neither wealthier nor happier nor healthier than before. He probably will be poorer, wiser, and weaker; but he will live, and he will be rid of the particular danger which threatened his life.

No government decides to launch upon war deliberately unless the chances of victory are great. This is particularly true of governments which aim at the increase of their power. If a country decides to fight, although its chances of success are small, it usually relies on the help of other nations or it estimates that its chances of recovery will be greater if it is defeated honorably in battle rather than conquered without resistance. *Chance* of victory should not be confused with *certainty* of victory. As a rule, aggressor governments will provoke war only if and when their immediate military superiority is such that they can defeat their opponents singly or jointly, either without interference of other more powerful nations, or so speedily that their conquest will be completed before third powers intervene. By the same token, if the chances of success are small, the aggressor government will hesitate to take the final, fateful step.

Hence the aggressor's logical course of action would be to arm secretly and far more rapidly than his chosen victims and opponents so that at a given time he will possess overwhelming *strength-in-being*. The logical action for the governments which want to avoid the war would be to arm continuously, in sufficient volume and at an adequate rate so that the day when the aggressor will have overwhelming strength-in-being never will arrive. In order to do so, peaceful governments must identify the aggressive intentions of other governments in time and take protective action without delay; they always must maintain so strong a defensive posture that the aggressor would experience great political and economic difficulties if he attempted to acquire striking power large enough to give him a sufficient chance of success.

Irrational decisions to go to war may result from the following possibilities, given here as mere illustrations: a government may overrate or underrate its chances of success; it may wrongly assess the attitude of its opponent or of third powers; it may overrate or underrate its ability to arm secretly or to catch up with the secret armaments of the opponent; it may not assess its military chances at all but go to war because of psychological, social, economic, or political pressures; or simply the ruler making the war decision may be out of his mind. Historically, the standard error is a slightly insane aggressor's overestimation of his own strength.

A government which makes the fateful decision to reduce its armaments and to entrust its security only to token forces must be very sure that there will be no threat of aggression for a long time to come. But no government can have such an assurance. It was possible for the United States to coast along with a minimum of armament at the time of its geographic isolation. But this historical exception cannot be considered a convincing precedent. For that matter, the United States usually maintained a respectable naval establishment and enjoyed, at no expense to itself, the protection afforded by the shield of Britain's mastery of the seas. No other great nation in history ever was able to reduce its armaments so drastically. The time when a defenseless America was a secure America is past.

The decision for all major powers is therefore not whether or not they must provide for their security interests but *how much* they must invest in their security and *how much* they can rely on the military help of other nations. Such a decision must be based on a calm and lucid identification of issues which indeed call for action, and on an accurate evaluation of one's capability by various actions abroad and at home, to prevent war or, if a war must be fought, to fight it at the right time, at the right place, and with the right means. Since armaments are costly, there usually arises a critical economic problem; a nation's productive potential may be insufficient to provide the necessary armaments, or a nation's weapons must be paid for by a reduction in living standards. Assuming that the armament needs were established in an objective manner, the nation of the first case would have to rely on foreign aid; the nation of the second case would have to tighten its belt. To reduce armaments to a level where they coincide with an imaginary ability to support them economically is as irrational as to pay $2,000 for an automobile but fail to pay another $150 for the tires and the battery. Depending on the risk, one has to pay a low or high insurance premium, but one cannot pay less than the full premium and still expect to be protected. To save money is sometimes an expensive luxury.

Ancient and persistent is the confusion beclouding the proper relationship between political and military leadership. Since war is a technique and not a purpose in itself and since the objectives for which a war is being fought must be defined by a political decision, it follows that political leadership must be supreme. This does not mean, however, that the military leader is simply an executor of the statesman's will. An industrial entrepreneur may have a good idea about a new product. He can ask his engineering staff to apply this idea and produce the new product, but if his "good" idea turns out to be technically impractical, there is little he can do about it. Similarly, a statesman may have clear ideas as to the policy he wants to pursue, but it does not follow that this policy is militarily practical. Hitler, for instance, wanted to invade the British Isles; but, having no amphibious equipment, the amateur strategist could not do what he wanted—and should have done in order to win the war. Xerxes ordered that the Hellespont be scourged with whips. He was not much sillier than many latter-day statesmen who entertained exaggerated notions of their powers of insight and of managing destiny.

There are two dangers which have been the bane of the ages: the politician dictating strategy, and the strategist dictating policy. Again and again, governments imposed on the military leadership the requirement of defending more territory than the military forces could hold, thus thwarting the proper conduct of the war. Often governments have demanded offensive or defensive operations when these were not feasible or were ill-advised. Frequently there has been interference with mobilization schedules, an unrealistic assessment of military requirements, and vain hopes of keeping the costs of blood and treasure down. Almost always civilian governments are reluctant to allow maximization of military effectiveness. Frequently governments denied their armed forces adequate funds in peacetime but expected immediate military success once the war broke out. The fundamental causes of such policies are that peoples fear the political soldier, the "man on horseback"—and, quite often, fear him with good reason—and harbor the mistaken idea that military power and political freedom are more or less incompatible.[5]

On the other side, there is the soldier or "militarist" who overlooks the power limitations of a nation, who ignores political problems unless they can be put in terms of victory or defeat, who is unwilling to cooperate with allied forces, who is willing to employ even the most extreme means when they are not necessary, who does not know when to stop fighting, who employs the methods of the barrack square in running a civilian economy, and who single-mindedly seeks to annihilate the opponent without paying heed to the fact that after the war the victor still has to live with the defeated. German history offers examples for both cases, political over military and military over political leadership. Bismarck overruled the military and made his decisions stick against the judgment of the general staff. Hitler was a politician who imposed military decisions which led to the destruction of his Third *Reich*. Ludendorff was a military man who strong-armed the civilian government and imposed on it policies which made a German defeat and humiliating peace inevitable.

The cliché according to which political leadership must prime military leadership misses the crucial point. Political leadership will be unsuccessful unless the military factors are taken fully into account. The statesman must have a thorough understanding of strategy, tactics, and military technology, and he must be able to grasp the military implications of his policy. Conversely, the military leader must be aware of the political implications of military action and also of necessary limitations which political considerations may impose on his freedom of action. To understand war and "its attendant rules and discipline" is the prime requisite for the statesman; [6] to understand politics, and, especially, international politics, is the prime requirement for the military commander. In addition, both statesman and commander should understand the workings of economics and sociopsychological forces.

War has its own logic. Once a security situation has become critical, military considerations may indeed prime political actions and desires. For example, the neutrality of a state may have to be violated; kowtowing to a reluctant ally may have to give way to plain and forceful speaking; people in one's own country may have to be dealt with harshly. Once open hostilities are in progress, the rules of the military art come into play. The principle of concentration must be observed even if it means temporary abandonment of territory. The principle of the offensive may ask its toll in blood, although that

---

[5] "Rome and Sparta lived armed and free through many centuries. The Swiss are heavily armed and have the greatest freedom." Niccolò Machiavelli, *The Prince,* 1513, Chap. 12.

[6] *Ibid.,* Chap. 14.

TABLE 23. WESTERN MILITARY PRINCIPLES

1. Selection and pursuit of objective	10. Offensive *
2. Unity of command	11. Indirect approach
3. Cooperation	12. Maneuver
4. Superiority of force	13. Initiative
5. Concentration of force	14. Flexibility
6. Economy of force	15. Simplicity
7. Maintenance of morale	16. Security
8. Center of gravity	17. Administration
9. Surprise	

* The principle of the defensive is nowadays without much honor. However, defensive strategies have been used effectively for the attainment of political objectives and in practically all modern campaigns were an integral part of any grand strategy leading to victory.

blood may cost the next election. Politics may have to defer to military strategy, however much it may remain the ultimate arbiter. If a strategic plan has been accepted, it is incumbent upon political leadership to support it by political action. Negotiations may serve as a cover for surprise attack, as did those initiated by the Japanese before Pearl Harbor in 1941. Diplomatic action may secure a needed base area more cheaply and conclusively than military action. Political warfare may be an integral part of the over-all strategy, as, for example, by fomenting a revolution in the enemy country.

In summary, decisions bearing on military problems may have the most far-reaching consequences of all political action. The habit of Western democracies is to ignore the problem of war until the shooting starts. War is something about which cultured folk do not talk. This negative approach is not only immature but dangerous. Most Western nations have equipped themselves with organizations designed to coordinate military with political and economic policy, a coordination function which in Stalin's Russia was handled by the Politburo and which the United States, since 1947, has intrusted to its National Security Council. Yet modern, literate, and prosperity-oriented societies have great difficulties understanding the nature of modern conflict and of war as an instrument of power. Proudly avowing their attachment to rationality, they indulge in emotional attitudes toward war. Hence Western security decisions rarely are informed by a sober understanding of the nature of war and its place within the political scheme of things. Machiavelli observed rightly: "The main foundations of all states . . . are good laws and good arms; . . . there cannot be good laws where there are not good arms."

INTERNATIONAL LAW—PACTA SUNT SERVANDA

The strands of international relations are woven into an intricate web of treaties, agreements, and conventions. Peace treaties were the first recorded solemn agreements made between peoples (3000 to 4000 B.C.), and gradually many other types of usages and agreements have come into existence. Without written or unwritten international conventions modern life would not be possible, even for countries like Nazi Germany or the Soviet Union. During the last 200 years or so, the volume of these conventions and treaties has increased greatly.[7] As far as international society is a reality, it rests upon a large body of "international law." Each frontier is the result of an agreement. International trade would not be feasible without large numbers of accepted usages, contracts, and treaties. Communication between governments would be practically impossible were it not for customs respecting the inviolability of diplomatic personnel. Contemplate treaties concerning international mail, navigation, air transportation, radio broadcasting, enforcement of criminal law, traffic in drugs, and health; neutrality agreements; nonaggression pacts; and military alliances; and it is indeed clear that the life of nations depends in large measure upon the observance of these various compacts!

However, unless words have lost their meaning, it should be apparent that these international compacts, whether they are in written form or are observed merely as time-honored usages, do not constitute *laws* in the proper sense of the word. They neither have been enacted like laws (except in rare cases) nor can be enforced like laws. A law, moreover, is an obligation which an authority imposes on itself, on subordinate authorities, or on individuals, while international "laws" apply to other authorities which are coequal in legal status and often far superior in material power. No particularly useful purpose is served by dissimulating these basic differences by semantic sleight of hand. International agreements are in the nature of *promises* and *not* of laws.

The utility of codified international understandings is so great that most international lawyers hold, and many governments assert, that treaty obligations must be fulfilled under any circumstances. Breach of faith often is described as the cardinal sin in international politics. The trouble with this theory is that international compacts cannot be compared meaningfully with private agreements, contract obligations or even promises by word of honor, and in actual fact cannot always be observed even if there were the will to live up to each stipulation of the instrument.

There scarcely is a treaty without loopholes and escape clauses. The wording of a treaty may have had a definite meaning at the time the treaty was drafted, but years later this meaning no longer may be so clear, assuming that there were not, from the very beginning, different interpretations of the text by the signatories. Clarification of the meaning of the written word through an international court would be a likely procedure, provided there are no contradictory obligations or secret amendments *in addition* to the text. Disregarding the fact that most treaties are not judiciable in this fashion, the international court at best could give an opinion; because of its lack of enforcement powers it could render judgment but could not make the sentence stick.

[7] For an exhaustive description of the network of international agreements, see Arthur Nussbaum, *A Concise History of the Law of Nations,* New York, Macmillan, 1947.

Another difficulty arises from the fact that many international contracts do not expire and are not canceled. Rather, they are allowed to lapse, with the result that they can be resurrected whenever this is expedient. In certain cases, agreements and treaties are in conflict with each other; for example, some of the signatories of the North Atlantic Treaty Organization are still bound by treaties of alliance to the Soviet Union. There are treaties which were imposed on one signatory under duress, most frequently in the case of defeat. Treaties which have been entered into freely may become obstacles to the free development of one nation, while they continue to benefit other signatories.

Nations caught in this maze of vagaries, contradictions, and downright hypocrisy have sought to regain their freedom by invoking a frankly relativistic doctrine in international law. According to this doctrine obligations must be fulfilled *only if* the situation in which they were concluded has not changed materially. A basic change of the situation invalidates treaties. This doctrine of the clause *rebus sic stantibus* has been attacked vigorously and vocally by the more enthusiastic schools of international law. In actual disputes, the validity of this clause is denied by the party which does not want to modify the treaty. The obvious argument is that, what with the incessant change of the international situation, all treaties would become practically worthless if the clause were admitted as categorically valid. The purpose of a treaty is to assume an obligation and to carry it out even against unfavorable circumstances; otherwise there would be no point in making the agreement. Acceptance of the clause *rebus sic stantibus,* it is argued, would knock out the very basis of "international law."

Suppose nation A concludes a military alliance with nation B. Suppose further that nation A is ravaged by a terrible epidemic which thins the ranks of its armed forces. It would be unable to live up to its treaty obligations regardless of the legal situation. Suppose, however, that A merely is the victim of a slight economic recession which it uses as a pretext to reduce its military forces, and that upon being called on by B to fulfill its obligations, it pleads the clause *rebus sic stantibus* on the grounds that it could not afford to maintain the armed force it promised to make available to the alliance: it would be welshing on its promise. Appeal to the clause would be abusive. It must be the purpose of "international law" to avoid such contingencies (although B would be ill-advised if it were to force A into action). Since it was the objective of both A and B to extend to each other mutual help, each signatory should be held to his given word.

Unfortunately, a nation's immediate self-interest may outweigh by far the more abstract interest of maintaining a reputation of scrupulousness and reliability. In so far as the Soviets are concerned, international law is considered as a means of the class struggle; hence communist states are not bound by their "commitments" except, of course, those which serve their interest. Coexistence in the legal sense between communist and "bourgeois" states can apply only to economic and related matters. Otherwise, "bourgeois" states are merely representatives of a single class and as such have no legal personality.[8]

The Soviet Union blithely violated its part of the Potsdam agreements of 1945 and thus compelled the Western allies to scrap, in self-defense, their own commitments under that monstrous document. Yet the Soviet Union insisted that the agreements—or, rather, those provisions that were to the Soviets' advantage—had to stand. As soon as the bad faith of the Soviets had become plain, the United States should have abrogated, by invoking the clause *rebus sic stantibus,* the Potsdam agreements—a step which, incidentally, would have gone far toward binding the Germans firmly to the West. That the United States did not do so can be ascribed, in large part, to that legalistic and abstract thought which still warps American perspectives of international realities, including the reality of evil.

The uninitiated should hold firmly to an important distinction, namely, that between international disputes which are justiciable and those which are not. Innumerable cases of nations against nations, individuals against states, and states against individuals have been adjudicated by international tribunals and national courts under the rules of international law.[9] A large number of treaties, agreements, and conventions between nations contain the stipulation that differences over their interpretation or execution shall be referred to special arbitration tribunals or the International Court of Justice, successor to the Permanent Court of International Justice under the League of Nations. The great majority of these contracts have been observed punctiliously; nearly all of the judgments of these tribunals have been recognized as binding, and virtually all have been complied with. International law is taught in law schools the world over; the practice of international law is a lucrative profession; no self-respecting ministry of foreign affairs feels at ease without a staff of experts on international law. It is these concrete tokens which sustain those who assert that international law exists, that it constitutes an important aspect of international relations, and that its uses are as manifold as they are rewarding. This claim is valid—as long as it is confined to the universe of what is justiciable. If it is expanded to include practical disputes over vital national interests, it impinges upon a field within which international law has, thus far, been conspicuous by failure to command observance of its rules. Sovereign states, locked in struggles for power, have invariably subordinated the use of courts to their interests. Under the cover of sovereignty, expressly recognized by every international treaty including the Charter of the United Nations, they can reject any procedure for the pacific settlement of disputes. The Permanent Court of International Justice held explicitly that "no State can, without its consent, be compelled to submit its disputes with other States

[8] See *ibid.,* p. 290; also T. Taracouzio, *The Soviet Union and International Law,* New York, Macmillan, 1935.

[9] See Amry Vandenbosch and Williard N. Hogan, *The United Nations: Background, Organization, Functions, Activities,* New York, McGraw-Hill, 1952, p. 50.

either to mediation or to arbitration, or to any other kind of pacific settlement." [10]

There is no dearth of treaties in which states agree to seek settlement of disputes by peaceful procedures—"under the rule of law." Such agreements are nearly always hedged by the stipulation that another agreement must be reached as to whether a case in dispute is covered by the treaty. In brief, submission of the dispute to jurisdiction beyond the authority of the sovereign contracting party depends on the consent of the latter. It is optional, not obligatory. Governments have devised a veritable arsenal of formulas under which they are authorized—or, rather, authorize themselves—to withdraw on principle whatever cases they may choose from international jurisdiction, and have couched the exemptions from international law in the impeccable language of international law. Among these are such elastic topics as territorial integrity, national independence, the right to decide what does and does not fall within the purlieu of domestic jurisdiction (most foreign treaties do), and arrangements with third parties (alliances)—in brief, all those political issues over which conflicts endangering the peace may be joined. To argue that these matters of vital national interest—change of the *status quo* must *always* affect vital national interests and reflects the very nature of international politics—can be left, or are already reserved, to the ministration of international law, is, at best, to play a joke on the eager student of international relations. At worst, it is an attempt to undermine the authority of governments over the national community within which law does supremely reign, and the authority of international law over that realm of international affairs, albeit narrow, within which it does exercise jurisdiction.

The question whether or not a given treaty obligation is to be fulfilled is not a legal but a political decision. It is always possible to find legal arguments *pro* and *con* for whatever decision a government wants to make. Treaties can be broken, with the assistance of able legal talent, quite "legally," and usually without very much effort. The significant question usually is *how* the contract is to be broken, whether openly or by legal subterfuge. In most cases it will be apparent that a defiant and unsophisticated breach of international obligation—like the one committed in 1914 by Germany when she invoked the "law" of military necessity, tore up the "rag of paper" guaranteeing Belgian neutrality, and blandly admitted that she had violated a solemn treaty—is most unwise. It gives the opponent a desirable pretext for action and a moral justification which he is eager to exploit, usually not without a larger or smaller dose of hypocrisy. When a treaty has been violated by one signatory, the other signatories are confronted by the choice of whether they should enforce compliance with the treaty through sanctions, silently agree

[10] Permanent Court of International Justice, Series B, No. 5, p. 27, as quoted by Werner Levi in his concise and sober assessment of international law and organization in *Fundamentals of World Organization,* Minneapolis, University of Minnesota Press, 1950, p. 63.

to the break by accepting the legal pretext, voice a platonic protest, attempt to negotiate, or replace the canceled obligation by other instruments. Again, these decisions are political in nature; the lawyer is needed merely to put the decision into the most appropriate form. While the partisans of international-politics-through-international-law dream about self-enforcing treaties and obligations without loopholes, governments usually refrain from signing agreements which would restrict their freedom of action in any substantive fashion.

Unwillingness to modify treaties, especially by nations which benefit from a given agreement, is a potent cause of international unrest. The nation which believes that it is entitled to privileges granted it by some legal definition of "right," is not interested in equity; but, understandably, the nation which is stymied by the inequitable arrangement—inequitable, albeit legal—is unimpressed by the sanctity of such "rights." The plot of *The Merchant of Venice* may serve as a pertinent reference for the analysis of such problems.

Treaties have been broken time and again. They cannot, therefore, be considered as reliable instruments of national security, although, no doubt, the resulting uncertainty must be a matter of keen regret. As a rule, aggressor states are not awed by the sanctity of international obligations, including written accords, and break the most solemn engagements without much hesitation once they deem such a step to be in their interest. In the past, such a procedure often ended by embroiling the aggressor in wars he did not wish to wage and, ultimately, exposed him to defeat. To this extent international law certainly has shown a wonderful vitality; it is an institution of vengeance. On the other hand, the unpleasant fact that numerous breaches of faith have gone unpunished must be given its due weight. The aggressor is not always wrong in thinking that he can get away with breaking the most solemn compact.

To governments which are basically interested in protecting their national interests and which are anxious to uphold a minimum of international order, the violation of treaty obligations is a far more serious matter. That agreements have been broken even by the most trustworthy governments is a fact. That these governments usually sin by omission rather than by commission (as did Great Britain in the case of two Soviet attacks against her "guaranteed" ally, Poland) also is true. And it is a galling fact that breaches of international agreements often are applauded by the prim devotees of international law in our midst, as happened in the case of Russia's attack on Japan in 1945. How responsible governments may be forced to break their obligations can be seen from the experience of France which, in 1940, had little choice but to abandon England and later violated her armistice agreement with Germany and reentered the war. This was as natural and as justified a political decision as was Italy's "betrayal" of Nazi Germany in 1943. Between 1919 and 1932 the Weimar Republic repeatedly circumvented the Versailles treaty, but the self-righteous condemnation of these violations by France and

Britain rang hollow, especially since the Western powers condoned, after Hitler's accession to power, far more dangerous and unjustified violations of the same treaty.

The decision to break a treaty obligation is therefore a difficult one. It is not an act by which a government can gain a unilateral advantage. It is an act for which a certain price must be paid. Sometimes this price may be excessive. But even if it were negligible, breach of contract should be risked only if other methods to renegotiate the agreement have failed. If the treaty must be torn up, the point should be driven home that there was no choice in the matter; that the step is not intended to weaken international law but is taken in conformance with higher rights than those compounded in the written treaty; and that breach of one agreement does not preclude the negotiation of another more satisfactory one. An aggressor state might violate its obligations in precisely the same fashion and still be given the benefit of doubt by world opinion, except that, in order to carry out aggression successfully, it must violate a whole series of treaties. The repeated use of such a procedure for purposes of dissimulation, fortunately, is impractical.

The point at issue is not this or that treaty, stipulation or modification. The nature of the problem is not legal. The whole argument over international law centers around the reliability of governments and the role of confidence in international relations. The confidence which a government instills in others is a formidable element of its strength; it is the prerequisite of effective international intercourse and alliance—*"Bündnisfähigkeit,"* as the Germans aptly call it. Governments which do not care about their reliability ratings, or about the confidence which other nations may repose in them, engage in a suicidal policy. To the statement of these axioms must be added the observation that, at the moment of this writing, hardly any government can be considered as highly reliable as regards observance of treaty obligations and, especially, of unilateral pledges which, too, are "international law." It is a fact that most nations of the world do not have the slightest confidence in the words and promises of any of the major powers, including the United States. The reason is not only that all nations have violated their most solemn undertakings—as, for example, the Atlantic Charter—or that they fail in punctilious observance of written obligations, but that the basic motivation of their conduct is expediency; their concepts of "right" change with constantly changing situations. The torrent of writings on "international law" which, these days, descends from our seats of learning, does not fill the gaping void caused by the fatal erosion of confidence. The claims of the partisans of a legal world order are in distinct contradiction to the behavior of nations. The obligatory character of promises (or treaties) is dependent on the acceptance of much more fundamental commitments.[11] "International law" cannot thrive in a world which does not recognize the norms of ethics.

[11] Alexander Sachs, "Rights, Promises and Property," in *Moral Principles of Action,* edited by Ruth Nanda Anshen, New York, Harper, 1952, pp. 228–302.

ETHICS AND INTERNATIONAL RELATIONS

During the Christian Middle Ages it was taken for granted that political action, like any other human action, was to be in conformity with ethical rules. Religion demanded of all mortals, including politicians, that they do good and shun evil. It also was taken for granted that statesmen will sin like any other human beings and that therefore unethical deeds would be perpetrated by politicians, but that such acts were reprehensible and had to be confessed and atoned for. The father-confessor was the constant companion of the medieval statesman. This did not mean that the statesman always listened to his father-confessor, or that the priest's advice always was ethically sound or otherwise apt; but it did mean that ethical considerations entered into practically all political decisions and that evil deeds were done with a consciousness of their true character. There was little effort to confuse the ethical categories and to misrepresent evil as good.

During the 15th century a different attitude, culminating in Machiavelli, emerged. Political science made its beginnings and tabulated its observations of actual happenings. Preoccupation with "oughts" and "don'ts" waned. Observation showed that statesmen commit numerous immoral and unethical acts as a matter of routine. If one looks closely enough, their behavior is in fact criminal, and often their crimes are more monstrous than those of common thieves and murderers. And yet not only are such statesmen not punished by regular legal proceedings—their punishment comes mostly in the form of crimes perpetrated against them—but it is a historic fact that success in political action is dependent to a large extent on ruthlessness and lack of scruples, or even on the very criminal tendencies of the politician. Success in politics, it is argued by the Machiavellians, is based on crime; [12] and quite often politics is nothing but institutionalized and "permissible" crime. Still, the paradox is that, as Goethe expressed it in *Faust,* the power who wills the evil often creates the good; while the opposite causal nexus manifests itself no less frequently. Hence to arrive and to survive, the new school of political science argued, the statesman must be a criminal, *i.e.,* a cheat, liar, thief, arsonist, robber, and assassin.

The analysis of the problems of the state showed, moreover, that a public organization *must* be run by rules of morality different from those pertaining to private individuals. For example, the state is entitled to deprive citizens of their money and even their lives, which the individual is not. Furthermore, it is incumbent on the statesman to care for the security and well-being of the citizens. Since security often is threatened by groups acknowledging no moral restraints, it is foolish to impose on defensive action limitations which would nullify their effectiveness. Hence the statesman cannot tell the truth openly; he must deceive his opponents; and he must not hesitate to liquidate persons

[12] Burckhardt, *op. cit.,* p. 242.

and situations which pose a threat to his plans. This, briefly, is the famous *raison d'état* which simply states that the state is entitled to undertake *any* action necessary for the achievement of its objectives and for the maintenance of its security. It does not impose on the state the requirement to proceed always by unethical action or to resort to crime if it is not inevitable or would entail serious consequences; [13] but if an action is clearly necessary and cannot be accomplished except by transgression of ethics, ethical rules of conduct should not be binding on the statesman. This, of course, is merely the political application of the old theorem that the end justifies the means, except that in political matters the end, too, may not be compatible with ethics, since it may be nothing else but the satisfaction of the power urge. The French summed up the theorem and its learned expansion in an earthy proverb: *À vilain, vilain et demi.*

The doctrine of *raison d'état* was taken up with alacrity by the statesmen of all nations. Yet this doctrine was not, at the time of its formulation, of a purely "unethical" character. It granted the validity of ethics, and it sought to define the limitations of ethics in so far as their norms bore upon the relation of man and state. It was, as it were, an attempt to formulate *public* as distinguished from *private* ethics.

Subsequently, however, the weakening of the religious beliefs on which medieval ethics were anchored led to an ever-increasing indifference about ethics. A high point in the process of erosion and corrosion was reached by Lenin when he wrote: [14]

For us, morality is subordinated to the interests of the class struggle of the proletariat. . . . Communist morality is the morality which serves the struggle, which unites the toilers against all exploitation, against all small property, for small property puts into the hands of one person what has been created by the labour of the whole society.

Thus, "ethics" to a communist consists merely in rigid devotion and service to the Communist Party: "For a communist, the interests of the Party must stand before all, otherwise he is not a communist. Before the Party, before his Party organization, he must be honest and straightforward always, in everything and to the end." [15]

The National Socialists, nihilists of another kind, viewed ethics in a manner not substantially different from Lenin. They asserted that *anything* that was useful to the German people also was *good* in a moral sense. Hitler had

[13] According to Napoleon I, evil in politics and war, even if it were within the "rules," is excusable only if and when it is "necessary"; unnecessary evil is a crime. Quoted in Burckhardt, *op. cit.*, p. 243.

[14] *Selected Works*, Vol. IX, pp. 476*f*. A nice paraphrase of this dictum can be found in *Kratkii Filosoficheski Slovar*, Article "Morality," Moscow, Gospolitizdat, 1941, p. 177. The anonymous philosopher quotes Lenin as follows: "From the point of view of Communist morality, 'moral' is only that which facilitates the destruction of the old world, and which strengthens the new, Communist regime."

[15] "Straightforwardness and Honesty," *Pravda*, Feb. 27, 1937.

no patience with any limitation ethics might impose on his freedom of action: "Terror is the most effective political instrument. . . . The most horrible warfare is the kindest. I shall spread terror by the surprise employment of all my measures. . . . The world can be ruled only by fear." In the mind of his subordinate, Hermann Göring, the precepts of morality assumed this lapidary form: "I have no conscience. My conscience is Adolf Hitler." [16]

These are merely the most extravagant formulations of such homely phrases as "Right or wrong, my country." Observations indeed indicate that the policies of nations are not strongly influenced by considerations of ethics. The ethical problem simply is ignored—except that most nations pay their respects to the moral forces by disguising their acts in such a way that ethical susceptibilities will not be hurt openly. This "pragmatic" attitude toward ethics is the result of a historical development in philosophy which led to the position that ethics could not be justified with any compelling reasons except that of "utility." In an epoch of "relativistic" thought it had become impossible to ascribe to ethics "absolute" values—hence, it was argued, there is really no substance in ethics.

In evaluating this state of affairs one is reminded of a remark made by the late Count Sforza, Foreign Minister of Italy. He was unable, he said, to understand why people believed that Machiavelli had written a handbook to political success. For at the time when he was penning his work, the man who had inspired him and whose actions he extolled, Cesare Borgia, was lying dead in a ditch in Spain, despised and abandoned by all, his once mighty realm shattered.

The problems posed by *raison d'état* do not imply a negation of ethics. Ever since Plato, these problems stood in the center of ethical discussion. Acts cannot be divided simply into good and bad acts, or acts for good and bad purposes. Nor can it be stated categorically that if, according to an accepted ethical definition, an act is considered bad, it never should have been committed. Plato discussed the example of a man who asked whither his friend had gone, and who asked he be given a knife, since he wanted to follow his friend and kill him. The person of whom this question was asked indicated the wrong direction and denied that he had a knife. In doing so he obviously lied. But it is also obvious that this lie was justified, since it prevented a greater evil, namely, murder. Similarly, Thomas Aquinas differentiated between lies for selfish purposes and lies for the benefit of others, among which he emphasizes the official lie or *mendacium officiosum*. While a lie remains a lie, there may be extenuating or aggravating circumstances, according to the character and intent of the liar. The official lie does not need to become a mortal sin. Thomas argued, however, that the official lie is permissible only if it aims at the benefit of others, and if it is not in contrast to *caritas*.[17]

[16] Hermann Rauschning, *The Voice of Destruction,* New York, Putnam, 1940, pp. 78, 81, and 83.
[17] *Summa Theologica,* Question 110, "De Vitiis Oppositis Veritati," Article IV.

Similar arguments can be made for all types of transgressions in the ethical field.

This is not the place to investigate the philosophical and anthropological foundations of ethics. Suffice it to point out that regardless of the particular justification which underlies ethical systems, all people at all places and at all times have been considering certain acts as good and other acts as bad.[18] This is an observable fact which is far more pertinent than the semantic humbug of whether there is an "absolute" justification of ethics. What is an "absolute"? By and large people consider those acts as bad which they do not want to have perpetrated against themselves and those acts as good of which they would like to be the objects, a situation which was interpreted philosophically by Immanuel Kant.

The legal codes of all nations are based on an almost identical interpretation of crime. There are differences, for example with repect to the circumstances wherein killing is permissible; but everywhere murder is considered a grave crime. Every society acknowledges that the individual possesses *some* rights, although these inalienable rights are defined somewhat differently according to cultural variations. There are variations as to the hierarchy of values and the meaning attached to various acts. The border line between permissible and illicit acts is movable. But every society has a system of ethics by which human actions are classified as to their value and justification. It is perfectly possible to understand the ethical evaluation of actions in culturally foreign and remote societies once the rationale behind the evaluation is clarified.

The "good" is not a substance which can be seen or touched like the Rosetta Stone. Nor is it an abstract entity which can be described in terms of eternal validity like a triangle. Acts are good or bad in concrete situations, and they are evaluated as to their goodness or badness by logical reasoning. Not all people may accept the result of this reasoning, but unanimity of judgment is not a requirement, nor is disagreement necessarily an indication that the dissenter disagrees on the fundamentals of ethical logic. Acts are responses to situations, and they usually constitute a choice among alternatives. Consciously or unconsciously, these choices are motivated by ethical judgments of a "spontaneous" nature (*i.e.,* induced by social conventions) or are the result of reflection. These acts are judged by others *both* on account of their material effectiveness and their ethical validity. The ethical evaluation is a continuous process, exactly as is the search for truth, but ultimately acts are "condemned" or "approved."

Whether or not he has firm ethical convictions, the maker of foreign policy must take into account moral forces even as he cannot disregard geography or economic factors. The inhibitions imposed on the maker of foreign policy by ethics are as intangible as the material limitations of military strength are

[18] Ralph Linton, "Universal Ethical Principles," in *Moral Principles of Action,* pp. 645–660.

concrete, but in this case the intangible is quite real—in the minds of people. However, while disregard of military or economic factors usually leads to swift punishment, the transgressor of ethics does not necessarily have to suffer for his doings. The temptation to gain unilateral advantages through unethical behavior is therefore very great, and since this is practically the only field where the offender may never submit to retributive sanctions, dynamic or aggressor governments rarely resist the temptation. It is the *one* method of scoring without pain. Nevertheless, even the most ruthless aggressor should scrutinize the historic record which shows that to spurn ethical principles is an effective method of politics *only* if it is employed rarely and with moderation. Consistent flouting of ethical convictions and conventions, the cynical disregard of intangibles as well as the worshipping of a pseudo-ethical code which acknowledges merely the rights of small elites and considers the rest of mankind obligated to that elite—such attitudes have proved to be the nemesis of practically all offending governments. By contrast, states which flourished for long periods exhibited standards of behavior more compatible with the dictates of human conscience. It is perhaps true that aggression may be eased by immorality; consolidation certainly is not.

Autocratic governments are not alone in disregard of ethics; the conduct of popular or democratic governments, too, is marred by peculiar lapses from ethical codes. They may not seek power for power's sake but as a means to achieve noble ends; yet they may not be true to their principles and may dishonor their promises. Their policies often are ruled by the axiom of the line of least resistance; they incline to shirk sacrifice. They are required by the very tenor of democratic debate to be more subtle; because consciences may not be offended openly, devious transgressions of honesty and decency occur frequently. However, in a state where law is enforced domestically, *i.e.*, where the government is not an arbitrary ruler, unethical conduct in the field of foreign policy is rendered difficult by the everyday restraints of accountability to courts and legislative bodies, except in conditions of emergency when legislation setting aside customary norms is enacted for the purpose of giving the government more freedom of action. Political conduct unfettered by ethical (and legal) restraints is possible, at all times, only in an autocracy. The autocratic government may do evil; the democratic government may fail to do good. The former may proceed through brutal crime; the latter may sin by omission and seek refuge in deceit.

Ethical or unethical conduct does not flow from abstract thought. The maker of foreign policy chooses between concrete alternatives, and his choice is dictated, among other things, by his ethical convictions or inhibitions. Ethical theories (or uncritical opinions) enter into any political decision, although in many cases those subjected to their influence are not consciously aware of them. The quality and consistency of political conduct would be improved if ethical orientation were the result of a reflective analysis of the ethical problem involved. Such an analysis ought to embrace both the ends and the means of political action. For example, what is the ethical reasoning underlying the proposition that security is more important than freedom (or vice versa)? What is the ethical argument behind the idea that it is more acceptable to fight a full-fledged war rather than to liquidate a warmongering statesman? Is not the killing of one man ethically preferable to the killing of many, and if not, why not?

Regardless of whether a decision is ethically valid or not, political conduct ought to conform to prevalent ethical notions, if for no other reason than that only thus can the statesman obtain prestige and moral support. If these prevalent notions happen to be fallacious and the government feels it should set some of them aside, it must be able to explain its conduct on the basis of convincing arguments. A need for such a revision of moral standards occurs frequently in countries which only recently have entered into the sphere of modern civilization. If time or arguments are lacking to accomplish such a reinterpretation, maneuvering the adversary into assuming the ethical onus may be the most appropriate course—a course which violates the ethics of means though not necessarily of ends.[19]

The objectives of a government or a nation must be analyzed with great care as to their ethical validity. It would be unwise to pursue objectives for which no ethical justification can be found. Objectives which correspond to ethical standards and which respond to the ethical aspirations of mankind will command respect and gain domestic and foreign support.[20] This means that objectives should always be compatible with basic human strivings, should satisfy the desires of a larger rather than a smaller group, and should not satisfy the power urges of but a small elite or even *one* nation but offer, as far as possible, general benefits to many nations, if not to all of mankind. As a corollary, these objectives must be pursued faithfully. They should be proclaimed with seriousness and gravity at all times and not be confined merely to high-sounding declarations and treaty preambles.

In formulating such objectives it must be borne in mind that human action never can be perfect. Hence, objectives can only conform to, but not be identical with, the highest ethical goals of mankind. By setting his sights too high, man must inevitably enter onto the road of broken promises and cynicism. It is therefore appropriate to formulate concrete rather than abstract objectives, and to clarify the reasons why these concrete objectives are ethically valid. As a corollary, it must be remembered that a government has obligations greater than merely defending national interests or pursuing its stated objectives. It is incumbent upon governments, as a continuing obligation, to pay tribute to the ideals of humanism and to carry out acts of charity and helpfulness.

It is inadmissible to select means by which the objective cannot be attained or through which the transcendent purpose of the pursuit of that objective

---

[19] See Charles Callan Tansill's chapter, "Japan Is Maneuvered into Firing the First Shot at Pearl Harbor," in his *Back Door to War, The Roosevelt Foreign Policy 1933–1941*, Chicago, Regnery, 1952.

[20] A. J. P. Taylor, *Rumours of War*, London, Hamilton, 1952, p. 240.

is negated. The incongruity of means and ends is a particularly noteworthy characteristic of revolutionaries and apostles of violence, who are willing to sacrifice hecatombs of human beings to establish paradise on earth. It would be an ethical, or, in any event, a reasonable demand to make sure not only that the promised state of bliss actually can be attained but also that the question will be answered whether the life and happiness of contemporaries ought to be sacrificed for the presumed happiness of future generations, and whether it is right to sacrifice one group of people for the benefit of other groups, especially if the victims are more numerous.

It is usually easy to *proclaim* plausibly ends which are impeccable ethically —even when a government has no other purpose than merely to increase its power. Not one of the least striking proofs of the contention that ethics are a potent factor in international politics may be found in the historical fact that exposure of such fraudulent claims usually arouses distrust and often leads to alliances against the guilty party.

The ethical quandary par excellence occurs in the area of means. Usually a democratic government is placed before the alternative of forswearing certain techniques or compromising its ends. Historically, many objections were raised against methods of nonviolent conflict, such as propaganda or political warfare. Such methods often are considered immoral, while military warfare, which has been a secular custom, is deemed beyond reproach morally. This is a classical example of a confusion between morals (not ethics) and habits. Similar uncritical judgments should not be binding on any government except that customs, too, must be taken into account as social forces.

Governments often place special emphasis upon certain techniques through which they hope to achieve their desired ends. These techniques may or may not be effective, and their adoption or rejection does not pose a problem of ethics. For example, a nation may be dedicated to the observance of human rights. It does not necessarily follow that human rights can be safeguarded, under all conditions, through the techniques of democracy, nor does it necessarily follow that elections are an effective method of introducing and maintaining democracy.

The dangers confronting governments on the "ethical front" are as follows:

1. *Overindulgence in Realpolitik.* The very rules of Machiavellism demand that governments behave as ethically as possible. To lie all the time is not only morally reprehensible but also politically inexpedient, because after a while no statement will find credence. To be effective, a lie must be believed, but in order to be believed, the liar must always speak the truth until the moment comes when he must make use of deception. Complete disregard of ethics is self-defeating.

2. *Verbal moralism.*[21] There is no point in indulging in moralistic and self-righteous policies when these are inapplicable in a concrete situation and when

[21] See George F. Kennan's *American Diplomacy 1900–1950* (Chicago, University of Chicago Press, 1951, Part I) on this species of diplomatic cant.

nothing is done to live up to the principles enunciated, or when principles contrary to those which were proclaimed are in fact put into practice.[22] It is even worse if a principle is applied under circumstances when this application will lead to results diametrically opposed to those intended, a dismal example being American insistence, after the First World War, on the principle of national self-determination. There is also the all too human temptation to condemn another nation's actions on moral grounds, without taking into consideration the practical necessities which led that nation to its actions. For example, the moral indignation heaped upon Japan's aggressiveness prior to the Second World War, especially her Manchurian and Chinese policies, failed to take cognizance of the economic needs of an overpopulated Japan. The criticism would have been more convincing if Japan had been offered satisfactory alternatives to aggression, as, for example, trading outlets.

3. *Tactics of expediency.* A concrete situation emerges which can be solved by two courses of action. Course A would be compatible with one's ethical beliefs and stated objectives, but would demand heavy sacrifices; course B would not demand any particular effort but would be incompatible with one's objectives and sense of justice. Course B is chosen. This was, during and immediately after the Second World War, the pattern of much of American foreign policy in its dealings with the Soviet Union. The United States acquiesced in Russia's territorial incorporation of Königsberg, which was incompatible with the stated objectives of the Atlantic Charter as well as traditional American defense of the principle of national self-determination; failed to protest Russian tactics in the Katyn affair and thus condoned, albeit tacitly, outright mass murder; abandoned faithful allies such as Mikhailovitch and Chiang Kai-shek; toyed with the Morgenthau plan; and agreed, though only during the brief honeymoon of American-Russian relations, to the impressment by the Soviets of millions of German civilians as slave laborers—perhaps the most radical divergence from the Bill of Rights in American history.[23]

The odious character of an opponent is not by itself a justification of unethical conduct. Little need be said to characterize the Nazis. But was there a justification for American acceptance of the mass expulsion of Sudeten Germans by the Czechs? For war-crime trials based on ex post facto "laws"? For failure to acquit many Nazi defendants of crimes which they did not commit (Katyn)? For attempting to force the Swiss government to break its trust to private investors and, despite Switzerland's hallowed tradition of neutrality, to surrender German financial holdings placed with Swiss banks? For the creation of a legal and ethical monstrosity such as "collective guilt" which extended moral responsibility from individuals to abstractions (a na-

---

[22] *Ibid.*, p. 36.

[23] Such policies in the foreign field rarely fail to be accompanied by transgressions at home. The treatment of American citizens of Japanese ancestry, who in clear violation of the Constitution were expelled from their homes and placed in detention camps, is an example in point.

tion or class or group) and punished individuals as presumable members of these abstractions for acts which they did not commit and which, had they known about them, they might not even have condoned? Perhaps some of these involutions of American policy were justifiable, but the ethical reasoning behind them remains obscure.

Tactics of expediency offer the greatest temptation to democracies to engage in unethical conduct. It is well to remember this imperfection, but it should be added that the prestige of nations like the United States, Britain, Switzerland, Holland, and Sweden is in a large part due to the fact that these nations are by and large trustworthy, that they at least seek to live up to ethical principles, and that they never denied the validity of ethical criteria. Occasionally, governments who acknowledge no ethical fetters are grateful that "honest brokers" are around to whom they can turn, without fear of betrayal, in their hour of need.

In summary, governments are confronted by situations in which they are presented with the alternative of taking expedient but morally wrong, or inexpedient but morally right, actions. They have the choice between respecting inalienable as well as acquired rights and disregarding them. It is quite unrealistic to expect, let alone demand, that governments always should shun expediency and abide by righteousness. At the time a decision is taken the alternative may be none too clear, several rights may be in conflict, and the price of righteousness may be excessively heavy. But governments should be aware of the ethical aspects of political problems. They should not only examine their objectives in the light of practical feasibility but also measure them by ethical standards.[24] Secondly, it is incumbent upon governments to realize that international stability depends to a large extent on the observance of basic ethical rules, on reliability, on the respect of rights, on faith with promises, and on the willingness to live up to obligations even in adverse circumstances.

Pseudoethical considerations often are used to prevent or provoke action. Measures that are proposed as suitable solutions to given problems frequently are censured on the ground that they are immoral, or, conversely, measures are advocated as imperative because they are demanded by ethics. For example, the idea of preventive war may be opposed or supported by such "moral considerations." On the one hand, it is supposedly immoral to initiate a war; on the other, it is immoral to allow an aggressive government to prepare a surprise attack or to permit a gangster government to exist. However, no action can be evaluated ethically without regard to its purpose and to the situation in which it is taken. Preventive war for unethical purposes un-

[24] "Statecraft is all that matters. Napoleon was unrivalled as a general; Bismarck as a diplomat; Lenin as a revolutionary. They went wrong only when they made mistakes. . . . Can we let it go at that? Is it enough to say: 'They did a fine job according to their lights'? Pursue this argument to its logical conclusion and the only wicked Nazis were the ones who tried occasionally to spare a political opponent or a Jew." Taylor, *op. cit.*, p. 11.

doubtedly is unethical. If the purpose is ethically defensible, preventive war would be immoral only if the purpose could be attained by less radical means. If indeed there is no other means to prevent the destruction of one's own nation except preventive war, it is not immoral at all to strike first and it might be quite immoral not to do so. Conversely, the need to initiate war can be justified only if it is reasonably certain that the enemy government has decided to launch a surprise attack and if it is improbable that this decision will be deferred. The mere existence of a gangster government with hostile intentions is an insufficient reason for a preventive war, because that government may change its character and intent.

It is often argued that peace per se is the highest ethical objective. Within the framework of a few ethical systems, this may be true, but it is not true of *all* ethical systems. Probably all ethical systems would agree that *under certain conditions* peace may be an overriding consideration and that under *all* circumstances peace is *one* of the highest values; but if peace comes in conflict with other values, for example, decency or freedom or conscience, opinions may differ greatly as to which value should become the supreme guide to action. *Each political conflict involves a conflict between ethical systems and value hierarchies.*

A "Gresham's Law" of International Morality? Must the unethical behavior of one state lower the ethics of all other states? Retaliation is an ethically acceptable practice; retaliation may cure the opponent of his aggressive mania. Except for its retaliatory nature, it is quite conceivable that the counteraction may have been as unethical as the unethical act which called it forth. Legally speaking, agreements which are consistently violated by one side become invalid. It is absurd, if not dishonorable, to continue recognizing such agreements. This consideration, however, may not always be decisive. To abrogate the agreement may serve no useful purpose and may even play into the hands of the transgressor. This was the argument of some of those who, at the occasion of the Congressional debates in early 1953, opposed the cancellation by the United States of the Yalta agreement.

Violation of ethical standards on the part of one government does not *necessarily* lower the ethical standards of all other nations; it *usually* does so. There is, however, no need to pour oil onto the flames or to forsake ethics. In such a case, politics should strive to reestablish proper standards. In the meantime, the law-abiding governments should attempt to halt the cumulative process of ethical disintegration by "insulating" the offender. It is inadvisable —and useless—to exact promises from, or conclude long-term arrangements with, governments which cannot be relied upon. The only practical way to engage in business dealings with unethical governments is to negotiate strictly on a *quid pro quo* basis and to restrict oneself to partial agreements which are self-enforcing. In private life, merchants deal similarly with customers who default on their payments. For example, instead of concluding a commercial treaty of a general nature and for a period of several years, one should agree simply on the exchange of x tons of coal against y head of cattle. To enter into over-all political settlements or alliances or disarmament treaties with governments notorious for their disregard of obligations is bound to be disappointing.

The sad fact is that there are always governments which do not hold with ethics. One cannot live obsessed with the delusion that all governments are ethically motivated, honorable, and reliable—and insure the safety of the state. The task of statesmanship is to abide by ethical standards and still to act effectively in a world in which immorality is rampant. This task may seem hopeless, were it not for the fact that ethics—or conscience—is one of the strongest forces motivating the behavior of men.

BIBLIOGRAPHY

Anshen, Ruth Nanda (ed.): *Moral Principles of Action*, New York, Harper, 1952.
Bourgeois, Émile: *Diplomatie secrète au XVIII siecle*, Paris, Colin, 1909.
Bryce, James: *International Relations*, New York, Macmillan, 1922.
Cambon, Jules, Richard V. Kühlmann, Sir Austen Chamberlain, Dino Grandi, Viscount Ishii, Karl Radek, and John W. Davis (contributors): *The Foreign Policy of the Powers*, New York, Council on Foreign Relations, Inc., 1935.
Chastenet, Jacques: *Vingt ans d'histoire diplomatique 1919–1939*, Geneva, Éditions du Milieu du Monde, 1945.
Die grosse Politik der europäischen Kabinette 1871–1914, 40 vols., Berlin, Deutsche Verlagsgesellschaft für Politik, 1922–1927.
Die internationalen Beziehungen im Zeitalter des Imperialismus: Dokumente aus den Archiven der Zarischen und Provisorischen Regierung 1878–1917, Berlin, Hobbing (publication not yet completed).
Documents diplomatiques français 1871–1914, Paris, Ministère des Affaires Étrangères, 1929–1935 (publication not yet completed).
Documents on German Foreign Policy, 1918–1945, many volumes, from the Archives of the German Foreign Ministry, Government Printing Office, 1948.
Gooch, G. P., and Harold Temperly (eds.): *British Documents on the Origin of the War 1898–1914*, 11 vols., London, H.M. Stationery Office, 1927–1938.
Hackworth, Green H.: *Digest of International Law*, 8 vols., Government Printing Office, 1940–1944.
Hartmann, Nicolai: *Ethics*, New York, Macmillan, 1932.
Green, Leslie C.: *International Law through the Cases*, New York, Praeger, 1951.
Kelsen, Hans: *Principles of International Law*, New York, Rinehart, 1952.
———: *The Law of the United Nations*, New York, Praeger, 1951.
Lauterpacht, Hersh: *International Law and Human Rights*, New York, Praeger, 1951.
Meinecke, Friedrich: *Die Idee der Staatsräson in der neueren Geschichte*, Munich, Oldenbourg, 1929.
Niebuhr, Reinhold: *The Irony of American History*, New York, Scribner, 1952.
Scheler, Max: *Etica*, 2 vols., Buenos Aires, Revista de Occidente Argentina, 1948. (Originally in German: *Der Formalismus in der Ethik und die Materiale Wertethik*, 3d ed., Halle, Niemeyer, 1927.)
Schwarzenberger, George: *A Manual of International Law*, New York, Praeger, 1951.
Voegelin, Eric: *The New Science of Politics, An Introduction*, Chicago, University of Chicago Press, 1952.
Wheeler-Bennett, John W.: *The Nemesis of Power: The German Army in Politics*, London, Macmillan, 1953.
Woodward, E. L., and Butler, Rohan: *Documents on British Foreign Policy 1919–1939*, London, H.M. Stationery Office, 1946–

Chapter 10

DIPLOMACY: THE FUNCTIONS OF DIPLOMATS

Diplomats have a twofold function: they represent their own nation abroad, and they report home the conditions prevailing in foreign countries. Since they conduct intergovernmental negotiations, collect intelligence, and discharge important, although mainly symbolic, ceremonial duties, diplomats should be expected to hold the center of the international stage. Yet the range of their influence varies not only with degrees of individual aptitude, but also with the times and, especially, with changing techniques of communications. In fact, it is difficult to say whether, how, or to what extent diplomats have shaped, and are now shaping, the course of history. The present functions of diplomats were succinctly described by André François-Poncet, former French Ambassador at Berlin and Rome: "En fait, j'étais surtout un informateur et un facteur." [1]

THE CRAFT AND THE MISSION

Collectively, diplomats were most important when, as in the negotiations leading to the termination of the Thirty Years' War and at the Conference of Vienna in 1814–1815, they were entrusted with the task of writing peace treaties. The art in which they excelled, namely, that of making compromises, supplied during that period an indispensable ingredient of statesmanship and contributed decisively to the creation of international systems which endured, but for minor alterations, for several generations. In this sense, the epoch between the Religious Wars and World War I may be called the Golden Age of Diplomacy. This is not to say that before and afterward diplomats did not execute missions involving the use of considerable discretion. Before the introduction of modern means of communication, ambassadors at faraway places were compelled, in emergencies, to make their own decisions

---

[1] "In fact, I was chiefly an intelligence agent and a mailman." *Souvenirs d'une ambassade à Berlin,* Paris, Flammarion, 1946, p. 12.

Compare this with the philosophy of an American nonprofessional Ambassador with strong liberal leanings: "An ambassador's job is no longer the relatively simple one of carrying out the policy of his government on a high level in the country to which he is assigned. As I see it, his job is also to reach the people and give them some understanding of the objectives and policies of the United States. And it is his job, too, to help work out programs of economic cooperation which would strengthen democracy in the country of his assignment." Chester Bowles, *Ambassador's Report,* New York, Harper, 1953, p. 16.

without consulting their governments. Up to a certain point, diplomats could, and did, commit governments; at Oriental posts, diplomats often possessed authority to order ship and troop movements and even to initiate military action. The advent of the telegraph, the telephone, the modern newspaper, and representative government greatly reduced the scope and responsibility of the diplomat.[2]

The role of the individual diplomat is usually of little consequence; yet, from time to time, a diplomat may change history. For example, in 1870, the French Ambassador to Prussia lacked, most historians agree, the elementary skills of his profession and managed to deceive, although unwittingly, his own government. It could be argued that a somewhat more adroit behavior on the part of this official might have prevented the War of 1870, a war which the Prussian Minister Otto von Bismarck could bring about only by clever, although unscrupulous, exploitation of the French diplomat's blunders.[3]

Benjamin Franklin achieved the French alliance for the fledgling United States, a diplomatic victory gained by personal prestige as well as by subtle negotiation. The brothers Pierre Paul and Jules Cambon, French Ambassadors to Great Britain and Germany respectively, contributed considerably to the framing of French alliances which saved their country in the First World War.[4] The American Ambassador to London, Walter Hines Page, in 1917 advised President Wilson of the authenticity of the dispatch sent in February, 1917, by Arthur Zimmermann, German Secretary of State, inviting Mexico to enter an alliance against the United States, and thus paved the way for America's entry into the war. Had his overriding purpose been to keep America out of the war, he might conceivably have convinced himself *and* the President that the intercepted dispatch, as shown to him by Sir Reginald Hall, Director of British Naval Intelligence, was a British fabrication designed to involve America in the war.[5] In the early twenties, the

[2] The influence which formerly a skilled diplomat was able to exert may be seen in Golo Mann, *Secretary of Europe, the Life of Friedrich Gentz, Enemy of Napoleon* (New Haven, Yale University Press, 1946), especially Part II. Compare with the impotence of modern diplomats as described in *Ambassador Dodd's Diary,* edited by William E. Dodd, Jr., and Martha Dodd (New York, Harcourt, Brace, 1941), and Sir Nevile Henderson, *Failure of a Mission: Berlin 1937–1939* (New York, Putnam, 1940).

[3] See Émile Ollivier, *The Franco-Prussian War and Its Hidden Causes,* Boston, Little, Brown, 1914, p. 271.

[4] A German officer, naval attaché in Constantinople and a personal friend of the Turkish statesman Enver Pasha, was one of the most important contributory causes of Turkey's siding with Germany during the First World War (see Ernest Jaeckh, *The Rising Crescent: Turkey Yesterday, Today and Tomorrow,* New York, Rinehart, 1944, pp. 118*ff.*).

[5] "Hall sent the first of these cables . . . to the British Prime Minister with a notation written across its corner calling attention to its importance in the relations between the Allies and the United States. Then he arranged for the decoding of the cable at the American Embassy in London with the copy of the German code book which he pos-

British Ambassador to Germany, Lord d'Abernon, counseled the German as well as his own government to pursue a policy of *rapprochement,* which bore fruit in the Pact of Locarno and the reemergence of Germany as a great power. In 1939, the American Ambassador to France, William C. Bullitt, strengthened the hand of the anti-Munich party and thereby helped to set the stage for the French declaration of war in 1939. The American Ambassador to Japan, Joseph C. Grew, advocated, for a long time, a conciliatory policy toward Japan, a policy fraught with as yet controversial but certainly fateful consequences for both countries.

There are cases on record when diplomats attempted to modify the set foreign policies of their governments. Prior to 1914, the German Ambassador to the Court of St. James's, Prince Lichnowsky, aimed at bringing about Anglo-German cooperation. He was unsuccessful. So was the German Ambassador to Moscow in 1941, Count von der Schulenburg, who, aware of the military strength of the Soviet Union, sought to dissuade Hitler from attacking Russia.[6] In 1940 America's Ambassador to Britain, Joseph C. Kennedy, on the other hand, believed that Britain had lost the war, an estimate of the situation not accepted as valid by the President on the basis of intelligence reports supplied by other sources. There are indications that Admiral Nomura, Japanese Ambassador to Washington in 1941, tried to prevent war between his country and the United States.

Perhaps the most critical mission which can be intrusted to a diplomat is to effect conciliation with a potentially hostile government. Ambassador François-Poncet was sent by the French government shortly before the outbreak of World War II to Rome, but achieved nothing. Sir Nevile Henderson has recounted in his *Failure of a Mission* his inability to appease Hitler.

World events are stronger than diplomats, who can do little to influence

---

sessed. To assure the American Government of its authenticity the original cipher text in the telegraph office in Washington was procured and relayed to the American Ambassador in London. Hall loaned our Ambassador his copy of the German code book and Mr. Bell, one of Ambassador Page's associates, himself deciphered the cable. President Wilson was convinced." (Admiral Sir W. Reginald Hall and Amos J. Peaslee, *Three Wars with Germany,* edited and illustrated by Joseph B. Simms, New York, Putnam, 1944, pp. 9–10.)

The text of the Zimmermann dispatch of January 16, 1917, is as follows: ". . . We propose to begin on the 1st February unrestricted submarine warfare. In so doing, however, we shall endeavor to keep America neutral.

"If we do not succeed in doing so we propose to Mexico an alliance on the following basis: Joint conclusion of the war, joint conclusion of the peace, generous financial support, Mexico to reacquire the lost provinces of Texas, New Mexico and Arizona. Your Excellency should for the present inform the President [of Mexico] most secretly upon the outbreak of war with the United States and suggest President's inviting Japan's immediate adherence. Also advise that our submarines will compel England to sue for peace in a few months. . . ." (Quoted from Hall and Peaslee, pp. 8–9).

[6] Allen Welsh Dulles, *Germany's Underground,* New York, Macmillan, 1947, p. 169. See also the interesting episode described in *The von Hassel Diaries 1938–1944: the Story of the Forces against Hitler inside Germany as Recorded by Ambassador Ulrich von Hassel, a Leader of the Movement,* New York, Doubleday, 1947, pp. 68–73.

them and, in most cases, serve only as "telephone girls of history." [7] Their main function is to transmit or accept "communications" and to "explain" the point of view of their government which, nowadays, is usually more forcefully explained by the newspapers.

INTELLIGENCE AGENTS

While diplomats neither make nor influence world history, they have rendered, and continue to render, valuable services to their governments, particularly as collectors of information. Alexander I of Russia counted on receiving all important news on French affairs from Count Nesselrode, Counselor of Embassy, and Colonel Chernyshev, military attaché, who later had to leave France because he became involved in an espionage plot. In 1940, the United States maintained an embassy in Vichy, France, not only to encourage resistance against Germany, but also to gather information about Germany. The American legations at Stockholm and Berne had, during the war, essentially the same major mission. For similar reasons, the Soviet Union, throughout her war with Germany, kept diplomatic representation in Bulgaria. The German legation at Dublin, Ireland, also served intelligence purposes. Germany's best source of information about conditions in England in 1940 and 1941 was the military attaché in the legation of a small satellite Axis country not yet at war with Britain.

Diplomatic stations, including venerable embassies, are frequently forced into intelligence work: a person who wants to sell secrets to a foreign nation but has no direct connection with a foreign intelligence service inevitably approaches accredited diplomats. Thus, the former Soviet diplomat Bessedovsky tells that his embassy was offered the purchase of the secret code of a south European power. The offer was made by a junior diplomat serving the very nation he wanted to betray—an intelligence function not counseled by the book of diplomatic etiquette. According to Bessedovsky, the Russians told the traitor-diplomat that they would have to check the documents, took them into an adjoining room, photographed them, and returned them with the remark that Soviet embassies would not buy such commodities.

The informational character of diplomacy was strongly emphasized early in 1940 when President Roosevelt sent Undersecretary of State Sumner Welles on a tour of the capitals of Europe to report on the war situation. This voyage in quest of facts proved to be an indispensable prerequisite for the formulation of an effective American policy.[8]

The "intelligence" function of diplomacy is not always clearly understood

[7] The expression "telephone girls of history" was coined by the Austrian quisling Seyss-Inquart, who engineered the annexation of Austria by means of telephone conversations with Berlin. These conversations are reprinted in Kurt von Schuschnigg, *Austrian Requiem* (New York, Putnam, 1946, pp. 297–314).

[8] Sumner Welles, *The Time for Decision,* New York, Harper, 1944, pp. 74–147.

by diplomats, and governments fail frequently in cogent evaluation of incoming information. Not all diplomats think it worth their while to learn languages. Yet possession of languages would not only make them well informed, but would also help them greatly in their ceremonial functions. Few American ambassadors ever troubled to learn Russian, German, or French, let alone Japanese or Chinese.

Diplomats have frequently engaged in political warfare, sabotage, and espionage—undertakings which, while highly "undiplomatic," prospered under the protection of diplomatic immunity. The German Ambassador at Vienna in 1934 acted as the leader of the Nazi revolt which culminated in the assassination of the Austrian Chancellor. A German diplomat, Abetz, directed before 1939 in Paris a highly successful propaganda campaign against French resistance to Nazi aggression.[9] In 1940, the British Ambassador to Spain, Sir Samuel Hoare, was assigned the mission of keeping Spain out of the war; he succeeded in so bolstering the antiwar forces and intimidating the war party that Spain's continued nonbelligerency must in no small measure be attributed to his efforts. The Allied landing in North Africa in 1942 was skillfully prepared by a number of American diplomats under the direction of Robert Murphy, who collected data indispensable for the planning of the landing and fomented a *coup d'état* which, though not entirely successful, insured the success of the operation.[10]

It is known from the revelations of former Russian officials, such as General Krivitski and Victor Kravchenko, that diplomatic Soviet missions are staffed with secret police agents whom the diplomatic personnel is instructed to support in their diverse undertakings. These activities may include the abduction of Russian citizens (General Miller) or even their execution (Trotsky)—a sinister innovation in the diplomatic "art." Russian diplomatic missions require specifically that all their members report accurately everything they see and hear in foreign countries—*i.e.*, to engage in intelligence activities as a matter of diplomatic routine.[11]

Certain intelligence functions are recognized as legitimate duties of diplomats. The mission of military attachés is plainly the collection of military data. In the realm of economics, commercial attachés report in peacetime on

[9] See J. Paul-Boncour, *Entre deux guerres; souvenirs sur la IIIe République*, Vol. III, "Sur les chemins de la défaite 1935–1940," New York, Brentano, 1946, p. 150.

[10] Sir Samuel Hoare, *Complacent Dictator*, New York, Knopf, 1947. Compare the comments by the former Spanish Foreign Minister, Serrano Suñer, on Hoare's memoirs in *Entre les Pyrénées et Gibraltar: dix ans de politique espagnole*, Geneva, Éditions du Cheval Ailé, 1947, pp. 242ff. See also William L. Langer, *Our Vichy Gamble*, New York, Knopf, 1947, especially pp. 328ff.; and Kenneth W. Pendar, *Adventure in Diplomacy: Our French Dilemma*, New York, Dodd, Mead, 1945, especially chapters 8–10.

[11] The best exposé of Soviet secret activities is contained in Royal Commission to Investigate Disclosures of Secret and Confidential Information to Unauthorized Persons, *The Report of the Royal Commission Appointed under Order in Council P.C. 411 of February 5, 1946*, Ottawa, E. Cloutier, Printer to the King, June 27, 1946. Also Igor Gouzenko, *The Iron Curtain*, New York, Dutton, 1948; and W. G. Krivitski, *In Stalin's Secret Service*, New York, Harper, 1939.

business conditions, but in wartime gather information required for waging economic warfare, such as production figures of strategic raw materials, exports by neutral countries, dates of sailings, and unusual transfers of currencies. Press or cultural attachés are "legalized" propagandists, but they, too, are collectors of information necessary for propaganda. However, espionage is not permitted by diplomatic rules, and the diplomat caught at it either returns voluntarily, as did some Japanese naval attachés accredited to the United States, or is withdrawn, like the Russian military attaché to Canada in 1946. It happens very rarely indeed that the *agrément* according diplomatic status to the offending official needs to be voided by the host country.

GOOD-WILL AGENTS

Diplomats are often assigned the mission of creating good will. The British, anxious to improve their relations with Russia, appointed, in 1940, Sir Stafford Cripps as Ambassador to Moscow, hoping that his political background, distinguished by avowed Marxist leanings, would enable him to bring Russia into the war before she was attacked by Germany. In order to obtain India's full cooperation in the Pacific War, Sir Stafford was later dispatched to India to solve India's constitutional problems. Sir Stafford failed in both tasks, not only because kindred political philosophies may be of small account in dealing with fanatics (to true believers such as communists, a small deviation in matters of political dogma is more offensive than forthright opposition), but also because mere "good will" does not set aside serious differences in political interests.

In 1807, Queen Louise of Prussia, relying on her charming presence, tried unsuccessfully to talk Napoleon into a "soft peace" for her defeated country. That Napoleon knew how to separate personal affairs from diplomatic intercourse, he proved again when he resisted the entreaties of Countess Walewska pleading for the independence of Poland; Poland could not have had a more convincing advocate than the beautiful Countess, who bore Napoleon a son, the later Count Walewski, Foreign Minister of Napoleon III. And yet Napoleon followed the *raison d'état* rather than the *raison d'amour*.

The aged Marshal Pétain was sent on many good-will missions. After Republican defeat in the Spanish Civil War, France wanted to establish friendly relations with Generalissimo Francisco Franco, in spite of previous ineffectual French opposition. Pétain, a personal acquaintance of Franco and not unsympathetic to the *caudillo*'s objectives, was appointed Ambassador. Neither his prestige nor his sympathies swayed Spanish policy to any appreciable extent. Ambassador Carlton Hayes, chosen by President Roosevelt for similar reasons as envoy to Spain, was more successful since he represented a more powerful country, had various means of pressure at his disposal, such as the embargo of American oil shipments to Spain, and—finally, abandonment of the policy of appeasement.

Some "good-will" ambassadors have indeed gained the esteem of their peoples—chiefly because their mission has been merely to improve already excellent relations. Lord Lothian was appointed British Ambassador to Washington, because it was felt that his record as previous sympathizer with Germany would make his support of the war most convincing, even to radical American isolationists. His successor Lord Halifax had a somewhat similar record. These two men contributed notably to British-American cooperation.

Diplomats are often called upon to mediate and to start peace negotiations between warring countries. Diplomatic contacts between hostile nations are, popular notions notwithstanding, never completely severed, although these are mostly maintained through neutral intermediaries. It is customary to negotiate various conventions between belligerents, such as regulating observance of international law, exchange of personnel, prisoners, and casualties, Red Cross and postal arrangements, etc. Sometimes it is via these innocuous channels that important secret negotiations are launched in order to seek out a basis for a peace by compromise. As a rule, these negotiations do not take place between ambassadors but mostly between junior members of the embassies. Once the exchange of views appears to lead to concrete results, it is likely to be continued by special emissaries.

During the Second World War, Finland's negotiations for a separate peace were carried on through the Russian ambassador in Stockholm, Mme. Kollontai. Marshal Badoglio, seeking to withdraw Italy from the war, sent his emissaries to Portugal, where they established contact with allied diplomats.[12]

Agents of the United States Office of Strategic Services, in charge of political and subversive warfare operations, arranged from Switzerland by secret negotiations for the surrender of the German army in Italy.

The armistice with Japan was preceded by secret contacts, some of which were allegedly conducted through the Vatican. It is known that Soviet Russia and Nazi Germany held various secret talks in 1943 and 1944, both in Sweden and Bulgaria. It is not known, in particular, whether the Russians engaged in the talks in order to conclude a separate peace and to reestablish a new German-Russian collaboration, or whether they used them to blackmail the United States into ever-greater concessions, or whether they simply wanted to know the German conditions.

[12] On separate peace negotiations during the First World War, see Potiemkine, *Histoire de diplomatie,* Paris, Médici, 1946, Vol. II, p. 319. See also Mermeix, *Les négotiations secrètes et les quatre armistices avec pièces justificatives,* Paris, Ollendorff, 1919. On the secret Italian negotiations, see Giuseppe Castellano, *Come Firmai l'Armistizio di Cassabile,* Milan, Mondadori, 1945; and Pietro Badoglio, *L'Italia nella Seconda Guerra Mondiale,* Milan, Mondadori, 1946, p. 97.

NEGOTIATORS

Negotiation is the diplomat's normal business. There are many minor things to negotiate every day, from commercial and tariff agreements to interventions to protect citizens abroad. Major negotiations, for example, for a military or political alliance, or for credits, or for the setting up of international organizations, are usually prepared by regular and accredited diplomats; yet, in most cases, such negotiations are concluded by foreign ministers and sometimes even by the chiefs of government or heads of state. For instance, Aristide Briand, as French Foreign Minister, participated in secret negotiations with the Central Powers in 1916–1917. Laval negotiated a French-Russian alliance by going to Moscow in 1935. Mr. Churchill negotiated personally with President Roosevelt after Pearl Harbor, and many times thereafter. Mr. Molotov went to London and Washington, Mr. Hull to Moscow. In fact, negotiations on the "top level" are usually necessary to speed and consummate important agreements.

In the wings of the diplomatic stage stand the secret negotiators without official status whose activities can always be disavowed. In order to attain their objectives, governments must often make use of the services of diplomatic "brokers." Tsar Nicholas II of Russia was very difficult to reach through ordinary channels and proved often inaccessible to accredited diplomats. The French accordingly used a broker if they wanted to get a communication through to the Tsar. This broker, a Dane by the name of Jules Hansen, had access to the Danish court and by this detour to the Tsar's mother, a Danish princess. Hansen was so skillful a negotiator that the French Foreign Ministry employed him for numerous secret missions all over Europe.

Before the Second World War, Britain enlisted the services of a Swedish industrialist who knew Göring and who hoped that he could persuade the Nazi Marshal to influence Hitler against war. (During the war, the Swedish Foreign Office approached the Germans through a Finn who happened to be Himmler's personal "physiotherapist.") On their part, the French, on the eve of World War II, sent a banker, M. Baudoin, to Italy to negotiate a *modus vivendi;* he was unsuccessful, but as he had supposedly established good relations with the Italian government and especially the Foreign Minister, Count Galeazzo Ciano, Marshal Pétain later appointed him Foreign Secretary of the Vichy government. In the earlier period of the Vichy regime, many secret negotiators, such as Professor Rougier, were sent to London to establish relations without knowledge of the Germans. Sometimes negotiators act on their own initiative, as Count Bernadotte of Sweden, representative of the Red Cross, who sought to end World War II early in 1945 by negotiating with Heinrich Himmler.[13]

[13] Louis Rougier, *Mission secrète à Londres: les accords Pétain-Churchill,* Geneva, Éditions du Cheval Ailé, no date. This book contains a thorough discussion of the official

DIPLOMACY-BY-ORGANIZATION

Since we live in an epoch that may well go down in history as the Administrative Age, it is not surprising that the organizational structure of foreign offices the world over has become an important aspect of foreign policy and is perpetually in flux. The problem is a twofold one: (1) the organization of the foreign office, and (2) the relation of the foreign office to other departments and branches of government. Especially in the organization-minded United States, preoccupation with administrative reforms has given rise to a bewildering succession of reorganizations, "streamlinings," and proposals of reform. As it now stands, the U.S. Department of State as well as the British Foreign Office is each a cross between functional and regional organizations. In the United States regional "bureaus," *i.e.*, Bureau of European Affairs, Far Eastern Affairs, etc., comprising "offices," *i.e.*, Office of Western European Affairs, Office of Eastern European Affairs, etc., handle foreign policy matters pertaining to major regions of the world, geographic areas within these regions and, on the next lower level of the organizational chart, individual states. One bureau's region, however, is as wide as the world; it is in charge of United States policies in relation to the United Nations. Each bureau is placed under an Assistant Secretary. Among the functional divisions are grouped Congressional Relations, Legal and Economic Affairs, etc., each headed by an Assistant Secretary. There are a Policy Planning Staff, a Counselor, and several Special Assistants. There is, finally, a public-relations (information and propaganda) organization, comprising broadcasting and press services and educational exchange services. The whole ponderous apparatus is supposed to respond to the control levers in the hands of the Secretary and Undersecretary, flanked by Deputy Undersecretaries and a Secretariat. The British scheme is about the same as the American, though the nomenclature is somewhat different.[14]

The purpose of these elaborate organizational devices is, among other things, to insure the firm control of foreign affairs in the hands of the foreign minister and yet to free him in the conduct of high policy from administrative details. Since the foreign offices of the great powers, within the last ten years, have grown enormously—the personnel at home and abroad of the State Department increased from 1,000 in 1940 to about 23,000 in 1953—solutions to the

---

British attempts to deny the existence of secret agreements with Pétain, especially p. 192. See also Winston Churchill, *The Second World War: Their Finest Hour,* Boston, Houghton Mifflin, 1949, p. 508.

[14] The reader interested in organization charts should consult Kurt London, *How Foreign Policy Is Made,* New York, Van Nostrand, 1949, especially charts opposite p. 110 and p. 122 (U.S. and Britain) and p. 133 and p. 148 (France and U.S.S.R.). See also *The Department of State Today,* Department of State Publication 3969, Government Printing Office, 1951. The reader, having consulted these charts, should, however, beware of taking them as final. Organization is not a static, but a fluid, concept.

problem of how to coordinate swollen ranks of officials and increasingly complicated policy matters are not easily found and, when found, even less easily applied.

The problem of the administration of foreign affairs is difficult enough when it is put in terms of foreign-office organization; if it is brought into relationship with the entire administration of a modern state it defies mere organizational ingenuity. In the past, international relations were the exclusive domain of the foreign office; the ministers closest to foreign affairs were those of army and navy, and even these ministries were hardly ever found poaching in the foreign minister's preserve. Other departments had hardly any connection with foreign affairs at all. Today, virtually all departments of government engage in international relations of one kind or another.[15] As regards these varied, often conflicting, departmental interests, the watchword has been "coordination."

That coordination is the prerequisite, though by no means the only one, of the efficient conduct of foreign policy, can be readily seen from the following hypothetical examples: The Ministry of Labor of country A is charged with keeping abreast of developments on labor organization abroad. It invites some prominent labor leaders in country B to visit country A. Yet A's official foreign policy supports in country B a government that is opposed by a political party allied with organized labor. The Ministry of Labor of country A may thus have gravely embarrassed A's Foreign Ministry, not to speak of B's Foreign Minister, who is held to account by his government and the ruling parties. Or, country A seeks to strengthen the military forces of country B, a faithful ally. The War Ministry of A, however, goes slow on releasing the needed weapons, because it has its own ideas about with whom and with what A should fight the next war. Country A's Foreign Minister is hindered in implementing the alliance with B. His colleague, the War Minister, may act from the highest motives, having his own deep convictions as to national security. The end result is that country B does not obtain arms at the right time and in the right amount, and that the policies of A and B as well as their responsible officials are plunged into confusion. These hypothetical examples, as everyone familiar with administrative processes knows, are not so hypothetical; examples drawn from life are supplied liberally by the daily press of all major countries.

The problem of coordination of decision making is now tackled mostly by the creation of supercommittees and supercouncils as, for example, the National Security Council in the United States of which the President, and the

---

[15] According to the Commission on the Organization of the Executive Branch of the Government ("Hoover Commission"), *Task Force Report on Foreign Affairs* (Government Printing Office, 1949), Appendix H, p. 44, forty-six out of fifty-nine major departments and agencies in the executive branch were concerned "with economic, social, military and other aspects of foreign affairs." In Britain, a similar expansion of ministries and boards, formerly considered as of purely domestic competence, into foreign affairs has taken place.

Secretaries of State, Defense, and Treasury are members; and the problem of coordination of operations is attacked by the creation of interdepartmental boards, as, for example, the Operations Coordinating Board in the United States, which is run by assistants to the Secretaries and a full-time staff. Coordination at the top, however, is not a substitute for lacking team spirit at the bottom. Frequently, coordination is rendered difficult or impossible by the simple fact that foreign policy has not been formulated clearly by the top officials and that, therefore, the lesser lights do not know what it is. Blind men leading blind men are unlikely to furnish leadership for coordinated undertakings. Diplomacy was always, and still is, an art: there are limits to what the best diplomatic organization can achieve in the way of successful foreign policy. Foreign policy is made by individual men and not by bureaus or tables of organization; the finest canvas and the most expensive brushes do not suffice to make a painter.

DIPLOMATS

Who are diplomats? How are they recruited? Until World War I, diplomats belonged to the "best society" and in many countries to the aristocracy; they were usually endowed with personal financial means. There were a number of solid reasons for the diplomatic monopoly of the aristocracy which, in many countries, are valid even today.

First of all, the envoy required considerable means to represent his country in an impressive manner; with rare exceptions (Great Britain), the salaries of the diplomatic personnel did not permit a high standard of representation. Secondly, the envoy had to be a man acceptable to "good society" and accustomed to move in such circles. Thirdly, he had to be a widely traveled man, possessing a broad education, language facilities, and a wide circle of acquaintances in foreign countries.

These characteristics were, in former times, possessed by members of the privileged classes only. At present, this is no longer true; nor is it advisable that the diplomat restrict his contacts to the "best society." On the contrary, "best society" being no longer a very powerful social force, the diplomat must become familiar with the members of all classes, including the most lowly. The typical diplomat of the old school may be, and often is, blind to social events of great importance and may evaluate conditions on the basis of inadequate knowledge or even prejudices. This is why it has recently been advocated that "labor" diplomats be appointed to countries where labor problems are important, and especially to countries ruled by labor governments, as well as to international organizations dealing with labor matters. On the other hand, errors of perspective may afflict "proletarian" as well as "bourgeois" envoys.

The advantages which a person of social standing and wealth possesses still are assets for the diplomat, yet "social position" is no longer an attribute of aristocrats alone. In modern times, industrialists, businessmen, scholars, and artists have acquitted themselves with distinction in diplomatic missions. Jacques Maritain, Thomist scholar, was appointed French Ambassador to the Vatican in 1945. The first postwar Ambassador of Poland to the United States was a mathematical economist of the University of Chicago, Oscar Lange. Carlton Hayes, the historian, represented the United States in Spain. A Chilean woman poet and winner of the Nobel Prize was appointed consul in Los Angeles. Although not a professional diplomat, the pianist Paderewski served as Poland's most effective good-will ambassador before the creation of the Republic and subsequently rose to the presidency of his country. Newspapermen are often chosen for diplomatic assignments, such as the "Walter Lippmann of France," Wladimir d'Ormesson, who served as Ambassador to the Holy See; the first postwar Italian Ambassador in Washington, Tarchiani, also was a newspaperman of high standing.

It can be said that virtually all countries select their diplomats from the "ruling class," although this class is no longer a "caste." Aristocratic privilege has been replaced by selection on the basis of examinations open to all qualified candidates. In this country as well as in Great Britain, many professional diplomats without private means have advanced from the ranks to important posts by sheer ability. However, individuals admitted to entrance examinations leading to appointment in the foreign service must be graduates of colleges or of other institutions of high learning. As a matter of record the bulk of the candidates is supplied by the middle or professional classes.

Diplomacy is a conservative profession. Diplomatic protocol is today still based on the order of precedence in rank established at the Congress of Vienna (1815) and Aix-la-Chapelle (1818). First come ambassadors plenipotentiary and extraordinary, then envoys extraordinary and ministers plenipotentiary, all accredited to heads of state and representing directly the heads of their own states. These dignitaries are followed by ministers and chargés d'affaires, ad hoc and ad interim, who are either permanently or temporarily in charge of a mission and accredited to the Foreign Minister, but not to the head of state. Formerly, only the great powers exchanged ambassadors with one another; they sent ministers to lesser states who, in turn, accredited ministers to the heads of the great powers. This custom lapsed. It is symptomatic of this inflationary age that the United States has by now raised nearly all its missions to the rank of embassy.

Consuls are not diplomats in the proper or protocol sense, though they sometimes engage in diplomatic activities. They are principally concerned with economic affairs and reporting and with the supervision of the export and import regulations of their own country. (U.S. consular officials see to it that goods shipped to this country are properly invoiced, i.e., identified in accordance with customs regulations.) Consular officers usually are in charge of visas, renewal or issuance of their own nationals' passports, and many notarial activities. Consuls are not "accredited" but are granted the "exequatur" by the resident government. In certain places, especially in Latin America and Asia, consuls of major nations are important officials, enjoying considerable local prestige and exercising quasi-diplomatic functions. Consuls enjoy certain immunities, though they vary from place to place. They are, as a rule, not granted extraterritorial status; extraterritoriality is a diplomatic privilege. The diplomatic agent's official residence is national territory and not subject to the jurisdiction of the country to which he is accredited, his person is inviolate even after war has been declared, and he cannot be subjected to legal proceedings no matter against which law he may have offended.

It can readily be seen why diplomacy appeals to individuals who are sensitive to the allure of position, prestige, and rank, and especially to scions of the middle and professional classes steeped in the tradition of graded, nonmaterial satisfactions.

DIPLOMATIC EDUCATION

In the United States, as well as in Britain, France, and most major nations, diplomats—political appointees excepted—are chosen by competitive examination. Candidates for the diplomatic service and for service in the foreign ministries present themselves for examinations which test their knowledge, and which also probe, though less formally, character, poise, manners, and looks, i.e., "personality." [16] The best candidates are selected and, after further instruction, sent on tours of service, usually alternating between service in foreign posts and service in the ministry. The foreign service career usually starts in out-of-the-way places or in subordinate positions at the more important stations. From then on, in theory, the more efficient diplomats rise to positions of increasing importance and responsibility, so that at the end of their career the ablest individuals hold the most important embassies.

In practice, of course, careers develop somewhat differently. Many diplomats stand for certain political orientation which may accelerate or retard their promotions. Diplomats whose views clash with those of the head of the ministry or government will rarely be intrusted with the "great embassies." Others whose abilities are not outstanding, but whose policies coincide with those of the department, are pushed forward. "Connections" and "political

---

[16] In the United States, any man or woman who has been a citizen for at least ten years, is not married to an alien, and is between twenty-one and thirty-one years of age may apply to the Board of Examiners of the Foreign Service to take the written entrance examination. If the candidate has passed the examination, which, of late, resembles more and more an intelligence test weighted on the side of liberal education, he is summoned to an oral examination. In the past, only a fraction of the applicants—10 per cent and sometimes less—passed both tests. If then security and loyalty checks do not disqualify the applicant, he passes into the Foreign Service. For the relationship of the Foreign Service to the State Department as a whole and proposed reforms, see James L. McCamy, *The Administration of American Foreign Affairs*, New York, Knopf, 1950; Commission on Organization of the Executive Branch of the Government ("Hoover Commission"), *op. cit.;* and Daniel S. Cheever and H. Field Haviland, "The Hoover Commission," *American Political Science Review,* October, 1949, pp. 966*f*.

pull" also play, needless to add, an important role. Sometimes a foreign country influences the choice of the diplomat accredited to it by informally indicating its desires. Sometimes, a diplomat attracts the attention of the public, which may help him in securing great positions, while sometimes it may make his life difficult. It is a frequent experience, not necessarily restricted to diplomacy, that the "man who was right" is persecuted by bitter enmity on the part of those who were wrong, and that "being right" does not always find its just rewards. Sometimes the ministries are split into various factions, each standing for a special policy. The standards by which the successes or the ability of individual diplomats are assessed are rarely completely objective.

For all these reasons, the selection of diplomats is not always what it should be. A diplomat who owes his job to special interests rather than to merit may perform adequately his ceremonial functions and represent correctly the "point of view" of his government. He may fail in his informational duties, misinterpret the intentions of the foreign government, and misunderstand significant events in the foreign nation's life.

That only too many diplomats have failed to attain the ideal standards of their craft can be ascribed to two principal causes. The first is the fact that diplomats rotate their positions and serve in the most varied countries. Since it takes many years to become intimately familiar with the politics, history, and language of a country, a diplomat has rarely a chance to acquire the knowledge prerequisite to being a competent observer. The impressions of *many* countries, cultures, and languages may, in the end, dull rather than sharpen powers of perception. It is understandable that many diplomats make only perfunctory attempts at acquiring specialized geographical and cultural knowledge. While it is advisable to give diplomats an "all-round" experience, a general education is not enough but should be supplemented by specialization.

The second cause of diplomatic failure is to be found in deficient education of diplomats. In most countries diplomatic training need not shirk comparison with other technical professions. The average diplomat has usually a good working knowledge of political science, international law, economics, history, languages, and administration. Former diplomats abound in the professions, and many a former diplomat, who through war and revolution "lost his country," gained renown as a university professor (as often professors turn diplomats). Yet the professional knowledge of the diplomats should not be compared to that of persons with functions of lesser responsibility but should be measured by the exigencies of their profession. General knowledge and a good academic education are not enough; knowledge of details and practical experience are essential.

The "old-school" diplomat is frequently unable to understand the particular psychology of a foreign nation or the dynamics of revolutionary movements. He knows little about military matters, technology, scientific research, applied economics—all subjects with which the diplomat should be familiar in this modern world where he may sometimes be called upon to evaluate engineering projects from the point of view of his country's interests, or guide political movements, or coordinate military operations. Of course, no one man can be proficient in all these subjects, but the diplomatic service as a team should approximate universality. This is not the case today in any country. The ignorance of an embassy about the significant events in the country where it works is often striking, as striking as is the belief widely held by professionals and laymen that a country's interests can be represented by purely verbal activities. Yet the staffs of embassies are often so small that real work cannot be done. Of course, there are countries whose diplomats are especially skilled in the political and informational arts, but if too great emphasis is laid upon these factors, such envoys may be unable to create and maintain friendly relations.

The ideal diplomatic service would combine the abilities of the ambassadors of Venice, namely, accurate and judicious observation, with those of the French foreign service before 1914, namely, effective cultivation of friends and allies prepared to support their country in an international crisis which that service was able to forecast accurately, and those of American diplomacy in North Africa in 1942—the active, more-than-verbal, and successful support of the friends of their country and the efficient outmaneuvering of their enemies.

CAREER DIPLOMATS AND POLITICAL APPOINTEES

Many diplomats are neither graduates of diplomatic schools nor the successful winners of a competitive career in the service; they are outsiders appointed to diplomatic posts because of special qualifications or political reasons. In former times, the aristocratic dignitaries of the state were nominated to high-ranking diplomatic posts as a matter of course. They were chosen because they had the confidence of their sovereign and possessed authority based on rank, experience in court life, easy access to the nobility of the foreign country—and because they liked to spend a few years in foreign capitals. In the era of America's economic expansion—the United States having acquired what could be called an aristocracy of wealth—wealthy businessmen, who could afford the expense and wanted the glamour of the diplomatic title, were often appointed to diplomatic positions, successors to the aristocracy of talent, Benjamin Franklin, Thomas Jefferson, John Adams, Arthur Lee, who represented the young Republic at the courts of Europe.

Among the political diplomatic appointees various different groups may be distinguished. Some individuals receive diplomatic appointments through the operation of the spoils system; in some form or other, this system operates in many countries, but most clearly in the United States, where it is customary for the President to appoint some of his campaign supporters or large contributors to the party funds to ambassadorial posts. This practice has by no means disappeared. It is, however, no longer accepted without murmur. Crass cases of partisan favoritism and appointments made plainly for reasons of domestic politics to the detriment, alleged or real, of foreign policy meet opposition, as illustrated by the Senate's refusal to confirm Ed Flynn, Chairman of the Democratic National Committee and political "boss" of New York City, as Ambassador to Australia.

Governments are likely to send personalities abroad whose abilities they value and whose policies they trust. Although the diplomatic service is theoretically independent of changes in domestic politics, diplomats who are in sympathy with the program of the administration are apt to rise more quickly than those who are unsympathetic or neutral. For example, Hugh Gibson, Ambassador to Belgium under President Hoover, was a typically "Republican" diplomat, while Sumner Welles, Undersecretary of State under President Roosevelt, gained prominence under an administration the general political outlook of which he seems to have shared.

Under the Hitler regime, the diplomatic service was more and more staffed with regular party members. Neville Chamberlain picked those diplomats who were most sympathatic to his policies, such as Lord Perth, Sir Nevile Henderson, and Lord Lothian, while others like Sir Robert Vansittart, dour foe of appeasement, were sidetracked.

Diplomatic appointments are often made on the basis of the appointee's political pedigree. Thus, France under Paul Reynaud made its foremost Catholic publicist Wladimir d'Ormesson Ambassador to the Vatican, while the conservative Léon Bérard was sent to Spain, and later, under Pétain, to Rome. Mussolini sent Baron Aloisi, reputedly a liberal and anti-German, to Geneva and the Germanophile Dino Alfieri to Berlin. Sometimes, however, persons are appointed who are not sympathetic to the country where they serve. Mussolini sent the Francophobe Guariglia as Ambassador to France after he had decided on a "dynamic" policy vis-à-vis that country. President Roosevelt sent William Dodd, a well-known liberal and scholar, to Hitler Germany, though he intended to appoint Walter F. Dodds, also a university professor, and appears to have confused one with the other.

In the hope that they may be more successful than the run-of-the-mill diplomat, high-ranking personalities are often selected for difficult and important missions. A classical mission of this type was that of Prince Bülow, former German Chancellor, to Italy in 1914. Bülow was married to an Italian woman and spoke Italian well. It was hoped that he would succeed in keeping Italy neutral and at the same time persuade Austria to sacrifice the South Tyrol, demanded by the Italian Irredentists, as price for Italy's neutrality.[17]

---

[17] The Russians are very adept at this method. For example, they sent Litvinov, who was married to an Englishwoman and, for unexplained reasons, often suspected of "liberal" tendencies, to reopen diplomatic relations between Russia and the United States in 1933 and again in 1941 when Russia needed lend-lease help. The selection of Soviet diplomatic personnel gives clues to their intentions: an expert in revolutionary technique, Oumansky, was sent as Ambassador to Mexico; a former boss of the Communist International,

Sometimes the very highest personalities engage in diplomacy. The President of the United States does this by the explicit authority of his office, as do the prime ministers of several other countries, although they do so usually under extraordinary and crucially important circumstances. During vital conferences—conclusion of alliances, peace negotiations—the diplomats are superseded, and the ministers, prime ministers, presidents, or sovereigns deal directly with each other. They travel into foreign countries—the foreign minister of A goes to B and his visit is returned a little later by a trip of the foreign minister of B to A. Such travels received high prominence during the Second World War—the Axis meetings on the Brenner Pass and the Allied meetings in the Atlantic, Moscow, Teheran, Washington, Casablanca, Cairo, Yalta, and Potsdam have become milestones in diplomatic history. Prior to the war, there was a yearly pilgrimage to Geneva, which after the founding of the United Nations was replaced by a pilgrimage to New York.

High diplomacy has always been a peripatetic business. Before the establishment of permanent diplomatic missions, special visits and meetings were, in fact, the principal occasions for transacting international business. Yet as modern means of transportation were perfected, a new kind of traveler made his appearance on the diplomatic scene. Edward VII, King of England, traveled repeatedly across Europe, preparing by his own initiative—and, incidentally, without precise constitutional authority—those alliances which led to the "encirclement" of Germany after the outbreak of the First World War in 1914. Wilhelm II tried by his own travels to undo Edward's work. During his short reign, Edward VIII attempted to emulate his illustrious grandfather.

Théophile Delcassé, the French statesman, exemplifies a rare blend of the "types" of diplomats enumerated in the above discussion.[18] To placate Germany, Delcassé was removed from office in 1905, an early victim of "appeasement." After his retirement, Delcassé not only maneuvered for a comeback as Foreign Minister, but also aspired to the presidency of France. Consequently, his competitors wished to eliminate him from the domestic scene. At the same time, the French Ambassador to Russia, Georges Louis, opposed to the Franco-Russian alliance, bungled his assignment and greatly endangered the workings of that vital alliance. After a new term as Foreign Minister from 1911 to 1913, Delcassé was appointed, in February, 1913, Ambassador to St. Petersburg in order to repair the damage, in which task he succeeded while sacrificing his ambitions. The reasons for his success were his great authority and skill as well as his trustworthiness from both the Russian and French points of view. Incidentally, he also contributed to the reduction of friction between Great Britain and Russia. His work shows that diplomats, if

---

Manuilski, became delegate to the U.N. General Assembly; and a most experienced "Nosayer" who, according to the *New Yorker,* acts like a descendant of many generations of pickles, Gromyko, went to the Security Council and the Atomic Energy Commission.

[18] See, for example, Pierre Renouvin, *La Crise européenne et la première guerre mondiale,* 3d ed., Paris, Presses Universitaires de France, 1948, p. 145.

they are truly experienced and skillful, can really accomplish many things, but this case also points up the extreme scarcity of diplomats of that caliber.

THE FOREIGN MINISTER

Despite the overwhelming importance of the position of the foreign minister, most appointments to this office are made in a somewhat haphazard manner. While a politician who accedes to a position of power in the national administration usually is adroit at handling domestic politics—an ability which provides at least some kind of a claim to high office—a politician placed by the workings of internal politics at the head of a foreign ministry is often a novice in the field of international relations. He is less well equipped for his task than his government colleagues holding domestic portfolios are for theirs. No wonder, therefore, that competent foreign ministers are scarce.[19]

The foreign ministers who "made history" and are held up by the historians as the great examples are usually those who correctly anticipated a war and concluded a defensive alliance in time, such as Delcassé, or who, like Bismarck, prepared the favorable constellation for an aggressive war. Few were ever successful in a policy aimed at preventing war. It may suffice to recall the names of Duc de Gramont, Sir Edward Grey, William Jennings Bryan, Aristide Briand, Chamberlain, and Bonnet—men whose peaceful intentions were beyond question but who could not maintain peace.

Among the brilliant exceptions from the rule is the Duc de Decazes, whose farsighted policy in 1875 enlisted British and Russian support, thereby discouraging Bismarck from renewed aggression against France. Lord Salisbury, as Foreign Secretary, and Disraeli, as Prime Minister, in the Berlin Congress of 1878, skillfully eliminated the causes of a British-Russian war. Whether the success of these men must be explained by the over-all conditions of the second half of the 19th century, or rather whether the long calm was due to their ability, may be open to serious debate. Yet there is in history no other instance of a group of foreign ministers so intently bent on peace and so consistently successful in preventing war. They were not guided by illusions, as were Hull, Bonnet, and Lord Halifax, but were hard realists who knew how to choose the right means for their policies.

The quality and the success of a foreign policy do not depend upon the abstract goals of that policy but upon its concrete execution. Most statesmen are committed as a matter of course to the popular objectives of peace and common welfare; however, only a few of them have accurate ideas as to how they can attain their goals. For most of them, foreign policy is a matter of precedent and preconceived notions.

[19] In the United States a primary consideration guiding presidential appointments to the secretaryship of state has always been the ability of the appointee to carry the Senate with him. Mr. Hull had been for many years before his appointment by President Roosevelt an important member of the Senate. Messrs. Byrnes and Acheson had at times strong support on the Hill.

Foreign ministers may be divided into two major groups: politicians and professional diplomats. The first group is more numerous because foreign ministers are appointed mostly for reasons of domestic politics. However able a diplomat may be, he rarely has the political backing requisite for high office; from the domestic point of view, he is rarely an asset in terms of partisan politics. A government takes over, and one among the party stalwarts is called to the post of foreign minister. In former times, when governments were recruited from the aristocracy and party lines in the proper sense either did not exist or hardly matttered, the newly appointed prime minister was wont to pick his foreign secretary from among professional diplomats. Yet in modern times the diplomat is regarded as a "nonpolitical" figure, the foreign ministry as the biggest political plum.

This is not to say that chiefs of governments do not exert some kind of selection, appointing those among their followers who, in the past, have shown interest in international relations or have gathered pertinent experience in previous positions. Franklin D. Roosevelt appointed Cordell Hull Secretary of State, not only because he wielded great influence in the political councils of the South, but also because he had, as a member of the Senate, sponsored enlightened tariff legislation and cordial relations with South America. At that time, both problems were among the most important in American foreign policy. In 1944, Mr. Stettinius was appointed successor to Mr. Hull because, as director of American lend-lease operations, he had gathered valuable experiences with foreign countries, presumably enlisting their good will, especially that of the Soviet Union. His colleague at San Francisco in 1945, Anthony Eden, Churchill's Foreign Secretary, possessed wide international experience, gathered first as Sir Austen Chamberlain's parliamentary secretary, then as minister in charge of Britain's dealings with the League of Nations, and then during an earlier tenure as Foreign Secretary. Before World War II he stood for a policy which, by timely opposition to Axis aggression, might have avoided that conflagration. John Foster Dulles, President Eisenhower's Secretary of State, had been the principal adviser on foreign affairs to Thomas Dewey, twice Republican candidate for the presidency, and served briefly in the United States Senate. His appointment brought to the Department of State not only the leading foreign-policy expert of the Republican Party but also the exponent of the "internationalist" wing of the party, which ensured General Eisenhower's nomination at the convention in 1952.

There is an endless procession of foreign ministers who had little or no qualification for that responsible position. In the twenties, an American Secretary of State so signally failed to grasp the nature of international relations that he abolished the code interception service in the Department of State. Under the Brüning government in Germany, Foreign Minister Curtius precipitated a purposeless and foreseeable crisis by concluding in 1931 a customs union with Austria. Since it resulted in the withdrawal of foreign credits, this wanton provocation of France and Britain accentuated the economic crisis in

Germany, aggravated unemployment, and ultimately brought the Nazis into power.[20] Sir John Simon, an eminent barrister and experienced parliamentary leader, was tragically miscast for the role of British Foreign Minister in times of permanent political crisis. The Polish Foreign Minister Colonel Beck, vastly overrating the military strength of his country, balked at establishment of friendly relations with Russia, thus exacerbating the tensions between the Soviet Union and the Western powers, and giving Russia a convenient pretext for concluding the alliance with Germany in 1939. Joachim von Ribbentrop, having gained dubious diplomatic experience as director of the "international research" bureau of the Nazi party, and later as Ambassador to London, advised Hitler in 1939 that England and France would not fight. During the war Ribbentrop, a narrow-minded toady, pursued a policy which made Germany's complete isolation and total defeat inevitable.

What diplomatic skill can achieve in the face of woefully inadequate military and economic resources is best illustrated by two foreign ministers of the Weimar Republic. It is to these two men that Germany owed her speedy recovery from defeat in World War I. The first was Walther Rathenau, assassinated by his grateful compatriots in 1922 after he had succeeded in extricating Germany from her isolation by signing the Rapallo agreement with the Soviet Union. Rathenau reestablished, against the vitriolic opposition of the German nationalists, friendly relations with England and France. He had gathered world-wide experience as an electrical engineer and builder of power stations in England, Holland, Argentina, Russia, France, and Switzerland, and traveled widely in Africa and Asia. Incidentally, it was Rathenau who invented the term and concept of "planned economy." [21]

Gustav Stresemann was called to the German Foreign Office after a witless government had brought Germany to the brink of a new war with France (*Ruhrkrieg*). Stresemann not only persuaded France to withdraw her troops from the Ruhr Valley but gained Germany's admittance to the League of Nations, thus recovering the status of equality among the great powers, a rank Germany seemed to have lost forever. Stresemann had learned to deal with foreign policy as one of the most influential members of the *Reichstag*. He had started out as a nationalist, but experience had taught him the wisdom of moderation. Unlike Rathenau, who had been appointed to the post of Foreign Minister mainly on the basis of sheer ability, Stresemann came to power by the mechanics of parliamentary party politics. It has often been asserted that Stresemann only feigned devotion to the ideals of the League but sought, in fact, to deceive the Western powers, a charge emphatically refuted by those who claim that he gave his life for the cause of peace. The fact remains that

[20] The true British attitudes toward the *Zollverein* attempt and the related Franco-British-German negotiations have now been revealed in *Documents on British Foreign Policy 1919–1939*, edited by E. L. Woodward and Rohan Butler, Second Series, London, H.M. Stationery Office, 1947, Vol. II, "1931," pp. 1–57.

[21] See Count Harry Kessler, *Walther Rathenau*, New York, Harcourt, Brace, 1930.

Stresemann restored to Germany international prestige and influence, objectives deemed wholly desirable by the great majority of the German people.

Revolutionary upheavals, such as the French Revolution and overthrow of the Tsarist regime, appear to release untapped talents in foreign politics just as in domestic and military affairs. Revolutionary governments, locked in the stark struggle for survival, do not hesitate to call on unusual and unconventional men to deal with perilous situations. Talleyrand, a former bishop and aristocrat, whose ancestors included many high officers, prelates, and ministers, guided for nearly twenty years the foreign policy of Revolutionary and Napoleonic France. Upon the outbreak of the Revolution, he went to England and the United States, returned and made his peace with the new powers, with the express purpose of assuming power himself. Significantly, he opened his campaign by an address before a scientific society on questions of foreign policy. He attained office by clever manipulation of domestic politics and influential women—such as the celebrated Madame de Staël—later supported Bonaparte's *coup d'état* of 18 Brumaire, and henceforth stayed in office because his skill as negotiator and urbane understanding of international affairs were invaluable to Napoleon. It was Talleyrand who in 1814–1815 extricated France from the worst consequences of defeat.[22]

The Soviets appointed Leon Trotsky as their first Foreign Commissar because his knowledge of languages and foreign countries as well as of the finer points of Marxist dialectics seemed to qualify him for the post. Trotsky, an unbending doctrinaire, proved a failure at Brest-Litovsk and was replaced by Chicherin, son of a career diplomat and an old-time Bolshevik with a thorough knowledge of diplomacy and diplomats. Litvinov started out as the Soviet representative at London, where he happened to reside at the time of the revolution. He later served in key positions in the Foreign Commissariat and led numerous diplomatic missions abroad. When he became Foreign Commissar, he was undoubtedly the Soviets' foremost expert in international relations.

To the second category of foreign ministers belong those who rise from the diplomatic ranks by virtue of professional skill. Among brilliant representatives of that type are Metternich (former Ambassador to Paris), Gorchakov (Ambassador to the Frankfurt Diet and Vienna), and Bismarck (Ambassador to Paris and St. Petersburg). At the moment of this writing, not a single important country can boast of a foreign minister who is a career diplomat.

The selection of foreign ministers, professionals or amateurs, is more often than not a matter of accident. Sometimes their choice is dictated by strange

---

[22] On Talleyrand's role in the saving of France, see Louis Madelin, *Talleyrand,* Paris, Flammarion, 1944, p. 238. A far more flattering portrait was painted by Guglielmo Ferrero in *The Reconstruction of Europe: Talleyrand and the Congress of Vienna 1814–1815,* New York, Putnam, 1941. In addition to Talleyrand's own memoirs, also consult Alfred Duff-Cooper, *Talleyrand,* New York, Harper, 1932.

involutions of political psychology. After Munich the Czechs appointed their Ambassador to Berlin, Chvalkovski, a notorious appeaser, as Foreign Minister, hoping that he would prove able and willing to appease Hitler. In April, 1945, Admiral Doenitz replaced Ribbentrop with Hitler's Finance Minister Schwerin-Krosigk, reasoning that this man, who had the reputation of being a supporter of Pastor Niemöller, would get better terms from the British and Americans. There is reason to believe that Secretary Byrnes was appointed chiefly because, under the legal provisions then in force, the presidential succession devolved upon the Secretary of State. Mr. Byrnes thus directed the international relations of the United States because he was considered the best available successor to the presidency.

In order to forestall the evil effects of "political" or random selection, virtually all countries developed the expedient of having career diplomats administer the department and "advise" the minister. These functionaries, called in some countries Permanent Secretary, in others Secretary General, and in others Undersecretary, are as a rule appointed from the service. Yet these officials are rarely immune to changes in the political climate; their "permanence" is as ephemeral as that of party politicians. Sir Robert Vansittart was removed by "promotion" to an insignificant office, created especially for this purpose, when he objected too strenuously to Neville Chamberlain's policy. When Paul Reynaud took over in 1940, he dismissed Alexis St. Léger, who had been Secretary General for nine years, and appointed Charles-Roux, at that time Ambassador to the Vatican. Mr. Sumner Welles, a most experienced diplomat who, during the prolonged illnesses of Mr. Hull, for long months on end was Acting Secretary of State, was dismissed for personal reasons. When Mr. Bevin became Foreign Secretary in 1945, he installed his own permanent secretary; the Undersecretary of State of Mr. Byrnes was not the same as that of Mr. Stettinius. Thus, while in theory the permanent secretary is supposed to counteract the hazards of the political appointment, in practice the undersecretary has also become a political appointee.

It may be concluded that choice for high office in the world's foreign ministries has not been, and is not, guided by selection of the fittest. The domestic power struggle determines the appointment of the foreign minister and his chief advisers. Domestic power competition thus enters into power competition on the international scale.

BIBLIOGRAPHY

Beaulac, Willard L.: *Career Ambassador,* New York, Macmillan, 1951.
Berndorff, Hans Rudolf: *Diplomatische Unterwelt,* Stuttgart, Union, 1930.
———: *Espionage,* New York, Appleton-Century-Crofts, 1930.
Brookings Institution: *The Administration of Foreign Affairs and Overseas Operations,* Government Printing Office, 1951.
Callières, François de: *The Practice of Diplomacy,* London, Whyte, 1919.
Cambon, Jules Martin: *The Diplomatist,* London, Allen & Son, 1931.

Courcy, John de: *Behind the Battle*, London, Eyre, 1942.
Craig, Gordon A., and Felix Gilbert: *The Diplomats*, Princeton, N.J., Princeton University Press, 1953.
Duff-Cooper, Alfred: *Talleyrand*, New York, Harper, 1932.
Forgac, Arpad: *Essai sur la diplomatie nouvelle*, Paris, A. Pedone, 1937.
Garden, Guillaume de: *Traité complet de diplomatie*, Paris, Treuttel et Würtz, 1833.
Genet, Raoul: *"Traité de diplomatie et de droit diplomatique,"* *Revue générale de droit international public*, Nos. 3, 5, 6, Paris, A. Pedone, 1931–1932.
Granet, Pierre: *L'Évolution des méthodes diplomatiques*, Paris, A. Rousseau, 1939.
Hankey, Sir Maurice: *Diplomacy by Conference*, London, Benn, 1946.
Hayward, Charles W.: *What Is Diplomacy?* London, Richards, 1916.
Kühlmann, Richard von: *Die Diplomaten*, Berlin, Hobbing, 1939.
Lion Depetre, José: *Diplomacia y diplomaticos*, Mexico, B. Costa-Amic, 1944.
Lippmann, Walter: *Stakes of Diplomacy*, New York, Holt, 1917.
London, Kurt: *How Foreign Policy Is Made*, New York, Van Nostrand, 1949.
Martens, Karl: *Le Guide diplomatique*, Leipzig, F. A. Brockhaus, 1866.
Nicholson, Harold: *Diplomacy*, London, Butterworth, 1939.
Pecquet, Antoine: *Discours sur l'art de négocier*, Paris, Nyon Fils, 1737.
Pradier-Fodère, P.: *Cours de droit diplomatique*, 2 vols., Paris, Pedone-Lauriel, 1881.
Royas Paz, Pablo: *Hombres y momentos de la diplomacia*, Buenos Aires, Atlantida, 1946.
Salemi, Leonardo: *Politica estera: Teoria, storia, diplomazia*, Palermo, 1936.
Satow, Sir Ernest M.: *A Guide to Diplomatic Practice*, 2 vols., London, Longmans, Roberts and Green, 1922.
Stuart, G. H.: *American Diplomatic and Consular Practice*, rev. ed., New York, Appleton-Century-Crofts, 1952.
———: *The Department of State*, New York, Macmillan, 1949.
Szilassy, Gyula, and Julius Pilis: *Traité pratique de diplomatie moderne*, Paris, Payot, 1928.
Thompson, James Westfall: *Secret Diplomacy*, London, The Century, 1937.
Tilley, Sir James, and S. Gaselee: *The Foreign Office*, New York, Putnam, 1933.
Wellesley, Sir Victor: *Diplomacy in Fetters*, London, Hutchinson, 1944.
Wesendonck, Otto Guenther von: *Diplomatie*, Radolfzell, Bodensee, A. Dressler, 1933.
Willert, Arthur: *The Road to Safety, A Study in Anglo-American Relations*, New York, Praeger, 1953.

Chapter 11

DOMESTIC POLITICS AND FOREIGN POLICY

It is not often that the reflections of high officials are exposed unedited to public view. It is only because of a grievous indiscretion that an American diplomat's observations destined for his immediate associates on the question of foreign policy versus domestic politics were published by the daily press. An effort was made in December, 1937, by the German Ambassador, Dr. Hans Dieckhoff, to negotiate a reciprocal trade agreement with the United States. American officials, who favored exploring the German offer in good faith, feared domestic political reactions in this country adverse to the administration in view of the feeling of many Americans against Hitler and his entire regime, and for that reason suggested that nothing be attempted until after the Congressional elections in the fall.

The effort of Ambassador Dieckhoff to improve German-American relations was set forth by Charles F. Darlington, assistant chief of the trade agreements division of the State Department in a long memorandum to his chief, which casts light not only on the formation of American foreign policy but also on the influence of domestic politics upon the routine conduct of foreign affairs.

Mr. Darlington observed that: "the maintenance of an unsympathetic attitude by this Government is not to the disadvantage of Germany alone; it has unfortunate consequences also for us."

Mr. Darlington argued that it would react against the moderates in Germany who were seeking to restrain the party extremists if German trade did not develop "with a minimum of regard to our formerly very great interest in the German market," and it would give American trade agreements policy "a two-faced appearance," casting a "shadow of discredit" upon it "in the eyes of those familiar with it at home."

Furthermore, Mr. Darlington contended, it would "strengthen Germany's feeling of encirclement" and give this feeling "more basis in fact." But in urging a constructive approach to the German offer, Mr. Darlington recognized the political factors here at home and suggested that for that reason nothing be attempted until after the fall elections. Mr. Darlington wrote: [1]

[1] Document released by the House Un-American Activities Committee, Dec. 16, 1948, as quoted by *The New York Times,* Dec. 17, 1948. The italics are Mr. Darlington's.

233

It is recognized that the first reaction of many will be that any commercial agreement with Germany would be *bad domestic politics in that certain groups would oppose it bitterly while the general public would show for it little enthusiasm.* Such an agreement might be expected for a period to cause the Administration embarrassment, and to reflect adversely upon the trade agreements program.

Certainly the best politics of all, at any time, is the politics of prosperity. An agreement with Germany, if at all comprehensive, could hold promise of greater gains for American exports, and particularly American agricultural exports, than an agreement with any other country.

If an agreement were concluded following next autumn's elections, a year and a half would still remain before the expiration of the Trade Agreements Act, and two years before the Presidential elections, in which its beneficial effects could be *influencing and softening public opinion.*

Such an attitude reveals a schizophrenic frame of mind. It also reveals a fundamental misreading of the obligations of representative government. The Constitution does not impose on the elected politician and his aids the duty to follow the dictates of public opinion. It is the essence of representative government that the politician is voted into office on the theory that he can defend the interests of the people better than the people themselves. In order to free him from the pressure of day-by-day fluctuations in opinion, he is not subject to recall during his term of office (except through impeachment). It is up to the elected statesman to act according to his best judgment but not according to the presumed dictates of a variable public opinion. It is true that he may fall in the line of duty, exactly as the soldier may fall; but his risk is considerably smaller. On the other hand, if his judgment is vindicated, his stature is bound to increase and his reelection is assured. From the personal career point of view, it is a doubtful policy to base one's decisions on the quicksand of public opinion; from the national point of view, it is disastrous.

The "influencing and softening of public opinion" is part of the policy maker's job in democratic countries as well as in lands ruled by despots. However, in democratic countries the pressure of public opinion is direct and is recorded with considerable immediacy and speed upon that sensitive negative, parliamentary representation. "The conscience of Congress," as one writer puts it, "is peculiarly sensitive to large numbers." Though a U.S. Senator has less cause to worry about the passing fancies of the public than his colleague in the House or even the President and may at times "be to a surprising degree deaf to the voice of public opinion," [2] he, too, is receptive to the wishes of the public—if that public represents "large numbers." Whatever may be one's opinion on the Senate's record in foreign affairs, that record is not the Senate's own but also that of the voter. That the voter may condemn his elected representatives for having acted in accordance with his

[2] Thomas A. Bailey, *The Man in the Street,* New York, Macmillan, 1948, p. 7.

wishes is not so much of a paradox as it may seem. It is a phenomenon familiar to psychologists and theologians.

THE SENATE AND U.S. FOREIGN POLICY

"Whipping a dead horse was ever a waste of effort," W. Stull Holt prefaces his book entitled *Treaties Defeated by the Senate*,[3]

yet not more so, many people would maintain, than proving that senators are influenced by considerations alien to the merits of the questions on which they vote. Everyone knows that the Senate has sometimes rejected treaties for reasons that have nothing to do with the wisdom of the foreign policy presented. Everyone knows that these extraneous reasons can usually be traced either to the struggle between President and Senate for the control of foreign policy or to the warfare of the President's political opponents who hope to secure some partisan advantage.

All this may be a dead horse, yet it is important to realize to what extent foreign policy may be decided by reasons of domestic and electoral politics and may become divorced from the true interests of the country. This state of affairs, an undue and unwarranted influence of domestic politics on foreign policy, by no means prevails only in the United States. However, the treaty-making power of the Senate is, for all practical purposes, a unique institution and exposes this country more than any other to the vicissitudes of domestic quibbling.

The Senate has acted as a brake to such an extent that virtually all Presidents have refrained from submitting treaties which, but for partisan reasons, would otherwise have been advantageous to this country. Repeatedly, various Secretaries of States expressed the belief that the Senate would not again accept a treaty of importance. During the ten years between 1805 and 1815 not a single treaty was submitted to the Senate, an extraordinary fact even if the United States' geographic remoteness from the principal theater of world politics is considered. It was a performance which was hardly ever duplicated in the history of any country.

The Louisiana Purchase stands out as the most important single diplomatic act in early American history. This treaty, which not only insured the political and economic future of the country but also removed the threat of war with France, was forced upon a reluctant Senate only by unusual pressure exerted by the Executive. In 1824, a treaty was signed with Great Britain for the suppression of the slave trade. The stipulations of the draft treaty conformed to senatorial wishes. Yet the Senate killed the treaty by writing into it a provision which authorized the United States to capture vessels off slave territory under British control, while Britain was denied a similar right off the coasts of the United States. The reason for the rejection, besides

[3] W. Stull Holt, *Treaties Defeated by the Senate,* Baltimore, Johns Hopkins Press, 1933, p. 1. The discussion is based on this excellent treatise.

partisan politics, was the opposition of many Senators to the abolition of slavery. In 1824, another antislavery treaty was concluded with Colombia. The terms of this treaty were identical with those which the Senate had approved in the treaty with Great Britain. Yet the treaty was defeated by a large majority, again because of its abolitionist implications.

Another senatorial puzzle was a treaty of commerce with Texas signed in 1842. After considerable temporization, the Senate eliminated from the treaty all clauses containing concessions made to Texas. For example, the Senate rejected the article which permitted Texas to market cotton in the United States free of duty for five years. This chicanery had little lasting consequences, yet it risked driving Texas into the hands of Great Britain and France who sought to enter into close relations with the new state.

In 1844 a treaty for the annexation of Texas was submitted. This treaty was killed for purely domestic reasons connected with a presidential election. The Senate action was one of the major causes of the Mexican War and is considered by some historians as an important link in the chain of events which ultimately led to the Civil War. The election proved the Senate to have misjudged the wishes of the country which desired the union with Texas, and the annexation was finally proclaimed. Holt writes that one "may well tremble at the narrow escape from disaster, for an independent Texas guaranteed by Great Britain and France would have been disastrous. . . . The risk was run by the United States . . . not because of any sincere difference of opinion among those in control of foreign policy but because of the hope of partisan advantage."

The purchase of Alaska from Russia, another step of extreme importance in American history, was approved by the Senate despite President Johnson's opposition. The Senate voted ratification in order to show its gratitude for Russian naval help during the Civil War. The picture of high-minded unanimity is slightly marred by the revelation that the Russian minister to Washington had made a "judicious distribution" of money "to newspaper writers and members of Congress."

In 1867, a commercial treaty was signed with Hawaii which would have been economically beneficial to both countries but would also have obligated the United States to offer protection to the island kingdom. The Senate postponed deliberations for more than a year, rejected the treaty, and in 1870 voted against a supplementary treaty extending the time of ratification.

At approximately the same time a treaty was concluded with Denmark for the purchase of two islands in the West Indies. This treaty was rejected despite its manifestly favorable conditions. The later history of this treaty is revealing as regards the Senate's pace and effectiveness in matters of foreign policy. In 1892 negotiations were resumed but proved futile. In 1902 a new treaty was signed and ratified, but this time the angry Danes refused ratification. In 1917 the purchase was accomplished but at a considerably higher price than had been possible fifty years earlier. The United States was able to consummate the transaction chiefly because Denmark pursued a policy of friendship and moderation. After the United States had refused to purchase the islands, Denmark was free to sell them to one of several great European powers. In this case, the United States would have been compelled to intervene or to suffer a flagrant violation of the Monroe Doctrine, in addition to being committed to the indefensible policy of depriving Denmark of the right to sell the islands but at the same time refusing to buy them itself. Moreover, a plebiscite conducted in the islands in order to determine the willingness of the people to join the United States was in the affirmative. Had Denmark not been a liberal power, the population might have been made to suffer for its stand.

In the period between 1869 and 1898 the Senate handled 134 treaties and turned down 20 of these. Only routine treaties were approved, while nearly all treaties which were of any political importance were defeated. Among these was a treaty with the Dominican Republic which was to have given the United States command of the Caribbean and the Isthmus and which President Grant considered urgent because a European power was known to be seeking a foothold in Santo Domingo. Senator Sumner opened his oration opposing this treaty with the following words which, although they seem singularly irrelevant as regards the issue at hand, may be taken as choice samples of partisan debate: "The resolution before the Senate commits Congress to a dance of blood."

Under Grant's presidency a naval officer secured, for a promise of protection and friendship, a treaty with a native chief on Tutuila, Samoa Islands, which granted the United States the right to establish a naval base in Pago Pago. This treaty died in the Committee on Foreign Relations.

In 1893 a new ruler came to power in Hawaii and concluded a treaty with the United States providing for the annexation of the islands. This treaty was submitted to the Senate during the last days of an outgoing administration, and the new President, Grover Cleveland, withdrew the treaty. He apparently had some doubt that the Hawaiian revolution was entirely spontaneous and was not engineered with American help. The main motive was the desire of Cleveland and his party to discredit former President Harrison and his administration. In 1897, when the revolutionary government was still in power, and while Cleveland was out of office, a second treaty for the annexation of Hawaii was signed. Yet the Senate refused ratification. The administration, therefore, planned to by-pass the Senate and to annex Hawaii by a joint resolution. However, before a decision was reached on this point, war with Spain broke out; the annexation was carried out as a war emergency measure and approved by large majorities in both Houses.

The United States was one of the champions of the policy of international arbitration and assumed leadership in the movement to substitute arbitration for the use of force in international affairs. In 1897, however, the Senate blocked the signing of arbitration treaties, for the simple reason that such treaties would deprive the Senate of some of its control over foreign affairs. In that same year, the Senate rejected a treaty signed between the United States and Great Britain which committed both countries to the adjustment of disputes by arbitration. In the words of Sir Julian Pauncefote, the Senate was "determined to retain absolute control over every case of arbitration, and for that purpose" destroyed "the treaty by amendments which reduced it to a mere agreement to arbitrate any dispute, provided it be with the consent of the Senate, and on such terms and on such conditions as a Senate might choose to prescribe." The Senate took this action presumably against the will of the majority of Americans; it acted in the sole interest of preserving its constitutional prerogatives.

When, in 1898, the peace treaty with Spain was submitted to the Senate, that august body had not approved any important treaty for more than twenty-five years. The Spanish peace treaty was saved through the exertions of Senator Lodge who, five minutes before the final vote, won over the second of four doubtful Senators; two more negative votes would have been sufficient to reject the treaty. Even so, it is doubtful whether any positive vote would have been secured without the resumption of fighting in Manila, and there is no doubt that, in order to get the treaty accepted, liberal use was made of patronage.

There is, however, an example in which the Senate succeeded in obtaining better conditions for the United States than had been secured by the administration in the treaty submitted. This is the first Hay-Pauncefote Treaty of 1900 designed to authorize the United States to build a canal through the Isthmus of Panama. This treaty had to take account of British rights secured in earlier agreements and it provided for neutralization of the canal and the prohibition of fortifications. The Senate rejected the treaty by amending it drastically. The British accepted the substance of these amendments in the second Hay-Pauncefote Treaty, acting largely in fear of the growing German naval threat. This treaty permitted the United States not only to build the Panama Canal but to integrate it in the American defensive system.

In 1905, President Theodore Roosevelt concluded a treaty with the Dominican Republic by which the United States was to supervise the finances of that country in order to prevent European states from collecting by force money owed them. This treaty was in line with the Monroe Doctrine and designed to forestall any violation of that basic American policy. Yet the Senate rejected the treaty. It was saved only by a subterfuge of President Roosevelt, who negotiated a temporary *modus vivendi* stipulating that supervision was to be carried out by individuals (and not by the United States government) nominated by the American President and appointed by the Dominican President. In the end the Senate signed a modified version of the original treaty in 1907.

President Taft also concluded treaties providing for supervision of the finances of certain Caribbean countries, most of which were defeated for purely domestic reasons. He was equally unlucky with various arbitration treaties, which were rejected because, as stated in a majority report of the Committee on Foreign Relations: "The constitutional powers of the Senate are taken away pro tanto and are transferred to a commission, upon the composition of which the Senate has no control whatever."

The action of the Senate with respect to the Versailles Treaty, the League of Nations, and later performances such as the Neutrality Act of 1935, are too well known to bear discussion.

The unratified treaties mentioned in the above discussion were merely selected as random examples. The list could be extended and many examples given when the administration did not even seriously consider a necessary step in foreign policy because it would not have proved acceptable to the Senate. It is not asserted here that the Senate acted unwisely in those cases where it opposed expansion of the United States. Expansion is not always beneficial. Yet the point must be made that in almost every instance when measures designed to enlarge the territories and influence of the United States were laid before the Senate, there were compelling reasons for adopting expansionist policies, including the desire to avert entanglements and war. In many cases annexation by the United States was desired by the inhabitants of the annexed territories. If the Senate had had its way, the United States would hardly have grown to be a world power. The most disappointing aspect of this story, however, is that the attitude of the Senators, though sometimes defensible, was in most cases based on considerations of domestic policies. It was the domestic politics, and not any doctrine of foreign policy, which determined and guided foreign policy. In practically all the cases mentioned, the senatorial rank and file cared more for what would be apt to sway their constituents at the next election than for the best interests of the United States in world politics.[4]

In fairness to the Senate it must be stressed that political considerations weighed heavily also on foreign policy decisions made by various Presidents. Nor would it be accurate to state that Congressional obstruction of a presidential foreign policy was always harmful to the best interests of the country; Congress did prevent many foolish acts, though unfortunately not enough of them. Lastly, it should be noted that there have been cases of administrative sabotage of foreign policy laws enacted by Congress. The failings of the Senate undoubtedly were the bane of the foreign policy of the United States during the 19th century. The failings of the Executive were fraught with grave consequences under many administrations in the 20th century.

For example, the recognition of the Soviet Union in 1933 was decided upon by President Roosevelt in practical disregard of the State Department's ad-

---

[4] Reduced to its simplest terms, the politician's dilemma is that of ambition and duty. "I have never been afraid of failing morally. The man who enters public life has always at command a sure resource against this danger, that is—retirement" (Prince Metternich, as quoted by Bertrand Russell in *Freedom versus Organization,* New York, Norton, 1934, p. 7).

vice. For many years communist propaganda had asserted that recognition would lead to an immediate and drastic enlargement of American trade with Russia. Nothing of the kind happened.[5]

Congressional criticism might have prevented President Roosevelt from making an agreement with Russia by which the possessions of a third state, China, were bartered away, without knowledge of or consent by that third government.[6] The Yalta dealings were secret diplomacy at its worst. President Truman's negotiations with the Russians during 1945, in the course of which he abandoned a large portion of the American conquests in Germany—western Saxony and Thuringia, as well as a land corridor to Berlin—for empty Russian promises, well might have been attended by less disastrous consequences had they been subject to Congressional scrutiny and approval.

Under modern conditions, the two-thirds rule of the Senate has lost much of its significance. The Senate has shown itself highly amenable to administrative leadership in foreign affairs, partly as a result of the vast propaganda machine by which any presidential policy is being supported, partly also because the Senate could not but respond to pressing security needs. The best illustration of this change may be found in the fact that the initiative for the North Atlantic Treaty Organization originated in a bipartisan Senate declaration. It is also a fact that the Senate accepted treaties submitted to it since 1945, usually with huge majorities. Examples are the NATO pact

[5] On July 27, 1933, the acting Secretary of State handed President Roosevelt a memorandum by the chief of the Division of Eastern European Affairs, Mr. Robert F. Kelley, in which the reasons against recognition were summarized. It was stated that the Soviet government was unwilling "to observe certain generally accepted principles governing the conduct of nations towards each other," such as the payment of debts. It was emphasized that the Soviet trade monopoly would produce considerable difficulties in the relations with the Soviet Union. The most important statement of the memorandum reads: "So long as the communist regime continues to carry on in other countries activities designed to bring about ultimately the overthrow of the government and institutions of these countries, the establishment of genuine friendly relations between Russia and those countries is out of the question. . . . It would seem, therefore, that an essential prerequisite to the establishment of harmonious and trustful relations with the Soviet government is the abandonment by the present rulers of Russia of their world revolutionary aims and the discontinuance of their activities designed to bring about the realization of such aims." U.S. Department of State Publication 4539, *Foreign Relations of the United States, Diplomatic Papers, the Soviet Union 1933 to 1939*, Government Printing Office, 1952, pp. 6–11. Whether the President ever read this memorandum or whether he took its argument seriously is not known. He decided upon recognition in two very casual conversations with Secretary of State Cordell Hull, who himself did not give the matter deep thought or study. See Cordell Hull, *The Memoirs of Cordell Hull*, New York, Macmillan, 1948, Vol. I, pp. 293, 297. It is remarkable that while in London, Hull tried to sound out the British Foreign Secretary Sir John Simon, to find out whether the British recognition of Soviet Russia had been a success. "But for some reason or other Simon would talk but very little" (*ibid.*, p. 239). The talkative American did not get the point his British colleague wanted to put across by silence.

[6] The efforts to bring Russia into the war against Japan were opposed as unwise and unnecessary by the U.S. Navy. See *Military Situation in the Far East*, Hearings before the Committee on Armed Services, U.S. Senate, 82d Cong., 1st Sess., Part 4, pp. 3055f. and p. 2731. See also William D. Leahy, *I Was There*, New York, McGraw-Hill, 1950, p. 318.

itself and the Japanese peace treaty. In some cases, such as the peace treaty with Italy which subjected that country to disarmament provisions quite incompatible with American security interests, it might have been wiser for the Senate to assert its prerogatives rather than be the rubber stamp of the administration.

FOREIGN POLICY AND THE U.S. CONSTITUTION

We must now give attention to one particularly difficult and vexatious problem that constantly plagues and sometimes obstructs American foreign policy, the constitutional problem. The Constitution of the United States does not authorize the executive department to carry out foreign policy alone. The executive department shares its powers with Congress. In Article II of the Constitution it is stated that the President "shall have power, by and with the advice and consent of the Senate, to make treaties, provided two-thirds of the Senators present concur." As we have seen, this so-called two-thirds rule of the Senate has, time and again, blocked treaties even though they would have been of great advantage to the welfare and security of the United States.

While diplomatic paralysis was not particularly dangerous during the 19th century, when the United States lived in almost complete isolation, times have changed. In the air age foreign relations have to be handled with speed. The Constitution of the United States—at least as it is generally interpreted —prevents speedy treatment of foreign problems; theoretically, the country may be confronted by the gravest danger, and yet Congress, basing itself on its constitutional rights, may forestall executive action.

This situation was highlighted in 1940, one of the most dangerous years in the history of Western civilization. France was about to fall, and the French Premier, Paul Reynaud, tried with all his waning strength to keep his country fighting. There was but one means to hold the European front against Nazism: the *active* help of the United States. Consequently, Reynaud sent a cable to President Roosevelt in which we read:

I beseech you to declare publicly that the United States will give the Allies aid and material support by all means short of an expeditionary force. I beseech you to do this before it is too late. I know the gravity of such a gesture. Its very gravity demands that it should not be made too late.

You said to us yourself on the 5th of October, 1937: "I am compelled and you are compelled to look ahead. The peace, the freedom and the security of 90 per cent of the population of the world are being jeopardized by the remaining 10 per cent who are threatening a breakdown of all international order and law.

"Surely the 90 per cent who want to live in peace under law and in accordance with moral standards that have received almost universal acceptance through the centuries, can and must find some way to make their will prevail."

The hour has now come for these.

M. Reynaud quoted aptly. He called upon America to make good its word and stand up and fight for the ideals which it championed. President Roosevelt answered as follows:

In these hours which are so heart-rending for the French people and yourself, I send you the assurances of my utmost sympathy, and I can further assure you that so long as the French people continue in defense of their liberty which constitutes the cause of popular institutions throughout the world, so long will they rest assured that matériel and supply will be sent to them from the United States in ever-increasing quantities and kinds.

I know that you will understand that these statements carry with them no implication of military commitments. Only the Congress can make such commitments.

The paralysis of American foreign policy that was climaxed by the fall of France lasted for another eighteen months until the day when bombs dropped on Pearl Harbor.

Many proposals have been worked out aiming at the reform of those constitutional processes which may hamper American foreign affairs.[7] Though this is not the place to discuss the merits or demerits of these proposals, it may be pointed out that most of them concentrate on the abolition of the two-thirds rule. Since there is little likelihood that such a change will be accepted and that the treaty rights of the Senate will be deleted from the Constitution, these ideas are of little practical interest in the present phase of American history. The more important problem, therefore, is this: what can be done within the framework of the American Constitution as it is *now* in force?

It should be obvious that the Constitution is a broad and general *outline* of the *principles* which govern American politics. It does *not* determine how these principles should be implemented. Foreign policy is conducted at present far more effectively than 100 or even 50 years ago. During the most recent past American conduct of foreign affairs has become increasingly flexible. It can be argued that the stalemate of 1940 was partly due to tactical errors on the part of Mr. Roosevelt and Mr. Hull. It is certain that their conduct was in part influenced by considerations of domestic politics and, in particular, of Mr. Roosevelt's impending campaign for reelection. However that may be, the flexibility of the Constitution must be recognized as of prime importance.

The power of Congress to declare war would severely limit the capabilities of the President in the conduct of foreign affairs, not only positively, but also negatively. Twice in American history, in 1812 and 1898, Congress provoked unnecessary wars, the first of which greatly endangered American

---

[7] See especially Kenneth Colegrove, *The American Senate and World Peace*, New York, Vanguard, 1944; Thomas K. Finletter, *Can Representative Government Do the Job?* New York, Reynal & Hitchcock, 1945; Henry Hazlitt, *A New Constitution Now*, New York, Whittlesey, 1942; Clinton L. Rossiter, *Constitutional Dictatorship*, Princeton, N. J., Princeton University Press, 1948. For a contrary view, see R. J. Dangerfield, *In Defense of the Senate*, Norman, Okla., University of Oklahoma Press, 1933.

independence. However, according to Article II, Section 2, the President is appointed Commander in Chief of the Army and Navy of the United States. By virtue of being the Commander in Chief, the President can send the armed forces of the United States wherever he pleases. Or as William Howard Taft, former President of the United States, defined it: "The President is Commander in Chief. Under this he can order the army and navy anywhere he will, if the appropriation furnish the means of transportation."

Presidents of the United States have ordered the execution of well over 100 military operations outside the borders of the United States. Some of these operations, whatever they were called at the time, were wars. From 1798 to 1800, there were large-scale hostilities with France. Two wars were fought against the Barbary States. The United States participated prominently in the repression of the Boxer Rebellion in China, during 1900 and 1901. Mexican-American hostilities in 1914–1917 were full-fledged wars, as were numerous other military "interventions" in Latin America. The Siberian expedition in 1918–1920 was a large-scale military operation.[8]

Attention may be invited to a provision in the Constitution which is usually overlooked in discussions of our problem: According to Article IV, Section 4, the United States "shall protect" each state of the Union "against invasions." It would seem that this sweeping provision gives the President wide freedom of action. In other words, while Congress has the right to *declare* war, the President has the right to *make* and *wage* war, and he can exercise this right as long as the forces and the money at his disposal last. Only if and when he runs short of soldiers and supplies would the President have to return to Congress for further authorization. It is noteworthy that Congress can declare war *by simple majority;* wars can be declared *without* a two-thirds majority of the Senate.

The most sweeping Constitutional provision obstructing speedy execution of foreign policy is the two-thirds rule. While this provision may seem very stringent and is often invoked as a pretext for inaction, actually it can be circumvented easily and legally. The Constitution fails to give a definition of the term "treaty." Nor does it stipulate the particular type of international action where a treaty is required. Any type of agreement can be concluded by the American government with any foreign government without using the instrument of a "treaty"—with the possible exception of peace treaties.[9]

[8] This whole problem was discussed *in extenso* by James Grafton Rogers in *World Policing and the Constitution* (Boston, World Peace Foundation, 1945). Rogers gives a complete list of these operations in the appendix to his book.

[9] McClure concludes his exposition with the statement that the President can do by executive agreement anything he can do by treaty. The President may need the cooperation of Congress, but there is a wide field of action where such cooperation is unnecessary and where Congress has no constitutional authority to dissent. "There is nothing that can be done by treaty that cannot be done by Congress-confirmed executive agreement." See W. M. McClure, *International Executive Agreements,* New York, Columbia University Press, 1941, p. 386; see also p. 363.

The only reason why a government should resort to a formal treaty is that it wants to give to its word the highest degree of solemnity and to increase its reliability vis-à-vis its partners. Practical reasons, therefore, sometimes suggest that a treaty be concluded. Practical reasons may *also* suggest that an agreement be *not* couched in the form of an official and formal treaty. The reason why many governments seek to conclude formal treaties instead of mere matter-of-fact agreements is that treaties are supposedly the strongest and only truly unbreakable commitment—according to the Constitution, treaties are the "supreme law of the land" (Article VI). This view overlooks the historical fact that other countries do *not* give so high a legal valuation to treaties.

Nor is it necessarily in the interest of the United States that an agreement with a foreign power be valued so highly that it becomes "the supreme law of the land." In view of the fluidity of foreign affairs, no government should bind itself to that extent.

In the absence of prophetic gifts, few responsible governments are ever ready to commit themselves over long periods of time. Treaties are usually concluded to take care of concrete situations even though they may be phrased in general terms. However, to reconcile the need of meeting a specific situation with the other (usually fancied) need of describing this situation in general terms, treaty texts are more often than not ambiguous and full of loopholes. This is particularly true of the overpropagandized North Atlantic Pact of 1949.

It can be said that no treaty has ever been concluded in modern times which would not have permitted any skillful international lawyer to extricate his government from the commitment. Many treaties become pointless shortly after their ratification, because fundamentally different situations arise. For example, when England in 1944 agreed to the dismemberment of Poland, she was still formally allied with that country. Throughout the Cold War with Russia and the Berlin blockade, both France and Britain were allied with Russia. Whatever the treaty provisions, a profound change in the international situation always gives the convenient and sometimes the valid pretext to invoke the clause *rebus sic stantibus* and thus to invalidate the treaty.

Less than two-fifths of the approximately 2,000 international agreements which the United States has entered into before 1934 have been made as treaties according to the constitutional procedure.[10] Most agreements were couched in the form of "executive agreements." *The use of such executive*

---

[10] See Henry S. Fraser, *Treaties and Executive Agreements,* S. Doc. 244, 78th Cong., 2d Sess., 1934. See also McClure, *op. cit.;* Green H. Hackworth, *Digest of International Law,* Government Printing Office, 1943, Vol. V. It should be added that various administrations usually made it a point to legalize important executive agreements by joint *resolutions* in Congress; for example, the annexations of Texas, Hawaii, and the Samoa Islands were endorsed by such joint resolutions (see David M. Levitan, *Executive Agreements,* Chicago, University of Chicago Press, 1940).

agreements has been upheld by the American courts, including the Supreme Court.

The first executive agreement in American history was concluded as early as 1792 and set up the postal service with Canada. In 1816, the first *important* executive agreement was entered into with Great Britain, limiting naval armaments on the Great Lakes.

The most important step in foreign policy which the United States undertook in all its history, the proclamation of the Monroe Doctrine—a commitment to defend the entire Western Hemisphere—was *not* a treaty. It was based on a more or less informal understanding with Britain. Legally, the Monroe Doctrine was nothing but a simple presidential announcement to Congress.

The United States annexed Texas and Hawaii and concluded the armistice with Spain in 1898 by executive agreement. The Open Door policy was worked out by a series of executive agreements. The United States joined the International Labor Organization and the Pan American Union by executive agreement. In the same manner, the United States exchanged with Britain fifty destroyers for Atlantic and Caribbean military bases, joined UNRRA, and adhered to the Four-Nation Declaration of 1943. This declaration came as close as anything to being an alliance. Actually, Secretary of State Cordell Hull stated that, originally, the Four-Nation Declaration had been drawn up in the form of a treaty but was changed because of the constitutional obstacle into an executive agreement.[11]

The far-reaching agreements entered into at Casablanca and Teheran, including the commitment of the United States to the "unconditional surrender" policy, were concluded without the benefit of the two-thirds Senate rule. The same is true of the even more consequential decisions of Yalta and Potsdam. The evidence is, therefore, very clear that in order to conduct its foreign policy the United States does not need to make use of treaties which have to be ratified by a two-thirds majority in the Senate but can resort to other types of legal and diplomatic instruments.

Even though the President has powers to conclude agreements which he may deem necessary, he cannot, of course, disregard Congress. In some way or other any agreement requires action on the part of the United States, and that action has to be financed. The President cannot risk that Congress will refuse him the means for his policy, let alone that Congress will pass laws which would invalidate the agreements (none of which, incidentally, need be made public). However, all the President needs is a *simple majority and nothing more.*

This statement may not be quite in accordance with the *written* word of the Constitution, but it agrees closely with the actual fact. To give just one example, one of the most important American actions in the field of foreign

[11] See Hull, *op. cit.,* Vol. II, pp. 1646*f*.

policy, the Foreign Assistance Act of April, 1948, was authorized by simple majorities in both Houses. It was *not* a treaty requiring a two-thirds Senate majority. The law authorized the establishment of a new government agency, the Economic Cooperation Administration, and assigned to it the funds necessary for its functioning. Yet it was essentially a "treaty" with numerous foreign nations.

As a rule, foreign policy can be formulated and executed with least hindrance and delay if it has at least the tacit support of a part of the oppositional party. Such support will hardly be lacking if the proposed policy is reasonable. While much criticism has been leveled at Congress, it should not be overlooked that the various administrations in American history contributed their share to the ineffectiveness of foreign policy.

To define and execute policy, the administration itself needs unity of purpose and direction. Too often, however, the American government was split between various departments working at cross-purposes; very often the State Department followed a different policy from the Department of Commerce or the military departments. At times, the President overruled the departments, and at other times the departments failed to act in accordance with presidential directives.

It must be conceded that many of the policies proposed and carried out by the Department of State were ill conceived. There have been times when Congress has shown a better understanding of the international situation than the Executive. While undoubtedly Congress can block a wise foreign policy, it also can substitute itself, at least partially, for an administration which fails to represent the interests of the United States.

Korean Complications. With the signing of the United Nations Charter by the United States, a new element was added to the constitutional problem. These complications derive especially from Articles 39 to 43. These articles provide that the United Nations Security Council, upon determination that a threat to the peace exists, shall "decide" upon countermeasures. The Security Council is entitled to "call upon the parties concerned to comply with such provisional measures as it deems necessary or advisable." The Security Council also may "take such actions by air, sea or land forces as may be necessary to maintain or restore international peace and security," while all members of the United Nations "undertake to make available to the Security Council, on its call and in accordance with a special agreement or agreements, armed forces, assistance and facilities, . . . necessary for the purpose of maintaining international peace and security." Article 43 qualifies these provisions by stating that the implementing agreements to be concluded between the Security Council and nation members "shall be subject to ratification by the signatory states in accordance with their respective constitutional processes."

It is quite clear that even if such special arrangements ever were to be negotiated (which is very doubtful), the United States Senate could not ratify them without abandoning one of its major prerogatives. Since such agreements have not been concluded, let alone ratified, the Security Council has no legal authority to *call* upon the United States for military support. Nevertheless, the United States did ratify the United Nations Charter. Hence the Security Council possesses a theoretical and limited authority to *ask* for the military support of the United States, but there are no provisions as to how this "authority" is to be exercised.

In 1950, in answer to the communist attack on South Korea, the Security Council did indeed ask the United States to intervene by force of arms. The American government complied with this request. It is, however, far more true to say that the American government *first* decided that such intervention was necessary, and that it *then* prevailed upon the Security Council to ask for American assistance. This policy was possible only because at that time the Soviet government did not participate in the deliberations of the Security Council. The Security Council passed from the Korean scene as soon as the Soviets returned to it. Instead of the Council exerting any authority, the United States was appointed executive agent in Korea and practically fought its own war. Very few nations complied with the Security Council's original demand for intervention, and even fewer sent more than "token forces" to Korea. Nevertheless, a precedent was set: the United States had gone to war upon the invitation of the United Nations.

Once the United States had intervened in Korea, the question arose whether Congress should declare war formally. The government, acting on the hypothesis that it was not fighting a war but simply a "police action," opposed such a step and opposed also a joint Senate-House declaration supporting American intervention. Whether this American policy was arrived at exclusively to avoid labeling the Korean conflict as *war,* or whether there was also the *arrière pensée* on the part of the administration of reducing the power of Congress in foreign affairs may be a debatable question. Congress appropriated all the military expenditures needed for the Korean conflict. Hence, regardless of the neat technicalities involved, the Korean conflict offers a case in which the United States went to war without an official declaration of war and still was able to secure continuous Congressional support. The question is, will wars henceforth be called "police actions"?

The establishment of the NATO structure—in particular the establishment of international military staffs, with American officers in key positions—also signifies a departure from the tradition inasmuch as American military and civilian officials, as a matter of routine, enter into numerous agreements without precise Congressional authorization. In a technical, legal sense these agreements may not be as binding as treaties, yet in practical life such military commitments, like reciprocal trade and economic arrangements, cannot be set aside easily. In brief, the constitutional structure of the United States is far less rigid than is generally assumed; moreover, it has been undergoing considerable change. These changes, naturally enough, have aroused Congressional opposition.

The National Security Council, established in 1947—and not to be confused with the United Nations Security Council—is another organ the creation of which has modified historic constitutional arrangements. The National Security Council serves two major purposes. First, it integrates foreign, military, and economic policies of the administration into a coherent whole and as such is the highest policy-making body within the American government. In addition, since the Vice-President who also is the president of the Senate is represented on the Security Council, there has been created an organ joining, albeit in a tenuous fashion, the legislative with the executive branch of the government. This arrangement assures some coordination between Congress and government of any long-range policy from its inception throughout its execution.

Minority Presidents. Under the American Constitution it is possible that the President may find himself in a parliamentary minority. This may happen as a result of off-year elections, and it is a contingency which has arisen more than twenty times in American history. But it is also possible that the President may lose support in his own party, or he may have such a small majority that due to the vagaries of parliamentary proceedings there is a danger that he may be outvoted.

Whenever there was during the 19th century a minority President, foreign affairs were paralyzed. Such a situation occurred also during the first Truman administration (1946–1948). At that time, however, as a result of the adoption of two-party cooperation as a considered policy of both parties, foreign affairs did not come to a standstill. In the European field this "bipartisan" system enabled the United States to carry out a broadly conceived foreign policy which culminated in the NATO Pact. In Asia, according to Senator Vandenberg, the two-party system did not operate during the take-offs, but was invoked invariably at the crash landings. The advantages of two-party cooperation and the avoidance of partisanship are great at all times, but it must not be overlooked that such a system tends to eliminate one of the most important features of a democratic government: the constant debate and criticism of policies. The bipartisan system is a medicine which can be taken only in limited doses. Otherwise it could develop into a one-party system.

What should a minority President do if he cannot enlist the support of the opposition party? If he is convinced that the opposition party will obstruct his course in the field of foreign policy in any event, he is therefore unable to do anything beyond his powers of concluding executive agreements and of commanding the armed forces as he sees fit. If, however, the obstruction on the part of the opposition is due purely to political reasons, and if the President believes that as soon as the opposition party were actually in power it would take the steps necessary for the protection of the United States, he could do the following things: He could remove either his Secretary of State or any other member of the Cabinet who belongs to his own party and appoint members of the opposition party as secretaries. (During his second administration, President Truman would have been far more successful if he had removed Secretary of State Dean Acheson, who incurred most of the oppositional criticism, and had replaced him by a Republican. In 1940, President Roosevelt weakened the opposition against his policies by appointing Republicans to be his Secretaries of War and Navy.) The appointment of a *true* coalition government or a government consisting almost exclusively of members of the oppositional majority party would be an unprecedented step which would be resisted strongly by the President's party machine. It will probably never be taken except in extreme emergencies. But this expedient, which would make the American system resemble more closely a parliamentary democracy, is legal and feasible. It is by no means inconsistent with the letter and spirit of the American Constitution, which makes no reference to political parties.

Or second, as an even more desperate measure, the President could dismiss his entire Cabinet and then convince the Vice-President to *resign* with him. The Speaker of the House, a member of the opposition party, would, according to the present succession law, accede to the presidency. Hence the stalemate would be broken through a change of government without the benefit of an election. This step, too, would be perfectly legitimate on the basis of the Constitution. Whether a President will ever succeed in convincing the Vice-President of the need of joint resignation is an entirely different matter. It would depend on the gravity of the situation and the patriotism of the minority party and the principal persons concerned.

These few remarks serve exclusively the purpose of refuting the erroneous idea that, for constitutional reasons, an effective American foreign policy cannot be conducted. Undoubtedly, the Constitution makes the conduct of foreign affairs more difficult in the United States than in most other countries, but it does not preclude efficient action.

The American government has the necessary legal authority to conduct foreign policy successfully. In crisis situations it can move with the same speed as foreign governments. If administrations in the past confessed themselves hamstrung by constitutional provisions, more likely than not either they were confused about their respective courses of action and hid lack of policy behind the constitutional smokescreen, or they were incapable of taking full advantage of the powers that were actually granted to the Executive by the Constitution. They were *fighting* the constitutional problem rather than using constitutional privileges.

THE INFLUENCE OF HOME POLITICS

In monarchical, feudal, and dictatorial states domestic politics impinge on foreign policy no less decisively and perniciously than in democratic countries. Napoleon I destroyed his empire with his own hands when he attacked Russia. Napoleon III went to war with Prussia largely because of domestic pressures which Bismarck had anticipated in his calculations and which he used with deadly dexterity for his own diplomatic strategy. While the Emperor, who was gravely ill and could no longer ride a horse except in great physical pain, wanted to avert the war, French public opinion clamored for a quick and decisive triumph over Prussia. Of greater importance was the intransigent attitude of the Empress, who wanted to assure the survival of the dynasty through a victorious war, especially a war against Prussia. The war destroyed the dynasty within four weeks.

In Ciano's diary there are many notations which indicate how the facts of domestic politics—in this case the mere existence of a dictatorship—may determine the question of war or peace and foreign policy in general. Ciano's entry for August 11, 1939, records his conversation at Salzburg with Joachim von Ribbentrop, German Foreign Minister: "The decision to fight is implacable. He [Hitler] rejects any solution which might give satisfaction to Germany and avoid the struggle. I am certain that even if the Germans were given more than they ask for they would attack just the same, because they are possessed by the demon of destruction." [12] The entry of May 10, 1940, the day when the Germans attacked Holland, Belgium, and France, reads in part: "The Duce repeated to me his certainty about rapid success of the Nazi armies, and also of his decision to intervene. I did not fail to repeat that, for the time being, we should wait and see. This is a long-drawn-out affair, longer than we can possibly foresee now. He didn't deign to answer me. My remarks served only to annoy him. . . ." [13]

Not only was the decision to intervene determined by the nature of Italy's internal political structure, but the ideological orientation of the Fascist state caused Mussolini to choose the losing side in a lost war. It was clear to many Italians, including many members of the government and the Foreign Minister himself, that a victorious Germany would treat an allied Italy no better than her enemies, and that for reasons of self-preservation, Italy should oppose German victory. Yet Mussolini joined Germany largely for ideological reasons, basing his alliance on the kinship of the domestic regimes, though not on popular sympathy for Germany.

[12] See *The Ciano Diaries 1939–1943: The Complete Unabridged Diaries of Count Galeazzo Ciano, Italian Minister for Foreign Affairs, 1936–1943,* edited by Hugh Gibson, New York, Doubleday, 1946, p. 119. See also Ciano's *L'Europa verso la Catastrofe, 184 Colloqui con Mussolini, Hitler, Franco, Chamberlain, Sumner Welles, Rustu Aras, Stoiadinovic, Goering, Zog, François-Poncet, etc.,* Milan, Mondadori, 1948, pp. 449, 454, 458.
[13] *The Ciano Diaries,* p. 246.

The history of Poland is perhaps the most replete with examples showing the catastrophic influence which bad domestic politics can have on the security of a country. Poland was one of the earliest European republics under a king. A parliamentary body, the Sejm, wielded a great deal of power. In the 17th century, the powers of the Sejm to act were restricted by two rules, to wit, that each delegate received complete instructions from the people whom he represented and that *each* member of the Diet could block the vote by his single veto: the *liberum veto* required that the voting be unanimous. This meant that the Sejm could never really govern the country.

Foreign nations exploited this situation fully. Both the King of Prussia and the Russian Tsar instructed their ambassadors as a matter of routine always to have a few noblemen in their pay in order that they might exert their veto rights in accordance with the wishes of their respective foreign benefactors. The climax of this sad state of affairs came in 1764 when the Russians, through "manipulation," secured the election to the Polish throne of Joseph Poniatowski, a former lover of Catherine II. During his reign, the first partition of Poland occurred. After this first spoliation, the Poles adopted a new constitution designed to cure the ills of the Polish state. Yet one of the foremost Polish noblemen, Potocki, who for all practical purposes was a sovereign ruler, opposed the new constitution on the grounds that it restricted his rights. He requested Catherine of Russia to intervene. The Empress acceded, and the second partition of Poland occurred in 1793. It is no exaggeration to say that the unhappy history of the Polish nation during the last 250 years has its roots in Polish domestic politics of the 18th century. But even before the Second World War, the lesson had not been learned.

IDEOLOGIES AND FOREIGN POLICY

Prior to 1914, a democratic France was able to come to terms with an autocratic Russia, because both countries considered Germany a supreme danger. In 1935 and after, the ideological schizophrenia of the French induced characteristic vacillation; France could not make up her mind as to whence threatened the greatest danger, from Germany or from Russia.[14] Had the Franco-Russian alliance not been allowed to lapse, it would have greatly facilitated the settlement of minor differences, such as the Polish-Czech dispute, and furnished a most persuasive argument against Hitler's aggressive schemes. Stalin, in turn, reared on Marxist and Leninist doctrine, was convinced that the "capitalistic" countries (including Nazi Germany) would ultimately come to terms among themselves in order to war upon the Soviet Union. It is reported that he expected a British declaration of war shortly after the German attack on June 22, 1941, an assumption consistent with

[14] The domestic squabbles which prevented the Franco-Russian alliance from becoming effective are described by Paul Reynaud, *La France a sauvé l'Europe,* Paris, Flammarion, 1947, Vol. I, pp. 108–135.

Lenin's teachings on the nature of "capitalist imperialism." Britain and the United States, however, decided that first things came first and that the challenge of Nazi Germany, measured by the potential threat from the Soviet Union, was not only the greatest, but also the most pressing, danger, and therefore supported Russia in spite of unbridgeable ideological and political differences.

This decision conformed to the best tradition of enlightened foreign policy. For under practically all circumstances, mere survival, *i.e.,* safeguarding of independence, is more important than ideologies. A sound foreign policy, therefore, has as its primary goal the security of the state, and only if survival is no longer in question can ideological differences be allowed to impinge on foreign policy. It is for this very reason that many Popes maintained diplomatic relations with the heathen Mongols, and ultimately ceased to oppose the establishment of a *modus vivendi* between the Moslem and the Christian worlds. By contrast, the domestic politics of the United States interfered frequently with the maintenance of diplomatic relations between the Vatican and Washington, although the existence of a permanent American diplomatic mission to the Vatican would hardly compromise the integrity of the Protestant faith, nor contravene the separation of state from the church, not to mention the fact that the Christian religions have more things in common than there are articles of faith separating them, and that all Christian religions are faced by common dangers.

INSTITUTIONAL CHANGE AND FOREIGN POLICY

The impact of domestic politics upon foreign policy and international relations is, however, of a far more fundamental nature and exceeds in importance the consequences of partisan or ideological prejudice. This impact results from the fact that the protagonists of foreign policy come to power, and stay in power, only by virtue of their domestic influence, and that, generally speaking, their policies must be in line with the desires of the citizens over whom they rule, especially if they may have to call upon these citizens to implement these policies at grievous personal sacrifice.

Geographically, France was the same country before and after 1789. Yet politically and militarily the French nation changed profoundly during the epoch of the Revolution. Pursuing activist policies in the domestic field and eager to carry the message of the Revolution to other peoples, France affronted every major power of Europe, and waged wars in Africa and Asia Minor. The "World Spirit on Horseback" (Hegel's designation of Napoleon) harnessed the dynamism of revolutionary France to the quest for world domination. In 1815, although exhausted and defeated, France was still the most powerful European country. Yet three generations later France had become a fundamentally conservative and peaceful country, the country of the timid *rentier* and petty politician in search of security.

The United States, which traditionally had opposed war as well as annexation by force, in 1898 went to war against Spain, acting under the influence of public opinion, or rather a powerful and unscrupulous press bent on arousing popular indignation. It is said that one great newspaper owner once boasted that it cost him only $5,000,000 to launch the Spanish War.

The aggressive tendencies of Tsarist Russia preoccupied the chancelleries of Europe, particularly the statesmen of Great Britain, until Russia's defeat by the Japanese in 1905 signaled a reversal of Russian policy. The policy of internal reform practiced by Count Stolypin was tied to a policy of peace in the foreign field. Early in 1914, the peace party was ousted from influential posts in the government, and Russia again was if not an aggressive power then at least one disinclined to compromise and moderation.

The importance of domestic politics was recognized in 1918 when Allied statesmen determined to dethrone the German Emperor. In his note to Germany of October 23, 1918, President Wilson wrote: [15]

It does not appear that the principle of a government responsible to the people has yet been fully worked out or that any guarantees either exist or are in contemplation that the alterations of principle and of practice now partially agreed upon will be permanent. The determining initiative still remains with those who have hitherto been the masters of Germany.

Thus was Germany advised by circumlocution that she would have to abolish the monarchy before she would be permitted to sue for an armistice.

For their part, wide circles in Germany, including the army and many conservatives, pursued the same goal on the grounds that a democratic Germany would appear to the Allies as a more reliable treaty partner than a monarchical *Reich* and would, therefore, receive better terms. It was the army who ushered in the social democratic regime in 1918, although its hand was forced by the sailors' mutiny of Kiel. The army was again instrumental in bringing Hitler to power in 1933. The Germanies of 1914, 1918, and 1933 are not the same countries. It could be said that in each case the *Reich's* domestic structure was adapted to the foreign policy which had become "necessary."

But the inverse case, namely, that foreign policy is dependent upon the existing domestic structure, also can be argued cogently. Clearly, the two factors are intertwined.

To understand the international importance of domestic politics, let us assume, for example, that instead of Italy, France had become a Fascist power and adopted a political structure similar to that of Germany; or let us assume that either Germany had become communistic in 1933, or Russia Nazi-Fascist in 1938. In all three hypothetical cases, the related regimes would

[15] Quoted from Leopold Schwarzschild, *World in Trance: From Versailles to Pearl Harbor* (New York, L. B. Fischer, 1942, p. 20), where there is also a pertinent discussion of the mingling of international and domestic politics prior to the armistice which ended World War I.

presumably have concluded alliances and without great difficulty gained control over Europe and perhaps Asia. With a Fascist France or Russia, or a communist Germany, the history of Europe would have been entirely different. It is true that historical disputes separate Russia and Germany, Germany and France; yet disputes of this order can be overcome once and for all, as were the historical disputes between Great Britain and the United States, or between Spain and France. Whether or not two countries march together or against each other depends at least in part on the domestic politics of the two nations. As a matter of fact, in each of these countries, Germany, Russia, and France, there were powerful forces which advocated precisely the alignment of our hypotheses.

A good example of ideological variability may be found in German-Polish relations before and after 1933. Before 1933, the intense nationalistic opposition and the unceasing anti-Polish propaganda made it virtually impossible for the *Reich* government to establish a sensible *modus vivendi* with Poland. When the Hitler government took over, it exercised so complete a control over the domestic field that it dared to carry out a highly unpopular reversal of policy, namely, cooperation with Poland. On the part of Poland, the German about-face was accepted with good grace, not only because the Polish government did not believe in the efficacy of French assistance in a serious German-Polish crisis, but also because it viewed the Nazi government with mild sympathy, partly for reasons of its kindred authoritarian nature, partly in view of the anti-Russian sentiments professed by Hitler. However, when the Poles sought to transform this change of sides into firm partnership and expressed willingness to enter into far-reaching agreements with the Germans, Hitler withdrew suddenly his chief negotiator, the President of the Danzig Senate Hermann Rauschning, and without completely revising his Polish policy, kept it within the narrow bounds of a nonaggression pact. The reason for this was that the Nazis were prisoners of their own propaganda and desired *no* understanding with the Poles. A determined pro-Polish and anti-Russian policy on the part of Germany might not have ended with the catastrophe of Stalingrad, as did the course Hitler actually chose. On the other hand, the Poles, too, were not ready to make territorial sacrifices on the altar of Germany's friendship. Had they taken the initiative in turning Danzig back to Germany, they would at least have acted in tune with their foreign policy and might have thus chosen the only alternative—barring an agreement with Russia—to fighting a hopeless war.[16]

As a rule profound changes in domestic political alignments signal changes in foreign policy. When Charles Fox succeeded the younger Pitt, the world knew that England would conclude peace with Napoleon. When Napoleon III attempted to convert the Second Republic into a monarchy, his followers propagated the slogan "L'Empire, c'est la paix" (the Empire is

[16] See Hermann Rauschning, *The Voice of Destruction,* New York, Putnam, 1940, pp. 118*ff.*

peace), while his opponents, in a more justified estimate of the situation, turned this around into "L'Empire, c'est l'épée" (the Empire is the sword). The campaign of General Boulanger had as its chief purpose the launching of a war of revenge against Bismarck's Germany. Boulanger was rejected by the French people; but when Hitler, some fifty years later, ran for election on a similar program in Germany, he was elected by the German people. In American history, the election of President Polk, for example, signified little else than war against Mexico.

Changes *within* a government may, at times, express not so much a change in foreign policy as such but the beginning of a new phase. When Hitler embarked openly on aggression, he replaced Neurath by Ribbentrop as Foreign Minister, while Mussolini proved his intention not to conclude a separate peace with the Allies by eliminating his son-in-law, Count Ciano, from the government.

Within dictatorial governments in general and especially within the Soviet government, a change in personnel practically always signifies a change in policy, that is, the change in policy is decided upon *first* and personnel is replaced *afterward*. Thus, when Stalin decided to abandon traditional communist policies, he purged the old party members; in 1939, when he made up his mind no longer to cooperate with the West but to seek a pact with Germany, he replaced Litvinov by Molotov as Foreign Commissar.

However, not every change in domestic politics entails a change in foreign policy. It is very doubtful whether the election of Wendell Willkie to the presidency of the United States in 1940 would have kept, as the Nazis hoped, the United States out of the Second World War. The policy of the Labor Government of Britain which took office in 1945 probably did not differ basically from the hypothetical policy which a Conservative Government would have pursued—except that a Conservative Government might have hesitated longer to grant independence to Burma and India and to renounce the Palestinian mandate.

It is widely held that states seek to channel pressures resulting from domestic troubles into aggressive foreign policies and, ultimately, into war, in order to compensate for their domestic failures by international successes. This is, in fact, an old device of ruthless statecraft. The idea was expressed succinctly by Maurice Joly when he put the following words into Machiavelli's mouth: "Every internal agitation must be countered by a foreign war; every imminent revolution [must be deflected] by a general war." [17]

It has often been said that Hitler had no choice but to go to war; after he had "abolished" unemployment through armaments, a peaceful foreign

---

[17] See Joly, Maurice, *Dialogue aux enfers entre Machiavel et Montesquieu* (originally published in 1864), Paris, Calmann-Levy, 1948, p. 61. Machiavelli-Joly adds these words: "In politics the words shall never be in agreement with the acts. The prince must be sufficiently skillful to disguise his true plans under contrary designs. He must always give the impression that he cedes to the pressure of public opinion, when in fact he carries out what he prepared by his own hand."

policy making the production of military equipment superfluous might have given rise to unemployment on a large scale. Whether theoretically true or not, this reasoning played an important role in "freezing" the policy which Hitler had adopted.

In a similar manner it can be argued that the Soviet government is constitutionally unable to desist from an aggressive policy; having adopted economic planning as the basis of its power, it *ipso facto* embraced an economic system which works most effectively in the field of heavy industry, but which would have to be modified if it were to attempt to satisfy the needs of the population as defined by that population. It is certain that a state system in which government activities have been maximized is far more inflexible than other systems in which the state functions have been held down to a minimum. The inertia of totalitarian regimes is great. Once they have embarked upon a policy—and they usually embark upon aggression—they encounter great difficulties changing it. In any event, modern history records no such change, and it is inevitable that, if such a change were to occur, it would have to be accompanied or preceded by far-reaching domestic adjustments, possibly entailing a complete overhaul of the entire government machinery.

The conventional Marxist theory assumes that the "inner contradictions" of the capitalist system must drive capitalist states inevitably to war. There is, in fact, no doubt that the economic situation of a country—which must be considered as a vital element of domestic politics—has a direct bearing on its foreign policy. It is a truism to say that states are eager to acquire wealth-producing regions. Thus, for example, many wars were fought during the 18th century for the Caribbean islands, at that time the world's foremost producers of sugar, then one of the most valuable commodities. Most colonial wars ended with trade agreements. The American Revolution was in great part caused by differences in economic interests. Expansion is in many cases directed toward sources of valuable raw materials, such as Germany's two attempts to seize the Ukraine, or Japan's dash to the Dutch East Indies. Lorraine iron, Rumanian and Persian oil, and Ukrainian manganese were coveted booty in the past, as African uranium may be in the future.

The territory known as "Gadsden Purchase" was acquired by the United States from Mexico because its possession was essential for the construction of a transcontinental railroad. If there had been no transcontinental railways, it may be presumed that the United States would have annexed Cuba to safeguard and improve sea communications between the east and west coasts.

A commercial policy which tends to cut imports to the minimum and to maximize exports is often connected with the establishment of barriers to migration. It is motivated in some cases by the special interests of individual producers or trade unions desirous of excluding competition, *i.e.,* considerations of domestic politics. Such a policy, which is contrary to the teachings of classical economics, nearly always hurts the country adopting it and always hurts other countries. For example, Germany's agricultural tariffs, while increasing the cost of living in Germany, deprived the Danube countries of their essential market; French tariff policies toward the Little and the Balkan Entente countries made it impossible to transform France's system of alliances into an effective bulwark against Germany; American tariffs incontestably aggravated the economic world crisis, especially in Europe. Precisely how much these policies of extreme economic nationalism contributed to war is impossible to say; it may suffice here to conclude that they were among the potent causes of the Second World War.

Governments which do not rest upon the broad basis of mass support and whose hold is menaced by widespread discontent often divert the political passions of the people into foreign conflict. A propaganda campaign, at first undertaken as a mere diversion, as, for example, Emperor Wilhelm II's "saber-rattling" prior to 1914, may result in cataclysmic consequences. If the social structure is threatened from outside or inside, recourse to arms may appear the simplest, because the most radical, solution of the social problem. The Boers, for example, feared that British policy in South Africa would overthrow their system, a racial caste system, and did not hesitate to go to war against a vastly superior power.

On the other hand, fear that the social system may be destroyed by a costly war, as existed, for example, in France in 1938, operates to deter energetic foreign policies and culminates in supine appeasement. By contrast, the need to take care of the unemployed has often furnished a compelling argument for increasing outlay on armaments and rousing the "martial spirit." During the 17th and 18th centuries, Britain recruited her armed forces mainly among the "beggars," the economic castoffs of English society, and employed them in overseas conquests. Japan's and Italy's expansionist policies were, at least to a degree, caused by agricultural overpopulation. The colonial empires of France and Holland were, in part, maintained by foreign legions recruited from the social debris of other nations.

Domestic politics exerts perhaps its strongest influence at moments when basic changes must be made in foreign policy. For example, it became clear to many German leaders as early as 1916 that continuing the policy which had united the world against them invited disaster. Yet they could not change their policy. Various factors preclude a change under such conditions: for one, there is social and intellectual inertia, which made it so difficult for American public opinion to understand before 1941 that the days of isolation were over; second, there is the reluctance of the leaders in power to acknowledge their errors and—as an inevitable consequence—to step down from their positions; third, there is the fear, partly justified, that a fundamental change may provoke a fatal crisis in military morale. Old antagonisms, such as that between the United States and Britain, linger on, and the politician seeking office is reluctant to brave the cherished preconceptions and idiosyncrasies of constituents, in the American case an image of rapacious, snobbish Britain. Politicians thrive on old hatreds and alleged predictions and promises. A party which has come to power on a program of disarmament, as did the French socialists under Léon Blum, usually is slow in making up its mind that the original program has become inapplicable. A speedy reversal of policy, so characteristic of the Cabinet diplomacy of the 18th century, is difficult to accomplish under modern conditions.

Without embracing the Marxist interpretation of international relations, it is still necessary to distinguish between more or less temporary party alignments and more permanent social or class cleavages. Whether domestic antagonisms are basic or superficial, virulent or moderate, these differences in degree bear upon foreign policy. Violent class struggles may be deflected into a foreign war, or they may cripple the nation as a potent factor on the international scene. A nation ruled by one powerful and intransigent class may oppose any other nation ruled by another class, or it may be bent upon changing the given social structure. The nature of a nation's foreign policy is determined in part by the character of its ruling class; the aggressive tendencies of Germany were due in part to the fact that that country had been governed a long time by its military families, while the policies of modern France can be explained partially by the fact that the military play a minor role in French politics, which are largely in the hands of lawyers, writers, and teachers. The psychology of the ruling class also exerts considerable influence; its policies will depend upon whether it is conscious of its prestige, jealous of its position, fearful of its future (as was the Russian aristocracy before 1917), or assured of its status. The same consideration applies to racial and cultural cleavages within a nation. In general, the better a social system works, *i.e.*, the more flexible is its mechanism for gradual adjustment, the less bitter will be its conflicts, the more stable its structure, and the broader the participation in the government. Such a nation is not bent upon aggression. But should war be forced upon it, its inner cohesion will give it the strength to meet formidable trials.[18]

In theory, foreign policy must be given primacy over domestic politics, for only if external security is maintained can there be domestic politics at all. In fact, both are reciprocal. "The first condition of good foreign policy," Gladstone said, "is a good domestic policy." The strife of the parties and factions is predicated upon the independence of the state, hence Britain's old saying that "politics stop at the water's edge."

PUBLIC OPINION AND FOREIGN POLICY

Perhaps the most controversial factor in international relations is that elusive and complex thing called "public opinion." It has become fashionable

[18] For a scientific discussion of the ambiguous term "class" and its social meaning, see Joseph A. Schumpeter, *Imperialism and Social Classes*, Oxford, Blackwell, 1951, pp. 133–221.

to gauge public attitudes by "polls," the results of which have, in the United States, undoubtedly influenced the President as well as the Senate in matters of foreign policy. Prior to Pearl Harbor, public opinion prevented a more active participation of the United States in the war, while after the war the same public opinion made it seem wise for the Senate to ratify American participation in the United Nations.

Public opinion has influenced world events long before Mr. Gallup sought to gauge it methodically. It was of the greatest importance in ancient Greece and Rome. The papacy relied on it when it banned offenders from the church and called upon Christendom to battle the infidel. For long years, it was Napoleon's greatest single element of power. In 1914, the German government would certainly have hesitated to plunge into war if it had encountered strong opposition among the German people. In the 1930's British public opinion clamored for sanctions against Italy, yet was not willing to implement that policy by paying for sufficient armaments, thus leaving the British Government to struggle with an impossible mandate.

During the Korean War, American public opinion exhibited a similar schizophrenic attitude. In general it was torn between the desire to stop and possibly destroy the communist threat and the desire to reduce armaments and stick to business as usual.

French public opinion after 1918 undoubtedly hindered the establishment of more friendly relations between France and Germany; but so did German public opinion, each kindling the suspicions of the other. Anglo-American relations often suffer from the nonsense which the two respective publics believe about each other.

Public opinion is apt to clamor for radical measures when moderation is more advisable. When, after the Battle of Königgrätz, Bismarck concluded a peace without annexation (in order to insure Austrian neutrality in case of war with France and to forestall a Franco-Austrian alliance), he was almost overthrown. After the Spanish-American War, President McKinley decided to keep the Philippines largely because of the popular outcry against "hauling down the flag."

The broadening of suffrage has made the rational conduct of foreign affairs increasingly difficult. British foreign policy until 1914, though by no means always cogent, nevertheless was practically always the result of rational deliberations among eminently qualified experts. In 1918, the Peoples Act doubled the electorate; the subsequent "Khaki Elections" compelled Lloyd George to embark on a foreign policy in which he did not believe, the policy of "Hang the Kaiser" and "Make the Germans pay." Unable to come out openly against this line, the British Government furtively and almost secretly violated its own officially proclaimed policy—inevitably with disastrous results. A somewhat similar situation obtained in France, where public opinion made impossible a reasonable settlement of reparation debts. After World War II, it certainly was fortunate that the peace with Japan was delayed for six years and that the quarrels with Soviet Russia precluded the imposition of a Carthaginian peace on Germany.

During the interwar period, the rule of the irrational, the nonreason, spread to all realms of public life. Being unable to guide public opinion rationally, governments must adopt expedients which are often worse than the evil they are supposed to cure. Public opinion often influences foreign policy indirectly, for example, when it clamors for tax cuts which lead to reductions in necessary armaments, and paradoxically tries to combine armament reductions with a "strong" foreign policy.[19] American public opinion in 1938 condemned the Munich agreement but refused to support England and France with deeds. The United States was long committed to a policy of "stop the aggressor," but for a long time little was done to put substance into that policy, or to prepare this country adequately to oppose aggression against its own possessions.

The education and guidance of public opinion in order to separate policy from passions and demagogy are thus most urgent problems of democracy. Needless to add, the establishment of a propaganda ministry would not be a solution. It has already been pointed out that according to the American Constitution public opinion should not influence policy; the chief function of the voter is to elect the makers of policy, but it is emphatically *not* to make policy himself. The point should also be made that public opinion may exert great influence *when it is overwhelmingly strong,* but that such a crystallization occurs only rarely.

Since, however, most governments feel that they need public support for their policies, they have developed secret means by which they influence the press and other public-opinion media. News may be released or withheld according to whether the facts would support or hinder its foreign policy. A number of public-opinion specialists are engaged busily in getting the government's interpretation of events to the people. The drumming up of "scares" about military or economic threats and about political crises which would result if the "helmsman" were thrown overboard is a common occurrence in modern life. The press, unfortunately, is far less independent than it claims. The slanting of news is far more frequent than the public realizes. Democracy has not yet found a truly reliable technique by which

---

[19] "Those programs are immediately most popular . . . which do not at once impinge upon the private habits of the followers. . . . All but the most exceptional leaders prefer policies in which the costs are as far as possible indirect. They do not like direct taxation. They do not like to pay as they go. They like long term debts. They like to have the voters believe that the foreigner will pay." (Walter Lippmann, *Public Opinion,* New York, originally published by Macmillan in 1922, reprinted by Penguin, in 1946, pp. 182*f.*)

"In many countries . . . if increases in taxes were to be submitted to referendum, they would always be rejected, even though they were of the most unqualified urgency and would be of the most obvious benefit to the public." (Gaetano Mosca, *The Ruling Class,* translation of *Elementi di Scienza Politica,* New York, McGraw-Hill, 1939, p. 158; see also *passim* on importance of domestic politics.)

a government can enlist the support it needs for its life-and-death decisions and yet avoid resorting to propaganda deceptions.

In most cases, it is impossible to determine what "public opinion" actually is with respect to a given issue. There are dozens of technical reasons—which cannot be discussed here—why public-opinion polling does not provide satisfactory and reliable answers. But in addition to these technical reasons which deal with methods of fact finding, measuring, interviewing, tabulating, etc., there is the fundamental reason that even the so-called "experts" in the field, called into conference to discuss precisely this very problem, could reach "no general agreement on what the public is and on what opinion is." [20] In addition to not knowing what public opinion really is, it so happens that the reliability of even the most accurate polls is "uncertain" and that their validity is variable.[21] Perhaps the disaster of public-opinion forecasting which occurred in the 1948 election is not really indicative of the effectiveness of the tool. Polls possibly help to determine, in a broad sense, what the opinion of people is. But this determination is valid only for the very short time in which the poll was taken. In Rogers' words, the polls have been precise "about matters of which you will remain ignorant." To make things worse, they have not been quite as precise as it is claimed; in fact, their alleged precision is due to the systematic confusion of percentages and percentage points. (If 50 per cent is predicted, and the result is 45 per cent, the error is 5 percentage points, but 10 per cent.)

Ever since polls have lost much of their fashionable appeal, public opinion again tends to be made by newspaper editorials and columnists. Politicians are inclined to consider as "public opinion" the opinions expressed by a small number of articulate political writers.

Hence we are in the position that, according to a widespread and uncritically accepted belief, public opinion does, or ought to, influence policy, but that in actual fact such an influence would mean the perversion of the American Constitution; that furthermore nobody knows exactly what it is that ought to exert this influence; and third, that even if we were to agree on what phenomenon we want to call public opinion, we are in no position to determine reliably the true opinion of the public. Add to this the hardly disputed facts that measurement can apply only to the opinion of yesterday or today but not of tomorrow; that opinion may change rapidly and that it is rarely articulate about the really important problems of foreign policy—most

[20] Lindsay Rogers, *The Pollsters: Public Opinion, Politics and Democratic Leadership,* New York, Knopf, 1949, p. 11. This book contains a devastating critique of the political claims of the "pollsters" and a restatement of the meaning of the Constitution vis-à-vis Gallupism.

[21] Leonard W. Doob, *Public Opinion and Propaganda,* New York, Holt, 1948, pp. 144*ff*. This book presents an excellent technical discussion of the various polling methods, their advantages and shortcomings. Doob, who is a foremost expert in the field, presents a definition of public opinion, but his views on public-opinion measurements are very critical. It is hardly an exaggeration to say that Doob believes that public opinion cannot be measured accurately.

of the vital decisions are made in secrecy, and even with respect to the open decisions, the public cannot be told the whole story—then we are indeed confronted by a totally unworkable theory of government and political action.[22] *Foreign policy cannot be conducted effectively by public opinion.*

The point is not that public opinion should be disregarded—obviously it should not—but that it be considered merely as *one* of the factors that go into policy making. It is, moreover, essential to enlist public support for one's policies. In this connection it is important to remember that public opinion must be given guidance. Guidance may consist of "information" but it is sometimes preferable and more effective *to guide by action*. Nations usually follow resolute and energetic leadership.[23] They react spontaneously to important events—there was not much dissension among the American public after Pearl Harbor. And while many people believe that public opinion (as determined by polls) trailed behind important decisions, the fact is that, at least in 1941 and again in 1947–1952, public opinion was far ahead not only of Congress but also of the Executive. Sometimes the man in the street behaves more rationally than the man in the Senate or in the State Department (and often, be it noted, Congress may be ahead of the government).

In other words, public opinion is a difficult problem, but it need not, and should not, be an obstacle to an effective and rational foreign policy. The familiar excuse that public opinion would not "go along" with a necessary policy is actually a cloak for unwillingness and irresolution. It is the politicians' way of "passing the buck" to innocent John Q. Public.

[22] With respect to the problem of reelection which allegedly governs the behavior of politicians, it should not be forgotten that elections are dependent not only on voting "records," but also on party alignments, voting traditions, personalities, patronage, public relations of the incumbent, etc. Politicians with a record which showed them wrong on most of their votes are nevertheless often returned for these "extraneous" reasons, and especially for the patronage which they can provide.

[23] Lippmann (*op. cit.*), "Fisher Ames . . . , in 1802, wrote to Rufus King: 'We need, as all nations do, the compression on the outside of our circle of a formidable neighbor, whose presence shall at all times excite stronger fears than demagogues can inspire the people with toward their government.'" But even great danger from the outside may not overcome the threat of the demagogues. The limitations of a democratic foreign policy which confounds representative government with a town hall meeting were given unwittingly by Lippmann: "Democracies in their foreign policy have had generally to choose between splendid isolation and a diplomacy that violated their ideals. The most successful democracies, in fact, . . . have had no foreign policy in the European sense of that phrase. Even a rule like the Monroe Doctrine arose from the desire to supplement the two oceans by a glacis of states that were sufficiently republican to have no foreign policy. Whereas danger is a great, perhaps an indispensable, condition of autocracy, security was seen to be a necessity if democracy was to work. . . . Insecurity involves surprises. It means that there are people acting upon your life over whom you have no control, with whom you cannot consult. . . . Every democrat feels in his bones that dangerous crises are incompatible with democracy, because he knows how the inertia of the masses is such that to act quickly a very few must decide and the rest follow rather blindly" (p. 205). It is the essence of representative government, as set up by the Constitution, that "few must decide."

The causes of an ineffective foreign policy are the same, regardless of whether they are to be found in public opinion or among professionals. They are intentional or unintentional disregard of pertinent facts, political prejudices and passions, inability to evaluate an international situation as a whole, and lack of foresight. Mr. Chamberlain and the British people were palpably *sincere* when, in 1938, they believed that the Munich agreement meant "peace for our generation." But they were catastrophically *mistaken,* the victims of ignorance and illusion.

A nation has attained political maturity when it is able and willing to discount social cleavages, personalities, and fluctuating opinions in discussion of foreign policy, to support that policy which serves the nation's interests best, and to oppose a dangerous or ineffective policy, regardless of its champions and regardless of the vagaries of public opinion. As Winston Churchill put it: "It is better for parties and politicians to be thrown out of office than to endanger the life of the nation."

BIBLIOGRAPHY

Almond, G. A.: *The American People and Foreign Policy,* New York, Harcourt, Brace, 1950.
Bailey, Thomas A.: *The Man in the Street: The Impact of American Public Opinion on Foreign Policy,* New York, Macmillan, 1948.
Barthélemy, Joseph: *Démocratie et politique étrangère,* Paris, Alcan, 1931.
Beard, Charles A.: *The Idea of National Interest,* New York, Macmillan, 1934.
Fleming, Denna Frank: *The Treaty Veto of the American Senate,* New York, Putnam, 1930.
Friedrich, Carl Joachim: *Foreign Policy in the Making,* New York, Norton, 1938.
Kindelan, General: *Ejército y Política,* Madrid, Ediciones Ares, no date.
Lasswell, H. D.: *World Politics and Personal Insecurity,* New York, McGraw-Hill, 1935.
Martin, Charles E.: *The Politics of Peace,* Stanford, Calif., University of California Press, 1929.
Myers, Denis P.: *Notes on the Control of Foreign Relations,* The Hague, Organisation Centrale pour une Paix durable, 1917.
Oncken, Hermann: "Über die Zusammenhänge zwischen äusserer und innerer Politik," *Gehe-Stiftung zu Dresden,* Vol. 9, No. 4, Leipzig, 1918.
Ponsonby, Arthur A. W. H.: *Democracy and Diplomacy: A Plea for Popular Control of Foreign Policy,* London, Methuen, 1915.
Poole, De Witt Clinton: *The Conduct of Foreign Relations under Modern Democratic Conditions,* New Haven, Yale University Press, 1924.
Schattschneider, E. E.: *Politics, Pressures, and the Tariff,* New York, Prentice-Hall, 1935.
Wisan, J. E.: *The Cuban Crisis as Reflected in the New York Press, 1895–1898,* New York, Columbia University Press, 1934.

Part Four

TECHNIQUES OF FOREIGN POLICY

Chapter 12

ISOLATION AND NEUTRALITY

Although foreign policy grapples with an infinite number of different situations, certain basic techniques and concepts recur throughout the ages. As in military strategy, where most operations aim at encirclement or breakthrough or at the destruction or attrition of the enemy armed forces, the fundamental techniques and concepts of foreign policy are but few in number. These few basic techniques can be applied in a variety of manners. The effectiveness of their employment depends in part on the skill of policy makers, but to an even higher degree on the appropriateness of the technique chosen to master a given situation. No foreign policy can be effective that does not operate on what could be called the "situation and time principle": at time t_1 and in situation a_1, a different technique may be called forth than at time t_2 and in situation a_2.[1] While the general objective—security and welfare—may remain immutable, techniques must change according to situational changes if the objective is to be pursued intelligently. Confusion of these techniques with the over-all objective may impede change in political *means*, a choice of new means being interpreted, especially by the propagandists of foreign powers, as a "betrayal" of one of the country's most cherished objectives (ideals). Yet none of these tools should be sacrosanct. Only *one* rule should be accepted as a permanent guide to action: to choose a technique which, in a given situation and at a given time, can bring the desired results and to apply it always with sufficient power. Two supplementary rules could be added: never to use at the same time techniques which are incompatible;

[1] See Alfred Korzybski, *Science and Sanity: An Introduction to Non-Aristotelian Systems and General Semantics*, 2d ed., Lancaster, Pa., The International Non-Aristotelian Library Publishing Company, 1941, pp. 192, 225*ff*.

and never to compromise present actions by carrying over into a new situation techniques used under other circumstances.

ISOLATION

A distinction must be made between isolation in fact and political isolation. Isolation in fact is caused by geography—it is simply a country's remoteness. Remoteness from where? Remoteness, first, from the main scenes of world politics, and secondly, from the sources of military power controlled by unfriendly nations. At the first glance, it would seem as though faraway islands like St. Helena or Madagascar could be considered as geographically isolated. Yet the sea, being in Mahan's words the "great common," makes their conquest by naval powers relatively easy. As long as there are no seafaring nations, or as long as fleets are deployed close to the centers of world conflict, such islands are safe, but in periods of intense world-wide sea-borne trade and naval expansion, they fall prey to naval powers seeking trading posts and anchorages. During the last 300 years, a great many of the world's remote islands were held variously by Holland, France, and Britain; at times Britain was not only an island empire in the sense that the main sources of British power were based on the British Isles, but also in the other sense that the British world empire was held together by a network of islands serving as coaling stations and anchorages for the Royal Navy. During the 19th century, Spain, who had lost the ability to control large continental areas such as South America, still kept control over a good many sizable islands, relying largely on the strength of her navy.

Geographical isolation is more pronounced in areas which are not accessible by sea and which can be reached by land only with great difficulty. There are, in fact, very few areas of that kind at the present time, and they are mostly situated in the arctic wastelands, the tropical jungles of Africa and South America, as well as in the deserts of central Asia. If the avenues of approach are as yet undeveloped, it is because in most cases the investment would hardly yield rewarding returns in raw materials and markets.

In former times, when transportation was primitive, many continental peoples lived in practical seclusion. For a very long period of time, the interior of Africa was geographically and politically isolated from the rest of the world. The Roman legions did not cross the Sahara into the Sudan; there existed no power which could have advanced into the continent either from the western or eastern coasts. Hence the peoples inhabiting these regions were left unmolested; some of them had been pushed back in early times by conquerors exactly as, for example, the Lithuanians had been pushed back into the forests of eastern Europe. The wealth of Africa was tapped by traders traveling along the caravan routes, as evidenced by the travels of the Arab ibn Batuta who, in the 14th century, crossed the Sahara to Timbuktu and the Niger. Yet no nation was *militarily* able to invade these territories; hence a number of native empires rose and flourished without outside interference. The most important of these empires was that of Kanem or Bornu which, situated around Lake Chad, endured for five centuries.

As transportation improved, African isolation was broken down, first, by the Arabs who had built up a sizable sea power in the Arabian Sea and expanded to the eastern coast of Africa, using Zanzibar and Ethiopia as their major bases of penetration; then, in North Africa, by Spanish and Portuguese troops, provided with firearms, and fighting under Moroccan leadership. The invaders destroyed the native culture and established a new reign which lasted in virtual isolation for 200 years. Later they were driven out by the Tuaregs who were temporarily expelled by the Fulah who, in turn, were subsequently defeated by the Tukulör. Ultimately, the Tuaregs resumed control and retained it until the French conquest in 1893. By that time, Europeans, masters of modern transport and scientific exploration, had advanced into the African continent along the river waterways. The isolation of Africa had yielded almost everywhere to the acquisitive curiosity of Europe.

The original pre-Columbian empires in America, the Aztecs, the Mayans, and the Incas, lived, grew, and declined in almost complete geographical isolation from the rest of the world. The Aztecs had built their capital city, Tenochtitlan, as an impregnable position in marshland, but this isolation was breached when sea power brought Spain to Mexican shores. Cortez's appearance seemed to fulfill a prophecy according to which the main deity of the Aztecs, Quetzalcoatl, "before departing this earth by descending into the West, had promised to come back to earth again by the East." That is why "Alfonso Caso writes, 'when the Spanish conquerors landed at Veracruz in the year 1519 . . . the Emperor Montezuma never had a doubt that Quetzalcoatl was returning to take possession of his Toltec Kingdom.' This accounts for the quickness of the triumph of Cortez." [2]

Geography seems to provide isolation only under certain historical and technological conditions. Mere distance from the scenes of world conflict is of small importance and does not offer protection except at times when potential aggressors do not covet outlying regions, are technologically unable to overcome geographical obstacles, or are unwilling to pay the high price which military expeditions into faraway regions entail. Yet a resolute invader can pass anywhere—if not at all times, then at least most of the time. During the 16th century the technologically backward Cossacks succeeded in penetrating one of the most forbidding regions on earth, the Siberian subarctic. If such an attack materializes, the hitherto isolated peoples will retain their independence only if they defeat the invader in battle. Backward peoples have often succeeded in repelling strong and well-organized invaders, as for example, the Koreans who defeated a French expedition under Admiral Roze in 1866, or the Ethiopians who, in 1896, defeated an Italian army at Adua. A similar mishap befell British power at its apogee: a British-Egyptian force

[2] F. S. C. Northrop, *The Meeting of East and West: An Inquiry concerning World Understanding,* New York, Macmillan, 1946, p. 21. The quotation is originally from Alfonso Caso's book, *The Religion of the Aztecs,* Mexico, D.F., American Book Store, 1937, p. 21.

was defeated in 1883 at El Obeid by the Mahdi Mohammed Ahmed, whose power was mostly nourished by religious-mystical enthusiasm and the willingness of his followers to die in a "holy war." As a result, the British and Egyptians saw themselves compelled to evacuate the Sudan. The Mahdi, despite promises to the British, massacred the garrison of Khartoum under General Gordon. Only in 1896—that is, thirteen years after El Obeid and eleven years after the loss of Khartoum—was the Sudan reconquered by Britain in a long and protracted campaign.[3] Isolation thus appears, even in the case of "remote regions," to be a military and political rather than a geographic factor.

In the course of the 20th century a great many hitherto inaccessible areas were developed and assumed economic as well as strategic importance. The Soviets, for example, established a regular sea route along the northern shores of Siberia, linking Murmansk and Vladivostok by navigation in Russian territorial waters. During the Second World War considerable military action took place in the arctic, subarctic, and tropics—only a generation ago the preserve of a few intrepid and eccentric explorers. Technological advances have focused strategic thought on the great-circle routes regardless of their location. In Asia, too, remoteness has yielded to organization armed by modern science. Trucks and jeeps have penetrated, via the old silk route, to Sinkiang.[4] The Himalayas and even Tibet have been forced to yield to aeronautical technology and motorization. One of the world's most forbidding areas, the Western Desert in Egypt and Libya, was one of the decisive battlefields in 1940–1943.

Isolation as Policy. Political isolation need not be a matter of geographical accident or subjective choice. A country which is not at all "remote" may be isolated by virtue of agreements concluded by *other* powers among themselves. For example, Abyssinia in the 20th century remained independent in its isolation because the major colonial powers controlling Africa could not agree as to who was to have and hold that country and because none of them wanted it badly enough to create a major crisis. This deadlock was broken as soon as Italy, without regard for the complications which might ensue, made her bid for the last remaining African prize. By 1935, one of the supposedly most inaccessible regions had become internationally so important that Italian aggression almost produced a full-fledged world war.

International alignments similar to the one which insured the survival of Abyssinia have repeatedly dictated the political fate of Turkey. Ever since the destruction of the Byzantine Empire, the Turks have controlled the Dardanelles, which are one of the most important strategic positions on the globe. The Straits were coveted by all the major powers, yet the Turks, being

---

[3] See George M. Trevelyan, *British History in the Nineteenth Century and After* (*1782–1919*), rev. ed., New York, Longmans, 1946, p. 416.

[4] On the paramount importance of the old silk route in antiquity when it afforded relatively close relations between Rome and China, see Frederick J. Teggart, *Rome and China: A Study of Correlations in Historical Events*, Berkeley, University of California Press, 1939, *passim*.

unable to defend them by their own means, always found security in the mutual jealousy of the powers, even at those times when, as during the 19th century, the Sultan eschewed active foreign policy and was continuously on the worst of terms with all major nations.

A similar "balance of jealousy" between the powers insured the independence of Siam, an easily accessible country controlling a highly important strategic bridge, the Isthmus of Kra. The highlands of Tibet, nominally a part of China, were created a political no man's land because an advance from the south or the north would have brought about Anglo-Russian conflict; communist China reasserted its hold over the country in 1951, without meeting any opposition. India, Britain's successor in the area, consented to China's increase in power. In all this, Tibet was just a pawn. Afghanistan, too, is a buffer country isolated by great-power agreement, the Anglo-Russian understanding of 1907 concerning the Middle East. Yet at times the policy of isolation was purposely and skillfully carried out by the Afghans themselves as, for example, at the end of the 19th century, when Shah Abd-er-Rahman played the British against the Russians and the Russians against the British, and thus stabilized the frontiers of the country.

Isolation as a reasoned and conscious policy was practiced by many Oriental states and empires, the most notable examples being China and Japan. A policy of strict seclusion was adopted as a means of preventing foreign infiltration and keeping the native culture and society intact. That policy was carried out rigorously and admitted of hardly any exception. Commerce with foreign nations was practically excluded; the little trade that was admitted was channeled through one port, Canton in China, and Hirado—later Deshima (Nagasaki)—in Japan. The volume of that trade was kept, in Japan, to two vessels a year. China refrained from expansionist ventures except various campaigns into nominally suzerain regions, such as Tibet, Nepal, and Burma. Foreigners were not admitted into either China or Japan except in rare and individual cases. In China, aliens were barred by law from studying the Chinese language. The "iron curtain" technique is nothing new.

Ambassadors were often refused admittance, as was the case in 1816 when Lord Amherst attempted to enter Peking. In turn, natives were not permitted to travel abroad or to return from foreign countries. In 1638, the Japanese Shogun Iyemitsu forbade the building of "large" ships of more than fifty tons, and put a stop to the lucrative piratical enterprises of Japanese sailors. These and similar exclusive practices were condoned by the Western powers as long as they were not greatly interested in opening China and Japan to their trade and political influence. Since Chinese and Japanese insulation against the international crosscurrents of ideas as well as trade retarded their technological development, the great empires of east Asia succumbed with surprising ease to the onslaught of Western imperialism.

It was by no means because of their mistrust of Western techniques alone that Oriental rulers looked askance at modern means of transportation. A characteristic case was Mohammed Ali's opposition to the building of the Suez Canal; he rightly feared that this canal would result in international complications for Egypt and ultimately lead to the loss of that country's independence. A similarly precautionary policy was adopted by Russia and Spain when these countries built railroads having a wider gauge than the railroads of other European countries. The Dutch constructed their system of canals in such a manner that they could flood the country in case of invasion, a method of strategic isolation. In the 1920's, Turkey enacted a law prohibiting *all* aerial flights through her air space, chiefly in order to prevent aerial inspection of the Dardanelles region. The keeping out of foreign literature is but another variant of the same policy, designed to reduce communications to a minimum.

Isolation of an involuntary character has often been brought about by a policy which runs contrary to the interest of all neighbors. This was, for example, the case of Germany during the two world wars, but especially prior to 1914. This policy consisted in stepping on everybody's toes and found its final expression in the bumptious slogan circulated in Germany during the First World War: *Viel Feind, viel Ehr'* (many enemies, much honor)! Germany's lonely eminence was not the result of an intelligent diplomacy but of saber-rattling truculence; Germany harbored, everyone thought, aggressive designs against practically all European countries. Basically, such a policy is founded on a belief that a country is strong enough to do whatever it pleases and that, if its friends do not want to go along, they may as well join the other side. It is a policy that is characteristic of the perennial "natural aggressor."

The isolation of "convalescence" recommends itself to countries recovering from exhausting efforts at war or internal reform. The policy of Cardinal Fleury in the early 18th century, after the ceaseless aggressive campaigns of Louis XIV had bled France white, was directed at giving the country respite from war. This policy was practiced at various times by Russia, for example, after the Crimean War when Count Gorchakov formulated it in these words: "La Russie ne boude pas; elle se recueille" (Russia does not sulk; she recovers). The same policy of diplomatic withdrawal was pursued after the Japanese War in 1905 by Witte and Stolypin, and was essentially the early program of Stalin (as opposed to that of Trotsky), a strategic retreat necessitated by Russia's weakness due to the ravages of war, revolution, civil war, and famine.

"Splendid Isolation." The true forms of isolationism should not be confused with what might be called "pseudo-isolation." This is a policy which keeps aloof of agreements with, and commitments to, other countries and bears ostensibly all the marks of isolationism but is, in reality, not isolationist at all. A good case in point is Britain's "splendid isolation," a position maintained throughout the 19th century and, especially, during the long tenure of Lord Salisbury. The logical foundations of this policy were simple: Europe became increasingly split into two rival camps, neither of which pursued a policy which coincided with Britain's interests. Nor could Britain have gained much by joining one of the camps; on the contrary, her interest would be best served by avoiding entanglement and by letting the others court British favor. Britain could not be attacked. Her "isolationist" policy was implemented by naval supremacy, and her physical isolation was safeguarded by deep water. So long as there were no obvious designs against Britain by any strong European power, Continental politics were of little concern to her. At the same time, Britain was free to expand and consolidate her African and Asiatic possessions. Whatever isolation there was, it derived from the fact that Britain was militarily unassailable and was not threatened by anybody at that time—"isolation" was speedily abandoned when Britain began to fear German aggression. Had Britain, faced by the threat of Germany's naval armaments, remained aloof, *i.e.*, isolationist, she would have courted the danger of Germany coming to terms with France or Russia, or both. Germany, secure against attack by the leading land powers, could have reduced her land armaments in favor of naval armaments and built a fleet stronger than the Royal Navy.

Britain's "splendid isolation," before her understandings with France and Russia in 1904 and 1907 respectively, was a foreign policy of great suppleness, a policy based upon *ad hoc* agreements. When England encountered difficulties with Russia or France, she moved closer to Germany; when Germany refused to yield, Britain leaned toward France and Russia. Together with France, Britain intervened in various Oriental crises, especially in the Mediterranean and the Near East. Britain and France repeatedly took parallel action in American matters. With Japan, Britain concluded an outright alliance directed against Russia. Britain took part in all major conferences, such as the Berlin and Morocco Conferences, and took an active share in all likely—and many unlikely—transactions of international politics. Her naval, industrial, and financial power, moreover, enabled her to play the role of arbiter. In any event, a country whose active policy was closely watched and taken into consideration by chancelleries all over the world can hardly be considered "isolationist." The label of "splendid isolation," though partially reflecting Britain's exceptional strategic position, served as a slogan adapted to the insular character of the British people, and also to its pragmatism which abhorred concluding binding agreements for contingencies which could not be foreseen. *In short, British policy was one of freedom of action, designed to gain the greatest possible advantage from any situation that might arise.*

The traditional foreign policy of the United States before 1941 must be classified as a case of "pseudo-isolationism." The United States maintained intimate trade relations with every and any country and was perennially prepared to fight for maintaining and increasing trade in the face of the most difficult circumstances. Second, the United States pursued a consistent policy of expansion Third, the United States was—and is—committed to the Monroe Doctrine (not to mention the unilateral declarations that the United States views the Atlantic and Pacific Oceans as American security zones), and that doctrine, although it may perhaps be defined as "hemispheric isolationism," encompasses in fact two continents and some twenty sovereign states. Fourth, the United States time and again cooperated closely with other nations, sometimes so closely that the dividing lines between mere friendship and alliance faded into the penumbra of purely verbal distinction. Fifth, United States policy was predicated during the 19th century upon British mastery of the seas; without the British navy, the United States would have been open to invasion and would have been compelled, had Britain withdrawn her protective shield, to adopt an altogether different foreign policy.

To be sure, the United States did not contract any permanent commitments in the form of alliances—if the Franco-American alliance during the War of Independence is disregarded. To use the traditional terminology, the United States avoided "entangling" alliances. In the historical controversies over American foreign policy the emphasis was usually placed upon "alliance" rather than on "entangling," yet the latter word is crucially important. It means, or implies, two things: there is no need for the "remote" United States to contract alliances of a character that might compel it to take up arms under circumstances which do not directly involve American interests—just as the French alliance seemed to do during the War of the First Coalition; secondly, for geographical reasons the existence of the United States was not dependent upon the strength or weakness, victory or defeat of specific European countries but, theoretically at least, the United States could join up with any country, or with none for that matter, *provided the balance of power was maintained on the other continents, and no single power rose anywhere in the world that would possess the military power to attack and defeat the United States.*

Quarrels in other continents, consuming the energies of other nations, enhanced the relative strength of the United States. In the 19th century, therefore, traditional American foreign policy served the interests of the United States. While in practice, *i.e.*, in case of an attack on the United States or the Western Hemisphere, the United States could have counted upon powerful allies, it did not become implicated in policies which were of no importance or direct interest to it. Thus the United States retained sufficient freedom of action; it could choose in each given issue that policy which actually or presumably fitted its interests most. Free from "entanglements," the United States saw no need for maintaining large and costly military establishments. American economy, unencumbered by heavy military expenditure, throve on the arts of peace. By the same token America's war *potential* increased at a fabulous pace.

This traditional policy was predicated upon a peculiar military situation. During its early history, an invasion of the United States constituted a very hazardous enterprise, because the United States could always muster a sizable military force within its own borders and spaciousness offered scope for a strategy of withdrawal similar to that of Russia in 1812. An invader would have had to attack with forces larger than any country of that epoch would have been able to transport and keep supplied across the ocean. Great Britain, had she bent all her efforts to this task, might have been the only exception, but even this is doubtful. It is a highly revealing fact that the United States maintained the most friendly relations with the only powerful country which, in the early 19th century, did not need to rely, as other powers, largely on sea communications but could mount an attack from a substantial adjacent land base—Canada. The demilitarization of the Canadian border signified the passing of the last real danger within the confines of the continent. As the United States grew more powerful, the possibility that a strong invader could defeat the American army within its continental borders vanished. Hence, with or without an unwritten alliance with Britain, the United States would always have been able to repel aggression by its own means. This fortuitous circumstance enabled this country to pursue a policy more independent than any other nation.

The United States was compelled to abandon its traditional policy whenever it seemed that military events in Europe and Asia would lead to the emergence of an aggressor more powerful than the United States, and therefore potentially able to invade this country and defeat it.[5] The military situation has changed; air power now enables an industrial aggressor to strike directly at the United States. The mere *possibility* that a war might be decided by air and atomic power alone, that it might be fought in American skies, and that a foreign nation might subject the United States to its will by smashing at the first blow the war potential of American industry, necessitated a change in traditional foreign policy. Moreover, during the Second World War, the distribution of power in Europe and Asia changed profoundly. It became considerably easier than at any time since the 18th century to concentrate superior military striking power for an overwhelming attack on the United States.

While the United States can no longer indulge in pseudo-isolation, it is still capable of choosing its foreign policy. By the force of circumstances, the United States retains greater freedom of action than most other countries, with the exception of the Soviet Union. The strength of the United States is such that in *any* alliance it will be the decisive power. Hence the United States can greatly influence the policies of its allies and steer clear of and prevent unnecessary quarrels. Being conscious of its material and unsure of its political strength, the United States occasionally permitted weaker states to influence its policies. The abandoning of the illusion of isolation has led

[5] The vulnerability of the United States to amphibious operations was recognized before 1901 by the German naval staff, and a discussion of such an attack was inadvertently published. See Alfred Vagts, *Landing Operations: Strategy, Psychology, Tactics, Politics from Antiquity to 1945,* Harrisburg, Pa., Military Service Publishing Company, 1946, pp. 474ff.

to the delusion that every member of the alliance, no matter how small, must be catered to. It is difficult to strike a balance between freedom from entanglement and freedom through cooperation.

NEUTRALITY

There are two types of neutrality: *ad hoc* neutrality adopted by a state toward competing or belligerent powers, and institutionalized neutrality as the basic and perennial policy of given countries. *Ad hoc* neutrality was, for example, the policy adopted by Great Britain during the Franco-Prussian War of 1870. The British Government chose to stay aside because, in their judgment, Britain's interests were not affected by victory or defeat of either belligerent.[6] During the various Franco-German crises from 1871 to 1914, Britain was no longer a neutral, since a second German victory over France would have established German power monopoly in western and central Europe, an intolerable threat to British security.

Through many years of its existence, the United States pursued a policy of neutrality. Indeed, it can be said that the United States was a traditionally neutral rather than an isolationist power. The United States was the protagonist of neutral rights which, in substance, are the right to carry on business and other international activities without hindrance by the belligerents —a doctrine which, although at times highly unrealistic, follows logically from the concept of neutrality.

While strong nations can abstain from participating in military and other conflicts, weak nations whose interests are not at stake try to avoid such participation because, no matter what side ultimately wins, the weak state, more often than not, suffers devastation and ruin. Only rarely can small states make a decisive military contribution. For example, if in 1940 Sweden had entered the war to support Finland against Russia, or Norway against Germany, she could not have prevented the defeat of either country but would have involved herself in a war which, as events showed, she was able to avoid without detriment to her national interest.[7]

On the other hand, the military power of small nations should not be underrated, since their resistance may slow down the aggressor and buy valuable time for the counterattack of friendly major powers whose mobilization is not quite completed. If all small nations had followed the example of Denmark in 1940, *i.e.*, had disarmed and refused to offer any resistance whatsoever to attack, Napoleon, Wilhelm II, and Hitler would, each in his time, have prob-

---

[6] Compare the singularly naïve and uninspired analysis by Britain's Foreign Secretary in 1870, John Earl Russell, *Recollections and Suggestions 1813–1873*, Boston, Roberts Brothers, 1875, p. 336.

[7] See the official publications of the Swedish Utrikesdepartement, *Förspelet till det Tyska Angreppet på Danmark och Norge den 9 April 1940*, Stockholm, Norstedt, 1947; also *Transiteringsfrågor och därmed sammanhängande Spörsmål April–June 1940*, and *Transiteringsfrågan Juni–December 1940*, both Stockholm, Norstedt, 1947.

ably subdued the entire world. In 1914, for instance, the stubborn fight put up by Serbia against Austria precluded a decisive *early* victory of the Central Powers over Russia. In 1941, the Yugoslav *coup d'état,* which provoked an unscheduled German attack, delayed Hitler's onslaught on Russia by about six weeks and thereby prevented the loss of Moscow—if not a Soviet collapse. By contrast, the Belgian army, which capitulated in the open field (May, 1940), numbered 500,000 men as against some 420,000 French and British troops fighting in Flanders. Without this defection, the Allied armies might have had a better chance to avert or, at least, delay the French collapse. Generally speaking, if the Belgian army had pursued a more effective strategy from the beginning of the battle on May 10, 1940, Hitler's astounding victory in the west would have lacked that conclusiveness which shattered French morale.[8] A small force may sometimes tip the scales, especially if geography helps and that force represents a large portion of the military strength within a crucial area.

The neutrality of a small nation is sometimes formally protected, or tacitly respected, by stronger powers. In 1914, the Germans did not attack Holland and Denmark because they believed that the continued neutrality of these states would be more advantageous to German strategy than their occupation. During their dash through the Balkans in the spring of 1941, the Germans did not push onward to the Dardanelles because violation of Turkish neutrality might have brought about an immediate Russian attack. The Allies, on the other hand, did not insist on belligerent cooperation from Turkey, for they, too, wished to avoid provoking a Soviet attack on that country.

Neutrality as a Policy. Neutrality is an ancient institution which, throughout history, could be *enforced* only by states which either were sufficiently strong or in possession of an easily defensible territory. However, the neutrality of states was often acknowledged by belligerents, even though these sometimes requested rights of passage. (Sweden granted Germany rights of passage after the defeat of Norway in 1940.) By the end of the 18th century, neutrality had become an institution only rarely violated by the strong. Guglielmo Ferrero believes that Bonaparte's violation of Parma's neutrality in 1796 marks a turning point in modern history—the hour, so to speak, of the birth of total war, and its concomitant, total fear.[9] It is certain that the observance of neutrality has become more and more perfunctory, until the Second World War degraded it to a legal fiction. The majority of the "neutral" states were directly or indirectly involved in the fighting.

[8] The illusions of a political, military, and economic nature which motivated the ill-fated Belgian policy of neutrality before the Second World War can be gleaned from the book by the former chief of the Belgian general staff, Lieutenant General Oscar Michiels, *18 Jours de guerre en Belgique,* Paris, Éditions Berger-Levrault, 1947, pp. 3–54.

[9] Guglielmo Ferrero, *Aventure: Bonaparte en Italie 1796–1797,* Paris, Plon, 1936, pp. 43*f.* The violation of Parmese neutrality entailed the violation of the neutrality of Venice by the Austrians; from that time on, neutrality was no longer a truly respected condition.

There are numerous reasons why neutrality is now only enforceable by strong states, if at all. First of all, the mechanization of modern war makes it necessary to fight in very large spaces. Furthermore, the smaller neutral state has little strength with which to oppose a major power; hence the temptation is too great not to forgo seizure of positions which may be of high value for the prosecution of the war. There are, however, exceptions to this: Britain's seizure of the Irish ports would have greatly improved Britain's position in the Battle of the Atlantic (1941–1943), yet the British abstained.

Neutral countries frequently control important raw materials (Rumanian oil, Congo uranium, Bolivian tin), industries (Czechoslovakia's steel plants), or transport routes (Norwegian coastal shipping and Egypt's Suez Canal) which the belligerents seek to deny to each other or to preempt as means of prosecuting the war. Numerous disputes arise between the belligerents and the neutrals about their respective rights. As a matter of fact, certain forms of warfare are carried out largely on neutral territory, such as economic warfare and, to a lesser degree, psychological warfare and the subterranean struggle of the intelligence services.

The fictional character of neutrality in modern times is glaringly apparent. Neither governmental policy nor public opinion remains really neutral but, more or less openly, supports one belligerent at the expense of the other. Thus, during both world wars Spain helped Germany, while Portugal supported the Allies.

The neutrality of great powers is characterized by the singular feature that, while fighting weakens the belligerent nations, it strengthens the neutrals sometimes not only relatively but also absolutely. The warring nations expend their wealth and weapons, while the neutral country accumulates power, wealth, and influence. The Italian Foreign Minister Count Ciano wanted to keep Italy neutral—or "nonbelligerent" as he put it—in order to make Italy stronger. In fact, Italy was never more influential and more advantageously placed than during her "nonbelligerency" from September, 1939, to June, 1940, when she received favors and handsome financial benefits from all sides. During the Second World War, Spain as well as Russia—in the phase of Soviet-German collaboration—profited in a similar way. The cunning neutrality policy pursued by the *caudillo* Francisco Franco insured his political survival after 1945.[10]

The fundamental reason why neutrality in the modern world is, at best, a precarious position and why sooner or later all great powers are forced into major wars is the intricate interdependence of industrial society. Formerly, a victory of A over B, or B over A, may have been of little concern to C, but today this no longer holds true, least of all in wars which are fought for ideological reasons or for world hegemony.

---

[10] See Serrano Suñer, *Entre les Pyrénées et Gibraltar: Notes et réflexions sur la politique de l'Espagne depuis 1936*, Geneva, Éditions du Cheval Ailé, 1948, p. 126.

Neutrality by Agreement. In every war some countries retain their neutrality, although they could be overrun without much difficulty. These countries have specific economic advantages to offer that would be annulled by seizure; or their occupation would be more costly than the operation warrants. Often the mere threat of occupation compels such countries to grant all concessions requested; occupation is then unnecessary. Political reasons may also play a role, as those which prompted respect of the neutrality of the Vatican. Neutral states serve the belligerents for a variety of purposes: they protect the nationals and interests of belligerents in enemy countries; they look after prisoners of war, arrange exchange of stranded diplomatic personnel, supervise repatriations, and maintain minimum postal communications. Most important of all, they are indispensable as listening posts for intelligence operations, for secret contacts, continued diplomatic communications, and preliminary armistice and peace negotiations. It could almost be said that war cannot effectively be waged without the existence of *some* centrally located neutral states.

Institutionalized neutrality obtains in the case of countries which have been created by the consensus of the major powers in order to prevent their territory from falling under the control of any one of them, upsetting the balance of power and unleashing war. Being the product of compromise, the newly created state must not violate the idea of the agreement by entering into alliances, thereby practically putting its strength and territory at the disposal of one power or one group of powers. Consequently, the new state undertakes to remain neutral in *all* contingencies, while the great powers, who are signatories to the birth-giving treaties, undertake to respect this neutrality. Two significant countries of this kind are, or were, Belgium—a "perpetually neutral state," according to the treaty of 1839—and Switzerland.[11] While the latter could maintain its neutrality, the former could not—except in the War of 1870. The reasons for this are fairly simple: Belgium is the main highway from northern Germany into France; if France is to be attacked in force, it is, for geographical and topographical reasons, almost imperative that part of the advancing armies march through Belgium, especially if and when the Franco-German border is strongly fortified. For an attack from central Europe against Britain, Belgium is an indispensable springboard; by the same token, any aggressive power controlling or attacking Belgium incurs the enmity of Britain. The fact remains that a staggering number of European wars and battles was fought in the Flanders plains.

[11] Edgar Bonjour, *Geschichte der Schweizerischen Neutralität: drei Jahrhunderte eidgenössischer Aussenpolitik,* Basel, Helbing und Lichtenhahn, 1946. The author is sufficiently realistic to ascribe the maintenance of Switzerland's neutrality to Swiss armaments (*bewaffnete Neutralität,* p. 331), but he has the strange illusion that Swiss security was strengthened when collective security was abandoned and that, *nur auf eigene Kraft sich stützend,* Switzerland could continue to defend her neutrality by her own means (p. 377). It should be obvious that Switzerland is not capable of defending itself long against any one of her neighbors with the exception of Austria and Liechtenstein.

The baneful effect of legal fiction upon a country's security is sadly exemplified by the case of Belgium. Under the impact of the events of 1914, Belgium forsook neutrality and in 1921 concluded an alliance with France. Prior to the building of the Maginot Line both governments agreed that the French and Belgian systems of fortifications be consolidated, saving France the expense of constructing permanent fortifications along her northern border. In 1935, Leopold III canceled these agreements and proclaimed Belgium a neutral state. The King was the victim of the delusion that meticulous neutrality would guard Belgium against an invasion in the case of another Franco-German war. After the start of the war in 1939, the Allies sought permission to enter Belgium *before* the Germans were prepared to strike. A last attempt was made in April, 1940, but the King took the position that he would call on the Allies only *after* the Germans had attacked. The Allied advance into Belgium ended in military catastrophe whereas a timely occupation of the Belgian lines would have permitted the Allies to consolidate their positions, coordinate their strategy, and integrate the Belgian war potential. No one can tell whether the Allies could have repelled the Germans. But it is certain that the policy of Belgium greatly facilitated German aggression while it did *not* spare that country the horrors of war and Nazi occupation.[12]

Switzerland is in a unique position. As regards passage from Germany to either France or Italy, better routes are available than the Swiss Alpine passes. The Swiss terrain is so difficult that attack even by vastly superior forces is a hazardous enterprise. An aggressor cannot hope to capture speedily the important passes, especially the excellently fortified Saint Gotthard. It is therefore not surprising that throughout history few armies marched through Switzerland, two notable exceptions being Russia's operations under Suvorov in 1799 and Austria's attack on France in 1814. Thus, Swiss neutrality was maintained not by the strength of legal agreement but by the inherent military strength and the relative impassability of the country.

A special case is the neutrality of the Vatican. In former times, the Papal states were not neutral in the proper sense of the word and actually took part in many wars; Papal territory was often invaded, and Popes were led into captivity. The Lateran Treaty of 1929 reestablished a small Vatican territory in Rome, which was confirmed by Republican Italy in 1947. The Vatican's neutrality was not violated during the Second World War, either by the Italians or by the Allies, or even by the Germans, obviously because such an affront would have alienated Catholics all over the world. The holocaust of World War II passed by such sacred places as, for example, Kyoto, Japan's Buddhist center, or Kairouan in Tunisia, a holy place of the Islam religion. But it is to expediency, rather than to piety and covenants, that the Vatican owed its safety from German and Fascist invasion, a grudging

---

[12] Belgium's unwillingness to cooperate had grave repercussions on Franco-British strategy in 1939 and 1940 (see General Gamelin, *Servir*, Paris, Plon, 1947, Vol. III, "La guerre septembre 1939–19 mai, 1940," pp. 135–186).

tribute not to the idea of neutrality but to the survival of a universal faith.
Only the future can reveal what lies in store for neutrality as a technique
and institution in the age of global air warfare. It may well be that the
strategy of "island hopping," so successfully employed in the Pacific War,
may supply the pattern of a future strategy of "country hopping." A country
by-passed by air-borne attack may find it possible to remain neutral.

As regards most countries, however, insistence on neutrality is an attempt
to stay out of the stream of history. It is not unlike the attitude of the man
who wished he had never been born. The technological and sociological conditions which, in a bygone age, made a policy of neutrality practical, if and
when the neutral power was willing to defend itself, no longer exist—except
fortuitously.

Bibliography

Isolation

American Council on Education: *American Isolation Reconsidered,* Washington, The
Council, 1941.
Brogan, Denis W.: *Is Innocence Enough? Some Reflexions on Foreign Affairs,* London,
Hamish Hamilton, 1941.
Buell, Raymond L.: *Isolated America,* New York, Knopf, 1940.
Herriot, Edouard: "An International Drama," *International Conciliation,* No. 290, May,
1933.
Latané, John H.: *A History of American Foreign Policy,* revised by David W. Wain-
house, New York, Doubleday, 1940.
Warburg, James P.: *The Isolationist Illusion and World Peace,* New York, Oxford, 1941.
Whitton, John B.: "Isolation: An Obsolete Principle of the Monroe Doctrine," *Interna-
tional Conciliation,* No. 290, May, 1933.

Neutrality

Bacot, Bernard: *Des neutralités durables,* Paris, Recueil Sirey, 1946.
Bemis, George: *American Neutrality: Its Honorable Past, Its Expedient Future,* Boston,
Little, Brown, 1866.
Buehler, Ottmar: "Neutralität, Blockade und U-Bootkrieg in der Entwicklung des
modernen Völkerrechts," *Schriften des Deutschen Institutes für aussenpolitische For-
schung,* No. 55, Berlin, Junker and Dünnhaupt, 1940.
Cohn, Georg: *Neo-neutrality,* New York, Columbia University Press, 1939.
Déak, Francis, and P. C. Jessup (eds.): *A Collection of Neutrality Laws, Regulations
and Treaties of Various Countries,* New York, Columbia University Press, Interna-
tional Documents Service, 1940.
—— and ——: *Treaty Provisions, Defining Neutral Rights and Duties,* Washington,
Carnegie Endowment, 1937.
Dulles, A. W., and H. F. Armstrong: *Can We Be Neutral?* New York, Harper, 1936.
Jessup, Philip C., Francis Déak, W. A. Phillips, A. H. Reede, and Edgar Turlington:
Neutrality, Its History, Economics and Law, 4 vols. New York, Columbia University
Press, 1935–1936.
Kunz, Josef L.: *Kriegsrecht und Neutralitätsrecht,* Vienna, Springer, 1935.
Phillips, W. Alison, and Arthur H. Reede: *Neutrality, Its History, Economics and
Law,* Vol. 2, "The Napoleonic Period," New York, Columbia University Press, 1936.
Politis, Nicolas S.: *Neutrality and Peace,* Washington, Carnegie Endowment, 1935.
Stimson, Henry L.: "Neutrality and War Prevention," *International Conciliation,* No.
312, September, 1935.
Suñer, Serrano: *Entre les Pyrenées et Gibraltar: Notes et reflexions sur la politique de
l'Espagne depuis 1936,* Geneva, Éditions du Cheval Ailé, 1948.
Turlington, Edgar: *Neutrality, Its History, Economics and Law,* Vol. 3, "The World
War Period," New York, Columbia University Press, 1936.
Wright, Quincy P.: *The Future of Neutrality,* Washington, Carnegie Endowment, 1928.

Chapter 13

ALLIANCES AND THE BALANCE OF POWER

ALLIANCES

Alliances will remain a subject of discourse as long as a multistate system exists. Public opinion in some countries is as much "for" alliances as, in other countries, it is "against" them. The reason adduced for the respective attitudes are rarely convincing; alliances are mostly discussed in the rarefied atmosphere of political metaphysics. For example, alliances are said to "freeze" groupings of nations into permanent hostile camps, or to make war "inevitable," or to provoke counteralliances. Ideas of a postwar Anglo-American alliance were, for instance, strenuously opposed by an eminent historian, because such an alliance would irretrievably split the world into two camps, and thus set the stage for a new war, while the absence of such an alliance would make it possible to adjust differences. There was no alliance, and the world was split, thus making defensive alliances of the West unavoidable.

It is true that alliances are effective means only for the solution of certain problems and are not a remedy to any and all international ills. In a world in which peaceful cooperation obtains between the major powers and where there is little danger of war, alliances for defensive purposes are not only superfluous but dangerous, as they make the other powers suspicious and incite counteraction. For example, prior to the Seven Years' War, Austria, Russia, and France concluded an alliance against Prussia. This alliance was originally of a defensive character, yet it had an offensive aspect which was not lost on Frederick II of Prussia. Hence when a suitable occasion presented itself in the form of a Franco-British war at the very moment when neither Austria nor Russia was able to fight offensively, Frederick attacked to forestall a surprise attack by superior forces. Whether Prussia would have launched her attack if there had been no hostile alliance is a moot question; the fact remains that this defensive alliance was followed by a general war.

If there is no obvious danger of war, the conclusion of alliances usually serves offensive purposes. History is replete with instances of various states entering into alliances as a first step toward preventive war. For example, in 1686 the League of Augsburg between the Emperor, Sweden, Spain, Savoy, Bavaria, Saxony, the Palatinate, Holland, and, upon the accession of William of Orange to the British throne, England, was directed against Louis XIV of France, who, after learning of the alliance's true character, promptly went to war. In 1699, Russia, Poland, and Denmark, seeking to curb Sweden's power in the Baltic, concluded a secret alliance and in the following year opened hostilities. This war, incidentally, started Sweden on the road toward the ultimate eclipse of her once considerable might and paved the way for Russia's ascendancy. In 1798, Russia, Britain, Austria, Naples, Portugal, and Turkey, under the leadership of Tsar Paul I, concluded an offensive alliance against revolutionary France and launched the War of the Second Coalition which very nearly subdued the French Revolution. Adolf Hitler concluded an offensive alliance with Japan and Italy, and unleashed a major conflagration.[1]

However there is a quite different type of alliance, one that is designed to *protect* a group of nations against impending aggression by combining their military forces. Even the severest critics of "power politics" hardly ever object to those alliances concluded, *de jure* or *de facto,* after aggression has taken place. In times of war no country will be so foolish as to reject help from others, even though their contribution may be as small as that of the Dutch East Indies during the first six months of the Pacific War. During wars alliances are quickly concluded—even between two countries which are ideologically at odds.

If wartime alliances are effective, it seems reasonable to assume that under certain conditions, prewar defensive alliances can be effective, too. Before such alliances become practical, it is necessary that nations be aligned in opposite camps, or at least that major divergencies be reasonably well defined. It would be hard to find an example showing that the conclusion of a defensive alliance in such a situation tends to sharpen antagonism and makes war inevitable. A defensive alliance which has been concluded *before* the opposite camp has forged an offensive alliance of its own, or clearly manifested its aggressiveness, is a contradiction in terms. There is, in troubled periods, invariably an expansionist power set on making war, provided a favorable opportunity presents itself. This being the case, the obvious countermove would seem to be *not* to present that power with such an opportunity. This precisely would be the purpose of a prewar defensive alliance. Hence, an alliance may be an effective means of stopping the aggressor, or, to paraphrase this thought, *whenever an aggressor arises, alliances are indispensable to avoid war* or, if this is impossible, to win the contest in the shortest time at the least cost.

History shows, indeed, that such alliances can stop aggression. For example, France after 1815 was several times on the brink of aggressive war as

---

[1] See Albert Sorel, *L'Europe et la Révolution Française,* Paris, Plon, 1927, Vol. V, pp. 392–448. On the manner in which modern alliances are being concluded, see Galeazzo Ciano, *L'Europa verso la Catastrofe,* Milan, Mondadori, 1948, pp. 433, 594, 610 and *passim.* See also U.S. Department of State, *Nazi-Soviet Relations 1939–1941, Documents from the Archives of the German Foreign Office,* edited by Raymond J. Sontag and James S. Beddie, Government Printing Office, 1948, pp. 215–259.

a means of ridding herself of the conditions she had been forced to accept in the Peace of Paris. These attempts never ripened into major conflict because France was opposed by a standing four-power alliance of Britain, Prussia, Austria, and Russia. In 1840, Adolphe Thiers, French Premier and Foreign Minister, eager to refurbish France's martial glory and having gained the support of French public opinion, involved France in the dispute between Mohammed Ali of Egypt and the Sultan of Turkey. He supported Egypt's claim to Syria; however, his main objective was to make France the predominant power in the Near East. This policy was countered by the Treaty of London concluded between England, Austria, Prussia, and Russia. The British navy sailed to Syria in support of the Sultan, while Mohammed Ali pleaded for the help of France. These events aroused French popular passions to a high pitch and created, in the words of Heinrich Heine, "a joyful bellicose enthusiasm rather than consternation: the most widely heard slogan of the day was 'war against perfidious Albion.'" However, the situation was obviously hopeless for France. When Thiers discovered that he could not drive a wedge between Britain and her Continental allies, he resigned. Europe stayed at peace.

In 1875, Bismarck, concerned over the speedy recovery of France and the reorganization of the French army, was about to provoke war in order to finish, once and for all, with France.[2] Bismarck later loudly disclaimed that he had harbored any warlike thoughts. The reason for Bismarck's peaceable disposition was that Britain and Russia had informed Germany unequivocally that they would not tolerate a further weakening of France. In 1870, British policy, which condoned the defeat of France, reflected the narrow vision of Gladstone, while in 1875 the tough realism of Disraeli prevailed. In 1911, during the Agadir crisis, and in 1912, during the Albanian crisis, England intimated that she would not remain neutral in the case of a German-Austrian war with France and Russia, and in both cases the Central Powers desisted from their aggressive designs and accepted diplomatic defeat thinly disguised as compromise.

Containment by Alliance. There is good reason to believe that in 1914 Germany would not have gone to war if she had known that Great Britain would side with France and Russia. Hitler might have halted on the road to European conquest if he had known that ultimately he would have to face the entire world. There is no conclusive proof that a Russian-British-French-

[2] Paul Liman, *Bismarck, Denkwürdigkeiten aus seinen Briefen, Reden und letzten Kundgebungen, sowie nach persönlichen Erinnerungen, zusammengefasst und erläutert,* Berlin, A. de Grousilliers, 1899, Vol. II, pp. 228*ff.* The British journalist de Blowitz, who was the medium through which the French Foreign Minister had revealed the German plan, absolves Bismarck and puts the blame on Moltke and the General Staff (see *Memoirs of M. de Blowitz,* New York, Doubleday, 1903, pp. 103–115). However, Blowitz may be mistaken, for Bismarck had not only instigated a press campaign against France but also had attempted to neutralize Russia through diplomatic means and thus to exclude Russian assistance to France in case of a German aggression.

American alliance in 1938 or 1939 would have contained German expansionism and prevented the Second World War. It is, however, a fact that, in 1934, when Italy, then militarily stronger than Germany and assured of support by the Western powers (an assurance later formalized in the Stresa Pact), opposed the seizure of Austria, Hitler backed down. In 1939, to the contrary, Hitler persisted in his plans because he counted on the discord among the Western powers, their failure to conclude hard and fast alliances, the continued policy of inaction of the United States, and, although perhaps none too confidently, on the neutrality of Britain. Indeed, he launched his attack against Poland only after he had made sure that Russia would not join the Western powers, but remain a benevolent neutral. *If the criticism leveled against defensive alliances were justified, then the policy of the Western powers should have averted the war. This it did not do.*

If prewar defensive alliances *can* prevent war, the question arises why, in certain cases, they have patently failed to do so. Why, for example, did the Franco-Russian alliance of 1892 fail to prevent the First World War? Why did the British-French guarantee of Poland and Rumania of April, 1939, fail to avert the Second World War? The answer is that in both cases the military strength which the alliance was able to muster was inadequate to deter the aggressor. Germany could in both cases reasonably hope that she could win the war, while in the second case she assumed that the alliance agreement would remain a dead letter. Alliances which do not assemble *superior* military power, or which do so only on paper because some of the allies have no readily available military strength, cannot be counted upon to avert war. This guarantee is given only by alliances which assemble *overwhelming* force. The chances of the NATO alliance—which, incidentally, is not automatic— ought to be examined in the light of these precedents.

What then is the value of alliances if they cannot accumulate sufficient deterring power? For example, was the conclusion of the Franco-Russian alliance of 1892 a wise decision in spite of the fact that Britain and the United States could not be persuaded to adhere to it? This alliance did not prevent the war but, in the case of France, it saved the French army from crushing defeat in 1914. Had the Russian army not engaged a large part of the German army, France could not have won the victory at the Marne and held the western front. The Franco-Russian holding action deprived Germany of victory. Seen from this angle, alliances are an indispensable element of security.

It may also be asked whether defensive alliances do not *accelerate* the coming of war. For example, there is much evidence to show that both in 1914 and in 1939 the Germans went to war because they surmised that a few years later the growing defensive strength of the Allied powers would have shifted the odds sufficiently to outweigh Germany's initial advantage. It is true that the extent of the deterring power of an alliance varies with time: when the power of the alliance is relatively weakest, the aggressor has his best chance of gaining a decisive victory. That chance may be his last. However, if there is no alliance, the chances of the aggressor are even better; if aggression is a foregone conclusion, a weak alliance is better than none because it increases the aggressor's risk. Only if the would-be aggressor surmises that the defensive alliance is likely to develop into an offensive compact despite his having renounced aggressive designs, only then might it lead to a preventive-defensive war by the "reformed" aggressor. This is a purely hypothetical case for which, to our knowledge, no historical precedent exists.

Alliances concluded between powers seeking to alter the *status quo* are by definition offensive; alliances between powers committed to the maintenance of the *status quo* are either plainly defensive or preventive. In most cases where a defensive alliance did not prevent war, no alliance at all would hardly have been more helpful for preserving peace. The argument that a compact between two states, although it was originally concluded largely for defensive reasons, denotes—because the allies are growing stronger—an offensive threat, will be advanced only by a government that is committed to or actually planning for war. If in 1914 and 1939 aggression had not been the basic motivation of the German government, its policy would not have been guided by the fear that a few years later certain European states would become militarily somewhat stronger. It must be borne in mind that this anticipated increase of strength merely would have reestablished the upset balance of power. This was of concern *only* because it would have prevented the successful execution of Germany's blitzkrieg strategy.

While the value of alliances can thus hardly be disputed, it need not be denied that they are far from perfect instruments of foreign policy. It has often been asserted that they engender intransigence in the policy of states which rely on the "automatic" aid clauses of alliance treaties and that they forestall compromise solutions which may avoid war. It has been said that without the system of alliances the First World War might not have broken out, because Austria would not have gone to such extremes of truculence toward Serbia had she not relied upon the support of Germany. Similarly, it is argued that Russia might have taken a far more conciliatory attitude if she had not relied on the French alliance. The first contention is true, except that in this case the mechanics of aggression are confounded with the mechanics of alliance: if Germany had not been ready in 1914, and if she had not relied on British neutrality, she would not have backed Austria. Austria's policy against Serbia was not determined by any "automatic" features of that alliance but by subsequent negotiations and agreements with the Germans.

The second contention is at best of doubtful validity, but, assuming it to be true, concessions on the part of Russia would have jeopardized what she considered to be her vital interests in the Balkans. This Russia might not have done under any circumstance; or she might have postponed the day of reckoning. It is true that Russia might have forsaken the French alliance, but in that case the war would not necessarily have been avoided. For the Germans had decided to wage war. Russia would have risked her own defeat in an isolated struggle in the east, to be followed by an overwhelming German onslaught on an isolated France.

The basic fact is that Germany, bent on fighting France, for reasons of domestic politics—the socialists had become the strongest German party and were unwilling to fight the West but willing to fight Tsarism—provoked the war with Russia.

Another consideration is more valid: the weaker members of an alliance often make life miserable for the stronger ones. Germany's hand was forced in 1914 because she feared Austria's domestic disintegration; yet Austria's military contribution was smaller than expected. Similarly, the Entente powers might have been better off without Italy's participation in the First World War. The weaker ally may not only be more reckless and irresponsible —as, for example, Mussolini's attack on Greece, 1940—he may also be more timorous and cautious—as, for example, the inhibitions which Britain and France placed on American strategy in Korea during 1951 and 1952.

Casus Foederis. No defensive alliance can be used for aggressive purposes unless the signatory powers deliberately transform it into a pact of aggression. *The self-operating nature of alliances is a mere myth.* Defensive alliances are formulated in such a manner that they cover only the specific *casus foederis* (case within the provision of the compact) for which they were designed, but do not give a contracting power the right to involve its allies over issues extraneous to that *casus foederis*.[3]

Russia concluded an alliance with Germany in 1873, according to which mutual assistance was to be given should any of the two parties be attacked by another European power. And yet, in 1875, when Germany was playing with the idea of attacking France, Russia not only did not permit herself to be dragged into this war as Germany's ally, but made it clear that in the case of such an aggression, Russia would join France *against* Germany. The in-

[3] On the way by which an alliance could be terminated *de facto* once it had fulfilled its main purpose, namely, to prevent war, see *Documents Relating to the Eve of the Second World War; Secret Documents from the Archives of the German Government Revealing Nazi Relations with Foreign Statesmen,* 2 vols., New York, International Publishers, 1948. (These are the documents published by the Soviet Ministry of Foreign Affairs in "answer" to the American publication of documents relating Nazi-Soviet relations.) On p. 122, we read in a report from the German Ambassador at London: "Sir Horace Wilson made the statement . . . regarding British encirclement policy, that it would become inoperative if a treaty of nonaggression were concluded with Germany." This term "encirclement policy" refers to the alliance with Poland; the statement was made in August, 1939. In another memorandum, later prepared from memory, the German diplomat wrote: "Again Wilson affirmed . . . that the conclusion of an Anglo-German entente would practically render Britain's guarantee policy nugatory. Agreement with Germany would enable Britain to extricate herself from her predicament in regard to Poland on the ground that the non-aggression pact protected Poland from German attack . . ." (p. 187). Sir Horace made the point that Britain had assumed her commitments "only against the event of attack. With the removal of the danger the commitments would also cease to be operative" (p. 118).

terests of states are not identical, nor do they necessarily run on parallel lines; yet some interests are common, and alliances become operative only if these specific *common* interests are in danger. Even when specific common interests are endangered and a *casus foederis* clearly obtains, the signatory powers always consult and coordinate their policy.

The Franco-British guarantee to Poland has been cited as an example to show how alliances draw the signatory as well as other powers into war—at an unpropitious moment to boot. It is true that this guarantee, which later took the form of a mutual assistance pact, was hastily concluded and inadequately implemented. In fact, it was a gesture rather than an alliance. Yet had this treaty never been concluded, the Western powers would have still been compelled to go to war against Germany. England and France realized that the moment had come to halt Hitler and that war could no longer be postponed, regardless of how well or badly they were prepared for it. Under these circumstances, the pact served two purposes: (1) it served notice on Hitler that future aggression would be answered by war—a warning which he did not take seriously in view of the British-French record of 1935–1939; and (2) it strengthened the hand of the Poles (which was somewhat unfortunate). Had the Franco-British guarantee not been given, Hitler would have attacked Poland just the same. When the crisis came, the French Cabinet discussed the question of whether the pact was to be honored or not.[4] They decided to go to war because, if they did not, Germany would attack France a few months later. Under the circumstances it was preferable to fight by the side of the Poles rather than to take up the challenge alone.[5] It was not the pact which brought about "automatic" French-British intervention; it was the identity of vital interests that created the pact and made it operative when the signatories faced the Polish crisis.

It can be said that the pact "did not work." Conceived as a warning, it did not convey the warning. Designed for mutual defense, it did not defend.

The failure of this pact must be traced to the collapse in 1938 of the French system of alliances in eastern Europe, *i.e.*, the Little Entente. An alliance with a weak state (Poland) which does not *counterbalance* the power of the aggressor cannot be expected to be effective, although—to be sure—even a small increment of force is useful in a life-and-death struggle against an overwhelmingly strong aggressor. Nor, for lack of offensive equipment, could the alliance be honored by energetic military measures from the west. Had the Western powers been able to mount an offensive against Germany in September, 1939, and had the other allies of France in eastern Europe, such as Czechoslovakia and Yugoslavia, still been capable of effective action

[4] See L. B. Namier, *Diplomatic Prelude 1938–1939*, London, Macmillan & Co., Ltd., 1948, Chap. 6; also pp. 244*ff.*, 293, 434–466. See also Georges Bonnet, *Fin d'une Europe, de Munich à la guerre*, Geneva, Éditions du Cheval Ailé, 1948, pp. 277*ff.*

[5] General Gamelin, *Servir*, Paris, Plon, 1946, Vol. I, "Les Armées françaises de 1940," p. 30.

(which as a result of Franco-British vacillation they were not), then the policy of alliances might have met the test for which it was designed: defense of the individual member and containment of the aggressor. *The true lesson to be learned from the series of dismal failures between 1933 and 1939 is that alliances which are not implemented by adequate political, economic, and military means, and are not backed up by adequate offensive striking power, are indeed "dangerous" alliances,* or, rather, they are no alliances at all. The lessons for the future are plain.

The value of alliances is attested by the fact that would-be aggressors usually concentrate, preparatory to attack, their energies upon destroying alliances. In 1870, Bismarck attacked when France was isolated, partly through his own efforts, such as those employed in the Convention of Alvensleben of 1863 in which he bought Russia's support for his aggressive wars by helping the Tsar crush the second Polish Revolution. Wilhelm II wrathfully accused France, Britain, and Russia of having "encircled" Germany and wooed now Russia, now Britain, now both. Hitler succeeded in isolating his intended victims before he overwhelmed them. If Austria, Czechoslovakia, Poland, Hungary, Yugoslavia, and Rumania had supported each other in the east and cooperated with the Western powers, Hitler would in all likelihood have stopped short of Vienna.

After World War II, Russia intervened to prevent the establishment of friendly relations among states on her western borders. Specifically, she defeated proposals for the establishment of a Czechoslovak-Polish federation proclaimed early during the war, the conclusion of an Italo-Austrian customs union planned in 1946, and the establishment of a federation of the Communist Peoples' Democracies in the Balkans propounded by a former General Secretary of the Third International, George Dimitrov. Russia supported frontier changes designed to perpetuate conflict among her-neighbors: Trieste and the Yugoslav-Italian border; the German-Polish frontier; the frontiers of Yugoslavia, Bulgaria, and Greece with respect to Macedonia. In addition, the Soviets tried to prevent the emergence and later the continuance of the NATO alliance—unsuccessfully, since their tactics were rather crude and hence self-defeating.

While alliances have shortcomings and dangers and do not operate effectively under all circumstances, *they are thus far the only available means of stopping a determined aggressor and of transforming him by forceful persuasion or by force into a peaceful member of the family of nations.*

Alliances and Affinities. There is a difference between temporary and permanent alliances or, since there is little that is permanent in history, between alliances of convenience and alliances of a more basic character. Countries with dissimilar interests may be thrown together by accident— chance companions in a particular situation. Such was the case of the German cooperation with Poland in 1934–1938 and with Russia in the early 1920's and in 1939–1941, the pro-German policy of Laval's Vichy France, and the cooperation of the United States with the Chinese Communist regime in Yenan. Such alliances disintegrate as quickly as they are formed. In some rare cases, an association formed under hostile pressure may lead to an alliance of more lasting character, as, for example, the Anglo-French Entente of 1904 which started out as a colonial settlement and developed into a close and almost permanent union.

Permanent or near-permanent alliances may have a geographical or an ideological character. Among the first are those which are determined by the location of the aggressor; for example, the formation—time and again—of a Franco-Russian or, more generally, a Franco-Slav alliance against Germany was determined by the latter country's central position in Europe. In many crises the United States and Russia have found themselves on the same side; there was, before 1949–1950, no case on record of American-German cooperation. Similarly, geography joined Russia and Austria, Austria and England, and Turkey and Great Britain during numerous phases of modern history.

In all these cases, there was, so to speak, no love lost between the allies; on the contrary, their political differences were quite marked. For example, Gladstone wrote a violent pamphlet against Turkish misrule (1876) at the very time that Britain supported Turkey against Russia. British public opinion was nearly always opposed to the Sultan, while the British Government practically always supported him.

By the end of the 19th century Russian public opinion held the "revolutionary" French in low esteem; it was considered a great event when the Tsar was present at the playing of the "Marseillaise" on the occasion of the visit of a French statesman to St. Petersburg. After the war, the conservative French professed themselves deeply shocked by the revolutionary Soviets. Despite all this, France and Russia, though not always on intimate terms and sometimes hostile to each other (as, for example, during the Russo-Polish War in 1920 and the Russo-Finnish War in 1939–1940 and the early phase of World War II in 1939–1941) found themselves nonetheless on the same side in many critical moments, or rather, they were repeatedly driven together by the logic of Europe's geography. The geographical position counted—the "where," not the "who."

Quite different are those alliances which are based, in addition to their strategic-geographical logic, on similar ideological or social structure. There are the alliances which are based upon "racial" or linguistic affinities, such as those between Germany and Austria, despite cleavages of interest and wars between Austria and Prussia; or the alliances between France and Belgium. On the other hand, linguistic kinship alone is not a sufficient basis of solid alliances, as can be seen from the failure of attempts to set up a "Union Latine" or merely to reconcile the "Latin sisters," France and Italy.

Anglo-American friendship or cooperation is based partly on language, partly on identity of interests. Yet these bonds are immeasurably strengthened by the associative elements of cultural and political structure and by the pull of common political ideals—particularly if and when these ideals meet the opposition of other powers. The organic bonds between the two countries are strong precisely because they grew gradually, and without artificial forcing, from shared experience. This is an alliance *de facto*. This alliance may be in an inoperative state when there is no crisis to activate it or when only limited interests of either partner are threatened. But as soon as the vital interests of both countries are at stake, the Anglo-American association becomes a vital factor, *the* most vital factor, as Bismarck predicted more than seventy years ago, in contemporary world politics.

Alliances which are based largely on ideological affinities, such as the Nazi-Fascist Anti-Comintern Pact, remain in force as long as the particular ideological regimes are in power. However, ideology alone is not sufficient as a basis of alliance; the Italo-German and the German-Japanese alliances, for example, never worked smoothly because of profound cultural differences, adverse geographical conditions, and mutually exclusive political interests.[6] Such cleavages may yet mar the Russo-Chinese alliance of 1950. Nevertheless, it remains true that states of a similar political philosophy are driven together by the force of an idea and usually cooperate with each other, forming a "bloc" in the field of foreign policy.

Yet to assume a factual alliance of all states of similar philosophies is to oversimplify the problem of ideas in politics. On the contrary, just as monarchies have fought each other, or republics have fought republics—as shown by the wars of the Italian Renaissance and events in the Western Hemisphere—dictatorships, too, may war against each other. Fascist Italy's most determined opponent was Greece, a Fascist dictatorship formed after the Italian model. The United Nations included a number of barefaced dictatorships and governments modeled after the Fascist pattern. On the other hand, the Axis powers found open or camouflaged support from some democratic countries and found an ally in democratic Finland. Socialist states may be hostile to communist states, and Yugoslavia's Tito has shown that conflicts between communist states are by no means inconceivable. In fact, it is inadmissible to confuse the Soviet "orbit" in Europe with a genuine alliance of Russia with Eastern European nations.

An alliance concluded by reason of the aggressor's geographical location is often opposed on ideological grounds as unnatural and unworkable. The simple truth, however, is that in international relations one cannot choose one's friends. The ideal ally does not exist—nor is one's own country ideal by everybody else's standards—and all friends and allies have many despicable characteristics and as bad a "record" as has, in their eyes, one's own country. The choice is one between lesser evils: whom does a country fear more, for whom does it care less? When in 1941 Hitler attacked Russia, the

---

6 The fundamental difficulties of the German-Italian alliance became obvious even before the first shot of World War II was fired. (See Mario Roatta, *Otto milioni di baionette: l'esercito italiano in guerra dal 1940 al 1944*, Milan, Mondadori, 1946, pp. 150ff.)

United States, heartily disliking both belligerents, had to decide whom it should help. The reasoning determining that choice was simple: if Germany had won, she would have united Europe and Asia, and gained a supreme power monopoly; nor would Germany have hesitated to destroy Britain in short order and then to attack the United States itself. No such threat was anticipated from the Soviet Union for the simple reason that it was assumed that the Soviet could not marshal similar offensive power. Disregarding how the situation did develop at a later date, *in 1941* Germany constituted a far greater threat to the United States, and a most acute threat at that. Hence the United States could not but aid Russia. The problems of 1950 could not be solved in 1941. Decisions in foreign policy must be made mostly on the basis of conditions actually obtaining and cannot be made solely, especially in emergencies, on the basis of anticipated conditions.

This does not mean that policy should be on a day-by-day basis and that likely future developments can be wholly disregarded. It means simply that a foreign policy which attempts simultaneously to solve two different and mutually exclusive problems will be vacillating, and will not, in the end, solve either. The most urgent and vital problem must be solved first, although in such a manner as not to prejudice the successful solution of a subsequent and anticipated major problem. Generally speaking, foreign policy can be effective *only if it is directed at one major problem at any one time.* If there are several problems to be solved at a given moment, compromise must clean the slate for the sake of the major problem's solution. If a country is beset by several serious problems, they are most efficiently dealt with in *succession.* Most attempts at simultaneous solution will produce a superior hostile coalition or, at best, leave *all* problems unsolved. Simultaneous solutions, incidentally, are enthusiastically advocated by ideologists; the realist eats his dinner in sequence from the hors d'oeuvres *via* the main dish to the dessert without omitting the accompanying drinks.

In conclusion, alliances are most effective—and indeed desirable—if countries whose geographical positions contribute to the emergence of similar interests, and whose political philosophies provide a similar outlook, are driven to make common cause against common danger. By concluding the alliance in time and thus accumulating greater strength than the would-be aggressor can muster, they may forestall war. By concluding it after war breaks out— "either we hang together, or we will all hang separately"—they may forestall defeat. Alliances directed against a common enemy and reinforced by geography but lacking a basis in similar philosophies may meet the test of war, are rarely concluded in peacetime, and fall apart during the peace negotiations. Alliances based exclusively on similar philosophy and not buttressed by geography are difficult to maintain. Offensive alliances are usually concluded between states with a similar philosophy and common interest against a common enemy; their strength or weakness is, however, largely determined by the geographical setting. While alliances have undoubtedly negative aspects and may drag peaceful countries into war, they are unavoidable in true crisis situations.

THE BALANCE OF POWER

It is frequently asserted that balance of power is a policy designed to keep peace. No less an expert than Sir Victor Wellesley, late British Deputy Undersecretary of State for Foreign Affairs, wrote, "The virtue of the balance-of-power doctrine lay essentially in its power to maintain peace." [7] The balance of power policy was practiced, from antiquity to our times, by innumerable states innumerable times. Since in innumerable cases it failed to maintain peace, the question must be asked whether the traditional explanation, "the balance-of-power maintains peace," is correct.

Two states, A and B, possess at a given moment approximately equal power; they are in balance. In most instances they will refrain from going to war against each other, since a contest between equal forces hardly ever leads to a clean-cut victory, but almost always to exhaustion. In that sense, balance of power may be said to maintain peace. Assume now that A becomes "dynamic" and either by conquest or organic growth becomes stronger and is suddenly superior in military strength to B. A would now be able to defeat B who, to forestall that peril, restores the upset balance by concluding an alliance with C. Hence the previous situation would obtain, and the balance of power would still preserve peace. However, reality does not conform to this pattern, because there is never a balance in the proper sense, *i.e.*, a condition where both parties are equally strong. Actually there are only approximate balances, and the dynamic power which has a small edge of military strength may resort to war at an "opportune moment," for example, when the relations between B and C are unsatisfactory. If within an approximate balance the would-be aggressor has a chance to win a war, the balance of power is unlikely to preserve the peace. Moreover, such balances are precarious and can be easily upset, for example, by an alliance between A and C.

Actually, the balance of power doctrine operates somewhat differently from this theoretical principle. Throughout many centuries, Great Britain contended for supremacy with France, then the strongest state on the Continent. At frequent intervals, Britain went to war in order to maintain the approximate balance of power; many wars of the 18th century were fought precisely in the interest of keeping the balance of power. Far from keeping peace by the application of this principle, war was often the only effective means of restoring the balance. Of course it might be correct to state that a *true* balance of power preserves peace, while the balance of power *doctrine* may lead to war. Yet this is quibbling about words, since there is never a "true" balance.

Not content merely to block the advance of France, Britain repeatedly pro-

[7] Sir Victor Wellesley, *Diplomacy in Fetters,* London, Hutchinson, 1945, p. 128.

ceeded to build up the strength of other nations in order to create a counterpoise. Thus Britain helped Prussia to become strong and did not oppose the unification of the German states—a policy which undoubtedly curbed France, but which, by the same token, transformed Germany into an aggressive power. It could be said that Britain's error was in backing a "young" and dynamic nation against a more mature people. But, disregarding the fact that until recent times France was certainly a dynamic and even an aggressive power, such an objection would entail a considerable modification of the balance of power doctrine. However that may be, the mechanical application of that doctrine by Britain after 1919—an application which failed to differentiate between apparent and real power—eased the comeback of Germany, and thus made possible the last war.

Yet if it be true that the balance of power is at best a precarious protection against war, the doctrine is not yet exposed as fallacious. *It is not the sole purpose of foreign policy to maintain peace. Up to the present time the highest goal of the foreign policy of virtually all states has been to preserve national independence and liberty.* It cannot be denied that the balance of power policy is an effective instrument to attain that goal.

Had England not pursued a balance of power policy at the time of Napoleon, France would have subjugated the entire Continent. Then France would have come into possession of military and naval power sufficient to invade England whenever that country did not obey the whims of the French ruler. Once Britain was subdued, Napoleonic France could and would have extended her power to America and the rest of the world, unless the French Empire were to have been overthrown from within. The same reasoning applies to the analysis of the period from 1914 to 1945 when Germany would have been able to subdue Europe and then the world. If today Britain and the United States were to forsake the balance of power, the inevitable result would be that Soviet power would extend over Europe and Asia, in which case both Britain and the United States would have to submit to Soviet rule or fight a war against hopeless odds.

The insecurity and all-pervading fear which has characterized the period after 1945 is explained largely by the fact that Russia *almost* upset the power balance of Europe and Asia. Whatever security there was left in that unstable world was due to the restablishment of the power balance by the United States on a *global* scale. The need to maintain this global balance is one of the fundamental reasons why the United States is unable to withdraw into isolation.

The Doctrine. The scope and depth of the British balance of power doctrine are nowhere revealed more clearly than in the lapidary sentences of one of Britain's most influential experts on foreign policy. Sir Eyre Crowe, Permanent Undersecretary for Foreign Affairs, wrote in January, 1906: [8]

---

[8] Sir Eyre Crowe, "Memorandum on the Present State of British Relations with France and Germany," *British Documents on the Origins of the War 1898–1914,*

History shows that the danger threatening the independence of this or that nation has generally arisen, at least in part, out of the momentary predominance of a neighbouring state at once militarily powerful, economically efficient, and ambitious to extend its frontiers or spread its influence, the danger being directly proportionate to the degree of its power and efficiency, and to the spontaneity or "inevitableness" of its ambitions. The only check on the abuse of political predominance derived from such a position has always consisted in the opposition of an equally formidable rival, or of a combination of several countries forming leagues of defence. The equilibrium established by such a grouping of forces is technically known as the balance of power, and it has become almost an historical truism to identify England's secular policy with the maintenance of this balance by throwing her weight now in this scale and now in that, but ever on the side opposed to the political dictatorship of the strongest single State or group at a given time.

If this view of British policy is correct, the opposition into which England must inevitably be driven to any country aspiring to such a dictatorship assumes almost the form of a law of nature.

How was Britain to carry out the policy prescribed by Crowe? In practice, he argued, only by harmonizing the national policy of Britain with "the general desires of mankind." [9] The first interest of all countries is the preservation of national independence. It follows from this that England "has a direct and positive interest in the maintenance of the independence of nations, and must be the natural enemy of any country threatening the independence of others, and natural protector of the weaker communities."

The establishment of one overwhelming power, of a dictatorial power monopoly, is thus the danger against which stands guard the balance of power doctrine. This danger is so real that all protestations and ostensibly quite different formulations of policy do not alter the fact that all governments observe, as it were instinctively, the balance of power doctrine. With the exception of the would-be world ruler, they are united in their desire to prevent the upsetting of the balance on a world scale.

The Balance of Power and Freedom. A global balance of power is an indispensable condition of political progress: the political independence and especially the rapid economic development of the United States would not have been possible under the domination of a world ruler, because he would not have permitted the emergence of a strong power liable to challenge his own supremacy.

By pushing this line of thought a little further, it can readily be seen that the world's wealth and social progress, too, depend upon the global balance of power; once a power monopoly is established, the monopolist would without fail proceed to make his position impregnable. The Germans openly an-

---

edited by G. P. Gooch and Harold Temperley, London, H.M. Stationery Office, 1928, Vol. III, p. 402.

[9] It is this ethical formulation of British foreign policy which prompted Hans Kohn's observation that England engaged in power politics but never *only* in power politics (see his *The Idea of Nationalism*, New York, Macmillan, 1944, p. 179).

nounced and actually carried out a policy of deindustrialization and depopulation in the lands they conquered. The Soviet Union pursued a similar policy in conquered Germany. Similarly, the monopolist of world power would deprive regions which he cannot closely control of all industrial war potential. Since the heavy, chemical, electrical, and light metal industries are not only the basis of military strength but also of improved standards of living, their removal in the interests of the ruler's continued power monopoly would lead to catastrophic impoverishment and cultural decline. As a Pan-German writer once put it, nothing would be left to the vanquished but eyes to weep. Global power monopoly would be the end of civilization.

Regionally, however, the balance of power problem presents itself in a different manner. For example, it would be obviously not in the interest of Mexico to attempt redressing the power balance against the United States, assuming this feat could be accomplished. Mexico would gain nothing, because the United States is not an aggressive power, nor does it plan to control its southern neighbor. Nor was it necessary for Austria, prior to 1933, to seek protection against Germany. If the regionally dominant power suddenly becomes aggressive, as did Germany under Hitler, the small regional powers may enter into an alliance of mutual protection. However, they may not be able to gather sufficient strength to balance the dominant power. The small Slavic states wedged between Germany and Russia, for instance, cannot—even in a perfect union—oppose unaided either of these strong neighbors.

The over-all global balance of power affects regional conditions. If a regionally dominant power takes over control of the entire region, it may upset the global balance and will thus call forth the opposition of the rest of the world—the result precisely of Germany's and Russia's attempts at regional hegemony. Consequently, small nations within a given region are protected by nonregional states. Indeed, it was extraregional power which restored the real or nominal independence of the small states which had succumbed to German aggression. While the disparity of strength usually leads the small regional powers to play up to the dominant state, the balance of power is maintained without their active cooperation and often without their active efforts at military defense.

In a world system under law, such as that envisioned by the proponents of world government, or great power condominium, or simply of domination by one great power, the balance of power doctrine in the classic sense of Sir Eyre Crowe no longer applies. Yet all viable political institutions are based on the principle of mutually balancing powers—those of the United States are unquestionably so based. The diversity of the multination system supplies the practical and moral justification for applying the balance of power principle to foreign policy. That this diversity would disappear soon and give way to a universal and uniform system was the belief of Cordell Hull, "the true heir of Wilsonism." [10] Unfortunately, illusions are not enough to change the world.

Occasionally the balance of power may be a means of preventing war "and safeguarding national security." *Under a system of diversity the only reliable, known way to avoid aggression is to oppose the aggressor in time by a united front of vastly superior military strength, i.e., by a clear imbalance.* By contrast, the balance of power is a policy designed to preserve the independence and freedom of individual nations even at the risk of war.

BIBLIOGRAPHY

Brinton, Crane: "The Threat of an Anglo-American Hegemony," *Social Research,* Vol. 13, 1946.

Chatham House Study Group (Donald McLachlan): *Atlantic Alliance, NATO's Role in the Free World,* London, Royal Institute of International Affairs, 1952.

Culbertson, Ely: *Total Peace: What Makes Wars and How to Organize Peace,* New York, Doubleday, 1943.

Dallin, David: *The Big Three: The United States, Britain and Russia,* New Haven, Yale University Press, 1945.

Davis, Forrest: *The Atlantic System,* New York, Reynal & Hitchcock, Inc., 1941.

Dupuis, Charles: *Le Principe d'équilibre et le concert Européen,* Paris, Perrin, 1909.

Fabre-Luce, Alfred: *La crise des alliances,* Paris, Grasset, 1922.

Fox, William T. R.: *The Super-powers,* New York, Harcourt, Brace, 1944.

Gentz, Friedrich von: *Fragments upon the Balance of Power in Europe,* London, M. Peltier, 1806.

Goblet, Yann Morvran: *The Twilight of Treaties,* London, G. Bell, 1936.

Gulick, Edward Vose: *The Balance of Power,* Philadelphia, The Pacifist Research Bureau, 1943.

Haushofer, Karl: *Weltpolitik von Heute,* Berlin, Zeitgeschichte, 1934.

Hume, David: *Of the Balance of Power: Essays Moral and Political* (various editions).

Langer, William L.: *European Alliances and Alignments 1871–1890,* New York, Knopf, 1931.

Schmitt, Bernadotte: *Triple Alliance and Triple Entente,* New York, Scribner, 1934.

Spykman, Nicholas J.: *American Strategy in World Politics: The United States and the Balance of Power,* New York, Harcourt, Brace, 1942.

Tardieu, André: *France and the Alliances: The Struggle for the Balance of Power,* New York, Macmillan, 1908.

Wache, Walter: *System der Pakte: Die politischen Verträge der Nachkriegszeit,* Berlin, Volk und Reich, 1938.

[10] See Alfred Vagts, "The Balance of Power: Growth of an Idea," *World Politics,* Vol. 1, No. 1, October, 1948.

Chapter 14

METHODS OF ADAPTATION

MEDIATION

Among the methods of adaptation to the environment of international politics—the multination world—perhaps the most important and certainly the most frequently used is mediation. Though some scholars and legal experts profess to distinguish between mediation and arbitration, the line of demarcation between mediation (voluntary and compulsory) and arbitration (voluntary and compulsory) is vague and can, at best, be drawn only by studying each individual case. Since no two conflicts between nations are ever exactly alike and international law is what nations make it, mediation, as often as not, turns out to have been arbitration, and what looked, on first glance, like arbitration is revealed as mediation. To make matters more complicated, what has been represented as mediation or arbitration frequently can be shown to have been neither but rather the unilateral policy of an interested power using the machinery of mediation in order to do what it would have done anyway—mediation or no mediation.

It is probably no exaggeration to say that statesmen are concerned with mediation almost every day. Almost every international dispute concerns parties other than those ostensibly involved. Almost every serious dispute of the last 500 years threatened to involve all nations. Hence all nations wishing to preserve the *status quo* or to alter it by diplomatic, and not military, action were eager to avail themselves of existing mediatory facilities.

The great international conferences, such as the Peace Conference of Westphalia, the Congress of Vienna, the Paris Peace Conference following the Crimean War, and, especially, the Congress of Berlin in 1878, supply case histories and technical innovations to the venerable compendium of mediation. In each of these conferences, the work of mediation and conciliation was eased by an unmistakable realignment of the balance of power, by a widespread recognition that further armed conflict could serve no one's best interests, and hence by a near-universal awareness of public interest. At Berlin, Bismarck confined himself to the role of mediator, the Honest Broker of Europe. Germany did not ask for a share in the redistribution of territories, and Bismarck's stake in peace was genuine—although for power considerations all his own. Bismarck, the mediator, had, however, at his back the might of the German army, the balance of power prevailing among the various parties to various disputes, and the "public interest," to wit, an agreement of public opinion of the major nations on the desirability of peace and the uselessness of war as an instrument of policy in the particular historical situation.

The history of mediation of international disputes under the auspices of the United Nations does not reveal substantive deviations from, or improvements on, the traditional diplomacy of mediation. To be sure, there is now a permanent machinery of mediation, or at least a facsimile of such a machinery. The United Nations Charter provides various methods for the settlement of international disputes, depending upon the nature of the dispute. In the case of so-called legal disputes, the Charter provides for recourse to the International Court of Justice. In Article 36 of the Statute of the International Court legal disputes concerning the interpretation of a treaty are recognized as disputes especially suitable for the settlement procedures of the International Court. Such disputes may be distinguished from those which, according to the Charter, are appropriate for settlement through the Security Council and the General Assembly. Under Chapter VI these organs handle disputes which are likely to endanger the maintenance of peace, *i.e.*, disputes likely to involve the international community. Therefore, the central political organs provide a service of settlement in the interests of the international community rather than in the interests of the litigants.[1]

In April, 1949, the United Nations General Assembly established an International Panel for Inquiry and Conciliation. Each member state was authorized to nominate five persons to the panel from which the Secretary-General, the President of the General Assembly, or the Chairman of the Interim Committee could select persons or commissions to perform tasks of inquiry or conciliation. It was provided that the members of the panel "shall not, in the performance of their duties, seek or receive instructions from any government."

When the conflict has entered the shooting stage, the Security Council or the General Assembly should presumably endeavor to stop it by a cease-fire. The parent organ determines the general procedure which should be followed with a view to settlement. These initial decisions may lay down the basis of negotiations, including measures to be taken by the disputants. These may include a return to direct negotiations, reference to the International Court, or establishment of subsidiary organs to assist in the settlement of disputes. The General Assembly and the Security Council have established such organs in connection with the Indonesian, Palestine, India-Pakistan, Balkan, and Korean questions.[2]

[1] See Elmore Jackson, *Meeting of Minds, A Way to Peace through Mediation,* New York, McGraw-Hill, 1952, pp. 82–83; and Werner Levi, *Fundamentals of World Organization,* Minneapolis, University of Minnesota Press, 1950, p. 61.

[2] As regards the Indonesian question, a Committee of Good Offices was established in accordance with the Security Council resolution of August 25, 1947. This Committee continued to function through 1948. Following the outbreak of hostilities at the end

Once we look closer at the case histories of United Nations mediation, we find that, but for changes in terminology, mediation—the substance of it— is administered along principles and lines of action that have been known for a long time. United Nations mediation in the Palestine conflict became effective only when the military contest had produced a new power relation- ship which had decisively altered the strategic state of things: the Israelis had won the war. The problem was how to ease acceptance by the Arabs of this ineluctable fact and to negotiate a truce which would, at least temporarily, consolidate the very real strategic gains Israel had won and the Arab states were too weak to annul. This does not diminish the achievement of the United Nations and especially of its able mediators, first Count Folke Bernadotte, and then, upon the latter's assassination, Dr. Ralph Bunche. Back of the United Nations, however, was firstly, the "public interest," to wit, the de- termination of the great powers to preserve the *status quo,* and secondly, the might, albeit invisible, of the United States. American material, diplomatic, and psychological aid had helped the Israelis to establish themselves upon territories sufficiently large and strategically secure to serve as a basis for their new state. Having helped Israel to repel the Arab states and to secure its frontiers, the United States did not wish to go further. One must assume that the United States made this clear, by unilateral diplomatic action, to all parties concerned. The United States, by what it did and did not do in its capacity as a great power, assisted most certainly the mediatory efforts of the United Nations and contributed decisively toward clinching a *de facto* settle- ment. Britain accorded her views with American policy. The Soviet Union was content to abstain from intervention, deeming the situation to be fraught with profitable opportunities for future exploitation. "Public interest" thus

---

of that year, the Committee was reconstituted as the United Nations Commission for Indonesia with additional terms of reference (January 28, 1949).

The United Nations Commission for India and Pakistan was established by the Security Council in the early part of 1948. On March 14, 1950, the Commission was replaced by the United Nations Representative for India and Pakistan. The first of the commissions established by the General Assembly to deal with the Korean question was the United Nations Temporary Commission on Korea (November 14, 1947). This Commission was to observe and report on elections in Korea. The United Nations Com- mission on Korea was established December 12, 1948. On October 7, 1950, the Assembly established the United Nations Commission for the Unification and Rehabilitation of Korea.

In handling the Balkan question, the problems arising from the Greek frontier inci- dents were first dealt with by the Security Council. When proposals based upon the report of the Council's commission of investigation were vetoed in the Council by the Soviet Union, the problem was transferred to the General Assembly. The Assembly established the United Nations Special Committee on the Balkans on October 21, 1947. The United Nations Palestine Commission was established at the next session of the Assembly as an integral part of the partition plan (November 29, 1947). The office of United Nations Mediator was created May 14, 1948. The Assembly established on December 11, 1948, the United Nations Conciliation Commission for Palestine. Under this resolution and resolutions adopted in 1949 and 1950, this Commission continued to seek a settlement of the Palestine question.

aligned itself in concert behind the United Nations mediator, and the truce was concluded. But one need not be unduly skeptic to ask the question, was formal mediation by the United Nations not in fact a case of great-power arbitration?

The Indonesian case was "settled" partly by the geographical distance separating the contenders, partly by the enfeeblement and weariness of the Netherlands, partly by the direct diplomatic (and mostly secret) pressures of the great powers. The Greek case was "settled" by the fortuitous defection of Tito from the Soviet bloc, which insulated Greece geographically against Soviet intervention. The "settlement" of the Kashmir dispute—an indefinite stalemate—was as precarious as it was inconclusive. A good case can be made for the contention that United Nations mediation has never produced significant results except in disputes over minor issues or between minor powers or as a face-saving device applied to major issues which *had* been settled by shifts in the balance of power.

Not a few international agreements contain specified provisions for arbitration; today, nearly all of them are subject to judicial review by international courts *provided* the sovereign states concerned agree to waive their sovereignty sufficiently to put the case to the competent court and abide by its decision. The most serious disputes arise over those issues which are not covered by agreement, which involve a substantial alteration of power relationships, and which invite the intervention of other powers. It is these that endanger the peace, and thus, public interest. When are these latter issues susceptible to mediation? These issues can be mediated when (1) a substantial change in power relationships has taken place *de facto;* (2) a crystallization of "public interest" has been completed, the major powers having arrived at a diplomatic agreement among themselves; and (3) a mediation machinery has been created and individual mediators have been selected who sensitively register (*a*) the change in power relationships, and (*b*) the crystallization of public interest. It is only after these conditions have been met that the worth of the "machinery" and the men must be considered an element in the fortunes of mediation. But without the *de facto* arbitration of the power relationships of the parties to the dispute and of the interested "friends of the court," mediation degenerates to a tedious farce.

APPEASEMENT

To appease is to pacify, to calm, to soothe. To pacify a defeated and vengeful foe, to calm the groundless suspicions and fears of any nation, to soothe the wounded pride of a people with whom one is linked by a long tradition of friendship, and, finally, to smother conflict by compromise without compromising vital interest—these practices form an essential part of routine diplomacy and lubricate the workings of world society. But for these ministrations of appeasement there would be incessant war. Appeasement is any policy designed to alleviate grievances through compromise and concession that otherwise may lead to war. It is a method of adaptation that is indispensable and recurrent in any foreign policy. Yet like any method, it can be used clumsily and inappropriately.

There are various forms of appeasement which must be carefully distinguished. For example, states may acquiesce in the expansion of other nations, which are deemed fundamentally nonaggressive, in order to make good some legitimate grievance or to divert some unrest which, were it not to find an outlet, might lead to dangerous tensions. The expansion of the United States was never seriously opposed by any other great power, for the occupation of such strategically important islands as Cuba and the Philippines endangered the security of no other nations. Similarly, when in 1911 Italy attacked Turkey in order to acquire Tripoli, she had already secured approval for this action from all other great powers, including Great Britain and Russia. Not only was this act of aggression unopposed by any third power but, on the contrary, there was general satisfaction that the Tripolitan coast had been put under a more "enlightened," *i.e.,* Western, administration. Again, French expansion in Tunisia and Indo-China was supported by Germany, France's main opponent; the makers of German foreign policy entertained the justified hope that France, engaged in ventures overseas, would have no energies left to expend on the Rhine and might ultimately be "appeased" for the loss of Alsace-Lorraine by gains elsewhere.

Appeasement in the proper sense does not involve a *quid pro quo.* It is an effort to pacify the aggressor or, in Churchill's picturesque simile, to feed the crocodile in the hope that it will stop being hungry. The futility of such a policy is nicely expressed by the French proverb: "L'appetit vient en mangeant," that is, the more the aggressor obtains without being compelled to fight, the more ambitious his objectives become.

History records practically only one important exception to that rule, that of the Indian King Ashoka (264–227 B.C.). That king, whose memory is still greatly revered in Asia, became deeply impressed by the horrors of war when, during his conquest of Kalinga (on the Indian east coast), 100,000 men were slain and many more people died.[3] Ashoka decided never again to wage war and henceforth devoted himself to spreading Buddhism by peaceful means, or as one of the old inscriptions states: "His Sacred Majesty desires that all animate things should have security, self-control, peace of mind, and joyousness." Ashoka did for Buddhism what Constantine and Charlemagne did for Christianity. His decision to forgo war was made at a moment when he controlled practically the entire Indian peninsula up to the Hindu Kush and the Himalayas, with the exception of the country's southern tip. His

---

[3] Jawaharlal Nehru, *Glimpses of World History: Being Further Letters to His Daughter Written in Prison, and Containing a Rambling Account of History for Young People,* New York, John Day, 1942, p. 63.

was therefore one of the largest empires of antiquity. How much legendary propaganda is woven into this traditional account of Ashoka is hard to tell.

Appeasement was freely practiced by the old Roman and Byzantine Empires, and occasionally during the Han Dynasty of ancient China, especially with respect to the "barbarians" living within their borders. These peoples were appeased by various means: land, gifts, food, wine, and money grants (the Chinese used silk as appeasement money), honors bestowed on their princes, and mutually beneficial marriages. The Chinese periodically opened the Great Wall to the barbarians so that they could enter for trading purposes. Barbarians were given important commands in the Roman army, as, for example, the Vandal Stilicho who became *magister militum* (commander in chief) under Emperor Honorius and married his daughter to the Emperor. The appeasement of the Vandals was not entirely successful, as they invaded Gaul and Spain and later established an empire in North Africa. Stilicho seems to have dissuaded them from invading Italy and conquering Rome, but fifty years after the establishment of their own empire on the former location of Carthage, they invaded Italy and sacked Rome. Appeasement had thus led to the emergence of a strong competing power, while a contrary policy might have averted the rise of the Vandal empire.

A most successful appeasement operation was carried out by Pope Leo I who in 452 persuaded the Huns under Attila to turn back from Italy.[4]

Similarly, the Indians succeeded in preventing an Arab invasion (712) and a Mongol invasion under Genghis Khan (1217) during the period when that dangerous invader pushed the limits of his realm to the gates of central Europe. Both Arabs and Mongols halted on the Indus River and turned back without having joined battle. They did so presumably because the Indians were militarily very strong—their weapons were fashioned of finely tempered steel.

Byzantium resorted frequently to the practice of buying off her enemies. The results of this policy were varied, and appeasement did not always lead to lasting adjustments. It could be argued, however, that without systematic appeasement, though interrupted by war, the Byzantine Empire could not have endured until 1452.

In modern times, Prussia appeased revolutionary and Napoleonic France from 1795 to 1806 but, despite repeated concessions, did not achieve peace. When it became evident that France proposed to conquer Europe, Prussia

---

[4] According to Gibbon, *The Decline and Fall of the Roman Empire,* Chap. 35, Attila was awed by "the pressing eloquence of Leo, his majestic aspect and sacerdotal robes." The Huns were willing to compromise, because "their martial spirit was relaxed by the wealth and indolence of a warm climate . . . and the progress of disease revenged in some measure the injuries of the Italians." The price of appeasement was the hand of the Princess Honoria and an immense dowry. After the immediate danger had been averted, the Romans were slow in delivering the dowry, and Attila threatened to resume the attack. Yet while waiting for Honoria, he succumbed to a hemorrhage. The Hunnish threat was ended before the Romans ever paid their ransom.

contemplated entering the war against Napoleon in 1805 on the side of Austria and Russia. However, after the battle of Austerlitz was lost by her prospective allies, Prussia relapsed into appeasement and ceded territory to France in exchange for Hanover. Shortly thereafter Napoleon offered to give Hanover back to Britain and at the same time seized additional Prussian territory. War broke out, and Prussia, which under the illusions of appeasement had neglected adequate military preparations, suffered crushing defeat.

Other countries, too, had tried to appease France, as, for example, Spain under the leadership of Manuel de Godoy, the "Prince of the Peace." Spain joined France in her war against Britain and fought on the French side in the Battle of Trafalgar. In 1801, on French instigation, Spain fought a war against England's ally, Portugal. Spain ceded Louisiana to France, and at the Bayonne Conference of 1808 Napoleon succeeded in inducing both King Carlos IV, as well as Carlos's successor, Ferdinand, to abdicate in his own favor. Yet Napoleon's plan, shrewdly designed to impose French domination upon the Spanish people step by step and with the aid of their own submissive princes, was thwarted by the resistance of the Spanish people who revolted against the French army of occupation. A long and difficult war ensued.

In 1864, 1866, and 1867, France under Napoleon III appeased Bismarck's Prussia in the hope that a united Germany would no longer be aggressive. The bill was paid in 1870.

The policy first of the Western powers and then, briefly, of Russia toward Hitler's Germany is thus no original contribution to the history of appeasement. The powers acquiesced in Hitler's plan to annex such territories as Austria and the Sudetenland, which, Hitler claimed, should "rightfully" have been Germany's. They did so on the promise that once these "legitimate" desires were satisfied, Hitler would make no further demands in Europe.[5] Hitler stated explicitly that he would never incorporate non-German peoples into Germany. Yet, in 1939, he took the Slavic parts of Czechoslovakia, invaded Poland, and started the Second World War.

"If anyone urges that King Louis yield Romagna to Alexander and the Kingdom of Naples to Spain in order to avoid war, I reply that one never ought to allow a disorder to take place in order to avoid war, for war is not thereby avoided, but only deferred to your disadvantage."[6]

Although it is true that appeasement is no staunch shield but an "umbrella policy" at best, because it does not deter the aggressor and, in addition, strengthens him materially and politically through concessions and capitulations, it is also true that often governments have no other choice and are compelled to appease the aggressor out of weakness.

---

[5] See Neville Chamberlain, *In Search of Peace,* New York, Putnam, 1939, especially p. 207. See also *Documents Relating to the Eve of the Second World War,* New York, International Publishers, 1948, Vol. 1, *passim* and pp. 264*ff.*

[6] Niccoló Machiavelli, *The Prince,* Chap. IV.

In 1706, Marlborough, Sir Winston Churchill's forebear, appeased Charles XII of Sweden, bribing in the process the King's chief counselor. Marlborough by this diplomatic sleight of hand prevented the Swedes from joining the French against the British in the War of the Spanish Secession. In 1707 a conflict between the Emperor and Charles over the treatment of Protestants in Silesia would have led to war—and thereby to Swedish intervention on the side of France—had not the British prevailed on the Emperor to give in. To clinch the transaction, Marlborough presented weighty arguments as to why Charles should go to war against Russia. Charles accepted these arguments and was beaten in 1709 at Poltava by Tsar Peter of Russia. Thus Sweden ceased to be a threat to Britain. This subtle combination of conciliation and diversion belongs to a category of appeasement which should not be confused with appeasement as practiced in the 20th century, the latter policy being based on the absurd assumption that the aggressor is, actually, no aggressor at all.

Alexander Nevski, prince of Novgorod and Vladimir, is rightly revered as one of the greatest Russian soldiers and statesmen. In a series of brilliant campaigns he stopped the advance of the Swedes on the Neva in 1240 and in 1242 defeated the Teutonic Knights on Lake Peipus. The Russians hoped that he would lead them against the Tatars and end Russia's subjugation. Various revolts took place to force his hand. Yet Nevski knew well that his strength was inadequate for such a task and that, for a long time to come, the Tatar's yoke had to be borne patiently by the Russian people, lest they be exposed to savage retaliation. Hence he crushed the insurrectionists and adopted a rigorous policy of submission. He thus insured the survival of western Russia and made possible Russia's later development.[7]

Temporary appeasement in order to complete military preparations for a war, the coming of which is clearly foreseen, is a relatively effective expedient of foreign policy. It derives its warrant from the simple axiom that a state should never accept a challenge which it cannot meet or wage a war in which only a doubtful victory can be secured at the cost of exhaustion. The decline of countries, as shown by the examples of Spain and France, is due to military exhaustion rather than to any other single cause.

There is no doubt that the appeasement policy of Britain and France in 1938 was in great part dictated by the military weakness of the two countries. At the time of Munich, French aircraft production was less than forty planes

[7] "Among the Russian princes there prevailed two general ideas as to how to regard the Mongolian power. Some princes espoused the policy of loyal submission to the Mongolian rule. This allowed them to defend the Russian lands from western attack and to strengthen their own authority. . . . An outstanding instance of a prince who followed this policy was Alexander Nevsky. . . . The policy of other Russian princes consisted in attempts to free themselves from the Mongolian yoke with the help of the West. This attitude was particularly characteristic of such western Russian princes as Daniel of Galicia." (See George Vernadsky, *A History of Russia,* rev. ed., Philadelphia, Blakiston, 1944, pp. 51*f*.) It was Russia's "permanent" alternative.

per month, and London was compelled to import a few modern antiaircraft guns from, of all countries, Hungary. Although the respite gained at Munich was not exploited to the full, or even very energetically, nevertheless, in the interim between Munich and the outbreak of the war, England introduced compulsory military service and created the strong fighter force which later won the Battle of Britain. France increased production and improved her methods of mobilization, although her efforts fell far short of requirements.

Whether or not Western policy toward Russia during 1945–1947 should be described as "appeasement" may be arguable. Russia was granted substantial territorial concessions—territories belonging to others—on the grounds that she was "entitled" to safe borders. As though other nations did not possess the same right! Possibly this was a devious way to reward the Russians for their contributions to the war against Germany. Whatever it was, it whetted their appetite. They might have comported themselves more peaceably had their greed not been aroused.

Perhaps the wisest application of that delicate device of statecraft, appeasement, is the victor's moderation at the peace table. Lord Castlereagh "appeased" defeated France at the Peace of Paris in 1815, insisting against the opposition of Russia and Prussia that France be permitted to retain the frontiers of 1789. Bismarck, in the face of popular pressure and the demands of the Prussian general staff, granted, in 1866, defeated Austria a lenient peace without territorial annexations. The noblest and the cleverest form of appeasement is, as Winston Churchill put it, "to war down the proud, but to be magnanimous toward the defeated."

PREVENTIVE WAR

The opposite of appeasement is preventive war, *i.e.*, an attempt to crush the prospective aggressor before he can become dangerous. It is, therefore, a method of keeping incipient conflict from developing into catastrophe. Preventive wars are extremely rare in history, and there is hardly a case on record when a strong potential aggressor was attacked by his presumptive victim. To some extent, the War of the First Coalition against France in 1792 was a preventive operation, for it was designed to stop the spreading of the Revolution. Even this is not a clear-cut example, for the French, on their part, contributed to the outbreak of the war. In the case of the Crimean War, England and France, even though they entered the conflict after hostilities between Turkey and Russia had actually begun, fought a preventive war to forestall Russian control of the Dardanelles. The significance of the Crimean War was summarized by Lord Cromer in these words: "Had it not been for the Crimean War and the policy subsequently adopted by Lord Beaconfield's Government, the independence of the Balkan States would never have been achieved and the Russians would now be in possession of Constantinople."

During the Napoleonic period, British naval attacks on the Danish fleet in 1801 and 1807 were preventive in nature, especially the second attack which was designed to forestall the surrender of the Danish fleet to Napoleon.[8] Napoleon, in turn, attacked Prussia after it had become clear to him that sooner or later Prussia would resort to the force of arms. Napoleon's attack on Russia was prompted, though not entirely, by preventive strategy. When Fouché visited Napoleon, from whose graces he had fallen, to dissuade him from the Russian project, the Emperor explained that a contest with Russia was inevitable and that, this being so, he preferred to fight this most difficult war while he was still in his prime. Nor did he propose to leave, Napoleon added, the legacy of this unsettled war to his son for, while he knew that he himself was a good and experienced general, he could not be sure that his son would be equal to the task.[9]

During the Second World War, a clearly preventive action was carried out by the Royal Navy in its attack on the French fleet at Mers-el-Kebir in 1940. This attack was designed to keep that fleet from falling into German hands. Not entirely successful and probably unnecessary, this attack greatly contributed to the difficulties between France and Britain. However, it did strengthen France's hand toward Germany so that the latter rescinded some of the military clauses of the armistice. Thus, in the last analysis, the attack on Mers-el-Kebir may have made some positive contribution.

Though the German attack on Russia in 1941 was brought about by a multiplicity of causes, nevertheless it was, in great part, a preventive war. As Hitler stated, the Germans were afraid that, after Germany had exhausted herself in the war against Britain, Russia would be the strongest Continental power and, moreover, that after a few years Russia's growing demographic superiority would terminate German hegemony. The year 1941 was considered by Hitler as the most favorable moment for a war which both Russia and Germany deemed inevitable.[10]

[8] The case for a preventive attack was succinctly summarized by Lord Nelson to the Commander in Chief of the Royal Navy, just prior to the attack on the Danish fleet: "The more I have reflected, the more I am confirmed in opinion, that not a moment should be lost in attacking the Enemy. They will every day and hour be stronger; we shall never be so good a match for them as at this moment." Nelson did not overlook the psychological handicaps arising out of a preventive attack and combined his military with a psychological strategy. In a note delivered to the Danes we read: "To the Brothers of Englishmen, the Danes. Lord Nelson has directions to spare Denmark, when no longer resisting; but if the firing is continued on the part of Denmark, Lord Nelson will be obliged to set on fire all the Floating-batteries he has taken, without having the power of saving the brave Danes who have defended them." (See Carola Oman, *Nelson*, New York, Doubleday, 1946, pp. 437, 447.)

[9] Louis Madelin (ed.), *Les Mémoires de Fouché*, Paris, Flammarion, 1945, pp. 351–365.

[10] See *Les Lettres secrètes échangées par Hitler et Mussolini*, Introduction by André François-Poncet, Paris, Éditions du Pavois, 1946, especially the letter of June 21, 1941, pp. 121*ff*. This letter was translated and commented upon in the *Infantry Journal*, August, 1947, pp. 14–16.

The argument for preventive war, which in the Machiavellian frame of reference grows out of considerations of power, becomes more persuasive as international tension mounts and the anxiety neurosis of large numbers of people raises the specter of "inevitable" conflict. Prior to the First World War, the British Admiral Lord Fisher advocated that the German *Hochsee-flotte* be "copenhagened" in Nelson's fashion.[11] The Austrian chief of staff, General Conrad von Hoetzendorf, favored a preventive war either against Serbia or against Italy which, he hoped, would stabilize the crumbling Habsburg Empire. In 1933, the Polish chief of state, Marshal Pilsudski, urged France to wage a preventive war against Nazi Germany. When the French did not accept the proposal, Poland concluded a nonaggression pact with the presumptive aggressor.[12]

During the Second World War, the Allies were urged to take preventive action against Vichy France at Dakar, which naval base, it was feared, could be used as a springboard for Axis aggression against the Western Hemisphere. After the war, a few voices were raised in favor of a preventive war against potential enemies of the United States in order to profit from the period of grace when the United States held a monopoly in atomic weapons.

Preventive war is, militarily speaking, a logical and reasonable idea: to strike the enemy before he strikes. It is the idea which directs all sound military planning. For example, in 1940 the Germans struck at the French and defeated them before they were ready, instead of waiting a few years until the French were prepared to resist the invader.[13]

Politically speaking, however, the idea of preventive war is based on a singular misreading of political realities and the psychology of nations. First of all, it can be applied only by dictatorships or other types of absolute regimes, but these are the very regimes against whom preventive war should be waged, they themselves being in most cases the aggressors.

[11] In a letter which Sir Maurice Hankey addressed to Lord Fisher, he reminded the latter of a prediction made in 1910, namely, that war would come in 1914, and adds: "I remember that my practical mind revolted against the prophecy, and I pressed for your reasons. You then told us that the Kiel Canal, according to experts whom you had assembled five to six years before to examine this question, could not be enlarged for passage of the new German Dreadnoughts before 1914, and that Germany, though bent on war, would not risk it until this date." (Lord Fisher, Admiral of the Fleet, *Memories and Records,* New York, Doubleday, 1920, Vol. II, p. 206.) Admiral Fitzgerald wrote an article in the *Deutsche Revue* of May 5, 1905 (a German magazine), in which he said: "I should regard a war between England and Germany as a great calamity: but I would sooner see such a war break out tomorrow than see it (if it really must come) postponed for a series of years, when Germany will be stronger by sea and it may be possible for her to obtain an advantage over us." (See Arthur J. Marder, *The Anatomy of British Sea Power: A History of British Naval Policy in the Pre-dreadnought Era 1880–1905,* New York, Knopf, 1940, pp. 498f.)

[12] See Potiemkine, *Histoire de la diplomatie,* Paris, Médicis, 1947, Vol. III, p. 480.

[13] See Office of United States Chief of Counsel for Prosecution of Axis Criminality, *Nazi Conspiracy and Aggression,* Vol. III, p. 584, Government Printing Office, 1946, where reasons are given in Hitler's own words why war against the Western powers should not be delayed.

Secondly, an advocate of preventive war must be very sure about the future. For example, while Lord Fisher and Marshal Pilsudski anticipated the course of future events correctly—both foresaw war with Germany—General Conrad von Hoetzendorf's proposals were very foolish indeed, since a preventive war as he wanted it would not have stabilized the Habsburg monarchy but would have accelerated its demise. The partisans of the Dakar action were wrong, too, since Dakar never fell into Axis hands. Had the proposed operation been undertaken, considerable force would have been diverted and the war needlessly prolonged. Moreover, it is very probable that the Germans would have countered by occupying French North Africa. Thus they would have greatly interfered with Allied strategy, preventing perhaps the North African campaign and very probably making Egypt untenable.

The current advocates of a preventive war against Russia would be on safe ground if (1) there was a possibility that the American people would go to war before being attacked; (2) there was an absolute certainty that war between the United States and Russia was inevitable which, among other things, would imply certainty that there would be no change in Russian politics and personnel over a period of ten to twenty years; (3) if it were certain that war could be fought at a lesser cost now than at a later date; and (4) if it were certain that, by waging preventive war, the United States would not suffer almost the same atomic devastation the action is designed to avoid. Nobody can possibly be sure about any of these conditions. Yet even granting that preventive war would be a wise policy—situations are conceivable where this would be true—such a course would be barred by constitutional limitations, although the American Constitution does not bar anticipatory action once it is obvious that the enemy is preparing to strike. These limitations may be deplored as unrealistic and dangerous. Indeed, in some cases they may obstruct timely action, while in other cases their restraint may prove beneficial. Considering the psychological climate engendered by the atomic threat, however, it cannot be ruled out that a democratic people, were it subjected to very long periods of tension and fear, would choose preventive war as a lesser evil. In 1939, the ultrapacifistic French found the continuous psychological terror unbearable and went to war with the motto "Il faut en finir" (Let's put an end to it). This, too, was the gist of Prime Minister Neville Chamberlain's remarks in the House of Commons on September 3, 1939. If war had not come in 1939 and the tension had been prolonged, the explosion might possibly have been set off by overwhelming public sentiment in France or England. These exceptions confirm the rule. Soviet harangues notwithstanding, democratic peoples abhor the thought of preventive war. Probably all sane peoples do. Bismarck said that a nation choosing preventive war in lieu of taking its chances with time was like a man who commits suicide because he is afraid to die.

EXPANSION AND WORLD STATES

The most likely and frequent cause of all international conflict is the desire of states to expand their territory and to incorporate regions into their dominion which belong to and are administered by other governments. The urge to expand is one of the primary facts of history and society. Although many do not think highly of it—and indeed its stark crudity is only too apparent—and propose that such an irrational instinct should no longer dominate mankind, the fact remains that this urge still persists and, like other urges, shows itself persistent and, alas, powerful.[14] Nor is this urge entirely irrational. Since, as Ratzel pointed out, space is power, expansion provides security through territorial accretion.[15]

In general, all other things being equal, the thesis of the German geographer is irrefutable; obviously Russia or the United States is more powerful than Belgium or Honduras. Why? Because their great spaces permit independent development and the raising of numerically very strong peoples. These spaces also produce numerous vital materials, and they can sustain large industries and large military forces—things which the small countries are unable to do.

However, Ratzel's theorem is a flagrant oversimplification. For example, Brazil or India possesses far larger spaces than France or Britain, but undoubtedly these latter countries are more powerful than the former. It would, of course, be different if all these countries had reached the same level of industrial and cultural development, but this shows merely that space is by no means the only decisive power factor. Nations may be very powerful without controlling large expanses of territory. During the Persian Wars, the Athenians, forced to relinquish their city, embarked on ships, leaving their country to the invader, whom they ultimately defeated. The Dutch and Venetians were at times restricted to a few roadsteads and yet remained great powers. In 1918, the Czechs controlled nothing but the Trans-Siberian Railroad; they participated in the strategic conduct of a major war and concluded treaties, yet they did not then possess a territory of their own. They took their country simply by arriving in Prague in a passenger train. That the Catholic Church as well as some other religious organizations are powerful forces which influence history, nobody will deny; yet they control practically no territory.

The Ratzel theorem is nothing but the expression of an idée-force which has bemused many rulers. The seemingly irresistible urge to gain more and more territory spelled the ruin of the great empires of the past. Suffice it to recall the names of Alexander, Napoleon, and Hitler, whose incessant con-

[14] See Bertrand de Jouvenel, *Du Pouvoir: histoire naturelle de sa croissance,* Geneva, Éditions du Cheval Ailé, 1947, especially the Introduction and Chap. VIII.

[15] Friedrich Ratzel, *Der Lebensraum,* Tübingen, Mohr, 1901, pp. 18–20.

quests led to exhaustion and dispersion of strength and made them vulnerable to counterattack. Even the Roman Empire's basic weakness lay in its size. Two of the greatest rulers of history recognized the fatal weakness of "too much": Diocletian in 285 divided the Roman Empire into two parts, or rather he parceled out his dominion to two "augusts," each of whom had a "caesar" as assistant. This solution—which, incidentally, was not applied too systematically—had its obvious dangers and, in the last analysis, led to the emergence of the Eastern and Western Empires. Yet the empire was no longer "administrable" from one single center and by one single man. In 1522, Emperor Charles V divided, although not yet nominally, his tremendous empire into two parts and intrusted the rule of Germany to his brother Ferdinand; upon Charles's abdication in 1556, the partition was made permanent. The continuing decentralization of the British Empire is a similar process. Even the young Soviet "empire" was compelled to pay the penalty of bigness when Yugoslavia recovered her independence; and the establishment of communism in China did not lead to one big two-continental empire but rather to the emergence of a modern replica of the two Romes.

Great aggressors usually aim at securing control of very large areas. Many have tried to establish supremacy over Europe. Yet history shows that none of them ever was successful and that they all succumbed ultimately to the balance of power mechanism. Nor did any one of them conquer by force of arms all the territories over which he ruled. On the contrary, a great part of these territories was added by settlement, treaty, and federation. Nevertheless, these agglomerations, wrought mainly by compulsion of one kind or another, rarely constituted durable political entities, and after a shorter or longer delay, the subjected and affiliated peoples insisted on recovering their independence.

The case history of attempts at world rule is pertinent to the question of world government as it is posed in current debate. Disregarding the fact that world government is recommended as a means of preserving peace but would have to be imposed by force, that is to say, by war on many nations, history seems to indicate that world government could not be organized in a loose federation, because in that case *competing* power centers would emerge or rather continue to exist and the danger of war, albeit civil war, would not be banished. A world government organized on a strictly centralized pattern would bear an embarrassing resemblance to a world imperium. Whatever the merits of the idea which is neither more nor less visionary or foolish than other utopian concepts, it must be mentioned here, because frequent references are made to so-called historical "precedents." The simple truth, however, is that there is no precedent for world government. There was never any political system extant even remotely approaching a global political organization. The Roman Empire is often referred to as the most important precedent. Actually, throughout Roman history there were powerful and independent nations in Asia—China, India, and Persia, not to mention many lesser ones in present-day Russia, in central Asia, Ireland, and Scandinavia. The "barbarian tribes" which lived between the Rhine and the Crimea were sufficiently well organized—the Goths on the Black Sea had managed to organize a genuine state—to undertake long military campaigns in areas remote from their bases and to defeat repeatedly the Roman legions. In point of fact, Rome could not extend her dominion over these regions, let alone over more highly integrated countries like Persia. It is probable that in Europe alone, Rome ruled not more than half of the population, if ever that much. Although exact population statistics are lacking, it is doubtful whether the roughly 70 million people which it is assumed Rome dominated were more than one-fifth to one-third of the world's population. The ancient world never was a two-power universe, though at times control was, for all practical purposes, divided between Rome and China. Most of the time there were numerous additional power centers. But there was never "one world." Nor is there now, as some thinkers postulate, some kind of "inner necessity" which makes world government "inevitable." True, modern technical civilization has decreased space-time dimensions. But it is politically neutral and does not evolve "logically" and "normally" toward a universal state which would be world embracing.[16]

Regardless of the validity of the "one-world" concept, it must be recognized that there is a strong trend to large regional power as well as to the acquisition of "forward bases." Power has been expanding in response to military needs rather than as a result of conquest. The great empires of the present possess holdings in many continents, and they could not survive otherwise. As they achieved direct or indirect control over most neutral positions, they were confronted by the alternative to "contain" or to destroy each other. Yet even if a conflict were to arise and leave one side in control of the world, it is highly probable that such a dominion would collapse and that numerous nations would recover their independence; the struggle probably would exhaust the victor. The trend to expand exists; but there still is an optimum size beyond which empires cannot grow safely. Moreover, global industrialization, which, within limits, seems inevitable, will tend to destroy the basis of the present power monopoly possessed by the great powers.

COLLECTIVE SECURITY

The expression "collective security," which is of Soviet origin, is a fig leaf for "alliance." It does not mean what it implies—that "collective security" is a specific technique for taming would-be aggressors—let alone that an

[16] For opposing views see Arnold Toynbee, *A Study of History, An Abridgement,* New York, Oxford, 1946, p. 207; "The Present Point in History," *Foreign Affairs,* September, 1947; and Edgar A. Mowrer, *The Nightmare of American Foreign Policy,* New York, Knopf, 1948, pp. 253–255. For a discussion of a world state or a world federation as a solution of the world problem *here and now,* see Chap. 28.

international "collective" offers a particularly effective type of security. It does denote, however, a particular type of alliance—one which (1) has numerous members, (2) imposes so light and ambiguous a military obligation that it is almost meaningless, and (3) is tied originally to a multinational organization of a "progressive" type.

The phenomenon—familiar though impalpable—constantly reappears in history, from the Greek leagues through the medieval empire, the Holy Alliance and the European Concert, to the League of Nations and the United Nations. In its essence the concept is a simple one: a peace-breaking government should be confronted by the joint coercive action of all law-abiding states. Theoretically, a strong alliance of "peace-loving" states, by virtue of the preponderance of the states so designated, could keep the peace forever.

In the light of historical experience, situations in which such a preponderant collective system functions effectively must be assumed to be short-lived. For the bond that holds such a system together is no stronger than is the common interest in the preservation of the *status quo*. Since the *status quo* of a particular moment is that order which has come into being as a result of an attempt to overthrow a preexisting order, it cannot be conceived of as being a static condition. In that sense *status quo* is a misnomer. For example, the League of Nations sought to "freeze" the *status quo* established as a result of the victory of the Allies over the Central Powers, though Article 19 of the Covenant provided the machinery for changing treaties which might become "inapplicable." Article 19 remained inoperative, and the *status quo* might have been preserved—had the Allies not fallen out among themselves and had the admission to the League of Nations of states who, in the nature of things, were opposed to the *status quo* not fostered within the League itself a "revisionist" opposition.

Leaving aside the question as to whether nations can or cannot subordinate their self-interest to a common good, it can be seen that collective security is an ambiguous concept. It does not mean the same thing to the defenders of the *status quo* as it does to the revisionist states, who, as a rule, are the very states who suffered a diminishment of power and hence a diminishment of *their* national security as a result of the establishment of the latest *status quo*.

In theory, it is easy to conceive of a situation where just one power seeks to overthrow the *status quo* and where all other "peace-loving" states rush to the defense of that *status quo*. In practice, there is always more than one dissatisfied nation; after World War I it was, among the members of the victorious Allies, first Italy and then Japan, and among the defeated, Germany, who opposed the main beneficiaries of the peace treaties, principally France and Britain. Because of the multiplicity of that opposition, the preponderance of the forces arrayed on the side of collective security was whittled down to parity—if not to inferiority—as compared with the aggressor powers. And this precarious balance did not signify "collective security" but the prelude to war. For the collective system must be able to marshal so unmistakable a preponderance of power that the aggressor, or alliance of aggressors, will not risk challenging the *status quo*. If this preponderance is not given or the defenders of the *status quo* are at odds among themselves, then the system of collective security is not only not a means of settling disputes among nations peaceably but a dangerous illusion for the defenders of the *status quo* and a vehicle for the aggressors' strategy of deception and prevarication.

The kind of mechanism which is set up for the solution of international conflicts is, comparatively speaking, of little importance. Under certain conditions a very imperfect mechanism can be made to work, while under other circumstances the best machine breaks down. Characteristically, these mechanisms are very loose, and the "security machinery" rarely has frightened an aggressor. Large membership is irrelevant except as it makes the "machinery" more ponderous and unworkable, a lesson which the Korean War ought to have driven home. "Collective security" has served in the past as a screen which either blinded states to their real security problems or was used by them to justify a foolhardy policy of disarmament. It rarely was a bona fide or realistic policy.

Still, the concept as such has some validity, being—if it were logically developed—an expansion of the argument for extending defensive alliances to a maximum number of states. If so, the prerequisite of collective security would be a basic understanding between the principal powers. This understanding must cover at least two points: that none of the major members proposes to change the *status quo*, with the exception of minor adjustments; and that none seeks to establish military or ideological supremacy.

To bind states together for joint undertakings—peace is such an undertaking, since it requires positive action—is possible only if there is a community of thought; it can be effective only if the members adhere to the same basic politicophilosophical doctrines, such as Christianity or liberalism. If multilateral alliances have held together in epochs when nations were not joined by unity of religious doctrine, then their durability and strength must be ascribed to the fact that they were rooted in unity of political philosophy linking the leading classes of the various nations.

Once such a unity exists, collective security may develop into an effective system of adaptation, as it did, for example, after 1815. Under such a system conflicts arise as under any other system, and it is not always possible to settle them by compromise. But conflicts are not willfully created or exploited for aggressive purposes. Peace is maintained, and a general atmosphere of confidence exists which permits, among other things, the maintenance of armaments at a low level and in some cases the elimination of the origins of possible future conflicts.

On the other hand, if no such community exists, and if one or two of the major powers are bent upon changing the *status quo*, collective security does not and cannot operate. Any attempt to create collective security by means of a mechanism, such as the League of Nations, must ultimately fail. In the absence of doctrinal unity and common political purposes as well as willingness to maintain the *status quo,* a policy of collective security has the paradoxical goal of making nations agree who do not agree. It is an invitation to the prospective aggressor to cooperate with the peaceful or *status quo* nations, but this invitation will be heeded only if the peace-loving nations have sufficient force to make it reasonably clear to the aggressor that he must abandon his policy. Thus, for instance, in 1924 the aggressive designs of Mussolini against Corfu were met by collective action, but in 1935 and 1940 the invitations addressed to him by the League did not persuade Mussolini to return to the system of collective arbitrament.

In a world which is rent asunder by conflicting ideologies striving for global dominance, and which is also split into various societies of different structure and into different, more or less closed, economic systems, collective security cannot obtain. Mere variety of racial, social, economic, and political differences does not, of course, exclude collective security or even federations or "more perfect" unions. If mere differentiation did exclude political concord or unity, political unions would never have been possible on the local, let alone the regional, level. The United States, the British Empire, Germany, Italy, the French Empire, the Russo-Ukrainian union would never have come into being or existed for more than a few years. The degree of the differences is decisive as well as the existence, or absence, of supplementary bonds of unity. If the differences are too deep, there is no basis for collective security. In that case, security can be achieved only *within* one group of kindred nations or between competing peoples *against* the most dangerous outside aggressor.

The quarreling Greek states composed their differences against the Persians, and the Christian nations united against Hun, Mongol, and Turk. Thus, systems of collective security were beneficial during their period of full life. Once the danger from which they arise passes, they tend to break down. Confronted by new ideologies, new situations and new aggressors, they fade away. A multilateral alliance is at its best when it is a specific alliance against a specific opponent; it is at its worst when it is set up as a mere "permanent" machinery with which it is proposed to forge the structure of eternal peace.

FEDERATIONS

A federation is the result of an associative process: a number of independent states establish common links in order to benefit each other economically and to set up effective joint defenses. The Thirteen North American States met in conference to discuss the problem of the Potomac waterway. Discovering that unification on more points than water transportation would benefit all of them, they ended up by establishing a more permanent and more comprehensive union. The advantages of the North American federation were threefold: the states who had begun to quarrel among themselves and were on the verge of war, largely concerning border lines, now composed these conflicts by the arbitrament of the Constitution. Secondly, federation ended economic provincialism and separatism, making it impossible for the states to maintain separate tariff and monetary systems; the act of federation lifted trade restrictions and established one free and large market. Thirdly, federation allayed the danger that individual states would enter into alliances with foreign powers or succumb to the attack of strong non-American states which might have established themselves on the continent.[17] Thus, a foreign policy effectively aiming at federation—a policy whose modern form may be said to have been invented by Alexander Hamilton—and which was adopted by, and partly forced upon, all Thirteen States was one of the mainsprings of the rise and the wealth of the United States. If a different foreign policy had been adopted, or if some of the states had not followed Hamilton's lead, the history of the United States would have been quite different and, in all likelihood, less fortunate. It is well to remember, however, that the American federation could be established because it was favored by suitable conditions, notably the lack of strong vested interests connected with the independence of each state; a common and brief history; joint success in a great undertaking, the Revolution; and to a large degree, a common culture, tradition, and language.

But is the United States truly a federation? Undoubtedly it was—till the Civil War. But it has become a national state—"one nation, indivisible," though it contains linguistic and cultural minorities. The member states have very little political significance except as administrative units. The national

---

[17] The foreign policy advantages of a more perfect union are discussed by John Jay in *The Federalist,* Nos. 3, 4, and 5. In No. 3, Jay shows that a union would obviate the danger of abject appeasement: "In the year 1685, the state of Genoa having offended Louis XIV, endeavored to appease him. He demanded that they should send their *Doge,* or chief magistrate, accompanied by four of their senators, to France, to ask his pardon and receive his terms. They were obliged to submit to it for the sake of peace. Would he on any occasion either have demanded or have received the like humiliation from Spain, or Britain, or any other *powerful* nation?" In No. 4, Jay discussed the possible causes of an aggressive war by strong foreign states on America. In order to avoid war, a situation must be created which "instead of inviting war, will tend to repress and discourage it. That situation consists in the best possible state of defence, and necessarily depends on the government, the arms, and the resources of the country." What would, by contrast, happen, if Britain would be split up and if instead of one British navy, England, Scotland, Wales, and Ireland would all have their independent "navigation and fleet"? It is easy to perceive how soon they would each dwindle into comparative insignificance. In No. 5, Jay quotes Queen Anne's letter of July 1, 1706, dealing with the impending union between England and Scotland: "An entire and perfect union will be the solid foundation of lasting peace: It will secure your religion, liberty, and property; remove the animosities amongst yourselves, and the jealousies and differences betwixt our two kingdoms. It must increase your strength, riches and trade; and by this union the whole island, being joined in affection and free from all apprehensions of different interest, will be *enabled to resist all its enemies.*"

state of the United States was born through a federation; at present, the United States is a federation only to the point that Puerto Rico is an "associated" free state.

The Germanic Federation of thirty-eight German states which, after 1815, took the place of the Holy Roman Empire—which had been an association of princes presided over by the Emperor—was made possible by a common language and culture, that is to say, by those factors which are of the utmost importance in an age when the idea of nationalism rules supreme. This Federation soon was split into two camps, one led by Prussia, the other by Austria. In 1819 the Kingdom of Prussia took the lead in transforming the political association into an economic union; after establishing a uniform tariff in all Prussian territories, Prussia slowly expanded the *Zollverein*. In 1829, Bavaria and Württemberg, the two largest states south of the Main River line, entered the tariff union, while Austria resisted this Prussian policy of economic expansion. In the end, Austria and her friends, Hanover, Oldenburg, Mecklenburg, and the three Hansa cities stayed outside the *Zollverein*, while Prussia gained economic supremacy within the German *Bund* and so strongly intertwined her interests with those of many smaller states that these, for all practical purposes, became members of the Prussian Kingdom. Thereupon Austria, perceiving the threat to her ancient hegemony, reversed her policy and attempted to enter the *Zollverein*. Prussia opposed her membership, and Austria then resorted to various unsuccessful attempts to break up the customs union. In 1853, the economic advantages of unification had become so obvious that Austria's allies, Hanover, Brunswick, and Oldenburg, joined the union. Thus the whole of Germany, with the exception of Austria, was economically united, but politically the German federation was more split than ever into the Austrian and Prussian camps. Both camps maneuvered for position by proposing various reforms of the *Bund*. In the end, Prussia violated the federal constitution by occupying Holstein which was joint federal territory. Most of the members of the federation, including Bavaria, Saxony, and Hanover, took Austria's side, but Prussia declared that the constitution had ceased to exist and attacked her Austrian competitor (1866). Austria was defeated and expelled from the federation. This left Prussia supreme in Germany, as Bismarck intended. A new union was formed, the North German Confederation, with the King of Prussia as its president; it included all German states north of the Main (1867). Prussia concluded military alliances with the three south German states. In 1871, the German Empire was created which was, in legal fiction, still a federation, but in practice a unified state under Prussian leadership.

From the beginning, the German federation was limited to German-speaking lands and *excluded* the non-German parts of the Austrian monarchy; thus an opportunity to organize central Europe and to provide that organization with supreme power was deliberately rejected. In the course of events, the federal idea was abandoned: many states, including the Kingdom of

Hanover, were incorporated into Prussia; German Austria was expelled; and the area even of the fictitious federation became more and more restricted. By the time of the Weimar Republic (1919–1933), the whole structure had changed into one more or less centralized edifice ruled and controlled from Berlin, only Bavaria retaining some semblance of political independence. There was one German army and one foreign office, and both were controlled from Berlin. So were the *Reich's* finances. The authority of the *Länder* was restricted to inconsequential and administrative matters.[18]

The story would be incomplete without mentioning that in 1931 Germany and Austria, then in the throes of the world depression, tried to overcome their economic difficulties by concluding a customs union. To their surprise the project was strongly attacked by France (with European federalist Briand as foreign minister) and Britain (with Labor leader Arthur Henderson as foreign secretary). The fundamental objections were political: fear of the rise of German power. Yet it was also argued that the *Zollunion* would deprive third states of the rights of the most-favored-nation clause laid down in the commercial treaties with Germany and Austria, and that the economic unity between the two Germanic states would preclude the realization of Briand's European union scheme. History has revealed the dishonesty of the latter argument. It must be conceded, however, that customs unions can be established more easily among preindustrial than among highly industrialized nations, and that economic arrangements of this type always have important political implications: they modify the distribution of power.[19]

The German example may be contrasted with the unification of Italy through Cavour. In both cases, a relatively large number of states joined and created a new and larger political entity. In the German case, one member state, Prussia, carried out the unification and also took over control of the federation, compelling all the other members to accept its policies and plans. In the Italian case, one state, Piedmont, brought about unification. But in the process Piedmont abandoned its political individuality; the member states dissolved themselves and merged into a new state, Italy. In the German case, federation was a disguise of Prussian imperialism; in the Italian case, there was a genuine merger. In neither case was there a federation.

The Soviet Union, which pretends to be a federation, followed politically the example of Prussia; in fact, Moscow established far more rigorous control than Berlin ever attempted. Soviet centralism is but Muscovite centralism

---

[18] Friedrich Wilhelm Förster, *Europe and the German Question,* London, Sheed, 1940, Chap. 2, especially pp. 31–35, and Chap. 5. Most Germans do not understand the meaning of federalism and confound it, often with good historical reason, with the provincial obstructionism of *Länder* governments.

[19] For the history of the Austro-German *Zollunion,* see E. L. Woodward and Rohan Butler (eds.), *Documents on British Foreign Policy 1919–1939,* second series, London, H.M. Stationery Office, 1947, Vol. II, pp. 1–57.

under a new management. While the treaty of Perejaslav (1654) provided for something like a federation between Russia and the Ukraine, the Ukrainian nation gradually was being subjugated. Other parts of Russia were conquered—just as France conquered Algeria or Hitler Czechoslovakia—especially the non-Slavic nations of the Caucasus and Central Asia. Most of "Siberia" (largely settled by Russians and Ukrainians) remained tied organically to Russia in the proper sense. According to Soviet fiction, the Soviet Union is a federation, whereas it is, in fact, a highly centralized state. The Soviets have made strenuous efforts to reduce the national diversity within their borders, resorting to Russification, resettlement, purges, and the splitting of large minority nations by fostering the development of what could be called "subnations" (for example, the splitting of Turkestan into several federated republics). The Soviet technique has been to force an alien nation into a loose association with Russia and gradually to strengthen Russian influence until the "federated" nation loses control over its affairs. Federation is considered to be a transitory step toward the "amalgamation" and "fusion" of nations "into a single common culture with a single common language." [20]

The future relationships among the peoples living within the Soviet Union are uncertain. Because of the cultural time-lag, the national awakening of these people has been delayed, but their national consciousness seems to be growing. On the other hand, these nations may have many economic interests in common, and some of them are so small that full independence may be difficult to attain and preserve. If history is any guide, a radical policy of Russification may yield the same results as the policy of Germanification in Austria-Hungary. The most logical solution within the context of a future settlement of the Russian question probably would be to take federalism within the Soviet orbit seriously, *i.e.*, to grant all nations living within Russia a maximum of autonomy and allow secession of those nations which aspire toward full independence. The maintenance of confederative ties and of economic unity would be a proper supplement to such independence. Yet the radicalism of Soviet *national* policy—a radicalism inherent in a system based on the strict power monopoly of a small group—may preclude a rational solution to a problem the very existence of which has been denied for years but which, partly as a result of Russian conquest of well-established nations like Poland, Hungary, Rumania, etc., can be ignored no longer. [21]

While the United States, Germany, and the Soviet Union became "federations" through agglomeration, other federations were created by secession.

[20] Josef Stalin, *Marxism and the National Question,* New York, International Publishers, 1942, pp. 207ff.; see also Josef Stalin, *Marxism and the National and Colonial Question,* New York, International Publishers (printed in Russia), no date, pp. 120ff., 129ff., 153, and especially p. 168 where it is stated that the right to self-determination must give way to the "right" of the working class to its dictatorship.

[21] See George F. Kennan, "America and the Russian Future," in *American Diplomacy 1900–1950,* Chicago, University of Chicago Press, 1951, pp. 134–137.

Austria-Hungary adopted, in 1867, a federal constitution in fact, though not in name, when the Habsburg realm was split into an Austrian and a Hungarian part with only the ministries of foreign affairs, war, and finance remaining the organs common to both states; the British Empire slowly transformed itself from one centralized body into a federation or, rather, confederacy, the Commonwealth, in which the Dominions, though still owing allegiance to the common Crown, have become independent, conducting their own foreign affairs and maintaining their own armed forces and currencies, although for reasons of security they continue to cooperate with each other.

Federations are very often imperfect structures which cannot resist the strains of severe conflicts. The wisest federal constitution could not have averted the American Civil War. The Dutch-Belgian union, created at Vienna in 1815, broke up in 1830 due to the nationalism of both members. The union between Norway and Sweden was dissolved in 1905, largely on account of Norwegian nationalist aspirations. The Austrian Empire collapsed, although it may be argued that its federal character was marred by imperfections and that it might have endured had the Slav population been permitted more freedom and independent representation. In the British Empire, the policy followed by Ireland during both world wars undoubtedly endangered the security of the British community as a whole. In 1948, Eire seceded formally from the Crown, thus severing an uneasy political connection, and assumed the status of a sovereign republic.

Yet the advantages of federations are obvious. Disregarding the economic benefits which derive from a large market, it is clear that a federation is stronger than each of its members and that it affords, therefore, each member greater security than does independence. If the Swiss cantons had remained independent, it is safe to say that they would have gradually been absorbed by their neighbors and that there would be no Switzerland today.[22] Britain retained her world position only because she did not stand alone. The United Kingdom as such is a federation, and it is united with a wide Empire which, though it is exposed to many internal strains, nevertheless makes England, South Africa, Australia, New Zealand, Canada, and, for that matter, India stronger than they would be in isolation.

While Austria-Hungary, despite its glaring faults and weaknesses, was a great power and capable of defending itself against any comer, the small successor states were subjugated twice in thirty years by a great power. The Czechs were unwilling to follow the policy of Vienna and to adjust their grievances within the Habsburg monarchy, yet they were compelled later to take orders from Berlin and subsequently from Moscow. Whatever independence the Czechs retained between 1919 and 1939, they did so by virtue of their affiliations with the Slovaks, the Ruthenians, and, to a lesser degree, with the Sudeten Germans, the Hungarians, and the Poles—a federation in

[22] See Denis de Rougement and Charlotte Muret, *The Heart of Europe,* New York, Duell, Sloan & Pearce, 1941, pp. 69–131.

all but the name. Even at a time when their independence was not threatened by anybody, the Czechs were too small a nation to subsist by their own means.

The same is true of the Serbs. That this fact was not recognized by either Czechs or Serbs, and that both engaged in domestic politics not compatible with the idea of federations, is another story. Neglecting to build up genuine federations, Czechs and Serbs exacerbated the ancient antagonisms of the Danube region and thus greatly eased the task of the aggressors.

It should be added, however, that federal states which—unlike the Commonwealth—are contiguous, ultimately must merge *all* their affairs, in addition to finances, foreign policy, and defense. The tendency of one dominant member to forge an ever greater internal unity is well-nigh irresistible, because circumstances usually demand the merger. In the end, only the cultural sphere, *i.e.*, language, may remain "independent," as shown by the example of Switzerland. Federation is more a method of founding a large state than a political organization for the preservation of local privileges.

Federations are neither an uncommon nor a modern political device.[23] Federations are in fact one of the oldest and most effective instruments of foreign policy. It is hardly an exaggeration to say that successful states are those who know how to federate. The process often began at the tribal level; for example, the origin of Germany can be traced back to the tribal federation which Arminius, chieftain of the powerful tribe of the Cheruscans, organized against the Romans. In the age of feudalism those families won out who "federated" most successfully, resorting to the technique of dynastic marriages; the Habsburgs were most skillful at this method of aggrandizement by connubial affiliations. Among the nation-states those won out who succeeded in merging several different nations into one. The Spanish nation is the result of the merging of the Catalans, Castilians, and Basques; the French nation comprises Bretons, Normans, Basques, Flamands, Provençals, Alsatians, and French; Russia grew through her union with the Ukraine.

If today the technique of federation were abandoned and nations presently federated were split according to the principles of nationalism or historical origin, every single large state would have to be broken up into numerous small parts, and peace, which now at least reigns within these states, would give way to the reemergence of countless long-forgotten feuds. On the other hand, if the establishment of new federations is contemplated, it should be borne in mind that, in the past, most federations were created by force and conquest. The federating process was more often than not incorporation pure and simple. The Swiss Confederation was forged, pleasing legends notwith-

[23] On the conclusive experiences of the Greeks, see G. Glotz, *La Civilisation egéenne,* Paris, La Renaissance du Livre, 1923, p. 442. Glotz, incidentally, points out that the first act of the Greek Union (*koinon*) which superseded the various confederacies and federations was to declare war on Persia—to wage an offensive war of conquest (p. 447). The German *Bund,* too, quickly embarked on aggressive war against Denmark. Every political system is suitable for the waging of war; no political system makes war impossible.

standing, by the expansionist and martial Bernese—much to the discomfiture of lesser cantons. Federation by agreement was comparatively rare.

BIBLIOGRAPHY

Mediation

Chase, Eugene P.: *The United Nations in Action,* New York, McGraw-Hill, 1950.
Jackson, Elmore: *Meeting of Minds,* New York, McGraw-Hill, 1952.
Langer, William L.: *European Alliances and Alignments 1871–1890,* New York, Knopf, 1931.
Leonard, L. Larry: *International Organization,* New York, McGraw-Hill, 1951.
Levi, Werner: *Fundamentals of World Organization,* Minneapolis, University of Minnesota Press, 1950.
Medlicott, W. N.: *The Congress of Berlin and After: A Diplomatic History of the Near Eastern Settlement 1878–1880,* London, Methuen, 1938.
Nicholson, Harold: *The Congress of Vienna: A Study in Allied Unity 1812–1822,* New York, Harcourt, Brace, 1946.
Ralston, J. H.: *International Arbitration from Athens to Locarno,* Stanford, Calif., Stanford University Press, 1929.
Temperley, Harold: *England and the Near East: The Crimea,* London, Longmans, Green & Co., 1936.

Appeasement and Preventive War; Expansion

Bonnet, Georges: *Fin d'une Europe,* Geneva, Éditions du Cheval Ailé, 1948.
———: *De Washington au Quai d'Orsay,* Geneva, Éditions du Cheval Ailé, 1946.
Churchill, Winston S.: *The Second World War: The Gathering Storm,* Boston, Houghton Mifflin, 1948.
Donosti, Mario: *Mussolini e l'Europea: La politica estera fascista,* Rome, Editioni Leonardo, 1945.
Fabre-Luce, Alfred: *Histoire secrète de la conciliation de Munich,* Paris, Grasset, 1938.
Feiling, Keith: *The Life of Neville Chamberlain,* London, Macmillan & Co., Ltd., 1946.
Fischer, Louis: *Empire,* New York, Duell, Sloan & Pearce, 1943.
Hobson, J. A.: *Imperialism,* New York, Pott, 1905.
Kordt, E.: *Wahn und Wirklichkeit: Die Aussenpolitik des Dritten Reiches,* Stuttgart, Union, 1947.
Langer, William L.: *Diplomacy of Imperialism,* New York, Knopf, 1935.
Langsam, Walter C.: *In Quest of Empire: The Problem of Colonies,* New York, Foreign Policy Association, 1939.
Lenin, Vladimir I.: *Imperialism, the Highest Stage of Capitalism,* New York, Vanguard, 1929.
Moon, Parker T.: *Imperialism and World Politics,* New York, Macmillan, 1926.
Namier, L. B.: *Diplomatic Prelude, 1938–1939,* New York, Macmillan, 1948.
———: *In the Nazi Era,* London, Macmillan, 1952.
Nearing, Scott: *The Tragedy of Empire,* New York, Island Press Co-operative, Inc., 1945.
Voigt, Fritz A.: *Unto Caesar,* New York, Putnam, 1938.
Weinberg, Albert K.: *Manifest Destiny: A Study of Nationalist Expansion in American History,* Baltimore, Johns Hopkins Press, 1935.
Weller, George: *Bases Overseas,* New York, Harcourt, Brace, 1944.
Wheeler-Bennett, John W.: *Munich, Prologue to Tragedy,* New York, Duell, Sloan & Pearce, 1948.
Wolfers, Arnold: *Britain and France between Two Wars; Conflicting Strategies of Peace since Versailles,* New York, Harcourt, Brace, 1940.

Empire; World State

Angell, Sir Norman: *Let the People Know,* New York, Harper, 1943.
———: *The Steep Places,* New York, Harper, 1943.
Birdsall, George A.: *A Proposed World Government,* New York, McGraw-Hill, 1944.

Crozier, John Beattie: *Considerations on the Constitutions of the World,* New York, Longmans, 1878.

Demangeon, Albert: *The British Empire,* New York, Harcourt, Brace, 1925.

Lord Elton: *Imperial Commonwealth,* New York, Reynal & Hitchcock, 1946.

Fairgrieve, James: *Geography and World Power,* 8th ed., London, London University Press, 1941.

Haushofer, Karl: *Raumüberwindende Mächte,* Leipzig, Teubner, 1934.

————: *Geopolitik der Pan-Ideen,* Berlin, Zentralverlag, 1931.

Kjellen, Rudolf: *Die Grossmächte und die Weltkrise,* Leipzig, Teubner, 1921.

Madariaga, Salvador de: *The Rise of the Spanish American Empire,* New York, Macmillan, 1947.

Ratzel, Friedrich: *Das Meer als eine Quelle der Völkergrösse,* Munich, Oldenbourg, 1900.

Rauschning, Hermann: *The Revolution of Nihilism: Warning to the West,* New York, Alliance, 1939.

Reddick, Olive Irene: *World Organization,* Philadelphia, Women's International League for Peace and Freedom, 1941.

Schuecking, Walter: *Die Organisation der Welt,* Leipzig, Kröner, 1909.

Triepel, Heinrich: *Die Hegemonie: Ein Buch von führenden Staaten,* Stuttgart, Kohlhammer, 1938.

Winslow, E. M.: *The Pattern of Imperialism,* New York, Columbia University Press, 1948.

Collective Security

Armstrong, George C.: *Why Another World War? How We Missed Collective Security,* London, G. Allen, 1941.

Beneš, E., J. Coulborn, and A. Fuller: *International Security,* Chicago, University of Chicago Press, 1939.

Beveridge, Sir William H.: *The Pillars of Security,* New York, Macmillan, 1943.

Bourquin, Maurice (ed.): *Collective Security: A Record of the Seventh and Eighth International Studies Conferences,* London, 1935, Paris, 1936.

Brugière, Pierre F.: *La Sécurité collective 1919-1945,* Paris, Pedone, 1946.

Eagleton, Clyde: *The Attempt to Define Aggression,* New York, Carnegie Foundation, 1930.

Jessup, Philip C.: *International Security: The American Role in Collective Action for Peace,* New York, Council on Foreign Relations, 1935.

Mitrany, David: *The Problem of International Sanctions,* London, G. Allen, 1925.

Rappard, William E.: *Cinq siècles de sécurité collective (1291-1798): Les experiences de la Suisse sous le régime des pactes de secours mutuel,* Paris, Recueil Sirey, 1945.

Rogge, Heinrich: *Kollektivsicherheit, Bündnispolitik, Völkerbund: Theorie der nationalen und internationalen Sicherheit,* Berlin, Junker and Dünnhaupt, 1937.

Salter, Sir Arthur: *Security: Can We Retrieve It?* New York, Macmillan, 1939.

Wheeler-Bennett, John W., and F. E. Langermann: *Information on the Problem of Security 1917-1926,* London, G. Allen, 1927.

Wright, Quincy (ed.): *Neutrality and Collective Security,* Lectures on the Harris Foundation, 1936, Chicago, University of Chicago Press, 1936.

Federations

Beveridge, Sir William H.: *Peace by Federation?* Federal Tracts, No. 1, London, 1940.

Bingham, Alfred M.: *The United States of Europe,* New York, Duell, Sloan & Pearce, 1940.

Brinton, Crane: *From Many One,* Cambridge, Mass., Harvard University Press, 1948.

Coudenhove-Kalergi, Richard N.: *Pan-Europe,* New York, Knopf, 1923.

Culbertson, Ely: *Summary of World Federation Plans,* New York, Doubleday, 1943.

————: *A System to Win This War and to Win the Peace to Come: The World Federation Plan,* New York, World Federation, Inc., 1942.

Deutsch, Karl W.: *Nationalism and Social Communication: An Inquiry into the Foundations of Nationalism,* New York, Wiley, 1953.

Egerton, H. E.: *Federations and Unions in the British Empire,* New York, Oxford, 1924.

Frantz, Constantin: *Deutschland und der Föderalismus,* Hellerau, Hegner, 1917.

Freeman, Edward A.: *History of Federal Government in Greece and Italy,* New York, Macmillan, 1893.

———: *History of Federal Government from the Foundation of the Achaian League to the Disruption of the United States,* London, Macmillan & Co., Ltd., 1863.

Hodé, Jacques: *L'idée de fédération internationale dans l'histoire,* Paris, Éditions de la Vie Universitaire, 1921.

Hoffmann, Ross J. S.: *The Great Republic,* London, Sheed, 1942.

Marriott, J. A. R.: *Federalism and the Problem of the Small State,* London, G. Allen, 1943.

Novicow, I. A.: *La fédération de l'Europe,* Paris, Alcan, 1901.

Owen, Ruth (Bryan): *Look Forward, Warrior,* New York, Dodd, Mead, 1942.

Ripka, Hubert: *Small and Great Nations,* London, Czechoslovak Ministry of Foreign Affairs, 1944.

Robbins, Lionel: *Economic Aspects of Federation,* London, Macmillan & Co., Ltd., 1941.

Sharp, Walter R.: *World Organization: Decentralized or Unitary?* New York, Council on Foreign Relations, 1944.

Smal-Stocki, Roman: *The Nationality Problem of the Soviet Union and Russian Communist Imperialism,* Milwaukee, Bruce Pub., 1952.

Streit, Clarence K.: *The Need for Union Now,* New York, Harper, 1940.

———: *Union Now: A Proposal for a Federal Union of the Democracies of the North Atlantic,* New York, Harper, 1939.

Chapter 15

FRONTIER MAKING: PEACEMAKING

The most common threat to international peace is that of the deliberate aggressor who for a multiplicity of reasons—lust for power, martial enthusiasm, religious or political ideologies—prepares for war and launches the attack as soon as a favorable situation arises. If relations between the aggressor country and its neighbors are good, the former will seek to worsen them and create artificially the tensions, conflicts, and incidents which inflame men's minds and ultimately lead to war. If relations are bad, the would-be disturbers of the peace will take advantage of existing conflicts; their game is facilitated by accumulated hatreds. A skillful aggressor can bend any given situation to his ends. Once a regime set on military conquest takes control of a powerful country, it is futile to attempt to prevent war by the amelioration of conditions or by the satisfaction of "just" claims.

For example, Hitler's demand for the Sudetenland may seem "justified" if nationalist doctrine is accepted as a yardstick.[1] Yet to argue in 1938–1939 the Sudeten question on the basis of the principle of national self-determination was to miss the point. Hitler was interested not in obtaining the cession by Czechoslovakia of the Sudetenland (which he accepted, of course, as an additional gain) but in breaking up Czechoslovakia as a powerful military base and in destroying the French system of alliances. His long-range stake in the Sudetenland was military; the destruction of Czechoslovakia increased his absolute and relative war potential and made possible subsequent attacks on Poland and France.

There is, however, another type of threat to international peace. This threat is not deliberately organized but emerges from authentic conflicts and

[1] Norman Hill, *Claims to Territory in International Law and Relations*, New York, Oxford, 1945, p. 55; this book discusses the various types of claims, including nonlegal, strategic, geographic, historic, economic, ethnic, legal, and miscellaneous. The conflicting nature of claims came up prominently during the Munich Conference: "The theory advanced by M. Daladier that economic, geographical and political factors must be taken into account when defining the frontiers seemed to Hitler dangerous, because it was precisely to this theory that the Czechoslovak State owed its origin in 1918. At that time an entity was created which was viable economically, but not viable nationally. Moreover, economic difficulties could be more easily settled than national difficulties . . ." This was in answer to Daladier's proposal to supplement "the Wilsonian principle of self-determination" by taking into account "geographic, economic and political realities." These quotations are taken from the German minutes of the Munich Conference made by Erich Kordt (see *Documents and Materials Relating to the Eve of the Second World War*, Vol. I, pp. 259*f.*).

untoward situations not artificially created. For various reasons the relations between two countries may be characterized by permanent crisis, "justified" grievances being harbored by both sides. Such a crisis may smolder for a long time, being sometimes more and sometimes less acute. There may be no intention on either side to settle the issue through war, and yet circumstances may suddenly arise which lead to military conflicts. Prolonged crises and conflicts facilitate the coming to power of demagogues and rabble rousers who, once they control the government, may turn the nation to deliberate aggression. While the timely elimination or the alleviation of conflicts cannot always be considered a safe means of preventing wars—because it may not deter the deliberate aggressor—such action may render more difficult the efforts of those who seek to fish in troubled waters. Elimination of international conflict would smooth domestic politics, *ipso facto* reduce the amount of armaments, and, by thus improving the standard of living, indirectly reduce the danger of war. Extremists rarely accede to power in "normal" and quiet times.

The question therefore arises, what can be done to reduce threats to world peace and, more specifically, to overcome existing tensions and conflicts? It is obviously the task of a foreign policy worthy of its name to develop rules and methods for the reduction of conflicts and the easing of tensions. Thus far, the foreign policies of all nations have miserably fallen down on this task. With only a very few exceptions, for example, the technical-assistance programs, nations have made no concerted, systematic, and permanent effort at conflict elimination. Foreign policy, as it is still practiced in a routine fashion everywhere, has hardly advanced from the model of 18th- and 19th-century diplomacy, and some of the human insights of that diplomacy have been lost. It is certainly not equal to the tasks which arise in the modern industrialized society. International organizations, such as the League of Nations and the United Nations, have been expressly designed to meet the world's need for an orderly system of international relations. But what good are organizations if one does not know what to do with them?

The basic contradiction of contemporary foreign policy is that it is conducted as though society were still divided into small, more or less independent, and more or less autarchic communities. In modern society very few nations, if any, control the keys to their own gates. Virtually all nations, including the strongest, are dependent for their own well-being on the conditions and activities of other nations. Modern industry and technology have given birth to an international community all of whose members are mutually dependent. This fact has given rise to proposals aiming at the abolition of "sovereignty." Disregarding the political, legal, and logical impracticability of such ideas—sovereignty, like matter, cannot be abolished—these proposals fail to recognize that communities, be they of a racial, religious, or economic character, still insist on remaining independent and do not choose to take orders from other communities.

The very complexity of modern conditions makes it inefficient to administer *centrally* very large units. Administration is the more effective the more it is decentralized under coordination. An all too simple formula is not a solution. While it is true that untrammeled sovereignty is obsolete, the relations between the various communities which now are called states cannot be improved simply by depriving them of certain rights and transferring these rights to a supergovernment. That all-powerful superstate would, for a very long period of time, command the allegiance of only a very few among the communities. For that matter, divergences of interest would continue to exist, and exist in many different fields.

The creation of a supergovernment would not solve a single basic conflict. At best, it would provide means to a solution. Yet there are no techniques of conflict solution which would differ from those that must be applied in a multistate society. Nor would the conflicts change in character. It is necessary to take each single class of conflicts and propose solutions to them. *There is no single settlement applicable to all issues.* Some international problems can be solved now, others defy solution in the foreseeable future, and it will be the measure of statecraft how well nations can live with these insoluble problems. Not to settle now the issues that can be settled and not to learn to live patiently with those that cannot be settled is to resign oneself to the inevitability of another war. It is a major task of foreign policy to eliminate or soften and isolate international conflicts and to execute that mission under the *prevailing* dangerous and complex conditions.

FRONTIER CONFLICTS

The range of international conflict is as wide as that of the clash of individual and group interests. To cover it exhaustively would involve a gigantic enterprise of historical analysis, supported by virtually every branch of science. In this section, the discussion will be limited to one major topic—frontiers.

Frontiers are, first of all, in themselves a source of frequent disputes: one nation may control territory which another nation deems to belong rightfully within its own boundaries. Innumerable wars have been fought to recover "lost" provinces, and virtually all wars terminate with a reassignment of frontiers. Secondly, frontiers are "artificial" in character, that is to say, they cut through economic, cultural, linguistic, or other entities, creating tensions in each area of social interest. A frontier which cuts a house into two parts may be inconvenient only for the owner, but an international frontier which separates coal from iron, as did the Franco-German border drawn in 1919; [2]

[2] For a similar case, see Stephen B. Jones, *Boundary-making: A Handbook for Statesmen, Treaty Editors and Boundary Commissioners*, Washington, Carnegie Endowment, 1945, pp. 28*ff.*

or industry from its markets, as did the frontiers dividing Austrian industries from the markets of Yugoslavia and Hungary; or a port from its hinterland, as did the demarcation of the Trieste Zone in 1919 and again in 1946; such a frontier, by impeding free circulation of persons and goods, is a standing provocation to conflict not only between the parties directly involved but also, because of its unsettling effect upon larger regions, between the great powers.

The most pernicious and pervasive influence of the frontier is, however, not of a material but of a psychopolitical kind: more than anything else, the frontier is responsible for the misconceptions which exist about neighboring countries, and it is only behind the modern, impenetrable frontier that governments and propagandists can spread falsehoods about other nations. Within each frontier society develops in a more or less arbitrary mold different from that in which the neighboring society is cast. These differences, especially when they are exaggerated and exploited, produce that basic incompatibility between nations which is at the root of antipathies and enmity. In contrast, while "open frontiers" may not eliminate friction, they would certainly make possible a process of gradual assimilation. Similarly, those *frontiers which are systems of communication and avenues of contacts rather than lines of separation and exclusion are factors making for peace.*

The Myth of the Natural Frontier. These observations are platitudinous. They lead, however, to the very real and pressing question: What are the right conclusions to be drawn from the above-stated premises? Up to now, it has been widely held that the difficulties inherent in frontier making could be, if not eliminated, at least alleviated by tracing natural or ideal frontiers. For many centuries statesmen have been trying to define the *natural* frontier, bending their most ingenious efforts upon drawing frontiers which, as far as possible, approximated the "ideal." Statesmen who did not seek to conform to the standards of the "ideal" or "natural" frontier were generally condemned, as, for example, those responsible for the creation of the Polish Corridor and the Free City of Danzig, while those who drew the "natural," *i.e.*, strategic, frontiers of Germany in 1871, for instance, were praised.

Two things should have become clear to the reader: First, valuations change, sometimes slowly and sometimes with breath-taking speed, and each change entails new attitudes toward the "is" and "ought" of frontiers. As soon, for example, as the contemporary zeal for nationalistic causes would slacken, while the importance of economic frontiers would be recognized, many of the presently acceptable frontiers might be considered intolerable. Hence a movement for the revision of frontiers might set in motion a development which, in due course, might lead to war in exactly the same manner as the elimination of feudal frontiers was accompanied by a long series of wars.

Second, a little reflection should show that the attempt to draw an "ideal" frontier is foredoomed to failure. The question is, what principle should be applied? It is quite clear that a frontier can be drawn according to many conceivable principles, but who can decide which principle is valid and which of the valid ones is most important? [3] Some of the criteria which may be used in tracing a frontier can be listed as follows:

1. Linguistic
2. Religious
3. Cultural
4. Military
5. Economic
6. Historical
7. Administrative
8. Ideological
9. Geographical
10. Racial
11. Sociological
12. Psychological

The list could be extended at random; moreover, within each category, dozens of subcategories could be established. In each concrete case, the contestants in a frontier dispute, even if they agree on the criterion of "arbitration," are bound to interpret the ideal, brought to earth by adjudication, very differently. For example, it may be agreed that a frontier should be traced in accordance with the history of a region. But history is changeable; practically all disputed territories have changed hands several times. In 1919, the Poles claimed a historical right to Breslau, because centuries ago they had settled in the Oder Valley. The Polish borders as drawn after World War II include Breslau (or, as it is called now, Wroclaw), but not because of Poland's historic claims; Russia annexed Eastern Poland and Poland was compensated with Eastern Germany—an arrangement of *divide et impera* for the benefit of Soviet Russia. The Jews claimed Palestine by right of occupancy during the reign of Tiberius, while the Italians, under Mussolini, abstained—surprisingly enough—from claiming London or Vienna or Paris or Cologne, although their ancestors had founded these cities; nor do the French now claim Louisiana and the Mississippi Valley, or the Province of Quebec, still today culturally and linguistically French. The Dutch have not recently claimed New York.

Not all historical claims need to be in the class of lunacy. For example, Corsica, in spite of its linguistic difference, has become an integral part of France simply because Napoleon was born there and Napoleon is an integral part of French history. New Mexico, Texas, and California, formerly Spanish and Mexican, "belong" to the United States, as does former "Russkaya Amerika"—Alaska. Yet which side can, on the basis of historical precedents, claim territories such as Alsace or Transylvania? [4] Since all the contestants

[3] Different types of "natural" frontiers are listed by S. Whittemore Boggs, *International Boundaries: A Study of Boundary Functions and Problems,* New York, Columbia University Press, 1940, pp. 25f.

[4] For a review of the protracted and stultifying controversy over Transylvania between Hungary and Rumania, see Joseph S. Roucek, *Contemporary Rumania and Her Problems,* Stanford, Calif., Stanford University Press, 1932, pp. 3–5; and, for the Hungarian case, Eugene Horvath, *Transylvania and the History of the Rumanians,* Budapest, 1935, pp. 5–9.

possessed these areas for long periods of time, all have valid historical claims.

The impossibility of tracing frontiers that are fully acceptable to *all* parties is most clearly apparent in the case of military frontiers. Assuming the contestants agree that their mutual frontier should provide both of them with a maximum degree of security, it is nevertheless inevitable that the military advantage of one party is the military disadvantage of the other. The commanding height, or the pass, which is given to one side is denied the other, and the only way to reduce somewhat the partiality of a military frontier is to demilitarize it.

In the case of economic frontiers, the dilemma may be posed by the fact that agricultural and industrial, regional and national interests may diverge. Lord Curzon, maker of the northwestern frontier of India, summed up the perplexities of political frontier making: [5]

It would be futile to assert that an exact science of Frontiers has been or is ever likely to be evolved; for no one law can possibly apply to all nations or peoples, to all Governments, all territories, or all climates. The evolution of Frontiers is perhaps an art rather than a science, so plastic and malleable are its forms and manifestations.

The Multiple Frontier. The most important cleavages of interest, however, occur in those cases where national, linguistic, and cultural interests do not coincide with economic interests; where, in other words, a group of people living in a disputed area desire to "belong" politically to state A, but are economically dependent upon state B. This was the case of the Saar Basin, Danzig, and Trieste and even of entire countries, such as Argentina, Canada, Ireland, Finland, Transjordan, and Denmark. It may be the case of a future Ukraine or a future Turkestan should they once grow into full-fledged statehood. Some countries which would greatly benefit by closer economic relations with their neighbors deliberately sever lines of profitable trade for reasons of military security, *e.g.*, the severance of east-west trade in Europe during the "Cold War."

Before the time of the French Revolution, boundaries were not well defined. In most countries techniques of map making were still too crude for representing accurately the shape of very large states such as the major nations of Europe. For technical as well as philosophical reasons, the linear frontier was not the common type of boundary that it is today. In fact, there were often several frontiers dividing two countries—political, economic, and military frontiers. Even today the Franco-Swiss border near Geneva is just such a multiple frontier; the political boundary does not coincide with the tariff boundary, two French districts enjoying the right to trade with Swiss Geneva without paying duty. Nor do military frontiers always coincide with political or economic frontiers. The demilitarized zone in Germany

[5] Lord Curzon, *Frontiers,* New York, Oxford, 1908, p. 53. See also Chap. 19.

after 1919 extended to fifty kilometers east of the Rhine. On the Franco-Swiss border near Huningue, there is a demilitarized territory.

If it is true that there is not one single frontier which would correspond to the ideal as defined in various fields, it may still be conceded that in *each individual field,* taken singly and with the exception of the military, a frontier could be drawn which comes close to the ideal. Yet an economic frontier would not necessarily coincide with the linguistic and the cultural borders, all of which might again be at variance with a line drawn according to geographical convenience, although each type by itself may be perfect. This being so, it could be argued that multiple frontiers within a frontier zone not unlike the typical boundary arrangements of the Middle Ages should be established, replacing the single linear boundary. In regions where there are no clear linguistic border lines and where people of various languages live closely together, frontiers can be drawn according to geographic features, such as rivers or watersheds. Such frontiers could accord to racial or linguistic groups all the cultural privileges they might desire. To give a practical example, if an Alsatian wished to pursue part of his studies in a German-language university in Germany, Austria, or Switzerland, he could be permitted to do so without prejudice to his rights as a French national; degrees granted by these institutions could be recognized exactly as though the candidate had completed his study in any recognized French university (with the exception of such localized disciplines, as, for example, jurisprudence).

An enlightened frontier policy should seek the elimination of modern *rigid* frontiers and the *replacement of barriers by contacts.* How this can be done depends on the concrete case and on the development of administrative techniques along entirely new lines, for which there exist today only a few precedents, as passage certificates for inhabitants of border areas. A frontier, on the whole, should indicate merely where a new country begins; it should define to which government a population has to pay its taxes and to whom it owes its allegiance in time of war.

To carry out such a modification of boundary functions various prerequisites are needed. To begin with, states should no longer have the right to decide questions which affect frontier problems by themselves and without consultation with other interested parties. Secondly, in all cases where there are disputed frontiers due to circumstances beyond human control, or where border conflicts already exist, frontier zones should be created embracing multiple boundaries. These zones should be administered jointly by all the border states and by representatives of an international organization. Some hardened cases of frontier strife call for administration by disinterested outsiders, just as, in the Middle Ages, Italian cities occasionally appointed foreigners as chief administrators (*podestà*).[6]

---

[6] Such a solution was suggested by the original U.N. proposal for the partition of Palestine. It was set aside in favor of linear boundaries, as, for example, the line allocating

Some conclusive observations on this eternal problem of frontiers were set forth by George F. Kennan: [7]

There are more important things than where the border runs, and the first of these is that on both sides of it there should be tolerance and maturity, humility in the face of sufferings of the past and the problems of the future, and a realization that none of the important problems of the future . . . is going to be solved entirely, or even primarily, within the country's national boundaries.

PEACEFUL CHANGE

It has been suggested that it is the function of an international organization to propose and carry out frontier revision. Indeed, the Covenant of the League of Nations contained, in Article XIX, specific provisions to that end. Lord Curzon wrote: "The opinion is widely held that certain injustices connected with frontiers are so obvious and absurd that sooner or later they will inevitably be removed. Hence, if war or violence is not to be arbiter of these injustices, they should be removed before trouble arises." This idea has merits, and, in fact, has been applied, although infrequently. Occasionally, agreements were concluded on the modification and delineation of frontiers, as, for example, between the United States and Canada–Great Britain and between such basically hostile countries as France and Germany. (The latter two nations twice during the interwar period revised their frontiers, in 1928 and in 1938.) Although such cases—involving as it were, the exchange of a few villages—may appear relatively trivial, vexatious (though petty) frontier frictions may spark major and international explosions.

A few of the more notable instances of peaceful boundary changes may serve as guideposts of sensible frontier policy. In 1890 Britain ceded the island of Helgoland to Germany, the latter renouncing in return claims to Uganda and the island of Zanzibar. In 1927, Belgium and Portugal exchanged territories in Africa; the purpose of the exchange was to permit Belgium to build a railroad to Leopoldville on the Congo and to enlarge the port facilities of Matadi. Portugal ceded 1 square mile of territory in return for which she received 1,350 square miles. Both parties were satisfied by the deal. In 1932, Turkey and Persia exchanged territory for linguistic and economic reasons.[8]

---

the modern section of the city of Jerusalem to the state of Israel. The linear frontiers demarcating Israel and the territories of its Arab neighbors were largely determined by the fortunes of the Israeli-Arab War in 1948 and only to a lesser extent by functional considerations, *i.e.*, the economic and cultural interrelationships of the area as a whole. Examples in point are the Egyptian enclave around Gaza and the Israeli bulge at Jerusalem. The United Nations Special Committee on Palestine (UNSCOP) recommended, in 1947, the partition of Palestine into independent Jewish and Arab states, the placing of Jerusalem under international trusteeship, and, most importantly, economic union.

[7] George F. Kennan, *American Diplomacy 1900–1950*, Chicago, University of Chicago Press, 1951, p. 143.

[8] During the 19th century the technique of peaceful change was expanded to embrace

A noteworthy example—although perhaps not a significant one, since it involved two states then controlled by Great Britain—was the modification of the boundary line between Egypt and the Sudan. The original line, established in 1899, was a geometrical-geographical boundary, following the twenty-second parallel north. It cut, however, right across tribal territories. A decree replaced it with a boundary which was better adapted to local conditions.

The Treaty of Lausanne (1923) provided for a population transfer between Greece and Turkey—the most important single case of peaceful change. The exchange involved the moving of some 1,250,000 Greeks and took place under the auspices of the League of Nations and the Red Cross. The operation was generally considered a success, some more skeptical verdicts notwithstanding, and undoubtedly made it possible for Greece and Turkey to maintain henceforth friendly and peaceful relations, despite a turbulent past.[9]

During the Second World War population exchanges were carried out on a large scale, mostly on the initiative of Germany and Russia. For example, a treaty was concluded between Italy and Germany for the voluntary removal of German-speaking persons from the southern Tyrol. A bilateral agreement between Austria and Italy, concluded in 1947, assured certain rights to the residual German-speaking minority in the Italian South Tyrol and thereby greatly eased the task of drawing up a peace treaty for Italy, since Austria desisted from pressing her claims to the Brenner Pass and the Pustertal.[10]

After the war ended, Czechoslovakia expelled 2,400,000 German- and 100,000 Hungarian-speaking citizens, and Poland expatriated several millions of Germans. Presumably, these constituted attempts to forestall a repetition of the events of 1938 and 1939. This action threw additional economic burdens on both Germany and Hungary while, at the same time, it gravely affected the economy of Czechoslovakia and Poland. Understandable though the Czech and Polish reaction may have been for political reasons, the expulsion of these people was a "solution" which worked severe hardship on all parties concerned. The expatriated minorities lost their homes; Czechoslovakia and Poland lost the labor of the most highly skilled elements of their respec-

---

more than frontier making. The Congress of Berlin was an example of peaceful change. The unilateral denunciation in 1870 by Russia of the Black Sea clauses of the Treaty of Paris and the annexation of Bosnia and Herzegovina were peaceful changes of another type. Note also the various attempts to settle differences concerning buffer states like Belgium, Rumania, Bulgaria, and Albania by putting into power members of the junior branches of houses ruling over major nations. On peaceful change between 1815 and 1914, see C. R. M. F. Cruttwell, *A History of Peaceful Change in the Modern World* (New York, Oxford, 1937). Postwar problems are discussed in Charles A. W. Manning (ed.), *Peaceful Change: An International Problem* (London, Macmillan & Co., Ltd., 1937). This book contains contributions by C. K. Webster, A. J. Toynbee, L. C. Robbins, T. E. Gregory, Lucy P. Mair, K. Mannheim, H. Lauterpacht, and C. A. W. Manning. See also Bryce Wood, *Peaceful Change and the Colonial Problem* (New York, Columbia University Press, 1940).

[9] See Sir John Hope Simpson, *The Refugee Problem: Report of a Survey,* New York, Oxford, 1939, pp. 11–28.

[10] See John C. Campbell, *The United States in World Affairs 1945–1947,* New York, Harper, 1947, pp. 128, 143.

tive populations; [11] the countries receiving the refugees incurred a vastly increased social burden.

Thousands of German-speaking persons were removed from territories taken over by the Soviet Union during the phase of German-Russian friendship, 1939–1941. Russia also carried out several population transfers from her newly annexed areas to the interior. Balts and Poles were removed in large numbers to Russia's eastern and Asiatic territories and replaced by Russians; 400,000 Volga Germans, and 600,000 Crimean Tatars, Kalmucks, and Checheno-Ingush, formerly organized as Autonomous Soviet Socialist Republics, were removed from their former habitat and dispersed over the less hospitable regions of Siberia.[12]

Population exchange as a method of frontier adjustment may be applicable in certain cases, yet it is obvious that it is economically impossible to shift large numbers of people throughout the world. Such shifts would greatly reduce the productivity of affected areas and neighboring areas. Migrations would be immediately resumed, especially if large low-pressure as well as high-pressure areas had been created. The remedy would be temporary in effectiveness and worse than the disease—not to mention the barbarity of the method, which must lead to the destruction of many human lives.

The idea of peaceful change of frontiers has another obvious shortcoming: as a common practice, it would make international relations even more unstable. No boundary question ever could be permanently settled; as soon as a settlement was reached, the party which considered the deal detrimental to itself would embark on a campaign to carry out peaceful change, that is, to undo the recently effected settlement. By its very nature, peaceful change can be a useful method only if used under exceptional circumstances. As a standard procedure in international relations, it would engender chaos.

Hence it can be argued that problems of frontiers should be solved without boundary changes and that this may be done by changing the *functions* of boundaries and adjusting obsolete boundary settlements to modern requirements. It should be the task of the United Nations to originate specific frontier reforms. Functions of frontiers should, on the United Nations initiative, be redefined along the lines discussed above and boundaries be simplified so that they constitute the least impediment to movements of goods and persons. Lastly, it would be advisable to form larger units, especially economic regions, or at least to remove those artificial obstacles which, though beneficial to vested interests, lower the general standard of living. These steps must be accompanied by measures designed to protect linguistic, religious, cultural and national groups. Such measures are fraught with formidable difficulties; there is no fully reliable method for protecting a minority from

[11] Joseph Fetter, *The Sudetens, A Moral Question,* New York, William Frederick Press, 1946.

[12] See Eugene M. Kulischer, *Europe on the Move, War and Population Changes 1917–1947,* New York, Columbia University Press, 1948, pp. 297–299.

persecution except the use of force against the persecutor. Fortunately, many cases are susceptible to peaceful settlement, and legal help (arbitration) as well as United Nations support may, in some instances, furnish the instrumentalities for effective change. Fear of nationalistic or cultural conflicts should not interfere with the making of frontiers that would provide for the efficient working of a common economy.

The Demilitarized Frontier. High on the agenda of international frontier reform stands the problem of making frontiers militarily less dangerous than most of them are today. The demilitarization of frontiers is one of the oldest devices of history. Caesar noted that the lands of the Suevi and Cherusci were separated by large and dense woods which acted "like a natural wall" and prevented military contacts (*De Bello Gallico,* liber VI). Korea and China were, for many centuries, separated by a broad and uncultivated tract of land in which nationals of neither state were permitted to settle. In 1390, a treaty was signed between Zurich and Austria exempting from warfare the valley of the Lake of Zurich; similar demilitarized zones were then called *Friedland,* or land of peace. It was out of such a beginning that the neutrality of Switzerland later arose. In 1815, the town of Cracow, with its territory, was declared to be forever a "Strictly Neutral City, under the protection of Austria, Russia, and Prussia"; it was stipulated that "no military establishment shall be formed that can menace the Neutrality of Cracow" and "no armed force shall be introduced upon any pretense whatever" (Articles VI, VIII, and IX of the treaty signed at Vienna on June 9, 1815). In November, 1846, the treaty was repudiated by the three protecting powers. Cracow had become the seat of revolutionary plotters, and the town was reincorporated into Austria, despite British and French protests—a somewhat ambiguous case both of demilitarization and "peaceful change."

A treaty concluded in 1858 between Costa Rica and Nicaragua contained the following article:

On no account whatever, not even in case of war, if it should unfortunately occur between the Republics of Nicaragua and Costa Rica, shall any act of hostility be allowed between them in the port of San Juan del Norte, nor on the river of that name, nor on Lake Nicaragua.

This clause was introduced in order to safeguard the traffic of a canal which was to have been built across the isthmus of Nicaragua. A treaty concluded in 1829 between Peru and Colombia created a demilitarized zone along the boundaries of both countries. Between 1885 and 1896, various land frontiers were demilitarized, such as those of the Congo (1885), Gold Coast (1888), Siam (1893), Burma-China (1894), Wakhan (1895), and Burma-Indo-China (1896).[13]

---

[13] For these and other examples, see James H. Marshall-Cornwall, *Geographic Disarmament: A Study of Regional Demilitarization,* New York, Oxford, 1935.

In 1864 the British Foreign Secretary, Lord Russell, when mediating the Danish-Prussian-Austrian War, proposed that the German Confederation, in return for the Danish provinces and as a condition for the future security of Denmark, should undertake "neither to erect nor to maintain any fortresses, nor to establish any fortified harbors, in the territory ceded by Denmark." This proposal was not accepted by the Confederation, one reason being that Germany had laid plans for the construction of the Kiel naval base.

In 1905, the Treaty of Portsmouth, ending the Russo-Japanese War, forbade the erection of fortifications on the island of Sakhalin and insured free navigation in the Straits of La Pérouse and Tartary. This treaty was observed—on the whole, faithfully—until the end of the Second World War. It was patterned after a treaty concluded in 1904 between France and Britain with respect to the nonfortification of the Moroccan coast. The Rhineland was demilitarized from 1919 to 1936.

The concept of the demilitarized zone is closely related to that of the buffer state. Russia was surrounded by a contiguous arc of buffer states, not only in Europe but also in Asia. It was separated from China by Outer Mongolia; from India it was separated partly by Tibet, by the Wakhan Corridor in the Pamir up to the headwaters of the Amu Darya, and by Afghanistan; from the Persian Gulf by Iran; and from the Mediterranean by Turkey. Such buffer states fulfill their "damper" function only as long as the competing major powers are interested in the *status quo*. As soon as this interest flags in one camp, the erstwhile buffer tends to fall into the hands of the other camp.

The advent of air power has changed the problem of regional demilitarization considerably. The existence or nonexistence of a narrow demilitarized zone now makes little difference, since noncontiguous states still are able to fight each other. Perhaps methods will be devised to demilitarize areas even in the age of air power, for instance by excluding certain cities, "open cities," from the lists of possible bombing targets. In Europe, the Vatican, and in the war against Japan, Kyoto and Nara were not bombed. Despite the emergence of air power, a ubiquitous increase in the number of demilitarized zones may have a beneficial effect.

At this stage it is impossible to formulate a clear program for frontier making in the future. The functions of frontiers will inevitably change, and no one can now say what precise form change will take. New types will develop by trial and error; they cannot be created by arbitrary decree. The foregoing discussion suggests two simple conclusions as starting points of a new frontier policy: (1) the traditional function of frontiers has become obsolete and, in fact, endangers international peace and economic progress; and (2) frontiers should be modified so as to become less rigid, less divisive, and more adaptable to changing conditions. It has become necessary to replace the line frontier by frontier *zones,* and the single frontier by *multiple* frontiers, divisive borders by *frontiers of cooperation.*

THE TECHNIQUE OF PEACEMAKING

All civilized men will agree that the transcendent aim of Western civilization is that of turning men toward universal and eternal peace. Yet, as long as armed conflict between alliances, blocs, or individual nations remains a possibility, it is dangerous and utopian to confound the idealistic goal of universal peace with the practical art of peacemaking. The right intention does not necessarily mean employment of the right procedure. Peacemaking, therefore, may be looked upon as a craft, requiring special knowledge and skills, instead of as a noble effort directed at reestablishing the allegedly "natural" state of things: peace. As practically each of the delegates to a peace conference entertains a different picture of that "natural" state of things, the problems of peacemaking cannot be solved by the application of generalities.

Hence, the art of peacemaking is centered upon the task of staking out a concrete area of agreement upon which necessarily divergent views can be reconciled. The delegate of a power presents his views, usually embodied in a draft treaty, in the very beginning. Thereafter a compromise may be hammered out, because in peacemaking, as opposed to commercial or other contractual negotiations, a solution must be found and agreed upon by all contracting parties. The acknowledged failure to find such a solution, or even the general recognition of the inadequacy of a solution, may mean the resumption of warfare or a prolonged "no-war-no-peace" situation. In 1814, Napoleon negotiated with the Allied powers at the Conference of Châtillon. The French delegate was unable to find a basis for discussion, as the divergences between Napoleon's and the Allies' peace views were clearly unbridgeable. The conference broke up; the campaign continued and eventually ended with the fall of the Emperor.

Generally, however, some kind of basis for agreement exists when the peacemaking powers assemble. Dramatic differences of opinion and approach are often greater and seemingly more insuperable than in other contractual negotiations. Yet in spite of the differences and the rancors they engender, the peace treaty *is* signed because, in contrast to other negotiations, the contracting parties are never on an equal footing: the stark reality of *relative power* dominates the scene.

Victors and Vanquished. The most important relation is that between victor and vanquished. From prehistoric times to our very day, every peace treaty was to a certain extent the victor's peace. Seldom did a war end in a stalemate. In 1885, a short war was fought between Bulgaria and Serbia. Military operations ceased soon after Austria-Hungary entered the scene as an energetic mediator. Not having been able to score decisive victories, the two warring powers quickly restored the *status quo ante bellum* with this tersely worded treaty: "Peace is restored." In 1748, the War of the Austrian Succession ended with the Peace of Aix-la-Chapelle. While there was a for-

mal distinction between victorious and defeated powers, the balance within
the warring alliances resulted in a peacemaking of compromise, where territories were swapped to and fro between the negotiating powers. International
intervention may stop a war in its stage of germination—as, for example,
League of Nations intervention resulted in settling such conflicts as those
between Peru and Colombia in the Leticia War of 1932 and in the Gran Chaco
War between Bolivia and Paraguay in 1933–1934. But in the last centuries
no important contest ended in a tie. Thus the problems of peacemaking consist of two discrete sets: the problems of the victors and those of the vanquished.

The Roman cry *"Vae victis!"* is echoed by the peacemakers of the ages.
The victorious peacemaker has always aimed at reaping all the fruits of victory and at obtaining safeguards against all kinds of probable or improbable
future attempts of the defeated to reverse the settlement. The peacemaking
of the defeated centers upon the immediate task of securing national survival and, in the long run, a possible regrouping of forces to restore the
vanquished's former power position. A typical victor's peace was the Peace
of Westphalia in 1648, by the conclusion of which France was able to prevent the unification of Germany for more than two centuries. A brilliant feat
of peacemaking on the part of the vanquished was accomplished by Prince
Talleyrand, who exploited the basic differences between Britain, Austria,
Prussia, and Russia and thus was able to secure the best possible conditions
for France in 1815, when that defeated country seemed to have irrevocably
forfeited her place as a major power.

In our century, which is dominated by ideological conflicts, irrational factors increasingly determine the approach to peace. The warriors of ancient
times took relish in demeaning their enemies and, in addition to having
extorted all the concrete advantages of the victor, staged abroad and at
home spectacular demonstrations, which were not only to manifest the annihilation of the opponent's military and economic might, but also to humble
his pride, prowess, morale, and virtue. Such an approach to peacemaking is
inevitable in world wars of conflicting ideologies, and the atavisms of primitive civilization have marred many a peace settlement in our era.

Territorial War Aims. Wars are fought in space and for space; hence
the main problems of peacemaking are territorial, although in modern times
peacemaking has assumed also *social* aspects: the destruction of entire societies and the dispersal of classes and even nationalities. The territorial aims
of the peacemaking powers are formulated before and during the war; these
aims may be professed openly or kept secret. Italy, immediately preceding
her entrance into World War I, secured secret agreements from the Western
Allies (Treaty of London) who promised Italy important Adriatic and
Mediterranean gains after the war.[14] Italy then entered the war and—when

[14] The story of the Treaty of London, as seen from Italy, is told by L. Aldrovandi
Marescotti, *Guerra diplomatica: Ricordi e Frammenti di Diario (1914–1919)*, Milan, Mondadori, 1937, pp. 57–80.

the victory of the Allies seemed to be certain—concluded two additional agreements for the enlargement of empire. Yet, after the war was over, commitments made by the Western Allies to other parties deprived Italy of many of the territorial gains which the Allies had held out as an inducement for Italian participation in the war against the Central Powers.

Thus, the actual aims and goals of the belligerent powers may gradually change as the war progresses. A great power may enter a war without having concretely defined its aims at the outset of hostilities; this may later lead to great difficulties. In the summer of 1798, the Maltese Knights appealed for help to Russia after Napoleon's Egyptian fleet had seized their island. This seemingly unimportant event influenced Paul I decisively; he made up his mind to join the Second Coalition against France. To the detriment of the Coalition, the Russian war aims emerged only gradually as the war progressed. Paul's successor, Alexander I, fought Napoleon in 1812 without having clearly formulated the aims of Russian policy beyond mere survival. Only when the French armies were defeated and the bulk of the Russians— against the advice of Alexander's commander in chief, General Kutuzov— crossed the Russian frontiers in pursuit of Napoleon in January, 1813, did Alexander's mind turn to territorial ambitions, which grew and diminished according to his military fortunes.

It often happens that a power, having stated its territorial war aims, decides subsequently to incorporate an additional region whose annexation was not envisaged at the outset of the campaign. Rumania joined the attack on Soviet Russia in June, 1941, in order to reconquer the lost province of Bessarabia. Yet, as the German and Rumanian armies pushed deep into the Ukraine, Marshal Antonescu decided to annex the territory between the rivers Bug and Dniester in addition to Bessarabia.

Under modern conditions of "sociological" warfare, territorial objectives have lost some of their former importance. The Western Allies meant it when, in the Atlantic Charter, they disclaimed territorial ambitions; all they were interested in, at least in Europe, was the destruction of the Nazi and Fascist regimes. The Soviets constantly have been aiming at territorial aggrandizement, but their *primary* objective has been the installation of communist or communist-controlled regimes which, regardless of the borders, ultimately will join the Soviet Union with their entire territory. The crux of all future peace settlements probably will be the question of what type of political (and economic) regime is to be established in the vanquished state.

Preliminaries of Peacemaking. As one power is prone to maximize its peace aims at the moment victory seems to be assured, another power inclines toward a compromise when victory seems to be remote, doubtful, or too costly. The first peace feelers are sent out through many likely and unlikely and circuitous channels. One most delicate operation of peacemaking is the choice of the most propitious moment for such action. The psychological factor enters here, too, as no power intends by initiating peace sound-ings to convey the impression that it is tired of warfare.

The next step toward peace is the armistice. In World War II, it was in November, 1942, when the tide seemed to have turned with the battles of El Alamein and Stalingrad, the North African invasion, and the halting of the Japanese advance, that the first tentative approaches were made in Lisbon and Ankara by certain Italian personalities and by the Hungarian and Ru-manian governments toward local British and American representatives. Such preliminary negotiations are usually initiated in neutral territories through neutral channels. It was the Soviet Ambassadress to Sweden, Mme. Kollontai, who negotiated with the Finns during the armistice talks of 1943–1944. In our times, short-wave radio assumes a decisive role as a means of negotiation; personal contact is often confined to the presentation of cre-dentials and to the formal signing of the armistice. In World War II, the romantic medium of eminent prisoners of war was used, just as during the Napoleonic Wars. For example, the British General Carton de Wiart, who had been taken prisoner in Africa, traveled from Italy to Portugal in August, 1943, in order to prepare the Italian armistice negotiations.

The word armistice defines a short period of time elapsing between the temporary halting and the later resumption of hostilities. Napoleon and his enemies often resorted to armistice as a purely technical measure, serving the advantage of both warring sides. The Armistice of Plaswitz in the summer of 1813 enabled Napoleon's opponents to regroup their armies and prepare for the decisive battle of Leipzig a few months later.

Nowadays it seems that such purely "technical" armistices are practically unknown, except when imposed by an international authority and accom-panied by threats of reprisal by a superior moral or actual force, such as the Palestine truce of 1948. In both wars, the term armistice was meant to define the cessation of hostilities without the implication of a probable future renewal of the fighting; in other words, while originally armistice meant a temporary interruption of warfare, more recent practice makes it a stage of transition from war to peace. The provisions of a modern armistice deal with such a variety of questions that they include almost all the provisions of the forthcoming peace treaties. The armistices of World War II with Italy, Rumania, Finland, Bulgaria, Hungary, and Japan contained practically the same conditions as the actual treaties of peace. It is not impossible that in the future armistice and peace may be merging into one function.

The armistice concluded with Germany in 1945 has not, at the time of this writing in 1954, been followed up by a peace treaty. Only the relations of the Western Allies with Germany were amended by a "contractual agree-ment," but Germany's relations with Russia remained in suspense, except that the Soviets exploited this confused situation to transform Eastern Germany into a "satellite." The armistice in Korea put an end to a three years' war. Yet the belligerents have thus far not concluded a peace treaty.

Old and New Diplomacy. While military matters and personalities dominate the scene of the armistice, the question of peacemaking is in the hands
of the diplomats. Whereas the armistice issues from a concrete military situation, the nature of the peace is predetermined by considerably less tangible
factors, among which not only the distribution of military power, but the
predispositions, attitudes, and power balances of the nations involved are of
paramount importance.

How such attitudes can dominate the actual work of peacemaking and
indeed make history for decades and perhaps centuries is shown in the brilliant writings of Harold Nicholson, who analyzed in a three-volume diplomatic history—of which Volume I is highly relevant to this discussion—the
"old diplomacy," "peacemaking," and "postwar diplomacy," covering approximately the years 1915–1925. After World War II, Nicholson published
a concise "study in allied unity" about the Congress of Vienna.[15] In these
books, the practices of "old diplomacy" are extolled, and while Nicholson
studiously abstains from any criticism of "new" diplomatic methods, it is
clear from his writings that he is recounting the deeds and prowess of "old-
style" peacemaking in order to leave it to the reader to contrast these with
the methods and actions of our days. Nicholson's path has been followed by
other eminent scholars.

Patently, modern peacemaking has failed, for the world cannot be said to
be at peace in an epoch of "Cold War." What, then, is the reason for the
failure of "new" diplomacy? The answer may be found in the irrational
atmosphere which surrounded the peacemaking of the two world wars and in
those circumstances which had transformed these wars between nations into
struggles between fighting ideologies. Ross Hoffman wrote: [16]

All wars, even the smallest, are revolutionary in the sense that violence is done and
the broken crockery of the *status quo ante bellum* is never pieced together again.
. . . But a war that is preeminently revolutionary in character is what is widely
called today an ideological war. It is much more than a collision between States
motivated by limited purposes which can only be achieved by force. There is in it
a challenge to all the world; on one side or both, there is an effort to vindicate or
propagate universally an ideological purpose. The *rationale* of a better world has
been revealed and there is an apocalyptic vision of the world remade and man reborn.

World War I, which started out as an imperialistic contest between nations, was transformed into an ideological war by 1918, when the Allies
adopted Wilson's Fourteen Points and "national self-determination" as their
supreme peace aims. World War II had been transformed into an ideological
war by January, 1943, when the English-speaking powers, who originally

---

[15] Harold Nicholson, *Studies in Modern Diplomacy,* Vol. I, "Portrait of a Diplomatist";
Vol. II, "Peacemaking"; Vol. III, "Curzon: The Last Phase"; and *The Congress of
Vienna,* London, Constable, 1947.

[16] Ross Hoffman, "Peacemaking after Ideological Wars," *Thought,* Vol. 20, No. 78,
October, 1945.

fought a war in the magnanimous spirit of the Atlantic Charter and hence for the purpose of redressing the balance of the world in order to free mankind from the menace of totalitarian ideologies, adopted the total formula of "unconditional surrender," a slogan which reflected the growing pressure of ideologically inflamed public opinion.

Our aim here is not a critique of "national self-determination" or of "unconditional surrender." These professed goals may be theoretically defended or assailed with equal justice from a purely ethical standpoint. Yet in practice, without a previously defined understanding as to how they were to be applied to concrete cases, they remained hollow and empty phrases. Two years after 1917 and 1943, respectively, the concrete tasks of peacemaking emerged, and it became evident that these lofty formulas not only were inadequate in the moment of victory but actually hampered the freedom of action of the Western powers, who discovered that their strict adherence to these phrases had strengthened the position of Soviet Russia to their own detriment.

The principle of self-determination was invoked in 1919 against Austria-Hungary and Turkey and led to the breakup of these balancing empires. It could not be applied to Germany, which remained the strongest continental power, or to Russia, which thus was given the opportunity to develop Bolshevism as a threat against the entire world. In World War II, the "unconditional surrender" of Germany created a power vacuum in Europe which almost upset the world power balance to the advantage of Soviet Russia. Yet it took almost four years before the Western Allies realized that they could not afford, for their own security interests, the destruction of Germany. The degradation of war aims by their own propagandists blinded the Western powers to the true nature of their own vital interests. The "punishment" of Germany became the self-punishment of the West.[17]

The Process of Peacemaking. Let us examine now the actual process of peacemaking.

Well before the assembly of the peace conference, extensive preparations are made by the interested powers. Roughly, these preparations may be divided into two categories: technical and diplomatic-political.

The technical preparation aims at the successful presentation of the case of the interested power at the peace conference. It consists of research, compilation, and elaboration of statistical and documentary material, in order to substantiate the points for which the delegation would be arguing. Experts elaborate claims for frontiers on the basis of population statistics, historical rights, economic relationships, and so forth. Most of the material is compiled long in advance, and much of it may turn out to be useless by the time the peace treaties are negotiated, as a shift in the relative power situation

---

[17] The slogan of unconditional surrender was based on the untenable concept of the "collective guilt" of the German people. Fallacious ideas are nearly always fraught with dangerous consequences.

may, in the meantime, have brought about a change in the peace aims of the power.

While the technical preparations are argumentative and center around the presentation of peace aims, the diplomatic-political preparations aim at the attainment of these peace aims by creating favorable alignment of powers at the peace conference. At the end of World War I, the interests of Yugoslavia and Italy, although fighting in the same camp, conflicted gravely on important territorial issues (Trieste and the Dalmatian coast). It was due to clever diplomatic preparations and a change of attitude on the part of the French that the Paris Peace Conference gave favorable consideration to the Yugoslav claims as against the arguments advanced by Italy. Diplomatic preparations are therefore of vital importance and are usually conducted while war is still being waged. There are cases, however, when diplomatic realignments may well occur immediately before or during the peace conference. Thus the representative of defeated France, Tallyrand, maneuvered so cleverly in September–October, 1814, that he was able to win British assent to his most important proposals just before the Vienna Congress sat down to work.

There is another phase of the preparatory work which, to a certain extent, combines the characteristics of both the technical and the diplomatic-political phase of preparations. This is the task of propaganda. Nowadays, when "public opinion" in most democratic states influences foreign policy directly and palpably, it is of great importance that the argument of a major or minor nation should receive a sympathetic hearing before the public of a powerful democratic country. When an influential newspaper or, in states where the radio is not nationalized, an influential radio commentator is willing to espouse the usually unfamiliar peace aims of another country, this may amount to the equivalent of a victory in battle. "Public opinion" is prone to formulate opinions in a certain stereotyped pattern, especially in fields of which it has but a superficial understanding. While during the last century even in democratic countries public opinion exercised but little direct influence on foreign policies, it had, in the peacemaking which followed the Spanish-American War of 1898, a decisive bearing on President McKinley's attitude.[18] Eight years later, when the United States was mediating between Russia and Japan at the close of the Russo-Japanese War, the genial Russian Foreign Minister Witte visited the United States and went out of his way to influence by his personal demeanor and fervent professions of good will various segments of the American public, that is, he won over the public opinion of the *mediating* power. It was an adroit campaign of successful propaganda waged by many central and eastern European nationalities, foremost among them

[18] In 1814–1815, British public opinion forced the Tory government to propose the abolition of slave trade at the Congress of Vienna. For the pressure exerted by the American public upon the formation of foreign policy, see Thomas A. Bailey, *The Man in the Street*, New York, Macmillan, 1948.

the Czechs, Poles, and Lithuanians, which convinced the American public that President Wilson was right in calling for "national self-determination."

Conversely, the awakening of American public opinion to the nature of communism imposed on the American government the need to resist Soviet claims concerning the peace treaties with Italy and Japan.

The selection of the place where the negotiations are to be held is again dependent on the relations between the victor and the vanquished. It is an age-old ambition of the victor to "dictate peace" in the capital of the defeated enemy; it was in the "preliminary treaty" signed in Versailles that Prussia imposed humiliating terms on France after the Franco-Prussian War in March, 1871. The final treaty was signed in Frankfurt two months later. In 1919, the French retaliated and made the Germans sign the peace treaty in Versailles. Hitler forced the French to sign the Armistice of 1940 in Compiègne, in the same railroad car where Marshal Foch received the German representatives at the Armistice of 1918. The United Nations peace with Japan (1951) was signed in San Francisco. The location of the peace conference may be a neutral place. For example, the War of 1812 ended with a treaty signed in Ghent, 1814. Often it is the mediating power which proposes to the belligerent powers to meet at a place within its own territory (Peace of Portsmouth, N.H., in 1906, concluding the war between Japan and Russia). Sometimes the mediating power or powers suggest a place not within their territories but in still another neutral country. France and Britain proposed the Swiss city of Lausanne for the peace negotiations between Turkey and Greece in 1923.

The treaties thus go down in history marked by the place where they were signed, and we think and speak about the Treaties of London, Aix-la-Chapelle, Kiel, and so on. The place name is not necessarily that of a city. For example, the Peace of Westphalia was signed in the towns of Münster and Osnabrück in the Westphalian region. The locality where the signatures are appended is not always identical with the place where the decisive negotiations are held. For example, in 1814–1815, the fate of Europe was dealt with in all of its details by the Congress sitting in Vienna, while the actual peace treaties marking the end of the Napoleonic era were signed in Paris. A century later, the Congress of Paris remade the map of Europe, while the various peace treaties bear the name of those Parisian suburbs where they were actually signed: Versailles, Saint-Germain, Neuilly, Trianon, and Sèvres.

Participation. The first task of the peacemakers is to determine the participants and to define the exact agenda of the peace conference.

Determining the participants is a much more complicated task than it may seem at first sight. It is, of course, logical that all powers who participated in the war should share in the making of the peace. It is equally logical that some powers would have to be granted broader rights at the conference table than others. Argentina and Turkey declared war on Germany in the spring of 1945. It would be a travesty if these two states carried as much weight in making peace with Germany as, for example, Britain. On the other hand,

Denmark, because of exceptional circumstances, did not maintain a formal state of war with Germany; yet the Danish contribution to the fight against Hitler was immeasurably greater than that of, for example, Chile; in addition, Danish interests are vitally affected by a German settlement. Russia could not be prevented from participating at the San Francisco Conference; but it was necessary to "neutralize" the activities of the Soviets completely lest the treaty not be signed at all or be signed on Soviet terms. In the summer of 1953, the General Assembly of the United Nations passed, after stormy debate, a proposal for a political conference which was to have settled the Korean War. The General Assembly rejected a Soviet counterproposal for a round-table conference with the participation of the Soviet Union, several Asian nations who had not fought in Korea, and Czechoslovakia and Poland as "neutrals." Had the Soviets had their way, the conference would have been stacked against those members of the United Nations who *had* fought North Korean and Chinese aggression, and the Soviets would have dominated the peace negotiations—although they pretended that they were "non-belligerents."

A most ticklish diplomatic task is that of determining invitations to a peace conference. In 1814, Austria and Britain objected to the presence of various Prussian and Russian "satellites" at the Congress of Vienna. They partially succeeded in eliminating these; however, France and Britain had to acquiesce in the fact that the King of Saxony was not invited to Vienna since he had been one of the allies of Napoleon. Thus the paradoxical situation arose that the universal enemy, France, was a full participant because of her change of sovereign and administration, while a former French satellite was unequivocally excluded from peacemaking. A somewhat similar situation occurred in 1946: Italy, Bulgaria, Rumania, Hungary, Finland, and the German puppet states of Croatia and Slovakia had been at war with Britain, the United States, and the Soviet Union.[19] The great powers disregarded the declarations of war in the case of Slovakia and Croatia, because these states had once been parts of Czechoslovakia and Yugoslavia. As these two latter states were recognized by the end of the war as full members of the victorious United Nations, the Slovaks and Croats were regarded by the peacemakers as mere components of the victorious democratic states, while Italy and the five other "satellites" had to sign peace treaties condemning them as collaborators of Nazi Germany. These treaties included terms which, in the case of Hungary, were to the advantage of the Slovaks and Croats.

The list of participants does not indicate who are the active peacemakers and who are the subjects of peacemaking, although that is the most decisive question. Both in 1919–1920 and in 1946, the minor allies of Germany had hardly an opportunity to present their case fully; the peace treaty depended

[19] Finland was not at war with the United States, and Bulgaria did not declare war on the U.S.S.R.

entirely upon the decisions of the great powers.[20] Because of the protracted difficulties in the way of proceeding toward a German peace treaty, the Potsdam Agreement of July, 1945, may well be considered today as the preliminary peace treaty for Germany; without sovereign government, Germany became the subject of peacemaking. If we suppose, however, that the July, 1944, attempt would have brought about the assassination of Hitler and the establishment of an anti-Nazi German government, this regime might have been permitted to present its case at the end of hostilities.

In the age of ideological wars, systems of government enter into the consideration of the great powers in their approach to peace settlements. Because the French Vichy regime was anti-British and Fascist, Hitler granted better armistice conditions to France in June, 1940, than he would have been willing to do had the French withdrawn to North Africa under their lawfully chosen government. Sometimes this procedure is reversed, and changes in regimes may be influenced by promises on the part of a great power or powers in regard to peacemaking. When the Soviets decided to remove the Liberal-Conservative Radescu government of Rumania in March, 1945, and supplant it with the Soviet stooge Groza, the acquiescence of the King was obtained not only by personal pressure but by hinting that, should the change occur smoothly, the Soviets would insist upon the complete restoration of Rumania's prewar western frontiers, an issue which had previously been left in doubt by Stalin.

The subjects of peacemaking are not necessarily warring powers; often, international arbitration may prevent the outbreak of a war. Arbitration is usually the result of intervention on the part of great powers, who offer their good offices to the quarreling minor powers, not so much because of their partiality to pacific solutions, but rather because an outbreak of hostilities would be against their interests. Thus the Axis powers mediated between Czechoslovakia and Hungary and Rumania and Hungary in the two Vienna Awards of 1938 and 1940 and were instrumental in bringing about the Dobruja settlement between Bulgaria and Rumania in 1940.

Agenda. There is ample occasion not only for minor preliminary skirmishes but for major diplomatic battles over the determination of the peace conference's agenda. It is here that questions of competence and problems of spheres of interest arise and that the basic differences in the peacemakers' concepts are revealed. The great peace conferences and congresses of history always had an exalted, universal character. The great problems of redesigning the world order, drawing frontiers, and restoring trade give rise to a

[20] On the role of the great and small powers in the peacemaking 1945–1947, see Campbell, *op. cit.,* pp. 64–74 and *passim*. The London Conference of the Council of Foreign Ministers of September, 1945, broke up on the issue of the satellite peace treaties, for the Soviet Union viewed the armistice agreements with Hungary and Rumania as *de facto* settlements requiring no more than formal ratification.

host of lesser questions. For example, the Congress of Vienna, amidst its tremendous and complicated labors involving the fortunes of great states and ancient dynasties, took time out to deal with such questions as slave trade and the problems of the German Jews. Incidentally, the Congress of Vienna dealt with these questions effectively and humanely.

With the growth of the modern system of international exchanges, economic questions gained gradually more and more importance on the peacemakers' agenda. The disposition of war booty is an age-old concern of the victors; economic problems came to preoccupy peacemakers from the 18th century onward. In the Treaty of Utrecht of 1713 Britain secured favorable provisions for her merchantmen in regard to the slave-trading monopoly in the Spanish colonies of America—the so-called *Asiento*. It was the Congress of Vienna which for the first time conceived the idea of economic sanctions. These sanctions were to be invoked against those nations who continued to engage in the slave trade. In 1817, Alexander I resorted to this device, using it as one of the weapons with which he planned to intervene against the rebellious South American colonies.

After the Franco-Prussian War, France was able to pay Germany within four years an indemnity of 4 billion francs. By contrast, the complexity and interdependence of modern world economy vitiated the economic provisions of the World War I peace treaties which had been stipulated without a clear notion of economic conditions and mechanisms.

The reparations imposed in 1947 by Russia on Germany's former allies became a vehicle for the economic subjugation of these countries. The dismantling of German industry enhanced the Soviet war potential and imposed upon German economy, severely strained by wartime dislocations, additional heavy burdens, with the result that the United States and Britain were compelled to help Germany with substantial sums—the victors paying tribute to the vanquished.

The experience of two world wars seems to indicate that the idea of economic reparations is impractical. Undoubtedly, the aggressor should pay for the economic loss which he caused in the countries he assaulted. Yet these payments can be made only at the detriment of the going concern of the defeated aggressor country's economy and, hence, its political stability. Within limits, the vanquished always will have to bring economic sacrifices. But insistence on "reparations" is indicative of a psychology preoccupied with the past. The peacemaker should rather concentrate on building the future.

When there are several peace treaties to be dealt with, one of the problems of the peacemakers is to define the so-called "greater agenda." In 1814, as well as in 1919, the Allies followed the practice of dealing with the major peace treaty first and then taking up the minor ones. The Peace of Versailles was concluded in June, 1919, and the five treaties of the Paris suburbs followed in succession from September, 1919, to August, 1920. After World

War II, the order was reversed; first came the so-called "satellite" treaties in 1946, and the German and Japanese treaties were left to follow.[21]

The main brunt of the work in the actual peacemaking procedure is borne by technical experts and professional diplomats. It is not unusual that a whole planning section is set up in a foreign office in order to deal with the conference preparations. The material is prepared with considerable care and secrecy, and the different arguments and facts are arranged before the conference—just as cannons are put in position on a battlefield. It is a usual practice of the various delegations to hold *résumés* every morning where the momentary situation is defined, new developments are taken into consideration, and the tactics of the day are outlined.

Although the delegations are mainly composed of professional diplomats and experts of long standing, they reflect to a certain extent the internal political balance of their respective countries, and it often occurs that only strict, self-imposed discipline can prevent the appearance of divergences between the various delegates' opinions. The delegations of most "satellites" to the peace conference held in 1946, for example, contained communist members who often pursued entirely different aims than the other members. Sometimes the dissensions within a delegation supply the comic relief of the serious business of peacemaking; in such cases, the responsibility falls upon the chief delegate. For example, in 1814–1815 Spain's chief delegate, Don Pedro Labrador, was the laughingstock of the Congress of Vienna. While incongruities within the peace delegations may have indeed unfortunate effects, divergent actions taken simultaneously on other stations of the diplomatic front may prove as embarrassing. Thus the whole Italian settlement of 1814–1815, which was sponsored by Britain's Castlereagh, was endangered by the fact that the British Minister to Sicily, Lord William Bentinck, an idealistic Whig and recalcitrant Liberal, pursued an anti-Austrian policy in exact opposition to Castlereagh's course in Vienna. This state of affairs only ceased with the Minister's removal from his post. The French Minister to Vienna in 1919, Allizé, opposed many of Clemenceau's ideas, yet his opinion, while listened to by some delegates, was not decisive enough to influence the general French conduct at the conference table.

The basis of the argument is elaborated by the various commissions. The commission-type handling of peace conference problems became a usage by the late 17th century. The central commission in the 18th and 19th centuries bore the name of "statistical commission" as in those times "statistics" included all the economic, ethnic, financial, and political data referring to a certain state or region. Expert commissions came into existence as technical political problems became more complicated and diverse. The experts serving on the commissions are not always chosen from among the country's best scholars, since considerations of partisan politics not infrequently determine

---

[21] It is interesting to note that the nations of the British Commonwealth concluded a separate peace treaty with the Japanese satellite Siam (Thailand) in 1946.

their selection. Although great strides have been made toward enlisting the best talent irrespective of party affiliation, mistakes occurred and do occur. Moreover the expert is frequently relegated to formulating an advisory opinion while the chief decisions are reserved to the policy-making delegates, professional diplomats who often are not well acquainted with the factual issues involved. On the other hand, it occasionally happens that a scholar-expert is given a leading role on the executive level; in such cases, lack of diplomatic training may put him at a serious disadvantage when facing other diplomats, who are more experienced in the intricacies of international negotiations. An expert may have his own political and ideological axes to grind. Such an "expert" may then not only fail to furnish helpful advice but also sabotage the right policy.

While commissions may do excellent work, their advice may still be largely disregarded. The French experts' commissions in 1919 were staffed by brilliant diplomats and scholars, but many of their recommendations were left unheeded. It may also happen that the experts' work on the commission is of questionable value. Many of the newly created eastern European states who voiced their claims in Paris in 1919–1920, produced "experts' data" which were neither "expert" nor reliable "data." The Czechs, for example, referred to a little creek as a "navigable river." As the Western Allies had but a few experts competent in eastern European geography and economics, many such "interpretations" were accepted.

Interpretation plays a decisive role when it comes to determining ethnic situations. For example, the Austrian census of 1910 was regarded with some justification as incorrect by Czechs, Rumanians, and Yugoslavs; the great powers were inclined to accept their views in 1919. In 1938, however, Lord Runciman and Ashton-Gwatkin during their examination of the Sudeten German question mistakenly questioned the reliability of the 1930 Czech census, thus supplying valuable propaganda ammunition to Hitler. In the 1919 peace settlement the Jewish and Saxon minorities of Transylvania posed a difficult problem: the Rumanians insisted that both be counted as non-Magyar nationalities, while the Hungarians argued that those Jews who spoke the Magyar language and proclaimed themselves Hungarians be defined as such. Ultimately, the Rumanian interpretation was accepted, as Bucharest was on the victorious side in 1920. The irony of the situation was that twenty years later, when the northern part of Transylvania was reassigned to Hungary under the second Vienna Award, it was the Hungarian government which, acting under German pressure, regarded the Jews as a strictly alien and non-Magyar ethnic minority.

The atmosphere of the peace conference is the incalculable and irrational factor of peacemaking. Gone are the days when haughty prince-diplomats walked through vast halls lit by crystal candelabra; gone also, indeed, are the days of amorous excursions and boudoir intrigues; gone are the days when "the Congress danced," and when "aristocratic statesmen and diplomats, victor and vanquished alike, met in courtly . . . disputation, and, free from the clatter and babel of democracy, could reshape systems upon the fundamentals of which they were all agreed." [22] Yet the "human" element in such a dramatic and tense atmosphere as that of a peace conference still remains an important, though frequently obscure, factor. Personal relationships and strange undercurrents exert a powerful influence; personal likes and dislikes of even minor statesmen may decisively affect the fate of millions of human beings. Benjamin Franklin's popularity in Paris made the French delegates stand by the American claims with unusual consistency in 1783; the personal dislike which President Roosevelt felt for General de Gaulle almost excluded France from the peacemaking when Stalin argued against French participation at Yalta in February, 1945. Social affiliations and personal friendships are and will remain invaluable assets in the business of peacemaking; the informal and extracurricular part of the international gathering may, in many instances, be far more important than the actual work itself.

The success of peacemaking thus depends on various and unpredictable factors. But the foremost prerequisite of success is that the authority and prestige of the peacemaking powers should remain unharmed during and immediately after the conference; that not the slightest doubt should arise as to the power and willingness of the peacemakers to validate their decisions; and that not the slightest rift among member nations of the victorious coalition should be revealed to the world. Without these requirements the work of the peacemaking powers may be doomed to failure from the outset. If possible, no territorial problems should be left unsolved. Provisional demarcation lines should be clearly and unmistakably recognized as such: occupation forces should not be withdrawn before a permanent settlement is reached. Late in 1920, the Poles defied the authority of the peacemaking powers, and their General Zeligowski marched into the disputed city of Vilnius (Vilna) which by an international agreement just previously concluded was to have gone to Lithuania. When this open defiance of their authority was tolerated by the peacemaking powers, not only was a new area of friction created between two neighbor states of eastern Europe, but a precedent arose which indicated that an eventual resort to arms would make it possible to change the peace charted by the great powers and that violation of international agreements would not be met by immediate reprisals. In turn, the Lithuanians took good note of this precedent and in 1923 occupied the Memelland which, according to the original terms of the Versailles Treaty, was to have had the international status of a Free City.

Territorially minded nations pursue the goal of territorial expansion, often at the cost of sacrificing ethnic unity or "natural" frontiers. The peace aims

[22] Winston S. Churchill, *The Second World War: The Gathering Storm,* Boston, Houghton Mifflin, 1948, p. 4.

which France pursued in her various treaties from 1659 to 1797 were territorial-strategic: in the east France strove to reach the Rhine, and in the south she sought to reestablish the Pyrenees as the French-Spanish frontier. France succeeded and thereafter maintained without major difficulties her hold upon these territories, especially after the main non-French part of her population was gradually assimilated culturally by the middle of the last century (Alsace). Thereafter the "ethnic" and "natural" boundaries of France largely coincided. In other regions, and especially in eastern Europe, it is considerably more difficult to reach a just solution, as ethnic islands exist here and there and the various nationalisms do not accept the criteria of "natural" frontiers.

Britain, with remarkable foresight, established her first Mediterranean bases in the Peace of Utrecht of 1713 when she secured Gibraltar and the island of Minorca (the latter she lost in 1783 but received in return Malta in 1801), long before the Suez Canal was built and the Mediterranean became part of the British lifeline. Bismarck in 1871 insisted on the cession of at least two of the four great French fortresses in the east: Metz, Toul, Belfort, and Verdun. Similarly, territorial policies are determined by economic geography, as, for example, the present French claim to the Saar. In 1940, the second Vienna Award established the new frontier between Rumania and Hungary in a straight line with the exception of a U-like dent about 20 miles wide around the village of Kissarmas. This was the so-called "Göring Gulf," leaving to Rumania a valuable piece of land containing rich natural gas in which Hermann Göring had acquired a financial interest.

Other powers, although they pursue certain strategic aims, are not necessarily territorially minded. Such nations seek security foremost, not by extending their frontiers but by establishing a presumably just and logical boundary which is the least likely to cause friction with their neighbors and disturb the equilibrium of a greater unit, a region, or a continent. Thus Denmark in 1919, although she was offered not only the northern but also the southern German-speaking region of Schleswig-Holstein, declined to accept that small stretch of land. This does not mean that unaggressive powers would not be willing to protect their rights. In 1857 Prussia was planning to incorporate the Swiss canton of Neuchâtel-Neuenburg into the Prussian provinces. The energetic refusal and fiery indignation of the small Swiss Confederation made the Prussians recoil.

A hundred and thirty years ago, Napoleon, brooding on the island of St. Helena, was at a loss to understand the meaning of the peace which Britain made in 1815. He scanned uncomprehendingly the opportunities which Britain seemed to have missed when total victory was achieved:

After twenty years of war, after all the wealth which she has expended; after all the assistance which she gave to the common cause; after a triumph beyond all expectation—what sort of peace is it that England has signed? Castlereagh had the continent at his disposal. What great advantage, what just compensations has he acquired to his country? The peace he has made is the sort of peace he would have made if he had been beaten. I could scarcely have treated him worse, the poor wretch, if it had been I who had proved victorious! . . .

Was it ignorance, was it corruption, that induced Castlereagh to take the line he did? Nobly, so he imagined, did he distribute the spoils of victory to the sovereigns of the continent, while reserving nothing for his own country. . . . Where did England find her equivalent? England, who had been the very soul of victory, who had paid the whole cost, must now reap the harvest of European "gratitude"; the harvest of the blunders, or the treason, of her plenipotentiary. . . .

Thus Napoleon. He was territorially minded and could not understand Britain's aims: peace through equilibrium, instead of forced security through space. The peace of 1815 ushered in Britain's period of greatness and Golden Age. Perhaps the position of the United States today bears a similarity to that of Britain in 1815. The lessons of the first half of our century indicate that the gist of effective peacemaking is still technical, moral, and legal—a practical approach to detailed problems, instead of dealing with fluid and glittering generalities. As in every aspect of human relationships, it is not only erroneous but dangerous to reach for universally valid and unassailably perfect formulas. If, after a series of more or less just settlements, a better equilibrium and with it the self-confidence of nations are restored, the next— indeed, greatest—phase in international development may follow: a gradual "thinning out," or perhaps disappearance, of national frontiers.

After World War II it proved impossible, probably for the first time in history, to end a major war by a proper peace settlement. Few things show more clearly than this failure of peacemaking the bankruptcy of the modern art of statesmanship. The Western people, intoxicated with ideas of "progress" and bemused by gadgets of international organization, will have to deem themselves lucky if they succeed in merely treading water instead of being swept to perdition by the torrents which they know not how to ride or harness.

BIBLIOGRAPHY

Birdsall, Paul: *Versailles, Twenty Years After,* New York, Reynal & Hitchcock, Inc., 1941.
Boggs, S. Whittemore: *International Boundaries,* New York, Columbia University Press, 1940.
Bonsal, Stephen: *Unfinished Business,* New York, Doubleday, 1944.
Bowman, Isaiah: *The New World,* 4th ed., Yonkers, N.Y., World, 1928.
Campbell, John C.: *The United States in World Affairs 1945–1947,* New York, Harper, 1947.
Curzon of Kedleston, Lord: *Frontiers,* 2d ed., New York, Oxford, 1908.
Ferrero, Guglielmo: *The Reconstruction of Europe: Talleyrand and the Congress of Vienna 1814–1815,* New York, Putnam, 1941.
Kalijarvi, Thorsten V. (ed.): "Peace Settlements of World War II," *The Annals of the Academy of Political and Social Science,* Vol. 257, May, 1948.
Kuehnelt-Leddihn, E. R.: "The Problem of Frontiers in Postwar Europe," *Thought,* Vol. 20, No. 76, 1945.

Mantoux, Étienne: *The Carthaginian Peace: Or the Economic Consequences of Mr. Keynes,* London, Oxford, 1946.

Morgenthau, Henry: *Germany Is Our Problem,* New York, Harper, 1945.

Moseley, Philip E.: "Peace-making, 1946," *International Organization,* February, 1947.

Muralt, Leopold von: *From Versailles to Potsdam,* Chicago, Regnery, 1947.

Nicholson, Harold: *The Congress of Vienna: A Study in Allied Unity: 1812–1822,* London, Constable, 1946.

————: *Curzon, the Last Phase 1919–1925,* Boston, Houghton Mifflin, 1939.

————: *Peacemaking 1919,* London, Constable, 1933.

Rudin, Harry L.: *Armistice, 1918,* New Haven, Yale University Press, 1944.

Tardieu, André: *The Truth about the Treaty,* Indianapolis, Bobbs-Merrill, 1921.

Temperley, Harold W. V.: *A History of the Peace Conference of Paris,* 6 vols., London, Frowde, Hodder & Stoughton, 1920–1924.

U.S. Department of State: *Making the Peace Treaties 1941–1947,* Government Printing Office, February, 1947.

————: *Paris Peace Conference 1946,* Publication 2868, Conference Series 103, Government Printing Office, no date.

————: *Papers Relating to the Foreign Relations of the U.S.,* Government Printing Office, 1933 *et seq.*

Part Five

TECHNIQUES OF REVOLUTION AND THE COLD WAR

Chapter 16

INTERVENTION AND NONINTERVENTION

THE PRINCIPLE OF NONINTERVENTION

The principle of nonintervention is one of the oldest concepts which determine the foreign policy of democratic nations, especially the United States. It is rarely observed by dictatorial states, nor, for that matter, is it consistently followed by all democratic states. It is a classical case of a policy which was formulated to meet a given need and which was uncritically retained when this need no longer existed.

Nonintervention as a considered policy was originally adopted by Britain under Castlereagh and Canning to thwart the interventionist policy of the Holy Alliance. Castlereagh took the position that Britain would never accept a principle which she would not permit to be applied to herself, namely, that other powers would interfere in her domestic politics and actually determine which government she might choose. The original meaning of nonintervention was therefore almost identical with that of self-determination: each nation should be free to choose the government it likes.[1] Nonintervention is a principle which is inherent in the democratic ideology; if it were not observed, the results of elections could be set aside whenever it pleased stronger outside powers.

Like any other principle in politics, it cannot be applied automatically everywhere, at any time, and under all circumstances. It cannot be inferred from the over-all validity of the principle that it should be applied when such application produces effects contrary to those intended. Specifically, the

---

[1] Britain intervened decisively in Italy (1860) to assist the Italian people in their struggle against Austria and for self-determination (Harold Temperly and Lillian M. Penson, *Foundations of British Foreign Policy,* London, Cambridge, 1938, pp. 219–225).

principle *does not* mean that a power C intervening in B should be permitted by A to impose its rule over B.

The principle was violated time and again.[2] The Western democracies pursued interventionist policies in practically all their dealings with the Sublime Porte, in the efforts to suppress slavery and slave trade in Africa, in their successful attempt to break up the Austro-Hungarian monarchy, in their negotiations with Germany in 1918 which led to the establishment of the German republic, in the Munich agreement, in the Yalta and Potsdam agreements, in the dealings with Chiang Kai-shek, and in the discussions between the United States on one side, and France and Germany on the other, concerning the European Defense Community treaty. These interventions were sanctioned by the idea that conditions which endanger national security or world peace or affront human dignity should not be tolerated. For example, the slave trader should not be protected by a principle designed to protect the slave.

A Test Case in Absurdity. During the Spanish Civil War (1936–1939) the principle of nonintervention was applied by the Western powers in what was surely a farfetched manner. The position was taken that no help was to be accorded to either side. The French socialist government, although sympathetic to the Loyalist side, did not support the Spanish government with armaments. In January, 1937, the United States Congress extended the Neutrality Act to the Spanish Civil War, despite the fact that the Spanish government was lawfully constituted and was within its right to repress rebellion and buy arms wherever it pleased. (Incidentally, the American military and naval attachés who had been accredited to the lawful government remained throughout the war on the Loyalist side. There was no American attaché with Franco's army, where alone important military information, for example, on German armaments, could have been gathered.)

Nonintervention discriminated against the Spanish government; it amounted to *de facto* intervention in favor of Franco. Italy and Germany actively intervened with material aid, troops, and naval operations on Franco's side,[3] and Russia intervened, though less actively and efficiently, on the Loyalist side. The successful Axis intervention helped to establish a regime which, at that time, was basically hostile to the West; while a successful Soviet intervention would have established a communist regime which also would have been hostile to the West and which, moreover, would have

---

[2] A simple cross-check showed that in 200 sample revolutions between 1900 and 1948, intervention took place in some form in about 100 cases and in about half of these cases more than one foreign power intervened. These figures do not take into account interventions that occurred in about 200 additional revolutions since 1900, or interventions carried out without connection with revolution (see Frank W. Bexfield, *Intervention as a Revolutionary Technique,* typewritten manuscript, Washington, Georgetown University, 1949).

[3] The Italian navy intervened even against British and Russian ships. See Count Ciano, *L'Europa verso la catastrofe,* Milan, *Mondadori,* 1948, pp. 206–209.

led, almost certainly, to international complications. This latter danger was so real that the Soviets decided merely to execute a sham intervention and later to withdraw their support; they did not choose to become involved in war at that particular time.[4] To safeguard their *own* interests, the Western powers should have intervened and seen to it that a truly democratic regime won out in Spain. This example clearly shows that under certain conditions there is no such thing as nonintervention, and what purports to be a policy of abstention is tantamount to intervention favoring one side.

TO INTERVENE OR NOT TO INTERVENE: A PROBLEM IN SEMANTICS

Nonintervention is a principle which is undoubtedly applicable to the relationships of civilized and democratic nations, but only to those—most of the time. While in the case of normal relations between nations the principle of nonintervention is the prerequisite of peaceful and friendly cooperation, that principle cannot possibly hold when international crises are brewing or when the world has entered upon general preparations for war. It is invalid in all cases where a change in government terminates an era of friendly collaboration and ushers in a period of tension, armaments, and war. As soon as potentially aggressive governments accede to power, they—by definition—no longer adhere to the principle of nonintervention. As a matter of record, "activist" powers have *always* intervened in the politics of other nations, while demanding that these very same nations continue in their traditional policy of nonintervention—a situation resembling a boxing bout in which one fighter uses both hands but insists that his opponent use only one.

A consistent policy of nonintervention in the face of aggression and the establishment of actively antidemocratic governments jeopardizes security as well as democracy. While at the time of the Holy Alliance nonintervention was a means of assuring political progress, situations may now arise where continued progress and peace can be safeguarded only by intervention. In point of fact the idea is now making headway that a principle of intervention should be applied to developments endangering general peace. A routine change in government would not be a reason for other states to abandon nonintervention, but the assumption of power by the Nazis in Germany would be a legitimate cause for intervention. Actually, should the Nazis regain power in the future, Articles 106 and 107 of the United Nations Charter would authorize intervention; moreover, according to Articles 39, 41, and 42, the Security Council can direct intervention against any "threat to the peace." Thus, the admissibility and necessity for intervention in certain cases has been legally acknowledged.

Forms of Intervention. Intervention can assume the most variegated forms and it can be practiced for the most different purposes. A nation may

---

[4] Franz Borkenau, *Der Europäische Kommunismus, seine Geschichte von 1917 bis zur Gegenwart*, Munich, Lehnen, 1952, p. 155.

practice intervention in order to protect its own nationals from violence or expropriation; intervention may be in the nature of a police action for the purpose of repressing rebellions or other forms of unrest. Intervention may be practiced to prevent a possible future aggressor from assuming power by revolution; or intervention may simply be camouflaged military aggression and territorial expansion. Technically speaking, open military attack is the easiest and most effective form of intervention. But, at the same time, it is the *one* form of intervention which almost certainly invites counteraction by other nations; therefore, self-avowed aggression is often shunned even by openly expansionistic states.

The annexation of conquered territory is not always the most effective method of expansion. While the objective of the victor may be to maintain control over conquered territory, such control may often be better exercised by indirect methods. Annexation may easily lead to opposition or counter-intervention by competing nations. Independence movements may spring up in the annexed areas. Aggressors find it, therefore, more expedient to rely on methods of indirect control and to leave a semblance of independence, *i.e.*, a quasi-independent government, to dependent territories. These indirect means may be purely economic in nature, as was the case of the control which Nazi Germany exerted over Yugoslavia and Bulgaria prior to 1941; or they may consist of diplomacy, cultural influence, propaganda, subversion, and political warfare; or they may be the implied or open threat of overwhelming military attack.

After the end of the Second World War, Soviet Russia ostensibly reestablished the independence of the Eastern European nations which it had helped to "liberate." Clearly the independence which Poland enjoyed in 1937 was different from the "independence" it was permitted to have after 1947. But rather than annexing Rumania or Hungary or Poland to the Union of Soviet Socialist Republics, or "federating" these states into the Union, the Soviet government preferred to rule them by means of secret, or not so secret, intervention. The Soviets may decide at a later date that, partly for reasons of centralized economic planning, outright incorporation may be advisable; for the time being, the Russians can rely on the effectiveness of indirect control.

RUSSIA'S ASIATIC CONQUESTS—CASE STUDIES OF INTERVENTION

While the Soviet Union did not expand in Eastern Europe through means of intervention but chiefly through war, it used intervention as an offensive instrument of expansion in Asia.

Mongolia. In 1912–1913, Russia established a *de facto* protectorate over Mongolia. This protectorate was recognized by China in 1915 through the Kyakhta agreement proclaiming the autonomy of Mongolia. After the First World War the Japanese penetrated into Mongolian territory behind the screen of the filibustering anti-Soviet forces led by General Ungern-Sternberg. After the Soviets had defeated the anticommunist forces, they convened, in 1921 and on Russian territory, a Mongolian "Congress Popular Party" which asked Soviet Russia "to liberate Mongolia from the foreign oppressors and to create a new democratic system." [5]

The Soviets promptly accepted this invitation; the Mongolian "Popular Party," supported by the Red Army, erected the Mongolian People's Republic and patterned it after the Soviet model. Again the fiction of Chinese suzerainty was upheld, but in 1936 when there was a danger of Japanese infiltration, the Soviets carried out an extensive purge of anti-Russian elements, including most of the local clergy. The Mongolian People's Republic and the Soviet Union concluded an alliance, and Mongolia became the second full-fledged satellite of Soviet Russia. During the Second World War, Russia did not withdraw from Outer Mongolia.

At Yalta it was agreed to preserve the *status quo* of Outer Mongolia. While this *status quo* clearly acknowledged the suzerainty of China over Mongolia, Stalin interpreted the text in his own fashion. The Soviets compelled the Chinese government to recognize the independence of Outer Mongolia on condition that a plebiscite would bear out popular desire for secession from China and for statehood. In that plebiscite, 98.4 per cent of the Mongolians cast their votes, and the vote was unanimously in favor of separation from China! In January, 1946, the government of China recognized Outer Mongolia as a separate and independent state.[6]

Manchuria. Russian intervention in Manchuria by means of small-scale infiltration and exploration dates back to the 17th century. In 1689 a treaty was concluded with China, at Nerchinsk, defining for the first time a border between China and Russia in eastern Asia. In the second part of the 19th century, the Chinese-Russian border was advanced to the Amur River.

The shortest line connecting Vladivostok on the Pacific Ocean with Siberian and European Russia leads through Manchuria. The Russians obtained permission from the Chinese government to build a railroad through Manchurian territory. Using this railroad as a lever for infiltration, they gradually encroached upon the country and established almost complete control. Russian penetration ultimately led to the war with Japan in 1904 and 1905 and to the virtual expulsion of Russia from Manchuria. After the revolution Lenin [7] stated that Russia would surrender all interests in the railroad concessions which had been extorted from China by force. This promise was not fully redeemed. But, since Japan controlled Manchuria, Russia, seeking to insure the defense of the Maritime Provinces, built a

[5] *Bolshaya Sovyetskaya Encyclopedia,* Vol. XL, p. 81, as quoted in an unpublished research paper by Jan Wszelaki, *Russia vs. Afghanistan, Sinkiang and Outer Mongolia,* Washington, 1949, p. 18.

[6] See David Dallin, *Soviet Russia and the Far East,* New Haven, Yale University Press, 1948, pp. 203f.; and Wszelaki, *op. cit.,* p. 19.

[7] George Creel, *Russia's Race for Asia,* Indianapolis, Bobbs-Merrill, 1949, p. 47.

railroad from Chita via Khabarovsk, *i.e.*, to the north of the Amur River.

During the 1920's and prior to the Japanese attack on China, both Japan and Russia intervened in Manchuria, largely by financing various chieftains of large bands of brigands, such as the famous "marshal" Chang Tso-Lin. These gangs were liberally supplied with Japanese and Russian money and arms, and induced to fight against each other and against Chinese government forces, Japanese detachments, White Russians, communists, and against any opponent of their current financial supporter. The Japanese intervened to take over Manchuria, the Soviets intervened to block Japanese intervention, and the Chinese government intervened sporadically to reassert its authority. The railroads were the main tactical objective of all contestants, and each claimed title to these railroads amidst a bewildering legal confusion over property rights. After many years of inconclusive fighting, the Soviets decided that they were not ready to risk a major conflagration in the Far East. They sold the Chinese Eastern Railroad to Japan for a nominal price.

Russia's return to Manchuria was sanctioned by the Yalta agreement (1945). According to this agreement, the port of Dairen was internationalized and the "preeminent" interests of the Soviet Union in the port acknowledged; Port Arthur was leased to Russia as a naval base. The Chinese Eastern Railroad and the South Manchurian Railroad were to be operated by a joint Soviet-Chinese company, "it being understood that the preeminent interests of the Soviet Union shall be safeguarded and that China shall retain full sovereignty in Manchuria."

This was intervention by a detour via the chief of a foreign government. The concession from China was not to be obtained directly by Russia but through the intercession of the United States; and the United States agreed to obtain the assent of China to a treaty concluded at China's expense but without China's foreknowledge of the terms of that treaty. The United States thus intervened on behalf of Soviet intervention.

The Soviet Union succeeded in preventing Nationalist China from establishing control over Manchuria and contrived to fasten upon that rich and strategically vital area the domination of the Chinese communists. Manchuria was developed as the main base of operations for the communists, who used it for training, weapons production, and the reconditioning of weapons which the Russians had seized from the Japanese or received from the United States. At the same time the Soviets dismantled the Japanese-built industrial plants and treated the area as conquered territory.

China. The communist conquest of China was largely the work of the Chinese communists. But Mao Tse-tung and his comrades could not have succeeded without effective help from the Soviet Union. This is not to say that the Russians never obstructed communist progress in China; they did. Nor is it to say that Chinese communist affairs did not get entangled with intraparty fights in the Kremlin; they did. However, if the Chinese communists had been left to their own devices, they hardly would have been able to capture China, the world's most populous country.

Soviet intervention began in 1921 when a "university" for the training of Chinese communists was founded in Moscow. There were two climactic phases of intervention: the first in the period from 1923 to 1926, and the second after 1945.

The communists realized, albeit hesitatingly at the start, that orthodox revolutionary techniques would not be applicable in China: China was a backward agrarian and not an industrialized country. In line with the Leninist doctrine that the "bourgeois democratic revolution" must precede a proper proletarian revolution, they decided to join forces with the Kuomintang, then still under the leadership of Sun Yat-sen. On January 26, 1923, the Russian ambassador to China, Adolf Joffe, concluded an agreement with Sun Yat-sen, on the basis of which the Chinese communists joined the Kuomintang party while the Kuomintang accepted Russian advisers. The Soviets disclaimed all intentions to establish communism in China. They averred that it was their aim to help the Chinese achieve "national unification" and to attain full national independence. They abrogated the treaties which Tsarist Russia had concluded with China and declared "categorically" that it was not the intention of the Soviet government "to work for Outer Mongolia's independence from China."

Sun believed these promises, and happily accepted the Soviet offer of help.[8] A Russian communist, Michael M. Borodin, who for many years had lived in the United States, became the party manager of the Kuomintang. Sun's most trusted assistant, Chiang Kai-shek, went to Moscow, where he studied Soviet organization and military science, both of which he introduced in China through the Whampoa military academy. Training of the Kuomintang forces was intrusted to the Russian general Galén, who later became known as Vassily Blucher (purged in 1938). The communist Chou En-lai, later Prime Minister under Mao Tse-tung, assumed a key role in the political leadership of the Kuomintang. Although the communists had joined the Kuomintang, they maintained their party organization and remained under the disciplinary orders of their communist superiors. These moves were a masterly application of Trojan-horse tactics, aiming at the infiltration of hostile political organizations, at the influencing or diverting of their decisions ("diversionism" in communist lingo, or policy sabotage), and ultimately at the capture of the infiltrated organization from within.

At first, the communists and the Kuomintang collaborated harmoniously. Both had the same purpose: the strengthening of the army. But then the question arose, how to use the army?

[8] For the text of the Sun-Joffe manifesto, see Conrad Brandt, Benjamin Schwartz, and John K. Fairbank, *A Documentary History of Chinese Communism*, Cambridge, Mass., Harvard University Press, 1952, p. 70.

Sun intended to use the army in order to spread his control to northern China, while the communists aimed at taking over China in its entirety. When two independent northern Chinese chieftains began to quarrel, Sun Yat-sen launched a military expedition to the north in order to conquer Peking. However, Sun died in March, 1925, in Peking where he had traveled to arrange a compromise with the northern rebels.

Since Sun had died without having designated his successor, Borodin thought the moment propitious for imposing his complete control upon the Kuomintang. Unwisely and hastily, he attempted to oust the anticommunists and Nationalists. Chiang Kai-shek awoke to the danger of the situation. He appointed loyal men to command positions wherever he could, and concentrated military power in his own hands.

Chiang sent Chou En-lai, then still his subordinate, to Shanghai, where the communist expert engineered one of the most brilliant *coups d'état* in modern history. Flushed by success, Chou turned against Chiang, but the Generalissimo had been forewarned by his excellent intelligence service, appeared in Shanghai with strong forces, put Chou to flight, and purged the communists from the ranks of his army. Another purge followed in Canton. The communists pulled in their horns, and Borodin, *de facto* Kuomintang boss, appointed Chiang as commander in chief.

The communists were now in a quandary. The more moderate wing wanted to support Chiang and did not want to press forward to full sovietization. They believed that Russian interests would be best served by a strong man, a Chinese Kemal Pasha, defending China's interests against Western and Japanese imperialism. The more radical wing pressed for all-out sovietization.

In 1926, Chiang Kai-shek's armies had won several decisive victories. The time had come when Chiang was able to establish himself as the ruler of the entire country. At this point Borodin conceived a bold plan. Chiang was about to resume his advance to the north and planned the seizure of Shanghai as a preliminary to the occupation of north-central China. Concluding that once Chiang had taken Shanghai it would be impossible to overthrow him at a later date, Borodin instructed Chiang's Soviet assistants to sabotage the advance to Shanghai and to contrive the *defeat* of the dangerous general.[9]

Certain Chinese generals, handsomely paid, had already promised to support Communism. The Red Guard were being busily trained at Shanghai. Borodin's plan was simplicity itself: to get Chiang Kai-shek's army beaten and put one of these pro-Communist generals in his place. Simultaneously the Red Guard at Shanghai was to mutiny and pursue Chang Tsu-chang's demoralized soldiers, among whom only the few White Russian squads could offer resistance. The revolt at Shanghai having succeeded, a revolutionary government of Soviet type would be established and the Red Army of China put on its feet.

[9] Grigory Bessedovsky, *Revelations of a Soviet Diplomat,* London, Williams & Norgate, 1931, p. 154.

To Borodin's misfortune, the dispatch containing his treacherous instructions was intercepted. Chiang took energetic countermeasures, disarmed the Red Guard, and dismissed the Russian instructors. The Soviet advisers retired to Russia, accompanied, incidentally, by the very personages who, after World War II, were to lead the communist rebels in Indo-China and Indonesia. The whole affair ended when Chiang occupied Shanghai and established a new government at Nanking (April 15, 1927). Stalin predicted, somewhat prematurely, the end of Chiang Kai-shek.[10] This fiasco of Soviet leadership became one of the points at issue between Stalin and Trotsky. In order to achieve a few sorely needed successes, Stalin first replaced Russian Comintern agents by Germans and Americans. Then he hastily instigated an uprising at Canton (December, 1927) under the leadership of a German communist, Heinz Neumann, dispatched especially for this purpose to China. In the following year, a new technique was used: peasant troops were to bring Soviet rule to the cities, as, for example, Changsha. According to the book, revolutions had to take place in cities. The Chinese communists under Li Li-san obeyed Stalin's orders.[11]

At this point, the Chinese communists reasserted themselves. Mao Tse-tung centered his efforts on the peasants. Abandoning the hopeless technique of city uprisings, he organized the countryside and established a tiny Soviet state in the mountains of Kiangsi and Fukien, a tactic decried in Moscow as "Trotskyism." The guerrillas maintained themselves from 1931 to 1934 but, on being hard pressed by the Kuomintang forces, retreated to the northwest, where they established a larger Soviet state in Shensi. With Trotsky out of the way, Stalin felt free to adopt new tactics. Mao Tse-tung became the acknowledged leader of Chinese communism—Russian domestic politics and interventionist techniques interacting upon each other. Nevertheless, the extent of the intimacy of Mao's relations with Moscow at that time is a matter of dispute. There seems to be little doubt that, by and large, Mao was following his own counsel. But did he receive material help? Probably, but only on a modest scale.

In December, 1936, Chiang Kai-shek was kidnapped at Sian by one of his subordinate officers but was released on communist advice. The upshot was that Chiang and the communists agreed to a truce and even to a "united front" for the purpose of fighting jointly against the Japanese. The Sino-Japanese war greatly helped the Soviets inasmuch as it lessened the pressure on Russia's Far Eastern flank, but it also helped the Chinese communists, who took advantage of the battle raging between the Nationalists and Japanese in order to expand their territory. The Russians did their best to keep

---

[10] *International Press Correspondence,* April, 1927, p. 544.

[11] For similar interventions by the Soviets in Germany, see Ruth Fischer, *Stalin and German Communism, A Study in the Origins of the State Party,* Cambridge, Mass., Harvard University Press, 1948. About Soviet interventions in France, Spain, and other countries, see Borkenau, *op. cit.*

Japan mired in China. From 1941 onward, the "united front" gave way to hostilities between the communists and the Kuomintang. This three-cornered war went on until 1945, when the Chinese communists emerged as a major power controlling about 100 million people and substantial territory.

It would be erroneous to assume that the Soviets helped the Chinese communists with large quantities of weapons. This was unnecessary. The Nationalists lost their armaments due to desertion and lack of replenishment from the United States; on the other side, the communists, with Soviet connivance, got hold of well-stocked Japanese arsenals. Yet the Russians undoubtedly helped with special equipment, training, and logistical support. Nor were many Soviet advisers necessary: the communists knew better than their Russian counterparts how to fight a war in China. Nevertheless, the switch from guerrilla fighting to large-scale military operations could not have been accomplished without experienced advice.

The biggest help which the Russian communists gave the Chinese was (1) all the resources of the communist world movement were mobilized in favor of the Chinese communists; and (2) Russia provided the Chinese communists with indispensable strategic cover. More specifically, the Soviets protected the communists against strong reactions from the United States. In this connection it is noteworthy that Mao Tse-tung launched his offensive revolutionary war late in 1948, coincident with the Soviet blockade of Berlin which diverted American attention from Asia, a case of indirect intervention.

Russia and Asia. The intermingling of races, the cleavages of classes and religious castes, the poverty and land hunger of the Asiatic masses have given Russia and world communism a fertile field for interventional tactics. With promises of land reform and national independence, the communists organized in many Asiatic countries, under Russian-trained leaders, guerrilla bands who supplied themselves by capturing weapons and food. Continuous guerrilla war interfered with economic production and required large-scale counter-operations, the repercussions of which were felt in Europe and in the United States. The ensuing unrest engendered reverberations all around the world.

Politically, the Soviets aimed at the "reorganization" of the Asiatic states. For example, the Soviet geographer Mstislavsky called attention to the "artificiality" of Afghanistan. In Mstislavsky's word, Afghanistan is an "artificial conglomerate of areas in no way welded ethnically or economically." [12] According to the Russians, out of the 12 million inhabitants of Afghanistan, more than 4 million are Tajiks and 750,000 Uzbeks; both Tajikistan and Uzbekistan are federated states of the Soviet Union. On the other hand, over 5 million genuine Afghans, the Pushtu, live, according to Soviet statistics, in northwestern India, in particular in Pakistan and Kashmir. These Afghans, therefore, are being "oppressed" by capitalist imperialism,

[12] *Bolshaya Sovyetskaya Encyclopedia,* Vol. IV, p. 83, as quoted in Wszelaki, *op. cit.,* p. 22.

while in Afghanistan proper, the Afghans, numbering only 3.5 million, on their part, "oppress" the Tajiks and Uzbeks.

The obvious inference from these allegations is that northern Afghanistan with its Turkestan, Tajik, and Uzbek minorities should be divided up among Turkmenistan, Tajikistan, and Uzbekistan, all members of the Soviet Union. In such a regional reorganization under Soviet aegis, the genuine Afghans living in Afghanistan would, presumably, be compensated for by the inclusion of a vast segment of Pakistan. And why go to all this trouble? Because, the Soviet Encyclopedia tells us, Afghanistan is the only *place d'armes* for the conquest of India.[13]

After the British withdrawal from India, the defeat of Japan, and the victories of Red China, the balance of power in Asia has been altered to the great advantage of Russia. Russia has, therefore, a more or less open field.

In the 19th century, the Russian government deemed pressure on India through Turkestan and Afghanistan the most efficacious method for putting pressure on Constantinople and the Dardanelles. Time and again throughout the 19th century, Russia elaborated plans to invade India, as, for example, when Alexander I was allied with Napoleon and when, during the Crimean War, Russia scanned her borderlands for a likely opening for a counter-offensive against Britain. The plans of General Khrulev in 1885, and of General Skobelev, in 1877, envisaged an attack on India, supported by the rebellious tribes of the northwest frontier.

There is some evidence that the Soviets have not abandoned the old dreams of their Tsarist predecessors. It has been reported that General Brusilov, one of the most important Tsarist generals who went over to the Soviets and who ended his career as a professor at the Soviet Military Academy founded by Trotsky (now called Frunze Academy), submitted to the Soviet rulers as early as 1921 the project of a strategy aiming at the destruction of the British Empire through the conquest of India. Brusilov believed that *Russia's future was in Asia.* He suggested that an attack on India be prepared. His plan was based on the idea that the campaign was to begin with a feinting attack against Persia. Once British forces had been diverted, an offensive into India proper was to follow. Military means were to be combined with revolutionary techniques.[14]

Afghanistan is the classical *place d'armes* for the invasion of India. Communism, however, has been approaching that major objective, the conquest of the Indian subcontinent, gradually through Tibet and the small states in the Himalayas. In Southeast Asia, the communists have been waging guerrilla wars in Indo-China, Burma, and Malaya, aiming at the breakup of these states as well as of Thailand. Southeast Asia possesses important mineral deposits, but, more important still, it is the world's foremost producer of rice.

---

[13] *Ibid.,* p. 71, as quoted in Wszelaki, *op. cit.,* p. 1.
[14] The authors are indebted to Jan Wszelaki for this information which he found in the American-Ukrainian newspaper *Svoboda,* issue of Mar. 25, 1949.

If it were to fall into communist hands, economic repercussions in India as well as in Japan would be considerable.

A former member of the Russian embassy in Teheran, Lev Vasiliev, revealed the secret Soviet methods of intervention in Iran. Essentially, the plan consisted of six parts:

1. The Soviets organized terror, such as an attempt on the life of the Shah and the assassination of the Prime Minister, Ali Razmara (1951).

2. There was systematic infiltration of spies and agents "into every channel of Iranian life." Iranian communists were trained at Moscow and upon their return were helped along in their careers. The objective was to place Soviet agents in a maximum number of control points, in order to gather information and to engage in tactics of "diversion" or policy sabotage.

3. The Soviets made full use of bribery and blackmail against Iranian public officials. According to Vasiliev, they paid the then Prime Minister $200,000 in order to obtain an oil concession in northern Iran. Whenever bribery did not work, blackmail was resorted to.

4. Soviet agents were enjoined to disrupt the Iranian economy. For example, the Soviet trade mission bought 30,000 tons of sugar and withheld it from the market. This created discontent and raised the price of sugar. After a while, the sugar was sold at a profit of several million dollars. Vasiliev claimed that Soviet agents contributed substantially to the expulsion of the Anglo-Iranian oil company from Persia.

5. Soviet agents organized large-scale mob actions and demonstrations. According to Vasiliev, an MVD technician attached to the Russian embassy planned and directed most of the riots throughout the country.

6. The Soviets made full use of propaganda, partly by subsidizing Iranian newspapers and magazines, and partly by bribing Iranian writers who supposedly were anticommunists. Moreover, a great effort was made to infiltrate and guide the Mohammedan clergy, who have the greatest influence with the Iranian masses.

The most interesting feature of the scheme was its financing. While according to Vasiliev, the Soviets poured, in one year, about 100 million dollars into underground operations in Iran, the money did not come from Russia but was raised locally through smuggling, black-market operations (partly with American lend-lease goods, such as automobile tires), stock-market speculation, and business ventures as, for example, the preemptive buying of sugar.[15]

Perhaps it may be argued that these conditions are typical only of the 20th century. There is no question that purpose and technique of intervention have changed with the emergence of national states and pseudoreligious political ideologies, like Nazism and communism. Yet ever since the Napoleonic period, this "modern" type of intervention was practiced by virtually

[15] Lev Vasiliev as told to Donald Robinson, "The Soviet Plot to Steal Iran," *Congressional Record*, Apr. 23, 1953, p. A 2272.

all major powers and by not a few small nations. Napoleon himself was a past master at this art. So were the statesmen of Austria, Germany, France, Britain, Japan, and, above all, Tsarist Russia.

These activities have not found the attention they deserve because the pertinent archives have not been opened. Intervention is one of the skeletons in the closet which is ignored with studied silence. However, there is ample documentation on one particular case which may serve to illustrate the generic type: the intervention of Russia in Bulgaria from 1879 to 1896.

In 1878 the Treaty of Berlin established the principality of Bulgaria. Russia was given the job of helping the young state organize itself. A favored nephew of the Tsar, Alexander of Battenberg, was elected prince. When Alexander did not play the role of the obedient puppet for which he had been cast, he incurred the enmity of Russia.

We need not examine here the details of this conflict and may restrict ourselves to a mere listing of the various techniques of intervention which the Russians employed in Bulgaria: support of Bulgarian political refugees living abroad and plotting against their country; supervision of anti-Tsarist Russian refugees; shadowing of political opponents; distribution of leaflets; production and use of false passports and documents; support of political parties favoring Russia and intimidation of political parties which opposed Russian intervention; financing of newspapers whose editors made explicit agreements with Russian officials; payments of lump sums of money and of regular allowances to Bulgarian partisans of the Russian cause; bribery of officials; the granting of Russian citizenship to Bulgarian politicians in order to protect them against legal prosecution; terrorization of political opponents; assassination of political opponents, including the assassination of Bulgarian diplomats abroad; selling of weapons within Bulgaria; recruitment, direction, and payment of armed bands; dispatch of Russian soldiers disguised as natives into Bulgaria and control of their activities; sabotaging of Bulgaria's official politics; moral, political, and financial pressure on the ruling prince and insistence on his abdication; bomb plots against the ruler; influencing and rigging of elections; declaring elections illegal when they were unfavorable to Russian policies; organization of conspiracy by high-ranking Russian officials—specialists in conspiratorial techniques—sent to Bulgaria for this particular purpose; distribution of false intelligence reports; negotiations and agreements with insurrectionists; support of insurrections; organization of *coups d'état;* organization of city and regional uprisings; attempts at general revolution; help to unsuccessful revolutionaries; naval blockade; military raids by freebooters launched from outside of Bulgaria; the mobilization of Bulgarian reserves by agents disguised as Bulgarian officers issuing faked mobilization orders; efforts, including large-scale propaganda, to substitute a Russian aristocrat as the elected prince of Bulgaria; inducing Bulgarian politicians to ask for a Russian protectorate; and, finally, break of diplomatic relations. It should be added that all these operations were executed by the Russians under loud protestations that they were adhering to the principle of nonintervention.

Perhaps the most interesting aspect of this affair is that this elaborate campaign of intervention failed in its purpose. Despite all the pressure which gigantic Russia exerted against little Bulgaria, the latter managed to retain its independence and ultimately forced the Russians out of the country. Though Bulgaria defended herself heroically, she was aided by counterinterventions on the part of Austria, Germany, and England. The Austrians, whose hand was more skillful in the fine art of intervention than that of the clumsy Russians, finally succeeded in installing Ferdinand of Coburg, an Austrian army officer, as the duly elected prince of Bulgaria.

It often has been said that the war of 1914 was caused, to a large extent, by the national jealousies of the Balkan peoples. It should be added that embers of these jealousies were fanned into flames by the interventions of the great powers, especially that of Russia, whose main purpose was to obtain an advanced base against Turkey.[16]

All in all, as long as nations resort to such methods, the principle of nonintervention belongs to the realm of abstract or utopian speculation rather than to that of political reality.

U.S. INTERVENTION IN THE PACIFIC AND EASTERN ASIA

During the first 150 years of American history, the United States foreign policy vis-à-vis Europe was characterized by a series of five "don'ts": don't become entangled, don't expand, don't arm, don't fight, and don't take sides —isolationism, anti-imperialism, antimilitarism, pacifism, and neutrality. The American policy vis-à-vis Asia and Latin America was, however, of an entirely different mettle. It was a policy of activity, action, and dynamism, a policy of "do" rather than of "don't."

Japan. The opening up of Japan by the United States was one of the most consequential events in history. The development of steam navigation, the growth of trade with China, and the needs of American whalers operating in the northern waters of the Pacific made it necessary to open ports of refuge in Japan. Commercial interest and requirements of navigation, therefore, prompted the American government to take action and to compel the Japa-

---

[16] See R. Léonoff (ed.), *Documents secrets de la politique russe en Orient 1881–1890*, Berlin, Wilhelm, 1893. See also Peter Pavlovich (ed.), *Avantyurii russkogo tsarisma v Bolgarii*, with a preface by V. Kolarov and a historical survey by A. Popov, Moscow, 1935. The interesting aspect of this last book is that it followed by a few months the famous Soviet directive of May 16, 1934, concerning the writing and teaching of history. This decree opened the phase of "Soviet patriotism" where books of the "debunking" type became strictly taboo. The book immediately was withdrawn and is now an extreme rarity; even the Library of Congress has no copy. See Bertram D. Wolfe, "Operation Rewrite: The Agony of Soviet Historians," *Foreign Affairs*, October, 1952, pp. 39–57. (The authors are indebted to Mr. Paul W. Blackstock for information on the Léonoff and Pavlovich books.)

nese to abandon their traditional policy of complete isolation as well as their inhumane treatment of foreign shipwrecked sailors. While Japanese coaling and supply stations were thus needed for maintenance and enlargement of already existing trade, it was obvious that the opening up of the Japanese Empire would produce a very substantial *additional* market.

American action was also prompted by the fact that the British had unlocked the gates of China and that the Russians had, for many years, sought to enter Japan.[17] Russian sailors and settlers had pushed into the Kuril Islands, Kamchatka, and Sakhalin, all of which were legally claimed by Japan. This expansion, incidentally, had compelled the Japanese to occupy, on their part, the island of Hokkaido and to fight a difficult war with the native population—an interesting side light on the futility of the most conscientious policy of isolation.

The threat that Russia or Britain might extend their domination to Japan and greatly increase their power in the Pacific, not to mention their trade, prompted the timing of American action.

We need not enter into the discussion of whether Commodore Perry was threatening the Japanese by force or whether he was simply "persuading" [18] them to change their laws, initiate trade with other nations, and end the voluntary isolation which had for centuries protected their society and customs. The instructions given to the Commodore were peaceable in nature; however, he was authorized to resort to force "in self-defense in the protection of the vessels and crews under his command, or to resent an act of personal violence offered to himself, or one of his crews."

Whatever the formalities, the American government did not leave any doubt that it intended its proposals to be accepted by the Japanese. The Japanese were not cognizant of Perry's ambiguous instructions and took Perry's arguments to be an ultimatum.[19] They may have misunderstood him, but it is likely that Perry wanted to be misunderstood.

Whether by persuasion or force, Commodore Perry's mission was an intervention in the domestic affairs of Japan, notwithstanding learned dissertations by conscience-stricken historians expatiating on Perry's instructions and overlooking Perry's warships. In any event, the results of Perry's "persuasion by force" radically changed Japanese life. The feudal society of the Samurai was crushed, the Shogunate was destroyed, the old economic system abolished, and Japan was transformed into a modern industrial nation.

---

[17] The Russians went about their Japanese plans with somewhat less than customary Tsarist indolence: Catherine II established a Japanese professorship at Irkutsk under the German Orientalist Klaproth who directed studies in Japanese language, geography, and sociology.

[18] Payson S. Treat, *Diplomatic Relations between the United States and Japan 1853–1895,* Stanford, Calif., Stanford University Press, 1932, p. 20.

[19] According to Japanese sources, Perry said: "If your country becomes an enemy, we will exhaust our resources if necessary to wage war. We are fully prepared to engage in a struggle for victory." (*Ibid.,* p. 15.)

Hawaii. In 1893, a revolution in the Hawaiian Islands was staged by resident Americans and native Hawaiians, with the help of American sailors landed at Honolulu from the cruiser *Boston*.[20] True, sailors and marines intervened without the consent or even the knowledge of the United States government; but their presence had the strong approval of the United States minister at Honolulu, for it afforded protection of American life and property. This intervention against the Queen of Hawaii gave rise to a lengthy controversy in domestic American politics. The Queen had been dethroned, a republic had been proclaimed, and the liberated Hawaiians expressed their desire to be incorporated into the United States. The acrimonious debates in the Senate and the scruples of President Cleveland delayed the outcome but did not affect the issue. Unauthorized or not, the intervention of the U.S. Navy secured the Hawaiian Islands for the United States.[21] The Islands were ultimately annexed during the Spanish-American War.

Siberia. An American intervention which could have had truly momentous consequences was the intervention in Siberia from 1918 to 1920. The original purpose of sending small numbers of American troops to Siberia was to relieve the Czechoslovak volunteer forces who, during their withdrawal along the Trans-Siberian Railroad, had been attacked by the Bolsheviki and found themselves in a perilous situation. It was the intention of the United States to help the Czechoslovak legions to reach Vladivostok and to repatriate them in order to put at the disposal of the newly established Czechoslovak Republic a nucleus of seasoned military forces. A second purpose of the intervention was "to steady any efforts at self-government or self-defense, in which the Russians themselves might be willing to accept assistance."[22]

By January, 1920, the Czechoslovak troops had been brought to safety. In the meantime, the United States government had become doubtful as to the wisdom of its policy of helping the Russian people to withstand Bolshevism. It was impressed with "the political instability and grave uncertainties" of the situation in eastern Siberia and disposed to view "that further military efforts to assist the Russians in the struggle toward self-government may . . . lead to complications which would have exactly the opposite effect, prolonging possibly the period of readjustment and involving Japan and the United States in ineffective and needless sacrifices." It was felt, accordingly, to be unlikely "that the second purpose for which American troops were sent to Siberia will be longer served by their presence there."[23]

The United States government had urged vainly the leader of the anti-Bolshevik forces in Siberia, Admiral Kolchak, to include in his government

[20] Charles A. Beard, *The Idea of National Interest*, New York, Macmillan, 1934, p. 77.

[21] The history of Samoa supplies an interesting case of American intervention directed against German intervention, and of a first-class international crisis resulting from these rival interventions.

[22] Department of State, *Papers Relating to the Foreign Relations of the United States, 1920*, Government Printing Office, 1936, Vol. III, p. 488.

[23] *Ibid.*, pp. 488*f*.

"progressive forces" rather than the "reactionaries" with whom he had surrounded himself. (Was this intervention or not?) But the true reason for the reversal of the American policy was that the 5,000 American soldiers stationed in Siberia were no longer sufficient to meet requirements. To send reinforcements

might involve the Government of the United States in an undertaking of such indefinite character as to be inadvisable. The amount of re-inforcement which might become necessary for the execution of such an agreement (for joint and enlarged American-Japanese intervention) might be so great that the Government of the United States would not feel justified in carrying it out.[24]

Hence the American troops were recalled.

The United States deplored this decision *not* because it made the victory of Bolshevism inevitable, but because it marked the end of a "cooperative effort by Japan and the United States to assist the Russian people." The emphasis was on cooperation with Japan! To make things worse, the War Department sent orders for evacuation without bothering to notify anybody else—including the State Department. The precipitate American withdrawal made it impossible for the Japanese to realign their forces; caused the rapid deterioration of the military situation in Siberia; led to the downfall of Kolchak, Bolshevik conquest of the Lake Baikal area, and the consolidation of Bolshevism. The fallacy of nonintervention had been valued higher than the obligation of a democratic nation to help other democratic forces fighting desperately against tyranny.

Chinese Revolution. Intervention need not always be carried out by the government itself or by government forces. One of the most successful and far-reaching American interventions was directed against the Manchu regime in China. Almost exclusively, this intervention was carried out by American civilians and private citizens, who never received a mandate from the American government but whose action was a most effective support of the Chinese Revolution.[25]

Sun Yat-sen's revolutionary party obtained a large portion of its funds from America. The Revolutionary Alliance, a revolutionary organization directed by Sun Yat-sen, assessed students studying abroad for $3 a month. The bulk of the party funds was gathered from donations by merchant members of the Alliance, many of whom lived in the United States.[26]

Another revolutionary group, the Protect Emperor Society, collected 50 cents per month from every American member. In February, 1905, alone,

[24] *Ibid.*

[25] In the Spanish Civil War foreign nationals fought as volunteers for the Loyalists; Americans, for example, formed a Lincoln Brigade. An American officer, General Chennault, organized a volunteer air force fighting for the Chinese against Japan.

[26] T'ang Leang Li, *Inner History of the Chinese Revolution,* London, Routledge, 1930, p. 51 and *passim.* See also S. Chen and R. Payne, *Sun Yat-sen,* New York, John Day, 1946, p. 73.

about $400,000 were collected from American dues-paying members, and this money was invested in South America, where it bore interest.[27] This money was not only used to finance the Revolution in China but also to smuggle American-trained revolutionaries into China and to finance visits of prominent Chinese leaders to the United States.[28]

Even more important was the military training which the Chinese revolutionaries obtained in the United States. A revolutionary society organized a number of efficient training camps that turned out about 2,100 officers for the revolutionary army.[29] Under the leadership of the well-known writer Homer Lea, a hunchback who became a lieutenant general in the Chinese army and chief of staff to Sun Yat-sen, uniform and effective methods of training were developed. Lea profited from the assistance and advice of a major general of the United States Army and obtained the services of a former first sergeant of the American cavalry who was an expert drill master. Training schools for Chinese revolutionaries were established in twenty-one major cities of the United States. Full-fledged maneuvers were conducted in the California mountains. Some American authorities were deceived by camouflage and cover organizations, but in many cases they knew full well what was going on. A former governor general of the Philippines as well as the Secretary of State Elihu Root were unofficially kept informed and failed to raise objections.[30] Without exaggeration it can be stated that American financing, training, and supplying of equipment were among the indispensable preconditions of the Chinese Revolution in 1911.

U.S. INTERVENTION IN LATIN AMERICA

While in Asia United States intervention was relatively infrequent, in Latin-American affairs it was one of the most constant factors. Here one intervention followed the other. Virtually all the expansionist moves of the United States southward into Florida, Texas, New Mexico, California, and Cuba were preceded by intervention and often by revolutionary uprisings engineered by groups operating from U.S. bases. In 1917, the U.S. Secretary of State Lansing signed his name to an agreement in which we read: "The Governments of the United States and Japan recognize that territorial propinquity creates special relations between countries." [31] This term "special

---

[27] Carl Glick, *Double Ten,* New York, Whittlesey, 1945, p. 130.

[28] Prior to the Revolution in 1911, Sun Yat-sen concluded an agreement with the British Foreign Office and with the French Foreign Office, according to which neither France nor Britain would make further loans to the Manchu government; an interesting case of economic intervention (see Chen and Payne, *op. cit.,* p. 73).

[29] See Henry S. Chisholm, *An Analysis of the Organization, Strategy and Tactics of the Chinese Revolution of 1911,* research paper, unpublished, Washington, Georgetown University, 1947, p. 20.

[30] See Glick, *op. cit.,* p. 59.

[31] Ruhl Bartlett (ed.), *The Record of American Diplomacy,* New York, Knopf, 1948, p. 421.

relations" makes only a fleeting appearance in American diplomatic texts. But it is of particular significance in U.S. relations with Latin America. Ever since the proclamation of the Monroe Doctrine, the United States had, indeed, a special relationship with the Latin-American nations. This special relationship was shaped by three factors: the desire of the United States to keep the European powers out of the Western Hemisphere; the security interests of the United States; and the need of the United States to protect its trade and its citizens.

Panama. The complications of that special relationship between the United States and its southern neighbors can best be shown by a concrete example. In 1846 the United States entered into a treaty with New Granada, later known as Colombia, and obtained the right of way and transit across the Isthmus of Panama. In compensation, the United States guaranteed "positively and efficaciously" to maintain and preserve the "perfect neutrality" of the Isthmus. In order that transit would not be interrupted or embarrassed by any disturbance, the United States guaranteed the rights of sovereignty and property which New Granada possessed in the territory of Panama.[32]

It so happened that at least one major disturbance per year occurred in the Panama Zone; altogether fifty-three insurrections and revolutions took place during the fifty-seven years which followed the signing of this treaty. Colombia was quite incapable of maintaining her sovereignty, let alone preserving order in the Panama territory. Only through the active intervention of the United States was it possible to maintain Colombian sovereignty. Without such intervention the Panama area would have declared its independence long before the close of the 19th century. And it goes without saying that the Colombian authorities not only tolerated but, time and again, actively requested U.S. intervention. At the request of the local authorities, the United States landed troops in Panama in 1856, 1860, 1861, 1873, and 1901; at the request of the central Colombian government in 1861, 1862, 1885, and 1900; and at the request of the United States consul in 1865, 1885, and 1902. In other words, the United States more often than not acted as the executive agent of the Colombian government.

By the end of the 19th century, it became obvious that the French company which had started constructing the Panama Canal was incapable of completing the work. The company sold its rights to the United States, which began negotiating a treaty with Colombia in order to complete the Canal. The Colombian government thought that it had the upper hand in the negotiations and tried to extort a price for its concessions which the U.S. government considered excessive. The price was indeed high; on the other hand, the seller of any commodity has the right to ask the highest price he wishes to get.

---

[32] In 1830 Panama had intended to ask for annexation by Great Britain but had been dissuaded by Simon Bolivar (see Charles E. Hill, *Leading American Treaties,* New York, Macmillan, 1931, p. 372.

After much haggling, the Colombian government signed a draft treaty. Unhappy about its stipulations, the Colombians approached Germany and Great Britain and offered them the Canal rights. Both governments declined. Thereupon the Congress of Colombia, which had not ratified the draft treaty, reformulated its conditions and made exorbitant demands on the United States.

As a consequence, the local population and the local authorities in the Panama area became thoroughly alarmed: it did not seem as though the Canal would be finished and the economic advantages which the Panamanians expected from the venture would materialize. The French company, too, was interested in the Americans' taking over the Canal construction.

The interests of the French and the Panamanians coincided, and both hatched plans for a Panamanian revolution. The Panamanians were sure that they could consummate the venture and secure their independence. However, they feared that, as in previous cases, the United States would step in and, in compliance with the 1846 treaty, put down the revolution and restore the sovereignty of Colombia. The important point, therefore, was to secure the "neutrality" of the United States. Time was running out. The concession of the French company was about to expire, and the U.S. government was bound, in case no satisfactory arrangements could be made with the French company and Colombia, by special legislation (the Spooner Act) to build a Canal through Nicaragua.

An emissary was sent to Washington to negotiate with the Secretary of State. Secretary Hay stated that it would be obviously impossible for the American government to support any revolutionary enterprise, even though the United States was dissatisfied with Colombia's decision not to ratify the Panama Canal treaty. The United States could not violate its treaty of 1846. This treaty stipulated the protection of free transit across the Isthmus and guaranteed Colombia's sovereignty against *foreign* aggression. But, Hay added, the treaty did *not* guarantee Colombian possession of the Isthmus against *local* and *domestic* revolution. That was the go-ahead signal for the Panamanian revolutionaries.[33]

When the revolution came, American forces did not intervene to put down the rising. One of the Colombian generals threatened to kill every American in town unless other Colombian generals were released. This induced the American railroad officials [34] to appeal to the American officer commanding the cruiser *Nashville* for protection. Promptly fifty American sailors and marines were landed; the local Colombian authorities failed to take stringent

---

[33] The inside story of the Panama revolution has been told by the Frenchman who more than anybody else guided developments: Philippe Bunau-Varilla, *From Panama to Verdun: My Fight for France,* Philadelphia, Dorrance, 1940, Chap. 5.

[34] One of the Americans allegedly represented the U.S. Army, Navy, and Treasury as an "expert in revolution" (*ibid.,* p. 126).

countermeasures. The presence of the U.S. cruiser prevented a Colombian counterattack by sea. The revolutionaries carried the day.

The American consul notified the Secretary of State that a *de facto* government had come into being. A few days later, the United States government authorized the consul to enter into official relations with this government. Thus, recognition was extended to the revolutionaries.[35]

In receipt of an official protest of the Colombian government, Secretary Hay conceded that the interest of the United States had been at stake during the Panamanian Revolution and that Panama had fought for this interest, while Colombia had opposed it. Hay added: [36]

Compelled to choose between these two alternatives, the Government of the United States, in no way responsible for the situation which had arisen, did not hesitate. It recognized the independence of the Republic of Panama, and upon its judgment and action in the emergency the powers of the world have set the seal of their approval.

Heretofore the United States had intervened *manu militari* in order to maintain the sovereignty of Colombia in the Panama territory. Now the United States stood aloof militarily and "intervened" by nonaction in order to remove the sovereignty of Colombia from Panama. Indeed, Talleyrand had been right when he stated: "The principle of nonintervention means more or less the same as the principle of intervention."

Other Interventions. Intervention was practiced by the United States in many forms, such as nonrecognition, diplomatic mediation, economic pressure, diplomatic intervention, dollar diplomacy, the refusal or granting of credit, manipulation of trade, threats, the support or nonsupport of subversive and revolutionary groups, arms embargo, naval blockade, the temporary landing of armed forces, and occupation over extended periods of time. Virtually every diplomatic act of the United States with respect to any country in Latin America could be construed as an act of intervention or nonintervention.

Did the United States recognize a revolutionary movement? By so doing the United States intervened. Did the United States refuse to recognize a revolutionary movement after it had seized power? This, too, was intervention. The United States granted a credit to state A; it interfered thereby in A's affairs. But this meant interfering also in the affairs of state B, simply because the United States did *not* grant a credit to that state. Intervention and nonintervention are a jungle of ambiguous terms from which no one can extricate himself without losing what is left of his diplomatic innocence.

The Latin-American states would never have acquired independence had it not been for the interventions of Britain during the Napoleonic Wars, the attacks by the British against Spanish possessions overseas, and the occupa-

---

[35] Hill, *op. cit.*, p. 376.
[36] *Ibid.*, p. 378.

tion of Spain by Napoleon. When Spanish sovereignty had been transferred to France as the occupying power, the old links of the overseas possessions with Madrid broke.

The wars of liberation were fought against loyal Spanish groups and, after the restoration of the Bourbons, against Spain trying to recover her possessions. Born itself of revolution, the United States did not come to the aid of the revolutionaries of South America. For a long time the United States did not recognize them. Hamilton, influenced by Francisco Miranda, stood ready to lead a United States Army to the liberation of South America. If such an expedition had been launched, a unified South America would have probably emerged instead of the present congeries of states.

When the liberation movement started, South America had a population of about 20 million, while the United States had less than 5 million. It is true that a united Latin America might have threatened the security interests of the United States; an instinctive mistrust of a strong Latin America probably dictated the policy of Adams, Jefferson, and Madison. However, it is quite probable that U.S. nonintervention stifled the development of Latin America, precisely as failure to transform the Confederacy through the Constitution would have arrested the growth of the United States. Thus, this first experiment in nonintervention of the United States entailed consequences of extraordinary historical importance: it prevented the emergence of a strong Latin America. Perhaps it fostered thereby the ascendancy of the United States. But by preventing the emergence of a supremely powerful, united American state, it may have, in the long run, limited severely the vistas of an "American century." [37]

The joint British-American intervention which took the form of the Monroe Doctrine prevented Spain from reasserting her sovereignty over the Latin-American countries. While virtually all of the Latin-American states owed their independence to the military genius of Bolivar and San Martín, it is nevertheless true that some states, for example, Uruguay and San Domingo, owe their independence to the interventions of Britain and France.

Only at a *later* date did the United States act as the guardian angel of South America. In 1867, the United States expelled the French from Mexico and reestablished the independence of the Mexican state which would never have been able to defeat by its own forces the military power of Napoleon III. With the blessing of the Senate, the United States supported an insurrection in Cuba against Spain; this insurrection was organized in the United States itself and led by Estrada Palma who later became the first President of Cuba.

[37] For a vigorous exposition of this thesis, see Carlos Davila, *We of the Americas,* Chicago, Ziff-Davis, 1949. It is undoubtedly true that the combined natural and manpower resources of North and South America would constitute the strongest power on earth, and that U.S. preoccupation with the development of countries that would be untenable in war not only retards Latin-American progress but also fails to develop what de Seversky calls the "air backyard of the United States," thus endangering U.S. security.

In 1871 Peru, whose independence had never been recognized by the motherland, enjoyed the protection of the United States in a war against Spain. The United States protected Venezuela in 1895 against Britain and again in 1902 against Britain, Germany, and Italy.

Occasionally the United States carried out intervention and arbitration jointly with other Latin-American states. For example, together with Mexico, it intervened in 1907 in a Central American war. In 1934, it joined other Latin-American nations in the arbitration of the Leticia conflict between Colombia and Peru. In 1935, the United States together with five Latin-American governments arbitrated the Chaco War.

In other instances, the United States acted alone. For example, between 1879 and 1884 the United States repeatedly and unsuccessfully tried to settle the War of the Pacific which raged between Chile, Peru, and Bolivia. In 1921, the United States mediated a conflict between Panama and Costa Rica. Even though Panama was closely allied with the United States, Washington settled the conflict in favor of Costa Rica. For many years the United States attempted to mediate the Tacna-Arica dispute between Chile and Peru (and Bolivia); the dispute was settled, however, in 1929 without United States participation.

For the sake of humanity it was disastrous that the United States did *not* intervene in the war which Paraguay waged against its neighbors between 1865 and 1870, and which left the little country completely exhausted and drained of manpower. This war reduced the male population of Paraguay to 28,000 and the female population to 200,000. No more "total" war was ever fought in modern history.

Time and again, the United States intervened in foreign countries in order to protect life and property and to prevent bloodshed. Often American intervention was requested by foreign governments. Often the United States intervened on its own initiative, just as any right-minded person would "intervene" if he came upon a band of ruffians administering a beating to innocent adolescents.

This, for example, was the case of the American intervention in Haiti in 1915, which occurred *after* two presidents of state had been murdered, more than a hundred of the leading citizens had been shot as hostages, and when an enraged mob threatened to kill scores of other people, including American citizens and diplomatic personnel. This was also the case in Nicaragua in 1926 where the rebellious General Sandino engaged in large-scale killings.

In other instances, timely American intervention *prevented* the outbreak of violence, as in Cuba in 1906 and in Honduras in 1919. The supervision of the elections in Cuba by an American general in 1920 probably saved that country from being plunged into an orgy of mass violence. Should not similar acts of preventive intervention find favor with those who praise the general principles of the United Nations Charter?

The United States compelled Caribbean states to carry out financial reforms, to modernize their tariff systems and to pay their debts. Similar interventions were mostly undertaken in connection with loans to be floated by these states on the American market, or in order to forestall intervention by European powers seeking to collect delinquent loans by force. Typical cases are the interventions in San Domingo in 1905; Nicaragua, 1911; and in Haiti, 1915–1922.

On numerous occasions the United States intervened patently for purely political reasons. In 1909, for example, it opposed the establishment of a dictatorial rule in Nicaragua; the would-be dictator had shown aggressive designs against Honduras and Salvador and was planning to establish a Nicaraguan overlordship over Central America. This American intervention was certainly in line with the wishes of the countries concerned and probably also in line with the desires of the Nicaraguan people.

In 1913 and 1914 the United States opposed the Mexican dictator Huerta, who was not only an accomplished cheat but a notorious murderer who had instituted a reign of violence and terror and flaunted aggressive anti-American tendencies to boot. President Wilson, refusing to recognize him, propounded a pious, though somewhat ambitious "corollary" to the Monroe Doctrine, namely, the resolution of the United States to "teach the Latin Americans to elect good men." While it is certainly true that the Mexicans have the right to their own dictators, it is also true that they did not freely elect Huerta.

In the course of its various interventions, the United States supported both liberal, "leftist," and conservative, "rightist," parties. In 1859 it recognized the liberal regime of Benito Juarez in Mexico. In 1924 it opposed a conservative dictator of Honduras. In 1930 it persuaded the president of Haiti to resign and to make room for liberal financial reforms. By contrast, in 1912 the United States protected a conservative government in Nicaragua against liberal attack. In 1913 the United States forestalled a leftist revolution in Cuba. In 1933 the United States refused to recognize the radical government of Grau San Martín in Cuba.

To be sure, there are cases when it is hard to see why American forces intervened. Sometimes there were false alarms, sometimes the magnitude of the disorders was greatly exaggerated, sometimes subordinate officials simply made a show of strength where none was necessary.

The military occupation of San Domingo between 1916 and 1924 seems to have been of doubtful benefit to the best interests of the United States. In 1916, an insurrection took place in San Domingo. By the consent of the Dominican president, the United States landed marines. A new president was elected, but the United States refused to recognize him unless he signed a new treaty providing for the collection of customs by American officials, the appointment of an American financial adviser, and the establishment of a constabulary force under American officers. The president refused to accept recognition on these terms, and the United States imposed upon the Dominican Republic a virtual financial embargo. In the end the Dominican Republic was proclaimed to be under the military administration of the United States.[38] While from the material point of view, the American rule undoubtedly proved beneficial—many roads, bridges, railroad installations, and other facilities were built—this intervention aroused indignation in Latin America and led to strong opposition in the United States itself. This conflict with San Domingo, because of its repercussions at home and abroad, was one of the incidents which, under the Hoover and Roosevelt administrations, led to a revision of the American policy of intervention.

For the sake of completeness it must be added that some of the more important U.S. interventions were carried out by individual American citizens against the expressed wish of the American government. This is particularly the case of the so-called filibusters, the most notorious of whom was William Walker. This colorful soldier of fortune conquered, in 1855, the entire state of Nicaragua. Walker's expedition was linked up with the quarrels among American financiers about railroad rights across the Nicaraguan isthmus. Walker attempted to undo the concessions which Cornelius Vanderbilt had obtained for railroads and other means of transportation. After Walker had almost succeeded in subduing Nicaragua and had himself elected president, the American minister immediately extended recognition to Walker's government, but he was quickly censured by Washington, which thus by "nonintervention" gave the impression of siding with Vanderbilt. Supported by Vanderbilt, the Central American republics formed an alliance against Nicaragua. Walker was forced to surrender (1856). His defeat was Vanderbilt's victory. It has been said that "it was American capitalists who set up the Filibuster regime in Nicaragua, and it was an American capitalist who pulled it down." [39]

Balance Sheet of U.S. Intervention. Very little purpose is served if we scan this vast canvas of American political action in Latin America with pat notions as to the "justification" of this or that action. Most certainly, not all actions were "justified." In 1912, for example, the American Ambassador to Mexico, Henry Lane Wilson, strongly disliking the Mexican President Francisco Madero, worked for his downfall, going so far as to request a needless concentration of American troops at the Mexican border. The immediate result of this uncalled-for measure was that Mexican bandits began to loot and terrorize with increased aggressiveness; they expected that the Americans would bring law into the country and thus terminate their lucrative trade.[40]

[38] Graham H. Stuart, *Latin America and the United States,* 4th ed., New York, Appleton-Century-Crofts, 1943, p. 294.

[39] *Ibid.,* p. 328.

[40] Edward I. Bell, *The Political Shame of Mexico,* New York, McBride, 1914, pp. 147ff.

Yet other American interventions were clearly justified on the grounds of common decency and humanitarian ideals. The assistance of American armed force made it possible for many Latin-American states to maintain their independence without incurring expenses for armaments. It is certainly no accident that the constitution of Panama, adopted in 1904, stipulated that the United States should not only guarantee the independence and sovereignty of Panama but should also have the right to intervene in order to maintain *domestic* order. (In 1936, this clause was abrogated.)

To understand the significance of American intervention in Latin America, it is necessary to realize that similar interventions were carried out by many states all over the world. Whenever there was unrest and prolonged disorder, one or the other of the great powers intervened, usually with the acclaim of world public opinion. If the United States had not intervened in Latin America, other European countries would have intervened in order to protect the life and property of their citizens. The result would have been that South America would have become a zone of major world conflict while, in fact, it remained a zone of neutrality and relative peace.

The Latin-American countries themselves practiced intervention against each other. In connection with Paraguay's wars of the last century, intervention was practiced on a very large scale by all the participants. Argentina, Paraguay, and Uruguay constantly intervened in each other's affairs. Virtually every revolution which breaks out in Latin America is supported by and from another Latin-American state.

Another important fact should not be overlooked. When the Latin-American countries gained their independence, not a few among them were backward countries culturally and economically. True, some of the larger cities were centers of culture and learning; the University of Mexico, for example, was the second oldest Spanish university after Salamanca. Some of the Latin-American regions were culturally and economically farther advanced than the United States: In the 17th and early 18th centuries Brazil was industrially ahead of North America. Yet there had been a great cultural and economic decline; moreover, the high standards remained geographically isolated in the major cities. Hence with the exception of the ABC and a few other states, the Latin-American nations and certainly most of the Caribbean countries (except Cuba) were not ripe for self-government. Throughout the continent illiteracy was, and still is, widespread. There was no stable government. Political intercourse usually took the form of violence.

It would have been a normal development if these states had been taken under the guardianship of mandating powers. Since this did not happen, it evolved on the United States to maintain a minimum of order and orderly government. American intervention was therefore a substitute method for colonialism and the ransom which the Latin governments paid for the privilege of being sovereign and independent at a time when they lacked the ability to rule themselves.

On the whole, the experiment was successful. The Latin-American nations were enabled to achieve great progress both in the economic and in the cultural fields. They reduced illiteracy and they "worked their passage home" to moderately efficient forms of government. Whatever occasional mistakes there might have been, the United States did not abuse, on the whole, its power of intervention for narrowly selfish interests.

Nor did the United States impose its rule over Latin America. Countries that were occupied in the course of intervention were, without exception, returned to full independence. As Secretary of State Hughes remarked: "The significant thing about American military interventions in Latin American republics was not that the United States went in, but that they came out." It is, therefore, somewhat difficult to take at face value the clamorous and fashionable indictments which not a few among our contemporary historians have hurled against the alleged crimes of American intervention in Latin America.

International Law. Intervention is a term with many legal meanings. According to one definition "intervention is the attempt of one or more states, even by use of force, to coerce another state in its purely state action. When a state directly interferes with the exercise of the lawful state authority in or by another state, it constitutes intervention." [41] It follows that if there be no lawful action by a lawfully constituted state, an act of interposition cannot be considered as intervention. [42]

Intervention loses its aggressive or warlike character if it is consented to by the states which are its objects. Moreover, intervention may take place for the express purpose of avoiding war. Intervention is legal if it is carried out for the purpose of self-preservation; if a breach of the law as between states has taken place; and also if the whole body of civilized states has concurred in authorizing the intervention. [43] Otherwise, intervention is a warlike act; sometimes it is war, pure and simple.

The practical meaning of all these definitions is that intervention is legal or illegal according to the argument which one chooses and according to the criteria which one employs. For a pacifist, intervention may be perfectly justified if it avoids war, be it at the price of completely changing the political structure of a nation. For a radical partisan of national independence, intervention is unjustified, even if nonintervention were to lead to full-fledged war. The difficulty is compounded by the circumstance that a *passive* as well as an *active* policy of a major state always, by necessity, constitutes some kind of intervention.

[41] George Grafton Wilson, *International Law,* New York, Silver Burdett, 1935, p. 91.

[42] *Report of the Delegates of the United States of America to the Sixth International Conference of American States, Havana, Cuba, 1928,* Government Printing Office, 1928, pp. 14*f.*

[43] William Edwards Hall, *A Treatise on International Law,* New York, Oxford, 1895, pp. 297*f.*

From the end of the 19th century onward, the Latin-American states fought a violent diplomatic battle against the United States' practice of intervention. This battle of words occasionally reached the height of absurdity, as, for example, when Argentina proclaimed that even diplomacy is a form of intervention. The Latin-American countries used the various Pan-American conferences to suggest so-called "doctrines" which they hoped would be codified into international law and restrict United States freedom of action. Specifically, they tried to elaborate a code of behavior to control the recognition or nonrecognition by the United States of governments which had come to power through revolution. Naturally, it proved impossible to find acceptable definitions. A political problem cannot be solved by sublimating it into a legal concept.

In 1933, at the Pan-American Conference of Montevideo, a subcommittee adopted the following definition of intervention: [44]

Any act of state, through diplomatic representation, by armed force, with a view to making the state's will dominate the will of another state, and, in general, any maneuver, interference or interposition of any sort, employing such means, either directly or indirectly in matters of the obligations of another state, whatever its motive, shall be considered as intervention, and likewise a violation of international law. It would seem quite unnecessary to state that the subcommittee was, and is, in perfect accord that any friendly act to offer good offices and mediation in the foreign relations of states in order to maintain peace is, by its very nature, outside the definition of intervention.

The Montevideo policy was influenced by the Argentine foreign minister, Dr. Saavedra Lamas, who championed a Pan-Latin instead of a Pan-American League and looked, in the hope that the United States could be excluded from hemisphere policy, to Europe for associations with the Latin-American countries. The principle of nonintervention was the main weapon in the arsenal of Argentine diplomacy. For all practical purposes, it was the legal tool by which the power and political initiative of the United States in the Western Hemisphere were to be neutralized.

The Seventh International Conference of the American States at Montevideo did not accept the subcommittee's definition but affirmed the fundamental principle that "no state has the right to intervene in the internal or external affairs of another." The Buenos Aires Conference of 1936 reinforced the principle and stipulated that direct or indirect intervention for whatever reasons was "inadmissible." This principle of the inadmissibility of intervention was reaffirmed in 1938 at the Conference of Lima.

---

[44] The real, though unspecified, target of this "doctrine" was the "corollary" of Secretary Olney who, in 1875, stated that "the United States is practically sovereign on this continent, and its fiat is law upon the subjects to which it confines its interposition." It is noteworthy that this corollary was contained in a note to Britain and was designed to *protect* Venezuela in a boundary dispute with British Guiana.

Good Neighbor Policy. In implementation of the policy of nonintervention, the United States adopted the good neighbor policy vis-à-vis the Latin-American countries. Applied to concrete situations this policy fell somewhat short of expectations. A test case came when Mexico expropriated the United States oil companies and, in Cordell Hull's words, "proceeded to outright confiscation of American property." This expropriation was "justified" by the highly original Cárdenas "doctrine," [45] which stated, in essence, that American citizens are not entitled to receive compensation because persons who emigrate to a foreign country should acquire local nationality and assume the rights and obligations of the citizens of the host country. Accordingly, since Mexican-owned oil property had been expropriated, American oil property in Mexico should also be expropriated.

This unilateral doctrine was a radical departure from traditional international law, and the United States government did not accept its validity. However, the Roosevelt administration was not inclined to press the point, let alone proceed to forceful intervention. The Mexican government was aware of this unwillingness. Since there was litigation, and since the various Pan-American treaties stipulated that disputes should be mediated or arbitrated, the United States proposed that the conflict be arbitrated by a third and neutral power. Mexico refused this offer. According to all the rules and codes of international conduct, Mexico was now in the wrong. Still, the United States refrained from taking strong action. Unexpectedly, however, and possibly without direction from the State Department or the White House, the U.S. Treasury stopped buying silver on the Mexican market and thus put the Mexican economy under a heavy strain. As a result, Mexico precipitately sought a compromise. The State Department failed to take advantage of the situation and negotiated an agreement which, except for minor concessions to the United States, was highly advantageous to Mexico. [46]

Allegedly the agreement prevented the total expropriation of American oil property. In actual fact, however, the so-called "compromise" was arrived at by the granting of an American loan to Mexico. It is difficult to explain why the American government did not compensate the U.S. oil companies by turning over the money to them directly. Is it not probable that if the suspension of silver purchases in Mexico had started at an earlier moment, the Mexican government would have become far more pliable? This, then, was a case when the principle of nonintervention was skillfully employed by a Latin-American state *against* the interest of the United States.

The U.S. government publicized the Mexican oil dispute as a test case showing the sincerity with which it now adhered to the principle of noninterven-

[45] See Salvador Mendoza, *La Doctrina Cárdenas,* Mexico, Botas, 1939, pp. 29ff.
[46] See Harry Hersh Shapiro, *The United States and the Principle of Absolute Non-intervention in Latin America with Particular Reference to Mexico,* unpublished doctoral dissertation, Philadelphia, University of Pennsylvania, 1949, Chap. 4.

tion. It is difficult to believe that President Roosevelt's social philosophy did not strongly influence his decisions or that he was overly concerned about the damage inflicted upon Big Business, *i.e.*, the oil industry.

The Mexican oil case may or may not have allayed the so-called "suspicions" of the Latin-American countries. It is probably impossible to allay suspicions which, in most part, are simply a convenient cloak for political intentions.

The fact is that Mexico very quickly entered into oil agreements with Japan and Germany and thus supplied the two aggressors with oil which they had difficulty in procuring elsewhere. American forbearance therefore threatened not only the security of the United States proper but the security of all the countries in the Western Hemisphere. Other countries have followed Mexico on the road of "nationalization" of foreign property (although Mexico itself gradually has come to modify its original uncompromising attitude). Obviously, an international system tolerating "nationalizations" cannot be at the same time a system favoring international economic development and capital export. International economic progress would be arrested if the nationalization craze were not stopped.

No less serious are the implications as regards the national security of this country. The United States has changed from an oil-exporting to an oil-importing country which must rely on the oil resources of the Caribbean area and of the Middle East. If the Mexican and Iranian examples were followed, matters far graver would be at stake than the financial losses of a few American oil companies; clearly the infatuation with expropriation need not be restricted to oil. Condoning of nationalization policies, albeit in the name of the principle of nonintervention, cannot be considered as a sound precedent for democratic action.

Balance Sheet of Nonintervention. The Second World War demonstrated the hollowness of the principle of nonintervention. To realize this it is sufficient to exercise one's imagination by visualizing the establishment, for example, in 1942, of a Nazi- or Japanese-controlled government in the midst of South America. Is there any doubt that the United States would have intervened energetically and that its initiative would have been supported by a large majority of the Latin-American states? As it was, a pro-Nazi government took over Bolivia in 1944. Collective nonrecognition followed; lend-lease arrangements and export-import plans were suspended, and economic pressure was applied. Thereupon, the attitude of the Bolivian government changed, and Bolivia manifested her sympathies toward the United Nations. Bolivia secured recognition and—thereupon happily returned the former pro-Axis sympathizers to power.

In 1944, the foreign minister of Uruguay, Guani, elaborated a new "doctrine" which stipulated that for the duration of the war the American republics should refuse to recognize any new government set up by force, pending an investigation regarding the methods of its establishment and its sincerity in fulfilling the inter-American responsibilities. This was the expression by circumlocution of the unwillingness of the American states to accept a Nazi- or Japanese-inspired government into their midst. Whatever the motivation and formulation, the states of the Western Hemisphere recognized the *need* for intervention under certain conditions. The chief difference was that, from now on, *many* were to participate in what previously had been condemned as an illegal act.

This unexpected development aroused new "suspicions" on the part of some Latin states, which then began to find fault even with the venerable principle of the recognition of *de facto* governments. The Act of Chapultepec, adopted in March, 1945, by twenty American republics in token of their wartime solidarity, could do little but again condemn intervention and ter- ritorial conquest and proclaim the nonrecognition of acquisitions made by force. It also stipulated the steps which should be taken in order to prevent war or to stamp out the threat of war. These steps were identical with the well-known "sanctions," which range from the recall of chiefs of diplomatic missions through the breaking of diplomatic relations and coercive economic measures to the defensive, or preventive, use of armed force. Whether these steps are called "sanctions" or "interventions," or anything else, is imma- terial.

The significant changes introduced by the Act of Chapultepec are that interventions or sanctions *can* be employed, but only in the case of a threat to peace or actual aggression; and that sanctions (or intervention) should not be undertaken unilaterally but upon *agreement* among the signatory states.

The future will tell whether the need for agreement for multilateral action will not impede the timely execution of sanctions. No one knows how the treaty is to be implemented. No rules have been established concerning the methods by which "agreements" should be reached. Will the voting be done by simple or two-thirds majority, and will there be a veto power on the part of the United States or of the Latin-American nations? Will the voting procedure be similar to that in the United Nations, and will it therefore conflict with the principles enshrined in the various Pan-American declara- tions? Or will there be equal voting rights in contrast to the United Nations Charter? The odds are that any serious test would expose the Act for what is: meaningless verbiage.

Pan-Americanism. The story of American intervention in Latin America is less confusing than it may appear at first glance. During the 19th and early 20th centuries the United States practiced intervention chiefly in order to maintain peace in the Western Hemisphere, to further progress, and to preserve good relations with the Latin-American nations. The choice of the tool, namely, intervention, was largely dictated by the conditions of the time.

During the last thirty years, the Latin-American countries have made great strides. The objective of United States policy is still the same—peace, progress, and friendship. But this objective can no longer be attained by the old methods. Instead, the United States now pursues this objective by the practice of nonintervention. Diplomatic forbearance took the place of military occupation; a policy of "don't" was substituted for a policy of "do."

The essential point is that the choice between intervention and nonintervention is a matter of expediency and not of *Weltanschauung*. Nonintervention was deemed expedient ever since the time of the Hoover administration, but no government should commit itself as to the choice of its *future* strategy and tactics. The principle of nonintervention does not impose on the United States the obligation *not* to defend its interests. If American interests were to require intervention, the United States would have to resort to this technique, if only as an ultima ratio.

In the last analysis, the controversy over intervention is one of the false issues that plague American foreign policy. It serves to becloud the fundamental failure of Pan-Americanism. Hemispheric solidarity is a pleasing slogan; the fact remains that of the eighty-odd conventions and treaties signed at the various Pan-American Conferences since 1881, only *one* treaty was ratified by, and is therefore binding on, all the American nations: this happy exception was the Sanitary Code, adopted in 1924 at Havana.[47]

Since 1826, when Bolivar convoked an American congress to Panama, over 200 inter-American and Pan-American Conferences have been held. These conferences resulted in little else but scholastic exercises in the drafting of sonorous phrases. Principles were enunciated; from one conference to the next, these principles were embellished. Yet one may well ask whether Pan-Americanism is a living thing outside of seminars in international law?

It has been said that "Pan-Americanism is merely a cooperative movement." Unfortunately, it is hard to see any area of truly profitable cooperation outside the sphere of speechmaking. When Secretary Blaine called the first Pan-American Conference in 1889, he hoped that the Americas would become united through a customs union, a monetary union, and an inter-American bank. It took fifty-one years before, in 1940, the least ambitious of these ideas was taken up—and killed. In 1948, a new proposal was made at Bogotá to create an inter-American bank, but the idea was again shelved for "technical" reasons. Regardless of whether Blaine's concept is still fully valid in the present era of neomercantilism, there is no concerted hemispheric economic effort. Despite great natural wealth, economic progress in Latin America has been lagging behind until recently. Pan-Americanism and hemispheric solidarity are myths.

This failure has been caused in part by the misconception that Pan-Americanism can come to life as a "cooperative" rather than a political movement and that hemispheric solidarity should manifest itself through negative legal regulations *rather than positive political and economic action.*

[47] See Davila, *op. cit.*, p. 170.

Communist-dominated Guatemala, albeit one of the smallest Latin-American states, sparked a major crisis when its Foreign Minister, addressing in March, 1954, the Tenth Conference of American States at Caracas, Venezuela, inveighed against United States "imperialism" and "intervention," although the United States had failed to take any serious steps to halt Guatemala's program of nationalization and infiltration by communists. Although Secretary of State John Foster Dulles persuaded eighteen Latin-American states to join him in a strongly worded anticommunist resolution, there was, under the provisions of Pan-American agreements, no practical procedure for enforcing this resolution against Guatemala. A diplomatic Rotary Club specializing in New Year's resolutions cannot become a force in the world of 1954. Without intense economic cooperation, there will be no real political unity in the Americas. Without a political solidarity *that can be tested in the fire of modern war,* there will be no Pan-Americanism.

The failure of Pan-Americanism is partly the responsibility of the Latin-American governments and their jealousies and regional power politics. But the United States, too, cannot escape responsibility. The United States, mistaking words for action, never realized the trap in the "Pan-American" or hemispheric concept. There is no reason why the United States should base its American policies on the agreement of *all* Latin-American republics; nor is there any reason why the proved method of bilateral or multilateral agreements should not be applied. By trying to get everybody into the act, even weak and hostile elements, the play never reaches the stage.

At a time when Siberia and Africa are being developed as major centers of military and economic power, the economic growth of Latin America must be accelerated with all means at the disposal of the United States. It is up to the United States as the leading American nation to strengthen its initiative and to secure the military safety of the American nations by developing their common economic and military strength to the maximum. As a first step there must be a close reexamination of the American policies of the United States.

BIBLIOGRAPHY

Bartlett, Ruhl (ed.): *The Record of American Diplomacy,* New York, Knopf, 1948.

Beard, Charles A.: *The Idea of National Interest,* New York, Macmillan, 1934.

Bemis, Samuel Flagg: *The Latin American Policy of the United States,* New York, Harcourt, Brace, 1943.

————: *A Diplomatic History of the United States,* New York, Holt, 1936.

Castillero-Pimentel, Ernesto: *Panama y los Estados Unidos,* Panama, Editora Panama Americana, 1953.

Fenwick, Charles G.: *International Law,* 3d ed., New York, Appleton-Century-Crofts, 1948.

Hyde, Charles C.: *International Law, Chiefly as Interpreted and Applied by the United States,* 2d ed., Boston, Little, Brown, 1945.

Jessup, Philip C.: *A Modern Law of Nations,* New York, Macmillan, 1948.

Nussbaum, Arthur: *A Concise History of the Law of Nations,* New York, Macmillan, 1947.

Office of U.S. Chief of Counsel for Prosecution of Axis Criminality: *Nazi Conspiracy and Aggression*, Vols. 1, 2, 5, Government Printing Office, 1946.

Oppenheim, L., and H. Lauterpacht (eds.): *International Law: A Treatise*, Vol. I, "Peace," Vol. II, "War," New York, Longmans, 1947.

Ostermeyer, Gerhard: *Die Intervention in der Völkerrechtstheorie und -Praxis unter besonderer Berücksichtigung der Staatenpraxis des 19. Jahrhunderts: Ein Beitrag zur Interventionslehre*, Würzburg, K. Triltsche, 1940.

Stuart, Graham H.: *Latin America and the United States*, 4th ed., New York, Appleton-Century-Crofts, 1938.

Taracouzio, Timothy A.: *The Soviet Union and International Law*, New York, Macmillan, 1935.

Whitaker, Arthur P.: *The United States and South America; Northern Republics*, Cambridge, Mass., Harvard University Press, 1948.

Wilson, George Grafton: *International Law*, New York, Silver Burdett, 1935.

Chapter 17

PROPAGANDA

The term "propaganda" has been rendered ambiguous by too frequent use. Prior to the First World War the term was virtually unknown except to specialists familiar with the *Congregatio de propaganda fide*—a cardinal's committee having charge of the church's foreign missions.

Nevertheless, propaganda was practiced in antiquity, long before the invention of the printing press and the radio. The oldest known piece of literature, discovered in 1947, is an ancient Sumerian epic.[1] The poem, entitled *Enmerkar and the Lord of Aratta,* far surpasses in age the classic Greek epics, the *Odyssey* and *Iliad.* It tells the story of a political victory more than 5,000 years ago in which King Enmerkar of Erech, one of the more important of the Sumerian cities, devised a stratagem of "war of nerves" much like that used today. The King sent his ambassador over seven mountain ranges to the city of Aratta located either in Persia or western India. Enmerkar first made sure that he had the support of the goddess Inanna—Sumerian counterpart of the Greek goddess Aphrodite. Then back and forth between Erech and Aratta his emissary traveled, applying political pressure both by threat and subtle persuasion until finally the morale of the people was broken, and the city fell and succumbed to the domination of Enmerkar.

Propaganda is an attempt to influence the minds and opinions, and ultimately, the behavior of people. Unfortunately, this definition is so broad that it takes in virtually all intellectual and emotional intercourse, oral or written, because in practically every transaction and discussion there is an element of "I want you to do so-and-so." John Stuart Mill, writing his *System of Logic,* undoubtedly wanted to influence people by explaining to them the meaning and the better use of syllogisms, yet while this may be a *reductio ad absurdum,* there is little doubt that his writings on economics and politics contained propaganda elements. In a very broad sense, therefore, any science, even mathematics, can be said to contain certain propagandistic elements, the natural sciences perhaps less (though there are historically important exceptions, such as Ernst Haeckel), and the social and political sciences more.

The term "propaganda" if used in a very broad sense has no meaning. While it is admittedly impossible to draw a clear line of distinction, propaganda designates specifically *any systematic effort at persuasion between po-*

[1] See *The New York Times,* Mar. 2, 1947, p. 20, column 1.

litical groups in order to achieve or forestall political changes.[2] Efforts at persuasion are generally directed by one hostile group against another, but propaganda is also applied against neutrals and friends. It is carried out by appeals to emotions, conditioned reflexes, and thought, and is basically a conscious attempt to produce political action or inaction.

Lies and falsehood, though a frequent characteristic of propaganda, are not a necessary one. In most cases a propagandistic presentation of a problem will resemble far more closely the plea of a skillful lawyer than the cool analysis of a scientist whose sole intention is to clarify assumptions; to ascertain facts, multiple causes, and effects; and to weigh accurately the importance of each factor. The propagandist, if and when he speaks the truth, will speak it forcefully, but he will rarely speak the *whole* truth; instead of an "interpretation," or a working hypothesis, he will have a "slant."[3] While the true scientist will take care to point out defects of and exceptions to a given thesis and mention assumptions which are not susceptible to proof, the propagandist will avoid any reference indicating that his assertions are not wholly beyond criticism. He will speak with the assurance of one who has the one and only answer. There will be no "ifs" and "buts," except when called for by the exigencies of the propaganda point of view. The unskilled propagandist may resort to falsehoods and bluntness—both of which, especially in their crude forms, are only seldom effective. *Yet the true art of propaganda consists in systematic and deliberate formulation, omission, and indirection, aiming to change, after an interval of time, the pattern of stereotypes in people's minds.*[4]

It is customary to inveigh against propaganda as evil by definition. However, propaganda may be the only means of arousing a people against dangers which confront them but which are either not recognized or are blinked at. By contrast, propaganda may transform itself from servant into master, an uncontrollable force pitted against reason. Conflicts which could easily be adjusted might degenerate into war because passion and hatred have been inflamed by propaganda.

Whatever its moral value, propaganda cannot be abolished, as has been naïvely proposed, by international agreement.[5] Propaganda cannot be closely defined, and for this reason alone it cannot be dealt with by international treaty. Even if nations dissolved their propaganda agencies, they would still be separated by differing concepts of political and social institutions, and they

---

[2] Kurt Baschwitz in *Du und die Masse* (2d ed., Leiden, Brill, 1951, *passim*) emphasizes that propaganda makes use of two basic devices: *activating* and *paralyzing* ideas.

[3] On slogans and symbols, see *Public Opinion and World Politics,* Lectures on the Harris Foundation, 1933, edited by Quincy Wright, Chicago, University of Chicago Press, 1933, pp. 116–136.

[4] On the significance of stereotypes, see Walter Lippmann, *Public Opinion,* New York, Harcourt, Brace, 1922, pp. 119–125.

[5] See James P. Warburg, *Unwritten Treaty* (New York, Harcourt, Brace, 1946, p. 157), where the author presents the drafts for a treaty on psychological warfare disarmament.

would seek to justify their actions by special pleading. Propaganda is simply an integral part of political action. The mills of propaganda will keep on grinding as long as people act politically.

FUNCTIONS OF PROPAGANDA

The Roman Empire was supported by three major propaganda devices: the concept of the *civis Romanus* served to enhance the prestige of the empire—as did the military emblems, the *fasces,* which symbolized the strength of the Roman legion. The Roman Empire protected all men, citizens and subject peoples alike, and provided a stable order with efficient administration, as well as the sober blessings of the *Pax Romana.* In dealings with other nations, the Romans, before resorting to the force of arms, always offered varying degrees of partnership rather than crude domination. It was their policy, whenever they established permanent relations with any people, to respect their customs as well as to transfer their gods into the Pantheon, the temple of *all* gods. In the later period the empire stood for Christianity.[6]

The medieval emperors stood for "unity" or "peace," the American revolutionaries for independence, self-government, and ultimately for the Bill of Rights, while the armies of the French Revolution propagated the concept of political freedom and equality. The stage of modern history is crowded with empires or "movements" pretending to represent a "mission" assigned to them by some mystical power such as Destiny or Dialectic. Thus, propaganda welds together states which depend for their very existence upon cohesive forces generated by propaganda—whether these cohesive forces are channeled into domestic integration or foreign aggression. Propaganda is a substitute for organic belonging together.

What is the function of propaganda in foreign relations?[7] Simply to influence a foreign government so that it will adopt a policy which is advantageous to one's own policy or, if that foreign government is impervious to propaganda, to deprive it of the support of public opinion.

A country may have a surplus of a commodity which it wants to sell; so it may embark on a propaganda campaign to familiarize other nations with the availability of that commodity and convince prospective customers that it would be beneficial to them if they would buy. Brazil, for example, employed publicity experts in several European countries to inculcate the coffee-drinking habit—and sell the surplus of its immense coffee crop. Commercial treaties are usually preceded by such propaganda as are practically all other

---

[6] See Alfred Sturminger, *Politische Propaganda in der Weltgeschichte: Beispiele vom Altertum bis in die Gegenwart,* Vienna, Bergland Buch, 1938, pp. 19ff.

[7] A short history of political propaganda may be found in Serge Chakotin, *The Rape of the Masses: The Psychology of Totalitarian Political Propaganda* (London, Routledge, 1940, pp. 128–159) ; also in Frederick E. Lumley, *The Propaganda Menace* (New York, Appleton-Century-Crofts, 1933, pp. 45–76).

agreements, including "giveaway" programs of the Lend-Lease and Marshall Plan type.

The adoption of any policy is usually the result of successful preparatory propaganda. This is true of loans, alliances, declarations of war, and attempts to make peace. Propaganda serves to condition the minds of one's own people and of one's friends and foes, as well as of neutral nations, to the ready acceptance of the proposed policy and to the rejection of unacceptable policies. It "makes the case" for the soundness of the policy and the necessity of one's acts.

PROPAGANDA IN DIPLOMACY

At present practically all governments intrust propaganda to special ministries or agencies. This does not mean, however, that prior to the establishment of these official organizations, governments did not engage in propaganda, or that these ministries and agencies monopolize a government's propaganda. Such an interpretation would be based on the erroneous idea that propaganda activities consist merely of dissemination of verbal appeals. These ministries engage merely in *one* specific kind of propaganda—public relations and advertising of the government as a whole. Yet diplomacy is permeated by propaganda which is contained in communications sent from one government to the other, in "notes," "requests," "protests," "publications," "demands for apologies," "declarations," official speeches, and the like.

A good example of the propagandistic content of many diplomatic exchanges may be taken from the correspondence between Emperor Wilhelm II and Tsar Nicholas II in 1904. At that time, Russia was involved in her disastrous war with Japan. France was the ally of Russia, but on account of the British-Japanese alliance and the Franco-British entente, in statu nascendi, France could not come to Russia's aid. In effect, in order to placate the British, on whose friendship they counted most, the French committed several rather unfriendly acts against Russia as, for example, refusing to sell them warships. This situation pleased Wilhelm, whose supreme hope was to split France from Russia. Hence we find the following passages in his letter to Nicholas of June 6, 1904: [8]

I had an interesting conversation about the war with the French military attaché who, on my remark that I thought it most astonishing that France, as your ally, "did not send down their fleet to keep Port Arthur open till your Baltic fleet had arrived," answered that it was true but that they had to reckon with other powers: after a series of allusions I found out what I always feared, that the Anglo-French agreement had one main effect in stopping France from helping you. *Il va sans dire* that if France had been under the obligation of helping you with her fleet, I would

[8] See *Die Grosse Politik der Europäischen Kabinette 1871–1914,* Vol. 19/1, "Der Russisch-Japanische Krieg," Berlin, Deutsche Verlagsgesellschaft für Politik und Geschichte, 1925, p. 183.

not have budged with a finger to harm her, that would have been most illogical on the part of one before whose eyes is always the picture "The yellow peril."

These remarks were followed by many others in subsequent letters. They were not entirely lost on the Russians. In September the Russian Foreign Minister Count Lamsdorf instructed his ambassador in Paris, in connection with a minor incident, to tell the French government that its "attitude produces an impression extremely unfavorable to France which is being accused of having an excessive fear of Japan." A short while later, when German deliveries of coal to Russian ships provoked British protests, Wilhelm wrote to Nicholas that "this new menace must be countered by Germany and Russia." This was, of course, the point Wilhelm tried to put over.

Similar incidents could be found in many other diplomatic exchanges, although few of them are so blunt and outspoken. Usually, diplomatic letters are written to show how beneficial cooperation would be or what greater advantages could be derived from ceasing to cooperate with a third power.

Far from using propaganda, diplomacy may be dominated by it. For example, by the end of 1931 when the powers were preparing the Lausanne disarmament conference to be convened early in 1932, it became quite clear that the moment was most unpropitious for the undertaking. Not only was there little hope of achieving an agreement on the reduction of armaments, but economic problems were much more pressing and should have been taken up first. Elections which probably would lead to changes in government were pending in France and Germany. Yet the disarmament conference had been given such a propaganda build-up that, in Dr. Beneš' words, "no government would suggest postponement of the conference without creating misunderstandings." Accordingly, the powers contrived to save the conference from immediate collapse. The chosen method was "to spin out proceedings and not to get down to business until after the French elections." Proceedings were spun out but the conference never got down to business.[9]

The crux of the disarmament discussions at that time was whether the Western powers would reduce their armaments to the level of Germany or whether Germany would be allowed to increase her armaments in order to reach the level maintained by the Western powers. The Germans based their case on the principle of equality, which the Western powers could not refute without coming into basic conflict with their own professed ideals. Especially the French, who have painted the word *egalité*—equality—on nearly all their public buildings, were hard put to oppose Germany's claims with plausible arguments. They attempted to emphasize "security" against "equality" but thereby made their bad case worse, Germany having been allowed far less "security" than any other power. In other words, French policy lacked the propaganda underpinning which policy needs in order to be successful.

[9] E. L. Woodward and Rohan Butler (eds.), *Documents on British Foreign Policy 1919–1939*, second series, London, H.M. Stationery Office, 1948, Vol. III, "1931–1932," p. 50f.

"Declarations" often are issued for propaganda purposes rather than as commitments. For example, during the Sudetenland crisis in 1938, the British Government at a decisive moment issued through the Foreign Office a declaration that if, in spite of all efforts, France and Czechoslovakia should become involved in war, they would be assisted by Russia as well as Great Britain.[10] However, this declaration was made almost furtively—it was made to the press by an "unnamed" official—so as not to constitute a British obligation. It was designed as a *warning* to Germany.

Of course, declarations must sometimes be more forceful to be really understood. Such a declaration was the famous British pledge of March 31, 1939, promising Poland help in case of attack. This pledge was predominantly a propaganda pledge because it was conceived as a last attempt to warn Germany that, by pursuing her policy, she would ultimately be opposed by British arms. Yet the pledge, to be propagandistically effective, had to be given legal validity.

Official government publications are more often than not composed and released for propaganda purposes. Outstanding among them are the "color books," [11] which from time to time are published either to justify a given policy or to expose the policy of an opponent; most important are the "color books" issued after the outbreak of a war and purporting to show how it came about. All such books contain actual documents, but they do *not* contain *all* the documents; nor are the printed documents always given in their full length. They are propaganda *by selection*. It will be remembered that shortly before the Argentine elections in 1946, the U.S. Department of State issued a publication showing the affiliation of certain Argentineans with Nazi espionage. It was widely believed that this publication was timed to coincide with the Argentine elections and that it was the purpose of the State Department to discredit one of the candidates, Juan Peron; if so, the attempt failed.[12]

Information concerning secret treaties concluded by opponents furnishes a government with unique propaganda opportunities. For example, in June, 1917, the German legation in Switzerland received, through a Swiss Cabinet

[10] This communiqué had originated with Churchill who wanted to show the "unity of sentiment and purpose between Britain, France, *and Russia* against Hitlerite aggression." It was released after a violent speech by Hitler. The "pith," to use Mr. Churchill's word, of the communiqué was worded as follows: "If, in spite of the efforts made by the British Prime Minister, a German attack is made on Czechoslovakia, the immediate result must be that France will be bound to come to her assistance, and Great Britain *and Russia* will certainly stand by France." The inclusion of the word "certainly," by a strange twist of grammar, deprived this communiqué of any legal validity that it might have had. The Russian government "certainly" had not authorized the British Foreign Office to speak in its name. (See Winston Churchill, *The Second World War*, Boston, Houghton Mifflin, 1948, p. 309.) Italics are the authors'.

[11] Harold Temperley and Lillian M. Penson (eds.), *A Century of Diplomatic Blue Books, 1814–1914*, London, Cambridge, 1938.

[12] See *Blue Book on Argentina: Consultation among the American Republics with Respect to the Argentine Situation*, Memorandum of the United States Government, Government Printing Office, February, 1946; New York, Greenberg, 1946.

member, vital information about a secret session of the French parliament. In this session the French government had informed the deputies that, according to a secret agreement between France and Tsarist Russia, the following territorial rearrangements would be made upon the termination of the war: In addition to Syria, France would receive Alsace-Lorraine and the Saar area, while it would obtain priority rights in the *Rheinprovinz* of Prussia, which was to be transformed into a buffer state. In other words, France would establish control over all German territories west of the Rhine. In return, Russia would be given the Dardanelles and Constantinople.

The German minister commented that, in his opinion, the publication of this secret treaty would cause considerable indignation in Russia and the United States, but he cautioned that the text must be published in such a way that the source would not be compromised. The minister suggested that the information be published in the newspaper *Berner Tagwacht* which, throughout the war, had served as the mouthpiece of Lenin's non-Russian comrades. (Up to April, 1917, Karl Radek was one of the chief editorial writers of this paper.) Publication in the *Tagwacht* would have the double advantage that it would be picked up immediately all over the world and that it would not compromise the indiscreet Swiss politician to whom this paper was strongly opposed. To cover tracks even more, the minister suggested that the article should indicate that the information had been received from socialists in Stockholm who were in touch with their friends in Petrograd. The German Foreign Office accepted this proposal and also made arrangements to familiarize the Petrograd socialists "who were working for peace" with the information.[13] The reverberations of this indiscretion proved very embarrassing to the Western governments. The Bolsheviks were so impressed by the effectiveness of this particular propaganda technique that, upon coming to power, they published many treaties and agreements concluded between Tsarist Russia and "capitalist" and "imperialist" nations in order to show the "rottenness" of bourgeois foreign policies; unfortunately, they have failed ever since 1918 to publish, for the purpose of comparison, any documents of their own foreign policy.

The speeches of statesmen almost always serve propagandistic purposes, not only in *what* is said but also in *how* and even *where* it is said. Propaganda is contained not only in the points made in a speech, and in the degree of moderation or violence, but the locality where the speech is delivered is also often very significant. For example, in December, 1938, Italy claimed concessions in Corsica and Tunisia; thereupon Premier Daladier of France visited these two areas and delivered several speeches which, though moderate, effectively conveyed the warning intended.

Any foreign policy to gain support must identify its concrete purposes with certain ideas or principles. The true aims of foreign policy can rarely be

[13] U.S. National Archives, *German Foreign Office Files, 1914–1918,* Microfilm Reel 2597.

publicized in their entirety—except at the risk of making these aims difficult or impossible of attainment. No country will declare that it desires to annex a certain territory; it will bare its unselfish intention of "liberating" the inhabitants of that territory or simply of extirpating a threat to general peace. Since propaganda invokes principles and does not and cannot admit the true motives of policy, there is an apparent lack of consistency which sometimes is apt to prove embarrassing.

Foreign policy is a series of acts for a purpose. In order to be successful this purpose must be understood and approved not only by one's own nation but also by other governments and peoples. Understanding and approval can be obtained easily for concrete objectives such as the alteration of a commercial treaty, but the more abstract and long-range objectives of a government often are quite incomprehensible. A long-range foreign policy will find popular acceptance when it can be couched in terms of a few simple ideas. This is the reason why official interpretations of foreign policy tend to be platitudinous. This is the reason, too, why it is necessary to accustom the audience to a few basic concepts which they will remember and use as criteria to judge the validity and success of any given foreign policy. For example, by the end of the Second World War not a few influential personages in Washington held the opinion that the world would have to move to the "left"; any policy interfering with this "inevitable" development was doomed to failure. The problems of Asiatic societies were to be solved by "agrarian reform"; those of the industrialized West by "nationalization" of the basic elements of production; those of internal and constitutional reform on the continent by the liquidation of "war criminals." The concrete steps of Russian foreign policy were made possible because a conceptual framework had been erected within which people could live, without any apparent strain on their critical faculties, with such assorted axioms as, for example, that Russia was standing for "progress" and "economic democracy," that she was entitled to more "security" than other nations, that she was truly "peace-loving," and that she was so strong that it was inadvisable to interfere with her plans.

A foreign policy is effective, then, when it can take advantage of simple ideas which find easy credence. Governments whose policies are derived from complex ideas which cannot be "put across" clearly, are apt to land themselves in a maze of contradictions and ultimately in hot water. Their propaganda clashes with their true interests, or they feel compelled to pay lip service to ideas in which they themselves do not believe. In general, even valid—"right"—ideas, once they have been taken up propagandistically, complicate policy; they mislead people into believing that there is a simple solution which can be applied consistently. *The great drawback of propaganda is that it prevents people from thinking; and yet, absence of propaganda would prevent them from doing.*

While propaganda never will be fully eliminated from foreign policy, its excessive use cannot but make international problems more and more complicated. Besides, too much propaganda, like a vaccine, produces virtual immunity against propaganda. By saying too much, propaganda merely devaluates all ideas and exposes its own government and people to cynicism and charges of hypocrisy.

It is perhaps the condemnation of propaganda by the general public and scholars as an evil device of "power politics" which explains the fact that few statesmen, diplomats, and soldiers have made a systematic study of this legitimate tool of their respective trades. A statesman as expert in the molding of domestic public opinion as President Roosevelt did not always prove as masterly and subtle a psychologist when dealing with problems of foreign propaganda.[14] For example, eager to prevent the Germans from hatching a new "stab-in-the-back" legend, President Roosevelt, at Casablanca in 1943, proclaimed the "unconditional-surrender" formula and declined to modify it after its hazards had become obvious. Despite the fears of the Allies, a new version of the selfsame legend spun by the German nationalists from the dubious evidence of World War I would hardly have been effective. Moreover, there is no way of preventing a resourceful propagandist from making capital out of *anything* his nation's opponents do or say. As it was, the opposite legend sprang up, namely, that, if the Allies had modified the unconditional-surrender formula and communicated its terms to the opposition in Germany, the *coup d'état* of July 20, 1944, would have been successful and the war would have ended ten months earlier. The exaggerated preoccupation with the idea that Germany's guilt for the Second World War must be proved (although empirically there could have been little doubt on this score) gave rise to some of the most unsatisfactory features of the war-crimes trials and furnished anyone who cared to pick them up with powerful arguments against Allied policies. The purpose—the legal identification and punishment of crime—could have been reached better through employment of proper means: the trial of the defendants by a German court for common crimes they actually committed, rather than for political crimes which are not listed in the criminal code of any country.

Another example of naïveté in propaganda matters was the uncritical acceptance by American diplomats and soldiers of the Japanese boast that "Japanese never surrender." A cursory survey of Japanese history would have

---

[14] President Roosevelt showed little interest in foreign propaganda. According to one observer, "The President . . . had been opposed to the creation of a propaganda service and had established OWI with considerable reluctance under pressure from his advisers whose primary aim was to provide an adequate flow of information to the American public. Once the organization was established, he did not want to be bothered about it. In his own right Roosevelt was a great propagandist . . . but he did not understand the systematic use of propaganda in total war." (Wallace Carroll, *Persuade or Perish*, Boston, Houghton Mifflin, 1948, p. 7.) Carroll also writes: "On every issue which arose, . . . the British had a policy. It was not always a sound or enlightened policy, but it was something with which you could make propaganda. On the other hand, American policy, while containing some good elements, was usually so abstract and negative that you could not turn it into effective propaganda." (*Ibid.*, p. 181.)

revealed that Japanese warriors, sensibly, did lay down their arms when confronted with overwhelming odds. More careful study might have brought to light the peculiar logic by which the Japanese mind manages to square the idea of surrender with that of national honor.[15] Apparently no such searching study was made and the "do-or-die" myth of the Japanese warrior continued to dominate American policy. This fascination was in part responsible for those portions of the Yalta agreement which surrendered the Kurils, Karafuto, and Manchuria, as well as Port Arthur and Dairen, to the Russians and which compromised the future of China.

During the Cold War, Western statesmen were bemused by two different propaganda images of Soviet Russia: one school was convinced that Russia was extremely weak, while the other group was sure that Russia had become all but invincible. The first group overemphasized the fact that living standards in Russia were very low. Unfortunately, a short supply of footwear or food does not necessarily indicate insufficiency of steel mills or of tank and airplane factories. Many conquerors of history have proved that poverty may be one of the greatest morale incentives. The second group fashioned a "20-foot Russian" simply by ignoring the weaker parts of the Russian economy and assuming that the dictatorial machine would work with clocklike precision, a scientifically constructed robot no longer subject to human whimsey or emotion. In actual fact, a monolithic dictatorship is a very inefficient political structure if only because the brain of *one* man, the dictator, is not big enough to handle the complex situations which must be decided by a modern government. Hitler's and Mussolini's experiences offer conclusive evidence on this point, and even in the case of Stalin the assorted evidence appears to indicate that he ended as a "tired old man." The historical record shows that the decisions of the Soviet dictatorship often were the result less of rational analysis than of intraparty strife. Moreover, there is a significant difference between what would appear "rational" to an outside observer and what is rational to the members of a particular group. It would have been rational for the Soviets to participate in the reconstruction of Europe including their own country as had been proposed by the original Marshall Plan offer—if their criteria had been those of a democratic society.

The impressions which a government creates about itself through its acts and which it creates through propaganda are an element of its strength or weakness. Conversely, the ideas which a government may nurse about its opponent may paralyze its actions or induce recklessness; in either event, policy is greatly handicapped.

---

[15] See Ellis M. Zacharias, *Secret Missions: The Story of an Intelligence Officer,* New York, Putnam, pp. 322*ff.* The basic assumption of the psychological warfare campaign directed by Zacharias against the Japanese was precisely that the Japanese would surrender if skillfully approached.

SOME PROPAGANDA TECHNIQUES

Slogans and catchwords · are important tools of propaganda. Urban II launched the Crusades with the cry *"Deus le volt"* (God wills it). The armies of the French Revolution, ill-clad, ill-trained, and ill-equipped, were victorious with the battle cry *"Ça ira"* (it will turn out all right)—a phrase allegedly used by Benjamin Franklin when he was asked about conditions in the United States. In the Spanish Civil War, the slogan *"No pasarán"* (they shall not pass) was widely used; it was a repetition of the phrase coined at Verdun, *"Ils ne passeront pas."* The German political comeback after 1919 was staged with the catchword *"Gleichberechtigung"* (equal rights). In India, "Amritsar" (the name of a town where British troops had fired on Indians) symbolized opposition against British overlordship. In American history the slogans, "Remember the Alamo," "Remember Pearl Harbor," "Fifty-four forty or fight," and "Make the world safe for democracy" are familiar. Such catchwords are not only war cries but capsular formulas of foreign policy and peacemaking. The identification of slogans with *concrete* objectives of foreign policy leads to the falsification of problems and accordingly to the adoption of crude and unworkable solutions. The terms self-government, democracy, free elections, security, minority rights, etc., are common coins in the market of political ideas. Many a political settlement purports to derive its sanction from tenuous ideas suggested by such slogans. While it is undoubtedly necessary to follow general ideas or principles, as directional devices, there is a great danger that the true nature of these ideas as *signposts* along the rocky road of reality is confounded with the nature of that road itself. Through sloganization, concrete programs become falsified and in time lose their original meaning. Once programs are no longer tools but assume the validity of absolutes, men fail to recognize that there are limitations in the application of the best ideas. A government committed to a certain idea or program rarely dares discard it even in cases where it is clearly inapplicable. If compelled by necessity to forsake that particular idea, it does so behind a verbal smoke screen designed to convey impressions contrary to unpalatable fact. The United States, for example, was prisoner of such a sloganized idea when, during the First World War, it insisted on the "freedom of the seas" at the risk of quarreling with Britain.

Sloganization compels a country to apply identical formulas for dissimilar situations. For example, while a democratic country like the United States may favor democracy everywhere, the means by which democracy can be introduced are not everywhere identical. In one country, free elections may restore the workings of democracy, while in other countries they may bring dictatorship into power. Statesmen themselves are not immune to contamination by propaganda, and after having repeated slogans often enough, ultimately end up by believing in their absolute and ubiquitous validity themselves. This happens, in particular, in countries where there is no public criticism to point out errors in thought. But even in countries unfettered by thought police, certain slogans take hold of public opinion, sacred taboos beyond the range of rational debate.

Once slogans have become accepted, foreign policy tends to become rigid and can no longer be adapted to changed conditions. In the course of international crises, slogans of the type of "the country's honor or national interest is at stake" tend to accentuate conflicts. While at the beginning they may serve as warning signals to the opponent that he should not go too far, they make it in the end impossible to arrive at a compromise settlement.

A good example is the story of the Ems dispatch in 1870. The King of Prussia conducted negotiations with the French Ambassador. These negotiations, arising from a Franco-Prussian dispute over the question of whether a Hohenzollern prince was to ascend the throne of Spain, were designed to put an end to the crisis. At one juncture, the King received a French proposal which he found unacceptable, though by no means offensive. The French Ambassador wanted to see the King again, but the King chose not to receive him, having nothing to add to the reply already given. Hence he had the Ambassador informed that, pending further information, he had nothing to say. The King was taking a cure and wanted his rest; he certainly did not intend to be offensive, let alone to break relations with France. Benedetti, the French Ambassador, repeatedly stated afterward that "at Ems there was neither offender nor offended." The French historian Albert Sorel pointed out: "At Ems the King did not seem to suspect that M. Benedetti had failed in proper respect to him, nor did M. Benedetti suspect that the King had insulted France in his person."

Bismarck, as the King's Minister, was kept informed of events and authorized to publish communiqués about them. When he received the dispatch from Ems relating the King's conversation with Benedetti, he felt that the negotiations were running unfavorably from his point of view, *i.e.*, toward amicable agreement. Hence he edited the text of the original Ems dispatch in such a manner that, to the unwary reader, it gave the impression that the Ambassador had offended the King and that the King had broken off negotiations; then Bismarck released the edited dispatch to the press. The text was phrased in such a way that no one doubted in Berlin that the King had been insulted, while in Paris everybody was convinced that the King had insulted France with the purpose of provoking war. Public indignation not only made war inevitable but brought it about so quickly that the French Foreign Minister, Duc de Gramont, was unable to establish the correct facts in time. As Bismarck had intended it, France was provoked into taking the initiative. Thus, the War of 1870 was provoked by Bismarck's propaganda maneuvers.[16]

[16] Bismarck did not hesitate to tell the story himself and tell it quite honestly. See *Bismarck, the Man and the Statesman: Being the Reflections and Reminiscences of Otto,*

PROPAGANDA VEHICLES

The means and methods of propaganda are as varied as is human ingenuity. They change with the time and situation. It is the mark of the skilled propagandist—and the successful statesman—that he can devise new means and methods. Propaganda is successful only if it is served in *new forms;* otherwise its character as propaganda is obvious and its effectiveness reduced.

Propaganda in its most common form is the spreading of news and rumors. Preoccupation with "news" is as old as history. In antiquity, states organized a network of "relay posts" which communicated with each other by word of mouth or signals, runners, or mounted messengers. Since news influences "morale" and political decisions, it always was and always will be a primary propaganda instrument.

Propaganda is also the dissemination of ideas. In ancient Greece, the theater, especially the comedy, served as a vehicle of political propaganda, a technique which the Chinese communists used effectively in our time. In antiquity, Demosthenes' speeches, disseminated throughout Greece, served to rally his nation against invasion, as did those of the philosopher Fichte in 1812 at Berlin. In the Middle Ages, religious sermons were widely circulated in order to publicize the point of view of the church on matters divine and profane.

The 17th and 18th centuries were the golden age of the political pamphlet. French writers went to Holland, then a perennial enemy of France, and published in safety their diatribes against Louis XIV. Sieyès's *Qu'est-ce que le tiers état?* contributed to the downfall of the old regime under Louis XVI. Benjamin Constant, novelist and poet, attacked Napoleon from Hanover, then a British possession.

In modern times, biographies of political figures such as Hitler and Evita Peron, histories of political movements, and pseudoscientific and occasionally even scientific books have become important propaganda vehicles. The communists have flooded the world market with literally millions of pseudoscientific books; the more sophisticated British are adept at presenting a closely reasoned and factual argument for their viewpoints in such dignified publications as those issued by the Royal Institute of International Affairs (Chatham House).

Creative writing is a most effective kind of propaganda. Dante's *Divine Comedy* is heavily charged with political argument. *Uncle Tom's Cabin* can be considered as one of the contributory causes of the American Civil War. The gifted German poet Ernst Lissauer concocted in 1914 an effective "song of hate against England." The German Hans Grimm's book *Volk ohne Raum*

Prince von Bismarck, Written and Dictated by Himself after His Retirement from Office, translated by A. J. Butler, New York, Harper, 1898, Vol. II, pp. 100*f.*

(people without space) provided the Nazis with a fetching slogan. Another German poet, Ernst Toller, used the drama to propagandize communism.

Satire has been one of the most effective propaganda weapons, from Aristophanes to Voltaire, Swift, and Beaumarchais to Shaw. That, in 1942, an adaptation of Sophocles' *Antigone* could still serve as powerful propaganda was proved in German-occupied Paris.

Great painters and caricaturists like Goya, Daumier,[17] David Low, and Arthur Szyk have provided very effective antiwar propaganda; many of Goya's best pictures were directed against the incessant Spanish civil wars. The propaganda value of sculpture and architecture lies in their timelessness and directness; monuments and arches of triumph are perhaps the most permanent forms of propaganda.

National anthems are often very poor poetry but effective propaganda, as, for example, the "Marseillaise"; satirical songs such as "Marlb'rough s'en va-t-en guerre" may assume political importance. Even opera did not escape the propaganda contagion. The aria "Amour sacré de la patrie" in Auber's opera *La Muette de Portici* became, when it was sung in Brussels in 1830, the signal for revolution. Verdi's *Ballo in Maschera* was banned from Naples, where the court considered it an incitement to political assassination. Verdi's name later became the battle cry for the liberation of Italy, as it presented an abbreviation of *V*ittorio *E*mmanuele *R*e *d'I*talia. The influence of the Wagnerian operas on German nationalism was very great. As can be seen from this list, some of mankind's greatest minds were zealous political propagandists.

France, the pioneer of cultural propaganda, founded, in 1883, the *Alliance Française,* a system of French educational centers spread over most of the world which contribute to upholding the prestige of French learning and art, and, implicitly, of French prestige and power. The *Alliance Française,* though not run as a propaganda agency, has been for this very reason an effective instrument of propaganda and one which, moreover, paid for its own upkeep.

Disclosure of secret and embarrassing information may convey a persuasive political message, as all readers of modern newspapers know who are accustomed to digest what are known as "inside stories." Julius Caesar made the first effective use of this literary propaganda device by publishing daily reports, *acta diurna,* about the secret proceedings in the Senate. In 1918, the American government published documents secured in Russia which showed the secret collaboration between the German government and the Bolsheviks.[18] In 1948, the American government published documents from the archives of the German Foreign Office concerning the negotiations between Soviet Russia and Nazi Germany from 1939 to 1941 in order to expose

---

[17] See Sturminger, *op. cit.,* p. 220.

[18] Committee on Public Information, *The German-Bolshevik Conspiracy,* War Information Series, No. 20, October, 1918.

Russia's contributions to the outbreak of the Second World War.[19] The Soviets countered with the publication of another series of German documents purporting to show that Britain had tried to involve Germany in a war against the Soviet Union.[20]

A favorite propaganda stunt is the fabrication of fraudulent documents such as the "testament" of Peter the Great and the Tanaka Memorial which outlined the aggressive strategy of Japan. (As of this writing, it has not been fully clarified as to whether the Tanaka Memorial is a fraud or not.) The various anti-Semitic campaigns since 1920 drew ammunition from that notorious hoax, the *Protocols of the Elders of Zion.* In 1924, the British Conservatives won an election by publishing the famous Zinoviev letter, which allegedly transmitted instructions from the Third International to British subjects and which contained suggestions for revolution.[21] As late as 1948, the Western powers were briefly duped by the famous "Protocol M," an alleged communist plot to wreck the Marshall Plan by strikes in Germany.[22]

Sometimes economic warfare may be used effectively for propaganda purposes. During the First World War, England and France bought large amounts of war matériel in the United States. German officials believed that these purchases were at the root of the pro-Ally sentiment in the United States, and suggested to the War Minister von Falkenhayn that he accede to the advice of the German Ambassador at Washington and place massive orders in the United States. Falkenhayn did not accept this idea on the ground that the matériel could be delivered only in three months and by that time the war would be over. (It never occurred to him that the Royal Navy might intercept the deliveries.) The reasoning of the German officials was singularly obtuse, but the story casts an interesting light on the bearing of economic warfare on popular attitudes. During the Second World War, Britain demonstratively continued with her exports and embellished boxes with slogans such as "Britain delivers the goods" in order to show that German bombing had not affected British industry.

During the Cold War, Russia repeatedly tried to bolster its waning political influence by promising advantageous commercial deals. The Soviets shipped small quantities of grain to France and India in order to enable local communists to acclaim these deliveries as proof of Russian good will and of Russian economic productivity. Since, however, even in those cases where com-

[19] Raymond J. Sontag and James Stuart Beddie (eds.), *Nazi-Soviet Relations 1939 to 1941*, Department of State Publication 3023, Government Printing Office, 1948.

[20] *Documents and Materials Relating to the Eve of the Second World War*, 2 vols., New York, International Publishers, 1948.

[21] An excellent discussion of the various outstanding historical frauds is contained in Henri Rollin, *L'Apocalypse de notre temps; les dessous de la propagande allemande d'après des documents inédits*, Paris, Gallimard, 1939. For an interesting discussion of the interrelationship of literary fraud and political truth, see Boris Mouravieff, *Le Testament de Pierre le Grand, Légende et Réalité*, Neuchâtel, Baconnière, 1949.

[22] "Protocol M" was reprinted by *The New York Times*, Jan. 16, 1949, p. 2. It had been published by the British Foreign Office.

mercial treaties had actually been concluded no sizable trade was done—except in timber, furs, and caviar—these business propositions were mere propaganda.

PROPAGANDA AND CONFLICT

At the dawn of history Homer described how in the Trojan War each side explained the whys and wherefores of the struggle. Such explanations are given virtually in every war; innumerable wars were accompanied by full-fledged propaganda campaigns.

When the Bohemian nobles threw the Imperial legates out of the window at Prague in 1618, an event which provoked the Thirty Years' War, they immediately published an "Apologia," or defense, to explain the reasons for their deed. The Imperial Court speedily answered with an "Information." The Bohemians then published a second defense. In 1621, both Imperialists and Bohemians captured secret state documents, including drafts for alliances, and published them, thus anticipating a propaganda trick which the communists used successfully in 1918. In the Thirty Years' War there appears the propaganda expert, forerunner of the information ministers of our time, the Protestant cause being represented by Dr. Ludwig Camerarius, and the Catholic cause by the Jesuit Father Jakob Keller.

The first modern statesman who recognized the importance of systematic "information" for the benefit of his subjects and foreign nations seems to have been Cardinal Richelieu. Richelieu intrusted the task of editing a newspaper to the Huguenot physician Renaudot who, on May 30, 1631, published the first issue of *La Gazette*. The purpose of the new venture, so it was explained, was to prevent the spreading of *false* information. Richelieu, as well as the King himself, wrote articles for the *Gazette;* the King specialized in stories of battles and campaigns.

Leaflets have, in more recent times, been used more and more prominently, for instance, in the American Revolutionary War when several attempts were made to induce the Hessians to desert from the British army.[23] Since the end of the 18th century, leaflets have been a regular feature in practically every war, but particularly during the two world wars when the rotary printing press, the leaflet-carrying shell or bomb, and the airplane made possible the distribution of leaflets in large numbers over large areas; during the Second World War alone several *billions* of leaflets were distributed by the belligerents.

Military communiqués have been given out, in one form or another, at all times. The art of denying defeats has long been highly developed. On the

[23] Carroll, *op. cit.,* p. 185, calls attention to the fact that Congress in 1776 showed great insight in the mechanics of propaganda when it accompanied propaganda words by material offers. Soldiers deserting the British were offered "a participation of the blessings of peace, liberty, property, and mild government" and, more important, 100 to 1,000 acres of land. At Bunker Hill, the Americans distributed "handbills" offering the would-be deserters seven dollars a month, fresh provisions, freedom, and a good farm.

black obelisk of the Assyrian King Salmanassar III (circa 780 B.C.) are inscribed reports of battles, including official versions of defeats suffered by the Assyrians.[24] Napoleon I proclaimed in his first communiqué that the Battle of Trafalgar had ended with the destruction of the British fleet. In the German communiqués of 1914, the Battle of the Marne never took place.[25]

Sometimes the truth will out, for example, when a province has been lost, but care is always taken to explain why this or that defeat was inevitable and why it was not serious. Since communiqués cannot supply detailed accounts of the event they publicize, being in substance merely brief information summaries, use of war correspondents appears early in the chronicles of history. Scipio Africanus employed Polybius as his war correspondent. Caesar acted as his own commentator. John Sobieski, King of Poland, who defeated the Turks before Vienna in 1683, employed war correspondents but sometimes took a hand at "improving" their reports. He remarked: "The salary of the news writer is to be increased in order to induce him, by this means, to tell the truth more often." Needless to say, in certain situations the soldier or the statesman may not be interested in the truth but may prefer his own version, to which, moreover, he seeks to give the widest possible dissemination.

Press campaigns have been conducted ever since the advent of the daily press. Campaigns against Napoleon, especially those led by the Catholic publicist Joseph von Görres in Germany, drove the French Emperor into several of his famous rages. Napoleon often took a hand in press campaigns against his opponents, especially against Pitt and other British ministers. Before the War of 1866, Austria had systematically bribed newspapermen and bought entire newspapers, especially in Prussia. A fund of 370,000 florins was to have been devoted to "influencing" the press. Two agents, acting as emissaries for the Austrian government, had concluded agreements with various newspapers, either acquiring a controlling interest in them or arranging to have them print articles submitted to them by the Austrians.

The War of 1870 was introduced by press campaigns on both sides. Bismarck masterfully orchestrated the German press, aided by two former newspapermen, Moritz Busch and Lothar Bucher, and dictated himself an article for the *Kreuzzeitung* which was supposed to have been written by a member of the "landed gentry living in a province of old Prussia." A second article of his was published in the *Kölnische Zeitung* and signed as though written by a correspondent in Paris. These maneuvers served to influence the French government and public opinion in all interested countries.

[24] See Sturminger, *op. cit.*, pp. 65, 122*f*. Incidentally, Sturminger devotes a chapter to discussing the use of postal stamps for propaganda purposes. On Napoleon, see Thérèse Ebbinghaus, *Napoleon, England, und die Presse, 1800–1803,* Munich, R. Oldenbourg, 1914.

[25] See the remarkable works by Jean de Pierrefeu on the art of writing communiqués. Pierrefeu wrote most of the French communiqués during World War I. One of his works has the self-explanatory title *Plutarque a menti;* it was translated as *French Headquarters 1915–1918,* London, Bles, 1924. On the Second World War, see the very prejudiced and pro-Nazi, but in many details quite accurate, book by Paul Allard, *La guerre du mensonge,* Paris, Les Éditions de France, 1940, pp. 50*ff*.

Prior to the war of 1914 as well as during the war, press campaigns played a great role. The Russian government bribed French newspapers—occasionally with the support of the French government—in order to enlist the support of French public opinion for the Franco-Russian alliance. The transactions were carried out by high Russian officials with the ambassador himself controlling the operations.[26] The Germans, too, were past masters at this technique and, during the weeks before the outbreak of the war, took great pains to influence public opinion in Italy and Rumania in order to keep these countries neutral.[27] In the midst of the war they tried to buy one Paris newspaper. The French succeeded, in 1915, in setting up in Italy a pro-French and prowar newspaper under the editorship of Benito Mussolini.

An interesting operation of a similar kind was organized by Germany in the United States. Between 1914 and 1917, German propaganda aimed at maintaining the neutrality of the United States and at preventing the delivery of munitions to the Entente powers. For the latter purpose Germany expended $200,000 on press manipulations aiming at the provocation of industrial strikes.[28]

The boldest German propaganda scheme was set forth in a letter from German Undersecretary of State Arthur Zimmermann to Count Bernstorff, German Ambassador in Washington. This letter, dated January 16, 1915, reads as follows: [29]

Until now Japan has abstained from sending troops to Europe for fear that the United States, particularly California, could exploit such a reduction of troop strength to enact anti-Japanese legislation. To create guarantees that Japan will continue to adopt this attitude in future, it is necessary to increase their concern. American circles have suggested to send a skillful personality with money to San Francisco to spread from there in every possible manner propaganda against Japan.

Under no circumstances must a German be entrusted with this task; Germany should not be mentioned in any manner or be recognized as having a hand in this. This agitation should stress in leaflets that, in the Far East, it is not a question of expelling the Germans but of the destruction of *Christian* culture, Church, schools and missions. These leaflets should show pictures in the American style, for example, of a Japanese soldier destroying a Christian Church and should be distributed in hundreds of thousands of copies. They should be written in America by an American and be printed in America.

[26] Many of the pertinent documents are reprinted in Friedrich Stiewe (ed.), *Im Dunkel der Europäischen Geheimdiplomatie: Iswolskis Kriegspolitik in Paris, 1911–1917*, Berlin, Deutsche Verlagsgesellschaft für Politik und Geschichte, 1926, Vol. II, pp. 11–29.

[27] Max Montgelas and Walter Schuecking (eds.), *Outbreak of the World War, German Documents, Collected by Karl Kautsky*, New York, Oxford, 1924, pp. 111, 117, 121, 167, 175, 218.

[28] United States National Archives, *German Foreign Office Files, 1914–1918*, Microfilm Reel 2587.

[29] *Ibid.*, Reel 2585.

Slogans: 1. The Fall of Tsingtao is not a defeat of Germany, but a mortal blow to Christianity in Eastern Asia. 2. Scores of Japanese students and tourists are flooding the United States every year to learn and see. This is nothing but a gigantic espionage system which, in due course, will be used against the United States. 3. America's interests in the Pacific: the danger of ever increasing economic influence by Japan in the Pacific Ocean area, including the Philippines. 4. Propaganda against the Japanese steamship company San Francisco–Nagasaki. 5. "We have enough colored citizens. No Japanese should become a citizen in the United States— in California there are already 60,000 Japs." 6. The yellow peril: The United States would not be capable of defending their west coast against the Japanese attack.

The organization should be directed by an American confidential agent from San Francisco. This agent should collaborate with some skillful newspaperman.

I ask your Excellency . . . to be particularly careful when selecting this confidential agent. Given the well known anti-Japanese attitude of Hearst, you might consider employing his good offices. Whether or not Hearst is sufficiently reliable is for you to decide. Please report your actions by highly secure means. [Signed] Zimmermann.

On March 21, 1916, Bernstorff wrote a letter to the German Chancellor Bethmann-Hollweg indicating that he had placed pertinent articles in the American press, using in particular the *Evening Mail* and the Hearst papers, which "on account of their Californian outlets were very receptive." However, the Ambassador informed Berlin that he had stopped this campaign in February, 1916, because in view of the incipient German-Japanese *rapprochement*—in the midst of war—there was a possibility that fear and hatred of Japan would drive the United States into the arms of Germany's enemies.[30]

Similar actions are taken, day in day out, by practically all governments in practically all countries whose public opinion is of importance. What happens at present can be deduced only through observation. But these past examples are based on documentary evidence and therefore provide us with reliable information about what foreign policy is in practice. We can only surmise, although not prove conclusively, that the German anti-Japanese campaign of the First World War was one of the causes, albeit remote, of the attack on Pearl Harbor.

PROPAGANDA IN WAR

Propaganda is of the highest importance in the strategy of political aggression and in war.[31] The aggressor employs propaganda, first of all, in order

---

[30] *Ibid.,* Reel 2592.

[31] Albrecht Blau, in *Propaganda als Waffe* (restricted document by Psychologische Laboratorium des Reichskriegsministerium, p. 56), states that it is an *"eiserne Notwendigkeit"* (an ineluctable necessity) to use propaganda and counterpropaganda in modern war.

to dissimulate his objectives, that is to say, he proclaims his peaceful intentions and denies all desire for war. At the same time, he uses propaganda to make some of his demands acceptable to the world and to gain allies.

Once war has broken out, it is the mission of the propagandist to absolve his country from responsibility for the war, to pin the guilt on the opponent, to gain new allies among the neutrals, to put the remaining neutrals in a friendly and cooperative frame of mind, and to minimize defeats or magnify victories. At a later stage, propaganda serves to shorten the war by convincing the beaten enemy that further resistance will not change the outcome but will be extremely costly in lives and treasure. Finally, propaganda serves to win the world's approval of the peace terms and to gain the submission of the defeated nation. The latter, in turn, uses propaganda as the only remaining weapon to modify the peace terms and ultimately gain readmission to world society on a basis of equality.

Domestic propaganda is the reciprocal of international propaganda and seeks to secure the nation's support for a given war policy. Without guidance via propaganda, the nation may favor a policy benefiting other governments or it may deny support for a policy representing its own interests.

Before 1914 German-English rivalry was sharpened by the German naval construction program. Responsible German statesmen, including the two Chancellors, von Bülow and Bethmann-Hollweg, were opposed to this program precisely because it would cause trouble with Britain, yet public opinion had been so much taken in by the propaganda of Admiral Tirpitz that the *Reichstag* voted increasingly large naval budgets. The German high seas fleet was not strong enough to defeat the Royal Navy, and its expansion put such a strain on Germany's resources that land armaments suffered. In other words, the naval propaganda of Tirpitz brought Germany into war with the British Empire and impaired Germany's chances of winning the war on land. To a certain degree, it made the war and Germany's defeat inevitable.

In France, the *revanche* propaganda—revenge for the defeat of 1871—had largely subsided after the eclipse of General Boulanger.[32] France was drawn into the war mainly because she feared that, if she did not stand by Russia, Germany would gain control of the European continent. Since the German war plan provided that in case of war with Russia France would have to be attacked first, France had little choice. Nevertheless, the *revanche* idea still agitated large sectors of French public opinion and weakened the French government's position as a possible and effective mediator.

Russian sponsorship of Pan-Slavism undermined the stability of Austria-Hungary. The assassination of Archduke Francis Ferdinand at Sarajevo,

---

[32] On the importance of press campaigns prior to World War I, see Rolf Arnold Scott-James, *The Influence of the Press*, London, Partridge, 1913. An excellent description of the role of the *revanche* ideology is contained in Friedrich Hertz, *Nationalgeist und Politik: Beiträge zur Erforschung der tieferen Ursachen des Krieges*, Zurich, Europa-Verlag, 1937.

which was the immediate cause of the war, was largely due to intensive propaganda.[33]

Both sides began the war with powerful offensives of falsehood. For example, on August 6, 1914, Havas, the French official press agency, asserted falsely that Germany had violated Dutch neutrality at Tilburg—which was an attempt of the Allied powers to draw Holland into the war on their side. A few days later, Reuter, the British agency, reported that the war had been provoked by the German *Kronprinz* in the Emperor's absence, and that the Emperor had slapped the *Kronprinz* upon his return. Both sides broadcast stories of atrocities, some of which had indeed been committed but which were reported with freely invented details and were said to have occurred in far larger numbers than accorded with actual fact.

Germany opened the war by including a blatant lie in the very declaration of war against France: the German government had the effrontery to state in that historic document that French planes had bombarded the towns of Karlsruhe and Nuremberg.[34] Twenty-five years later, the Germans started the Second World War with the lie that Polish soldiers had attacked the German radio station at Gliwice; it was shown in the Nuremberg trial that such an attack had in fact taken place but that it had been organized by the Nazis themselves. German propaganda had thus progressed from the lie to the faked incident.

As soon as World War I was in full swing, an intensive propaganda battle was touched off by the controversy over war guilt. This question was of extreme importance, domestically and internationally, for both sides sought by marshaling moral and legal arguments to enlist the good will and cooperation of the "nations at arms" and of neutral countries. As time went by, this issue was to plague victor and defeated alike and finally to serve as one of the propaganda levers by which Germany removed the most onerous impositions of the Versailles Treaty.

The Allies gained their early headstart in this contest largely because the German Chancellor Bethmann-Hollweg had made the blunder of saying that a "scrap of paper" (the treaty guaranteeing Belgium's neutrality) need not obligate Britain to go to war. Bethmann-Hollweg also furnished the classical example of official ineptitude in public relations. On August 4, 1914, he said in the *Reichstag:* "Not kennt kein Gebot" (Necessity does not recognize laws). "Our troops occupied Luxembourg, and have perhaps entered Belgian territory. This is contrary to rules of international law." There is hardly another case where a responsible statesman openly admitted that he had intentionally violated international law. In fact, the preoccupation with propa-

---

[33] Eugen Lennhoff, *Politische Geheimbünde,* Zurich, Amalthea-Verlag, 1931, Vol. I, pp. 486ff.

[34] Bethmann-Hollweg, the German Chancellor, informed the German Ambassador in Paris that "Yesterday French airmen dropped bombs on the railroads near Karlsruhe and Nuremberg. Thus France forced us into the war." In 1914, airplanes were not equipped to drop bombs; no French plane had the range to reach Nuremberg.

ganda and "diplomacy" is everywhere such that great efforts are made to prove the compatibility of one's political and military acts with law and custom, and to show that aggression has become necessary because the opponent has violated the law which the aggressor proposes to redress. (For an unsurpassed exposition of how such proof can be developed, see Shakespeare's *King Henry V*, Act I, Scene 2.)

The greatest success of strategic propaganda was scored when the United States finally entered the war on the side of the Entente. For almost three years the United States had stood aside from the conflict, although it was supporting Britain and France economically. British propaganda in the United States tried to show that a German victory would be highly disadvantageous to American interests. German blunders, such as the sinking of American ships and the perpetration of sabotage acts, gradually estranged American public opinion from Germany. The United States decided, however, to enter the war *only after* the British admiralty had intercepted a dispatch from the German Foreign Office in which Secretary of State Zimmermann instructed the German minister in Mexico to embroil Mexico and Japan in a war against the United States. This was political warfare on the part of the Germans; the revelation to the American government of the intercepted message was a master stroke of British propaganda.

The United States, after entering the war, embarked on a great propaganda campaign which culminated in President Wilson's Fourteen Points, designed to clarify the peace conditions of the Allies, to drive a wedge between the governments of the Central Powers and their peoples, and to counter Soviet propaganda. Nine months after the proclamation of these points, the Germans surrendered by invoking them. Yet the Germans afterward made capital out of the alleged failure of the Allies to redeem their "promises." (Incidentally, as long as the First World War lasted, the Allies had a clear-cut advantage over the Germans, because the British controlled the Atlantic cables. After the war, the Germans were more successful in presenting their point of view.)

On the tactical level, propaganda was used in many different and ingenious ways. The main intention was to spread defeatism in the enemy camp, convince enemy soldiers and workers that the war could not be won, and induce them to desertion and capitulation.

Propaganda was also used to prevent the enemy from using certain weapons. For example, the Allies presented a considerable propaganda barrage against the use of submarines and poison gas. Although they did not succeed in outlawing these weapons, they at least aroused most neutrals against Germany's conduct of the war.

After the war, the Germans organized a world-wide propaganda campaign directed toward the repeal of the economic clauses, reparations, territorial cessions, and the disarmament conditions imposed upon them by the Versailles Treaty. They had no hopes of succeeding quickly, hence they concentrated upon a campaign of persuasion by installments. Ultimately, a large part of the world actually came to believe that the Versailles Treaty imposed uncalled-for hardships on the German people. The French concern for military security was ridiculed and no longer taken too seriously by France's former Allies, and the conviction grew that the Versailles Treaty should be abrogated. Inside Germany, the Nazi party grew stronger because of its vocal anti-Versailles stand.[35]

The first result of this propaganda barrage was the reduction of Germany's war debt and the granting by the United States of large credits. The second was the premature termination of the Allied occupation of western Germany. The third was the permission given Germany to discontinue reparations payments (Lausanne Conference, 1932). In 1932, the Germany of Weimar was just about to obtain considerable concessions concerning armaments; the clauses prohibiting civil aviation and the construction of civil aircraft had been abrogated long before. Democratic Germany would probably have been permitted to increase the size of its army from 100,000 to 200,000 men, in which case she would have had, with a population only half as large, an armed force of a size equal to that of the United States. Yet before this concession was granted, Hitler came to power.

At that juncture the power of propaganda became plain: although it should have been obvious to the entire world that the Hitler regime had no other major objective than to make war, attention was still centered on the alleged griefs of Germany. Hence Hitler met with none but purely verbal opposition when he broke all those clauses of the Versailles Treaty which hindered him in carrying out his program. The British went so far as to agree officially to German naval rearmament.

At the same time, Germany conducted large-scale and systematic propaganda operations to convince the world that she had no aggressive designs. This propaganda proved so successful that the German annexation of Austria, a patent act of aggression, was widely considered as a positive good—the joining of "blood brothers." In the United States, German propaganda convinced large parts of the population that Germany's aggressions in Europe did not concern America and did not threaten American security.[36] This propaganda succeeded: America's entry into the war was greatly delayed.

German propaganda prevented the prospective victims of aggression from arming themselves in time and from uniting with one another to stop aggression by joint action. Propaganda provided the strategic cover for German rearmament and incipient aggression. Without the success of that propaganda, Germany would not have been able to win any significant military victories. The time lead in armaments gained by propaganda was compounded by the

[35] See Lindley M. Fraser, *Germany between Two Wars: A Study of Propaganda and War-guilt*, New York, Oxford, 1945.
[36] See Leonard Doob, *Propaganda, Its Psychology and Technique*, New York, Holt, 1935, p. 272.

successful propaganda campaigns which Germany had conducted inside enemy countries and which had so weakened their powers of resistance that even the military strength which they possessed was not used in an efficient manner.

During the Second World War, propaganda was employed by all belligerents on a most extensive scale, yet nobody has as yet made claims concerning its effectiveness that would even approach the claims made about the propaganda of the First World War. The present "expert" opinion is that propaganda was a useful "auxiliary" of the military weapons. This expert opinion is based on the manner in which the Western powers used the propaganda weapon. With the exception of the period after 1940 when the British had little with which to oppose the Nazis except propaganda, and of the American propaganda campaign to induce the early capitulation of Japan in 1945, Britain and the United States indeed employed propaganda merely as an "auxiliary" tool. While propaganda, like any other type of strategy, requires generalship and creative direction, the Allies did not understand fully the characteristics of this weapon and entrusted it to bureaucratic management. They scored not a few tactical successes, but the war against Nazi Germany was not shortened, nor was the appeal of Nazism nullified. On the contrary, the Nazis proved able to turn Allied propaganda about unconditional surrender against the Allies, using it as a prop to uphold the waning morale of the heavily bombed and tightly encircled Germans.

Nazi war propaganda has been described as outstandingly successful. Yet this was not always the case, with the one exception that the Nazis' propaganda *about* their own propaganda was so effective that most governments actually were in a state bordering on hysteria about this imaginary danger. It is sufficient to recall the strategic objectives of the Nazis to see the utter failure of their propaganda methods. In 1939, they wanted to keep Britain and France out of the war and to get Italy into the war. In 1940 Hitler wanted to conclude peace with Great Britain. At the beginning of the war against Russia, the Nazis scored initial gains in obtaining Ukrainian and even Russian popular support against the communists. They managed by their brutish behavior to turn the Russian population, which was only too willing to greet them as liberators from the communist yoke, against themselves and failed to break up Russia from within, as they might well have done. During 1941 and 1942 the Nazis failed to draw Franco's Spain into the war against the Western Allies. Between 1943 and 1945 the Nazis, who estimated correctly that, sooner or later, Russia would fall out with Britain and the United States, failed to break up a most unnatural alliance. Any one of these objectives—including, conceivably, the continued neutrality of the United States—might have been obtainable by propaganda means. But Nazi words proved most unconvincing—if not actually a hindrance to Nazi deeds.

The effectiveness of skillful propaganda can be gleaned from the example of de Gaulle who, though opposed by Roosevelt and Churchill, waged successfully, in 1942 and 1943, a psychological-warfare campaign against the United States and Britain. He reached all his political objectives while Washington and London were compelled to abandon theirs. Without military strength, de Gaulle took over as head of the French provisional government *against* the will of America and Britain, who held de Gaulle's purse strings and possessed a crushing *superiority in military power*.[37]

The Soviets proved themselves past masters of propaganda during World War II. They contrived to put across their arguments without the propagandees realizing that they were being propagandized. The Soviets succeeded in extorting from the United States lend-lease materials in such quantities that the Red Army was greatly strengthened and the growth of the Anglo-American forces was retarded and impeded; they influenced Western military operations to *their* strategic advantage with the result that Russia now controls the Balkans and Central Europe, while a more judicious Western strategy could have secured for these areas the blessings of self-government; and they obtained large territorial and economic concessions in Europe and Asia which left the Soviet Union as the only victor of World War II.

In the postwar world the Soviets achieved considerable success by preventing the Western powers from interfering with the step-by-step sovietization of Eastern Europe and the seizure of China. Some of their greatest successes were achieved in various Asiatic countries opposing colonialism and clamoring for agrarian reforms. On the other hand, the communists suffered defeat in their propaganda campaigns in Germany and, despite deceptively large communist votes, even in France and Italy where, for a time, they participated in the government. They were conspicuously unsuccessful in Britain and the United States. Their clumsiness sparked the American containment policy and growth of the NATO alliance, and ultimately, perhaps, adoption of an active policy aiming at the gradual liberation of the countries prostrate under the Soviet heel. Soviet propaganda had been effective as long as it was imperceptible and could be covered up by the peculiar political and psychological conditions under which World War II had been fought. As soon as communist propaganda maneuvers became transparent, their effectiveness decreased.

Nevertheless, Soviet propaganda technique has reaped a rich harvest. Since the Soviets consider propaganda as one of their chief weapons, it is necessary to study their techniques continuously. Soviet propaganda is directed at two major audiences: noncommunists and communists. To the noncommunists, the Soviets emphasize that the capitalist system inevitably leads to war. By contrast, the Soviet Union is described as the staunch defender of peace, the dedicated protector of the poor and as the greatest

[37] See Carroll, *op. cit.*, Chaps. 2–6.

military power in the world. It should, therefore, be to the advantage of all people to side on all issues with the communists and to prevent hostile acts against the communist system.

In addition, the communists employ what could be called "false-flag appeals." Since communism per se nowhere displays great powers of attraction—which, considering its program and achievements, is not too surprising—the communists have latched on to promises which are exactly contrary to what they are actually planning. They proclaim that they are working for democracy, when actually they want to establish a dictatorship. They present themselves as partisans of civil rights, when they allow no such rights in the Soviet Union. They profess to favor national independence of allegedly subjugated peoples, while they themselves keep national minorities in bondage. They clamor for agrarian reform, while they work for the expropriation of agrarian ownership.

In their appeals to communists or prospective communists they play up the inevitability of capitalist collapse and communist victory. Gradually, as the *Communist Manifesto* was replaced as the basic textbook by the *Short Course*, idealistic appeals were superseded by appeals to the power urges of a future elite. It is no longer the golden future of mankind; it is the career of party members Tom, Dick, and Harry.

In recruiting members for their organization, the communists do not rely on the effectiveness of verbal appeals alone. Communist propaganda and organization are one. Organization is necessary to carry the communist message to the audience and to accomplish the brainwashing techniques suitable for the conditioning of the protocommunist and communist mind. Continuous propaganda, in turn, is necessary to enlarge the membership of the organization. Reliable communists are used to set up special organizations by which "false-flag appeals" can be propagated under the cover of respectable newspapers and political fronts. This *perpetuum mobile* is energized by a never-ending stream of broadcasts, books, and pamphlets emanating from the Soviet Union and other propaganda centers.

The broad propaganda attack of the communists has forced the United States and Great Britain to engage in defensive propaganda and counterpropaganda. Both countries are heavily engaged in broadcasting and, to a lesser extent, in publication efforts. The effectiveness of American propaganda has been criticized and, to some extent, criticized with justification. The attaching, in 1948, of propaganda activities to the authority of the State Department was less than a stroke of genius. Diplomacy by propaganda is as improper and ineffective as is propaganda by diplomacy. These two distinct functions cannot be married without resultant detriment to both. In 1953, the U.S. Information Agency became an independent organization receiving only general guidance from the State Department. On the other hand, a democracy by its very nature cannot imitate simply the propaganda techniques of dictatorial governments. Democracy must work out its own techniques.[38] It must not ape its opponents by engaging in the dissemination of uniform "party lines" or brainwashing, let alone in systematic "false-flag appeals" and deceptions. Democracy must appeal to human reason. Its difficulty lies precisely in the fact that appeals to emotions and prejudices win over mass audiences far more easily than do syllogisms. To compound the difficulty, democracy should speak—nay, cannot help speaking—with many voices. Perhaps the obstacles can be overcome only when democracy returns to its 18th-century militancy. Whatever the ultimate answer may be, the fact remains that democracy has not yet solved satisfactorily its propaganda problems because its efforts lack that degree of plausibility which only faith, conviction, and enthusiasm can attain.

The record of propaganda will be pondered carefully by tomorrow's aggressors. A country that plans aggression and schemes to achieve a lead in armaments—an indispensable precondition of successful attack—must resort to propaganda to lull its prospective victims into a sense of safety. It must also seek to forestall concerted action on the part of those marked out for conquest. It would be erroneous to believe that such a propaganda will not have valid points to make. On the contrary, no propaganda can be effective that does not contain many elements of truth.

Although it is always and everywhere possible to criticize existing conditions with cogent arguments, the question arises *why* such points are raised and why they are *magnified* into international issues intractable by peaceful negotiations. In concrete cases, it is very difficult to distinguish propaganda from genuine complaints or efforts at adjustment. Yet the point must be borne in mind that *the arguments used are of less importance than the motives which prompt the use of these arguments.*

Propaganda may serve to redress real wrongs, and no country can be blamed for trying to improve its lot. It is a danger signal, however, if propaganda of that type is accompanied by propagandistic efforts to pin blame on a given country or group, to seek alibis for future aggression, to undermine military preparedness, to sap existing friendships, and to intensify the cleavages that may exist within one nation. It is another danger signal if the propaganda of a given country systematically employs the technique of identifying scapegoats such as the "Jews," the "capitalists," the "communists," the "warmongers," etc.

It would be naïve to assume that foreign propaganda must necessarily be of foreign origin. On the contrary, propaganda favoring an actual or poten-

---

[38] For an interesting discussion of propaganda in a democracy see *Truth Is Our Weapon* (New York, Funk & Wagnalls, 1953) by Edward W. Barrett, former Assistant Secretary of State and Chief of the U.S. "Campaign of Truth." According to Barrett, there are no universally effective propaganda terms. The propaganda of the United States should be based on truth, though it has to be put across in terms which conform to the aspirations and educational standards of the target peoples. Is there a universal *political* truth? If so, how is it to be determined? Mr. Barrett's confusion casts a revealing light on the ineffectiveness of U.S. propaganda.

tial opponent is most effective if it emanates from domestic groups. Sometimes such groups may take their clue from abroad, but sometimes they may act on their own initiative. This distinction is relatively easy to establish; one need only compare the propaganda line of a given political group, as well as the motives and objectives of that line, with the propaganda spread by a foreign country.[39]

DEFENSE AGAINST PROPAGANDA

Is protection against propaganda possible? Since democracy is a political system in which, on principle, all opinions and points of view should have the right to be presented, democracy is obviously exposed to propaganda attacks. A dictatorship can, to a certain degree, exclude propaganda, but by doing so, it subjects the nation to its own undiluted propaganda, a process which leads to distortions, eliminates constructive criticism, and ultimately engenders general incredulity and weakens national morale.

It is instructive to review some of the attempts made in history directed at keeping out "dangerous propaganda." In 1559, Pope Paul IV ordered the establishment of the *Index librorum prohibitorum*. The organization of the *Index* appears to have been prompted by the increasing importance of the printing press and to have been directed essentially against the reading of "dangerous" books by the *broad masses*. After Napoleon had come to power, he prohibited on January 17, 1800, the publication of more than 1,000 newspapers and authorized the circulation of only thirteen papers. His Bourbon successors were deeply troubled by the unruly press, and King Charles X caused to be published on July 26, 1830, five ordinances abolishing press freedom on the ground that "at all times, the periodical press is, by nature, nothing but a tool of disorder and seduction." It so happened that the editors of the leading Paris newspapers assembled for a demonstration of protest. It was this demonstration which touched off the July Revolution— the unique case of a revolution which was made by the brawn of the newspapermen instead of by their brains.

Napoleon III used public funds for improving his relations with the papers, exerted pressure on the papers through the news monopoly of the Agence Havas, himself wrote articles and *feuilletons*, and fostered intimate relations between the press and the stock exchange. Those papers which did not dance to his tune he seized.[40]

[39] On the methods of propaganda detection and the identification of propaganda origins, see Harold D. Lasswell, Nathan Leites, and Associates, *Language of Politics, Studies in Quantitative Semantics,* New York, Stewart, 1949, especially pp. 173–232.

[40] On censorship in war, see the very instructive article "Censorship" in *Encyclopædia Britannica*, 12th ed., Chicago, 1922, Vol. XXX, pp. 591*ff.;* also Douglas Brownrigg, *Indiscretions of the Naval Censor*, New York, Doubleday, 1920; also Byron Price, *Censorship*, Washington, 1943; and H. C. Lea, *A History of the Inquisition of the Middle Ages*, 3 vols., New York, 1887–1888.

Modern democratic governments maintain sufficiently close and friendly relations with important newspapers to insure having their point of view represented. They cannot, however, prevent the expression of other points of view, and sometimes the opposition—even that of foreign origin—prevails. In the United States procedures are being elaborated designed to compel propagandists to reveal their sources of money and to indicate plainly their political affiliation. Various security laws aim at preventing, for example, communists from masquerading as democrats, progressives, and reformers. Nevertheless, there is no possibility in a democracy of excluding competing opinions. Even in dictatorial states which monopolize all public means of information and expression, opinions of opposition can prevail, especially when public opinion is formed spontaneously and without the help of any "means" of information or expression. The plain fact is that not only the masses but also the articulate groups, including the so-called "elites," are highly vulnerable to propaganda. No means is as yet known which would provide a safe protection against the effectiveness of a well-planned and well-executed propaganda or, for that matter, against unplanned spontaneous shifts in public opinion.

PROPAGANDA AND NATIONAL SECURITY

The relatively best defense against propaganda in a democracy is education in the principles of foreign policy in particular and of national interest in relation to security and the scheme of politics among nations in general. National interest need not be understood as a narrow chauvinistic thing, nor should it be conceived of as opposed to the adoption of solutions which may offer better prospects than the old system of sovereign states. It should be clear, however, that it is in the national interest to preserve national and individual freedom, to insure order and progress. To arrive at a definition of national interest at a given moment, the following questions must be asked:

1. Is there at present a country which may be planning aggression? Since at most times in history there has been a nation bent upon aggression, one must have convincing reasons to conclude that today there is none. If there is some doubt as to the intentions of one or the other foreign nation, simple prudence would demand the assumption that that nation either harbors aggressive designs or will put such designs into effect whenever the intended victim's weakness favors aggressive action.

2. Assuming the need of preparation against planned or only conceivable aggression, any proposed policy must be tested as to whether it will put the country in a more vulnerable position or whether it will reduce the country's vulnerability.

3. Citizens of a democracy should always bear in mind that, while the policies of their government never are perfect, they have been nevertheless decided upon by legislators and administrators who derived their power

from the voters and whom the voters can evict from office. In most instances these policies are representing the will of the electorate. Most of these policies were arrived at after mature reflection. If they are designed to advance special rather than national interests, this fact will be noted and discussed by many observers and by newspapers of various political inclinations. While these policies should be improved constantly, there is a prima-facie argument for the assumption that these policies are neither as malevolent nor as ineffective as hostile propagandists assert.

4. As a general rule of thumb, it can be presumed that if in a democracy a faction advocates policies calling, here and now, for the wholesale scrapping of traditional institutions and existing social and property relationships, that faction is bent upon the destruction of democracy, for democratic institutions operate through compromise and gradual adjustment. This does not mean that radical solutions may not at some time become necessary. But if so, they would enhance the power of democracy only if they were to be applied to specific problems and *not* to the system as a whole. A person may feel that democracy should give way to another form of government. If so, he should realize that the advocacy of such ideas in peacetime is quite a different proposition from their propagation during an international crisis or in wartime. He should realize that, whether he wants it or not, he is helping the enemy and in so doing is hurting his own cause. A movement which wins through the help of a foreign power will be compromised forever and be destroyed either in its substance or its personalities. Nor will the foreign victor prove to be its reliable ally.

Hostile propaganda can become dangerous only if foreign policy is not conducted according to a system of priorities. The major objectives of foreign policy should be to reduce the country's vulnerability from surprise attack and to maintain a military establishment adequate for dealing with the most likely or possible aggressor. If such a priority is adhered to, foreign propaganda cannot jeopardize the security of the nation.

Often a nation is befuddled by the proclamation of foreign-policy objectives which are unrealistic and unattainable; the disillusionment arising from an unsuccessful policy gives the opponent many propaganda openings. In other words, if foreign policy is formulated mainly according to propaganda dictates, as were, for example, recent "peace-aim" formulas, foreign propaganda can exploit the gap between ideal and reality. It is relatively easy to guard against this danger by avoiding the proclamation of high-sounding, meaningless programs and by seeking instead public support through sober appreciation of facts and by a gradual education in the realities of international life. Concentration on security as the primary aim of foreign policy does not mean that reliance on force alone is the proper method for attaining that end or that no attention should be given to international organizations. Excessive armaments may endanger real security by imposing intolerable strains upon the national economy. The minimum level of armaments necessary to security is given by the following factors: (1) the capacity of the strongest potential aggressor and his allies to launch a surprise attack; (2) the strength necessary to repel such an attack and to take immediate countermeasures designed to forestall large initial successes of the enemy; (3) the requirements of *rapid* mobilization of the armed forces and industry; and (4) the investments required to keep abreast with, or to lead in, technological progress.

There is no need to go beyond these requirements. It is obvious that the size of national armaments, therefore, should to a large extent be dependent upon the size of other nations' armaments. In other words, military policy cannot be safely determined by the exigencies of propaganda. Assume, for example, that it has been calculated that the security of the United States is assured if American armaments are kept at x per cent of the armaments of countries A, B, C, and D; then this relationship is the principal criterion of American security policy. If armaments in these countries decline, American armaments can also be reduced; however, if these armaments rise, those of the United States should be increased without delay.

The propagation of truth is not dangerous from whatever source it may flow. If valid ideas should happen to be in disagreement with state policy, the security of the nation would require not that they be kept out but, on the contrary, that the false policy be scrapped. It is questionable whether a democracy is entitled to suppress the propaganda of ideas which are essentially antidemocratic. Suppression and censorship are inadequate means at best.

It is a popular and comforting supposition that a more or less intelligent person should be able to distinguish between truths and falsehoods. Unfortunately, there are very few people able to do so. This fact indicates a glaring weakness in our educational system. This weakness is, briefly, that the critical mind is not being developed and that, while facts are being presented, their interrelationship is rarely properly underscored; not to speak of dubious criteria for the selection of facts. The greatest danger is, as the modern sciences of general semantics and phenomenology attempt to show, that wrong methods of thinking are being taught and continuously applied. Discussion of this subject is not within the scope of this book, yet it may be pointed out that the main faults of our habitual thinking include the failure to demand sufficiency of cause, *i.e.*, that any explanation given is really valid, and that the cause indicated really explains the *entire* effect, while the effects should not be reduced to one inadequate cause; second, inadequate abstraction, consisting mainly in the omission of elements essential to comprehensive analysis; third, disregard of the time element; fourth, improper identification, *i.e.*, things are identified with each other which are by no means identical.[41]

[41] On the possibilities of defense against propaganda through semantics, see *Papers from the Second American Congress on General Semantics, University of Denver, August,*

The first error, for example, leads to the theory that war is "caused" by the profit motive alone; the second error is illustrated by the assumption of American officials that Russia would continue to cooperate with the United States in the postwar period, an assumption based on autosuggestion by propaganda and the limited experience of wartime alliance unverified with respect to its historical and psychological validity. A sample of the third error is the mistaken evaluation by Britain and the United States, in terms of 1919, of the military strength of France in 1939. The fourth error warps political judgment in such a way, for instance, that all "bourgeois" or all "socialists" or all "Britishers" or all "Nordics" are lumped together into one category.

Unfortunately, most people, including rational beings and scientists, do not always think rationally and scientifically, even though they may know how to do so. Political decisions and acts are more often than not prompted by drives and urges rather than by reason. Sometimes a person adheres to a movement or a propaganda line *first* and provides an explanation for his attitude *later*.

Political convictions and propagandas are often—if not always—*derivative* in nature. Even if refuted in their entirety, their strength and their hold over people may remain unimpaired. In this case, the individual can be kept in line only by means of social or physical *compulsion*.

While it is true that propaganda always played an important role in history, it is no less true that it never exerted as great an influence as it has for the last 200 years. The reason probably is that, with the increase in literacy, people have become more susceptible to verbal appeals and hence are tending to become politically conscious. Through modern means of communication, from the daily newspaper via the radio to television, they can be reached by appeals which in former times were addressed only to small numbers. Since literacy continues to increase, and since more and more

---

1941, Non-Aristotelian Methodology (applied) for Sanity in Our Time, edited by M. Kendig, Chicago, Institute of General Semantics, 1943, Book II, Part 2, section B, pp. 325ff. A frequent trick of propagandists and lawyers is to invite the opponent to prove that a certain contention is not true and to deduce from his inability to do so that the contention is right. This trick is technically known as the fallacy of *ad ignorantium* (p. 339). On p. 351, Edwin Green, himself a practical newspaperman, in his "Notes on the Construction of Chaos; an Extensional Analysis of Journalism," describes a typical newspaper which "provides the student of general semantics with sufficient examples of identifications, objectification, description by inferential terms, confusion of orders of abstraction, two-valued orientation, etc., for an exhaustive study, from the psychiatric point of view, of neuro-semantic transference of pathological projections through the public prints." (See Morris R. Cohen and Ernst Nagel, *An Introduction to Logic and Scientific Method,* New York, Harcourt, Brace, 1934; and Vilhjalmur Stefansson, *The Standardization of Error,* New York, Norton, 1927.) Aristotle, incidentally, is the father of the science of propaganda, which in his time was called rhetoric and which he defines as follows: "Rhetoric may be defined as the faculty of observing in any given case the available means of persuasion" (*Rhetoric,* Book I, chapter 2). He is also the father of counterpropaganda which he developed (*ibid.,* Book II, chapter 25 in the *Organon* and especially in "On Sophistical Refutations").

people come in touch with modern communications, the effectiveness of propaganda and the resulting disturbances may be expected to grow.

But the question may be asked whether the effectiveness of propaganda is not due to a time lag rather than to the efficacy of its techniques and vehicles. Education has taught people how to read but not how to evaluate the meaning of what they read. Political consciousness has not yet developed into political maturity. The disturbing effectiveness of propaganda is caused, at least to some extent, by the lack of propaganda sensitivity on the part of journalists and radio script writers, especially in countries where press and radio do not serve informational needs but are primarily organs of political parties. Exactly as hygiene can be taught in school and serve as a protection against disease, so detection of propaganda as well as the evaluation of evidence can be taught in the educational process. Such education hardly would give a foolproof protection, just as people instructed in hygiene may become infected as a result of their negligence. But it would be a long step forward. The original purpose of the classical education was precisely to instill into people a sense of discrimination between true and false and good and evil, as well as a sense of proportion and civic responsibility. Modern education, allegedly so practical, has left modern man exposed to the lures of the lie. Falsehood and skulduggery can and should be taken out of propaganda. There will always remain the need for a proper art of persuasion which the state must master if its policies are to be successful.

BIBLIOGRAPHY

Akzin, Benjamin: *Propaganda by Diplomats,* Washington, Digest Press, 1936.
Allport, Gordon W., and Leo Postman: *The Psychology of Rumor,* New York, Holt, 1947.
Barrett, Edward W.: *Truth Is Our Weapon,* New York, Funk & Wagnalls, 1953.
Bauer, Wilhelm: *Die öffentliche Meinung in der Weltgeschichte,* Potsdam, Athenaion, 1930.
Bernays, Edward L.: *Propaganda,* New York, Liveright, 1928.
Carr, Edward H.: *Propaganda in International Politics,* New York, Oxford Pamphlets on World Affairs, No. 16, 1939.
Carroll, Wallace: *Persuade or Perish,* Boston, Houghton Mifflin, 1948.
Creel, George: *How We Advertised America,* New York, Harper, 1920.
Doob, Leonard W.: *Public Opinion and Propaganda,* New York, Holt, 1948.
Farago, Ladilas: *German Psychological Warfare,* New York, Putnam, 1942.
Hunter, Edward: *Brainwashing in Red China: The Calculated Destruction of Men's Minds,* New York, Vanguard, 1951.
Irion, Frederick C.: *Public Opinion and Propaganda,* New York, Crowell, 1950.
Koop, Theodore F.: *Weapon of Silence,* Chicago, University of Chicago Press, 1946.
Lasker, Bruno, and A. Roman: *Propaganda from China and Japan,* New York, Institute of Pacific Relations, 1938.
Lasswell, Harold D.: *Propaganda Technique in the World War,* New York, Richard R. Smith, 1938.
Leighton, Alexander H.: *Human Relations in a Changing World,* New York, Dutton, 1949.
Lerner, Daniel: *Syke War, Psychological Warfare against Germany, D-Day to VE Day,* New York, Stewart, 1949.
Linebarger, Paul M. A.: *Psychological Warfare,* Washington, Infantry Journal, 1948.
Miller, Clyde R.: *The Process of Persuasion,* New York, 1946.

Mock, James R., and Cedric Larson: *Words that Won the War: The Story of the Committee on Public Information, 1917–1919,* Princeton, N.J., Princeton University Press, 1939.

Münzenberg, Willi: *Propaganda als Waffe,* Paris, Carrefour, 1937.

Padover, Saul K.: *Experiment in Germany,* New York, Duell, Sloan & Pearce, 1946.

Petersen, H. C.: *Propaganda for War: The Campaign against American Neutrality, 1914–1917,* Norman, Okla., University of Oklahoma Press, 1939.

Schönemann, Friedrich: *Die Kunst der Massenbeeinflussung in den Vereinigten Staaten von Amerika,* Stuttgart, Deutsche Verlagsanstalt, 1924.

Semmler, Rudolf: *Goebbels: The Man next to Hitler,* London, Weshouse, 1947.

Speier, Hans: "The Future of Psychological Warfare," *Public Opinion Quarterly,* Spring, 1948.

————: "Magic Geography," *Social Research,* Vol. 8, New York, 1941.

Steed, Henry Wickham: *The Fifth Arm,* London, Constable, 1940.

Sturminger, Alfred: *Politische Propaganda in der Weltgeschichte,* Salzburg, Bergland Buch, 1938.

Thimme, Hans: *Weltkrieg ohne Waffen,* Stuttgart, Cotta, 1932.

Chapter 18

POLITICAL WARFARE

Clausewitz, theoretician of war, wrote that war is the continuation of foreign policy with other means. This phrase is often misquoted and misunderstood. Hence it is given here in full: [1]

War is only a part of political intercourse, therefore by no means an independent thing in itself. We know, of course, that war is only caused through the political intercourse of governments and nations; but in general it is supposed that such intercourse is broken off by war, and that a totally different state of things ensues, subject to no laws but its own. We maintain, on the contrary, that war is nothing but a continuation of political intercourse wtih an admixture of other means. We say "with an admixture of other means," in order thereby to maintain . . . that the main lines along which the events of the war proceed . . . are only the general features of policy which run on all through the war until peace takes place. And how can we conceive it to be otherwise? Does the cessation of diplomatic notes stop the political relations between different nations and governments? Is not war merely another kind of language for their thought? It has, to be sure, its own grammar, but not its own logic.

Political relations between nations cannot be broken off entirely even during war. Continuous official and unofficial, direct and indirect negotiations concerning such matters as conditions of peace, prisoner-of-war exchanges, interpretations of international law, and agreements on "open cities" bear eloquent testimony to the resiliency of political relationships even under the most adverse conditions. Despite war, there is maintained a similarity and often identity of some interests among the belligerents. Occasionally the two enemies may be united by common interests in opposing a third state which is an ally of the first and an enemy of the second belligerent.

A situation of this kind is best illustrated by the following example: in May, 1916, France and Britain, employing the Catholic Church as their intermediary, proposed to Germany that, while the war should continue on all fronts, the Western powers and Germany should cooperate on *one* particular point against Russia. France and Britain, disturbed by Russia's intentions to seize Constantinople, decided to prevent their ally from reaching the Dardanelles. Since they had not enough military forces in the area and since, obviously, they could not oppose their ally openly, they invited the

[1] Karl von Clausewitz, *On War,* New York, Modern Library, 1943, p. 596.

Germans to prevent the Russians from reaching the Straits. The Western powers undertook, as their end of the bargain, not to attack Bulgaria and Rumania and declared their willingness to remain on the defensive in Greece. They asked that the main Turkish forces be concentrated in the Caucasus and promised that they would not interfere with these operations. They expected that pressure in the Caucasus as well as German pressure in southwest Russia would prevent the Russians from attacking Constantinople.[2]

The Germans were dumfounded by this offer. So fearful were they that the Allies were setting a trap that they failed to take advantage of this unique opportunity of splitting the Entente, perhaps to the extent of obtaining a separate peace with Russia. Yet the Western offer, tricky as it was, probably was genuine: The Western powers simply could not tolerate the presence of Russia at the Dardanelles, especially after a war in which the Central Powers presumably would have been beaten. Nor could they afford to deny their ally the right to seize a vital objective which was not only a perennial objective of Russian foreign policy but also the capital of a hostile state. They reasoned correctly that there was a community of interests between Germany and themselves concerning Constantinople. While this particular overture was barren of results, it might be presumed that if a real Russian threat to Constantinople had materialized, a realignment of powers would have taken place. The incident illuminates what probably was the basic reason why after the Bolshevik revolution the Western powers failed to crush the Soviets and why they did not object to President Wilson's demand of 1918 that the Germans evacuate immediately all areas they occupied in Russia—a demand which, more than anything else, enabled the Bolsheviks to stabilize their tottering regime.

Wars are fought to impose one's political will on a foreign state. But military techniques are not the only ones to achieve this objective. Propaganda and political warfare can be defined as *a continuation of war with the admixture of nonmilitary means of pressure.* The purpose of this pressure is to make war *unnecessary;* or to create the *most favorable conditions* for the implementation of one's own policies and military plans should war become inevitable.

Political warfare, briefly, is a systematic activity, mostly of a secret nature, to influence and direct the policies of other nations. The ultimate objective of political warfare would be reached if the government of nation A would make not only its own decisions but also the decisions for nation B, and do so *without resorting to coercion by force or military occupation.*

Political warfare is abetted by the simple fact that a government and its nation never constitute a true unity—a monolithic block—but are split into many groups and subgroups and cliques opposing each other because of divergent personal and group interests, beliefs, and strategic and tactical concepts. These divisions may be ephemeral or enduring, moderate or intense,

[2] United States National Archives, *German Foreign Office File, 1914–1918,* Microfilm Reel 2592.

critical or relatively unimportant. The significance, scope, and permanence of these cleavages determine the odds of political warfare.

The purpose of political warfare may be to strengthen some of the competing groups or to weaken others; to organize forces whose activities can be directed toward desired ends; to support groups for as long as their objectives conform to one's own; and to help fully controlled and semicontrolled groups and personalities to reach positions of power and influence and eventually to take over the government. These methods can range all the way from simple manifestations of sympathy to the financing, organizing, and equipping of political movements, and from personal friendships between statesmen to the infiltration or capture of politically important agencies in the target country and the fomenting of mutinies, civil wars, and revolutions.

Theories and doctrines of international security are meaningless if they do not acknowledge the reality of continued "war in peacetime," or of the unceasing struggle which is fought with psychopolitical weapons. It is misleading to define peace as absence of organized violence in international relations. Abeyance of military warfare does not mean that there is no war—war understood in the sense that one nation seeks to further its own interests and ambitions and *impose* its will on other nations. Peace can only be defined as a state where no nation seeks to prevail over any other nation. If one nation attempts to remove its competitors or to influence the decisions of a foreign government in its own interest, there is, at least, a state of nonpeace whether the issue is joined on a battlefield or merely in human minds and political and economic contests.

On the average, the great powers of history have spent approximately half of their life span at war; about one-third of the 20th century was spent in open warfare. If the periods of undeclared psychopolitical wars are added, it would appear that *international society exists in a permanent state of war*. Not all the great powers participate at all times in this permanent war; single nations, or even regions, can therefore enjoy longer or shorter periods of peace. But there is always war somewhere. For *all* countries, the periods of open and psychopolitical war are sufficiently frequent so that foreign policy must be conceived of as a predominantly warlike operation.

The techniques of political warfare are as old as history. The first description of these methods comes to us from an unknown Chinese writer of the pre-Christian era who gave his contemporary prince the following advice: [3]

Disorganize everything that is good in the enemy's country, try to entangle representatives of the highest spheres in criminal undertakings, compromising their position and afterwards, according to opportunity, give publicity to their transgressions. Enter into contact with the lowest and most objectionable individuals in your enemy's country. Hamper the activities of the government of the country. Propa-

[3] Quoted by Włodzimierz Bączkowski in *Towards an Understanding of Russia: A Study in Policy and Strategy*, Jerusalem, Liphshitz, 1947, p. 19.

gate disagreement and dissatisfaction among the citizens. Instigate the young against the old. . . . Introduce sensuous music; loosen the old customs. Send licentious women to complete the work of degradation. Be generous in your offers, in your gifts, whenever it becomes necessary to obtain information on what is going on in the enemy's country. . . . You should keep spies everywhere. Only a man who has such tools at his disposal, . . . who knows how . . . to disseminate dissolution and dispute everywhere, only such a man is entitled to govern. He is . . . the pillar of the state.

Political warfare is essentially an offensive undertaking and, on the whole, can be successful only if waged offensively. Benjamin Franklin, master of political warfare, though in this capacity neglected by a long line of American statesmen who were unskillful amateurs at the game of political warfare, wrote the first American text on the subject. It is entitled *On the Means of Disposing the Enemies to Peace,* and contains the following observations: [4]

Warres, with whatsoever prudence undertaken and conducted, do not always succeed. . . . Northerne People . . . are ofttimes more easilie to be governed and turned by Skill than Force. There is, therefore, always Hope that, by wise Counsel and dexterous Management, those Advantages, which through cross Accidents in Warre have been lost, may again with Honour be recovered. In this Place I shall say little of the Power of Money secretly distributed among Grandees, or their Friends or Paramours; that Method being in all ages known and practiced. If the minds of Enemies can be changed, they may be brought to grant willingly and for nothing what much Gold would scarcely have otherwise prevailed to obtain.

Franklin goes on to explain how "menne of learning" should spread defeatism through sermons, discourses, writings, poems, and songs.

. . . All who are in Places, fear to lose them, or hope for better; all who are out of Places, and hope to obtaine them; . . . these, with all the Weighte of their Character and Influence, shall join the Crie for Peace; till it becomes one universal Clamour, and no Sound, but that of Peace, Peace, Peace, shall be heard from every quarter. . . . Then shall your Majestie's Termes of Peace be listened to with much readiness.

STRATEGY OF DIVISION

The Trojan horse is the standard precedent of political warfare. Adam Mickiewicz, the Polish national poet, wrote a famous poem entitled *Konrad Wallenrod* (1828) in which he described how a Pole had entered the hated Teutonic Order, faithfully served his enemies until he became one of their military leaders, and then, taking advantage of his situation, led the knights to defeat in battle. Mickiewicz's poem was actually directed against Russian overlordship in Poland; he insinuated that the appropriate strategy would be

---

[4] *The Complete Works of Benjamin Franklin,* compiled and edited by John Bigelow, New York, Putnam, 1887, Vol. III, pp. 133–137. The paper, written in 1760, was addressed to the King of England.

to maneuver Russia into a defeat by destroying Russian leadership from the inside. Significantly, Mickiewicz prefaced his poem with a motto from Machiavelli: *"Bisogna essere volpe e leone."*

In modern times the "fifth column" need no longer be smuggled into the enemy's camp; in most cases it is already available among the nationals of the country marked out for penetration.

Political warfare was practiced widely throughout the ages. In feudal warfare malcontent members of princely houses, pretenders, or ambitious noblemen contracted alliances with foreign states against their own sovereign. Great nobles fought against their own people. One of the last incidents of political warfare under feudal conditions was Cinq-Mars' conspiracy against Richelieu in 1642, which was to be coordinated with a Spanish offensive against the heart of France.[5]

The only successful invasion of the British Isles in modern times was that of William of Orange. It was successful precisely because the commander of King James's navy did not wish to fight William. A number of important army officers, including Lord Churchill, later the Duke of Marlborough, deserted the King. Hence William was not faced by armed resistance and had little difficulty in consummating that dynastic transaction, the Glorious Revolution of 1688.[6]

The American War of Independence was greatly influenced by the pro-American attitude of leading British soldiers and politicians. Lord Howe, for example, sought to avoid a fighting war, and his scruples may account for some of his military blunders. American political warfare was conducted brilliantly by Benjamin Franklin, who made effective use of his British and French connections and of Masonic organizations. While the main victories of the Revolution were undoubtedly won on the battlefields (where incidentally American weapons proved superior to British ones), there is no denying the fact that American political warfare weakened the British Government's determination to fight the war to a finish and induced Britain to conclude a peace long before Britain's military forces were exhausted.

In 1797, during the first of the wars of the French Revolution, the large-scale mutiny in the British navy anchored in the Nore was mainly due to the intolerable conditions then prevailing in the fleet, yet it was given a distinct political flavor by the Irish sailors on British ships. The mutiny was under the leadership of Wolfe Tone, who had organized the Irish surgeons in the British ships as the cadres of the mutineers. Tone was brought into contact with Carnot, then civilian head of the French army, and a plan was developed for a French invasion of Ireland; the Royal Navy was to be incapacitated by large-scale naval desertions. The scheme was well designed

[5] See Auguste Bailly, *Richelieu,* Paris, Fayard, 1939, pp. 310*ff*.

[6] Katherine Chorley, *Armies and the Art of Revolution,* London, Faber, 1943, pp. 34*ff*., 88.

and might have worked had the French been able to carry out their side of the bargain.[7]

Political warfare schemes directed against the French Revolution and Napoleon, though mostly organized by French *émigrés*, usually found support in foreign countries, especially in England. French *émigré* "legions" were linked to partisan groups in France. Napoleon is the inventor of the modern type of combined or broadened strategy,[8] to wit, the joint employment of subversive and military attack. When the French decided to undertake an expedition into Egypt, it became necessary to take, as a preliminary, the island of Malta, then under the rule of the Knights of St. John. The island-fortress was virtually unconquerable. Napoleon infiltrated agents and established contacts with a powerful fifth column on the island. The peace party got the upper hand over the war party; Napoleon took Malta without resistance (1798).[9]

In Egypt, Napoleon thought for a while that he could master the Orient by the device of taking Aleppo and then accepting, together with his army, the islamitic religion. His successor as French ruler of Egypt, General Menou, in fact became a Mohammedan, but the gesture did not strengthen his position, since the French military situation was by then gravely compromised. (In 1937, Mussolini brandished the sword of Islam and proclaimed himself protector of the Moslems.) Napoleon may have missed his greatest opportunity of political warfare when, in 1812, he failed to proclaim the liberation of the Russian serfs—a step by which he might have gained the wholehearted support of the Russian people.[10]

The troubled period of 1792 to 1815 saw a great extension of political warfare methods. Under the impact of the French Revolution, republican and antimonarchical parties sprang up in many states of Europe and collaborated with the French. During the same period, the oldest method of political warfare, the bribing of officials, reached a peak in the deals which Prince Talleyrand, French Foreign Minister, transacted with various powers. In 1800, Napoleon destroyed the Austrian army. A crushing peace would have been

[7] See T. H. Wintringham, *Mutiny: Being a Survey of Mutinies from Spartacus to Invergordon,* New York, Fortuny's, no date, pp. 63–97.

[8] On this important concept, see Hermann Rauschning, *The Voice of Destruction,* New York, Putnam, 1940, p. 7.

[9] Henri Rollin, *La Revolution russe,* Paris, Delagrave, 1931, Vol. II, "Le parti bolsheviste," pp. 300–309.

[10] See Eugen Tarlé, *Napoleon's Invasion of Russia 1812,* New York, Oxford, 1942, pp. 256ff. Tarlé writes: "We are confronted by a paradox: the peasants who loathed their servitude, who protested by murders of landowners . . . and by revolts . . . the same peasants met Napoleon as a fierce enemy, fighting with all their strength. . . . And yet there is definite evidence that as early as 1805–1807, and at the beginning of the invasion of 1812, rumours associating Napoleon with dreams of emancipation circulated among the Russian peasantry. . . . The French command promptly crushed the peasants and restored all the feudal rights. . . . The Russian serf peasantry soon realized that no liberation could be expected from Napoleon . . ." (pp. 256–259). These observations apply, but for a few minor modifications, to Hitler's Ukrainian campaign in 1941.

signed but for the fact that the Austrians bribed Talleyrand with a substantial sum of money. The result was that Austria escaped lightly (Peace of Lunéville, 1801). Subsequently, the structure of Germany, as it had been devised at the Peace of Westphalia, was remade; many of the states were abolished, and the bigger states lost or gained territories according to Napoleon's whims. Prussia, which had the foresight to bribe Talleyrand, made considerable territorial gains.

Talleyrand was a master of a technique which in modern times has become known as "policy sabotage" (in communist parlance, "diversionism"). Once he understood that Napoleon's megalomania would lead to the destruction of France, he made up his mind to thwart his policies. In 1808, Napoleon concluded an alliance with Russia. When difficulties arose, he decided that this alliance had to be strengthened and that Austria, the last remaining Continental military power, had to be disarmed. Talleyrand realized that the accomplishment of this plan would perpetuate Napoleon's rule; hence he decided to work against it. Napoleon met Tsar Alexander at Erfurth and almost won him over to his scheme. Talleyrand told the Tsar that he should not be persuaded by Napoleon, and, above all, that he should avoid hostile measures against Austria. The Tsar replied that Napoleon had offered very convincing arguments. Talleyrand assured the Tsar that he, too, could advance many telling points and suggested a policy which was exactly contrary to that envisaged by Napoleon, slyly intimating that the Franco-Russian alliance might not last and that the Tsar might, one day, need Austria as an ally. On the following day, Talleyrand visited Alexander and told him: [11]

It is up to you to save Europe. You will not succeed in this task except by opposing Napoleon. The French people are civilized but their sovereign is not civilized. The sovereign of Russia is civilized but his people are not civilized. Hence the sovereign of Russia should become the ally of the French people. The Rhine, the Alps and the Pyrenees are the conquest of France. But all the rest are the conquests of the Emperor. France does not care about those.

Metternich, Austrian Ambassador in Paris, knew about Talleyrand's ideas, and supported his anti-Napoleonic policies at Vienna. In addition, Talleyrand entertained close personal relations with the French Ambassador in St. Petersburg through whom he continued to influence the Tsar and to counteract Napoleon's policies toward Russia. He was able to carry out this plot because the Minister of Police, Fouché, formerly his bitter enemy, had joined forces with him and failed to report Talleyrand's activities to the emperor. In many ways Talleyrand was manipulated by Metternich, who in this situation saved Austria through a typical maneuver of political warfare.

In March, 1848, the population of Milan, restive under Austrian rule, was galvanized into action by the news of the revolution in Vienna. The revolutionaries, secretly backed by France and taking advantage of the Austrian

[11] Louis Madelin, *Talleyrand,* Paris, Flammarion, 1944, p. 215.

government's paralysis, struck and expelled in a five-day revolutionary battle the Austrians from the city—and thus supplied an example of perfect timing, even though after consolidation of the Vienna government, Milan was again won back by Austria.

Sometimes the plots of political warfare are as tricky as those of French comedy. In 1892, France and Russia agreed in principle to sign a military alliance; however, powerful anti-French forces in Russia succeeded in delaying the drawing up of the military convention. The anti-French party advanced an argument that greatly disturbed the Tsar: that a country which tolerated revolutionary movements could not be trusted as a Russian ally. In fact, they intimated that the anarchists who had murdered Alexander II had been trained in France. Proalliance Russians secretly urged the French to repress the anarchistic movement, but the Chamber refused to vote the required laws.

In this impasse it seems that somebody thought of frightening the deputies into action. A reputed anarchist threw a bomb in the Palais Bourbon. Though no great damage was done, the politicians had been greatly frightened; the laws were voted, and the French-Russian alliance was ratified forthwith. At the time great admiration was expressed about the courageous behavior of Charles Dupuy, who had just resigned as Prime Minister and who kept the panicky Chamber under control by roaring with a stentorian voice through the fumes of the explosion: "Le séance continue." Thirty years later, however, several high officials of the French police published their memoirs. It appeared that the bomb plot had been organized by the police itself and probably at the suggestion of Dupuy who, driven by his Russian friends, wanted to leave no stone unturned to conclude the Russian alliance.[12]

POLITICAL WARFARE AND WAR IN THE 20TH CENTURY

During the Russo-Japanese War of 1904–1905 a number of revolutionary disturbances occurred in various parts of Russia. Precisely how far the Japanese supported the Russian revolutionaries has not been fully established. Yet the following facts are known: the Paris section of the Okhrana was convinced that the Japanese maintained very close contacts with the revolutionaries, and they believed that the Japanese supported in particular the Finnish socialist Konni Zilliacus. However, the accuracy of these reports is open to doubt. On the other hand, it *is* known that the future Marshal Pilsudski, then leader of the Polish Socialist party, went to Japan during the war and probably obtained help. It is also known that the Japanese general staff accorded financial help to revolutionary movements and that it maintained an excellent intelligence service among the revolutionaries.[13]

---

[12] See Henri Rollin, *L'Apocalypse de notre temps: les dessous de la propagande allemande d'après des documents inédits,* Paris, Gallimard, 1939, p. 429.
[13] *Ibid.,* pp. 459, 506.

Political warfare was waged on a lavish scale in Eastern Europe, especially by Russia, Austria, and Serbia. The Russians built up controlled political parties abroad. In Austrian Gallicia three such parties were working toward the secession of that province from Austria and its incorporation into Russia. The Austrians countered by supporting various nationalist Polish and Ukrainian parties agitating for the "independence" of Poland and the Ukraine (under Austrian princes), and socialist parties aiming at the overthrow of Tsarism.[14] In supporting these Polish parties, Austrian staff officers of Polish origin were not always guided by the interests of the Austro-Hungarian monarchy alone but took their inspirations from the idea of a truly independent Poland. Poles by conviction, they exploited Austrian policy for their own purposes—a remarkable case of double loyalty and of political warfare modeled after the Chinese box within a box.

Under Russian influence, the Serbs set up various organizations which operated in the Slavic regions of southern Austria-Hungary. Whether or not the Serbian government had foreknowledge of, and controlled, the operation which culminated in the assassination of Archduke Francis Ferdinand and which led to the outbreak of the First World War, is a debated question; probably they did not. The fact remains that *after* their creation these organizations developed their own momentum. Key officers of the Serbian army supported their activities, probably with the intention of provoking the military conflict with Austria on which the future of a "greater Serbia" depended. This was another case of policy sabotage not of the negative type practiced by Talleyrand, but of an *aggressive* type aimed at forcing the hand of a reluctant government.[15]

The First World War gave rise to an almost unbelievable proliferation of political warfare procedures. At the very beginning, German agents in Turkey and Bulgaria took steps to involve these two countries in the war against the Entente. They scored a rapid success in Turkey where the Germans had maintained excellent relations with politicians of the Young Turk movement.

The involvement of Bulgaria in the war against the Entente proved to be difficult. Yet in the end, the Germans prevailed, despite the fact that it was clearly to Bulgaria's national interest to remain neutral. One of the main devices used was the financing of Bulgarian *Komitadji* bands and the fostering of a large insurrection in Macedonia which embroiled Bulgaria in war with Serbia. The cost of the operation was 30,000 francs.[16]

German operations in Greece proved less successful. Although the King was pro-German, the government was pro-Entente. The Germans were spending considerable sums of money to influence public opinion and elections. For example, on June 21, 1915, the German Secretary of State for foreign

---

[14] Max Ronge, *Kriegs- und Industrie-Spionage, 12 Jahre Kundschaftsdienst*, Zurich, Amalthea, 1930, *passim*.

[15] Albert Mousset, *L'Attentat de Sarajewo*, Paris, Payot, 1930, *passim*.

[16] German Foreign Office File, Reel 2587.

affairs sent a letter to the German treasury demanding that 1 million francs be made available to the German Minister in Athens for political warfare purposes.[17] The Germans splurged; the Entente powers displayed greater skill. They succeeded in overthrowing the King and installing a pro-Entente government which took Greece into the war against Germany.

During 1916, the Germans suspected that Spain, which had been neutral, was moving closer to the Entente. The Germans sought to bring about, at no matter what cost in money, the removal of the Spanish Prime Minister, Count Romanones. The German Foreign Office, deeming it inadvisable that Germany should show her hand too openly, decided to entrust the operation to pro-German Spaniards and to revitalize the old Carlist movement. For this purpose, the Carlists were to be supplied by submarine. The plan proved to be impractical,[18] partly because moribund political movements cannot be easily revived.

In their political warfare against Britain the Germans supported the Irish revolutionaries. In 1914, Sir Roger Casement, one of the Irish leaders, left New York for Germany. In Germany he organized an Irish brigade and laid plans for coordinating a revolutionary attempt in Ireland with German strategy on the Continent. The Germans promised financial help and deliveries of weapons and equipment and in 1916 sent Casement by submarine to Ireland, where he was to lead the rising.[19] However, two munitions ships were intercepted, and Casement was captured shortly after landing on Irish soil. The Easter Rebellion, timed to coincide with the Battle of Verdun, was suppressed.[20] Had the German plan succeeded, the British would have been compelled to curtail their military effectives on the Continent at a most crucial time and to stop the offensive on the Somme.

The Germans hatched many schemes to foment revolutions within the British Empire. They built up a large Indian organization and attempted unsuccessfully to supply anti-British elements in India with weapons from the United States.[21] They organized Egyptian groups (while in Egypt T. E. Lawrence, on behalf of Britain, organized the Arabs against Turkish rule)

[17] *Ibid.*, Reel 2588.

[18] *Ibid.*, Reel 2594.

[19] The treaty which Casement concluded with the German government contains the following provision: "(1) With a view to securing the national freedom of Ireland with the moral and material assistance of the Imperial German Government, an Irish Brigade shall be formed from among the Irish soldiers now prisoners in Germany, or other natives of Ireland. The object of the Irish Brigade shall be to fight solely the cause of Ireland, and under no circumstances shall it be employed or directed to any German end. . . ." This document which, incidentally, was written in English, was signed by Casement and Zimmerman on December 27, 1914. (Denis Gwynn, *Traitor or Patriot: The Life and Death of Roger Casement,* London, J. Cape and Harrison Smith, 1931, pp. 329–331.)

[20] The best account of this rebellion is found in W. B. Wells and N. Marlowe, *A History of the Irish Rebellion of 1916,* Dublin, Maunsel & Co., Ltd., 1926.

[21] For German aid given to Indian revolutionaries in the shape of a $200,000 credit and shipments of weapons, see Franz von Papen, *Der Wahrheit eine Gasse,* Munich, List, 1952, p. 63.

as well as various movements in French North Africa. Persia and colonies in Central Africa were not overlooked. These intrigues hardly affected the outcome of the war; they created unrest and weakened the position of the European powers in Asia and Africa.

In France, the Germans supported radical and defeatist-pacifist movements, maintained contacts with influential politicians, including—through remote intermediaries and therefore perhaps unknown to him—relations with the former Prime Minister, Joseph Caillaux. The Germans fostered "negative defeatism" (humanitarianism, pacifism, disbelief in victory), "active defeatism" (desertion, rebellion, mutiny, sabotage, high treason), and "positive activism" (national independence and revolutionary movements, establishment of subversive armed forces, overthrow of governments).[22] France, though demoralized through these attacks, was not defeated. The wounds, however, which she suffered from these "secret weapons" were deep and more grievous than they seemed in the first flush of victory.

German political warfare against Russia proved highly successful. All kinds of techniques, old and new, were used. There were attempts to come to terms with pro-German and antiwar elements in the imperial court. These attempts failed but rumors about secret negotiations, some of which were highly exaggerated, undermined the moral position of the Tsar and, especially, of the Tsarina. The Germans attempted to operate through financial and industrial circles, some of which had close German connections (*e.g.*, the textile and electrical industries). The Germans sent into the fray influential Swedish and German businessmen (as, for example, the German industrialist Stinnes and the banker Warburg), but the Russian government usually got wind of these negotiations and was able to stop them.[23] Ironically, German attempts to weaken the Tsar paralleled British maneuvers to replace Nicholas II by Grand Duke Cyril Vladimirovich. Whether these activities which allegedly were directed by the Ambassador at Petrograd, Sir George Buchanan, aimed at replacing an ineffective by an effective government or at the weakening of Russia as a factor in future peace negotiations may be debatable.[24]

The Germans endeavored to employ the services of pro-German members of the noble class. In the summer of 1916, the Germans negotiated with a Russian prince for the purpose of buying the *three leading Russian newspapers,* including a semiofficial organ. The whimsical idea was to slant these newspapers in such a manner that one would have influenced the political right, one the center, and one the left-of-center bourgeoisie. The cost of the operation was estimated at 10 to 25 million rubles. However, the scheme

---

[22] See Paul von Lettow-Vorbeck (ed.), *Die Weltkriegsspionage,* Munich, Moser, 1931, p. 529.

[23] In addition to numerous items in the German Foreign Office File, see Victor Chernov, *The Great Russian Revolution,* New Haven, Yale University Press, 1936, pp. 30–49.

[24] See Anna Viroubova, *Memories of the Russian Court,* New York, Macmillan, 1923, p. 202*f.*

languished, either because the Germans judged it impractical or because they had decided in favor of a revolutionary change in Russia.[25]

Support to separatist movements was a second line of approach. At the very beginning of the war, the Germans, operating from Turkey, excited independence movements in the Caucasus region. Both Austrians and Germans made major efforts to achieve the independence of the Ukraine and of Poland. To be on the safe side, they organized various national political parties ranging all the way from the extreme left to the right. The Austrians set up a Polish Legion, a military force which was under the command of Joseph Pilsudski, later a marshal and dictator of Poland. The Germans supported the independence movement of Finland and asked German socialists to organize a Finnish "revolution." [26] When this scheme failed, they transported, by "underground railroad," young Finns to Germany where they trained for military service. By 1917, German support had been extended to the Mohammedan nations of Russian Asia and a link established with German operations in support of anti-British Moslem movements in the Middle East.[27]

The main German political warfare effort against Russia was based on the systematic support of the socialist revolutionary movement. From the beginning of the war, the imperial government, which needed the support of the Social Democratic parties of Germany, had set up a working arrangement with the socialists, the so-called *Burgfriede*.[28] The socialists' contribution to German political warfare was threefold: they compiled revolutionary publications in support of the German war effort; they attempted to influence socialists in Western Europe and the United States in order to bring about an early peace of compromise; and they worked toward the destruction of the Tsarist system in Russia.[29]

The mastermind of the German Social Democratic party, a Russian-born socialist named Alexander Helphand but more widely known under the pen name "Parvus," elaborated the requisite theory: the German army was the best tool for the destruction of Russian Tsarism and therefore the natural, though temporary, ally of the socialist movement.[30]

[25] German Foreign Office File, Reel 2593.

[26] Philipp Scheidemann, *The Making of New Germany,* New York, Appleton, 1929, Vol. I, pp. 232f.

[27] German Foreign Office File, Reel 2160.

[28] See Hans W. Gatzke, *Germany's Drive to the West, A Study of Germany's Western War Aims during the First World War,* Baltimore, Johns Hopkins Press, 1950, p. 18.

[29] On the reasons which led the imperial government to cooperate with the Social Democratic party, see Prince Bernhard von Bülow, *Memoirs,* Boston, Little, Brown, 1932, Vol. III, "The World War and Germany's Collapse, 1900–1919," p. 187. For the reasons which induced the Social Democrats to give their consent to an aggressive war, see Scheidemann, *op. cit.,* and Gustav Noske, *Aufstieg und Niedergang der deutschen Sozialdemokratie,* Zurich, Aero-Verlag, 1947.

[30] See various articles by "Parvus" in *Die Glocke* (monthly), Vol. I, August, 1915–June, 1916, pp. 35, 77–85, 148–155. Parvus was a close personal friend of the leaders of the Social Democratic party, including the later *Reichspräsident,* Friedrich Ebert.

The *official* German policy was formulated on December 6, 1915, by the German Minister at Copenhagen, Count Ulrich von Brockdorff-Rantzau. While his diplomatic position did not entitle Brockdorff-Rantzau to make national policy, his influence, based on a superior intellect and an extraordinary diligence, was such that he must be ranked as the framer of Germany's policy toward Russia during the entire period of 1914–1926. (He later was almost appointed *Reich* Chancellor and became German Foreign Minister and then Ambassador to Moscow.) In an *aide-mémoire* to the *Reich* Chancellor, Theobald von Bethmann-Hollweg, he wrote that it was a moot question whether or not the Tsar could or would make a separate peace:

It would be a disastrous error to consider seriously continuing our traditional relations with Russia, i.e., with the House of Romanov. By its base ingratitude, the House of Romanov has forsaken the traditional friendship to which we have stood in fateful hours. The struggle threatens our very existence. Once we hesitate, the cynical and clever plans of England would be realized and Germany, utterly exhausted, may be forced to accept the conditions dictated by the Entente.

Yet victory, and as its prize the first place in the world, would be ours if it were possible to revolutionize Russia in time and by this means to destroy the coalition.

The *aide-mémoire* continued by recommending that "Parvus" be employed for the implementation of this program: [31]

I believe that we should use his [Parvus's] services before it is too late, and pursue a policy toward Russia which will gain Germany the permanent friendship of the Russian people. This objective cannot be reached before the tsarist empire in its present form has been overthrown. Considering our present position, I believe that we must take the risk. . . . Should we be able to achieve a definite decision in our favor by military means, this [military] method would be preferable. Otherwise, according to my conviction, there is no other solution. Our existence as a great power is at stake—and perhaps even our very survival.

Brockdorff-Rantzau had not gained these insights by his own ratiocinations; "Parvus," then living in Copenhagen, had been his intellectual mentor. The experienced socialist had convinced the diplomat of the feasibility and desirability of the Russian revolution; the diplomat now saw in the revolution a method to secure German world dominion. "Parvus" hoped that the Russian revolution ultimately would lead to a socialist revolution *in Germany*, while Rantzau and his friends hoped that socialism would be a tool of German imperialism, to be destroyed after use. To which must be added that revolution in Russia was feasible only because of the abysmal stupidity of the Tsarist government: after his overthrow Nicholas II told Kerensky that Wilhelm II consistently advised him against a liberal policy which presumably could have forestalled the revolution.[32]

---

[31] German Foreign Office File, Reel 2590. Compare the similarity of phrasing in Rantzau's and Talleyrand's statements: the Russian tsar and the French nation, the German emperor and the Russian nation.

[32] Maurice Paléologue, *An Ambassador's Memoirs,* New York, Doran, no date (1926?), Vol. III, p. 284.

The German government extended support, through many intermediaries, to revolutionary movements. Particular attention was given to Lenin and his Bolsheviks, then living in exile, whom the Germans helped, upon the outbreak of the Russian revolution in March, 1917, to travel to Russia. Lenin launched a massive campaign for the immediate cessation of the war. There is a great deal of evidence to the effect that the Germans financed many of the political and propagandist activities of the Bolsheviks. Synchronization between military operations at the front and revolutionary operations in Petrograd ultimately culminated in the Bolshevik seizure of power in November, 1917. Three weeks later, Lenin offered the Germans peace on the Eastern front.[33]

Although they had brought their minions into power, the onerous conditions which the Germans imposed on the Russians made it almost impossible for Lenin to conclude the peace. At one point negotiations were broken off and the German army was ordered to advance. At this point German political warfare scored its greatest success: Lenin and Krylenko, the commander of the Russian army, who in all likelihood was an outright German agent, dissolved the existing army, proposed to replace it by a Red Army—although they kept the reasons to themselves why this replacement had to occur at precisely that crucial moment—and ordered the still existing Russian army units to offer no resistance and to fall back before comparatively light German pressure. The Bolsheviks thus "proved" that resistance against German demands was hopeless. The peace of Brest-Litovsk was signed, and Russia was delivered into the hands of Germany.[34]

Once the peace was secured, the Germans were confronted by the question as to whether they should continue the Bolsheviks in power or should replace them by a more acceptable regime which would stabilize conditions in Russia. The decision was made to maintain the Bolshevik dictatorship and to keep out all those elements who conceivably might have put the country back on its feet.

We should have at present only one purpose in Greater Russia: to further the disintegrating forces and to keep the country weak. . . . It is therefore to our interest that the Bolsheviks stay in power. . . . The Russian system of transportation, industry and commerce must be controlled by us. We will succeed in exploiting the Eastern territories.[35]

[33] All this does not mean, of course, that Germany "made" the Bolshevik revolution. This revolution was due to much more complex and profound reasons than German political warfare, but German strategists certainly made the most of their opportunities, and the connection between Bolsheviks and Germans was, to say the least, intimate.

[34] Communist writers assert that Lenin had no choice but to accept the German demands. For the true facts as they emerge from communist literature itself, see George Spiro, *Marxism and the Bolshevik State,* New York, Red Star Press, 1951, pp. 284–348.

[35] United States National Archives, *Gröner Papers,* unsigned memorandum, no date, box 27, index 254 II.

The Germans contemplated, in the words of General Wilhelm Gröner, then German governor of the Ukraine, a "complete marriage with the Bolsheviks." By the time this policy was being reconsidered and steps prepared to oust the Bolsheviks (August, 1918), Germany's armies had been beaten in France and the Germans were no longer capable of remaking the Russian government to their liking.[36]

On a world-wide scale, the German government gave full support to the international socialist movement. This support culminated in the organization by Germany of the international socialist peace conference at Stockholm in 1917 which, surprisingly, was attended by many national independence leaders from many colonial countries. Not so surprisingly, Germany's subversive activities extended to the United States. The Ambassador at Washington, Count J. H. von Bernstorff, wrote on July 13, 1915, to the German Foreign Office that he had established contacts, through an intermediary, with the American Federation of Labor and particularly Messrs. Gompers and Mitchell. He stated that, in the opinion of these personalities, American labor should cooperate with the European workers' movement in order to bring about peace. This cooperation would force the United States government or Congress to declare an embargo on weapons and munitions. (This would not have harmed Germany but would have hurt Britain and France; it might have led to a German victory.) However, to execute this plan in the United States, there would be needed $400,000 to $500,000, and it was suggested that Germany should supply most of this amount.

The Ambassador informed the intermediary that the German government never would pay money for such evil purposes. But having delivered this hypocritical reply and presumably having appeased his conscience, the Ambassador agreed that perhaps the German labor movement (rather than the government) might get the money together. If so, the American partners must guarantee that the transaction remain secret. Bernstorff continued:

I gained the impression that these declarations were sincere. To confirm this impression, I have asked cautiously for the advice of the former secretary of commerce and labor, Charles Nagel, who is sympathetically inclined toward this movement, both for the sake of peace and of the German cause. . . . I believe that organized labor is in effect politically strong enough to impose a weapons embargo on Congress.

Bernstorff added that the American socialist labor movement also could be drawn into this activity and might be able to obtain financial support from Catholic circles (sic!). He asked that $200,000 be made available by German labor for this purpose. "Where the labor movement finds these means would be a question which is of no concern to anybody." The Ambassador con-

[36] When the Germans launched "operation Lenin," they had no assurance that this particular stratagem would work. Hence they laid the groundwork for substituting either anarchist forces or anti-Western elements among the Mensheviks and Social Revolutionaries for the Bolsheviks should these fail or decide to work against German interests.

cluded that Berlin should not be worried about security leaks; his contacts were in a form which made it impossible that the embassy be incriminated.[37] Moreover, the American labor movement was politically so strong that there was no chance of its being investigated!

It is dangerous to play with fire. The Germans were soon to discover this truth; the German revolution of 1918 was a direct consequence of the Bolshevik revolution in 1917 and of the impetus given to the socialist movement by these various political warfare activities. The breakup of Russia stimulated the revolutionary movement in Germany. Repatriated German prisoners, imbued with the new ideology, leavened the domestic revolutionary elements. Revolutionary agents filtered into the German army on the eastern front. As a matter of fact, the Bolshevik government embarked upon a systematic attempt to overthrow the imperial government of Germany, not only in order to liberate Russia from the chains of the Brest-Litovsk Treaty but also to further world revolution. The Russian Ambassador to Berlin, Joffe, admitted in January, 1919: "It is necessary to emphasize most categorically that in the preparation of the German revolution, the Russian embassy worked all the time in close contact with the German socialists." The Germans expelled Joffe shortly before the Kaiser's overthrow and later, in a radiogram to the Russian government, officially accused him of having acted in bad faith. They complained that Joffe had engaged in propaganda and had purchased arms and ammunition for German revolutionaries, spending for this purpose 105,000 marks (at that time a ridiculously low sum). Joffe answered on December 4, 1918: [38]

With reference to the radiogram of December 3 . . . , which accuses the former embassy of the Soviet government in Berlin not only of spreading Bolshevik propaganda but also of purchasing arms, I wish to state that the said propaganda was carried on with the help of the Independent Social-Democratic party. As regards the purchase of arms . . . the amount mentioned in the radiogram is not correct. Minister Barth received not 105,000 marks but several hundred thousand marks for the purpose of acquiring arms. I desire to make known the real facts in the case and consider it to my credit that by means of my above-mentioned activities . . . , I contributed to the full extent of my power to the triumph of the German revolution.

The Allies, on their part, insisted on the Kaiser's abdication and thus contributed to the revolution in Germany and to the final collapse of German resistance. During the same year, the Allies entered into various agreements with the Slavic nations of the Austrian monarchy. These agreements set the stage for the establishment of foreign legions and provisional governments in exile; wholesale desertions, revolutions in Prague and Zagreb, and the breakup of the Austro-Hungarian Empire followed.

[37] German Foreign Office File, Reel 2589.
[38] James Bunyan, *Intervention, Civil War, and Communism in Russia, April–December, 1918, Documents and Materials,* Baltimore, Johns Hopkins Press, 1936, p. 156.

POLITICAL WARFARE IN WORLD WAR II

The history of the Austrian *Anschluss* in 1938 traces with exemplary clarity the pattern of political warfare. The number of Nazis in Austria had been increasing rapidly as a result of the silent, though effective, support of Germany. Nevertheless, the Austrian Nazi party was illegal, and it was clearly not within its own power to overthrow the government. In the winter of 1937, the Austrian government uncovered several illegal Nazi organizations, two of which were busily plotting an armed revolt. Yet before energetic repressive measures could be taken, the German government stepped in and maneuvered in such a manner that Chancellor Schuschnigg saw himself compelled to visit Hitler at Berchtesgaden. The upshot of the negotiations was that "pro-German" ministers were taken into the cabinet, one of them obtaining the Ministry of the Interior with control over the police. Once the police were neutralized, the Nazis launched mass demonstrations and established control over the streets in all Austrian towns and villages. Gradually the campaign of terrorization was stepped up until chaos prevailed. By that time the Austrian government was demoralized and, being far too weak to resist an invasion by the German army, capitulated to Nazi demands.

This pattern was repeated again and again with slight variations. After the Sudeten crisis, for example, the Germans advised the Czechs that there could be peace only if President Beneš were ousted; *i.e.,* that he be replaced by a man less liable to oppose their further designs. Beneš resigned, and the Germans had thus paved the way for the total annexation of Bohemia.

Intervention in the affairs of the small kingdom of Albania was described by Mussolini's son-in-law and foreign minister, Ciano. After having conferred with the secretary-general of the Fascist party on April 2, 1939, he made the following entry in his diary: "I got ready to send him to Tirana with a small band of men as enterprising and boastful as himself, in order to create the incidents which are to take place . . . if the King . . . has not . . . the kindness to capitulate." [39]

On April 12, 1939, when Albanian opposition to a union with Italy developed, Ciano wrote: "I have long discussions with many chiefs; the most stubborn are those from Scutari (who have been incited by the Catholic clergy) whom it will be easy to convince, however, as soon as I distribute bundles of Albanian francs, which I have brought with me." [40]

National minorities are often effectively used for political-warfare purposes. In the United States, particularly during the First World War, the attitudes of these racial minorities were of great importance in domestic poli-

[39] See *The Ciano Diaries 1939–1943: The Complete Unabridged Diaries of Count Galeazzo Ciano, Italian Minister for Foreign Affairs, 1936–1943,* edited by Hugh Gibson, New York, Doubleday, 1946, p. 57.

[40] *Ibid.,* p. 65.

tics and hence in foreign policy. How an unscrupulous politician proposes to exploit irredentist sentiments is revealed by Ciano's entry of April 21, 1939: [41]

I have a conference with Sthyka, Albanian ex-Minister to Belgrade. He furnished information on the problem of the Cayovosi [Albanians under Yugoslav rule], that is, eight hundred and fifty thousand Albanians . . . enthusiastic at the idea of a union with their mother country. It seems that the Serbs are in a panic over it. For the moment we must not even allow it to be imagined that the problem is attracting our attention; rather it is necessary to give the Yugoslavs a dose of chloroform. Later on, it will be necessary to adopt a policy of real interest in the Cayovo question; this will cause an "irredentist" problem in the Balkans that will absorb the attention of the Albanians themselves and will be a dagger thrust into the back of Yugoslavia.

Political warfare cannot always be applied in this simple fashion, especially if the victim country is militarily strong. Yet it is often possible to weaken an existing government from within—be it by economic pressure, political demonstrations, infiltration into army and police, or military blackmail—and to engineer the accession to power of that faction which will come to terms with the aggressor.

The Abortion of the Greatest Coup. For many years the world was at a loss to explain for what reason Stalin, in 1936, suddenly arrested the entire high command of the Red Army and had some of his most prominent generals, including Marshal Tukhachevski, shot. The official Soviet version was that the generals had turned traitors and had plotted Stalin's overthrow. Since the Soviet story contained many contradictions, and since it is hardly plausible that the entire high command of a modern nation should betray its own country in the interest of an ideological and racial enemy, the world remained incredulous and assumed that Stalin had simply intended to eliminate competitors or to stamp out opposition. Churchill later told the story that in 1936 President Beneš of Czechoslovakia had been informed by the Germans that a political change was impending in Russia; warned by this hint, Beneš discovered that "communications were passing through the Soviet embassy in Prague between important personages in Russia and the German government." These communications were part of a conspiracy to overthrow Stalin. Beneš "lost no time" in warning Stalin.[42]

Data have now turned up which throw a different light on this affair. It seems that in 1936, Heydrich, one of the top men in the Gestapo, obtained specimens of the handwritings of the Russian generals who were later executed, employed handwriting experts, and kept in custody four agents of the Russian GPU. Several months after the execution of Tukhachevski, Heydrich was to boast to Admiral Canaris, chief of German Intelligence who in turn told the story to some of his confidants, that he, Heydrich, *had eliminated the*

---

[41] *Ibid.*, p. 69.

[42] Winston Churchill, *The Second World War: The Gathering Storm*, Boston, Houghton Mifflin, 1948, p. 225.

leadership of the Red Army. Forged documents were produced indicating an alleged plot by the Soviet generals in cooperation with the German general staff: ". . . a comprehensive exchange of communications between the Tukhachevski group and the German *Reichswehr* chieftains had been duly forged. These damaging, incriminating documents were played through GPU agents via the Czech General Staff into the hands of Stalin." And Heydrich added: "The idea came from the *Führer* himself." [43]

Incredible though the story may sound, it is given some degree of plausibility by the fact that there is at least one precedent: the famous Dreyfus scandal in France. Some evidence has come to light according to which the documents which led to the conviction of Captain Dreyfus for espionage, had been *planted* by the German military attaché who knew that the contents of his wastepaper basket were given daily to the French *Section de Statistique.*[44] The attack by Hitler on Tukhachevski is quite in line with Hitler's theories on *geistige Kriegführung*—a term for which there is no appropriate English translation, and which means warfare with weapons of the mind. It is also in line with the favorite Nazi device of *Rufmord,* character assassination, or rather elimination of a dangerous opponent by destroying his reputation.

Political warfare is not waged exclusively for the benefit of what could be called sympathetic parties. If one cannot get the government one likes, one tries to eliminate the government one dislikes. For example, the Germans feared President Roosevelt as their most formidable opponent. They supported in 1940 Wendell Willkie and in 1944 Thomas E. Dewey as the lesser of two evils. This support was not too effective, but it is unlikely that pro-German Americans voted for Roosevelt. On the other hand, the Russians preferred Roosevelt. Hence pro-Russians hardly ever voted for Roosevelt's opponents. Similarly, the Germans attempted to keep Munich men in power in Great Britain and especially to prevent Churchill from entering the Cabinet. In France, they concentrated their opposition against Paul Reynaud.

During the "Cold War" phase preceding World War II, the Germans and Italians supported many movements in many lands, Nazi and Fascist as well as anti-Semitic. They apparently paid considerable sums of money to some of their French confederates as, for example, Fernand de Brinon, Darquier de Pellepoix, and to newspapers like *Je suis partout,* advocates all of German policies. During the Vichy period these men came to power.[45] Axis support

---

[43] See Melvin J. Lasky, "Did Hitler Help Stalin in the Frame-up?" *The New Leader,* Dec. 25, 1948. Lasky's source is a German officer using the pseudonym of "Horst Falkenhagen." Lasky checked this story and was "reassured that the author was *earnest* and *possessed* credentials and although that in no way puts [him] in a position to vouch for his revelations, it is a warrant for this report." See also the version of K. H. Abshagen, *Canaris, Patriot und Weltbürger,* Stuttgart, Union, 1950, p. 167*ff.;* and Walter Hagen, *Die Geheime Front,* Zurich, Europe, 1950, pp. 54–68.

[44] Rollin, *op. cit.,* pp. 308*f.*

[45] The various German attempts to rule France through their pro-Nazi French friends and the continuation of political warfare in France after the collapse of 1940 are described in *Pétain et les Allemands, Memorandum d'Abetz sur les Rapports Franco-Allemands,* Paris, Gaucher, 1948.

was given to the Mufti of Jerusalem and the Indian Nationalist leader Subhas Chandra Bose.

A *coup d'état* which was cleverly coordinated with military operations secured Norway in 1940 for Germany. Strange as it may sound, the initiative for this coup did not come from the Germans but from their Norwegian sympathizers. The scheme took shape only after Vidkun Quisling, a former Minister of War and leader of the Nasjonal Samling party, established contact with the Germans and suggested to them active operations in Scandinavia. As summarized in a memorandum by Alfred Rosenberg, Quisling explained that "ten per cent of the population . . . is in favor of cooperation with Germany" and that action against the government might be possible. Rosenberg's undated memorandum ends with the following significant paragraph: [46]

A plan for possible procedure has been suggested. According to the plan a number of picked Norwegians will be given training in Germany for this particular task. They will be told exactly what to do, and will be assisted by seasoned National Socialists who are experienced in such matters. These trained men are then to be sent back to Norway as quickly as possible, where details will be discussed. Several focal points in Oslo will have to be occupied with lightning speed, and simultaneously the German Navy with contingents of the German Army will have to put in appearance at a pre-arranged bay outside of Oslo in answer to a special summons from the new Norwegian Government. Quisling has no doubt that such a coup, achieved simultaneously, would at once meet with the approval of those sections of the Army with which he now has connections.

On December 11, 1939, Quisling called on Grand Admiral Raeder, commander of the German navy. Quisling depicted "the dangers to Germany arising from a British occupation of Norway . . . in great detail," and continued: "The National Party desires to anticipate any possible British step in this direction by placing the necessary bases at the disposal of the German armed forces. In the whole coastal area men in important positions (railway, post office, communications) have already been bought [*sic*] for this purpose."

On the following day, Raeder saw Hitler and reported on the Quisling negotiation. He emphasized that "it is impossible to know with such offers how much the people concerned wish to further their own party schemes." Yet "it must be made impossible for Norway to fall into British hands, as this could be decisive for the outcome of the war." Hitler agreed that the British occupation of Norway—for which there was no other proof than Quisling's

---

[46] See Office of Naval Intelligence, *Supplement to War Diary of Commander in Chief, Navy: Führer Conferences on Matters Dealing with the German Navy,* Washington, 1947, Vol. 1939, p. 59. Also *Trial of the Major War Criminals before the International Military Tribunal, Nuremberg, November 14, 1945–October 1, 1946,* Nuremberg, Germany, 1947, Vol. XXV, pp. 26–34. Rosenberg's complete statement is given in Anthony Martienssen, *Hitler and His Admirals,* London, Secker & Warburg, 1948, pp. 45f. Martienssen thinks that the memorandum was written about December 8.

assertion—was unacceptable.[47] He decided to talk to Quisling personally "in order to form an impression of him." Raeder then suggested that "if the *Führer* is favorably impressed, the Armed Forces High Command be permitted to make plans with Quisling for preparing and executing the occupation either: (1) by friendly methods, *i.e.*, the German armed forces are called upon by Norway, or (2) by force." Hitler approved these orders.

In April, 1940, while German forces approached Norway, the Norwegian Nazis put most of the coastal defenses of the country out of commission. Without this stratagem of political warfare, the hazardous landings in Oslo and Narvik fjords would have been impossible. Quisling's plan was carried out—on the whole, successfully.

The Germans would have had an excellent chance to organize political warfare against the Soviet government of Russia. However, due to ideological blindness, they did not exploit this opportunity until it was too late. The pros and cons of political-warfare policy in Russia were debated hotly by the various Nazi services, while Hitler usually took the position that he wanted to achieve a purely military victory over the Soviet Union. In the end, various political movements were organized, the most important of which was under the leadership of the Russian General Andrei A. Vlassov. The story makes fascinating reading. It provokes speculation as to how the course of modern history would have been changed if the Nazis had not suffered from a chronic inability to understand Russia, the world, and German national interest. The lasting historical significance of Vlassov's tragedy is that it proved the political vulnerability of the Soviet dictatorship.[48]

During the Second World War, the Allies, too, mastered the difficult art of political warfare. In 1941, a *coup d'état* overthrew the Yugoslav government, which had adhered to the German-sponsored Anti-Comintern Pact, and compelled the Germans to go to war against Yugoslavia.[49] This unforeseen event postponed the date of the German attack on Russia by approximately six weeks, a crucial delay which may have prevented the Germans from taking Moscow and winning the war in the East. The Yugoslav guerrillas, supplied by the Allies, never ceased to plague the Germans, draining resources from all German fronts and hampering German strategy in Italy and Russia.

In 1942 the American diplomatic representative in French North Africa, Robert Murphy, organized a *coup d'état* with the help of French anti-Vichy organizations and part of the French army and succeeded in paralyzing the

[47] Gamelin, in Vol. III of *Servir*, "La Guerre (septembre 1939–19 mai 1940)," (Paris, Plon, 1947), reveals (p. 201) that the Supreme Allied War Council met on February 5, 1940, and that Chamberlain proposed an operation against Narvik. The foolhardiness of this idea was well recognized by most responsible soldiers and statesmen (p. 199). The Allies mined the Norwegian coastal waters just prior to the German attack (pp. 308*ff.*).

[48] See George Fischer, *Soviet Opposition to Stalin: A Case Study in World War II*, Cambridge, Mass., Harvard University Press, 1952.

[49] See David Martin, *Ally Betrayed, The Uncensored Story of Tito and Mihailovich*, foreword by Rebecca West, New York, Prentice-Hall, 1946, pp. 17*f.*

Vichy authorities in Algiers, thus permitting the landing of the Allied forces which were so small that they might have been repulsed by the French had it not been for political preparation.[50] Without this American essay in political warfare, completion of military operations might have been delayed long enough to permit the Germans to move in force into French North Africa and defeat the Allied landing.

In 1943, the Allied landings in Salerno, Italy, were timed to coincide with Marshal Badoglio's break with Germany, prepared by a skillful campaign meshing political with military warfare and culminating in the overthrow of Mussolini. It was one of the neatest political strokes of modern history.

In Spain the British counteracted the activities of German agents and succeeded, largely thanks to the subtle manipulations and cool self-assurance of Sir Samuel Hoare, in keeping Spain neutral. American agents penetrated into the pro-Japanese Burma government and checked Japanese influence in Siam.[51]

The Russians were helped by various *coups d'état* in adjacent countries, such as Rumania, Bulgaria, and Hungary; while in the case of the Warsaw rebellion, they intentionally left their Polish allies to battle the Germans alone, unaided by the nearby Red Army. The Soviet Union preferred Poles of another political orientation to Poles who were loyal to the Polish government-in-exile in London. In the United States, the Soviets conducted a vigorous political campaign in order to accelerate the opening of a second front across the Channel, to prevent an Allied campaign through the Balkans, and to insure the continued provision of lend-lease materials in exchange for no tangible commitments on the part of the U.S.S.R.

In 1945, the Allied ultimatum to Japan issued at Potsdam as well as the dropping of the atomic bomb were followed quickly by a *coup d'état* in Tokyo, eliminating the military die-hards from control over Japan's destinies, thus paving the way to the early cessation of hostilities. The Allies did not take a hand directly in the transformation of the Japanese political scene; pro-Allied Japanese elements sprung into action as soon as they received the assurance they demanded, namely, the preservation of Japanese sovereignty and the Emperor institution.[52]

[50] Renée Pierre-Gosset, *Algiers 1941–1943: A Temporary Expedient*, London, J. Cape, 1945, pp. 63*ff*.

[51] Stewart Alsop and Thomas Braden, *Sub Rosa: The O.S.S. and American Espionage*, New York, Reynal & Hitchcock, 1946, pp. 184*ff*.

[52] In February, 1945, the Japanese Emperor initiated interviews with elder statesmen to clarify the situation. On February 14, Prince Konoye, twice before Prime Minister, talked to the Emperor and recorded the conversation: "I think that there is no longer any doubt about our defeat. A defeat is, of course, a serious strain on our history, but we can accept it, so long as we can maintain our Tenno system. . . . What we have to fear, therefore, is not so much a defeat as a Communist revolution which might take place in the event of defeat. . . . A majority of younger officers seem to think that the present form of the Japanese Government is compatible with Communism. . . . Under such circumstances, the longer we continue the war, the greater will be the danger of revolution. We should therefore stop the war as soon as possible. . . . I must urge Your

TERROR

Terror is one of the most common, and most effective, political warfare weapons. When in 1934 the Austrian Nazis, under German leadership, sought to join Austria to the *Reich*, they attacked the government buildings in Vienna and assassinated the Chancellor Engelbert Dollfuss, believing that after his death resistance would collapse. In 1939, the Iron Guard—the Rumanian Nazis—assassinated the anti-German Prime Minister Călinescu, in the hope that they would be able to seize power. Whether this attempt was made with German knowledge is as yet unconfirmed by documentary evidence, but it was timed to coincide with German military operations exactly as in 1941 an abortive *coup d'état* in Iraq coincided with German infiltration into Syria.

Political warfare by assassination is not a Nazi invention. In the 11th and 12th centuries, the "assassins" or Hashīshīn of the Near East, the eponyms of political warfare by murder, sought to terrorize their opponents by means of assassinating individuals.[53]

One of the politically most successful, though physically unsuccessful, murder plots was that of Felice Orsini in 1858 against Napoleon III. Orsini was a highly cultured, though radical, Italian nationalist and a former friend of Giuseppe Mazzini. He was motivated by the conviction that Napoleon was the chief obstacle to Italian self-determination and independence. The Emperor and the Empress escaped, but the attempt so terrified Napoleon that he espoused the cause of Italian freedom, being fearful that unless he did so he would ultimately be assassinated.

In 1900, the assassination of the German Minister to Peking, Baron von Ketteler, led to an international intervention against China. In 1938, the Nazis discussed the advisability of murdering the *German* minister to Prague in order to create an incident justifying intervention against Czechoslovakia; the project was dropped for practical—not for moral—reasons.

The assassination, at Sarajevo in 1914, of the Austrian heir apparent, Archduke Francis Ferdinand, launched the First World War. The assassination of Admiral Darlan in 1942, predominantly a matter of domestic politics, compelled Britain and the United States to modify their foreign policy toward France. Darlan's elimination eased de Gaulle's assumption of power in North Africa and later in France.

Majesty to make a serious decision to that end." (See The United States Strategic Bombing Survey, *Japan's Struggle to End the War*, Government Printing Office, July 1, 1946, pp. 21*f*.) The Emperor accepted this advice, and after the Okinawa landing, which presented a perfect opportunity, appointed a trusted Admiral and long-time courtier, Suzuki, as Prime Minister. Suzuki proceeded by imperceptible means to "reform" the army and navy, that is, to infiltrate them with trusted men. For all practical purposes, an invisible revolution was effected from above.

[53] Max Lerner, *Encyclopedia of Social Sciences*, "Assassination," New York, Macmillan, 1937.

In 1942, the German overlord of Czechoslovakia, Heydrich, was murdered by Czech patriots who had been parachuted into their country from England. This assassination led to the notorious massacre at Lidice and, temporarily at least, to heavy measures of repression against the Czech people. It has been suggested that the Czech government at London was perturbed about the relatively good relations of the Czechs with the occupying power; the Germans were doing their best to obtain the "collaboration" of the Czechs, and many Czechs were being taken in. Heydrich's assassination was to reverse this trend through the provocation of Nazi terror. If this was the intent behind the mission of the Czech patriots, the strategy was successful.

After the end of the Second World War, Jewish terrorists in Palestine conducted foreign policy in the manner of the Hashīshīn. They assassinated Lord Moyne, British Minister Resident in the Near East, in November, 1944; later they waged a ruthless campaign of terror and sabotage; and, in 1948, they murdered the United Nations mediator, Count Folke Bernadotte. Although this deed hurt their moral cause, it helped them to achieve their desired end, the independence of Israel.

In 1947, a mass murder of almost the entire government took place in Burma, an act which was probably designed to prevent the establishment of a *modus vivendi* with Britain.

COMMUNIST TECHNIQUES OF POLITICAL WARFARE

While most nations have employed political warfare when it seemed to them desirable and expedient, the communists have chosen this particular technique as their basic weapon system. Their purpose being the overthrow of governments, this end tends to become synonymous with the means. They were helped greatly in this strategy by the fact that from the very beginning they proclaimed themselves to be "internationalists." A Frenchman collaborating with Germany violates the tenets of his own nationalist convictions and offends the conscience of his countrymen. Yet a French communist collaborating with Soviet Russia can pretend that he remains loyal to his primary allegiance; his only *patrie* is the "fatherland of socialism." The fact that communist successes enhance the power of Russia as a country and diminish the power of France is considered no more relevant than the bad taste of a medicine needed to restore health. The communist dictionary explicitly defines an "internationalist" as anyone who would side with, and fight for, the Soviet Union even against his own country. In such a mental climate political warfare can attain its fullest bloom.

In addition to having the appropriate mentality, the communists also possess an organizational structure with which they can wage political warfare continuously and practically everywhere. This structure is the Communist Party organization. Schematically put, communists organize a party in each country where they are able to do so, regardless of whether this party carries the official communist label or not. Wherever they are unable to organize a Communist Party, they will set up a party which comes as close to the standardized Party pattern as the law and the political situation will permit. Only in few dictatorial, "one-party" countries have they proved unable to establish legal organizations.

These parties are supported by three elements: (1) outright communist subparties of specialized types such as youth,[54] women, veterans, and professional organizations, occasionally trade unions, and in democratic countries, parliamentary factions; (2) front organizations which are directed by professional communists and follow the Party line just on a few particular issues (e.g., a foreign-policy front advocating "understanding" of the Soviet Union) but comprise numerous noncommunist members, the purpose being to bring such noncommunists under communist influence and direction; (3) illegal "cells" in noncommunist organizations and agencies of all types, such as armed forces, government departments, noncommunist trade unions, educational institutions, newspapers, or any other social organization which the communists can penetrate.

National Communist Party structures and their suborganizations are directed, more or less rigidly, from area centers; for example, the communist parties of Western Europe, for a long time, were run from Berlin, while Paris was once responsible for the American Communist Party which, in turn, supervised the Chinese Communist Party. These area commands are under the centralized control of Moscow and, in the case of many parties on the Asiatic continent, probably of Peiping. This regional control system, however, undergoes many changes and often is nothing but camouflage for tight Moscow control.

This international structure originally took the organizational form of the Communist International,[55] which later was replaced by the Communist Information Bureau and the partisans of peace movement. In addition there are international organizations of artists, mutual-aid societies, committees dealing with special and temporary issues (e.g., a law case)—a whole cosmos of political stars, fixed stars, novae, dead stars, planets, satellites, meteors, and comets, all bathed in a steady stream of books, booklets, magazines, newspapers, speeches, and radio broadcasts. Parts of this literature are identical for the whole movement and are translated into numerous languages, with key organs being published in four to six key languages; parts are slanted so as to be suitable for local use only and are withheld from circulation in other countries.

Control is exerted by a triple chain of command consisting of a political line for political activities, a military line aiming at securing intelligence and

---

[54] See Gerd Friedrich, *Die Freie Deutsche Jugend, Stosstrupp des Kommunismus in Deutschland,* Cologne, Rote Weissbücher, 1950.

[55] On the beginnings of this novel device of foreign policy, see Branco Lazitch, *Lénine et la IIIe Internationale,* Neuchâtel, Baconnière, 1951.

setting up paramilitary forces, and a control line largely in the hands of the secret police, which also aims at obtaining intelligence but whose primary task is to maintain discipline within the world-wide structure.

The main functions of these organizations can be summarized as follows: (1) the overt and covert propagation of operational ideas which the communists want to put across, aiming in the last analysis at governmental or mass action; (2) the influencing of the minds and convictions of nations as a whole and of important subgroups; (3) the infiltration of reliable communists into the governmental and other public and semipublic agencies and the secret recruitment of government and other officials into the communist movement; (4) the organization of industrial strikes and other methods of economic warfare, including sabotage; (5) the acquisition of intelligence on all aspects of national life; (6) the weakening of the armed forces by agitation, espionage, and infiltration; (7) the capture of *de facto*, though camouflaged, control by hard-core, disciplined communists of agencies and organizations within the attacked nation; (8) the organization of unrest, individual and mass terror, local uprisings, and guerrilla operations; (9) the influencing of decisions of governments, partly through parliamentary activities, in the direction desired by the Russian and other communist governments; (10) if possible, the destruction of the established government and its replacement by a communist or cryptocommunist government.

While this elaborate organization has not always scored successes and while its purposes often were confused and self-defeating, it has given extensive scope to the application of political warfare methods. The Communist Party of France, for example, exploited its parliamentary strength to influence government decisions in the military and foreign policy fields. Its activities greatly and adversely affected French military strength. Before 1932, the German communist party, through its Moscow-dictated parliamentary maneuvers, contributed to the accession to power of the Nazis. During World War II the British and American communist parties and innumerable front organizations conducted an intensive campaign on behalf of the Soviet Union. They urged that unqualified support be given Russia and helped to make acceptable the program of lend-lease through which the Russians obtained 12 billion dollars' worth of weapons and other goods. The international political warfare apparatus of the Communist Party was of great aid to the Soviet Union in establishing its control over Eastern Europe. Its operations were a factor, though not the only one, in creating the pressures which induced the United States to demobilize prematurely in 1945–1946. It was the instrument through which the pacification of the world after the Second World War was prevented and the Cold War launched.[56]

[56] On many additional examples, see Franz Borkenau, *Der Europäische Kommunismus, seine Geschichte von 1917 bis zur Gegenwart,* Munich, Lehnen, 1952; Ruth Fischer, *Stalin and German Communism,* Cambridge, Mass., Harvard University Press, 1948; and Possony, *A Century of Conflict, Communist Techniques of World Revolution, 1848–1950,*

Unlike German exploits, very few communist operations of this type can as yet be analyzed through documentary evidence. Yet *one* such operation has come under close scrutiny by a United States Senate Committee: the influencing of the American Far Eastern policy after 1945 by a pro-Russian or procommunist "cell" within the Institute of Pacific Relations, a reputable research institution, largely financed by American industrialists, corporations, and educational foundations. In making its analysis, the committee made use of a collection of 20,000 documents and pieces of correspondence taken from the institute's file, as well as numerous witnesses.

According to the committee's findings, this cell within the Institute of Pacific Relations had come under the influence of the Far Eastern Division of the Communist International at Moscow. It succeeded in setting up "actively cooperative and confidential relationships with persons in government involved in the determination of foreign policy." It was able "to place in government posts both persons associated with the IPR and other persons selected by the effective leadership of IPR." This group of persons "disseminated and sought to popularize false information including information originating from soviet and communist sources." It "exerted a substantial influence on United States Far Eastern policy" and, between 1941 and 1945, succeeded in changing "the United States policy so as to accommodate communist ends and to set the stage for a major United States policy change, favorable to soviet interests," and "favorable to the Chinese communists." Finally, "during the period 1945 to 1949, persons associated with the Institute for Pacific Relations were instrumental in keeping United States policy on a course favorable to communist objectives in China." [57] This is a summary of the committee's unanimously adopted conclusions based on more than 5,000 pages of printed evidence.

The potentialities of communist political warfare techniques include *conquest without war*. This feat is possible if communist organizations succeed in fomenting successful uprisings or, more likely, in carrying infiltration to its logical end by participating in so-called "coalition governments." This is the simple device of gradual and imperceptible revolution. Given a suitable international or parliamentary constellation, communists enter into the Cabinet. With the support of the entire national and international communist apparatus and *ad hoc* fabricated issues and crises, they gradually enlarge their positions of influence and control. One by one, they take over additional Cabinet posts until ultimately they are able to establish control over the government as a whole. The device can be applied to propel semicommunists or pro-Russian or anti-anti-Soviet elements, such as neutralists, into power, with a resultant increase in Soviet international influence. Soviet purposes would be

---

Chicago, Regnery, 1953; also Charles A. Willoughby, *Shanghai Conspiracy: The Sorge Spy Ring,* New York, Dutton, 1952.

[57] *Institute of Pacific Relations,* Report of the Committee on the Judiciary, 82d Cong., 2d Sess., Government Printing Office, 1952, pp. 223–225.

served admirably if active anticommunists were kicked out of governments and were replaced by nothing more dangerous than passive noncommunists.

In summary, the influencing from abroad of political organizations and parties, the engineering of *coups d'état*, coalition governments, and revolutions as well as sabotage, terror, political assassinations, and paramilitary operations in the interest of foreign nations must be considered in the present historical period as commonplace means of an aggressive foreign policy.

The philosophy of ruthless violence is summarized by one of its most notorious adepts, V. I. Lenin, as follows: "War and revolution are two events which almost always occur in pairs. Either war causes revolution, or revolution culminates in war." Or, differently put, wars are a means of bringing about revolution, and revolutions are a means of winning wars or making them unnecessary. Since war is today not only extremely costly but also dangerous for the aggressor, and since revolutions may be more easily and cheaply organized, it would be a miracle indeed if we did not see other examples of foreign policy by revolution.

BIBLIOGRAPHY

Adams, Brooks: *The Theory of Social Revolutions,* New York, Macmillan, 1913.
Angell, Sir Norman: *The Public Mind: Its Disorders; Its Exploitation,* New York, Dutton, 1927.
Brinton, Crane C.: *The Anatomy of Revolution,* rev. ed., New York, Prentice-Hall, 1953.
Chorley, Katherine: *Armies and the Art of Revolution,* London, Faber, 1943.
Dulles, Allen W.: *Germany's Underground,* New York, Macmillan, 1947.
Elliott, Mabel A., and Francis E. Merrill: *Social Disorganization,* rev. ed., New York, Harper, 1941.
Faÿ, Bernard: *Revolution and Freemasonry 1680–1800,* Boston, Little, Brown, 1935.
Fischer, Ruth: *Stalin and German Communism,* Cambridge, Mass., Harvard University Press, 1948.
Hadamovsky, Eugen: *Propaganda und nationale Macht,* Oldenburg, Stalling, 1933.
The Institute of Pacific Relations, Hearings before the Committee on the Judiciary, Internal Security Subcommittee, U.S. Senate, 82d Cong., 1st and 2d Sess., 14 vols., Government Printing Office, 1951–1952.
The Institute of Pacific Relations, Report of the Committee on the Judiciary, 82d Cong., 2d Sess., Government Printing Office, 1952.
Kintner, William R.: *The Front Is Everywhere: Militant Communism in Action,* Norman, Okla., University of Oklahoma Press, 1950.
Langer, William L.: *Our Vichy Gamble,* New York, Knopf, 1947.
Le Bon, Gustave: *The Crowd: A Study of the Popular Mind,* New York, Macmillan, 1925.
Leites, Nathan: *The Operational Code of the Politbureau,* New York, McGraw-Hill, 1951.
Malaparte, Curzio: *Coup d'Etat: The Technique of Revolution,* New York, Dutton, 1932.
Micaud, Charles A.: *The French Right and Nazi Germany 1933–1939: A Study of Public Opinion,* Durham, N.C., Duke University Press, 1943.
Neumann, Sigmund: *Permanent Revolution,* New York, Harper, 1938.
Ortega y Gasset, José: *The Revolt of the Masses,* New York, Norton, 1942.
Peterson, A. C.: *Propaganda for War: The Campaign against American Neutrality, 1914–1917,* Norman, Okla., University of Oklahoma Press, 1939.
Pettee, George S.: *The Process of Revolution,* New York, Harper, 1938.
Rauschning, Hermann: *The Voice of Destruction,* New York, Putnam, 1940.
Rossi, A.: *Les communistes français pendant la drôle de guerre,* Paris, Iles d'Or, 1951.
Schumacher, Rupert V., and H. Hummel: *Vom Kriege zwischen den Kriegen: Die Politik des Völkerkampfes,* Stuttgart, Union Deutsche Verlagsgesselschaft, 1937.

Selznick, Philip: *The Organizational Weapon: A Study of Bolshevik Strategy and Tactics,* New York, McGraw-Hill, 1952.

Sorokin, Pitirim A.: *Social and Cultural Dynamics,* 4 vols., New York, American Book, 1937.

Tarde, G.: *L'Opinion et la foule,* Paris, Alcan, 1901.

West, Rebecca: *The Meaning of Treason,* New York, Viking, 1947.

Wright, Quincy (ed.): *Public Opinion and World Politics,* Chicago, University of Chicago Press, 1933.

Chapter 19

IDEAS, IDEOLOGIES, AND INTERNATIONAL POLITICS

Geography, economic resources, and social structures define the framework in which men make history. National relations are indeed conditioned by material factors. Yet these factors are of a plastic quality and can be shaped into the most diverse patterns. How men use the "external" factors, that is, how they accommodate themselves to each other on the globe, is largely dependent upon their mental processes. In so far as international politics is concerned, these mental processes fall into three major categories: ideals, ideas, and ideologies. The bond of reason unifies mankind; yet man does not always use his mind according to the dictates of reason. Human motivations and beliefs are not necessarily influenced by the verdict of logic and by factual proof or disproof. Hence the limits of the power of reason as moderator in conflicts between men and states.

IDEALS

Political ideals are images in our mind of the "good society." While ideals may not specify the details of society in a state of perfection, they may serve as the lodestars of political action; they give meaning and purpose to man's political activities.

Political ideals are developed as contrast images of reality. The unhappiness and frustrations here and now are transformed into their opposites, and political ideals have been born. While political ideals refer to each basic field of human activity, they are few in number. The politically most important ideals concern human rights, the structure of society, and material opulence. Spiritual ideals in the proper sense are politically neutral—one can be a mystic even·in chains—but religions, since they can be professed only within a suitable political framework, stand in significant relationship to political institutions. Moreover, religion and ethics supply the yardsticks by which politics is judged. They project an image of man which determines the image of the society he proposes to create.

Throughout the ages there has been a remarkable similarity between the political ideals of most people at most times and most places. By and large they all are contained in the descriptions of paradise vouchsafed by the various religions and utopian writings. The golden rule is common to all world religions; similarly all world religions recognize the brotherhood of mankind.[1] There is no government or political party which would take exception openly and unequivocally to the principles laid down in the preamble of the United Nations Charter. Some governments may consider these principles beyond man's reach or inexpedient, but none has ever believed them to be false. The ideals of all races and peoples are concerned with happiness of the individual and of the social group, and with peace and plenty. Not all peoples' ideals of personal freedom conform to Western terms, but all envisage a life unencumbered by restrictions and frustrations. It never has been claimed by any large group of people that unhappiness, misery, slavery, or perpetual war are "ideals." In fact, it is difficult to find even individual exponents of such an inverted "idealism." Misery can be explained as a necessary evil, or as a state through which man can attain true happiness inasmuch as he must free himself from all earthly desires so that he may earn his rewards in the hereafter. Yet misery never was proclaimed as a goal to be striven for on its own merit. In the same sense war may have been described as divinely ordained but only because it would contribute to man's ultimate salvation. There never has been a body of beliefs or ideals which, in one way or another, does not deal with the salvation and happiness of man.

Despite the great similarity between ideals, very important differences exist. These bear on the following major points:

1. *The exact meaning of ideals.* Is it proposed to secure the happiness of the individual or of a social group, and if the latter, which social group? Or is happiness to be conceived of as being of a spiritual, cultural, or predominantly material nature? If the latter, does material happiness reside in wealth, or social security, or leisure?

2. *The limitation of ideals.* Must peace be preserved unequivocally, everywhere and always, and regardless of the issue, or are there issues which justify war? Is freedom absolutely irreconcilable with controls and obstructions, or should freedom so be limited that, in Fichte's words, "the other man beside you also may be free"? [2]

3. *The inclusion or exclusion of certain human purposes among ideals.* For example, is the ending of sex frustration a general ideal, or is it an evil which should be resisted?

4. *What is the hierarchy of various ideals?* Is it more important to achieve full individual freedom than material opulence, or more important to achieve peace before freedom, or is it preferable to secure religious salvation rather than peace?

5. *Which ideals can be realized (or approximated) by political action and which must remain the concern of private activity?* For example, should production and distribution of goods be left largely to individual action or be

---

[1] For a concise comparison of these ideals, see Norman Cousins, *Who Speaks for Man?* New York, Macmillan, 1953, pp. 232–241.

[2] Johann Gottlieb Fichte, *Sämtliche Werke,* Berlin, Veit, 1845, Vol. III, p. 15.

regulated by political action? Should the educational ideal be striven for by political or individual action or by a mixture of both?

Societies always profess a specific set of ideals; they have their own answers to these questions. These answers define the common purpose without which society would fall to pieces.

In a broad sense, societies may be divided into those professing norms which are spiritual-religious (only the soul and the hereafter count), idealistic (perfecting man on earth), and sensate-materialistic (satisfaction of desires, wealth). Some societies evolve historically from one set to another set of ideals, usually moving from the idealistic to the sensate principle.[3]

The profession of ideals often is an aggressive act. Hence these differences in ideals frequently are basic to the conflicts between societies. Historically, the most important cleavage in the field of ideals has been the fight between those societies which proclaim the individual's right to happiness and those which subordinate the individual to the state: the pursuit of happiness as distinguished from the quest for power.

It often has been said that ideals are not subject to proof or disproof. Hence conflicts about ideals are presumed to be irreconcilable as well as inevitable. In the past, this certainly has been true, and it probably will remain true that preferences of individuals or societies as, for example, that for economic plenty as against spiritual peace, will remain a matter of choice. However, many conflicts over ideals were due to misunderstandings of an intellectual and semantic kind; faulty logical reasoning; an inadequate elucidation of the meaning; insufficient testing of the implicit assumptions underlying ideals; contradictions of ideals professed simultaneously; and misconceptions as to the practicality of beliefs. The most potent of the sources of conflict was the inclination to invest given formulations of ideals (which should have been considered as perfectionable rather than as perfected) with absolute validity.

There is no question but that the application of the scientific method could modify disputes about ideals. Most choices of ideals are made on the basis of emotion and tradition. As soon as the ideals are analyzed logically and their true and full meaning is revealed, a nation will contemplate tolerantly other nations' convictions. The need of an ultimate purpose remains, but this purpose no longer necessarily includes the rejection of competitive purposes. Bathed in the light of reason, most purposes suddenly acquire a strange similarity. In other words, disputes about human ideals are a reflection of human immaturity, almost to the same extent as would be "disputes" over arithmetic.

Far more basic, and hence probably more permanent than the quixotic tilting about ideals, is the conflict between political "idealists" and "realists." Idealists are those who believe in some set of ideals and who aim, through

[3] For a similar classification, see Pitirim A. Sorokin, *Society, Culture and Personality, Their Structure and Dynamics,* New York, Harper, 1947, pp. 620*f.*

their political acts, at bringing society closer to the state of perfection. Realists are those who feel that each political act should aim at a concrete objective defined by the over-all or momentary requirements of the state or of the groups which they represent. Politics is conceived just like any practical or technical job. Its success is to be measured in power increments and other practical achievements but not in terms of a "state of perfection." It is pointless to chase after elusive ideals. Talk about freedom and similar subjective, hence undefinable, values is mere verbiage; the task is to improve the road system or promote trade in peanuts.

The idealist often is inclined to "move in the clouds." He pays inadequate attention to reality and is likely to oppose practical steps which fall short of his ideals. Being of the declamatory kind, he may be less interested in avoiding tomorrow's war than in building a world society of *eternal* peace. By contrast, the realist stands in danger of ignoring the ultimate purposes of human action and often behaves like a man who is running very fast but has no idea of where he is going or why he is making the effort.

Among the realists, there must be counted a large group of "political businessmen" who consider politics as a business or as an enterprise of social status insurance. They are in the profession to make a living or to represent their interests, and they care nothing about the perfection of society or even its gradual improvements. To them political ideals are meaningless mouthings, although they may make use of them to make their actions palatable.

The Practicality of Idealism. Politics as a profession has dominated history in most of its phases. This probably was inevitable in periods when there was a great scarcity of goods and skills and a minimum of political consciousness. As soon as life became more abundant, men began to ask themselves how society should be organized in order to bring it closer, if not to perfection, then at least to a reasonable mean. Unfortunately, disputes over organization quickly assumed a metaphysical and irrational character. The awakening of political consciousness was not yet paced by the awakening to rationality. This is one of the fundamental reasons of contemporary world crisis.

Politics should be a mixture of administration and development; administration of existing societies and their development toward a perfect state. The imperfections of the political world are such that transformations and changes take place continuously. These changes can be exploited for the purpose of improvement, provided the goals are well understood. A policy which aims at unattainable goals is wrongly described as "idealistic"; it has no greater practical value than the antics of Don Quixote. It is by no means superior to a cynical *Realpolitik* which limits itself to administration, at best aims at reaching short-range objectives, and which scorns attempts at more basic improvements of the institutional framework.

True idealism is not to pursue unattainable goals or to proclaim "maximalist" programs, but to make the best out of a given situation. A truly idealistic policy is one which steadily aims at improvements and adjusts its plans and actions to reality. Such a policy can be labeled *Realpolitik* of idealism, in contrast to a *Realpolitik* of the power urge.

IDEAS

A political idea is a concept of social organization. Such an idea may embrace plans of action aiming at the establishment of the desired organization. It then traces a diagram of political behavior and describes the institutions to be set up or the modifications to be applied to existing institutions in order to implement a given set of ideals. For example, democracy is conceived of as the institution by which the ideals of "good society" based on individual freedom can be approximated.

Most of the political ideas of significance are described by words ending in "ism" such as socialism, pacifism, republicanism, nationalism, racism, and those ending in "cracy" such as autocracy and democracy. There are, however, plain verbal descriptions such as "free trade" and "federation." Much misunderstanding as to the validity of political ideas arises from the fact that they are not conceived of as organizational schemes and that their *functional character* is not clearly seen. For example, a lengthy discussion about the validity of Pan-Germanism or Pan-Slavism resolves nothing if it does not clarify what ideal state of society a Pan-Germanic or Pan-Slavic organization is supposed to secure. Nor is the organizational practicality of such concepts ever tested with care; how does one go about organizing Pan-German, Pan-Slavic or any other kind of panracist institutions? It is not surprising that discussions about "isms" tend to be meaningless.

If the battle over political ideas or organizational concepts does not produce much light, it certainly generates much heat; there are misunderstandings as to the exact meaning of terms. For example, a democracy proposes to organize society by the separation of powers and by decentralization of authority. It envisages periodic changes of government through elections and continual supervision of the government's action through parliamentary control. Government must govern by laws and adhere to firmly established patterns. But does democracy prevail when the percentage of voters is very small in relation to all those entitled to vote, or when the government operates through emergency legislation? How do democratic organizational principles apply to the interrelationships between a democratic and a dictatorial state? Can a democratic government temporarily abridge diverse rights, such as freedom of opinion and habeas corpus, in order to meet a serious foreign threat? How temporary is temporary?

No institution is impervious to historic development. For example, Britain for a long time has been described as a democracy (although it also is a constitutional monarchy). Yet between 1900 and 1950 the *composition* of the electorate has changed considerably; moreover it grew in *size* from about 3 million to almost 29 million actual voters. "If the population had not changed, it would still be true to say that of every four voters to whom the politicians must now appeal, only one would have been entitled to vote in 1900." [4] Obviously, this must mean a change in the composition and size of government. Democracy is dependent upon the educational level of the population. In 1900, British children were leaving school at twelve years of age; in 1950 they left school at fifteen. Total expenditure per pupil rose from less than 3 pounds to 51 pounds. If such comparisons were made internationally, it would appear readily that there are basic differences among British, French, and American democracy and among the various concepts underlying the respective political institutions.

Thirdly, conflict arises from the fact that various nations are agreed on one concept yet at odds on others. For example, both liberalism and socialism fundamentally aim at the same objective, the increase of economic well-being. Yet in order to achieve this same objective, one proposes to organize society in a manner vastly different from that propounded by the other. Theoretically, it should be possible to evaluate the merits of each organizational scheme on the basis of logic and experience. It should be easy to determine, in broad outline, the costs of each organizational solution in direct expenditures and sacrifices as well as in the loss of competing values. Yet protagonists of an organizational idea must have a certain amount of faith in their proposal. This faith is not susceptible to proof or disproof, if only because the validity of the solution depends in part on the skill with which it would be applied.

Finally, differences emerge because situations vary. An economic system which is based on individual initiative does not function properly in a society of religious fatalists, just as a system of checks and balances does not work in a highly stratified society which is run by a closed caste. On the other hand, organizational solutions which were successful in one society rarely are entirely inapplicable to other societies. It *is* possible to learn from other nations' experiences.

This battle of ideas increasingly disturbs the circles of international politics. It is fought over the question of how the international community and all its subcommunities are to be organized. Medieval society was rent by the cleavage between temporal and spiritual powers. The idea of universal monarchy retained its luster throughout the entire epoch, yet relations between states were regulated on the basis of feudal, legal, and personal relationships, and the universal monarchy succumbed to the endless power struggles of the feudal lords. Following the American and French revolutions the world has been organized in nation-states. Empires were reared on the basis of linguistic and cultural affinities (for example, the German Reich) or on the domination of allegedly superior over inferior races (colonialism). Structures which did not conform to these ideas, such as Austria-Hungary, were swept

4 *The Economist,* Coronation Number, May 30, 1953.

away. As erstwhile colonial empires such as the British and the French grew into multinational organizations, they tended to break apart; they did not conform to the "accepted" or "modern" pattern of ideas.

At any given time, peoples and states can be divided into those who are anxious to improve the existing organizations and those who are content to operate within the existing international and national framework. Among those who are interested in improving the organizational structure, there are again two major categories: revolutionists and evolutionists. The former propose to change existing organizations radically and speedily and to experiment with new organizational ideas. The latter, while proposing to improve the framework, are aware that change and reorganization, especially if they are to be accomplished quickly, may engender conflict and violence. If transformations are brusque and basic and the ensuing conflict cannot be contained within the framework of traditional society, the new organizational scheme will be warped by the fierce passions of the struggle and can no longer be tested properly. Changes in the basic situation will make the original scheme inapplicable.[5] By contrast, if transformations are carried out gradually, spread over many years, and restricted only to those parts of the social structure that really need change, the reorganization may serve its purpose. Similarly, while some movements aim at positive and over-all changes, including the establishment of new institutions, others are content to eliminate those features of the existing institutions which have become useless or odious. The pruning of the tree of society may be a greater service to mankind than the seeding of new trees or the felling of live, though old, ones.[6] Yet gradual change may not be fast enough to respond to the urgency of a given problem. In that case a process of transformation is set in motion in which the validity of an idea becomes far less significant than its usefulness as a political weapon.

IDEOLOGIES

Political formulas are indispensable props of organized society. A state professes a certain set of ideals and proposes to live up to these ideals through a certain organizational scheme. This political formula demands faith and allegiance. If the state is to be a going concern, the formula cannot be questioned continuously. Some of its aspects thus may be placed beyond

[5] A situation *a* requires a solution *L*. As *L* is being applied, *a* changes into *b*. *L* undergoes modification, and becomes *L'*; as such it is successful. Hence *b* is paired with *L'*, while *a* should have been paired with *L*, or *b* with *M*. Often a solution *L* which was developed as a result of experience with situation *a* is applied many years later to a situation *d*. A British commitment such as that made in 1939 to Poland might have stopped, if applied in 1914, the First World War; a NATO pact concluded in 1939 might have stopped the Second World War—and so forth and so on ad infinitum.

[6] On this fundamental idea, which has escaped the attention of modern reformers, see Wilhelm von Humboldt, *Ideen zu einem Versuch, die Grenzen der Wirksamkeit des Staates zu bestimmen* (originally 1792), Berlin, Deutsche Bibliothek, no date.

criticism. Yet as soon as the *entire* formula, or more particularly, a given interpretation, is no longer subject to continuous appraisal, reinterpretation and modification, the gap between formula and reality must widen, for the nature of reality is change. The state no longer functions effectively. A workable political formula must be a living and a growing thing. If it dries up and hardens into a mere ceremonial rite of the mind, it transforms itself into an "ideology."

Ideals and ideas degenerate into ideologies either because they have been reduced to clichés or because they have been extended to fields where they have no applicability. For example, the socialist formula of "public ownership" may or may not be apposite at certain times and places, and in relation to certain types of property. For anyone but an ideological socialist it stands to reason that this cannot be a desirable solution at all times, at all places, and for all types of ownership. Moreover, if the socialist scheme for the organization of the economy is applied, for example, to artistic creativity, it obviously transgresses the bounds of its applicability. Whenever organizational ideas are treated as *fundamental* concepts instead of as practical procedures which may or may not work, which are subject to limitations and degradation, and which entail costs as well as gains, we are confronted by ideologies. Wherever we find a cure-all solution, we have found an ideology.

Many a political idea contains tenuous ideological elements, though in other respects it can be argued on firm logical grounds. For example, it may or may not be desirable, as the Nazis asserted, that Germany should have reorganized Europe on the *Führer* principle. This is an organizational idea which can be analyzed in the same manner as, let us say, a proposed reorganization of the General Motors Corporation. But this concept was justified by a theory of race which was scientifically buncombe and equivocated on the terms "race" and "nation." Similarly, it may or may not be true that the establishment of a Pan-Slavic empire would yield great material and cultural benefits to Europe and the world. But it is untrue that all Slavs are "blood brothers," belong to one and the same "family," and commune in one and the same culture. All that can be claimed is that Slavs speak languages which have more or less the same word roots and a similar syntax.[7]

At any given time a society suffers from greater or smaller imperfections which are disturbing to its members and which, under stress, endanger cohesion. For example, a society may aspire to economic well-being, yet it may not have rescued some of its members from abject poverty. Or a society may proclaim its devotion to equal rights, yet it may not have abolished the grosser forms of discrimination. In such circumstances, society develops

[7] The opposite of non-sense is not necessarily sense. In 1849, Marx and Engels, criticizing Pan-Slavism, wrote: "Except for the Poles, the Russians and, at best, the Slavs in Turkey, no Slavic people has a future, for the simple reason that all the other Slavs lack the most basic . . . prerequisites for independence and vitality." Karl Marx and Friedrich Engels, *The Russian Menace to Europe,* ed. by Paul W. Blackstock and Bert F. Hoselitz, Glencoe, Ill., Free Press, 1952, p. 72.

interpretations which explain away these imperfections, minimizing their importance or promising their early disappearance. As de Sade said: "When the strong wished to enslave the weak he persuaded him that a god had sanctified the chains with which he loaded him, and the latter, stupefied by misery, believed all he was told." [8]

The political thinking of all states, parties, and societies always contains ideological elements. As long and in so far as ideologies exist, they are believed in with firm convictions, with the result that if ideologies meet, competition or conflict must ensue. Like all thought, however, ideologies have a history. They are, at first, developed by a few individual thinkers and do not find ready acceptance. Once accepted they are held strongly, usually during the lives of one or two generations. After a lapse of time, their hold over the mind diminishes. Ultimately, they are replaced by a new ideology. Ideological conflict is most violent when the competing ideologies still are in their prime. By contrast, when ideologies have weakened, their clash may be attended by consequences no more serious than an academic debate and a tacit agreement to "coexist." Clashes between a "young" and an "old" ideology may lead to historical catastrophe or the death of the aging creed.

As the ruling ideologies of a given society or geographic region follow each other in time, certain basic beliefs tend to become fixed. For example, a straight line of descent links medieval attitudes toward money lending at interest to the modern criticism of "capitalism," the Calvinistic doctrine of predestination to economic determinism and doctrines of race superiority. As each society undergoes its historical development, it tends to reinforce certain dominant types of behavior, and in turn, behavior is reflected in its ideology. For example, predominantly agricultural societies tend to be conservative and autocratic, while societies engaging in trade and industry incline toward democratic institutions. The more crushing has been in the past the weight of poverty upon a society and the greater the fascination of other-worldly creeds, the more it leans in modern times toward dogmatic and radical ideologies. Societies which found it difficult to structurize themselves often establish institutions to the rigid specifications of ideological models to which they conform with determination, while societies which have shown a great adaptability to changing conditions are more suspicious of intellectual blueprints. The ideology a nation adopts is not an accident but is rooted deeply in that nation's history and the "character" of its people. No nation, however, adopts just one ideology at the exclusion of all others; within each nation, several ideologies are in vicious conflict, fought out openly or in the hidden recesses of the mind.

[8] See Geoffrey Gorer, *The Devil's Disciple,* Paris, Le Ballet des Muses, 1933, p. 137. "When we wish to impose on others we must accustom them little by little to see in us what really doesn't exist; otherwise they will see us as we are and we will infallibly lose." *Ibid.,* p. 134.

It is apparent that mental processes as they refer to politics should not be lumped together under the term "ideology." Ideals, ideas, political formulas, and ideologies are not one and the same thing. Ideology is basically faulty or mechanical thinking. Its logical or factual absurdity does not, however, render it politically or emotionally ineffective. On the contrary, ideologies are among the prime movers of history. People have been much more ready to fight and die for "absolutes" than for ideals and ideas staking less comprehensive claims. In fact, it often is necessary to transform a proper political idea into an ideology in order to trigger action; even a reasonable goal may have to be garlanded with "myth" if the idea is not to remain just an idea on a piece of paper.[9]

While ideologies engage men's minds at all times and places, they are variables and not constants. They themselves undergo changes, and they may change with changing political institutions and personnel. New governments, if they are not merely the products of routine changes in administration, usually modify the prevailing political formula to some extent. By the same token, if the political formula or the ruling ideology no longer carries conviction, the life expectancy of the government in power is short.

A distinction must be made between ideologies which are of short and of long duration. The Nazi ideology, at least in its Hitlerian version, was of exceedingly short duration, while the communist ideology has been relatively long-lived. A defunct political formula may survive as an ideology for a considerable period but ultimately go under, while an ideology by ridding itself of its volatile and unstable components may condense into a workable and viable political formula. The first case, for example, is that of the feudal monarchies of 19th-century Europe, which clung to the mystical concept of ruler "by the grace of God" and were duly swept to their doom. The opposite process transformed in Britain the highly ideological type of monarchy into a representative monarchy and the highly successful political formula of the British Commonwealth. International politics are influenced strongly by this crazy-quilt pattern of rising, changing, fighting, and dying ideologies.

Changes in the Political Formula. The development from a decentralized feudal regime to the absolute monarchy of the 18th century was paralleled by the growth of trade and transportation which called for a more uniform administration of large territories. However, absolute monarchy left intact many of the feudal privileges and arrangements, with the result that the *ancien régime* was a hotchpotch of administrative systems and overlapping authority. This confusion begot many social injustices. The French nation accepted this situation until its foremost intellectuals convinced them that it was unreasonable,[10] until Adam Smith proved that the existing organiza-

---

[9] See Georges Sorel, *Réflexions sur la violence,* 10th ed., Paris, Rivière, 1944, pp. 32–36.
[10] See Louis Madelin, *La Révolution,* Paris, Hachette, 1920, p. 9.

tion hampered economic progress, and until the American Revolution demonstrated that intolerable conditions could be changed successfully. Once the new political formula was found, it spread all over Europe. The result was that many states and feudal principalities disappeared and that a new state system emerged. In part, the new ideological and organizational formulas of the French Revolution were elaborated by an international political organization, the Freemasons. Its appeal transcended historic loyalties, and it was used widely as a tool of political warfare.

The new political formula guided statesmen in the attempt to redefine the boundaries of modern states. The concepts of the linear and natural frontier replaced the practice of multiple frontiers and interlacing boundary areas. Before the end of the 18th century multiple frontiers were the rule rather than the exception. The feudal system conceived of political frontiers as having the same nature as the boundaries of the noble estates. The Duke of Lorraine, a subject of the King of France, married an Austrian princess and was elected Emperor of the Holy Roman Empire. As proprietor of his estate, situated in the territory under the sovereignty of the King of France, he remained a French subject, while a number of French nobles owed him allegiance. Yet as emperor, he outranked the King. Two nobles with adjoining possessions often worked out special economic and military arrangements which were at variance with the over-all policies of their respective overlords. Political frontiers did not coincide with economic and administrative frontiers. These anachronisms of boundaries within boundaries and states within states were swept away by the French Revolution.

Napoleon revolutionized the ideology of boundary making. At the Peace of Campoformio with Austria in 1797—the peace which marked the end of Venice as an independent state—he introduced the linear boundary. In his later treaties he eliminated numerous small states and created the nuclei of national states, the Kingdom of Lombardy (Italy), the Duchy of Warsaw in 1807 (Poland), and the Illyrian Provinces in 1809 (Yugoslavia). Linear frontiers replaced multiple frontiers. Since then exclaves such as demilitarized zones have been rare exceptions from the universal rule.

Napoleon's reforms seemed reasonable at the time, so much so that his principles were adopted by other states. Tsar Alexander, for example, instructed, in 1804, his special envoy to London, Count Vorontsov, to include in a project for the creation of an international organization the principle of "proper frontiers." What are proper frontiers?

It would be necessary to follow those which nature itself indicated, such as mountain chains, seas, or on the other hand give the states those outlets which they need for the export of their agricultural and industrial products. At the same time, each state should be composed of homogeneous peoples, who can get along among themselves and live harmoniously with the government which rules them.[11]

[11] See Jacques Ancel, *Géographie des frontières*, Paris, Gallimard, 1938, *passim*.

The idea of the "natural frontier" had been suggested first by Rousseau. It became a political reality in 1793 when Danton proclaimed that France's natural frontiers were the Ocean, the Rhine, the Alps, and the Pyrenees, and that, although the constitution of 1791 had renounced war as an instrument of conquest, the French frontier should be carried forward to those lines. Since that time, the ideology of the "natural frontier" has exerted a powerful influence.

The location of a "natural frontier" can be traced easily in countries like Italy or Britain. But in other regions, areas which are defined vaguely by nature may be inhabited by peoples of different languages, cultures, and social and political structures. "Hereditary enemies" may live together in a "natural" habitat. It is obvious, therefore, that the applicability of this organizational scheme is limited. Yet this fact notwithstanding, it served, and still serves, as a justification of conquest.

Nationalism has been perhaps the most important idea that has gone into the making of the political formula of modern states. Its philosophy was expounded with particular vigor by 19th-century Italians, especially by Mancini and Mazzini. It can be summarized as follows: A group of people speaking the same language and living together in contiguous areas form a nation. Nations should not be subjected to the overlordship of other nations (as many of them were during the early 19th century in eastern Europe and many of them still are, to this date, in Asia and Africa). Their consciousness of unity should be aroused, and their individuality should be expressed freely and within the proper political setting. One nation should not be partitioned politically among several states but should be unified under one government of its own stock or, if it is too small or too dispersed, enjoy complete cultural and linguistic autonomy within a "foreign" state. Each national state should acquire its natural boundaries. All states should be constituted as national states. Legally, all nations are equals.

The first result of the ascendancy over men's minds of this new political formula was the dissolution of supranational states such as the Ottoman Empire. The second result was the creation of small nation-states. Either they rose from the ruins of empires (Czechoslovakia), or they broke away from large states (Estonia and Latvia), or large states split into national component parts (Holland-Belgium, Sweden-Norway, India-Pakistan). Furthermore, nationalities which lived dispersed all over the earth started to organize so-called "pan" movements ranging all the way from Pan-Germanism to Zionism and Pan-Africanism, with a Pan-Chinese and a Pan-Hindu movement still to come.

States created after 1919 which did not conform to the national formula—Czechoslovakia, Poland with its corridor, the free state of Danzig, and the quasi condominium of the Saar—were short-lived. In Asia, where the formula is still new, decomposition has barely begun. But as the formula grows in popularity, many states such as Burma, Afghanistan, India, Indo-China,

Indonesia and even China may suffer the fate of the Ottoman Empire and Austria-Hungary. The cohesion of the Soviet Union, too, is assailed by the forces of nationalistic disintegration.

The decline of colonialism is another consequence of the change in ruling ideas as well as ethical norms. During the 18th and 19th centuries it was taken for granted that the purpose of colonization was to confer advantages upon the colonizer. During the 20th century, the concept took root that colonization should primarily, if not exclusively, confer advantages upon the dependent peoples. The "right" of a colonizing power to have and to hold a colony must now be justified by how much it invests in the colony. If it does not do "enough," it must depart and free the dependent people. This new mentality—which is the penalty the colonizers must pay for their own ludicrous propaganda in praise of the "white man's burden"—has changed the entire relationship between white and colored peoples. It will cause infinite trouble until it is replaced by the realization that the interests of the colonizer and the colonial people are interdependent.

Ideologies as Drives. Charles Merriam has made the important distinction between *credenda* and *miranda*. *Credenda* are ideas or political formulas to be believed, while *miranda* are ideas to be admired. The *miranda* ideas or myths are those which drive nations to actions and sublime sacrifices. The Napoleonic soldier, for example, was content to live as a pauper and was willing to sacrifice his life for the glory of France and the heroic epos of Napoleon's conquests. The fanatics and heroes of all times, the Roman legionnaires, the Christian martyrs, the crusaders, the warriors of Mohammed, the explorers and the political reformers, the enthusiastic Nazis as well as the Japanese followers of Shinto and the hard-core communists, in brief, the builders of churches, states, and empires, always have been driven by a powerful urge to lay down their lives for their creed and to make it triumph over all other creeds. They are ravaged by the "fire," as the Biblical term goes. They may even sacrifice themselves in an empty gesture of defiance. But their zeal, according to the French historian Ernest Renan, is the virtue which history rewards. Josef Goebbels put it more crudely when he said that people die willingly only for ambiguous ideals.

Perhaps Napoleon's soldier was not motivated by the psychology imputed to him by romantic and highly literate historians. Perhaps his high morale was due simply to the excellence of Napoleon's military leadership or of the commissary which tended to the bodily needs of the *Grande Armée,* similarly as Genghis Khan's troops appear to have been innocent of any ideological motivation. Yet there is little doubt that persons who firmly believe in a political faith are strongly motivated.[12] Hence they are capable of shouldering

[12] During May, 1942, Hitler remarked that a Soviet division on Kerch peninsula was fighting bravely until death. Clearly, he added, this was an ideologically motivated force, a *Weltanschauungsdivision.* And he consoled himself with the reflection that, fortunately, there were not too many of these divisions: Stalin had been unsuccessful in inculcating

the burdens of protracted conflict much better than those who lack any motivation but personal interest. People who care only for their physical survival make poor soldiers—and poor reformers. The French soldier marched under the banners of a country which in 1790 had hung up a poster at the bridge of Kehl bearing the inscription *"Ici commence le pays de la liberté,"* and which on July 22, 1807, imposed a constitution on the Duchy of Warsaw, Article 4 of which read: "Slavery is abolished. All citizens are equal before the law." He proved more than a match for troops who had been indoctrinated with the idea that they should fear their commanding officers more than their enemy.

But ideas that move nations cannot always be contrived at will and by teams of clever experts in public relations, morale building, social psychology, and propaganda. The time must be right for a motivating idea. During the 19th century Pan-Slavic writers sought to fire the Russian soldier with the idea that the Orthodox church with its concept of *sorbornost*—"togetherness," or the close community of all church members united in mutual love—was far superior to Catholicism, which allegedly sacrificed liberty for unity, and to Protestantism, which presumably sacrificed unity for liberty. They claimed that Russia would bring to the world brotherly love which had been crushed by Western civilization, and that Russia was destined to become the center of Christianity, ruling through moral consciousness rather than coercion. One Pan-Slavic Russian poet declared: "One cannot understand Russia by reason and measure her by a common yardstick, she has a peculiar nature, one must simply believe in Russia." [13]

At the turn of this century, French conservative writers of the *Action Française* sought to inculcate a similar spirit in the French. The skeptical French did not respond to the entreaties of neoroyalist and authoritarian intellectuals. But similar concepts found acceptance in Nazi Germany and later, dressed up in more crudely spun nationalistic garments, in Soviet Russia—at least if one judges this acceptance by strictly external evidence.

The ideology of expansion feeds upon the very scope of the expansionist design; the vaster the latter, the more powerful the drive. The great empire builders, from Alexander the Great onward, fired the imagination of their soldiers and people, even when there was no rhyme or reason for expansion. There may be excellent reasons for the expansion of territory, as when Italy, after its unification, seized Rome, its "natural" capital. It is understandable when a country wishes to reconquer a province inhabited by its own nationals and which has been lost to the expansionism of a more successful neighbor; or when nations want to control territory which is vitally important to their economic existence. But there is also a spirit of expansion for expansion's

---

the entire Red Army with the communist creed. See Henry Picker (ed.), *Hitlers Tischgespräche im Führerhauptquartier 1941–1942*, Bonn, Athenaeum, 1951, p. 156.

[13] See the brilliant study by Hans Kohn, *Pan-Slavism, Its History and Ideology,* Notre Dame, University of Notre Dame Press, 1953, pp. 212, 128, 156.

sake, dramatically expressed in a poem entitled "Russian Geography" by Fedor Ivanovich Tyuchev: [14]

Moscow, Peter's city and Constantine's city—these are the sacred capitals of the Russian empire. But where are its limits? where its boundaries? . . . The future is destined to discover it. Seven inland seas and seven great rivers . . . from the Nile to the Neva, from the Elbe to China, from the Volga to the Euphrates, from the Ganges to the Danube, behold the Russian realm, and never will it end, as the Spirit foresaw and Daniel foretold.

In the 20th century, mystical expansionism no longer commands a following. Instead nations claim the right to *Lebensraum*—living space—without stopping to think that the space which they conquer for themselves must be denied to other nations, and that no nation can conquer enough space to satisfy all its economic needs, let alone conquer it without greatly overextending its strength. Other nations believe that they must expand their political system to other areas and thus insure security from other societies; they seek to make the world "safe" for democracy or communism or planning or whatever the formula may be and do not take into account that in this fashion they greatly increase international tensions and force other nations into a war which the whole operation was designed to avoid in the first place.

Modern nations are swayed by metaphysical notions such as the "inevitability" of cultural decay or of the ultimate "victory" of a race, a nation, a group of nations, or a social system. They accept readily "historic missions" and are inclined to assume that there are chosen nations or chosen classes which must carry the burden of civilization and progress.

There are ideologies of reform, such as the belief that nations must be united, perhaps even forcefully, into larger, more efficient units, to enhance trade or to prevent war. Eschewing violence as contrary to divine ordinance or simply man's higher nature, pacifism and diverse nonresistance ideologies assert that the aggressor should not be met by force, even if he should extend his writ over entire continents. (To make their case more plausible, pacifists —like other ideologists—often resort to the simple device of tampering with the evidence, trying to prove, for example, that the prospective aggressor really is a peace-loving and endearing fellow.)

The danger of these ideologies, which scientifically and objectively are plainly nonsense, is the obfuscation of real political problems. Moreover, such ideologies lead to meaningless conflicts and unnecessary wars. Ideological crusades may end in unlimited struggles. Here a great paradox arises: ideologies motivate people to undertake vast projects and overcome heavy obstacles, yet they lead the mind into error. *Hence the historical experience that the ideological crusader wins initially and succumbs in the end—unless he sheds his ideology and recovers his objectivity.* Even as a motivating force, ideology ultimately loses its power. The virtues of the Napoleonic soldiers were great

[14] *Ibid.,* p. 127.

and many. It should not be forgotten, however, that by 1813 desertion had become so widespread that Napoleon no longer was able to recruit strong armies and that, as he did not desist from continuing the war, his remaining troops gradually melted away.

Sample Ideologies. In 1815 Britain adopted the Corn Laws, which in essence prohibited the importation of cheap bread cereals. The purpose was to secure high prices for British agricultural products and thus to increase home production. Since British population rose very rapidly and since harvests had failed, the result was that the urban population became economically depressed. The abolition of the Corn Laws was fought on the grounds that it would entail famine and the ruin of British agriculture. This argument was advanced, in part, under the cover of patriotism, for did not the international-ist idea of free trade fly in the face of the most sacred national traditions? The argument was most certainly based on faulty economics. It was disproved by actual events when the abolition of the Corn Laws put British agriculture on a sound basis and led to a general upsurge of British commerce and productivity. This example does not prove, incidentally, that under different conditions the abolition of the Corn Laws would have proved as beneficial, or that the unequivocal stimulation of free trade, for example, between Western Europe and the Soviet bloc, inevitably must serve useful economic (or political) purposes.

Throughout most of his rule, Bismarck was opposed to the establishment of German colonies. Colonies, he held, served above all as magnets to emigration; he opposed losing Germans to overseas areas. He was willing to support the establishment of commercial colonial enterprises and trade posts, provided difficulties with Britain could be avoided. Finally he agreed that private entrepreneurs could engage in colonial ventures at their own risk. His successor, Georg Caprivi, stated that he could think of nothing worse than that the whole of Africa would be given to him as a present. However, the next *Reichskanzler,* Prince Chlodwig zu Hohenlohe-Schillingsfürst, in his first speech before the *Reichstag* on December 11, 1894, committed Germany to an aggressive colonial policy. To justify the change, he adduced various reasons. The economic reasons were that colonial trade, though it was still very small, was somewhat increasing, and that perhaps in the future, after heavy investments, German emigrants might prosper in the colonies. He added that colonial policy must be the result of a strengthened national consciousness. The *Reich* must find a new field of activity in order to satisfy its strong national urges. "The colonial movement . . . is a valuable reinforcement of the spirit of unity. No government can or wants to reject this new and strong tie which will bind together the various parts of the nation and the various classes of the people." And then, of course, there were religious reasons and idealistic motivations: it would be to the detriment of German honor if Germany were not to participate in that praiseworthy "cultural mission" which was the abolition of slavery [15]—in 1894! In other words, there was no good reason why Germany should become a colonial power, except the desire to assuage the aspirations of nationalist ideology.

The basic assumption underlying the economic policies of *laissez faire, laissez passer* is that individuals will act according to their self-interest and that the sum total of the satisfaction of individual self-interests will produce the greatest common good. It was alleged, for example, by Bastiat and Carey that, in the last analysis, there is a preestablished "harmony" between individual interests, however competitive they may appear to be. It is clear that such a hypothesis cannot be supported by any facts and that, even if it is admitted that individual interests need not be contradictory, it would be "ideological" or nonsensical to assert that individual interests *never* could be contradictory. This doctrine of mid-19th-century liberalism, whatever its validity in the economic field, cannot be transposed to domestic or international politics; yet many schemes of world reform are based on the assumption that "fundamentally" there is no real conflict between national interests.

Let us now take an example from the first part of the *Communist Manifesto:* "The price of the commodity, and also of labor, is equal to its cost of production. In proportion, therefore, as the repulsiveness of the work increases, the wage decreases." Even if the first sentence were correct, the second sentence would not follow, since repulsiveness does not change the cost of production. While according to the first sentence wages are determined by the costs of producing labor, according to the second they are determined, in an inverse proportion, by repulsiveness. Of the two explanations, one must be wrong. No proof can be adduced for either, and incidentally, in order to deduce a conclusion, *i.e.,* arrive at a "therefore . . . ," it would be necessary to argue from two premises rather than one.

The *Communist Manifesto* continues: "In proportion as the use of machinery and division of labor increases, in the same proportion the burden of toil increases, whether by prolongation of the working hours, by increase of the work enacted in a given time, or by the increased speed of the machinery. . . ." This means "the more machinery, the longer the working hours and the greater the toil"—a complete misstatement of facts. The speed of the machine may increase and thus lead to an increase in output but not necessarily to an increase in toil. The introduction of machinery has led to a reduction and not to a prolongation of working hours. The *Communist Manifesto* is shot through with similar fallacies, technically known as "equivocations," and innumerable factual errors. Yet it has served as the ideological platform of the strongest international movement in the current period of history.

What, for that matter, is the goal of communism? According to Engels, men have been making their own history but *as yet* not according to a uni-

[15] *Handwörterbuch der Staatswissenschaften,* 2nd ed., Jena, Fischer, 1900, Vol. V, p. 201.

versal will or according to an over-all plan. The proletariat has been the passive and powerless object of the historic process. But, we are told, it is the *only* class which can acquire consciousness of the entire society. Therefore, it alone is able to assume leadership over society as a whole. It does so by destroying the bourgeois ideology, ending the isolation of the individual proletarian, developing proletarian "class consciousness," and organizing itself politically. "The conscious universal will is the communist party." [16] In the words of the *Communist Manifesto,* the Communist Party has no interests which diverge from those of the working class. It understands the historic role of the proletariat in its entirety and aims at defending the interests of the working class as a whole, liberating in the process the rest of mankind. Ultimately, applying violence, the working class under party leadership would leap from the realm of necessity into the realm of freedom. The proletariat would become the first "subject of history," and for the first time mankind, through the class-conscious proletariat and its party, could take history deliberately into its own hands. The true history of man as man would begin. History could be directed by an over-all will and a universal plan.

Without bothering to discuss this compound of mystification and specious argument in detail, be it pointed out that (1) the hope of becoming the "subject of history" was tersely expressed by the words of the scriptures: *eritis sicut deus.* Hence, eschatological communism is nothing but secularized theology, a derivation from the teachings on salvation, and an inversion of the God who became Man; (2) class consciousness is used here in the same fashion as the Nazis used race consciousness or *Blutsgemeinschaft;* (3) to the consciousness of many people is ascribed a concrete reality—an error known as *hypostasis*—and, more absurdly still, an identical and necessary content; (4) a mystical communion is established between a universal will, the party, the proletariat, and mankind; and (5) one particular social group is credited with the exclusive faculty of understanding the social process, while other groups are denied this capacity, not because they are too stupid, but because they are nonproletarians. This last is logically not different from the theory that there *must* be superior and inferior races. All this, incidentally, goes by the name of "scientific Marxism."

A last example: In a discussion of the "social reconstruction" taking place at the present time, Karl Mannheim, a celebrated continental sociologist who —some years ago—achieved popularity in American and British academic circles, tried to show that the difficult problems confronting society and personal freedom can be solved only by "planning." Up to now, he stated, history was allowed to follow its own unplanned course, but now mankind itself must take history in its hands and begin to regulate its affairs, an argument which shows the influence of Marxist thought on academic scien-

[16] Georg Lukács, *Geschichte und Klassenbewusstsein,* Berlin, Malik, 1923, p. 318; see also pp. 181, 188, 189, 217, 224, 234, 251, 254, 257, 260, 318, 321, 328.

tists. At this point someone asked Mannheim: "We have progressed so far as to be able to plan society and even to plan man himself. Who plans those who are doing the planning?" Without bothering to refute the evident untruth of the first sentence, Mannheim asked a second question: "Which of the existing groups shall plan us?"

Mannheim admitted that the longer he reflected on this question, the more it haunted him. He conceded a disturbing possibility:

We are possibly acting according to our own plan, but in reality we are acting according to a law which is imposed on us and which lies beyond us. We can indeed direct and control the rational and irrational forces in certain spheres, but after a certain point they are beyond our reach and dominate us. . . . The planners can recruit themselves only from already existing groups. Everything will, therefore, depend on which of these groups with existing outlooks will produce the energy, the decisiveness, and the capacity to master the vast social machinery of modern life. Is it to be those human groups in which traces of primitiveness . . . operate without restraint or those which have, through gradual education, developed their rational and moral capacities so far that they can act not only for a limited group, but also for the whole of society, and bear the responsibility for it?

Mannheim admitted that "no one has planned the planners" and that "we live in a world of unsolved problems." Hence it would be "less useful to give an optimistic answer than to conclude with an open question." From all this it could be reasonably deduced not only that Mannheim has *not* solved the key problem of his own concept, but also that the concept does not make sense. What is left of "planning" the entire society if significant rational and irrational forces must remain beyond our reach and continue to dominate us, and if planners cannot be selected properly but acquire their planning capacity through an unplanned power struggle, as, incidentally, always has been the case? It would seem, therefore, that if the fate of mankind could be improved, planning would not be the answer. Yet wide strata of thinking people all over the world make their political decisions in the belief that planning is *the* solution they are looking for.[17]

At the end of his life, Stalin apparently caught on to this significant point when he wrote in his last published writing: [18]

It is possible to limit the sphere of operations of the economic laws; it is possible to prevent their destructive effects if, of course, such exist, but they can be neither reformed nor destroyed. . . . The laws of political economy under socialism are objective laws . . . proceeding irrespective of our will.

Nicholas Berdyayev, the Russian philosopher, said: [19]

[17] Karl Mannheim, *Man and Society in an Age of Reconstruction,* London, Kegan Paul, Trench, Trubner & Co., 1942, pp. 74*f*.
[18] *Bolshevik,* September, 1952, p. 24.
[19] Quoted by Aldous Huxley as a headnote to *Brave New World,* New York, Bantam Books, 1952, p. v.

Utopias appear now to be far nearer to reality than we used to believe. And we find ourselves confronted by an entirely different and troublesome question: How can we prevent their realization? . . . Perhaps in a new century, the intellectuals and the educated classes will dream about ways to keep utopias from happening on this earth, in order to return to a non-utopian, less "perfect" society which, however, will be freer.

Ideologies as Tools. Ideology as a drive dominates the mind not only of the followers but also of the leaders. Ideology as a tool is used consciously by leaders or governments in order to enlist support for their actions. They do not themselves believe in the ideology propagated by them—unless this happens spontaneously through autosuggestion. Ideology as a tool serves to produce *credenda*-images which people ought to believe because this would be useful for the execution of political plans.

In their international dealings, governments employ ideologies as flexible tools. The British, for example, convinced themselves that Mao Tse-tung could be split from Soviet Russia if he were handled properly. They decided to recognize his regime and to send an ambassador to Peiping. When this policy met with opposition in the United States, the British took refuge behind the ideology of self-determination. They argued that each nation has the right to choose its own government and that, moreover, Mao was in *de facto* control of China. The point of self-determination would seem to be that a nation is entitled to a government of its own choosing; hence the methods by which a government assumed power and stays in power must have some bearing on recognition. Who knows whether the Chinese "wanted" Mao? Legitimate governments should be recognized. But what is the test of legitimacy? Incidentally, does it not appear as though the principle of self-determination demands that each nation should be ruled by *democratic* methods? Otherwise, how can the determination take place? Almost simultaneously, however, the British took exception to the activities of the Iranian government culminating in the expropriation of the Anglo-Iranian Oil Corporation. The explanation given was that the Iranian nationalist movement was not "genuine." And in the case of the Suez Canal crisis, 1952–1953, it was claimed that a solution would have to be found by which Western and NATO security interests could be protected.

When Hitler sought an alliance with Scandinavian countries and with Britain, he played heavily upon the theme of the Nordic, blond, blue-eyed, Aryan supermen. But when it became necessary to conclude an alliance with Japan, the Mongolian quickly was made over into an "honorary Aryan." Similarly, the United States took a strong position against dictatorship during the Second World War. Included in this category—dictatorship, totalitarianism, tyranny—were the Axis powers and, to some extent, Spain but *not* Portugal, Turkey, and Brazil; definitely excluded was the Soviet Union, which was described as an "economic democracy." In other words, there always is some ideology handy with which one can justify what needs to be done. If the professed ideology does not fit, it can be reinterpreted, or if this involves intellectual somersaults which might frighten the customers, it can be superseded temporarily by another ideology.

It is not necessary that he who uses ideologies as tools must have professed them openly for a long time. Napoleon, who viewed ideologies skeptically and consciously used them as weapons, remarked that François I, who "was well placed to adopt Protestantism at his birth," could have become, by declaring himself Protestant, the "Chief in Europe." He should have done so, Napoleon argued, because his rival, Charles V, pursued an uncompromising Catholic policy. François I, as leader of a Protestant alliance, would have found many allies in Germany proper. Napoleon thought that such a course would have been preferable to the French-Turkish alliance concluded by the French king. Moreover, he added, this course (which François, in Napoleon's opinion, did not reject on account of religious scruples, but simply because he did not think of it) would have spared France the devastating Religious Wars of the 16th century.

Napoleon seriously played with the idea of embracing the islamitic religion, an act which, he hoped, would allow him to conquer the Orient. He decided against it, because it might have hurt his chances of gaining the mastery of France. But it is not surprising that, upon leaving Egypt, he instructed his successor, General Menou, to become a Mohemmedan.

Napoleon, when he invaded Russia, did not live up to his own ideology as he had done in Poland where he abolished serfdom. The reason for this breach with the tradition of the French Revolution was that Napoleon hoped to limit the war and therefore did not want to break definitely with the Tsar.

Edward Gibbon said: "To the intellectual skeptic all religions are false, to the devout all are true, to the politician all are useful." Ideologies are indeed useful tools in the hands of unscrupulous mass leaders. In former times the politicians used the ideologies that already existed. Nowadays it is possible to follow Voltaire's advice "to invent God if he did not exist": it is now possible, thanks to modern means of communication, to construct ideologies synthetically.

The credit for this portentous invention must go to Adolf Hitler. To be sure, he had predecessors. During the French Revolution, for example, an attempt had been made to create a "religion of reason" (1793) and to base it on a decree abolishing the worship of God. In the place of God there was to be "reason"—and terror; the place of the old religious symbols was taken by a scantily dressed and comely female who was paraded as the "Goddess of Reason" through the streets of Paris.

The synthetic nature of the ideology invented by Hitler is illustrated by the very name of his party. First called German Workers' Party, the new title—National Socialist German Workers' Party—was consciously designed to combine the two major ideologies of the time, nationalism and socialism, and thus to outdo both. This combination was first attempted in Bohemia where the Czechs founded a National Socialist party in 1898. The idea was taken over by a Viennese agitator, Georg von Schönerer, who strengthened the nationalist element of the combination by racist appeals and the socialist element by his avowed hostility against the "plutocracy" of Vienna and the Jews, adding to the concoction violent anti-Catholic and anti-Habsburg slogans.[20] In his youth, Hitler was among Schönerer's enthusiastic admirers.[21]

Having acquired the support of the *bourgeoisie* by nationalism and of the lower middle class by anti-Semitism, the crucial problem was to obtain the help of the workers; hence special emphasis was laid by the Nazis on forming a *workers'* party. The same synthetic diligence went into the designing of a flag, the swastika, which combined the old national black-white-red with the red field of the proletarian flag. The first of May and the ninth of November became the two Nazi holidays. And the party program of twenty-five points contained appeals to every conceivable ideology, including, last but not least, to Zionism. Contradictions were of no concern. The combination of nationalism and socialism which had been considered incompatible was a stroke of impudent political genius, the more so since Hitler in his cynicism did not believe in either ideology, but made the combination merely as a move in his strategy of power accumulation. This performance was in full accord with Hitler's dictum: "The German has not the faintest notion of the way the nation has to be swindled if one wants mass support."[22] Could it be that other nations can be duped as effectively as the Germans?

The lesson was not lost on the communists who, however, introduced an improvement. Complete cynicism is self-defeating; there must be an ideological core which will remain immutable and command the unswerving allegiance of the group in power. There must be an ideology, *i.e.*, Marxism, which can hold convinced communists; but there must also be a number of ideologies to recruit, as time and conditions may warrant, the support of noncommunist groups and to neutralize the opposition of hostile groups. There must be Marxism as the strategic ideology defining motive and objective, but in addition there must be other ideologies to be used as tactical weapons.

No discussion of Marxism should omit the very considerable changes which have been made in the original concepts of Marx and Engels, and even in those of Lenin. Marx and Lenin anticipated that, shortly after the communist revolution, the state would "wither away." The modern communist believes, on the contrary, in the necessity of a strong and, apparently, perennial dictatorship. In Marx's definition of historic materialism, economic forces are the prime mover of society while intellectual events are merely epiphenomena.

[20] Kohn, *op. cit.,* p. 186.
[21] Adolf Hitler, *Mein Kampf,* Munich, Eher, 1942 (originally 1925), p. 107.
[22] Hermann Rauschning, *The Revolution of Nihilism: Warning to the West,* New York, Alliance, 1939, p. 89. This book contains the best description of synthetic ideology making.

Stalin, by contrast, acknowledged the great role of nonmaterial factors.[23] Marx and Engels anticipated a classless society, while Soviet society has become highly stratified. According to many formulations in early socialist literature, the workers would own and administer factories. According to the Stalinist version, factories are owned by the state and administered by government-appointed managers. To give a last example: While Marx and Engels were not very much impressed by chauvinism, modern Russia places great emphasis on so-called "Soviet patriotism." Thus the Soviets made the same discovery as the Nazis, namely that communism and nationalism can be merged profitably. This discovery stood them in good stead in their foreign policy.

Ideologies which are not Marxian in character but have been used by the communists deliberately as tactical weapons include all types of nationalism, pacifism, agrarian reform movements, civil-rights movements, Pan-Slavism, and the Orthodox Church. In recent times anti-Semitism could be added to the list. The Soviets, with an eye on the Middle and Near East, did not persecute severely the islamitic religion. This is saved for a later day.

The Soviets are proponents of "controlled ideologies." This means that they are not satisfied with letting ideologies develop spontaneously. They take a hand in fabricating the ideology they want or activating an existing ideology they temporarily like. For this purpose they are engaged in a vast enterprise of book publishing, not only at home, but also abroad. The scope of this operation—for which they maintain special organizations—is unknown. It was brought out in hearings before a U.S. Senate Committee that the Soviet government assisted in the publication of books on Mongolia, with the purpose of obtaining for Mongolia membership in the League of Nations and thus counter Japanese influence in eastern Asia. It also was revealed that Soviet government officials helped the well-known British socialist writers Sidney and Beatrice Webb to write the second procommunist edition of their widely read *Soviet Communism: A New Civilization*.[24] According to the witnesses, the bulk of the materials for this book was prepared by the Soviet

---

[23] Marx wrote: "It is not the consciousness of men that determines their being but, on the contrary, their social being that determines their consciousness." Stalin, echoing this thought, explained that the "chief force in the complex of conditions of material life of society which determines the physiognomy of society . . . is the method of procuring the means of life . . . , the mode of production of material values." But he also emphasized "the tremendous role of new social ideas" which "organize and mobilize the masses. . . . The spontaneous process of development yields place to the conscious actions of men." During the war, Stalin expanded this thought into his theory of the "constantly operating factors" which include "morale of the army, quantity and quality of arms" and "the organizational abilities of the army commanders." By emphasizing these "organizational abilities," Stalin finally married Marx to Carlyle with his theory that history is made by men. Josef Stalin, *Dialectical Materialism*, New York, International Publishers, 1940, p. 27 and pp. 43*f.*, and *The Great Patriotic War of the Soviet Union*, New York, International Publishers, 1945, p. 41.

[24] Sidney and Beatrice Webb, *Soviet Communism: A New Civilization*, 2 vols., New York, Scribner, 1937.

foreign office, the secret police taking a hand in chapters dealing with concentration camps. The Webbs acknowledged in their preface that Soviet authorities answered willingly their innumerable questions and that they gathered much material from officials and other Russians including "discontented intelligentsia and disgruntled revolutionaries." From looking at their footnotes it is indeed plain that the Webbs were assisted by well-informed, though not exactly impartial, parties.[25]

A more interesting example, perhaps, is that of the great Soviet world atlas. The work on this atlas started in the early 1920's at the request of Lenin, who wanted to reform the teaching of geography along Marxist lines. According to a report of December, 1934, made for the internal use of the Institute for Pacific Relations, "The aim of the atlas is to give a Marxist-Leninist cartographic picture of the world, *i.e.*, a comprehensive picture of the epoch of imperialism and particularly of the period of the general crisis of capitalism."

When the atlas was published a few years later, it gave, from the technical and scholarly point of view, the impression of a remarkable piece of work. In a review, published in *Pacific Affairs* (September, 1938) and signed O.L., we read: [26]

The historical message . . . , of which special mention is made in the introduction, is extended to demonstrate the superiority of socialism as practiced in the Soviet Union with the deliberate purpose of arrival at a future communism over the capitalism of the rest of the world. The method, it must be conceded, is formidable. It is not vulgar propaganda, but scientific argument on a plane that commands full intellectual respect.

Some examples of how the intended purposes were achieved by cartographic means were brought out in the Senate hearings. It should be added that statistics too have been used for similar political objectives. Nobody knows how many allegedly scientific and scholarly works have been prepared and influenced by the practitioners of "controlled ideology."

The future will not see a letup in this obnoxious practice. In his political "testament," Stalin called upon the comrades to produce a Marxist textbook on political economy which "is needed not only for our soviet use; it is particularly needed for the communists of all countries and for people who sympathize with the communists. . . . What is required is a textbook which can serve as the handbook of revolutionary use not only inside the country but abroad." [27] It would be a worthy companion piece to the notorious *Short Course*.

Fortunately, it is still characteristic of the Western mind to despise the use of ideologies as tools. Ideological loyalties are supposed to be a matter

---

[25] *The Institute of Pacific Relations,* Hearings before the Committee on the Judiciary, U.S. Senate, 82d Cong., 2d Sess., Part 13, Government Printing Office, 1952, pp. 4509–4519.
[26] Quoted from *Institute of Pacific Relations,* Hearings . . . , Part 8, p. 2703. The peculiar wording of the first sentence is given here as it appears in the Hearings.
[27] *Bolshevik,* September, 1952, p. 24.

of honest convictions. Ideological professions are meant to be sincere. Even more so, scientific books and treatises are expected to be written by impartial servants of truth, according to their best insights and with the help of the scientific method. It is only lately that the Western world has come to realize that there are in circulation not only counterfeit monies but also counterfeit thoughts—and counterfeit books.

The Dangers of the Ideologization. The ultimate importance of ideologies lies in their power: they have the power to move men and to destroy and create society. The competition of political ideologies and formulas is a part of the over-all conflict of power. Political ideas and ideologies give direction to the physical resources of nations.

The "ideologization" of modern politics has reached a point where rational solutions to political problems are becoming more and more difficult. *Ideologies,* rather than *political ideas* or formulas in the proper sense, have tended to monopolize political thought. This situation seems to be accepted widely without too much protest or soul-searching. Indeed, political proposals often are criticized on the ground that they lack ideological content. Proposals are being made constantly to oppose hostile ideologies with "more attractive" ideologies, *i.e.,* counter a lie with a bigger, more marketable lie.

"Ideologization" involves grave dangers. It leads to cliché thinking and to analysis of the black-white, either-or type. Ideologists are prone to over-look facts which do not fit into their patterns. They are therefore unable to evaluate political situations correctly and realistically. The ideologist, since he is prone to misinterpret the political situation, is apt to choose wrong means for the attainment of his ends. Another danger of "ideologization" is that it creates conflicts which benefit no one and could have been avoided altogether. Minor differences may be blown up into fundamental conflicts which are not susceptible to compromise; conflicts over limited objectives can-not be composed before the "unconditional surrender" of the opposing party. Last but not least, since the exposure of the hollowness of an ideology leads to the loss of a government's prestige and influence abroad, and also to the diminution of its support at home, considerable efforts are being made to keep an outworn ideology alive—a hideous mummy of the collective mind. A fatal degeneration of thought becomes inevitable.

Ideology, a two-edged sword, is, therefore, a potential danger to one's own security. The foreign policy of the democratic nations, including the United States, is not always worked out by scientific methods but is strongly influ-enced by ideology. Whether or not it is possible to free "public opinion" of ideological fetters may be open to doubt; the fact is that a determined cam-paign to restore the rule of reason in place of ideology was never and is not now being attempted on a large scale and with appropriate means. However, top-level statesmen and diplomats should possess sufficient scientific training to avoid the pitfalls of ideological thinking.

Generally speaking, ideology in foreign policy means faulty thinking characterized by assumptions of doubtful validity, disregard for the meaning of words and definitions, misrepresentations of facts, omissions of facts, general conclusions drawn from specific premises or conclusions based on only one premise, predictions on the basis of insufficient data, conclusions drawn *per analogiam* without due regard for differences impairing the over-all validity of the analogy, disregard of the time element, and disregard of the laws of thinking in general.

This list could be extended at random. Evidently an effective policy cannot be evolved by faulty logic. But while foreign policy should be cleansed of ideological elements, this does not mean that it should abandon the quest for improvement and attainment of ideas and ideals in general. The terms "ideology," "idea," "ideal," and formula should not be confounded. The goals of the preservation of Western civilization, or of economic welfare, or world peace require no adumbrating ideologies. Ideals are formal terms, "horizons" or very generalized abstractions lacking concrete content. Foreign policy makes sense only if it aims at concrete objectives. It becomes ideological when mental images are taken for reality, when the choice of means is influenced by preconceived notions, or when one ideal is used as an absolute and single criterion to the exclusion of other criteria.

There is no ideology to end all ideologies. Only the adoption of the scientific method as the intellectual way of life can bring relief. Perhaps this is utopian; yet mankind undoubtedly has progressed on the road to rationality. So long as the rational way of life has not been adopted by *Homo politicus,* it remains necessary to expose ideologies and to explain patiently that mankind is beset by many *different* problems which cannot be solved all at once, by one and the same cure-all solution. It must be demonstrated furthermore that there *are* proper methods of problem solving and that the application of these methods is the *only* way to progress. These truths are self-evident. Arithmetic has finally come to be understood all over the world. Teachers and students in institutions of higher learning should effortlessly perceive the analogy.

It is true that not all problems can be solved speedily and easily, and that many problems may be forever insoluble. But this still would be true no matter what ideology—the most attractive, the least absurd—we may embrace. Once mankind understands thoroughly that ideological solutions lead to disaster and that the *only* salvation lies in the continuous, ubiquitous, and vigorous application of the scientific method to whatever problem needs solution—even then the danger of ideologization will not yet have been overcome, for the scientific method, too, can lead to error. But there are tried procedures for minimizing the errors which dodge the scientist. Only when these procedures have been adapted to politics will democracy function efficiently and ideologization no longer impair democratic processes.

It may be argued in rebuttal that such a program neglects to give the *irrational* forces their proper weight, and that, even if it were successful, it would be a long time before the leading nations would achieve sufficient maturity to rid themselves of their ideological blinkers. This may be so. Yet nations have, under the impact of nazism and communism, grown much more mature than most observers dared to believe a generation ago. There certainly is in Europe a strong tendency away from ideological clichés and a pronounced turn to political pragmatism. But even if ideological infection were to spread, statesmanship still would not consist in meeting ideology with ideology, just as modern science does not deal with the irrational in man by irrational methods. Confusion need not be twice compounded. It would be disastrous if the foreign policy of the Western powers were to intensify the tendency toward the mystification of the "masses" and were not designed to reduce the impact of ideology on international relations. As long as alien and hostile ideologies remain a threat, reason offers a more powerful defense than a synthetic ideology. The "battle for the mind of man" must be fought and won. In that battle slogans and counterslogans are the least suitable weapons.

Needless to say that "reason" must be presented in such a form that it is intelligible to the "masses." The gist of an argument must not be crushed beneath ponderous academic language lest the argument lose the power to convince. Television, for the first time in history, offers a real opportunity for visual, political education. *The threat of the ideological opponent must be met by ideological exposure—and by adequate power.*

It is highly doubtful that communism, as a militant *ideology* and distinguished from a military threat, presents a real ideological challenge. As a political philosophy it is obsolete, and intellectuals are turning to greener fields of social speculation. Intellectually, communism has remained sterile. If tomorrow the power basis of the Marxist ideology should disappear, it is likely that this ideology, too, would wither; it has no authentic hold over the minds of mature people. No greater treason could be committed by scientists and intellectuals than if they were to abandon the concept of truth. Truth can be applied with devastating effect against the dishonesty and untruths of the communist ideology. For truth is still the most powerful weapon on earth.

BIBLIOGRAPHY

Adler, Georg: *Die Bedeutung der Illusionen für Politik und Soziales Leben,* Jena, Fischer, 1904.
Benedict, Ruth: *The Chrysanthemum and the Sword,* Boston, Little, Brown, 1946.
Carr, Edward H.: *Nationalism and After,* New York, Macmillan, 1945.
Delaisi, Francis: *Political Myths and Economic Realities,* New York, Viking, 1927.
Hayes, Carlton J. H.: *The Historical Evolution of Modern Nationalism,* New York, Macmillan, 1948.
Hertz, Friederich: *Nationality in History and Politics,* New York, Oxford, 1944.
Huxley, Aldous: *Brave New World,* originally 1932 (various editions).
Kohn, Hans: *Prophets and Peoples,* New York, Macmillan, 1946.
————: *The Idea of Nationalism,* New York, Macmillan, 1944.

Mannheim, Karl: *Ideology and Utopia, An Introduction to the Sociology of Knowledge,* New York, Harcourt, Brace, 1936.

Mosca, Gaetano: *The Ruling Class,* New York, McGraw-Hill, 1939.

Orton, William Aylott: *The Liberal Tradition,* New Haven, Yale University Press, 1945.

Pareto, Vilfredo: *The Mind and Society,* 4 vols., especially Vol. 3, "The Theory of Derivations," New York, Harcourt, Brace, 1935.

————: *Les Systèmes Socialistes,* 2 vols., 2d Ed., Paris, Giard, 1926.

Roepke, Wilhelm: *Civitas Humana,* Paris, Médicis, 1946.

Rougier, Louis: *Les Mystiques politiques contemporaines et leurs incidences internationales,* Paris, Recueil Sirey, 1935.

————: *La Mystique sovietique,* Brussels, Collection Équilibres Cahiers Périodiques, 1934.

————: *La Mystique démocratique,* Paris, Flammarion, 1929.

Rueff, Jacques: *L'Ordre social,* rev. ed., Paris, Médicis, 1949.

Spencer, Herbert: *The Man versus the State,* originally 1884, Caldwell, Idaho, Caxton, 1940.

Stratton, George M.: *Social Psychology of International Conduct,* New York, Appleton-Century-Crofts, 1929.

Sulzbach, Walter: *National Consciousness,* Washington, American Council on Public Affairs, 1943.

Unwin, J. D.: *Hopousia or the Sexual and Economic Foundations of a New Society,* New York, Piest, 1940.

Part Six

INTERNATIONAL ECONOMICS

Chapter 20

INTERNATIONAL ECONOMICS: FOREIGN TRADE AND THE NATIONAL ECONOMY

The most important function of a foreign policy aiming at the maintenance of peace and the well-being of the nation, next to national security, is to improve the economic conditions of one's own country and of other countries. Economics is concerned with the demand for and the supply of goods and services satisfying human wants. Nowadays, the satisfaction of these wants hinges to an ever-increasing degree upon a nation's participation in international trade. No nation can obtain from domestic sources all the goods and services upon which its economic well-being depends; virtually all nations must trade abroad in order to fill by imports the gaps of the domestic economy. The rising demand for raw materials on the part of the industrial countries, and for manufactured goods and, in particular, for industrial equipment, on the part of the backward countries, has heightened the importance of international exchanges to all countries.

Though opinion may vary as to what kinds of goods which are not or cannot be produced at home are indispensable to a nation's well-being—what is the index of the indispensability to the United States of, let us say, the Belgian Congo's uranium and English shaving lotions?—there is no denying that a minimum of foreign trade is indispensable in order to procure all those commodities which cannot be produced by the national economy. Yet it is misleading to assess, as is often done, the importance of foreign trade in percentages of a country's total production. The importance of foreign trade can be determined only by means of a "multiplier," because the need for imported goods is diffused throughout the entire production process, and exports, in addition to being indispensable for the acquisition of imports, may provide the marginal profit which maintains a producer in business.[1]

Rather than calculate percentage values, it is advisable to consider foreign trade as an integral part of a machine. Spark plugs cost less than 1 per cent of the total price of an automobile, yet without them the car does not run. In most countries foreign trade has a far greater proportionate importance than appears on the trade balance sheet; the invisible returns—freight charges, interest, tourist trade, etc.—must be included in order to estimate realistically the share of revenue from international exchange in the national income. There is little doubt that discontinuance of foreign trade would ruin some countries, greatly reduce the standard of living in others, and deprive all of some of the most important standard commodities. One country might have to do without automobiles and airplanes, another without telephones, a third without electricity and radios, and most of them would have to cut down considerably on their diet, some countries to the point of mass starvation.

Since international interdependence in the economic field is but the corollary of economic progress and since trade cuts across all national boundaries, it follows logically that organizing the world as one economic unit would serve best the interests of mankind. This logical deduction underlies the argument for free trade. In the eyes of the free trader the interdependence of individual national economies is their greatest virtue. For it is this interdependence that sparks demands, hence, productivity, and, beyond the purlieu of economics, promotes closer relationships between peoples in all spheres of human concern. The usages and conventions of free trade constitute norms of international conduct, hence of international order; economic relationships between nations may have been the very cause of the development of international law.[2]

That world-wide free trade redounds to the greatest benefit of the greatest numbers is an axiomatic truth beyond controversy. It is, however, a hotly debated question as to whether individual nations would gain were the present system of trade, which is far from free, transformed into a true world economic unit. With every individual free to produce and to trade as he pleases, and with all individuals, whatever their nationality, held to be of equal worth, it would be purposeless and practically impossible to determine the gains from international trade or their distribution among the individuals

---

[1] The multiplier concept, introduced into economic theory by R. F. Kahn and elaborated by J. M. Keynes, is an expression of the quantitative relationship between an increment in net investment or new money put to work and the increase in aggregate income induced by such an initial outlay; see J. M. Keynes, *The General Theory of Employment, Interest and Money,* New York, 1936, pp. 114–117. This concept becomes increasingly important for many economic problems, see Fritz Machlup, *International Trade: The National Income Multiplier,* Philadelphia, Blakiston, 1943, pp. 212*f.*

[2] See Werner Levi, *Fundamentals of World Organization,* Minneapolis, University of Minnesota Press, 1950, p. 92*f.*

involved.[3] Since under present circumstances the analysis of the contribution which international trade makes to the satisfaction of human wants must take its cue not from individual or global, but from particular, interests —the interests not of mankind but of humans joined in national communities—the question of gains from trade must be put in national terms. National interest calls for a national economic policy, *i.e.*, a positive economic policy devised and executed by the state. Trade between nations has never been free—if by free is meant the independence of trade from political considerations and, hence, from the authority of the state. If governments have refrained from intervening in international exchanges they have done so because they deemed this policy compatible with the best national interest and not because they were impressed by the objective validity of economic theory.

The foreign economic policy of a nation is largely determined by two independent and often contradictory forces: its domestic economic interests and its foreign political interests, including that of its military security. If the aims of a nation's economic activity, at home and abroad, were purely economic, there conceivably might be no contradiction between domestic economic policy and its foreign policies, its economic foreign policy included. Free trade necessarily makes available to the community as a whole a greater physical—"real"—income in the form of more of all commodities, for free trade tends to develop internationally that same specialization of production which, within the community, makes for increased production at lower costs; everybody specializes in what he knows how to produce best, and all commodities so produced are hence available to everybody most advantageously. This is the gist of the doctrine of comparative costs. Translated into the language of international trade, this doctrine maintains that, under the regime of free trade, each country in the long run tends to specialize in the production and exportation of those commodities which it is able to produce at a comparative advantage in costs, and to import commodities which can be produced at home only at a comparative disadvantage, and that such specialization is to the advantage of all countries participating in the arrangement.[4] The arrangement would be a perfect one—were it the primary policy objective of all states to maximize the real income of their respective peoples and of the international community as a whole. This, patently, is not the case. It is here that the contradictions enter which impinge upon the economic foreign policies of all states, the United States included.

In this age of protracted international and civil wars and social revolutions, the primary and secular policy objectives of nations have been to increase

[3] See Frank D. Graham, *The Theory of International Values,* Princeton, N.J., Princeton University Press, 1948, p. 214.

[4] See Jacob Viner, *Studies in the Theory of International Trade,* New York, Harper, 1937, p. 438.

national security, hence national power, and to strengthen the domestic socio-political order, hence to safeguard that order against disruptive forces from within and without, especially against foreign and domestic economic crises. Economic dependence upon others, in a system of sovereign states, means a diminishment of political independence, hence of sovereignty, and thus entangles, by definition, sovereign states in intolerable contradictions. No wonder that every nation has pursued the goal of national economic self-sufficiency—and the possession "within itself," as Alexander Hamilton put it, of "all the essentials of national supply." [5] The case for free trade succumbs to the argument of power, the power of the state to make its foreign policies prevail in relation to those of other states and to adjust its domestic economic policies to prevailing domestic power relationships. Economics, just as every other phase of national life, is dominated by the quest for power.

In terms of power, the possession of one vital commodity which is denied to others yields great though perhaps temporary political advantage. The social and economic privileges of the feudal classes undoubtedly retarded their own enrichment as well as the advancement of the other classes of medieval society. Nevertheless, economic monopoly provided the feudal classes with precious political power. The concentration of industry in western Europe and North America is, from the economic point of view, far less desirable than a globally diffused industry. Yet it provides the industrial nations of the West with power supremacy over the world. The world of economic theory may be full of harmonies, but the world of power is beset by cacophonous dissonances. This is one of the crucial problems in national and international economic relations. The frank acknowledgment of the power aspects of economics is the first step toward allaying the semantic confusion which reigns in this sphere of international relations and thus toward creating a more rational order.

FREE TRADE VERSUS PROTECTIONISM: A POLITICAL ISSUE

The ideal of free trade has, in America, acquired a new luster at the very moment it has been fading in the country which for a century lived by it and supplied its classical formulation, namely, Britain. Paradoxically, it is the United States, the country which most persistently maintained its protection-ist position throughout the classic epoch of free trade, the 19th century, and benefited most spectacularly from that deviation, which now champions the principles of free international competition.

Since 1923, the United States has steadily supported the principle of unconditional most-favored-nation treatment of foreign commerce, that is, equality of treatment of imports and of exports without regard to their source or destination. Since the beginning of the depression of the 1930's, however,

[5] Henry Cabot Lodge (ed.), *Works of Alexander Hamilton*, New York, 1885, Vol. 4, p. 69, as quoted by Levi, *op. cit.*, p. 108.

the trend over most of the world has been strongly in the opposite direction —toward bilateralism, or the limitation by countries of the imports which they will permit from any particular other country to some agreed proportion of their exports to this country.

American determination to reduce trade barriers and expand world trade was revealed as early as February 23, 1942, with the signing of the Lend-Lease agreement with Great Britain. This document, which became the master Lend-Lease agreement and was later signed by the Soviet Union, China, and nine other nations, included in Article VII America's postwar trade aspirations. It specified that the final settlements between the United States and the signatory should include a provision for action directed to: ". . . the elimination of all forms of discriminatory treatment in international commerce, and to the reduction of tariffs and other trade barriers." Article VII also stipulated that at "any early convenient date" conversations were to be initiated among all "like-minded Governments" to attain these objectives.[6] This stipulation was not mandatory under the Lend-Lease Act, signed on March 11, 1941. The Act itself merely stated that the terms and conditions upon which any foreign government receives aid "shall be those which the President deems satisfactory." The initiative for the tie-in between Lend-Lease and participation in a future international trade organization came from the executive branch. It did not commit Congress in any way to approval of the proposed trade program.

The most ambitious scheme for the restoration, after World War II, of international free trade was embodied in the Charter of the International Trade Organization. It owed its existence to the leadership of the United States. It called for the establishment and maintenance by "mutual agreement [of] an 'open' or multilateral system of trade relations between members of the organization," for equal treatment, for reduced tariff barriers, for the elimination of quantitative restrictions (quotas) and, in brief, for all those measures which add up to the total of a system of free trade in the image of the classical school. Not so surprisingly, the Charter contained innumerable loopholes, inserted under the pressure of nations less eager than America to introduce free trade here and now, through which member states can escape back into the cosy shelter of protectionism. It is illustrative, however, of the ambiguity of principle and practice that, in the very year (1948) when the United States fathered the International Trade Organization, its representative advised the General Assembly of the United Nations that export controls imposed by the United States were "for the purpose of securing an equitable distribution of commodities in short supply and of assisting the European Recovery Program in the interest of national security," and that in general, American foreign economic policy was guided by "considerations of national

---

[6] See Edward R. Stettinius, Jr., *Lend-Lease, Weapon for Victory,* New York, 1944, p. 340.

security." [7] Since national security is a subjective criterion, "the difficulty of applying any principles of general validity and of reaching agreements on economic practices can easily be envisaged." [8]

Although the foreign policies of the United States aimed at the removal of trade barriers between nations, it did not revise its own tariff legislation in any important respect. Its own foreign-trade policy remained protectionist; the best its lawmakers managed to do was not to repeal the Trade Agreements Act of 1934 (as amended in 1951), which act, though intended to diminish by the means of reciprocal concessions the obstacles to America's international exchanges, falls short of being a Magna Charta of free trade. The ideals of *laissez passer*, of free competition for profit, and of a minimum of state intervention still enjoy in America a sway which they have lost elsewhere. To permit goods and factors of production, including labor, to move freely across one's borders, would be merely to project these ideals into the rest of the world. Yet, patently, the United States has stopped short of the consummation of this ideal scheme. De la Rochefoucauld wrote: "Man's spirit draws him in one direction, his heart leads him imperceptibly in another one."

The issue of free trade versus protectionism is basically a political rather than an economic issue. The free-trade system which evolved between the Napoleonic Wars and the First World War—the one and only free-trade system that one knows anything about—was no more purely economic in nature than any other type of economic system. It was a system of power nourished by political, social, cultural, and ethical forces of such complexity that the system as a functioning whole is clearly revealed only now when many of its wheels have stopped turning.

FREE TRADE: PAX BRITANNICA AND THE LIBERAL SPIRIT

In 1786, Pitt concluded a commercial treaty with France which removed many of the prohibitions and duties that had previously obstructed legitimate trade between the two countries. After the Napoleonic Wars, the accelerated growth of Britain's population created a demand for imported foodstuffs, and, at the same time, the growth of industrial productivity favored the freeing of trade as likely to expand export markets. In 1846, Sir Robert Peel carried in Parliament the repeal of the Corn Laws, *i.e.*, duties on imported grains. In 1860, Gladstone eliminated the last protectionist restrictions on Britain's trade. Britain's example and readiness to embody the principles of her new trade policy in commercial agreements tended to liberalize the trade policies of other nations, especially France and Germany where active free-trade movements had developed. The age of the flowering of free trade opened, roughly,

[7] United Nations, General Assembly, *Official Records*, Plenary Meetings, 3d Sess., Part I, Sept. 27, 1948, p. 169.

[8] See Levi, *op. cit.*, p. 108. For ITO and the General Agreement on Tariffs and Trade (GATT), negotiated by ITO in 1947, see Chap. 28.

with the 1840's and lasted well into the 1870's. In the 1870's began a long wave of depressions which subsided only in the 1890's. During this period, there was a regression to protectionism among the important trading nations of the European continent. The policy of the United States became, after the Civil War, increasingly protectionist. These retrogressive developments, however, did not gravely impair the flow of international trade: the tariffs which had been imposed were relatively low; a large part of the world, securely tied to Britain's political and commercial system, had weathered the storm without resorting to protectionist devices; and the return to prosperity of the world economy in the 1890's scotched further moves toward protectionism. The system did not survive World War I. Its official demise can be dated 1921–1925, when Britain herself surrendered to the universal tide of protectionism by introducing prohibitive elements into the tariff, especially by the Safeguarding of Industries Acts.

What were the factors, the "strategic" factors, which must be considered in evaluating the operation of the system?

1. In general, the 19th century was an epoch of unprecedented economic expansion. The enormous increase of world trade resulted from (a) the intensification of economic relations between the established trading and industrial nations; and (b) the extension of capitalism to new areas of the globe.

2. The world economy was an interdependent and multilateral system. The world market was virtually a unit. Some slight disparities notwithstanding, traders could buy in the cheapest and sell in the dearest market. Customs duties, transportation costs, and handling charges could be integrated in transactions which were otherwise free, connected the national market to world markets and reduced national price differences to a minimum. The multilateralism of world trade enabled (a) industrial nations to procure their raw materials via roundabout exports to third, fourth or more countries without any problem arising concerning "access to raw materials" or currency "shortages"; and (b) countries producing raw materials to sell them on a uniform world market without any problem arising of "gluts" or "blocked accounts" and to service their foreign debts without chronic difficulties in transferring amounts owed into the creditor's currency.

3. The world economy was a world payment community or "union." The operation of the gold standard adjusted changes in the exchange value of currencies so that they did not enter as a new element in trade transactions. But for a few unimportant exceptions, the currencies of all nations had a fixed value in relation to gold. Any merchant could change one currency into another. A trader who wished, for example, to buy British goods could secure through a bank in his own country a "bill" drawn on a British bank by a British trader who had bought goods abroad. Only when supplies of national currency fell below the demand of this currency were transactions settled in gold. On the basis of fixed parities within the narrow margins of "gold points" (*i.e.*, rates at which it was advantageous to purchase gold, ship it, and con-

vert it into another currency, rather than convert a currency directly into another currency), the different currency systems always could be reduced to a common denominator.

4. The world economy was not only a process of relatively free exchanges of goods but also one of free movements of capital and labor. These movements were eased by (*a*) the comparatively low risk of long-term investment, due to the workings of the gold standard and the stabilizing factors which will be discussed below; and (*b*) the absence of migration restrictions. The great capital markets were in close communication with each other. The flow of capital *and* labor reduced comparative cost disadvantages and tended to equalize average returns on capital (interest rates) and labor (wages).

5. The heart of the world economy was the free-trade area of Britain. Not only had Britain taken the lead in the international movement toward free trade, but her bankers and merchants also perfected the methods and usages of commerce which had developed from the practices of many centuries and in many lands and refined them into a handy system. This system could be used by everyone in all lands because its terms were as simple as they were precise—a kind of Esperanto of international business. The free-trade area of Britain, nucleus of world trade, operated as the balancing wheel of the mechanism as a whole. British imports were balanced by exports, by capital investments abroad, and by payments earned for "services" such as British shipping, insurance, and banking facilities. The balance of British exports and imports created the "sterling standard" which was virtually identical with the "gold standard." The pound sterling, the currency in greatest demand for world trade, was never out of balance. In this sense, all nations formed part of a "sterling bloc" which was as wide as the world.

6. The integrated system which we call free trade was closely linked to noneconomic integrating factors. Economic and noneconomic factors reinforced each other. To confine the discussion of historical free trade to economics is about as meaningful as undertaking a production of *Hamlet* from which the Danish prince has been excised together with all his lines. The international order which in the beginning of the 19th century gave scope to the unprecedented expansion of world trade was created by Britain's victory over Napoleon. After the battle of Trafalgar (1805), the British Navy exercised a mastery of the high seas which was not contested until World War I. British balance of power policy forged the diplomatic instruments which, together with the primary instrument of force, the Royal Navy, maintained the predominance of British power. Yet the *Pax Britannica* would not have become as readily acceptable to other powers and could not have been as easily enforced as actually was the case at the apogee of the epoch of the long peace from 1815–1914, had it not satisfied the interests and aspirations of all major Western nations, if not of all of mankind. The fact that the principal objectives of British policy became increasingly the collective objectives of all major nations can only be explained by (*a*) the collective and concrete

benefits of the system; and (*b*) the philosophical and moral consensus which drew the ruling classes of these nations into a community of intellectual outlook and of sentiment. To the political and economic integration of the world corresponded its intellectual and moral integration. It was this unity which gave the world peace, security, and a code of loyalties. The philosophy of liberalism—*laissez faire* and *laissez passer*—gained ascendancy over the minds of the ruling classes, especially the *bourgeoisie*. It should not be overlooked, however, that this philosophy derived from an understanding of the natural order and man's place in it which was permeated by Christian ethics. No matter how cleverly designed were the purely economic or "nonmoral" theories of the laissez-faire system, free trade could not have thrived except in an environment where contractual loyalties, the sanctity of contract, the code of the gentleman, and a host of other moral sanctions commanded the respect of the ruling classes.[9]

INTERNATIONAL ECONOMIC DISINTEGRATION

The international economic system of the 19th century carried, like all historic systems, seeds of its own destruction within itself. Its very nature—a self-operating system—induced a false sense of security. Its fabulous material achievements—unprecedented acceleration and expansion of exchanges, universally rising standards of living and accumulation of vast individual fortunes—obscured the nonmaterial assumptions underlying the historical laissez-faire doctrine. The secularization of liberalism culminated in that extreme economic materialism which ignored religious and ethical restraints upon the competitive urges of the market place. These pathological developments of the capitalist system, which naturally manifested themselves most forcefully in the international competition of capitalist nations, have been topics of endless post-mortem debate. It has been rightly said that "free trade, once established, will contribute to the integration of the world" but that this is different from maintaining that in a nonintegrated world ". . . free trade will lead to integration . . . [for] an integrated world is a condition of the successful introduction of free trade." [10]

This analysis applies retrospectively. Free trade, as we have known it, was buried under the disintegration of the world in which it had flourished.

1. The First World War destroyed vast wealth. It impoverished several of the greatest trading nations, especially Britain, France, and Germany. The

[9] See for the historical, political, and social milieu of free trade Karl Polanyi, *The Great Transformation*, New York, Farrar & Rinehart, 1944, pp. 3–30. See also the same author's discussion of the role of international banking—*haute finance*—in the late 19th and early 20th century, although some of his conclusions seem overly dogmatic. See for a brilliant analysis of the economic and social factors underlying free trade, its doctrine and practice, W. Roepke, *International Economic Disintegration*, London, Hodge, 1942, pp. 12*f*. and 69*f*.; and *Gesellschaftskrisis der Gegenwart*, Zurich, Rentsch, 1942, pp. 65–103.

[10] Levi, *op. cit.*, p. 93.

seemingly rapid reconstruction, in the 1920's, did not restore the financial reserves, especially in the form of middle-class savings, which heretofore had furnished European capital exports and a cushion against depressions.

2. The First World War unleashed the Russian revolution. This cataclysmic event resulted in the excision of the Russian market from the body of international economic organization. The repercussions of the Bolshevik revolution engendered not only a shrinkage of the world trade area but also social disturbances throughout the world which, in the economic sphere, expressed themselves in a crisis of confidence and increasing timidity of investors. Moreover, the Bolsheviks made it their business to jam deliberately the workings of the world market wherever they could.

3. The rise of new nation-states in central and eastern Europe was accompanied by a resurgence of protectionism in that part of Europe where free trade had been least firmly established. These new nation-states, more often than not hostile toward each other and fearful of the retaliation of the states from which their territories had been torn, notably Germany, Russia, Hungary, and Turkey, sought desperately to establish their economic independence and, especially, self-sufficiency in munitions. To protect their "infant" industries—mostly war industries—they raised tariffs far beyond those rates which, though they increasingly hampered exchanges, world trade could, before 1914, take in its stride.

4. The collapse of the international balance of power which prevailed up until 1914 created a vacuum which the League of Nations could not fill. The increasing strains upon the British Empire entailed, aside from direct economic consequences, crucial political and strategic developments. *Pax Britannica* was superseded by a hollow system of collective security. The resultant widespread sense of insecurity and weakening of the checks and balances which had kept power politics within tolerable limits, were the principal causes of international economic disintegration. The policeman of the world market, the Royal Navy, no longer could cover the lengthening and increasingly hazardous beat.

5. Because of the obsolescence of British machines and industrial methods, the result partly of a slackening of the British people's vital energies and competitive ardor, partly of the wear and tear of the war years, partly of the contraction of the world market (see above), the terms of trade—the ratio of export prices to import prices—changed in disfavor of Britain. In other words, Britain was losing out in the international competition for export markets, particularly markets for those industrial products with which she had established her position as the world's leading trader.

6. The pound sterling ceased to be the standard currency of world trade. The importance of London as the center of world trade declined; with it declined the prestige of those practices and usages which supplied the conventional framework of free trade. After the twenties and thirties, the American dollar became the currency in demand.

7. The United States emerged as the major economic power of the world. However, because (*a*) American productivity had grown immensely; (*b*) Americans bought less than they sold; (*c*) the United States, despite its transition after World War I from the status of a debtor to that of a creditor nation, did not lower its tariffs; and (*d*) foreign goods could not clear the American tariff barriers, dollars were always in demand. The heritage of world economic leadership had fallen to the United States. But the United States refused to assume that part of it which consisted of Britain's doctrine of free trade.

8. The demise of the gold standard was one of the most important casualties of the great depression of 1929. That crisis can now be seen for what it was, namely, not so much the culmination of the inherent "contradictions" of capitalism as a delayed reckoning. The bill for World War I, its destructions and revolutions, finally came due. It was not that the gold standard was failing to do its job, but that governments, which increasingly intervened in the management of national economies, refused to employ the gold standard and pay the cost of operating this device. To rely upon the gold standard to bring about the necessary readjustments of trade balances would have called for a high degree of self-restraint. Yielding to the mounting political pressures upon them, governments discarded, one by one, the mechanisms which heretofore had restored the economic equilibrium. The principal argument for abandoning the gold standard was that only thus could the vicious cycle of deflation and unemployment be broken. It is doubtful in the light of the dismal history of currency devaluations in Germany, France, Britain, and the United States that currency devaluation can effect more than a temporary relief from ills. Devaluation is no remedy at all but merely a temporary palliative that weakens the patient. A good case can be made for the contention that the great crisis had run its course, that the world economy was righting itself *before* the new devices (abandonment of the gold standard, currency devaluations and government spending) were tried, and that the new devices—which in fact were not so new—retarded rather than hastened international recovery. Be that as it may, the gold standard was discarded and discarded for good, and with it fell one of the principal props of international free trade.

9. The conditions under which World War I had been fought and the consequences of the war, notably the Russian revolution and its repercussions throughout the world, brought about profound changes in the "social climate." World War I was fought as the first "total" war in modern history. The entire national society was mobilized; virtually all phases of social life were subjected to stringent controls such as rationing, censorship, and travel restrictions. Virtually all governments felt compelled to include in their peace aims more or less vague promises to the masses of social and economic improvements. The various socialist parties, Marxian and non-Marxian, had cam-

paigned for these goals long before the war. During the war, however, even the most conservative governments made these objectives their own, for the tremendous sacrifices in blood and sweat which were demanded of the masses had to be represented as down payments not merely on victory over the enemy but also on a brighter future. The Russian revolution and communist agitation greatly intensified the social ferment. (The Peace Treaty of Versailles gave modest recognition to the aspirations of the masses: it created the International Labor Organization charged with the defense of the workingman's interests, albeit not endowed with compulsory powers.)

The inflationary catastrophes unleashed by the war which wiped out the savings of millions of peoples of all classes, especially in central Europe (Germany and Austria) and, to a lesser extent, in Western Europe (France and Italy), gave rise to an all-pervading sense of insecurity. The economic crisis of the 1930's deepened this sense of helplessness and frustration—millions of men lost their jobs because of no fault of their own and because of the workings of a market mechanism which they could not understand—and increased the pressures for "social justice," that is, for *security*, security against chronic unemployment, against poverty in old age, and against poverty in ill health. These pressures found their articulate expression in the catchwords of the political parties which rode to power upon the tide of mass discontent. Their programs emphasized just distribution rather than increased production, stability rather than "boom or bust," security rather than risk, public spending rather than balanced budgets, and the virtues of planning over those of the free market, of a government-controlled economy over a competitive free economy.

This further shift away from the free competitive economy and toward a more or less controlled economy was greatly eased by the administrative experiences of the First World War. The war had been, so to speak, a dry run in directed economics. The new age of planning opened with a surprising unanimity which seemed to join the most diverse political movements into a kind of "international" of controlled economies; the German Nazis paid handsome tribute to certain enactments of the New Deal, and not a few New Dealers called for the respectful reexamination of the achievements of Bolshevik Russia. It is not surprising, however, that these theoretical agreements did not lead to increased exchanges of goods *between controlled economies*. To the contrary, as each government expanded its authority over the domestic economy and projected ever more comprehensive plans into the future, it sought to guard the experiment against the interference of those extraneous factors which it could neither control nor plan. Among the most important was, of course, the world market of commodities, currencies, and gold. The collapse of the London Conference in 1933, called by the President of the United States (who then disavowed an agreement entered into by his own delegation), was but the logical consequence of a process which, once set in motion, could not be arrested even by its own progenitors.[11] The demonetization of gold, devaluation of currencies, and commodity controls (parities, output restrictions, quotas, etc.) were not mere accidents due to "emergencies"; they were the necessary conditions for the introduction and operation of state controls. The trends toward increasing state interference in the economic sector of society were more pronounced in Europe than in the United States and most pronounced in central and eastern Europe, where neither liberalism nor democracy had sunk its roots as deeply into the social soil as it had in Britain and France. In the United States, the ideals of self-reliance and individual enterprise still retained their luster despite a spate of reforms which sought to restrict the power of the entrepreneur and regulate economic activity. The great natural resources of the United States, the vastness of the internal market, and the very real achievements of the free-enterprise system—high average standards of living, a great variety of mass-produced goods at low prices, rapid technological progress, and generous opportunities for advancement from rags to riches—greatly contributed to the relative staying power of the free-enterprise system in the face even of severe "cyclic" tests. But even in the United States the ideals of free enterprise and free competition appeared to have lost some of their attraction.

INTERNATIONAL TRADE AFTER WORLD WAR II

What have been the economic consequences flowing from World War II? The Second World War reinforced the trends issuing from the first. Again, vast wealth was squandered irretrievably upon destructive undertakings. The physical damages to capital investments of every kind were even greater than in World War I. The area of the world market shrank still further; the absorption in the Soviet orbit of most of Eastern Europe, Eastern Germany, and the Far Eastern mainland closed these regions to international exchanges except on the reduced scale of government-supervised barter deals.

Britain, in order to pay for imported arms and ammunitions, divested herself of many overseas investments; British shipping suffered heavy losses from enemy action; and Britain's industrial plant was subjected to bombing as well as to the wear and tear of peak production under wartime conditions. Diminishing returns from foreign investments and services resulted in a further deterioration of Britain's financial position. The obsolescence of her industrial equipment and its inadequate replacement by modern techno-

[11] See Raymond F. Mikesell, *United States Economic Policy and International Relations,* New York, McGraw-Hill, 1952, pp. 52–53. See especially the passage quoted from *Memoirs of Cordell Hull* (2 vols., New York, Macmillan, 1948): "There were some signs of approaching trouble in the fact that the new agencies, National Recovery Administration and Agricultural Adjustment Administration were coming into being with their new remedies of recovery. *Basically they believed in cutting the United States off from the rest of the world* . . ." (p. 54). (Italics supplied by the authors.)

logical devices, particularly in coal mining, resulted in a further worsening of Britain's competitive position in export markets. In addition, Britain had gone heavily into debt. She now owed staggering sums to her Dominions, particularly India. Because wartime needs had already reduced British gold and dollar reserves, these debts could not be paid through transfers of gold and dollars. Instead, they were carried as "blocked sterling accounts," held for these countries in London. British goods shipped in payment against these accounts were dubbed "unrequited" exports, since Britain received, in return, neither goods nor foreign exchange.

The pound sterling registered these cumulative deleterious developments. Despite a postwar devaluation (September, 1949) which lowered the exchange rate of the pound sterling by roughly one-third in relation to the dollar, Britain was forced to impose stringent currency restrictions; the pound sterling ceased to be a "hard" currency.

The creation of the "sterling area" marks the culminating point of international economic disintegration; fifty years ago the whole world was a "sterling area." Pegged to a working gold standard, the pound was freely convertible at a fixed value and held as a reserve by the world's trading nations. Two world wars and the rise of economic nationalism, the shift in the balance of power, and the rise of the dollar as the world's strongest currency broke the supremacy of the pound. It should be emphasized, however, that this process of contraction and decline had long been in the making. Countries which had been good British customers and purveyors of raw materials were beginning, long before World War I, to industrialize, raising the price of raw materials and hence the price of British imports. The Statute of Westminster reflected the growing movement within the empire not only for political but also for economic autonomy. The most significant action of the members of the Commonwealth, having now achieved all but formal independence of the Crown, was the raising of trade barriers against goods from the United Kingdom. Britain's answer to the Commonwealth competition and the world economic crisis of the 1930's was the creation of the Imperial Preference system agreed upon by the Commonwealth at Ottawa, Canada, in 1932. With this system of "closed" trade, today's "sterling area" was born; the free-trade world upon which Britain's power depended had already ceased to exist.

The new-nation states of Asia and a number of "backward" countries followed in the footsteps of the new nation-states of eastern Europe spawned by World War I. Nearly everywhere, national independence asserted itself in the shape of tariffs discriminating against foreign imports and protecting native industries, and of "nationalization" recte expropriation of key industries, particularly those built by the overseas investments of the Western trading and colonial powers. Iran "nationalized," in 1950, the oil industry (Anglo-Iranian Oil Company); and the Union of India, in 1953, some basic industries. The Republic of Indonesia possessed itself of a large part of the holdings built up over centuries by Netherlands capital. Bolivia nationalized the tin mines developed by foreign capital. These examples, drawn at random from a rich compendium of nationalizations, may suffice to illustrate the present state of that international capital market which, once upon a time, was the alter ego of international free trade. It was the *private* investor in Europe and the United States who supplied the bulk of the capital for the development and industrialization of the rest of the world. He did so because he was reasonably confident to see his risk rewarded and his capital returned. That confidence was badly shaken after World War I; if it is not dead now, it most certainly is moribund.

The international economic "system" which emerged from World War II, consisted of (1) the sterling area; [12] (2) the dollar area including all "hard currency countries such as Switzerland and Canada (despite the latter's political affinities with the sterling area); (3) multicurrency Europe with its complex relations with both the sterling and dollar area and its own payment union of which the United Kingdom is a member; and (4) the ruble area including the Soviet Union and its satellites. Though these four areas are linked with each other by a labyrinthine system of trade treaties, barter deals, currency clearing arrangements, and preferential agreements, bilateral and multilateral, this fuzzy patchwork does not constitute a "world market" in any acceptable sense of the term.

At the close of World War II, ambitious projects for world organization suggested new approaches to world economics. If the planners of the new world order had learned one lesson from their predecessors at the end of World War I, it was that a political organization of the globe which did not rest upon solid economic foundations, could not endure. Before turning to an examination of their schemes and practical achievements, it is necessary to review the theory and practice of tariffs, for it is the tariff policies of states which pose, here and now, the most immediate problem of international trade.

THEORY AND PRACTICE OF TARIFFS

There are three basic types of international tariffs: tariffs imposed in lieu of taxes; tariffs as a means of economic warfare; and tariffs which purport to serve the strengthening of the domestic economy.

Whether it is advantageous to use tariffs as an instrument for collecting revenue is a matter of expediency. In some undeveloped Latin-American countries taxation through tariffs was the only practical procedure for raising

---

[12] The sterling area is composed of the United Kingdom, Australia, New Zealand, India, Pakistan, Ceylon, Southern Rhodesia, Burma, Iraq, Iceland and Ireland. South Africa, possessed of considerable reserves of gold and dollars, is an "associate" member. The currencies of Egypt, Scandinavia and Greece are closely tied to sterling.

the government's revenue.[13] This type of tax tends to put heavier burdens on the richer classes. In economically and socially advanced states taxation by tariff has the same disadvantages as an indirect tax—it is a device to make the tax burden *appear* smaller than it actually is. Tariff rates are, however, rarely high, chiefly for the reason that the state must seek to adjust its tariff policy to demand in order to maximize its revenue.

Tariffs can be introduced for the express purpose of hurting a foreign power or to create and protect industries needed in war. Such measures will be discussed below; it will be noted merely that these are not economic but political measures, although carried out with economic means. Whether they are advantageous or not is exclusively a matter of political and military judgment rather than a question of economics.

For conventional import tariffs (export tariffs are uncommon and serve only special purposes) the claim is usually made that they protect the national industry, that they procure employment, and make high wages possible. According to the virtually unanimous opinion of the economists, they do nothing of the kind. They do, however, restrict consumption and prevent the most advantageous use of capital. They may create unemployment. If they keep wages high, they do this with nominal and not with *real* wages. Income cannot be adequately measured by its money value but, in order to be meaningful, must be expressed in purchasing power: what does a certain sum buy in terms of commodities? It is in the nature of things that the price level is higher behind a tariff wall than in an economy that works without tariffs.

There are exceptions to the rule. John Stuart Mill, himself one of the most prominent partisans of free trade, accepted the "infant industry" argument as valid. An industry may have to be protected in its infancy; once such protection has been given, the industry may grow to produce at no cost disadvantage, and without such a protection the industry might never be created. Under certain circumstances a temporary tariff may afford legitimate protection to an industry when it produces at too high a cost and may thus ease cost readjustment, for example, retooling. A tariff may permit the gradual liquidation without hardships to an industry that has become unprofitable. A temporary tariff may allow an industry to expand so that it reaches the zone of "external economies," with the result that from that moment on it can produce at lowered cost. In sum, therefore, there are cases where a temporary and small *specific* tariff may provide some advantage, but, be it repeated, economic theory considers such cases as exceptions to the general rule that tariffs, and especially high and permanent tariffs, are harmful to a country's welfare. Tariffs reduce a nation's real income.

The theoretical arguments in favor of specific and temporary protection appear far from conclusive if considered in the light of experience. The infant

---

[13] When, after 1870, the free-trader Napoleon III was succeeded by the protectionist Thiers, tariffs were reintroduced on the ground that they would help to pay the war debt. After the debt had been paid, tariffs not only remained but rates were increased in 1881.

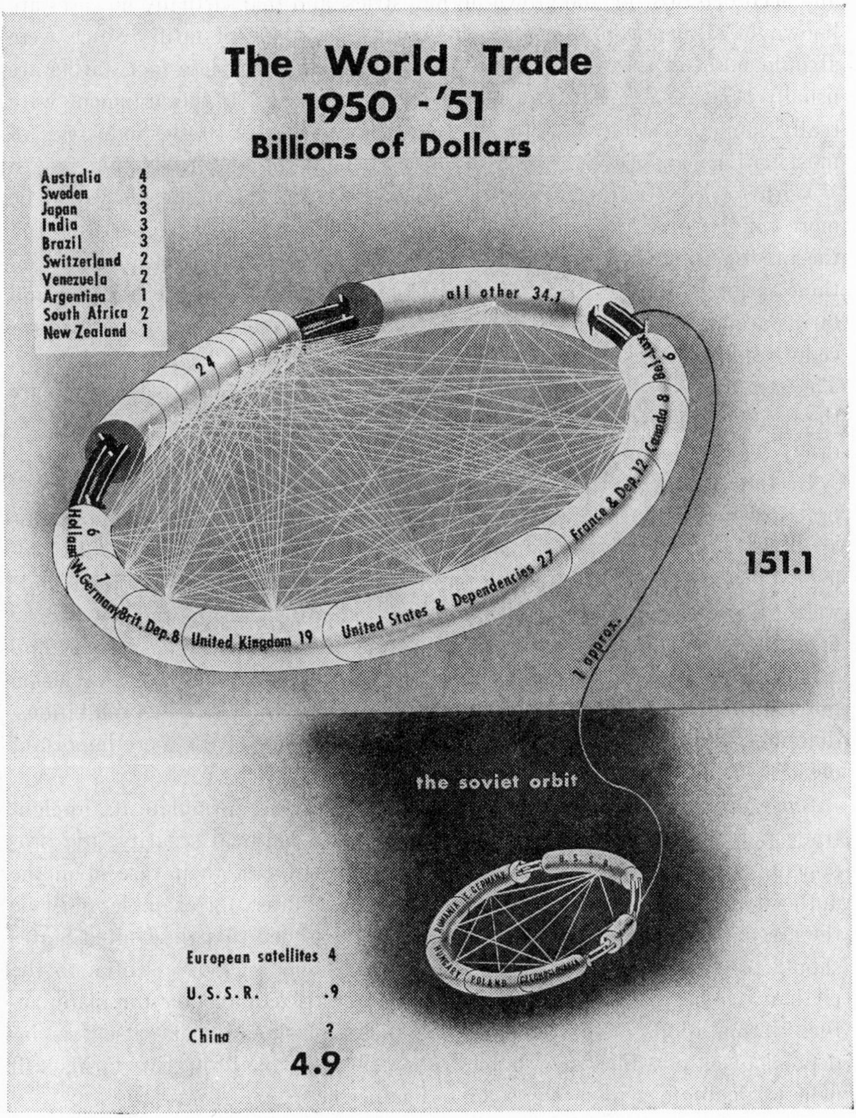
The World Trade
1950 -'51
Billions of Dollars
Australia 4
Sweden 3
Japan 3
India 3
Brazil 3
Switzerland 2
Venezuela 2
Argentina 1
South Africa 2
New Zealand 1
all other 34.1
24
Bel-Lux. 6
Canada 8
France & Dep. 12
United States & Dependencies 27
United Kingdom 19
Brit. Dep. 8
W. Germany 7
Holland 6
151.1
1 approx.
the soviet orbit
POLAND
European satellites 4
U.S.S.R. .9
China ?
4.9

industry argument, for example, is controverted by the fact that would-be producers rarely, if ever, secure tariff protection, that such protection is usually accorded *existing* and grown-up industries, and that virtually no cases are known of authentic infant-protecting tariffs, let alone of tariffs which were abandoned after the "infant" had reached maturity. In plain fact, tariffs are usually a means of protection for *declining* industries. If the argument were really sound, it would be difficult to explain how most of the industries of most nations could ever grow without the benefits of such protection.

With respect to other allegedly beneficial tariffs, the argument would be more convincing if there were a reliable method to establish the need for and the precise amount of such tariffs and if there were a mechanism to discontinue tariffs no longer beneficial. There is no such method or mechanism; and tariffs are adopted not in consonance with even a semblance of scientific procedure but are the result of *political* pressure exercised by interest groups. The stronger these interests are politically, the higher and the broader are the tariffs; to which it must be added that the interests of the consumers are rarely represented and have never yet anywhere exerted noticeable pressure.[14]

In the past moderate tariffs had only moderately bad effects. For all practical purposes, they were in fact but a part of the freight cost, but this artificial boost in transportation costs was partly compensated for by technological progress which continually reduced freight rates. If international trade were today impeded only by moderate or "scientific" tariffs, there would be little to worry about. Actually, far more nefarious practices have come into use, such as prohibitive tariffs, specifications of merchandise for exclusion purposes, barter agreements, quotas, trade monopolies, outright prohibitions, dumping, and currency controls, to mention only some of the more important devices.

Since no government can, under present conditions, formulate its foreign-trade policy without giving full consideration to national security, the proponents of high tariffs and national self-sufficiency rest their case upon the authority of war economics. Because the United States, for example, must be the arsenal and base of the free world it can be argued that the United States should produce upon its own territory all consumer's goods essential to the civilian economy in times of war and all materials required for the manufacture of munitions. The United States therefore should make itself as independent as possible from sources of supply abroad. Protective tariffs will help to maintain a high degree of self-sufficiency.

[14] The contention that tariffs are largely the result of vested-interest groups pressuring for specific short-range as contrasted to national long-range advantages was proved by a wealth of historical data by E. E. Schattschneider, *Politics, Pressures and the Tariff: A Study of Free Private Enterprise in Pressure Politics, as Shown in the 1929–1930 Revision of the Tariff* (New York, Prentice-Hall, 1935). In 1922, the United States made an attempt to establish a "scientific tariff": it was to be determined how much tariff was needed to equalize production costs in the U.S. and abroad. Since trade is the result of differences in cost, such a tariff would, in effect, have abolished trade altogether. The experiment was soon abandoned.

In order to determine the merits of this argument, three questions must be answered: (1) Can the United States or any other country attain self-sufficiency or anything approaching it? (2) What would be the cost of self-sufficiency if material and technological resources were available to attain it? (3) If there were indeed no other practical solution to the economic problem of national security, would a protective tariff supply the means for obtaining self-sufficiency?

1. The leading powers, including the United States, are far from self-sufficient now and are becoming steadily less so. At present, the United States, for example, accounts for nearly one-half of the materials consumption of the free world, although its population is only one-tenth of that outside the iron curtain.[15] It was estimated that by 1975 the requirements for all materials of the United States will be about one-half larger than they are now, with mineral requirements nearly double the present consumption. Since no other country this side of the iron curtain enjoys anything near the *relative* self-sufficiency of the United States and since even the Soviet Union is dependent on the importation of important raw materials, the chances of attaining absolute self-sufficiency within any national territory appear slim —except at the cost of a severe curtailment of average living standards and, ultimately, of military power.

2. While it is unlikely that self-sufficiency can be attained at all as regards certain materials, there is the possibility of developing substitutes by the use of "synthetics" and new methods for employing materials which are in plentiful supply. But here the problem of cost arises, and these costs must be calculated not only for each particular product but also in relationship to the economy as a whole.

Considerable confusion befogs the controversy over the production of substitutes, *i.e.*, the production of commodities, such as rubber and nitrate, which are not available in their natural state upon the national territory. The creation and subsidization by the state of these "synthetic" industries is advocated frequently by arguments as spurious as those advanced in rebuttal.[16] Economists can easily show that substitute production is costly and unprofitable. Yet they cannot always prove that it should therefore not be undertaken. True, in certain cases substitute production actually endangered a country's war-making ability. For example, Italy's attempt to produce textiles from milk only reduced that country's small milk supply and almost upset its

[15] "By the midpoint of the twentieth century we had entered an era of new relationships between our needs and our resources; our national economy had not merely grown up to its resource base, but in many important respects had outgrown it. We had completed our slow transition from a raw materials surplus nation to a raw materials deficit nation." A Report to the President by the President's Materials Policy Commission, *Resources for Freedom*, June, 1952, Vol. 1, p. 6. See Chap. 7.

[16] Ernst Hoch, *Die Wehrkraft der Wirtschaft: Beiträge zur Methodik wehr- und kriegswirtschaftlicher Lagebeurteilungen*, Hamburg, Hanseatische Verlagsanstalt, 1937, pp. 43f.

food economy.[17] In Germany, the introduction of substitute textiles depleted the country's clothing reserves, for the new substitutes proved of inferior quality and offered inadequate protection against the rigors of the north European winter. Germany would have fared better had she continued to import high-grade textiles, clothed her population properly, and kept a stockpile to be used in case of war (see Chap. 7).[18]

These are clearly cases of ill-conceived policies of economic self-sufficiency by means of domestically fabricated substitutes.[19] But not all policies of economic self-sufficiency are so ill-conceived. If in 1913 Germany had not introduced nitrogen fixation as an alternative to importation of Chilean saltpeter, Germany would have been defeated early in 1915. If Germany had not engaged in the production of synthetic gasoline from 1934 onward, Hitler could never have dared to war upon mighty industrial nations.

There are many instances where one material can safely be substituted for another and without any marked difference in cost. For example, steel alloys are, to a degree, interchangeable; hence it is entirely within economic reason if a country uses an alloy metal which it finds in its own territory rather than one which it has to import. It is true that costly production of a commodity which could be cheaply imported is economic waste. Britain did not produce many agricultural commodities but imported them, marshaling her manpower for the manufacture of industrial goods. Yet as soon as shipping became scarce, Britain had to enlarge her agricultural production. The United States imported the antimalaria drug atabrine from Germany; but during the war it could no longer obtain atabrine from Europe. The alarming spread of malaria among U.S. forces engaged in the Pacific War immensely increased the demand for that drug. If the United States had been able to supply atabrine from the domestic production, it might have waged Pacific warfare more effectively during the first year of the fighting.

These examples may suffice to indicate at least the complexity of the problem. No modern industrial country is capable of producing *all* the materials it needs; no country can engage in large-scale substitute production without lowering the quality of its goods and reducing its war potential. On the other hand, each country is in dire need of procuring a number of "critical" or "strategic" commodities produced abroad. There is no set rule for best assuring access to these goods. In some cases, it may be advisable to start domestic production, possibly of a slightly modified product. In other cases

[17] See Luigi Lojacono, *L'Independenza Economica Italiana,* Milan, Hoepli, 1937, pp. 273, 292.

[18] Germany's autarchic policy is well described from the technological points of view in Anton Lübke, *Das deutsche Rohstoffwunder: Wandlungen der deutschen Rohstoffwirtschaft,* Stuttgart, Verlag für Wirtschaft und Verkehr, Forkel & Co., 1938. Lübke treats agricultural questions on pp. 387–401; textiles, pp. 313–358, and synthetic oil on pp. 203–254. See also Anton Zischka, *Wissenschaft bricht Monopole: Der Forscherkampf um neue Rohstoffe und neuen Lebensraum,* Leipzig, Goldmann, 1936.

[19] On the general economics of self-sufficiency, see P. H. Asher, *National Self-sufficiency,* New York, Nelson, 1938.

outright substitute production may be called for by the circumstances. Sometimes, however, stockpiling may be the best answer. Yet the problem cannot be dodged by pointing out that these procedures are not "economical." Nor can the economic argument, *i.e.,* the argument of relative costs, be disregarded altogether. While money may be of little importance in modern war, no country can afford to squander its industrial resources. In short, one and the same solution can never be adopted for all types of deficit commodities.

3. Even for those products which are of such importance to national security that to rely on foreign sources of supply would entail intolerable risks, there is the further question whether tariff protection is a desirable means of achieving self-sufficiency.

To the extent that tariffs are used to encourage production of exhaustible materials that could be imported (and imported more cheaply), the depletion of such materials is accelerated, and dependence on foreign sources of supply is progressively increased. In the case of some products, however, it is argued that supplies in an emergency need to be available actually, rather than merely potentially, and that a going industry finds and develops new resources.

So far as nonexhaustible products are concerned, actual experience throws some doubt on the belief that tariffs assure sufficient production in emergency and that they are effective in reducing reliance upon foreign sources. For example, from 1943 to 1946, American production of sugar, a highly protected commodity, was 20 per cent less than prewar, and 30 per cent short of the targets which were set. If Cuba had not covered the deficit, there would have been a severe shortage. Similarly, wool is an auxiliary product of many sheep growers. As meat prices rose, producers became more interested in meat than in wool production, which fell from 202 million pounds in 1942 (19 per cent of American needs in that year), to a twenty-year low of 155 million pounds in 1946. American textile production relied largely on foreign wool.

Consequently, if the objective is to insure domestic production of a given amount of a commodity, it is necessary to consider the conditions of production of that particular commodity. In some cases maintenance of standard capacity and retention of skilled personnel are doubtless desirable. There are, however, alternate ways of assuring readily available supplies, of which tariff protection is only one. These alternatives include (1) stimulation of technological progress; (2) in case of a situation critical to national security, the granting of government subsidies to noncompetitive industries; and (3) stockpiling. Such methods may be less expensive than protective tariffs to taxpayers as well as consumers, and usually they are infinitely less harmful to the international trading community.

ATTEMPTS AT ECONOMIC INTEGRATION

At the close of World War II, at the high noon of Allied amity and when hopes for a better world to come were high, the attention of the architects of victory and planners of the new order turned to economic matters. So closely interwoven had been the economic policies of the leading powers with their political and military policies and so sweeping had been the authority of centralized economic planning that it seemed only logical to project concepts of international economic cooperation, planned and executed by governments and intergovernmental boards, into the philosophy of the new order and especially the crowning edifice of the new order, the United Nations.

The First World War had been the first "total" war. Yet it became "total" when traditional social and economic organization proved incapable of accommodating the insatiable and all-inclusive demands of the war machine. The Second World War was, from the very outset, waged by mass societies. Some of these were organized as totalitarian states on a permanent war footing long before the war began; others, especially the Western democracies, transformed themselves speedily into highly organized and bureaucratic nations-in-arms. The psychological leaven of the war effort was supplied by avowed peace aims conceived in the image of mass aspirations. In this respect, the propaganda aims of the Nazis, communists and the democratic states were distinguished from each other by tenor and ideological peculiarities, but not by substance. The third freedom of President Roosevelt's famous speech, namely freedom from want, stood high on the propaganda agenda of all the belligerents. It was a freedom upon the desirability of which the working classes of the Western nations could effortlessly agree with the toiling masses of Russia, the backward and colonial peoples of Asia, and the self-styled "have-not" nations such as Germany, Italy, and Japan.

It occurred to no one at the beginning of World War I to claim that the war was being waged for higher average standards of living or "social justice." Even the Covenant of the League of Nations was reticent on such matters as organized economic cooperation between nations and all those aspects of economic and social existence which did not seem directly relevant precisely because they were economic and social and therefore not political in the narrow sense of the term. By contrast, the United Nations Charter is permeated by the universal consciousness of the indivisible nature of international order. A large part of the Charter is taken up with provisions designed to insure the economic well-being of the world community. The Economic and Social Council was created as the matrix of world economic organization. That part of the Charter which deals with economic and social matters represents, just as do all other parts of the Charter, a compromise not only between the most diverse interests of the various member states but also between diverse political ideologies. This spirit of compromise pervades the constitutions of the several specialized agencies, charged with the implementation of the general aims of the Economic and Social Council. Whatever forthright agreement there was among the founding members is chiefly confined to the desirability of an international economic organization. But since that agreement does not include a binding definition as to where precisely international economics stops being international and becomes the domestic concern of the sovereign state, its implementation poses a formidable problem.

A good case can be made for the contention that much of the thinking which went into the making of the specialized agencies and the various related projects for organizing international trade in key commodities was predicated on the assumption that governments would continue to exercise a high degree of control over domestic markets, that is, on a universality of state socialism in substance, though not necessarily on a universality of doctrine. The speedy dismantling after World War II of internal controls by certain countries, notably the United States, inserted a wedge into the unanimity that prevailed among the peace planners when all the participating governments were still in the full enjoyment of their powers to plan, control and regulate. Thus, much of America's foreign economic policy appeared in the eyes of nations having espoused one or the other collectivist doctrine not only as the unilateral and brash assertion of American power but also as a fall from ideological grace. The United States was now viewed as the representative *par excellence* of the capitalist system. The avowed devotion of the United States to international free trade was deemed to stem not so much from American awareness of the oneness of the world but from addiction to laissez-faire economics, to wit, unbridled competition at home and abroad. Was not, as Friedrich List, a German economist writing a hundred years ago on Britain's economic dominance, put it, "free trade the weapon of the strongest"? It is these basic tensions arising from fundamental ideological disagreements and institutional differences which supply the key to the failure of all recent attempts (ITO, GATT) to reintegrate the world economy by international organization.

UNITED STATES FOREIGN ECONOMIC POLICIES

If American foreign economic policies at the end of World War II were more forthrightly directed toward the reintegration of world trade into a truly global system than those of any other major country, their evolution during the postwar years reveals the full extent to which the attempt has failed. No major power placed so much trust in the efficacy of the economic approach to world problems as did the United States. This emphasis upon economics over politics reflected American tradition. In the United States, the protection of trade had been considered by generations of Americans as the sole mission of American diplomacy. Nowhere else did political leaders, businessmen, and academic economists proclaim as fervently that economic problems, mismanaged and neglected so absurdly in 1919, should take precedence over all others in the task of postwar reconstruction; that political problems, such as readjustments of frontiers and ideological differences, were unimportant or, at best, secondary; and that, in brief, if economics were taken care of politics would take care of themselves. (This, incidentally, was decidedly not the view of the Soviet Union, a state supposedly informed by a materialistic doctrine placing economics above all other social activities.)

Right after the war, the principal vehicle of American economic initiative was UNRRA (United Nations Relief and Rehabilitation Administration), charged with the task of supplying emergency aid to the war-ravaged countries of Europe and Asia. UNRRA's most important financial backer was the United States. By about 1947 the usefulness of this arrangement, at least from the point of view of the United States, had come to an end. Not only had Europe not recovered its prewar productivity, but the "dollar gap" —the excess of U.S. exports over imports from Europe—exceeded 11 billion dollars. The United States was confronted by two interrelated problems: (1) how to raise Europe's productivity and exports, and (2) how to halt the deterioration of European politics which stemmed from economic crisis, the growing power of the various communist parties, especially the French and Italian, and the increasing hostility of the Soviet Union. The American answer to the challenge, a political and a military one as well as an economic one, was first a 400-million-dollar grant, approved by Congress in May, 1947, to Greece and Turkey (to be spent on economic and military reconstruction) and, about a year later, the Foreign Assistance Act of 1948, authorizing the appropriation of 5.3 billion dollars for the operation of the European Recovery Program, in addition to the relatively minor sums allocated to China, Greece, and Turkey. The administration of the program was placed in the hands of the Economic Cooperation Administration (ECA). ECA had dispensed by December 3, 1951, when ERP came to an end, a total of about 12.3 billion dollars.[20]

ERP envisaged large-scale help to European nations on condition that this help be used to modernize industrial equipment and launch international economic cooperation, including joint exploitation of resources. ERP "spark-plugged" European recovery. The communist parties in Western Europe, seconded and abetted by the Soviet Union, sought to prevent the plan's success. Their stratagems failed. The European governments, however, showed themselves little disposed toward "putting their house in order." American help, therefore, perpetuated an unsatisfactory *status quo*, maintained too high a wage level for too low a productive return, and in fact may have subsidized strikes, top-heavy bureaucracies, and unwise social and economic "experiments."

[20] On the genesis of the Marshall Plan, which saw the light as Public Law 472, 80th Cong., see the speech of General George C. Marshall, Secretary of State, at Harvard University on May 8, 1947, rendered in full in *Documents on Foreign Relations, 1947*, Boston, World Peace Foundation, 1948. See also *The European Recovery Program: Basic Documents and Background Information*, S. Doc. 111, 80th Cong., 1st Sess., Government Printing Office, 1947.

No European country initiated a really comprehensive program of economic self-help. There were no comprehensive agreements for pooling of labor, no substantial efforts for the joint development of electric power, no compacts on selection of complementary crops, no significant lowering of tariffs, no satisfactory removal of trade obstacles, and no creation of customs unions. Even the tariffs union between Holland, Belgium, and Luxembourg (Benelux), agreed upon by formal treaty—the only trace of economic sanity in the world—could not be put into operation.

The most solid achievements, in the realm of intra-European economic cooperation, of ERP were the creation, in 1945, of the Organization of European Economic Cooperation (OEEC) in which all European recipients of American aid joined for the purpose of facilitating intra-European trade and stabilizing currencies, and, in 1950, of the European Payments Union (EPU) designed to act as a clearinghouse for currency transactions. Yet these innovations, desirable as they were, fell far short of the explicit purpose of American Congressional action, namely, to employ ERP as an instrument of European economic unification or, as ECA's administrator, Paul Hoffman put it, European "integration."

The European nations were waiting for America to take the initiative, as though it were not their own survival which was at stake. In turn, American policy—naïvely trying to avoid giving substance to communist accusations of "imperialist intervention"—did not enforce compliance with the avowed purpose of economic aid, namely, the economic unification of Europe.

Whatever the merits of large-scale American assistance projects of the type of the ERP, no lasting positive result is possible unless the recipient states (1) improve the domestic management of their respective economies, and (2) help themselves collectively by discontinuing harmful trade practices and initiating joint development projects. If a program of large-scale assistance merely perpetuates the *status quo* in economic practice, the results must be more harmful than had no assistance been given at all. Assuming that American production is adequate to permit, for several years, massive shipments of goods abroad, large-scale transfer of wealth cannot but negatively affect the growth of American industry. Such a program, therefore, entails a reduction of America's future war potential without offering any certainty that this reduction will be compensated by the strengthening of America's allies. If reduction of United States armaments is the price of the recovery program, American security would be endangered. While help to some nations is undoubtedly necessary for humane as well as political reasons, an enormous and continued diversion of American resources barren of material returns must weaken the United States not only militarily but also socially. The peace of the world might be safer if American economy and armaments were kept intact and if foreign investments were made according to sound business criteria rather than by the ideological precept of fighting communism by bolstering inefficient governments.

In this sense, the third phase of American foreign assistance policies can be called "ECA with the bloom off." The Mutual Security Act, which in 1952 superseded ECA, created another letter agency in the endless chain of letter agencies—MSA, the Mutual Security Agency.[21] This new agency was charged with the task of coordinating three heretofore distinct programs: (1) military aid to America's allies who had joined in the North Atlantic Treaty Organization (NATO); (2) economic-aid programs administered by ECA (which was to be absorbed by MSA); and (3) the technical-assistance program administered by the State Department and launched by the celebrated "Point Four" of President Truman's inaugural address of January 20, 1949, in which the President proposed that "we should make available to peace loving peoples . . . our store of technical knowledge" and ". . . should foster capital investment in areas needing development."

The relative figures of the allocations show that military considerations now outweighed economic ones: nearly 6 billion dollars were set aside for military aid and only 1.44 billion for economic aid. Strictly speaking, MSA was designed not so much as an instrument of American foreign economic policy as a means for subsidizing allied forces and thus supplementing American military power.

Though MSA, reflecting as it did the grim realities unveiled by the Korean War, served American purposes probably better and more faithfully than did ECA, the questions must be asked (1) whether it did not impose, because of the sudden shift away from economic aid and toward accelerated rearmament, burdens upon the European economies which they were not as yet able to bear; and (2) whether it did not push into the background a problem that should have been dealt with on a footing equal to that of rearmament, the problem of American-European trade relations. This problem, which Britain's Chancellor of the Exchequer, Mr. R. A. Butler, paraphrased as "Trade, not Aid," is none other than that of international economic integration. Will the United States permit Europe to earn dollars by imports to the United States rather than to draw them against "gift" allocations, and will the United States thus live up to its avowed devotion to principles of free trade and competition?

American foreign-aid programs served to provide products which America's allies need but cannot buy because of their inability to earn enough dollars to cover their import requirements. Hence American tariff policy is directly related to the scope of American aid programs, economic as well as military. It is true that tariff reductions alone would not close overnight the "dollar gap." The question is whether tariff reductions together with other measures, notably the removal of obstacles to private investment and the procurement of weapons for America's allies from their own productive

[21] Public Law 165, 82d Cong., 1st Sess. See also Department of State Publication 4236, Government Printing Office, 1951.

facilities, would not (1) ease the load of the American taxpayer, and (2) increase the productivity of America's allies and thus reduce, ultimately, their dependence on dollar imports.

This question is especially pertinent to America's relationship to the greatest trading area of the free world, the sterling area. This relationship is painfully complex, and tariff reductions alone will not solve its many problems.

Problems of American-British Trade. Any curtailment in world trade adversely affects Great Britain. For example, Britain relies upon Russia for supplies of grain which she cannot afford to buy from dollar sources. For these reasons, the American legislative riders (Battle Act and Kem Amendment) to aid programs, enjoining recipients of American aid from trading with the Soviet Union, were not kindly received in sterling area quarters. In the Far East, Britain would much prefer that Japan be permitted to trade with Red China and Manchuria rather than be encouraged by the United States to sell in Southeast Asia, traditional export market of Britain and Britain's Dominions. In Europe, a reorientation of German trade to its traditional central European markets (now preempted by the Soviet bloc) would be preferable to facing German competition in South America and the Middle East. Trade considerations also influence British attitudes toward European union. An economically unified Europe could produce more goods at lower costs. Britain has so far been unable to produce any scheme whereby the sterling area, already rent by political dissatisfactions, can lower *its* costs. Sir Stafford Cripps, speaking for the Labor Government, said in December, 1949, that ". . . if [European integration] means some sort of linking up of the economies . . . which might jeopardize the position of the sterling area as a whole, then I think we should not want to go in for such close linkages." [22] This position was not abandoned by the Conservatives.

Proposed solutions to Britain's economic problems are usually tied to the question of how to achieve convertibility of the pound sterling. It is doubtful that any economic solutions could attain the *political* objectives of maintaining Britain's system of legislative social benefits and Commonwealth ties.

So far as United States policy is concerned, the solution to world economic problems, including those of Great Britain, is an expanding world economy, freed of national trade barriers. On the basis of this policy, the United States has championed a unified Europe, including Britain, and sponsored the International Monetary Fund and the General Agreement on Tariff and Trade. The British, by contrast, look upon the maintenance of the sterling area as a legitimate policy objective. Here, however, lies the paradox: the sterling area is officially described as a "multilateral trading area." This it is— between its members. Yet it is also a "closed" trading and high-cost pro-

---

[22] Sir Stafford Cripps, "Britain's Battle for Survival," *U.S. News and World Report*, Dec. 16, 1949, p. 36.

duction area in so far as the rest of the world is concerned. This deadlock can be broken only by the United States. If the United States, with the world's strongest economy, cannot bring itself to eliminate tariff protection and run the risks of marginal unemployment, it is highly improbable that less wealthy economies will give up "protection" they find in such arrangements as the sterling area.

The case for "Trade, not Aid," though its advocates not infrequently have weakened it by patent and partisan oversimplifications, is strong. It is strong not only on grounds of long and sobering economic experience, enriched by the case histories of several world depressions, but also psychologically. It would hold out to America's friends the prospect of wider markets and serve as a solid token of America's devotion to avowed principles. Not a few of the increasing political tensions which have arisen between the United States and its allies derive from the reality of American protectionism, which belies America's avowed fidelity to free-trade principles.[23]

The failure of the countries of the free world to restore within its vast area a measure of free trade and the resiliency of protectionism have been grist to the dialectical mills of the Soviets. Stalin reaffirmed in an article published in *Bolshevik* on October 3, 1952, his belief in inevitable growing conflicts in the non-Soviet world. He wrote: [24]

The most important result of the Second World War in its economic consequences must be considered the disintegration of a united, all-embracing world market. This circumstance determined further the deepening of the general crisis of the capitalist system. . . . But from this it follows that the sphere of application of the forces of the chief capitalist countries to the world resources will not expand but will contract, that conditions of the world market of sale for these countries will grow worse, and idleness of enterprises in these countries will increase. In this, properly speaking, there consists a deepening of the general crisis of the world capitalist system in connection with the disintegration of the world market.

As far back as 1928 Stalin presented the Sixth World Congress of the Comintern with a program based on world economic trends and drew attention to the "centrifugal tendencies within the premier maritime and colonial empire—Great Britain (Canada, Australia, South Africa, etc.)." Stalin looked forward to exploiting these tendencies as well as "antagonisms between America and the rest of the world." Reiterating Lenin's prophecies of 1920, Stalin observed of America, ". . . everybody is now in debt to her . . .

[23] For an exhaustive, yet admirably brief, discussion of American trade policy, see Chamber of Commerce of the United States, *International Trade Policy Issues* (prepared under the direction of Harry C. Hawkins), Washington, February, 1953. This study does not deal with the problem of free trade in the abstract. It centers upon the trade problems of that part of the world which is free, *i.e.*, outside of the ruble bloc. In this sense, international integration means the creation of a trading area composed in the main of the Americas, the Commonwealth, and Western Europe.

[24] Stalin's statement in *Bolshevik*, as quoted by *The New York Times*, Oct. 4, 1952.

[and] she is becoming more and more hated." [25] Again, beginning roughly in 1946, Soviet journals have published articles portraying Anglo-American differences as an inevitable outgrowth of their rival "capitalisms." [26]

In the face of the Soviet threat, the United States employed its economic and military might to strengthen the free world. It failed to take the *one* step which its political and social ideals seemed to dictate: *the creation of a free trading community centered upon the great market of the United States itself, just as, a generation ago, world trade was centered upon a Britain that had cast off the tight armor of protectionism.*

BIBLIOGRAPHY

Barber, Hollis W.: *Foreign Policies of the United States,* New York, Dryden, 1953.

Bidwell, Percy W.: *The Invisible Tariff,* New York, Council on Foreign Relations, Inc., 1939.

Buchanan, Norman S.: *International Investment and Domestic Welfare,* New York, Holt, 1945.

Chardonnet, Jean: *Les Conséquences économiques de la guerre 1939–1946,* Paris, Hachette, 1947.

Clark, Colin: *The Conditions of Economic Progress,* London, Macmillan & Co., Ltd., 1940.

Condliffe, J. B., and A. Stevenson: *The Common Interest in International Economic Organization,* Montreal, International Labor Office, 1944.

Diebold, William, Jr.: *Trade and Payments in Western Europe,* New York, Harper, 1952.

Ellis, Howard: *The Economics of Freedom,* Council on Foreign Relations, New York, Harper, 1950.

Eucken, Walter: *Grundsätze der Wirtschaftspolitik,* Bern-Tübingen, Francke-Mohr, 1952.

Ezekiel, Mordecai (ed.): *Towards World Prosperity,* New York, Harper, 1947.

Feis, Herbert: *Seen from E. A.,* New York, Harper, 1947.

———: *The Changing Pattern of International Economic Affairs,* New York, Harper, 1940.

———: *Europe, the World's Banker 1870–1914,* New Haven, Yale University Press, 1930.

Graham, Frank D.: *The Theory of International Values,* Princeton, N.J., Princeton University Press, 1948.

Haberler, G.: "The European Recovery Program," *American Economic Review,* Vol. 38, No. 4, 1948.

Hahn, L. Albert: *The Economics of Illusion: A Critical Analysis of Contemporary Economic Theory and Policy,* New York, Squier, 1949.

Haight, Frank A.: *A History of French Commercial Policies,* New York, Macmillan, 1941.

Harris, Seymour (ed.), "International Economic Relations," *The New Economics: Keynes' Influence on Theory and Public Policy,* New York, Knopf, 1948.

Hauser, Henri: *Économie et diplomatie: Les Conditions nouvelles de la politique étrangère,* Paris, Recueil Sirey, 1937.

Heilperin, Michael: *The Trade of Nations,* New York, Knopf, 1947.

Hoover, Calvin B.: *International Trade and Domestic Employment,* New York, McGraw-Hill, 1945.

Jouvenel, Bertrand de: *L'Amérique en Europe,* Paris, Plon, 1948.

Kindleberger, Charles P.: *The Dollar Shortage,* New York, Wiley, 1950.

[25] *Program of the Communist International, adopted by the Sixth World Congress of the Comintern, Sept. 1, 1928,* New York, Workers' Library Publishers, pp. 28–58; and V. I. Lenin, *Selected Works,* Vol. VIII, New York, International Publishers, 1943, p. 289.

[26] See, for example, *Mirovoye Khozaistvo i Mirovaya Politika,* No. 12, December, 1946, pp. 3–17; also E. Varga, "Anglo-American Economic Relations," *Bolshevik,* No. 3, February, 1946, and "The Foreign Trade of England and Conditions Aggravating Anglo-American Antagonisms," *Vneshnaya Torgovlya,* June, 1950, No. 6, pp. 10–17.

Lasswell, Harold D.: *World Politics Faces Economics: With Special Reference to the Future Relations of the United States and Russia*, New York, McGraw-Hill, 1945.

Metzger, L., and W. L. Neumann, Jr.: "The Havana Trade Conference," *American Perspective*, Vol. 1, No. 10, March, 1948, pp. 591–611.

Mikesell, Raymond F.: *United States Economic Policy and International Relations*, New York, McGraw-Hill, 1952.

Parks, Wallace J.: *United States Administration of Its Economic Affairs*, Baltimore, Johns Hopkins Press, 1951.

Robbins, Lionel: *Economic Planning and International Order*, London, Macmillan & Co., Ltd., 1937.

———: *The Consequences of Economic Nationalism*, International Conciliation, No. 323, October, 1936.

Roepke, Wilhelm: *International Economic Disintegration*, London, Hodge, 1942.

Rougier, Louis: *Les mystiques économiques*, Paris, Médicis, 1938.

Ruestow, Alexander: *Das Versagen des Wirtschaftsliberalismus*, Düsseldorf, Küpfer, 1950.

Sharp, Walter R.: *International Technical Assistance*, Chicago, Public Administration Service, 1952.

Staley, Eugene: *World Economic Development*, Montreal, International Labor Office, 1944.

———: *World Economy in Transition: Technology vs. Politics; Laissez Faire vs. Planning; Power vs. Welfare*, New York, Council on Foreign Relations, 1939.

The Sterling Area: An American Analysis, Economic Cooperation Administration, Government Printing Office, 1952.

Tew, Brian: *International Monetary Co-operation, 1942–1952*, New York, Longmans, 1952.

Tinbergen, J.: *International Economic Cooperation*, New York, Elsevier, 1945.

A Trade and Tariff Policy in the National Interest, A Report by the Public Advisory Board for Mutual Security, Government Printing Office, February, 1953.

Viner, Jacob: "Conflicts of Principle in Drafting a Trade Charter," *Foreign Affairs*, Vol. 25, No. 4, July, 1947, pp. 613–628.

———: *Studies in the Theories of International Trade*, New York, Harper, 1937.

Williams, B. H.: *Economic Foreign Policy of the United States*, New York, McGraw-Hill, 1920.

Zeeland, Marcel van: *Revision des Valeurs: Essai de synthèse sur certains problèmes fondamentaux de l'économie contemporaine et leurs réactions politiques*, Brussels, Renaissance du Livre, 1937.

Chapter 21

ECONOMICS AS A WEAPON

National security is the foremost obligation of any government. Hence each government regulates its economic life in view of its defense requirements. The purpose of such regulatory policies is to strengthen a nation's own economy and to weaken the economy of prospective opponents. By strengthening is meant not only the securing of all raw materials which might become necessary in case of war, but also the acquisition of finished products, weapons, ammunition, technological know-how, financial support and the establishment of an international network of economic auxiliaries, while at the same time denying all these advantages to the opponent. The economic weapons also can be used for the acquisition of political friends and the development of alliances.

It is quite true that international trade, if unobstructed, flourishes spontaneously and that this spontaneous growth would strengthen the economic posture of all trading nations. Yet the play of the free market may make a nation rich in consumers' goods while depriving it of those items which are indispensable in wartime. A free-trade organization is the logical economic structure of a world at peace. In periods of conflict, however, trade must be controlled, at least partially, in order to maximize a nation's military power.

Similarly, the sale of commodities in a peaceful world is highly advantageous for a nation's living standard. Yet when a prospective opponent wants to buy commodities in order to strengthen his war potential, economic logic must be displaced by military logic. For example, Japan bought in the United States large quantities of scrap iron. Normally the sale of scrap iron would have been highly advantageous to the United States. Yet Japan used American scrap iron to build up its war machine. Hence the United States ultimately was compelled to embargo the sale of scrap iron.

One of the most important means of economic warfare consists in attacks on the opponent's financial strength for the purpose of diminishing the exchange value of his currency. These attacks can take the form of withdrawal of credits, dumping of large amounts of currency in order to compel the target country to pay in gold, manipulation of international currency exchanges, and sometimes simply psychological means which undermine confidence in the victim's financial honesty or economic strength.

CURRENCY AND CREDIT MANIPULATIONS

During the 17th century, the British, French, and Dutch were haunted by fear lest Spain accumulate overwhelming financial strength through the removal of gold from America. Two methods were developed to drain the Spanish gold supply. The first, called "interloping," consisted in seizing a port close to the American continent and transacting from there contraband trade with the Spanish colonies, thus circumventing Spain's trade monopoly and restrictive regulations.[1] British Jamaica and Dutch Curaçao were the principal bases of this economic warfare. The second means was to supply the Spaniards with the commodities they exported to America, and to ship these commodities under the Spanish flag to America but then to capture the gold received in payment from Spain and divert it to England, Holland, and France. This three-cornered gold warfare engineered by private bankers and traders led ultimately to the exhaustion of Spain and the astonishing power growth of Great Britain.

During the First World War the Western Allies were in dire need of American financial help. When the war was over, England and France and their European allies had obtained from the United States the then staggering sum of 14 billion dollars. They obtained this money by a variety of means. First, they shipped to the United States approximately 1 billion dollars' worth of gold.[2] Second, the United States purchased its own securities held abroad and thus transferred to the European countries between 2 and 3 billion dollars. Third, the American banks arranged private loans to the extent of about 3 billion dollars. The rest of the money was in the form of American government loans which were granted after the United States' entry into the war in 1917.[3] Without these huge financial transactions, the Western powers unquestionably would have lost the war.

Before the United States became a participant in the war, the European powers had great difficulties securing the desired loans. In the beginning the American government discouraged such transactions on the ground that these would violate American neutrality. However, these obstacles were removed speedily, partly because the American government came to realize that its interests demanded an Allied victory, partly because Allied propa-

---

[1] Bertrand de Jouvenel, *Napoléon et l'économie dirigée: le blocus continental,* Brussels, Éditions de la Toison d'Or, 1942, pp. 15*ff.*

[2] This great influx of gold into the United States presented Britain with the danger that American banks, in order to avoid credit inflation at home, would reexport this gold to neutral countries for investment purposes and in the process buy up British holdings. In order to prevent such a contingency, the British made use of their control of shipping and put obstacles against American gold shipments, especially to Argentina and Spain. Hearings before the Special Committee Investigating the Munitions Industry, U.S. Senate, 74th Cong., 2d Sess., part 30, Government Printing Office, 1937, p. 9555.

[3] *Ibid.,* part 32, p. 10188.

ganda changed American public opinion, and partly because close financial collaboration definitely was in the American interest.[4]

A second obstacle was that the Allied nations had not set up proper purchasing channels and were competing with each other, not to mention the competition among the various departments of one nation. This difficulty was overcome, in part at least, by the British Government's accepting a proposal by J. P. Morgan to the effect that the Morgan bank was to coordinate British purchases.

As a third obstacle, the danger of currency inflation had to be removed. This was done by a group of American banks who under Morgan's leadership undertook to peg the British pound. The firm of Morgan had a wide experience in these operations, having during the Franco-German war of 1870 raised war loans for France (while British bankers had supported the war effort of Prussia).[5]

At first, it was possible to float only small loans. As a second step, so-called "secured loans" were brought on the market, which meant that the American investor bought bonds issued by municipalities and preferred securities issued by industrial enterprises such as railroads. As a third step some of the Allied gold was used for the purchase of American securities for the purpose of reaping the benefit of dividend payments. Finally, in October, 1915, France and Britain were able to float a loan of 500 million dollars—at that time an enormous sum. While this loan ultimately was placed successfully, full subscription was achieved only by high-pressure publicity (for which the Allies allocated a certain sum). There were many anxious moments in the course of the experiment.

During the fall of 1916 the Allies again needed money. It was estimated that between October, 1916, and March, 1917, about 1.5 billion dollars would be required. This amount was so "staggering" that American banking circles became alarmed.[6] Even J. P. Morgan himself was far from clear how these requirements could "possibly be met." American bankers were divided into a strongly pro-Allied group under the leadership of Mr. Morgan, a pro-German group under the leadership of German-born Paul M. Warburg, and a neutral group. Reflecting these apprehensions the Federal Reserve Board, in December, 1916, issued a statement saying "practically in so many words

---

[4] For example, *The New York Times* on Sept. 16, 1915, pointed out that fluctuating exchange rates interfered with American export trade. "It is quite impossible to make commitments in the ordinary way when a sudden drop in exchange before purchases can be made to meet the engagement may sweep away all the profits or even bring actual loss. . . ." Hence war loans were "manifestly in our own interest as well as in the interest of our foreign customers." (Hearings . . . Munitions Industry, part 30, p. 9656.) The *Times* concluded that it was not a question of a "war loan" but that the interests of the wheat grower of the Northwest, the cotton grower of the South, the cattle and pig farmers everywhere were at stake, and that a depreciation of the sterling would produce an economic crisis. This was propaganda; but it was also true.

[5] Hearings . . . Munitions Industry, part 30, p. 9643.

[6] *Ibid.*, pp. 9609*f.*

that the British and French treasury bills would not be paid at maturity." The result of that announcement was "a definite marked decline in the market value of all the British and French securities selling in the United States." [7] According to contemporary interpretations, this announcement was either a piece of pro-German propaganda put over by Mr. Warburg; or a move on the part of President Wilson "to make the allies long for peace on the ground that they can't get any more money to continue fighting"; or a maneuver against the Morgan interests.[8]

The German Ambassador in Washington soon found out about these difficulties. On January 16, he wrote a letter to the Foreign Office in Berlin in which we read: [9]

Since probably England can be forced to make peace only as a result of economic collapse, the following proposal ought to be taken under consideration. I guarantee for the discreet handling of the matter. An American banker, a personal friend of mine, not of German origin, has suffered from the terror methods of the Morgan group. He is ready to lead a campaign against the English loan which probably will be floated within the next few weeks. His idea is, without arousing attention, to buy bonds of the first English war loan and to throw these on the market on the day following the issue. In the opinion of my friend, this would lead to such a drop in the price of the old bonds that the new loan inevitably must fail. This would mean the end of the British credit in the United States. To implement this plan, it would be necessary to deposit at least 1 million dollars at the Leipzig bank of Knauth, Nachod and Kuehne for their New York branch. The rest would be done here. Since German names must not appear, only my friend and a partner of his firm know about this plan. His firm will be in charge of the operation. The two gentlemen estimate that, at worst, 20 per cent of the amount might be lost, a sum which is negligible if the purpose were attained. Request instructions. [Signed] Bernstorff.

In Berlin the Foreign Office asked for the advice of the German treasury which on January 24, 1917, approved the proposal. In addition, the Foreign Office asked for the opinion of Max M. Warburg, a Hamburg banker and close relative of New York's Paul M. Warburg. On January 24, 1917, Max wrote the following letter:

I do not know more about the planned English loan than what I read in the papers. Unquestionably, it is a fight between the Federal Reserve Board on the one hand and the Morgan clique on the other. The Federal Reserve Board issued a sharp warning against further investments in foreign values. But the Morgans, the National City Bank, and others have taken a different view. It looks as though the Morgans will have their way. I am firmly convinced that, should they try, they will experience failure [*ein Fiasko erleben*].

[7] Letter by J. F. Curtiss to Benjamin Strong, Dec. 16, 1916, *ibid.*, part 30, p. 9545.
[8] *Ibid.*, p. 9544.
[9] U.S. National Archives, *German Foreign Office File,* Reel 2596.

On the basis of this letter, the German treasury advocated the allocation of 2 million dollars to this operation. Ultimately only 1 million dollars were sent, which arrived in New York early in February, 1917. Nevertheless, the British got their money. If the Germans had not in the meantime declared unrestricted *U-boat* warfare and thus made inevitable the war with the United States, and if they had used a larger sum, perhaps 10 million dollars, the maneuver might have had a better chance of success.[10]

Speculation against the currency of a hostile power, or against that of a "friendly" power, is a standard device of economic warfare in peace and war. When, in 1923, the French occupied the Ruhr against the opposition of Britain, measures were taken by London against the French franc which resulted in a sharp decline of that currency. When, in 1931, Germany and Austria concluded a customs union, France withdrew her short-term credits from both countries, a tactic which bore fruit in the bankruptcy of the major private banking institution of Austria, the Kreditanstalt. Appeals by the Austrian government for credit were turned down by France. However, Britain, seeking to prevent French control over Austria, granted an emergency credit. The repercussions of the Austrian financial crisis spread to Germany. Within a few short weeks Germany had to relinquish about one-fourth of her gold and foreign currency reserves. Interest rates were increased sharply, with the result that the economic life of the nation was crippled.

At this point President Hoover suggested that a moratorium be declared which for one year would relieve Germany of the need to pay her debts. At the same time negotiations were started to give Germany a long-term credit of about 500 million dollars. These two measures undoubtedly would have stabilized the situation and would have permitted Germany to liberate herself from the crisis. However, the French delayed their acceptance of President Hoover's proposal, trying to capitalize on their strong economic position in the hope of forcing Germany to abandon the *Zollunion* (customs union) with Austria, to disband various paramilitary formations, to discontinue the naval construction program, and to obligate herself for the further payments of reparations. While the French were delaying their answer, withdrawal of gold and currency from Germany continued at an accelerated pace—foreign creditors wanted to get their money before the moratorium would be declared. When, in the end, the French accepted the moratorium plan, it was too late. The German banking system had collapsed.

Still the French had it in their power to grant Germany a sufficiently large credit and thus to restore the financial balance. At that time the French had hoarded most of the world's gold outside of the United States, about 3.5 billion dollars in bars and coins. They were the only European power capable of making a substantial loan. Yet they did not do so. The

[10] *Ibid.*

German crisis was permitted to take its course, either because the French government was politically so weak that it was incapable of creative action —even the French socialist party opposed effective help to Germany—or because it chose its course deliberately to destroy Germany, which had staged a remarkable comeback since her defeat in 1918.

The German crisis set in motion an economic chain reaction all over the world. The British were forced to abandon the gold standard on September 21, 1931, almost simultaneously with a mutiny in the Royal Navy and with the start of Japanese aggression in Manchuria. There is no question but that this economic catastrophe was the basic reason for Hitler's accession to power. The French failed to benefit economically and politically from their policy.[11] Within less than nine years they paid the heaviest penalty for their folly: the Nazi conquest of France.[12]

It should be added that the world depression which began in November, 1929, with the New York stock-exchange crash need not have been so grave a dislocation as it turned out to be. Early recovery was possible and upward trends were observed by the end of 1930. The very gravity and duration of the depression resulted from the fact that France had attempted to exploit an economic recession and a financial crisis for her own power-political interests.

Financial sanctions were applied to a limited extent against Italy during the Ethiopian crisis in retaliation for Italy's defiance of the League, but they failed to achieve important results. Nazi Germany forestalled attempts to draw off gold by legislation halting gold and hard currency transfers abroad. With the exception of short-term commercial credits Hitlerite Germany was denied foreign financial assistance. Yet this did not, as it had been hoped, delay German rearmament.

Between 1933 and 1940, the United States pursued an extraordinary policy of gold and silver hoarding, though it did not seek deliberately to corner the world supply of these metals. During that time the gold reserve increased from 2.5 to 17 billion dollars. This policy was largely dictated by domestic political pressures, and the peculiar psychological circumstances of the post-depression era precluded clear recognition of its disastrous international consequences. It is difficult to say whether or not, and to what extent, American gold hoarding aggravated economic difficulties over the world. It had considerable though unforeseen military and political consequences. On the one

[11] Needless to add that the deflationary policy of the German government which contracted credit and inflated the interest rate as the gold was flowing out, and kept up this policy after this efflux had been stopped, contributed its share to the German debacle. See Walter Eucken, *This Unsuccessful Age, Or the Pains of Economic Progress,* London, Hodge, p. 65. For additional details on German conditions, see Ferdinand Friedensburg, *Die Weimarer Republik,* Berlin, Habel, 1946, pp. 298–309.

[12] F. A. Hermens, *Der Staat und die Wirtschaftskrise,* Wien, Österreichischer Wirtschaftsverlag, 1936, pp. 63*f.,* 68–70, 81*f.,* 86, 88, 103*f.;* and E. L. Woodward and Rohan Butler, *Documents on British Foreign Policy 1919–1939,* second series, London, H.M. Stationery Office, 1931, Vol. II, pp. 96, 106, 109, 175, 181, 193*f.*

hand, virtually unlimited purchases of gold by the United States made it possible for Britain and France to buy arms, or rather equipment required for arms manufacture, in the United States for which otherwise they would have had to pay with export commodities. On the other hand, since they feared to deplete their stocks of gold and foreign exchange, England and France chose to pay for their purchases by proceeds from increased exports of goods. Therefore, Britain and France did not in time, that is, in 1937 and 1938, convert their entire economy to war production.

The gold policy of the United States greatly assisted Japan in her war against China. Between 1937 and 1940, the United States bought 640 million dollars' worth of gold from Japan and thus supplied Japan with the exchange required for the purchase of considerable quantities of war material. Without this liberality, Japan would have been much harder put to maintain herself for many years at war.

By contrast, acquisition by the United States of 1 billion dollars' worth of silver originally helped China. Inasmuch as it maintained and increased the price of silver, it prevented a collapse of Chinese currency and for a time preserved China's purchasing power abroad. However, as the silver purchases continued, the metal reserves of Chinese banks became depleted and the Chinese price structure was affected adversely. The Chinese government imposed a tax on silver exports which proved ineffective because of the activities of smugglers. Finally the Chinese government nationalized silver and forced its citizens to exchange their silver holdings for bank notes. In the end, the American silver policy dislocated Chinese foreign trade and weakened China's powers of resistance against Japanese pressure.[13] If the support of Chinese purchasing power had been an objective of American policy, it could have been reached more effectively by other means. Moreover, silver was also bought from Japan. The American gold and silver policy failed to discriminate between potential friends and foes of the United States.[14]

Mere financial techniques, pitted against the complexities of modern economic organization and the intricacies of legislation designed to safeguard the national economy against foreign financial interference, cannot meet the requirement of modern economic warfare. Financial strength and denial of

---

[13] Charles Callan Tansill, *Back Door to War, The Roosevelt Foreign Policy 1933–1941*, Chicago, Regnery, 1952, pp. 149*f*.

[14] Kenneth E. Boulding (*Economic Analysis,* New York, Harper, 1941, p. 344) states that the "monetary policy of the United States belongs perhaps to the realm of economic psychopathology rather than to economic analysis." He calls attention to the fact that the government's gold policy was based on the desire to raise the dollar price of gold which, on statistical "evidence," was supposed to raise all other dollar prices. The statistical evidence was that in the 19th century there had been a connection between the price of gold and the price level. But the conditions in which this correlation had been valid no longer existed. Hence the expected result did not materialize. This is a good illustration for the contention that the study of logic may be of some use. The framers of that policy had overlooked the difference between correlation and causation, and they were unaware of the pitfalls of conclusions by analogy.

such strength to the enemy are still potent levers. But financial power is but one weapon in the arsenal of economic warfare.

One of the simplest, though least savory, practices is forgery. In 1926, Hungarian counterfeiters, probably with the connivance of their government, forged French franc notes and applied the proceeds to the dual purpose of financing the restoration of the Habsburgs and undermining the exchange value of the French currency. The Nazis were great experts in the art of forgery, employing for this purpose experienced engravers whom they held in concentration camps. They used counterfeit money in their secret operations, especially for the payment of spies.[15] The Soviets, too, engaged in the manufacture of foreign bank notes, particularly dollars, and applied the returns to financing the international communist movement in the early twenties.[16]

ECONOMIC PENETRATION

Nations may acquire economic interests in a given country and through economic pressure determine its policy. Such a policy can be most successfully applied against smaller and underdeveloped states. Foreign economic interest thus manipulated the politics of the Near East. But even in a large country foreign-owned firms can exert pressure on the government, as the history of Russia before 1914 and of Germany between 1919 and 1930 shows. For that matter, in the late 19th century British capital was influential in the United States, and prior to the First World War German capital played a minor, though by no means negligible, role in shaping the course of American foreign policy.

British capital in Argentina often oriented the country's policy toward British interests. The economic penetration of Austria, Czechoslovakia, and Hungary by German industrial firms and banks during the 1930's created powerful pro-German factions and prepared the eventual annexation of these countries. The technique is not a new one; the various "charter companies" organized by west European countries in the 17th and 18th centuries initiated the conquests of immense territories in the Orient—the trade preceded the flag.[17] Today, Soviet-controlled "joint stock companies" are instruments of Soviet political domination of Hungary and Rumania.

Investments in foreign countries play a great role in the use of economics as a weapon. These investments serve subversive, political, financial, techno-

[15] The valet of the British Ambassador to Turkey, who sold Allied war secrets to the Germans, was paid 300,000 pound sterling in counterfeit money. See L. C. Moyzisch, *L'Affaire Cicéron,* Paris, Juillard, 1950, p. 249.

[16] See Walter G. Krivitzki, *In Stalin's Secret Service,* New York, Harper, 1939, pp. 116ff.

[17] The personnel of such charter companies was often trained by economists of the highest achievement. Malthus, for example, taught the cadets of the East India Company for more than thirty years; see James Bonar, "The Malthusiad: Fantasia Economia," in *Economic Essays: Contributed in Honor of John Bates Clark,* edited by Jacob H. Hollander, New York, Macmillan, 1927, p. 237.

logical, and industrial purposes. Foreign investments can be made openly in the name of the true owner, whose nationality would be admitted, or ownership can be camouflaged. For example, a German firm may own openly a firm in the United States, or it may possess a large amount of stock in an American firm. If open ownership is not advisable, the German firm may set up a holding company which ostensibly is of Swiss nationality, as did the I.G. Farben when it founded the so-called I.G. Chemie Basel. This company took over all the foreign investments of the German I.G. Farben which, in turn, did *not* "own" even one share of I.G. Chemie Basel.[18] Control was maintained through private and personal commitments. Or again a German firm would send a few associates to the United States where they would found a company, in due time become American citizens, and thus end up with an "American" business enterprise. Or finally, a German firm would finance American friends to establish themselves in business without ever assuming legal title to the property.

Foreign investments can be exploited for subversive purposes and may serve the attainment of three objectives: (1) propaganda which would be paid for by the proceeds from the investment; (2) espionage which, among other methods, could be accomplished through the firms obtaining classified orders; and (3) economic sabotage which could take various forms, including slowdowns of output, stimulation of strikes, defective production, etc.[19]

The political purpose of foreign investment is to exert influence on the host country's political orientation. Foreign investments can be used to influence a country's monetary and credit policies, while in addition, financial holdings abroad can be exploited to help the mother country financially. Investments abroad allow insights into foreign production techniques and are therefore an essential condition of technological progress. Finally, foreign investments secure needed imports, for example, through ownership of mineral deposits abroad (Britain's ownership of foreign oil fields), or through control of commercial and transportation facilities. Such ownership or control makes it unnecessary to yield the profits of international trade to foreign nationals, while at the same time it reduces the risk that the desired commodities, because of political machinations, may not be for sale.

Foreign investments can take various forms, although under modern conditions investments usually are in the form of outright ownership or possession of a controlling block of securities. Traditionally, various nations specialized in different types of foreign investments. The Germans participated in practically all chemical and pharmaceutical industries the world over. The communists often go into the publishing, real-estate, insurance, and entertainment businesses, which are most suitable for their subversive operations.

---

[18] Hearings . . . Munitions Industry, part 12, p. 2888.
[19] For examples, see Yuan-li Wu, *Economic Warfare,* New York, Prentice-Hall, 1952, pp. 166*f.*

The French have extensive banking connections, while the British, in addition to banking, specialize in transportation. The United States, with a private and government investment abroad of 37 billion dollars (1952), participates in many foreign automobile industries, in airlines, oil, consumer goods (Coca-Cola), agricultural machinery, fibers, electrical and office machinery, electric-power generation, and also pays great attention to the mining industries.

Geographically, foreign investments often are concentrated in one particular region. During the 19th century France specialized in the eastern Mediterranean and Russia; while Germany invested heavily in Latin America. To this date Sweden has retained a particular interest in Abyssinia, and Denmark in Thailand and in the Virgin Islands. By contrast, British, Dutch, Swiss, and American investments are strung out over many areas.

Many countries could not maintain their living standards except by means of foreign investments. This is particularly true of some small nations such as Switzerland, Belgium, and Holland who derive a large income from their investments abroad (for example, Holland's foreign oil and electronics enterprises), and who specialize in foreign business which they transact for other nations. Britain is the classical case of a large country which can continue as a great power only by virtue of its foreign investments. From the strictly military point of view, foreign investments helped, for example, the Germans during 1919 and 1932 when they were able to carry out secret armaments in German-owned or German-controlled firms in Sweden, Finland, Holland, and Spain,[20] and when, through their international connections, they were able to secure the training of German technicians in the British and American aircraft industries. The military significance of British foreign oil holdings does not need to be elaborated; not only did British ownership or control of large oil firms such as Shell secure for them all the fuel they needed, but they also were able to prevent Germany from obtaining some of the fuel the Nazis wanted to buy. In any event, the German navy in 1940 blamed Shell for its lack of fuel reserves.[21]

It has been reported that in the United States the largest optical firm—which, for all practical purposes, held a monopoly in that field—was controlled by the German firm of Zeiss. After the outbreak of the war in 1939, when France and England sought to place with the American corporation highly important and urgent military orders, these orders were turned down through German influence. Even the United States government had difficulties in placing its orders, until it resorted, on its part, to the exercise of pressure.[22]

[20] See *Trials of War Criminals before the Nürnberg Military Tribunals,* Vol. IX, "The Krupp Case," Government Printing Office, 1950, pp. 240–348.

[21] See *Führer Conferences,* 1940, Washington, 1947, Vol. I, p. 30.

[22] Joseph Borkin and Charles A. Welsh, *Germany's Master Plan: The Story of Industrial Offensive,* New York, Duell, Sloan & Pearce, 1943, pp. 286*f.* See also Wendell Berge, *Cartels: Challenge to a Free World,* Washington, Public Affairs Press, 1944, pp. 142*ff.*

In other cases, firms were founded in foreign countries in order to take out and thus control patents as a means not of starting production but of *preventing* another country from manufacturing a given product. This was the stratagem employed by the Germans to delay the production of magnesium [23] and plastics outside of Germany. Sometimes it is not even necessary to found a special firm for this purpose; it is enough to take out a patent and to reveal little, or give out misinformation, about the production process so that the patent is unusable. This technique was frequently employed by the German chemical industry before the First World War.

CARTELS AND MONOPOLIES

Perhaps no topic of international economics is as important and as hotly debated by the experts as is the question of international cartels. Very little is known about their actual operations and in particular about their connections with individual governments. In most cases it is probably safe to say that cartels operate in order to maximize profits. Yet sometimes their activities appear to further deliberately the political objectives of governments. In other cases, governments take political advantage of the economic situation created by the cartels.

Statistically speaking, there were in 1939 somewhat less than 200 international cartels, with about one-third of international trade under some form of marketing control. About 75 per cent of these cartels provided for the division of international markets, while 44 per cent provided for licensing and mutual use of patents.[24]

There are two characteristics of cartels which are of great military and political consequence. First, firms which are members of an international cartel usually pool their patents and inform each other of technical procedures. Therefore firms participating in international cartels can procure intelligence about the economic, technological, and military preparations of foreign countries. For example, I.G. Farben supplied the German *Wehrmacht* with information about British chemical factories.[25]

Second, cartel agreements entail the reduction of output in various areas and sometimes lead to the discontinuance of production. A country which is the base of an international cartel can thus acquire important patents and, at the same time, inhibit the production of military matériel in hostile countries. While such a procedure may be somewhat difficult to apply in democratic countries, it has been used effectively by countries operating under dictatorial controls. The Nazis succeeded in deriving great technical advan-

---

[23] In 1940 the United States produced only 30 per cent of the total of the German magnesium output. See Wu, *op. cit.*, p. 556.

[24] *Ibid.*, p. 172. The number of national cartels is far greater. In Germany it rose from 385 in 1905 to about 2,500 in 1925.

[25] See *Trials of War Criminals before the Military Tribunals,* Government Printing Office, 1953, Vol. VII, "The Farben Case," pp. 676ff.

tages from various German-controlled cartels; when it was their turn to live up to agreements entered into by these cartels with foreign firms, they hid behind the excuse of officially imposed restrictions and *ad hoc* legislation. In this fashion, they obtained foreign patents but refused to disclose their own by the simple device of classifying them as military secrets. They also insisted upon limitations of output, but themselves produced as much as they chose, sometimes by keeping the production secret, sometimes by paying the penalties prescribed in the cartel agreement. Generally speaking, the Germans were most successful in this tactic with respect to the production of aluminum, the output of which they were able to curtail in the Western countries.[26] Maximizing their own production, they gained a very considerable advantage in aircraft production. Similarly they gained a head start in the manufacture of medical drugs.

Perhaps one of the most interesting episodes in the international competition for supremacy in the technological field prior to and during the First World War was the capture by Germany of the lead in the manufacture of dyes. The German chemical industry took advantage of the invention of the Englishman Perkin who showed how coal tars could be transformed into aniline dyes, and whose discoveries were not put to use by his countrymen. The German chemical industry had grown by leaps and bounds during the last third of the 19th century. Soon the world market for dye and derivative products was virtually under German control. The growth of competitive chemical industries abroad was deliberately stifled by patent manipulation, price cutting, cartel output agreements, buying up of installations, refusal of delivery of intermediate products, and similar practices.[27] While chemical factories were built in the United States, Britain, and France, the Germans either gained partial control or diverted them to the production of finished goods so that they were dependent on German imports for their requirements of so-called "intermediates" or semifinished products, sold to them at very high prices.

Late in the fall of 1913 the German chemist Fritz Haber informed the German general staff that it was possible to produce *synthetic* ammonia and that a plant for this purpose had been made ready at Oppau. Hence, Germany no longer was vulnerable to an English naval blockade which would cut her off from Chile saltpeter, then the basic raw material for the production of explosives. There is little doubt that this information played a great role in Germany's decision to go to war in 1914.[28]

When the First World War broke out, the German chemical industry was vastly superior to any other. This superiority was one of the main factors in

[26] A somewhat different view is taken by Louis Marlio, *The Aluminum Cartel*, Washington, Brookings, 1947, pp. 95*ff.*; see also Erwin Hexner, *International Cartels*, Chapel Hill, The University of North Carolina Press, 1946, pp. 133*ff.*; also Berge, *op. cit.*, p. 222.
[27] Victor Lefebure, *The Riddle of the Rhine: Chemical Strategy in Peace and War*, New York, Chemical Foundation, 1923, Preface and Introduction by Marshals Foch and Wilson, p. 146; see also Hearings . . . Munitions Industry, part 11, pp. 2560*ff.*
[28] Hearings . . . Munitions Industry, part 11, p. 2564.

Germany's resistance for more than four years against the combined on-slaught of the Western nations and Russia. The chemical industry supplied the Germans with substitutes for many goods which were denied them by the naval blockade, and explosives in larger quantities than those available to their enemies, thus retaining for Germany a decided military advantage al-most up to 1918. Last but not least, chemical superiority permitted Germany to resort to chemical warfare (poison or toxic gases and flame throwers) with little fear of effective retaliation. German military experts believed that, with-out gas production, Germany would not have been able to resist the Allies so long and so effectively. In point of fact, the Germans remained in the lead not only quantitatively but also qualitatively, inasmuch as they managed to introduce new types of gases, repeatedly taking the Allies by surprise.

While the connection between war potential and such industries as the chemical industry becomes painfully clear on the battlefield, economic and industrial strength endow a country also with vast capabilities in the field of the "Cold War" or in any other attempt to obtain the fruits of war without fighting. A German chemist, who during the First World War engaged suc-cessfully in preemptive buying of explosives in the United States, confided his conclusions in a treatise entitled *The Chemists' War*.[29] He wrote:

The farmers who cultivated the madder root and the planters who raised indigo were first inclined to jest when they were apprised of the fact that German chemists had succeeded in reproducing in the laboratories the dyes which their crops fur-nished. But when the manufactured materials drove the natural products from the markets and left the farmers and planters without a job, they did not view their plight with hilarity.

But even more important would be the development of a chemical fertilizer which would be in great demand everywhere as a boost to agricultural pro-duction.

What an enormous power will be exercised by a nation possessing such a universal fertilizer and practically world-wide monopoly of potash salts! It will have some-thing to sell that every farmer in the civilized world cannot do without.

It does not require much imagination to see that the possession of such monopolies would endow a nation with controlling power over a large part of the globe. It is a significant fact that Karl von Krauch, top executive of the I.G. Farben, the German dye trust, became not only a top planner of Ger-man economy during the period when Hitler openly prepared for war and, later, of the economic integration of Nazi-occupied Europe, but also head of the office of economic development which directed research and development.[30] The German chemical industry exploited its technological superiority for

[29] See Borkin and Welsh, *op. cit.*, p. 70. See also Lefebure, *op. cit.*, pp. 199ff.

[30] On Karl von Krauch and the governmentlike organization of the I.G. Farben, see Delbert Clark, "The Fabulous Farben Empire Faces Trial," in *The New York Times Maga-zine*, Aug. 10, 1947, p. 12. See also Howard W. Ambruster, *Treason's Peace: German Dyes and American Dyes*, New York, Beechhurst, 1947.

military purposes. This superiority was not entirely due to the excellent organization of and the large investments in chemical research and development; it was achieved in part by a ruthless cartel policy.

Many other industries would lend themselves to a similar exploitation for power purposes. International cable lines were exploited during the early part of the 20th century with telling effect by the British.[31] In a period where victory or defeat may be dependent upon the quality of electronic instruments, the electronics industry undoubtedly could play a key role. The same is true of aircraft and missile engines and, last but not least, of the atomic industry which, once it were developed for use of atomic energy in transportation, electric power, and possibly agriculture and medicine, could accomplish far more than even the chemical industry, assuming that its potentialities were to be applied according to the principles of *The Chemists' War*. A hypothetical future monopolistic owner of artificial photosynthesis would wield extraordinary power, especially in a period of food shortages and increasing agricultural prices.

It would be an error to assume that what could be called "monopoly pressure" can be exerted only in the economic field. A technological monopoly, sole possession of one or more instruments or inventions, may provide virtually irresistible political and military power. The Turks defeated dozens of culturally more advanced nations because they possessed a near monopoly in the form of heavy artillery. In a similar way, Britain, France, Germany, and Belgium conquered in the 19th century a territory of 7.5 million square miles, with small forces and at small cost, although up to that time colonial wars had been almost as difficult as other wars and although the natives showed themselves frequently to be superior fighters. The simple explanation behind that feat of imperialism was that at that time the Western troops were in possession of the breech-loading rifle.[32]

The invention of airpower and nuclear explosives, and to a certain extent of submarines, rendered all nations not equipped with these weapons powerless. Whether intercontinental guided missiles will confer a military monopoly on their first user only the future can tell.

EXPLOITATION OF STRATEGIC ECONOMIC POSITION

Economic power based on the seller's or the buyer's monopoly (monopsony) wields great and, at times, decisive political influence. The War between the

[31] For example, in October, 1935, the British postal authorities refused "to relay through the radio-telephonic circuit between London and New York a speech made by Baron Aloisi at Geneva." Aloisi was the Italian delegate to the League of Nations arguing against British policy. This refusal was in contrast with treaty obligations. See Tansill, *op. cit.*, p. 230.

[32] See J. F. C. Fuller, *Armament and History: A Study of the Influence of Armament on History from the Dawn of Classical Warfare to the Second World War*, New York, Scribner, 1945, p. 119.

States deprived the world of most of its cotton supply, an event which both belligerents exploited to gain military and diplomatic advantages; if the North had not deprived the South of its export outlet, it might have lost the war. In 1905, the Austrians waged a "pig war" against Serbia.[33] Pigs were that little country's most important article of exportation, and Austria was practically its only customer. Since political relations between the two states were strained, the Austrian government hit upon the heroic device of stopping the importation of Serbian pigs. This measure was intended to create such economic dislocation in Serbia that the stricken country would be ultimately compelled to comply with Austrian demands. The Serbs, disappointing Austrian expectations, succeeded in reorienting their exports. Serbia, however, had suffered great economic damage, a circumstance which contributed to the radicalization of Serbian domestic politics and, indirectly, by aggravating Austro-Serbian antagonism, to the outbreak of the First World War.

Under modern conditions, rice-exporting countries like Burma and Thailand could exert considerable pressure on India or Japan, since both of the latter countries are heavily dependent on the importation of rice. Similarly, Russia has used her dominant position in manganese to obtain advantages from the United States. Improper use by Malaya of its tin resources could have vast repercussions on the preservation of food and thus affect practically the entire world.

In 1667, the French statesman Colbert invented the powerful weapon of "tariff war" and instituted a tariff rate which prohibited imports of manufactured goods from Holland. With the end of the age of mercantilism, tariff wars fell into oblivion. But by the end of the 19th century they had again become fashionable; France waged tariff wars against Italy and Spain, and Germany and Russia engaged in a particularly fierce one between 1893 and 1894.[34] Another example is the tariff war in 1932–1936 between Ireland and Britain, which broke out after the Irish stopped making payments to which, in British opinion, they had obligated themselves. The Irish suffered considerable economic loss; the conflict was finally settled, though not without having given rise to animosity on both sides.

The enactment by the United States of the Smoot-Hawley tariff act under President Hoover was not an act of economic warfare. It was designed to revive America's economy by reducing unemployment. This purpose was not achieved. On the contrary, many Americans who had made investments in foreign countries suffered loss; the disruption of international trade aggravated the world depression. Hence, regardless of its purpose, the Smoot-Hawley act was tantamount to economic warfare waged by the United States against nations of Europe. In a petition which more than 1,000 American economists submitted to Congress and to the President and which implored

[33] See Sidney Bradshaw Fay, *The Origins of the World War*, 2d ed., New York, Macmillan, 1931, Vol. I, p. 359.

[34] Herbert Heaton, *Economic History of Europe*, New York, Harper, 1936, pp. 389, 677.

the government not to enact the tariff law, we read the following prophetic words: "The higher duties proposed in our pending legislation . . . plainly invite other nations to compete with us in raising further barriers to trade. A tariff war does not furnish good soil for the growth of world peace."

Sometimes governments conclude what amounts to cartel agreements in order to assure the "just" distribution of a given product yet at the same time restrict output in order to maintain prices. Similar restrictive agreements were, for example, concluded by the main wheat-producing nations with respect to that grain. They are designed to promote the welfare of vested-interest groups and serve purposes largely of domestic politics. Their results in the international field are far-reaching, since such agreements place in the hands of the "have" nations important levers of control over other peoples. Moreover, by restricting total output, the supply for poorer countries remains limited.

Modern international life has been characterized by the employment of many discriminatory devices such as price fixing, dumping, quotas, exchange controls, and export and import taxes, which in their combined effect on international trade are far more serious than conventional tariffs. These devices usually are adopted to protect the national economy against dislocations and more particularly against unemployment. They rarely are conceived as measures of economic warfare, *i.e.*, their primary purpose is not to hurt the other nation but to protect one's own people. Nevertheless, these measures weaken the powers of resistance of foreign nations, especially of those nations which are dependent on foreign trade, and they always can be used to exact political concessions from a foreign nation.

An illustrative example of monopolistic practice may be found in the case of quinine. This drug was discovered by the Incas and then distilled on the plantations of the Jesuit order. The order distributed the drug free to the poor, but took its weight in gold from the rich. Since demand far surpassed supply, the quina tree slowly disappeared in South America. The trade in this valuable drug was taken over by the Dutch Quinine Syndicate which improved the tree, preserved various secrets of quina botany, including how to peel the bark without killing the tree, and maintained a tight monopoly from 1865 to World War II. Before 1941 there was one closely guarded plantation in Java which, with its 37,500 acres, supplied 95 per cent of the world's quinine. The policy of this syndicate was to ration out the small amount of quinine produced, and in case of a production larger than the total quotas, to store the bark or burn it. Moreover, the price was maintained at an excessively high level. As a result, no help could be brought to tens of millions of native malaria sufferers. Though this policy may have eased the "white man's burden," it was uneconomic as well as immoral, since it impeded production of wealth in the malaria-ridden countries.[35]

---

[35] See Borkin and Welsh, *op. cit.*, p. 171. For other cases in the fields of medicines, synthetic hormones, and vitamins, see Berge, *op. cit.*, pp. *52ff.*

BOYCOTT

In modern practice, *boycott* means the refusal to buy commodities offered by a state or group against which pressure is to be applied. Boycott practiced domestically against the government assumes usually the form of refusal to pay taxes.[36]

The Irish, from whom the term *boycott* is derived, during the 19th century applied that device of economic warfare with telling effect against the British landholders. In the 20th century, the Indians boycotted British goods, notably textiles, and although they harmed themselves in the process, contributed to the emergence of the "depressed areas" in Britain. The United States and Britain, responding to the anti-Semitic bias of the Nazi government and their policy of boycotting Jewish firms in Germany, made half-hearted attempts to boycott German trade in the international market. The effects on German trade were slight. But the Germans became alive to the danger of a "cold blockade." They concluded a number of bilateral trade agreements which made their export outlets as well as their lines of import virtually unassailable by private boycott initiatives.

By selling German marks to foreign travelers at 40 per cent of their value, to cite only one of the Nazi antiboycott measures, the Germans attracted great numbers of travelers who at a higher cost of tourism would have "boycotted" Germany. In this fashion, Hitler obtained large amounts of international currency and incidentally subjected many foreign tourists to effective Nazi propaganda. The same device was employed by Italy.

Boycotts of Soviet and Japanese goods were overcome by both countries through the device of "dumping," *i.e.*, selling export articles at a price much lower than the cost price, the deficit being covered by the government. Dumping not only harmed competitive industries in the Western countries, but also provided Japan and Russia with international currency which was used for the strengthening of their war potential. The Germans, incidentally, invented the most grotesque type of dumping; they sold at a "loss" vast quantities of mouth organs, aspirin tablets, and cameras, and persuaded many nations, particularly those of eastern Europe, to buy these articles in exchange for vital raw materials. The success of these strange operations was partly due to the attraction of the German market with its 70 million consumers, partly to the then prevailing glut of world commodity markets, and partly to German political pressure.

[36] See Robert Michels, *Le Boycottage international: boycottage économique et crises politiques,* Paris, Payot, 1936; see also David Henry Thoreau, "Civil Disobedience," in *Anti-slavery and Reform Papers,* edited by H. D. Salt, London, 1890.

ECONOMIC WARFARE

Economic warfare is an integral part of war. In one way or another, it has been waged at all times and in all climes. Many wars serve predominantly economic purposes. The nomads must conquer territory to live. In a society based on slave labor, the supply of the labor force must be maintained by war. The time-honored strategy of the attack upon the enemy's supplies and food reserves, destruction of crops, stealing or killing of cattle, plunder, and pillage—all these thrusts against the fabric of a people's wealth are economic warfare.

Economic motives are among the most potent causes of war. To give a lesser known but highly illustrative example, a memorandum written by an unknown French official in 1747 explains why British control of America would make Britain unconquerable, since America would furnish Britain gold and silver as well as trading outlets and thus the material resources required for the construction of a large navy. The memorandum concludes: "The balance of money in the hands of the British entails the balance of power. They would be the masters of the sea through their navy, and the masters of the land through their wealth. They would draw the means from America to dictate the law to Europe." Sainte-Croix, 18th-century historian of the British navy, explained the reason why the logic of the situation compelled France to support American independence: [37]

If she were to possess an immense and fertile country whose population doubles every twenty years, what high degree of power would England reach? What counterweight of force would be necessary to oppose against her? Was not the independence of the universe menaced? By taking the side of the Anglo-Americans, France helped general welfare as well as her own safety.

Blockade and Contraband. In modern times, the most telling weapon of economic warfare is naval blockade, *i.e.*, the halting of a country's maritime imports and exports of vital commodities. The purpose of naval blockade was defined as early as 1601 by Queen Elizabeth. Seizing upon Spain's dependence on overseas trade, she said: "The stopping, hindrance and impeading of all commerce and traffick with him [Philip II] in his territories of Spain and Portugal will quickly in likelihood give an end to these bloodie unnatural warres which disturb the generall peace and quiet of all these parts of Christendome." [38]

Napoleon centered his strategy against Britain largely in blockade of British exports to western Europe. This blockade served to develop French industry against British competition. Napoleon imposed the "Continental blockade," that is, he interdicted all European coasts to British trade. Though

[37] Quoted from Jouvenel, *op. cit.*, pp. 22–23.
[38] David L. Gordon and Royden Dangerfield, *The Hidden Weapon: The Story of Economic Warfare*, New York, Harper, 1947, p. 1.

never fully effective, that policy could be enforced as long as Russia adhered to it. The decisiveness of Britain's ultimate victory over Napoleon tends to obscure the fact that she had come perilously close to economic collapse.

Fortunately for Britain, difficulties soon plagued Napoleon's ambitious scheme. European economies were dependent on colonial and industrial supplies. French industry (including the industries controlled by France, like those of Holland and Saxony) could not provide for the needs of all of Europe. After a while, the industries themselves suffered from shortages of raw materials. Many factories were shut down. Consequently, the smuggling of British and colonial commodities assumed such proportions that Napoleon abandoned, though tacitly, the Continental blockade. Blocking British exports meant blocking French imports—and practical experience taught Napoleon the fallacy of the mercantilist school according to which imports were nefarious and wasteful.

In the council of July 17, 1810, Napoleon adopted an entirely new policy, although he still pretended that the Continental blockade remained in force. Napoleon's ingenious argument can be summed up as follows: it is absurd that the French consumer and industrialist should pay three times more than the market value for goods which must be bought from overseas. This enormous profit goes into the pockets of smugglers and merchants. It is time, Napoleon concluded, to open French ports for indispensable commodities. Since the people have been accustomed to paying high prices, they will continue to do so, with the difference that the profit will no longer be garnered by smugglers but will henceforth be collected by the French government, to be applied to the expansion of the French navy. Hitler and Schacht invented nothing new!

Napoleon's new policy revolved on a tacit agreement with the enemy, Britain, to deliver goods to France. In actual fact, profit was to be shared by both countries to the detriment of the rest of Europe. Supplies to Europe as well as their prices would henceforth be controlled from Paris and London. In other words, Napoleon had abandoned the idea of ruining British trade and substituted for it the exploitation of Europe.

This policy could not fail to rally Europe against him. The imposition of economic hardship is a sure way to lose allies. When, in 1811, he requested Russia to confiscate every ship carrying colonial goods under whatever flag, hostile or neutral, Russia balked. Actually, Napoleon attempted to prevent Russia from engaging with Britain in that very commerce from which he derived lucrative profits for France. In reply to Napoleon's insolent demands Russia opened, in December, 1811, her ports to *all* ships.

Thus, war between France and Russia became inevitable. It culminated in the coalition of practically all European states against Napoleon. Had Napoleon been as good an economist as he was a military strategist, he would never have been defeated. It need hardly be pointed out that both Hitler and

Stalin faced economic problems of conquest similar to those which doomed Napoleon.

Modern Naval Blockade. During the First World War the naval blockade of Britain against the Central Powers caused decisive shortages in oil and foodstuffs.[39] German strategy during the Second World War, adapted to the lessons of the first, was directed at defeating the naval blockade which Britain again, by automatic reflex as it were, imposed upon her adversary. The pursuit of that objective forced Germany to adopt an economy of substitutes and stockpiles, led to expansion into the Balkans and Scandinavia, and finally to German attack on Russia.

Naval blockade involves a highly complicated technique and a nice sense of discrimination between essentials and nonessentials. It is impractical to throw a line of ships around the blockaded country, seeking thereby to prevent the passage of every ship. Blockade runners will often break through the blockading patrols. Neutral states must be permitted a minimum of trade. A continental country always has access to supplies via land routes. None can be completely blockaded from the sea. Naval blockade must, therefore, be supplemented by measures designed to prohibit the reexport from neutral countries of sea-borne supplies, and to reduce the sales to the enemy of commodities originating in adjacent neutral states.

In the 19th century a distinction was evolved between absolute and conditional contraband. The distinction was not always clear, but in 1909 an international agreement on the meaning of the term was reached: absolute contraband consisted of every type of *war* material, while conditional contraband comprised goods needed for the civilian population but which, under certain conditions, could be used for military purposes; if there was evidence of such a use, they could be confiscated. During the subsequent wars, which were contests between the industrial capacities of the belligerents, this separation lost its validity, simply because virtually every important commodity must now be used for war production. The distinction was all but abandoned during the Second World War.

It made its reappearance during the Korean War when most trading nations, with Britain in front, sold to China commodities which allegedly were not of military significance. During the Cold War in Europe East-West trade in "civilian" goods also was continued without letup. These trading arrangements were criticized widely because, in modern times, there are barely any commodities which directly or indirectly cannot be put to military use or be used to enhance a nation's warmaking capacity. Undoubtedly, medicines and low-octane gasoline shipped to China were not unwelcome to the Chinese armies fighting in Korea against the very nations which traded with them.

In its most pronounced form, the economic weapon can be used against the basic needs of peoples. Naval blockade usually reduces the food supply

[39] See M. W. W. P. Consett, *The Triumph of Unarmed Forces 1914–1918*, London, Williams & Norgate, 1923.

of a blockaded area. The Germans did not make great efforts to improve the diet of the population in the occupied territories because ill-fed men are politically less dangerous than well-fed persons, who enjoy great nervous energy. By contrast, the United Nations (UNRRA) used food to accelerate the reestablishment of devastated areas. The donation of food is an old tradition of the United States which has usually enlisted the good will of other nations and greatly strengthened American prestige in the world.

The Covenant of the League of Nations contained provisions for countering aggression by economic sanctions, *i.e.*, by denial of exports to an aggressive country. Sanctions can also be applied according to the United Nations Charter. Economic sanctions, decreed by the League, were applied against Italy in 1935 in retaliation for Italy's attack on Ethiopia. These sanctions hampered Italy but little since the most important commodities, such as oil, were not placed under embargo.[40] It is doubtful whether sanctions *without war* can ever be effective, except when applied to weak countries which depend for a large part of their income on foreign trade.

It should be remembered that economic sanctions often have been acclaimed as a method of punishing the aggressor and even as a means of preventing war. In pure *theory*, economic sanctions, *i.e.*, the blockade on land and sea of a country in peacetime, must have dislocating effects on its economy. The cutting off of all exports and imports must lead to a catastrophic decline in consumption and production. In *practice*, however, many countries will refuse to participate in the sanctions, as Germany, Austria, Hungary, Japan, and, to a lesser extent, Russia and the United States did in the case of the Italian conflict. Hence Italy was able to import whatever she needed. To make sanctions complete and effective, they would have to be supplemented by embargoes on trade with third nations. This measure, since it would produce dangerous crises, must be considered as impractical. It also would be useless because the greater the area, the less the economic effects of sanctions. Even if *all* nations participated in sanctions, their effect would be slow, especially if the country against which they were applied were less vulnerable to economic pressure than Italy. However, upon being confronted by a threat of this kind, the offending country may resort to arms, particularly if the nations imposing the sanctions are militarily unprepared. It therefore would be necessary to cool that nation's military ardor by maintaining superior military power. But if the peace-loving nations are militarily stronger than the aggressor and are resolved to use their power whenever the aggressor moves, peace can be preserved in any event, and sanctions are superfluous.

To return to the naval blockade in the proper sense: [41] at the end of World War I, a device was introduced which was to be widely used during World

[40] Herbert Feis, *Seen from E. A.*, New York, Knopf, 1947, pp. 193–308.

[41] Tansill, *op. cit.*, pp. 165–261, gives an exhaustive history of the comedy of errors and deceit which from 1935 to 1936 under British leadership revolved around "sanctions" against Italy.

War II, the so-called "navicert," or navigational certificate. This document entitled a nonenemy ship to carry its cargo to a neutral country. No ship that failed to obtain a navicert was permitted to proceed. World-wide intelligence systems were employed to report immediately the departure of any ship from any port and as to whether or not it had taken out a certificate. Though provided with a navicert, ships were liable to search. As time went by, ships were compelled to stop at designated Allied ports before they were permitted to continue through blockaded areas. Extensive mine fields made it imperative to take pilots on board and thus precluded evasion from control.

Issuance of navicerts was made contingent upon investigation as to whether the individual recipients of permissible goods were bona fide users. If the recipients were found to be firms owned or controlled by enemy nationals, they were denied the navicert. Such firms were then "blacklisted."

Trade connections under this elaborate system were maintained only with countries which assumed the obligation of halting reexports and, in general, reducing the level of their exports to the enemy countries. For example, supplies were permitted to reach Sweden and Switzerland on condition that these countries reduce the exportation of goods vitally needed by Germany. Switzerland was limited in its exports of electric power to Germany. Since both Sweden and Switzerland were dependent on German coal and since Germany on her part exploited this dependency for her own purposes, trade between these states and the Axis could not be stopped entirely by the navicert technique.

Preemption. Hand in hand with rationing went "preemption." [42] This euphemistic term means simply the purchase of a goods produced in a neutral country in order to forestall its delivery into hostile hands, lest it increase the enemy's war potential. Country A prevents country B from buying a product by buying itself that product regardless of price and regardless of whether it can be put to use or not. During the First World War the Germans bought several chemicals in the United States which the Allies were trying to secure for the production of explosives and gases. When preemption proved impossible, German agents resorted to sabotage as, for example, in the famous Black Tom case when they blew up ammunition ships lying in New York Harbor.

During the Second World War, the Iberian Peninsula was the principal theater of preemptive warfare; the bone of contention was the mineral wealth of Spain and Portugal. Copper and iron mines were largely in British possession, and therefore no great difficulty was encountered by the Allies in repelling German buyers of these metals—a good example of the military importance of capital holdings abroad. Yet the wolframite (tungsten) mines in Spain and Portugal were not owned by Allied nationals; some of them were actually in German hands. The flow of wolframite extracted from these

[42] See Geoffrey Crowther, *Ways and Means of War*, New York, Oxford, 1940, p. 58. See also Wu, *op. cit.*, pp. 83*ff.*

mines to Germany was not altogether halted, though the control exercised through navicert reduced it. The Allies acquired some mines. Nevertheless, it became necessary to buy the output of the remaining mines. As the Allies bought the ores, prices rose disproportionately. The total cost of the operation ultimately reached fantastically high figures. Nevertheless, the Germans were deprived of great quantities of this vitally needed alloy and forced to reduce drastically the production of tungsten steel, thus lowering the quality of their ammunition. Similar operations were carried out with Turkish chromium and, at the beginning of the war, with Yugoslav copper and bauxite. In the case of Swedish ball bearings an entire yearly output of the principal factories was bought and purchases of future output guaranteed.

The method of preemption also can be employed effectively in the field of technology. For this purpose patent laws can be used. For example, the exploitation, though not the purchase, of a patent can be denied to foreign nationals. The Soviet for many years systematically acquired knowledge about patents issued in industrialized countries, but they denied similar information about their own patents to foreign nationals and, in fact, have failed to publish any information about Russian inventions.[43]

Even during the war, however, economic relations with the enemy do not cease altogether.[44] There are sometimes joint properties in neutral countries which must be jointly administered, and exchanges continue in the twilight zone of officially sanctioned "illicit" trade precisely in order to support the war effort. During the First World War, this trade allegedly extended to goods like barbed wire and ammunition parts. During the Second World War, in 1939, the French are said to have covered part of their coal deficit by shipping iron ore through Belgian intermediaries to Germany, receiving German coal in return. Tools were repeatedly traded by the same route. Trading across the lines was a standard practice in China, for had the Chinese not sold rice to the Japanese, the latter would have taken the rice-growing area as well as *all* the rice. In addition, this trade improved China's financial position and aided Allied intelligence in the gathering of information.

[43] On German methods in this area see *Trials of War Criminals before the Military Tribunals,* Vol. VII, "The Farben Case," pp. 1273–1295. See particularly Farben memorandum of January 25, 1940 (*i.e.,* after the outbreak of World War II), which reads: "There are agreements and arrangements between the German production companies (I.G. Farbenindustrie A.G. and Ruhrchemie) and the large oil companies such as Standard Oil, Shell, et cetera, with regard to mineral oil. Among other things, these agreements provide for the exchange of know-how with regard to mineral oil between the parties to the contract. This exchange of know-how, which is still being handled in the usual way by the neutral countries abroad even now and which is transmitted to us via Holland and Italy, first gives us an insight into the development work and production plans of the companies and/or their respective countries, and at the same time informs us about the progress of technical developments with regard to oil. . . . Up to now, we have carried out this exchange in such a way that from our side we have only sent reports . . . which contained only such technical data as concerned facts which are known or out of date according to the latest developments."

[44] On the continued trade between the belligerents, see Lehmann-Russbuelt, *Die blutige Internationale der Rüstungsindustrie,* Berlin, Fackelreiter-Verlag, 1933, pp 31*ff.*

A belligerent government usually grants permission for "trading across the lines" on the basis of national interest, although private commercial interests have not infrequently influenced the official policy. The questions which must be answered are, does the proposed "illicit" trade benefit one's own side more than the opponent's, and can these benefits not be obtained by other means? The problem can be illustrated best by the example of East-West trade during the late forties. In general, the Western powers were anxious to cut trade with the Soviet orbit and thus to prevent the Russians from increasing their economic war potential. However, France was compelled to import coal from Poland; there was no other coal available to France at that time. Without Polish coal France would not have freed herself from the vicious circle of a shortage of steel induced by a shortage of coal and a shortage of coal induced by a shortage of steel. Thus coal imports from Poland were the prerequisite for French recovery. In compensation for coal imports France had to sell those commodities which the Soviet orbit needed most. Not all of the West's exports to the Soviets served merely to cope with emergency situations arising from wartime dislocations. A large part of trade with the Soviets as, for example, the sale of jet aero engines, natural rubber, and chemicals, could be justified by no other consideration than profit. These commodities could have been sold elsewhere—though perhaps not quite so profitably. Hence these sales furthered Soviet interests far more than those of the West.

Another kind of "preemption" consists of restriction on personal movement; a government prevents a scientist or technician from going abroad and thus from selling his invention to foreign interests. This is a time-honored device. It was used during the early part of the Industrial Revolution, when investors and artisans were sometimes threatened with the penalty of death if they were to sell their inventions to foreign governments or go abroad.[45] In 1913, the German inventor Rudolf Diesel sailed for England to sell his patents there; inexplicably he vanished during the crossing. The Russian atomic scientist Peter Kapitza, who had been living in England, paid a visit to Russia but was not allowed to return.

When preemption fails, the last resort is recourse to military means. For example, the Allies in April, 1940, tried to block the "iron route" from Narvik to Germany by the laying of mine fields. Conversely, one of the motives which prompted the French to build the Maginot Line was to protect the iron mines in Lorraine and prevent their early seizure by Germany.

Stockpiling. To defend themselves against blockade and preemptive buying, nations often resort to the stockpiling of vital commodities. In previous times stockpiling extended mostly to raw materials, but under the threat of modern air war there is a tendency to stockpile machine tools and finished products, including weapons. Stockpiling must be undertaken in peacetime,

[45] Heaton, *op. cit.*, p. 390. Contrary to present practices, mercantilism considered immigration good, but prevented emigration.

or during the very first weeks of a war before blockade arrangements have been completed.

The difficulties of an adequate stockpiling program are very great. Most of the commodities needed are in short supply. This leads, first, to a considerable increase in the price of the commodity and therefore to economic dislocation affecting all nations habitually buying the particular commodity. Second, it leads to an overexpansion of production facilities. Once the stockpiling program has been completed, inevitable retrenchment must be paid for by unemployment and financial loss. Third, if the threat of war has receded and the government decides to release its stockpiles, prices will fall. Necessary though stockpiling may be, it is a dislocating factor in world economy. This became obvious shortly after the outbreak of the Korean War, when the acceleration of the American stockpiling program produced repercussions all over Europe. One method to reduce the adverse effects of stockpiling is to fix prices by international agreements; another is to carry out the program over a long period of time, taking advantage of drops in prices and periods of overproduction as they occur in the economic cycle. But if large purchases have to be made rapidly, and if there is no time to arrive at intergovernmental agreements, grave disturbances are inevitable.

Economic Subsidies. Economic warfare in wartime includes "supply programs." Unlike activities designed to *deny* supplies to certain countries, these programs serve to *support* neutrals which are to be influenced. At the beginning of the Second World War, the Allies maintained trade with Italy, a token demonstration of the profitability of neutrality. Vichy-controlled North Africa was supplied with sugar in order to keep the natives well disposed toward the Allies and facilitate continued control by the French. In addition, North Africa was supplied with all kinds of materials, including fuel, in order to increase French power of resistance against German pressure. Food was delivered to France and Greece to stave off famine among a friendly population. If Turkey could have been abundantly provisioned with military materials, she might have entered the war at a strategically opportune moment; as it was, Turkey was inadequately equipped for waging war against as formidable an enemy as Germany.

The Anglo-Saxon powers also helped to confirm Spain in her neutrality by providing her with foodstuffs and oil—positive economic warfare, as it were.[46] The German high command credited this policy with keeping Spain "nonbelligerent." Yet a similar policy against Japan failed; American scrap and oil shipped to Japan, in order to insure Japanese neutrality, actually made possible Japanese aggression. Russia's strategy to supply Germany with raw materials, foodstuffs, and oil failed and redounded to Russia's own detriment.[47]

During World War II lend-lease operations contributed greatly to Allied victory. The assertion has been rashly made that lend-lease was a historically

[46] See Sir Samuel Hoare, *Complacent Dictator,* New York, Knopf, 1947, *passim.*
[47] See *Nazi-Soviet Relations,* pp. 85, 119, 196, 199, and 339.

unique operation. Economic subsidy is a time-honored means of war, employed whenever a rich state sought to induce poorer states to fight its battles or to replenish its effectives with troops from abroad. Subventions always played an important role in coalition warfare. During the 17th and 18th centuries they were used on a large scale, chiefly by Britain, Holland, and France. Countries such as Prussia waxed powerful because they had been liberally subsidized; between 1674 and 1688, the Grand Elector received almost 900,000 thalers, while his successor Frederick I amassed 14 million. During the Seven Years' War, Frederick the Great received altogether 27 million thalers from Britain. While direct subventions fell into disrepute during the 19th century, credits were given by the Western powers to smaller European countries and Russia, and by the United States to England and France. Since some of these debts remained unpaid, they must be considered as subsidies in fact, though not in name.

In fact, large credits frequently have political connotations. The unity of Italy was financed by English bankers. In 1871–1875, English banking firms assisted France in paying her 4-billion-franc war indemnity to Germany. Foreign "lending" also can be a means for preventing international economic disturbances which may lead to political repercussions. After the First World War the central banks of England and France, the Federal Reserve Bank of New York, and the German Reichsbank helped to stabilize the currencies of Belgium, Poland, and Rumania. In 1925, Wall Street agreed to support England in protecting its gold reserve if she were to return to the gold standard. Credits and investments made on purely economic grounds may ultimately provide the creditor with political power. For example, British investments in Argentina and especially in Argentine railroads, coupled with the fact that Britain was the foremost buyer of Argentine meat, provided Britain with a measure of influence upon Argentine politics.

Sabotage. A most radical means of economic warfare is physical sabotage, *i.e.*, destruction of industrial plants by clandestine agents. During the First World War, the United States was the target of a German sabotage campaign.[48] During the Second World War the French often resorted to effective physical sabotage. The Russian technique of scorched earth must also be mentioned in this connection.

During a shooting war it is not always possible to resort to physical sabotage. More subtle methods of sabotage have often been applied effectively. Chief among them is the instigation of strikes and wage troubles. The German collapse in the First World War started with two major strikes by the munitions workers. When the Western powers decided to support Poland in

[48] See Franz Rintelen von Kleist, *The Dark Invader: Wartime Reminiscences of a German Naval Intelligence Officer*, New York, Macmillan, 1933. See also the instructive book by Henry Landau, *The Enemy Within: The Inside Story of German Sabotage in America*, New York, Putnam, 1937, *passim*, and especially the chapter "Black Tom Blows Up," p. 77.

the war against Russia in 1920, dockers' strikes in many European ports, fomented by Soviet agents, prevented the shipping of ammunition. The strike weapon can be applied with telling effect during periods of nominal peace— a substitute for outright military attack and a weapon the use of which involves no undue risks. Strikes and other types of economic unrest, including black markets organized by foreign agents, are most effective in paralyzing a national economy, and thus possibly paralyzing a hostile nation. In 1926, the Soviets lent financial assistance to striking British coal miners—their strike all but brought to a standstill the economy of Britain and Western Europe. Time and again this weapon was used after 1945 to delay recovery of the democratic nations. Strikes in the British-occupied Ruhr were instigated by communists in an attempt to discredit the Western powers and enlist German sympathies.

After the Second World War the Soviets participated in setting up the World Federation of Trade Unions which, for all practical purposes, has remained ever since under communist control. One of the main purposes of the W.F.T.U. is to instigate industrial and transport strikes. For example, the communists organized strikes to halt the shipment of American munitions to European nations under the military-assistance program. It is likely that, in case of war, the communists will seek to provoke strikes in areas where raw materials of world-wide importance are being produced, such as Latin-American oil. Another means of communist economic warfare is agitation for the nationalization of industries, with the purpose of reducing the war potential of their opponents. The nationalization of the French aircraft industry in 1936 contributed greatly to the destruction of French air power.[49] The crypto-communist Tudeh party played an important part in the agitation leading to the nationalization of the Anglo-Iranian Oil Company.

The agricultural companion piece of the strike, the hoarding of foodstuffs, is a stratagem effective both in war and peace. While political and ideological propaganda may persuade the farmer to withhold his produce from "profiteering middlemen" and sundry "exploiters," it is usually enough to point out to him the economic advantages which he can derive from hoarding.

Agitation against profits, while of little significance in wartime when profit margins are usually limited by war and when patriotism often proves stronger than economic motives, is an effective brake on economic expansion and improvements in time of peace. Agitation against high taxes is an excellent method of interfering with armaments.

Armaments Trade. Trade in weapons and munitions has been, ever since the industrialization of war, a flourishing, albeit malodorous, business. It derives its zest and highly lucrative returns from two kinds of demands. On the one hand, many of the smaller nations, especially of the agricultural type, do not possess armaments industries and therefore must equip their armed

[49] Marcel Ventenant, *L'expérience des nationalisations, premier bilan,* Paris, Médicis, 1948, especially pp. 82–96.

forces with weapons purchased abroad. Besides governments, there are such private customers as revolutionaries, civil-war factions, and industrial firms setting up paramilitary units charged with protection of plants. On the other hand, industrialized nations are eager to market arms because (1) the armaments trade is as profitable as is any other kind of trade; and (2) the military security of these nations demands that armaments industries be maintained at a larger size than can be utilized in peacetime.[50] Since the armaments industries must look for markets in order to survive, the international armaments trade is a factor of military security. Moreover, military powers are compelled to keep their armaments up to date. This means that from time to time they must get rid of their stocks of obsolete weapons. Whenever the military are able to sell these out-of-date armaments to foreign countries, their budget situation is improved.

It is clear that the armaments trade has many political implications. The purchasing country enters into a special relationship with the selling country, and for its future security is dependent upon the continuing delivery of ammunition and spares from the seller. Each transaction provides the customer, be it a government or a revolutionary party, with additional power, especially so if the purchase price is kept low. For example, in a letter from the Soley Armament Corporation Ltd. to the American Armament Corporation dated February 3, 1934, we read: [51]

We are really the sole selling channel for small arms, etc., which belong to the British War Office. We are to a very great extent controlled by the varying policy of the government. . . . The stocks we control are of such magnitude that the sale of a big block of them could alter the political balance of power of the smaller states, involving corresponding complications from the point of view of finance and industry. . . . Under these conditions we have to submit to fairly strict control by the authorities concerned.

This simply means that through the control of the armaments trade it is possible, to a certain extent, to interfere in the policies of small states,[52] and this indirectly affects the position of larger countries. It also is possible through this trade to foment unrest and civil war, as, for example, in China during the twenties.[53] The preferred means of such a deliberate intervention is the sale of weapons at low prices to a selected revolutionary organization. The denial of armaments to the government of a target state is a less certain means of intervention because the armaments trade is highly competitive, with

---

[50] See Hearings . . . Munitions Industry, part 12, p. 2862, where we read in a du Pont memo dated March 21, 1924: "The U.S. Army and Navy being unable to give orders sufficient to keep the du Pont military smokeless-powder plant in operation and yet being exceedingly anxious for reasons of national defense to have the use of that factory in emergency, have requested the du Pont Company to get military foreign business and have helped the du Pont Company to obtain such business as it has got."

[51] Hearings . . . Munitions Industry, part 3, p. 672.

[52] See, for example, *ibid.*, part 38, p. 13064.

[53] See, for example, *ibid.*, part 10, pp. 2307*ff.*

the result that governments usually are able to buy all the weapons they need.

It should be noted, however, that a large part of the armaments trade has no political significance and falls under the category of plain business. For example, in 1926 the Chinese army bought small arms from Germany, Italy, and Japan; explosives from Norway, Denmark, and Germany; antiaircraft guns from Italy; field artillery from Russia; and airplanes from France.[54] A lively trade in armaments often serves the purpose of economic penetration, leading, as it were, to the establishment of banking firms, repair installations, transport arrangements, etc. The transactions of armament deals usually require the establishment of firm relations with government officials in charge of export and import controls.[55] Naturally such relations are often established by means of bribery or "percentages," but, in the end, they usually further the enlargement of trade.[56]

International Networks. To wage economic warfare effectively a nation must have a world-wide net of business interests dealing in credits and vital commodities. This net must be serviced or controlled by persons friendly to the nation engaging in economic-warfare practices. These sympathetic individuals must have had at their disposal large financial means and an influential propaganda apparatus.[57] *Economic warfare can therefore be waged effectively only by nations which build up their international trade or, failing this, by nations which maintain, like Russia, an international political movement. Economic warfare merges with the other techniques of penetration, such as intervention in foreign countries, psychological and political warfare, and policy sabotage.*

The Spoils of War. From time immemorial, the victor imposed on the vanquished economic tributes. Wars which are fought for economic profit aim at little else but spoils, whether they are in the form of slaves, money, goods, rights, or territories. In wars which are not fought primarily for economic profit, the victor still will seek to recoup the expense of his operations. A city conquered by a foreign army must support the garrison and pay tribute; even

---

[54] *Ibid.*, p. 2380.

[55] In 1924 the Chinese parliament accepted a premier-designate only if members were compensated financially for their vote. Situations like this give great scope to "economics as a weapon." See *ibid.*, p. 2371.

[56] Armaments are usually priced so as to allow for "palm oil." See *ibid.*, part 3, p. 640; for an extensive discussion of trading methods in the Balkans and in Latin America which (once upon a time) required strange methods of salesmanship, see *ibid.*, part 11, pp. 259ff. and 2601.

[57] As an example of propaganda which was not conceived by academic experts, a du Pont memo of May 9, 1922, is recommended reading: "The Bethlehem Steel Company has found our State Department of very little assistance in handling any of their problems in which it might be expected that our State Department would be of assistance. For instance, there is ample evidence at hand to show that the British naval attaché for South America is deliberately making false statements regarding the Bethlehem Steel Company's 14″ naval guns, for the purpose of injuring Bethlehem sales and possibly hoping to aid British ordnance firms in making sales." See *ibid.*, part 10, p. 2370.

in our times, cities were turned over to the troops for pillage. If an armistice is concluded, the vanquished often is required to deliver rolling stock, cattle, coal, ammunition, and weapons, partly to cover deficiencies in the equipment of the victorious army, partly to preclude resumption of hostilities.

Once peace is established, the victor usually forces the vanquished to pay indemnities, a procedure frequently justified by the argument that the vanquished was the aggressor and hence must be held accountable for the destruction he caused. Indemnities may be paid in money or commodities. In the first case, the indemnity may be paid in the currency of the vanquished, a method fraught with inflationary consequences; or financed through credits which the vanquished nation receives from a third party; or paid out of the current proceeds of the vanquished's international trade. If reparations are paid in commodities, the vanquished may transfer to the victor specified quantities of finished products already in existence such as locomotives; or he may transfer capital goods such as machine tools or factory installations; or may make goods available out of current production. Payments also could be made in the form of slave labor; prisoners of war often have been used to make "reparations."

Regardless of their moral and political justifications, reparations, whatever their form, introduce elements of dislocation into the world economy. The nation forced to pay the indemnity must reduce its standard of living and, therefore, becomes the center of political unrest. It also ceases to be a customer; at the same time, it must seek to maximize its export trade, thus affecting the trade balance of third nations. The delivery of large quantities of commodities tends to create unemployment in the receiving nation. Hence, paradoxically, the latter may grow unwilling to accept the reparations.

After the First World War Germany was asked to pay a sum which would have imposed the burdens of reparations upon more than three generations. At the same time all kinds of barriers were raised against German trade. Originally, German reparation payments were set at 54 billion dollars or 226 billion goldmarks, several times the German national income. In 1921, this sum was reduced to 132 million goldmarks or about 31 billion dollars, to be paid in annual installments of about 2 billion marks plus 25 per cent of the value of German imports. In 1924 a new arrangement was negotiated by an American financial expert Rufus C. Dawes. This agreement envisaged German payments for an *indefinite* period! So unrealistic were its provisions that the agreement accorded to Germany a loan with which to pay the first Dawes annuity. Naturally enough, the Dawes agreement was superseded by the so-called Young Plan which, in 1929, imposed on Germany the payment of an annuity of about 2 billion marks for fifty-nine years. Again it was necessary to float a loan in order to enable Germany to pay the first installment. Finally, in 1932 the Lausanne agreement reduced the German debt to 3 billion marks, *i.e.*, to 1.3 per cent of the original sum. In fact, however, no reparations of any kind have ever been paid since 1931.

For that matter, Germany never paid reparations in a true economic sense. Whatever she did pay had been loaned to her by American investors (many of whom lost their investment after the 1931 crisis). Between 1924 and 1931 Germany paid out 11.4 billion marks in reparations, yet during the same period received 15.4 billion marks through capital imports.[58] Nevertheless, the reparations issue complicated international relations, created many unnecessary difficulties for Germany, and hindered the resumption of normal relations between Germany and France. Moreover, the successive reparations agreements did very little to accomplish the purpose for which they had been concluded, namely, to speed up the recovery of the devastated areas, especially in France and Belgium. Economics had gotten entangled hopelessly with politics and popular emotions.

To avoid a similar fiasco, the Allies, after the Second World War, abstained from imposing financial reparations on Germany. Instead Germany was compelled to surrender commodities, especially industrial installations. The purpose of the arrangement was not only to force Germany to repair the damage she had done in foreign countries, and to destroy her powerful armaments industry, but also to help the industrialization of other European nations and at the same time reduce German industrial superiority. Before long, to avoid dangerous social and political disturbances in Germany, very large credits were granted the Germans by the United States and Britain. Dismantling of plants gradually was abandoned, and new investments were encouraged. This meant that Germany's industrial power actually was being restored. As Allied policy shifted from the demilitarization of Germany to the remilitarization of the *Bundesrepublik*, the question was no longer how to wreck the house Herr Krupp had built, but how to put it back in working order. Theory and practice obviously did not accord with one another.

Whether or not the nations receiving the industrial equipment torn from German factories actually benefited from the transaction is highly doubtful. In individual cases, nations acquired industrial installations which they could use to good purposes. But in most cases, dismantled factories could not be put in operation because there was not enough skilled labor to reassemble them. In the few cases where the recipients managed to start the production of the "dismantled" factories they were plagued by shortages of spares, supplies, and labor.

In summary, under the conditions of an interdependent world economy the gathering of the spoils of war is a very difficult undertaking. The larger the reparations the less easily can they be collected. A vanquished nation undoubtedly can transfer parts of its wealth to the victor. But such transfers must be kept within narrow limits and cannot be continued for more than a few years. Otherwise large dislocations and outright losses must ensue, affecting *all* members of the world economy. Reparations are harmful po-

[58] See Gottfried von Haberler, *The Theory of International Trade with its Applications to Commercial Policy*, London, Hodge, 1936, p. 112.

litically. They are of dubious value economically. The vanquished cannot pay, since war and defeat have devoured his reserves. Nowadays it is rather the victor who pays "tribute" to the vanquished.

Soviet Techniques of Exploitation. In the postwar world, the Russians have exhibited a new streamlined method of exploiting occupied territories. Although they have followed the pattern set by the Nazis, they developed their own "improved" techniques. The Russians, just like the Germans before them, have used foreign people for forced labor, thus supplementing their productive manpower reserves. Second, they removed whole industrial installations to Russia, hoping thus to increase the Russian war potential.

Of a different, though not less destructive, nature were Russian activities designed to "communize" countries under their control. The old entrepreneur classes were decimated by deportation and political purges. Since these means can, in the presence of foreign observers and a population as yet only half subdued, be applied only against individuals (for example, through war-crimes trials) and not against large groups, economic extermination proved more efficient; the middle classes can be ruined by rapid and excessive wage increases to the masses or by inflationary assaults upon middle-class reserves. These methods can take the place of outright and open expropriation, although in most cases they merely supplement the "nationalization" of key industries such as banking, electric power, oil, insurance, transportation, steel, and coal. In the early stages of the process, these measures are popular with the masses, who expect from them an immediate increase in their living standards.

In Rumania, expropriation was achieved in the following manner: the National Bank was nationalized, and thus the Soviet-dominated government obtained control over the country's credit. Credit was then denied to private owners of factories who, after exhaustion of their cash reserves, were forced to close their plants. Since they were creating unemployment or engaging in "sabotage" by shutting down their plants, their properties were transferred to public ownership.

At the highest level, the economies of the occupied countries were tied in with the economy of the Soviet Union, especially by means of agreements whereby the Russians absorbed the entire exportable surplus in addition to reparations for war damages. Needless to say, a nation dealt with in this profitable fashion, yet not wholly integrated in the Soviet scheme of things, would be difficult to control, if the Soviet army were to withdraw behind the borders of Russia. Yet sovietization through socialization is *de facto* control, though it be also remote control.

It may be mentioned in passing that in 1946 the American authorities delivered to the Russians the printing plates of German currency, thus enabling the Russians to print as many marks as they wanted. The money so freely created was then used by the Soviets to engage in preemptive buying in the Western zones, accelerating the inflation all over Germany, and thus greatly impeding Western policy. It is, therefore, not surprising that in 1948 Soviet insistence on Russian control over the emission of a single currency for Berlin was one of the main stumbling blocks in the negotiations between the three Western powers and Russia on a settlement of the Berlin crisis.

The Honest Broker. In the past many states have lived by trade *and* prospered by the judicious practice of economic warfare. The best examples are Carthage and Venice, which waged economic warfare almost incessantly. In modern times, their place was taken by Portugal, Holland, and Britain. At present, no major state lives through and by economic warfare, yet several smaller countries owe their political importance largely to the fact that they carry out some of the most important economic transactions for the account of warring states and act as trustees for great powers seeking to maintain, though locked in military conflict, economic and political contact with one another. Such countries are Switzerland and, to a lesser extent, Sweden, Belgium, and Holland, states which are not only financially strong but also leading in industrial technology and, in the case of Switzerland and Sweden, in military technology. An important though enigmatic role is played by dwarf states such as Liechtenstein and Monaco, homes of numerous "holding companies" and, by virtue of legislation especially drawn to attract cosmopolitan capital in quest of security and discretion, scenes of vast international transactions.

BIG BUSINESS IN INTERNATIONAL POLITICS

Today, some of the most important international units of power are no longer organized as states but have assumed the form of large international cartels. These cartels are administered somewhat in the manner of a modern government; several of them are administered more elaborately and efficiently than are most states. The management of large cartels is, in all but the name, a government with division of power. There is a supervisory board of directors exercising the functions of the legislature. There is the executive, otherwise known as the managing board of directors. Within the latter board (the I.G. Farben may serve as the sample of cartel government), policy is made by a central committee which might be compared to the War Cabinet of Britain. There are various "ministerial" posts. In the I.G. Farben organization administration was divided among the following "ministries": directorate of domestic and foreign sales, directorate of construction and physical plant development, directorate of commerce, directorate of intelligence, chief production planning office, directorate of political and economic policy, directorate of labor, chief of chemical research, and chief counsel. To these must be added several "undersecretaryships," such as regional production, inorganics and organics committees, the nitrogen syndicate, and the development of poison and explosives.

That I.G. Farben was fully aware of the power which it possessed may be highlighted by an episode in its colorful history. In 1920, the I.G. Farben invented the drug Germanin Bayer 205 which was a remedy against sleeping sickness.[59] This disease prevented, and still obstructs, the white race from colonizing the African continent. I.G. Farben offered that drug to the British Government in trade for the return of Germany's lost colonies. The British declined.

Some cartels, especially armament firms, maintain large propaganda organizations which, by supporting nationalistic aspirations, generate demand and large orders. For example, prior to World War I, Krupp supported the German *Flottenbund* which made propaganda for a large navy; after the war Baron Krupp von Bohlen acquired the Scherl Company, a large newspaper- and book-publishing concern, and, through his collaborator Hugenberg, control of the largest German film enterprise (Ufa).[60] It is interesting to note that the Berlin newspaper which, on August 1, 1914, printed alarmist and mendacious news of the Russian mobilization, the *Lokalanzeiger,* was controlled by Krupp. The power of some international cartels is indeed considerable. By contributing 400,000 marks to the Nazi party, the I.G. Farben abetted, at a critical moment, Hitler's consolidation of power and thus helped to set the stage for the Second World War. This payment was made, prior to the decisive elections of March, 1933, as part of a 2-million-mark contribution which leading German industrialists made the Nazi party fund. The subscribers included the German General Electric Company, Telefunken, and several mining and machine tool cartels.[61]

The reasons why large business firms participate in politics and thereby greatly influence international relations may be divided into two broad categories. In the first place, they may hope that, by supporting a given political party, they will further their business interests. In 1932, for example, I.G. Farben was confronted by the necessity of closing its synthetic gasoline plant. In view of this contingency the firm sent emissaries to Hitler (who was as yet only a mere party leader) to sound him out about his attitude concerning the German fuel economy. Hitler stated that Germany had to become self-sufficient in gasoline, thus reassuring the company, which immediately became a faithful ally of the Hitler movement. I.G. Farben increased the output even before Hitler was appointed Chancellor.[62]

The other motive is simply to buy political protection. German industrialists, for example, were concerned lest continued political unrest endanger the

---

[59] See Berge, *op. cit.,* p. 55.

[60] See Bernhard Menne, *Blood and Steel: The Rise of the House of Krupp,* New York, Citadel, 1938, p. 162. For general background on this, see Eckart Kehr, *Schlachtflottenbau und Parteipolitik 1894–1901: Versuch eines Querschnitts durch die innenpolitischen, sozialen und ideologischen Voraussetzungen des deutschen Imperialismus,* Berlin, E. Ehering, 1930.

[61] See *Trials of War Criminals before the Military Tribunals,* Vol. VII, "The Farben Case," pp. 565–568.

[62] *Ibid.,* pp. 539, 547.

survival of private ownership.[63] Since large corporations often are the butt of political criticism, they incline to support parties which, they hope, will silence the critics either by suppressing them or by buying them off. Last but not least, businessmen may wish to buy "political insurance." They believe that they can purchase this elusive commodity by financing various types of political movements ranging all the way from the left to the right. For example, in 1932, the Flick concern spent about 950,000 marks to help President Hindenburg to win reelection as *Reichspräsident* against Hitler.[64] Yet they also supported several right-wing parties, including the Nazis (to whom allegedly they gave only a small amount of money), and for good measure, the left-wing parties, including the Social Democrats. The documents suggest faintly that Flick may have given money even to the communists, yet this interesting question was not elucidated in the war-crimes trials which brought these transactions to light.[65]

Big industrial firms cooperate with governments by putting at their disposal large sums of money which are to serve their joint interest. Often when a government or a ministry does not care to reveal its operations, it will draw on private funds. Thus, for example, the Nazi Minister of the Interior and chief of the S.S., Heinrich Himmler, maintained a so-called *circle of friends* who annually paid out to him about 1 million marks to assist him in his "special tasks." These contributions came from the steel, coal, oil, chemical, and metallurgical industries and from banking firms.[66]

Moreover, in order to further their own interests, such firms collaborate closely with governments, for example, by supporting government propaganda abroad and maintaining political contacts. They may handle finances of secret operations—this apparently was the method by which Lenin and his party were financed during World War I. Occasionally, embassies receive their funds from business enterprises operating in foreign countries. During the Second World War, for example, the German embassies in Brazil, Colombia, China, Chile, and Argentina were supported largely by the proceeds of the I.G. Farben affiliates operating in these areas.[67]

It should be added that the above illustrations are taken from German history merely because they are well documented. Similar practices have been current in practically all other countries, but in the absence of reliable and full documentation, they cannot be discussed profitably.[68]

[63] See *Trials of War Criminals before the Nürnberg Military Tribunals,* Government Printing Office, 1952, Vol. VI, "The Flick Case," pp. 230, 286.

[64] *Ibid.,* pp. 385*f*.

[65] *Ibid.,* pp. 348, 382*ff*.

[66] *Ibid.,* pp. 270, 281.

[67] *Trials of War Criminals before the Military Tribunals,* Vol. VII, "The Farben Case," pp. 701*f*.

[68] Some examples of how American armament firms tried to influence the policies of the U.S. government, especially with respect to embargoes, may be found in Hearings . . . Munitions Industry, parts 10 and 12.

Large firms may send their key men into the government or themselves employ influential politicians. What Krupp and I.G. Farben were in Weimar Germany, the Suez Canal Co. and the Comité des Forges were in France, Vickers and Imperial Chemical in Britain, Ansaldo in Italy, and Juan March in Spain. The influential banker Rouvier, whose firm had engaged in many transactions with German concerns, pursued, as Prime Minister of France, a straight pro-German policy. The German politician Helfferich, one of the chief exponents of the Baghdad railroad project, was a director of the *Deutsche Bank,* financial backer of the plan.[69] Dr. Schacht, long-time German economic director, had been picked by a number of influential bankers, allegedly with the consent of British financial circles. Walther Rathenau, German Foreign Minister, was also director of the AEG (German General Electric Co.). The influential cabinet member Erzberger was connected with the Thyssen firm, controlling steel mills and collieries. The German Chancellor, director of the *Reichsbank,* and Ambassador to Washington, Hans Luther, was connected with the house of Krupp. Another Krupp employee, Wiedfeldt, was made Ambassador to Washington, negotiated loans for Krupp, and then resumed his position as a Krupp director.

On the other hand, high-ranking officers and officials often join important cartels. When in 1902 Friedrich Krupp committed suicide to escape prosecution for sexual irregularities, he left no male heir; Emperor Wilhelm picked a young diplomat, von Bohlen und Halbach, as husband for Krupp's daughter and as director of the concern. Admirals who had been in charge of matériel procurement found their berth at Krupp's; so did a former Prussian minister of railroads who, after having bought rails from Krupp for the state, then sold rails to the state for Krupp.

In the United States the phenomenon is not unfamiliar. It is sufficient to cite the names of Mellon, Straus, Rockefeller, Stettinius, Harriman, Davies, Clayton, Knudsen, and Draper; yet in this country, democratic control is sufficiently strong to enforce a neat separation of private interests and public policy. Whenever there is doubt as to an appointee's detachment from private business interests, vigorous criticism in the press and Congressional scrutiny preclude that individual's confirmation in office. It was only when Charles E. Wilson, former president of the General Motors Corporation, divested himself of his holdings in that concern that the Senate confirmed, in 1953, his appointment to the post of Secretary of Defense.

In small countries, such "personal unions" may assume great significance. Prime Minister Colijn of Holland had been a chief official of the Royal Dutch concern, to which he returned between terms of public office. This firm was an international political factor of prime importance since Sir Henri Deterding, chairman of Royal Dutch, financed the anticommunist move-

[69] See Parker Thomas Moon, *Imperialism and World Politics,* New York, Macmillan, 1927, p. 253.

ments in many lands, including—it is asserted—the Nazis. The most important agreement concerning rights to the oil fields of Iraq was concluded between various governments and one private firm, owned by the Armenian magnate Gulbenkian, as equal partners.

Hence there is no dearth of examples for the team play of powerful international financial combines and governments. Britain would not have gained possession of the Suez Canal shares but for the private loan made by Rothschild to Disraeli. Krupp was an excellent source of intelligence for German diplomats who often learned their secrets from the local Krupp agent. Cecil Rhodes conquered an African empire for Britain, and Carl Peters acquired East Africa for Germany. During the First World War, when the German government decided to create a raw-material control office, the Hamburg-American Shipping Line (HAPAG) created that office with its own personnel and administrative machinery.[70]

The Firestone Company, domiciled in the United States, practically runs an entire state—Liberia.[71] The United Fruit Company ruled Costa Rica almost like a government till 1898; in 1908 it subjected the government to economic blockade and imposed its conditions. The Mitsui and Mitsubishi concerns and other large firms influenced Japanese policy and were, before the establishment of military dictatorship, in turn influenced by British and American capital. The South Manchurian and Chinese Eastern railroads (both formerly Japanese) ruled Manchuria and, to a lesser extent, parts of China. It is asserted that, in Mexico, Standard Oil supported the Madero rebellion against Porfirio Diaz, who allegedly favored British oil interests, and that the Huerta rebellion in 1923 was backed by Royal Dutch.

In France, relations among international bankers were effectively exploited by the Pétain government, especially through the intermediary of the Banque Worms, to achieve various *de facto* concessions from Germany, although these were made not so much by the Nazi government as by private German industry and finance.[72] This French bank was in liaison with the then largest German financial institution, the Dresdner Bank, slated to become, in the case of a Nazi victory, the financial "leader" of the entire European continent.

In the postwar world, Swiss chemical concerns have fallen heir to some of I.G. Farben's dominions. Switzerland's Brown-Boveri and Oerlikon and Sweden's Bofors now fulfill some of Krupp's former functions. The greatest and possibly the most influential concern now operating in numerous countries, a concern which has become a major European power with its own

[70] On all these and other cases, see *ibid.*, and Eugene Staley, *War and the Private Investor: A Study in the Relations of International Politics and International Private Investment*, New York, Doubleday, 1935.

[71] See Staley, *op. cit.*, p. 108. On Costa Rica, see Moon, *op. cit.*, p. 428.

[72] On Banque Worms and the concept of "synarchy," the somewhat mysterious and unproved international conspiracy of industrialists, bankers, and high officials, see H. du Moulin de Labarthète, *Le Temps des illusions: Souvenirs (Juillet, 1940–Avril, 1942)*, Geneva, Éditions du Cheval Ailé, 1946, pp. 311ff.

independent policy, is the Dutch firm of Philips, the world's foremost electronics specialist. In view of the decisive influence of electronics in the Second World War—it won the Battle of Britain, the Battle of the Atlantic, and made strategic bombing possible—it may perhaps be said that Philips could possibly hold the power to pick the winner of a future war.

Russia exercises a foreign-trade monopoly. The trade between the outside world and Russia is channeled through it. The objective of the Soviet trade monopoly was defined by its creator, Leonid Krassin: "The Red Army must defend our country against possible military attacks. The monopoly of foreign trade must repulse all economic and financial intervention from abroad." [73] It goes without saying that such an organization need not remain defensive. In fact, the Soviet monopoly has acquired considerable offensive capabilities. Through its mere size it must achieve political power in all countries where it does large business, especially if and when the Russian foreign trade monopoly is assisted by monopolies of satellite countries.

The exact measure of the influence of large firms and especially international cartels on the shaping of modern history is as yet largely a matter of guesswork. Only on rare occasions has the veil been lifted.[74] While "capitalism" does not engender war any more frequently and lightheartedly than other economic systems, and while wars are mostly due to political causes, economic warfare is being waged incessantly by capitalist and noncapitalist systems. This warfare serves economic as well as military interests. Heretofore too little attention was given to these problems. Without awareness of their existence, international relations cannot be properly understood.

RELIEF AND POLITICS

Commercial treaties must be closely coordinated with the over-all policy of a nation and especially with its security policy. The same is, unfortunately, necessary with respect to the humane and charitable policies, which some countries, but most particularly the United States, pursue for no other reason than generosity and compassion. It is true that giving food to hungry people should not be a matter subject to political considerations and that no differences should be made between people who suffer. Charity does not distinguish between race, creed, class, color, and ideology. Yet not all governments and peoples are guided by these principles. Often charity is demanded merely in order to exploit the benefactor nation. What is worse, charity is requested by governments who desire to maintain themselves in power, to continue practicing inhuman domestic policies, and to wreak their vengeance

[73] Quoted by Alexander Baykov in *The Development of the Soviet Economic System: An Essay on the Experience of Planning in the U.S.S.R.*, New York, Macmillan, 1947, p. 28. The quote is originally from Krassin's book *Voprosy vneshney torgovli* (Questions of Foreign Trade), Moscow, 1928.

[74] See Moon, *op. cit.*, p. 210.

on the wealthy giver. When charity is extended to such "needy cases," it is proportionately reduced for other peoples who need it almost as badly and who would accept it in a friendly spirit.

The story of food relief in communist Russia supplies a highly instructive example. In 1919 Herbert Hoover proposed to President Wilson his plan of feeding Russia. He urged generous relief not merely for purely humanitarian reasons, but also because he believed that, as a result of relief, ". . . the pendulum will yet swing back to some moderate position when bitter experience has taught the economic and social follies of present obsessions. No greater fortune can come to the world than that these foolish ideas [of Bolshevism] should have an opportunity somewhere of bankrupting themselves."

Intervention was not believed by Hoover to be the right means for swinging the "pendulum from the extreme left back toward the right." But if pressure be reduced by feeding, this pendulum "will find the point of stabilization based on social instincts that could never be established by outside intervention" (Memorandum of March 28, 1919). In other words, the feeding of the hungry was recommended as a policy that would eliminate the Bolshevik danger, and not merely for reasons of charity; Hoover believed that the moderation of communism through relief would "save our country [the U.S.] from further entanglements." [75]

This policy did not attain its political objective, but (1) helped to stabilize communist power and (2) permitted the Bolsheviki to continue their policy of exterminating the former ruling classes. Not only were the humanitarian objectives not attained but, to the contrary, the consolidation of the Bolsheviki was the direct cause of greater human suffering. For all that, no good will was created toward the United States. American food relief was discontinued in 1923 after it turned out that the Soviets, in order to obtain foreign exchange, actually *exported* food and relied on the United States to cover this additional deficit. Upon remonstration, the Soviets declared themselves willing to discontinue food exports provided they were given a substantial loan! There is no doubt that many innocent lives were saved by the Hoover relief mission. But who can tell how many equally innocent lives were lost because the Soviets stayed in power and were not cast out by a policy that would have been more effective than feeding?

The lessons of this experiment were not heeded in the conduct of American lend-lease operations. More often than not lend-lease aid was granted without asking for any political or material return. Undoubtedly, American lend-lease policy attained its principal objective, namely, strengthening allies in the war against a common enemy. In that respect American performance was as effective as it was grandiose. The 12-billion-dollar lend-lease goods to Russia helped to turn the tide in the war in Europe. However, in many instances,

[75] See H. H. Fisher, *The Famine in Soviet Russia, 1919–1923: The Operations of the American Relief Administration,* Stanford, Calif., Stanford University Press, 1935, see especially pp. 10–14.

too, lend-lease materials were requested which were not needed at all or were earmarked for postwar reconstruction.

This lesson was lost on policy makers when the United States made the largest contribution to the UNRRA organization, and materially helped to *consolidate* Soviet power in eastern Europe. None of the communist governments, graciously supported by the United States, would have rushed aid to the United States in the case of an American famine. It is—in a world which is rent asunder by latent and open aggressiveness—a dangerous as well as a futile gesture to engage in relief activities without regard to the nature of the recipient nation's ruling class (which can nowhere be excluded from determining who is and who is not a "needy case") and their political intentions. It is a futile gesture because those most in need cannot be helped; it is a dangerous one because it may strengthen the hand of tyrannical governments and thus compound the very tensions which find release most readily in war. This is not an argument against relief as such; American generosity is one of America's most potent weapons in the struggle for the world's allegiance to the cause of democracy. It is, however, a simple dictate of democratic statecraft to make certain that relief is not used by recipient nations to bolster totalitarian, militaristic, and unfriendly regimes.

Prophylactic Economics. After the Second World War the United States pioneered in a new method of international economics: the supplying of systematic and large-scale economic help to countries in the throes of economic difficulties and menaced by political and social upheavals. The philosophy behind prophylactic economics is very simple; it is assumed that unrest is intimately connected with economic dislocation and, in particular, with shortages of consumers' goods. It is furthermore assumed that these hardships cannot be alleviated simply by relief measures but that in addition large investments must be pumped into the national economy of the needy country. Given the volume of these investments, it is impossible that the capital be raised by private investors. Instead, it must be raised by the government through taxation. Once the foreign economy has been improved through the combined impact of relief and investment, the threat of political revolution will fade away.

In line with this philosophy the United States has spent during the postwar years many tens of billions of dollars, especially in Europe. These operations —UNRRA, ECA, etc.—have already been discussed. Here it is merely necessary to point out that a very large part of these appropriations was spent on capital investment in foreign countries. For example, France was helped in the enlargement of her electric-power industry, while Italy was aided in the modernization of her shipping industry. The purpose was to stimulate the further economic development of the recipient nations. In addition, the so-called underdeveloped areas received aid, largely through the technical-assistance program. The purpose of this program was to spur productivity, not by means of capital investment but by the export of production skills.

In view of the fact that inexpensive changes (rotation of crops or the use of different seeds) can boost production, the technical-assistance program aimed particularly at the adoption of such modern techniques.

The application of prophylactic economics is new in the sense that it *organizes* the spread of technical know-how and makes large-scale investments more or less independent of favorable "market conditions." [76] In the past, international investments took place gradually, on a relatively small scale, and if and when there was an opportunity of considerable and early profit. Technical know-how was supposed to spread by a kind of international osmosis; often it did not spread at all. The new policy telescoped economic developments which, in previous times, would have lasted centuries, into the short span of a few years. This policy was based squarely upon the enormous productivity of the American economy and upon the high humanitarian motivation of American citizens, who were willing to pay ever higher taxes for the alleviation of economic needs abroad. If the various recipient governments had not indulged in policies of currency control, nationalization, confiscation, etc., this program of economic cooperation could have been left in the hands of private investors. It might then have proceeded perhaps at a slower pace, but quite probably it would have been restricted to sound investments, *and it would have been self-generating, which the government program was not.*

The difficulty of the cooperation program lay in the fact that it aimed at overhauling the local economy and putting in motion an economic process of reform through investment and education. However, economic structures and traditions cannot be changed rapidly, even by the most enlightened education or the largest investment. In some countries where graft was rampant, a large portion of the investment never was put to use. In other countries where the tax structure was out of date, the investment did not yield full benefits. In tradition-bound countries, the new skills were not welcomed. In many countries the new capital structure was top-heavy in comparison with native purchasing power, which could not be raised so long as the local banking system was not modernized and an effective system of installment buying introduced. All in all, prophylactic economics still have a long way to go before they can be handled reliably and successfully. Nevertheless, they started a process of international economic modernization, which is fraught with political and social consequences of vast, yet unpredictable, scope.

[76] The figures are approximately as follows: From the end of the war to January 1, 1952, the U.S. government made foreign grants in the amount of about 30 billion dollars. It also made investments and gave credits to the tune of 14 billion dollars. Private investment abroad stood, by 1952, at about 23 billion dollars; however, some of these investments had been made before 1945. Dividends on these investments averaged about 7.4 per cent, but since there were heavy local reinvestments, the American investor actually received only about 5.5 per cent. This is too low to attract capital into *risky* foreign investments. This low return is not due to insufficiency of demand for credits but largely to restrictions and heavy taxation imposed by foreign governments.

THE VISION OF THE FUTURE

As these various assistance programs were applied to isolated problems in individual countries, it gradually came to be understood that there was a need of reorganizing the basic structure of world economy. The economic malaise is *not* identical with the sum of single deficiencies but is due to the disruption of the basic economic order and to the malfunctioning of the main economic processes taken as a whole. Rather than curing isolated symptoms, it is necessary to reestablish a workable system.[77]

There is, first, the problem of whether or not such an international economic system can be established at all so long as nations live under a regime of centralized economic planning. Should this question be answered in the negative, as it probably must, the next problem that arises is whether existing economic structures which do not lend themselves to international integration can be modified, and in what way they should be reorganized. Even if the problem of the Soviet "orbit" and communist economic warfare were disregarded, there still would remain the need for adjusting the various systems of taxation, labor, industrial and credit policies, social security, production standards, etc., of the non-Soviet nations in order to join them in a properly run international economy. Finally, there is the everlasting problem of war and the impact of the military threat on economic organizations.

At the time of this writing, these immense problems are not yet clearly understood, let alone soluble. Yet it is with these problems that the makers of economic policy must come to grips. Once the objective of a workable economic *system* is grasped fully, it will be possible to apply economics as a weapon, not for the purpose of hurting other nations—which usually yields the result that one's own nation also suffers damage—but against poverty and thus for the purpose of improving the living standards of *all nations*.

BIBLIOGRAPHY

Alexandrowicz, C. H.: *International Economic Organizations*, New York, Praeger, 1953.
Borkin, Joseph, and Charles A. Welsh: *Germany's Master Plan*, New York, Duell, Sloan & Pearce, 1943.
Brockway, Thomas: *Battles without Bullets: The Story of Economic Warfare*, New York, Foreign Policy Association, 1939.
Caspary, Adolf: *Wirtschaftsstrategie und Kriegsführung*, Berlin, Mittler, 1932.
Clark, J. M., W. H. Hamilton, and H. G. Moulton: *Readings in the Economics of War*, Chicago, University of Chicago Press, 1918.
Consett, M. W. W. P.: *The Triumph of Unarmed Forces 1914–1918*, London, Williams & Norgate, 1923.
Einzig, Paul: *Economic Warfare*, London, Macmillan & Co., Ltd., 1940.
Ellis, H. S.: *The Economics of Freedom*, New York, Harper, 1950.
Engelbrecht, H. C., and F. C. Hanighen: *Merchants of Death: A Study of the International Armaments Industry*, New York, Dodd, Mead, 1934.

[77] By contrast, the Mutual Security Agency till 1952 based its work on the slogan, "one country, one program."

Eucken, Walter: *This Unsuccessful Age or the Pains of Economic Progress,* London, Hodge, 1951.
Gayer, Arthur D.: *The Control of International Cartels,* New York, Council on Foreign Relations, 1944.
Gordon, David L., and Royden Dangerfield: *The Hidden Weapon: Story of Economic Warfare,* New York, Harper, 1947.
Heckscher, Eli F.: *Mercantilism,* 2 vols., London, G. Allen, 1935.
Heilperin, Michael A.: *The Trade of Nations,* New York, Knopf, 1952.
Hexner, Erwin: *International Cartels,* Chapel Hill, The University of North Carolina Press, 1946.
Hirschmann, Albert O.: *National Power and the Structure of Foreign Trade,* Berkeley, University of California Press, 1945.
Howard, Frank A.: *Buna Rubber: The Birth of an Industry,* New York, Van Nostrand, 1947.
Jack, D. T.: *Studies in Economic Warfare,* London, King, 1940.
Jewkes, John: *Ordeal by Planning,* New York, Macmillan, 1948.
Lauterbach, Albert K.: *Economics in Uniform,* Princeton, N.J., Princeton University Press, 1943.
Lefebure, Victor: *The Riddle of the Rhine,* New York, Chemical Foundation, 1923.
Lewinsohn, Richard: *The Profits of War through the Ages,* New York, Dutton, 1937.
Marx, Daniel: *International Shipping Cartels,* Princeton, N.J., Princeton University Press, 1953.
Mason, Edward: *Controlling World Trade,* New York, McGraw-Hill, 1946.
Mendershausen, Horst: *The Economics of War,* rev. ed., New York, Prentice-Hall, 1943.
Menne, Bernhard: *Blood and Steel: The Rise of the House of Krupp,* New York, Citadel, 1938.
Neumann, Robert: *Zaharoff, the Armaments King,* New York, Knopf, 1935.
Noel-Baker, Philip: *The Private Manufacture of Armaments,* London, Gollancz, 1937.
Robbins, Lionel: *The Economic Causes of War,* New York, Macmillan, 1940.
Roepke, Wilhelm: *Explication économique du monde moderne,* Paris, Médicis, 1940.
Sasuly, Richard: *I.G. Farben,* New York, Boni & Gaer, 1947.
Sombart, Werner: *Krieg und Kapitalismus,* Munich, Duncker & Humboldt, 1913.
Sonneman, Theodor, *Die Wirstschaft als Kriegswaffe,* Berlin, Junker und Dünhaupt, 1943.
Staley, Eugene: *War and the Private Investor: A Study in the Relations of International Private Investment,* New York, Doubleday, 1935.
Stedman, M. S.: *Exporting Arms,* New York, King's Crown Press, 1947.
Vagts, Alfred: *Mexiko, Europa und Amerika, unter besonderer Berücksichtigung der Petroleumpolitik: Eine wirtschaftsdiplomatische Untersuchung,* Berlin, W. Rothschild, 1928.
Viner, Jacob: *The Customs Union Issue,* Washington, Carnegie Endowment, 1950.
———: "International Finance and Balance of Power Diplomacy, 1880–1914," *Southwestern Political and Social Science Quarterly,* Vol. 9, No. 4, March, 1929, pp. 407–510.
Winslow, E. M.: *The Pattern of Imperialism,* New York, Columbia University Press, 1948.
Wissmann, Hellmuth: *Das Gold in Wirtschaft und Politik,* Leipzig, Wilhelm Goldmann, 1940.
Wu, Yuan-li: *Economic Warfare,* New York, Prentice-Hall, 1952.
Zischka, Anton: *La guerre secrète pour le pétrole,* Paris, Payot, 1933.

Part Seven

THE AGE OF CONFLICT

Chapter 22

SOVIET CONFLICT MANAGEMENT

BASIC MOTIVATIONS

Since the termination of the Second World War, the political fate of the world and certainly world peace have been dependent on the foreign policy of the Soviet Union. This policy is rooted in doctrinal beliefs and operational practices of long standing. To understand these is to know why Soviet policy has become the crucial factor in international relations.

In the *Communist Manifesto* (1848), Marx and Engels wrote that the communists disdain to conceal their aims. This is one of the few frank and truthful statements ever penned by dedicated communists. The communists never have hidden their purpose of destroying the existing social order the world over; indeed they loudly have proclaimed this intent.

The stated rationale underlying the communist objective has been the aim of establishing a system based on the public ownership of the means of production. Communists claim that such a system—communism or socialism —would usher in an era of plenty and create a society without oppression. They have failed to explain the reasoning behind this contention; nor has the argument been proved that the emancipation of mankind can be achieved in this manner, and only through the methods proposed.[1] Yet despite the lack of plausibility of the communist program, despite the utter failure—in terms of human betterment—of the communist achievement in Russia, despite the certainty that the establishment of a Soviet economic system would be preceded and accompanied by the establishment of a Soviet political dictatorship, this ideology or pseudo-religion had become the powerful drive behind

[1] See also the discussion in Chap. 19.

THE AGE OF CONFLICT

the actions not only of the present government of Russia, but also of its numerous followers and dupes all over the world.

The student of international relations must register the fact that the Soviet leaders, for more than thirty-five years, have with unswerving dedication served their spurious cause; that a vast store of written and factual materials supply the evidence for the Soviets' determination to achieve world hegemony; and that the free world rejects the benefits of communism and hence resists the imposition of a communist world rule. These three facts are basic to the conflict between the Soviet orbit and the free world.

The West is prone to underestimate the importance of ideology and theory in the Soviet scheme of things. There is no evidence that Soviet leaders have lost faith in the efficacy and cogency of their doctrine, although, without doubt, they are rationalizing and modifying the original theory. The point is academic, since Soviet leaders can no more divest themselves from their intellectual baggage than the United States government can divorce itself from the political concepts of democracy. Intellectual frivolity is not one of the failings of the Russian heirs of Karl Marx.

While virtually everything may be plausibly argued with the help of pertinent quotations from Marx, Engels, Lenin, and Stalin, and while Leninist-Stalinist doctrine is so flexible that it can justify numerous tactical shifts, there is nevertheless a hard core of communist thinking which never has been diluted or varied by verbal manipulations. It is possible to justify leftist or rightist courses, to explain victories and defeats, offensives and defensives, but there have not been variations of Soviet doctrine concerning, for example, the inevitable violent downfall of capitalism or the necessity of a dictatorship of the proletariat after assumption of power by the communists.

Regardless of its many reinterpretations, the Marxist-Leninist-Stalinist doctrine has become an integral part of the Soviet power machine. It is the magnet which holds together the communist world movement and attracts its many sympathizers. It is the political formula with which the Bolsheviks justify their rule to their hapless subjects. In the doctrines of Marx, Engels and Lenin, the Bolsheviks found

the justification of their instinctive fear of the outside world, for the dictatorship without which they did not know how to rule, for the cruelties they did not dare not to inflict, for the sacrifices they felt bound to demand. In the name of Marxism they sacrificed every single ethical value in their methods and tactics. Today they cannot dispense with it. It is the fig leaf of their moral and intellectual responsibility.[2]

Without this façade, the Soviet leaders would stand exposed as the most wanton oppressors of history. This doctrine, and only this doctrine, provides

[2] Excerpts of a dispatch by George F. Kennan, as quoted in *The Forrestal Diaries*, Walter Millis (ed.), New York, Viking, 1951, p. 137.

the Soviet rulers with that legitimacy without which their power could not endure.

THEORY

The all-embracing philosophical framework of Soviet ideology is *dialectical materialism*. This concept is a synthesis of several strands of thought: Ricardo's economic analysis, Saint Simon's social physics, the idealistic dialectic—"the theory of the union of opposites"—of Hegel, and the "inversion" of Hegelian idealism by Karl Marx and Friedrich Engels. This eclectic and none too systematic philosophy was put to the test under the specific conditions of Russia. The result of this application of theory to refractory realities is Soviet ideology.

To think dialectically is, according to Marxian doctrine, to think historically, *i.e.*, not only to accept change, but also to seek its patterns and to discern the forces moving within any particular historic phase. At the center of the communist philosophical system is the concept of *class struggle*. All history is seen as a struggle of classes. A class is defined as a group of persons holding such a common relationship to the means of material production as to bring them into conflict with another group standing in some other common relationship to the means of material production. At this stage of history the *bourgeoisie* is being challenged by the proletariat. The resulting class struggle will be resolved by the victory of socialism—a progressive organization of society and its work—over capitalism. History is in a constant state of flux, and there is no such thing as a stable social order. Capitalism, by seeking to retain its hold on society, vainly attempts to swim against the tide of historical inevitability. Evolution is not confined to quantitative change. Evolution proceeds from an accumulation of imperceptible *quantitative* changes to abrupt and open *qualitative* changes, *i.e.*, *revolution*. This means, translated into terms of contemporary social conflict, that the oppressed proletariat overthrows its capitalist exploiters. Thus socialism replaces capitalism in the march of history.

The transition from capitalism to socialism cannot be brought about by reforms introduced by democratic (bourgeois) republics, but only by qualitative change, that is, overthrow of the capitalist order by violence.

The main force in the social process is change in the productive forces, especially the means of production. Capitalism developed large industrial plants and techniques of mass production. In this process, however, it built up the contradiction to which it will eventually succumb. The contradiction results from the fact that in its efforts to industrialize, capitalism gathers great numbers of workers together in enormous factories and in this way makes them aware of themselves as a social class and of their relation to the means of production. The primary contradiction of capitalism is that it is based on the one hand on cooperative production, and on the other hand on the private ownership of the means of production. According to Soviet theory this contradiction is the cause of overproduction and recurring capitalist crisis. The new productive forces require a change in ownership in order to realize their potentialities.

It is not possible here to examine this theory, presented in rudimentary fashion, for its validity. Suffice that the "contradiction" that allegedly opposes "capitalists" and "proletarians" is a semantic humbug. What is important here is the use to which this theory was put by the Bolsheviks and how it was modified in the struggle for power, first between the Bolsheviks and their opponents in Russia, then between Bolsheviks and Bolsheviks, and lastly between the Soviet Union and the rest of the world.

OPERATIONAL PRINCIPLES

The Basic Principle. Soviet doctrine is not merely a set of ideological beliefs. It is also a compendium of operational principles, a concept of conflict management. It is this aspect of the matter which ought to be of particular interest to the student and practitioner of international politics.

Marx, who thought he knew exactly how the world revolution would come about, expected that "capitalism" would be weakened by the "contradictions" of its own development. The poor would become ever poorer and the rich ever richer. Conditions ultimately would become so unbearable that the proletariat, which by that time would comprise the near-totality of the population, would rise, destroy the *bourgeoisie*, expropriate the means of production, and establish the communist state (which, Marx professed to believe, would wither away after a while).

However, historical events did not conform to Marx's prophecies. "Capitalism" developed into something quite different from what it was 100 years ago. There was no increasing misery, but a constantly improving living standard. There were no self-destructive "contradictions," but continuous development and growth. And the Western proletarian did not hanker for revolution.

This failure to conform to the dogma posed a difficult problem to Soviet leadership. The sacred texts could not be sacrificed without destroying the foundations of the communist faith, nor could they be used as action guides without destroying communist power. The Soviet leaders sought to escape this dilemma by using Marx's basic theorem as a working hypothesis: *if* there were insufferable and continuous misery and unemployment, *if* the economic system were to benefit only a small number of profiteers and impoverish the overwhelming majority of the people, *then* the free-world system must collapse. Accordingly, since these conditions did not come into being spontaneously, as Marx had taught, the anomy of the social structure must be created artificially.

Since the proletariat has nowhere risen to power in conformity with the original Marxian tenet, Marxian premises obviously must have been false.

Thus Soviet strategy must seek to validate Marx's premises—by turning them upside down. The strategy of modern communism depends not upon Marx's original construction, but upon the following variant: the destruction of capitalism must be accomplished, not by historical or economic erosion, but by revolutionary strategy and tactics. The communist movement should not let itself be pulled by the locomotive of history but must engineer its own success. Modern Soviet communism expects success not as the product of an unpredictable and uncontrollable historical process, but as the consequence of sociological warfare.[3]

The Concept of World Revolution. Marx expected the revolution to arise spontaneously from the disintegration of the social structure. The latter-day communists decided that this disintegration must be planned and systematically brought about by social-fission operations, uprisings, and war. Stalin gave to this sociological-military concept an additional sociological-geographic meaning: the mission of the Russian communists is to team the proletarian revolutions in the West with the peasant revolutions in the East (and in other "dependent" areas). The proletarian no longer is considered as the main force of the revolution. Revolution will be made by proletarians, peasants, intellectuals, soldiers, uprooted and alienated people of all kinds, with professional revolutionaries and military forces operating in joint action.

The various discontented social forces, organized in instruments of political and military combat and strategically supported by, or operating jointly with, the armed forces of the Soviet states, contrive the anomy and ultimately the collapse of the attacked state. Once a "revolutionary crisis" has been created, it must be exploited by a "revolutionary act"—communist seizure of the attacked government. It is immaterial by what means the crisis is brought about (violent or nonviolent methods, insurrections, or wars) and by what means it is exploited (political capture, revolutionary seizure, or military capitulation), *provided* the operation poses no undue risks to the survival of the Soviet dictatorship.

[3] Discussions on communism frequently degenerate into an exegesis of an indigestible amount of communist writings, which usually are quoted out of context. The result often is that the reader sees the trees but not the forest. Since the scholarly apparatus to support the discussion is easily accessible, the authors will happily resist the temptation to clutter this text with the *dicta* by Lenin and Stalin. Those skeptical readers who wish to verify the synthesis given in these pages may, under their own power, plough through the communist classics or, if this seems too tedious, consult William R. Kintner, *The Front Is Everywhere: Militant Communism in Action,* Norman, Okla., University of Oklahoma Press, 1950; Timothy Taracouzio, *War and Peace in Soviet Diplomacy,* New York, Macmillan, 1940; Nathan Leites, *The Operational Code of the Politbureau,* New York, McGraw-Hill, 1951; Waldemar Gurian, *The Soviet Union: Background, Ideology, Reality,* South Bend, Ind., University of Notre Dame Press, 1951; Ebed van der Vlugt, *Asia Aflame, Communism in the East,* New York, Devin-Adair, 1953; Franz Borkenau, *European Communism,* London, Faber, 1953; Anthony T. Bouscaren, *Imperial Communism,* Washington, D.C., Public Affairs Press, 1953; and Stefan T. Possony, *A Century of Conflict, Communist Techniques of World Revolution, 1848–1950,* Chicago, Regnery, 1953.

Organization. The creation of conditions which will lead to the collapse of the free world is the task of communist organization, strategy, and tactics. To the communists, organization (and not economic or even military power) is the strongest of all social and political forces. Organization serves to create and maximize material and political resources which can be thrown into the struggle. Internally, Soviet organization aims at the destruction of all political opposition, the indoctrination of the population, the maintenance of the economy at high levels of military readiness, the creation of large military forces, and the impulsion of the Soviet state machinery by *one* strong and aggressive will. Externally, the Soviets obtain organizational control over communist and cryptocommunist parties which they employ for psychological, political, and economic warfare as well as for the infiltration of foreign governments. These organizations are built up through propaganda and agitation. The process is designed as a chain reaction: the more propaganda, the more organization; and the more organization, the more propaganda. Combined, the external and internal organizations provide the Soviets with states, military armies, "political armies" (parties), revolutionary forces, infiltration cells, and psychological, political, and economic warfare units, as well as with indirectly controlled organizations, and thus with a *unique* power structure which can influence events in all corners of the globe.

Strategy. The Soviets aim, first and foremost, at the security of their base and their system. By security of base is meant not only the security of Russia against hostile activities, but also the security of the Soviet regime itself regardless of whether the threat is domestic or foreign, or of a military, economic, political or ideological nature.

Offensively, the Soviets expand, first, through local revolutions. These revolutions may assume the form of traditional uprisings, of mass infiltration leading to the political conquest of the target state, or of civil war. They can be undertaken through openly acknowledged, covert, or indirectly controlled communist elements. The Soviets expand, second, by means of limited wars waged by themselves or by their satellites. Such wars include guerrilla, civil, defensive, and offensive wars. While limited in terms of geography, they are fought to dislocate the social and political structure of wider areas. Third, major opponents, as the United States, may have to be eliminated by all-out war. A fourth method is to foment war among the capitalist countries and contrive the fatal weakening of all belligerents. The exhaustion once brought about would be exploited by the Soviet orbit through dictated peace, revolution, or occupation.

Each of these strategies has its advantages and disadvantages. Full-fledged war, for example, poses the greatest risk to the security of the Soviet base, yet it also holds the greatest promise of success. Expansion through local revolutions poses the least threat, but it offers the smallest opportunity and requires too much time. Limited wars may develop into all-out wars at the wrong time and place. The technique of fomenting wars among the "capitalist" nations and inducing them to dig their own grave was Stalin's preferred method which he reemphasized in his last public pronouncement: [4]

Some comrades hold that, owing to the development of new international conditions since the Second World War, wars between capitalist countries have ceased to be inevitable. They consider that the contradictions between the socialist camp and the capitalist camp are more acute than the contradictions among the capitalist countries; that the United States has brought the other capitalist countries sufficiently under its sway to be able to prevent them from going to war among themselves and weakening one another; that the foremost capitalist minds have been sufficiently taught by the two world wars and the severe damage they caused to the whole capitalist world not to venture to involve the capitalist countries in war with one another again—and that, because of all this, wars between capitalist countries are no longer inevitable. These comrades are wrong.

Stalin's legacy was to engineer fatal cleavages among the Western powers and between the West and dependent peoples, thus to bring about the most desirable conflicts of all—wars between noncommunist and, better still, anticommunist states. The binding directive on all good communists is to accomplish this objective through the effective use of such tools as infiltration, intellectual subversion, provocation, uprisings, and civil wars. But the limitations of this strategy should be obvious—unless we assume that Germany will war again upon the West or that Britain and the United States will fight each other. However, if we assume that Stalin may have been thinking rather of conflicts between "capitalist" powers and "dependent" colored peoples, then tne scope of this strategy becomes more clearly apparent.[5]

The Soviets are not bound to any one of these strategies but will use them as they always did, according to opportunity: singly, jointly, and successively.

The point is that they propose to employ, in any given situation, the *one* strategy which can accomplish most for the least cost and risk. Political conquest may take the place of uprising. Revolution may take the place of war or render war less costly. Or war may have to be substituted for revolution.

Soviet Geographical Strategy. The geographic objectives of Soviet strategy have been (1) to secure full domination over the areas which formerly belonged to the Russian empire; (2) to develop the "empty" spaces within Russia, especially the arctic areas; (3) to control, indirectly or directly, the key countries of Europe and Asia—Germany and China; (4) to gain control over the Middle East; and (5) to capture all and every area vulnerable to seizure.

Strategy against Germany and China has been characterized by a typical "dialectical" approach; while allegedly maintaining friendly relations with

---

[4] J. V. Stalin, *Economic Problems of Socialism in the USSR,* Information Services of the U.S.S.R., Embassy of the U.S.S.R., Washington, 1952, p. 15.

[5] *Ibid.,* p. 15. See also Eugen Varga, *Osnovnye Voprosi Ekonomiki i Politiki Imperializma posle Vtoroi Mirovoi Voiny* ("Basic Economic and Political Problems of Imperialism after World War II"), Moscow, Gospolitizdat, 1953.

the governments in power, the Soviets at the same time built up authentic communist and revolutionary forces in both countries. The objective of the first method was to influence these governments through diplomatic means, while the second method was applied in order to exert pressure on them if they were slow in following Soviet suggestions. Whenever the Soviets were rebuffed in their attempts to cooperate with Germany, they veered toward cooperation, albeit halfhearted cooperation, with France. Since the fall of China, India has become the Soviets' main preoccupation on the Asiatic continent. Several attempts to take over parts of the Middle East were never yet pressed home with resolution.

Until recently, the Soviets considered Britain and Japan as their main enemies. The destruction of the British Empire was a cherished goal, presumably because such an event would accelerate revolution in a large number of countries. Since the sources of British power were beyond Soviet grasp, attacks upon Britain were launched circuitously and by proxy, for example, by stirring up unrest in the Middle East, organizing large-scale strikes in the United Kingdom, espionage, subversion of officials, and fomenting war between Germany and England. Japan, too, was beyond the geographic reach of Soviet power. The attack against Japan was conduced partly by embroiling that country in a war with China (to which maneuver the Japanese foolishly lent themselves) and partly by limited wars in the Manchurian area.

More recently, the United States has been raised to the rank of major enemy of the Soviet Union. The Soviets have made every effort to separate the United States from its European and Asiatic allies and to disperse American strength by fomenting limited and peripheral wars. The ultimate purpose, it seems, was to contrive the isolation of the United States while, at the same time, encircling North America by building up Soviet "positions of strength" on the Pacific and Atlantic shores and in the arctic, and planting cryptocommunists in various bureaus of government, labor unions, and educational institutions as well as in the armed forces.

Tactics. Soviet tactics are based on the "dialectical" principle that all social and political entities are composed of contradictory and mutually hostile forces. Hence the fundamental tactical rule is to exacerbate the contradictions within social and political units, widen and exploit the cleavages between opposing forces, and bring about the disintegration of the target body.

Additional tactical rules are as follows:

1. Tactics must be flexible. The criterion is success, not conformity with a preconceived plan of action.

2. Tactics always should make the most of the element of surprise, the purpose being to prevent the opponent from putting up an effective defense.

3. In the course of operations, violent means *must* be employed, usually during the decisive phase of the struggle. However, violence never should be applied without concurrent employment of nonviolent means of combat. Non-

violent means, especially propaganda and infiltration, weaken hostile military forces, confuse public opinion, and dislocate government activities.

4. Communism cannot advance everywhere at the same time. It should concentrate its forces against that component of the free world which is the weakest.

5. Pressure against the opponent should never cease. The initiative should never be abandoned, particularly not in a difficult situation which requires a temporary switch to the defensive or a retreat.

6. The choice of offensive or defensive tactics depends on the over-all world situation. There are revolutionary ebb and flow periods. In flow periods the communists can advance their positions easily due to crisis, conflict, and war or war's aftermath. When opposing systems are relatively stable and take appropriate countermeasures, the revolutionary tides are ebbing. The communists act offensively during flow periods and defensively during ebb periods. Both types of situations are temporary. Whenever the Soviets are capable of creating a revolutionary flow period, they are bound to exploit the opportunity. Ebb periods must be put to use by strengthening the Soviet forces and preparing for later battles. Defensive tactics do not necessarily signify the discontinuance of attack but rather the suspension of frontal assaults.

7. Soviet tactics always must aim at deceiving the opponent. One of the standard methods of deception is the employment by the Soviets of pseudo-peace propaganda. The nature of this deception was explained quite candidly by M. Waldeck-Rochet, a leader of the French Communist Party. Speaking in Limoges (October, 1951), he said: [6]

You will say: "Why does not the Soviet Union intervene in Korea?" It would throw the Americans into the sea—that is true. But it would start a world war, which for the time being is contrary to the peace policy of the Soviet Union. . .
A year of peace is a year utilized to the utmost by the Soviet Union to re-inforce its army and the armies of the popular democracies. It is to permit this rearmament, this development of the Soviet Union's strength, as well as the strength of the popular democracies, that we must actively continue our propaganda in favor of peace. It is this movement for peace that will undermine the imperialist armies and delay the outbreak of war [and] assure the destruction of our enemies. *The Soviet Union will choose the right moment and the imperialists will have no say in the matter.*

8. Attacks on major enemies never should be launched when these are militarily, socially and politically strong. Decisive attacks should be delayed till the opponent is weakened internally through espionage, crisis, infiltration, disarmament, or war. But once the major opponent is readied for the kill, he must be struck with overpowering force. The atomic bomb surely is not an unwelcome addition to the Soviet arsenal of weapons; and perhaps it may

[6] Quoted by Lewis Corey in "War as a Soviet Policy," *The New Leader,* June 25, 1952, p. 15. (Italics added.)

be substituted, some time in the future, for the social dislocation which, according to present doctrine, must precede attack.

DOCTRINE AND DIPLOMACY

What ought Soviet diplomacy and foreign policy to be, according to official doctrine? Fortunately the Soviets have revealed forthrightly what role they assign to diplomacy in their political endeavors. No less a person than Eugene Tarlé, foremost Russian historian, member of the Academy of Sciences, and coauthor of the official *History of Diplomacy,* edited under the chairmanship of Vladimir Potiemkine, former Soviet Deputy Foreign Commissar, has taken the trouble to define the mission of Soviet diplomacy. Writing in the *History of Diplomacy,* Tarlé pointed out that Friedrich Engels called the attention of those "who fight in the political arena" to the need of studying military science: military science, or the art of war, plays "a capital role in the fight for a better future of humanity." [7] (The communists have always despised pacifism.) However, studies in military matters are not enough, says Tarlé. It is equally important to study the art of diplomacy. The fighter for that better future of humanity must know thoroughly "the tactics and the ruses employed by the adversary on the battlefield as well as in diplomatic controversies." The adversary is, of course, the *bourgeoisie.* And Tarlé goes on to describe the tactics of "bourgeois diplomacy."

Summarizing his findings, the Russian historian states that bourgeois diplomacy virtually always follows the dictum of the celebrated Swedish Chancellor Oxenstierna: "Simulantur quae non sunt, quae sunt vero dissimulantur" ("Feign what is not, and conceal what is"). According to Oxenstierna, the diplomat has two devices at his disposal: simulation and dissimulation. And those devices, Tarlé insists, still serve the bourgeois diplomat, but apparently not the Soviet statesman.[8]

According to Tarlé the standard tricks of bourgeois diplomacy are as follows: [9] Aggression is hidden behind the pretext of defense; aggression can be camouflaged by allegedly disinterested motives; pacifist propaganda is used to deceive the opponent and to lull him into a feeling of false security;

[7] See V. Potiemkine, *Histoire de la diplomatie,* Paris, Médicis, 1947, Vol. III, p. 727.

[8] See *ibid.,* pp. 732ff.

[9] Lenin, in his *"Left-wing" Communism: An Infantile Disorder: An Experimental Talk on Marxian Strategy and Tactics* (Moscow, Cooperative Publishing Society of Foreign Workers in the U.S.S.R., 1935) stressed that the communists must be masters of *all* methods of warfare and politics (p. 95) and must display artful flexibility (p. 101). The book was written to show how democratic parliaments and elections can be abused "in a revolutionary manner, in a Communist manner" (p. 62). The general line of argument can be gleaned from this quotation which is in the best Machiavelli style: "The surest way of discrediting a new political (and not only political) idea, and of damaging it, is to reduce it to absurdity while ostensibly defending it. For every truth, if it is carried beyond the limits in which it can be actually applied, can be reduced to absurdity, and, under the conditions mentioned, is even inevitably converted into an absurdity" (p. 59).

treaties of friendship are concluded in order to put vigilance to sleep; conflicts are localized to make possible the destruction of countries by successive aggression (otherwise known as the "artichoke strategy"); internal dissensions in the opponent's country are utilized to facilitate aggression; national disputes and contradictory interests among the opponents are exploited; aggression is prepared by demagogic appeals for a fight against imperialism; and the protection of weak states is used as an excuse for their occupation. Other standard tactical means are threats, terror, lies, and blackmail (pressure). If Tarlé were to be believed, bourgeois diplomacy never uses other methods.

It is beside the point whether or not this is an accurate description of "bourgeois diplomacy." It is true, to be sure, that such practices were used time and again and by all countries, including the Soviet Union. However, such diplomacy is much more characteristic of Messrs. Chicherin, Litvinov, Molotov, and Vyshinski [10] than, for example, of Messrs. Hughes, Stimson, Hull, and Byrnes. Yet Tarlé has supplied the official Soviet interpretation of the diplomacy of such countries as the United States and Great Britain. This interpretation has been, and in all likelihood still is, the guide of Soviet diplomats. Is it far-fetched to assume that these are the very techniques which characterize Soviet diplomacy?

SOVIET FORCES

Many observers experience difficulties in perceiving the true proportions of the Soviet threat. They hesitate to credit the Soviets with bold ambition to achieve world rule, a goal which no power has ever attained. If history retains its deeper meanings the Soviet *hubris* indeed will be punished exactly as was the unseemly pride of previous would-be conquerors. Yet new instruments now serve the ambitions of the conqueror. Atomic weapons and air power will endow a future aggressor with a strength no previous conqueror ever could dream of. Moreover, the total power structure of the Soviet orbit, in size and capabilities, is quite exceptional in the annals of history. The Soviets now control

The strongest power base, in terms of resources and manpower, of any historically known aggressor

A far larger portion of the globe's power resources than any previous aggressor

A strong state organization which provides for militarization from the cradle to the grave for all the inhabitants of the Soviet orbit

[10] The entire line of thought was aptly summarized by Bakunin who was a great expert in the matter: "The Russian peasant would think that he is slipping if he does not deceive when he has a chance to do so" (quoted by Henri Rollin in *La Révolution russe —ses origines—ses résultats*, Paris, Delagrave, 1937, Vol. II, "Le Parti bolcheviste," p. 167).

A position of near-hegemony in Europe and Asia

A very strong military force together with a weapons technology of unprecedented destructiveness

Organized political communist forces abroad

Organized paramilitary forces abroad

Rebellious peasant forces abroad

National liberation movements (to varying degrees)

Forces to carry out demoralization, infiltration, sabotage, economic dislocation, disintegration, and provocation abroad

The list could be lengthened. Some of these forces can be maintained without cost to the Soviet government. There is a danger in exaggerating communist strength and thus yielding to fear; there is an even greater danger in underrating the strength of America and the free world. Nonetheless, there is food for thought and for some bitter reflections in the fact that the communists succeeded in building up their might within a third of a century and that their power still is growing. Not even Japan's rapid rise to power can compare with the Soviet accomplishment.

The Defense of the Soviet Bloc. It has been asserted frequently that the Soviets are "defensive-minded." How a group of people working at revolutionizing the entire world can be "defensive-minded" is a little hard to explain, and certainly no evidence has ever been adduced to support the contention. If we take our bearings by acts rather than words, we shall note that the Soviets have consistently pushed forward the borders of the areas under their control. As a result of this expansion, the strategic problem of the Soviets has changed. Previously they needed to concern themselves merely with dangers that arose in Europe. Beginning in 1931, they were compelled to strengthen their defenses in the Far East, but even so it was quite impossible for the Japanese to pose a real (as distinguished from a peripheral) threat to Soviet security. Under present conditions, the defensive task of the Soviets has grown immeasurably: they must provide proper defenses for vital areas in Asia; their glacis in Europe has become vulnerable to rebellion as may in future Soviet possessions in the Caucasus, in Central Asia, and even in the Ukraine; and they have to guard against a threat which may come from the north. The Soviets find themselves placed in a difficult position somewhat similar to that of the British Commonwealth burdened with the operational problem of how to coordinate the interests of many far-flung nations. The defense problem is becoming increasingly unmanageable for the Soviets. If they should consider it insoluble, they may bethink themselves of the venerable axiom that offense is the best defense.

Inevitability of Conflict. There are numerous official communist statements documenting the conviction of the Soviet leaders that violent conflict with the free world, including the United States, ultimately will be inevitable. There are quite a few statements to the effect that such a conflict would be desirable. On the other hand, in a few rare interviews with foreign newspapermen Stalin professed the belief that the "capitalist" countries and the Soviet world could coexist peacefully. Not one of these interviews for foreign consumption has proper standing within the permanent communist literature. Not one of the statements which Stalin addressed benevolently to his awed interlocutors really says what it is supposed to say. In Stalinist thought, coexistence means a temporary state of affairs in which there is *no open* conflict between the Soviet Union and the Western powers. Coexistence periods —"ebb" periods—are conceived as preludes to violent conflict. They are to be exploited by fostering "revolutions" in the East and in the West. Not once have Soviet leaders committed themselves to calling off their tactics of social fission and to desisting from their preparations for the ultimate test. Never have they attempted to organize their power as an instrument of peace rather than as a tool for war.

Regardless of the intentions of Soviet leadership, much will depend on whether the internal strains and stresses of the Soviet system will force them into outward aggression or to eschew foreign adventures. It is next to impossible to build up tension and hatred for many years, to live by a revolutionary code of aggression, to spark conflagrations in many areas of the world, and then to halt the juggernaut before it reaches its destination. It is characteristic of militant elites—and the Soviets *are* a militant elite—that they never know when to stop. It is foolish to expect gamblers to quit while they are still winning and while they have yet enough chips to continue the game.

It is futile to disregard facts; Soviet leadership, by its intent and action, has committed itself to a life-and-death struggle against the free world and strained every muscle and exploited every resource to prepare itself for a gigantic contest.

LEADERSHIP PROBLEMS

Russian Nationalism. As the medieval papacy needed the sword of the Emperor, so communism must rely on the military strength of Russia, Eastern Europe, and China. In the early phases of their existence, the communists believed that communism would prove ideologically stronger than nationalism. But in the 1930's they came to realize that their strength did not depend on the members of the Communist Party alone but on the Russian people as a whole and that they could not safely antagonize the innate patriotism of the Russian nation. Hence they decided to play up to patriotic sentiments and to stimulate the basic and instinctive urge to defend one's own fatherland as a sure method of increasing Soviet military power.

Since communism operates from Russia as its major base, the policies of the Soviet Union must show a Russian face and display some of the geographic and operational characteristics which previously graced Tsarist policies. Russian nationalists, moreover, may condone and serve Soviet rule on the ground that it advances the cause of Russia. Communists the world over may support Russia because Russia champions the cause of communism. But the objective is not to further the glory of Russia but to impose the communist dictatorship on the rest of the world. Even in the cultural field, the communists do not support Russian nationalism per se. Their objective is to create a new *Soviet* culture into which the various national cultures are to be fused or dissolved. Soviet patriotism—*not* Russian nationalism—is supposed to be the psychological response of affection toward the new type of society. It is to reflect the "superiority" of the Soviet system over other systems and to express the proud love which "Soviet man" ought to feel toward socialism. While the manifestations of this "patriotism" rarely are different from the manifestations of old-fashioned and purblind chauvinism, it would be a great error to confuse it with nationalism in the Western style. The Soviets never became Russian nationalists. They harnessed the force of Russian nationalism to the interests of furthering communism.[11]

In seizing Eastern Europe the Soviets were confronted with the problem of how to avoid arousing antagonisms among the Eastern European nations. The clumsy postwar policy of enforced Russification has rekindled the national hatreds which have been traditional in the area. The Soviets found it difficult to make the subjugated people understand the subtle difference betweeen Russification and sovietization. The difficulty is compounded by the fact that some of the subjugated peoples are just now emerging into full nationhood and have tasted, albeit briefly, the joys of national independence. It is not surprising that, at the time of this writing, the Soviets have not even tried to undertake the cultural integration of Russia with China, although they succeeded in infiltrating that country. Nevertheless, the problem of integration cannot be side-stepped; and it holds the key to the future. To create an international state, a unifying bond must be forged. The communists hope that "Soviet patriotism" can be developed as such a unifying, international bond, and that loyalty to socialism organized in a multinational system of states will overcome old loyalties to national independence and statehood. This feat might conceivably be accomplished were the Soviet system to satisfy the aspirations of its citizens. As it is, the ideal of a unifying Soviet culture does not shine brightly. The attempt to manufacture and spread that synthetic "culture" may contribute heavily to the final undoing of Sovietism.

Cleavages among Soviet Leaders. Soviet propaganda tries to create the impression that Soviet leadership is united and "monolithic." That Soviet leaders have shown in the past a high degree of solidarity is indisputable. Yet this unity was achieved not by persuasion but by the elimination of all groups which disagreed with the group exercising the monopoly of power. Historically, conflicts among Soviet leaders have arisen for the following reasons:

---

[11] See P. Fedosseyev, "Sotsialism i patriotism," *Kommunist*, No. 9, 1953; also John S. Reshetar, Jr., "Der Bolschevismus und die nationale Frage," *Ost-Probleme*, No. 31, 1953; and M. D. Kammari, *The Development by J. V. Stalin of the Marxist-Leninist Theory of the National Question*, Moscow, Foreign Languages Publishing House, 1951.

1. Different concepts concerning operations: offensive or defensive? Violent or nonviolent? Revolutionary or military?

2. Differences as to how and where the conflict should be waged primarily: in Europe or in Asia? Through proletarian or peasant forces? Through class wars or united fronts?

3. Differences on domestic politics: should the terror be reinforced or relaxed? Should there be more or less slave labor? More or less "democracy"? More "nationalism" or more "internationalism"?

4. Ideological differences: to what extent should Marxism be reinterpreted? To what extent is it wise to rewrite history surreptitiously? Should it be acknowledged frankly that the old concepts are out of date? For that matter, to what extent do the Soviet leaders recognize that their axioms and thought patterns have become obsolete? To what extent has communism stopped being a drive ideology and become a tool?

5. Differences on economic policy: should there be more emphasis on armaments or on goods for consumption? Should the collectivization of agriculture be pushed further or be relaxed? Should internal trade be liberalized or be controlled more tightly? Should there be more or less foreign trade? Should the satellites be industrialized or their industrial equipment be cannibalized for use within Russia?

6. Differences on relations with the outside world: should the basic conflict be intensified or relaxed? Is the ultimate struggle to be waged at an earlier or a later date? In this connection, the most difficult question on the agenda of the Soviet government probably is this: how is the immense power of the United States to be broken, by direct or indirect, military or nonmilitary means? Should the United States be tackled at all?

7. Differences among the Soviet leaders in their competition for power: They fashion their arguments, tactics, and strategies, at least in part, according to the demands of the internal power struggle. The influence of this struggle on their policies must be enormous, since policies are often being adopted not for their suitability but for their appropriateness as means of a Soviet politician's physical survival.

In evaluating the foreign policy of a dictatorial system, one should never forget that, despite appearances, its flexibility is far less than that of an efficient democratic government. Men who reach high command posts in an established dictatorship are brought in by cooption, and not by genuine, competitive political struggle; they succeed because they possess a conformist mentality. Yet if the old generation dies and the dictatorship perpetuates itself, then a younger generation is bound to infuse a new life into the system. Before such a transformation takes place, there will inevitably be a conflict between the older and the younger generation. As a matter of course, such conflicts end either with the extermination of both contestants or with the victory of the young.

Whatever the ideological fervor which inspires a group of men, professional politicians are habitually consumed by strong power urges. In practically every case (including that of the most fanatical theoretician) personal power is more important than theory. The men who hold the levers of command want to keep them; their policy is constantly influenced by their intention to defeat their opponents. Some of these opponents themselves hold important posts of command. At the heights of internecine conflict, paralysis grips the government. Whenever power struggles wax intense, as, for example, during the period of the treason trials of 1936–1938 and after Stalin's death in 1953, and whenever the loser may lose his life—a not unusual occurrence in the Soviet Union—the machinery of government tends to stall. While this may not delay decisions on important issues of foreign policy, it is conducive to the making of foolish and dangerous ones. Both Russia and the rest of the world may be made to suffer for the neurosis of power-hungry, competing cliques mutually frightened of each other.

So much for the struggles among the Soviet leaders in Russia. Ever since the emergence of a Soviet orbit, there have occurred struggles between Russian and non-Russian communists which usually ended in purges of the foreign communists. In the case of Tito, however, the contest ended with the defection of Yugoslavia. The biggest problem will be how the Russian communists will get along with the Chinese communists and to what extent differences of concept and interest will weaken the orbit's unity of purpose.

Personal struggles between Russia's communists and the leaders of communist parties in the free world also reduce the Soviet conflict machine's over-all capability.

The ultimate outcome of these incessant struggles between power-hungry and fearful leaders, rebellious peoples, contrary ideological ambitions, national hatreds, rival party organizations, economic interests, and military strategies is most uncertain. We can *hope* the Soviet regime will become more moderate and that it will evolve into a more stable *modus vivendi* with the West. We certainly cannot rely on such a contingency, nor can we be sure that such an evolution, if it were to occur, would not be accompanied by extraordinary convulsions. The Soviet regime may grow senile—*mors certa est*—but then the question will be how the present regime can be liquidated and how it can be made to yield up the conquered areas without setting the world on fire.

Heretofore, Soviet leadership always has been able to compose its difficulties. The death of Stalin may have resulted in the rejuvenation of Soviet leadership and hence in an increase of the danger. The only hopeful conclusion that can be drawn with a reasonable degree of assurance, but by no means with certainty, is this: if the Soviets are denied promising opportunities for carrying their aggressive and offensive policies to a victorious conclusion, they may be compelled to cooperate, or risk destruction. But if opportunities continue to present themselves, the Soviets will not be halted on their forward march. It would be foolish to expect it.

Perhaps the Soviet leaders realize that the continuation of their policies will have to be paid for by their own doom. But can they extricate themselves from this dilemma? If they were to embark on a true and honest policy of peace, they would have to adapt their system to their changed intent. This they probably cannot do without risking their eviction from power. The image of the sorcerer's apprentice comes to mind. It conjures up an almost compulsive threat to the peace of the world.

BIBLIOGRAPHY

Beloff, Max: *Communism: Its Strength and Its Future,* Toronto, Canadian Association for Adult Education, 1948.
Borkenau, Franz: *European Communism,* London, Faber, 1953.
Carr, Edward Halett: *Studies in Revolution,* London, Macmillan, 1950.
———: *The Bolshevik Revolution, 1917–1923,* 3 vols., London, Macmillan, 1950–1953.
Chamberlin, William Henry: *The Russian Revolution, 1917–1921,* New York, Macmillan, 1935.
Dallin, David: *The Rise of Russia in Asia,* New Haven, Yale University Press, 1949.
———: *Soviet Russia and the Far East,* New Haven, Yale University Press, 1948.
———: *Russia and Postwar Europe,* New Haven, Yale University Press, 1943.
———: *Soviet Russia's Foreign Policy, 1939–1942,* New Haven, Yale University Press, 1942.
——— and B. I. Nicolaevsky: *Forced Labor in the Soviet Union,* New Haven, Yale University Press, 1947.
Deutscher, Isaac: *Stalin: A Political Biography,* New York, Oxford, 1949.
Fischer, Louis: *The Soviets in World Affairs,* 2 vols., 2d ed., Princeton, N.J., Princeton University Press, 1950.
Gruliow, Leo (ed.): *Current Soviet Policies,* New York, Praeger, 1953.
Hunt, R. N. Carew: *The Theory and Practice of Communism,* New York, Macmillan, 1952.
Lasswell, Harold D.: "Inevitable War: A Problem in the Control of Long-range Expectations," *World Politics,* October, 1949, Vol. II.
Lens, Sidney: *The Counterfeit Revolution,* Boston, Beacon Press, 1952.
Meissner, Boris: *Russland im Umbruch, Der Wandel in der Herrschaftsordnung und sozialen Struktur der Sowjetunion,* Frankfurt, Verlag für Geschichte und Politik, 1951.
Milioukov, P.: *La Politique extérieure des Soviets,* Paris, Giard, 1934.
Monnerot, Jules: *Sociologie du communisme,* Paris, Gallimard, 1949.
Pareto, Vilfredo: *Les Systèmes socialistes,* 2 vols., Paris, Giard, 1926.
Possony, Stefan T.: *A Century of Conflict, Communist Techniques of World Revolution, 1848–1950,* Chicago, Regnery, 1953.
Schwarz, Solomon M.: *Labor in the Soviet Union,* New York, Praeger, 1952.
Scott, Andrew McKay: *The Anatomy of Communism,* New York, Philosophical Library, 1951.
Seifert, Josef Leo: *Die Weltrevolutionäre: Von Bogumil über Hus zu Lenin,* Vienna, Amalthea, 1931.
Selznick, Philip: *The Organizational Weapon: A Study of Bolshevik Strategy and Tactics,* New York, McGraw-Hill, 1952.
Shub, David: *Lenin,* New York, Doubleday, 1948.
Swarup, R.: *Russian Imperialism, How to Stop It?* Calcutta, Prachi Prakasham, 1950.
Timasheff, Nicholas S.: *The Great Retreat: The Growth and Decline of Communism in Russia,* New York, Dutton, 1946.
Towster, Julian: *Political Power in the U.S.S.R., 1917–1948,* New York, Oxford, 1948.

Vagts, Alfred: "Russian Diplomatic History—N.S. or O.S.?" *World Politics,* Vol. 2, October, 1949 (a critical review of Potiemkine).

Varga, Eugen: *Osnovnye Voprosi Ekonomiki i Politiki Imperializma posle Vtoroi Mirovoi Voiny,* Moscow, Gospolitizdat, 1953.

Wolfe, Bertram D.: *Three Who Made a Revolution: A Biographical History,* New York, Dial Press, 1948.

Chapter 23

SOVIET FOREIGN POLICY: A CASE STUDY

> To destroy the danger of foreign capitalist intervention, the capitalist
> encirclement would have to be destroyed.
> History of the Communist Party of the Soviet Union.

The study of Soviet policy can be pursued by two different methods: by developing an over-all analysis of this policy and its manifestations at different times and places; or by analyzing comprehensively one particular case of Soviet conduct in international politics. The choice between the universal-historical and the case-study method is dictated by space limitations; only an illustrative case study can be fitted into the framework of a general text on international relations.

The selection of the Nazi-Soviet pact of 1939 and, in a more general way, of German-Soviet relations as the subject of this case study was prompted by the authors' belief that this pact is a key to the understanding of Soviet policy. The Nazi-Soviet pact was not just an improvisation, but the crowning piece of Stalin's statesmanship. Moreover, it was one of the most crucial events of modern history.

In 1939, Russian foreign policy first reached the summit of ambiguity, and then became clearly and aggressively pro-German. Russia's *professed* policy aimed at stopping the aggressor. This avowed policy did not change after the Munich pact of 1938; on the contrary, Russia participated in many conferences to strengthen her ties with the Western powers. Secretly, however, the Soviets conducted negotiations with the Germans. While they did not exert themselves to come to an agreement with the West, they made far greater efforts to come to an understanding with Nazi Germany.[1] According to the published record, they were far less suspicious of German than of British intentions.

[1] The difference in attitude on the part of the Soviets is well illustrated by a letter from the German Ambassador in Moscow to the German Foreign Office: "Concerning the political negotiations up to now [with France and Britain], we hear that throughout Herr Molotov sat like a bump on a log." To this Ambassador Count von der Schulenburg added the marginal note: "He has been very different toward Hilger and me of late; very communicative and amiable." The letter continues: "He hardly ever opened his mouth, and if he did it was to utter only the brief remark: 'Your statements do not appear to me entirely satisfactory. I shall notify my government.' The British and French ambassadors are both said to be completely exhausted." (Department of State, *Nazi-Soviet Relations 1939–1941*, Government Printing Office, 1948, p. 42.

The crux of the Russian-German relationship always has been that each had much to offer to the other. If Russia were to dominate Germany and her great technological resources, she would *ipso facto* dominate Europe and hence be close to the domination of the world. Similarly, had Germany dominated Russia, she would have been the world's leading power. Defensively, each was able to provide the other with protection against a two-front war. It is not surprising, therefore, that in their early plans the communists dreamed of a Russo-German "amalgam" which would constitute the insuperable power base of world revolution.

The difficulty of this concept has been that the "amalgam" can be brought about only through a true and trusting collaboration between two basically different peoples. As long as the "amalgam" would have meant *de facto* German rule over Russia, it was unacceptable to Russia. As soon as the "amalgam" became tantamount to Russian rule over Germany, it grew unacceptable to the Germans.

Russo-German collaboration in the past has been popular with the rulers of both countries. It usually was effective as a defensive arrangement. As an offensive threat, it served as an instrument of blackmail but, more importantly, it also tended, at crucial moments, to upset the policies and strategies of the West. Thrice in this generation, the Western governments negotiated and cooperated with Russia only to discover to their surprise and dismay that secret agreements of Russia with Germany had forestalled them. During the First World War Lenin, acting in accord with Germany, took Russia out of the war and thus almost contrived a Western defeat in 1918. After the First World War, the surprise pact of Rapallo prevented a settlement between Germany and the West. In 1939, the Western powers underwent the disenchanting experience of the Nazi-Soviet pact. And there might have been a fourth incident of this type if after 1943 Hitler had accepted Stalin's offers to negotiate a separate peace.[2]

THE SOVIET-GERMAN CONNECTION, 1918–1939

Between 1918 and 1925 Germany and Russia were very close to each other. During those years, the two "outcast" nations did not maintain international relations in the true sense of the word; they were isolated from the other great powers. Their mutual relationship was the only chink in the curtain of isolation. The conclusion of the Locarno pact (1925) opened to Germany the doors of the League of Nations and restored the German republic to international equality, at least formally. It did not signify the termination of Germany's special relation with Russia. Even with the rise of Adolf Hitler, influential groups in both countries championed, for various reasons, close

[2] Peter Kleist, *Zwischen Hitler und Stalin 1939–1945*, Bonn, Athenaeum, 1950, Part III. Kleist quotes Ribbentrop to the effect that "the old Rapallo fright" is always good enough to force the Western powers into *any* concession (p. 273).

German-Russian cooperation. Western statesmen were prone to overlook the fact that the Bolsheviks were Russians as well as Marxist-Leninists, and that the Nazis were Germans as well as Nazis. Historical environment is not so easily transformed by new ideologies. Germany's greatest statesman, Prince Otto von Bismarck, always strove to prevent conflict between Russia and Germany. Bismarck, the "honest broker" of the Congress of Berlin (1878) which upset the gains Russia had made in a victorious war against Turkey, applied his diplomatic skill to the appeasement of Russia—he sought to guide Russian expansionism toward Asia: "Russia has nothing to gain in the West; she only contracts nihilism and other diseases; her mission is in Asia; there she stands for civilisation." [3] Bismarck's policy was based on the fact that both Russia and Germany shared common monarchical traditions and that both ruled over areas which were inhabited by Poles. While the First World War ended with the overthrow of monarchical government in both countries and while Poland became a sovereign state, Germany and Russia still maintained close and friendly relations with each other.

The collaboration between the Germans and the Bolsheviks probably antedates by several years Lenin's famous journey—by sealed railroad car—in 1917, from Switzerland across Germany to Russia. In all likelihood, Lenin and other Bolsheviks had for many years collaborated closely with Germany. Most certainly, it is thanks to German connivance that Lenin succeeded in taking command of the Russian revolution.

When the Bolsheviks had gained control of the Petrograd-Moscow area, they negotiated the Brest-Litovsk Treaty with Germany which removed the fledgling Soviet state from World War I. According to official communist historiography, this treaty gave Lenin the "breathing spell" he needed to consolidate the revolution in Russia. True, Russia suffered grievous losses. She lost 34 per cent of her population, 32 per cent of her agricultural land, 85 per cent of her best sugar land, 54 per cent of her industrial undertakings, and 89 per cent of her coal mines.[4] Despite these losses, the base of the first proletarian state in the world was secured. Without these sacrifices, communist historians tell us, it would have perished before the onslaught of the German or White Russian forces. This theory sounds convincing enough except for the fact that Germany was militarily unable to evict the Bolsheviks from Russia and was moreover determined to maintain Lenin and his cohorts in power. The true motives which prompted Lenin to accede to German demands can only be guessed. That they were complex and "dialectic" is beyond doubt. For while Lenin was playing along with the German government, he also made some efforts to stimulate a revolution in Germany.

To many German generals, the Brest-Litovsk Treaty appeared to realize their long-cherished dreams of German self-sufficiency in raw materials and

[3] Quoted by Sir Bernard Pares in *A History of Russia,* New York, Knopf, 1930, p. 409.
[4] John W. Wheeler-Bennett, "The Meaning of Brest-Litovsk Today," *Foreign Affairs,* Vol. 17, No. 1, October, 1938, p. 139.

foodstuffs, since most of Germany's shortages could now be met from the surplus of territories ceded by Russia.[5] The dual prospect of autarchy and freedom from a two-front war combined to make the Brest-Litovsk Treaty attractive to even such an arch-Bolshevik-hater as Ludendorff—"involuntary savior of bolshevism for Europe."[6]

Following Germany's defeat in World War I, official German-Soviet collaboration did not start until 1922 with the signing of the Treaty of Rapallo; however, there was mounting evidence of clandestine collaboration between these two powers long before the launching of the Rapallo policy. In 1919, Sir Halford Mackinder, the well-known geographer and then British High Commissioner to South Russia, reported to the Foreign Office that the "Bolshevik army is rapidly adopting German methods of fighting" and that German diplomats were "entering into negotiations with the Soviet government," then virtually outlawed by international society.

It has often been asserted that the Germans are behind the bolshevik policy, and the younger officers in Denikin's army undoubtedly believe that Germany has only to utter the word and the bolshevik advance would stop. It may well be that there are subterranean German agencies, probably through Jewish channels, and there is now much more definite evidence than before that German soldiers of fortune are obtaining scope in the bolshevik army, but I can obtain no mass of evidence that the German government is at present directing bolshevik policy. This, however, does not affect the serious fact, which has become very evident during the recent bolshevik advance, that the bolshevik army is rapidly adopting German methods of fighting. . . . The new fire tactics, the new strategy of attacking at the joints between armies, the assaults just before dawn, and many other phenomena, afford conclusive evidence of a very different kind.[7]

[5] ". . . For Germany it was essential to concentrate all available troops on the Western front as soon as possible in order to insure the success of the spring offensive against the Allies on which the high command had staked their all. Hindenburg and Ludendorff therefore demanded a speedy conclusion of the negotiations. . . . There opened before their eyes too, the opportunity to exploit the rich black soil of the Ukraine, whence grain could be exported to feed the army and population of Germany, brought near starvation by the Allied blockade." *Ibid.*, p. 138.

[6] *Ibid.*, p. 142.

[7] Sir Halford Mackinder, "Report on the Situation in South Russia," *Documents on British Foreign Policy,* London, H.M. Stationery Office, 1919, Series 1, Vol. 3, pp. 776–777. Mackinder later added an appendix to his report (*ibid.*, p. 798) providing a documentary basis for his fears that such collaboration existed: "When I was on the point of leaving Novorossik on my journey home General Lukomsky made the following statements to me:

"1. Krassin makes frequent journeys to Berlin.

"2. Madame Kharitonenko, wife of the proprietor of a sugar factory, went from Malta to Geneva some one or two months ago. At Geneva she met by accident in a drawing room Bülow * and Allersleben (? Alvensleben).† They told her they had received plenipotentiary powers to go to Moscow, and to get into relations with the Soviet government. . . . I see no reason to doubt the accuracy of General Lukomsky's report of what she had told him, though it seems curious that such a meeting should have taken place by accident. . . .

* "Possibly Herr B. W. von Bülow, formerly a member of the German Peace Delegation at Versailles. . . .

† "H.M. Minister at Berne had reported in May 1919 that Count Alvensleben owned

Preliminary negotiations between Russia and Germany were started as far back as 1921 by General von Seeckt, chief of the *Reichswehr*.[8] The Polish question was the godmother of the alliance between the *Reichswehr* and the Red Army, an alliance which pushed ideologies to the side and countered French diplomacy in eastern and southeastern Europe. The *rapprochement* was speeded by economic considerations. Already in 1922, German business groups were pointing to the potentialities offered a resurgent German industry by the Russian market. The industrial interests of the Ruhr eyed hopefully plans for the reconstruction of the Russian railway system. While these groups gave domestically every assistance to the anticommunist right-wing parties, they stood steadfastly in opposition to attempts aimed at overthrowing the Soviet government in Russia.[9] The political representative of these groups was the German National People's Party. That party's spokesman was Otto Hoetzsch, a professor at the University of Berlin and member of the *Reichstag*. In a *Reichstag* debate, Hoetzsch made this revealing statement: [10]

As an adherent of the capitalist system and of our present state system, I oppose the Russian system without compromise. For many years, however, I believe that the coexistence of a capitalist and a soviet-socialist state system is possible because it is necessary. I am an ardent opponent of all intentions, groups and ideas seeking to join Germany to the anti-soviet front notwithstanding the motives of those who advocate such a policy. We would be foolish to join such a combination.

It was in March, 1921, that Seeckt began to negotiate with Russia for the establishment of German factories in Soviet Russia, with the obvious intention of violating the Versailles Treaty which prohibited the manufacture of military aircraft and tanks by Germany. There was a reciprocal advantage for Russia because her own rearmament effort was now aided by German industry. Krassin and Radek, Lenin's closest collaborators, and other high Soviet officials journeyed to Berlin for the purpose of quietly and secretly laying the groundwork for the Rapallo policy. The Rapallo Treaty was the result of considered German and Soviet policies; it was not concluded to provide an outlet for the ill humor of two neglected sulking nations. It was also at this time that Seeckt organized the "Special Branch R" in the *Reichswehr* Ministry. General von Schleicher, later a Chancellor of the *Reich*, placed his Berlin residence at the disposal of high Soviet officials for use as a meeting place and then went secretly to Moscow.

---

a villa by the Lake of Geneva and was reported to have been summoned to Berlin with a view to proceeding to Petrograd and entering into relations with the Soviet government."

[8] Walter Goerlitz, *History of the German General Staff*, New York, Praeger, 1953, pp. 228–233.

[9] Ernst Fraenkel, in "German-Russian Relations since 1918," *Review of Politics*, Vol. 2, No. 1, January, 1940, pp. 52–53, points out that the pro-Russian tendencies of the German general staff were supported by German business.

[10] *Ibid.*, pp. 53–54. The National People's Party led the fight against communism in Germany. Despite this, Hoetzsch was invited to Russia every year. Ironically, the German socialists were not allowed to enter Russia, while the German nationalists were welcomed with open arms.

Seeckt promised benevolent neutrality to Russia should she be attacked by Poland. Germany was to provide Russia with military advice. In return, Russia allowed the German general staff to test and perfect weapons and thus to circumvent the Versailles Treaty. This arrangement enabled the Germans to give on-the-spot training to specialists in various weapons, far from the eyes of the Allied control authorities in Germany.[11]

Two organizations were created for the purpose of acting as intermediaries between the *Reichswehr* and Russia. One was the *Gesellschaft zur Förderung gewerblicher Unternehmungen* (Society for the Development of Industrial Enterprise); the other was the *Bersol-Aktien Gesellschaft,* located in Russia, where it engaged in the production of poison gas. Junkers opened two aircraft factories—one near Moscow and the other in Kharkov—where the construction of military aircraft was begun.[12] Thus cooperation between Russia and Germany was well under way when the signing of the Rapallo Treaty in 1922 put the official stamp of approval on it. The treaty was drafted by Baron von Maltzan, a prominent exponent of the "Eastern" school of postwar German diplomacy, and was signed on April 24, 1922, by Walter Rathenau and G. V. Chicherin, who had slipped quietly away from the Genoa Conference to the nearby town of Rapallo, Italy.

The Treaty of Rapallo ushered in a period of ten years of the most intense cooperation between Germany and Russia. Under the provisions of Article 116 of the Versailles Treaty, France had tried to acquire reparations payments due Russia from Germany as a means of settling Russia's prewar debt to France. This scheme, known as the "Barthou Plan," was rejected by Russia when she signed the Rapallo Treaty which renounced all of Russia's reparations claims against Germany. The Rapallo Treaty made Russia the first nation to favor revision of the Versailles Treaty and Germany the first nation to recognize the Bolshevik revolution. To solidify the new pro-Eastern orientation of German policy, Count Brockdorff-Rantzau, another member of the "Eastern" school, was appointed ambassador to Russia.[13] Following the signing of the treaty, "Special Branch R" of the *Reichswehr* Ministry sent its first group of officers to train in Russia during 1922. In 1923 a tank school was established in Kasan and a school for combat fliers at Kharkov. Joint maneuvers by German and Russian officers were conducted in Russia and East Prussia, and at the same time, Russian officers were being trained in Germany. Among those receiving such training were the future Chief of Staff of the Russian army, Tukhachevski, and Marshal

[11] Goerlitz, *op. cit.,* pp. 231–232.

[12] For the question of illegal rearmament see Goerlitz, *op. cit.;* W. M. Knight-Patterson, *Germany from Defeat to Conquest 1913–1933,* London, G. Allen, 1945, pp. 397–403; and Helm Speidel, "Reichswehr und Rote Armee," *Vierteljahrshefte für Zeitgeschichte,* No. 1, January, 1953.

[13] Fraenkel, *op. cit.,* p. 38.

Zhukov of World War II fame and presently Deputy Defense Minister of the Soviet Union.[14]

During this time some rightist papers in Germany were strongly pro-Russian. The desire to avenge the defeat of 1918 was far more important to some brands of the German Right than the threat of Bolshevism. Symbolic of the rightest press attitudes toward the question of Russia was a statement by Count Reventlow in the *Reichswarte:* "An anti-Russian policy is an anti-German policy." [15] Some nationalists, working both sides of the street, inveighed against the danger of Bolshevism in Germany and assured Western audiences that Germany was Europe's bulwark against communism. While German leaders belabored the "red threat," Germany continued to cooperate fully with Russia.

Ironically enough many of the factories set up on Russian soil were financed by capital procured in Western states. Although the Rapallo Treaty did not lead Germany and Russia into a formal military alliance, it did prepare the ground for close military cooperation.[16] During the *Reichstag* session of December 17, 1926, the socialist deputy Scheidemann contemptuously told the communists that from now on, should they be killed by the *Reichswehr*, they would have the pleasure of knowing that it was done with Soviet grenades.[17]

Adolf Hitler came to power in 1933 partially through the parliamentary support of the German communists. On the Russian side, there was no indication of any desire to abandon the Rapallo policy of the previous ten years. Despite the oratorical conflict which followed Hitler's rise to power, the Politburo was anxious to continue the Rapallo policy.[18] In the propaganda conflict Germany was clearly the aggressor. The Soviet leaders in-

[14] Goerlitz, *op. cit.,* p. 233, asserts that Tukhachevski was plumping for a Russo-German alliance in 1937, and, pointing to the Spanish War, argued that the Western powers were seeking to exploit for their own benefit the hostility between Germany and Russia. He allegedly declared for an alliance with Germany which would give Russia a free hand in the Baltic countries, Poland, Rumania, and Bulgaria.

[15] Knight-Patterson, *op. cit.,* p. 408. Seeckt shared the same sentiments. In his book *Wege deutscher Aussenpolitik,* written in 1931, he said: "[Russia] is obliged to consider the representatives of the great capitalist powers (France, Britain, and behind them, America) as the chief obstacles to her projects. From this emerges a certain community of interests between Russia and Germany, which are both menaced by the claims of these powers."

[16] "Rapallo was not, as indignant British and French commentators insisted, a soviet-German 'alliance.' But it was a rapprochement between outcasts, each of which thereby enhanced, however slightly, its bargaining power in dealing with London, Paris and Rome." Frederick L. Schuman, *Soviet Politics at Home and Abroad,* New York, Knopf, 1949, p. 190. The official Soviet view today would seem to be that the military collaboration was a secret conspiracy between Trotsky and the *Reichswehr*. This thesis is obviously untenable. See E. H. Carr, "The Road to Rapallo," *Soviet Studies,* University of Glasgow, Vol. 1, No. 3, January, 1950, p. 234.

[17] See Ruth Fischer, *Stalin and German Communism,* Cambridge, Mass., Harvard University Press, 1948, p. 530.

[18] See Isaac Deutscher, *Stalin: A Political Biography,* New York, Oxford, 1949, p. 409.

variably emphasized their desire to remain on amicable terms with the Germans.[19]

On the German side, important factions were still working for an alliance with the Soviet Union. The most important of these was the group gathered around General Karl Haushofer, professor of geopolitics at the University of Munich. Haushofer's global thought was strongly influenced by Sir Halford Mackinder, the celebrated English geographer mentioned above.[20] Mackinder saw Russia in control of the "heartland" of Asia: [21]

As we consider . . . the broader currents of history, does not a certain persistence of geographical relationships become evident? Is not the pivot region of the world's politics that vast area of Euro-Asia which is inaccessible to ships, but in antiquity lay open to horse-riding nomads, and is today to be covered with a network of railways? There have been and are here the conditions of a mobility of military and economic power of a far-reaching and yet limited character. Russia replaces the Mongol Empire. Her pressure on Finland, on Scandinavia, on Poland, on Turkey, on Persia, on India, and on China, replaces the centrifugal raids of the steppemen. In the world at large she occupies the central strategical position held by Germany in Europe. She can strike on all sides and be struck from all sides, save the north. The full development of her modern railway mobility is merely a matter of time. Nor is it likely that any possible social revolution will alter her essential relations to the great geographical limits of her existence. Wisely recognizing the fundamental limits of her power, her rulers have parted with Alaska; for it is as much a law of policy for Russia to own nothing overseas as for Britain to be supreme on the ocean.

Mackinder had wished to warn his countrymen of the dangers of a Russian-German alliance; Haushofer welcomed Mackinder's doctrine as the heaven-sent formula by which Germany would escape her world political dilemma.[22] The policy followed in the early 1920's by Germany vis-à-vis

[19] See Max Beloff, *The Foreign Policy of Soviet Russia 1929–1941,* London, Oxford, 1947, Vol. I, p. 94.

[20] See Hans W. Weigert, *Generals and Geographers,* New York, Oxford, 1942, p. 116. Mackinder dubbed an area stretching from the Volga to the Yangtze and from the Himalayas to the Arctic Ocean the "heartland of the world." The "world-island" consists of the continents of Europe, Asia and Africa, around which the lesser land areas of the world are grouped. "When our statesmen are in conversation with the defeated enemy, some airy cherub should whisper to them from time to time this saying: Who rules East Europe commands the Heartland: Who rules the Heartland commands the World-Island: Who rules the World-Island commands the world." Sir Halford Mackinder, *Democratic Ideals and Reality,* New York, Holt, 1919, p. 186.

[21] Sir Halford Mackinder, "The Geographical Pivot of History," *Geographical Journal,* Vol. 23, January–June, 1904, p. 436. Haushofer's ideas consisted largely in taking the very factors on which Mackinder counted as the props of stability and using them to upset, in Germany's favor, Mackinder's postulated stabilization between Britain and Russia. Mackinder, in his 1904 paper, wrote that "the oversetting of the balance of power . . . would permit the use of vast continental resources for fleet-building, and the empire of the world would then be in sight." This might happen if Germany were to ally herself with Russia.

[22] See Robert Strausz-Hupé, *Geopolitics,* New York, Putnam, 1942, p. 167.

Russia accorded perfectly with the Haushofer view.[23] The signing of the Anti-Comintern Pact was a reversal of the Haushofer policies. In 1939, Haushofer's star was again rising.

If Germany feared a two-front war, so did the Soviet Union. To the east of the Soviet Union stood her old antagonist Japan. But other than strictly geographic and economic relations played their role in bringing the Soviet Union and Germany together again. Among the factors determining Soviet policy perhaps the most important was the position Germany had always held in the Soviet scheme for world revolution. In Bolshevik philosophy Germany always had been the classical example of the "antithesis" of capitalism and revolutionary socialism. Her industries had developed rapidly; the working class had grown numerically, and the time for sudden "qualitative changes" seemed to be near.[24] Germany seemed to be the test case for the cogency of Marxian dialectics. Thus Soviet policy in the 1920's made "staking everything on Germany" a basic principle of world revolution.[25]

When in 1921 Germany seemed to sink into chaos, the Soviet leaders were convinced that Germany's only escape from the noose with which the Allies had sought to strangle her economy was by the road of revolution. In 1923 hopes were high that the time for revolution was ripe. The elections in Germany showed communism in the ascendancy. The tide of revolution was flowing. Under pressure from Moscow the uprising was set to take place in Hamburg on October 23, 1923.[26] The revolt was crushed.

Upon the failure of revolution in Germany, the Soviets attempted to replace Germany in their world revolutionary scheme first with England and then with China. Both proved unworthy successors: Britain's general strike petered out in 1926, and Chiang Kai-shek purged the communists from the Kuomintang. Stalin, who at this time had assumed control of the Politburo, persisted in viewing Germany as the land most likely to follow Russia's example. As late as 1924 he said: [27]

[23] In the days leading up to the Nazi assumption of power, Karl Haushofer and Oswald Spengler were active in Munich. Spengler appears to have influenced Haushofer and thus the pro-Russian orientation of many Germans. Spengler's *The Decline of the West*, predicting the rise of Russia, was published in 1919. In his *Hour of Decision*, published in 1933, Spengler argued that Russia was unconquerable from outside; sheer distance had never been conquered; and any offensive against Russia would be like a thrust into empty space. See Max Beloff, *op. cit.*, p. 95. On the close attention given by the Soviets to *Geopolitik*, see Strausz-Hupé, *op. cit.*, p. 137.

[24] See Historicus, "Stalin on Revolution," *Foreign Affairs*, January, 1949, p. 179. "The process of evolution is not simply one of quantitative growth; 'insignificant and hidden quantitative changes' repeatedly accumulate to a point at which radical and 'open qualitative changes' suddenly occur . . ." Thus the numerical growth of the working masses in Germany pointed toward a sudden qualitative change from capitalism to socialism.

[25] See David J. Dallin, *Russia and Postwar Europe*, New Haven, Yale University Press, 1943, pp. 51–52. For an understanding of the ideological importance of Germany within the Soviet scheme of international revolution, this work is the best available. See especially Chap. 2.

[26] *Ibid.*, p. 56.

[27] *Bolshevik*, No. 11, 1924, pp. 51–52, as quoted by Dallin, *op. cit.*, p. 58.

Of all European countries Germany is the one most pregnant with revolution; a revolutionary victory in Germany is a victory all over Europe. If the revolutionary shake-up of Europe is to begin anywhere it will begin in Germany. Only Germany can take the initiative in this respect, and a victory of revolution in Germany is a full guarantee of victory of the international revolution.

In 1930, the Soviets again looked toward Germany as the country most likely to collapse under the onslaught of international economic crisis and to revolt against the capitalist order, for Germany's Communist Party was the largest in the world. It was able to muster 4 to 5 million votes at the polls, it controlled important media of publicity and propaganda, and it was well organized. In addition, the strength of the Social-Democratic Party, the communists' leading rival, was rapidly declining, and communism and National Socialism seemed to be moving toward an inevitable clash. In September of 1932 a new revolutionary tide seemed to be rising. Moscow, convinced of the sharpening of the class struggle in Germany, instructed the German communists to sit on their hands as the Weimar Republic went to pieces. In Moscow the official organ of the Communist Party commented as follows: [28]

In Germany the proletarian revolution is nearer to realization than in any other country: and victory of the proletariat in Germany means victory of proletarian revolution throughout Europe, since capitalist Europe cannot exist if it loses its heart. . . . He who does not understand the German question does not understand the path of the development of proletarian revolution in Europe.

Wilhelm Pieck, later communist boss of East Germany and then a guest of the Kremlin, asserted: "We are fighting for a soviet Germany. We will conclude a fraternal alliance with the U.S.S.R., arm all the toilers, and create a mighty revolutionary Red Army." These predictions, though their error was soon to be disclosed, bespoke the high hopes which Soviet Russia placed upon Germany. It was Adolf Hitler, not Stalin, who changed Soviet Russia's orientation from its pro-German course.

Until Hitler broke the Rapallo thread, Soviet-German collaboration was uninterrupted; however, the record of the relations between the Soviets and the Western states was marred by hostility and painful incidents. Litvinov alluded to this fact when he reported, in 1928, to the Central Executive Committee that "unlike some countries, Germany and Italy never complained about interference of the Soviet Union in their internal affairs." He specifically referred to the unsatisfactory relations between the Soviet Union and Britain and France:

Efforts to destroy these relations [with Germany] are directed by the states which have been unwilling or unable to establish similar relations with us. . . . But the forces directed at a severance of Germany from the Soviet Union can offer her

[28] *Bolshevik,* Dec. 31, 1933, as quoted by Dallin, *op. cit.,* p. 62.

as compensation only assurances and promises which are incompatible either with their general policies or with the system of the Treaty of Versailles.

An interesting commentary on the Soviets' unshakable faith in what may be called the German-Russian community of interests is supplied by Stalin's conversation in 1933 with Emil Ludwig, the well-known German biographer-journalist. Ludwig reported that, having told Stalin that everywhere in Russia he had observed "an extraordinary respect for everything American, even a worship of everything American," the latter replied:

You exaggerate. . . . We have no special respect for everything American. . . . If one is to speak about our sympathies for any nation or, to be more correct, for the majority of any nation, one would, of course, speak of our sympathies for the Germans. There can be no comparison between these sympathies and our feelings for the Americans.

There seems hardly any doubt, in view of the long collaboration between Russia and Germany, that the Soviet-Nazi pact corresponded more closely to Soviet expectations and projections than would have a Soviet-Western pact.

The question must, however, be asked, why did the Russians ever negotiate with the West at all? Soviet tactics leading up to the Soviet-Nazi pact of 1939 were identical with those which bore fruit in the Rapallo Treaty of 1922. Both operations are excellent examples of Soviet diplomacy in action. In both cases the Soviets negotiated secretly with the Germans while openly they negotiated with France and Britain. In both instances, while they secretly sought to extract a pact from the Germans, they feigned that they were close to signing a pact with France and Britain. The memoirs of Viscount D'Abernon throw considerable light on the Rapallo negotiations which closely paralleled the negotiations preceding the 1939 pact. Then the Soviet agent conducting the secret negotiations with the Germans was Karl Radek, who had slipped into Berlin in January, 1922, just prior to the Genoa Conference. His mission was to discuss with German authorities and business circles the best attitude to adopt at the Genoa Conference. D'Abernon wrote: [29]

. . . To all he tells the same story, that France is seeking a secret agreement with Russia, to whom she could promise trade credits, diplomatic support at Angora, economic aid for reconstruction purposes, and the payment by Germany of a war indemnity in accordance with Article 116 of the Versailles Treaty. . . . "Now, if you don't want us to be driven into the arms of France, make us a counter-offer: give us a loan, and agree to resume full diplomatic relations at once, before the Genoa Conference meets . . ."

It seems likely that the real reason behind the well-publicized Soviet negotiations with the West was to force the errant Adolf Hitler back into an

[29] See Viscount D'Abernon, *Versailles to Rapallo, 1920–1922,* New York, Doubleday, Doran, 1929, pp. 263–265. See also Carl Joachim Friedrich, *Foreign Policy in the Making,* New York, Norton, 1938, pp. 144–146.

alliance with the Soviet Union. In order to guide Hitler back onto the Rapallo track it was necessary to raise the fear of the two-front war which had always haunted the Bismarckian, the "Eastern," school of German diplomacy.[30]

That the Soviet leaders, on their side, were banking heavily on the traditional eastern orientation and fear of a two-front war seems obvious from a statement Litvinov made in 1937 to an American journalist: [31]

Hitler and the generals who control Germany read history. They know that Bismarck warned against war on two fronts. They know that he urged the reinsurance policy with Russia. They believe that the Kaiser lost the First World War because he forgot Bismarck's admonition. When the Germans are prepared at last to embark upon their new adventures, these bandits will come to Moscow to ask us for a pact.

It is possibly true that Stalin might have signed a pact with the British and French if the Germans had not signified their readiness to come to terms with the Soviet Union. Whatever faith the Soviet Union ever may have had in the will of the French to fight would appear, however, to have been short-lived indeed. In 1935, the Franco-Russian pact was signed. Yet in 1937 Litvinov, the promoter of collective security and reputedly the great friend of the West, confided to an American publicist that France was through and would never fight. Litvinov, replying to the question as to whether France and Britain would oppose Hitler's next move in Czechoslovakia, said: [32]

Don't tell me about our treaty with Czechoslovakia. I drafted that treaty. Read the text again more carefully and you will see that you are wrong. We are obliged to come to the aid of the Czechs under the League of Nations machinery and then only if France has assumed her obligations. . . . Well, France won't fight. France is through.

The widely touted assertion that the Soviet Union would faithfully cooperate with the West for any length of time is unsupported by communist statements with the exception of an occasional oblique reference to the possibility of coexistence or to revolution not being "for export." Only one state

[30] The German Foreign Office was still manned by those Junker diplomats to whom Bismarck's counsel was command and who thought Germany's natural orientation to be eastward. Count Schulenburg, German Ambassador to the Soviet Union during the 1939 negotiations, was considered by the Nazi leaders so pro-Russian that it was necessary in 1941 to keep Germany's impending attack on Russia secret from him while preparations were being made. (Schulenburg was a victim of the mass executions of leading Germans implicated in the plot on Hitler's life, July 20, 1944. The plotters planned to sign an alliance with the Soviet Union.) Goebbels wrote: "Our Ambassador in Moscow, Count von der Schulenburg, hadn't the faintest idea that the Reich was determined to attack. He kept insisting that our best policy would be to make Stalin our friend and ally. He also refused to believe that the Soviet Union was making tremendous military preparations against the Reich. There is no doubt that one does best if one keeps the diplomats uninformed about the background of politics. . . ." Louis P. Lochner, *The Goebbels Diaries,* New York, Doubleday, 1948, p. 87.

[31] See John T. Whitaker, *We Cannot Escape History,* New York, Macmillan, 1943, p. 268.

[32] Whitaker, *op. cit.,* p. 269.

in the capitalist world ever held a permanent position in the *Weltanschauung* of Soviet communism—and that state clearly was Germany.

THE PACT OF 1939

It is not known which side initiated the German-Russian negotiations leading to the pact of 1939.[33] The State Department publication *Nazi-Soviet Relations 1939–1941* gives the impression that the Russians took the first fateful step,[34] but this is not necessarily the case with respect to preliminary and unofficial negotiations between secret emissaries. When negotiations were started at the level of the foreign offices, both the Russian and the German press had already effected some kind of truce in what had been for years a ferocious war of invectives.[35] This remarkable reconciliation could not have been brought about without prior intimate and friendly contacts, and hardly without an informal agreement on a "personal basis."

Once the Russians had initiated the high-level discussions, they quickly made arrangements clearly indicating their desire to come to an agreement. The most important of these "hints" was the dismissal, in May, 1939, of Foreign Commissar Litvinov, reputedly the representative of a pro-Western orientation, and his replacement by Molotov—a few days after Britain had rejected a Russian counterproposal to the original British draft of an assistance agreement. This change in personnel was intended to impress upon the British that they would have to make greater efforts if they wanted to gain the support of the Russians, and indicated to the Nazis that the person of Litvinov, a Jewish citizen of the Soviet Union, was not to stand between Germany and Russia. As soon as Litvinov had been dismissed, the Soviet Chargé at Berlin went to the German Foreign Office and "tried without asking direct questions to learn whether this event would cause a change in our [German] position toward the Soviet Union." [36]

Russian statesmen, like political experts in the West, had believed—or, at least, had acted as if they believed—that solidarity between East and West would stop Hitler. They joined the League of Nations, supported the policy of "collective security," offered France a military convention (after having previously concluded a political accord), and insisted on a joint policy against the aggressors. During the Sudeten crisis, Foreign Comissar Litvinov

[33] The French Ambassador in Berlin reported early in May, 1939, that a Soviet-Nazi *rapprochement* was in the making and might result in a new partition of Poland [*French Yellow Book, Diplomatic Documents (1938–1939)*, New York, Reynal & Hitchcock, 1940, p. 145].

[34] The very first document of *Nazi-Soviet Relations,* a memorandum by State Secretary Weizsäcker on a visit by the Russian Ambassador states: "It had appeared to me that the Russian press lately was not fully participating in the anti-German tone of the American and some of the English papers" (pp. 1*f.*).

[35] The Bulgarian Prime Minister predicted the Russo-German pact in the fall of 1938 to the French Minister. See John A. Lukács, "Political Expediency and Soviet Military Operations," *Journal of Central European Affairs,* Vol. 8, No. 4, January, 1949, p. 394.

[36] *Nazi-Soviet Relations,* p. 3.

stated on September 21, 1938, at Geneva: "Even composed as it is today, the League of Nations is still strong enough by its collective action to avert or arrest aggression. All that is necessary is that . . . the machinery of the League of Nations be at least once brought into action in conformity with the Covenant." Similarly, in a speech at the eighteenth congress of the Communist Party of the Soviet Union in March, 1939, Stalin expressed his displeasure at the vacillating policy of the "non-aggressive states, primarily England, France and the U.S.A.," and stated: "We stand for the support of nations which are the victims of aggression and are fighting for the independence of their country." The Soviet Union negotiated with France and Britain for the conclusion of a military convention.

When the Soviets signed their pact with Germany in August, 1939, they knew perfectly well that war would follow immediately. Hitler did not at all hide his intention to attack Poland. From the very first, this pact was conceived and written down in black and white not as a nonaggression pact—as it was labeled—but as an agreement for dividing Eastern Europe between the Soviet Union and Germany,[37] or, as the text of the secret agreement runs, for "the demarcation of the spheres of influence of either party." [38] Article I envisaged "politico-territorial change" in the Baltic states; Article II forecast a similar change "in the territories belonging to the Polish state." Therefore, when the Soviets signed the pact, they knew that they were initiating an immediate German attack on Poland in which, incidentally, they soon participated.[39]

By contrast, might they not have deterred Hitler from attacking Poland had they signed a pact with Britain and France? To be sure, this was not certain. However, only a few trained observers doubted in 1939 that a Russian-Western agreement would, at least, reduce the chances of war. Hence, it can be concluded that the Soviets initiated a policy which certainly *increased* the danger of war and most probably made war inevitable.

Confronted with the triple choice of defending Poland, of keeping neutral by doing nothing, or of sacrificing Poland, they sacrificed Poland. Having

[37] In the conversation with Stalin during the night of August 23 to 24, 1939, Ribbentrop, according to his own report, informed Stalin that "indignation against Poland was so great that every single man was ready to fight. The German people would no longer put up with Polish provocation. In the course of the conversation, Herr Stalin spontaneously proposed a toast to the Führer, as follows: 'I know how much the German nation loves its Führer; I should therefore like to drink to his health.' " (*Ibid.*, p. 75.)

[38] Secret Additional Protocol, August 23, 1939, as published in *Nazi-Soviet Relations,* p. 78.

[39] The Secret Protocol contains the following agreement: "The question of whether the interests of both parties make desirable the maintenance of an independent Polish state and how such a state should be bounded can only be definitely determined in the course of further political developments. In any event both Governments will resolve this question by means of a friendly agreement" (*ibid.,* p. 78). The true Russian attitude concerning Poland was revealed by Molotov when he boasted: "One swift blow to Poland, first by the German army and then by the Red Army and nothing was left of this ugly offspring of the Versailles treaty which existed by oppressing non-Polish nationalists."

finally convinced the Western powers of the dangers of appeasement, they themselves adopted that policy at the precise moment when it was completely abandoned by the West. Instead of intimidating Hitler, they encouraged him.

The question, therefore, arises: Why did the Soviets abandon the policy of collective security for a policy of war? Why did they choose war instead of peace? Why did the Soviets deliberately provoke World War II?

It is unfortunately impossible to give a fully documented answer to these questions. The Soviets have not yet opened their archives, even though thirty years ago they inveighed against "secret diplomacy" and published the documents of the Tsarist and provisional governments. Nor have Soviet statesmen written their memoirs. We are, therefore, compelled to proceed part of the way by deductive reasoning.

There are, on the whole, three basic hypotheses which may explain the causes of Soviet Russia's diplomatic reversal.

Byrnes's Thesis. The first hypothesis was advanced by former Secretary of State James F. Byrnes, who suggested [40] that Stalin

must have reasoned that, if the Non-Aggression Pact prevented the Western powers from coming to Poland's aid, general warfare would be averted and the Soviet Union would have more time to develop its military strength. On the other hand, if the Western allies did go to war the balance of strength would be such that Russia would still have time to train and equip its armies.

This hypothesis is rather implausible. Stalin must have known that, in August, 1939, the Western powers were irretrievably committed to come to the assistance of Poland. As a matter of fact, Russia's own policy had encouraged Western firmness to such an extent that, in August, 1939, it was no longer possible for England and France to leave Poland to her own fate. It was, therefore, most improbable that the nonaggression pact would "buy" a limited war as against a general war. Was not also the theory of "indivisible peace" one of the principal ideas of Russian foreign policy?

Second, the purely military interests of Russia were incompatible with a policy which would have led to a common German-Russian border, the military strengthening of Germany, and the disappearance of the "cushion" of Poland *without a concurrent neutralization of German military strength* in the West.

Nor can the intention of strengthening Russia's armament have been the motive of the Molotov-Ribbentrop pact. If military preparations against Germany had been Russia's primary aim, it could have been attained much more effectively through a pact with the West. The Soviet economy was mobilized for large-scale armaments only on June 27, 1940, that is, *after* the French collapse. On that day the eight-hour working day was reintroduced, a seven-day week ordered, and mobility of workers prohibited. If Russia

[40] James F. Byrnes, *Speaking Frankly,* New York, Harper, 1947, p. 285.

wanted to gain time, she would not only not have accelerated, but would have *delayed* the outbreak of war between Germany and the Western powers.

A Stalin Thesis. The second hypothesis was presented by Stalin himself in the course of "an after-dinner conversation at Yalta": "The soviet government would never have entered into the Non-Aggression Pact with Germany had it not been for the attempt at Munich to appease Hitler and the failure of Britain and France to consult the Soviet Union on the subject." [41]

There is no doubt that the Munich agreement had angered the Soviets. Still, such picayune reasons cannot have been the motive of a far-reaching and fateful decision by a responsible and powerful government. If Stalin had judged that it was in his interest to combine with the West, he would have done so even if the snub had wounded his pride more grievously. Actually, in March, 1939, he himself explained his attitude toward moralistic criticism of the Munich policy: "Far be it from me to moralize on the policy of non-intervention, to talk of treason, treachery and so on. It would be naïve to preach morals to people who recognize no human morality. Politics is politics. . . ." [42] Stalin was certainly not so naïve as his statements at Yalta would imply. He was using propaganda arguments suited to the occasion.

In any event, Stalin's explanation at the Yalta tête-à-tête seems to contain a great deal of belated wisdom, for it must have taken almost eleven months to find out that lack of consultation and appeasement of Germany by France and Britain in 1938 deserved to be punished by a German-Russian pact in 1939. For that matter, the Western appeasement policy was officially terminated on March 17, 1939, *i.e.*, five months before Ribbentrop's trip to Moscow. Russia agreed in April, 1939, to enter into a military agreement with France and England, and to this effect started negotiations in Moscow, which ended only *after* the conclusion of the Ribbentrop-Molotov pact.

These military negotiations were, undoubtedly, unskillfully and dilatorily conducted by the Western powers. The main stumbling block was Russian insistence on incorporation of the Baltic countries into the Soviet Union and, as during the Munich crisis, on free passage of Russian troops through Poland.

It should have been obvious that the solution of the Baltic problem was an issue to be settled by a peace treaty rather than a defensive military alliance. Moreover, an alliance concluded to maintain the territorial *status quo* could not very well be based on a redistribution of territory. The Russians knew this, of course, and it is difficult to understand why they should have raised the question at all and thereby delayed the negotiations—if not precisely in order to achieve such a delay. The fact remains that the draft

---

[41] *Ibid.*, p. 283.

[42] *The Land of Socialism Today and Tomorrow. Reports and Speeches at the Eighteenth Congress of the Communist Party of the Soviet Union, March 10–21, 1939*, Moscow, 1939, p. 18.

treaty initialled by France, Britain, and Russia on July 24, 1939, yielded to the Soviets on this point.

By contrast, Molotov had thrice stated a Soviet desire to create a "political basis" for Russo-German negotiations, namely, on May 20, on June 28, and on July 3. Moreover, the Soviet Chargé at Berlin conveyed through the Bulgarian Minister the following hints to the German government on June 15, 1939: [43]

The Soviet Union faced the present world situation with hesitation. She was vacillating between three possibilities, namely the conclusion of the pact with England and France, a further dilatory treatment of the pact negotiations, and a *rapprochement* with Germany. This last possibility . . . was closest to the desires of the Soviet Union. . . . If Germany would declare that she would not attack the Soviet Union or that she would conclude a nonaggression pact with her, the Soviet Union would probably refrain from concluding a treaty with England.

The pact with Germany was, then, Russia's main desire; *and she negotiated with the West in order to extract the agreement from the Nazis.* The various discussion points raised by the Soviets were "red herrings" to delay the negotiations till late in summer when the Germans had to make up their mind, or delay the war.

Gafenco's Thesis. The third hypothesis explaining the causes of the Russian *revirement* was set forth by Grégoire Gafenco, former Rumanian Minister of Foreign Affairs and in 1940–1941 Ambassador at Moscow. He wrote: [44]

Russia was afraid of Germany. . . . Stalin did not believe any longer in the possibility of containing Germany by a collective effort. He feared that the Western Powers . . . had abandoned Eastern Europe to Germany. In order not to be subjected to the first shock of the German troops, when Russia was alone, it was necessary quickly to oppose an eastern "realistic" policy to the egotistical policy of the West. . . . Stalin no longer fought to prevent the war but only to divert it from his own borders.

It would seem that this explanation is somewhat contradictory; if Russia had feared Germany, she would have made every effort to acquire powerful allies. Moreover, if she feared the Nazis, this also meant that she did not trust them; hence what could she gain by the pact? It seems to be true that Stalin suspected the motives of Britain and France, but did he suspect the motives of Hitler any less? The theory of distrust does not explain why he preferred one suspected partner over the other suspected partner. Nor does it explain why he should have suddenly become so distrustful of Britain and France in August, 1939, when most of the reasons for the distrust had disappeared; and why he was less suspicious at an earlier date, for example, in

---

[43] *Nazi-Soviet Relations,* p. 21.
[44] Grégoire Gafenco, *Préliminaires de la guerre à l'Est,* Paris, Egloff, 1944, p. 52.

October, 1938, when he continued to cooperate with the West. It is true that Stalin temporarily diverted the war from his frontiers, yet he sacrificed the Polish army, which could have operated as a buffer, and established a common frontier with Germany. He also sacrificed the French army and thus helped to deliver the Germans from the threat of a two-front war which they dreaded. If Gafenco's premises are admitted, the logical policy would have been for Russia to stay out of any agreement of alliance or cooperation, but certainly not to lure the Nazis onto the warpath, let alone directly and indirectly contribute to the strengthening of Germany's military power.

For these reasons it seems improbable that Gafenco accurately describes Stalin's thinking. Nevertheless, there is a grain of truth in this hypothesis. In March, 1939, Stalin had defined one of the tasks of the communist party in the sphere of foreign policy: "To be cautious and not allow our country to be drawn into conflicts by warmongers who are accustomed to have others pull the chestnuts out of the fire for them." [45]

This meant that Russia did not want to enter into an alliance in which she would have to bear the brunt of offensive fighting. Since it became clear during the military negotiations at Moscow that France could not take the offensive for several years to come, Russia would have been the only member of the tripartite pact which could have attacked Germany. Stalin obviously had no intention of weakening or exhausting himself in such an effort, or of permitting the Western powers to become stronger so that, ultimately, they might dictate the peace.[46] On this basis, his refusal to enter the alliance with the West was entirely logical. But the conclusion of the pact with Hitler remains unexplained.

Stalin's Estimates. The over-all logic of Stalin's policy depended on a specific assumption as to the defensive strength of the Western powers. In effect, if Stalin expected France to be easily crushed by Germany, he would, in order to assure his military survival for reasons explained above, have been compelled to enter into a system of multipartite security, whether or not he would have been obliged to take the offensive. By contrast, if he assumed that France and Britain could withstand the German onslaught, he had nothing to risk. The Western powers would weaken Germany, though not defeat her conclusively. Germany's capabilities against the Soviet Union would be reduced and the Russians would still be able, in case of attack, to count on the *de facto* military help of the resisting Western powers. The alliance could then be concluded at a later date, after France and Britain had "pulled the chestnuts out of the fire" for Russia.

Fortunately, there are texts available which indicate that Stalin had made an estimate of the situation according to which the Western powers were stronger than the aggressors. In his speech of March 10, 1939, he stated

[45] *The Land of Socialism, Today and Tomorrow,* p. 16.
[46] As early as 1925, Stalin predicted the war and Russia's active participation. *"We must attack, but attack last." Sochineniya,* Moscow, Ogis, 1947, Vol. VII, p. 14.

explicitly: "Combined the non-aggressive democratic states are unquestionably stronger than the fascist states, both economically and militarily." On the following day, Manuilski was even more outspoken:

The world reactionaries are deliberately creating the legend of the might of German fascism in order to weaken the people's determination to resist. Fascist Germany is not prepared for a big and serious war—she has not enough raw materials and foodstuffs; her financial position is critical; her coasts are vulnerable to naval blockade; her army is inadequately officered; her rear is a dangerous one for fascism. The superiority of material force is undoubtedly on the side of the so-called democratic states."

Manuilski spelled out precisely how superior were the "so-called" democratic states, among which he included the United States. Then he added: "If the so-called democratic states pursued a firm policy of resistance to the fascist aggressors, combined with economic pressure, this would be a quite effective means of forcing the fascist states to retreat."

In view of the fact that these were policy-making speeches delivered to the congress of the Communist Party, there can hardly be any doubt that the above quotations represent the official estimate of the situation as made by the Soviet government in 1939.[47] Actually, these estimates reflect merely the professional and public opinion about German strength as of 1939. Realization of the true German strength came everywhere only in 1940.

But why, despite Germany's fancied inferiority, should the Soviet government not have made an effort to delay war with the possibility in mind that, after completed rearmament of the West and Russia, war would never come? In July, 1935, the Soviet Ambassador in Paris, V. Potiemkine, visited the French Minister of War Colonel Fabry and proposed that Russia and France conclude a military convention after the pattern of the secret alliance of 1892. Fabry answered rather stupidly: "You talk about war. Does war frighten you?" Potiemkine replied: "Why should war frighten us? The Russia of the Soviets emerged from the last war, the Europe of the Soviets will emerge from the next." [48]

As a second quotation, we may again refer to Manuilski's speech. Discussing the communist movements in capitalist countries, he cited the official *History of the C.P.S.U. (B)-Short Course* and its distinction between just and unjust wars: "Just wars, wars that are not wars of conquest but wars of liberation, [are] waged to defend the people, from foreign attack and from attempts to enslave them, or to liberate the people from capitalist slavery, or, lastly, to liberate colonies and dependent countries from the yoke of

---

[47] In his conversation on August 23, 1939, with Ribbentrop, Stalin stated that "England, despite its weakness, would wage war craftily and stubbornly." "Herr Stalin expressed the opinion that France . . . had an army worthy of consideration" (*Nazi-Soviet Relations*, p. 74).

[48] As quoted in Paul Reynaud, *La France a sauvé l'Europe*, Paris, Flammarion, 1947, Vol. I, p. 117.

imperialism." Thus, a war fought to liberate peoples from capitalism is considered a "just war." Soviet policy is, therefore, not pacifist. There would be no hesitation to wage a just war which would result in a "Europe of the Soviets." [49]

With these two passages in mind, let us go one step further. It seems that the new Russian policy, as expressed in the nonaggression pact, was announced and explained for the first time to a Politburo meeting on August 19, 1939, a few hours after the signing of the commercial treaty with Germany.[50]

Stalin allegedly made the following points: If the pact with Germany were signed, war would break out immediately; after the destruction of Poland, Germany would attack the West. Stalin did not think that the West would be defeated but that the war would continue for a long time. Germany would be greatly weakened, but this would also be true of the Western powers. The contest would culminate in mutual exhaustion.

If Germany were beaten very quickly, the Western powers would be able to march to Berlin and crush the communist regime that would emerge as a result of a German defeat. Accordingly, Germany should be supported economically by Russia in order that the war *be protracted;* in that case, the Western powers would be unable to destroy communism in defeated Germany. If, on the other hand, war were avoided by a Russo-Western pact, Germany would be compelled to establish a *modus vivendi* with the West and Poland; such a development would constitute a danger for the Soviet Union.

Stalin is said to have admitted that, in case of war, a German victory would also be dangerous for Russia; but he allegedly minimized this danger by pointing out that Germany would be too exhausted for a war with the U.S.S.R. and would, moreover, have her hands full keeping France and England down, and administering her newly acquired overseas territories. Stalin believed that, in the case of a Western defeat, France would turn communist.

[49] On August 23, 1915, Lenin wrote an article on the "United States of Europe Slogan" in which he stated (*Selected Works,* New York, International Publishers, 1943, Vol. V, p. 141) that victory of socialism in a few or even in one single country is possible. "The victorious proletariat of that country . . . would *confront* the rest of the capitalist world, attract to itself the oppressed classes of other countries, raise revolts among them against the capitalists, and in the event of necessity, come out even with armed force against the exploiting classes and their states." This passage was quoted by Stalin in every edition of the *Problems of Leninism.* Historicus (*loc. cit.,* p. 199) indicates that Stalin used the passage in other works also, and adds: "This repetition in widely circulated works is added evidence that Stalin means every word." Stalin also frequently used a passage from Lenin's March 18, 1919, speech (*Selected Works,* Vol. VIII, p. 33): "We are living not merely in a state, but in a system of states, and the existence of the Soviet Republic side by side with imperialist states for a long time is unthinkable. One or the other must triumph in the end. And before that end supervenes a series of frightful collisions between the Soviet Republic and the bourgeois states will be inevitable. That means that if the ruling class, the proletariat, wants to hold sway, it must prove its capacity to do so by military organization also" (quoted by Stalin, *op. cit.,* p. 156).

[50] Reynaud, *op. cit.,* p. 588; also Winston Churchill, *The Second World War: The Gathering Storm,* Boston, Houghton Mifflin, 1948, p. 392.

In sum, if everything went according to Stalin's plan, Russia would emerge as the dominant power in Europe, and the communist system would be introduced in a number of European states.

This was also the official line of the central committee of the German Communist Party, which in October, 1939, stated that it had always believed that the liberation of the German nation could not be carried out except by war.[51] As a matter of fact, this idea of revolution though war is part and parcel of traditional Leninism-Stalinism.[52] In August, 1939, the Soviets merely had their first excellent opportunity to spark that climactic process culminating in world revolution, a world war, without, at the same time, having to assume overtly the responsibility for this act.

Regardless of earlier statements, these ideas were very much alive in 1939. For example, the connection between war and revolution was pointed out in Stalin's speech of March, 1939: "The bourgeois politicians know, of course, that the first imperialist world war led to the victory of the revolution in one of the largest countries. They are afraid that the second imperialist world war may also lead to the victory of the revolution in one or several countries." [53] Stalin's party congress statement contained also the other crucial

[51] A parallel document containing the secret instructions sent by the Russian Communist Party to the communist parties in eastern Europe was given by the Rumanian Prime Minister Călinescu to the French Ambassador. (It is reprinted in Georges Bonnet, *Fin d'une Europe: de Munich à la guerre,* Geneva, Cheval Ailé, 1948, pp. 411f.) Bonnet calls attention to the fact that this Comintern document does not, in any way, charge France and Britain with the responsibility for the failure of the pact negotiations.

[52] The idea was, for example, clearly expressed as early as 1907 in the Resolution adopted at the Seventh International Socialist Congress at Stuttgart. After declaring that wars are "part of the very nature of capitalism," it goes on: "In case war should break out . . . , it is their [the working classes'] duty . . . to utilise the economic and political crisis created by the war to rouse the masses and thereby to hasten the downfall of capitalist class rule" (quoted from V. I. Lenin, *Collected Works,* Vol. XVIII, "The Imperialist War; the Struggle against Social-Chauvinism and Social-Pacifism 1914–1915," New York, International Publishers, 1930, p. 468). The entire volume is full of comments by Lenin on the relationship between war and revolution (see, for example, pp. 347, 358 and 395). The resolutions of the Sixth World Congress of the Comintern (1928), entitled *The Struggle against Imperialist War and the Task of the Communists,* which has been rightly called the Soviet *Mein Kampf,* discussed this relationship at full length. The main point is that war militarizes the workers and trains them in the use of arms. Thereby "imperialism creates the prerequisites for the victory of the proletariat in the civil war."
In his *magnum opus* Stalin mentions the connection between war and revolution by stating that wars lead to "the mutual weakening of the imperialists, to the weakening of the position of capitalism in general, to the acceleration of the advent of the proletarian revolution and to the practical inevitability of this revolution." If this statement is turned around, it would follow that, in the absence of war, revolution is not "inevitable" and that, in fact, it can be avoided. Since war may produce revolution anywhere, and therefore also in the country of the warmaker, *he will be inclined to produce the war among foreign nations, and to keep out of the fray if he possibly can.*

[53] See *The Land of Socialism,* p. 14. Potiemkine's and Stalin's statements contain a key to Soviet thought. Almost textually these same words were used again by Georgi Malenkov in his speech commemorating the thirty-second anniversary of the Russian revolution. According to this interpretation, the Second World War "led to the establishment of people's democratic regimes in a number of countries of Central and Southeast Europe, and to the victory of the great Chinese people. Can there be any doubt whatever that . . .

ideas of his apocryphal Politburo speech. The meaning of his March statement, as it ultimately applied to his secret August policy, becomes quite obvious if, in the text, "France and Britain" are substituted for "Soviet Union," and "Germany" for "Japan."

The policy on non-intervention means conniving at aggression, giving free rein to war, and, consequently, transforming the war into a world war. The policy of non-intervention reveals an eagerness, a desire, not to hinder Japan, say, from embroiling herself in a war with China, or, better still, with the Soviet Union; to allow all the belligerents to sink deeply into the mire of war, to encourage them surreptitiously in this, to allow them to weaken and exhaust one another; and then, when they have become weak enough, to appear on the scene with fresh strength—and to dictate conditions to enfeebled belligerents. Cheap and easy!

There was, after all, no reason why Stalin should not himself practice such a "cheap and easy" policy, when he saw an opportunity to put it into effect.

It is self-evident that Stalin's logic was valid only on one major condition: namely, that Russia was strong enough for the gamble and that she could risk the eventuality of a Nazi victory. In his March speech he presented his estimate of the situation in the following terms: "We are not afraid of the threats of aggressors, and are ready to deal two blows for every blow delivered by instigators of war who attempt to violate the Soviet borders."

If Stalin had not believed in the accuracy of his forecast and in the sufficient strength of the Red Army, he would have ordered most massive armaments already in 1939. It may be presumed that he based his estimate of the situation on a comparison of the numbers of German and Russian divisions, and the quantities of equipment, and did not allow adequate weight to technological and qualitative factors.

Let us now try to express the 1939 alternatives of Russian policy in two sets of syllogisms:

Alternative One: Tripartite pact with England and France. In a first variant, the major premise would be that this pact would lead to war between Germany and Russia; Russia would be compelled to come to the support of Poland, or, were she to declare war against Germany but stay on the defensive, would expose herself to the full force of a German offensive. *Minor Premise:* Russia would become exhausted in this fight; there was a danger that the West might ultimately support Germany to crush Bolshevism. *Conclusion:* The West would emerge as the dominant power group. This alternative was clearly unacceptable.

In a second variant of this alternative, the major premise would be that the tripartite pact would prevent war; in this case (minor premise) the West, owing to its rearmament, would become the dominant influence in Europe. *Conclusion:* Either Germany would combine with the West and

a Third World War . . . will be the grave not only for individual capitalist states, but for the whole of world capitalism?" *The New York Times,* Nov. 7, 1949, p. 15.

ultimately oppose the Soviet Union with Western support, or the *status quo* would be maintained. According to this variant, Russia would run a risk without a concomitant territorial and political gain. If, moreover, it was basic Soviet policy to upset the *status quo,* whether to strengthen the relative power of Russia or to further world revolution, this variant would also be unacceptable.

Alternative Two: Nonaggression pact with Germany. *Major Premise:* Germany is not strong enough to defeat the West, nor would she constitute, in the case of an unexpected victory over France and Britain, a dangerous threat to Russia; the war with the West would have been too exhausting. *Minor Premise:* The signing of the pact makes immediate war inevitable, Germany having announced her intentions, and the Western powers being unable to default on their treaties of alliance and declarations of guarantee. *Conclusion:* The result of the war would be fourfold: Germany would be weakened; the Western powers would exhaust themselves in the struggle; by contrast, the relative and absolute strength of the Soviet Union would grow immensely; communism would spread into the territories to be annexed by Russia and possibly also into the territories of the belligerent nations, especially Germany.

Chestnut Strategy. At this point we may advance our investigation by tagging Stalin's policy with a descriptive label. A good label was supplied by Stalin himself when he said that the Soviets did not want to pull the chestnuts out of the fire for others. Mindful of the use of inverted "Aesopian" language by the communists, we may assume that Stalin really wanted others to pull the chestnuts out of the fire *for him.*

Let us therefore call Stalin's technique of 1939 "chestnut strategy." It consists, ideally, in stacking the cards in such a manner *that the kibitzer wins the game.* In practice the kibitzer may be compelled to participate in the game; if so, he will try to enter it at the last possible moment when the others have already lost their pants and when he still has a big heap of chips.

It is a gamble for the highest stakes with the least risk. Stalin wanted to get the chestnuts but he wanted France, Britain, Poland, and Germany to burn their fingers. This interpretation fits whether the stake for which Stalin was gambling was the expansion of communism or the accumulation of Mother Russia's power.

Chestnut strategy was not invented by Stalin. Its essential features were analyzed as early as 1920 by Lenin himself, in a speech delivered on November 26. Lenin said:

The fact that we were able to hold on, this miracle, was entirely due to the fact that we took proper advantage of the hostility between German and American imperialism. We made a tremendous concession to German imperialism [Brest Litowsk], and by making a concession to one imperialism we at once safeguarded ourselves against the persecution of both imperialisms. . . . The example of the Brest Peace has taught us a lot. We are at present between two foes. If we are unable to defeat them both, we must know how to dispose our forces in such a way that they fall out among themselves; because, as is always the case, when thieves fall out, honest men come into their own. But as soon as we are strong enough to defeat capitalism as a whole, we shall immediately take it by the scruff of the neck. . . .

To leave not the slightest uncertainty about the way in which his mind was working, Lenin added the following key sentences: [54]

What could have saved us still more would have been *a war between the imperialist powers*. If we are obliged to tolerate such scoundrels as the capitalist thieves, each of whom is preparing to plunge a knife into us, *it is our direct duty to make them turn their knives against each other*. [Italics are the authors'.]

For all practical purposes, this Lenin quote supplies a coherent and logical explanation of Stalin's strategy in 1939. It paraphrases the old proverb of the *tertius gaudens*.

CONTRADICTIONS OF SOVIET PROPAGANDA

It is clearly impossible, without authentic Russian documents, to reconstruct the thinking of the Soviet government in all its details. It is certainly noteworthy that the Soviets did not see fit to publish any documents and that they publicly interpreted their policy only by spurious and contradictory arguments. Why did they never publish a plausible interpretation? [55]

[54] According to Bukharin, Lenin expounded in 1918 the theory that "one can use the weapons of any foreign power against those of any other foreign nation." Chestnut strategy was practiced time and again by Britain and Italy; the expansion of both countries was partially made possible by the struggles among their opponents.

[55] On August 31, 1939, Molotov made a speech giving several explanations. In Potiemkine's book several mutually exclusive interpretations were given of the pact which, of course, differ widely from the explanations given by Stalin himself to Byrnes and Churchill.

To Churchill, Stalin pointed out that he had formed the opinion that Britain and France did not want to go to war if Poland were attacked, although it is hard to see how this opinion was arrived at: it was first expressed by Zhdanov in an article in *Pravda* published on June 29, 1939. Stalin also explained his pact by the military weakness of France and Britain (Churchill, *op. cit.,* p. 391).

Potiemkine quotes Stalin's speech of July 3, 1941, according to which an offer of a non-aggression pact by a neighboring power simply could not be declined by any peace-loving government; this on the condition that the territorial integrity, independence, and the honor of the peace-loving government were not put in question. Yet Germany was not a neighbor; Stalin had previously declined numerous offers of perhaps more profitable pacts; and the pact destroyed the independence of Poland.

Then Voroshilov is quoted to the effect that the negotiations with France and Britain were not broken off because of the pact with Germany but, on the contrary, the pact with Germany was concluded because these negotiations had been unsuccessful.

Finally A. M. Pankratova and Potiemkine themselves expound their own theory (Potiemkine was then Deputy Foreign Commissar), namely, that the pact upset Anglo-French projects to isolate the Soviet Union and direct German aggression against Russia. Not the slightest proof is offered for this theory. It is contradicted by the actual behavior of the Western powers. On the strength of the actual behavior of the Soviet government, it can be argued much more plausibly that the Russians tried to direct German aggression against

The very confusion of the explanations given by the Russians themselves shows that they have not seen fit to divulge the *true* motives which led them to conclude the pact with the Nazis. Two explanations come to mind: either the Soviet government blundered; or the revelation of true motives would endanger the effectiveness of Soviet policy in the future. Whatever the reasons, the fact remains that the Soviets concluded a pact with Germany which launched the Second World War and by which they waged, jointly with Nazi Germany, an aggressive war against Poland. It is a fact, too, that the Soviets, at the most crucial moment in the interwar period, abandoned the policy of collective security in order to support and participate in aggression.

The most charitable view one may take is that the Soviet government based its decision on a faulty interpretation of British and French intentions. Stalin may have reasoned that the British and French wanted Russian support in case they were drawn into the war, but that they were unwilling to give the same guarantee to the Soviet Union. Allegedly the Western powers refused to guarantee the Russian borders; nor did they promise *their* support of the Soviets in case of aggression against Russia proper.

As early as May 9, 1939, Prime Minister Chamberlain pointed out in the House of Commons that this Russian interpretation of the British-French offer was quite incorrect. He even went so far as to say that Great Britain and France were prepared to allow Russia to reserve the right to enter the war *after* England and France had already done so. Hardly any precedent will be found in history of so generous an attempt to allay the alleged suspicions of another government. Nevertheless the Russians did not abandon their "suspicions."

Did the Russians really believe, as it is stated in Potiemkine's book, that England and France attempted, under the camouflage of their negotiations with the Soviet government, to isolate the Soviet Union and "by refusing to assume the obligation of mutual assistance, hoped to deflect the German aggression against the U.S.S.R."? [56] If so, their policy and, for that matter, one of their most important decisions, was based on faulty knowledge of British and French intentions. It was also based on an inadequate forecast concerning future German actions, capabilities, and timing.

By contrast, if the Russians were honestly convinced of the sinister designs of the Western powers, why then did they counter with an equally sinister scheme and, by refusing to support the West, deflect German aggression against France? The Russians applied precisely the same policy which they

---

the West. V. P. Potiemkine (ed.), *Istoria Diplomatii v Period Podgotovski Vtoroi Mirovoi Voiny,* 1945, Vol. III, pp. 711*ff*.

[56] Potiemkine, *op. cit.,* p. 690. This version is flatly contradicted by the text of the Franco-British-Soviet Agreement, July 24, 1939, published in Bonnet, *op. cit.,* pp. 401–403. In this document the United Kingdom and France pledged mutual defense against "direct and indirect" aggression as unequivocally as did the U.S.S.R.

accused the West of practicing. The theory according to which the Russians acted on poor intelligence has probably some merits, yet intelligence alone, be it poor or excellent, never explains a policy. Policies are predicated on *intentions;* intelligence is merely one of many factors that must be considered.

SOVIET-GERMAN COLLABORATION 1939–1940

The German-Russian nonaggression pact constituted direct support of German aggression. Regardless of the motives of the Soviet government, this was its actual effect. On October 18, 1939, Ribbentrop wrote to the German Ambassador at Moscow concerning his negotiations with Stalin in August. According to this version, Ribbentrop had opened the discussion by remarking that he did not come to ask for armed assistance in case of war. (This was a slap at the British and French.) The Germans were strong enough to win a war against Poland and the Western countries combined. To this Stalin is alleged to have replied "with his characteristic clarity and precision." [57]

Germany was taking a proud attitude by rejecting at the outset any armed assistance from the Soviets. The Soviet Union, however, was interested in having a strong Germany as a neighbor and in the case of an armed showdown between Germany and the Western democracies the interests of the Soviet Union and of Germany would certainly run parallel to each other. The Soviet Union would never stand for Germany's getting into a difficult position.

Loyally observing this pledge, the Soviet Union lent Germany valuable military support. They supplied Germany with badly needed raw materials, especially oil, iron ore, scrap iron, chromium, manganese, platinum, phosphates, foodstuffs, cotton, and lumber. Second, the communist parties were directed, through the Comintern, to facilitate German military operations. In France, the communists did their best, or worst, to undermine national morale and to delay armaments. Even in the United States not a little of the labor trouble during those years was traceable to the communists—and the trouble ceased as if by enchantment on the day following Germany's attack on Russia. Third, Russia supported German military operations. Russia facilitated German communications with Japan and lent diplomatic support to Germany's attack on Norway and Denmark. Russia profited from the alliance with Germany by taking Polish territory and defeating Finland.

The record shows that the Russians, while they aided and abetted German aggression, from time to time also made difficulties. Prior to the Norwegian invasion, for example, they suspended oil and grain shipments to Germany. They also made it difficult for the Germans effectively to use their "North Base," the anchorage near Murmansk. The German Ambassador could not explain this sudden negative attitude since, as he pointed out in a memorandum of April 11, 1940, nothing at all had happened to make the Russians

[57] *Nazi-Soviet Relations,* p. 125.

angry. He suspected that Allied psychological warfare had had its effects and that the Soviet Union "feared being forced by the Entente into a great war for which it is not prepared." The sudden termination of the Finnish War was believed by the Ambassador to have come about from similar considerations. Yet after the Norwegian invasion, there was "a complete about-face" on the part of the Russians which the Germans explained by the theory that the capture of Norway had relieved the Soviets of a "great burden of anxiety," namely, of becoming involved in a war with the West.[58]

It seems that the Soviet government reconsidered its pro-German policy after the Germans had defeated France within a few short weeks. In fact, the collapse of the Western front showed very clearly that Germany possessed immense military capabilities and that she was much stronger than had been believed previously by virtually all governments, including that of the Soviet Union. In the words of the Russian Minister to Sweden, Mme. Kollontai, as reported to the German Foreign Office on June 13, 1940, "it was to the common interest of the European powers to place themselves in opposition to German imperialism. It had become evident that the German danger was far greater than had been believed."

It is only from this moment on that the Soviet government greatly accelerated its armaments and took action to strengthen its frontiers by incorporating the Baltic States and Bessarabia. At the same time, the first serious issues of conflict with Germany emerged. First, German trade deliveries to Russia lagged behind; while the Soviets had delivered their raw materials, the Germans had failed to live up to the stipulations of the contract. Second, territorial disputes arose. Russia desired to annex Rumania's Bucovina, yet because of German objections had to be content with half of the coveted territory.

In August, 1940, the Germans and Italians arbitrated frontier disputes between Hungary and Rumania and imposed on them the so-called Vienna Award which, in substance, dismembered Rumania. The Russians objected strenuously on the grounds that Germany had violated her pact with the Soviet Union and that Russia should have been consulted. The Russians were on firm ground, and the Nazis could offer only a few lame excuses.

To top everything, the Germans and Italians concluded an alliance with Japan (September 27), the meaning of which, for simple geographical reasons, was quite obvious [59]—it was to "promote the prosperity of their peoples"—but which they took pains to describe to the Soviet government as an alliance directed against the United States and designed to bring the American "warmongers" to their senses. The Soviets professed to accept that in-

[58] *Ibid.,* p. 140.
[59] The alliance followed, within a few days, Hitler's decision to abandon the invasion of Britain. The German general staff had started working on operational plans against Russia sometime in August.

terpretation, again showing their eagerness to "trust" the Nazis more than anybody else.

There were many minor irritations. One day, the Germans obtained from Finland rights of passage, but did not inform the Russians. On another day they sent troops into Rumania, allegedly as a defense against England! Then the Germans cut down their industrial deliveries even further.

When Nazi-Soviet relations had reached an impasse, the Germans invited Molotov to come to Berlin—possibly as a cover for their preparations for an attack on Russia, but possibly also as a "last attempt" to arrange a settlement on Nazi terms. In Berlin, the Germans offered Molotov a deal, to wit, a division of their respective *Lebensräume*.

The Germans invited the Soviets to enter the Tripartite pact between Germany, Italy, and Japan. According to the Nazi version, this was an offer to Russia to participate in the crusade against Britain and the United States. The Russians agreed to this proposal "in principle." Then the Germans produced a draft treaty according to which the Soviet Union was to declare its readiness "to cooperate politically," that is, not militarily, with the three powers. To the draft agreement was appended a secret protocol which provided for the division of spoils.

According to this draft agreement "the Soviet Union declares that its territorial aspirations center south of the national territory of the Soviet Union in the direction of the Indian Ocean." [60] Clearly, to satisfy these aspirations the Soviet Union would have been compelled to take up arms. A second secret protocol stipulated that the Montreux agreement concerning the Dardanelles was to be abrogated and that the Soviet Union was to obtain the right of unrestricted passage of its navy through the Straits at any time while no other nations, with the exception of the Black Sea countries, were to have that right.

Within less than two weeks after Molotov's return to Moscow, the Soviet government declared that it was prepared to *accept* the draft of the four-power pact, but it stipulated the following conditions: withdrawal of all German troops from Finland; permission to conclude a mutual assistance pact between Russia and Bulgaria; establishment of a land and naval base "within the range of the Bosporus and the Dardanelles by means of a long-term lease"; recognition that the Persian Gulf area south of Batum and Baku constituted the "center of the aspirations of the Soviet Union"; and abandonment by Japan of her concessions in northern Sakhalin. There was also to be a stipulation for military and diplomatic measures to be applied against Turkey should that country not "agree" to the proposed Straits convention. [61]

With this counterproposal, Soviet foreign policy not only openly sided with Germany against the Anglo-Saxon countries, but also aimed at the

[60] *Nazi-Soviet Relations,* "Secret Protocol No. 1," pp. 250, 257.
[61] *Ibid.,* p. 258.

despoliation of the British Empire, Turkey, and Iran; and possibly of Finland and Bulgaria. There was not even a pretense at a "democratic" or "peaceful" foreign policy. There was no resistance against, but participation in, aggression. There was no resistance against "fascist aggression" but support, assistance, and participation in "fascist aggression." Not a shred was left of the concept of collective security.

But was it perhaps an attempt to gain time and to improve Soviet positions vis-à-vis Germany? If so, the Soviets would have acted more wisely if they had shown less intransigence and had compromised with the Germans, for obviously the Soviet conditions were unacceptable to Hitler. It seems as though the Soviets considered the proposed territorial division as a settlement that would last for a very long period of time, and that they sought to obtain a maximum share in prospective territorial redistribution.

The Germans did not accept the Soviet conditions, and intensified their war preparations. The Russians apparently did not realize that the situation had changed completely, and for a while relations continued to be relatively good. Contacts with the Axis became again somewhat closer on the occasion of the Japanese Foreign Minister Matsuoka's visit to Berlin and Moscow. A few weeks later, however, the Soviet Union took a none too friendly stand during the Yugoslav crisis in April, 1941, and concluded a nonaggression pact with Yugoslavia prior to the German attack.

The Soviet government received numerous warnings that Germany would attack Russia, including warnings from London and Washington. Yet the Soviet government failed to take these warnings seriously. Did they not come from the democratic countries whose policy it was to embroil Russia in a war with Germany? The German attack on June 22, 1941, was a military surprise. The Soviets, it seems, had closed their eyes and proceeded on the a priori assumption that Hitler was a trustworthy fellow. Whatever the explanation, the military surprise cannot be argued away. One fact is not controversial: Soviet policy in 1941 was based on woefully inadequate intelligence.[62]

GERMAN-SOVIET RELATIONS DURING THE SECOND WORLD WAR

To recapitulate, the Soviet Union was willing to participate with Germany and Japan in an alliance against Britain and the United States. Through this alliance they hoped to gain control over the Middle East, from the Black Sea to India, and to arrange a *modus vivendi* with Germany in Eastern Europe. They probably also hoped that Germany, Japan, Britain, and the United

[62] "Stalin said that the Russian Army had been confronted with a surprise attack: he himself believed that Hitler would not strike but he took all precautions possible to mobilize his army. Hitler made no demands on Russia, hence they were forced to organize a defensive line of battle." Report to Roosevelt by Harry Hopkins, 1941, as quoted by Robert Sherwood in *Roosevelt and Hopkins*, New York, Harper, 1948. If this is an accurate report of what Stalin told Hopkins, it shows a great deal of confusion in Stalin's mind.

States would destroy each other in an unending holocaust while the Soviet Union would grow stronger. That Hitler attacked the Soviet Union was not Stalin's fault. The communist leader did his best to avoid the conflagration. However, the attack was due to the inner logic of Germany's problems; Germany never could win European hegemony, let alone world dominion, without destroying Russian power, and it could not defeat Britain without controlling Russian bases and resources (any more than it could defeat Russia without being helped by Britain). There is hardly any doubt that the German attack demolished many of Stalin's ambitious projects.

From June, 1941, when the fateful attack came, to the end of the battle of Stalingrad in January, 1943, the relations between Nazi Germany and communist Russia were those of bitter and deadly enemies. On the German side this hostility against all things Russian went so far as to reject the co-operation which anticommunist Russians and Ukrainians offered against the Soviet regime, not to mention the ferocity with which the Nazis went after Communist Party members. Only the German army, which was suffering from manpower shortages and which had a more accurate understanding of the military situation than the Nazi politicians, tried to reconcile the population of the occupied territories. The German army employed millions of nationals from the Soviet Union as auxiliary forces.

After the German defeat at Stalingrad several significant changes occurred. In the first place, Stalin tried to negotiate a separate peace with Germany, although he never brought himself to offering really advantageous terms. Second, the Soviets created, from the prisoners taken at Stalingrad, the so-called Free German Committee. The purpose of this committee, which comprised quite a few high-ranking officers, was to propound the advantages of a future German policy in the spirit of Bismarck and Rapallo and on this platform perhaps to bring about the large-scale defection of German military forces fighting in the east. Another purpose apparently was to threaten the United States and Britain with the ghost of Rapallo.

The Free German Committee disappointed Soviet expectations.[63] The plan never was implemented in a proper fashion, partly because the hatred against Germany had grown to a point where policies of this kind were inapplicable. It was very difficult for the committee to function in the front lines. In addition, the appeals of the Free German Committee did not strike responsive chords in the German soldier's breast, and the expected large-scale defection did not take place. The reason for this was not only the stubbornness of the German commanders but the failure of the Soviets to develop their relations with the committee into a real and honest policy as distinguished from a propaganda stunt. The Soviets were vacillating between several policies; they never trusted the committee fully. Nevertheless, the committee was not dis-

[63] Heinrich von Einsiedel, *I Joined the Russians,* New Haven, Yale University Press, 1953.

solved. It was used as a sort of training school for noncommunist German collaborators.

On the German side, a parallel and similarly abortive operation was undertaken aiming at the political collapse of the Soviet system and at the defection of the Red Army. There was the attempt to set up legions of Russian minority nationalities, such as the Tatars, and, above all, the experiment with an all-Russian liberation movement under the Russian General Andrei A. Vlassov. There was a great deal of close cooperation between these various anticommunist organizations and subordinate German elements, but what the real effectiveness of Vlassov's contingents would have been is conjectural, since they never were put to a real test. German leadership was afraid to give Vlassov free rein for fear that he would put the Russian house in order and thus ultimately re-create the Russian threat. The one solution which Nazi leadership was willing to advance was entirely unacceptable to the Russian opposition: the destruction, or at least radical diminution, of Russian state power. When in the end the Nazis decided to modify this policy, they had lost the war.

SOVIET IDEAS OF PEACE

Thus neither Russia nor Germany could operate a policy of collaboration successfully even when that policy commanded the support of a controlled opposition organized within the other country. Hence the war was fought to the bitter end. Soviet forces conquered Eastern Germany including, thanks to the assent of the West, the capital city of Berlin. This conquest was almost as bloody and brutal as the earlier Nazi conquest of western Russia. The Soviets, bent upon revenge, came as military victors and political oppressors. They proposed to make the Germans pay for the injustices they had perpetrated. The Soviets championed a Carthaginian peace for Germany. Königsberg and the northern portion of Eastern Prussia were annexed to the Soviet Union. The remaining parts of Eastern Germany east from the Oder-Neisse line, including Breslau and Stettin, were turned over to Poland. The Soviet Union, and not Poland, was responsible for this monstrous settlement. The Soviets tolerated and caused the expulsion and evacuation of Germans and *Volksdeutsche* from all states overrun by the Red Army, including Czechoslovakia. They removed numerous industrial plants, exacted reparations, imposed forced labor, carried out expropriations, collectivized agriculture, and opposed any Western move aiming to reduce the burdens on Germany. They imposed a rule of terror, the popularity of which can be gauged from the fact that within about eight years of communist performance approximately 10 per cent of the East German population went into exile.

At the various postwar conferences, such as Moscow and London in 1947 and Paris in 1949, the Soviets continued to advocate a draconian peace, asked for reparation payments to the tune of 10 billion dollars, opposed even the most urgent economic reforms and refused to allow Germany political self-rule. By contrast, the Western powers speedily abandoned any ideas of the harsh peace they originally had advocated, gradually but resolutely took a stand against the Russian policy of destruction, initiated and partly financed German reconstruction, and ultimately became the champions of German freedom and independence. They disassociated themselves completely from Soviet policy, resisted extreme Soviet pressure—as, for example, the Soviet blockade of Berlin—made it clear that they would not abandon Germany to the tender mercies of the Soviets, and in spite of threats and menaces allowed the formation of the *Bundesrepublik Deutschland* (May 20, 1949). Thus a sovereign German state reemerged, and with it the hope of a better German future. On October 11, 1949, the Russians established in their zone of occupation the so-called German Democratic Republic ruled by the proxy of a "government" composed of communists and Soviet appointees.

THE IMPASSE

The Soviets were confronted by a series of quandaries for which they were unable to produce solutions. Using graduates from the Free German Committee to staff the government of Eastern Germany, they tried to develop a viable political structure. They failed lamentably. Their collaborators were anything but trustworthy. Repeated halfhearted schemes for setting up military or "police" forces in East Germany had to be discarded. The Soviets were plainly afraid that such German military or semimilitary units might turn against them. A solution in the style of Korea, *i.e.*, an attack by East German forces against the *Bundesrepublik,* was inapplicable, and this not only because the presence of American and British forces made it so. The Soviets not only were unable to enlist the political cooperation of the population, but also managed to alienate the Germans to such an extent that open rebellions occurred (summer, 1953), an unprecedented event in a modern dictatorship. While under the Soviet heel, East Germany turned into one of the most anticommunist countries on the globe. In Western Germany too, the strength of communism declined to the vanishing point.

Yet while through their actions the Soviets were arousing antagonism of the Germans, at the same time they naïvely hoped to enlist their help by political trickery. The basic objective of Soviet policy vis-à-vis Germany was to bring about "unity." Such "unity" did not mean so much the unification of the two Germanies as the expulsion of the Western powers from Western Germany and the expansion, directly or indirectly, of the Soviet orbit to the borders of France, Belgium, and Holland. The Soviets posed as champions of true German "unity" in order to gain the support of public opinion against the Western powers, which allegedly stood for the *status quo., i.e.,* the *Zerreissung* (ripping apart) of Germany.

Stalin's congratulatory telegram addressed, on the occasion of the founding of the German Democratic Republic, to Messrs. Pieck and Grotewohl (president and premier respectively of the republic) contained the following suggestive passage: "The experience of the last war has shown that the German and the soviet peoples have been making the greatest sacrifices and that both peoples possess the greatest potentialities for the accomplishment of deeds of worldwide significance." [64]

It is not surprising that the *Berliner Zeitung* accorded Stalin's message an enthusiastic reception, for this newspaper was—and, at the moment of this writing, still is—the mouthpiece of the communist-controlled government of Eastern Germany. It is, however, of more than passing interest that the editorial on Stalin's message was entitled *1922 and 1949*. It greeted the birth of the German Democratic Republic, blessed by Stalin's congratulations, as "Russia's return to the policy of Rapallo." The Germans, on their part, so *Berliner Zeitung* assured its readers, would resume the Rapallo policy on "a higher plane." [65] In view of the peculiar character of the *Berliner Zeitung,* ostensibly the organ of the East German government and actually the mouthpiece of the Communist Party and its Russian masters, the meaning of these ruminations on the "Rapallo policy" is crystal clear: an official Soviet invitation to the German nation to resume the Soviet-German connection.[66]

However, the realities of the situation militated strongly against a Rapallo on "a higher plane." Disregarding the fact that the Western powers were most unlikely to fall for this Soviet bluff, such a policy no longer can be executed. It would have to be based on the willing cooperation of the German nation; yet for a long time such a cooperation will not be forthcoming. Too many Germans have suffered from the depredations of communism, too many have lost home, shop, and family, and too many have seen the Soviet paradise with their own eyes to lend themselves willingly to schemes which so transparently serve the Soviet purpose alone. Nor will the Soviets for a long time be able to trust the Germans. Hence they can obtain German unity as *they* want it only through transforming Germany into a satellite. This ob-

---

[64] For the complete text see *Neue Welt* (Berlin), Vol. 4, No. 19, 1949, p. 3.

[65] See *Berliner Zeitung,* Oct. 14, 1949.

[66] For a detailed and carefully documented account of the step-by-step advance of Soviet policy from the Stalin-Truman-Churchill meeting at Potsdam (with its emphasis of the punishment of war criminals, reparations, and denazification) to the nineteenth congress of the Communist Party at Moscow, October, 1952, see Boris Meissner, *Russland, die Westmächte und Deutschland: Die sowjetische Deutschlandpolitik 1943–1953,* Hamburg, Nölke, 1953. This book also contains an interesting account of the two schools of thought on German policy within the Politburo: according to the author, Beria backed a "national front," *i.e.,* a strong *national* German state no matter what its ideological coloration, whereas Molotov favored the sovietization of Germany and the elimination of the "imperialist," *i.e.,* conservative-nationalist, elements in German society. There is an interesting discussion of why the communist leaders rejected the neutralist movement in Germany (p. 224). See also the blueprint for a new "Rapallo policy" by Joseph Wirth in "Die Reise hinter den Eisernen Vorhang," *Dokumentation der Zeit,* 1952, pp. 1166–1174. Wirth was German Chancellor in 1922, the year of Rapallo.

jective can be attained only, if at all, through war. To obtain even a minimum of cooperation from the Germans, the Soviets would have to change radically their policies in Eastern Germany. They would have to return at least part of the East German territory. Even if they were willing to do so, such a step would produce difficulties with Poland and Czechoslovakia and necessitate large-scale population movements from and into Eastern Germany.

Thus German unity under Soviet control is blocked. German unity in the form of an independent and "neutral" Germany would require a contraction of the Soviet orbit, with concomitant reduction of Soviet power. A return to Rapallo, *i.e.*, to a Russo-German alliance, would require as a prerequisite the partition and resettlement of Poland, without thereby necessarily attaining the Soviet objective. Under the circumstances it was logical that, time and again, the Soviets reverted to the policy of Potsdam—*i.e.*, to the partition of Germany and the retention of East Germany as a satellite. This was the gist of the Soviet reply to President Eisenhower's address of April 16, 1953, and to the British plan submitted by Anthony Eden during the Berlin Conference early in 1954 laying down the conditions for a general settlement. Russia's German policy had run into contradictions which could not be resolved in a rational manner. As a result, the Soviets have no choice but to live with the problem until there arises an opportunity which may allow them to make a new approach.

EVALUATION

In evaluating the record of Soviet-German relations it is necessary to remember that the Soviet Union is confronted by many problems in addition to the German question. Moreover, our knowledge of Soviet policy is incomplete. No one outside Russia—or rather, outside the Kremlin—knows for sure why, for example, Stalin concluded a pact with Hitler in 1939 and why during 1931 to 1933 he ordered the German Communist Party to engage in those bizarre maneuvers which made Hitler's accession to power inevitable.

These reservations notwithstanding, the Soviet record in Germany provides a good insight into the mechanics of Soviet operations, which consisted of a mixture of diplomacy, propaganda, subversion, political warfare, revolutionary uprisings, provocation, and war. On the credit side, the alliance between communists and Germans enabled the communists to come into power in Russia and to consolidate their world position. It led to the Second World War from which the Soviet Union emerged as the only victor, to a large extent to the detriment of Germany herself. On the debit side, the Nazis almost destroyed the Soviet regime. The Soviets, in 1945, grievously impaired their chances when—instead of establishing themselves as the champions of German survival—they indulged their vindictive urges and thus blocked the road to peaceful collaboration. In their gamble for Germany the Soviets overplayed their hand and thus forfeited their advantage to the West. By advancing deep into the heart of Central Europe as conquerors, lugging behind themselves an unworkable social system, they overextended their position and blundered into a situation which curbed severely their freedom of action. Being "contained" in the West, it was only natural that they again turned their attention to Asia, where they still had elbowroom for strategic maneuver.

For the time being, Soviet policy in Germany has been forced on the defensive. By 1954 their objectives simply were to prevent the integration of Western Germany into the European Defense Community, to forestall West German rearmament in any shape or manner, and to hold on to their possessions in Eastern Germany. The Soviets, with their characteristic tenacity, were waiting for, and preparing future opportunities to resume ultimately, an offensive German policy. If such opportunities should fail to materialize, their position may become increasingly precarious, and the cancer of Berlin may spread throughout the Soviet orbit in Europe.

The German workers are today the least likely among the world's proletarians to precipitate a communist revolution. In effect, the Soviets' old allies in Germany were the nationalists, not the proletariat—which explains perhaps why, in German domestic politics after the Second World War, Soviet appeals were increasingly slanted toward German industrialists, pining for East European markets, and the unregenerated Nazis. If anywhere in the world communism as an intellectual movement is played out, it is so in Germany. The deep revulsion of the German working classes and of the great mass of the German people against Soviet ways of living and destroying may, in the end, spell the greatest defeat suffered by world communism.

In so far as the Germans were concerned, many of them had learned their lesson: the World War I policy of collaborating with the communists was a grave mistake; the policy of Rapallo prevented a settlement with the West and did not yield Germany any tangible results in the east; the pact of 1939 was paid for dearly by defeat and contributed greatly to the emasculation of German independence and power; Russian behavior since 1945 has shown clearly that collaboration with the Soviet Union cannot be advantageous to any of the basic interests of Germany; and lastly, cooperation against the West between a gigantic Soviet Union and an enfeebled Germany is possible only if Germany were willing to forgo her national independence, reduce her living standards, abolish her economic and social system, and become a communist satellite. By spring of 1954, the spirit of Rapallo was but a wan ghost. It is unlikely that a Rapallo policy in the proper sense will again be possible before the Russians have evacuated Eastern Germany or at least transformed by an entirely new approach the present crudely repressive system into one operated by discreet and remote controls.

There is no doubt that the Germans would be prepared to make many concessions if they could persuade the Soviets to leave their country. But the essential concession would have to be made by the Soviets: the contraction of the Soviet orbit.

Soviet policy in Germany reveals much about Soviet objectives in general. There has been, however, a profound change in emphasis; the great stakes of Soviet policy have now become the conquest of Asia. The conquest of Asia and the domination of its former colonial and backward areas signify near world domination and, ultimately, the annihilation of American power. To be sure, in order to attain these goals, the Soviets must solve the problem of Germany in their own inimitable fashion. But this problem is now derivative; in order to expand in Asia and deal with the United States, the strategic position of the Western powers in Europe must be made untenable. This requires the restoration of the situation of 1939, or if not the exact replica of that situation, then at least one that allows similar opportunities for maneuver —a West uncertain of its course and rent by internal divergences, and a Germany that, as a minimum objective, can be manipulated into blocking Western moves directed against Russia and kept out of a Western system of alliance or, as a maximum objective, can be absorbed into the Soviet system by standard techniques applied by the Soviets to "friendly" countries alienated from the West by the bait of Soviet markets and by appeals to German *revanche* sentiments. That the old recipe was still a favorite one with the master—thirteen years after he had paved the way for a world war with the best of intentions of staying out of it until the capitalist states had finished each other off—can be gleaned from Stalin's political testament (see Chap. 22).

Yet at the moment of this writing, the Soviets appear to be no nearer to their goal than they were at the start of their struggle with the West over the dismembered body of Germany. In fact, the goal appears to have receded, for, by 1954, Soviet policy in Germany had reached an impasse. Whether the Soviets can extricate themselves by sagacious retreat (a feat unprecedented in Soviet annals), or by making a detour through Asia or Western Europe, or by launching intercontinental warfare, these are the questions that intrigue and baffle Western statesmanship. History, as is its wont, may bring forth an entirely unforeseen situation invalidating the alternatives which are so plainly visible at the time of this writing.

BIBLIOGRAPHY

Beloff, Max: *The Foreign Policy of Russia, 1929–1941,* 2 vols., New York, Oxford, 1948–1949.

Bluecher, Wipert von: *Deutschlands Weg nach Rapallo, Erinnerungen eines Mannes aus dem zweiten Gliede,* Wiesbaden, Limes, 1951.

Carr, Edward Hallett: *German-Soviet Relations between the Two World Wars, 1919–1939,* Baltimore, Johns Hopkins Press, 1951.

Castex, Raoul V. P.: *De Gengis Khan à Staline, ou les vicissitudes d'une manoeuvre stratégique 1205–1935,* Paris, Société d'Éditions Géographiques, Maritimes et Coloniales, 1935.

Cressey, George B.: *The Basis of Soviet Strength,* New York, Whittlesey, 1945.

Deutscher, Isaac: *Russia: What Next,* New York, Oxford, 1953.

Ebon, Martin: *World Communism Today,* New York, Whittlesey, 1948.

Degras, Jane (ed.): *Soviet Documents on Foreign Policy*, New York, Oxford, 1951–1952, Vol. I, "1917–1932."

Grunwald, Constantine de: *Trois siècles de diplomatie russe*, Paris, Calmann-Lévy, 1945.

Hilger, Gustav, and Alfred G. Meyer: *The Incompatible Allies: A Memoir-History of German-Soviet Relations, 1918–1941*, New York, Macmillan, 1953.

Lobanov-Rostovsky, Andrei: *Russia and Europe 1789–1825*, Durham, N.C., Duke University Press, 1947.

————: *Russia and Asia*, New York, Macmillan, 1933.

Lovestone, Jay: *Soviet Foreign Policy and the World Revolution*, New York, Workers Age Publishing Company, 1935.

Lukacs, John A.: *The Great Powers and Eastern Europe*, New York, American Book, 1953.

Maisky, Ivan M.: *Soviet Foreign Policy*, London, Anglo-Russian Parliamentary Committee, 1936.

Mehnert, Klaus: *Stalin versus Marx*, London, G. Allen, 1952.

Meissner, Boris: *Russland, die Westmächte und Deutschland*, Hamburg, Nölke, 1953.

Moore, Barrington, Jr.: *Soviet Politics*, Cambridge, Mass., Harvard University Press, 1950.

Prokopovicz, Serge N.: *Histoire économique de l'U.R.S.S.*, Paris, Flammarion, 1952.

Radek, Karl: *Die Liquidation des Versailles Friedens: Bericht an den 4. Kongress der Kommunistischen Internationale*, Hamburg, Verlag der Kommunistischen Internationale, 1922.

————: *Die auswärtige Politik Sowjet-Russlands*, Hamburg, Hoym, 1921.

Rossi, A.: *A Communist Party in Action: An Account of the Organization and Operations in France*, New Haven, Yale University Press, 1949.

————: *The Russo-German Alliance*, London, Chapman & Hall, 1950.

Rothstein, Andrew (transl.): *Soviet Foreign Policy during the Patriotic War: Documents and Materials*, 2 vols., London, Hutchinson, 1946.

Seraphim, Hans-Günther: *Die deutsch-russischen Beziehungen 1939–1941*, Hamburg, Nölke, 1949.

Seton-Watson, Hugh: *From Lenin to Malenkov: The History of World Communism*, New York, Praeger, 1953.

Smith, Walter Bedell: *My Three Years in Moscow*, Philadelphia, Lippincott, 1950.

Sontag, Raymond J., and James S. Beddie (eds.): *Nazi-Soviet Relations 1939–1941: Documents from the Archives of the German Foreign Office*, U.S. Department of State, 1948.

Thorwald, Juergen: *Wen sie verderben wollen, Bericht des grossen Verrats*, Stuttgart, Steingruben, 1952.

Von Laue, Theodore H.: "G. V. Chicherin, Peoples Commissar for Foreign Affairs, 1918–1930," in *The Diplomats 1919–1939*, Gordon A. Craig and Felix Gilbert (eds.), Princeton, N.J., Princeton University Press, 1953.

Chapter 24

IMPERIALISM AND COLONIALISM

Almost instinctively, Americans are opposed to imperialism and colonialism. They hold "empire" and "imperialism" in low esteem and deem all nations by nature capable of self-government and hence entitled to self-determination. Hence colonialism—the rule of one nation over another and, more specifically, the rule of an advanced over a backward nation—is considered evil. Ever mindful of the origins of the United States, Americans favor the abolition of all colonial empires, forgetting all too easily that the Americans who obtained their independence from Britain were culturally and politically as advanced as their rulers, militarily superior, and led by an "elite" whose sagacity and acumen were of the highest order. Only a few colonial peoples of the 20th century measure up to these standards. This fact notwithstanding, the United States has lived up to its high principles and popular convictions. In 1946, it granted independence to the Philippines. Yet this gesture did not signify the end of colonial empires, including that empire under the American flag. Their survival poses multiple and difficult problems.

MOTIVES AND HISTORY OF IMPERIALISM

Any one or several of many powerful motives may induce a state to expand its frontiers. The demands of military security or economic welfare may compel an otherwise peaceful state to venture upon the conquest of territory. Sometimes nations expand into sparsely populated or even "uninhabited" territories for the purpose of settlement and of securing the frontier population's lives and property against brigandage, tribal wars, and frontier raids. It is to suppress unrest and to establish the rule of law that the power of the state reaches into the frontier society, as shown by the history of the American West, India's northwestern frontier, Russia's Siberia, and South Africa's veld. These types of expansion are not properly called imperialism. Imperialism is rather the tendency of a state to expand *without any particular reason* in an *unlimited fashion* toward an *unrestricted* and *undefinable* objective. It is expansion for its own sake.[1]

[1] See Joseph A. Schumpeter, *Imperialism and Social Classes,* with an introduction by Paul M. Sweezy, Oxford, Blackwell, 1951, p. 7.

Expansion of this kind usually is the work of a power-hungry elite teamed with a strong military organization created originally by wars of survival, but now requiring the practice of war in order to keep fit—a society, in brief, which looks upon war as if it were a national industry, as Mirabeau remarked of Prussia, or a kind of WPA for otherwise unemployed warrior castes. Examples of expansionist societies in ancient history are Egypt, Persia, and, above all, Assyria for which kingdom war, like a royal hunt, was an end but not a means. Similarly, the Arabs, while ostensibly fighting for the propagation of a new creed, Islam, were not overeager to convert the vanquished to the new faith, lest they would have been compelled to award to others the very privileges they wished to reserve unto themselves. Arabic society was a nomadic society which waged everlasting war. The Arabs, far from taking to the sword because they embraced the new faith, accepted that prophet who was willing to proclaim the sanctity of eternal war.[2] Mohammed was a product of his society, not the other way around; yet once the new faith was accepted, it became a stimulant of extraordinary strength.

Systems have been described erroneously as imperialistic because the real motives of their expansionist politics did not become clear to their contemporaries or to the historians. The German Hohenstaufen emperors, for example, have been condemned, especially by latter-day German historians, for their policy of conquest in Italy and their neglect of the German realm. It is argued that, instead of seeking glory in the south, they should have administered Germany and expanded the German *Siedlungsraum* (area of settlement) to the east. The fact of the matter is that the Hohenstaufens warred in Italy for reasons of domestic policy; only by keeping the feudal lords busy in war, and only by exacting tribute from Italy, then the wealthiest country, were the Hohenstaufens able to stay in power. Their policy was to rule Italy through the German knights and to rule Germany through Italian money.[3]

If imperialism is defined as the quest for more power without any other objective but power, imperialism in the proper sense of the word may, in this century, have gone out of business. Nowadays a different interpretation of the phenomenon has been accepted widely: imperialism and, specifically, the establishment of colonies in areas inhabited by "colored" or "backward" peoples are explained as the quest for economic gain. Consciously or unconsciously, this interpretation derives from Marxian theory, which argues that the "capitalist" system must expand its markets continuously. Economic growth allegedly is not possible in a closed capitalist system. In order to insure the growth of the system, large investments must be made. Yet the capitalists will not and cannot invest unless they find expanding markets for their products. Since markets cannot expand domestically, new territory must be pulled into the capitalist economy. The "surplus" of the capitalist produc-

[2] *Ibid.*, pp. 52–55.
[3] *Ibid.*, p. 63.

tion thus is seen as being wrung from the conquest of precapitalist societies. While on the one hand, imperialistic competition leads to international wars, on the other the "extension of capitalism into new territories was the mainspring . . . of the 'vast secular boom' of the last two hundred years." [4]

There is no question that the economic opening up of new territory has yielded great economic advantages. But this "secular boom" was due, above all, to the industrialization of the Western powers and to the expansion of their domestic markets triggered by increase of population and purchasing power. The colonies were never significant purchasers of industrial products. It is only recently that the colonial areas have become important suppliers of vital raw materials. The raw materials on which the industrialization of the 19th and early 20th century was based, by and large, came from the industrial countries themselves. This is, to a large extent, true even of cotton. Only when oil, rubber, and tin assumed importance did dependence on colonial or underdeveloped areas become more marked. In the field of foodstuffs, dependence on tropical cane sugar was reduced greatly when industrialized countries began to cultivate sugar beets. In the future, however, the raw-material riches of the underdeveloped areas indeed will become crucially important for the progressive industrialization of the world.[5]

Historically, "imperialism" is a complex phenomenon. The origins of present-day imperial systems may be sought in the period of the Crusades. Venice and other Italian cities sought to acquire ports along the Oriental trade routes. It should be borne in mind, however, that the spices of the East, for example, were indispensable for the conservation of meat and, therefore, for the survival of the population; hence the spice trade was not merely a question of "profits." Furthermore, establishment of advanced bases became necessary as a defense against the Turks.

The next phase of imperialism began with Columbus' discovery of America. Regardless of the motives which led to the expedition, the discovery was to have immense economic consequences. The Spaniards carried off large quantities of gold which transformed the European economy. Although primarily spurred by the quest for gold, the conquistadors were founders of empire in their own right. Yet their empires did not last. Their most significant "accomplishment" was the destruction of native societies such as the Inca and Mexican states.

Other maritime powers, especially Britain, seeking to halt the flow of gold to Spain and to divert it to themselves, embarked on a secular war of piracy

[4] See Joan Robinson in her Introduction to Rosa Luxemburg, *The Accumulation of Capital* (originally 1913), New Haven, Yale University Press, 1951, p. 28.

[5] The facts of this development have been characteristically garbled by Marxist theoreticians. It simply is not true, as Lenin asserted, that the First World War "was a war for the division of the world, for the partition and re-partition of colonies." See V. I. Lenin, "Imperialism, the Highest Stage of Capitalism," preface to the French-German edition, *Selected Works,* New York, International Publishers, 1943, Vol. V, p. 7. See also E. Varga and L. Mendelsohn, *New Data for V. I. Lenin's Imperialism, The Highest Stage of Capitalism,* New York, International Publishers, 1940.

—naval guerrilla war—in the course of which their sailors occupied many islands and anchorages. Settlers sometimes followed, sometimes preceded, the traders and warriors. Thus were founded the early tropical colonies.

These colonies supplied the first practical means for satisfying one of the most urgent nutritional needs of Europe: the production of sugar. Ever larger tracts were taken under cultivation, but since there were not enough Europeans to work the sugar fields—and, for that matter, no Europeans at all who could do sustained and heavy physical labor under tropical conditions— the natives were forced into bondage. The unsuitability of the West Indian natives for hard labor and their stubborn resistance to enslavement led to their extermination—one of the darkest chapters of European history. To improve their lot, Father Bartolomé de las Casas suggested that it would be more humane to free them and recruit plantation labor from more robust African Negroes. The demand for manpower thus led to the expansion of the slave trade and the establishment of slave-trading posts in Africa.

Concurrently with these developments, a large expansion of trade with the Oriental and colonial countries took place. Most of the trading nations operated through trade monopolies, such as those created by Britain's navigation acts. The ensuing competition between trade monopolies was settled not by price wars but by military means. In response to military requirements, ports and whole subcontinents were incorporated in these growing empires by military force or diplomatic negotiation and closed to the competitor's trade. Trade exchanges with Asia, especially with India, were highly profitable to both sides. European nations and trading companies entered into protective and commercial arrangements with local states. They often participated in regional conflicts, some of which they themselves had excited but some of which they fought in order to protect their vassals and allies against pillage and enslavement.

The religious struggles in Europe profoundly influenced the history of imperialism. People who wanted to escape religious discrimination or persecution looked for new homelands. The quest of religious freedom was the origin of much of the white settlement of North America and the Caribbean islands. On the other hand, the Christian church encouraged missionary work among the "heathens." Some Catholic countries, especially France, entered into relations with overseas and Oriental countries. Though in these missionary activities as, for example, those of France in Southeast Asia during the late 17th and early 18th century, the commercial element was not absent, religious fervor predominated over all other motivations.

Strictly military considerations accelerated the race for empire, albeit not as decisively as the quest for gain and freedom. Modern navies no longer depended on mere anchorages but on permanent supply bases whence they could replenish their stores of fresh vegetables, water, and ammunition. These bases and the settlements growing around them required the protection of garrisons. The garrisons' demand for local services stimulated the growth of the trading population and hence of the settlements. The first move set in motion a slow and often wholly unforeseen chain reaction; trade followed the flag as much as the flag followed trade.

The wars which European powers waged in Europe and for European possessions engendered repercussions overseas. The belligerents extended hostilities to all their possessions; Frenchmen and Englishmen fought their battles not only in Europe but also on the North American continent, in the Caribbean and in India. Naval strategy had its own fluid logic. Naval operations encompassed all the world oceans. Nelson pursued the French navy from one end of the Mediterranean to the other and across the Atlantic into the West Indies. Peace arrangements among the European powers involved cessions and exchanges of colonial possessions. European powers often entered into alliances with native tribes and princes. Native manpower became a significant addition to European military strength. Since now their very security was at stake, the European powers continually stirred up troubles in each other's colonial possessions. Local colonial wars occurred independently of European conflicts. The French revolution provoked many revolts— *Jacqueries*—in colonial areas, some of which, like Haiti and San Domingo, achieved "independence."

Once the process had started, it developed its own momentum—as a result perhaps of the instinct of imitation and competition or because politics, like all of nature, abhors a vacuum. The challenge-response course of the development was well described by a French observer. In 1774, the French Foreign Minister Vergennes, in his *Réflexions politiques et secrètes,* wrote: [6]

The conquests the English are making in India give them a great advantage over the French in the financial and political affairs of Europe. Some means must be found to procure for France positions in Asia, which will counterbalance these [English] advantages.

Another memorandum reads as follows: [7]

The English have established a post in the vicinity of Borneo in order to export gold, paper, camphor, the spices of the Moluccas, and other commodities the sale of which is extremely profitable in Europe, as well as in China and parts of India. . . . It appears that nothing remains but Cochin China which has escaped the eyes of the English. But can we delude ourselves into believing that they will delay in advancing thither? If they decide to step in ahead of us, we will be excluded forever. If they were to establish themselves there, they would regard us as their vassals upon every Asiatic coast.

By the beginning of the 19th century, the Western Hemisphere had been settled by whites and Negroes; several colonial products had become in-

---

[6] Quoted by Charles B. Maybon, in *La Relation sur le Tonkin et la Cochinchine,* Paris, E. Champion, 1920, p. 170.

[7] Charles B. Maybon, *Histoire moderne du pays l'Annam, 1592–1820,* Plon-Nourrit, 1919, p. 170; and Albert Septans, *Le Commencement de l'Indochine française,* Paris, 1887, Challamel, pp. 65*ff.*

dispensable to the European economy; a huge amount of trade was being done with the Orient; and colonial possessions had assumed great military significance.

Empires circled the globe, yet nowhere had anyone troubled to devise a grand design for empire building. There always was some specific and sufficient reason why this or that European nation acquired this or that colony. The wisdom, however, of acquiring huge colonial possessions was much in doubt, especially since empires imposed on their motherlands heavy economic burdens. Napoleon abandoned France's large holdings in North America. The Spaniards and Portuguese lost practically all their American possessions. Only the British, and to a lesser extent the Dutch, were able to derive profit from their colonies, for they possessed the chief prerequisite for colonial operations, namely, sea power. But even in Britain, there raged a controversy as to whether or not the colonies were, as Disraeli put it, "millstones" around the British people's necks. The abolition of slavery destroyed the economic basis of white settlement and, for two or three generations, the economic usefulness of the colonies. Yet the British, undaunted, proceeded to stamp out slavery—a telling comment on the accuracy of the economic interpretation of history.

In the 19th century, the pace of imperialist expansion perceptibly quickened. Again, the forces impelling individual states were most complex. France ventured into Algeria partly in order to divert domestic unrest— the Bourbons, having made themselves exceedingly detested by the populace, sought to retrieve their popularity by martial deeds—and partly because piracy in the Mediterranean had become an intolerable nuisance and world opinion called for an end to the infamies of the Barbary States. The conquest of Algeria had not been planned but came about as a by-product, so to speak, of military operations. Similarly, Britain acquired bases in the Arabian Sea not so much for the sake of permanent aggrandizement as for the humane purpose of wiping out the slave trade. When, in the Orient, various British and Dutch trading companies displayed administrative ineptitude as well as economic and military weakness, the home governments stepped in and took over. They handled—as protective powers—foreign and military affairs. They did not interfere with the domestic affairs of their wards, except to curb savage customs and advance education.

Troubles with China arose from the desire to open up trade with that large and sophisticated country. The Opium War was an early and important step toward drawing China into the mesh of world trade. Trade in opium was unquestionably a deplorable kind of commerce—but once China's barriers had fallen, trade in more conventional commodities became far more important; the "imperialist" powers joined forces to suppress the international narcotics trade. In any event, Western imperialism was not expansionistic; there was no attempt to conquer space. True, peripheral areas such as Tonkin were conquered, international settlements and free ports were secured; Western administrators took over certain functions of the Chinese government, such as the collection of customs revenue; and the Western powers discussed, off and on, the partition of China. These encroachments notwithstanding, China's independence was left intact. Nor did the West impinge upon the integrity of Japan. In other words, countries with highly advanced civilizations, while they were drawn into world trade, did not succumb to "colonialism" in the true sense of the word.

The expansion of European holdings in Africa followed upon the disintegration of the Ottoman Empire. Political and military penetration was not infrequently triggered by violence and sundry mischief perpetrated by natives against European traders and settlers as, for example, in Egypt. The African stakes of Western imperialism grew immensely with the discovery of important mineral deposits, especially gold and diamonds in South Africa. Often the explorer paced imperialist expansion. Geographic exploration opened "free territory" which was claimed for European countries. Entrepreneurs as, for example, Cecil Rhodes and King Leopold I of Belgium, followed hard upon the heels of the explorers and developed the wealth of Africa's virgin areas. The history of the Congo, a mixture of exploration and business, is characteristic of this development. Toward the end of the century, the quest for new territory had become more or less an end in itself. Countries like Germany, which for a long time had refused to engage in colonial ventures, suddenly felt that they could not do without colonial possessions if they were to maintain their status as true world powers.

Once imperialistic competition had started, nations grabbed territory to round out their possessions, to improve their strategic lines of communication overseas, and to forestall the expansion of other nations. Imperialism reached its peak in the competition of the European powers for Africa at the end of the 19th century, and in the carving up of Asia into spheres of influence between Russia and Britain at the beginning of the 20th century. In the course of this process of acquisition and redistribution, tempers often grew short and international crises occurred with disturbing frequency. But the powers never subordinated their European interests to colonial aspirations. Metropolitan security remained the prime consideration. Moreover, trade exchanges among the imperial powers exceeded by far their trade with the dependent areas.

There is no doubt that many colonies were established by brutal force and for the purpose of exploitation. But many colonies and dependencies were founded by peaceful means. Quite a few came into being as a result of treaties, some through liberation from an oppressive native ruler or decadent imperial power, such as the Ottoman Empire. Frequently, weak and defenseless native societies solicited the aid of imperial powers against dangerous neighbors. Not a few native societies themselves took the initiative in entering into close commercial and political relations with European nations or traders.

Hence it is quite impossible to talk about the "colonial system" as though there were only one imperial structure of uniform genesis and uniform social organization. The various dependent nations are at different levels of social and cultural development, ranging all the way from primitive tribal societies to ancient and complex civilizations. Economically, they may yield income to the motherland or to a small group of businessmen, or they may eat up taxes paid by the population of the motherland. Politically, the status of colonies differs from one of complete subjection to foreign rule to almost full self-government in all domestic matters and considerable freedom in foreign and military affairs. Some dependent areas are being administered by the Trusteeship Council of the United Nations. On the other hand, many "sovereign" nations, especially in Central and South America, which enjoy formal independence, are in fact colonies inasmuch as they rely for their capital needs, their defenses, and their administration upon foreign powers.

EVALUATION OF COLONIALISM

There are fundamentally two arguments against colonialism. The first asserts that colonial arrangements deny to the subjugated nations the right of self-determination. Though this is formally true, it is not always meaningful. Quite a number of colonies originally were built by the imperial powers from practically nothing. For example, when Britain leased Hong Kong, it had a population of 7,500 persons; the demographic and commercial growth of the colony occurred under British rule, in response to British trade. The history of Singapore displays a similar pattern. The aboriginal population of the West Indies no longer exists; peoples live there today who are composed of Negroes, mulattoes, East Indians, Chinese, Syrians, and Europeans. These new peoples grew up in the cultural, linguistic, and religious orbit of the mother country and cannot, therefore, in view of the enormous differences among them, be considered as entirely distinct "nations."

Whites have settled in some colonies for as long a time as, and occasionally even a longer time than, the so-called "natives." They undoubtedly possess rights which must be protected. This is also true of the economic stakes which millions of white settlers acquired in many dependent areas, for example in North, East, and South Africa where they have cultivated the land, built the cities, organized transportation, established public utilities, and set up the educational and health services. The granting of complete independence could endanger the position of the white minorities.

On the other hand, there are cases, especially in Asia, where colonial rule is not much different from the subjugation of one European nation by another. Yet, the principle of national self-determination, just as it has proved its limitations in Eastern Europe and in the Balkans, cannot be applied mechanically in Asia without creating more inequities than it is supposed to remove. In some of the colonial areas the intermingling of many different races and cultures, the simmering of "melting pots," and long histories of cultural and regional rivalries make it likely that the withdrawal of the peace-enforcing imperial powers would be followed by racial and cultural strife. The overlordship of the white might be followed by the overlordship of another group, as happened in Indonesia where one group of Javanese assumed hegemony. Solutions through which every individual nation or tribe, or every typical mixture of races such as mulattoes, can obtain complete security in the absence of a dominant power are hard to find. Obviously, before such solutions are in sight, or before the native peoples achieve sufficient maturity and race wars become improbable, the withdrawal of imperial controls would be inadvisable.

The second argument asserts that colonies are the object of unilateral and hence inequitable economic "exploitation." In the past colonial exploitation has taken the form of the payment of extremely low wages to native labor, the exploitation of regional resources largely for the profit of absentee owners, the imposition of trade monopolies, the exaction of high interest rates on loans from the mother countries, high taxation, and, above all, failure to reinvest profits made locally. This kind of "exploitation," especially the paying of low wages, occurs in all lands, not only in colonies. It is partly a function of "productivity," and partly of conditions of labor wherever workers lack the protection of trade unions and legislation, and is largely the result of "underdevelopment" regardless of political form.

However great may be the loss in terms of human welfare or conservation of natural resources caused by exploitation of colonial areas, it is balanced by the huge investments which the imperial powers have made in their possessions for transportation, housing, public utilities, trade, industries, and health and educational services. Even the most backward colonies of the leading imperial powers have now road systems, reasonable medical care, primary education, and rudimentary local industries. But for some rare exceptions, population in the colonial areas has been rising rapidly for the last hundred years and the average life expectancy has improved considerably. Standards of living continue to be relatively low but are improving steadily. Quite a few colonial areas have reached higher per capita incomes than such western countries as, for example, Bulgaria, Yugoslavia, and Italy's Sicily.[8] The salient fact of colonial history since the end of the First World War is that a great deal of capital has been flowing into the colonial areas and that much of that capital was not in the form of loans and venture capital for profit but of grants. It is no longer accurate to talk of "exploitation" of the colonial possessions by their motherlands. In fact, in many cases, the

[8] R. Strausz-Hupé, "Italian Foreign Policy," *Current History*, April, 1953, p. 217.

(nominal) debtors "very successfully exploited their [nominal] creditors." [9]
In any event, to use the Marxian lingo, much of the surplus produced in the
mother countries found its way into dependent areas, where it was invested
à fonds perdu, showing no return of any kind, not even of good will. A few
examples may suffice:

The American Red Cross poured into French Equatorial Africa during the
Second World War 118 million dollars. After World War II, the United
States made grants to Indonesia to the tune of 84 million dollars and, in addition, advanced loans totaling 63 million dollars. The Philippines received
716 million dollars in grants and 97 millions in credits.[10] While the American
government's program of aid was widely publicized, Britain, France, and
Holland also have spent considerable and unsung sums of money over a
period of many years. Western philanthropic foundations (which were
endowed by capitalists) poured hundreds of millions of dollars into the
good works of education and medical care. In addition, industrial and
commercial firms as, for example, the Haut Katanga Mining Company
in the Belgian Congo, have built education and health facilities as well as
roads, power stations, and harbors without reaping monetary profits from
such ventures. This does not mean that these firms did not profit from their
regular business. They benefited, however, the areas where they operated.
The native populations have as yet neither the ability nor the resources to
build up trade and industry themselves. If they had the resources and technical know-how, it is doubtful that they would pay higher wages or display
greater social consciousness than Western enterprise.

Unfortunately, no over-all statistics of the total investment in colonial
areas are available, but there can be no question that the sums are huge.
Whether, on balance, the colonies have been "exploited" or "developed" is
perhaps impossible to determine, given the ambiguous meaning of the term
"exploitation." Undoubtedly, the colonies have given up wealth to the motherland, but undoubtedly, too, they are immeasurably wealthier now than they
were at the beginning of the colonial period. The wealth they gave up was
first developed by the European countries; later it was exchanged in trade.
The term "exploitation" does not describe properly such complex and varied
situations. Actually the imperial system has drawn the colonial areas into the
world economy and has enriched these areas as well as the motherlands and
the rest of the world.

The colonial system must plead guilty to *one* accusation: it undermined
native civilizations, destroyed the structures of native societies, and partly
supplanted local political and economical usages by the undesirable as well

[9] See M. J. Bonn, *Whither Europe: Union or Partnership,* New York, Philosophical
Library, 1952, p. 29.
[10] U.S. Department of Commerce, *Foreign Aid by the United States Government, 1940–
1951,* Government Printing Office, 1952, p. 84.

as the desirable practices of Western civilization. Undoubtedly, some precious values were destroyed in the process. Perhaps the rugged imperialists of the 19th century would have suffered pangs of conscience if they had believed less firmly in the ideology of "progress." No doubt, the most sordid conquest of the West was made by Hollywood and technical gadgetry, and the admirer of Asiatic culture and spirituality is welcome to deplore the change.

Though one may harbor some skepticism as to the values of the Western World, one need not take too seriously the invidious comparison of Western materialism and the spirituality of this or that "exploited" people, especially if it is advanced (as it usually is) by persons of liberal convictions. Every single one of these civilizations was the concern only of a very small elite, and practically all were stagnant. Hardly any native society conforms to the critics' own standards. It may be debatable how many Indian widows the British saved from the funeral pyre. It may be questionable how widespread was cannibalism in Africa and elsewhere. There is no gainsaying that, before the coming of the West, slavery, torture, inhumane punishment, uncontrolled disease, lawlessness, squalor and arbitrary government were, in Africa and Asia, the rule rather than the exception. These ancient ways may be romantic in books; their disappearance does not warrant an indictment of colonialism.

The imperial powers did not succeed in eliminating these scourges entirely, but they reduced them greatly. They introduced almost everywhere the concepts of justice and of the inalienable rights of the individual. These "Western" concepts have been revolutionizing the "inscrutable East"—and all tribal societies—and it is they who furnished material and moral strength to various independence movements directed against Western domination. That these Western-made improvements coincided with the desires of the native populations, once they understood the worth of these improvements, will be confirmed by any observer who has seen the natives save money to buy shoes, radios, motorcycles, and books and appeal to the local policeman and judge. Even if "imperialism" had done nothing but abolish slavery and replace it by economic "exploitation" and Western law, it would have done a glorious deed; it would have transformed chattels into persons. Without the works of imperialism we could not talk today about a *world* economy, let alone discuss the concept of "one world." Imperialism was a historical phenomenon; it began, it had its day, and it must end. It displayed many unpleasant features. On the whole, it was a progressive force. The question before us is not whether imperialism could have done better, but what other force can in the future carry forward its civilizing mission.

COLONIAL INSTABILITY

Despite political, economic, and cultural progress in the colonial areas, the world colonial system has become unstable. The colonial peoples have been growing more mature and experienced, while losing the psychological handicaps of tribalism, serfdom, and illiteracy. They are acquiring a properly educated leadership, while at the same time displaying greater cultural and racial uniformities due to urbanization, racial and cultural co-habitation, and inter-marriages. Social and status differences no longer are quite as extreme. In a word, the populations of some colonial areas tend to integrate themselves into more cohesive societies. Some of these societies could be described as nations-in-formation. It would have made little sense, 50 or 100 years ago, to talk of an Indonesian or Jamaican "nation," and even today there is a certain affectation about such terms. Yet they do describe an emerging reality.

A process of national integration is going on in Latin America, where nations have been acquiring distinct physiognomies developed from specific mixtures of particular Indian tribes with particular types of Negroes and particular types of whites, all blended into a particular type of society and economy. Heretofore these nations (with the exception of Brazil), by virtue of the quasi identity of the Spanish ruling class, conveyed the impression that they were all "the same." The transformation of the Latin-American "one world" into a cosmos of many national worlds is an astonishing process. Perhaps its most astonishing aspect is the degree to which originally "similar" nations tend to differentiate themselves from each other, even when they are as small and live as close to each other as the nations of Central America.

In Africa a similar process is under way, although it is as yet not so far advanced as is the Latin-American metamorphosis. Here tribal societies are amalgamating into larger social groupings, which could be described as "protonations." Each such group is simultaneously growing together and growing more differentiated in respect to other groupings. Everywhere these two simultaneous developments are accompanied by emergent trends toward private ownership, commercialization, universal use of money in lieu of barter, acquisition of technical skills, gradual adoption of the Western system of material values (*e.g.*, living standards) and gradual conversion to one of the world religions. The emergence of a broader political conscience is paired with growing political ambitions which, as a result of the stimulation of human energy by improvement in diets, are being pursued with increasing aggressiveness. As the amorphous masses of aborigines, natives, former slaves, outcasts, traders, settlers, and colonial masters develop into an articulated society, they acquire the fundamental prerequisites of representative self-government.[11]

Contrary to the legend, the imperial powers are rarely interested in denying self-government to such societies but rather are anxious to turn the local obligations over to them at the earliest practical moment. If anything, the

[11] "Articulation . . . is the condition of representation." This vital point is usually overlooked in the contemporary debate about colonialism. See Eric Voegelin, *The New Science of Politics,* Chicago, Chicago University Press, 1952, p. 41.

process has been too precipitate; democratic self-government presupposes the attainment of certain educational and cultural levels and elementary grasp of political, economic, and governmental facts, especially the crucial fact that in order to receive one must be willing and able to give. The historical experience of Russia and Eastern Europe shows clearly that semiliterate peoples who know just enough to embrace radical programs are as yet unfit for democratic self-government. Democracy is not a matter of constitutions but of learning; less a matter of "programs" than of attitudes; not a system of class or race warfare but one of compromise and mutual adjustment. A premature imposition, by fiat and from "above" rather than "below," of "democracy" must lead to radicalization and gigantic upheavals. The Burmese experience of independence bears this out; so does the record of Iran. Yet other nations like India (despite Kashmir) and Indonesia (despite continued domestic difficulties) should, thanks to specific circumstances among which the long association with Western ways and institutions is not the least significant, fare better. Whether they will indeed use their patrimony wisely, only the future will tell.

The support given by many Western groups to the so-called "nationalism" of colored peoples is based on an equivocation of the term "nation." The Indians, for example, are not *one* nation, a fact which received its first recognition in the partition of India and Pakistan. Languagewise, the Indian subcontinent is inhabited by about twelve "nations," and the number may be higher if other divisive factors, such as religion and social structures, are considered. Nor are the Chinese a "nation." Recent events have driven home the fact that erstwhile "Chinese" areas such as Tibet, Tonkin, Mongolia, and Sinkiang were not stable components of Chinese national domain and that their peoples remained outside the Chinese cultural orbit. But there is some reluctance to acknowledge the fact that Manchuria is not really a part of China and that the "Chinese" themselves are not a unity but consist of several groups, similarly as the French, Italians, and Spaniards all speak Romance languages but do not form one nation. The chief Chinese language, Mandarin, is spoken by only one-half of the Chinese, just as Russian is spoken by only one-half of the inhabitants of the Soviet Union. The dominant languages, Hindustani in India and Mandarin in China, are being imposed in the same fashion as German and Hungarian were imposed on the peoples of Austria-Hungary, and presumably with the same perplexing results. To accept the fiction that India or China represents *one nation* is simply to support the "imperialism" of Hindus and Mandarin Chinese; it is most certainly not in conformity with the doctrine of self-determination. These dominant population groups have progressed farther on the road to national maturity than the other groups within the geographical regions called India and China which are still largely in statu nascendi. This situation is analogous to that of Austria in the 18th and 19th centuries.

Whenever dependent areas move closer toward independence, consciousness of national identity may impede rather than hasten the coming of the day of emancipation. Thus, in the Anglo-Egyptian Sudan, the pagan and semi-Christian southern area, which is roughly one-third of the country, threatened to revolt if, upon withdrawal of the British, it were handed over to the Islamic northern Sudanese politicians of Khartoum. The issue still exists as a threat to an eventual independent Sudan. The southern Sudanese demanded continued protection of the British, while the Islamic northern Sudanese pressed for quick independence in a state in which they will be predominant. Islamic northern Nigeria, making up something like 12 million out of a population of 30 million in Nigeria, rose against southern demands for quick self-government and independence in a state in which the semi-Christian semipagan south would be predominant. Islamic Nigeria demands continued protection of the British. It may or may not be politically wise to keep India or China, the Sudan or Nigeria, "united," but it must be realized that such a policy does *not* flow logically from the acceptance of the principles of nationalism or self-determination.

Should the independenec of these nations have been delayed? As new social situations arose, the old political forms revealed themselves as out of date. The motherlands were too weak to hold by force colonies which wanted to break away; nor did they think that to do so would have been worth their while economically. The United States took a somewhat childish delight in working toward the severance of imperial ties. The postwar crop of ex-colonies becoming independent states owes its existence chiefly to the shifting fortunes of the war, especially the weaknesses of the colonial powers before Japanese aggression, and to the emotional gambits of American foreign policy, not to reasoned and careful policies.

In those areas which remained under colonial regimes, important changes took place. The gradual introduction of local and, in certain cases, of national self-government engendered an ever greater participation of colonial peoples in political life and afforded them first experiences in the practices of representative government and trade unionism. In many instances the primary effect of these developments was the clamor for the acceleration of the process. The result has been more in the nature of unrest than of order, as could have been expected.

In addition, the various colonies and ex-colonial states now entered upon closer relations with each other. Formerly, each colony maintained close relations with its mother country but had little intercourse with neighboring colonies or other dependent areas. At present, increased migration among the various colonies and the expansion of intercolonial trade bespeak the growing interdependence of the colonial peoples. There are, moreover, joint security problems which require coordination.

These trends have given rise to movements for regional groupings among the colonies such as, for example, a British West Indies federation, a Malayan federation including Singapore, and an East African dominion. These tendencies are strengthened by the efforts of the motherlands to reorganize their empires into systems of preferential trade, commonwealth structures, and political unions. They are resisted by some colonies which fear that they would lose whatever control over their internal affairs they were accorded by the motherland. For example, British Guiana and British Honduras are cool toward the idea of West Indian federation because they anticipate and fear large immigration from the more densely populated Caribbean islands, although an increase of population is the prerequisite for their own economic development. The inequality of treatment accorded various colonies within one empire and the differences of treatment between the various colonial systems—some of which, for example, granted select colonial areas the status of metropolitan territory and the right of parliamentary representation in the motherland (France) [12]—as well as the fact that a number of former colonial areas *have* achieved independence, have created in practically all colonies strong movements aiming at constitutional and political reforms.

Economic developments accentuate this political instability. Increasing population pressure requires the introduction of new forms of ownership, especially land tenure, and production. The supersession of traditional exchange systems by a modern financial and monetary structure has increased social and geographic mobility in colonial societies as well as the power of the dependent peoples. The influx of capital, the establishment of industrial and mining facilities, and the demand for salaried labor have not only stimulated the economic consciousness of colonial peoples but also evoked strong pressures for economic concessions and were conducive to a more sophisticated understanding of the inequities of colonial economic systems. The traditional emphasis on monocultures had to yield to the poise of more evenly balanced economic systems, and with it went, to a degree, the particular vulnerability of the colonial societies to the economic "cycle." At the same time, there emerged typical phenomena of modern industrialized societies such as blue- and white-collar workers, the urban unemployed and, perhaps most important, political parties. The colonial societies are in transition. Small wonder that they are politically unstable!

[12] The French Empire, the *Union Française,* consists of "metropolitan France" and "France overseas" (*France d'outre-mer*). The President of the French Republic is its head; it has both a High Council and an Assembly. The High Council is composed of delegates of the French government and of representatives of the associated states. One half of the assembly consists of representatives of metropolitan France; the other half, of deputies from the "overseas *départements* and territories" and the "associated states." Overseas France comprises Algeria, the overseas *départements,* the overseas territories, and the French associated states. The latter are the protectorates of Morocco and Tunisia, and the federation of Indo-China. Algeria's three *départements* are treated as part of metropolitan France. The "overseas territories," mainly in Western and Central Africa, are run as dependencies, somewhat like the Congo or Nigeria. The protectorates and the associated states are governed by native rulers under more or less discreet French surveillance.

THE COLONIAL MENTALITY

The modernization of colonial societies differs in many ways from the social and economic transformations which are wrought by scientific advancement and industrialization in Western countries. In the West, the progression from a rural and feudal society through medieval city economies and the Industrial Revolution on to the world market evolved organically, inasmuch as it followed the inner logic of Western development. The process corresponded to the thought and behavior patterns of Western man; it spanned several centuries. By contrast, the development of the colonial societies involved the destruction of preexisting social structures, the adoption of different and alien thought and behavior patterns, and the telescoping of the entire process into a short period. Moreover, the relationship between the ruling and the ruled clasess was entirely different from that obtaining in the motherlands. To this day, the ruling classes of most colonial countries are racially and culturally alien elements whose primary concern is their own survival and the retention of their privileges rather than the development of the society as a whole.

The white ruling classes have developed a specific colonial mentality which is one of the greatest obstacles to the peaceful development of the colonial areas. In the first place, the whites are imbued with a feeling of racial superiority. Hence they keep themselves segregated from the native populations, whom they try to "keep in their place." It is true that the bars of segregation have broken in many of the colonial areas where white and colored now enjoy practically equal status. Yet regardless of official policy, the white ruling class makes every effort to maintain its separate status and is unwilling to abandon any privilege which race and history may have conferred on it. This racial cleavage is one of the most powerful motives driving the colored peoples to oppose the colonial status and, more specifically, the continued presence of whites in colored areas.

Secondly, while the whites in the colonial areas are in a hopeless minority, they are addicted to Malthusian practices although they may have never heard about that population expert's theories. They discourage the influx of additional white settlers, whether they be businessmen, farmers, and professionals or whether they be industrial workers. In many cases they are unwilling to accept whites of "inferior" nationality as their equals. Actually they often resist immigration even of those whites, for example, refugees from totalitarian regimes, such as physicians, nurses, teachers, technicians, who could contribute valuable services to white settlers as well as natives. Their exclusion is usually defended by the argument either that the market for these professional services is saturated or that the natives should not be deprived of jobs, an attitude which is either condoned or strongly supported by the officials to whom motherlands intrust the administration of their colonies.

Thirdly, the whites are unwilling to abandon the various economic privileges which they were able to acquire throughout the years. They seek to maintain market monopolies and to keep wages low. The economic colonial system displays some shocking injustices which the governments themselves are slow in remedying. For example, the price of gasoline produced in Trinidad from local oil deposits is higher than the price for which the same gasoline is sold in Britain; sugar production on Martinique and Guadeloupe has been for years in a depressed state because the French government discriminates in favor of the metropolitan sugar-beet producers; the sale of Antilles rum is kept to a minimum in order not to hurt the interests of the French and Algerian winegrowers. The colonies do not always profit from their ties with the motherland even in cases where their imports would not compete with metropolitan producers; every year the British buy large quantities of timber from Russia, while they do little to exploit the timber resources of their own colonies, for example, British Honduras and British Guiana.

The colonial mentality reveals itself most blatantly in economic policies. The colonial powers built roads and schools and provided for many basic necessities of life; but otherwise, while they do not stifle economic progress, they do little to enhance it. Medical services in most colonies are still inadequate. In 1950 Indo-China had only one physician for 49,000 inhabitants; the ratio of physicians to inhabitants in France is 1:1,300. The British colonial administration, undoubtedly the most progressive of all, was staffed at the end of the Second World War by about 800 service doctors and 600 agricultural and veterinary specialists, and it had altogether less than 3,000 technicians and specialists on its payroll. Even ten times this total of 4,400 would not meet the demand for trained personnel. Yet these deficiencies could have been remedied easily through employment of non-British Europeans as well as through the acceleration of higher education in the colonial areas themselves. Many English physicians who allegedly are practicing in the colonies are listed as "temporarily absent," but only a few non-British candidates are admitted to take their place. A few medical schools, colleges, and universities have been established, especially after 1945, but the educational facilities of dependent areas still compare unfavorably even with backward independent countries. In the French Union, Malthusianism and exclusionism were driven to the extreme of discouraging voyages to, and sojourns in, the colonies by Frenchmen although some of these possessions are legally *"départements"*: The French traveler must deposit a large sum of money so that the government, if it so desires, can send him home. Thus, Frenchmen are not allowed to move freely between the various parts of their "metropolitan" domain. Needless to add, French venture capital does not move to where it is urgently needed.

Similarly, the development of credit and savings banks has been slow. While the banking facilities of the colonial areas, at least of the British Empire, compare favorably with some independent countries such as Iran, where interest rates are catastrophically high, the fact remains that the native peasant has to carry a heavy, often a usurious, interest burden and does not enjoy the services of those rural banks or cooperatives which, in Western countries, have done so much to put agriculture on a sound and stable basis. To be sure, the governments put limits on interest rates, but rules are not enforced, and, since the development of banks is being hampered, the local moneylender enjoys a monopoly. For example, in 1939 the official interest rate in Indo-China was 8 per cent per year, but actually the peasants paid between 8 and 10 per cent per month.[13] In so far as businessmen are concerned, it is difficult for them to obtain loans, especially if the color of their skin is not the requisite white. Although the situation is improving, development in the colonial areas is still dependent on decisions made by the banking houses in Western Europe. These absentee bankers are reluctant to underwrite industrial and commercial ventures in the colonies and prefer investments at home. They should not be blamed too severely: the colonial empires are not economic units within which capital, labor, and goods can flow freely, unhampered by currency and other controls. In some ways, investment in a colony is not much different from investment in foreign countries. But why then, one may ask, maintain the system in the first place?

Numerous reports have been issued by various commissions and study groups which, but for rare exceptions, tend to minimize the economic potentialities of the colonial countries. Although reliable statistical data are lacking on which over-all prognoses could be based, and although the productivity of the colonial areas has grown much faster than the "experts" expected, such reports almost invariably end up with the recommendation that the economic development of the colonies must be "directed," "gradual" or even "slow." Underlying such recommendations are assumptions dressed up as statistics concerning, for example, the ratio of arable land and population. If these assumptions had been made in 1200 they would have indicated that Europe was uninhabitable east of the Vistula. If they had been made in 1800 they would have placed the maximum "carrying capacity" of the United States at 15 million, at best. The philosophy underlying these studies and recommendations constitutes a most unfortunate marriage of old-fashioned paternalism with socialistic planning. Colonies are regarded as greatly retarded children, who must be made to grow up in the protective atmosphere of neomercantilism. Instead of inviting the flow of venture capital and calling in enterprising immigrants, colonial administrations keep their wards insulated

[13] See Philippe de Villiers, *Histoire du Viêt-Nam de 1940 à 1952,* Paris, Éditions du Seuil, 1952, p. 48.

even from each other, with each little colony—unless this is forbidden by statutes such as those enacted in some African colonies—being pressed into the strait jacket of self-sufficiency. Again, of what earthly use are imperial systems?

As Dr. Malan and his South African party see it, the native's lot is to supply cheap labor to white enterprisers and farmers. In all other respects, he must be kept entirely segregated from the whites and be deprived of political rights. The corollary of this policy, namely, that foreigners and foreign capital of any form, shape and description must be kept out, reflects faithfully the colonial mentality which deliberately prefers economic stagnation to the surrender of the white man's privileges and jeopardy of his "racial security." [14]

In most colonial societies, the ruling class lately has comprised a colored element consisting either of half-castes or of wealthy colored people who, in some way or another, achieved positions of eminence. There have developed fine gradations of acceptability according to the various shadings of color and racial origins, such as East Indian and Arabic which are more acceptable than American Indian and Negro. Even within pure and independent Negro societies, such as Haiti, there are social differences related to skin color. The light-colored Negroes usually constitute the elite, but when they are out of political power the darker "ins" proclaim that they are of purer race and are not averse to organizing pogroms against the lighter-shade "outs."

In the dependent areas where the ruling class consists of whites, the colored elite tries either to assimilate itself into the white elite or to share power with it. In other cases, the native elite assumes leadership over the natives and then confronts the whites with a real threat. An Englishman, resident of Kenya, commenting on opinions aired in the English press on the Mau Mau rebellion in 1952–1953, wrote as follows: [15]

Why does British policy in Africa tend to drive the educated ambitious African into opposition to it? Why do the natural leaders become extremists determined to oust British rule? . . . We in Kenya can only feel irritated when told by people at home that Mau Mau is a political and economic rebellion and that the correct and only cure is more politics and higher wages. The fact has to be faced that the tribe that has come to hate us with a hysterical loathing is the wealthiest in Kenya. It is also the tribe with the highest percentage of literates. It is the tribe most closely integrated in the economic life of the country and the most intelligent, enterprising and industrious of all the tribes. . . . We have not governed these people. We have not even studied them. Hardly any one of us speaks their language. Our education, lacking any policy, has destroyed their tribal restraints and tradition and

---

[14] It would be an interesting task to rewrite the history of the much-maligned Boer War from the point of view of recent experiences with Afrikander policies. This war was waged by the British to keep the most extreme manifestations of the colonial mentality in check.

[15] *The Economist* (London), May 9, 1953, p. 356.

given them little in exchange except a moderate standard in the three R's. As far as one can tell, Government has never asked itself what happens to the African when he leaves school. There is no place in our society for the educated African. . . . Occasionally from amongst the educated Africans arises a man of outstanding character and ability. What hope that he will be loyal? I watched Jomo Kenyatta when he was on trial. There sat a man obviously born to rule, a man of fascinating personality. . . . What scope was there for a man of his ability and character in Kenya? None whatever. . . . Men must fulfill themselves or become bitter. There are potential Jomos growing up all over Africa. They must inevitably take leading social positions or become agitators. As yet, the former positions are barred to them; the latter road is wide open.

For a while Dutch colonial policy aimed at stimulating the growth of half-caste groups which were to serve as a bridge between the natives and the whites, but this policy did not work or did not go far enough. Half-castes, as in South Africa, often find themselves in the unhappy position of being liked by neither of their parent groups. All in all, the acuity of the colonial problem derives from the circumstance that the cleavages between economic interests and social status of the various "classes" are intensified by the cleavages between "races."

The economic difficulties could be overcome by a change in colonial policies. It is simply a matter of removing barriers to development and of washing Malthus's ghost out of the hair of the colonial administrators. The racial problem in the colonial areas, however, cannot be solved except by a radical deemphasis on the significance of racial differences. This is fundamentally a long-range program of education which, unfortunately, may not be practical so long as there are strong differences in cultural patterns, professional skills and educational standards which tend to perpetuate racial antipathies. In this connection, it is particularly unfortunate that the white colonial elites are the foremost victims of race prejudice.

Other social factors should not be overlooked: The isolation of the whites from the surrounding society; the traditional, though attenuated, master-servant relationship; the debilitating climate of some colonial areas; economic hardship; alcoholism; lack of cultural activities; and the residue of psychological characteristics which led to the white settler's departure from the mother country. These conditions have often caused what has been called the degeneration of the white settler in the tropics. Although the natural causes leading to degeneration have been partially eliminated by air transport, air conditioning, radio, and modern hygienic and dietary practices, the fact remains that the white ruling classes in the colonies constitute a quasi-feudalistic society which lacks profound understanding of modern political and industrial trends and, above all, recoils from creative action because of its overriding and not entirely unwarranted fear of race extinction.

Colonial societies stand in dire need of outside help. Unlike Western societies, which can be relied upon to solve their own problems themselves, at least ultimately, colonial societies may not be capable of reforming from within. Possibly this is too pessimistic an evaluation. But the transition from a stagnant, closed society to a healthy, viable, and open society would be much less painful and dangerous if it were to occur under the aegis of liberal forces brought to bear upon the colonial problem from without. Such aid and inspiration are becoming the future tasks of the imperial powers.

THE COLONIAL QUESTION IN ITS INTERNATIONAL SETTING

The conflicts assailing colonial systems do not take place between the peoples of the colonies and the motherland alone. They are an integral part of the world crisis. The example of Indo-China may serve to illustrate the point. Between 1862 and 1883, France took over Annam, Tonkin, Cambodia, Cochin-China, and Laos in a series of wars, conquests, cessions, and establishments of protectorates. Regardless of the various pretexts which made these conquests politically acceptable, French claims to these Asian territories were, to say the least, flimsy. The best that can be said is that these conquests involved relatively little violence. The subjugated peoples were culturally advanced. They were bound by cultural traditions to China, which remained independent and continued to exert some influence over its neighbors. Lastly, Indo-China was situated at an extreme distance from France which, given French maritime weakness, made it unlikely from the very beginning that France could establish herself securely over Indo-China.

The wisdom of the seizure of Indo-China was questioned even in France. Some of the more realistic among French statesmen argued that Indo-China could not be defended effectively. Clemenceau, for example, warned his countrymen that Indo-China (and other distant colonies) would divert resources from the defense of France's European frontiers. It was, indeed, for this very reason that the Germans encouraged French colonial ventures in Asia and Africa. French financial strength was inadequate to build up the huge resources of the overseas empire. Priority had to be given to the North African possessions. Under these circumstances it is not surprising that French investments in Indo-China fell far short of meeting requirements. It is true that even less capital would have been available had the French not established a relatively reliable and trustworthy regime and had foreign capital not been assured of fair returns at acceptable risks. On the other hand, a comparison with independent Thailand shows clearly the lack of economic development under the French regime. On the basis of official exchange rates and the few available figures, the following comparison can be made:

	1951, in millions of U.S. dollars	
	Thailand	Indo-China
Government expenditures	200	120
Foreign trade	660	150

Since the population of Indo-China is about 28 million as against 18-odd million for Thailand, it appears that, relatively speaking, Thailand's government expenditures (20 per cent of which is set aside for education) are 2.5 times higher and its foreign trade 6.6 times larger than the respective expenditures of Indo-China. Furthermore, the rice yield per acre is 0.5 tons in Indo-China as against 0.7 tons in Thailand (and 1.6 tons in Japan). It should be noted, however, that Indo-China has been suffering from prolonged war and that Thailand has received larger loans from the International Bank than Indo-China received from all sources. It is nonetheless a startling fact that Thailand's income is about $100 per head of population and, according to the latest available figure, by one-fifth higher than that of Indo-China. Thailand's record thus compares favorably with France's accomplishments in Indo-China—all the more remarkable an achievement since "next to Japan, Indo-China has the best physical basis of any Asiatic country for the growth of modern light industry." [16]

One of the reasons for France's poor performance in Indo-China is that the French colonial administration has been unusually inefficient, not only because of its antiquated organization but also because it became a political football of the party struggles in France. Two banks established tight control over the country's economy. The few French business firms which shared among themselves Indo-China's trade enjoyed, despite huge returns, considerable tax privileges and failed to reinvest much of their profits. Though some improvements in transportation and health services were made and a small university was established, Franco-native relations were far from cordial. The white ruling class in Indo-China—unlike the white settlers in other French colonies, who are noted for a minimum of race friction—developed a pronounced case of the sahib complex.

The question must be asked: even assuming that France can protect such states as Laos and Cambodia against aggressive neighbors, what advantage is there for Indo-China to stay within the French Union? The same question

[16] *Indo-China: The War in Southeast Asia,* Department of State Publication 4381, Government Printing Office, 1951, p. 9.

can be asked as regards many other dependent areas. The dependent peoples will not be interested in remaining members of a union or a commonwealth unless they can see clearly their advantage in an arrangement which falls short of complete independence.

The recent history of Indo-China may serve to illustrate the colonial dilemma.

Prior to the Second World War, Japan flooded the country with Pan-Asiatic propaganda. Simultaneously, the Indo-Chinese students in France eagerly absorbed the ideas of national independence, and many joined Marxist movements. In turn, the socialist and communist parties of France encouraged various radical movements in Indo-China. The colonial service included socialist and communist officials, quite a few of whom reached high and influential positions.

After the collapse of France in 1940, the Japanese asked France to agree to their occupation of Indo-China. Since Britain and the United States were unable to help the French administration, the latter had to give in. Though French officials, under the close supervision of the Japanese occupation forces, continued their administrative functions until a few months before the end of the war, French rule lost much of its prestige.

By the end of 1940, Thailand attacked Indo-China, inflicting a stinging defeat upon the French troops, and forced France to cede considerable territory. As the Second World War lengthened, the economic situation grew steadily worse. By 1942, Nationalist China gave support to Indo-Chinese guerrillas under communist leadership. From 1943 onward, the Allies supplied these guerrillas with weapons which, they hoped, would be turned against the Japanese. On August 15, 1945, the Japanese declared the full independence of Indo-China—a crucial event.

Upon termination of the conflict the country was not immediately reoccupied by the French. The northern part was taken by the Chinese and the southern by the British. French troops arrived with a delay of several months. The French lost what remained of their ailing prestige when the de Gaullist and the anti–de Gaullist forces entered into a deadly fratricidal struggle. The French administration virtually ceased to function, yet France was slow to grant political concessions. At last Paris consented to the formation of the Republic of Viet-Nam. Since the French government itself then stood to the left, it did not object to Ho Chi-minh as the first premier of the new state. Was he not an authentic "nationalist" leader? Thus the imperial power itself placed a trained and disciplined communist at the head of its possessions. Not so surprisingly, the arrangement was short-lived. Ho soon set up, with the arms which the Allies had shipped to Indo-China during the war, a communist guerrilla base from where he launched revolutionary military operations.

France's political and economic maneuvers, the experiment with the restoration of the Annamite (Viet-Nam) monarchy under Bao Dai, the transformation of Indo-China into a system of associated states within the French Union, and the protracted war against the communists, need not detain us here. However, three points must be made:

1. The success of communism in China greatly stimulated the revolutionary movement in neighboring Indo-China.

2. The colonial mentality of the French ruling class in Indo-China and business interests in France stubbornly persisted in the face of mounting crisis. French businessmen deemed it nothing but proper that they should make whatever profits the traffic would bear and pay the least taxes for as long as they could stay in Indo-China.

3. Despite antiquated French military tactics and despite an undoubtedly strong desire by large segments of the population to see the French leave, Ho Chi-minh's forces were less successful than could be expected. Ho's communism was nicely camouflaged, yet not all Indo-Chinese were duped by Ho's brand of Asian nationalism masterminded by Moscow and Peking.

The case of Indo-China points to the conclusion that it would be mistaken to ascribe even to the strongest colonial independence movements a power and strength of purpose which they do not possess. Their strength is derivative. It increases as the effectiveness and power of the motherland declines. Moreover, part of this strength is generated outside of the dependent area by communist Russia and China and, last but not least, by various anti-imperialist groups in the West, those in the United States not excluded. Be that as it may, the relative power of the independence movements is likely to grow. A great conflagration is in the making. The West has not yet found the means to smother it. The communists are busy pouring oil into the flames.

THE PROBLEM OF COLONIALISM RESTATED

Three basic facts have to be faced:

1. Colonies have become increasingly vital parts of the world economy because of the wealth of their raw materials and future agricultural possibilities. Their control is indispensable for the military safety of the West. Their contribution is essential to the continued industrial development of the entire world. They are *the* great undeveloped market. The rise of living standards *everywhere* is dependent on the development of these resources and markets.

2. Soviet Russia and the world communist movement have adopted a strategy which aims at bringing colonial areas under communist control or, as a minimum objective, at ejecting the Western powers from directly or indirectly controlled areas and, in any event, at fomenting cataclysmic political disturbances throughout the colonial world. Not all colonial conflicts are communist-inspired, nor must concessions to dependent peoples necessarily benefit the communists. The communists, however, will exploit all colonial conflicts, will claim the credit for all concessions, and will take ad-

vantage of every possibility to weaken the Western powers through colonial involvements and secessions.

3. The motherlands have lost much of their power, both absolutely and relatively. Their military power has weakened and so has their economic strength. Concurrently, the over-all power of many colonial peoples has increased. Communist political inroads in colonial areas—as, for example, communist parliamentary majorities in British Guiana and the election of communist deputies from Martinique to the French metropolitan parliament —engender repercussions in the motherlands. Communist movements in the British Empire, which are controlled from London (rather than Moscow),[17] and in the French Union lead to a strengthening of communism in Europe and, conversely, powerful European communist parties foment unrest in the colonies.

It is nowadays fashionable to argue that this thorny problem would be solved instantly by the granting of full independence to all colonial and dependent areas. The question must be asked whether even thornier problems would not be created in the process. Disregarding a few exceptions, the colonial empires issued from the workings of fundamental historic forces. Many of these forces, in addition to new ones, continue to operate. Let us suppose, for example, that Algeria (which is considered part of metropolitan France and is closely integrated into the French economy) were to be given "independence," and that the 7 million Arabs were to proceed to expropriate the 1.1 million Europeans and Jews and perhaps toy with the more conclusive political device of genocide. Or let us suppose that the Congo, having cut loose from Belgium, were to be seized by a communist government which would sell the entire uranium output to the Soviet Union. It is inconceivable that in such cases the European powers would not intervene and that in some way or another they would not be obliged to reestablish controls over the areas. In other words, independence may lead straight to war.

It should be obvious that the granting of full independence is impractical where people have not developed a society capable of self-government. Societies riven by deep racial or economic cleavages would, upon withdrawal of the imperial power, plunge into prolonged civil war. In some colonial areas, the property and settlement rights of the former mother country would be endangered; in others, holdings may be exposed to seizure and settlements may be destroyed. Some native societies would ring in the grant of independence by resorting speedily to the establishment of home-grown types of oppression such as slavery. In each of these cases the net result of emancipation would be regressive developments, including a dramatic reduction of health and educational standards.

One merely need compare the development of Haiti with that of Jamaica to arrive at some reservations about the wisdom of independence at all costs.

[17] *Ost-Probleme,* Jan. 22, 1953, pp. 131*f*.

The situation in independent Haiti grew so intolerable as to call for American intervention. Dependent Jamaica was spared the political and economic chaos of independent Haiti. A comparison of Abyssinia before, during, and after the Italian occupation may serve, too, as an instructive example, regardless of the fact that Italy's attack on Abyssinia in 1935 was a wanton as well as a foolish act of aggression. Yet the Italians did abolish slavery. Upon their ejection, independent Abyssinia reverted to that peculiar institution. This manifestation of sovereign independence was accompanied by a drop in health and educational standards.

There are, on the other hand, cases where the granting of independence may become advisable, especially if it can be effected in the tried and proved form, devised by Britain, of dominion status. This would be the case in areas where no large foreign interests are involved or where there is obvious willingness and ability to safeguard these interests as well as the interests of the natives. Peoples who are clearly capable of self-government can be associated more securely with the Western world if rights to which they are plainly entitled are granted fully and without unwarranted delays. It is probable that self-governing nations develop faster than nations which remain under foreign control.

Considering the historical and sociological background, it is obvious that not many colonial peoples should be granted independence in the foreseeable future. In areas where there are large white settlements or promising possibilities of large-scale immigration and development and cultural ties with the motherland are close, independence may never be the suitable solution to the problem of imperialism. But this does *not* mean that the maintenance of the colonial *status quo* is practical or advisable. Continuation of traditional colonial methods, especially if they are not backed by considerable military and economic strength, must lead to disaster and perhaps ultimately to a global race war.

Necessary reforms must be sought along the following lines:

1. *Improvements of the techniques of colonial administration.* Administrative machinery in many colonies is out of date, especially in the French, Spanish, and Portuguese colonies. More important than the change of the techniques themselves would be a modification of the philosophy informing the colonial administration, and the abandonment of restrictive Malthusian, mercantilistic, and paternalistic ideas. The United Nations Trusteeship Council could be most helpful in this task.

2. *The breaking down of the present colonial mentality.* This task concerns especially the improvement of racial relationships and of educational standards, and the broadening of cultural activities throughout the colonial areas. UNESCO would have a full job cut out for itself in this domain.

3. *The opening up of the colonies to economic development and the gradual relaxation of restrictions on investment, trade, and immigration.* This task could be accomplished partly through private initiative, partly

through the technical agencies of the United Nations dealing with agriculture, food, health, labor, and refugees, and partly through intergovernmental schemes as, for example, the Colombo plan.

4. *The establishment of a strong banking system specializing in low-interest assistance to farmers and the development of credit policies compensating for the financial weaknesses of the respective motherlands.* Within such a scheme of economic development—which falls ideally within the competence of the International Bank—it would be most important to stimulate the growth of native capital and the education of native management personnel.

5. *The intensification of foreign trade with and among the colonial areas.* The expansion of colonial trade calls for the development of large economic units, created not on paper but in reality, and for a break with the protectionist mentality. All in all, the imperial ties which heretofore have stimulated the development of the colonial nations, must not strangle them in the future, as they inexorably must unless there is a change in basic policy.[18] *Not only must membership in a commonwealth accelerate development but it must confer clear and massive advantages which cannot be obtained except through this membership.*

Undoubtedly there will be situations where a motherland cannot continue carrying the burden of colonial rule and responsibilities or where relations between the colonial people and the motherland have deteriorated to such a point that the partnership cannot be continued decently and successfully. In such cases the Trusteeship Council may be a suitable agency to take over—provided, needless to say, that communist and other revolutionary influences aiming at a further deterioration of the situation can be excluded.

In summary, the Western world and the colonial areas are mutually dependent upon each other for their security as well as for their economic well-being. In the long run, the dependence of the West on these areas will continue to grow. Given the increase of population and of industrial production, the trend is irreversible, unless the West, succumbing to suicidal mania, deliberately hastens its own decline. The time when individual Western nations were able to control the colonies according to their own short-sighted interests has passed. In that sense, colonialism is dead. Yet the old colonial system, disregarding a few exceptions, cannot be replaced by a system of weak, chaotic, independent nation-states. Imperial systems can be transformed into international structures. Colonialism should give way to a *system of partnerships* not only between a motherland and its colonies but also between all the Western nations and all the dependent

[18] The Belgian Congo, upon which the Berlin Conference (1885) imposed the "Open Door," is, unlike many other colonies, not tied to the metropolis by a system of preferential agreements. Some colonial empires have been closed empires; their trade was more or less restricted to dealings with other members or with the mother country. Others, like the British Empire in the free-trade era, were open empires; foreign countries enjoyed equality of opportunity in both colonial and metropolitan markets; colonial produce had to compete in home markets with foreign produce.

areas. The entire resources of the West should be thrown into the joint venture of building up the "underdeveloped" countries. This process of building commonwealths from the fragments of empires has been triggered by the necessities of defense and the launching of technical-assistance programs. The meaning of this process is not yet fully understood by those who set it in motion: nothing less than the economic and political future of the entire world is at stake.

Marx thought that, in the proletarian, he had found the predestined revolutionary. He was wrong, but only because economic progress transformed the Western worker into a conservative. The colonial native has better reasons to be a revolutionary than the Western industrial worker. Colonial man, whether he be a land-hungry peasant, a hungry coolie, or an uprooted urban white-collar worker, labors under infinitely worse conditions than the "proletarian." He suffers social discrimination, especially in caste societies such as that of India. He is wracked by racial and religious antagonisms. He feels that he is deprived of national freedom. *The combination of economic poverty, social frustration, racial hatred, cultural alienation, and national aspiration makes colonial man the most explosive revolutionary force world history ever has known.*

Unfortunately, the urgency and significance of the problem has not been realized. Little is being done to forestall a revolutionary assault of unprecedented violence.[19] Between naïve American clamor for a global policy of full independence and unimaginative European insistence on continuation of conventional practices, there is being gathered up enough stuff to set off explosions of truly global dimensions. To be more specific, without full American cooperation and understanding of the true problem, satisfactory solutions may not be reached. The United Nations, once the potentialities of this organization are clearly grasped and the dangers of its subversion by destructive forces met, could play a key role in the transformation of colonialism into a system of cooperation. Even then the transition will not be smooth. It probably will be painful, lengthy, and disappointing. In many instances no solutions will be found except to live, as well as one may, with the unsolved problem. But the West can neither shirk the responsibility nor throw away the opportunity.

BIBLIOGRAPHY

Boeke, J. H.: *Economics and Economic Policy of Dual Societies as Exemplified by Indonesia,* New York, Institute of Pacific Relations, 1953.
Caribbean Commission, *Caribbean Land Tenure Symposium,* Washington, 1946.

[19] An indication of this lack of understanding may be found in the distribution of American aid after 1945. About one-fifth of this aid (1945–1953) went to the colored and colonial areas. If help to China, Japan, and Korea is deducted, it appears that these areas received less than 7 per cent; Indo-China received less than 0.1 per cent! These figures are not quoted to suggest that economic aid alone would solve the colonial problem but simply to show to what extent the importance of Western Europe (which received about three-quarters) is exaggerated and that of the colonial areas underrated in contemporary political thinking.

Christian, John L.: *Burma and the Japanese Invader*, Bombay, Thacker, 1945.

Demangeon, Albert: *The British Empire, A Study in Colonial Geography*, New York, Harcourt, Brace, 1925.

Dunbar, Sir George: *India and the Passing of Empire*, New York, Philosophical Library, 1952.

Lord Elton: *Imperial Commonwealth*, New York, Reynal & Hitchcock, 1946.

Furber, Holden: *John Company at Work*, Cambridge, Mass., Harvard University Press, 1948.

Furnitall, S. S.: *Colonial Policy and Practice*, Cambridge, Cambridge University Press, 1948.

Knorr, Klaus E.: *British Colonial Theories, 1570–1850*, Toronto, University of Toronto Press, 1944.

Kolarz, Walter: *Russia and Her Colonies*, New York, Praeger, 1953.

Langer, William L.: *Diplomacy of Imperialism, 1890–1902*, New York, Knopf, 1935.

Lewis, W. Arthur: "The Industrialization of the British West Indies," *Caribbean Economic Review*, May, 1950.

Madariaga, Salvador de: *The Rise of the Spanish American Empire*, New York, Macmillan, 1947.

Mus, Paul: *Viet-Nam, Sociologie d'une guerre*, Paris, Éditions du Seuil, 1952.

Panikkar, Kavalam M.: *Asia and Western Dominance*, New York, John Day, 1954.

Partners in Progress, A Report to the President by the International Development Advisory Board, Government Printing Office, March, 1951.

Prescott, William H.: *History of the Conquest of Mexico*, New York, Modern Library, no date.

———: *History of the Conquest of Peru*, New York, Modern Library, no date.

Proudfoot, Malcolm J.: *Population Movements in the Caribbean*, Port of Spain, Trinidad, Kent House, 1950.

Rance, Hubert: *Development and Welfare in the West Indies, 1947–1949*, Port of Spain, Trinidad, Kent House, 1950.

Royal Institute of International Affairs: *The Colonial Problem*, London, Oxford, 1937.

Singh, Baljit: *Federal Finance and Underdeveloped Economy*, Bombay, Hind Kitabs, 1952.

Stamp, L. Dudley: *Africa: A Study in Tropical Development*, New York, Wiley, 1953.

Stern, Jacques: *Les Colonies françaises, passé et avenir*, New York, Brentano, 1943.

Thayer, Philip W. (ed.): *Southeast Asia in the Coming World*, Baltimore, Johns Hopkins Press, 1953.

Winslow, E. M.: *The Pattern of Imperialism: A Study in the Theory of Power*, New York, Columbia University Press, 1948.

Chapter 25

SOURCES OF U.S. CONDUCT: PERNICIOUS ABSTRACTIONS

> Problems which bear directly on the future of our civilization cannot be disposed of by general talk or vague formulae—by what Lincoln called "pernicious abstractions."
>
> Secretary of State Marshall, April 29, 1947.

"THE EXTENSION OF LOCAL PRACTICES TO THE INTERNATIONAL PLANE"

Perhaps no major government in the world has such an urgent need to re-examine its principles and political ideas as the government of the United States of America. No government on earth now shoulders a greater responsibility for the future of mankind. Yet the American government, on the strength of its record, has done little to equip itself with the intellectual weapons needed for the successful discharge of this responsibility. At the threshold of American history stand some of the greatest political geniuses of all times, the authors of *The Federalist,* perhaps the sanest book on politics ever written. In the course of time the government has stagnated and has now become the victim of its own public relations experts whom it mistakes for original political thinkers, and whose shopworn stereotypes it employs in the vain hope that they have magic power.

If the U.S. government is to stand the test of the present struggle, it must proceed to *intellectual rearmament.* Where is this rearmament to start? This same question was once asked of Confucius. The Chinese sage answered: "It is necessary to rectify terms." And he gave the following reasons for this surprising answer:

If terms be not correct, language is not in accordance with the truth of things. If language be not in accordance with the truth of things, affairs cannot be carried on to success. When affairs cannot be carried on to success, ritual and music will not flourish. When ritual and music do not flourish, law and justice will not be proper. When law and justice are not proper, the people will be unable even to move their hands and feet.[1]

According to popular legend the foreign policy of the United States and the sources of the conduct of the American government in international

[1] See Lin Mousheng, *Men and Ideas; An Informed History of Chinese Political Thought,* New York, John Day, 1942, p. 39.

637

affairs are fundamentally different from the foreign policy of other nations. It is true that every nation has its own foreign policy which fits its own particular circumstances. Since the United States is different from most other nations, and since it has existed under conditions of geographic isolation and exceptional economic well-being, while at the same time dominating and controlling an entire continent, it is obvious that its foreign policy must be different from that of nations not so situated. The emphasis on the "otherness" of American foreign policy is usually based upon the written and spoken word rather than upon actual facts. If we take the official pronouncements of American foreign policy at their face value, the United States has consistently striven for the betterment of economic well-being all over the globe, for peace and for stability, for friendship and for good-neighbor relations. In short, it has stood for the "good" and has opposed the "evil." It is important to know what nations say about themselves. But it is by far more important to know what people actually do.

For example, the United States, in the words of Vice-President Truman of February 22, 1945, engages in a "ceaseless crusade for a just and durable peace." And there is the altruistic American politician who is "willing to sacrifice temporary nationalistic advantages for the ultimate benefit of all." [2] Most Americans will voice approval of Mr. Truman's sentiment expressed by quoting Emerson to the effect that "nothing can bring you peace but the triumph of principles." Therefore, "America must live up to its highest principle; otherwise peace and security become impossible." The Liberal British Prime Minister Asquith once asked: "What are principles?" Nobody has as yet been able to answer this pertinent question.

Since there can be no "good" except by contrast with "evil," the latter is properly represented and duly exorcized in the misdeeds of those atypical Americans who annexed Texas, California, and the Hawaiian Islands to the United States; who preached the importance of military strength; who used American power actively by means of the "big stick"; who practiced "dollar diplomacy"; who wrought American sea and air power; and who, in sum, refused to believe that mere principles are enough in the world of war and power relationships. These were the men who replaced the high principles of the Confederacy with the allegedly "dictatorial" Federal Constitution; who opposed the secession of the Southern states—although secession may be deemed perfectly legitimate if the principle of self-determination is pushed to its extreme conclusion; waged war against the Secessionists; and established a highly centralized government, which, if not in theory then in actual fact, leaves to the states a mere shadow of sovereignty. These were the men whose political actions were motivated by their concern for the military, economic, and political security of the United States.

The idealistic—or should we rather say illusionistic?—approach of most

[2] Vice-President Harry Truman, quoted in *The New York Times,* Feb. 23, 1945.

Americans to foreign policy is due to a particular environment which is quite different from that of most Europeans and Asiatics. America was, and still is, the land of the future. The men who left the old European continent and its age-old struggles did not only want to quit something that was essentially bad, but looked forward to the creation of something essentially good.

The term "New World" denotes more than the mere fact that Columbus discovered a new hemisphere in 1492. It denotes a new *society,* a life freed from the evils of European traditions, hatreds, and quarrels—an island utopia situated at a safe distance from the turmoil of political upheavals and economic misery. As a counterimage to the Old World, the New World was to combine the pleasures of economic well-being with the satisfactions of full mental development, religious tolerance, and maximum personal freedom. It was to be a society in which class stratifications were replaced by the leveling action of general progress.

It is a society in which ancestry counts for little and money power counts for much; Americans, like Napoleon's nobles, are "ancestors" and not "descendants." It is an "open society," to use an expression of Henri Bergson, and not a closed society such as prevailed in Europe 150 years ago and is still believed by many to exist today.

The contrast between American and European society extends into many spheres; let us try to summarize them:

New World	*Old World*
Great social mobility	Low social mobility, except downward
High standard of living	Generally low standard of living and widespread poverty
Full employment punctuated by short-term unemployment; decreasing agricultural population	Permanent large-scale unemployment; agricultural overpopulation
Small "proletariat"	Mass proletariat
Self-identification of labor with middle class	Self-identification of labor with the proletariat
No fundamental difference between city and country people	Fundamental difference between "city" and "land"
High degree of equality in habits, comforts, and outlook	Vast difference between classes
Moderate friction between majority elements and racial minority groups	Sharp nationalistic cleavages
National history as success story	Doubtful national successes, often arrested development and decline
Simultaneous political and economic progress	Political *or* economic progress
No permanent enemies	Hereditary enemies
No permanent threat of invasion	Permanent threat of invasion
No militarism	Militarism as an influential political factor
Melting pot and habits of intergroup cooperation	Cultural isolationism and mutual suspicion

New World	Old World
Moderately nationalistic: pride of own country, tempered by self-criticism; administration always in hands of moderates	Intensely chauvinistic: hatred of other countries; self-criticism identified with treason; government or "power" often in hands of radicals
Voting for men	Voting for programs
Political competition	Tendency to suppress opposition
Political stability	Political instability
Undoubted validity of fundamental political philosophy	Extreme relativism of all political values

Is it surprising that the characteristics of American society are reflected in the foreign policy of the American nation? Is it surprising that Americans feel the urge to expand a system which proved so highly successful [3] into areas afflicted by political systems far less successful and often downright detrimental to individuals, nations, and even the entire world?

A product of a growing and dynamic society, the average American has a basically optimistic outlook. He believes that steady progress is actually taking place in most areas of the globe, that technology must inevitably accelerate the rate of progress anywhere, and that any regression which may occasionally occur is nothing but an unfortunate relapse into the past, ultimately destined to be overcome by the universal force of progress.

By contrast, the European and Asiatic is inclined to be pessimistic: he can be hardly anything else unless he becomes a revolutionary; even then he usually ends up as a cynical power politician. The man of the Old World will deny that fundamental changes, whether they be caused by technology or thought, are ever likely to occur in society and human nature, and that whatever progress may occur is temporary and deceptive.

Thus, the European instinctively must favor a foreign policy of defense and security; while the American, also instinctively, wishes to use foreign policy as a means of social and economic progress.

For the average American, foreign policy is, in the words of Vice-President Truman of February, 1945, "an extension of local and national practices to the international plane." Foreign relations are subject to compromises and "deals," to give and take, to arbitration, and to a delineation of mutual interests, providing each nation with its "due share." Essentially, foreign policy is a specialized form of "business."

To the non-American, foreign policy is more likely a phase of a life-and-death struggle. It is an attempt to ward off invasion, to win the current or future war, or to liquidate, with a minimum of damage, the last conflict. It is controlled by the instinct for self-preservation, as manifested in society, national governments, and individuals.

[3] American policy makers may still peruse profitably Chap. 4 in John Stuart Mill's *Representative Government,* entitled: "Under what Social Conditions Representative Government Is Inapplicable."

When President Truman addressed the United Nations Conference on April 25, 1945, he defined the goal of American striving as follows: "We must build a new world—a far better world—one on which the eternal dignity of man is respected." Of all the non-American nations only Soviet Russia is out to build what the communists consider a "better world." The rest of the world is concerned, almost exclusively, with survival.

AMBIVALENT IDEALISM

In the course of history the idealistic or illusionistic aspiration of American foreign policy has materialized in two different forms. During the 19th century and again in the interwar period of the 20th century, American idealism inspired isolationist foreign policies. By contrast, at the end of both world wars American idealism labored for international organization and for a global policy of good neighborliness and cooperation. In both cases, the American idealist stood for disarmament and arbitration as against "power politics."

Isolationism manifested itself in opposition to the expansion of the United States into Texas, California, and Oregon. After having violently rejected the Louisiana Purchase, the intervention in and subsequent purchase of Florida, and later the purchase from Russia of Alaska, the isolationist idealists opposed the opening up of Japan and purchase of the island of Okinawa, today one of the most important bases in the Pacific area. Isolationism opposed the annexation of the Hawaiian Islands, which ultimately were joined to the American Union by executive order, the building of the Panama Canal, and the political preparations for the construction of that waterway which consisted in fomenting a revolution. This revolution, as already discussed, took the form of a secession by Panama from Colombia; the American government *approved* this secession as quickly as it had *opposed* the secession of the Confederate states. The newly established Republic of Panama was speedily recognized, quite in contrast to the nonrecognition by the United States of many other revolutions in Latin America, for example, that of Costa Rica in 1917.

Isolationism opposed the acquisition of vital bases such as the Virgin Islands in the Caribbean area. The reduction of the U.S. Navy, after the American Civil War, from the strongest naval force then existing to token size for almost thirty years, gratified isolationist sentiment. Before both world wars, isolationism opposed the participation of the United States in either conflict, for it was of no concern to the American nation, so the publicists of isolationism averred, whether or not aggressive nations established a hegemony over the European Continent.

Recapitulation of the objectives for which isolationism stood is the most conclusive proof of the *impotence and ineffectiveness of American isolationism during the last 100 years.* While time and again isolationism obstructed the conduct of effective and rational foreign policy, delaying the execution of necessary measures, isolationists have a conspicuous record of failure and defeat. They opposed the growth of the American Union. Yet that Union now covers about 3 million square miles in the Western Hemisphere alone. It extends across the Atlantic and Pacific Oceans to the China Sea and the confines of Japan. It controls the air space from the North Pole downward to the latitude of Samoa, not to mention the U.S. claims in Antarctica. Florida, Texas, and California have become as much part of America as isolationism itself; so have Alaska, Hawaii, and the Panama Canal. And the air bases in the North Atlantic and Africa stand a good chance to become in fact, if not in law, part of the dominion of the American nation.

WOODROW WILSON AND THE JUST PEACE

The "internationalist" line of American idealism can be traced back to the arbitration treaties which had come to preoccupy increasingly the diplomacy of the United States in the period immediately preceding World War I. Among the antecedents of this policy were the pacifist movement of the first half of the 19th century, the systematic campaign against "entangling alliances," and the idealistic aspects of the Pan-American movement. It found its *Magna Charta* in President Wilson's Fourteen Points and the subsequent Four Principles, Four Ends, and Five Particulars.[4] The main ideas embodied in these various declarations are open covenants openly arrived at by public and open diplomacy, for "all international agreements and treaties of every kind must be made known in their entirety to the rest of the world"; absolute freedom of navigation upon the seas alike in peace and war; removal of economic barriers; impartial adjustments of colonial claims in a manner satisfactory to both the population concerned and the government whose "title" is to be determined.

The most sweeping provision of Wilson's program was the first of his Four Ends: "The destruction of every arbitrary power anywhere that can separately, secretly and of its single choice disturb the peace of the world; or, if it cannot be presently destroyed, at least its reduction to virtual impotence." At the same time, however, armaments were to be reduced, not by any means to the level necessary for a country's defense, let alone to the level necessary to carry out this program of the Four Ends, but to the minimum consistent with "domestic safety."

President Wilson devised for the establishment of permanent peace a plan of extraordinary simplicity. First, World War I was to be concluded by "just" settlements. Second, upon signature of the peace treaties, international relations were to be conducted by "open" means in the same manner as

---

[4] The various declarations of President Wilson are easily accessible in Walter Lippmann, *U.S. War Aims,* Boston, Little, Brown, 1944.

individual citizens conduct their private and business relations—or, more accurately, foreign policy was to be executed by methods which even in private life are employed only infrequently and then usually unsuccessfully. Third, peace was to be secured by economic means and by the satisfaction of "well-defined" national aspirations. Fourth, armaments were to be reduced substantially. Fifth, peace was to be maintained by an organization of peace, a "tribunal of opinion" to be endowed by "means of discipline and control." Upon establishment of that organization, nations should no longer conclude special agreements—such as "alliances"—among themselves. Sixth, to crown the edifice, every arbitrary power "anywhere" was to be destroyed or rendered impotent.

Thus, settlements had to be "just." Nations had to behave according to the maxims of altruism and self-abnegation as though they were guided only by the loftiest religious belief. There were to be neither armaments nor alliances. Aspirations of any kind, nationalist and economic, were to be satisfied even if they were mutually exclusive. An international organization was to arbitrate conflicts and possibly to impose sanctions, should struggles occur despite the satisfaction of these aspirations. The main danger to peace, arbitrary power, was to be eliminated. Yet in a world so ordered and so disarmed, a crusade was advocated not against a specific arbitrary power but against *any* such power *anywhere*. In theory, Wilson offered a program of peace. Yet in actual fact, tacitly and implicitly, he also advocated aggressive, preventive war on a global scale.

For almost thirty years his program has influenced the political thinking of the United States. Yet it would be difficult to find a more incoherent and contradictory program serving as the lodestar for the foreign policy of any major nation. It is a tribute to the strength of the United States that it increased its sway in world politics despite Wilson's program. It is an indictment, however, of American political education that it continued to pay lip service to Wilson's intellectual concoction which offers nothing of value, except that *superficially* it expresses the American dream. Although it should be inspired by ideals, foreign policy, to be effective, must always remain the art of the practical; instead of a policy of the apt word and the emotional appeal, only a policy of the greatest skill applied in the pursuance of ideals can be truly successful.

Doctrine of National Self-determination. The doctrine which has made Wilson more famous than his other activities is the principle of national self-determination. In a speech to Congress on February 11, 1918, Wilson stated that "self-determination is not a mere phrase. It is an imperative principle of action which statesmen will henceforth ignore at their peril." (Actually, the word "henceforth" ignored the fact that "self-determination" was nothing but the regurgitated concept of the "consent of the governed" advocated by a centuries-old political philosophy.) On the same day, Wilson amplified this idea in his Four Principles, stating that "all well-defined national aspirations shall be accorded the utmost satisfaction." This blanket endorsement was qualified by the addition that this satisfaction was to be obtained "without introducing new or perpetuating old elements of discord and antagonism that would be likely in time to break the peace of Europe and consequently of the world."

These self-defeating qualifications were overlooked by the public. Wilson became the champion of self-determination, chiefly on the strength of his Fourteen Points which proclaimed this principle with respect to the peoples of Austria-Hungary, the Balkan States, Turkey, and Poland. Later, Wilson reasserted the principle of self-determination in his draft for a League of Nations Covenant, Article III, which envisaged territorial readjustments "by reason of changes in the present racial conditions and aspirations or present social and political relationships, pursuant to the principle of self-determination." [5]

It is little known that Wilson himself, in his practical dealings, did not adhere to the principle of self-determination, except as it was applicable to *special* conditions. The principle was to be applied against Austria-Hungary, and the "Congress of Oppressed Habsburg Nationalities" duly met at Rome in April, 1918, and initiated a propaganda campaign for the dismemberment of the Habsburg monarchy.

The principle had thus been used as *a means of psychological warfare*, as an instrument for *destroying* political units but not as a creative idea on which to build.[6] This is a fundamental difference. In actual fact, Wilson had considered, in February of 1917, reassuring the Austrian government that Austria-Hungary would *not* be dismembered, that is, that the principle of self-determination was *not* to be applied. "It is the President's view that the large measure of autonomy already secured . . . is a sufficient guaranty of peace and stability in that part of Europe so far as national and racial influences are concerned." [7]

In response to violent remonstrances by various Allied statesmen, Lansing wrote on December 30, 1918, a memorandum in which he clearly outlined the destructive nature of the principle: there would be "danger of putting such ideas into the minds of certain races. . . . Will it not breed discontent, disorder, and rebellion? . . . The phrase is simply loaded with dynamite.

[5] See Robert Lansing, *The Peace Negotiations: A Personal Narrative,* Boston, Houghton Mifflin, 1921, p. 93.

[6] See Sir Campbell Stuart, *Secrets of Crewe House: The Story of a Famous Campaign,* London, Hodder, 1920, *passim.* See also Harold D. Lasswell's *Propaganda Technique in the World War,* New York, Richard R. Smith, 1938 (originally 1927), pp. 217f., where he praises Wilson's "matchless skill" as a propagandist, but adds: "Just how much of Wilsonism was rhetorical exhibitionism and how much was the sound fruit of sober reflection will be in debate until the World War is a feeble memory. . . ."

[7] Publications of the Department of State, *Papers Relating to the Foreign Relations of the United States, 1917; Supplement I, The World War,* Government Printing Office, 1931, p. 40.

. . . It will . . . cost thousands of lives." [8] Wilson relented and softened his stand, striking out the principle of self-determination from his draft for the League of Nations Covenant.

More important still, *Wilson opposed the principle very strongly when the attempt was made to apply it to Russia, and to support the self-determination of the Ukraine, Georgia, Armenia, Azerbaijan, and the Baltic States.* He favored that the integrity of Russia be conserved—communism or no communism—and he was willing to grant self-determination *only* to Poland and Finland. (Poland was to include many alien races, and Finland almost fought a war with Sweden over the possession of the Åland Islands inhabited by Swedes.)

In the end the principle was violated with the prominent help of Wilson himself in central Europe. Germans were put under Polish and Czech overlordship, Tyrolians under Italian, Hungarians under Austrian, Yugoslavs under Greek, and Poles under Czech rule; the Sudeten Germans and the Austrians were not permitted to join Germany. In Asia, Kiaochow was turned over to Japan, and so was, for "economic development," the entire province of Shantung.

In other words, the application of the principle of self-determination was used to disorganize central Europe and to destroy a useful, balancing, and no longer dangerous political unit, the Habsburg protofederation. The nonapplication of this principle served to stabilize the aggressive and most dangerous empire of the Bolsheviki.

The point in all this is *not* that departures from principles are wrong. The point is that Wilson "by his acts proved that 'self-determination' " *is* "a 'mere phrase' which ought to be discarded as misleading because it cannot be practically applied." [9] Unfortunately, the impression was perpetuated as though self-determination was an immutable principle of general validity and that the American government was committed to it. This principle fanned the nationalistic passions of many European and Asiatic nations and supplied the ammunition for Hitler's first salvos. It contributed to complacency when Germany militarized the Rhineland and annexed Austria and the Sudetens. With the exception of neomercantilist economics, nothing contributed as much to the disorganization of Europe and to the crisis which culminated in the Second World War as did Wilson's formula. *The principle of national self-determination was never repudiated.* However wrong it may be, no government ever abandons principles which it once espoused. This is an unwritten "moral" code. The politician fears nothing more than the criticism that he is untrue to his own principles. The creation of chaos is deemed of smaller import than this reproach.

Pact of Paris. The impossible was achieved and Wilson's ideology was outdone by one principle which was even more removed from reality. Upon

[8] Lansing, *op. cit.*, p. 97.
[9] *Ibid.*, p. 100.

the suggestion of the American Secretary of State, Mr. Kellogg, the Pact of Paris was drawn up in 1927. The signatories of this pact renounced war as an instrument of national policy and agreed that "all disputes or conflicts of whatever nature or whatever origin" were to be settled by peaceful means. Mr. Kellogg made it clear that the pact did not impair the inherent right of self-defense. Still, it was believed that this platonic renunciation of war would ultimately lead to war's abolition.[10]

As could have been foreseen, war outlawed by the Kellogg pact was henceforth fought "illegally." In 1931 Japan attacked China, an event which evoked the enunciation of a new doctrine. This doctrine introduced a new principle into the armory of idealist principles, the principle of nonrecognition. This doctrine was formulated in the American note addressed by Secretary of State Henry L. Stimson to Japan and China on January 7, 1932. According to this document "the American government . . . cannot admit the legality of any situation, treaty or agreement which may be brought about by means contrary to the covenants and obligations of the Pact of Paris." Yet the American government abstained from enforcing the legality of the Pact of Paris by such means as were envisaged in Articles X or XVI of the League of Nations Covenant. In fact, the principle of nonrecognition is an excellent self-characterization of the "idealist" ideology; that ideology refuses, on principle, to recognize unpleasant facts.[11]

CORDELL HULL: SELF-RESTRAINT AND ABSTINENCE

Foreign policy played a subordinate role during the first administration of President Roosevelt. The United States participated in the World Economic Conference at London in 1933, but in one of the most dramatic reversals to old-line isolationism, President Roosevelt, though celebrated for his internationalism, torpedoed the Conference. In contrast to this, Secretary of State Hull pursued a foreign economic policy aiming at the removal of barriers—tariffs, quota systems—obstructing free international trade.

The first term of President Roosevelt coincided with the accession to power of Adolf Hitler and German rearmament. The American public and policy makers alike were confused about the real meaning of the Nazi dictatorship: subconsciously they felt that another world war was in the making. Instead

[10] "Mentally ill are often characterized by . . . this capacity for building themselves fictitious worlds in which they can find refuge from actual life. If we, who live outside of asylums, act as if we live in a fictitious world—that is to say, if we are consistent with our beliefs—we cannot adjust ourselves to actual conditions." (Alfred Korzybski, *Science and Sanity: An Introduction to Non-Aristotelian Systems and General Semantics,* 2d ed., Lancaster, Pa., The International Non-Aristotelian Library Publishing Company, 1941, p. 87.)

[11] "For the schizophrenic the world of day-dreams where all his wishes come true without effort or risk to himself . . . becomes far more attractive and satisfactory than the world of reality. . . ." (*Van Nostrand's Scientific Encyclopedia,* 2d ed., New York, Van Nostrand, 1947, pp. 1277f.)

of approaching the war danger realistically and instead of devising methods by which that conflagration could have been averted, the attempt was made to prevent American involvement in war by legislation, that is, by verbal effort alone. There was the widespread belief, largely unverified by factual proof, that wars are brought about by the munitions makers, who secretly "control" the governments. This dubious premise suggested the conclusion that restrictions imposed on these sinister conspirators, the "merchants of death," would prevent a repetition of the events of 1917. It was stated in the preamble to the Neutrality Act of 1937 that the United States desired to preserve its neutrality and to avoid involvement in war, but that at the same time the United States did not waive any of its own rights or privileges. The contradiction seems to have escaped the lawmakers.

On July 16, 1937, Secretary Hull defined the fundamental principles of international policy:

This country constantly and consistently advocates maintenance of peace. We advocate national and international self-restraint. We advocate abstinence by all nations from the use of force in pursuit of policy and from interference in the internal affairs of other nations. We advocate adjustment of problems in international relations by process of peaceful negotiation and agreement. We advocate faithful observance of international agreements. Upholding the principle of the sanctity of treaties, we believe in modification of provisions of treaties, when need arises, by orderly process, carried out in a spirit of mutual helpfulness and accommodation. We believe in respect by all nations for the rights of others and performance by all nations of established obligations. We stand for revitalizing and strengthening of international law. We advocate steps toward promotion of economic security and stability the world over. We advocate lowering or removing excessive barriers in international trade. We seek effective equality of commercial opportunity and we urge upon all nations application of the principle of equality of treatment. We believe in limitation and reduction of armament. Realizing the necessity for maintaining armed forces adequate for national security we are prepared to reduce or increase our own armed forces in proportion to reductions or increases made by other countries. We avoid entering into alliances or entangling commitments but we believe in cooperative effort by peaceful and practicable means in support of the principles herein before stated.

This statement reveals how the American government thought other governments should, but quite obviously did not, behave. It is undeniable that the world would be a better place if these principles were observed; but it would be another world.

For the practical statesman, however, the most relevant question reads: "What is?" Only with the knowledge of existing circumstance can an effective foreign policy be formulated and applied in this world. We may or may not "advocate" self-restraint. The question is, what should we *do* in order to reach our objectives provided certain governments do *not* exercise self-restraint? Likewise, we may "advocate" noninterference in the internal affairs of other nations. But what should our line of *action* be if, regrettably, foreign governments actually *do* interfere?

In one point Mr. Hull's doctrine showed development beyond President Wilson's ideas: Hull no longer advocated the reduction of armaments to the minimum required for domestic safety, but acknowledged the necessity of maintaining "armed forces adequate for national security." Unfortunately, while this principle was enunciated, it was not followed. The United States rearmed in earnest only three years later.

In this connection, an important question arises: was the sudden upsurge of American armaments after the destruction of the French army not a *de facto* recognition of the then dependence of American security on the combined military power of France and England? It is easy to say that "we avoid entering into alliances" when, in reality, the United States relied on a protection provided by other nations. Whether they wanted it or not, France and England protected the European flank of the United States. The United States profited from this *de facto* and one-sided alliance and reduced per capita expenditures for armaments to the lowest level of all great powers.[12]

IDEOLOGY AND THE WAR

On September 3, 1939, on the very day the Second World War started in Europe, President Roosevelt said in a radio address: "You must master at the outset a simple but unalterable fact in modern foreign relations. When peace has been broken anywhere, peace of all countries everywhere is in danger." Hence the peace of the United States was in danger. One would expect that this fact should have led to the reevaluation of past American policies. Yet when on September 21 Mr. Roosevelt sent a message to Congress, he merely said: "For many years the primary purpose of our foreign policy has been that this Nation and this Government should strive to the utmost to aid in avoiding war among other nations. But if and when war unhappily comes, the Government and the Nation must exert every possible effort to avoid being drawn into the war." How was this policy to be reconciled with the "unalterable fact" stated eighteen days earlier?

On November 23, 1939, Assistant Secretary of State George S. Messersmith summarized the "cardinal points" of American foreign policy. He stated that it is our "earnest desire" and hope that peace will be *restored* on other continents. While war is in progress, the United States and other governments would try to keep the Western Hemisphere "free of warlike activities." The United States would continue to practice its good-neighbor policy. "Where and when practicable we shall seek to promote a sound and healthy

[12] In 1937, the U.S. spent $7.69 per capita for armaments; Germany, $58.82; Japan, $15.91; Britain, $26.87; Russia, $29.91; France, $21.64; and Italy, $19.77. In total dollar expenditure, the U.S. was fifth among the great powers (see Quincy Wright, *A Study of War*, Chicago, University of Chicago Press, 1940, Vol. I, p. 672).

reconstruction of international economic relationships." The United States would also assist "in the establishment of conditions which will assure stable peace." America stands ready to "discuss" the situation in the Far East; and finally, "We are ready to discuss with other nations the problem of limitation of armaments by international agreement." This latter point was made at a time when the aggressor already had swallowed Austria, Czechoslovakia, Memel, and Poland—not to mention Albania, Abyssinia, Manchuria and North China—and when Britain and France had at last accepted the military challenge.

These "cardinal points" of American foreign policy had no practical relation to the actual international situation. To formulate a program which even at the time of its enunciation was not applicable in one single point, and to advocate reduction of armaments in the midst of war—at the very moment, incidentally, when the United States itself was, of course, obliged to increase armaments—is the ultimate triumph of the nonrecognition of facts.

Anniversary of the Pact of Paris. On August 29, 1940, shortly after the collapse of France and at the very moment when Hitler was trying to knock out the Royal Air Force as a prelude to the invasion of Britain, Mr. Hull proclaimed, at the occasion of the twelfth anniversary of the signing of the Kellogg-Briand Pact, that the soundness of the pact's "underlying principles has in no way been impaired by what has taken place since then. Sooner or later, they must prevail as an unshakeable foundation of international relations unless war with its horrors and ravages is to become the normal state of the world and mankind is to relapse into the chaos of barbarism."

Like an obsession, an ideology is never disproved by facts; rather, the ideology disproves the facts. One remark in Mr. Hull's statement was slightly out of tune in a commemoration of the Pact of Paris: "*Only* by vigorous and adequate preparation for self-defense can any country, including our own, hope to remain at peace." [13]

It is true that the coming of war did not disprove the validity of the principle, if it can be called such, that peace should be preserved. Nor does a disease disprove the advantages of health. To appreciate the advantages which peace offers over war, the world need not wait for Messrs. Kellogg, Briand, and Hull. The only novel principle which can be detected in the Kellogg-Briand Pact is that a solemn declaration and a verbal renunciation of war as an "instrument of national policy" and an "agreement" that conflict should be settled by pacific means is sufficient to eliminate the scourge. But precisely this novel "principle" had been disproved by the mere fact of war.

By January, 1941, events had forced a more active course on the United States. Up to that date, American foreign policy had been characterized by a clearly passive and negative character—do *not* recognize, do *not* interfere,

---

[13] Italics added.

do *not* take the initiative, do *not* act. At best, it had been a policy of passive defense based on the Monroe Doctrine. Now it became obvious that a policy of "don't" could not suffice to protect the United States and would have to be replaced by a policy of "do's."

Accordingly, a policy of material help was developed which Roosevelt explained on January 6, 1941: "We are committed to full support of all those resolute peoples, everywhere, who are resisting aggression, and are thereby keeping war away from our hemisphere. By this support, we express our determination that the democratic cause shall prevail; and we strengthen the defense and security of our own nation." President Roosevelt stated at the same time that American policy sought to secure the preservation of four essential human freedoms: freedom of speech and expression, freedom of every person to worship God in his own way, and the freedoms from want and fear. Freedom from want means "economic understanding which will secure to every nation a healthy peacetime life for its inhabitants," to which one may add the comment that such understandings had not been feasible for about twenty-five years, partly because there *was* danger of war; partly because they were precluded by the selfishness of many nations, including the United States; and partly because the world's largest country, Russia, engaged in closely controlled foreign trade.

President Roosevelt explained that freedom from fear "means a world-wide reduction of armaments to such a point and in such a fashion that no nation will be in a position to commit an act of physical aggression against any neighbor." In Hull's understanding of American policy, it was to be safety through strength; in Roosevelt's interpretation of that same policy it was safety through nonstrength. Needless to add that in a situation of complete international disarmament, even kitchen knives and hunting rifles would enable a resolute nation to commit acts of "physical aggression."

THE ATLANTIC CHARTER: COMPENDIUM OF PRINCIPLES

On August 21, 1941, the Atlantic Charter was signed. The reasons which prompted President Roosevelt to insist on publication of this document were in part entirely practical. It has been suggested that the Atlantic Charter was actually an attempt to make the Soviet Union—which had just been attacked—adhere to a postwar program compatible with that of the Western powers, to shackle, in other words, the Soviets with fetters of paper. The Atlantic Charter was also designed as a counterideology against National Socialism.

The Charter stipulated that the signatories did not seek aggrandizement, "territorial or other," and desired no "territorial changes that do not accord with the freely expressed wishes of the peoples concerned." All peoples were to have the right to choose "the form of government under which they will live." Sovereign rights and self-government were to be restored to those who had been deprived of them. In the economic field, equal access to trade and raw materials was to be furthered for the "enjoyment by all States." Full economic collaboration was to be brought about "with the object of securing, for all, improved labor standards, economic advancement, and social security." The peace to be established after the destruction of Nazi tyranny was to afford to *all* nations "the means of dwelling in safety within their own boundaries" and give "assurance that *all* the men in *all* lands may live out their lives in freedom from fear and want." [14]

In the concluding section of the Charter, the belief was expressed that, "for realistic as well as spiritual reasons," all the nations of the world "must come to the abandonment of the use of force." The point was furthermore made that "pending the establishment of a wider and permanent system of general security," the disarmament of nations "which threaten, or may threaten" aggression outside of their frontiers was essential. Practicable measures "which will lighten for peace-loving peoples the crushing burden of armaments" were to be encouraged.

Taken literally, the Charter meant very little. It did not contain one single concrete commitment, with the one exception that the signatories "seek no aggrandizement" which, grammatically speaking, constituted only a relative commitment, since one may get what one does not "seek." The other points were phrased cautiously: the signatories "desire," "respect the rights," "wish," "will endeavor," or they simply "hope" and "believe." The signatories nowhere obligate themselves. The Charter was neither a policy nor a program, *for a program is the selection of clearly defined, concrete, and attainable objectives, and a policy is the selection of appropriate means to reach these objectives.*

The abandonment of force or the disarmament theme reappeared in a new variant: aggressor nations were to be *disarmed*, while "peace-loving" peoples would merely have to *reduce* their armaments. In 1941, it was quite clear that the Nazis were aggressive and their victims "peace-loving," although in 1939 the Russians did not show an abiding love for peace when they invaded Poland and Finland, nor was the United States "peace-loving" in 1898 when it attacked Spain. No signatory could honestly boast of persistent love of peace. The first love of all the signatories had been war.

In any event, a clear-cut distinction, such as "peace-loving" and "aggressive," does not necessarily exist except for very brief periods. No practical policy of peace in peacetime—that is, when no country has yet given clear evidence of aggressiveness—can be built on such a criterion. The only aggressors that can be disarmed are those nations which, whether they were aggressors in actual fact or not, were defeated in the *last* war. Yet the aggressors of the *next* war, even if they were known beforehand, cannot be disarmed prior to their defeat—in war. Hence "preventive disarmament" is not an effective method of preserving peace. This idea, then, is nothing but

[14] Italics added.

an unconscious program of preventive war which is quite in contrast to the spirit of the Charter.

The Charter actually, though somewhat obliquely, advocated the disarmament of nations which "may threaten" aggression. Taken at face value this would amount to recommending a program of preventive wars against all *possible* aggressors. Somewhat inconsistently, that program was advocated in the same paragraph where "all nations" were urged to abandon force. Since every nation "may" one day threaten aggression, and since for this very reason every nation must retain armaments which, in turn, would facilitate aggression, *the eighth point of the Atlantic Charter implicitly proposes an all-round preventive war against every nation on earth.*

Aggrandizement. Let us take up the one relatively "binding" commitment of the Atlantic Charter—the assurance that the signatory countries "seek no aggrandizement, territorial or other." To begin with, what meaning can the word "other" have? It seems logical that the purpose of war is to defeat the enemy. Yet as soon as the enemy's military strength has been eliminated by defeat, the victorious nations inevitably "suffer" from an aggrandizement of power. They also inevitably "suffer" from an aggrandizement of prestige, moral influence, and, in many respects, economic strength. There is no sphere of human activity where, in case of victory, the victorious powers—and the signatories of the Atlantic Charter indeed expected to be victorious—could have avoided relative or absolute "aggrandizement."

The promise not to seek territorial aggrandizement served to assure the world that the Allies did not fight for conquest. Undoubtedly, this morally commendable promise had propaganda value, but it was an inaccurate forecast of future events. As a program, it was impractical, even though a program of territorial annexation may have been inadvisable.

If the enemy nations interpreted this promise to mean that they would not suffer territorial diminishment, they must now rue their credulity. Italy, Japan, Germany, and all their satellites lost territory. It is not argued here that these changes in territory were not justified—some of them were, others were indefensible on ethical, economic, and political grounds. The fact is simply that, contrary to point one of the Atlantic Charter, these changes led to the territorial aggrandizement, open or disguised, of some Charter signatories.

It is, however, more surprising that frontiers were revised *to the detriment of allies* rather than enemies. It is true that aggrandizement of that kind was perpetrated only by the Soviet Union and by Soviet satellites, yet the identity of the sinner is relatively immaterial. The fact remains that territories *have* changed hands and that therefore the "better future of the world" does not differ materially from the past.

The main objection against this promise of the Atlantic Charter is somewhat more fundamental: the defeat of powerful states creates a vacuum that must be filled. The demise of great nations creates an entirely new military situation (as does rapidly advancing technology), and the new balance of power *requires* territorial realignment. It is entirely immaterial whether this alignment is made in the form of "annexation,"—a formality which can well be dispensed with. It is possible to effect territorial changes without disturbing the local *status quo*. Yet this does not alter the fact that realignments had to take place, and actually took place.

For example, the expulsion of Italy from Ethiopia restored to that country its former independence. Yet as that country is dependent upon other nations for its defense, markets, and internal developments and as, on the other hand, Britain is shifting the center of its Empire from Asia to Africa, and more specifically to East Africa, Ethiopia moved into the British "orbit." According to a treaty concluded with Britain, the Ethiopian army is being trained by a British military mission. A United States concern obtained a fifty-year oil concession. To be sure, there was no annexation. Yet an area from which Italian power was withdrawn was pulled into the Anglo-American sphere of influence.

The United States, in turn, established control over both the Atlantic and Pacific Oceans. In the Atlantic, it leased a number of bases. In the Pacific, the United States has taken over a number of island bases conquered from the Japanese. A deal was made with Russia which supported American claims to Pacific islands in return for the Kurils and Sakhalin. There are American bases in the Philippines, and that country, although it gained its independence, remains within the U.S. orbit.

By the medium of private enterprise, the United States acquired a number of oil concessions in the Middle East. In order to protect these interests, the United States extended its sphere of influence to the eastern Mediterranean, to the Black Sea, to Arabia and the Persian Gulf. While all this may not fall under the heading of "aggrandizement," it certainly cannot be labeled nonaggrandizement.

The Peoples' Wishes. Nobody will take exception to the Charter's second provision—the "desire to see no territorial changes that do not accord with the freely expressed wishes of the peoples concerned." But is this statement more than a platitude? Obviously, one would wish that any change that does befall a people would meet with their agreement. In private life, for example, if one changes a job, it would be most agreeable if such transactions were always voluntary and if the new position were always an improvement. There are, however, many changes which run counter to the wishes of the parties concerned and yet are inevitable.

What does this second point of the Atlantic Charter really mean? Territories whose transfer is under discussion usually are not inhabited by people with clear and unequivocal sentiments of allegiance. The inhabitants of Paris, Rome, London, or Berlin (or Breslau and Königsberg, for that matter) would under no circumstances express the wish to become separated from France, Italy, Britain, or Germany, respectively. The attitudes of the inhabitants of Alsace, southern Tyrol, northern Ireland, Upper Silesia, or Macedonia are by no means so unequivocal. Territories under dispute are usually inhabited by a mixed population in which there are to be found at least three major groups: those who favor incorporation into country A, those who would choose country B, and those who prefer "independence" or "neutrality." Splits of such a kind are often due to linguistic, religious, cultural, economic, or merely historical reasons. These very cleavages are frequently the chief cause of frontier dispute.

Moreover, in a composite population, allegiances change. The inhabitants of a disputed territory may vote today for country A, but they may change their mind at a later date. For example, in 1919 Austria voted for the *Anschluss* with Germany, but in 1923 a party came to power which was opposed to incorporation into Germany. In 1931, there was a new pro-*Anschluss* tendency (tariff union) which ended abruptly when the Nazis took over in Germany. In 1938, a majority of Austrians was perhaps in favor of the accomplished *Anschluss*, but subsequent events produced a strong majority for Austrian independence. Similar fluctuations occurred in many other regions, such as Alsace, Schleswig, Translyvania, Slovenia, Macedonia, the Ukraine, Tunisia, and diverse Asiatic countries, such as Sinkiang, Mongolia, and Korea. If the desires of border populations were taken as basis for the allocation of disputed territories, boundaries would have to be changed continuously.

It is, therefore, very difficult to determine the will of the "peoples concerned." But who *are* these peoples? The use of the plural in the Atlantic Charter would suggest that not only the local population but also *other* peoples should decide the fate of disputed territories. What other peoples? Up to now, plebiscites were only held among the *local* population and nowhere has a different method been suggested.

For example, the population of Danzig was German and did not desire to become Polish. However, Poland desired no less emphatically a port at the estuary of its lifeline, the Vistula River. Moreover, while Danzig was German, the country around the city was inhabited by Slavs. Therefore, it was a question of the wishes of a few thousand Danzigers versus the vital interests of several million Poles. There is a similar situation in Trieste. The city population is largely Italian. The Italians are determined to retain the city, and the great majority of the city inhabitants probably desire to stay with Italy. Yugoslavia, on her part, can point to her urgent need of at least one good port with good railroad connections; only Trieste is available. Since Italy has many excellent ports, Italy would not suffer a great economic loss. Yet the separation of Trieste creates psychopolitical tensions which are only alleviated, but not eliminated, by setting up Trieste as a free territory. In such conflicts the wishes of the local residents are relatively irrelevant; nor would it be practical to have Yugoslavia and Italy, or parts of both countries, decide this question by vote, last but not least because Italy, having a larger population, could always muster a majority of the votes. To solve similar questions, criteria other than the *wishes* of the local, border, or national population must be consulted—and do in fact nearly always determine the adjudication of the dispute.

Evidently, the Atlantic Charter does not err in pointing to the necessity of taking into account the wishes of the "peoples concerned." These wishes are a highly important factor and, wherever possible, should be satisfied. This *one* factor, however, is not the *only* one that is relevant in deciding territorial changes. There are cases where the wishes of the local population must necessarily be disregarded. The principle of self-determination, expanded into one of unlimited validity, has engendered friction and led many governments, signatories of the Atlantic Charter, to go back on their written word.

Equal Access to Raw Materials. On October 8, 1942, Undersecretary of State Sumner Welles discussed the Atlantic Charter. He pointed out that the "Atlantic Charter does not propose to aid aggression. It proposes, on the contrary, to make sure that aggression does not happen." This assurance is to be given by creation of the "necessary" instruments which "this time . . . will be effective instruments and must be firmly used." What are these "necessary" and "effective" instruments? Since no answer was, and can be, given to this crucial question, it seems a rash undertaking to commit the United States to act as though such assurances actually exist, let alone to claim that the U.S. government will "make sure" that aggression does not happen.

The ideological mechanism set in motion by solemn "charters" develops somewhat as follows: a promise is made that situation A is going to be brought about, and this promise is repeated over and over again until the public begins to believe that situation A already has been created; subsequently action is taken which is predicated on the firm belief that situation A already has existed for quite a while; these actions would fit A excellently, had A ever existed.

The ideological confusion can be illustrated by still another remark in Mr. Welles's speech. He recalled that point four of the Atlantic Charter promises "to further the enjoyment by all States, great or small, victor or vanquished, of access, on equal terms, to the trade and to the raw materials of the world which are needed for their economic prosperity." This was a programmatic note which had been struck recurrently in many prewar conferences, though up to the present moment no one has ever suggested how equal access to raw materials could be granted in a manner different from the traditional one of buying the raw materials from the producer and exchanging them for other goods. No state was ever prevented from buying, in time of peace, those raw materials which it needed, or from obtaining, in case that it did not possess sufficient ready money to pay for raw-material imports, the necessary credits.

Equal access to trade is a more complicated problem, and in many respects a more real issue. Mr. Welles himself asked the question: "How do they [the United Nations] propose to make it real?" Strangely enough, Mr. Welles gave no answer to his own question.[15]

THE POLICY OF THE GOOD NEIGHBOR

On July 23, 1942, when the military fortunes of the United Nations were at their lowest ebb, Mr. Hull, speaking on the radio, said:

From the time when the first signs of menace to the peace of the world appeared on the horizon, the Government of the United States strove increasingly to promote peace on the solid foundation of law, justice, non-intervention, non-aggression, and international collaboration. With growing insistence we advocated the principles of a broad and constructive world order in political, economic, social, moral, and intellectual relations among nations—principles which must constitute the foundation of any satisfactory future world order. We practiced these principles in our good neighbor policy, which was applicable to every part of the earth and which we sought to apply not alone in the Western Hemisphere but in the Pacific area, in Europe, and everywhere else as well.

If the United States government strove to promote or to maintain peace with the help of certain principles of allegedly world-wide validity, and if peace was not maintained but war broke out on a world-wide scale instead, one would assume that the United States government had gone about its job in the wrong way. If in physics an experiment is made and the expected result is not achieved, there would be no doubt that the experiment failed.

Not so in foreign policy. Since war had come, one should have expected that Mr. Hull would explain how basically sound principles had been inadequately or wrongly applied or how experience had demonstrated that these principles were unsound or temporarily inapplicable. Quite to the contrary, the principles were restated in so dogmatic a manner that no one would suspect that something had happened to disprove or question their validity.

Mr. Hull may have come to realize that the principles cherished by him are applicable only if other nations *also* play the game according to the same rules. The principles of nonaggression and international collaboration are excellent, to be sure; but it is necessary that other nations adopt them in their dealings. *The existence of one strong aggressor is a compelling reason to apply a policy different from the policy applicable in a situation where there is no aggressor.* Is it not self-evident that while a policy of collaboration

[15] In his *The Time for Decision* (New York, Harper, 1944, p. 176) Mr. Welles recounts Churchill's statement that "he was not empowered constitutionally to enter into any commitments of this character without the consent of the other members of the British Commonwealth of Nations." Therefore it was finally agreed that the signatory countries will only "endeavor" to "further" the enjoyment, etc., and that "with due respect for the existing obligations." Mr. Welles does not mention the lack of the same constitutional powers on the part of the President of the United States. The fact remains that the promise of "equal trade" has never been concretely defined as a practical international policy (as distinguished from a mere theoretical wish).

is effective *if* and *when* there is a general desire to collaborate, the existence of a strong aggressor must be countered with a policy of "containing the aggressor"? In both cases, policy would strive for the same over-all goal, namely, the maintenance of peace; but different situations necessitate the choice of different action guides.

Mr. Hull stated that the "good-neighbor policy . . . was applicable to every part of the earth." If so, why was it not applied? Clearly, the answer seems to be that it was not applicable. The most elementary knowledge of scientific methodology would have required that the conditions would have been stated under which the good neighbor policy actually functions in the Americas, and then to have asked whether or not these same conditions existed in "every part of the earth." Some of these conditions are as follows:

First, in the Western Hemisphere the United States possesses what amounts to a monopoly of military power and has applied for more than 100 years a policy, the Monroe Doctrine, which is expressly designed to bar any other nation from military competition with the United States in the Americas. Thus, competing power groups—the chief condition of military conflict—do not exist in the Western Hemisphere.

Second, none among the Latin-American nations possesses the material means for launching a major aggression. Nor is there any pressing conflict over *Lebensraum* in a continent which, for all practical purposes, still contains vast empty spaces. Third, the Latin-American countries speak, with the major exception of Brazil, the same language; all have similar cultures and the same religion. Thus, if peace could not be maintained in the Western Hemisphere, one would have to despair that it could ever be maintained anywhere.

Yet none of these conditions exist, for example, in Europe or Asia. In Africa, peace was maintained because two imperial powers, Britain and France, controlled practically the entire continent and cooperated with each other: the peace of Africa was broken when a third major power, Italy, established control over some African regions and declined to cooperate with the other European powers. What Mr. Hull failed to explain was how a good neighbor policy can be applied among bad neighbors.

THE SEVENTEEN POINTS

On March 21, 1944, Mr. Hull issued a memorandum to the press on the "Bases of the Foreign Policy of the United States," known as the "Seventeen Points."

Mr. Hull's ideas can be summarized as follows: Foreign policy must serve our true national interests. Once victory is won over the Axis, the national interests of the United States are national security and social and economic well-being. These interests can best be safeguarded by international cooperation. This cooperation is to be achieved by the establishment of an international organization backed by force; furthermore, by the settlement of political differences through discussion, negotiation, conciliation, and good offices; by adjudication of threats to the peace by an international court of justice; reduction of arms; cooperation between Russia, Britain, China, and the United States on the basis of the Moscow Four-nation Declaration; the elimination of spheres of influence, alliances, and balance of power; surveillance over aggressor nations; the reduction of excessive trade barriers; free exchange of national currencies at stable rates of exchange; adherence to the principles of the Atlantic Charter on the basis of reciprocal obligations; sovereign equality of nations; free choice of the form of government; nonintervention; duty to fight for liberty and right of the "qualified" nations to enjoy liberty; assistance to dependent peoples so that they may prepare themselves for self-government and attain liberty.

This document of state invites searching examination. Mr. Hull believed that the pledge of the Atlantic Charter "will give every nation, large or small, a greater assurance of stable peace, greater opportunity for the realization of its aspirations of freedom, and greater facilities for material advancement." This is in line with earlier thoughts, yet this time Mr. Hull added an important qualification: the pledge of the Atlantic Charter "implies an obligation for each nation . . . to fulfill scrupulously its established duties to other nations, to settle its international differences and disputes by none but peaceful methods, and to make its full contribution to the maintenance of enduring peace."

In other words: the Atlantic Charter cannot possibly work if any one nation does *not* carry out its obligations as they are implied in the Charter, or if nations make merely a halfhearted instead of a "full" contribution to the maintenance of peace. Thus, the system of the Atlantic Charter is predicated on the acceptance *everywhere* of identical principles of political action. The system would fail were certain nations to adhere to different standards of valuations and sets of principles, or if fundamental differences in the interpretation of these jointly accepted principles should arise. Clearly, a general principle cannot be used as a guide of common practical action unless agreement has been reached about its concrete meaning or, to put it differently, "principles" are so vague in nature that they can be used to justify diametrically opposed courses of action.

In purely logical terms, it is stated:

Peace needs cooperation.

From this it allegedly follows:

Cooperation brings peace.

Obviously, such a conclusion cannot be made because *there is no middle term.* Logically speaking, there is no syllogism but merely an inversion of *one and the same proposition;* not a syllogism but a tautology. A meaningful syllogism would run as follows:

> Peace needs cooperation.
> Cooperation can be established.
> Established cooperation may bring peace.

The conclusion must be a contingent proposition because the major premise is not of a universal character, stating only one and not all of the requirements of peace. If the middle term were fully or partially negative and ran "Cooperation cannot be achieved" or "Cooperation can be achieved regionally," the conclusion would be either "Peace cannot be achieved," or "Peace can be achieved regionally."

If one eschews this exercise in logic, one may question the validity of the major premise and investigate whether peace really needs cooperation, or whether cooperation is merely *one* of many factors needed for peace. The cooperation which is required, according to Mr. Hull, is one in the spheres of international law and political philosophy. Yet is this really the *conditio sine qua non* of peace?

The fallacy of similar syllogisms can be seen if, on the basis of historical evidence, we turn them around:

> There was no cooperation in the sense of Mr. Hull's
>   definition between 1893–1913 and 1920–1938.
> Peace was maintained during these years.

The inevitable conclusion from these two premises is that peace is *not* always dependent upon cooperation. During the two periods mentioned, peace was maintained through the action of *other* factors. To determine these other factors and put them to work would appear to be a primary mission of the policy makers.

"STABLE AND PROGRESSIVE GOVERNMENTS"

There is another aspect in Mr. Hull's interpretation which requires comment. He stated that the pledge of the Atlantic Charter "implies an obligation for each nation to demonstrate its capacity for stable and progressive government." This amounts to saying that the program of the Atlantic Charter can be carried out only with, and among, certain types of governments, but is inapplicable should nations be ruled by types of government not covered by this definition. The two criteria given by Mr. Hull are vague. Is a stable government one which stays in power for an indefinite period of time, like the Soviet dictatorship, or one which rules for a period of time predetermined by law, like the Swiss government? What is a progressive government? Is it not true that, according to the standards presently prevailing on the Continent, the U.S. government would not necessarily be classed as progressive?

But regardless of the terrifying ambiguity of these terms, the fact remains that the types of government vary in time and space. Consequently, if Mr. Hull's premise were correct, a different conclusion could be drawn: to apply the principles of the Atlantic Charter, it would be necessary that only governments of the required type and of no other type would ever come to power. In addition to being a radical abandonment of the principle of nonintervention, reasserted by the Atlantic Charter itself and these very Seventeen Points, this is simply a program of continuous preventive war.

Mr. Hull's proposition is simply the tautology that the Atlantic Charter can be applied only if it is being applied, or that we can maintain peace only if we are peaceful. The difficulty of a policy of peace is precisely that the world is split by fundamental cleavages of interests and ideas; if there were unity, peace would be self-operative, and the diplomats and secretaries of state would be unemployed. *The mission of foreign policy is to maintain peace in a disunited world.*

Let us take Mr. Hull's point with respect to the surveillance of aggressor nations. How long is this surveillance going to last? "Until the peoples of Germany, Japan, Italy, and their satellites give convincing proof that they have repudiated and abandoned the monstrous philosophy of superior race and conquest by force and have embraced loyally the basic principles of peaceful processes." It would be more logical, though less practical, to keep under surveillance those nations which do not accept the basic principles of peaceful processes, but which have not been defeated. It would also be necessary to demonstrate that the real danger to peace lies in a given philosophy and not in other factors, for example, in the disarmament of the prospective victims of aggression.

Yet granting Hull's assumptions, the question arises, what is "convincing proof" that a nation has repudiated such philosophy? An impressive, though not necessarily valid, case could be made for the contention that the nations of whom Mr. Hull spoke never actually embraced the philosophy of superior race and conquest by force. The Nazis, for example, never gained a majority before they themselves controlled the results of elections.

It is impossible to give the required "convincing proof." Moreover, ideologies change. Something quite different from Nazism may threaten American security in future. The basic error is to assume that the threats to security can be eliminated once and for all, while in fact *such threats succeed each other in spontaneous creation.* The nature of threats cannot be anticipated, and the elimination of one threat from the past will not eliminate threats of the future.

What Mr. Hull indirectly and implicitly suggested in his program was that American security, and more generally world peace, should be based on the acceptance of a certain philosophy, or rather ideology, by the former enemy nations. Numerous criteria are needed to determine when the occupation of the enemy countries should cease. Yet, to the pained surprise of the ideologists, the decisive problem of occupation was suddenly no longer the attitude of the former enemies, but the status of Russo-American relations. Termination of occupation became dependent not on the repentance of the Germans and Japanese, nor on the conversion of the Nazis and the radical Shintoists, but upon a Russo-American settlement.[16] Russia cannot leave Germany without delivering the German people up to the "capitalists," and the United States cannot leave Germany without abandoning the former enemy to communism and thereby sacrificing Europe. Occupation has become a problem of global power politics in which the "philosophies" that influenced the minds of the now occupied nations some years ago, play now only a minor role.

As a last point we may briefly discuss Mr. Hull's idea that "as the provisions of the Four-nation Declaration are carried into effect, there will be no longer need for spheres of influence, for alliances, for balance of power,, or any other of the special arrangements through which, in the unhappy past, the nations strove to safeguard their security or to promote their interests." Thus, the Four-nation Declaration was, indubitably, the gravedigger of the "unhappy past"; but was it the midwife of a new and happy future?

It is hard to understand why the Four-nation Declaration should have been elevated to such a high prominence. This declaration dealt largely with problems of war, surrender, and disarmament of the enemy. The four nations pledged themselves to continue "their united action . . . for the organization and maintenance of peace and security" and agreed to "confer and cooperate with one another . . . with respect to the regulation of armaments in the post-war period." The chief importance of this declaration (aside from its practical military value) was that it constituted the marriage license of the parents of the United Nations. It promised continued "united action" among the great powers; and it was not the first or the last promise broken in history.

Actually, this pledge was nothing but the familiar paralogism: united action can be forthcoming only *if, when,* and *where* there are common interests. Such interests existed in 1943, but in 1944 the Polish conflict revealed disturbing divergences in points of view. If there are few identical interests, and if some vital interests are incompatible, united action is impossible. It was therefore meaningless to promise it unless one believed in the identity of basic interests. No statesman can possibly have been naïve enough to entertain such a belief.

[16] In his Stuttgart speech of 1946, Secretary of State Byrnes said: "It is not in the interest of the German people or in the interest of world peace that Germany should become a pawn or a partner in a military struggle for power between the East and the West." A modern attempt to square the circle: If Germany is not to become a pawn, she must be rearmed, but if she has been rearmed, it would be inevitable that, in a "military struggle" between East and West, she would become a partner of one side.

PRINCIPLES AND PERSISTENCE OF POWER POLITICS

What does it mean that there is "no longer a need for spheres of influence"?
A sphere of influence is not something that has been created artificially and
can therefore be abolished if one wants to. A sphere of influence is as natural
a phenomenon as the influence which an able and intelligent person exercises
over his friends, or the influence which, contrary to the book, a wife or a
mother-in-law often exercises over the family. It is, first of all, a question of
spontaneous leadership which a nation assumes, and often reluctantly assumes,
simply because the nation is more powerful, wealthy, and able than other
peoples within a given area.

As long as nations are different in power, there will be differences in the
"influence" exercised by them. A very powerful nation automatically exerts
influence, and in certain zones that influence is inevitably greater than in
· other areas. The United Nations cannot alter this situation by its mere
existence. The United Nations organization is based on the principle of equal
sovereignty of nations. If instead it were based on the (entirely impractical
and fantastic) principle of equal *power*, and if each member of the United
Nations were reduced or increased to a predetermined level of power—as
proposed by innumerable eternal-peace projects—then there would conceivably be no other than intellectual spheres of influence.

To be sure, there is also a more dynamic aspect of this "influence." The
great powers entertain intimate economic relations with those nations with
whom they can trade profitably and whence they import strategic raw materials and finished goods. They will go to great lengths to insure that these
trade relations will not be disrupted by political changes. Trade will therefore always be accompanied and supported by an organized interexchange of
cultural influences and by propaganda.

The spheres of influence are also of military importance. A country may
lie within the sphere of influence of a great power merely on account of
economic or cultural reasons, yet be of little military importance to its "protector." There may be other countries with whom the great power has little
economic or cultural relations, but whose geographical position is militarily
of vital importance. For example, Bolivia is economically closely linked to
the United States, yet militarily it is of minor importance to the defense of
the United States. By contrast, Greenland has barely any cultural or economic relations with the United States, and yet it is militarily of extreme
importance for the defense of this country. In such "military outposts,"
active policies are being applied in order to keep them within one's own and
outside other orbits. By the force of circumstances, such a policy often de-
parts from the principle of nonintervention.

The Charter of the United Nations is designed merely to forestall *minor*
wars but does not provide a mechanism to prevent *wars between the great*

powers. Consequently, the creation of the United Nations has not obviated the necessity for the great powers to provide for their own military safety. This requires, among other things, an active policy of spheres of influence. Actually, the United Nations Charter acknowledged this state of affairs by permitting "regional" security arrangements. The United States was the first country ever to set up a *continental* sphere of influence (the Monroe Doctrine), and it has now one of the largest "orbits" on the globe.

Part of the opposition against orbits seems to stem from the feeling that spheres of influence invalidate the principle of sovereignty and self-determination. So they do. If a nation were *fully* sovereign, *ipso facto* it would not live within the power orbit of another nation. It must be recognized that there are degrees of sovereignty and self-determination. A fully sovereign nation is one which has sufficient power to be the master of its decisions. In the past, there were many nations who were sovereign in the true sense of the word. Today, there are probably only two or three, but certainly not more than five or seven.

The lack of sovereignty of the smaller nations is not due to the fact that they lie within a sphere of influence; it is simply a result of their weakness. Their dependence on greater powers is the result of the nature of modern military technology and is not necessarily the result of an imperialistic policy. It is lack of true military power which compels smaller nations to *seek* protection from larger ones. As the small nations feel themselves compelled to attune their foreign policy to that of the "orbit power" and as this circumstance is reflected in their domestic politics, with or without open and direct interference from outside, their degree of self-determination and self-government is reduced. Whether or not one likes these things, they do exist and have to be taken into account.

Self-determination of weaker nations is possible only *within* a given power orbit. Some "dominant" powers will enlist the good will of the small nations by permitting them a maximum of self-determination, others will transform self-determination from a reality into a sham. There is no small nation, except buffer states, which can maintain itself outside a sphere of influence. Sooner or later it will be drawn into or volunteer to enter an orbit. The question is simply, into which orbit? That, alas, is very often a question not of preference but of geography.

Spheres of influence have obvious shortcomings. Yet how are these to be overcome? Certainly not by proclaiming that there is no longer any "need" for the orbits. As a democratic nation, the United States follows the practice of allowing full self-determination within its orbit, even though from time to time it opposes governments which it does not like. On the whole, it uses the only method available to reconcile its philosophy with the brute facts of global power distribution. Only the establishment of workable and fair ground rules, and not the negation of spheres of influence, can bring about a change for the better.

PRESIDENT ROOSEVELT'S LAST SPEECH

Some of the themes of Mr. Hull's Seventeen Points were taken up by President Roosevelt's speech to Congress on March 1, 1945, which was to be his last general pronouncement on matters of foreign policy. He stated that world peace would have to rest on the cooperative efforts of the whole world and that it should be based "on the sound principles of the Atlantic Charter." This was said at a time when territorial aggrandizement had already, in some cases, been agreed to, and a few weeks before the United Nations Charter (Article 77, 1., *b.*) envisaged that "territories . . . may be detached from enemy states as a result of the Second World War." If these principles were so sound, why were they not transferred into the Charter? These principles were not incorporated into that document because, less than a few years after enunciation, they were no longer acceptable to some important foreign nations. If so, why should they be considered "sound"? [17]

The crucial part of Mr. Roosevelt's speech reads as follows:

I think the Crimean Conference was a successful effort by the three leading nations to find a common ground of peace. It spells, it ought to spell, the end of the system of unilateral action and exclusive alliances and spheres of influence and balance of power and all other expedients that have been tried for centuries and have always failed. We propose to substitute for all these a universal organization in which all peace-loving nations will finally have a chance to join.

There are now several distinctions between the legally equal and equally sovereign nations. There are, first, "leading nations," a term which would imply that there are also spheres of influence. For what is a sphere of influence other than an area where a "leading nation" assumes leadership? Yet while the first sentence acknowledges the "leading nations," the second excommunicates their leadership.

There are, second, "peace-loving nations" which would imply that there must be war-loving nations. If so, the proposed organization could not be "universal" and would have to be a protective union against dangerous nations, to wit, an alliance. That Mr. Roosevelt was not too much convinced of the validity of his own reasoning may be seen from his rather cautious phrasing: "It spells, it ought to spell." Nor did he proclaim the end of alliances but merely the end of "exclusive alliances" without giving a definition of this term. An alliance is always "exclusive" since it must exclude the nation against which it is directed. Shortly after this speech, the United States

[17] The story was told about Kaiser Wilhelm's experiences as a naval architect. One day he completed the blueprint for a battleship and showed it to an experienced shipbuilder. The expert said: "Your Majesty really did a remarkable job. This ship is not only the biggest and fastest of all battleships in the world, it has also the strongest protection, and it can shoot further than any ship now serving. Now if you could improve your design in such a way that the ship could float, too, the German navy would undoubtedly become the master of the seas." So much on "sound principles."

signed the Act of Chapultepec which, in substance, was an "exclusive alliance" among the American nations.

The "universal" organization which was to substitute for all these evil practices embodied every single one of them.

The United Nations Charter did not end the system of unilateral action, as it acknowledged the right of self-defense without defining it (Article 51) and clearly authorized such action against former enemy states (Article 107). It did not spell the end of alliances, since "regional arrangements" are encouraged by Chapter VIII. Again there was no definition of the term, but the Charter evidently did not prohibit the Franco-Russian and the Anglo-Russian treaties. The existence (not of an "expedient" but of the "fact") of the balance of power was acknowledged in Chapter V of the Charter setting up the Security Council, splitting it into permanent and nonpermanent members (Article 23) and giving the veto right to the former (Article 27). The trusteeship system, as set up by Chapter XII, tacitly acknowledged even the existence of spheres of influence.

When the President spoke, the Charter had not yet been drafted in its final form, although its contents were already known in a general and preliminary manner. The question therefore arises, was the Charter a complete surrender of the American position? Then, why is so much value attached to it, and why is this surrender not acknowledged? If, however, the Charter incorporated the American position, then why was this position described in completely different terms and why, moreover, were these different terms interpreted as describing the "common ground" on which the three "leading nations" wanted to build peace?

NAVY DAY SPEECH

On October 26, 1945, Mr. Truman spoke in New York to celebrate Navy Day and to explain why the United States needed "armed might."

Mr. Truman presented a list of the twelve fundamental points of American foreign policy. Some of these points are familiar: good neighbor policy in the Western Hemisphere, economic collaboration, preservation of peace through the United Nations, nonrecognition of any government imposed by force, and freedom of all peoples in all continents "who are prepared for self-government to choose their own form of government by their own freely expressed choice."

Some of the old acquaintances reappear in new disguises or with some variations: the principle of the freedom of the seas—which, it will be remembered, brought the United States into trouble when it was neutral, and was always disregarded by the United States after it entered war—was reaffirmed.

Equal rights of navigation were extended to "boundary rivers and waterways and . . . rivers and waterways which pass through more than one country." It may be added in passing that this preoccupation is justified by the overwhelming economic importance of transportation. Yet water transportation is only *one* form of transportation, and by no means the most important one. The amount of freight carried by rivers and seas is far smaller than the freight carried by railroads. Hence, if international transportation is to be improved, it would be necessary to give greater emphasis to rail and air transport, and to solve the various transit and tariff problems connected with *all* media of transportation. The preoccupation with water transport has little logical meaning.

The idea of access on equal terms to the trade and the raw materials of the world also reappeared, but this time the privilege of access was to be given only to "states which are accepted in the society of nations." Did this mean the United Nations? This would be an unlikely interpretation. The United States certainly made huge presents of raw materials and other commodities to Japan, Germany, and Italy when none of them was a member of that organization.

This point patently did not aim at former enemy nations who were not to be deprived of trade and raw materials, for Article 11 of the Potsdam ultimatum to Japan, which formed the legal basis of the Japanese surrender, stated explicitly that "access to, as distinguished from control of, raw materials shall be permitted. Eventual Japanese participation in world trade relations shall be permitted." The promise contained in point four of the Atlantic Charter "to further the enjoyment by all states . . . of access, on equal terms, to the trade and to the raw materials of the world" was explicitly extended to "victor or vanquished." Whoever would be deprived of the benefits of equal trade terms, and therefore of raw materials, actually would be blockaded. According to international law, blockade is a form of aggression, and in this case, the aggression would be carried out without specific cause. It seems clear that a country deprived of raw materials and trade cannot exist, let alone become democratic and "peace-loving."

Some principles had not appeared in previous statements. There is, for example, the pledge that "We shall try to attain a world in which Nazism, Fascism, and military aggression cannot exist." Mr. Truman omitted to say that we try to attain also a world in which disease, crime, and unhappiness cannot exist. Unfortunately, it was not said how such a world could be brought into being.

The United States will "continue to strive to promote freedom of expression and freedom of religion throughout the peace-loving areas of the world." This is a commendable policy. Does this principle demand that the United States embark on an active policy to promote freedom of expression, for example, in the Soviet Union, and what should this active policy be? Would not freedom of expression and religion be beneficial *particularly* to non-peace-loving areas?

Mr. Truman continued: "We shall approve no territorial change in any friendly part of the world unless they accord with the freely expressed wishes of the people concerned." This was a *fundamental* modification of the Atlantic Charter, in so far as territorial changes were now admitted even in *friendly* parts of the world. Needless to say, this modification deprived the original position of its entire validity. It implied that the United States would approve territorial changes in "unfriendly" parts of the world, even if they do *not* accord with the freely expressed wishes of the people concerned. What, for that matter, is, *after* the end of the war, the distinction between friendly and unfriendly? A distinction based on the alignment during the *last* war comes to mind, yet some of the former enemy nations joined the United Nations on the battlefield and cannot therefore be considered as "unfriendly," nor would it be in American interest to consider them still as potential enemies.

The United States did approve, whether reluctantly or not, territorial changes in friendly parts of the world which were carried out with no opportunity for the people concerned "freely" to express their wish. It also recognized, contrary to point six of Mr. Truman's declaration, the forceful imposition of governments "upon any nation by the force of any foreign power." For example, the United States recognized the governments imposed on Hungary and Rumania; yet it continued its opposition against a similar, though legally somewhat different, imposition on the Baltic States.

The Ten Commandments, the President said, have not yet been universally achieved over these thousands of years; he thus held out the hope that ultimately his twelve principles of foreign policy would be accepted universally and implied that these principles have actually controlled American foreign policy. A foreign policy everywhere based on the twelve principles "may take a long time, but it is worth waiting for, and it is worth striving to obtain." The slight difference is that the Ten Commandments are practical and logical, and that the twelve principles are not. Difficult though it may be, one *can* live according to the Commandments, but Mr. Truman's principles *cannot* be used as guides for practical political behavior. Even a very long waiting period will not improve them.

UNITED STATES FOREIGN POLICY IN A WORLD DIVIDED

In 1946, the foreign policy of the United States concentrated mostly on the atomic problem. Few general pronouncements were made, especially since the various sharp disputes with the Soviet Union had imposed a great deal of caution on the American government. However, early in 1947, these disputes could no longer be glossed over, and the American government saw itself compelled to take a positive line of action. On the whole, this policy dates from President Truman's speech to Congress on March 12, 1947, in which he discussed the need for financial help to Greece and Turkey. After having shown the economic plight of the two Mediterranean countries, Mr. Truman continued to say that the United Nations is designed "to make possible lasting freedom and independence for all its members."

The United States must be

willing to help free peoples to maintain their free institutions and their national integrity against aggressive movements that seek to impose upon them totalitarian regimes. This is no more than a frank recognition that totalitarian regimes imposed on free peoples, by direct or indirect aggression, undermine the foundations of international peace and hence the security of the United States. The peoples of a number of countries of the world have recently had totalitarian regimes forced upon them against their will.

Mr. Truman mentioned Poland, Rumania, and Bulgaria, and continued:

At the present moment in world history, nearly every nation must choose between alternative ways of life. The choice is too often not a free one. One way of life is based upon the will of the majority, and is distinguished by free institutions, representative government, free elections, guarantees of individual liberty, freedom of speech and religion and freedom from political oppression. The second way of life is based upon the will of a minority forcibly imposed upon the majority. It relies upon terror and oppression, a controlled press and radio, fixed elections and the suppression of personal freedoms.

What should be the policy of the United States in view of this conflict?

I believe that it must be the policy of the United States to support peoples who are resisting attempted subjugation by armed minorities or by outside pressure. I believe that we must assist free peoples to work out their own destinies in their own way. I believe that our help should be primarily through economic and financial aid which is essential to economic stability and orderly political processes.

On March 21, Mr. Acheson amplified the President's statement: "Greece needs financial help to carry on essential imports, to organize and equip her army in such a way that order can be restored, to start economic reconstruction, and to pay experienced American administrative, economic and technical personnel as advisers."

Mr. Acheson also explained the administration's ideas as to what would happen if aid to Greece and Turkey were not forthcoming: if the integrity and independence of Greece were lost, "the effect on Turkey is inevitable." There would be disastrous effects on the countries to the east and south of Turkey, some of which "are just emerging into statehood." Such developments would make it very difficult for them to solve their problems "in ways compatible with free institutions and individual liberty. . . ." The effect on the entire Middle East of a Greek or Turkish collapse would be enormous, "especially if [it] . . . should come about as a result of the failure of this great democracy to come to their aid." On the other hand, if Greece and Turkey were helped, the effects throughout "the vast area from the Dardanelles to the China Sea" would be beneficial to its "morale."

These convincing arguments could have been applied with even greater force to China, but the administration pursued policies in the Near and Middle East different from those it followed in the Far East. Consistency may not be a political virtue, but if a basic policy—or, at least, a policy that has been represented as basic—has been abandoned in one particular respect, it might be useful to know the reasons for the deviation.[18] It is unnecessary to stress the fact that the stakes in China were far greater than those in Greece or even Turkey. Yet American help given to Nationalist China was relatively far smaller than the help given to the two Mediterranean countries. Inexplicably, this aid was described officially as far greater than it actually was. Whatever help was extended was rendered in the fashion of too little and too late. No attempt was made to administer it along the lines which had proved so effective in Greece, namely, through a proper organization and through adequate numbers of supervisory and training personnel.

In Europe, the United States opposed communist participation in governments, chastened by a short unhappy experience with so-called "coalition" governments in France and Italy to which originally American diplomacy had given its blessings. This opposition was imaginative and forceful. Yet General Marshall was sent to China to prevail upon Chiang Kai-shek to make his peace with the communists. According to one instruction, he was to make sure that the communists would be represented in the Chinese legislature, while according to another one, he was to convince Chiang that he should accept them into his government.

The special conditions of China, which had suffered from an eight-year war and from partition into four different parts, never were clearly recognized. For example, on January 12, 1950, Mr. Acheson stated that "no one in his right mind suggests, that . . . the Nationalist government fell because it was confronted by overwhelming military force which it could not resist." He then proceeded to discourse on recent Chinese history. After the war, he said, "Chiang Kai-shek emerged as the undisputed leader of the Chinese people." Chiang hardly could be expected to concur with this statement. He never was able to establish control over Manchuria or to set up an effective administration over the rest of China, for he had neither the requisite administrative personnel nor sufficient economic resources. The sudden withdrawal, late in 1945, of American logistical support left the Nationalist regime suspended in mid-air. Secretary Acheson still insisted that Chiang had "overwhelming military power, greater military power than any ruler ever had in

---

[18] On this point the following statement was made by Secretary of State Dean G. Acheson (January 12, 1950): "There seems to be a great interest in many quarters in trying to point out a logical inconsistency. They say if you do so and so in Greece, why don't you do so and so in China? The idea is that we must always act exactly the same way in every country in the world, and if you don't somebody rings up score one on the cash register. That, I think, is not a helpful way of discussing foreign policy and it is a very false trend. The United States in my judgment acts in regard to a foreign nation strictly in regard to American interest."

the entire history of China." Whether Chiang had greater military power than the Chinese rulers of, say, the 15th century (which was undoubtedly true) was quite immaterial. The point at issue was his *relative* military power, his effective strength in *comparison* with that of his opponents. To describe Chiang's *relative* military power, the only type of military power which counts, as "overwhelming" was to do violence to the facts. To state, moreover, that Chiang had "tremendous economic and military support and backing from the United States" is an assertion which is not supported by American statistics. The facts are that between 1945 and 1949 China received per head of population effective aid of 75 cents, or less than 19 cents per year and person. At the same time, the United States allocated to individual European countries sums that were much larger than the total of Chiang's share. These European nations were then at peace; China was still at war.

Mr. Acheson also stated: "Only one faction, the Communists, up in the hills, ill-equipped, ragged, a very small military force, was determinedly opposed to [Chiang's] position." The facts are that, within a few short weeks after the conclusion of the war against Japan, the communist "faction" no longer was "in the hills" but had advanced to the coast and the plains. The communists controlled approximately 100 million people or about one-fourth of the Chinese population. Their military force was not "very small" but very substantial and, what is more significant, very well organized and extremely well led. The communists were ill-equipped, it is true, but early in 1946 they acquired, through the connivance of the Soviets, large stocks of arms from the Japanese Kwantung army and began to take possession of the industrial installations of Manchuria. General Marshall saved them from military defeat twice by imposing a truce on Chiang Kai-shek.[19]

In February, 1950, Mr. Acheson supplied a searching analysis of communist tactics in China and a scrupulously fair assessment of the forces arrayed against the Nationalist regime. He said:

There has never, in the history of the world, been an imperialist system that compares with what the Soviet Union has at its disposal. . . . What they did was to invite some Chinese leaders who were dissatisfied with the way things were going in their country to come to Moscow. There they thoroughly indoctrinated them so that they returned to China prepared to resort to any means whatsoever to establish Communist control. They were completely subservient to the Moscow regime. . . . These agents then mingled among the people and sold them on the personal material advantages of Communism. They talked to the people in their own language. They promised to turn over the land to them. . . . The arsenal of the Communists is varied. I need not describe in detail the uses which they make of force, threats, infiltration, planned chaos, despair and confusion, and the enslavement of the people they dominate by a shrewd use of informers.

[19] The methods which the communists employed in their seizure of China are described by Stefan T. Possony, *A Century of Conflict*, Chicago, Regnery, 1953, pp. 298–351.

Mr. Acheson continued that the United States "must be prepared to meet wherever possible all thrusts of the Soviet Union." He described how the Soviet "thrust" was halted in Greece and Turkey. "The Greeks were able, with our assistance, to meet military force with military force." Both Greeks and Turks were determined "to protect their independence against communist aggression." But resistance against communists in China failed. Why?

The Communist threat succeeded because the Chinese people were not convinced that the national government was concerned with their welfare. I do not think that threat could have been prevented so long as the Chinese people felt that we were supporting a government that they did not believe to be serving their interest.[20]

How could anyone know what this mythical entity, the Chinese people, believed and desired? In the light of Mr. Acheson's own analysis of the policies pursued by the Soviet "imperialist system," it is difficult to see how the Nationalist government could have governed efficiently and increased the welfare of the people. Even assuming it to be true that the Nationalist government could not have been saved, why was a *positive* policy never developed to prevent China from falling into communist hands? Had not the United States taken a hand in Chinese politics in order to defend not only the integrity of China but also its own interests?

But now that China had fallen, what could be done about it? Mr. Acheson's answer was:

What is happening in China is that the Soviet Union is detaching the northern provinces of China from China and is attaching them to the Soviet Union. This process is complete in Outer Mongolia. It is nearly complete in Manchuria and I am sure that in Inner Mongolia and in Sinkiang, there are very happy reports coming from Soviet agents to Moscow. . . . It is the detachment of these whole areas, vast areas —populated by Chinese—the detachment of these areas from China and their attachment to the Soviet Union. . . . This fact that the Soviet Union is taking the four northern provinces of China is the single most significant, most important fact, in the relation of any foreign power with Asia. . . . Nothing that we can do and nothing that we say must be allowed to obscure the reality of this fact. . . . The only thing that can obscure it is the folly of ill-conceived adventures on our part. . . . We must not undertake to deflect from the Russians to ourselves the righteous anger and the wrath and the hatred of the Chinese people.

Although Mr. Acheson now grasped the Soviet nettle firmly, he still held that the United States was to do nothing; America must act like a man whose friend is being beaten by a thug but who does not interfere on the grounds that afterward the friend will be all the more grateful to him because *he* did not beat him.

There is a tendency among American policy makers to base policy on "estimates," "trends," and "forecasts." It is overlooked that human *will* prevails

[20] Dean G. Acheson, *Strengthening the Forces of Freedom, Selected Speeches and Statements,* Department of State Publication 3852, Government Printing Office, p. 17.

against odds deemed impossible by the most savant estimates. *The will to succeed is a more important factor than opportunity.* True, the Chinese situation was going from bad to worse. But did the United States government have the firm will to hold China? And, if it did, did it implement this will with sufficient means and sufficient energy? The only way to make foreign policy is to make it, and not to sit by as somewhat restless and vocal observers and wait till the "dust settles," to use Mr. Acheson's descriptive phrase.

THE MARSHALL PLAN

On June 5, 1947, Secretary of State Marshall announced the intention of the United States to make substantial economic contributions to the recovery of Europe, provided the Europeans would get together and inform the United States about their needs. He stated that the United States government could not design and carry out unilaterally "a program to place Europe on its feet economically. This is the business of the Europeans. The initiative, I think, must come from Europe. The role of this country should consist of friendly aid in the drafting of a European program and of later support of such a program as far as it may be practical for us to do so."

General Marshall specifically disclaimed any ideological purposes of this plan. "Our policy," he said, "is not directed against any country or doctrine but against hunger, poverty, deprivation and chaos." Accordingly, the Soviet Union was invited to participate in the program but, fortunately for the success of the scheme, the Soviet government decided, after some hesitation, to reject the offer. Apparently, the Soviets reasoned that a large mutual-aid program would punch too many holes in the iron curtain. The plan was adopted by sixteen European nations outside of the Soviet orbit.

Although Secretary Marshall stated that his policy was to combat hunger and poverty, the selection of the first countries to receive American aid, namely, Greece and Turkey, was dictated largely by *strategic* reasons; the United States saw itself compelled to defend its sphere of interests in the eastern Mediterranean and to prevent these countries from being overrun by the Soviet Union.

The Marshall Plan was designed to defend Europe against Cold War methods practiced by the Soviet Union. The purpose of the plan was *not* to alleviate hunger or poverty; this was only the means. The purpose was to stop Soviet expansion in Europe.

In a speech of January 8, 1948, Secretary of State Marshall talked about the *reconstruction* of Western Europe. The subsequent economic cooperation agreements committed the signatories to promote the economic *integration* of Europe. Economically and sociologically, the program was far more ambitious than a holding action against hunger or chaos. Yet the real scope of the program never was made explicit and perhaps never was analyzed fully. Hence the plan's requirements as well as its implications never were understood properly, either by the program's promoters or by its beneficiaries.

Mr. Truman stated that in the present world situation "nearly every nation" must choose between two camps. The question arises why the program as outlined by Secretary Marshall, though it was predicated on the *global* character of the conflict, suggested that American intervention be confined to a number of select countries. Hence, if Mr. Truman's estimate was accurate, American policies did not conform to Mr. Truman's conceptions. But if this policy *was* in line with his true estimate he must have taken a far more alarming stand publicly than he did in his secret councils. A global conflict, one must presume, is more dangerous than a regional struggle. Either alternative ought to give pause for contemplation. But suppose that Mr. Truman's public estimate was right; it would then follow that the United States waged a world-wide struggle on a limited front. What else could be the outcome but that this struggle *might* be won on one front but *must* be lost on other fronts?

This was by no means the only inconsistency in the program. President Truman stated his belief that American help "should be primarily through economic and financial aid." Hence there was the paradox that the United States proposed to fight an *ideological* conflict with *economic* means. No responsible official explained why economic weapons could decide the ideological conflict.

But *was* it an ideological struggle? In some statements the communist danger was defined as an ideological and, occasionally, as a propaganda threat. In others, it was held to be a threat of subversion and revolution. According to still other interpretations the threat appeared to be that of Russian imperialism. On January 12, 1950, Mr. Acheson said: "Communism is the most subtle instrument of Soviet foreign policy that has ever been devised and it is really the spearhead of Russian imperialism"; on April 22, 1950: "This fanatical doctrine [communism] dominates one of the greatest states in this world"; on February 8, 1950: "In part, the Soviet government is ideological and, in part, it is imperialistic." On March 16, 1950, Mr. Acheson identified the opponent as "the leaders of international Communism" and added: "Here is a moral issue of the clearest nature. It cannot be evaded. . . . We can see no moral compromise with the contrary thesis of international Communism." Does this mean that compromises with communism would be immoral or merely that no compromises are possible in the moral field?

The confusions of the Democrats in power were not more astonishing than the confusions of the Republicans in opposition. The Republicans, confronted by impressive proofs of Soviet bellicosity, including the attack on Korea, attempted to argue away the military threat of communism. Let us take just two representative examples. Senator Taft, on January 5, 1951, expressed the belief that the Soviets intended to take over Europe by "infiltration and persuasion." "I do not believe it is at all clear that the Russians contemplate the military conquest of the world. . . . I believe they know it is impossible. It would take them at least 100 years to build up their sea power to enable them to get across the seas." Why? The two-ocean United States Navy was built in about seven years; considering their smaller industrial capacity, the Russians should be able to duplicate such an effort in twenty years or less. The point is academic, since the communists hardly consider fighting the United States with sea power, but the argument is typical of its kind. Mr. John Foster Dulles said: "The soviet communist party has consistently taught that the military establishment of a state is primarily an instrument of defense, and that offense is primarily the task of the party, to be carried out by its methods of class war, civil war, penetration, terrorism and propaganda." The communists taught nothing of the kind. Mikhail V. Frunze, the most outstanding of Soviet commissars of war, described the Red Army as the *main weapon* of the proletarian revolution; *this* has been the consistently taught communist doctrine.[21]

Nowhere was an official statement made by the American government or by the opposition party in which the *over-all* threat was described in *all* its elements. The official statements at best deal with *segments* of the threat—and sometimes with the unimportant ones. Piecemeal analysis must lead to piecemeal and hazardous policies. Thus, Mr. Truman and his advisers originally ignored the military aspects of the communist threat. They assumed that the Soviets would not be able to acquire atomic bombs before 1953, when actually the first Russian bomb exploded in 1949. Even when the first Soviet atomic blast was reported, the country was told by official spokesmen, including General Omar N. Bradley, then chairman of the Joint Chiefs of Staff, that nothing much had happened (although the American atomic program was enlarged almost immediately). American armaments were kept at a low level—about $80 per head of population.

The most discouraging aspect of this misjudgment was that, thirty years earlier, the American government had had a perfectly clear understanding of the nature of communism. On December 1, 1919, Secretary of State Lansing wrote a memorandum to President Wilson in which he discussed a basic difference between the "Bolsheviks" and "Bolshevism." In his terminology, Bolshevism was "a popular state of mind growing out of the war and past abuses. It is compounded of demoralization and protest." It is a *social* condition typical of a war-ravaged country. The Bolsheviki, by contrast, were a *military* dictatorship. Lansing emphasized that "against this machine it may be that only force will prevail." [22]

---

[21] John Foster Dulles, *War or Peace*, New York, Macmillan, 1950, pp. 12*f.* For details on Frunze, see Possony, *op. cit.*, p. 124.

[22] Department of State: *Papers Relating to the Foreign Relations of the United States, 1920*, 1936, Vol. 3, p. 441.

Yet while the analysis was sound, the American government did not act on it. It gave substantial economic assistance to the Russian people, hoping to alleviate the conditions which gave rise to Bolshevism as a state of mind. Actually this help enhanced the strength and power of the Bolshevik apparatus and the Red Army, and thereby achieved the very opposite of what was intended. Far from solving *half* of the problem, this piecemeal approach made the *entire* problem insoluble.

The men who framed policy between 1948 and 1950 had reached manhood in the period from 1919 to 1922 when this particular American policy failed. It could have been expected that they would remember the lesson and pay attention to the precedent. This they did not do. The United States again embarked on an attempt to stop force and forestall armed conflict by economic measures alone.

This time, however, the communists themselves rectified the American terms by seizing Czechoslovakia, creating a conflict with Yugoslavia, instituting the blockade of Berlin, and launching a military offensive in China. The American government was compelled to consider the distasteful problem of force; the answer was to be the North Atlantic Treaty Organization (NATO). A pact was concluded between the United States, Canada, and Britain on the one hand, and various Continental nations on the other. The hope was expressed that this alliance would counterbalance the Soviet threat. The trouble was that this alliance included many states which militarily were of small significance.

The alliance was another attempt to come to grips with a *global* program of conquest by developing a *regional* arrangement. At the very time when the North Atlantic Treaty Organization was being established, the United States went on one of its habitual disarmament sprees; it was argued that this country could not "afford" an adequate military budget. The bipartisan advocates of reduction in military expenditures quoted Lenin to the effect that the communists would destroy the United States by forcing it to spend itself into bankruptcy. Lenin never said this, but the politicians who invoked his authority never took the trouble to verify the quotation, let alone reason out the economic "theory" behind it. The question was not asked how it was that the Soviet Union with its backward economy could "afford" larger armaments than the wealthy United States. The Korean War, for a while, led to increased (though still inadequate) armaments. Preparedness was boosted to more than $200 per head of population.

The neglected, though capital, point was *the need for American power as the basis of NATO strength.* Instead, the as-yet-nonexistent NATO forces were taken as a substitute for indigenous American power-in-being. This misconception gave rise to another strange idea, namely, that in order to keep the alliance together, United States policy should conform to the wishes and fears of the more timid and weaker members of the alliance.

This confusion as to basic purpose of the alliance became obvious in the debate which raged over General MacArthur's (and later, Senator Taft's) proposal to "go it alone." Obviously, it would be foolish to "go it alone" if an alliance could strengthen the military power of the United States and the free world and thus diminish the relative power of the Soviet Union. But if by "going it together" this military power is not increased but reduced in its effectiveness, spread too thinly or over too many theaters of action, and hampered in its employment, and if moreover, in such an actual conflict as the Korean War, the United States—for all practical purposes—*was* "going it alone," then clearly the wrong question had been put. The right question would not be, should the United States go it alone, but, how can it best employ the power it has? How can the alliance be made into the strongest deterrent against aggression? Actually, the real meaning of the debate was whether American policy should conform to British and French wishes, or whether American leadership should prevail.[23] A good case might have been made that in the Korean dispute the United States should have complied with the wishes of its European allies. But this case should have been argued on its *specific* merits, and *not* on the grounds of an abstract argument of complete self-reliance versus unquestioning compliance with the wishes of weaker allies.

THE OBJECTIVE OF AMERICAN FOREIGN POLICY

It has become banal to say that the United States with its social structure and way of life, as well as freedom all over the world, have been put in jeopardy by communism operating from Russia, China, and Eastern Europe as its bases. Confronted with such a threat, the first requirement was to *stop* its further encroachments. This was the purpose of the so-called "containment" policy enunciated by George Kennan in 1947.[24] This policy was implemented in the economic and military fields by the Marshall Plan and by NATO respectively. It concentrated on Europe while, before the Korean

[23] George Catlin, one-time adviser to the British Foreign Office, renowned advocate of Atlantic Union, and most certainly no isolationist, wrote: "In terms of America's national interest, the patent conclusion would seem to be that America should 'go it alone,' especially in the Pacific theatre. . . . It is doubtful if the NATO agreement is worth the paper it is written on, since it produces the illusion of a security which does not exist." ("Why Europe Is Neutral," *New Leader*, Nov. 2, 1953, p. 2.) Mr. Catlin's verdict may be all too harsh, yet he puts squarely a question which cannot be answered by simply denying that it exists. For a candid statement on Anglo-American divergencies on Korea by an Englishman, see G. F. Hudson, "Will Britain and America Split in Asia?" *Foreign Affairs*, Vol. 31, No. 4, July, 1953. For Britain, the Far East is less important strategically than it is commercially; for the United States, the major Pacific power, the order is exactly the reverse. What remains of Britain's status as world power is based on the solidarity of the Commonwealth, including restive India; the United States is committed to the defense of Japan, Formosa, the Philippines, and Indo-China. It is quite conceivable that on a number of these issues Britain and the United States will, nay *must*, "go it alone."

[24] See George F. Kennan, "The Sources of Soviet Conduct," *Foreign Affairs*, Vol. 25, No. 4, July, 1947. See also his speculative estimate "America and the Russian Future," *Foreign Affairs*, Vol. 29, No. 3.

War, little was done to contain communism in Asia. In general, "containment," or holding the line, was restricted to the halting of hostile "expansion," but did not concern itself with nonmilitary conflict techniques. No effort was developed to counter the Soviet organizational weapon.[25]

After the proclamation of the containment policy, the remnants of democracy were destroyed in Czechoslovakia, China fell, Tibet was lost, and the United States prepared to abandon Formosa. On the credit side of the ledger must be entered the following accomplishments: the communist attack on Greece was defeated and Yugoslavia was given strategic cover after Moscow had expelled that country from the Cominform; the United States, with some support from other nations, foiled the communist attack on South Korea; and France and Viet-Nam resisted the communist offensive in Indo-China. Hence, here and there, Soviet expansion *was* stopped (spring, 1954). The question is, has it been halted permanently or temporarily? All students of communist power are convinced that, given a favorable opportunity, Soviet expansion will be resumed.

Should the United States seek to appease the Soviets? This approach was tried in 1943 and 1947 and failed. Will the leopard change his spots? When Kennan first presented the formula of the containment policy to the public, he wrote: [26]

Who can say with assurance that the strong light cast by the Kremlin on the dissatisfied peoples of the Western world is not a powerful afterglow of a constellation which is in actuality on the wane? This cannot be proved. And it cannot be disproved. But the possibility remains . . . that Soviet power . . . bears within it the seeds of its own decay, and that the sprouting of these seeds is well-advanced.

If this contention can neither be proved nor disproved, the question must be asked, on what assumption should American foreign policy be based? On the assumption that the Soviet threat will recede as forces from within weaken Soviet power, or on the assumption that the Soviet regime will stay firmly in the saddle and its hostility will remain a dire threat to the free world for a long time to come?

If American policy is based on the second assumption, as it obviously must be if national security is not to be exposed to intolerable risk, then the question arises, how is the United States to cope with a threat that for all practical purposes is permanent as long as its source exists? Secretary of State Acheson's answer was to build "positions of strength" which would become impregnable against Soviet drives.[27] But what positions? The entire free world? Only part of the free world? Can the rest then be held, and has the United States the strength to maintain such a universal defensive posture? Neither the Secretary nor, for that matter, President Truman made it clear

---

[25] See Philip Selznick, *The Organizational Weapon, A Study of Bolshevik Strategy and Tactics,* New York, McGraw-Hill, 1952.

[26] Kennan, "The Sources of Soviet Conduct," *op. cit.,* p. 580.

[27] *Strengthening the Forces of Freedom,* p. 3.

in what respect this building of "positions of strength" was different from the policies which materialized in the building of the Chinese great wall, the Roman *limes,* Prussia's belt of fortresses, and France's Maginot Line. What is a "position of strength" in the atomic age? Where, for that matter, could a "position of strength" which could command the respect of Russian *military* power be built *except* in the United States? Areas like Western Europe, Scandinavia, and Japan can be strengthened, but can they become true "positions of strength," *i.e.,* become stronger than Russian power?

The criterion that American foreign policy must satisfy is whether it can promote the interests of the United States and the free world and *preserve peace* in a world in which the opponent of the United States pursues objectives contrary to those which the American leaders would *like* him to pursue. The policy of containment and coexistence leaves the initiative in Soviet hands. The Soviets make use of the time and resources which they have won by their dynamic strategies to build up the power of a bloc of 700 to 800 million people. They strive toward making themselves stronger than the United States and its allies. Conversely they seek to weaken the free world by employing the techniques of disintegration which they have perfected in nearly forty years of ceaseless political warfare.

In the long run, containment and coexistence can be successful only if there will be a change of heart in the Kremlin. What is the American government going to do if such a change of heart (or, what would seem the prerequisite of such a change in foreign policy, namely, a change of the Russian government) does not occur spontaneously? In speeches during the 1952 presidential campaign, Secretary of State John Foster Dulles launched a new concept: "liberation." The objective seemed to be to eliminate Soviet power from the satellite areas. President Dwight D. Eisenhower appeared to have raised the concept of "liberation" to the dignity of a major foreign-policy objective when he said in an address on April 16, 1953:

We are ready not only to press forward with the present plans for closer unity of the nations of Western Europe but also, upon that foundation, to strive to foster a broader European community, conducive to the free movement of persons, of trade, and of ideas.

This community would include a free and united Germany, with a government based upon free and secret elections.

This free community and the full independence of the East European nations could mean the end of the present unnatural division of Europe.

Nine months later, Secretary Dulles alluded, albeit somewhat negatively and cryptically, to the United States' concern with the lot of the satellite peoples when he said on January 12, 1954:

If we rely on freedom, then it follows that we must abstain from diplomatic moves which would seem to endorse captivity. That would, in effect, be a conspiracy against freedom.

At the moment of this writing the practical policies for leading the captive peoples into freedom have not been spelled out. Secretary Dulles, in his speech of January 12, rejected the idea of strategic containment and insisted: "The way to deter aggression is for the free community to be willing and able to respond vigorously at places and with means of its own choosing." Although such a policy, had it been adopted by the preceding administration, might have conceivably forestalled the wars in Korea and Indo-China, it could not, by itself, have brought about a decisive reversal of the prevailing power relationships between the free world and the Soviet empire. The United States would have gained its strategic freedom—in order to contain more effectively. It would not have come nearer to the goal of "liberation."

The critics of the concept of "liberation" have argued (1) that a liberation policy is but a mild version of preventive war strategy, and (2) that no one as yet has shown a way by which liberation can be brought about. The partisans of "liberation"—of a dynamic versus a static policy—have countered these arguments by pointing out that any strategy requires suitable opportunities, but if the objective has not been defined, the opportunities may slip by unused, as has happened all too often in the past. By experimenting with "coexistence" American foreign policy very justifiably attempted to eschew war as a solution of the problem of security against Soviet aggression, but it did not thereby assure—as a matter of course—peace or survival. The concept of containment was never translated into a set of understandable, concrete, and workable propositions. The partisans of containment have yet to explain what they propose to do in order to halt or balance the rapid growth of the Soviet power machine or how, under the threat of atomic war, a policy of defensive and passive coexistence can preserve democracy and safeguard what Mr. Acheson called "the very existence of all civilization . . . and the safety of the free world." Possibly there are answers to these questions, but they have not been given. By contrast, the concept of liberation, so its partisans argue, has logic and reality on its side. Liberation simply means that each concrete policy decision would aim at reducing and ultimately eliminating Soviet power rather than granting it an inviolate zone of influence.

In the light of the Monroe Doctrine, the War between the States, the Spanish-American War, the two world wars, and American attitudes on "colonialism," liberation can be described as the classical concept of American foreign policy.[28]

Both policies—"containment" and "liberation"—entail risks, the former because time is not necessarily on the side of the United States, the latter because time is not necessarily on the side of the communists and the Soviets might go to war rather than watch their empire falling apart under the pressure of the militant forces of freedom. The explosion of a hydrogen

[28] See James Burnham, *Containment or Liberation? An Inquiry into the Aims of United States Foreign Policy*, New York, John Day, 1953.

bomb on March 1, 1954, supplied a forceful reminder of how great are these risks. Whether the development of nuclear weapons has strengthened the cause of freedom, or has left the United States and the Soviet Union no alternative other than indefinite contemplation of a stalemate, or has swung the balance in the Soviets' favor—these questions can be answered only by events and not by fallible man. Life in this century has been fraught with hazards more terrible than those confronting mankind in all of its previous history. No matter which policy the United States chooses, the risks are as great as are the stakes: the survival of the nation, of human freedom, and, perhaps, of the human race. To make foreign policy is to take risks. This has always been so. The United States cannot escape the terrible dilemma by avoiding all risks—lest it accept defeat before the issue is joined.

THE MIRACLE

At this point, the reader may pause and marvel at a unique and strange phenomenon. Here is a country whose government, obstructed by mental blinders, has all too often failed to give dynamic and farsighted leadership and limped behind events. Here is a nation which would have fallen victim to catastrophe and national extinction had it followed its preconceptions. Here is a country which at its birth was conceived by political genius but which confounded the form of its political tradition with its content.

Yet this same country, though abandoning itself to the illusions of peace and progress, did not succumb to invasion. Divorcing its actions almost completely from its doctrine, the nation dimly sensed that instinct is a better guide to action than faulty reasoning. Putting trust into the practical and distrusting their own theories, the American people marched on at giant paces, accumulated power which they did not desire and, without plan or design, emerged as the greatest empire of the modern world.

Had the American nation followed the beck and call of its abstractions, it would long ago have ceased to be a major power. It would have remained a pawn on the chessboard of world history; at best, it would have grown to be a larger and more centrally located Australia. By singular good fortune the American nation disproved Napoleon's somber prophecy: "The cannon killed feudalism; ink will kill the modern society." With its extraordinary talent of unsophistication, *the American nation perceived that the chief political problem in this world is to survive as a community, and that, in order to survive and to escape foreign domination, that community must grow and grow stronger,* and, unafraid, must face and subdue the most deadly of threats.

From its entry into history the American nation accumulated wealth and power. It procured for itself an absolute and unparalleled security within its own immediate habitat. In order to achieve this objective, America did not trust in "international cooperation," but waged war against the British,

Spanish, and Mexicans; and through money and pressure it forced France and Russia to withdraw from the North American continent.

In its hemisphere, the United States established an undisputed and, again, unparalleled power monopoly. For more than 100 years it has prevented any hostile and strong force from menacing United States security from bases in the Western Hemisphere.

On a world scale, the United States opened up Japan; participated in the development of China, the Near East, and Africa; and invested large sums of capital in Europe. The United States fought the First World War to forestall the changing of the balance of power to its detriment. Yet the United States, separated by no more than four generations from the founders, its instinct of survival dulled, entered the Second World War *after* it had been attacked—the only *defensive* war in U.S. history, and the one war where *offensive* American action would have saved untold lives—probably the only war in American history where *offensive* action would have been in full accordance with American ideals.[29]

To preserve its security and to expand its strength, the United States practiced various methods. It engaged in international cooperation, economic and psychological warfare, subversion, the establishment and maintenance of spheres of influence, the balance of power policy, military threats, military alliances, and military action. With some nations, the United States cooperated almost always on the most friendly terms, but often intervened by force in the affairs of other peoples to bend their conduct to its will.

Situated far from the strategic battlefields of the world, the United States could afford to prosper with a minimum of expenditures for armaments. Practical and hardheaded in business affairs, the American nation spent no more for security and expansion than was necessary. Today this country has become history's biggest prize for an aggressor. The United States is now compelled to maintain, for the duration of the Soviet threat, a huge military establishment to deter aggression and ward off nuclear destruction.

The United States was, and still is, one of the most accomplished practitioners of "power politics" in all its forms. The United States consistently denied that it engaged in power politics, but precisely because of its vehement denials, the United States was able to use power techniques with exceptional success—and with an untroubled conscience. The main intellectual task before the American people is to develop a new sense of reality in order to walk upright upon its path through a world of decaying cultures and crumbling empires, which, in its entirety, is being rent asunder by revolution.

[29] Even if it were true that President Roosevelt provoked the Japanese into attacking Pearl Harbor, as has been suggested by careful analysts of the events of 1941, the above statements would still be true psychologically. The provocation, if any, was necessary because the nation did not want to fight.

BIBLIOGRAPHY

Barber, Hollis M.: *Foreign Policies of the United States,* New York, Dryden, 1953.
Bundy, McGeorge (ed.): *The Pattern of Responsibility:* Edited by McGeorge Bundy from the Record of Secretary of State Dean Acheson, Boston, Houghton Mifflin, 1952.
Adams, Ephraim D.: *The Power of Ideals in American History,* New Haven, Yale University Press, 1926.
Adams, James Truslow (ed.): *Jeffersonian Principles and Hamiltonian Principles,* Boston, Little, Brown, 1932.
Beard, Charles A.: *The Idea of National Interest,* New York, Macmillan, 1943.
Bolles, Blair: *Who Makes Our Foreign Policy?* New York, Foreign Policy Association, 1947.
Chamberlain, Lawrence H., and Richard C. Snyder: *American Foreign Policy,* New York, Rinehart, 1948.
Colegrove, Kenneth: *The American Senate and World Peace,* New York, Vanguard, 1944.
Dennison, Eleanor E.: *The Senate Foreign Relations Committee,* Stanford, Calif., Stanford University Press, 1942.
Elliot, William Y.: *The Need for Constitutional Reform,* New York, Whittlesey, 1935.
Feis, Herbert: *The China Tangle,* Princeton, Princeton University Press, 1953.
Fleming, Denna F.: *The Treaty Veto of the American Senate,* New York, Putnam, 1930.
Gibson, Hugh: *The Road to Foreign Policy,* New York, Doubleday, 1944.
Godshall, Wilson L. (ed.): *American Foreign Policy: Formulation and Practice,* Ann Arbor, Mich., Edwards Bros., 1937.
Henderson, Roy W.: *Foreign Policies: Their Formulation and Enforcement,* Government Printing Office, 1946.
Johnson, Walter: *The Battle against Isolation,* Chicago, University of Chicago Press, 1944.
Jones, Joseph M.: *A Modern Foreign Policy for the United States,* New York, Macmillan, 1944.
Kennan, George F.: *American Diplomacy 1900–1950,* Chicago, University of Chicago Press, 1951.
Leonard, Larry L.: *Elements of American Foreign Policy,* New York, McGraw-Hill, 1953.
Lippmann, Walter: *U.S. Foreign Policy: Shield of the Republic,* Boston, Little, Brown, 1943.
McCloy, John J.: *The Challenge to American Foreign Policy,* Cambridge, Mass., Harvard University Press, 1953.
Morley, Felix: *The Foreign Policy of the United States,* New York, Knopf, 1951.
Perkins, Dexter: *Hands Off: A History of the Monroe Doctrine,* Boston, Little, Brown, 1942.
Poole, DeWitt Clinton: *The Conduct of Foreign Relations under Modern Democratic Conditions,* New Haven, Yale University Press, 1924.
Taft, Robert A.: *A Foreign Policy for Americans,* New York, Doubleday, 1951.
Westphal, Albert C. F.: *The House Committee on Foreign Affairs,* New York, Columbia University Press, 1942.
Wright, Quincy: *A Foreign Policy for the United States,* Chicago, University of Chicago Press, 1947.

Part Eight

THE QUEST FOR PEACE

Chapter 26

WAGING THE PEACE

THE FAILURE OF THE ORGANIZATIONAL SOLUTION

The fact that disarmament is not an effective and reliable method of preserving peace is too obvious to pass unnoticed. So an alternate idea was suggested: to use armaments in order to oppose and punish the aggressor, or to put it differently, in the absence of cooperative means of preventing war, to enforce peace through military methods. This idea is by no means so new as its protagonists believe. Nor is the record of its application very encouraging.

Almost a thousand years ago, Bishop Gui d'Anjou initiated one of history's great attempts to secure peace. He proclaimed a Truce of God and issued instructions limiting the use of arms. To the surprise of many, the Bishop succeeded in curbing violence in his diocese; so impressive was his success that other French bishops emulated his example. In the year 1000, a council at Poitiers adopted the motto, *Guerre à la guerre,* and passed a resolution which obligated the princes of the church to oppose war by forceful means, that is, by the intervention of troops under religious leadership. At a synod in Limoges in 1031, it was resolved to excommunicate violators of the peace. It was also decided that, should moral coercion prove insufficient, military force was to be used against any breakers of God's truce. Under the energetic leadership of Archbishop Aimon of Bourges several punitive expeditions were carried out against rebellious knights; the Archbishop may, in fact, be considered as the earliest predecessor of the commander of a modern international armed force. Unfortunately, Aimon's peace force was soon annihilated by a group of knights who were more expert in the art of war than the 700 clerks whom they killed.

The principle of *active* maintenance of God's truce was proclaimed time and again. Pope Urban II, in preparation of the Crusade, decreed a general pacification of the Occident to be imposed by associations of nobles. Pope Alexander III (1159–1181) decreed that "peace and concord . . . must be proclaimed and begotten," the word "begotten" being a euphemism for "coerce." [1] The Council of Toulouse perfected the legal framework for the maintenance of the Truce of God; it was ordered that:

1. Every person over fourteen years of age was to pledge himself with a solemn oath not to violate the Truce of God and not to assist any violator of the peace.

2. This oath was to be repeated every three years, and a person refusing to renew the pledge was to be treated as a breaker of the law.

3. Alliances between nobles were forbidden.

4. Any violator of the peace was to be attacked forthwith by all the others who had pledged themselves to maintain peace; his territory was to be cut off from communications and traffic; his stronghold was to be besieged and stormed; the aggressor and his men were to be punished severely and their property confiscated.

5. The violator of the peace was to be excommunicated (a sanction which frequently entailed economic ruin and even physical destruction).

6. The subjects of the aggressor were formally ordered to revolt against their master and to obstruct his aggression.

In some regions of France, it also became customary for the knights who had obligated themselves to protect the Truce of God to accept personal responsibility for any breaches of the peace. Fighting was limited to the period between Monday morning and Thursday evening; the Truce of God reigned on Fridays, Saturdays, and Sundays. Certain groups of persons and institutions enjoyed a perpetual peace of God—clerics, monks, nuns, pilgrims, women, children, and workers, as well as churches, monasteries, cemeteries, and tools of work.

We do not know by how much the Truce of God diminished the frequency and intensity of war. Powerful princes often disregarded the limitations imposed upon them and observed the law only when it was in their interest to do so. But we also know that the Truce and Peace of God were strictly observed in many regions. Peace was enforced by the spiritual power of the church, accompanied by strong economic and sometimes military sanctions. But later the church's power declined and it was no longer able to impose its law. Secular power then assumed the task of pacification. In France, Saint Louis IX issued his famous *ordonnance* which outlawed "private warfare," an edict enforced by the might of his sword. In Germany, Rudolph of Habsburg ended the lawless chaos by declaring the *Landfrieden.*

[1] Ernest Sémichon, *La Paix et la trêve de Dieu,* 2d ed., Paris, Albanel, 1869, Vol. I, pp. 35*ff.*

The maintenance of internal peace had become the duty as well as the *raison d'être* of the secular state.[2]

At the beginning of the 14th century, the question arose whether international war could not also be limited. While the ideal of peace was, of course, known to previous centuries, it is nevertheless correct to say that the roots of modern pacifism go back to that period. Scholastic philosophy, under the leadership of Thomas Aquinas, had insisted on the difference between just and unjust war. But now the idea was pronounced that war is always an evil and that society thrives best in the tranquillity of universal peace.

Yet how should peace be preserved? Dante wanted to gain universal peace through the establishment of a universal monarchy. Pierre Dubois rejected this idea, but proposed instead a congress of princes to rule the affairs of Europe. Union and federation still compete as alternative patterns of world organization; the political inventiveness of mankind is small.

Dante pointed out that disputes between princes cannot be settled because the litigants are equal in rank, whereas the monarch is most powerful and can impose his will to maintain peace. The idea of international military coercion was implicitly argued by Dante; there would be no point in establishing a universal monarchy unless the monarch had the power to eliminate aggression.

While Dubois argued that universal monarchy could not lead to peace—continuous wars would have to be waged to establish and maintain the universal system—he recognized that the establishment of his system in the contemporary world also would require a series of preventive wars in the Holy Land, Italy, and Germany. Within the league, peace was to be settled by arbitration, the Pope being the supreme arbiter; the judges were to be appointed by papal council. If peace was violated, the aggressor, called *bellum ferens,* was to be subdued by an international army formed from the troops of all confederate states.

The writings of Dubois were soon forgotten, and even Dante, whose treatise could have served as a program for an expanding imperial institution, was almost totally neglected.

From Campanella to James Madison. The 17th century witnessed the publication of a number of peace projects. The series was opened by Campanella's *De Monarchia Hispanica Discursus,* a treatise which placed the burden for the enforcement of universal peace on Spain, then the most powerful country. In 1625, an anonymous French statesman, in a book titled *Le Caton du siècle, un conseil salutaire d'un ancien ministre d'État pour la conservation de la paix universelle,* realizing that one country will always be too weak to establish a universal system, advocated a sort of federal union between France and Spain.

---

[2] For precedents in ancient Greece, Rome, and the early Middle Ages, see Lord David Davies, *The Problem of the Twentieth Century: A Study in International Relationships,* London, Benn, 1938, Chap. 2, and the literature quoted therein.

In the same year, Grotius wrote in his famous *De Jure Belli ac Pacis:* [3]

. . . It would be useful and in some fashion necessary that the Christian powers should make between themselves some sort of body in whose assemblies the troubles of each should be determined by the judgment of others not interested, and that there should be sought means of constraining the parties to come to an agreement under reasonable conditions.

In his *Mémoires,* written between 1617 and 1638, the Duc de Sully elaborated an ambitious project.[4] The "Grand Design" suggested that Europe should be divided equally among the Powers in such a manner that none of them could impose his will upon the others; no state was to seek aggrandizement by conquest. The reallocation of land was to eliminate causes of international friction. The European states were to be ruled by a general council to be named by the princes, including the Emperor and the Pope. The council would have at its command military and naval contingents to enforce its decisions and to preserve the peace. "The greater powers," wrote Sully, "should force the lesser into [peace] by assisting the weak and oppressed; this is the only use they ought to make of their superiority." [5]

In the period of the Thirty Years' War, the organization of peace was a widely discussed subject, and since then each major conflagration has been accompanied by a flood of ideas about the art of "peacefare." The Treaties of Osnabrück and Münster reflected this tendency and contained provisions to assure the stability and permanence of peace. Paragraphs 114–116 of the Treaty of Münster determined that any person breaking the convention or public peace, either intentionally or otherwise, would incur the punishment prescribed for such violations. Despite violations, the peace would remain in force; all signatories to the treaties were obligated to defend and protect each other as well as the laws or conditions of the peace against whomever it might be, without distinction of religion. If violations occurred, an attempt was to be made to settle the dispute by friendly means or legal procedures; if, however, after three years the dispute could not be settled by peaceful means, all the interested parties were bound to help the victim.

In 1693, William Penn, in his *Essay towards the Present and Future Peace of Europe, by the Establishment of an European Diet, Parliament or Estates,* suggested the organization of an international tribunal and a diet of the European sovereigns.[6] This tribunal was to settle disputes which could not be resolved by diplomacy. "Refusal to refer by one party or refusal to respect the decision subjected the offender to the exercise of force by the others." [7]

[3] Quoted by Jackson H. Ralston in *International Arbitration from Athens to Locarno,* Stanford, Calif., Stanford University Press, 1929, pp. 118–119.

[4] *Ibid.;* also Davies, *op. cit.,* pp. 72–76. *The Grand Design,* in the version by the Abbé de l'Ecluse des Loges, was reprinted by the Grotius Society.

[5] Sully, *Mémoires,* Book XIV, quoted by S. C. Vestal in *The Maintenance of Peace,* New York, Putnam, 1920, p. 288.

[6] Davies, *op. cit.,* p. 77.

[7] Ralston, *op. cit.,* p. 120.

All the members of the European Parliament were to unite against the aggressor to "compel the submission and performance of the sentence."

The end of the War of the Spanish Succession brought forth the publication of one of the most renowned peace projects, the *Projet de Paix Perpetuelle,* by the Abbé de Saint-Pierre. Saint-Pierre envisaged, like others before and after him, a European senate or council, yet his project is interesting for the methods of coercion it suggested. In his Fundamental Article VIII we read the following sentences: "The Sovereign who shall take up arms before the Union has declared war, or who shall refuse to execute a regulation of the society, or a judgment of the Senate, shall be declared an enemy to the society, and it shall make war upon him, 'til he be disarmed, and 'til the judgment and regulations be executed."

Saint-Pierre also attempted to determine the aggressor by defining him as the sovereign who attacks suddenly or who refuses to conform to the decisions of the Union. In his Fundamental Article IV, the Abbé linked peace clearly and unequivocally to the maintenance of the *status quo:* "All the sovereignties of Europe shall always remain in the condition they are in, and shall always have the same limits that they have now."

Saint-Pierre's scheme became very well known during the 18th century. It was known to Benjamin Franklin, who may have had it in mind when he proposed his Albany plan. The problem of coercion was discussed thoroughly by the drafters of the American Constitution. Both the so-called Virginia and New Jersey plans contained provisions for enforcement against recalcitrant states and against those members of the Union who should fail to fulfill their duty under the articles of the Constitution.[8] These proposals met, however, the strenuous opposition of Madison and Hamilton. Madison thought that force should not be applied to people collectively but individually and pointed out that enforcement would lead to war and to the destruction of the Union. Speaking militarily, he observed,

> Could the national resources, if exerted to the utmost, enforce a national decree against Massachusetts abetted perhaps by several of her neighbors? It would not be possible. A small proportion of the Community in a compact situation, acting on the defensive, and at one of its extremities might at any time bid defiance to the National authority.

He called the idea that the central government could force its will upon the states "visionary and fallacious." Hamilton added that foreign powers would "not be idle spectators" during enforcement operations, and summed up his opinion, "To coerce the states is one of the maddest projects that was ever

---

[8] James T. Lowe, *The Origins of American Diplomacy,* unpublished manuscript, Chap. 1. See also James Brown Scott, *The United States of America: A Study in International Organization,* New York, Oxford, 1920, pp. 203 ff. Compare *The Federalist,* Nos. 15 and, especially, 16. These same arguments later played a major role in the Senate debate of 1919 concerning the League.

devised. A failure of compliance will never be confined to a single state. This being the case, can we suppose it wise to hazard a civil war?"

Practical Attempts. During the 18th century, war was accepted as a matter of course. Yet two political attempts at peace preservation deserve attention. After the War of the Spanish Succession, the European Cabinets pursued a rigorous policy of peace and appeasement. To avoid a conflict in the Low Countries, Britain, Austria, and the States-General in 1715 signed a "Locarno" treaty at Antwerp, called the Barrier Treaty.[9] From our point of view, the main stipulation was that part of the Austro-French frontier was to be ·guarded by Dutch troops, acting as a sort of international police. However, the Dutch international police never became operative. ". . . On the only occasion when it was seriously wanted, in the war of the Austrian Succession, the Dutch garrisons were withdrawn from the fortress in 1745 in order that the Dutch should preserve their neutrality."

In 1717, an unforeseen danger menaced the peace of Europe—the aggressive policy of Alberoni's Spain, which aimed at the destruction of the system created by the Peace of Utrecht and more specifically at the conquest of Sardinia, Sicily, and southern Italy. In 1718 the Utrecht powers (Britain, France, Austria, and the United Netherlands) concluded an alliance, promising each other mutual support in case of attack. Spanish aggression was forestalled by the annihilation of the Spanish fleet off Cape Passero by the British, acting in behalf of the Quadruple Alliance—a most successful "archetype" of peace enforcement action. It was perhaps this event which, in 1736, led Cardinal Alberoni to propose a peace project of his own in which military enforcement was to play a prominent role.

THE HOLY ALLIANCE

The most elaborate attempt at peace preservation prior to the 20th century was undoubtedly the system which resulted from the liquidation of the Napoleonic Wars and which is wrongly known as the "Holy Alliance." This system was constructed on several levels and can be understood only if it is considered in its complex totality.[10]

The basis of the system was the Holy Alliance proper, a treaty suggested by Tsar Alexander I and signed by all European states with the exception of England, Turkey, and the Papacy. Although "a piece of sublime mysticism and nonsense" (Castlereagh) and so vague that it can hardly be called a legal, let alone an enforceable, document, the treaty precluded war between the legitimate sovereigns, or rather it codified the fact that, under the circumstances, such war was a very remote possibility. Article I stated that the

[9] R. B. Mowat, *A History of European Diplomacy, 1451–1789*, New York, Longmans, 1928, p. 209.
[10] *Memoirs of Prince Metternich, Vol. IV, 1815–1829*, New York, Scribner, 1881, pp. 182–188.

signatory powers "will, on all occasions and in all places, lend each other aid and assistance." Article II proclaimed:

The sole principle of force, whether between the said Governments or between their Subjects, shall be that of doing each other reciprocal service, and of testifying by unalterable good will the mutual affection with which they ought to be animated, to consider themselves all as members of one and the same Christian nation.

While the Holy Alliance bound the European states against unspecified dangers, there was unanimity among the leading powers that France was the country most likely to start a future war. Accordingly, Britain, Austria, Russia, and Prussia signed a specific military alliance to protect each other by intervention against French aggression. In 1818, France entered the alliance, thus signifying her purpose to adhere to a policy of peace; to be protected against any eventuality, the four original signatories renewed by a secret treaty their mutual defense pact.

Mindful of recent French history, statesmen of the time believed that revolution must inevitably engender aggression. Any uprising or insurrection, especially when it led to the dethronement of the legitimate ruler, signer of the Holy Alliance, was considered a potential threat of war. Hence, if peace was to be preserved, revolutions had to be crushed. This, to be sure, was not the only reason why Metternich and Alexander were opposed to revolution; yet, grasping the intricate relationship between internal and external peace, they acted to maintain both in order to preserve the internal as well as the external *status quo*. This was the third level of the system.

Metternich's experiences within the German Confederacy led him to believe that the treaties would be useless unless threats to peace were terminated by immediate intervention. In July, 1820, a revolution broke out in Naples; by virtue of the Pact of 1815, a conference convened in Troppau at the end of which Austria, Russia, and Prussia—but neither France nor England—signed a protocol promulgating the principle of intervention for the maintenance of peace. The text of the protocol is as follows: [11]

States which have undergone a change of government due to revolution, the result of which threatens other states, ipso facto, cease to be members of the European Alliance, and remain excluded from it until their situation gives guarantees for legal order and stability. . . . If, owing to such alterations, immediate danger threatens other states, the powers bind themselves, by peaceful means, or if need be, by arms, to bring back the guilty state into the bosom of the Great Alliance.

The three eastern powers were strongly opposed by England. Metternich was unable to convince Castlereagh that the new principles were merely the logical conclusion of the premises to which England was already committed. Castlereagh's answer was that Britain could never accept a principle which

[11] Carlton J. H. Hayes, *A Political and Cultural History of Modern Europe,* New York, Macmillan, 1932, Vol. I, p. 733.

she would not permit to be applied in her own case; England, he wrote,[12] "cannot and will not act upon abstract and speculative principles of precaution." Nevertheless, a breakdown of the alliance was avoided; while objecting to intervention, England admitted that Austria had special interests in Italy and interposed no objection to the Austrian intervention in Naples and Piedmont.

In 1822 a revolution in Spain necessitated a new conference, which convened in Verona. The Tsar offered to march 150,000 Russians to Piedmont, where they would serve as an international police against revolutions in western Europe—a proposal rejected by all the other states. Russia, Austria, and Prussia agreed, however, to support France in intervening in Spain; this intervention took place in 1823 and reestablished the legitimate monarchy.

Great Britain was afraid that the French intervention might serve as a pretext for European powers to seize territory in South America. In fact, it had been suggested at Verona that Spain should recover some of her former possessions, but in addition there was an informal understanding between France and Russia to take Buenos Aires and establish naval control in the Pacific. England threatened immediate war if France or Russia should attack South America, and communicated with the American government which, shortly afterward, proclaimed the Monroe Doctrine. The Verona Conference also decided to recall the enforcement contingents from Naples and Piedmont in order to demonstrate clearly that the interventionists had no secret design of annexing territory. Nevertheless, the "Congress system" was at its end; Metternich had been unable to win acceptance of the enforcement principle.

Navarino. Yet while Metternich's system was dead, his idea lived on and soon found an important application, this time in the interest of liberalism. When the Greek insurrection broke out, Alexander, true to the principles of the Holy Alliance, condemned the revolution, although it had been prepared with Russian help. The Tsar sympathized with the Greeks and felt morally obliged to support them against the Sublime Porte, not only for religious reasons but also because, apparently, he was a member of the secret Greek organization which prepared the uprising.

As time went by, Russia forsook the Holy Alliance and openly supported the Greeks; in 1827 the former Russian Foreign Minister Capo d'Istria, himself a Greek, was elected President of Greece. While the powers were unwilling to permit Russian action against Turkey, the Greeks, in a clever move of political warfare, put themselves under British protection. Thereupon, Russia and Britain, later joined by France, concluded the Treaty of London (1827), requesting Turkey immediately to conclude an armistice, threatening otherwise to support the Greeks. When the Turks refused, British, French, and Russian naval forces destroyed, in an international peace enforcement action, the Egyptian-Turkish fleet at Navarino. Though Turkey's naval

---

[12] Golo Mann, *Secretary of Europe: The Life of Friedrich Gentz, Enemy of Napoleon,* New Haven, Yale University Press, 1946, p. 271.

power was thus broken, Turkey was not ready to yield. England and France showed no intention of further intervention, but Russia declared war and, in a hard campaign in which she almost suffered defeat, advanced to Adrianople.

At that stage, of course, the war assumed an entirely different character; the question was no longer Greek but Turkish independence. Further Russian advances toward Constantinople would have compelled Britain to intervene against Russia. The Battle of Navarino had greatly damaged British interests. The elimination of the Turkish fleet had upset the naval balance, thereby menacing British security. When, after initial enthusiasm, this unexpected result became clear, British public opinion was enraged. Admiral Codrington, the commander of the allied intervention squadron, was recalled and a Cabinet crisis was barely avoided. Russia hastened to make peace with Turkey.

In Greece the basic principle of the Congress of Vienna, namely, the sacrosanctity of the *status quo* and legitimacy, had been violated by the powers themselves. Metternich stated that with the maintenance of all legal rights "alone can general peace be possible." Peace is thus the preservation of the *status quo,* which must be maintained by crushing all forces liable or willing to upset existing conditions. Obviously, such a solution must sooner or later lead to ultrareaction and radically stifle political progress. The Holy Alliance would have become an instrument of "reaction" even if Metternich had been a "liberal."

Enforcement Actions. Despite Navarino, peace enforcement was not entirely discontinued. Significantly, it was exclusively employed against *weak* countries. In 1832, Franco-British land and naval forces intervened against Holland to secure Belgium's independence. In 1835, England and France blockaded the Argentine coast; ten years later, in order to check expansionist tendencies of Argentina against Uruguay, French and British troops occupied the latter country and blockaded the Rio de la Plata. In 1896, the Armenian massacres led to a British proposal for intervention, but Russia declined to join in the action and prepared instead to seize Constantinople and the Straits should the intervention take place—an interesting indication of the complications which may result from peace enforcement.

In 1897, an insurrection in Crete threatened to cause civil war in Macedonia; the powers requested both Greece and Turkey to withdraw their troops on pain of "measures of constraint"; rejection of the note was answered by blockade and occupation of the island. A new uprising occurred in 1905, the insurrectionists claiming union with Greece. Though this union was opposed by the powers, it was proclaimed by Crete. The powers withdrew; they had been unable to impose the will of "Europe."

In 1900, an international army was sent to China to repress the Boxer uprising. Taken by itself, the intervention was successful; yet it gave the Russians an opportunity to occupy Manchuria, an event which was the chief cause of the Russo-Japanese War. The intervention, therefore, was a remote cause of the Russian Revolution of 1905 and the emergence of Japan as a world power.

In addition to these actions, there were some others which, though ostensibly carried out for the cause of peace, actually had different motivation. There was the intervention against Mohammed Ali of Egypt in 1840 which put an end to his quarrel with the Sultan and compelled him to return the Turkish fleet to Turkey, but which had the more important result that it strengthened England's position in the eastern Mediterranean and redressed the naval balance that had been upset at Navarino. In October, 1848, the Russians, in agreement with the Turks, occupied the Danubian principalities which had become rebellious; Russian forces stayed until 1851. In 1849, a revolution broke out in Hungary; the Tsar's offer of help was accepted by the Austrian Emperor, and Russian and Austrian forces crushed the rebellion.

The Twentieth Century. The first person of outstanding international stature to bring up the idea of peace coercion in the present century was Theodore Roosevelt, proponent of the "international sheriff." He spoke of such a scheme in a message to Congress in 1904. In an address delivered to the Nobel Prize Committee at Oslo in 1910, he advocated a forceful combination of "those great nations which sincerely desire peace."

In June of the same year, a resolution was submitted to Congress by Mr. Bartholdt from Missouri and Mr. Bennet from New York, and received the consent of both Houses. To limit armaments, mankind was invited ". . . to consider the expediency . . . of constituting the combined navies of the world in an international force for the preservation of universal peace, . . ." [13]

The First World War. Shortly after the outbreak of World War I, the idea of peace coercion made new headway. Theodore Roosevelt restated his position; Hamilton Holt suggested a league endowed with force for the administration of sanctions; the Dutchman Hendrik Dunlop published a little book in which he suggested that an "international *gendarmerie*" ought to be established with a strength of 1 per cent of the population, with contingents in every country; 25 per cent of the contingents were to consist of police troops native to the territory where the contingents were located.

The idea of peace coercion found a particularly good reception in the United States where a "League to Enforce Peace" was created under the leadership of former President Taft and A. Lawrence Lowell, president of Harvard University.[14] At a conference in Philadelphia in June, 1915, a program was adopted which called for compulsory arbitration and the appli-

[13] *Congressional Record,* Part 8, 8545, 1910.

[14] Ruhl T. Bartlett, *The League to Enforce Peace,* Chapel Hill, The University of North Carolina Press, 1944. This book deals also with American prewar pacifist activities, including proposals for international forces and later American developments connected with the founding of the League of Nations. (See also Theodore Marburg, *Development of the League of Nations Idea,* New York, Macmillan, 1932; Sylvester John Hemleben, *Plans for World Peace through Six Centuries,* Chicago, University of Chicago Press, 1943.)

cation of economic and military force by all states against any state resorting to war without submitting its disputes to pacific settlement.

THE LEAGUE OF NATIONS

Preliminaries. During the discussions about the Covenant of the League of Nations, Clemenceau and Léon Bourgeois, the French delegate, suggested that the League be provided with a powerful executive. In some form or other, most drafts for the Constitution of the League envisaged military sanctions, *e.g.,* the plans of Phillimore, Smuts, Cecil, and Hurst-Miller, the German and Italian schemes, the project of the League to Enforce Peace, and that of the Fabian Society. The French plan, which was the most elaborate, dealt with military sanctions in the following manner:

The execution of the military sanctions on land or at sea shall be entrusted either to an international force or to one or more Powers, members of the League of Nations, to whom a mandate in that behalf shall be given.

The International Body shall have at its disposal a military force supplied by the various member States of sufficient strength: (I) to secure the execution of its decisions and those of the international tribunal; (II) to overcome in case of need, any forces which may be opposed to the League of Nations in the event of armed conflict.

The strength of the international force and the national contingents was to be fixed by the "International Body." The League army was to be distributed over the globe and to be commanded by a permanent general staff of the League. The activities of national armies were to be controlled by the League, which had the right "at any time to require that the member states introduce any alteration into their national system of recruiting which the staff may report to be necessary."

This idea had been conceived by Clemenceau as a device to improve France's military security; because, fully aware of France's inner weakness, the French leader wanted to prevent British and American disarmament which he foresaw and dreaded. Whatever the motivation might have been, President Wilson refused to discuss the project on the ground that "the United States would never ratify any treaty which put the force of the United States at the disposal of such group or body." The idea that, instead of a League army, the member states should put troops at the League's disposal, was equally vetoed by Wilson. "The only method lies in our having confidence in the good faith of the nations who belong to the League." [15]

The Covenant. It is in the nature of things that an all-embracing international treaty designed for the maintenance of peace must contain some stipulation about unified action in case of aggression. In spite of Anglo-

[15] Leopold Schwarzschild, *World in Trance: From Versailles to Pearl Harbor,* New York, J. Fischer, 1942, p. 89.

American abhorrence against obligations which may commit them to military action under unforeseen circumstances, the Covenant contained, in addition to several random references, Articles 10 and 16 which deal with peace enforcement. Article 10 was almost entirely of American origin and was, incidentally, one of the chief reasons why the Senate refused to ratify the Covenant. It reads as follows:

The Members of the League undertake to respect and preserve as against external aggression the territorial integrity and existing political independence of all Members of the League. In case of any such aggression or in case of any threat or danger of such aggression the Council shall advise upon the means by which this obligation shall be fulfilled.

In Article 11 any war or threat of war was declared to be "a matter of concern to the whole League, and the League shall take any action that may be deemed wise and effectual to safeguard the peace of nations."

It is hardly necessary to belabor the vagueness of these Articles; speaking legally, this very vagueness would have entitled the Council to advise even military coercion. However, while in domestic politics few governments will hesitate to take the fullest possible advantage of all the rights conferred upon them by law, in international treaties general authorizations, such as Article 10 of the Covenant, carry no weight; their loopholes are interpreted so as to permit a policy of "wait and see."

The framers of the Covenant felt this themselves and, making a concession to the French proposal, included Article 16, which stated that any aggressor should be "deemed to have committed an act of war against all other Members of the League"; to oppose the aggressor, the League was to order economic sanctions.

Article 16 stipulated clearly that these economic sanctions were to be complete, that is to say, that *all* trade or financial relations were to be severed and that *all* financial, commercial, or personal intercourse was to be prohibited. According to the mandatory language of this Article the imposition of only partial sanctions, as occurred in 1936, was excluded, although it could be justified by various other Articles and, in practice, by the unanimity rule. In addition to economic sanctions, Article 16 envisaged the use of military power. The pertinent paragraph follows: "It shall be the duty of the Council . . . to recommend to the several governments concerned what effective military, naval or air force the Members of the League shall severally contribute to the armed forces to be used to protect the Covenants of the League."

In a very indirect and oblique manner, this Article speaks of armed forces for the protection of the League covenants. The Article did not *direct* that military force was to be used against the aggressor. Nor were the conditions determined wherein the Council would have been obliged to recommend military coercion. Moreover, the seemingly forceful wording of Article 16 was voided by Article 5 which stipulated that the Council could make recommendations only upon *unanimous* approval. In practice, therefore, the Council was prevented from recommending military sanctions.

The Record of the League. The League was not entirely unsuccessful; out of sixty-six, it settled thirty-five international disputes. It was able to settle disputes if and when both litigants wanted to accept the arbitration awards and if and when, as in the Swedish-Finnish conflicts about the Åland Islands, they did not exploit their disputes as a pretext for aggression. When, however, one country was determined and able to carry out aggressive plans, the League was powerless and usually ended up by pronouncing Solomonlike judgments which legalized the aggressor's conquest. An example was the occupation of Vilnius by Poland, in connection with which an abortive attempt was made to create an international force to supervise a plebiscite. The idea was quickly dropped when Russia, at that time not a member of the League, declared that the presence of an international army close to its borders would constitute a *casus belli*. Apparently the Kremlin did not believe that peace enforcement could ever be made for the sake of peace alone.[16]

ATTEMPTS TO STRENGTHEN THE LEAGUE

The refusal of the United States to ratify the League of Nations and to enter into a security agreement with Great Britain and France left France in a very precarious military position. Great Britain, feeling that her own security was intimately linked to that of France, opened negotiations for a mutual security pact. These negotiations soon encountered difficulties; yet as other nations also were interested in security, the discussions were transferred to the League.

In 1922, the third Assembly of the League adopted the famous Resolution XIV which called for a defensive treaty open to all countries and based upon a plan of military and mutual defense. Accordingly, the draft "Treaty for Mutual Assistance" was submitted to the Assembly in 1923. It suggested a general pact supplemented by regional military agreements; the Council was to determine the military forces which each member was to provide in case of aggression and was to appoint a commander in chief under whose orders the military contingents were to fight. The draft was not favorably received. Strongest opposition was made by the British (Conservative) Government which made the objection, among others, that the unanimity rule would paralyze the Council and dangerously delay its intervention.

In view of this criticism, a new document was prepared which became known as the "Geneva Protocol," and whose official title was "Protocol for

[16] For these and various other cases, see E. H. Carr, *International Relations since the Peace Treaties*, London, Macmillan & Co., Ltd., 1940, pp. 103*ff*. For a complete survey of League disputes including statistics of success and failure, see Quincy Wright, *A Study of War*, Chicago, University of Chicago Press, 1940, Vol. II, pp. 1429–1431.

the Pacific Settlement of International Disputes." The Protocol was to make possible implementation of the disarmament provisions of the Covenant. The disarming states were to be assured that the reduction of armaments would not impair their security.

The Covenant had proclaimed the "moral solidarity of the new era," but it had failed to provide for compulsory arbitration or effective international jurisdiction. The Protocol, essentially a proposal for the amendment of the Covenant, was to remedy this "great omission of the Covenant." [17] It was also to correct the previous draft treaty which had conferred too much discretionary power upon the Council, particularly with respect to the determination of the aggressor. It was felt that the aggressor should not be determined *ad hoc,* on the basis of actually existing circumstances, but according to general criteria previously established in a binding legal form.

The Protocol is an ingenious piece of work and still remains a most logical plan for the elimination of war. The basis of the Protocol was an agreement between all signatory states "in no case to resort to war" (Article 2) and, for certain cases, to "recognize as compulsory ipso facto and without special agreement, the jurisdiction of the Permanent Court of International Justice" (Article 3). Cases not covered by the Statute of the Court were to be submitted to the Council. Failing unanimous decision (minus the votes of the litigants), the Council was to appoint a committee of arbitrators whose recommendations were to be binding (Article 4, paragraphs 2, 3, and 6). The Assembly, too, was entitled to arbitrate disputes by majority vote, or if no majority could be obtained, to remit the case to arbitration (Article 6).

In case of dispute, as well as before and during proceedings for pacific settlement, the quarreling states were to abstain from taking "any measure of military, naval, air, industrial or economic mobilization, or, in general any action of a nature likely to extend the dispute or render it more acute" (Article 7). The Council was entitled to investigate and inquire into any complaint arising from this provision and to "decide upon the measures to be taken with a view to end as soon as possible a situation of a nature to threaten the peace of the world" (Article 7). Moreover, it was recommended that the litigants create demilitarized zones between their forces and place them under the Council's supervision (Article 9). Under modern conditions of aerial warfare the usefulness of demilitarized zones separating hostile ground forces has declined. The various peace plans of the 1920's and 1930's were based on the implicit assumption of a slow-moving and lengthy war.

The Protocol then proceeded to define the aggressor (Article 10):

Every State which resorts to war in violation of the undertakings contained in the Covenant or in the present Protocol is an aggressor. Violation of the rules laid

---

[17] David Hunter Miller, *The Geneva Protocol,* New York, Macmillan, 1925, p. 201; P. T. Noel-Baker, *The Geneva Protocol for the Pacific Settlement of International Disputes,* London, King, 1925; Wehberg, *The Outlawry of War,* Washington, Carnegie Endowment, 1931, pp. 26–32.

down for a demilitarized zone shall be held equivalent to resort to war. In the event of hostilities having broken out, any State shall be presumed to be an aggressor, unless a decision of the Council, which must be taken unanimously, shall otherwise declare.

If the Council does not at once succeed in determining the aggressor, it shall be bound to enjoin upon the belligerents an armistice, and shall fix the terms, acting, if need be, by a two-thirds majority, and shall supervise its execution. Any belligerent which has refused to accept the armistice or has violated its terms shall be deemed an aggressor.

This was a masterly way to preserve the unanimity rule and yet to enable the Council to act if no unanimous decision could be reached. Whatever the merits of the conflict or the interests and policies of the various states, the Council was obligated to enforce an *armistice* and thereby to end hostilities in a practical, though not in a legal, manner. It was mandatory to designate as aggressor any state which did not comply with the armistice terms; no unanimity rule applied for the determination of armistice violations. That it may be open to interpretation whether or not a state complied with the Council's orders, is another question. No provision was made for the voting procedure should any disagreement develop with respect to this point.

Once the aggressor had been determined, the Council was to "call upon the signatory States to apply forthwith against the aggressor the sanctions provided by Article 11 of the present Protocol." These sanctions were those of Article 16 of the Covenant, but Article 12 of the Protocol prescribed that, to avoid improvisation, effective plans for economic and financial sanctions should be drawn up *in advance*. Article 13 specified the nature of military sanctions. According to this article,

The Council shall be entitled to receive undertakings from States determining in advance the military, naval, and air forces which they would be able to bring into action immediately to ensure the fulfillment of the obligations in regard to sanctions which result from the Covenant and the present Protocol. . . . The said States may, in accordance with any agreements which they may previously have concluded, bring to the assistance of a particular State, which is the victim of aggression, their military, naval and air forces.

Although a considerable strengthening of the Covenant's Article 16, this Article still left to the individual states the right to determine for themselves the strength of their contingents.

Other shortcomings may be reviewed briefly. In a report of the British delegates to the Prime Minister, it was explained how, by preserving the unanimity rule, action could still be guaranteed by making the test of aggression automatic and "presuming" a certain state to be the aggressor; this "presumption . . . is to hold good until the Council has made a unanimous decision *to the contrary*. If the presumption stands it is considered sufficient to justify the application of sanctions." [18]

[18] Miller, *op. cit.*, p. 244.

This solution, it was claimed, eliminated the difficulty of a "procedure by a majority vote" which "might have resulted in a State being obliged to apply sanctions against its own judgment."

However, it can be readily seen that it did no such thing; if a state believed that sanctions were injurious to its own interests, it might not obey the injunctions of the Council whether the attacking nation were "deemed" or merely "presumed" to be the aggressor.

The obligations of the Protocol were, in the words of Dr. Beneš, *"imperfect obligations* [19] in the sense that no sanctions are provided for against any party which shall have failed loyally and effectively to co-operate in protecting the Covenant and resisting every act of aggression."

This is, of course, the crux of the whole matter; the problem of peace coercion reappears on a higher level. Yet on this level this problem can be "solved" only by ignoring the noncooperative state—in which case there would be no coercion; or by presuming it to participate in aggression; or by forcing it to participate in the enforcement action. In both latter cases, the original aggressor would be gratuitously provided with an ally.

The Protocol contained no provisions for the maintenance of basic military strength. The possibility that under conditions of general disarmament as well as under other conditions the aggressor may be the strongest Power was not considered. Nor was it taken into account that surprise attack may make possible the rapid and cheap execution of territorial conquest by the aggressor. Like other peace projects, the Protocol sanctified the *status quo*.[20]

On the other hand, if a majority of the signatory Powers had become opposed to the existing international arrangement, aggression might have been approved by the Council. In 1914, Germany was about to demand that France, as a token of her peaceful intentions, should permit German troops to occupy Toul and Verdun, the two strongest fortresses in the French defense belt. A Council which is in favor of the aggressor may impose similar terms on the victim country on the ground that noncompliance with the "just" demands of the attacker constitutes aggression.

Austen Chamberlain pointed out that the discontinuation of military preparations and activity during settlement proceedings would frequently benefit the aggressor. Before starting his operations, he may arrange his timetables in such a manner that compliance with the Council's request would not weaken, but further increase, his striking power. By contrast, the victim, not having expected the onslaught, would have made no preparations. The perpetuation of this condition during the "cooling-off period" would actually penalize the victim country. Alternately, by resisting such a development, the victim country may technically become an aggressor. Furthermore, as

---

[19] Italics added.
[20] For a justification of *status quo* treaties, see Salvador de Madariaga, *Disarmament,* New York, Coward-McCann, 1929, *passim,* particularly p. 130.

Bismarck and Hitler have shown, the victim often can be forced to make the first attack.

Whatever the merits or demerits of the Protocol, it never came to life. England under the Labor government had already voiced its opposition to the principles laid down in the document. Ramsay MacDonald took the position that "our interests for peace are far greater than our interests in creating a machinery of defense. A machinery of defense is easy to create but beware lest in creating it you destroy the chances of peace." He pleaded confidence in human nature but, as Jules Cambon rightly commented, the British Prime Minister forgot Pascal's word that justice without force is powerless.

The Labor government was soon succeeded by a Conservative government which took the attitude that it could not accept an unlimited obligation of arbitration in its own disputes and would not ask other nations to accept such an obligation.

To replace the Protocol, Chamberlain suggested that those nations whose conflicts and differences were most likely again to lead to war should bind themselves not to attack each other and to submit their disputes to arbitration. This suggestion was the origin of the Locarno Pact.[21]

THE FRENCH PROPOSALS OF 1932

Despite these setbacks, the idea of military peace enforcement continued to be discussed. In 1929, Nicolas Politis declared in the Preparatory Disarmament Commission that the establishment of an international force was an essential prerequisite for the reduction of armaments. In 1930, Lord David Davies published his book, *The Problem of the Twentieth Century*, wherein he argued with an imposing array of historical facts that peace cannot be preserved except by an international police. In September, 1931, Poland, in an official communication to the Preparatory Disarmament Commission, suggested the creation of an international army.

At the beginning of the Disarmament Conference, France again came forward with a plan for an international armed force which was to secure peace and disarmament. The proposal was presented by André Tardieu on February 5, 1932. It envisaged: "(1) An international police force to prevent war. (2) A first contingent of coercionary forces to repress war, and to bring immediate assistance to any State victim of aggression."

The police force was to be ". . . permanently available with complete freedom of passage to occupy in times of emergency areas where a threat of war has arisen. . . ." It was to be composed of contingents furnished by

[21] Various attempts to amend the Covenant and to establish world security (*e.g.*, the Pact of Paris, the Litvinov Protocol, the "model treaties," the Convention for Improving the Means of Preventing War, etc.) are described by J. W. Wheeler-Bennett in *Disarmament and Security since Locarno 1925–1931* (London, G. Allen, 1932).

each of the contracting parties. It was a special feature of the French project that offensive weapons, such as heavy artillery, warships with a displacement exceeding 10,000 tons, heavy bombers, and large submarines, were no longer to be part of national armaments but were to be put at the exclusive disposal of the international police. Civil aviation was to be internationalized under the League's control.

The French proposal received a very cool reception. The English paper *Manchester Guardian* suggested that it had been put forward to wreck the Disarmament Conference. The representatives of many countries considered the proposals as theoretically sound, albeit impractical.

Maxim Litvinov, Russian Foreign Commissar, attacked the idea as such and tried to prove its futility. An international police force, so he stated, would neither prevent war nor offer effective assistance to the victim of aggression. In the past, no aggressor ever desisted from his projects merely because he had to fight several nations. So it will remain in future. It is all a question of relative strength. The international police cannot be very strong—a few hundred thousand men against the millions of a strong aggressive nation. Hence the aggressor will only have to modify his strategy to protect himself against sanctions. After having made several critical remarks about the League's ability to determine the aggressor or to assist victims of aggression, Litvinov showed concern lest the nation which, by virtue of its alliances, agreements, or general influence, came to dominate the League might use the international police for its exclusive benefit—a circumlocution for his fear that the League army would lead an attack against the Soviet Union.

Shortly afterward the French dropped the project. In November, 1932, a new plan was presented by Herriot. The proposal envisaged that

Each of the contracting Powers will place permanently at the disposal of the League of Nations, as a contingent for joint action, a small number of *specialized units* consisting of troops serving a relatively long term and provided with the powerful materials prohibited for the national armies . . . these specialized contingents will be kept constantly ready for action.[22] [Italics supplied.]

Like Metternich's system, the plan contained security provisions to be carried out on different levels—general obligations to be assumed by all signatories, and continental and regional arrangements, the obligations becoming increasingly stronger and more definite as the area is narrowed.

Hitler's accession to power put an end to all discussions about international organization. The idea of peace enforcement was abandoned as a practical possibility when France, in 1933, refused the Polish Marshal Pilsudski's proposal to intervene against German rearmament, and when, in 1936, England was unwilling to honor the Locarno Pact against the reoccupation of the Rhineland. Officially, the idea of peace coercion did not reappear

[22] Davies, *op. cit.*, p. 797.

before the Conference of Dumbarton Oaks in 1944. Even the most inveterate pacifists realized that it was futile to discuss peace or peace enforcement in a world that was rapidly heading to Armageddon.

THE UNITED NATIONS CHARTER

The Charter reveals the effort that has been made to avoid some shortcomings of the Covenant and the Geneva Protocol, although not all the strong points of these documents were salvaged. The new document shows weaknesses of its own. From the point of view of peace enforcement, the Charter has fewer "teeth" than the Protocol.

The outstanding feature of the Charter is the authority that it bestows upon the Security Council. It is stipulated that the Security Council shall "be able to function continuously" (Article 28). The United Nations "confer on the Security Council primary responsibility for the maintenance of international peace and security, and agree that in carrying out its duties under this responsibility the Security Council acts on their behalf" (Article 24). "The Members of the United Nations agree to accept and carry out the decisions of the Security Council in accordance with the present Charter" (Article 25). This sweeping provision implies that a country may be obliged to abide by a decision to which it is no party and which runs counter to its intentions and interests.

The Council is entitled to investigate any international dispute and even any *situation*—note the widening of scope—either on its own initiative, or upon invitation or complaint of any member or nonmembers. The General Assembly "may call the attention of the Security Council to situations which are likely to endanger international peace and security" (Article 11, paragraph 3). Yet "while the Security Council is exercising in respect of any dispute or situation the functions assigned to it in the present Charter, the General Assembly shall not make any recommendation with regard to that dispute or situation unless the Security Council so requests" (Article 12).

This virtually unlimited authority of the Security Council stands in marked contrast to the rights of the Assembly, which in security matters is merely allowed "to discuss, debate, reveal, expose, lay open—to perform, that is to say, the healthful and ventilating functions of a free deliberative body, without the right or duty to enact or legislate." [23] With less verbiage it could be said that the General Assembly has no rights and but one duty—to talk, and it may discharge that duty during international disputes only if the Security Council grants permission (Article 12). The Security Council, as the executive, has no legislative counterpart; it has to make the laws itself, but in many instances it has also to act as the judiciary—a construction

[23] Edward R. Stettinius, Jr., chairman of the United States Delegation to the United Nations Conference at San Francisco, Letter of June 26, 1945, to the President, Department of State, Conference Serial No. 72, p. 7.

without checks and balances which runs counter to democratic-liberal ideas, but which is consistent with absolutistic constitutional law.

The Security Council may, whenever it chooses, "recommend appropriate procedures or methods" of adjusting a dispute or a situation (Article 36), with the proviso that "legal disputes should as a general rule be referred by the parties to the International Court of Justice." Hence the Council has primary jurisdiction over political and nonjusticiable disputes.

The most far-reaching powers are conferred upon the Security Council by Article 39 which reads: "The Security Council shall determine the existence of any threat to the peace, breach of the peace, or act of aggression and shall make recommendations, or decide what measures shall be taken . . . to maintain or restore international peace and security."

Before making recommendations or decisions, however, the Security Council may call upon the parties "to comply with such provisional measures as it deems necessary or desirable" (Article 40). This seems to be a broader as well as a vaguer formulation of the Protocol's provisions for the creation of demilitarized zones. Article 51 accords to any state "the inherent right of individual or collective self-defense if an armed attack occurs." Since, however, aggressive acts are often termed "acts of defense," this Article may leave wide leeway to a diplomatically and propagandistically skillful aggressor. One danger is avoided, another courted; the squaring of the circle is not more difficult than the legal construction of eternal peace.

Besides the right to make recommendations, the Council may decide upon the employment of nonmilitary measures of coercion, such as "complete or partial (*sic!*) interruption of economic relations and of rail, sea, air, postal, telegraphic, radio, and other means of communication, and the severance of diplomatic relations" (Article 41). It may also order military measures of coercion "as may be necessary to maintain or restore international peace and security. Such action may include demonstrations, blockade, and other operations by air, sea, or land forces of members of the United Nations" (Article 42). In short, the Council has the power to order military intervention or, in traditional parlance, war. In its military decisions, the Council would be advised and assisted by a technical Military Staff Committee, which would include the chiefs of staff of the permanent members or their representatives.

The members are obligated to carry out the decisions of the Security Council even if they do not agree with them. Yet like the Covenant and the Protocol, the Charter contains only "imperfect obligations" in that no action is stipulated that may be taken against members refusing to abide by the Council's decisions.

In theory, the Council may commit any country which is not a permanent member of the Security Council to warlike acts without that country's desire or declaration of war. The right to declare war may thus no longer be considered as the exclusive prerogative of national sovereigns. However, the text is extremely vague. How far will warlike acts carried out at the order of the Security Council legally commit the countries of origin of the military contingents? The position could very well be taken that once a military unit has come under the jurisdiction of the Security Council, it is no longer part of the armed forces of its native country. Such an interpretation would mean that while the members may subscribe to the policies of the Security Council *qua* members of the United Nations, they can disavow them *qua* independent national states.

The International Police. Articles 43 and 45 endow the Security Council with the means necessary to enforce its decisions. These articles stipulate that "all Members of the United Nations . . . undertake to make available to the Security Council, on its call and in accordance with a special agreement or agreements, armed forces, assistance, and facilities, including rights of passage" (Article 43). To make possible "urgent military measures, Members shall hold immediately available national air force contingents for combined international enforcement action" (Article 45).

Special agreements shall fix "the numbers and types of forces, their degree of readiness and general location, and the nature of the facilities and assistance to be provided" (Article 43). The Security Council can plan for the combined action of the national air-force contingents only "within the limits laid down in the special agreement or agreements" (Article 45). It is true that the agreements shall be negotiated at the initiative of the Security Council, but they "shall be subject to ratification by the signatory states in accordance with their respective constitutional processes" (Article 43).

The Security Council and Peace Enforcement. Enthusiastic supporters of the United Nations claim that these provisions offer a satisfactory mechanism through which world peace should be preserved. If this were true, mankind indeed would have entered a new phase of its history. If it were untrue or only partially true, there would be created a false sense of security which ultimately would harm rather than help the cause of peace. It is necessary, therefore, to test the provisions of the Charter with sober objectivity and to beware of misunderstanding and illusions.

It may be granted that the United Nations Charter makes it possible to stop war as long as the Security Council takes action. Decisions by the Security Council can be made by the affirmative vote of seven of its eleven members. However, on substantive as distinguished from procedural matters, each of its "permanent members," China, France, the Soviet Union, the United Kingdom, and the United States, must cast an affirmative vote. (The questions as to whether the concurring vote of *all* members is required in order to give the Security Council the power to act, and whether absence or abstention of a permanent member is equivalent to a negative vote, arose when the Security Council voted, in 1950, to recommend the use of military force against aggression in Korea during the walkout of the Soviet representative. Not so surprisingly, the various official interpretations as well as law experts are widely disagreed. The drafters of the Charter, it appears, did

not foresee such a situation. See below.) The veto or unanimity rule according to which Security Council decisions concerning the coercive settlement
of disputes (under Chapter VI of the Charter) must be made with the concurrent votes of the permanent members does not apply to the provisions for
the pacific settlement of disputes (Chapter V of the United Nations Charter).
Decisions under this heading are to be made with the party to the dispute
abstaining from voting. These provisions mean that so long as the Security
Council negotiates an amicable settlement, a permanent member involved in
the quarrel cannot make use of his right of veto. Yet the veto still may be
invoked by other members of the Council.

By contrast, if the Security Council discusses "action with respect to the
threat to the peace, breaches of the peace, and acts of aggression," and if it
deliberates about the use of sanctions and military force, the great powers
may make full use of their rights of veto. Each of the permanent members
has the right to block decisions of the Security Council. Any permanent member of the Security Council, whether a party to a dispute or not, can prevent
the United Nations from taking coercive action. He can condone aggressive
measures on the part of friends and forestall sanctions against himself should
he indulge in acts of aggression. However, should the permanent members
adopt an identical policy on a security issue and unite in their desire to stop
the conflict, they would have the legal power as well as the military strength
to do so.

It follows that a coercive Security Council decision can be obtained only
if (1) none of the permanent members is a party to the dispute, indirectly
participates in the conflict, or supports one of the litigants; and (2) the conflict does not affect the interests of any of the permanent members. Clearly,
such cases will be exceedingly rare. In practice, the veto precludes the possibility that a great power ever will be coerced by collective United Nations
action to keep the peace.

The veto may be justified on the ground that enforcement action without
participation or approval of the "leading nations" would lack military striking power as well as truly supranational authority desirable for common
international action. The present voting procedure, no doubt, is a little more
workable than the unanimity rule of the Covenant of the League of Nations
which permitted any small country to block decisions. Yet while the voting
rule of the Covenant practically prevented enforcement action, the rules of
the Charter provide that the Security Council can act only on *secondary
issues.*

Threats to world peace do not arise from small nations except in so far
as a small state may fire the first shot with the backing of a major military
power. Aggression of world significance cannot occur if the big military
powers are united in their intent to prevent war. It occurs *only* if the aggressor has succeeded in splitting the major powers, or if the aggressor is himself a first-class military nation, or if at least one major power has decided

that the time has come to go to war. The Charter may offer protection against small dangers, but *conflicts which can be settled by the Security Council do not constitute a threat to world peace* except, perhaps, indirectly.

There is only one exception to the axiom that world peace is menaced only if and when there is a conflict involving at least one permanent member of the Security Council: conflicts involving great powers such as Germany or Japan which are not presently members of the United Nations, or nations which in the future may become powerful and which, like India, are not permanent members of the Security Council. In fact, any of these three nations is potentially about as powerful as France or China. If this contingency should arise, it is likely that at least one of the permanent members would condone or even support the peace violation. The days of World War II are over, and no common interest unites the five permanent members against Germany or Japan (or India). While legally the veto does not apply to action against states which were enemies of any signatory of the Charter during the last war (Article 107), this provision has become meaningless.

In short, whenever there will be a real international crisis, the Security Council will be inoperative because of the veto. He who reads a different interpretation into the Charter must make the assumption that, at the crucial moment, one or more of the permanent members will vote against their own interests, oppose their own policies, and act against themselves.

"Uniting for Peace." In 1950, the United States, Britain, France, and four smaller nations tried to amend the United Nations Charter. Acknowledging that the Security Council cannot fulfill the functions for which allegedly it was designed, they attempted to bestow the necessary authority on the General Assembly. They submitted a resolution entitled "Uniting for Peace" which provided that,[24]

If the Security Council, because of lack of unanimity of the permanent members, fails to exercise its primary responsibility for the maintenance of international peace and security in any case where there appears to be a threat to the peace, breach of the peace, or act of aggression, the General Assembly shall consider the matter immediately with a view to making appropriate recommendations to members for collective measures, including in the case of a breach of the peace or act of aggression the use of armed force when necessary, to maintain or restore international peace and security.

The resolution, which passed by a vote of 52 to 5, stipulated that the General Assembly was to meet on twenty-four hours' notice on the request of any seven members of the Security Council or of the majority of all the United Nations members. A peace-observation commission and a collective-measures committee were formed to study and recommend measures to be taken under the resolution. Members were invited to allocate military forces for employment under the United Nations.

[24] For the complete text see the *United Nations Bulletin,* Nov. 15, 1950, pp. 508*f.*

It is highly questionable whether, legally, technically and politically, this resolution changed matters. For example, while the peace-observation commission supposedly would be sent into litigant states to study there "international tension the continuance of which is likely to endanger the maintenance of international peace and security," it can do so only with the consent of the state it proposes to visit. Furthermore, the provisions concerning the veto in the Security Council remain in full force. Thirdly, supposing an overwhelming vote in favor of peace enforcement by all the small and medium powers, it still would be impossible to generate substantial military strength unless at least *one* of the major powers complies with the vote. Yet if it does so, it may unleash counteraction by other major powers.

The fundamental problem remains: how can the General Assembly impose on member states compliance with its vote, especially as the Charter contains the glaring discrepancy that on the one hand, it imposes on members of the United Nations the obligation to carry out decisions by the United Nations but on the other (Article 2, 1) acknowledges "the sovereign equality of all its members"?

The practical meaning of the "Uniting for Peace" resolution is that *if* a major military power wants to engage in enforcement action, it might be able to obtain from the general assembly a vote authorizing this undertaking. This would be a moral and political asset. Moreover, through this vote, the enforcing state may be able to acquire associates for the operation or as it were, to conclude an *ad hoc* alliance. On the other hand, no major power will engage in an enforcement action unless it feels that its interests are at stake. In this respect then, the familiar situation has been reestablished; it always was customary for states to take action if they felt that their interests were menaced. This remains true, Charter or no Charter, although the intervention now may be given a more pleasing name. But, contrary to the stipulations of Article 1, such interventions would *not* constitute "effective collective measures for the prevention and removal of threats to the peace and for the suppression of acts of aggression." The action would not be "collective" but unilateral or multilateral, as of yore. The action would be designed not to remove threats to the peace but to subdue threats to a particular big nation's interests, also as of yore. And the operation could not be run as a process of prevention unless unilateral or multilateral *preventive war* were to be approved by the General Assembly—an unexpected result indeed.

So what remains? On the strength of the "Uniting for Peace" resolution, unilateral or multilateral actions on the part of great powers henceforth may be "authorized" by an approving vote of a world forum. Against this dubious advantage, an enforcing nation which subjects itself to General Assembly control could find its political, economic, and military freedom of action curtailed dangerously.

The handicaps of such a situation were experienced by the United States during the Korean War. Actions under the banner of the General Assembly lack the advantages either of a truly collective enforcement action or of a closely knit alliance. The arrangement gives small nations undue influence over the military and political decisions of the powers bearing the brunt of the fighting, with the result that they prevent these powers from carrying out their mission successfully. Yet they may make almost no contributions to the struggle. It is unlikely that the pseudocollective action of the Korean War ever will be repeated. After all, the test of this affair was not whether the United States would be supported by Britain, Turkey, Thailand, or Peru but whether the North Koreans and Chinese could be persuaded from desisting from aggression and whether the Soviet Union could be induced to withhold help from the aggressor or to contribute itself to the halting of the aggression. In this test, the only one which counts, the United Nations failed lamentably.

Can the Veto be Abolished? Since the legal standing of the "Uniting for Peace" resolution is highly doubtful, we must revert to a discussion of the Security Council.

The opinion is often voiced that through the abolition of the veto the United Nations may be transformed into a reliable instrument of peace preservation. Yet while it may be possible to abolish the veto *de jure,* it is questionable whether it can be abolished *de facto.*

It is axiomatic that a nation which vetoes an enforcement action can neither be expected nor be compelled to put military forces at the disposal of the United Nations; it would withhold its military contingent from participating in that particular action. Suppose, for example, that six nonpermanent members and one permanent member resolve to coerce an aggressor of significant military strength. Although they may be supported by a few other small nations, the military superiority of the international force would hardly be sufficient to stop the aggressor. If one or several of the permanent members were to oppose the action, it certainly could not be carried out, except by risking full-fledged war which, for that matter, might be lost. Nor may, for geographical reasons, the "international police" of a rump Council always be able to get at its opponent. For example, China as a permanent member, supported by some European, Central American, and Near Eastern nations, could not coerce the Argentine.

In the Korean case the facts of the military equation were that the United States, though it was the world's strongest military power, thought it could *not* deploy in Korea strength sufficient to subdue the aggressor; and believed that it could neither withdraw forces from other theaters nor carry the war to a definite conclusion without risking the counterintervention of hostile "permanent members."

It is conceivable that the Charter can be amended to the effect that the permanent members may vote by *absolute* majority. The veto of one great power could then be overruled and would not be sufficient to block decisions by the Security Council.

Whether the Council could act if supported by only four great powers is dependent upon the case. If, for instance, Portugal were the aggressor and Russia vetoed coercion, it would undoubtedly be possible for the remaining great powers, together with other members of the United Nations, to restrain Portugal by force, even against opposition by the Soviet Union. If, however, Honduras were the aggressor and the United States did not want interference, the four permanent members of the Security Council, even jointly with other nations, could not effectively engage in coercive action. To stop Honduras they would be compelled to cross the Atlantic and fight the United States—but none of them has adequate long-range power to make such a policy practically feasible.

Similar examples could be construed *ad libitum*. Whenever a great power lodges a veto and is willing to uphold its position by force, the veto can be overruled by superior force only. Whenever one of the "Big Three" becomes an aggressor, it can be restrained only by a total war that must be fought to the finish. Consequently, the success of the "enforcement action" depends on the relative military strength and preparedness of the aggressor and his opponents. Victory of the international police over a great power aggressor cannot be achieved if the latter is militarily the stronger.

Voting by absolute majority among the great powers would give positive results in all those cases where the vetoing nation does not feel that its vital interests are involved and restricts itself to a verbal demonstration. In all other cases, a voting procedure which permits peace enforcement against the will of one of the permanent members would reduce or eliminate the military superiority of the international force and lead to such a tension among the great powers that war might easily be the result. While, fundamentally, the abolition of the veto is advocated in order to facilitate the maintenance of peace, its removal may in fact make war inevitable.

The double danger that war could not be averted and that the United Nations might become utterly ineffective would be even more pronounced if the Security Council were to make decisions by the affirmative votes of three permanent and four nonpermanent members.

Three typical situations may occur:

1. The dispute is of vital importance to the vetoing power or powers, but only moderately important to the other great powers; hence the vetoing powers will take a very firm stand, while the others will be vacillating.

2. The vetoing powers' interests in a dispute are less vitally affected than those of other great powers.

3. A dispute affects the interests of both sides to an equal degree.

In case 1, an amended voting procedure would result either in war or in the open failure of the United Nations. It is virtually certain that the least interested great powers would not join in military action but rather be inclined to support the veto. Hence the veto would be likely to stand. In case 3, the form of voting procedure would be immaterial. War would be inevitable unless one side capitulated. However, any kind of majority vote may prove to be a complicating factor or provoke rather than prevent war.

Only in case 2 would a voting procedure without a veto be advantageous, because only then would it be materially and militarily possible to overrule the veto and to enforce peace. However, it is debatable whether this is at all a likely case and whether it would be in the interests of world peace to adopt a voting procedure that may be useful in exceptional and presumably quite inconsequential conflicts, but embarrassing and outright dangerous in most other disputes.

Atomic Veto? The same arguments hold true with respect to the proposal that atomic violations ought to be followed up by immediate punitive sanctions without any nation having the right to interpose a veto.

If the great powers were to remain in agreement about the inadmissibility of atomic violations, the existence or nonexistence of the veto would make no difference. Substantial violations will occur *only* in the case of basic disunity among the great powers.

While an agreement may be reached providing for immediate punishment of any violator of atomic agreements, the powers on whom enforcement action would devolve cannot possibly renounce their right of veto. They will, by legal authorization or not, feel free to decide for themselves whether they should participate in the sanctions and the possibly ensuing war. It is a foregone conclusion that they will refrain from acting should they believe that punitive attacks were not in accordance with their own national interests or would involve them in a costly or hopeless war. No sovereign state can ever be deprived of its right to "veto" its own active participation in military action. In the last analysis, everything depends on the willingness of three or four great powers to attack one or two other great powers—and to go to war in order to maintain peace, possibly against heavy atomic odds.

It is, indeed, true that the existence of the veto will in many instances prevent the United Nations from stopping incipient or actual aggression. Yet the right of veto, being a factual rather than a legal right, is more easily criticized than abolished. As long as human society is organized in states and as long as military power remains unequally distributed over the globe, and is not necessarily possessed by a majority of nations, any international organization will suffer from the weakness that collective peace enforcement can be blocked by the nonparticipation or opposition of some of its more powerful members. The brutal fact that actually a minority of nations possesses a monopoly of military power cannot be "abrogated" by international law.

The present Security Council voting procedure is nothing but a recognition of the basic fact that world peace *can be maintained only as long as there exists a minimum of "unanimity" among the great powers*. Whether or not "unanimity" can be preserved in spite of tensions engendered by acts of aggression does not depend on voting procedures.

The Military Agreements. Speaking purely legally, the United Nations Charter provisions for the enforcement of peace will not be completed until the special agreements concerning the availability to the Security Council of international armed forces have been negotiated. The fact is that these agreements have not even been drafted.[25] There is no chance whatever that in the present world situation such agreements will be forthcoming.

It would be a fallacy to assume that the drafting of the agreements of implementation is a mere technicality or that purely military problems of an international force can be solved with relative ease. In fact, these problems are at least as complex as those of disarmament; while it would be wrong to say that disarmament failed because its technical problems were not solved, the fact remains that no generally satisfactory solution was found or even suggested. There are numerous difficulties inherent in setting up an international force which, if they can be overcome at all, will require organizations and arrangements so highly complicated that their sabotage, or misuse, should be a relatively easy matter.

If a modern international force becomes very strong, the persons who command it or the nations who control the international commanders may impose their will on the rest of the world. If the force is not overwhelmingly strong, it cannot fulfill its primary function. If the international force is concentrated within one region, it will exert very strong influence there, but its presence may not influence events in distant parts. Concentration at one place makes possible a devastating attack against the international force, yet dispersion—no strength anywhere, weakness everywhere—will be tantamount to emasculation. There is the problem of how to prevent abuse of command posts for personal or national interests. During more than 2,000 years, governments have made attempts to solve similar problems typical of coalition war, and no generally applicable solution was ever found.

In modern war the army equipped with technically superior weapons possesses a great and frequently decisive advantage. But what degree of technical perfection will the weapons have which are put at the disposal of the international force? If one nation relinquishes its best arms to the force, it will *ipso facto* inform other nations, including a possible enemy, of its military secrets and thereby jeopardize its own security. Not all nations will desire to reveal their secrets. There can be no law to compel them to do so, not even on the basis of a second-level enforcement superimposed on ordinary enforcement.

Violations in this field are easy. As soon as the mere suspicion exists that one nation keeps its secrets, all others must follow suit. Yet an international

[25] There is available merely a statement of 1947 on *General Principles Governing the Organization of the Armed Forces Made Available to the Security Council by Member Nations of the United Nations* (see *United Nations Yearbook, 1946–1947,* pp. 424–443). This statement was not adopted unanimously by the nations participating in the military staff committee and hence has no legal standing.

force equipped with yesteryear's weapons will have little chance of stopping the aggressor who, incidentally, will have guarded his military secrets most jealously. The French proposals of 1932 were logical: to arm the international police with the best weapons.

Logistics and supplies interpose other tremendous obstacles. Immediately available strength may be of relatively little importance. If a force consisting only of troops with their organizational equipment (but not with an assured supply line) were thrown against a strong aggressor, it could not sustain its attack; after a few desultory engagements it would cease to exist. The international force can remain a military force only on condition that it is kept *continuously* supplied with new equipment and replacements, but even if the nations agree and desire to do so, their ability to fulfill this obligation depends on the state of their own industrial mobilization. Without continuous industrial mobilization, the international force simply cannot be kept adequately supplied. Without control of industry by the Security Council or its staff, the international force is, at best, capable of fighting *one* battle.

Proponents of the international force usually overlook the crucial importance of logistics and supplies. Whether the international force possesses, for example, 1,000 or 2,000 planes is not the question at all; *the question is at what strength the international force can be maintained*. The original strength will be quickly destroyed, especially if the aggressor possesses superior aircraft. Yet to maintain a force with real striking power, at least partial industrial mobilization in one or more large industrialized countries is required. Even assuming that no political obstacle would be interposed, supplying the international force with adequate power could begin only months after D Day. But what good would an international force do if it could not become an effective military force at the very moment of aggression?

To be sure, some of these limitations may be overcome through the use of the atomic bomb. Yet as the United Nations has been attempting to outlaw this weapon, such a contingency may not be likely. Even if no legal restrictions were placed on the employment of the atomic weapon, the United Nations could not very well set a precedent legalizing atomic warfare. In any event, the concept that atomic weapons would be an effective means of enforcement had validity only while there was an atomic monopolist. Future aggressors probably will be in possession of atomic weapons. The result would be that the many weak members of the United Nations which possess neither bombs nor defenses frantically will try to prevent the employment of such weapons. Moreover, the chances of survival of the international force would be small indeed if the aggressor, expecting atomic enforcement, were to strike a surprise nuclear blow at its bases. In practice this may mean that military enforcement actions would be condemned to failure even before they start.

So much for the topical difficulties. But how were these problems attacked by the United Nations? In the first place, the discussions of the military staff committee were predicated on the assumption that on account of the veto

(Article 27) peace can be enforced only against countries of minor military strength.[26] It also was determined that the creation of an international army consisting of contingents of *all* members of the United Nations and therefore requiring command arrangements in dozens of languages, the integration of a multitude of logistic systems, and the welding together of highly divergent armaments was a military impossibility. There was no way out but to put a major share on the shoulders of the great powers. So in practice the two principles of world peace and truly collective action were abandoned.

The next question which arose dealt with the composition of the international force. The Soviet Union proposed that the permanent members of the Security Council should contribute equally to the international force. This would have meant that the size of the international force never could be greater than five times the contribution of the weakest member. It would mean, for example, that the Chinese should contribute as much air power as the United States,[27] or that the Russians should be contributing as many aircraft carriers as the United States (when in fact they have not a single one), or that France, with its 40 million inhabitants, should make available as much infantry as China with its 450-odd million people.[28] No way out from that impasse was found. Clearly, the military problems of peace enforcement revealed themselves as insoluble even before the practical discussions were started. Another failure in the long history of futile ideas! [29]

THE ACCOMPLISHMENTS OF THE UNITED NATIONS

The Iranian Case. During its existence the United Nations has had to deal with various international conflicts. The first issue of importance arose in 1946 when the Soviet Union failed to withdraw its troops from Northern Iran where they had been stationed on the strength of wartime agreements. The Soviet occupation forces were supporting a local uprising the purpose of which was to declare the "independence" of Iranian Azerbaijan. Iran, not without encountering considerable difficulties, succeeded in placing the issue before the Security Council. After the dispute finally reached the Council and

[26] See *The New York Times*, Mar. 24, 1946.

[27] The absurdity of this problem becomes self-evident if it is remembered that the permanent member, China, for many years practically meant Formosa, and that the weapons on Formosa came from the United States. Even if China had been China, it could not have contributed aircraft unless it would have been permissible to throw in weapons originally acquired (by purchase or grant) from another state. But would these be *modern* weapons? Would the principle of equality also apply to the *quality* of weapons?

[28] See Hollis W. Barber, *Foreign Policy of the United States,* New York, Dryden, 1953, p. 457.

[29] It is notable that proponents of "international forces" rarely make an attempt to study the military aspects of their proposal. If an engineer omitted analyzing the strength of the materials which he wanted to utilize and, for example, proposed to build a railroad bridge of cardboard, he would be considered incompetent, if not insane. Political scientists are judged by more tolerant standards.

Russian activities were given an airing, the Soviets staged an angry walkout. They put considerable backstage pressure on the Iranian government, with the result that Iran withdrew its complaint. Nevertheless, the Soviet Union recalled its troops and abandoned support of the Azerbaijanian rebels. Whether this change of Soviet policy was due to the debates before the Security Council and to the realization by the Soviets that they were alienating the United States and other nations at the wrong time for no tangible return is unknown. But presumably this settlement can be described as a success of the United Nations in its character as an international forum where international public opinion could concentrate its pressure.

The Indonesian Case. In 1947, a dispute arose between Holland and Indonesia when the Dutch government commenced military action in Java and Sumatra to support its interpretation of the Linggadjati agreement of 1946. The Security Council issued cease-fire orders and established a committee of good offices, subsequently rechristened the United Nations Commission for Indonesia. A peaceful agreement was negotiated by which Holland transferred sovereignty to Indonesia. This agreement hardly would have been reached but for strong American pressure on both contestants. Moreover, Holland is a nation which always can be depended upon to do its utmost to comply with its commitments, to work out reasonable compromises, and to avoid war. Under the circumstances the United Nations proved highly effective, which is another way of saying that the effectiveness of that organization is largely dependent on the attitude of the litigants.

The Greek Case. The support given by Yugoslavia, Bulgaria, and Albania to communist guerrillas in Greece was brought before the United Nations by the Greek government in 1946. A commission of investigation reported in 1947 that the guerrillas, who then were fighting a civil war, were receiving support from the three communist states. Due to a Soviet veto the Security Council, unable to take substantive action, removed the topic from its agenda, an "action" which was "procedural" and therefore not subject to veto. Subsequently, in September, 1947, the question was taken up by the General Assembly. A new committee was created which was given the task of terminating guerrilla warfare in Greece. Poland and Russia refused to serve on this committee which, however, went to work undismayed and reported that illegal aid continued to flow to the guerrillas. The committee did a good reportorial job and described the conflict to the world in a truthful fashion. But otherwise the United Nations was unable to take effective action. Ultimately, the guerrillas were subdued because, upon the break between Tito and Stalin, Yugoslavia withdrew its military and logistical support and because the Greek armed forces, reinforced by massive American military and economic help, were able to defeat the guerrillas in battle. The guerrillas had removed many Greek children to communist territory where they were held as hostages. This matter was brought repeatedly before the United Nations, but despite the revolting character of this violation, the United Nations was unable to do anything about it; with a few exceptions, the children never returned home.

The Palestine Case. For many years the United Nations tried to effect a settlement of the Palestinian issue. The Jewish-Arab war led to the establishment, by force, of Israel, while Jordan incorporated the Arabian parts of the small country or, rather, those parts which Jordan claimed as Arabian. While the United Nations was helpful in imposing a cease-fire, it proved unable to work out a permanent settlement. No status for Jerusalem was established. The problem of the Palestinian Arabs displaced by the war was handled only with indifferent success. Above all, the splitting of Palestine into two parts (instead of setting up a federation) cannot be considered a feat of statesmanship. The state of war between Israel and Arab countries, including Egypt, was not terminated for several years.

The Case of Kashmir. With respect to Kashmir, the United Nations talked India and Pakistan into a cease-fire, but no settlement was reached. The armies of the two states, at the moment of this writing, still face each other in a no-war-no-peace situation. A final settlement appears to hinge on the success of bilateral Indian-Pakistan negotiations rather than on United Nations mediation. In any case, the Kashmir issue can be scored as a failure as far as United Nations intervention is concerned. For that matter, it engendered hostility between India and the United States.

The Case of Berlin. In so far as the conflict about Berlin was concerned (1948), attempts to achieve a settlement through the Security Council were blocked by Soviet veto. The Berlin blockade was terminated after the United States and the Soviet Union had reached a *modus vivendi* through direct negotiations. Again, a United Nations failure.

The Case of Korea. The United Nations role during the Korean conflict was complicated. On June 25, 1950, the Security Council met and requested North Korea to withdraw its armed forces from South Korea. It also called upon members "to render every assistance to the United Nations in the execution of this resolution and to refrain from giving assistance to the North Korean authorities." This resolution was passed for the simple reason that the Soviet Union had staged a walkout and did not participate in the Security Council meeting. On June 27, after North Korea did not comply with the Security Council's resolution, the United States gave military support to South Korea. On the same day, the Security Council, at the suggestion of the United States, adopted a further recommendation "that the members of the United Nations furnish such assistance to the Republic of Korea as may be necessary to repel the armed attack and to restore international peace and security in the area." In addition to the United States, sixteen nations sent military and support forces, but fundamentally the fight was taken up *only* by South Korea and the United States. In essence, the United States decided *first* to fight, and *then* obtained the United Nations' blessing for the intervention.

Article 27, 3 of the Charter states clearly that substantive decisions of the Security Council "shall be made by an affirmative vote of the permanent members." Thus, it would seem as though the Security Council cannot make a decision *unless* it is specifically approved by all permanent members. Conversely, if a permanent member fails to cast a vote, the Security Council can make no decision. In the Korean case the Security Council acted as though the concurrent vote of the Soviet Union was not required, so long as no negative vote was cast.[30] While the Soviet Union raised objections, it was unable to modify the Security Council's decision. The Korean case furnished another proof—if further proof were still required to confirm the cogency of a self-evident proposition—that written texts of agreements, whether agreements between nations or Covenants or Charters, are less significant than actual alignments of power. It must be added, however, that Soviet action at the beginning of the Korean crisis can be interpreted in two ways: either the Soviet Union made a tactical blunder in walking out from the Security Council at the wrong time; or it did not object to an enforcement action embroiling the United States in a Far Eastern war. The odds are that the Soviets simply blundered. In any event, it is most unlikely that the Security Council action on Korea has set a precedent; nations henceforth will make it a point to be present when important issues are voted upon.

Shortly after the Korean War was in full swing, the Soviet Union returned to the Security Council and took up its old tactics of blocking decisions. The Russians vetoed a resolution condemning North Korea for continued defiance of the United Nations. When, by the end of 1950, the Chinese communists struck, the Soviets vetoed Security Council actions on this new threat to the peace. Hence, the "Uniting for Peace" resolution. The United States succeeded in referring the new conflict to the General Assembly. On February 1, 1951, the General Assembly declared that the Chinese communist government was guilty of aggression in Korea. (The United Nations had not previously declared North Korea to be an aggressor.) An arms embargo was imposed on China and North Korea. Whether or not the embargo was observed faithfully by most members of the United Nations is a hotly debated question. The effect of the embargo was almost zero; the communist forces in Korea continued to be supplied from the Soviet Union. The futility of the "Uniting for Peace" resolution was demonstrated by the fact that hardly any nation was ready to engage in enforcement action against communist China, the declared aggressor. Nor was there any eagerness to implement the resolution calling for the unification of Korea. The upshot of these parliamentary maneuvers was that the Korean War proved the im-

[30] According to a carefully prepared brief by the late Leo Gross, international law expert, the action of the Security Council, *i.e.*, to equate absence with abstention, was contrary to the "unambiguous terms" of Article 27, paragraph 3 of the Charter. See his "Voting in the Security Council," *Yale Law Review*, Vol. 60, No. 2, February, 1951, p. 249.

potence of the General Assembly as well as of the Security Council. Unfortunately, American eagerness to placate the sentiments of the General
Assembly, which predominantly was opposed to really effective action,
stymied American conduct of military operations and armistice negotiations.

The task of evaluating the United Nations record does not pose insuperable rational obstacles. The judgment that the United Nations "has not
solved a single political question which could not and would not have been
settled by the traditional processes of diplomacy if the United Nations had
never been created" may be too harsh.[31] Yet it is beyond argument that the
performance of the United Nations was at best insignificant. The heart of
the matter is that the United States and many other nations, in their practical
activities, ceased to rely, securitywise, on the United Nations organization. Not only did they carry out huge armament programs but they also
concluded military alliances. It is all very well to justify, for example, the
North Atlantic Treaty Organization on the basis that Article 52 of the
United Nations Charter specifically authorizes "regional" security arrangements for the settlement of "local" disputes. The fact is that an area which
stretches from Okinawa, across the Western Hemisphere and Western Europe
to the southern shores of the Black Sea hardly can be described as a "region."
Nor is NATO designed to settle merely "local" disputes. Or have words lost
their meaning? Moreover, while the discussions about international forces
under the United Nations were suspended, great efforts were put into the
establishment of an international armed force in Western Europe. Thus,
the pretense that a *world* organization was being established was given up,
except in official declarations and speeches. Instead, efforts were made to set
up a security system embracing about *one half of the world*. The difference
is one of essence, and not merely of quantity.

Those who are disappointed about this state of affairs should remember
that the weaknesses of the Charter, as well as the political and military
limitations of the concept which underlies it, were pointed out many years
ago. Those whose hopes came to grief should have made, in 1945, a proper
analysis of the Charter; they would have been spared their discomfiture.
Those who are still "optimistic" about the future of the United Nations *as
the protector of world peace* had better take a second look at the Charter and
the realities behind it, including the backstage politics and strange activities
indulged in by many of the United Nations delegations. They also should
analyze the motives which prompt the Soviet Union in its activities within
the United Nations.

It still remains true that the United Nations may serve as a forum for the
discussion of international issues. Public debate of aggressive acts undoubtedly will be helpful in many cases. The focusing of attention upon burning

[31] Chesly Manly, "The Truth about the United Nations," *American Mercury*, June,
1953, p. 89.

issues may dissuade some nations from engaging in violent action. Yet international negotiations cannot always be conducted in public. Lord Balfour said: [32]

How is the task of the peacemaker to be pursued, if we are to shout our grievances from the house-tops whenever they occur? The only result is that you embitter public feeling, that the differences between the two states suddenly attain a magnitude they ought never to be allowed to approach, that the newspapers of the two countries have their passions set on fire and great crises arise which may end, have ended sometimes, in international catastrophes.

Whatever the United Nations may be—and it is a useful organization to further the pursuits, among friends, of peace: health, trade, education, and communication—it is not an instrument of international security. It is not designed for, and it is not capable of, maintaining world peace. International security cannot be patterned after the model of domestic security. Whether or not it is feasible to design an organizational device of collective peace enforcement which theoretically, *i.e.*, *if* it were applied in good faith by all nations, could subdue the threat of war, is an irrelevant question. Whenever a dangerous crisis occurs which splits nations into hostile camps, the chances are that *this very crisis would destroy the device*. The preamble of the Charter promises that "armed force shall not be used, save in the common interest." Yet there would be no common interest during such a crisis; hence armed force cannot be used *except* in the pursuit of particular interests. An international force of all great powers within a divided world is an irreducible paradox.

INTERNATIONAL AND DOMESTIC SECURITY

It cannot be claimed that the basic soundness of the idea of peace coercion has been established. This idea was conceived as an analogy to that of domestic peace and security. Unfortunately, the analogy between the sheriff and the international gendarme is tenable only within limits. Some wars may be of a criminal nature, but war cannot be compared to crime. While the criminal clearly violates laws and customs, war may actually be a valid and necessary expression of a nation's will. International relations cannot be regulated in the same way as safety is organized in a town.

Let us point out a few essential differences between national and international security:

1. While the behavior of individuals is prescribed by an all-inclusive body of law which defines clearly whether or not an act is illicit and punishable, no such law exists in the international sphere. The decision not to incorporate into the Charter objective criteria for determining acts of aggression is an admission that international society cannot be administered like a national

[32] Quoted from *ibid.*, pp. 94*f*.

community. It also implies that the principle *nullum crimen sine lege* does not obtain in international relations.

2. Bertrand Russell once said that "the use of force is justifiable when it is ordered in accordance with law by a neutral authority in the general interest." While it is an essential tenet of domestic justice that the judges should not be parties to a dispute, no such rule can be applied in international disputes. The Security Council, hybrid legislator-judge-sheriff, is composed of "interested parties" whose own vital interests may be at stake and who are unable to judge any case *sine ira et studio*. They cannot speak in the name of general interest, except by arrogation. Even with the best intentions, the members of the Security Council must decide in accordance with their individual political interests. Such decisions would be tantamount to intervention in the domestic lives of nations. An interventional policy amounts, in the last analysis, to the imposition of government upon nations and to the abrogation of the right of self-determination. To be sure, the manner in which this right may be exercised could be defined more clearly in order to avoid the adoption of policies detrimental to other nations. But exhumation of the Holy Alliance type of intervention may drive small nations to follow, as they did during the last century, a policy which was expressed by the Hungarian poet Petöfi: "Life is dear to me, love dearer still, but I would give them both for liberty."

3. The life of nations follows other rules than the life of persons. There is such a thing as a *bellum iustum*, at least according to the fundamental beliefs of the nations waging it. Nations may resort to war to gain national independence, to remove conditions which obstruct progress or condemn them to poverty, or they may fight in the pursuit of what they consider their highest ideals.

4. We have seen that attempts to outlaw war must, in some way or other, be based upon the sanctity of the *status quo,* at least as long as there are no effective methods of "peaceful change." Law can be enforced in domestic life because the principles of justice change extremely slowly and because the law, especially as regards criminal offenses, does not fluctuate. Yet in other fields, the *status quo* cannot be maintained even domestically.

Democracy is a superior system precisely because it permits continuous adaptations. Intranational violence is still recognized, for example, in the form of strikes. The domestic enforcement of law is possible because the individual may advance through labor, service, trade, organization, and marriage. In modern societies, hardly anybody is compelled, for his subsistence, to kill and rob. Yet in the international field, the *status quo* often can be broken only by brute force.

Can National Sovereignty Be Curtailed? The idea is frequently advanced that, to make the Security Council militarily and politically powerful, nations should transfer elements of their sovereignty to the international authority. Nations should indeed restrain themselves in exercising their prerogatives, but sovereignty is not merely a legal concept or a right that may be bestowed upon or taken away from a nation. Sovereignty is a *fact* in the same sense that power is a fact.[33] It simply means that some nations possess the material strength to make vital decisions without taking counsel from anybody. When they so choose, their decisions may run counter to the interest of other nations. The establishment of an international authority would not alter the geographical power distribution on the globe. It is an inherent weakness of the international force that it can possess derivative power only; it may control some instruments of coercion, but not the sources of power; it may have weapons and troops, but *no war potential*. As long as the majority of nations uphold the principle of self-determination and are unwilling to hand over control of their industries and other resources, the international force can act only through agencies of *national* power. Hence the sources of its strength may dry up.

PEACEFARE: A POLITICAL TASK

Throughout the ages more than 8,000 peace treaties and hundreds of peace plans have been worked out by some of history's greatest thinkers and by many of history's intellectual impostors. Some arrangements have been successful and lasted for two or three generations. Elaborate peace plans and arrangements often proved more fragile than improvised peace treaties bearing on a few concrete issues and often less enduring than an informal *modus vivendi*. Among the elaborate peace structures that stood up against the ravages of time and power politics, the Holy Alliance shines as a rare success: it lasted for half a century.

If certain types of conflict were removed from the arena of war, it was usually not because they were legislated out of existence but because the social and political causes of conflict disappeared. Wars between small social units (tribes, feudal lords) were replaced by wars between large units (nations and groups of nations). During some periods of history (the early Middle Ages and the 19th century), the incidence of war diminished, while during others (20th century) it increased. Whether the future will be more peaceful than the past, no one can tell. It is certain that organizational schemes of peace preservation will influence the course of events but little.

There is a fallacious assumption underlying much of the heavy thinking on peace: that war is a great evil and that most people recognize it as an extreme misfortune. Granting that war is a negative value, the practical choice rarely lies between a good peace and a bad war. There are many reasons why people go to war, and some of them are foolish. But not infrequently people decide on war because they want to terminate a situation

[33] The impossibility of "surrendering" sovereignty is discussed in Jacob Viner, "The Implications of the Atomic Bomb for International Relations," in *Proceedings American Philosophical Society*, Vol. 90, 1946, p. 53.

which, rightly or wrongly, they consider to be more disadvantageous than armed conflict. The inmate of a slave-labor camp in Siberia or the member of an ethnical group which suffers oppression views war with sentiments different from those of the owner of a prosperous business in a free country. If a situation is deemed so intolerable that men do not hesitate to sacrifice their own lives in order to remedy it, they rarely put much stock in the argument that war, since it is destructive, must be avoided. People who sacrifice their all in defying a hated conqueror or a despised political police are contemptuous of pacifism which, rightly or wrongly, they equate with cowardice. They hold the conviction—and under many circumstances hold it rightly—that war is the only technique of social change which can bring about the desired improvement. Far from being a clinching argument against war, the atomic bomb might become a powerful argument *for* war; it makes possible a fast and conclusive victory and therefore might transform war from a dull into a sharp and effective instrument.

The point that war is destructive and therefore pointless is more convincing to the skeptic than to the fanatic. A person who thinks that all values are relative will indeed find few reasons to offer his own life for an ideal the validity of which seems doubtful. He whose attitude grants to the hostile ideal as much truth as to his own, or ascribes to it advantages which his own ideal does not display, is forever ready to "talk it over" but always unwilling "to shoot it out." A man who believes strongly in his ideal or political concept and who holds that, in a given conflict, far more is at stake than political or philosophical abstractions usually acknowledges moral obligations toward his convictions. He does not necessarily overlook the high price which must be paid for "standing up and being counted." Undoubtedly, men guided by the teachings of the great moral philosophies, if intellectually competent, will give consideration to the dire implications of extreme violence. But few will be inclined to accept the maintenance of peace as the sole criterion of political decisions. The fact is that pacifists are in a minority, especially during a serious crisis menacing the foundations of a way of life.[34] The second fact is that, at most times, there are situations and conditions which must be changed drastically but which can be changed only through military surgery. Even a government which prefers peace to war often is confronted by the choice of weighing the disadvantages of war against the disadvantages of the continuance of an intolerable situation.

War as a technique of social change is accepted readily by alert and active minds operating within the framework of a dynamic state and a high-tension society. Therefore the case for war usually is represented with far greater vigor than the case for peace, which all too often is argued by cautious and hesitant individuals operating within the framework of a saturated society

---

[34] Experience shows that in times of stress "pacifists" easily become proponents of a crusade and reject the idea that a war should be fought for "only" limited objectives. In their opinion, nothing can justify war except the salvation of mankind.

in which there are only minor tensions. The militant personality has greater strength of character and purpose, and usually possesses more positive virtues, than the defender of peace and of the *status quo*. The history of the 19th century seems to indicate that peace is defended well only when its defense lies in the hands of statesmen who had been great warriors, or even aggressors, like Metternich, Wellington and Bismarck, and for whom peace is not an abstract idea but the concrete and limited objective of maintaining an acquired position. Whenever the problems of peace are to be discussed usefully, the argument should begin with analyzing these fundamental factors.

It is unlikely that the cause of peace has been served well by the emphasis on the destructiveness of war. Much of this destructiveness must be ascribed not to war as such, but to the lack of proper defenses. A far more plausible argument could be based on the fact that, in many cases, war as a technique of social change is an improper tool. It rarely can achieve the goal for the sake of which it was employed. In a nomadic society, war may be a means of accumulating wealth; in a modern industrialized society, war causes the destruction of wealth. War as a means of world conquest has failed historically time and again. War as a means of freeing people from foreign subjugation has been successful repeatedly, yet it may not be so successful in the future if the people who are to be freed would be destroyed in the process. War as a means of making revolution in foreign countries may be effective, yet it is unpredictable whether or not this same war would not produce also social transformations in the state initiating the conflict. Many of the objectives for which modern wars have been waged could have been reached through peaceful means. The aims of many wars were unattainable both by military *and* by nonmilitary techniques. It is a fact that in modern times most of the regimes which instigated wars did not survive the conflict.

It stands to reason that the functions of war must change as human society gradually is transforming itself from an extremely pluralistic system to a more integrated order whose members are mutually interdependent, not only for their economic subsistence but also for their cultural, scientific, and intellectual development. The brittleness of modern international institutions is due in part to the fact that this changing function of war has not been assessed correctly by those numerous organizations and movements which are working assiduously for basic and radical change. On the other hand, the techniques of war cannot be discarded until society develops a technique for executing changes as they become necessary. The marriage of peace to *status quo* politics is deadly for both.

Statistics show that our present century has seen the greatest development of war since the dawn of history. Wars have become more frequent. They have involved a larger number of people and nations. They have entailed the most profound social transformations and, at least in absolute terms, have taken more human lives than previous military conflicts. Paradoxically, this astonishing and perturbing spread of war has been accompanied by loud criticism of war, by continual discussion about peace, and by numerous attempts to organize peace and "outlaw" war. It is perhaps true that the *frequency* of war during the 20th century has been the effect of the extraordinary social, economic, and technological dynamism of modern society. But it is certainly no less true that war has been one of the root causes of accelerated change. It is hardly unfair to suggest that the high incidence of war must stand in some causal relation to the methods which governments presently employ to preserve peace. The suggestion that the inadequacy, and perhaps occasional dishonesty, of these so-called peace policies may have contributed to the frequency of war is perhaps an iconoclastic heresy. But before the thought is rejected it should be studied with objectivity.

An examination of the various 20th-century attempts to legislate peace brings to light several impressive facts. First, we observe that many peace proposals and peace plans were submitted with ulterior motives, for the purpose of assisting the state that avowed itself the champion of peace under law. These schemes were not designed to bring peace, but to enhance the security position of the proponent.

Second, it should be noted that the inspiration of most peace plans comes either from Great Britain or the United States. Most of the other nations, with the possible exception of a few Continental democracies, do not take these ideas too seriously, just as they are unimpressed by Anglo-Saxon preoccupation with birth control. This Anglo-Saxon infatuation with peace undoubtedly has some relation to the religious background and the predominantly economic attitudes of the Anglo-Saxon nations. But it is also tied in with their tradional invulnerability to military attack, as well as their dominant position at sea.

Third, while the organizational aspects of peace have been analyzed thoroughly, the best solution which was developed never has been adopted by the nations: the Geneva Protocol. Both the League Covenant and the United Nations Charter fall far short of the provisions of this document, although even the Geneva Protocol could not be relied upon to guarantee the maintenance of peace. In comparison with the Protocol, the Charter is a long step backward, as evidenced, for example, in its failure to supply a definition of aggression.

Fourth, the preoccupation with the peace problem and the illogical and unreasonable emphasis on disarmament have given the aggressors of the 20th century additional relative power and therefore have contributed greatly to the outbreak of both world wars. It is simply not true that these two wars were preceded by an "armaments race." Both wars were preceded by Germany's acquisition of heavy superiority in military strength, due not only to massive German armaments but also to the halfhearted, slow, and parsimonious armament programs of Germany's prospective enemies. If there had been a true armaments race, in the course of which German armaments had been balanced or overtaken, it is probable that neither war would have occurred.

Fifth, almost everyone agrees that wars do not occur on account of minor incidents but are due to more fundamental causes, especially intellectual, social, political, and economic maladjustment. Very little has been done, however, in the field of gradual adjustment of unsatisfactory conditions, aiming at the removal of basic causes of conflict. American assistance programs really are the first step in this field, but unilateral American action, restricted, by and large, to economic problems, cannot possibly fill the gap between the *status quo* and the aspirations of mankind.

In view of (1) the demonstrated incompetence, and occasional impotence, of modern governments, (2) existing maladjustments, (3) the rapid transformation of modern societies, and (4) the existence and military preparations of resolute would-be world conquerors, the odds against peace are high. If this vital, or deadly, problem continues to be handled in an amateurish and illusionary fashion, the future outlook indeed would be forbidding. Yet if this problem were handled competently and realistically, war would be by no means inevitable. Since competent and skillful statesmen have been able to avert wars in the past, there is no reason to assume that similar accomplishments should not be possible in the future. To familiarize oneself with the practical techniques of the avoidance and prevention of war, it would be advisable to study such precedents as the crises of 1875 and 1905 rather than waste one's time on the exegesis of theoretical peace plans or anemic international charters.

An effective policy of peace preservation consists of the following steps:

1. Its formulation must be based upon the unequivocal recognition that in this age the danger of war has not diminished. If war comes, it will not "break out" like a thunderstorm but will be a deliberate act of aggression by a state or group of states. As long as this danger of war exists, a nation's policy must be attuned to it, or to put it differently, although people may talk about peace, they should not act as though peace were an assured reality rather than an objective.

2. War is not an abstract phenomenon but a specific act by a specific nation, or group of nations, in a specific situation, undertaken because of specific causes and for specific objectives. Physicians do not cure "disease" but they treat a specific sickness with which a specific patient is afflicted. Nor are economists confronted by an abstract phenomenon called "economic depression," but by a specific depression which is due to specific causes. The causes of World War I were different from those of World War II. The causes of World War III, should it occur, will reveal themselves as different from those of its predecessors. Hence, to prevent World War I, other methods than those which might have prevented World War II would have been necessary. This means that, fundamentally, the preservation of peace is not susceptible to an organizational solution. The effectiveness of an organiza-

tional solution would be dependent on the regularity of the phenomenon, *i.e.*, if the causes of war always were more or less identical, an organizational solution fitted to this regular pattern would be workable. Such a regular pattern exists, for example, in automobile traffic; hence the traffic police is able to apply organizational devices with a high degree of effectiveness. Since in the case of war we have to deal with a variable and, to a large extent, an unpredictable phenomenon, the prevention of war is a *political* task to be solved by political means. The objective cannot possibly be to negate an abstraction called "war," but to prevent a *specific* war undertaken by a specific state. Over-all peace would result through the prevention of all *specific* wars.

3. It is quite true that such political action can and should take advantage of existing organizations and that international organizations should be created in order to facilitate preventive political action. But the crux of the matter is whether or not the aggressor is identified early enough for proper counteraction and whether this counteraction, whatever it be, will be taken in due time. On the basis of the historical record, the identification of the prospective aggressor should present no difficulties. Aggressors usually do not hide their intentions and sometimes they even advertise their bellicose preparations. It is true that the identification of the aggressor cannot be final before acts of aggression actually have been committed. Yet regardless of the potential aggressor's intent, suspicious actions on his part must be followed up by proper counteraction.

4. The most basic counteraction consists of a systematic effort at balancing the aggressor's armaments. It is not necessary under all circumstances to exceed his military power. In most cases it would be sufficient to reach such a level of strength that the aggressor could not launch a successful surprise attack and would be deprived of the chance to win cheaply and easily. The same argument applies to the aggressor's efforts in the field of propaganda warfare. In addition to countervailing military and nonmilitary armaments, the peacefaring nations should unite in an effective alliance and thus make the aggressor's task militarily, politically, and economically hopeless. It must be recognized that the peace camp may not be in a position to balance the aggressor's armaments and to join together in an alliance, and that the would-be aggressor may have the support of many allies. If the peace camp is in a minority or weaker than the war camp, it will be confronted by the alternative to fight or surrender.

5. Assuming that the aggressor's preparations have been counterbalanced, or that the counterbalancing effort proceeds on schedule without the aggressor's having as yet the capability to attack, the peace camp has it in its power to negotiate with the would-be aggressor in order to remove the causes of justified complaint. In such a negotiation the peace camp undoubtedly would have to make concessions. But the issues may be compromised to mutual satisfaction. It must be recognized, however, that if the would-be

aggressor is unable to attain satisfaction, he probably will play for time and attempt to bring about the reduction of counterbalancing armaments as well as the dissolution of the peace alliance, unless he finally decides that the game is not worth the candle.

6. If the peace camp is confronted by a "natural aggressor" whose avowed grievances are mere pretexts and who is not interested in compromise but eager to conquer, the peace camp must take full advantage of the protection afforded by its counterbalancing armaments, expose the would-be aggressor's objectives, and apply the techniques of psychological, political, and economic warfare against him. Such a decision would be predicated on the realization that "coexistence" with a natural aggressor is not possible and that ultimately, despite counterbalancing armaments and alliances, peace cannot be maintained *unless* the aggressive government has been modified. This modification could be a partial replacement of the ruling clique and a gradual evolution of the entire system; or it might have to take the form of a change of system. Needless to add that these techniques may not be successful in their objective and that they may bring about the war they are to avert, but in such a situation the peace camp has few other choices; if it wants to avoid a shooting war, and if it cannot contain the aggressor, it must seek its salvation in nonviolent techniques of conflict. The only other solution would be to sit tight and let time take care of things. If the peace camp is willing to remain heavily armed for a long period, and if it is able to stave off hostile penetration and disintegrationist tactics, this unspectacular conduct ultimately may bring the desired result. This course of action may be the least risky and the least costly—if it works. But studied inaction usually leads to the dissolution of the alliance and to the reduction of armaments. This solution requires forbearance, patience, and the ability to handle limited conflicts without losing one's nerve. It requires constancy of political purpose for long periods. And it always is an unpopular solution.

There is no cure-all against war. Yet there is the hope that war is becoming obsolete and that the expanding community of mankind will lead to the reduction of cultural and mental "incompatibility" [35] and will absorb the forces and structures which in the past have made for war. We are still far distant from such a culmination of cooperative tendencies. We are living in an expanding community; war between some members of that community has become a remote possibility; and war has been changing its function. We need not, however, speculate whether human conflict will come to an end or reemerge in a different form. It is not our problem to labor eternal peace, if only because human work is temporal. Yet it *is* our task to do our level best *to prevent a war in the middle of the 20th century, and yet to prevent war in such a fashion that our freedoms and values will remain unimpaired today*

[35] On the influence of "incompatibility" and social disintegration on the frequency of war, see Pitirim Sorokin, "The Causes of War and Conditions of a Lasting Peace," *Approaches to World Peace,* edited by Lyman Bryson, New York, Harper, 1944, p. 90.

so that they may live and grow tomorrow. This is not an abstract task, nor is it an effort which must be undertaken against an unidentified threat. There may be many threats, but the nature of the current *main* threat is a challenge to practical and creative statesmanship. This current threat may not be a lasting one; it may be superseded by another as yet unidentified threat. If so, the nature of the practical task will change. But it can be predicted with certainty that at no time will it be our task to prevent an abstract war. We must defend ourselves against *concrete* threats.

BIBLIOGRAPHY

Altman, Victor: *The International Police and World Security,* London, Alliance, 1945.
Barber, Hollis W.: *Foreign Policies of the United States,* New York, Dryden, 1953.
Bedford, Hastings, and Sackville Russell: *Total Disarmament or an International Police Force,* Glasgow, 1944.
Cheever, D. S., and H. F. Haviland: *Organizing for Peace,* Boston, Houghton Mifflin, 1954.
Davies, Lord David: *The Problem of the Twentieth Century,* London, Benn, 1930.
Dunn, Frederick S.: *War and the Minds of Men,* New York, Harper, 1950.
Evatt, Herbert V.: *The United Nations,* Cambridge, Mass., Harvard University Press, 1948.
Ferrero, Guglielmo: *The Unity of the World,* New York, Boni, 1931.
Haviland, H. Field: *The Rise of the General Assembly,* New York, Carnegie Endowment, 1951.
Hemleben, Sylvester John: *Plans for World Peace through Six Centuries,* Chicago, University of Chicago Press, 1943.
Kelsen, Hans: *The Law of the United Nations,* New York, Praeger, 1950.
Lange, Christian: *Histoire de l'internationalisme jusqu'à la Paix de Westphalie, 1648,* New York, Putnam, 1919.
Marriot, Sir John A. R.: *Commonwealth or Anarchy? A Survey on Projects of Peace from the 16th to the 20th Century,* London, G. Allen, 1937.
Meulen, Jacob Ter: *Der Gedanke der internationalen Organisation in seiner Entwicklung, 1300–1800,* The Hague, M. Nijhoff, 1917.
Miller, David Hunter: *The Drafting of the Covenant,* 2 vols., New York, Macmillan, 1928.
———: *The Peace Pact of Paris,* New York, Putnam, 1928.
———: *The Geneva Protocol,* New York, Macmillan, 1925.
Orton, William Aylott: *The Liberal Tradition: A Study of the Social and Spiritual Conditions of Freedom,* New Haven, Yale University Press, 1945.
Rappard, William E.: *Cinq siècles de sécurité collective, 1291–1798,* Paris, Sirey, 1945.
Reves, Emery: *The Anatomy of Peace,* New York, Harper, 1946.
Roepke, Wilhelm: *Civitas Humana,* Paris, Médicis, 1946.
———: *Internationale Ordnung,* Zurich, E. Rentsch, 1945.
Rousseau, J. J., Thomas More, Francis Bacon, Thomas Campanella: *Famous Utopias; the Complete Text of the Social Contract, Utopia, New Atlantis, City of the Sun,* New York, Tudor, no date.
Russell, Bertrand: *Freedom versus Organization 1814–1914,* New York, Norton, 1934.
U.S. Department of State: *Arming the United Nations,* Bulletin Supplement Vol. XVII, No. 422A, Aug. 3, 1947.
Vandenbosch, Amry, and Willard N. Hogan: *The United Nations: Background, Organization, Functions, Activities,* New York, McGraw-Hill, 1952.

Chapter 27

FUNCTIONAL ORGANIZATION OF THE PEACE

The scope of functional cooperation between nations is severely limited by the nature of their political relations. Activities which are intrinsically non-political become in a tension-laden atmosphere, so to speak, politically "ionized." Under such circumstances the functional approach breaks down. To the extent that the habit of international cooperation in nonpolitical matters is developed, human associations so formed may weather the storms of political conflict. In fact, the benefits accruing from these cooperative ventures may be carried over into the sphere of politics.

INTERNATIONAL FUNCTIONAL ORGANIZATIONS

Despite all the disunity and the struggles between states, nations are compelled to live together. Accordingly, many problems arise which require joint solutions or which cannot possibly be solved except through collaboration. For the purposes of solving such problems, nations have been creating, during the last 100 years or so, international organizations. Popular preconception notwithstanding, the League of Nations, the United Nations, and the Pan American Union are not the only important or the only existing international organizations. Numerous additional organizations are indeed keystones of world order under law because they accomplish the many purely technical functions of international life. It is not possible to determine precisely how many international organizations exist now, or how many existed in the past. In 1946, the U.S. Department of State published a survey of international agencies and listed 216 such organizations, stating that "complete data were not available . . . for the greater number of the 216 organizations listed." [1] Of the 216 organizations enumerated 52 no longer functioned, 20 were, in 1946, in the formative state, and 143 were more or less active. How many thousands of international organizations existed in the course of history? Nobody seems to know the answer to this question.

The international agencies were grouped by the State Department according to the following categories: agricultural, 12; commercial and financial, 17; commodity, 29; educational, scientific, and cultural, 33; political and

[1] Department of State, *International Agencies in Which the United States Participates*, Publication 2699, Government Printing Office, 1946.

legal, 48; social and health, 38; transport and communications, 39. Let us survey the functions of some of these bodies.

There is, for example, the *Central Bureau of the International Map of the World on the Millionth Scale* at Southampton, England. The purpose of this Bureau is to publish a series of maps on a uniform scale and according to standardized techniques in order to provide satisfactory map coverage of the entire world. It was set up in 1913; the United States did not join until 1926. With the exception of the Soviet Union, practically all important countries participate in it.

The *International Bureau of Weights and Measures,* located at Sèvres, France, was created in 1875. Its function is to establish weights and measures according to uniform standards, which can be used by all countries. It has the custody of international prototypes, undertakes periodical comparisons of national standards, and develops new standards that may become necessary, for example, in the electrical field. Membership includes practically all nations.

The *International Hydrographic Bureau* is located at Monte Carlo, Monaco, and serves to develop, standardize, and improve hydrographic work all over the world. Relatively few states are members, the reason probably being that hydrographic information may, under certain conditions, assume military importance. Nations appear to harbor no such misgivings with respect to the *International Meteorological Organization,* Lausanne, Switzerland, in which virtually all the meteorological services of the world participate. Although weather data may also be of military importance, the usefulness of an international meteorological agency is so great for every nation that none can afford to forgo participation.

Other international bodies of a strictly functional and nonpolitical character include the *International Bodies for Narcotics Control.* Beginning in 1912 agreements were concluded to regulate the trade of narcotics and to limit and control the manufacture and distribution of narcotic drugs. Narcotics control is now exercised by the *Commission on Narcotic Drugs* of the United Nations, which possesses strong enforcement powers. As long as nations are interested in the suppression of narcotics trade, these bodies will continue to work efficiently. The joint effort in the narcotics field was and is one of the outstanding successes of international cooperation.

The *International Criminal Police Commission* was established in 1924 and works for the suppression of international crime. It concentrates in the fields of counterfeited currency; forgery of checks, securities, and passports; traffic in women and children; immoral publications; and extradition and methods of identification. It maintains communications between police authorities designed to facilitate the apprehension of international criminals.

A number of international agencies devote themselves to the regulation of international transport and communications. Prominent among these are the *Universal Postal Union,* founded in 1863 and now embracing all states of the world; the *International Telecommunication Union;* the *European Central Inland Transport Organization,* the *United Maritime Authority,* the *International Railways Union,* and the *Permanent International Association of Navigation Congresses.* The purpose of these bodies is to facilitate, in fact to make possible, international movements of commodities, persons, and messages.

Useful work is also done by international agencies dealing with agricultural, economic, and financial matters. *The Inter-American Institute of Agricultural Sciences,* Turrialba, Costa Rica, is intended "to encourage and advance the development of agricultural sciences in the American Republics through research, teaching and extension activities in the theory and practice of agriculture and related arts and sciences." The Institute has developed, for example, a new tomato for the tropics; established methods for the control of cattle insects; investigated the possibilities of coffee pulp as cattle feed; experimented with the production of hybrids; and tested fertilizers. The *International Institute of Agriculture* at Rome has surveyed the agricultural sciences and produced excellent statistics on world agriculture. The *International Union for the Protection of Industrial Property,* Bern, Switzerland, created in 1883, serves as a clearinghouse of information on patent laws, drafts and supervises conventions on related matters, and seeks to promote uniform rules for national patent registration statutes.

The *International Sugar Council,* London, was established in 1937; its origins date back to the Brussels Sugar Convention of 1902. It seeks to negotiate arrangements in order to assure an adequate supply of sugar on the world market "at a reasonable price not to exceed the cost of production, including a reasonable profit, for efficient producers." It also attempts to promote increased sugar consumption in states where consumption is still low. The *International Tin Committee* dates back to 1931 and exercises control over tin exports in order to avoid a slump in tin prices. The Committee is associated with the *International Tin Research and Development Council* which initiated a "research scheme" aiming to promote the use of tin through research, development, and statistics.

International agencies for financial transactions and reconstruction are also operative. The *Bank for International Settlements* at Basel, Switzerland, was founded to transact the payment of reparations arising from World War I; it also served for any other kind of international money transfers and for clearing purposes.

One of the oldest international agencies, and one that is unique of its kind, is the *International Labor Organization,* located at Montreal and Geneva. Historically, the Organization dates back to a proposal made in 1818 by the manufacturer and "utopian" socialist Robert Owen to the Congress of Aix-la-Chapelle, for an institution which would serve to improve the conditions and standards of labor. In 1890, the German Emperor convened a conference dealing with the health and welfare of the working class which led to the establishment of the International Association for Labor Legislation at Brussels in 1897. Adopting a proposal emanating from a commission composed of employers, workers, and government representatives, the Peace Treaty of Versailles—which launched the League of Nations—adopted several provisions calling for an international labor organization.

There are literally scores of international agencies in addition to those mentioned. They deal with virtually all aspects of human life, from wildlife preservation to fisheries, soil conservation, copper, hides, skins, leather, textiles, coal, and paper; from astronomy, radiology, geodesy, physiology, art and music, to slavery, childhood protection, demography, eugenics, horticulture, medicine; from causes of death, liquor traffic, prisons, and codification of law to navigation, lighthouses, ocean observation, maritime safety, radio static, and highways. There are international agencies administering internationalized zones, such as the *Sanitary Council* of Teheran or, formerly, the *International Settlement* at Shanghai, or the *Tangier Control Committee*. The *Allied Control Commissions* for Bulgaria, Hungary, and Rumania would have had an important function, had they not been stymied by Soviet politics. There are special *ad hoc* missions to supervise elections, such as the mission (and international police force) supervising the plebiscite in the Saar during 1934–1935 and the mission observing the Greek elections in 1946; committees to settle boundary conflicts, population exchanges, reparations agencies, and international military tribunals, like the Nuremberg and Tokyo War Crimes Courts. There are bilateral agencies, such as the *U.S.-Canadian Joint Agricultural Committee,* the *Mexican-American Commission for Economic Cooperation,* the *Alaskan International Highway Commission,* and the *U.S.- St. Lawrence Advisory Committee,* and dozens of similar agencies regulating certain phases of the lives of contiguous states.

There are about 100 or more important international organizations in which the United States does not participate. Among these are the following: the *African Telecommunication Union, Central Commission for the Navigation on the Rhine, European Commission of the Danube,* similar commissions for the navigation on the Elbe and Oder Rivers, *European Conference on Timetables, European Freight and Timetable Conference, Central Office for International Railway Transport, European Telecommunication Union,* and other agencies dealing with long-distance telephone communications, bridge building, alcoholism, intelligence on locusts, unification of criminal law, whaling statistics, chemistry, agricultural engineering, scientific exploration of the Mediterranean, olive growing, protection of telecommunications lines and subterranean cables, railway wagons, contagious diseases, venereal diseases, leprosy, tuberculosis, wine growing, poultry science, and sanitary equipment. Finally, there are bodies whose function it is to adjust legal international disputes; among these are the *Inter-American Panel of Mediators,* the *Permanent Court of Arbitration,* and the *International Court of Justice,* an integral part of the United Nations structure, as well as the *Interparliamentary Union for the Promotion of International Arbitration* and the defunct *United Nations Committee of Jurists.*

Many of these international agencies work effectively; most of them have inadequate resources at their disposal and do not receive full support from the member states. Some of them were founded, then passed through a brief period of intensive activity, and then became "dormant." Others, however, have done good work and have made valuable contributions to the raising of international standards of safety, knowledge, decency, and general well-being.

Most successful has been the work done by international agencies in the fields of transport, communications, disease and vice control, and, to a lesser extent, science. Without this work there could be no scheduled international railroad and air traffic, no unimpeded navigation on international rivers and seas, no foreign mail, telephone, and telegraph; even radio listening would be virtually impossible in many states. Without these agencies the ravages of disease would be far greater, the control of epidemics would break down, and white slavery and opium trade would corrupt the world. And without the *International Red Cross* war would be even more cruel than the perverse ingenuity of man has made it.

It is quite clear that a great deal of useful work still remains to be done along similar lines, for example, in the fields of malaria, sleeping sickness, and rinderpest; industrial techniques; disposal of surplus production; international transport routes; and so on. But there is no doubt that the value of international organizations already has amply been proved by the success of these pioneer agencies. Imperfect though they are in operation and limited though they may be in scope, our modern life, as we know it, would not be possible without that network of international cooperation which they have woven, albeit in a rudimentary and haphazard fashion.

THE UNITED NATIONS AND THE WELFARE OF MANKIND

Universal international organizations of the type of the League of Nations and the United Nations are designed primarily to carry out peace enforcement. In the second place, the United Nations is designed to function as an organization for developing "friendly relations among nations based on respect for the principle of equal rights and self-determination of peoples, and to take the appropriate measures to strengthen universal peace." It is within the area staked out by this broad dispensation that those organs of the United Nations which are not specifically charged with the implementation of collective security against aggression may operate and seek to eliminate the causes of armed conflict, if not armed conflict itself.

Third, the United Nations is a center where governments can maintain permanent liaison and thus by personal contact thrash out many problems that may arise, and improve cooperation in the economic, social, cultural, and humanitarian fields. By its mere existence, the United Nations can uphold the idea of the "fundamental freedoms for all without distinction as to race, sex, language, or religion." All in all, the United Nations is designed as a "center for harmonizing the actions of nations in the attainment of these common ends" (Article 1, paragraph 4).

Not all of these manifold functions of the United Nations have found adequate attention. Hence little coordinated effort has been undertaken in those fields where great successes could actually be achieved. During the first years of the United Nations comparatively little use has been made, for instance, of Article 13 which reads:

The General Assembly shall initiate studies and make recommendations for the purpose of:

a. promoting international cooperation in the political field and encouraging the progressive development of international law and its codification;

b. promoting international cooperation in the economic, social, cultural, educational, and health fields, and assisting in the realization of human rights and fundamental freedoms . . .

Article 55 stipulates that the United Nations shall promote higher standards of living, full employment, and conditions of economic and social progress and development as well as cultural and educational cooperation. According to Article 62, the *Economic and Social Council* "may" make studies and recommendations with respect to international economic, social, cultural, educational, health, and related matters. It might have been indeed advisable to make it mandatory for the Council to make such studies and recommendations.

Fourth, the United Nations is designed to function as the mother organization of subsidiary, technical international agencies. It is hoped that in due time the numerous existing international agencies can be coordinated and additional ones established to cover systematically fields which require international treatment. In effect, even if the United Nations should fail in its peace-enforcement mission, its existence would still be of great advantage to mankind as long as cooperation is maintained, for example, in the fields of economic and social activities.

Yet despite all these provisions the United Nations has concerned itself little with the solution of nonpolitical, technical problems. This does not mean that no work has been done in the technical fields. On the contrary, the technical bodies have been in frequent session, but their work is inefficiently organized. Technical reports either are of too general a nature or deal with too insignificant or too immediate a problem. No over-all global research program has been established. Budgets and programs are confused and insufficient. Little sustained interest is shown by governments and nations alike. Generally speaking, the great usefulness of the technical work and the overwhelming need for basic research are not recognized.

If we glance at the over-all organization of the United Nations, we can readily see that the fate of mankind would be considerably improved if the United Nations were to operate efficiently. Leaving aside the Security Council and the Secretariat, which runs the administration of the United Nations, many of the basic fields of human endeavor could be advanced through the organization; and many of the basic problems of human life could be alleviated by international cooperation supported and guided by the United Nations.

The *General Assembly* can make recommendations of any kind and propose over-all policies. The *Economic and Social Council* operates under the authority of the General Assembly but specializes in economic and social matters. Both, therefore, have the power to propose any step that may redound to the benefit of mankind. The *Trusteeship Council* administers mandated territories, territories detached from enemy states after the Second World War, and territories voluntarily placed under its administration. The Trusteeship Council has the organization and authority necessary to work out the most effective methods of political administration applied anywhere on the globe. These methods, proved by experiment, may then be adopted by individual nations. Theoretically, many territorial disputes could be solved simply by putting the disputed lands under the Council. Thus, international territories would arise, the existence of which could facilitate the establishment of federations as well as of the world authorities.

The *International Court of Justice,* as the principal judicial organ of the United Nations, has two types of responsibilities. It decides cases brought before it and gives advisory opinions on legal questions. Only states may be parties before the Court. It can decide equitably some political and any non-political conflict. Its radius of action is limited by many implicit and explicit reservations contained in the Charter itself and by the general nature of international law.

There are also specialized commissions under the various councils, in particular those on economics, social matters, and human rights; these commissions may serve to improve the conditions of individuals.

The Economic and Social Council and the Specialized Agencies. In addition to the various organs of the United Nations proper, there are specialized agencies affiliated with the U.N. The *Economic and Social Council* functions, or is supposed to function, as the intermediary between and coordinator of the Specialized Agencies. It is the entire complex of the Economic and Social Council with its own functional commissions [2] and its specialized

[2] The *Economic, Employment and Development Commission* was discontinued in 1951. ECOSOC's eight commissions are: the *Fiscal Commission; Commission on Human Rights; Commission on Narcotic Drugs; Population Commission; Social Commission; Statistical Commission; Commission on the Status of Women;* and *Transportation Commission;* and three regional commissions domiciled in their respective areas, namely, *Economic Commission for Europe* (ECE); *Economic Commission for Asia and the Far East* (ECAFE); and *Economic Commission for Latin America* (ECLA). Several of these commissions estab-

affiliates which, by its elaborateness and scope, constitutes *the most significant advance beyond the domain of the League of Nations* and reflects the recognition of the problems created by modern mass societies and the awakening of the colonial and backward peoples. The preamble to the Charter pays tribute to the rise of social welfare to the level of international concern, the members having agreed to "promote social progress and better standards of life in larger freedom." This resolve is spelled out in Chapter IX of the Charter, and it is the principal mission of the Economic and Social Council to translate that high purpose into practice.

The Charter provides that the Economic and Social Council may negotiate agreements under which various international unions (administrations), upon ratification by the Assembly and the representative body of the union (henceforth designated "specialized agency"), shall be "brought into relationship with the United Nations." That relationship is one of cooperation rather than control. The specialized agencies are autonomous bodies. The Economic and Social Council is authorized to "coordinate the activities of the specialized agencies through consultation with and recommendations to such agencies," but not to control them directly. Nor does the Council or the Assembly exercise binding control over their budgets. Coordination is thus largely achieved by series of interlocking agreements concerning reciprocal representation at conferences, exchange of information, and pledges to cooperate and consult in the other United Nations organs. The entire structure is extremely loose, a characteristic which, given the stress on voluntary cooperation and functional autonomy, could be its virtue—were it not for the ponderousness of the proceedings of the parent body, the United Nations, perpetually agitated by national sensitivities, as well as the international tendency toward bureaucratic diffusion and overorganization. Over certain agencies as, for example, the International Bank and the International Monetary Fund, ECOSOC exercises no control whatsoever, being prevented by the agreements of affiliation even from proffering advice on certain important matters.

The International Bank for Reconstruction and Development. The Bretton Woods Conference in June, 1944, which gave birth to the twin institutions, the International Monetary Fund and the International Bank for Reconstruction and Development, was concerned with the drafting of an international financial charter for the postwar world.

The Bretton Woods Conference devised an international monetary constitution for the world as it would be after it had been "reconverted" to peacetime conditions. This reconversion would consist of more than mere reconstruction in the sense of rebuilding and reshaping the mechanical apparatus of production. Instead, the International Bank was conceived as a mechanism to foster international investment. It was to take over the special risks inherent in international investment during the reconstruction period by giv-

---

lished subcommissions, and only by daily on-the-spot observation could the ramifications and frequently overlapping jurisdictions of these bodies be traced.

ing its guarantee to private investors or by making loans out of funds borrowed from private investors. Its capital, of which only 20 per cent was to be paid up (18 per cent out of the 20 per cent in local currency), was meant to enable the Bank to run risks the private investor would not take. The Bank was not, however, to indulge in transactions that would not have the character of investment. Its task would be to break the vicious circle formed by the impossibility for reconstruction to get under way without international investment, and the reluctance of the private investor to lend money as long as the success of reconstruction was uncertain. The Bank could base its lending policy on the assumption that reconstruction would succeed. But it should only give or guarantee loans that, on the basis of that assumption, could be expected to be serviced and repaid. Barring a general failure to get the world on its feet again, the Bank was to pay its own way. Eventual losses were to be met in the first place out of a reserve built up by levying a special commission from all its borrowers. The Bank's capital was not to be involved in covering other losses than those caused by a major political or economic crisis.

The Bank's capital was put at the figure of 10 billion dollars (in 1952, actual subscriptions reached around 8.5 billion dollars), to be subscribed by the various countries in proportion to their financial and economic strengths.

The International Bank began its organization when plans for the reconstruction of Europe were being made. It became clear, however, that without the European Recovery Program, underwritten by the United States, reconstruction could not possibly succeed.

As a consequence of the working of ERP, the dividing line between the two aspects of the Bank's task, reconstruction and development, became less sharp. The further reconstruction proceeded, the less it had the character of rebuilding something that had been destroyed.

Europe has to adapt itself to the structural change in world economy caused by the war. Europe's development problem has very different aspects from the development of Latin America, Africa, or Asia. But in essence it is also a development problem. Development programs, wherever they are devised, are closely interrelated and dependent on each other's success. The "development" of Europe is a condition of the success of all of them. The Bank's task, seen originally as divided into a temporary part, reconstruction, and a permanent one, development, can now be defined as an indivisible one: the enlistment of surplus productive capacity, wherever it is to be found in the world, for the further development of the world's productive resources.[3]

The International Monetary Fund. The purposes of the Fund, broadly stated, are to cooperate closely with the Bank (IBRD); to promote international monetary cooperation and exchange stability, maintain orderly exchange arrangements among members and avert competitive exchange depre-

---

[3] See J. W. Beyen, "The International Bank for Reconstruction and Development," *International Affairs*, Vol. 24, October, 1948, p. 541.

ciation, assist in the establishment of a multilateral system of payments and in the elimination of foreign exchange restrictions, make available to members funds in order to correct maladjustments in the balance of payments, and generally improve the techniques of international payments. The Fund draws for the execution of these tasks upon a gold and currency pool valued at about 8.8 billion dollars.

Since the United States supplied by far the largest quota of the member subscriptions to both Bank and Fund and the headquarters of both Bank and Fund are located in Washington, it is not surprising that the policies of both have come under the fire of the most diverse criticism, particularly on the part of candidates for loans and currency support respectively. Both Bank and Fund, it is alleged, reflect the attitude of conservative American bankers ("Wall Street") and the indifference to "full employment" which is supposedly innate in conservative bankers. Conversely, it is argued by the friends of the management that it is precisely the task of both organizations to stabilize the international economy and to cure some of its acute ills, especially the inflationary ones, and, as far as the Bank is concerned, to promote investments for development schemes that can stand searching investigation and, in the long run and with the help of very low interest rates, pay for themselves. These purposes can be achieved only by sound banking and fiscal practices and not by "giveaway" schemes.

The International Trade Organization.[4] Obviously, one of the most urgent tasks of current international politics is the reactivization of international trade. This need was generally recognized and a Preparatory Committee of the International Conference on Trade and Employment was called. It sat at Geneva from April to October, 1947, and elaborated a proposal for an international trade charter. This charter is as detailed as it is ambitious. It proclaims the need for increased trade and accelerated economic development through the reduction of tariffs and trade barriers and advocates the abolition of restrictive trade practices. But these excellent principles were voided by numerous amendments and escape clauses. Moreover, when the United Nations Conference on Trade and Employment at Havana considered the charter in November, 1947, additional "amendments" were proposed and carried. Some progress was made, yet the problem of international trade was very far from being solved.[5]

The most important achievements of ITO were a series of tariff agreements. The first of these was negotiated at Geneva in 1947. The General Agreement on Tariffs and Trade (GATT), ratified by the United States, Great Britain, and France and virtually all other major trading nations accounting for three-fourths of world trade, resulted in 123 bilateral agreements for the reduction of tariffs. The United States, for example, granted reduc-

---

[4] See Chaps. 20 and 21.

[5] See Laure Metzger and William L. Neumann, Jr., "The Havana Trade Conference: Some Basic Problems," *American Perspective,* Vol. 1, No. 10, March, 1948.

tions to importers valued at about 1.7 billion dollars and received concessions valued at about 1.5 billion dollars. At subsequent conferences further agreements were reached. The network of these bilateral agreements now covers many thousands of items and represents a considerable advance from the conditions obtaining after the end of the war. This did not mean, however, that nations would not take refuge behind ITO's sundry escape clauses whenever the pressure of special domestic interests became politically articulate enough. Indeed, the United States in 1952 raised tariff rates on Turkish figs and Dutch and Danish cheeses, relatively small items in America's over-all imports but vitally important ones in the trade balance of the exporting countries. Praiseworthy as were ITO's achievements, they fall by a long distance short of closing the "dollar gap" which poses the world's principal trade problem.

It would seem that no better results can be expected so long as discussions on international trade are not based on solid scientific data and statistics indicating clearly the consequences of trade barriers. As it stands now, attempts are made to persuade nations to lower their trade barriers despite the conviction of their governments and large and influential groups within these nations that this would be disadvantageous to them. Obviously such attempts are foredoomed to failure. Unless it can be proved statistically that the removal of trade barriers will prove an advantage to *all* countries, and unless a method is worked out by which transition losses—which will inevitably occur, but which are rarely mentioned—can be compensated for, progress will remain very difficult. It is up to the United Nations to provide the scientific data for a profitable discussion of the trade problem. If the United Nations fails in this task, which can be solved only on a global scale, nobody else will or can do the job.

The Food and Agriculture Organization of the United Nations. The Food and Agriculture Organization aims to increase the world's food supply, improve distribution of food, and ultimately make available a minimum sanitary diet to all people on earth. One of the important achievements of this organization was the conclusion of an intergovernmental agreement on the distribution of wheat. In 1948, all major producers, except Argentina and Russia, agreed on quotas for sales and purchases of wheat; established maximum and minimum prices for these quotas; and undertook to create and maintain buffer stocks for the purpose of achieving price stability. The principal difficulties which arose over this particular agreement, and which still dog the steps of the FAO in its quest for further commodity agreements, reside in the constantly shifting price situation of many commodities. One country has a good crop and tries to get rid of its surplus; crop failure may suddenly force a habitual export country into the ranks of occasional importers; planning quotas and maximum and minimum prices is hazardous because crop predictions are subject to many uncertainties; and producers, especially in free-enterprise countries like the United States, are numerous and highly individualistic and cannot be easily persuaded to enter long-term, binding agreements. Yet the idea of a world food board is a sound one. An international institution is necessary to facilitate the year-by-year exchanges between food-surplus and food-deficient countries.

The International Civil Aviation Organization. Aside from providing technical advisory services and obtaining agreements concerning the introduction of devices and practices for the improvement of international air transportation, the Council has been authorized to act as arbiter in the settlement of all kinds of international disputes on aviation and to furnish advisory opinion on legal aspects of civil aviation, a great many of which raise problems for which there is virtually no precedent in existing codes of law. The Council, while it was unable to reconcile differences with respect to commercial rights—especially the so-called "fifth freedom," or the right of an airline to carry passengers and freight between points situated in foreign countries (cabotage)—made great progress in air navigation, transit, communications, safety rules, and other technical fields. Particularly useful was an agreement on ocean weather stations which enlarged the scope of meteorological information and which greatly contributed to flight safety.

The International Labor Organization. Organized in 1919 as an intrinsic part of the peace settlement of Versailles and operating independently of the League of Nations, ILO contributed more solid achievements to the promotion of "social justice" than any other international organization. What there is of international uniform standards governing labor legislation in virtually all civilized countries—except, of course, the Soviet Union and its satellites—has been largely the achievement of the ILO.

ILO concerns itself with the physical, moral, and intellectual well-being of industrial wage earners. It attempts to define standards and to introduce into national legislations provisions concerning the right of association of employees and employers, minimum wages, the eight-hour day and forty-eight-hour week, night work, abolition of child labor, equal wages for men and women performing work of equal value, protection of migrants, social insurance, sickness and unemployment insurance, vacations, inspection of working conditions, labor hygiene and safety, and so on. The Organization worked out an international labor code and helped with the adoption of sixty-seven conventions and international labor treaties. Seventy-three of its recommendations have been accepted by various governments for incorporation into national laws. The Organization has, in fact, created a "network of mutual obligations" aiming at the maintenance of labor standards. On the whole, the International Labor Organization has made a significant contribution to the solution of what generations ago was known as the "social question." [6]

[6] A fair illustration of ILO's operations is supplied by the résumé of an agreement on minimum standards of work covering the multinational personnel of international river navigation. "The Rhine serves a number of countries in its course and the boatmen work-

The International Maritime Consultative Organization. IMCO, domiciled in London, is to function as a clearinghouse for information, chiefly on such technical matters as safety regulations and navigational rules of the road. Its further purpose is to negotiate agreements and conventions for the elimination of discriminatory regulations which hinder maritime shipping and, though frequently disguised as safety regulations, simply serve to protect national shipping interests against foreign competition.

The International Refugee Organization. IRO was an offshoot of the United Nations Relief and Rehabilitation Administration, better known as UNRRA. The task of this Administration was to provide immediate relief to areas ravaged by the war and in particular to provide, on an emergency basis, food, fuel, clothing, shelter, medicaments, and other basic necessities and services. UNRRA gave help to hundreds of thousands of persons in more than a score of areas suffering from the war. In many cases, it provided not only basic necessities and immediate relief but also machinery and industrial equipment needed for rehabilitation.

Like UNRRA, IRO was a temporary agency created for an *ad hoc* purpose. Over 1,250,000 refugees and displaced persons, the hard core of the many millions of uprooted peoples scattered over the world at the end of World War II, were placed in the charge of IRO. The United Nations General Assembly, acting upon the recommendation of ECOSOC, instructed IRO to undertake the legal protection and the resettling of the homeless and nationless "displaced persons" who had lost their "place" in their native lands and were barred, because they either could not meet transportation costs or could not qualify under the provisions of national immigration legislations, from finding new homes in other lands.

The IRO operated under great difficulties. Very few nations were willing to help it accomplish its mission. Funds voted by the General Assembly of the United Nations were not fully appropriated by individual nations. The United States defrayed nearly two-thirds of the IRO's total expenditure of 400 million dollars. Few nations offered to accept refugees. Various other nations were openly hostile to the agency. This is particularly true of the Soviet Union, which objected to IRO policy of resettling persons who fled from Russia or the satellite countries and who did not want to return to the paradise lost. The United States also proved reluctant and took cover behind its archaic immigration laws. However, in 1948, three years after the end of the war, Congress voted to accept 202,000 "carefully selected" refugees. In 1953,

ing on it are drawn from all the bordering countries. Often they move from ship to ship and flag to flag and thus work under divergent conditions and different schemes of social security, which give rise to difficulties over the transfer and maintenance of accrued rights. A meeting of the states concerned was held this year under ILO auspices and agreements were reached on minimum standards of conditions of work and coordination of social security schemes. . . . This represents a major practical step through concerted international action toward the security and well-being of some 50,000 men." *United Nations Bulletin*, Jan. 1, 1951, p. 27.

another refugee law authorizing the admittance of 214,000-odd refugees was adopted. Perhaps the most generous support of IRO's plan for resettling refugees and displaced persons has come from Britain which admitted in addition to thousands of IRO wards the remnants of the Free Polish Army. Small, arid Palestine admitted many thousands of homeless Jews. Only a few "empty" countries cooperated fully.

In spite of many obstacles, IRO supported many "displaced persons" in European and Middle Eastern camps and provided aid to almost a million people living outside the camps. By 1952, IRO had cared for settling more than 2 million people—mass expulsion and mass flights from Eastern Europe having swelled the original contingent—and had succeeded, by one means or another, in resettling about 1,050,000 people. IRO provided effective help to D.P.'s, who, without help, would have perished in large numbers. Yet a great deal of criticism was directed against IRO for the indifferent success of its efforts. It is true that the administration of IRO was cumbersome and that it operated sometimes with bias, especially against D.P.'s of German origin or language. Actually, criticism ought to be leveled against the sovereign nations which supported or, rather, hampered the agency.

In 1952, IRO's activities were transferred to the U.N. High Commissioner of Refugees (UNHCR). IRO went out of existence; the problem of refugees did not. The Commissioner was now confronted with more than a million D.P.'s *i.e.*, about as many as were originally intrusted to the care of IRO. His wards now consisted chiefly of escapees from behind the iron curtain and refugees from the wars in Palestine, China, and Korea. UNHCR is a stop-gap measure. The Commissioner's budget is smaller than that of IRO. The problem of the D.P., a problem that is symptomatic of the inhumanity of our epoch, is with us, and will remain with us as long as the struggle between freedom and dictatorship lasts. There is a crying need for an international migration and resettlement authority, endowed amply with funds, operated as a permanent institution, and staffed by the best experts in the many fields of its concern.

The United Nations International Children's Emergency Fund. UNICEF, though formally not a specialized agency because of its status as a section of the U.N. Secretariat, is complementary to those of IRO and the latter's successor, UNHCR. Its task is not only to assist children directly, but to care for parents so that they, in turn, can rear healthy children. UNICEF has undertaken a vigorous campaign, encompassing millions of adults and children, against tuberculosis, malaria, and venereal diseases. Like most U.N. agencies, it is perpetually hampered by inadequacy of funds. Its precarious existence is, to a large extent, dependent on year-by-year appropriations granted by unpredictable national legislatures. Since UNICEF does not know what its financial resources will be from one year to the next, it cannot develop the long-range and comprehensive program which its task—child and family care on a world-wide basis—requires.

The United Nations Educational, Scientific, and Cultural Organization.
UNESCO has been somewhat impaired by a fatal penchant to mix politics
with its technical work. Moreover, it has initiated too many projects rather
than concentrating on those of real importance. Nevertheless, good results
may ensue ultimately from projects such as the analysis of textbooks for objectivity of content, from a universal copyright convention, and in the field
of natural sciences, from projects such as the *International Institute of the
Hylean Amazon* which is to encourage research on development possibilities
in this vast region, but whose status has become uncertain.

The single most important job of UNESCO lies in the field of fundamental
education. It should contribute to the raising of educational levels, particularly in countries with a high rate of illiteracy. Two regional conferences on
fundamental-education needs have been held, in Nanking in September,
1947, and in Mexico City in November, 1947, to discuss means of broadening this program in those areas where the need exists. Small "pilot projects"
in fundamental education were launched in South and Central America. Yet
out of UNESCO's budget of from 7.6 to 9 million dollars annually, only
about $350,000 annually were devoted to the purpose of fundamental edu-
cation. A great deal of money is devoted to press, radio, and film activities.
It would be far more in the interests of the United Nations if a concentrated
effort were undertaken in the fields of basic research, scientific and library
exchanges, and coordination of scientific results as well as general education.

The World Health Organization. WHO is the successor of the International Office of Public Health at Paris. The IOPH had a very large membership. It was set up "to collect and bring to the knowledge of the participating States facts and documents of a general character concerning public health and especially regarding infectious diseases, notably cholera, plague,
and yellow fever, as well as the measures taken to check these diseases." In
addition to these diseases, exanthematous typhus, smallpox, and dengue fever
have been declared diseases the incidence of which must be signaled to the
Office. The Office engaged in the study of disease control and held conferences for the revision of sanitary conventions. To a certain degree, it supervised and suggested methods of health control for ships and aircraft.

WHO also inherited the mission and facilities of the League of Nations
Health Section, including the Epidemiological Intelligence Station at Singapore. WHO has set up regional intelligence and information centers in the
Americas and Asia which supply what may be called an epidemiological
warning service. WHO concentrates on certain "key diseases" such as malaria, tuberculosis, and venereal diseases. Since annually about 300 million
people are affected by malaria and about 3 million are killed by it, and
about 5 million die of tuberculosis, WHO's strategic approach appears fully
justified. The death rates of venereal diseases are unknown but also run
into millions. WHO's global attack upon venereal diseases received the support of UNICEF, with which WHO is closely teamed in a number of under-

takings (vaccination of about a hundred million children against tuberculosis). WHO is pioneering in the introduction of mental-health services to many lands. WHO still suffers from the endemic disease affecting all specialized agencies: inadequate funds and the noncooperative attitude of certain nations, especially Russia, which is not a WHO member.

The Universal Postal Union. Perhaps the best proof of UPU's truly universal usefulness is supplied by the fact that even the Soviet Union belongs to it. Founded in 1875, it has accommodated itself so successfully to changing political as well as technological conditions that it must be viewed as the ideal example of functional relations between nations. No one would think of blaming it for partiality in its dealings or suspecting it as a vehicle of espionage or ideological penetration. No one wants to shoot the international mailman. But UPU has done its job so smoothly and self-effacingly—self-effacement being virtue No. 1 of any international specialized agency—that hardly anyone knows that UPU exists.

The International Telecommunication Union. The ITU descends from the International Telegraph Union of 1865. One of its most important tasks is now the allocation of radio frequencies. Since agreements on radio, telephone, and telegraph communications across international boundaries involve political (propaganda) and military considerations, ITU's existence has not been as untroubled by "nonfunctional" interference as has been the Universal Postal Union. The Soviet Union, which prefers isolation to communication, is understandably not a member.

The Technical Assistance Board and the Technical Assistance Committee. TAB, consisting of the Secretary General and the heads of the specialized agencies, and TAC, delegated by ECOSOC to handle the technical-assistance program in a supervisory and policy-making capacity, constitute the principal parts of the U.N. machinery set up to supply member nations with expert advice in the various fields of economic, social, and cultural development. The general purposes of the U.N. program are identical with the so-called Point Four program of the United States, and the two programs run parallel to one another. For the fiscal year 1952, Congress appropriated 206 million dollars for these purposes. The American program was administered for a time by the Mutual Security Agency, which was succeeded by the Foreign Operations Administration.[7] Part of this Congressional appropriation, 16 million dollars for 1952, was allocated to the United Nations as the American quota of the U.N. technical-assistance program. Since the American share of the budget (29 million dollars for 1953) of the United Nations technical-assistance program was the largest individual contribution, there were in fact, *two* Point Four programs, one run by the United States as a unilateral venture and one run by the United Nations on a cooperative basis

[7] Charles P. Kindleberger, *International Economics,* Homewood, Ill., Irwin, 1953, pp. 446–447. See also a concise summary of the technical assistance program in Hollis W. Barber, *Foreign Policies of the United States,* New York, Dryden, 1953, pp. 544–550.

backed by American funds. The contribution of the United States amounted to more than half of the total of all other countries' shares in the program. This ambidextrous arrangement was, in all likelihood, suggested by President Truman's pledge that "the old imperialism—exploitation for profit—has no place in our plans . . ." and is designed to allay the fears, real or feigned, of the new nation-states of Asia that Point Four may prove the back door to the "old imperialism" which they expelled or which departed voluntarily by the front door.

"Technical assistance" is conceived as a pinpointed attack upon the political and social problems raised by the vast differentials in standards of living throughout the world. The programs of the United States and of the U.N. are designed as a means of supplying backward countries not so much with capital equipment as with expert advice, chiefly furnished by the technicians dispatched to the problem areas. Both the United States and the U.N. set up programs for training native personnel in the needed skills. Some remarkable work has been done—several hundred projects having been launched in some 40 countries—and has stirred through an ingenious publicity campaign the imagination of the public, especially the American public ("exportation of American know-how"). Yet the effects to date of "technical assistance" upon the economy of those 1.5 billion people, whose average standard of living is so considerably lower than the American, have been about as impressive as the elephant's response to the blows of an umbrella.

Not considering the International Bank, the Monetary Fund, the Food and Agriculture Organization, and the technical-assistance program, the United Nations and the specialized agencies operate on a budget of less than 40 million dollars per year.[8] Of that amount, about two-thirds defray the costs of the United Nations proper, that is, largely of the Secretariat, the General Assembly, and the Security Council. The rest is distributed among the specialized agencies.

This means that few of the specialized activities can be carried out efficiently. It is doubtful whether investments in the strictly *political* activities of the United Nations (*e.g.*, the Security Council) will ever pay. But if the adequate financing of research, experimentation, and technical executive agencies made possible the augmentation of the food supply of the world, if world health could be improved through the functioning of a truly effective and duly endowed health service, if educational levels could be raised everywhere but especially in the backward countries, and if there were a satisfactory exchange of scientific information, international organization clearly would have proved its worth.

A federation of technical services would have come into being which could not fail to lead to improved cooperation in the political field. Perhaps, the

[8] The General Assembly, in 1952, approved a budget for the United Nations' financial year 1953 of 38 million dollars. This does not include the budgets of UNESCO, ICAO, ITU, WHO, and U.N. Children's Emergency Fund.

solution to many baffling political problems may lie in a technical integration of national societies. In any event, the United Nations could make a far greater and more lasting contribution to the happiness of the world if it succeeded in reducing the number of those sick with tuberculosis or malaria and if it increased the food consumption of the average world inhabitant rather than by stopping a minor war between Begonia and Lusitania. At least, this would be so according to vital statistics. Though the United Nations cannot do in the political realm what it is intended but not equipped to do, *it can, in the field of functional cooperation, advance the welfare of mankind.* Habits of international cooperation are as deeply rooted as the associations of men in a large number of common activities and as vital interests are intimate, interrelated, and matter-of-fact.

BIBLIOGRAPHY

Barber, Hollis W.: *Foreign Policies of the United States,* New York, Dryden, 1953.
Chase, Eugene P.: *The United Nations in Action,* New York, McGraw-Hill, 1950.
Eagleton, Clyde: *International Government,* New York, Ronald, 1948.
Finer, Herman: *The United Nations Economic and Social Council,* Boston, World Peace Foundation, 1946.
Fry, Varian: *Bricks without Mortar: The Story of International Cooperation,* New York, Foreign Policy Association, 1938.
Goodrich, Leland, and Edward Hambro: *The Charter of the United Nations: Commentary and Documents,* rev. ed., Boston, World Peace Foundation, 1949.
Hill, Martin: *The Economic and Financial Organization of the League,* Washington, D.C., Carnegie Institution, 1946.
Leonard, L. Larry: *International Organization,* New York, McGraw-Hill, 1951.
Levi, Werner: *World Organization,* Minneapolis, Minn., University of Minnesota Press, 1950.
Mitrany, David: *A Working Peace System: An Argument for the Functional Development of International Organization,* London, Royal Institute of International Affairs, 1943.
Potter, Pitman B.: *An Introduction to the Study of International Organization,* New York, Appleton-Century-Crofts, 1951.
United Nations, Department of Public Information: *Measures for the Economic Development of Under-developed Countries,* Document E/1986.
U.S. Department of State: *United States Participation in the United Nations: Report by the President to Congress for the Year 1948,* Publication 3437, Government Printing Office, 1949.
———: *Participation of the United States Government in International Conferences,* July 1, 1945–June 30, 1946, Government Printing Office, 1947.
———: *International Agencies in Which the United States Participated,* Government Printing Office, 1946.
Vandenbosch, Amry, and Willard N. Hogan: *The United Nations: Background, Organization, Functions, Activities,* New York, McGraw-Hill, 1952.
Walters, F. P.: *A History of the League of Nations,* New York, Oxford, 1952.
Wertheimer-Ranshoffen, Egon: *The International Secretariat,* New York, Columbia University Press, 1946.
White, L. C., and M. R. Zocca: *International Non-governmental Organizations,* New Brunswick, N.J., Rutgers University Press, 1952.

Part Nine

THE GOOD SOCIETY IN THE MAKING

Chapter 28

THE UNITY OF THE WEST

THE IDEA OF WORLD GOVERNMENT

It is possible, though by no means certain, that the world would remain forever at peace were it feasible to abolish national sovereignties and establish a world government under a constitution which—to paraphrase Alexander Hamilton—would "operate on individuals" in the same manner as do now the laws of the sovereign states This proposition is simple enough to satisfy those who view history as a progression from smaller to larger units, from diversity to uniformity, and from anarchy to order, or those who deem that the potentialities for mass destruction latent in modern technology constitute an irrefutable argument in themselves for the abolishment of violence perpetrated by nations upon nations and that nothing less than world government *here and now* will furnish the sole alternative to the annihilation of civilization together with most of mankind.

Nowhere has the idea of world government received wider public attention than in the United States, where diverse movements for world government sprang into existence virtually simultaneously with the founding of the United Nations organization. This phenomenon is explained partially by the sway in that country of doctrines of progress deriving from the rationalist philosophy of the 18th and 19th centuries, partially by a growing sense of frustration over the inadequacies of the two most recent world organizations, and partially by a complex interaction of guilt feeling, fear, and related psychological responses triggered in the collective mind by the introduction to warfare of new techniques of mass destruction.

It is not possible here to explore the sources in reason and emotion which have nourished the movement for world government in the United States nor their divergences as regards specific features of the world government-to-be. There is, however, agreement on one point: the world state is to be federal and not a world imperium established through conquest by one dominant power. The suggestive analogy of the American Constitution and the ethos of American society preclude any other but the federal solution. The growth of world government is thus conceived as the extension of a beneficent process to which the United States owes its national well-being. The establishment of world federation, patterned on the American example, involves the *voluntary* surrender of national sovereignty while allowing for a considerable degree of local autonomy. Nations, big or small, are facts of nature and culture, and it is not in the power of any state to destroy them. Hence a world federation offers a basis of compromise between the centralization of power required for enforcing the federal laws, *i.e.*, principally maintaining the peace of the world against any or all aggressors, and the right to national self-determination proclaimed by Woodrow Wilson. It is here that the argument for a federal "world order under law" or "limited" world government runs into formidable objections.

If the modern nation-states, which concentrate far greater powers in the hands of government than did the states of old, are incapable of keeping the peace, whether by their individual policies or by such collective action as that envisioned in the League Covenant and U.N. Charter, where is the organizing principle of world government to be found? Since the nation-state is inherently aggressive and militant, by what dialectical leap can it gain that higher ground upon which it can slough off its competitive characteristics, yield itself up to the world community, and release its citizens or subjects to the rule of a higher law? Evidently, if nation-states could at will so transform themselves, no world government would be needed for the enforcement of laws against aggressors, for the regenerated nation-states would be peace-loving as a matter of course. If nation-states possessed the capacity for self-abnegation, the problem of world government would not exist; if they did not, it would have to be shown by what means they could be persuaded to release their citizens or subjects from their respective allegiances to the rights and duties of world citizenship. For the latter case, the answer, search as we may, looks suspiciously like coercion by force. That it may be the great majority of nation-states who would coerce by force a small minority, perhaps only one, of their fellow nation-states to release their peoples from the bondage of sovereignty, does not constitute a moral warrant for coercion. A federation so created would start its existence with a flagrant violation of minority rights. Moreover, this particular kind of persuasion would, more likely than not, entail war, and that is what the entire operation is intended to prevent.

The question arises as to whether the great mass of individuals *wish* to be released from the allegiances they now bear their respective nation-states. Anyone even slightly familiar with the history of foreign-trade legislation in the advanced industrial countries, diverse national policies designed to "stabilize" domestic employment, wages and markets, and world-wide restrictive barriers to migration designed to keep the "foreigner" out, will be hardly predisposed to answer the question in the affirmative. That a great mass of men may at one and the same time profess ardent desire to see world government established forthwith and yet be unprepared to yield a fraction of their stake in the area of national protection is no contradiction. It is consistent with the contradictory nature of man.

The towering fact of modern politics is the abject helplessness of the individual facing the "complexity" of industrial civilization and his consequent dependence on a host of collectivities within collectivities. The highest and most effective of these is the state, for it not only dispenses the multitudinous services on which modern man has come to rely in his struggle against baffling economic uncertainties, but also supplies the only form of security he knows, and ever knew, against a host of dangers, real and imagined, lurking beyond the national frontiers. These are not the sole claims of the state to the loyalty of its citizen, but they are the ones which make all the other privileges of citizenship effective and all its burdens tolerable.[1]

The "Functional" Approach. It has been argued that the problem of international political cooperation could be eased by "functional" cooperation, *i.e.*, cooperation in "nonpolitical" matters such as specific economic and cultural activities. Professor Mitrany, perhaps the most persuasive exponent of the "functional" approach to the obstinate problem of equal sovereignty, holds "that by its very nature the constitutional approach emphasizes the individual index of power; the functional approach emphasizes the common index of needs," and that, since many such needs cut across national boundaries, a beginning could be made by providing joint government for them.[2] This means that if by joint efforts people were fed, clothed, and housed, and industries developed for common use while trade barriers were broken down, general peace would prevail. The real problem is to persuade some hundred sovereign governments to do just that. There is no hardship in exchanging cultural "goods" between, let us say, Britain and China or the United States and India. In areas, however, where existing inequalities are very great or generally considered very important, the functional approach runs into the same difficulties which beset the constitutional or political approach to world government.

It is possible, though not always easy, to persuade peoples of not too dissimilar living standards to pool their resources, as, for example, the pooling of hydroelectric power by France and Italy, or the exchange of Austrian electric power in summer against Czechoslovak coal in winter. But "functional" partnership in peacetime between high-living-standard and low-living-stand-

[1] See Raymond Aron, *The Century of Total War*, New York, Doubleday, 1954, pp. 262–271.

[2] "The Functional Approach to World Organization," *International Affairs,* Vol. 24, No. 3, July, 1948, pp. 350–362.

ard countries involves, if it is to come to grips with the vital issues of international conflict, a sharing of wealth and trading opportunities.

Such sharing, while highly desirable from the point of view of classical economics, flies in the face of the protectionist doctrines dominating the economic policy of every major country. For the sovereign power of every major state is chiefly employed in the defense of existing "inequalities," to wit, a high standard of living which is *not* equal to that of the poor countries. Wherever "functional" arrangements entail large, though perhaps only temporary, sacrifices of cherished "inequality," their ratification by popular approval stands no more chance than do such "functional" proposals as tariff agreements and agreements on population movements in general.[3]

In brief, the functional solution is practical only when there exists a similarity or community of interests. That similarity or community of interests can be reinforced by functional organizations; it cannot be created by them. Moreover, the circuitous road to peace by way of "functional" cooperation is a long one, whereas the danger of war is near.

History throws some light on the question. When the Thirteen American Colonies had succeeded in gaining independence from Britain as sovereign states, they were faced by the double danger of invasion from Europe and also of wars with each other. Jealous of the sovereignties that George Washington had won for them, they tried to solve their problem by a functional approach in various directions. Washington induced them to face the question whether their newly won freedom could be preserved unless they agreed to merge their sovereignties in the United States. He forced them to face the fact that this could only be done by making Congress responsible not to thirteen sovereign governments but to the electors from whom those governments derived their authority. Having faced *and solved* the *political* problem, Americans *then* found they could solve their economic and functional problems. *The political settlement was the key to the functional problems.*

South Africa offers the most interesting case of all. That medley of colonies, republics, and native states was again and again involved in wars. The functional approach was tried in vain, till in the 20th century Lord Milner, in his commanding position as British High Commissioner of South Africa, was able to persuade them all to adopt a customs convention. For a few years it seemed that this functional approach had averted the drift toward another war until self-government was restored to the conquered republics. These governments quickly realized that the governments of the coast colonies had been using their sovereign power to evade the customs convention in favor of themselves. The Transvaal government at once denounced the convention, and everyone felt that events would move to another catastrophe in a country where rifles go off with remarkable ease.

Lord Selborne, who followed Milner as High Commissioner, published a memorandum in which he showed with unanswerable logic that unless the

[3] See Chap. 20.

four colonies merged their sovereignty into one South African Union, they would soon be fighting each other again. Not many politicians believed that a union was then possible. But Generals Botha and Smuts, supported by Dr. Jameson, the Prime Minister of Cape Colony who was recognized as leader of British South Africans, and also his opponent F. S. Malan, leader of the Afrikander Bond in the Cape, supported Lord Selborne's thesis in public speeches. When people at large realized that the leaders of both races felt that another South African war could only be averted by union, a national convention was demanded by public opinion. The Union of South Africa was an accomplished fact within two years.

The functional approach thus led to union, but only by the breakdown of the customs convention which forced politicians to realize that functional problems can only be dealt with when the political problem has been solved.

South Africa had merely repeated the experience of the German states in the previous century. Napoleon reduced some hundreds of German states to less than forty, of which Prussia was the largest. After his downfall the Prussian bureaucracy induced the others to enter a customs convention. The difficulty of dealing with more than thirty governments was such that Bismarck announced that unless they agreed to establish a national legislature based on manhood suffrage, which could fix the tariff for Germany as a whole, Prussia would break up the *Zollverein*. Everyone knew that war would follow, and the states accepted the federation devised by Bismarck. The German states accepted union as the only alternative to another intestine war.

The functional approach is useful to this extent, that it seems to be necessary to convince politicians by its breakdown that political problems are prior to functional problems.

The fact is that the people at large are less tenacious of sovereign rights than the politicians, for an obvious reason. The sovereign power vests in the people; but is wielded in fact by the politicians, who therefore prize the power they hold in their hands more than the people to whom it belongs. It is only when some outstanding leader—a Washington, a Bismarck, a Botha—tells the people that the maintenance of national sovereignty will end in war that the ordinary politicians realize how the common people value peace more than their national sovereignty.[4]

WESTERN UNION

It seems that the federalist as well as the functional approach to world government is based on a far too simple and superficial interpretation of the problem of war and peace. The devil theory of national sovereignty rests upon a platitude. Moralists, notorious for their dogmatic bent, are agreed that the best means of establishing the rule of good is to cast out evil. National sovereignty as such is an empty term. It acquires meaning only by the identification of interests which it embraces. These interests, entrenched be-

[4] Lionel Curtis, *The Master-key to Peace*, New York, Oxford, 1947, pp. 17–21.

hind national frontiers and within the national society, engender tensions whenever interests similarly entrenched threaten "interference." It is these tensions which at various times and places have sought release in war. National sovereignty *per se* does not "cause" war; hence its abolition will not bring peace. This conclusion may do violence to the cherished preconceptions of the advocates of world government as an ultimate political panacea. It will hardly surprise the student of the history of revolutions, a history as crowded and violent as that of wars between nations.

The very reasons which speak against superficial universalism argue forcefully for the case of regionalism in a general way and that of Western unity in particular. The term "regionalism," be it noted, must not be understood here as denoting a concept purely based on geographical characteristics, but rather on a community of interests, reinforced by strategic geography. Loose as this definition may seem, it acquires a lively meaning when it is tested on the realities of the world in which we live—and on the preconceptions of "one world" universalism.

It is the tenacious hold of these latter preconceptions on the minds of American statesmen which impeded for nearly three precious years, 1945–1948, the speedy organization of *what can be organized because it exists,* and diverted American policy toward the pursuit of a formal internationalism which cannot make up by pleasing legal constructions for nonexistence of historical formations. The rejection of historical experience was all the more surprising because the war which just had been fought had taught a stern lesson in strategic "priorities."

The leaders of the United States had had the foresight and the courage to fight the war according to their judgment of the comparative importance of strategic objectives and to fight it as a *coalition war.* The decision was to vanquish Germany first, then conquer Japan. Strategic exigencies impelled the United States to defend the Atlantic community, to support its principal ally, Britain; rescue its ally, France; liberate Western Europe; reinforce Russia in order to mount a concentric attack against Germany, and, only after the Atlantic community had been secured, to throw its full weight against Japan. And the alliance with Russia was a means to that end: defense of the Western community. It was not forged as part of the grand design or in deliberate pursuance of the distant goal of world order under law, but as an *ad hoc* partnership in which the primary stake of the United States was the defense of the West in what President Roosevelt called, in 1942, a "war for survival."

In this sense, the attempt to wrest from that bold and necessary improvisation a permanent arrangement, to wit, the great-power unanimity which is the "cornerstone of the United Nations," transcended the primary objective. It was the second phase in a scheme in which first things had been rightly judged as coming first. The great problem today is again—or is it still?—

how to prevent war. Foreign policy shaped in the crucible of strategic exigencies is an austere discipline. By dire necessity it is guided by the principle of the greatest economy of effort. First things still come first, and the primary issue of American foreign policy remains the defense of the Western community.

The Western community, in contrast to the figments of the political and moral "oughts" spawned by universalist imagination, is an impressive historic, economic, and political reality. Every state of the Americas stems from Europe. Its Western ideals and institutions originated in the immensely fertile soil of Hellenic and Judaeo-Christian civilization. From the 15th century onward the Anglo-Saxon, French, Spanish, Portuguese, Dutch, and Danish conquerors and colonizers extended the sway of Europe to the western reaches of the Atlantic. By the beginning of the 19th century, the Atlantic had been transformed into the Mediterranean of Western civilization. The spread of British, French, and American ideals of liberty and constitutional government has made the region of this vast inland sea the "citadel of what today is rather loosely called Democracy." [5]

Its underlying strategic unity is shown by the fact that since the Thirty Years' War every great European conflict has embroiled all the states of the Atlantic region; and twice in this century a coalition of virtually all the members of the Atlantic world met the challenge of German imperialism. European capital investment broke the ground upon which arose the American national economies. When the United States, in turn, became a source of capital funds, it placed four-fifths of its foreign holdings in Great Britain, the British Dominions, Latin America, and Western Europe. The distribution of the foreign lending of the United States reflected the distribution of its trade: more than nine-tenths of American exports went to Britain and her Dominions, Europe, and Latin America. These are the lands who received the bulk of American lend-lease supplies; it is they who are the recipients of the bulk of American aid advanced under the European Recovery Act of 1948.

It is no accident that trends originating on one hand in the postwar problems of European economic rehabilitation and, on the other hand, in the political and strategic problems arising from the advance of Russian power into the heart of Europe, converged in a series of developments which posed anew the problem of Western solidarity. For the former were revealed as insoluble except within the broad context of the economic interdependence of the Western European countries themselves and, in the last resort, their dependence on American resources; and the latter as insoluble except in terms of systems of alliances, pooling the strategic resources of Western

---

[5] See Ross Hoffman, "The Atlantic Community," *Thought,* Vol. 20, No. 76, p. 25. This important and prescient essay projected the idea of the Atlantic Pact long before the concept aroused the interest of practicing American and European statesmen.

Europe, and, in the last resort, aligning the entire Western community in a defensive system against the East.[6]

The first steps toward the creation of a Western political and strategic system were taken in the Anglo-French Treaty of 1947 and subsequently by Great Britain, France, and the Benelux states (Holland, Belgium, and Luxembourg) who, on March 17, 1948, signed a fifty-year alliance, providing for consultation on any situation constituting a threat to the peace "from whatever quarter" and for mutual military aid under Article 51 of the U.N. Charter, "if any of the high contracting parties should be the object of an armed attack in Europe." On the same day, President Truman, speaking in New York City, dispelled whatever doubts may have lingered in the United States as to the efficacy of mere economic aid to Europe, by stating that "economic rehabilitation was not enough," and called for the prompt enactment of universal training and selective service legislation. On June 11, 1948, the United States Senate resolved that

this Government should pursue the following objectives within the U.N. Charter:

1. Voluntary agreement to remove the veto from all questions involving pacific settlements of international disputes and situations, and from the admission of new members.

2. Progressive development of regional and other collective arrangements for individual and collective self-defense in accordance with the purposes, principles, and provisions of the Charter.

3. Association of the United States, by constitutional process, with such regional and other collective arrangements as are based on continuous and effective self-help and mutual aid, and as affect its national security.

4. Contributing to the maintenance of peace by making clear its determination to exercise the right of individual or collective self-defense unler Article 51 should any armed attack occur affecting its national security. . .

On April 4, 1949, at Washington, the Foreign Ministers of Belgium, Canada, Denmark, France, Iceland, Italy, Luxembourg, the Netherlands, Norway, Portugal, the United Kingdom, and the United States signed the Atlantic Pact. They were joined, in September, 1951, by Greece and Turkey. In the classical language of the great military alliances of history, the Pact specified the obligation of the signatories to "consider an armed attack on any one of the Parties as an attack against all and, consequently, to take such individual and collective action, including the use of armed force, as each party considers necessary to restore and maintain the security of the North Atlantic area."

According to the White Paper issued by the U.S. government, the Pact does not represent a violation of the U.N. Charter: [7]

---

[6] For a forceful and profound statement of the forces which have brought the great community into existence, the reader is referred to R. J. S. Hoffman's *Durable Peace,* New York, Sheed and Ward, 1944.

[7] See the White Paper issued by the U.S. Department of State, Mar. 20, 1949.

The Atlantic Pact is a collective self-defense arrangement among countries of the North Atlantic area who, while banding together to resist armed attack against any one of them, specifically reaffirm their obligations under the Charter to settle their disputes with any nations solely by peaceful means. It is aimed at coordinating the exercise of the right of self-defense specifically recognized in Article 51 of the United Nations Charter.

This claim has never found favor with the Soviet Union, which—concentrating its fire on Article 52, also invoked by the State Department—holds that

It can only be claimed in mockery that the North Atlantic Pact is a regional arrangement. He who respects Article 52 of the United Nations Charter will not take this view, as the North Atlantic Alliance was formed, not on the basis of Article 52, but as a direct violation of the Charter and the fundamental principles of the United Nations organization.[8]

Soviet protests failed to deter the Western powers from their cooperative undertakings. Indeed, Soviet conduct furnished the most convincing argument for seeking strength in union. Regardless of legalities, the Atlantic Pact was made inevitable because (1) the Atlantic nations continued to be apprehensive of Soviet designs, and (2) the United Nations clearly did *not* provide the security that had been expected. And when President Truman signed the Military Aid Program on October 6, 1949, it signified American recognition of the military implications of the Atlantic Pact, although not to the full extent of Western Europe's defensive needs. (Of the 1.3 billion dollars allocated to MAP, only 1 billion was reserved for Western Europe.[9])

The North Atlantic Pact was a step forward on the road of Western survival. It was a more solemn and binding commitment than in peacetime ever bound the Western nations together. Its danger was that it induced a feeling of false security. The text of the treaty left enough loopholes for the legal evasion of obligations assumed. The large number of signatories did not veil the unpleasant fact that few of them possessed significant military strength. The Pact had the geographic weakness that distance prevented the speedy concentration of the Allies' armed forces. The basic condition of the Pact's

[8] "Official Text of U.S.S.R. Statement on North Atlantic Pact," *U.S.S.R. Information Bulletin*, Feb. 11, 1949, p. 85.

[9] The North Atlantic Treaty provided for a council to head the treaty organization. Originally composed of the foreign ministers of the signatory powers or their representatives, it was enlarged in 1951 to include defense, economic, and finance ministers. First, a Council of Deputies was formed to serve as a permanent agency of coordination. It was replaced by the Permanent Representatives sitting in Paris under a Chairman and an International Secretariat representing not an individual government but NATO itself. The military organization was placed under the supervision of the Military Committee composed of the chiefs of staff. Supreme Headquarters Allied Powers in Europe (SHAPE) was set up as top military planning agency. The command of the Allied forces in Europe was placed in the hands of a Supreme Allied Commander in Europe (SACEUR). The successive chiefs, all of them Americans, were General Dwight D. Eisenhower (1951–June, 1952), General Matthew B. Ridgway (to June, 1953), and General Alfred M. Gruenther.

functioning was that the signatories would remain true to its spirit and that not one or the other nation would embark on a course of appeasement. The Atlantic Pact, in short, merely defined the framework within which the defense of the West could best be undertaken. It did not by itself provide security. It did not alter the fundamental fact that Western security—and world peace—were dependent upon the strength of *American* military power.

The North Atlantic Pact did not launch a ready-made "Atlantic Community"—just as neither American exhortations nor the official responses of European governments brought forth European "integration." New institutions will prove successful only if they derive their warrant from necessity and from public recognition that it is they, and they alone, which can solve pressing problems. It is not surprising that the bold schemes for the unity of Western defense and the political integration of Europe should have run into formidable difficulties: the obstacles to be overcome were—and are today and will be for years to come—apathy, factionalism, and sheer malice and, in some countries, economic and political weaknesses paralyzing action. The record of the North Atlantic Treaty Organization's achievements reflects these difficulties; the goals set when NATO started operations—fifty-five to sixty-two divisions in Western Europe by the end of 1953—have not been reached. Despite agreement in 1950 on German rearmament, "in principle," there was no German army in 1954. At the Lisbon Conference in February, 1952, the European NATO members, spurred by American urgings and the implications of the Korean War, made plans for a European army of 1.4 million men and 4,000 planes. In mid-winter 1952–1953, the European governments conceded that these plans had been overoptimistic. At the time of this writing, the NATO powers have not discovered the formula for bridging the gap between what military men say is necessary to defend Europe and what financial experts say these countries can afford for this purpose.

The growth of European unity is inseparable from the development of American-European cooperation; the former shared in the vicissitudes of the latter. Both European unity and the Atlantic community sprang from the same soil: Europe's need for the support of the United States and the need of the United States for a strong Europe, guardian of the Atlantic approaches and partner in world economic development. In 1949, Congress called for the "unification of Europe" as an explicit objective of the United States. The Mutual Security Act of 1951 provided that the funds authorized for economic and military assistance should be used "to further encourage economic unification and political federation of Europe." In the MSA Act of 1952, Congress "welcomes the recent progress in political federation, military integration and economic unification in Europe and reaffirms its belief in the necessity of further vigorous efforts toward these ends as a means of building strength, establishing security and preserving peace in the North Atlantic area."

Without American material support and moral impulsion, Europe might not have mustered the energies that went into the making of the new, supranational institutions. Without the stirring of European imagination and the spontaneous surge of Europe's creative forces, American aid and suasion might have fallen upon barren soil. The instinctive search for Western unity, impelled by common fears and hopes, thus called forth simultaneously Atlantic and European institutions which were interdependent and rooted in the same necessities.

Divergences arose over degree and timing rather than over the purpose of the efforts which were to lead to the making of a West united. It was, however, precisely these divergences on the *how* rather than the *what,* which weakened the West in the face of powerful divisive forces within and of the diplomatic and propaganda strategy of the Soviet Union aiming precisely at the defeat of that one project which would kill the communists' hope in Europe: the unification of a free Europe including Germany.

Perhaps the most important source of the tensions which assailed the system of Western alliance was the disparity of power between its members. The ancient military powers of Europe, Britain and France, had emerged from the war far weaker than they themselves—and, for that matter—the United States had realized in the flush of victory. The very preponderance of American power and the awareness of Europe's relative weakness engendered among Europeans a psychological condition which can be likened to the "inferiority complex" of individual psychology. European nations looked to American power as the guarantee of their own security and yet feared that America would use that power to press for changes they viewed as too radical, or for the pursuit of objectives, especially as regards the Soviet Union and the Far East, which they deemed too perilous. This ambiguity haunted the makers of the institutions which were to transform the new regionalism from a grand design into a working concern. The United States advocated vigorously what Europeans should have wanted to do themselves for their own good and now were hesitant to do precisely because the United States advocated it. The United States urged speedy action where European states wished to move slowly because, being more conscious of the intricacies of ancient historical issues, they deplored American haste as tending to oversimplify complex issues and thus to render them less tractable than they had been before American diplomacy had seized upon them.

No wonder that the general advance upon the goal of integration has been broken by local retreats and has been stalled at various points!

PROGRESS TOWARD EUROPEAN "INTEGRATION"

The Council of Europe. The (embryonic) Western Union of the Brussels Treaty was barely one year old when it was superseded by the Council of

Europe. In October, 1948, the Consultative Council of the Foreign Ministers, created by the Brussels Pact, set up a committee representing the signatories of the treaty to "examine and propose the measures to be taken with a view to realizing a greater degree of unity between the countries of Europe." A decision was made to set up a Special Committee to recommend measures aimed toward this end. This Special Committee first met on November 26 in Paris. On January 20, 1949, it reported the failure of the British delegation to agree to a European consultative assembly, the British holding out for a ministerial council. The British feared an assembly would become a mere "talking shop" and that, by the French method of voting, communists could not be kept out. Upon the recommendations of the Committee, the Consultative Council agreed to a solution which compromised, at least for the time being, the differences of the French and the British project for European political integration. The Consultative Council finally agreed upon the establishment of a Council of Europe. The Council is composed of a committee of ministers and an advisory assembly. The committee is to function as an upper chamber but has greater powers than the lower chamber whose agenda it determines by two-thirds majority. It negotiates secretly, and is composed of members of ruling cabinets. The members of the assembly—their number, ranging from 3 (Luxembourg, Iceland, the Saar) to 18 (France, Germany, and the United Kingdom), was fixed at 132 by an amendment in 1951—deliberate publicly and are named by the parliaments of the participant nations. They have no legislative powers. The decisions of the committee are dependent upon the policies of individual governments. The committee is empowered to make decisions for all member states except in the field of national defense, but each member retains the right of veto. Sessions are to be held once a year for a period of less than one month. As can be seen from this constitution, the Council is by no means a supergovernment of the participating nations. It is essentially a body of coordination and discussion. The retention of the right of veto by members and the limited duration of its operations make the Council merely a symbol. The statute of the Council of Europe was signed on May 5, 1949. Strasbourg, France, was chosen as its seat.

The European members of the Council were not identical with the European signatories of the North Atlantic Pact. At the time of the former's founding, Sweden, Eire, Greece, and Turkey participated in the Council but were not then parties to the Atlantic Pact, while Portugal adhered to the Atlantic Pact but did not join the Council of Europe. The Council was founded by Belgium, Britain, Denmark, France, Italy, Holland, Ireland, Luxembourg, Norway, and Sweden who on August 8, 1949, were joined by Greece, Iceland, and Turkey, and later by West Germany, and, as an associate member, the Saar. The Council obviously was misnamed; it should have been called Council of Agglomerated States in Europe. However, it was hoped that by 1952 all the governments of OEEC would become members. Indeed, the European Consultative Assembly voted on September 3, 1949, for a European Economic Union.[10]

The European Payments Union—a first step toward economic union, though by no means a decisive one—was created in July, 1950. It was designed as a multilateral clearing system for intra-European payments. The United States made an initial capital contribution to get EPU under way.

Schuman Plan. The precise form in which institutional unity in Europe could be effectively molded remained undetermined—largely because British and French concepts on European unity were at odds. This is one reason why ambitious proposals for an all-embracing federation have floundered. It was only slowly, within the framework of the security and economic assurance of a developing Atlantic Community, that six countries of Europe came to agree in 1951 and early 1952 to cessions of sovereignty that have laid the foundations for the building of a "European Community of Six."

The Coal and Steel Community (CSC), the first—and in some respects the most significant—step in this direction, was launched by the Foreign Minister of France, Robert Schuman, in May, 1950. He proposed that the coal and steel industries of France and Germany, together with those of any other European country willing to participate, be merged into a single production and market area and that supranational institutions be established to carry into effect their collective purposes. By August, 1952, this proposal, in the form of a treaty, had been accepted by the governments of France, Belgium, Italy, Netherlands, Luxembourg, and West Germany, ratified by the parliaments, and come into operation.[11]

[10] Great emphasis is laid on the need for customs unions. Under modern conditions customs unions can have only *limited* effect unless they are accompanied by the abolition of other planning devices, such as quotas, price controls, allocation of materials, and by a unification of currency, credit, investment, and wage policies. A return to at least a limited *laissez faire* is a prerequisite of economic unification as is the establishment of common economic policies in the fields that cannot be "decontrolled." Clearly, as Professor Haberler said, "economic unification is impossible without political unification." The probability that the European nations will gradually abandon "planning" is fairly low. Hence it would seem to follow that there will be neither a political nor an economic unification unless it is imposed by force or forceful persuasion. Small wonder that Professor Haberler concludes that "there will be no European union now or in our time"! See Gottfried Haberler, "Economic Aspects of a European Union," in *World Politics,* Vol. 1, No. 4, July, 1949, pp. 431–441.

[11] See Donald C. Stone, "The Impact of U.S. Assistance Programs on the Political and Economic Integration of Western Europe," *American Political Science Review,* Vol. 46, No. 4, December, 1952. The original Schuman Plan, brain child of France's chief economic planner, Jean Monnet, was much modified in the process of intergovernmental negotiations. The CSC, as it now functions, is a federal-type organization. Its main organs are (1) a High Authority; (2) a Common Assembly; (3) a Council of Ministers; and (4) a Court of Justice. The High Authority is a kind of board of managers. Of its nine members, eight are chosen by the Council of Ministers, the ninth member by the other eight. The Common Assembly, which held its first session in September, 1952, can, by a two-thirds vote, compel the members of the High Authority to resign. This is its chief substantive power. The Assembly meets once a year to hear the report of the Authority and to question its members. The High Court has the power to annul decisions of the High Authority and Common Assembly and has jurisdiction over appeals from decisions or recommendations of the High

The Coal and Steel Community reflects at once the progress of the European idea *and* the ambiguity which dogs each step of its advance. Like the Council of Europe, it was planned as a truly autonomous, supranational, and federal body, linked to the peoples of the member states rather than to their respective governments. The High Authority was to have been truly sovereign within its domain. The interposition of a Council of Ministers, which had not been contemplated by the initiators of CSC, opened the door to the reaffirmation of the interest of governments as against the interest of the supranational community. It is provided that "in all situations not expressly provided for in the treaty, decisions and recommendations of the High Authority are to be made subject to the unanimous concurrence of the Council." It is this provision as well as other modifications of the original concept which considerably diminished the scope of the High Authority and gave rise to the criticism that the competence of CSC does not go much beyond the power exercised, albeit informally or clandestinely, by the private coal and steel cartels flourishing before World War II.

Moreover, the creation of CSC appeared to emphasize the emergence of a Little Europe within the Europe which is only one-half of all Europe. Great Britain, which first sought to hinder by diverse tactics the making of CSC which might become a formidable competitor of Britain's own steel industry, and then accepted a place as interested and accredited observer at the High Authority's proceedings, is not a member and had declared its determination not to join CSC under any circumstances. Britain's abstention tends to increase the preponderance of German industrial capacity. From the French point of view, one of the chief merits—perhaps the principal merit—of the original Schuman Plan was that it would have transformed the International Ruhr Authority, set up after World War II to control Germany's mighty arsenal, into a collective and permanent body with voluntary German membership, thus creating a counterpoise to Germany's power potential. The Coal and Steel Community, since Britain had not joined it, attained only part way the principal objective of French policy; the problem of Franco-German relationships, the core problem of European unity, remained suspended in mid-air. This unsolved problem was at the root of the difficulties besetting the European Defense Community, designed by René Pleven, M. Schuman's ministerial colleague, as the pendant piece of the Schuman Plan. If the political implications of the latter could be submerged in its economic-functional purpose, those of the Pleven Plan remained impervious

---

Authority submitted not only by the Council of Ministers or a member state but also by a private coal or steel company or association. CSC's principal task is to create a single market of coal and steel products, to eliminate restrictions within that six-nation market, and to regulate investments, price scales, production quotas, and, under certain conditions, wages. The text of the draft treaty is rendered in full in *The Schuman Plan Constituting a European Coal and Steel Community,* Department of State Publication 4173, European and British Commonwealth Series 22. Jean Monnet was named first head of the High Authority, which is seated at Luxembourg.

to "functional" solutions because military matters involve, first and foremost, political considerations; the military security of the nation *is* the primary political concern of its government.

The European Defense Community. The organizational framework of the European Defense Community was closely patterned after the Schuman Plan. An agreement was signed at Paris in February, 1952, by the foreign ministers of the Community of Six to merge their national forces into a single European Defense Force in which basic national units of troops of a unit strength of around 13,000–15,000 men would be integrated at the army-corps level.[12] The supranational institution, the EDC, would be empowered to raise, equip, train, command, and finance such a force.

The Consultative Assembly and Committee of Ministers at Strasbourg had given the scheme its blessings in December, 1951. The Foreign Ministers of France, West Germany, and the Benelux states agreed one month later to propose to their governments that a federal parliament be established—in the image of the Schuman Plan—to supervise both the operations of the Coal and Steel Community and the Defense Community. At the Lisbon meeting of NATO, the North Atlantic Council approved the plan for the European Defense Community and agreed to link the Defense Community to NATO by a system of "cross-guarantees." Upon the signing of the European Defense Community Treaty, the signatory governments proceeded to seek its parliamentary ratification—and here the real difficulties began. Ratification, though it met with the vocal resistance of the opposition parties in the Benelux countries, was obtained by the respective governments. In Germany, Chancellor Konrad Adenauer won the *Bundestag*'s approval of the treaty (May, 1953). The general elections (fall, 1953), contested mainly on the issue of Western Germany's participation in EDC, gave overwhelming victory to Adenauer's coalition government. The *Bundestag* voted (February, 1954) a constitutional amendment which empowered the government to proceed with the rearmament of Germany. Germany could go no further until France gave her assent.

In France, parliament thus far—summer, 1954—has failed to ratify the treaty. After the fall of the Pinay government and the retirement of Robert Schuman, a succession of cabinets retreated farther from the treaty and promised the opposition, the de Gaullists as well as the left, that the treaty would be renegotiated or embellished by protocols. The issue of the Saar, a territory detached from Germany in 1945 and in economic and foreign policy matters linked to France, entered the French as well as the German debate of the European Defense Treaty. The French opposition to the treaty insisted that clarification of the status of the Saar, *i.e.*, Germany's irrevocable ratification of the Saar *status quo*, was to be sought as a precondition of French

[12] EDC is to be governed by a Commissariat, an Assembly, a Council of Ministers, and a Court of Justice. The Political Consultative Assembly is to meet once a year and will be the same body as for the Coal and Steel Community.

ratification of the EDC treaty. Parliamentary opposition and the entanglement of the EDC treaty with all kinds of extraneous issues reflected (1)
widespread popular reluctance to plunge into an adventure fraught with
fundamental changes in traditional national attitudes, and (2) perhaps more
important still, changing popular attitudes toward the overarching issue of
world politics, *i.e.*, the American-Russian conflict. Many Frenchmen could
not shake off their fear of a resurgent, vengeful Germany; others appeared to
believe that France should withdraw from a global conflict between giants,
lest she be crushed—no matter which side won. And not a few Frenchmen
insisted that France should revert to her alliance with the Soviet Union.

The United States placed, especially after the outbreak of the Korean War,
the greatest emphasis upon balancing Soviet military power in Europe and
hence upon the rearmament of Germany. From the French point of view—
and that point of view did not differ greatly from that of millions of Europeans who were not German—the major problem was how to balance a revived
Germany's military power, once Germany was permitted—or invited—to
rearm. In this sense, French diplomacy can be said to have been concerned
single-mindedly with the inclusion of Germany in the West European community for the very purpose of preventing a detached Germany from becoming a menace to France and her neighbors. This was, politically, the gist of
the Schuman and Pleven Plans.[13]

It is the very profusion of functional schemes for the "integration" of
Europe—the Little Europe of the Six and the half-Europe of Strasbourg—
which tends to obscure the fundamental problem hampering European unity.
The fundamental problem of Europe is not economic or even military; it is
political.

It is then to the political problems of European unity that we must turn
in order to grasp the transcendent purpose of scattered economic and military measures designed to defend Europe against threats from within and
from abroad. It is this transcendent purpose—the making of a cohesive
political structure—which is the warrant for piecemeal measures such as
American subsidies, regional defense pacts, and customs unions. Without accomplishing that purpose the costly efforts which have gone into the prop-
ping up of a score of national economies and the military defenses of Western
Europe will not achieve a durable settlement and will have to be repeated
over and over again—until exhaustion puts an end to the aimless waste of
dwindling resources.

The Atlantic Community is a mighty reality; strategic and economic exigencies have traced its outlines. However, these outlines are as yet vague.

---

[13] For a thorough airing of French hopes and fears as regards Germany's role—if any—
in EDC, see the parliamentary debates over the European Defense Treaty as reported by
the *Journal Officiel,* Assemblée National, First Session (February, 1952, p. 585 and *passim*).
For the views of two eminent leaders of the opposition to the EDC treaty—one a German
socialist, the other a de Gaullist deputy—see Carlo Schmid and Jacques Soustelle, "Organizing Europe: Dissenting Opinions," *Foreign Affairs,* Vol. 30, July, 1952, pp. 531–553.

They cannot be otherwise because the most important questions concerning the scope of that community still remain to be answered: (1) Are Atlantic Community and European Union mutually compatible systems? (2) What is the position of the British Commonwealth with relation to either of these hypothetical systems? (3) What role is to be assigned to Germany? These are, to be sure, not the only questions—the problems of the Iberian Peninsula and of Asia within the context of that of the Western striving for unity may be considered almost as pressing—but if the first three questions are not answered, the others will most certainly not be answered at all.

THE EUROPEAN DILEMMA RECONSIDERED

The first question can be rephrased as follows: What is Europe? And what is that part of Europe that belongs to the Atlantic Community whereas the rest of Europe does not? [14]

The French proposals submitted to the League of Nations on May 17, 1930, by Aristide Briand [15] described European Union as a "federal bond establishing between them [the twenty-seven European states which were members of the League of Nations] a system of constant solidarity." Briand's proposal specifically recognized that the federal union "may in no case affect the sovereign rights" of the member states; its primary objective was that the nations inhabiting a certain geographical area should in some way cooperate, but not necessarily integrate their social and political systems.

Briand's Europe broadly embraced an area reaching from the Aegean to the North Cape, from Lisbon to Tallinn, Riga, and Warsaw. Since it was to be subordinated to the League of Nations, the Soviet Union (which was elected a member only in 1934) was virtually excluded. Briand's plan emphasized regional military security as the main aim of the proposed European organization. It met with small sympathy in London, where the Labor party under Ramsay MacDonald had returned to office in 1929 and sought to improve Anglo-Russian relations. The project did not get beyond the stage of discussion. Its conception and failure, however, can still serve as criteria to judge the validity of the Pan-European concept.

[14] For the exposition of the case for European Union, see Alfred M. Bingham, *The United States of Europe,* New York, Duell, Sloan & Pearce, 1940; Lord David Davies, *A Federated Europe,* London, Gollancz, 1940; W. Ivor Jennings, *A Federation for Western Europe,* New York, Macmillan, 1940; Abraham Weinfeld, *Towards a United States of Europe,* Washington, American Council on Public Affairs, 1942; Richard N. Coudenhove-Kalergi, *Crusade for Pan-Europe,* New York, Putnam, 1943; and for the rebuttal see Ross Hoffman, "The Atlantic Community"; Rudolf Schlesinger, *Federalism in Central and Eastern Europe,* London, 1945, especially Chap. 16; W. T. R. Fox, *The Super-powers,* New York, Harcourt, Brace, 1944; and Raymond Aron, "Can Europe Achieve Political Unity," *Modern Review,* Vol. 1, No. 7.

[15] *Mémorandum sur l'organisation d'un régime d'Union Fédérale Européenne,* League of Nations Document, 1930, VII, 4. The answers of the European governments are contained in League of Nations Documents, 1930, VII, A 46.

Where does Europe begin, where does it end? No one thus far has been able to define categorically the limits of Europe because no one could say convincingly—now less convincingly than ever—where Europe ends and Russia begins. If Russia is deemed a part of Europe, Soviet Asia too is a part of Europe and so may be Soviet China and Soviet Korea—patently an absurdity. If the Soviet Union and its Asiatic possessions and appendages were to join a European Union, then it would no longer be European but would be Soviet, and the operation would be climaxed by the absorption of the variegated United States of Europe by the monolithic Soviet state and its own steel-riveted, centrally governed "federation." This was precisely the scheme for Eurasian unification of German *Geopolitik,* which would have made Soviet Eurasia a dependency of Europe. True, the Soviet Union, not Germany, would now play the role of "federating power"—if such a development could at all be dignified by the label "federation." As far as Britain and the United States are concerned, the results would be the same: the Eurasian Empire of which Napoleon dreamt and which Hitler came dangerously close to creating.

The dilemma of the Soviet Union's relation to Europe suggested a formulation which may be considered basic to the concept of European Union as it was understood, at the eve of World War II, by its most influential exponent: "The eastern frontier of western culture lies along the Polish-Russian boundary, as does the frontier of Christianity and of the European economic system." [16] This definition begs more questions than it answers. Not only the Russian boundary, but also the frontiers of the Soviet social and economic system have advanced deep into Europe.

If in the east the frontiers of Europe are blurred by the sweep of Soviet power, they are no more sharply defined in the west. For it is difficult to characterize Great Britain as being more "European" than is the Soviet Union. Undoubtedly Great Britain is one of the Western European nations. But are her cultural and economic affinities with Rumania, Hungary, and Poland, not to speak of Russia, closer than those which link together the English-speaking peoples throughout the world or perhaps even the Indian peoples, united as they are by India's *lingua franca*—English—with the peoples of the British Isles? As the Soviet Union embraces northern Asia, so Great Britain reaches across the world. A British world system that would federate with the European continent would be placed in a position analogous to that of the Soviet Union faced by the same contingency. It would either be absorbed by Europe or it would absorb Europe. The first alternative is the one England has rejected repeatedly by force of arms since the days of Cardinal Wolsey; the second alternative would mean the integration into that world system of the 200 million peoples of Central and Eastern Europe, a process which, were it not wholly beyond the physical resources of the

[16] Richard N. Coudenhove-Kalergi, "Europe Tomorrow," *International Affairs,* Royal Institute of International Relations, September, 1939.

70 million people forming the white population of the British Common-wealth, conflicts with their historic and cultural outlook, and what is perhaps more important, with the strategic arrangements which Britain and her Dominions have come, by trial and error, to rely upon in supreme common danger. Neither Russia nor Britain could organize Europe without losing themselves in Europe or subjugating Europe, nor would they tolerate the organization of Europe by the strongest Continental state except by being forced to do so by defeat in a world war.

The peoples of Latin Europe, who are as much Mediterranean, African, and trans-Oceanic as they are European, have not been able to defend or regain their independence in two world wars by their own efforts; they were saved—as was all Western Europe—by the intervention of the English-speaking powers. This holds true not only of France and Italy, but also of Spain and Portugal who, had Germany been victorious, would have had to take whatever place Hitler had been pleased to allocate to them in his Pan-Europe.

Germany twice launched, within the lifetime of one generation, upon the venture of uniting Europe. More than any other state heretofore engaged in European conquest, she has been able to derive advantage from her ideal position at the crossroads of the European peninsula and athwart the north European plain which facilitates movement from east to west and west to east. A united Europe, of which a united Germany peopled by the largest and most vigorous race of the Continent forms part, again may serve as a launching site for German ascendancy. All the experiences of the European peoples cry out against this solution. It may be the logical one from the point of view of economic "functional" efficiency—and much can be said in its favor if Europe is viewed as a system of economic reciprocity—but it meets insuperable objections: the psychological conditioning of Germany's neighbors in the school of German aggressiveness and mastery, and the psychological conditioning of the German people themselves "who suffer the standing temptation to seek leadership of an organized continent." *A united Europe of which a united Germany forms part and Britain does not and is not linked by firm bonds—economic, strategic, and cultural—to the United States, is acceptable to no one but the Germans; a united Europe which has no place for Germany is a contradiction in terms.* This, stripped of ideological décor, is the real dilemma of European Union.

The Idea of European Unity. The longing for a united Europe is not confined to a few thinkers and statesmen nor to any particular European nation; the idea that that unity should be safeguarded by political and economic integration, be it even at the sacrifice of long-cherished sovereign rights, has won a large and increasing following among the broad public in many European lands. So strong and spontaneous has been the public response to this idea, which ten years ago agitated no one except a handful of intellectuals, that statesmen now acknowledge themselves deeply concerned with the problem of European federation, little enamored as they may be of the scheme.

Some of the nostalgia for the unity of Europe is born of the decline. The age of European political hegemony and quasi monopoly of technology, and consequently of modern armament, has closed. Europe, from Warsaw to the Atlantic, is covered with ruins of cities, of national economies, and of states. Europe is a defeated continent. Though the true victors owe their science, technology, and ethical doctrines to Europe—just as the Roman-Hellenic world "descended" from Greece—they are younger than Europe. Both the Soviet Union and the United States are countries of great spaces and bear a lighter burden of historic past. Their civilizations are essentially futurist and optimist. Thus they stand apart from small and crowded Europe, whose peoples are bent over the past and mourn its lost splendors. The feeling that Europe is in danger is aroused not so much by the dissolution of old European colonial empires as by the rise of the two Superpowers, each embracing continents. It is in relation to the overawing might of the United States and the Soviet Union that thinkers and leaders propound the unity of Europe and seek to rouse the European peoples to awareness of their common cause.

Perhaps no one has expressed the longing and the will to European unity more eloquently than has Salvador de Madariaga, Spanish historian and representative of Republican Spain in the League of Nations. Madariaga wrote in 1945: "Much of what is now happening may be explained as a process whereby Europe is endeavoring to create herself. . . . This war is a world event and cannot be explained in mere European terms; but insofar as it is European, it is one of the birthpangs of the European nation." [17]

Madariaga's united Europe is the culmination of unitary trends of culture. In the period between the 13th and 14th centuries Europe was very much aware of herself, owing mostly to the prevalence of the Latin language throughout her territory. When Latin lost its European status—perhaps the most grievous, though indirect, consequence of the Reformation—Europe lost her sense of unity. Hence the sense of European unity must assert itself across the language frontier as well as across any other frontier.

In this way, the process of European unification may be best compared with that of the unity of nations such as Switzerland, which has four language groups, or Belgium, which has two, or Spain, which has three. A nation which is built over several language frontiers and which, despite them, maintains her unity for reasons grounded on common sense and historical tradition is more in harmony with the spirit of progress than the naïve nationalism which, like certain forms of extremist Flemish, Catalan, or Basque separatism, bases its claim to separate nationhood on mere community of language.

Madariaga concluded:

[17] Salvador de Madariaga, *Victors Beware*, London, J. Cape, 1946, p. 153.

The European appeal which the nazis advertised was in part sheer camouflage. But only in part. The spirit of unity is in the air of our epoch. . . . We must create a European commonwealth. The respite, the second great armistice which we must endeavour to transform into a permanent peace, must be imbued with a strong European sense. Nothing short of a European standard must be allowed to move in Europe after the war.

To this fervent plea may be added the observation that, though it is probable that the rise of the United States and the Soviet Union was inscribed in the nature of things, the logical consequence of superiority of population and material resources, Europe did not decline because of a drying up of the creative powers which had carried European civilization to the four corners of the world. In the arts and the sciences, in philosophy and literature, the most original and important contributions came, in our times, still from Europe. The utilization of atomic energy was realized by the United States, but this feat was performed with the help of European scientists and as a result of their labors in the field of abstract research. Until 1939, in any case, modern civilization bore the dominant impress of Europe. Europe's breakdown was not caused by senility. It was the result of the anarchy of her immense creative forces, turning, as it were, back upon themselves. It was also the result of Western Europe's military weakness.

But against these arguments, which seem so persuasively to call Europe to unity for the sake of the very survival of its rich culture, stands the indisputable fact that *Europe, at the height of its powers, never had the consciousness of itself as a political reality.* There did exist a feeling of community up until the end of the 18th century; the European "concert" was linked to the similarities of monarchical regimes and agricultural economies. Among the aristocrats of birth and wealth who governed the great powers in the 19th century, there still existed the idea of a common civilization or, rather, social order. But that common order of things was rent in our times by the clash of ideologies which divided Europe between communist, fascist, and democratic peoples. Within the last thirty years new social groupings took over nearly everywhere from those that were crushed by economic crises, revolutions, and foreign conquest. The opposition between Western democracy and communism does not only divide the Continent, but also the society of each nation. And there are many additional cleavages; for example, those between socialism and liberalism, between religious groups, acute "class" struggles, and demographical complexities.

Perhaps the peoples of Europe have more in common than they think; but awareness of that community is the crucial factor in the process of organizing it. As things stand, the European exponents of Western democracy *and* European Union have a precise idea of what kind of community a united Europe is to be; so have the communists. It may, at some future date, suit the strategy of the Kremlin to call for the formation of the Union of European Soviet Republics. But the communists will fight tooth and nail against

European unity *now* under the tutelage of Western democracy, for they believe, quite rightly, that European Union is not large enough a term to embrace both Western democracy and Oriental despotism.

But is there not a compromise solution: Europe as an ideological Third Force? Indeed, the idea of Europe as a neutral ground or "bridge" between East and West has found great favor among the intellectual circles in France, Britain, and Germany[18] who envision the gradual transformation of the domestic social order by the workings of a Third Force, the coalition of moderate Marxist and non-Marxist (Christian-Socialist) parties. It is conceivable that Europe can work out, by parliamentary processes, a common system of partial socialization of the means of production and of state planning synthesized with private ownership in certain sectors of the economy and guarantees of individual liberties. For reasons inherent in the techniques and politics of "planning," gradually increasing socialization would counteract the tendency to economic and political unification.

That solution, moreover, could appease neither domestic communists nor the Soviet Union. Communist orthodoxy does not allow for alternatives to the communist blueprint of social evolution; social democracy is the unspeakable heresy of communist theology. The more Western socialism came to appear as the valid form of European social integration, the more the Soviet Union would denounce it as a philosophical deviation and a counterrevolutionary movement. That point is clarified with characteristic vigor in one of the letters addressed in 1948, by the Control Committee of the Soviet Communist party to that of the Yugoslav Communist party: "The peaceful development of capitalist elements alongside Socialism is a rotten and opportunist theory."

Whether in the domain of ideologies or in that of power politics, the idea of a united Europe is beset by the same contradiction. A divided Europe, buffeted by opposing forces, cannot move toward one pole without provoking a violent reaction from the other. Although the United States may accept a Europe for the Europeans on the sole condition that it not be communist, the Soviet Union will not tolerate a Europe that is organized without her, since she is certain that such a Europe will not only reject the salvation which Soviet orthodoxy seeks to press upon all peoples, but will be as menacing as was the Europe of Napoleon and Hitler.

European Union versus European Economics. It may be objected that Europe even today, split as it is along the Stettin-Trieste line, is an economic unity. Does not the United Nations Economic Commission for Europe still officiate in Geneva, despite Russia's refusal to permit Eastern Europe

---

[18] Walter Dirks, "Ein falsches Europa?" *Frankfurter Hefte*, Vol. 3, No. 4, August, 1948. See also R. Strausz-Hupé, "European Attitudes towards United States Foreign Policy," *Proceedings of the Academy of Political Science*, 1949; and the same author's *The Zone of Indifference*, New York, Putnam, 1952.

to participate in the Marshall Plan? [19] Do goods not move in large volume across the lines of power-political cleavage? Do not the Franco-Polish, Anglo-Polish, and Anglo-Yugoslavian trade agreements, concluded during the first year of the ERP, bespeak the economic interdependence of Europe and specifically, its dependence on "East-West Trade"? Did not, during the height of the Berlin crisis, December 1, 1948, the American military government on behalf of Western Germany conclude with Czechoslovakia a $40,000,000 trade agreement? It is not proposed here to resume the discussion on the virtues and vices of "functional" integration. Cases on record are plentiful showing that nations warring upon each other managed to trade with each other, utilizing for the exchange of vital commodities the services of neutrals or of their own nationals engaged in smuggling, as did France and Britain during the Napoleonic Wars. Activities of this kind, needless to say, are wholly irrelevant to the topic of economic integration.

Both the Marshall Plan and the so-called Molotov Plan [20] were posited on the assumption of the revival of East-West European trade. The Marshall Plan countries were dependent upon the flow of grain, lumber, and coal for their economic development, while the Molotov Plan countries were dependent on the supply of machinery from the West for their plans of development. The proportion, however, of trade from the East in the total trade of the Western nations would be considerably less than the proportion of Western trade in the total trade of Eastern Europe, if the prewar flow of trade were to be revived.

In the short run the nations of the Eastern bloc will encounter many difficulties. The pattern of the Molotov Plan begins to emerge in outline somewhat along these lines: Russia will provide the industrial raw materials whereby East Germany, Czechoslovakia, and Poland, as "workshops" of Eastern Europe, will industrialize the Balkan countries. Of the latter, Rumania and Hungary will be most closely tied to the Soviet Union, which they supply with certain industrial raw materials.

There is nothing in the nature of things to prevent the creation of an Eastern bloc as a single economic unit. It has been said that such a project could never be achieved since the economies of Russia and the Danubian countries are not complementary, both having exportable surpluses of such products as grain and timber. If the industrialization of Eastern Europe proceeds and population increases, and if the population of the Soviet Union expands as it

[19] The Soviet delegate on the U.N. Economic Commission for Europe proposed in May, 1948, that a special subcommittee for the revival of East-West intra-European trade be set up ("E.C.E. Reaches Important New Decisions," *United Nations Bulletin,* Vol. 4, No. 11, June 1, 1948).

[20] See "Trade Pattern for Eastern Europe," *Business Week,* No. 857, Feb. 2, 1947; Vera Micheles Dean, "Economic Trends in Eastern Europe I–II," *Foreign Policy Reports,* Vol. 24, Nos. 2 and 3, Apr. 1 and 15, 1948; "Czech-Soviet Trade Post," *Central European Observer,* Vol. 24, No. 14, Aug. 15, 1947; and H. H. Dayrell, "Bulgaria's New Economy," *ibid.,* Vol. 24, No. 6, Apr. 3, 1947.

is projected, it is quite certain that the Eastern bloc of Europe will need every bit of food and minerals it produces. There is little reason why in the long run these two areas, as the diversification of their economies proceeds, should not be able to merge into a single economic bloc with perhaps a few common surpluses, such as timber, and a few extraneous needs. Besides, economic unification can be carried out even if there is *no* complementary trade. Both the Ruhr and Silesia produce coal and are therefore "competitive." Yet the two regions were joined in the one great industrial potential of Germany.

The term "trade pattern" is commonly used as though these "patterns" were something immutable. When trade patterns of long standing are disrupted, there is no reason why new patterns cannot be established. Before the First World War Russia supplied many European nations with grain; after the war Russia no longer exported foodstuffs. Its former customers turned to southeast Europe and the Western Hemisphere. Such adjustments are painful but not impossible. After World War II the reestablishment of East-West trade remains a desirable goal, but even if there were no Cold War, it would still be doubtful whether the countries of Eastern Europe could produce a substantial exportable surplus. The various agrarian "reforms" may cut down agricultural production precisely as they did in the Soviet Union. There is no question that the economies of the Eastern European nations are being reoriented toward the production of capital goods and armaments and toward the supplying of the Soviet Union. Yet the "trade pattern" would have changed even if there had not been the barrier of the "iron curtain."

All available evidence points to a far-reaching reorientation of East European trade and integration of East European national economies within the Soviet orbit.[21] Soviet theory and Soviet practice accord primacy to politics over economics, and nothing in the record suggests that Soviet policy will yield to economic logic—be its arguments ever so persuasive as regards the "natural" correspondence of East European agricultural surpluses and the industrial export capacity of Western Germany. To gamble on the revision of autarchic policies now vigorously pushed by the Soviet Union wherever its political power predominates, is to gamble on a revolutionary change in Soviet thought, if not in the Soviet regime itself.[22]

The need for European unity exists; the lack of power to realize it and the world political schism, too, are facts. The antithesis is real; it is posed by historic realities and the divided personality of European man. It is possible, though not probable, that the contradiction can be overcome by another generation, and here the functional approach may prove its worth. Within the near future, however, the political unification of Europe is impossible— except by war. As a matter of fact, the slogan of European Union is a seman-

[21] See Nicolas Clarion, *Le Glacis Soviétique,* Paris, Somogy, 1948, pp. 160–176.
[22] For a presumably authoritative statement of the nature and objectives of Soviet economy, see N. A. Voznesensky, *The Economy of the U.S.S.R. during World War II,* Washington, Public Affairs Press, 1948, especially pp. 107–115.

tic flourish, and the most intelligent advocates of a federal solution for Europe proceed on the assumption that *all* of Europe *cannot* be united. Thus, for example, Senator J. William Fulbright, sponsor of a resolution calling for a United States of Europe, plainly proposed a *Western* European federation, to wit, a federation of those European states who belong to the Atlantic Community.[23] That, too, is the frame of reference within which the integration of Britain and the British Commonwealth can be meaningfully discussed.

BRITAIN, THE DOMINIONS, AND WESTERN UNION

Britain's foreign policy is now, as it has been for three centuries, to safeguard her position in Europe and to maintain the security and well-being of her Dominions and possessions. The task of reconciling these two interests proves now, when the available resources of Britain are strained to the limit of her capacity, more difficult than ever. Yet its successful achievement is the condition of Britain's survival as a great power and, consequently, determines categorically Britain's attitude toward Western European Union. For Britain, the problem of her dual role is what it always has been, and geography limits severely—even in the air-atomic age—the alternatives of British foreign policy. Thus the aim of British policy is to preserve her integrity as a European power and secure and strengthen her overseas connections.

When, in World War II, the threat of German victory receded, notably after the landing in Italy, British policy turned, for various reasons sooner and more deliberately than that of the United States, to the problems which Germany's defeat would create in Europe. It was evident that Germany's collapse would leave a power vacuum in Europe. Significantly it was a Dominion premier who first suggested how that vacuum could be filled. Field Marshal Jan Smuts of South Africa, addressing the Empire Parliamentary Association on November 25, 1943, proposed closer cooperation between Britain and the states of Western Europe. The Empire statesman said:

We have evolved a system in the Commonwealth which opens the door for developments of this kind. Today in the Commonwealth we have a group of sovereign States working together, living together in peace and in war, under a system that has stood the greatest strain to which any nations could be subjected. They are all sovereign States, they retain all the attributes and functions and symbols of sovereignty. Other neighbouring nations, therefore, living the same way of life, and with the same outlook, can with perfect safety say: "That is our group; why are we not there? With full retention and maintenance of our sovereign status, we choose that grand company for our future in this dangerous world."

Since France and Belgium together with Britain are also Europe's major African colonial powers, Marshal Smuts's proposal envisioned in effect the

---

[23] J. William Fulbright, "A United States of Europe," *Annals of the American Academy of Political and Social Science*, Vol. 257, May, 1948.

creation of a European-African empire with a population close to 400 million. Marshal Smuts emphasized the retention of full sovereign status. What he contemplated in 1943 was "a Union in Western Europe which would leave each member state a full master in its house." [24]

Though Mr. Bevin, in his pronouncement in Parliament on January 22, 1948, did not reiterate Marshal Smuts's emphasis on national sovereignty and formally embrace the idea of Western Union, his words left the impression of "judiciously considered imprecision." Manifestly, Western Union, in view of the "breach between East and West, is a 'League for defense.' " But was it likely to fuse into an organic, federal union, superseding national sovereignties? This question the Secretary of Foreign Affairs did not answer. "If," he said, "we are to have an organism in the West it must be a spiritual union. While no doubt there must be treaties, or at least understanding, the union must be primarily a fusion derived from the basic freedoms and ethical principles for which we all stand. . . . It is more of a brotherhood and less of a rigid system." It is not surprising that this particular artifice of "judicious imprecision" failed to elicit a favorable response on the part of France, the principal Continental power of Western Europe *and* the United States, the principal sponsor of Western Union.

Britain's Problem. Foreign Secretary Bevin, goaded by criticisms emanating not only from France and the United States but British parliamentary circles irrespective of party affiliations, made, on September 14, 1948, a spirited defense of Britain's role in fostering Western European unity. His defense was partly that the United States was overlooking the great British contributions to the Western European Union but mainly that European unity was practical only step by step over a long period and with the cooperation of the whole British Commonwealth.

Both Mr. Bevin's speech and the leading speech from the Conservative opposition by Anthony Eden, which preceded it, traced the postwar British conception of a new world-wide balance of power in which domination either by the United States or the Soviet Union would be made impossible through the existence of a great Third Force, consisting of the British Commonwealth and Western Europe.

From these speeches emerges with startling clarity the British scheme for a Western Union as a Third Force. That Third Force, however, bears no resemblance to a European Union advocated under the same label by French and German thinkers and politicians. It is Atlantic, and not Continental; it is pragmatic, and not ideological. It cleaves with great fidelity to the scheme propounded by Field Marshal Smuts. Britain's spokesmen carefully avoided a reference to the institutional forms of the Union, contenting themselves with the elastic term "association." They could not do otherwise, because the Dominions, although they had made it clear that they welcomed

[24] Nicholas Mansergh, "Britain, the Commonwealth, and Western Union," *International Affairs*, Vol. 24, No. 4, October, 1945, p. 493 and *passim*.

all steps taken by the United Kingdom to help to restore "the shattered fabric of Western European economy, security and civilization," had different ideas about Western Union, for the simple reason that it would in all likelihood affect them in different ways.[25]

The position as regarded European union of the Conservative government did not differ in any significant respect from that of its predecessor. Prime Minister Churchill's statements on the Schuman Plan and the European Defense Community repeated in substance what the Labor government had said, in response to American exhortations, on the Council of Europe.[26] Britain, in order to assure France and to appease American public opinion, declared herself willing to maintain forces by the side of a European defense force, but not to become a member of the European Defense Community. Prime Minister Churchill's position was that a European Union, for which he had campaigned so vigorously in 1946 as offering the only possible bulwark against Russia, had been superseded by the development of NATO embracing the United States and Canada and therefore appealing more to the British than a purely Continental combination.

It is a matter of conjecture as to whether Sir Winston Churchill's call, May 11, 1952, for a four-power conference (Britain, the United States, France, and the Soviet Union) "at the highest summit" and his allusion to a new "Locarno" was an attempt to assert Britain's diplomatic leadership, or whether he intended to take the sting out of EDC, *i.e.*, to assure the Soviets of the nonaggressive character of the arrangement. Sir Winston said: [27]

... I do not believe that the immense problem of reconciling the security of Russia with the freedom and safety of Western Europe is insoluble. . . .

The Locarno Treaty of 1925 was in my mind. It was the highest point reached between the two wars. . . . It was based upon the simple provision that if Germany attacked France we should stand with the French, and if France attacked Germany we should stand with the Germans. The scene today, its scale and its factors, is widely different and yet I have a feeling that the master thought which animated

[25] For an analysis of Dominion reactions to the Atlantic Pact, see "Commonwealth and the Pact," *The Economist*, Mar. 26, 1949, pp. 545–546.

[26] See the Labor Party's pamphlet, *European Unity* (the "Dalton Brown Paper") issued in 1951: "Britain cannot join a European Union because of her Commonwealth ties. . . . Furthermore, there can be no British commitment to a Plan [Schuman Plan] which will include the unnationalized industries of other nations. *Western Europe cannot unite until there are socialist governments in power* in those nations desirous to unite." (Italics are the authors'.) See also Aneurin Bevan, *In Place of Fear*, New York, Simon and Schuster, 1952, for British (left wing) Labor's case against European Union, against United States leadership in the affairs of the West, and against American emphasis on arms rather than economic aid. For a British view of EDC as a kind of waiting room through which Germany must pass in order to gain admission to NATO and for Britain's relation to EDC as well as European federal government, see Chatham House Study Group (Donald McLachlan), *Atlantic Alliance*, London, Royal Institute of International Affairs, 1952, pp. 102 and 126*f*.

[27] Sir Winston Churchill, as quoted by Byron Dexter, "Locarno Again," *Foreign Affairs*, Vol. 32, No. 1, October, 1953, p. 34.

Locarno might well play its part between Germany and Russia in the minds of those whose prime ambition is to consolidate the peace of Europe as the key to the peace of mankind.

British popular sentiment—fear of atomic and thermonuclear war, growing restiveness under United States pressure and wide Anglo-American divergences on the problem of Korea—may have prompted Sir Winston's initiative. In all likelihood, his try for a negotiated settlement with the Soviets reflected not only British home opinion but also Commonwealth sentiment.

This brief survey, though it hardly scratches the surface of the complicated and shifting alignments of that vast, informal and, not infrequently, ineffable organization, the British Commonwealth, does not suggest a synthesizing conclusion. Here, too, as in the case of the idea of European unity, the task of finding a common denominator of political integration is beset by formidable contradictions between "is" and "ought." The British dilemma transcends European problematics.

Mackenzie King, the former Premier of Canada, drove to the core of Britain's postwar problem when he spoke of "leagues of free peoples" for which Western Union should be the pattern. However, Western Union would be the keystone of a larger system. It is precisely the immense scope of the concept of Atlantic Community which accommodates a security system in which Western Europe, the Commonwealth peoples, and the United States can unite and reconcile their varied interests, leagues within a "league of free peoples."

The quandaries of British policy were not reviewed here in order to diminish the importance of Western European Union or to declare it impossible of achievement. It is an evolutionary step without which other steps leading to the execution of a larger design cannot be taken. It is not impossible; it is, as Foreign Secretary Bevin put it, "a long and tedious and difficult job." If the Atlantic Community is taken as the master plan, then the odds and ends of the scheme for Western European Union fall into their place, just as the concept of the Atlantic Community resolves the basic contradiction of British policy.

THE WEST AND GERMANY

Though the analogy takes considerable license with peoples and places, it can be said that what Commonwealth relationships are to Britain, the German problem is to Western Europe. For the German problem, too, engenders a species of schizophrenia. Germany is no less a country of Western Europe than, let us say, Holland, and the Rhine is indubitably Western Europe's most important river and joins its waters to those of the Atlantic Ocean. Yet Germany is also of the East, and the plains of Prussia merge, without serving any warning that the geographer can perceive, into the Baltic plains which, in turn, broaden into the vaster plains of Russia.

As regards her cultural and political history, Germany exhibits characteristics which are no more or less "Western" than are those of, let us say, Portugal, Spain, Italy, and, for that matter, France—depending what historical epoch one chooses as the most significant one for striking a sensitive balance. Germany, her cultural landscape as well as her philosophy, literature, and art, bears the impress of Western Christianity; yet the barbarian has breached, in our times, the fragile walls of the ethical citadel, and it was Hitler's Germany that struck the most vicious blow at Western civilization and opened the gates of Europe to Asian despotism in its modern guise. It is not proposed here to press further along these lines of reasoning. They lead to dilemmas as complex and as profound as is the problem of Western man, cast adrift from the haven of eternal verities onto the turbulent currents of materialist civilization. Politically, they lead nowhere.

The political and strategic questions which have to be answered *now* are these: Must Germany be integrated into a Western European Union in order that that Union may "live"? Can Germany be so integrated? and, if not all of Germany, how much of Germany? Thus baldly stated, the German problem lacks some of its exciting philosophical implications as, for example, the vaporous emanations of the collective "German Mind," but it becomes tractable. It differs in this respect only little from the general problem of international politics, which is to solve the problems that can be solved and to improvise arrangements for living on tolerable terms with problems that cannot be solved.

In a fashion, the working arrangements devised under the Marshall Plan already answered the question as to whether Western Europe can or cannot exist without Germany. Patently, Western Europe cannot. The geological formation of northwestern Europe, the juxtaposition of Rhineland coal and Lorraine iron ore, meshes the heavy industries of Germany, France, Belgium, and Holland into an economic unity. That unity is reinforced by interconnected waterways, rail and road systems which, in large measure, conform to topographic formations. The power system of Western Europe has been developed as a combine of German, French, and Swiss thermoelectric and hydroelectric resources. More important still, the distribution of plants, labor force, and skills form a pattern which can be altered only by interventions requiring colossal investments.

In this respect, German heavy industry in its capacity as producer as well as consumer is of vital interest to such "intermediate" and specialized producers as Holland, Belgium, and Switzerland. France, of all European countries, can least afford to forgo imports from Western Germany. Germany stood first in Britain's trade with the Continent, and the bulk of that trade was in manufactured products and industrial raw materials. To insist on Germany's contribution to the economic life of Western Europe is to labor a truism. But it is necessary in order to decide whether Germany does or does not "belong" to Western Europe and hence to the Atlantic Community.

Can Germany be integrated in a Western European Union, and, if not all of Germany, how much of Germany? Soviet foreign policy and the incorporation of the Eastern German "popular democracy," proclaimed as the German Democratic Republic on October 7, 1949, into the Soviet orbit gave a categoric answer. At the time of this writing, the answer still stands. The partition of Germany cut off the 48 million inhabitants of Western Germany from one-half of the arable land of prewar Germany. It is the diversion of the agricultural surplus of Eastern Germany and Eastern Europe away from Western Germany, formerly the most important market for that surplus, which accounted for the chronic food shortages of the West German industrial centers. Countries of Western Europe, such as Holland, Britain, and Norway, are now more dependent than in prewar years on overseas food imports. Their food supply was and will be tied to their overseas trade. The food deficit of Western Germany introduced an unprecedented element into the postwar economic situation of Western Europe.

It is unrealistic to assume that the food surplus—if any—to the east of the European partition line will again revert to its prewar markets.[28] Soviet commercial policies in Eastern Europe merely hastened long-standing trends which were inscribed in the population statistics of Eastern Europe and its pattern of progressive industrialization and urbanization. In this sense, Hitler's attempt to conquer Eastern Europe was an attempt to capture markets and sources of supply that were slipping from Germany's grasp.

Thus there remains, by the force of circumstance, only one alternative, and that alternative suggests a new form of European economy: the integration of Western Germany with Western Europe and, in the last resort, with the Atlantic trading sphere. The question put into economic terms is this: can 48 million Germans, in order to gain their livelihood and contribute to the well-being of their Western neighbors, replace the markets they lost in the East by new markets in the West?

The question put into political terms is this: can the Western neighbors of Germany, especially Britain, be expected to accede to the consequent expansion of German trade and industry? For such expansion is fraught with obvious risks not only to their own respective competitive position in world markets but also to their military security.

The Marshall Plan and subsequent American grants, EPU and CSC, were addressed to the first question with considerable success up to date, though no one can now say whether American economic policies *and* the coordinating efforts of Western Europe will succeed in answering the question conclusively. The second, the political, question can only be answered politically, that is, by political and military guarantees. To expect that Germany's Western neighbors will yield vital national interests, political and military, to a common and exacting task, without being guaranteed against military and po-

---

[28] This is the assumption stated in the *Report of the Paris Conference on the Marshall Plan,* Chap. VI, Article 119, as published by *The New York Times,* Sept. 24, 1947, pp. 25–28.

litical aggression, is to ignore not only European aspirations in particular but human nature in general.

It is a truism to say that coexistence within a geographically and economically interdependent area of peoples belonging to the same culture requires voluntary collaboration. Yet this truism sums up the Western European-German problem. That problem, pared down to practical politics, is first and foremost that of Franco-German relationships.

Germany: The French Point of View. The French approach to Germany is matter of fact. Compared with the wide swings, if not to say, the dramatic reversals, of American and Soviet policies toward Germany, the French attitude stood out because of its consistency and directness. No responsible French politician proposed the razing of German industries and transformation of Germany into an agricultural country; no French statesman promised the Germans "unity," to wit, the reestablishment of the *Reich,* or the restoration of their prewar industrial capacity. French demands remained the same throughout three postwar years enlivened by violent gyrations not only in U.S.-Soviet relations, but also in the course pursued by the United States and the Soviet Union in Germany.

These demands were control, decentralization, and reparations. The principles of control and decentralization were incorporated in the London Recommendations on Germany of June 7, 1948, agreed upon by the United States, Britain, France, and the Benelux states. To a large degree these French demands were met by the Bonn constitution, ratified by the West German states (Länder) on May 20, 1949, by the virtual splitting of the *Reich* into two Germanies, and by the establishment of the International Authority for the Ruhr. Yet the constitutions and policies of both Germanies leave little doubt that the Germans still strove for German unity.

Though France stuck to her principal demands, French policy evolved considerably. When asked for his views, General de Gaulle, then still President of the French Provisional Government, declared with commendable bluntness: "We do not want any more Reich," and Georges Bidault's MRP, incidentally backed on this issue by the French communists, demanded the political separation of the Ruhr and the Rhineland from Germany. By contrast, French policy in 1948 and 1949 signified a realistic adjustment of French demands not only to the Anglo-American points of view, but also to the novel position of Western Germany as an important member of the West European recovery team.

It can be argued that French policy revealed a deplorable astigmatism. Was Germany still the principal threat to France in a Europe that was contested ground between the extra-European superpowers? Has Germany not become France's "natural ally"? [29]

[29] For a more comprehensive treatment of these problems, see R. Strausz-Hupé, "France and the German State," *Yale Review,* Vol. 38, No. 2, 1949; and William Diebold, Jr., "The Choice in the Ruhr," *Foreign Affairs,* Vol. 27, No. 1, 1948, pp. 117–128.

Each of these questions implies more or less formidable objections to what may be called the "French point of view" on a German settlement. Yet these objections do not impinge materially on the tenacity of the French conception if one recognizes its roots in the deep subsoil of European experience.[30]

A united Western Europe without Germany is a contradiction in terms, and the great majority of Europeans—be they French, Dutch, or Norwegian —recognize full well the role the German people will have to play in a viable Western European community. Yet their fear—which, be it noted here, is by no means typical only of the French—lest the potential energies of the largest European population group be again gathered in a new bid for domination, is a fact beyond dispute. Hence the degree to which a German settlement eschewed those features—a heavy industry freed of all external controls, and a *Wehrmacht* with its own general staff—which were considered, rightly or wrongly, as the conditions of organization for aggression, was taken by Germany's neighbors as the criterion of Germany's qualification for membership in a Western European Union. The provisional Bonn constitution was considered sufficiently "safe" to admit Western Germany as an "associated" member of the Council of Europe. Germany's adherence to the Schuman Plan was considered sufficient guarantee against the use by Germany of her industrial potential as an instrument of political domination.

GERMANY AND THE DEFENSE OF THE WEST

So long as large Soviet forces remain in Europe, Western Europe needs defense in depth. This means holding Germany as far east as possible. Thus military plans for the defense of Europe must necessarily include Germany.[31] It is obvious that without the German area of maneuver and German industrial and manpower resources, defense in depth is impossible. If attacked, the forces of the Western Allies, unsupported by the Germans, would have to withdraw beyond the Rhine and possibly the Pyrenees. The Allied forces in Germany depend for their lines of communication on the good will of the German people and their government. The position of NATO forces in Europe is not secure as long as Germany has not become a loyal ally of the West. No one knows this better than the Soviets; the chief long-term aim of the Soviets in Europe is to win Germany as an ally or as a subservient neutral through offers of unity, markets, and frontier adjustments at Poland's expense and through threats of devastation, if not total annihilation in a third world war.

Soviet policies accord with the hopes and fears of many Germans of whom only a negligible number are communists. Soviet offers strike responsive chords in the hearts of those Germans who as patriots would pay any price

[30] See René Courtin, "French Views on European Union," *International Affairs,* Vol. 25, No. 1, January, 1949, pp. 8–22.

[31] M. J. Bonn, *Whither Europe,* New York, Philosophical Library, 1952, p. 135.

for the reunification of the fatherland even if it were to entail what they believe would be only temporary concessions to communism; who side intellectually and morally with the cause of the West but resent the inequalities of Germany's status in the Western community and view German unity as the precondition of Germany's resumption of her rightful place in the world; who abhor war and view even subservience to Russia as the lesser of two evils; and who hope for the restoration of the lost provinces to the east to their rightful owners, the millions of refugees now eking out precarious existences in Western Germany. And there are finally those Germans who believe that they are clever enough to strike an advantageous deal with Russia and that a united Germany would be strong enough to keep her independence and remain safe if both Western and Russian troops withdrew. In brief, if Western statesmanship cannot resolve the problem of Germany within the context of Western unity and if a German government were to insist on working for German unity, even on the terms offered by the Russians, then the Western Allies may be confronted by movements of political resistance in Germany which would make their position to the east of the Rhine untenable.

It is this consideration which triggered the efforts of the United States to bring Germany into the Western camp and keep it there. This objective could be achieved by either of the two approaches: (1) to bring a rearmed Western Germany directly into NATO; or (2) to bring Western Germany into a West European military combination and to link that combination by diverse arrangements to NATO. The second approach was chosen. It was chosen because, had Germany been given full NATO status, France would not have ratified the Treaty of Germany or any other treaty according Germany sovereign status and the right to rearm. The circuitous approach of the European Defense Community represented the victory of the French point of view.

The French with virtual unanimity concluded that Germany, were she allowed to join NATO, would obtain complete freedom of military action and would be entitled to demand a general staff and a defense industry. And this is precisely what French public opinion rejected categorically. In EDC, the Germans were asked to forgo these demands because the other members themselves agreed to accept restrictions upon their military freedom. Yet all members, except Germany, were members of NATO. In NATO councils, they could hence discuss problems affecting Germany without Germany being represented. This arrangement, which was hardly improved by the proposal that EDC and NATO should hold joint sessions and that the Germans should be represented in matters concerning them, *but only in those,* was patently absurd. Germany was invited to furnish nearly one-third of the EDC contingents, yet not to raise her voice in the deliberations of NATO, the top organization of Western defense. The only basis on which Western Germany could be expected to agree to this discriminatory provision was that EDC would be absorbed in the ultimate federation of its members, if not in that of all the members of the Strasbourg Council. The principal burden of the responsibility for completing the structure which they themselves designed and advocated, rested upon the French. Admittedly, EDC was a means for bringing Germany into Western defense and yet balancing her power by the joint power of France and her Western neighbors, *i.e.*, to make German rearmament "safe." [32] In EDC, Western Germany accepted military and political conditions which, in a matter of a few years, would place her on terms of equality with France. To seek to revise these conditions downward and to perpetuate, by diplomatic means or simply passive resistance, Western Germany's status as a defeated former enemy rather than an ally played into the hands of those German factions who opposed closer ties with the West, and thus into the hands of the Soviet Union.

EDC could solve the problem of how to join German power to the aggregate of the free world's power in Europe without embittering the Germans and repeating the mistakes which, after World War I, weakened the Weimar Republic and alienated the German masses from democracy as well as cooperation with the West. For EDC would safeguard Germany's neighbors against the unilateral employment of a reconstituted German army. Behind the EDC project was the political movement for European unity, the Council of Europe, the Coal and Steel Community, and plans for the pooling of transport facilities and agricultural production. Behind EDC stood not only NATO but the greatest productivity and the greatest purchasing power of the world. Integration of Western Germany into a larger European political and economic framework would call for a termination of those politics and economics of fear which have belied what has been creative and "European" in the French diplomatic response to the challenge of the German problem. The French have been mistaken in ascribing their defeats at the hands of the Germans to German industrial and military superiority rather than their own inability to organize their own considerable resources effectively and to recapture the moral vigor which once made France all other nations' peer.

Yet to burden France with the sole responsibility of solving the German problem, whether by "sublimating" German power in EDC and accepting even the contingency that EDC's spokesman in NATO councils might be a German, or by compromising the Saar issue, is to dispose all too lightly of the responsibility that rests upon the United States and Britain. It is by no means certain that European integration can compensate Western Germany for the temporary renunciation of German unity, which, in German eyes, is a terrifying price to pay for political equality with their Western neighbors and for the two-edged concession of remilitarization. It is certain that European integration cannot compensate Western Germany for the markets lost in the East and cannot supply the outlets for an economy that must not only

[32] Bonn, *op. cit.*, p. 146.

provide for the livelihood of a population standing 20 per cent above the prewar level but also keep alive Western Berlin, the isolated, but morally strongest, bastion of the West. The survival of Western Germany as a viable economic unit and as a democracy, politically, militarily, and spiritually securely tied to the West, depends on the most intense cooperation with the entire Western world and not merely with her Continental neighbors. The restoration of free trade throughout the free world, the removal of trade restrictions, especially those imposed by the United States and British Commonwealth, and free access of German goods and skilled manpower to world markets, especially the markets of the Americas and the underdeveloped countries, these are conditions as essential to the solution of the "German problem" as is the transcendence of narrow and obsolete concepts of national security by French statecraft.

It can be seen from the above discussion that the German problem, as it appears to Germany's neighbors to the West, is fraught not only with enormous economic difficulties—the reorientation of German trade—but also with psychological complications—the anxiety neurosis engendered by German aggressiveness.

Analyzed against the background of current conditions, with Russia standing poised at the Elbe River, these controversies about Germany have become purely academic. Granted all the worst assumptions about innate German aggressiveness, the sober fact remains that even a reunited Germany does not possess the war potential of 1939. Poland took away about one-third of Germany's warmaking powers. Nor does the Saar any longer constitute a part of Germany. For the duration of the Russian danger, there will hardly be a German reunion—except under Soviet overlordship or as a result of profound change in United States and European views as to the nature of Soviet intentions and how to cope with them, in which case NATO and EDC will have lost their meaning. Hence the only Germany that could join the Western nations is the Germany of Bonn, and the war potential of Bonn Germany is smaller than that of France and Benelux combined. The resurrection of a *genuine* German threat must be preceded by the elimination of the Russian threat and by the retreat of Russia behind the Pripet Marshes as well as by a new partition of Poland in which Germany regains the Oder territories and Silesia. These are possibilities of the far distant future for which nobody can plan today. True, every solution of the German problem entails great dangers, but the security and well-being of Western Europe must be planned against the *primary* threat which comes from Moscow and not from Berlin, let alone Bonn. The future cannot be built by perpetuating the tensions of the past. There must be an end to every conflict. The time is ripe for the liquidation of the hereditary Franco-German enmity.

The inclusion of Western Germany in a Western European Union has become imperative. Yet the joining together of the German economy and the economies of Western Europe is not a matter of simple arithmetic. It is a revolutionary process which creates new opportunities and new wants.

The problem of Germany viewed as a European problem is no longer as refractory or as absurd as it is when treated in isolation—as it was at Versailles in 1919 and at Potsdam in 1945. But it still looms forbiddingly on the broader plans of Western European integration. Under the broad canopy of the West—Western Europe, the Americas, and the British Commonwealth —48 million Germans can find their place; the German settlement will be a "long and difficult and tedious job" but one which the 400 million peoples of the Atlantic Community together with the majority of the world's resources can manage. To fail in this "job" would not only imperil their security, but spell out their abdication as a creative civilization—as advertised by Soviet propaganda and, not so long ago, by Nazi propaganda.

Germany: Europe's Neutral Ground? But can it not be argued that the "job" need not be done at all, and that the most practical expedient—most practical because it would rid both the United States and the U.S.S.R. of the German problem—is to exclude Germany from the Western *and* the Eastern orbit? This solution, the neutralization of Germany, is based on the assumption that by withdrawing their forces simultaneously from Germany, the United States and Russia would leave Germany a neutral ground, and that it would be in their mutual interest to insure the permanent demilitarization of Germany.[33]

The inference this solution suggests is that West and East would find in the common task of controlling Germany that ground of collaboration which had crumbled under the pressure of the conflicting policies of their respective military governments in Germany. Germany is conceived as a sort of vacuum which is to insulate West and East from each other.

But is not the vacuum which was left by the collapse of power in central Europe among the potent causes of the East-West crisis? And is it not the nature of a vacuum that pressures from outside converge upon it? The maintenance of a neutralized Germany would call for a degree of self-restraint on the part of the great powers which they have so far not exercised and which great powers are generically incapable of exercising—even when they are not, as they are now, animated by ideological antagonism.

---

[33] See Walter Lippmann, *The Cold War: A Study in U.S. Foreign Policy,* New York, Harper, 1948, p. 5. See also James P. Warburg, *Germany—Bridge or Battleground,* New York, Harcourt, Brace, 1947, pp. 234*f.* For the French case for a neutralized Germany, unarmed and uncommitted to West or East, see the running commentary of *Le Monde,* Paris, the leading French neutralist daily journal, advocating not only neutralization of Germany but—presumably by a U.S.-British-French-Russian pact—of all of Europe in the West-East conflict. See especially *Le Monde's* discussion of EDC on Feb. 9 and 11 and Oct. 19 and 20, 1952. For the English case, see the mischievous *New Statesman and Nation,* Feb. 9, 1952. For the German case, see Schmid and Soustelle, *op. cit.,* and Fritz Baade, "Entscheidung zwischen drei Deutschland-Konzeptionen," *Aussenpolitik,* September, 1952.

Moreover, this solution reflects a sovereign but dangerous indifference toward the aspirations of the German people. The only way in which their aspirations could be safely ignored would be to impose on Germany a quarantine far more stringent than has been suggested by the Morgenthau school of thought. Under less rigorous conditions the internal political alignments of Germany would inevitably seek contact with corresponding alignments abroad, and, inversely, major political movements abroad would, by this osmotic process, impinge on German domestic politics.

In brief, the same centrifugal forces which, as we have seen, strain against the unification of Continental Europe, would upset Germany's internal balance. Germany would thus become not Europe's "neutral ground" but its cockpit, its ideological Balkans. Obviously, this problem would not exist were the tension between the East and West to subside. At present, the East-West rift is, to say the least, not confined to the conflict between the Western powers and Russia over the future of Germany but cuts by its vertical and horizontal extension through political society *everywhere*.

A country can stay neutral only when (1) it is so strong that it can defend itself successfully against its potential antagonists and thus defend its neutrality with its own might, or (2) its geographical position is so strong that violation of its neutrality would be too costly (Switzerland), or (3) its geographical position is too remote to matter in the conflict between major antagonists (Afghanistan). In each case the whole population must *desire* to stay neutral in order to make the most of the basic condition *permitting* the country to stay neutral. None of these basic conditions apply to Germany, and the German people, or even a slim majority of the Germans, are *not* neutral in the East-West conflict.

The neutralization of Germany would require the withdrawal of Western and Soviet forces from German soil. This, precisely, has been the principal aim of Soviet policy in Europe. For the withdrawal of Western forces would (1) reduce the area of Western military domination in continental Europe by one-third, while Russia would give up a negligible fraction of its European domain; [34] and (2) unleash open political and social conflicts which are now contained by the presence of armed forces and which the far-reaching changes in the social and economic structure of Eastern Germany, inspired and enforced by the Soviets, may have rendered irreconcilable. [35] Germany would be imbedded between two hostile economic systems. Germany would have to be either self-supporting or would have to be so modest an economic prize as not to tempt either the West or Russia to seek it. These conditions

[34] See Erich Dethleffsen, "The Chimera of German Neutrality," *Foreign Affairs*, Vol. 30, No. 3, April, 1952, p. 369.

[35] On the widening gap between the economic and social systems of Western and Eastern Germany and its ominous implications for German unity which might turn into unity-in-chaos, see Peter Nettl, "Economic Checks on German Unity," *Foreign Affairs*, Vol. 30, No. 4, July, 1952, pp. 554–563.

do not apply to Germany. If vigorously enforced, economic neutrality would mean that Germany could not obtain large-scale investments from the West, *i.e.*, from the only party to her neutrality that has capital to spare. The result would be a decline in the German standard of living and the strengthening of the forces that could drive Germany into the arms of communism. German neutrality has little to recommend it to the Germans, except a temporary respite from world conflict, entails none but adverse consequences for the West, and is pregnant with immense potential advantages for Russia. No wonder that the neutralization of a united Germany, even an armed one, was the theme song of successive Soviet peace offensives. It will remain the principal objective of Soviet diplomacy and propaganda designed to split the Western alliance, to drive U.S. power from Europe, and to establish in Germany the forward base for the drive toward the domination of all of Europe.

The German problem must be analyzed also from the point of view of preventive diplomacy, which is no less important than creative diplomacy. The West may be unable to decide what *it* should do with Germany; there should be no doubt as to what the West does *not* want Russia to do about Germany. An alliance with Germany has been a recurrent objective of Soviet foreign policy. A German-Russian alliance would constitute the supreme danger to the survival of the Western world and to the independence of the Western nations—regardless of the ultimate development of Russo-German relations. Such an alliance encounters many obstacles which are similar in nature to the difficulties obstructing cooperation among Western nations and Western understanding with Germany. Yet a dictatorship is less inhibited in overcoming such hindrances than a democracy which operates by consultation. In the past, despite frequent close cooperation, the dream of the Russo-German fusion never materialized, essentially because the Russians did not want to be dominated by the Germans. They need no longer fear such a possibility. A future Russo-German alliance would be dependent on the willingness of the Germans to play second fiddle. Hence German psychology is a major key to the practicality of such an alliance and to the future of peace in the West. Under these circumstances, Western policy must avoid provoking a psychological reaction which would make a Russian alliance palatable to the Germans. If the West discriminates against the Germans, whether as traders in world markets or as soldiers in Europe's defense, the emergence of a pro-Soviet attitude may follow as a matter of course. The German boat must be anchored to the West lest it float to the East. There is a community of interests between Germany and the West; it will not be used to advantage by half measures and by looking backward to past aggressions. Policy must be directed to the future. Last but not least, the democratization of Germany, a foremost Western war aim, cannot be effected except through the integration of Germany into the Western system.

THE WESTERN COMMUNITY

The postwar world has witnessed confusing and muddled attempts to organize the "good society." With bewildering speed the Western nations adopted and discarded "solutions." They started out enthusiastically to build the United Nations, only to realize that it would not work under the conditions of a bipolar political world. France and Britain concluded alliances with Russia, only to discover that they had bought no security. Bilateral alliances in Western Europe were transformed into the Western Union of Britain, France, and Benelux. But it became apparent that the Western Union could not solve its problems, and more specifically could not devise a system of Continental defense, without the support of the United States and Canada. Hence the Atlantic Pact. That Pact in turn revealed the shortcomings of any modern, *purely military* alliance: namely, that such an alliance cannot attain its end without political, economic, and military integration. Hence the Council of Europe, the Schuman Plan, and EDC. The end is not yet. These various organizations—and a host of others, including the Pan-American defense scheme—have not been, and cannot be, coordinated. They left many vital problems unsolved, including their administrative and political machineries, which are as yet unworkable. It is easy to condemn these improvisations as the gropings of muddle-headed politicians. Yet these frantic efforts also show that the Western community is wakening to its responsibilities and trying to solve its problems through *experimentation*. They exhibit all the characteristics of creative endeavor, together with its disappointments and slow progress. It is not easy to wrest order from chaos. The only question is, will there be enough time to complete the creation?

Not only philosophers in general but political philosophers in particular are prone to discover a formula of progress, showing that the world is gradually becoming more and more to their liking. The procedure is simple; the philosopher first decides which are the features of the existing order which accord with his preconceptions and which do not. Then, by a careful selection among the facts, he persuades himself that the process of change is subject to a general law leading to an increase of what he likes and to a decrease of what he dislikes in the existing order of things. Having formulated the law of progress, there is little else for him to do but to design a system. Then he turns to the audience and invites it to participate in the new system, ratify its ideal constitution, and live happily for ever after under that system, and condemns all those who do not grasp the inevitability of things to come as he sees them as numbskulls and reactionaries.

Lest this particular and unlovely kind of utopianism be imputed to the foregoing arguments on the prospects of the Western community, let us hasten to say that it is not inevitable and that it would not necessarily—should it come into existence—establish a world order under law and thus universal, lasting peace. Since Western civilization has never achieved political unity, no precedent exists. The forging of closer political union would necessitate a sacrifice of sovereign rights on the part of some of the world's oldest and proudest nation-states and, perhaps more important still, a high degree of self-abnegation on the part of those groups whose interests are vested in sovereign rights and who stand to lose economic advantages, administrative jobs, and honorific emoluments.

For such feats of national and personal unselfishness there is hardly any precedent. The difficulties caused by Europe's historical diversity; the frailties of the British Commonwealth, the most effective international organization yet devised; and the ambiguities of even the most perfect settlement that can be imagined for Germany, have been reviewed all too briefly in the preceding pages. None of the difficulties are insuperable in logic. None can be overcome without an abiding sense of purpose, by keeping "the great objective of union in sight." [36] No one can now say whether, given that sense of purpose, they can be overcome with a degree of simultaneity in order to close ranks against the rising pressure of opposing forces. Though each of these problems calls for the sober skills of statesmanship, the ultimate question of Western unity has to be given by an act of faith. Each novel form of social organization springs from an *an act of faith*. There was little precedent to guide the makers of the United States. The Republic was born from a chance encounter of necessity and accident transformed into a meeting of destiny by a creative act of faith.

The successful creation of viable institutions presiding over the military safety, economic well-being and cultural development under freedom is not foreordained. It will not solve all world problems. But it can solve the one which Western civilization faces here and now: the problem of life and death.

A More Perfect Union. Federation is one of the great inventions of political theory. It has been developed and perfected in America. It served admirably such new political associations as the thirteen newly created states which first joined together to fight the War of Independence and then made common cause in order to surmount the economic and political crisis that war had left in its wake. Federal experiments are, as a rule, inspired by a sense of kinship and a will to unity. Or the federal experiments are imposed from above, as in the case of the Soviet Union, which managed to transform the Tsarist state, dominated by Russian autocracy, into a "federation" of national states, each dominated by a state Communist Party controlled in turn by the party hierarchy of the Union and thus the autocrats of the Kremlin.

[36] Barbara Ward, *The West at Bay,* New York, Norton, 1948, p. 261. This brilliant book advances a compelling argument for a close political and economic association of the Western nations of Europe, in close cooperation with the United States, and calls for a "reaffirmation of faith" in the Western idea of freedom.

The ideas of federalism and concentration of powers (centralism) are contradictory terms. It is the foremost liberal task of our times to strengthen the power of the free nations while guarding jealously that separation of powers which sets bounds to arbitrary government and guards the right of peoples, be they great or small; of social groups, be they strong or weak; and of men of all creeds, classes, and professions.

The West is still far from achieving that diversity in unity and that unity in diversity which would give it strength in war and prosperity in peace, and safeguard human freedom at all times. So much has been achieved toward the meshing of Western resources that it is easy to cultivate a false sense of comfort and security. However, the indisputably remarkable advances on the road toward unity will prove to have been made in vain if the ultimate goal has not been reached. At the time of this writing, it seems as if energies were flagging and the Western peoples were straying from the road that could lead them into a new epoch of their history. Perhaps the West has fumbled its greatest opportunity. Perhaps it is true that all that men can learn from history is that men never learn from history.

What are the lessons which the last few years can teach us? They are these:

1. Unification must be a major and deliberate political act.

2. Unification cannot be achieved by piecemeal and roundabout approaches.

3. Unification cannot be brought about as long as its manifold implications have not been thought through and proper methods have not been devised for dealing systematically with its principal problems.

The proliferation of institutions has served to becloud rather than to clarify the basic issue: political unification versus functional "integrations" from which sovereign states can withdraw whenever they choose to exercise their sovereign discretion. Perhaps this issue could have been met had the United States, at the height of its influence after World War II, pressed single-mindedly for Western unity; perhaps the issue would not have arisen had not the West European states, dissimulating their reservations, sidetracked the quest for unity onto roads which, notwithstanding their elaborate markings, lead nowhere. There is a Council of Europe; it does not govern Europe. There is a European Payments Union; Europe's economy is still divided into national currency and tariff systems. There is the blueprint of a European Defense Community; there is no European army. More important still, the two countries that should be the pillars of the Western Community, the United States and Britain, have failed not only to accord their views on the kind of unity—Atlantic, European, and world-wide—they want, but also to coordinate their diplomatic, economic, and military policies. The difficulties of reconciling the interests of the United States and the British Commonwealth, with its informality of association and aversion to rigid commitments, are great and numerous; the difficulties of reconciling the interests of the English-speaking peoples with the nations of continental Europe are staggering. But to admit defeat would be to accept the decline and fall of the West. *Western unity is not one of several alternatives. It is the one and only alternative to defeat. Hence the task of creating a real, a working Western Community is the ultimate test of Western statecraft.* To pursue the ultimate goal calls for purposefulness, but also for great elasticity of method and tolerant urbanity. The statesman who will lead the way will have to wrestle with innumerable known and unknown difficulties. By the time he has reached his destination, he will have shed the excess baggage of formulas and blueprints with which he set out on the road.

The goal is the unity of the Western Community. That community is a reality, just as communist Russia and contested Asia are great realities. A maze of economic agreements, defensive alliances, and political pacts now covers, albeit untidily and oddly, the Atlantic region. Beneath it we can dimly perceive new forms of political organization. It was the comfortable delusion of a utopian philosopher that the need creates the organ, and that necessity, recognized by intelligence, realizes itself inevitably. Circumstances obstruct as much as they favor new developments. The record of the past tends to determine the present—until circumstances intervene. The final answer to the unique challenge now confronting the West must be given within a brief span of time by *this* generation of Western peoples.

THE POSITION OF THE UNITED STATES REAPPRAISED

The United States succeeded in revitalizing Western democracy, its policies and power, by a series of bold and grand measures. The Marshall Plan, NATO, and Point Four are superb examples of imaginative statesmanship. Since 1947, the United States pursued a policy toward Europe that was courageous as well as sensible because it recognized, despite formidable opposition—sometimes vicious and devious, sometimes merely obtuse, but always unrelenting—the key position which Germany holds in the system of European defense. The United States has reached some of its objectives and come within sight of the others. Yet somewhere at the halfway mark of the course set by American policy, the success of the entire undertaking seems in doubt. Stalin died. His successors launched what by then should have been a familiar offensive combining peace appeals with political and military operations. The ranks of the Western alliance wavered. Clamorous voices called for a four-power conference, for a relaxation of the armament effort, and for "independence" from United States initiatives. The American President's speech of April 16, 1953 ("The Chance for Peace"), spelled out on what basis an agreement with the Soviets could be reached. Though the clamor subsided, fissures in Western unity, heretofore hidden beneath formal diplomatic unanimity, had become visible to all who cared to look. What are the causes which underlie what seemed like Europe's ominous estrangement from the United States?

Disparity of Power. Following World War II, Europe found itself faced with problems, particularly economic, which were insoluble without the assistance of the United States. Recognizing its dependence, Europe began to resent its position, and to seek independence from the benefactor. Traditionally, Western culture has meant the pursuit of individual freedom. Economic well-being and independence have been sought as a prerequisite for the enjoyment of that freedom. National self-determination and national "sovereignty," its international counterpart, have been accepted as expressions of that freedom. However, as these policies toward which Europe is driven, and which are associated with American policy, are seen to entail *less* self-determination and, because of the costs of rearmament, *less* economic well-being, as well as increased dependence economically and militarily upon the United States, the defense of Western culture becomes less meaningful to America's European allies. Europe is disillusioned by World War II, is fearful of becoming the battlefield of World War III, and mourns her failure to solve such internal problems as overpopulation, inflation, inadequate housing, unemployment, and the "dollar shortage." She finds it, therefore, more difficult to rally to the support of American programs for the defense of Western culture. Special-interest groups find it easy to advance their own ends behind the cultural and ideological smoke screens of anti-American propaganda and the growing ranks of its eager audience.

Psychologically, Europe may be diagnosed as suffering from an inferiority complex. This complex seeks a psychological release: Europe seeks to prove not merely her "equality" but her "superiority" to the United States in those fields which still permit competition, *i.e.*, culture and diplomacy. This desire has been channeled by European political factions into two distinct movements closely akin to each other—nationalism and neutralism. Europe's extreme Right and Left are, paradoxically, nationalist *and* neutralist. They converge upon the common ground of questioning or opposing American leadership in Europe and throughout the world. Nationalism and neutralism are themselves ideological products of the divisive forces which threaten the internal stability of European society, *i.e.*, the growing pressure of overpopulation, the continuing proletarianization of the middle classes, the weakened state of organized religion as a spiritually and politically cohesive force, and the masses' loss of a belief in the future.

Both these movements seek the creation of a Third Force in Europe which would theoretically attain two objectives, namely, independence from the United States and avoidance of war with the Soviet Union. It is significant that opposition to American judgment is most emphatically formulated by those nations which once enjoyed substantial power—Great Britain, Germany, and France. It is *comparatively* negligible in Italy, despite a large communist party in that country. It is even less of a factor in the Scandinavian countries, which, like Italy, do not draw revenue and prestige from overseas sources as do Britain and France, or possess the strength of Germany's strategic bargaining position.

Divergence on Policy. It is the Soviet threat that drives Europe into further dependence upon the United States and, therefore, into resentment of American policies designed to meet that threat. Europe, faced with internal unrest, would *like* to feel that the threat could be met without large-scale rearmament, without a curtailment of the supposed benefits of East-West trade, and without the resurrection of competitive German economic and military strength. This political quandary suggests all kinds of more or less fantastic solutions. For example, according to the Labor Left in Britain, the Soviet threat is primarily economic, social, and political—and only secondarily military. It is contended that the Atlantic Pact, which is called an American guarantee of Western Europe, is already adequate to deter the Soviet Union militarily. The situation is basically the same in Western Germany. German nationalists and neutralists take different stands as regards U.S. policy, but they do so for identical reasons: both exploit popular resentment against the policies which the U.S. pursues in order to "contain" Russia, and the risks and sacrifices those policies entail for Germany.

Objections to American policies in Japan, China, and the Middle East derived, although more obliquely, from the same basic attitudes and reasoning. For example, the British insisted that America was not dealing properly with the issue of recognizing Red China, despite the fact that the latter has systematically snubbed the envoy Whitehall so hopefully dispatched. The British were further disturbed by the fact that the United States persuaded Japan to recognize Nationalist China while Japan was still under American control and before the restoration of full sovereignty gave her the independent power to choose between the two Chinas. Behind this reproach was the British desire to save investments in China and to channel Japanese economic competition into the larger market of China, thus allowing Britain, the sterling area, and the Commonwealth a wider opportunity to better their economic position and free themselves of dependence upon American aid. Moreover, Europeans (chiefly the British) were highly critical of American conduct of the Korean War and feared that American policy would lead to World War III. In the Middle East, both Britain and France faced an increasing loss of economic resources and prestige as the United States refused to align itself with their colonial policies in those areas.

The fact that European attitudes toward American policies may be traced to a felt loss of national sovereignty, to resentment of economic dependence upon the United States, or to a pernicious combination of the two, points up the need for a more articulate expression of the Western culture in whose defense these policies have been formulated. European countries, as well as the United States, might be brought to make greater sacrifices of "sovereignty" and narrow economic "advantages" if a stronger psychological bond could be drawn between them. The failure of the United States to relinquish vested economic advantages, as reflected in its tariff and immigration practices, reinforces the attraction of economic determinism and of those "disintegrationist" philosophies which fatten on Europe's real ills and are exploited by Soviet propaganda. Economic determinism and disintegrationist philosophies drain from Western culture its intrinsic social and political values. Without belief in these values, United States–European relationships appear as a mere struggle between the decaying empires of Britain and France and German territorial ambitions on the one hand, and an emerging American global hegemony on the other.

Some of the tensions might have been alleviated if the United States had consulted more frequently with European powers over particular issues and publicized diplomacy-by-consultation. The timing of American moves, as well as the wording of official statements on policy, did not always receive adequate consideration in terms of European sensibilities.

The United States conveyed the impression that the Soviet threat was the principal motivating factor behind its European policies. Since the assumption of continued Soviet aggressiveness was not susceptible of rigorous proof or refutation, it was a tempting target for the irresponsible attacks of various European factions such as the British "Bevanites," the French and German neutralists, the German socialists, and the followers of diverse neofascist and anti-American movements. It was argued that the United States must come to the aid of Europe in its own interest and that, therefore, Europe's military security was guaranteed no matter what domestic and foreign policies Europeans may choose. These groups appeared to argue that it is only they who can make their respective countries strong enough to be independent of the United States, while paradoxically they assumed that the latter must guarantee Europe's territorial integrity. *The fallacy of this argument should have been exposed to Europeans.* To do so, the United States should have revealed its own underlying assumptions, namely, that the building of a Western community, irrespective of the Soviet threat, was a good move in and of itself, and that America's rise to a position of leadership marked the present point in the cultural development of the Western community. Such assumptions will not be proved valid by the synthetic creation of a new ideology. The validity of these assumptions will be borne out by what the United States does and does not do.

The best propaganda for winning and keeping friends, as well as for confounding one's enemies, is the propaganda of the deed. This does not mean that the United States should not speak with a strong voice. But it must speak clearly. Americans cannot inveigh against the iniquities of totalitarian bureaucracy and, at the same time, speak to Europe through the thousand mouths of a resident bureaucracy, which, though not totalitarian, exhibits a propensity for red tape hardly surpassed by its counterparts on both sides of the iron curtain. Americans cannot proclaim their devotion to freedom if they lock their own borders to immigration and trade. The United States cannot assume, in Africa, the pious pose of anticolonialism, and, at the same time, admonish its friends to do battle for those of their colonial possessions in Asia which happen to be strategically important in the American scheme of defense.

That American policies have sometimes been too hastily conceived and too brusquely implemented and that the United States has, by its own hands, helped to compose a picture of truculent and bureaucratic arbitrariness that does not correspond to the real and engaging character of the great mass of its citizens, does not mean that the United States must don sackcloth and ashes and abdicate its leadership. It most certainly cannot surrender leadership to Britain. The balance of power policy pursued by Britain in the interwar period, playing a resurgent Germany against an exhausted France, bears a great, if not the principal, responsibility for the disaster of World War II. Whether British statesmanship can resist the temptation to maneuver for a winning position between the United States and Russia depends in part on Britain's discretion and, to a far greater extent, on the resolution and skill of American statesmanship. Neither Britain's policy in 1938 toward Hitler and Germany's rape of Czechoslovakia, nor Britain's policy in 1950–1954 toward Mao Tse-tung's China, furnishes a guidance that the United States should follow in its relations to the Soviet Union and the world.

The United States may have fewer staunch friends than Americans would like to believe. All the more reason that they be given American support and that the United States should not seek to buy what cannot be bought: friendship, loyalty, and strong hearts in common danger. The prevention of war demands an effective alliance of the strong. At the root of NATO's weakness is American hesitation to affront the susceptibilities of the weak and to transform a (theoretical) system on paper, hampered by the irresolution of the least effective members, into a fighting alliance capable of guaranteeing the security of the strong *and* the weak. The weak may become strong; old and proud military nations may recapture their traditional vigor and will. But the United States cannot safely adjust its pace to that of the halt and the lame but rather must seek to create conditions under which the strong can deploy their strength so that the stricken nations can reconvalesce and recover.

Perhaps no other country in history was ever confronted by so vast a task as the making of Western unity and its defense against terrible dangers in this age of conflict over the very future of mankind. This is a task requiring deep understanding of the souls of nations, the resolution to lead the way and the willingness to set that living example that is the most solid token of leadership.

BIBLIOGRAPHY

Adenauer, Konrad: "Germany and Europe," *Foreign Affairs,* Vol. 31, No. 3, April, 1953.
Aron, Raymond: "Can Europe Achieve Political Unity," *Modern Review,* Vol. 1, No. 7, September, 1947.
Baldwin, Hanson W.: *The Price of Power,* New York, Harper, 1947.
Bonn, M. J.: *Whither Europe,* New York, Philosophical Library, 1952.
Boyd, A. F.: *Western Union,* London, Hutchinson, 1948.

Brinton, Crane: *From Many One,* Cambridge, Mass., Harvard University Press, 1948.
Coudenhove-Kalergi, Richard N.: *Crusade for Pan-Europe,* New York, Putnam, 1943.
———: *Pan-Europe,* New York, Knopf, 1926.
Dawson, Christopher: *Understanding Europe,* New York, Sheed, 1952.
Friedrich, Carl J.: *Inevitable Peace,* Cambridge, Mass., Harvard University Press, 1948.
Frisoff, V. A.: *The Unity of Europe,* London, Lindsay, Drummond, 1947.
Haas, Ernst B.: "The United States of Europe: Four Approaches to the Purpose and Form of a European Federation," *Political Science Quarterly,* Vol. 58, No. 4, December, 1948.
Hoffman, Ross: "Europe and the Atlantic Community," *Thought,* Vol. 20, No. 76, March, 1945.
———: *Durable Peace,* London, Sheed, 1944.
———: *The Great Republic,* London, Sheed, 1942.
Kohn, Hans: *World Order in Historical Perspective,* Cambridge, Mass., Harvard University Press, 1943.
Kohr, Leopold: *Customs Unions: A Tool for Peace,* Washington, Foundation for Foreign Affairs, 1949.
Lanux, Pierre de: *European Manifesto,* New York, Creative Age, 1945.
Layton, Lord C. H.: *Western Union,* London, Gollancz, 1948.
Lehmann-Russbueldt, Otto, and Alexander Hirsch: *Europa den Europäern,* Hamburg, F. Oetinger, 1948.
Lippmann, Walter: *The Cold War: A Study in U.S. Foreign Policy,* New York, Harper, 1947.
———: *U.S. War Aims,* Boston, Little, Brown, 1944.
Mackay, R. W. G.: *You Can't Put the Clock Back,* Chicago, Ziff-Davis, 1948.
Madariaga, Salvador de: *Victors Beware,* London, J. Cape, 1946.
Mansergh, Nicholas: "Postwar Strains on the British Commonwealth," *Foreign Affairs,* Vol. 27, No. 1, October, 1948.
Mitrany, David: "The Functional Approach to World Organization," *International Affairs,* Vol. 24, No. 3, July, 1948.
———: *A Working Peace System,* London, Royal Institute of International Affairs, 1944.
Morgenthau, Hans J.: *Politics among Nations,* New York, Knopf, 1948.
———: *Peace, Security and the United Nations,* Chicago, University of Chicago Press, 1946.
Newfang, O.: *World Federation,* New York, Barnes & Noble, Inc., 1939.
Patterson, E. M.: "NATO and World Peace," *The Annals,* Vol. 288, July, 1953.
Reves, Emery: *The Anatomy of Peace,* New York, Harper, 1946.
Roberts, Owen J.: "U.S. and European Union," *Freedom and Union,* Vol. 2, No. 3, March, 1947.
Russell, Bertrand: *Philosophy and Politics,* London, National Book League, 1947.
———: *Freedom and Organization, 1814–1914,* London, G. Allen, 1934.
Schlesinger, Rudolf: *Federalism in Central and Eastern Europe,* New York, Oxford, 1947.
Schuman, Frederick L.: *The Commonwealth of Man,* New York, Knopf, 1952.
Schuman, Robert: "France and Europe," *Foreign Affairs,* Vol. 31, No. 3, April, 1953.
Strausz-Hupé, Robert: *The Zone of Indifference,* New York, Putnam, 1952.
Streit, Clarence K.: *Union Now,* New York, Harper, 1939.
United Nations, Department of Economic Affairs: *Customs Unions: A League of Nations Contribution to the Study of Customs Unions,* Lake Success, N.Y., 1947.
Ward, Barbara: *The West at Bay,* New York, Norton, 1948.
Young, Sir George: *Federalism and Freedom,* New York, Oxford, 1942.

Chapter 29

THE WEST AND THE WORLD

A recent study defined the long-term aim of the Atlantic alliance as the "hegemony of the West." [1] There will be no security for the free world in the foreseeable future unless its forces are stronger than those of its totalitarian opponents. This means that the power of the United States and its allies must be not only equal but superior to that of the Soviet Union and its allies. As for material resources and reserves of skilled manpower, technological equipment and scientific knowledge, the West can more than hold its own compared with its antagonists. But these are latent potentialities that must be brought to life in order to create power-in-being. The West has not yet marshaled its resources efficiently. It has not yet created military and political organizations that are incontestably superior to those with which totalitarian dictatorship wages its wars of varying temperatures. Nor has the West been able to take the moral and intellectual measure of the forces confronting it.

The West is *not* united. The best that can be said about the situation here and now is that the West is groping for the organizational formula which could give it strength in unity. A beginning has been made to solve imaginatively problems which *can* be solved and should be solved in concert so that the West may become aware of itself and acquire the habit of common action in a common crisis. NATO, the defense of Asia, technical assistance to underdeveloped areas, Pacific Pact—these are the training fields of the Western team. But these tender shoots of unity-to-be are constantly in danger of being blighted by even a light frost spread, in the forms of peace offensives and sundry strategies, by the Soviets. The hope for "coexistence" does not die easily.

"Coexistence" on the basis of the present distribution of forces is impossible. Peace can be kept only if (1) the distribution of potential forces is changed decisively in favor of the West, and (2) the Soviet regime changes or Western initiative succeeds in changing it by pressure and persuasion. If these changes cannot be brought about, there is only one other alternative: the free world will undergo change until it ceases to be free. Since the West, not to speak of the rest of the free world, has not attained unity in the face

[1] Chatham House Study Group (Donald McLachlan), *Atlantic Alliance,* London, Royal Institute of International Affairs, 1952, p. 134.

of the common threat, it is only the United States that can cut the Gordian knot of the problems posed by "coexistence."

In the present stage of "coexistence," the state of the free world is highly unstable. The European half of the Atlantic system creaks and groans ominously under pressures that are not so much political and military as psychological. The countries of the Middle East and in South and Southeast Asia, with their inchoate political structures and economic backwardness, are so many tempting targets for Soviet aggression and penetration. If the weakness and disunity of the free world were less pronounced than is argued in these pages, even then it could not be shown how the peoples of the free world could "coexist" with the Soviet bloc without the material contribution and the political leadership of the United States. Thus the problem of "coexistence" comes to rest at the doorstep of the United States; no one else can solve it. To accept "coexistence" and with it the present highly unstable state of the free world is but to abet its further disintegration.

"Coexistence" of the United States and the Soviet Union, *i.e.*, avoidance of war in the present world situation, is dependent on the intentions of the two governments, on their ability to live up to their intentions, on their policies, on developments in other parts of the world, and on the changes which these governments and their regimes undergo as time goes on. To a certain extent, the United States has the capability to enforce "coexistence," *i.e.*, Soviet abstention from aggression, through superior military and economic strength. It is doubtful, however, whether the Soviet government has the capability to adopt a policy of true peace, as distinguished from a policy in which nonviolent conflict techniques are employed for the purpose of Soviet expansion. Such a policy would require internal relaxation in Russia, including reduction of armaments and greater concentration on the production of consumers' goods, and hence some decentralization of political and economic power. Whether the Soviets can take this risk, which might force far-reaching political reforms and entail the overthrow of the regime, is doubtful. If they do, the structure of the Soviet regime would have undergone substantial change. There is little historic evidence showing that an ideological and minority dictatorship is capable of basic reforms. The past offers many examples showing that oppressors must keep on being oppressors until they disappear.

Developments in other countries, such as the war in Korea and disturbances in East Germany in 1953, may have repercussions on American or Soviet policies, depending on the interests involved. The world situation is in flux, and the Soviets do their share to keep it so. If they should turn singlemindedly to the many problems of their own country, gradually release the subjugated peoples from their rule, and disband international organizations like the communist parties and communist-controlled peace movements, the world situation would improve and the chances of "coexistence" would grow.

Coexistence with *Russia* is possible, but whether it will be possible also with the *Soviet government* depends on the development of that regime. This regime is undergoing some modification, but the direction of these changes is uncertain and their extent is as yet insignificant. So long as the Soviets continue to push forward with their various programs of expansion, coexistence in the sense of a permanent policy of "live and let live" remains fundamentally impossible. Before a different estimate can be made, the Soviets would have to do more than issue propaganda statements for external consumption and negotiate endlessly about trivialities. They would have to reduce drastically their programs of conflict management, ranging all the way from indoctrination at home to violent operations abroad. They would, in fact, have to cease to be communists.

For the time being, "coexistence" between the United States and the Soviet Union is a highly ephemeral condition. It is not a *modus vivendi*. "Coexistence," adopted by the United States as a policy, cannot preserve peace, for it is a unilateral American desire and not a Soviet promise. "Coexistence" cannot be negotiated with the Soviets, nor will they ever sign an enforceable treaty which embodies a mutually agreed code of "coexistence." It is therefore not a practical political program. Nor is the term a meaningful one if it is supposed to connote a fixed and long-lasting Russo-American relationship. For that matter very few international relationships can be stable in a rapidly changing world, and these few relationships hardly include those between the United States and the Soviet Union.

American weakness will invite Soviet attack regardless of what the situation before the Soviets will have struck is called, be it "coexistence," "no-peace-no-war," "armed truce," or something else. Ultimately, war can be avoided only if the Soviet regime changes. Before that happens there is only *one* method to reduce the risk of war: to complete American military preparedness and preserve it at a maximum. Crushing military superiority will not by itself bring peace, but it is the essential prerequisite of peace. The idea that "coexistence" can be achieved with the present Soviet regime is as dangerous an illusion as Neville Chamberlain's hope that, at Munich, he had achieved peace for our time.

"NEITHER EAST NOR WEST"

The stark realities of the power struggle which goes by the name of "coexistence" weigh oppressively upon mankind. It is not surprising that men in all lands should seek to escape it either by designing clever stratagems for riding the balance of power or by retreating into spiritual and intellectual isolation from the facts of international life. Neutralism feeds from many sources. It is the catchall of bare-faced selfishness and humanitarian idealism, of cowardly appeasement and nonresistant heroism. It is an ethical philosophy as well as a political ideology. Its political formula is simple: the creation of a Third Force independent of both the United States and the Soviet Union. The best way of solving the problem of "coexistence" is by separating the two superpowers so that they cannot rub against each other, *i.e.,* to contain them both. "This line of reasoning," as Raymond Aron wrote, "takes it for granted that both the great powers are equally responsible for the present world situation; that both are equally undesirous of war, but that each if left to his own designs, natural impulses, or fears, is equally likely to end up by unleashing one; and that the countries in the middle should therefore do the two brainless giants the favor of keeping them apart." [2]

We attempted to show, in the preceding chapter, what are in the case of Germany the prerequisites of neutrality. The statement can be expanded to cover *all* the countries outside the Soviet bloc, individually, or combined in regional groups, or consolidated into one world bloc. A Third Force in Europe or in Asia or formed by all the countries of Europe and Asia has much to recommend it—except the fact that it does not possess the strength to enforce its neutrality. Assuming that Soviet conduct can be explained solely in terms of fear and defensive strategy—for which there is in Soviet history and doctrine no supporting evidence—it is the United States alone whom the Soviets fear, not the countries of Western Europe or Yugoslavia or India or Indonesia or all of them combined.

It is a corollary of neutralist doctrine that the United States and the Soviet Union should be induced—presumably by the diplomatic finesse and moral prestige of the older countries of Europe and Asia or simply by a sit-down strike of the Third Force—to negotiate a global settlement. Such a global settlement can only be negotiated on the basis of the acceptance by the United States and the Soviet Union of the division of the globe into two power orbits relatively equal in strength. This would mean that the West would have to accept (1) in Europe, the sovietization of Eastern Europe in return for the promise that the Soviets would not interfere in the Western orbit, and (2) in Asia, the sovietization of China, Tibet, and Mongolia in return for a Russian-Chinese assurance not to disturb the *status quo* in Japan, South Asia, and the Middle East. In addition to the West's agreement on some sort of neutralization of Germany and the *de facto* abandonment of the European Defense Community project, *i.e.,* a substantial reduction of Western armament goals, the Soviets would obtain the guarantee of the permanent demilitarization of Japan. In brief, the West would have to forgo the creation of the two regional "situations of strength" which its best military opinion viewed as essential to its safety. The Soviets would give the kind of assurances which they have given before and have not kept, *i.e.,* the promise not to intervene in the affairs of other nations. It is doubtful that they could keep such promises even if they wanted to do so, given the dynamism of communist-fomented peasant rebellions in Asia and the momentum of diverse

[2] See Raymond Aron, "Can We Negotiate a Settlement Now?" *Commentary,* June, 1952.

subversive forces, such as local communist parties, "fronts," etc., which they have set in motion in the Western world during the last thirty-five years. Such a settlement would be a hoax. It would ratify a partition of the globe which already exists and, therefore, need not be negotiated. It could straighten a frontier here and there; it could not—even were the Soviets inspired by unwonted good will toward the "monopolist-capitalist states"—relieve the latter of dealing with the problems of collapsing colonial rule in the East, peasant wars in South Asia, and their own domestic communist parties. These problems would remain just as thorny as they had been before a Western-Russian pact was signed.

This does not mean that the Soviets in a period of internal crisis will not resort to ebb tactics and employ, among other means, diplomacy in order to win a breathing spell. Such episodes occurred before in Soviet history; the Soviets negotiated settlements of all kinds of issues and observed agreements which recorded prevailing power relationships. They kept some of these agreements and broke others—again depending on existing power relationships and the advantages they derived from keeping or breaking a specific agreement. Not to negotiate with the Soviets over specific issues and thereby to fail to take advantage of favorable situations, *i.e.,* not to use the diplomatic tool where it is appropriate, would be as foolish an omission as it would be in regard to any other state. It should be noted, however, that the Soviet Union, being a dictatorship, can initiate diplomatic negotiations and, once they are initiated, again call them off more easily than democratic states in which public opinion cannot be shunted at a moment's notice from one track to the other by the government and where public pressures are apt to force the diplomatic negotiator's hand. A good case can be made for the contention that the West has been clumsy in the use of the diplomatic tool; that local settlement here and there could be made and local tensions could be ameliorated, thus reducing over-all tensions; and that it is the business of diplomacy to negotiate as long as, and whenever, there is something to negotiate about. But the idea that a lasting, over-all settlement can be reached by conference whereby the free world and the Soviet Union can settle down to each other's peaceful contemplation is a footless and dangerous idea.

It would be a great error to suppose that Soviet Russia is the *sole* cause of international crisis or that Soviet "imperialism" and international communism are identical in every respect. It is often argued, therefore, that mankind is beset by many international problems, of which the conflict between the West and the Soviets is but one; that communism derives its strength from many forces, some of which would operate were the Kremlin inhabited by stockbrokers and conscientious objectors; that the "Revolt of Asia," the "Tide of Asian Nationalism," and the "Emancipation of the Backward Peoples" were inscribed in the history of Western colonialism and would harass the West no matter what the Soviets do or do not do; and that hence the

West's, especially the United States', preoccupation with the Soviet threat reveals a deplorable and dangerous astigmatism.

This is true in part. Like all half truths, this particular oversimplification slurs over important facts that call for a more complex, though more accurate, evaluation. Moreover, this explanation evokes the image of irresistible and anonymous forces, "Asia-out-of-control," the unanimous demand of hundreds of millions of Chinese and Indians for social and economic security, the collapse of Western colonial power everywhere, and similar cataclysmic and massive occurrences which the West can do nothing about—except roll with the punch—and must not even question. Yet the present crisis did not originate in some metaphysical or preordained condition, but in a concrete and definable situation.

ASIA: A THIRD FORCE?

The present crisis stems from the way the Second World War was fought and ended. In Europe the immediate consequences of the war were the collapse of Germany, the sovietization of half of Europe, and the presence of Soviet military power at the gates of Western Europe. In Asia, the present situation stems from the collapse of the Japanese Empire, the expansion of Soviet power in the Far East, the unleashing of anticolonial and anti-Western revolutionary forces, and the unfolding of a well-organized communist conspiracy. The pattern of political relationships is woven from these different yet intertwined strands; to overlook one is to miss altogether the meaning of the whole.

The Japanese in 1941–1942 ejected the Dutch from the islands that now form the independent state of Indonesia, and the British from Hong Kong, Malaya, Burma, and their island possessions in the Western Pacific. The Japanese occupied the key centers of Indo-China; the pro-Vichy French colonial government cooperated until 1944 with Japan. When the French, taking their cue from the liberation of the motherland, attempted to resist, they were disarmed by the Japanese and put in concentration camps.

In India, the presence at the borders of Japanese forces (including an Indian Nationalist Army led by Subhas Chandra Bose, former president of the Indian National Congress and, in that post, a successor of Mohandas K. Gandhi and Jawaharlal Nehru) and risings in the Central Provinces, Bihar, and the United Provinces forced the hands of the British. Upon Sir Stafford Cripps' return from India, Britain offered India Dominion status after the war. The offer was rejected, in August, 1942, by the All-India Congress Committee. The British used force in repressing ubiquitous disorders and arrested Gandhi and Nehru. Yet the issue no longer was in doubt. Confronted by the alternatives of an Indian revolt coinciding with a major Japanese push across the eastern frontier, and accommodation with the Indian nationalists and, incidentally, with American public opinion, the British chose the latter. From

1943 on, the Indian nationalists knew that the British would quit, the only open question being the nature of the settlement: would India remain united, or could the question of the religious communities be settled only by partition?

It can thus be seen that the Western colonial rule was not overthrown by indigenous nationalist movements but largely by the military power of Japan and the relative weakness of the West, caused mainly by the internecine struggle in Europe. The ascendancy of Asian nationalist movements coincided with the disintegration of Japanese military power. The defeat of Japan created a vacuum; the Japanese had left and the Western powers had not yet returned. It was during this interregnum that native nationalists seized the government in Burma and Java and that Ho Chi-minh, with Chinese Nationalist support, established his revolutionary Viet-Nam regime, now called Viet-Minh to distinguish it from the French-sponsored Viet-Nam (second edition), in Indo-China.

Virtually everywhere, Asian leaders, who now established themselves as national rulers, collaborated with native communist parties or, if they did not do so actively, were linked to communism by past affiliations and affinities. In China, Sun Yat-sen had, some thirty years earlier, cast his lot, albeit not without rending inner conflict, with the Soviet Union and invited communist advice and support. Chiang Kai-shek had, in 1927, evicted the communists from the Kuomintang, but remained, until his withdrawal from the Chinese mainland, chained to the dilemma bequeathed to him by his predecessors: to collaborate or not to collaborate with the communists in order to secure the national independence of China. The Chinese pattern now repeated itself in Burma and Indonesia. Burma owed her independence in no small measure to the activities of communist-led guerrilla troops, armed by the Western Allies to fight the Japanese occupation forces. The communists, later split into a Stalinist and a Trotskyite faction, led several revolts and, in 1947, assassinated the first Prime Minister, Aung Sang. Though his successor, Thakin Nu, took energetic measures against the communists, their power was not broken. Burma still balances on the razor's edge.

The Republic of Indonesia was established in 1945 during the six weeks which elapsed between the Japanese surrender and the first landing of British —not Dutch—troops in the Netherlands East Indies. Its first leaders, Achmed Soekarno and Mohammed Hatta, had held positions under the Japanese. Their colleague, Amir Sjarifuddin, who for a time was Minister of Defense and Internal Security in a Cabinet headed by Soetan Sjahrir and then succeeded to the post of Prime Minister, was a communist. The Dutch, their military operations against the Indonesians stalemated by inadequate supplies and manpower reserves, accepted the *fait accompli* of Indonesian independence in the Linggadjati agreement of 1947. The Indonesian Republic became formally a part of a United States of Indonesia associated with the Netherlands Commonwealth through the Dutch crown. This arrangement was modified substantially by the agreement reached in 1949 at the Hague; the independent republic of the United States of Indonesia was proclaimed by Queen Juliana as a sovereign partner in a Dutch Indonesian union. A year earlier, the hot breath of the Cold War had touched Indonesia; the communists under Sjarifuddin had revolted. Though Sjarifuddin was executed by his former associates—the pattern of the split in the Chinese Kuomintang being repeated Javanese style—and the revolt was crushed, Indonesia since then has known no peace. Communist guerrilla and underground activities coupled with the centrifugal tendencies of a multination-state (the Indonesian leaders having sought to impose a centralist regime on what was supposed to be a genuine federation) have kept Indonesia in a perpetual state of disorder.

Ho Chi-minh, the first president of the Indo-Chinese Democratic Republic —the original Viet-Nam as opposed to the French version—was himself a communist; so was his Defense Minister and commander-in-chief, Vo Nyugen Giap. To the day of this writing, Indo-China is in the throes of a communist revolution and full-fledged civil war.

In India, the liquidation of colonial rule was accomplished in 1947 at the price of partition. Of the two succession states, the Union of India and Pakistan, the former is three times larger, mainly Hindu with a Moslem minority, and the principal target of communist penetration in Asia.

Though the communist party of India is small—its active membership is said to be only 50,000—it polled in the first national elections 5½ per cent of the total vote and managed to gain control of certain key states as, for example, Travancore-Cochin. There are, according to a shrewd and eminent observer, "communist pockets" all over India.[3] The communist party is— as it is everywhere—well organized and can count on the stand-by reserves of many groups that ostensibly are uncommitted, especially intellectuals and white-collar workers, trade-union leaders, and ambivalent nationalist extremists. More important still is the pull of communism as a model system for the industrialization and agricultural development of Asian societies. Its show windows are Asian Russia and China, where it is supposed to be bringing the blessings of progress-by-planning to the masses. Communism has a "plan," and that plan, whatever it is, is the opposite of the mode of Western-capitalist development. The new political and intellectual elite of India may be divided on whether or not communism, the Soviet model, can be reconciled with the "Indian way of life." It is virtually unanimous in its devotion to the ideology of planning and its rejection of the free-enterprise system. In India the line of demarcation between various shades of Marxism is by no means so clear as it is in Europe.

Prime Minister Nehru took measures to curb what he called the "extra-territoriality" of the communists and had individual ones arrested; but rarely

---

[3] See Adlai Stevenson, "Will India Turn Communist?" *Look,* July 14, 1953, p. 39.

did he miss any opportunities to extol the virtues of Soviet progressivism, and his own philosophy of economic development owed as much to his explicit admiration of Soviet performance under planning as to his Western socialist antecedents. It is possible that Indian leaders of Nehru's intellectual width and cultivated sensibilities can maintain the balance between what they consider best and therefore useful to India in Soviet communism on the one hand, and in Western democracy on the other hand. It is uncertain, to say the least, that great masses of their followers can do so—and, if they could, would care to do so. "There is an intellectual elite," a recent study by an American political scientist concluded, "rapidly growing in size, which is embracing [communist ideology] with frightening enthusiasm." [4]

It is not surprising that the mood of Asia, contemplating the struggle between West and East, is neutralist. Should nationalism be the teammate of communism or its foe? Should the new states choose Western democracy or Soviet dictatorship as an organizational formula? What side should they take in the international conflict? Hardly any of these questions has been answered politically or even intellectually. Indian foreign policy reflects these dilemmas; it can be said that it has constructed a doctrine from these dilemmas without resolving them. Indian foreign policy is "independence"— independence in the older sense, *i.e.*, national emancipation from Western imperialism and self-rule, and independence in its more recent meaning, *i.e.*, a noncommittal attitude toward the global conflict between the Western democratic camp and the Soviet bloc. This concept is rooted not so much in a cool assessment of the international balance of power as in emotion. In March, 1939, the All-India National Congress adopted the following resolution on India's foreign policy, written by Jawaharlal Nehru: [5]

The Congress disassociates itself entirely from the British Foreign Policy. . . . The Congress is opposed to Imperialism and Fascism alike and is convinced that world peace and progress require the ending of both of these. In the opinion of the Congress, it is urgently necessary for India to direct her own foreign policy as an independent nation, *thereby keeping aloof from both Imperialism and Fascism and pursuing her path of peace and freedom.* . . . India as well as the rest of the world certainly stands to suffer greatly if Fascism dominates the world. India does not suffer if British imperialism fades away. . . .

By substituting in this statement American for British foreign policy and communism for fascism, the foreign policy concept of India can be brought up to date.[6] It was the impact of the West that made Asian peoples aware of themselves and fostered Asian nationalism. Without the foil of Western

---

[4] See Werner Levi, *Free India in Asia,* Minneapolis, University of Minnesota Press, 1952, p. 136.

[5] Taraknath Das, "India and the Present World Crisis," *Amerasia,* Vol. 3, No. 8, October, 1939, p. 378. Italics are the authors'.

[6] For a more metaphysical explanation, drawing upon Indian philosophy of nonviolence and predilection for mediation rather than for taking sides in fights, see F. S. C. Northrop, *The Taming of Nations,* New York, Macmillan, 1952, p. 56.

imperialism, Indian foreign policy would lack that sense of righteousness which permitted Nehru—in 1953 just as in 1939—to call "a plague on both your houses" and enlist the support of the Indian masses, united in their hatred of Western domination and divided on almost every other issue.

As colonialism gradually recedes from Asia there remains only one major issue on which a measure of popular agreement can be obtained: the racial question. It is increasingly difficult, now that Asians are masters in their own house, to pin local economic problems on Western imperialism—except by somewhat circuitous reasoning inaccessible to the thinking of the average peasant and laborer. The race issue, however, has lost none of its zest. Moreover, it is close to the hearts of the Asian leaders, most of whom may have found their way to the diverse nationalist movement by the road of resentment against the white man's racial and social snobbery rather than against his political and economic practices. That the rallying point is shifting increasingly to the race issue can be gleaned from many signs and portents, particularly India's attempt to assume the leadership of the international movement for racial justice. Prime Minister Nehru, speaking on July 6, 1953, before the All-India Congress Committee at Agra, pledged India to "back the fight of the colored races throughout the world short of war, . . ." and, referring to the African situation as "scandalous," predicted that if "there is no solution to this problem very soon, the whole of Africa might be ablaze." Leaving aside the question of motives, it appears that Indian foreign policy parallels the policy of the Soviet Union.

SOVIET STRATEGY AND THE COLORED RACES

The early concept of Bolshevism was to employ the Western proletariat as the chosen instrument of world revolution. This concept was modified by the (Leninist and Stalinist) emphasis on wars between the imperialist nations. The second change bore on the sociology of communism; the proletariat no longer was considered as the one providentially chosen class which would make the revolution. The poor peasantry now was deemed to possess the greatest revolutionary energy. This shift of revolutionary emphasis to the peasantry began after the 1905 revolution. It resulted in the Bolshevik success in 1917. It characterized Soviet strategy in Eastern Europe and Asia.

The impoverished and frustrated but ambitious intelligentsia is another group which, in current communist thinking, possesses great potentialities. In the underdeveloped areas, the communists put great hope on those members of the educated classes, who under present conditions cannot find congenial employment but fancy that one day they might become the "managers" of a planned economy.[7]

[7] G. F. Achminov, *Die Macht im Hintergrund, Totengräber des Kommunismus*, Ulm, Spaten, 1950.

The Soviets have reawakened to the potentialities of nationalism, particularly nationalist independence movements. They realize that the slogans of "exploitation" and "oppression" cannot be brought to life among highly paid industrial workers but that they are dynamite in areas where nationalist sentiments are growing or where independence is partly or wholly denied.

The third change was geographic: a shift from Europe to the dependent areas as the main target of expansion. This shift was also in the making before World War I, but took form only during the Baku conference in 1920. Lenin's political testament admonished the comrades to insure the success of the world revolution by carrying the revolutionary onslaught initially against China and India. This strategic concept was codified during the Sixth World Congress of the Comintern (1928), which (1) presented the communist program; (2) outlined the tactics concerning the exploitation of war by the communists; and (3) showed how unrest in the colonial and dependent areas could be exploited between the imperialist powers themselves.

These changes have been integrated in the following manner: Revolutions in the dependent areas are conducted through civil war by means of "regular" peasant armies. These peasant revolutions necessitate military interventions on the part of the Western powers. In the course of these interventions, the Western armies are dispersed and demoralized. The loss of overseas territories weakens the Western powers economically and politically, and strengthens the local communist and nationalist forces, and the conflicts arising out of these interventions lead to dissensions, and possibly wars, among the Western powers. Needless to add, such conflicts must be exacerbated by operations in the West which may take the form, for example, of "anti-imperialist" propaganda or policy sabotage. Indeed, Anglo-American and Franco-American tensions over colonial policies and policies concerning the aspirations to self-rule of dependent peoples are matters of increasing concern to all NATO members. In all this, the Soviet Union proposes to play, and frequently does play, the role of the *tertius gaudens*.

It should not be deduced from the above that domination of the Western world—and especially of Germany—has ceased to be the communist objective, nor that proletarian uprisings are written off as impractical. The point is that no actual or potential revolutionary force is neglected and no method of power seizure is left unused. Race *and* class war are to be used in combination. It is a matter of enlarging the strategic scope.

At present, the road to world domination, in communist estimation, lies in the "dependent" areas. These areas are the "weakest link in the capitalist chain," and the "main blows" always must be directed against the weakest links. As soon as these regions cease to be the weakest links, strategy will have to be redirected.

The question arises as to how the dependent areas can be exploited most effectively for revolutionary purposes. The revolutionary importance of the peasant, intellectual, and nationalist is taken for granted; there is, nevertheless, one issue fraught with potentialities which far outweigh all others: the race issue. This issue appeals to the largest number of people in the largest number of dependent areas; gives cohesion to the various revolutionary forces (while nationalism may tend to split them apart); raises the maximum of opposition against the Western world, especially against its Anglo-Saxon component; and reaches right into the heart of the United States. It is a fact that Western economic dependence, as regards strategic and critical raw materials, on the "colored" areas is growing. These areas are undergoing tremendous social and economic changes; they are becoming "energized" as a result of improved diet, reduction of endemic disease and large-scale capital investment. It is also a fact that the Western powers are most vulnerable to the race question.

Race hatred is the most effective device by which a maximum of people can be turned against the West, and especially against the United States. The Soviets find it simple to incorporate the race slogan in their program. The dependent colored peoples are the largest group of underprivileged persons in the world. Hence, the most effective method for the Soviets to enlist the support of Asia, Africa, and South America is to become the champions of the "exploited races" and to foment race war on a world scale.

This policy is partly necessitated, partly simplified, by the emergence of communist China and the tremendous revolutionary impetus of Chinese communism. In fact, the Russian communists, now in their second or third generation, have lost much of their former crusading spirit and are tending to become cynical bureaucrats. In China, by contrast, the crusading spirit seems to be growing. There the communist leadership, which naturally does not think in conventional nationalistic terms, cannot fail to see that their cause would be served best by making maximum use, all throughout Asia, of this revolutionary impetus. This may have been the basic, long-range strategic reasoning behind the Korean War.

Whether the Russian communists will be able to remain in this struggle on the side of, and lead, the colored races, or whether the colored races will, in their thinking, lump the Russians together with the other whites, is for the future to unfold. At this stage, the main point is to comprehend that there is an exceedingly strong trend toward universal race war. This trend gradually may merge with the current conflict between Soviet communism and the West. The Soviets will try hard to capitalize on this new situation. If, however, this diagnosis of future events should be accurate, it charts a development which requires, for its completion, a considerable span of time. Hence, the West should be able to develop in time the required counterstrategy.

THE WEST AND ASIA

It is not at all certain that the "Asian Century" has begun or that the "Revolt of Asia" is the "greatest single event in human history," [8] if only for the reason that Asia has been in "human history" for a long time and has risen before to power and impinged upon the affairs of other continents, and that no one can read the future. More important still, the question must be asked, what is Asia? Asia is a geographical expression; politically, socially, economically, and culturally, it is a myth. Whatever Asian solidarity there is, is the creation of a tiny group of Asian leaders and intellectuals, most of whom were steeped in Western thought. It is a solidarity *against* foreign—Western—encroachment rather than *for* common tasks. The cleavages of national interest between independent states are in Asia as wide as they are elsewhere and are growing wider as the one common rallying ground —the fight against colonialism—shrinks. India and China, despite the occasional exchanges of amenities between Delhi and Peiping, are both contenders for Asian leadership, and most other Asian states, particularly Pakistan, the Philippines, Thailand, and Ceylon, show no enthusiasm whatever for being led by either. Even the racial issue cannot focus upon itself the undivided attention of the Asian and, for that matter, the African peoples. Afghans, Thais, Filipinos, Iranians, and Saudi Arabians in Asia, Ethiopians, Moroccans, and Ismaelis in Africa may have many grudges against the West; the race issue concerns them but mildly, if at all. Some, as, for example, the Japanese, deeply resent racial discrimination at the hands of whites but deem themselves racially—as in other respects—superior to other Asian races, and are, because of their clannishness, themselves the object of resentment.

Culturally, ethnically and linguistically, the Asian peoples are *more heterogeneous* than are the peoples of the West. The rift between Islam and the Hindu and Buddhist religions is probably deeper than that separating the Western faiths from each other. There is no "International" of the black, yellow, or the brown man, just as there is none to which the white man can transfer his allegiance.

Politically, the Pan-Asian movement has been a failure, first under Japanese and, after World War II, under Indian management. The Asian-wide conferences called by India, one in 1947 and the other in 1949 (to present an all-Asian front opposing the Netherlands intervention in Indonesia), did not go beyond a repetition of anti-Western slogans. They drafted resolutions of a most general and innocuous kind. Unexpectedly, the smaller powers voiced their fears not of Western but of home-grown Asian (Chinese and Indian) imperialism. The Baguio Conference, called to discuss a common Asian stand on the Korean issue, revealed the brittleness of Asian solidarity.

[8] See Robert Payne, *The Revolt of Asia,* New York, John Day, 1947.

The Asians, it appeared, were even more divided on Korea than were the United States and its principal allies.

If in the foreseeable future a united Asia and a common front of the "colored" peoples were to emerge, they could do so only because Western statesmanship committed colossal blunders. Even then, the "colored united front" remains an improbability.

It is true that the backward peoples throughout the world, and those of Asia in particular, can tip the scales of the balance of power in the conflict between Western democracy and Soviet dictatorship. But the formation of an Asian (or "colored") bloc is impossible at this stage. Within the foreseeable future, the visible tendencies are in the opposite direction, not only regionally but also within the larger states. Neither India nor China nor Indonesia is a nation; each is burdened by serious minority problems. Not the least important among the questions confronting Western statesmanship is: should the West, having not only accepted but actually advanced the withdrawal of Western dominion from Asian peoples, now desist from intervening in those cases where one liberated Asian nation has established domination over other Asian nations? Some Asian peoples merely exchanged rulers and, in some instances, efficient and kindly ones for slovenly and cruel ones, as is the case in Indonesia. If the ideal of national self-determination has not lost luster in American eyes, it may well be worth keeping it in the Asian policies of the United States. The balance of power operates in Asia as it does elsewhere, and the opportunities are the West's for the taking.

The problems of Asia and Africa are many. The idea that they can all be solved by Western economic aid and imported Western ingenuity is not only a fallacious but also an arrogant one. A great deal of special pleading to the contrary, many—if not most—of these problems are not of the West's making. Neither Asian nationalists nor European communists can be converted to Western democracy or bought off by American economic aid laced with professions of admiration and good will. Mistakes that have become clearly apparent in Europe need not be repeated in Asia or Africa. In justice to the Soviet approach to the struggle for the domination of Asia and, in due course, of Africa, it must be conceded that it is an integrated approach. The Soviets—avowed materialists though they may be—know better than anyone else that poverty is not the sole "cause" of communism and that it can neither be spread nor fought with economic weapons alone. They also know full well the limits of propaganda, be it directed at the intellectual turmoil beneath the burning brow or at the empty feeling below the belt. They know that the struggle is world-wide, that it cannot be won in Europe if it is lost in Asia, and that the shortest road to losing both is to lose one. They can teach the West several lessons which it once knew and then forgot: that the source of all power is the power of the human will; that problems which are inherently political call for political solutions; and that political solutions can be had only for a price on which the first down payment is the military power to enforce them, if need be.

The West has a rich tradition of political sagacity ennobled, as Soviet doctrine is not, by "a decent regard" for the aspirations of mankind. It has most certainly the natural and technological resources that can be forged into instruments for enforcing its political solutions. These political solutions may not lead straightaway to utopia, but they may give mankind the breathing spell it needs to adjust itself to those technological and economic changes which necessitate the transformation of obsolescent political structures into a universal Good Society. These political solutions lie within the reach of Western man. Has he the will and the fortitude to do what he knows must be done?

BIBLIOGRAPHY

Brown, Norman (ed.): *India, Pakistan and Ceylon,* Ithaca, N.Y., Cornell University Press, 1951.

Bryson, Lyman: *Foundations of World Organization: Political and Cultural Appraisal,* New York, Harper, 1952.

Burnham, James: *Containment or Liberation,* New York, John Day, 1953.

Chatham House Study Group (Donald McLachlan), *Atlantic Alliance,* NATO's Role in the Free World, London, Royal Institute of International Affairs, 1952.

Kahin, George McTurnan: *Nationalism and Revolution in Indonesia,* Ithaca, N.Y., Cornell University Press, 1952.

Levi, Werner: *Modern China's Foreign Policy,* Minneapolis, University of Minnesota Press, 1953.

————: *Free India in Asia,* Minneapolis, University of Minnesota Press, 1952.

Mowrer, Edgar Ansel: *Challenge and Decision: A Program for the Times of Crisis Ahead— for World Peace under American Leadership,* New York, McGraw-Hill, 1950.

Muller, Herbert J.: *The Uses of the Past,* New York, Oxford, 1952.

Northrup, F. S. C.: *The Taming of Nations,* New York, Macmillan, 1952.

Panikkar, K. M.: *The Future of South-East Asia: An Indian View,* Macmillan, 1943.

Possony, Stefan T.: *A Century of Conflict,* Chicago, Regnery, 1953.

Sabattier, G.: *Le Destin d'Indochine,* Paris, Plon, 1952.

Stamp, Dudley: *A New Geography of India, Burma and Ceylon,* Bombay, Orient Longmans, 1948.

Strausz-Hupé, Robert: *The Zone of Indifference,* New York, Putnam, 1952.

Toynbee, Arnold: *The World and the West,* New York, Oxford, 1953.

————: *Civilization on Trial,* New York, Oxford, 1948.

Turner, Arthur C.: *Bulwark of the West,* Canadian Institute of International Affairs, Toronto, Ryerson, 1953.

Van Mook, Herbert J.: *The Stakes of Democracy in South Asia,* New York, Norton, 1950.

EPILOGUE

The world is out of joint. Many of our generation cry with Job: "Let the day perish wherein I was born, and the night in which it was said, There is a man child conceived . . . I was not in safety, neither had I rest, neither was I quiet; yet trouble came."

Our trouble will not end soon. The turmoil—created by the phenomenal feats of modern technology; the decline of European power and incipient integration of the Atlantic Community; the awakening, revolt, and transformation of Asia; the expansion of communism; the economic unbalance; the relativity of moral values; the decline of religious faith; the rise of American air power; the involutions and lapses of democratic procedure; and the faltering of the faith in the Good Society—cannot subside simply because of our abhorrence, nor will it abate without crises and upheavals yet to come.

The unification of the world may be in the making. This unification is a process of conflict and war, of destruction and ruin, of tragedy and mourning. It is in the nature of the historical process that the debris of decaying institutions serves as fertilizer for the growth of the future order. And it is in the nature of history that the end is undetermined: It may be what we wished or what we feared—or it may be the unexpected and the unforeseeable. Today's logic sows the seeds of tomorrow's crisis.

Yet let us not indulge in the introversions of self-pity which have been stultifying the creative forces of our era. Other generations had their troubles and rewards; we have ours. Civilization is *always* on trial. Survival is *always* in question. The crisis of humanity began shortly after the seventh day of the Creation. It will not end before the Day of Final Judgment.

We cannot win, nor survive, with fear and anguish. If the present tasks seem insuperable, it is because the growth of our character did not keep pace with the growth of our knowledge.

The problems before us, though difficult, can be mastered. If our actions be wise, the inevitable changes will be slow, relatively painless, and will preserve the values deeded to us by the generations; if our actions be foolish, they may bury the achievements of 3,000 years of cultural endeavor in cataclysmic catastrophe. We must will the solutions to our problems. We must will the means required for these solutions. We must accept the hardships and sacrifices which the solutions and the means impose on us. Let us not deceive ourselves into thinking that progress has no cost.

And then, when we have completed the chore, we must stand ready to face new problems and overcome new dangers. It is the task of Political Man to re-create society daily, to nurse it through simultaneous becoming and passing away, and to lead it, by small steps, toward the goal of perfection.

Knowledge is the shield of Political Man. But his sword is forged of moral strength, courage, and faith in human destiny. Adversity is his challenge and his opportunity. *Sursum Corda!*

INDEX

d'Abernon, Lord, 58, 212
Abetz, Otto, 214
Abyssinia, 633; foreign policy, 176; isolation, 268
Acheson, Dean G., 227*n.*, 249, 668–672
Adenauer, Konrad, 759
Afghanistan, 334, 362–363; political isolation, 269
Africa, communications, 76–77; European imperialism, 614; isolation, 266–267; national development, 619; population, 111; raw materials, 133, 138, 150–152
African Telecommunication Union, 730
Agadir incident, 282
Aggression, 187–189, 203, 323–324, 562–563; "aggrandizement," 652–653; alliance factor, 283–284; causes, 5–7, 255–256; control of, 723–726; geographic factor, 53; "natural aggressor," 6; propaganda factor, 405–414
Aimon, Archbishop of Bourges, 683
Air communication, 76–77
Air invasion, 58
Air power and boundaries, 334
Air warfare, 95–96
Aix-la-Chapelle, Congress of (1818), 221, 729; Peace of (1748), 335–336, 385
Alaska, purchase by U.S., 236
Alaskan International Highway Commission, 730
Albania, 282, 437
Alexander the Great, 82
Alexander I, Tsar, 213, 345, 427, 460, 688
Alexander III, Pope, 684
Alfieri, Dino, 225
Ali, Mohammed, 692
All-India Congress, 800–801

Alliance Française, 400
Alliances, 192–198; of containment, 282–285; defensive, 280–287; geographic factor, 35–36, 52, 177–178, 288–291; ideology factor, 177–178; military, 36; offensive, 280–281, 284; permanent and temporary, 287–291; wartime, 281–282
Allied Control Commissions, 730
Allizé, 346
Aloisi, Baron, 225
Alsace, 326
Alvensleben, Convention of, 287
American Armament Corporation, 536
American Federation of Labor, 435
Ancel, Jacques, 460
Anglo-Iranian Oil Company, 142, 535
d'Anjou, Bishop, 683
Anne, Queen, 314*n.*
Anti-Comintern Pact, 441
Appeasement, 299–304; examples of, 300–304; forms of, 300; Munich, 183, 303–304, 306, 323*n.*, 354, 386; temporary, 303
Approaches, geographic, 53–62, 72; policy of, 58–62
Arab states, 298
Arabs, expansion, 609
Arbitration, 296–299
Arbitration treaties, 237–238, 642–643
Arctic, 60, 62, 81
Argentina, 342, 378, 392, 534, 691
Aristotle, 418*n.*
Armaments, 190; and national security, 416–417; reduction of, 189, 641–642, 648; trade in, 535–536
Armistice, 338
Aron, Raymond, 795
Ashoka, King, 300
Ashton-Gwatkin, 347

2000